Longman Annotated English Poets

GENERAL EDITOR: F. W. BATESON

THE POEMS OF

JOHN MILTON

EDITED BY

JOHN CAREY AND

ALASTAIR FOWLER

LONGMAN
London and New York

Longman Group Limited London

Associated companies, branches and representatives throughout the world

Published in the United States of America by Longman Inc., New York

First published 1968
Second impression, with corrections 1980

ISBN 0 582 48443 X

Printed and bound in Great Britain by
William Clowes (Beccles) Limited, Beccles and London

Contents

Illustrations ix

Preface x

Abbreviations xv

Chronological Table of Milton's Life and Chief Publications xvii

THE MINOR POEMS AND SAMSON AGONISTES

Edited by John Carey

Textual Introduction

1 A Paraphrase of Psalm cxiv

2 Psalm cxxxvi

3 Carmina Elegiaca [Elegiac Verses]

4 Ignavus satrapam . . . [Kings should not oversleep]

5 Philosophus ad regem . . . haec subito misit [A philosopher on his way to execution . . .]

6 Apologus de Rustico et Hero [The Fable of the Peasant and the Landlord]

7 On the Death of a Fair Infant Dying of a Cough

8 Elegia prima ad Carolum Diodatum [Elegy I, to Charles Diodati]

9 In Obitum Praesulis Eliensis [On the Death of the Bishop of Ely]

10 In Obitum Procancellarii Medici [On the Death of the Vice-Chancellor, a Doctor]

11 Elegia secunda. In Obitum Praeconis Academici Cantabrigiensis [Elegy II. On the Death of the University of Cambridge Beadle]

12 In Proditionem Bombardicam [On the Gunpowder Plot]

13 In Eandem [On the Same]

14 In Eandem [On the Same]

15 In Eandem [On the Same]

16 In Inventorem Bombardae [On the Inventor of Gunpowder]

17 In Quintum Novembris [On the Fifth of November]

18 Elegia tertia. In Obitum Praesulis Wintoniensis [Elegy III. On the Death of the Bishop of Winchester]

19 Elegia quarta. Ad Thomam Junium ... [Elegy IV. To Thomas Young ...]

20 Naturam non pati senium [That Nature does not suffer from old age]

21 De Idea Platonica quemadmodum Aristoteles intellexit [Of the Platonic Ideal Form as understood by Aristotle]

22 Elegia septima. [Elegy VII]

23 At a Vacation Exercise in the College

24 Elegia quinta. In adventum veris [Elegy V. On the Coming of Spring]

25 Sonnet I

26 Song. On May Morning

27 Sonnet II

28 Sonnet III

29 Canzone

30 Sonnet IV

31 Sonnet V

32 Sonnet VI

33 The Fifth Ode of Horace, Lib. I

34 On the Morning of Christ's Nativity

35 Elegia sexta [Elegy VI]

36 The Passion

37 On Shakespeare

38 On the University Carrier ...

39 Another on the Same

40 An Epitaph on the Marchioness of Winchester

41 L'Allegro

42 Il Penseroso

43 Sonnet VII

44 Ad Patrem [To my Father]

45 Note on Ariosto

46 Arcades

47 At a Solemn Music

48 On Time

49 Upon the Circumcision

50 Comus. A Masque presented at Ludlow Castle, 1634

51 Psalm cxiv

52 Haec ego mente ... [A post-script to his love poems]

53 Lycidas

54 Fix here

55 Ad Leonoram Romae canentem [To Leonora singing at Rome]

56 Ad Eandem [To the Same]

57 Ad Eandem [To the Same]

58 Ad Salsillum poetam Romanum ... [To Salzilli, a Roman poet ...]

59 Mansus [Manso]
60 Epitaphium Damonis [Damon's Epitaph]
61 Translations from 'Of Reformation'
62 Translation from 'Reason of Church Government'
63 Translations from 'Apology for Smectymnuus'
64 Sonnet VIII. When the assault was intended to the City
65 Sonnet X. To the Lady Margaret Ley
66 Sonnet IX
67 Translation from title-page of 'Areopagitica'
68 Translation from 'Tetrachordon'
69 In Effigiei eius Sculptor [On the Engraver of his Portrait]
70 Sonnet XIII. To Mr H. Lawes
71 Sonnet XII. On the Detraction which followed upon my Writing Certain Treatises
72 On the New Forcers of Conscience under the Long Parliament
73 Sonnet XIV
74 Ad Joannem Rousium Oxoniensis Academiae Bibliothecarium [To John Rouse, Librarian of Oxford University]
75 Sonnet XI
76 Psalms lxxx-lxxxviii
77 On the Lord General Fairfax at the Siege of Colchester
78 Translation from 'Tenure of Kings and Magistrates'
79 Translations from 'The History of Britain'
80 Epigram from 'Defensio pro Populo Anglicano'
81 To the Lord General Cromwell
82 To Sir Henry Vane the Younger
83 Sonnet XVI
84 Samson Agonistes
85 Psalms i-viii
86 Verses from 'Defensio Secunda'
87 Sonnet XVII
88 Sonnet XV. On the late Massacre in Piedmont
89 Sonnet XVIII
90 To Mr Cyriack Skinner Upon his Blindness
91 Sonnet XIX
92 From title-page of the second edition of 'The Ready and Easy Way'

PARADISE LOST

Edited by Alastair Fowler

Introduction 419

93 The Poem 457

PARADISE REGAINED

Edited by John Carey

Introduction 1063

94 The Poem 1077

Bibliography of References Cited 1168

Index of Titles and First Lines 1177

Illustrations

PLATES *facing page*

1 Milton aged 10. Oils, probably by Cornelius Janssen 202
(Courtesy of the J. Pierpont Morgan Library, New York)

2 Milton aged 21. Oils, by an unknown artist. Acquired in 1961 by the National Portrait Gallery and identified as the so-called Onslow portrait, formerly assumed lost; see David Piper, *Catalogue of Seventeenth-Century Portraits in the National Portrait Gallery, 1625–1714* 203
(Courtesy of the National Portrait Gallery)

3 *Lycidas*. From a facsimile of the Trinity manuscript 234
(Courtesy of the British Museum)

4 *Comus*. From a facsimile of the Trinity manuscript 235
(Courtesy of the British Museum)

5 *Paradise Lost*. Pierpont Morgan manuscript 1034
(Courtesy of the J. Pierpont Morgan Library, New York)

6 *Paradise Lost*. Pierpont Morgan manuscript 1035
(Courtesy of the J. Pierpont Morgan Library, New York)

7 Milton aged about 62. Engraving by William Faithorne. From *The History of Britain* 1670 1066
(Courtesy of the British Museum)

8 Bust of Milton. Plaster cast of original in Christ's College Cambridge, attributed to Edward Pierce 1067
(Courtesy of the National Portrait Gallery, London)

TEXT ILLUSTRATIONS *page*

Title page of *Poems &c.*, first edition, 1645 289
(Courtesy of the British Museum)

Title page of *Poems &c.*, second edition, 1673 290
(Courtesy of the British Museum)

Title page of *Paradise Lost*, first edition, 1667 424
(Courtesy of the British Museum)

Title page of *Paradise Lost*, second edition, 1674 425
(Courtesy of the Bodleian Library)

Preface

In preparing the text we have throughout this volume followed a somewhat unusual plan. We have modernized old spelling, but have reproduced old punctuation with diplomatic faithfulness. Usually a different, even an opposite, plan is followed. A modernized text is commonly modernized throughout; and it is even possible to find cases where an editor has retained old spelling but modernized the punctuation. But we believe that if the matter is considered in the light of linguistic theory the plan adopted in the present edition will normally appear preferable. Of course some readers need freely modernized texts, just as scholars for certain purposes need texts scrupulously diplomatic. In general, however, it is best to modernize only the spelling.

Spelling and punctuation present quite separate problems to an editor for the good reason that they have quite different functions linguistically. Punctuation, like word order, inflection and function words, is a class of grammatical symbols. It is an organic part of the grammatical system, and as such its mode of operation is subtle and complex. Not only does it obey conventions of logic but also others whereby it renders the pauses and junctures and tones of spoken language (see the emphasis laid in, e.g., D. W. Brown, W. C. Brown, and D. Bailey, *Form in Modern English* (1958) or H. Whitehall, *Structural Essentials of English* (New York 1956)). Consequently we ought to be almost as reluctant to alter the punctuation of an old text as we would be to alter, say, its word order. Moreover, punctuation is less standardized than the other types of grammatical symbol; which means that the gain from modernizing is reduced, while the difficulty of finding exactly equivalent modern conventions is increased. And unless he finds exact equivalents the modernizing editor must continually falsify the meaning (not to mention the rhythm) of the text. With subtle complex poetry such as Milton's, decisions will have to be made about tone, juncture and logical structure for which there is no basis in the punctuation of the early editions, and distinctions introduced that the poet himself may have taken care to exclude. Time and again ambiguities will have to be removed and enhancing suggestions lost. Yet even these are not all the problems with which the modernizing editor is faced. For he has next to maintain a sensible rank-ordering or relative frequency among the modern punctuation points he uses. He could make some sort of version of the meaning of *Paradise Lost*, for example, if he allowed himself a very high relative incidence of dashes or of commas. But this he may not do; since the overall effect would be breathy and talkative in the one instance, unrhythmical and pedantic in the other.

Our aim, then, has been to provide a text that retains evidential value with respect to punctuation, equally with word order and the other grammatical symbols. The cost that has to be paid for this (and we regard it as a relatively low cost) is that the reader may at first experience an occasional temporary difficulty in making out Milton's syntax. But when he overcomes the difficulty it will at least be Milton's syntax he has understood, and not the editors'.

The linguistic function of spelling is by comparison much cruder and simpler. It is not a grammatical symbol but a vocabulary symbol. That is to say, all that can generally be expected of orthographic signals is that they should enable the reader to make the right vocabulary selection. Now modern spelling is perfectly well able to do this for a seventeenth-century text. It is usually easy to find exact modern equivalents for old spellings, because orthographic signals are essentially simple binary signals. True, spelling also conveys some information about how words sound. But in English the relation between orthography and the phonetic pattern it renders is remote. Certainly with our knowledge of the pronunciation of the seventeenth century in its present state there can be few instances where the old spelling indicates the sound to a modern reader better than the new. (We have drawn attention to some of these instances in the notes.) The typical case, on which editorial practice must be based, is instead exemplified by *eternity*, *PL* viii 406, where the early editions have *eternitie*. It is probable that Milton intended a pronunciation something like *etarnity*: or perhaps even *etarrnity*, since (according to Aubrey) 'he pronounc'd the letter R very hard'. But how are we to tell this from the old spelling?

Some will object that while in general it may be all very well to treat punctuation and spelling differently, it will not do for Milton. What about his special orthographic rules and his preferences for certain current forms rather than others? A great deal of attention was focused on these matters by Helen Darbishire's and Bernard Wright's editions, in which the spelling purported to be normalized in accordance with Milton's wishes. Each text was based upon an ingenious system of idiosyncratic spellings; and between the two systems there was an impressive area of agreement. If either could be mastered, it seemed reasonable to hope for a better grasp of the intentions of the author of the spellings. The special rules of spelling and capitalization fell into five main groups (1) those distinguishing homophones; (2) those making grammatical distinctions, especially between the preterites (ending in *-d*) and past participles (in *-t*) of certain weak verbs; (3) those indicating prosodic stress; (4) those preferred for their phonetic value, etymological value, modernity, or cultural flavour; and (5) those distinguishing emphatic forms of the personal pronouns–*mee, hee, wee, yee* or *you, their*–from unemphatic *me, he, we, ye, thir*. Much of the information that could be gleaned from the special rules was, it is true, redundant; and almost all of it was complicated by doubts as to whether one was dealing with a blunder on the printer's part or a finesse on Milton's. But there were a good many places where the special rules had some bearing, even a bearing on interpretation of the meaning.

Miss Darbishire's edition, of which the first volume appeared in 1953, provoked controversy. Uneasiness was expressed at the readiness with which she attributed to Milton's printer or amanuenses only the many exceptions to the spelling rules, and not the rules themselves. Then in 1955 Robert Martin Adams's *Ikon: John Milton and the Modern Critics* questioned the whole theory of special orthography. Arguing closely on the basis of internal evidence, he seemed to many to demolish the theory, particularly with respect to the distinction between emphatic and unemphatic pronoun spellings (Adams 61–76). However, the Preface to Professor Wright's edition in 1956 set out a modified, and in some ways even more complex, system of idiosyncratic spellings. The *coup de grâce* to the special orthography theory was not delivered until 1963, by John T. Shawcross's modestly titled 'One aspect of Milton's spelling: idle final "E",' *PMLA* lxxviii (1963) 501–10. Neither Miss Darbishire nor Professor Wright had cared to test the statistical bases of their theories. But Shawcross's statistical comparison of Milton's own holograph spellings and the spellings of the printed editions showed that the latter could only reasonably be attributed to amanuenses or compositors, since they were completely at variance with Milton's own practice. The same applies to the spelling corrections at the press, including the notorious alteration of *we* to *wee* at *Paradise Lost* ii 414. The issue seems as settled now as any in literary criticism.

Accordingly we have paid no attention in the present edition to spelling variants in the early editions. The early punctuation, on the other hand, for reasons explained above, is reproduced with diplomatic faithfulness; though this should not be taken to imply that it is necessarily Milton's punctuation. In the few instances where a clear misprint in the early editions has had to be corrected, a note calls attention to the emendation.

For the rest, we have retained the early spelling of proper names, as well as of other words that have changed their form in a way that might have a bearing on sound or sense (e.g. *ammiral*; *highth*), even if the obsolete form is probably only a spelling variant. A very few obsolete words and words intended by Milton as archaisms are also inevitably given in old spelling; but the forms are those selected as commonest in *OED*, and have no evidential value. Similarly with obsolete verb terminals, which for uniformity and intelligibility are given in standard spelling, regardless of contractions and elisions, unless the modern spelling is likely to confuse the reader by suggesting an extra-metrical syllable: thus *diest* is printed for 'di'st' (*PL* vii 544) *winged* for 'wing'd' (*Comus* 729); but *Bless'd* (*Psalm i* 1) and *sat'st* (*PL* i 21). Similarly 'the' is printed for 'th''. Old hyphenated words now amalgamated are given their new form. Where old spelling indicates two words and modern spelling one, however, the old word division is kept for its potential prosodic or other interest (e.g. *mean while*). Italicization of proper names is not retained: it is a typographical accidental not found in the MSS. But a note is given where its presence or absence may have a bearing on, for example, personification.

(The above refers only to the text, and to quotations from M.'s poems. In the notes generally, the spelling and italicization of the edition cited are retained, with *v*, *u*, *i*, *j*, *s*, and *ſ* normalized in the usual way.)

Our textual policy may seem an oversimplification. But editorial policy is bound to be decided in terms of broad simple issues; even though it is a different matter with editorial practice in individual cases. And if the policy seems a compromise, this too is inevitable. For no text is completely modern unless the editor is prepared to change word order and vocabulary; and none is completely diplomatic unless he resorts to photographic facsimile (perhaps not even then). We have tried to arrive at the best practicable compromise between the demand for evidential value and the demand for readability.

In the headnotes and footnotes, the titles of works that we have had to cite fairly frequently have been abbreviated to the author's or editor's surname. Where similar abbreviation has been needed for a second, third or fourth work by the same author or editor, we have used the surname followed by the appropriate arabic numeral above the line. A list of these abbreviations will be found at pp. 1168–75.

Reference-books that we have used include: D. H. Stevens, *A Reference Guide to Milton* (Chicago, Ill. 1930); Harris F. Fletcher, *Contributions to a Milton Bibliography 1800–1930*, University of Illinois Studies in Language and Literature xvi (1931); Calvin Huckabay, *John Milton. A Bibliographical Supplement 1929–1957*, Duquesne Studies Philological Series i (1960); John Bradshaw, *A Concordance to the Poetical Works of John Milton* (1894); Lane Cooper, *A Concordance of the Latin, Greek, and Italian Poems of Milton* (Halle 1923); A. H. Gilbert, *A Geographical Dictionary of Milton* (New Haven, Conn. 1919); E. S. Le Comte, *A Milton Dictionary* (1961); J.

Milton French, *The Life Records of John Milton* (New Brunswick, N. J. 1949–58); and Harris F. Fletcher, *The Intellectual Development of John Milton*, Vols. i and ii (Urbana, Ill. 1956–61).

In preparing our edition we have greatly profited from the pertinent observations of Mr F. W. Bateson, general editor of the series of Annotated English Poets. We have received generous assistance from Professor Richard Beck of the Royal University of Malta, who placed his unpublished edition of *Paradise Regained* at our disposal. Learned advice as well as kindly interest was offered by Mrs E. E. Duncan-Jones of Birmingham University; Mr George Merton; Mr B. D. H. Miller, the Revd L. M. Styler, Mr D. L. Stockton and Mr J. V. Peach of Brasenose College; and Mr J. C. Maxwell of Balliol College. For instruction on some points in Milton's Greek and Italian poems and translations from Hebrew we applied to Mr W. S. Barrett of Keble College, Professor C. Grayson of Magdalen and the Revd L. H. Brockington of Wolfson. We should like to express our gratitude to each. The remaining errors, needless to say, are ours.

St. John's College J. C.
Brasenose College A. D. S. F.
Oxford
August 1966

In the present edition we have had an opportunity to make a number of corrections, some of them affecting the text. We owe many of these improvements to the vigilance and kindness of scholars who have communicated information: particularly Masahiko Agari, Gordon Campbell and Jasper Griffin.

Oxford J. C.
Edinburgh A. D. S. F.
August 1979

Abbreviations

The following abbreviations will be found, in addition to standard abbreviations for books of the Bible, classical works and literary periodicals.

1637 = *A Maske Presented at Ludlow Castle* (1637).
1645 = *Poems of Mr John Milton* (1645).
Ed I = *Paradise Lost.* First edition (1667).
1671 = *Paradise Regain'd. A Poem in IV Books. To which is added Samson Agonistes* (1671).
1673 = *Poems, &c. Upon Several Occasions* (1673).
Ed II = *Paradise Lost.* Second edition (1674).
Trin. MS = The Trinity Manuscript.
MS = The Manuscript of *Paradise Lost* i.

Ad Pat = *Ad Patrem.*
Dam = *Epitaphium Damonis*
Id Plat = *De Idea Platonica quemadmodum Aristoteles intellexit.*
Leon = *Ad Leonoram Romae canentem.*
Natur = *Naturam non pati senium.*
PL = *Paradise Lost.*
PR = *Paradise Regained.*
Prae E = *In obitum Praesulis Eliensis.*
Proc Med = *In obitum Procancellarii medici.*
Prod Bomb = *In Proditionem Bombardicam.*
Prol = *Prolusion.*
Q Nov = *In quintum Novembris.*
SA = *Samson Agonistes.*
Salsill = *Ad Salsillum poetam Romanum aegrotantem. Scazontes.*

Columbia = *The Works of John Milton*, ed. F. A. Patterson *et al.* (New York 1931–8).
EB = *Encyclopaedia Britannica.* Eleventh edition (1910–11).
F.Q. = *The Faerie Queene.*
Migne = *Patrologia Latina*, ed. J. P. Migne (Paris 1844–55).
Migne *P. G.* = *Patrologia Graeca*, ed. J. P. Migne (Paris 1857–66).
Yale = *The Complete Prose Works of John Milton*, ed. Douglas Bush *et al.* (New Haven 1953–).

Selected Journal Abbreviations

AR	*American Review*
CQ	*Classical Quarterly*
E & S	*Essays and Studies by Members of the English Association*
EC	*Essays in Criticism*
ELH	*A Journal of English Literary History*
EM	*English Miscellany*
HLQ	*Huntington Library Quarterly*
JEGP	*Journal of English and Germanic Philology*
JHI	*Journal of the History of Ideas*
JWI	*Journal of the Warburg and Courtauld Institutes*
KR	*Kenyon Review*
MLN	*Modern Language Notes*
MLQ	*Modern Language Quarterly*
MLR	*Modern Language Review*
N & Q	*Notes and Queries*
PMLA	*PMLA: Publications of the Modern Language Association of America*
PQ	*Philological Quarterly*
RES	*Review of English Studies*
SP	*Studies in Philology*
TLS	*The Times Literary Supplement*
TRSL	*Transactions of the Royal Society of Literature*
UTQ	*University of Toronto Quarterly*
UTSE	*University of Texas Studies in English*

Chronological Table of Milton's Life and Chief Publications

1608 (*9 December*) Born at his father's house, The Spreadeagle, Bread St, London.

1615 (*24 November*) Brother Christopher born.

1618 Portrait painted by Cornelius Janssen.

1620 Enters St Paul's School, under Alexander Gill. The date is uncertain: some would put it as early as 1615, but see *Defensio Secunda* 'after I was 12 years old I rarely retired to bed from my studies till midnight' (Columbia viii 119). Friendship with Charles Diodati begins. Either now, or earlier, begins to receive tuition at home from, among others, Thomas Young.

1625 (*12 February*) Admitted to Christ's College, Cambridge, under tutorship of Chappell.

1626 Perhaps rusticated temporarily. Removed to tutorship of Tovey.

1627 Unpopular with fellow-students: dissatisfied with Cambridge syllabus (see *Prolusions* i, iii and iv, Columbia xii 118–49, 158–99 Yale i 218–33, 240–56).

(*11 June*) Lends future father-in-law, Richard Powell, £500.

1628 (*June*) Writes verses for one of his College fellows (*Id Plat*?).

1629 So-called Onslow-portrait painted, also portrait painted by unknown artist (now in Christ's College).

(*26 March*) Takes B.A.

1630 Portrait, said to be M., painted by Daniel Mytens (now in St Paul's School: the date is uncertain).

(*16 April*) Charles Diodati matriculates at Geneva.

(*10 June*) Edward King given a fellowship which it has been assumed (without evidence) M. expected or desired.

1631 (*November*) Brother Christopher admitted to Inner Temple.

1632 *On Shakespeare* published.

(*3 July*) Takes M.A.

Retires to Horton for life of study; see *Defensio Secunda* 'I left with most of the fellows of the College, by whom I had been cultivated with more than indifference, a regretful desire for my presence. At my father's house in the country, to which he had gone to pass his old age, I gave myself up with the most complete leisure to reading through the Greek and Latin writers; with this proviso, however, that I occasionally exchanged the country for the town, for the sake of buying books or of learning something new in mathematics or music, in which I then delighted' (Columbia viii 120).

1634 (*29 September*) *Comus* acted.

1637 *Comus* published.

(*3 April*) Mother dies.

(*September*) Thinking of entering an Inn of Court (see letter to Diodati dated 29 September, Columbia xii 28, Yale i 327).

1638 *Lycidas* printed in *Justa Edouardo King Naufrago*.

(*1 February*) Lends Sir John Cope and others £150 at 8 per cent.

(*April*) Meets Sir Henry Wotton; is kindly treated (see Wotton's letter to M., Columbia i 476–7, Yale i 339–43).

(*May*) Sails for France; meets John, Viscount Scudamore, in Paris; calls on Hugo Grotius.

(*June–July*) To Nice, Genoa, Leghorn, Pisa.

(*27 August*) Charles Diodati buried.

(*August–September*) Arrives in Florence; makes friends (see *Defensio Secunda* 'There I quickly contracted intimacy with many truly noble and learned men. I also assiduously attended their private academies, an institution which is most highly to be praised there ... Time shall never efface the memory of you, James Gaddi, Charles Dati, Frescobaldi, Cultellino, Bonmatthei, Clementillo, Francini, and numerous others', Columbia viii 122). Visits Galileo (see *Areopagitica*, Columbia iv 329–30).

(*October*) To Siena, Rome. Meets Lucas Holstein, one of the Vatican librarians. Attends Barberini concert. Entertained in English College.

(*December*) To Naples. Meets Manso.

1639 Receives news of Diodati's death. Gives up plan of crossing to Sicily and Greece (see *Defensio Secunda* 'The sad news of the English civil war recalled me; for I thought it shameful, while my countrymen were fighting for their liberty at home, that I should be peacefully travelling for culture', Columbia viii 124).

(*January–February*) Revisits Rome.

(*March*) Returns to Florence. Again reads poems at Svogliati academy.

(*April*) Excursion to Lucca (home of Diodati family). To Bologna, Ferrara, Venice (stays a month, and ships parcel of books home).

(*May*) To Verona and Milan. Travels through Lombardy.

(*June*) Visits theologian John Diodati in Geneva (uncle of Charles)

(*July*) Returns home.

1640 Moves to St Bride's churchyard: begins tutoring nephews. Takes 'a large house' to contain self, books and pupils, who include 'the Earl of Barrimore ... Sir Thomas Gardiner of Essex, and others' (Darbishire 24–5).
Occasionally leaves this secluded 'pretty Garden-House ... in Aldersgate-Street, at the end of an Entry' and drops 'into the society of some young sparks of his acquaintance, the chief whereof were Mr Alphry, and Mr Miller, two Gentlemen of Gray's-Inn, the Beaus of those times,' with whom he likes to 'keep a Gawdy-day' (Darbishire 62).
Poem on Hobson printed in *A Banquet of Jests.*
Epitaphium Damonis printed? The first edition is undated but probably belongs to 1640.
(*30 June*) Takes Powell's lands in Wheatley by mortgage.

1641 (*May*) *Of Reformation* published.
Of Prelatical Episcopacy published.
(*July*) *Animadversions* published.

1642 (*February*) *The Reason of Church Government* published.
(*May?*) *Apology For Smectymnuus* published. Marries Mary Powell ('At Whitsuntide it was, or a little after, that he took a Journey into the Country; no body about him certainly knowing the Reason: ... after a Month's stay, home he returns a Married-man, that went out a Batchelor', Darbishire 63).
(*July?*) Mary returns home.
(*October?*) M. sends for her without success.
(*21 October*) Brother Christopher's name on Reading muster-roll: supporting Royal cause.

1643 Brother-in-law Richard Powell doing intelligence work for Royalists.
(*1 August*) *Doctrine and Discipline of Divorce* published.

1644 (*2 February*) *Doctrine and Discipline of Divorce* (second edition) published.
(*5 June*) Tract *Of Education* published. About this time M.'s attempts to seize the Powell property for debt begin: they continue till 16 July 1647, when he obtains the writ he requires.
(*6 August*) *Judgment of Martin Bucer Concerning Divorce* published.
(*13 August*) Divorce books attacked by Herbert Palmer in sermon before Parliament.
(*24–26 August*) Stationers petition against his divorce books.
(*September*) Begins to notice failure of sight (cp. letter to Philaras, 28 September 1654, Columbia xii 66).
(*23 November*) *Areopagitica* published.

(*28 December*) Summoned before the House of Lords for examination: 'soon dismissed' (Darbishire 24).

1645 Plans to marry 'one of Dr Davis's Daughters, a very Handsome and Witty Gentlewoman' (Darbishire 66). Wife returns.

(*4 March*) *Tetrachordon* and *Colasterion* published.

(*September?*) Moves to larger house at Barbican.

(*6 October*) *Poems of Mr John Milton, Both English and Latin . . . 1645* registered for publication.

1646 (*2 January*) *Poems . . . 1645* published.

(*29 July*) Daughter Anne born.

1647 (*1 January*) Father-in-law Richard Powell dies.

(*13 March*) Father dies, leaving M. the Bread St house and a 'moderate Estate' (Darbishire 32–3).

(*16 July*) Obtains extent on Powell's property in Oxfordshire.

(*September-October*) Moves from Barbican to a smaller house in High Holborn 'among those that open backward into Lincolns-Inn Fields, here he liv'd a private and quiet Life, still prosecuting his Studies and curious Search into Knowledge' (Darbishire 68).

(*20 November*) Takes possession of Powell property at Wheatley.

1648 (*25 October*) Daughter Mary born.

1649 (*13 February*) *Tenure of Kings and Magistrates* published.

(*13 March*) Invited to be Secretary for the Foreign Tongues by the Council of State.

(*15 March*) Appointed Secretary (at £288 p.a.). Ordered to answer *Eikon Basilike.*

(*11 May*) Salmasius's *Defensio Regia* appears in England.

(*16 May*) *Observations on the Articles of Peace* published.

(*6 October*) *Eikonoklastes* published.

(*19 November*) Given lodgings for official work in Scotland Yard.

1650 (*8 January*) Ordered by Council of State to reply to Salmasius.

1651 (*24 February*) *Defensio pro populo Anglicano* published.

(*16 March*) Son John born.

(*17 December*) Moves, for the sake of health, to 'a pretty Garden-house in Petty-France in Westminster . . . opening into St James's Park' (Darbishire 71).

1652 (*28 February*) Becomes totally blind at about this date.

(*2 May*) Daughter Deborah born.

(*5 May*) Wife dies.

(*16 June*) Son John dies on or about this date.

(*August*) Pierre du Moulin's *Regii Sanguinis Clamor* published, in reply to M.'s *Defensio*. M. ordered to reply by Council of State.

1653 (*21 February*) Writes letter recommending Andrew Marvell to John Bradshaw (this is the first evidence of M.'s acquaintance with Marvell).
(*3 September*) Salmasius dies.

1654 (*30 May*) *Defensio Secunda* published.

1655 Allowed substitute in Secretaryship (Darbishire 28). Takes up private studies again. Starts compiling Latin dictionary and Greek lexicon; works on *De Doctrina*, and possibly on *Paradise Lost* (Darbishire 29).
(*17 April*) Salary reduced from £288 to £150, but made pension for life.
(*8 August*) *Defensio Pro Se* published.

1656 (*12 November*) Marries Katherine Woodcock.

1657 (*19 October*) Daughter Katherine born.

1658 (*14 January*) Lends Thomas Maundy £500 and takes mortgage on property in Kensington as security.
(*3 February*) Wife dies.
(*17 March*) Daughter Katherine dies.
(*May?*) Edits and publishes his MS of Sir Walter Raleigh's *Cabinet Council*.

1659 (*16 February?*) *A Treatise of Civil Power* published.
(*August*) *The Likeliest Means to Remove Hirelings out of the Church* published.
(*20 October*) Writes *Letter to a Friend, Concerning the Ruptures of the Commonwealth* (not published until 1698).

1660 (*3 March*) *Ready and Easy Way to Establish a Free Commonwealth* published.
(*April*) Publishes *Brief Notes Upon a late Sermon* in reply to Matthew Griffith's *Fear of God and the King*.
(*May*) Goes into hiding in friend's house in Bartholomew Close to escape retaliation (Darbishire 74).
(*16 June*) Parliament takes steps to have M. arrested and *Defensio pro populo Anglicano* and *Eikonoklastes* burned.
(*27 August*) Copies of M.'s books burned by hangman in London.
(*29 August*) Act of Indemnity does not exclude M.
(*September*) Takes house in Holborn, near Red Lion Fields. Moves from there to Jewin St (Darbishire 74–5).
(*October?*) Arrested, and imprisoned.
(*15 December*) Parliament orders that M. should be released.
(*17 December*) Andrew Marvell protests in Parliament about M.'s excessive jail fees (£150).

1662 Becomes acquainted with Thomas Ellwood: begins tutoring him (see *The History of the Life of Thomas Ellwood*, ed. C. G. Crump (1900) 88–90).

(*June?*) Sonnet to Sir Henry Vane published.

1663 On bad terms with children: 'a former Maidservant of his told Mary one of the deceased's [M.'s] Daughters . . . that shee heard the deceased was to be marryed, to which the said Mary replyed . . . that that was noe News to Heare of his wedding but if shee could heare of his death that was something, – and further told this Respondent that all his said Children did combine together and counsell his Maidservant to cheat him . . . in her Markettings, and that his said children had made away some of his bookes and would have sold the rest of his bookes to the Dunghill women' (from Elizabeth Fisher's deposition on M.'s will, 15 December 1674, French iv 374–5).

(*24 February*) Marries Elizabeth Minshull.

(*February?*) Moves from Jewin St to 'a House in the Artillery-walk leading to Bunhill Fields' (Darbishire 75). New wife allegedly severe to M.'s daughters, 'the two eldest of whom she bound prentices to Workers in Gold-Lace, without his knowledge; and forc'd the younger to leave his Family' (from a letter of Thomas Birch, 17 November 1750, French iv 388).

1665 (*June?*) Thomas Ellwood takes house for M. in Chalfont St Giles, to avoid plague.

1666 (*2–6 September*) House in Bread St destroyed by fire.

1667 (*August?*) *Paradise Lost* published.

1669 (*June*) *Accedence Commenced Grammar* published.

1670 Portrait by William Faithorne.

(*November?*) *History of Britain* published.

1671 *Paradise Regained* and *Samson Agonistes* published.

1672 (*May?*) *Art of Logic* published.

1673 (*May?*) *Of True Religion* published.

(*November?*) *Poems, &c. upon Several Occasions . . . 1673* published.

1674 (*May*) *Epistolae Familiares* and *Prolusiones* published.

(*6 July?*) Second edition of *Paradise Lost* published.

(*8–10 November*) Dies in Bunhill house. The exact date is not known.

(*12 November*) Buried in St Giles, Cripplegate.

The Minor Poems
and *Samson Agonistes*

Edited by

JOHN CAREY

Textual Introduction: the Minor Poems, *Samson Agonistes* and *Paradise Regained*

There were two editions of M.'s collected minor poems in his lifetime: *1645* and *1673*. In *1673* thirty-two poems were added: 6 (*Apologus de Rustico et Hero*), 7 (*Fair Infant*), 23 (*Vacation Exercise*), 33 (*The Fifth Ode of Horace*), 70 (*Sonnet XIII*), 71 (*Sonnet XII*), 72 (*On the New Forcers of Conscience*), 73 (*Sonnet XIV*), 74 (*Ad Joannem Rousium*), 75 (*Sonnet XI*), 76 (*Psalms lxxx–lxxxviii*), 83 (*Sonnet XVI*), 85 (*Psalms i–viii*), 87 (*Sonnet XVII*), 88 (*Sonnet XV*), 89 (*Sonnet XVIII*), 91 (*Sonnet XIX*). For these poems *1673* is the only authoritative text, and has been followed.

The other poems in *1673* appeared also in *1645*. In twenty-three of them (1, 10, 12–16, 19, 21, 25, 28, 29, 35, 37, 38, 49, 51, 52, 55–57, 59, 69) the two texts do not vary significantly. There remain, however, thirty-six poems in which significant differences between the *1645* and *1673* texts occur. Which should be followed? The differences are not numerous, and usually involve punctuation, not words. It is clear that the poems in *1673* which are common to both editions were set up from a copy of *1645*. This would be a reason for following *1645*. There are variants, however, which indicate that at some time the copy of *1645* used was corrected by M. or under his direction (the most obvious are at *Nativity Ode* 143–4 and *Solemn Music* 6). If some of *1673*'s divergences from *1645* are evidently M.'s, it would appear unsafe to assume, without evidence to the contrary, that all are not.

It has been claimed that such evidence is particularly strong in *L'Allegro* 104, and in *Comus* 166–8 and 546. In the first of these instances *1645* introduces a new subject after the 'She' of l. 103, reading 'And he by friar's lantern led', where *1673* reads 'And by the friar's lantern led' making the girl tell the story of Robin Goodfellow and his cream-bowl, as well as that about Fairy Mab and the junkets. Perhaps the kitchen-detail of the cream-bowl made the tale seem more suitable for a girl; and Jonson, in a passage M. may have remembered, associated Robin Goodfellow's 'drudgerie' with country maids (see l. 105*n*). At any rate there seems as much to be said for the *1673* reading as for that of *1645*, and I have retained it. It seems possible, too, to defend the *1673* version of *Comus* 166–8 (see note), as representing M.'s final intention, particularly in view of the attitude he had developed towards 'the jingling sound of like endings'. In *Comus* 546, however, where *1645*'s 'meditate' becomes 'meditate upon', it seems likely that the *1673* printer has automatically followed English idiom, though M., as at *Lycidas* 66 (see note) is imitating Latin. Here I have adopted the *1645* reading.

Some have argued that since M. was blind in *1673* he could not have supervised the printing efficiently, and so *1645* should always be followed except in cases of indisputably Miltonic emendation. This objection to *1673* is weakened by the fact that at *In Quintum Novembris* 149–50 (where *1673* reads *Perpetuoque leves per muta silentia Manes / Exululat, tellus & sanguine conscia stagnat.*) the *1673 Errata* calls for 'a Comma after *Manes*, none after *Exululat*'. *1645* had read *Exululant* at the beginning of 150. The change to the singular *Exululat* in *1673* means that *Manes*, which had been the subject of this verb, becomes one of the subjects of a previous verb, *videntur* (l. 147), and *tellus* becomes the subject of *Exululat* (as of *stagnat*). The *Errata* removes the comma before *tellus* which would otherwise separate the new subject from its verb. One way of explaining these alterations would be to say that *1645*'s *Exululant* was the correct reading, that the *1673* compositor misprinted *Exululat*, and that some hasty reader undirected by M., perhaps Edward Phillips, getting together a list of *Errata*, noticed *tellus* divided from the nearest singular verb by a comma, assumed it was the subject of that verb, and shifted the comma. The trouble with this explanation is that whoever got together the *1673 Errata* list must surely have had the *1645* copy from which *1673* was set up, or at any rate some copy of *1645*, at hand. A quick glance at this would have shown him that there was no need to move the comma: all he had to do in the *Errata* list was restore the *1645* reading. That no such action was in fact taken makes it difficult to believe that anyone but M. was originally responsible for the change from plural to singular in the verb, and consequent change of meaning, in *1673*. Since the punctuation given in the *1673 Errata* list supports this change, the inference is that the compiler of the list was acting in accordance with M.'s wishes, and this suggests that M. was too closely connected with the production of *1673* for any editor to jettison *1673* variants even when there is superficially little to choose between *1645* and *1673* readings.

For these reasons I have adopted *1673* as copy text for all poems appearing in it, but have abandoned it for *1645* in the few places where the arguments for that text seem conclusive, as, for example, when a word has obviously been garbled by the *1673* compositor (e.g. 14 l. 4, where *1673* prints the impossible *corona* for *1645*'s *cornua*). I have also left *1673* on a few occasions when its punctuation, compared with that of *1645*, seriously hampers the modern reader's understanding of M.'s meaning (e.g. 17 l. 43, where *1673*'s full stop after *possunt* divides the subject from the rest of the sentence). Any such divergences from the copy text are clearly indicated in the *Publication* section of the headnote of each poem.

In the same section of the headnote I have listed all *1645* variants. In each case the reading adopted in the text is given first, and then the variant in the edition under discussion. For example, in the headnote to 2:

Publication. 1645 (*10.* Who]That *similarly 13, 17, 21 and 25*) means that *1645* reads 'That' in the lines specified where my text (following *1673*) reads 'Who'.

Of the poems in both *1645* and *1673* five had appeared in print before 1645: 37 (*On Shakespeare*), 39 (the second Hobson poem), 50 (*Comus*), 53 (*Lycidas*) and 60 (*Epitaphium Damonis*). The pre-*1645* text of the second of these (see headnote) is incomplete and of no authority. For the others I have listed in the *Publication* section of each headnote all verbal variants of the pre-*1645* texts, and summarized the punctuation variants (of which full details may be found in Fletcher[3]).

Of the minor poems in neither *1645* nor *1673*, four (3, 4, 45 and 54) were not printed in the seventeenth century, and are printed here from M.'s autograph. Ten (61–63, 67, 68, 78–80, 86, 92) were first printed in various of M.'s prose works, and the text followed here is that of the first editions of those works. Three (77, 81, 90) were first printed, in poor versions, in Edward Phillips's edition of the *Letters of State* (1694). They also exist, however, in fair copies in the Trinity MS, which the present text follows. The remaining poem (82) was first printed in George Sikes's *Life and Death of Sir Henry Vane* (1662), which the present text follows.

Several of M.'s early poems are found, some in more than one version, in the Trinity MS, either in his own hand or that of an amanuensis. *Comus* is also in the Bridgewater MS. The footnotes of the present edition give full details of the verbal variants of each MS version (though not of punctuation variants, since the punctuation of the MSS is so sparse that this would multiply footnotes excessively), and also of all MS corrections and deletions. In doing this, the following conventions have been used: *italics* denote that the item italicized is crossed out in the MS; SMALL CAPITALS denote that the crossed-out item has later been reinstated in the MS; insertion marks \ / denote that the item between them has been inserted in the MS; square brackets and dots [. . .] denote that a section has been cut or torn away from the MS. E.g. *Comus* 4–5:

> *Trin. MS*: Amidst the *gardens*/ Hesperian gardens, ON WHOSE BANKS *where the banks*/

means that 'gardens' has been inserted into the line, then deleted; and that 'on whose banks' has been deleted and 'where the banks' substituted, then 'where the banks' deleted and 'on whose banks' reinstated. In *Comus* 79:

Trin. MS: adventu` ` 'rous

means that the 'u' of 'adventurous' has been deleted in the MS and an apostrophe inserted.

Samson Agonistes and *Paradise Regained* were published together in 1671. This was the only edition in M.'s lifetime. The present text follows it.

J.C.

1 A Paraphrase on Psalm cxiv

Date. 1624. Headnote in *1645* reads: 'This and the following Psalm were done by the Author at fifteen years old.'
Publication. *1645* and *1673* (no significant variants).
Modern criticism. Metrical versions of the psalms became so common in the late sixteenth and early seventeenth centuries (206 versions of the complete psalter were published between 1600 and 1653) that something approaching a traditional phraseology grew up. M. H. Studley, *PQ* iv (1925) 364–72, examines the effect of this on M. (see headnote to *Psalms lxxx–lxxxviii* p. 306 below). M.'s ignorance of Hebrew in 1624 forced him to depend on previous translations, among them, probably, Buchanan's Latin metrical psalter (1566). For M.'s translation of this psalm into Greek see p. 229 below.

When the blest seed of Terah's faithful son,
After long toil their liberty had won,
And passed from Pharian fields to Canaan land,
Led by the strength of the Almighty's hand,
Jehovah's wonders were in Israel shown,
His praise and glory was in Israel known.
That saw the troubled sea, and shivering fled,
And sought to hide his froth-becurled head
Low in the earth, Jordan's clear streams recoil,
As a faint host that hath received the foil.
The high, huge-bellied mountains skip like rams
Amongst their ewes, the little hills like lambs.

¶ 1. *1. faithful son*] Abraham–an example of faith in *Heb*. xi 8–9: *faithful* has particular force–Terah was an idolater.
3. Pharian] Egyptian. Sylvester (Du Bartas 14) coined the adj. from Pharos, the island off Alexandria. Buchanan's Latin has *arva Phari* here.
8–9. Echoing Sylvester (Du Bartas[2] 954): 'Cleer Jordan's Selfe . . . was fain to hide his head.'
10. foil] defeat.

Why fled the ocean? And why skipped the mountains?
Why turned Jordan toward his crystal fountains?
Shake earth, and at the presence be aghast
Of him that ever was, and ay shall last,
That glassy floods from rugged rocks can crush,
And make soft rills from fiery flint-stones gush.

2 Psalm cxxxvi

Date. 1624: see headnote to previous poem.
Publication. *1645* (*10.* Who] That *similarly 13, 17, 21 and 25*), and *1673* (the text followed here, except in *65* where *1673* misprints a full stop after 'host').
Modern criticism. W. B. Hunter observes, *PQ* xxviii (1949) 141, that though each line should contain four iambic feet the unstressed syllable in the first foot is frequently lacking. This is also found in *L'Allegro* and *Il Penseroso* but, Hunter remarks, there are no comparable examples in the Puritan psalters.

Let us with a gladsome mind
Praise the Lord, for he is kind
  For his mercies ay endure,
  Ever faithful, ever sure.

Let us blaze his name abroad,
For of gods he is the God;
  For, &c.

O let us his praises tell,
Who doth the wrathful tyrants quell.
  For, &c.

Who with his miracles doth make
Amazed heaven and earth to shake.
  For, &c.

Who by his wisdom did create
The painted heavens so full of state.
  For, &c.

14. Echoing Sylvester (Du Bartas 61): 'Toward the Crystall of his double source / Compelled Jordan to retreat.'
17. Sylvester has 'glassie' (Du Bartas 59) as epithet for water, and 'crush/gush' rhyme (Du Bartas 38) in a description of rain.

Who did the solid earth ordain
To rise above the watery plain.
  For, &c.

Who by his all-commanding might,
Did fill the new-made world with light.
  For, &c.

And caused the golden-tressed sun,
All the day long his course to run.
  For, &c.

The horned moon to shine by night,
Amongst her spangled sisters bright.
  For, &c.

He with his thunder-clasping hand,
Smote the first-born of Egypt land.
  For, &c.

And in despite of Pharaoh fell,
He brought from thence his Israel.
  For, &c.

The ruddy waves he cleft in twain,
Of the Erythraean main.
  For, &c.

The floods stood still like walls of glass,
While the Hebrew bands did pass.
  For, &c.

¶ 2. *22. watery plain*] Found in Spenser, *F.Q.* IV xi 24, Drayton, *Polyolbion* xv 110, and Phineas Fletcher, *Purple Island* iii 28.
29. golden-tressed] Sylvester gives the sun 'golden tresses' (Du Bartas 107, 452). Buchanan's Latin translation has *solem auricomum* here.
33–4. In Sylvester the moon is frequently 'horned' (Du Bartas 51, 103) and the stars 'spangles' (Du Bartas 17, 91). Shakespeare has stars which 'spangle heaven' (*Taming of Shrew* IV v 31) and 'spangled starlight' (*Midsummer Night's Dream* II i 29). 'Horned moone' occurs in Spenser, *F.Q.* IV vi 43.
41–2. Sylvester calls Pharaoh's hands 'fell' (Du Bartas 453), and rhymes 'fell / Israel' (Du Bartas 447, 473, 598).
46. Erythraean] Adjective from Greek, ἐρυθρός (red), used by Herodotus, i 180, ii 8 and 158, to denominate the Red Sea. Sylvester makes God's voice 'cleave the bottom of th' *Erythraean* Deepe' (Du Bartas 61), and refers to 'the *Erythraean* ruddy Billowes' (Du Bartas[2] 967).
49. In Sylvester the Red Sea divides to form 'Two Walls of Glass' (Du Bartas 454)

But full soon they did devour
The tawny king with all his power.
For, &c.

His chosen people he did bless
In the wasteful wilderness.
For, &c.

In bloody battle he brought down
Kings of prowess and renown.
For, &c.

He foiled bold Seon and his host,
That ruled the Amorean coast.
For, &c.

And large-limbed Og he did subdue,
With all his over-hardy crew.
For, &c.

And to his servant Israel,
He gave their land therein to dwell.
For, &c.

He hath with a piteous eye
Beheld us in our misery.
For, &c.

And freed us from the slavery
Of the invading enemy.
For, &c.

All living creatures he doth feed,
And with full hand supplies their need.
For, &c.

Let us therefore warble forth
His mighty majesty and worth.
For, &c.

53–4. Echoing Sylvester's 'But contrarie the Red-sea did devower / The barbrous tyrant with his mighty power' (Du Bartas 21).
54. tawny king] Fairfax's translation of Tasso iii 38 has 'Affrikes tawnie kings'.
65–6. Buchanan's Latin translation has *Amorrhaeum* . . . *Seonem* here and *Quique Amorrhaeis Seon regnavit in oris* in *Ps.* cxxxv. Sylvester uses 'Ammorrean' for Amorite (Du Bartas 372).
89. Sylvester has 'warble forth' (Du Bartas 1).

That his mansion hath on high
Above the reach of mortal eye.
For his mercies ay endure,
Ever faithful, ever sure.

3 *Carmina Elegiaca*

[Elegiac Verses]

Date. 1624? The verses were discovered *c.* 1874 by A. J. Horwood at Netherby Hall, Longtown, Cumberland. The MS leaf on which they are written bears M.'s name and contains also *Ignavus satrapam* . . . (p. 11) and the prose theme on early rising (Columbia xii 288–91). Horwood found the leaf among the papers of Sir Frederick Graham, loose in the same box as M.'s Commonplace Book. H. C. H. Candy has argued that the leaf is autograph in *Library* xv (1934–5) 330–9 and prints a reproduction of part of it. There is an autotype reproduction in the Public Record Office (Autotypes Milton &c./Fac. 6/Library/Shelf 156a), and a photograph of this autotype in the BM (Add. MS 41063 I, ff 84–5).

Reasons for regarding the contents of the leaf as grammar-school exercises, belonging to M.'s St Paul's days, are given by Clark (178–80, 230–7), and by Maurice Kelley and D. C. Mackenzie (Yale i 1034–6).

Publication. First printed in Horwood 62–3. The text printed below follows M.'s autograph. Note the scanty punctuation.

Surge, age surge, leves, iam convenit, excute somnos,
Lux oritur, tepidi fulcra relinque tori
Iam canit excubitor gallus praenuntius ales
Solis et invigilans ad sua quemque vocat
Flammiger Eois Titan caput exserit undis
Et spargit nitidum laeta per arva iubar
Daulias argutum modulatur ab ilice carmen
Edit et excultos mitis alauda modos
Iam rosa fragrantes spirat silvestris odores
Iam redolent violae luxuriatque seges

¶ 3. *1. excute*] M. first wrote *arcere*, then inserted *excute* over the top, without deleting *arcere*.

7. Daulias] The swallow, which Ovid calls *Daulias ales* (*Her.* xv 154) because Daulis, a city of Phocis, was celebrated as the scene of the fable of Tereus, Philomela and Progne (*Met.* vi 438–674), at the end of which Progne is turned into a swallow.

Ecce novo campos Zephyritis gramine vestit
  Fertilis, et vitreo rore madescit humus
Segnes invenias molli vix talia lecto
  Cum premat imbellis lumina fessa sopor
Illic languentes abrumpunt somnia somnos
  Et turbant animum tristia multa tuum
Illic tabifici generantur semina morbi
  Qui pote torpentem posse valere virum
Surge age surge, leves, iam convenit, excute somnos
  Lux oritur, tepidi fulcra relinque tori.

Get up, come on, get up! It's time! Shake off these worthless slumbers: it's getting light. Come on out from between the posts of that warm bed. The cock's crowing already: the guardsman cock: the bird that forewarns us of sunrise. He's wide awake and calling everyone to work. Fiery Titan is rearing his head above the eastern waves, and flinging bright sunlight over the gay fields. From her oak-tree perch the Daulian bird[7] trills a piercing song, and the gentle lark is pouring forth exquisite harmonies. Now the wild rose breathes out sweet perfumes; now violets scent the air, and the standing corn frisks and dances. Look, fruit-bringing Venus[11] is decking out the fields in fresh turf, and watering the ground with dew as bright as glass. You sluggard, you're not likely to find such sights as these in that downy bed of yours, where feeble lethargy closes your tired eyes. There your idle slumbers are racked by dreams, and a host of griefs troubles your spirit. That is where the germs of corroding disease are bred! How can an inactive man be healthy? Get up, come on, get up! It's time! Shake off these worthless slumbers: it's getting light. Come on out from between the posts of that warm bed.

4 *Ignavus satrapam . . .*

[Kings should not oversleep]

Date. 1624? See headnote to previous poem: these lines appear on the MS leaf directly beneath *Carmina Elegiaca*, without a separate heading. The metre is the Lesser Asclepiad.
Publication. First printed in Horwood 63. The text printed below follows M.'s autograph.

11. Zephyritis] Venus. Arsinoe, Ptolemy II's queen, was deified, identified with Aphrodite, and given a temple on the promontory of Zephyrium east of Alexandria, from which she took the title Aphrodite Zephyritis. M. probably found the name in Catullus lxvi 57 (a translation from Callimachus's *Aetia* IV cx), where Zephyrus, the west wind, appears as Aphrodite-Arsinoe's attendant.
15. somnos] M. first wrote, in error, *somnum.*
19. excute] M. first wrote *arcere,* then deleted it and inserted *excute.*

Ignavus satrapam dedecet inclytum
Somnus qui populo multifido praeest.
Dum Dauni veteris filius armiger
Stratus purpureo procubuit strato
Audax Euryalus, Nisus et impiger
Invasere cati nocte sub horrida
Torpentes Rutilos castraque Volscia
Hinc caedes oritur clamor et absonus.

To a famous governor, who is responsible for the many and various concerns of a nation, idle slumber is a disgrace. While old Daunus's soldier son[3] lay stretched in his luxurious bed, bold Euryalus and energetic Nisus craftily attacked the Volscian camp and the drowsy Rutilians, under cover of thick darkness. The result: slaughter and a confused clamour.

5 *Philosophus ad regem quendam qui eum ignotum et insontem inter reos forte captum inscius damnaverat* τὴν ἐπὶ θανάτῳ πορευόμενος, *haec subito misit.*

[A philosopher on his way to execution sent these impromptu verses to a certain king who had unknowingly condemned him to death when he happened to be taken prisoner–unrecognized and innocent–in the company of some criminals]

Date. 1624? There is no certain evidence. Clark 206 suggests that this epigram may have been written to 'fulfill the requirements of a moral theme in Greek verse, if such an assignment were imposed on M. in the Eighth Form' at St Paul's. If not written at school the epigram must be post-1634 (see *Psalm cxiv* headnote, p. 229). W. R. Parker (Taylor[2] 128–9) dates between Dec. 1634 and 1638 (on the assumption that the order of poems in *1645* corresponds to the order of composition). He adds 'the poem could indirectly allude to Gill's unfortunate clash with Laud and the Star Chamber, and his subsequent pardon by King Charles (Nov. 30, 1630)'.
Publication. 1645 (4. *Μαψιδίως*] *Μὰψ αὔτως*   *τεὸν πρὸς θυμὸν ὀδυρῇ*]

¶ 4. *3. Dauni . . . filius*] Turnus, whose camp is attacked by Nisus and Euryalus in *Aen.* ix 176–449.

χρόνῳ μάλα πολλὸν ὀδύρῃ 5. πόλιος] πόλεως) 1673 (the text followed here).

> *Ὦ ἄνα εἰ ὀλέσῃς με τὸν ἔννομον, οὐδέ τιν᾽ ἀνδρῶν*
> *Δεινὸν ὅλως δράσαντα, σοφώτατον ἴσθι κάρηνον*
> *Ῥηϊδίως ἀφέλοιο, τὸ δ᾽ ὕστερον αὖθι νοήσεις,*
> *Μαψιδίως δ᾽ ᾽ἀρ᾽ ἔπειτα τεὸν πρὸς θυμὸν ὀδυρῇ,*
> *Τοιόνδ᾽ ἐκ πόλιος περιώνυμον ἄλκαρ ὀλέσσας.*

King, if you destroy me, a law-abiding man who has done no harm to anybody at all, you may easily, let me tell you, take away a head of great wisdom, but afterwards you will realize what you have done, and you will lament, then, in vain to your own heart [*1645*: and in time then you lament very greatly, all in vain] that you have deprived your city of a bulwark of such renown.

6 *Apologus De Rustico et Hero*

[The Fable of the Peasant and the Landlord]

Date. 1624? Harris Fletcher has demonstrated, *JEGP* lv (1956) 230–3, that M.'s fable is a close imitation of one in Mantuan's *Opera* (Paris 1513) 194v. Fletcher considers the *Apologus* a grammar school exercise.
Publication. First printed in *1673* (the text followed here).

> Rusticus ex malo sapidissima poma quotannis
>   Legit, et urbano lecta dedit domino:
> Hic incredibili fructus dulcedine captus
>   Malum ipsam in proprias transtulit areolas.
> Hactenus illa ferax, sed longo debilis aevo,
>   Mota solo assueto, protinus aret iners.
> Quod tandem ut patuit domino, spe lusus inani,
>   Damnavit celeres in sua damna manus.

¶ 5. *4*. ὀδυρῇ] M. must have intended the future, 'you will lament'. In *1645* he accents as present, ὀδύρῃ; in *1673* as future, ὀδυρῇ.
5. Cp. *Prov*. xxiv 3–6: 'Through wisdom is a house builded; and by understanding it is established. . . A wise man is strong; yea, a man of knowledge increaseth strength. For by wise counsel thou shalt make war; and in multitude of counsellors there is safety'; also Comenius, *Didactica Magna* tr. M. W. Keatinge (1896) p. 453, 'With truth did the sainted Luther write . . . "Where one ducat is expended in building cities, fortresses, monuments and arsenals, one hundred should be spent in educating one youth aright. . . For a good and wise man is the most precious treasure of a state, and is of far more value than . . . gates of bronze and bars of iron."'

Atque ait, Heu quanto satius fuit illa coloni
(Parva licet) grato dona tulisse animo!
Possem ego avaritiam frenare, gulamque voracem:
Nunc periere mihi et foetus et ipsa parens.

A peasant had an apple-tree from which he picked, each year, fruit of really exquisite flavour. He presented the choicest specimens to his landlord, who lived in the city. The landlord, fascinated by the unbelievable sweetness of the apples, transplanted the tree to his own little pleasure-gardens. Although it had borne fruit up till now, the tree was really very old and weak, and once moved from its accustomed soil it withered and became barren. Eventually, when the landlord realised what had happened, and saw that he had been deluded by a vain hope, he cursed himself for being so swift in his own undoing.

'Alas!' he said, 'how much better it was to accept my tenant's gifts with gratitude, small though they were! If only I could have kept my avarice and my ruinous gluttony under control! Now I have lost both the fruit and the tree.'

7 On the Death of a Fair Infant Dying of a Cough

Date. Winter 1625–6. Headed *Anno aetatis 17* in *1673* (i.e. Dec. 1625–Dec. 1626). Edward Phillips, writing in 1694, confirms that *Fair Infant* was written at seventeen, but also claims that its occasion was 'the Death of one of his Sister's Children (a Daughter), who died in her Infancy' (Darbishire 62). W. R. Parker, *TLS* (17 Dec. 1938) 802, taking Phillips at his word, concludes that the only child of M.'s sister who could have been the poem's subject was Anne (baptized 12 Jan. 1626, buried 22 Jan. 1628–when M. was nineteen, not seventeen). However, two-year-old Anne cannot have been the poem's subject, since the 'infant' of whom M. writes did not outlast even a single winter (*3–4*). If, then, we accept Phillips's and M.'s dating, there is one piece of corroboratory evidence: M.'s references to the horrors of the plague (*64–70*). The great plague year was 1625 (see *Elegia III* 6–7*n*, p. 49 below). As F. P. Wilson says (*The Plague in Shakespeare's London* (Oxford 1927) p. 174), the next London plague of any importance did not occur until 1636.

Publication. First printed in *1673* (the text followed here; but emended in these instances: *3.* outlasted]outlasted, *12.* blot]blot, *40.* were)] were.) *49.* head?]head. *53.* youth?]youth! *54.* crowned]cown'd *56.* good?]good. *63.* aspire?]aspire. *69.* smart?]smart).

Modern criticism. Allen 47–52 examines *Fair Infant* and finds it 'a vivid indication of the poet's mature technique. . . Pagan myth, with Christian undertones, leads to universal philosophical abstractions that open the door to Christian legend.' Following up Allen's analysis, H. N. Maclean, *ELH* xxiv (1957) 296–305, finds that from the viewpoint of the Pagan-Christian antithesis *Fair Infant* marks an intermediate stage in M.'s development between *Elegia III* and *Prae E* on the one hand and *Nativity Ode* on the other.

I

O fairest flower no sooner blown but blasted,
Soft silken primrose fading timelessly,
Summer's chief honour if thou hadst outlasted
Bleak winter's force that made thy blossom dry;
For he being amorous on that lovely dye
    That did thy cheek envermeil, thought to kiss
But killed alas, and then bewailed his fatal bliss.

II

For since grim Aquilo his charioteer
By boisterous rape the Athenian damsel got,
He thought it touched his deity full near,
If likewise he some fair one wedded not,
Thereby to wipe away the infamous blot
    Of long-uncoupled bed, and childless eld,
Which 'mongst the wanton gods a foul reproach
        was held.

III

So mounting up in icy-pearled car,
Through middle empire of the freezing air
He wandered long, till thee he spied from far,
There ended was his quest, there ceased his care.
Down he descended from his snow-soft chair,
    But all unwares with his cold-kind embrace
Unhoused thy virgin soul from her fair biding-place.

¶ 7. *1–2.* Probably echoing the pseudo-Shakespearean *Passionate Pilgrim* x 1–4: 'Sweet rose, fair flower, untimely pluck'd, soon vaded, / Pluck'd in the bud and vaded in the spring! / Bright orient pearl, alack too timely shaded! / Fair creature kill'd too soon by death's sharp sting!'
2. timelessly] unseasonably; the first recorded occurrence of the adverb in *OED*.
6–7. In Shakespeare's *Venus and Adonis* 1110 the boar 'thought to kiss him, and hath kill'd him so'.
8–9. Ovid *Met.* vi 682–710 describes how Boreas (also called Aquilo), the north wind, carried off Orithyia, daughter of King Erechtheus of Athens.
15. icy-pearled] Sylvester calls hail 'Ice-pearls' and 'Bals of Ice-pearl' (Du Bartas 389 and Du Bartas[2] 1096).

IV

Yet art thou not inglorious in thy fate;
For so Apollo, with unweeting hand
Whilom did slay his dearly-loved mate
Young Hyacinth born on Eurotas' strand
Young Hyacinth the pride of Spartan land;
  But then transformed him to a purple flower
Alack that so to change thee winter had no power.

V

Yet can I not persuade me thou art dead
Or that thy corse corrupts in earth's dark womb,
Or that thy beauties lie in wormy bed,
Hid from the world in a low-delved tomb;
Could heaven for pity thee so strictly doom?
  O no! for something in thy face did shine
Above mortality that showed thou wast divine.

VI

Resolve me then O soul most surely blest
(If so it be that thou these plaints dost hear)
Tell me bright spirit where'er thou hoverest
Whether above that high first-moving sphere
Or in the Elysian fields (if such there were)
  O say me true if thou wert mortal wight
And why from us so quickly thou didst take thy flight.

VII

Wert thou some star which from the ruined roof
Of shaked Olympus by mischance didst fall;
Which careful Jove in nature's true behoof
Took up, and in fit place did reinstall?

23–7. Ovid, *Met.* x 162–216 tells how Apollo accidentally killed Hyacinthus, son of Oebalus, king of Sparta (which stands on the river Eurotas), with a discus, and made a flower of bright colour (*purpureus color*) spring from his blood. Allen 49 notes that in Servius' commentary on Virgil, *Ecl.* iii Boreas, not the more usual Zephyrus, is blamed for diverting the discus. Thus these lines are linked with ll. 8–9.

25–6. Probably echoing Spenser, *Astrophel* 7–8: 'Young Astrophel, the pride of shepheards praise, / Young Astrophel, the rusticke lasses love.'

31. Shakespeare, *Midsummer Night's Dream* III ii 384 has 'wormy beds'.

39. high first-moving sphere] The *primum mobile* of the Ptolemaic universe (see *Vacation Exercise* 34–5*n*, p. 77).

40. Elysian fields] The abode of the blessed in Greek myth, described by Homer, *Od.* iv 563–8. See p. 225 ll. 980–1*n*.

Or did of late Earth's sons besiege the wall
  Of sheeny heaven, and thou some goddess fled
Amongst us here below to hide thy nectared head?

VIII

Or wert thou that just maid who once before
Forsook the hated earth, O tell me sooth
And cam'st again to visit us once more?
Or wert thou that sweet smiling youth?
Or that crowned matron sage white-robed Truth?
  Or any other of that heavenly brood
Let down in cloudy throne to do the world some good?

IX

Or wert thou of the golden-winged host,
Who having clad thyself in human weed,
To earth from thy prefixed seat didst post,
And after short abode fly back with speed,
As if to show what creatures heaven doth breed,
  Thereby to set the hearts of men on fire
To scorn the sordid world, and unto heaven aspire?

X

But O why didst thou not stay here below
To bless us with thy heaven-loved innocence,
To slake his wrath whom sin hath made our foe
To turn swift-rushing black perdition hence,
Or drive away the slaughtering pestilence,
  To stand 'twixt us and our deserved smart?
But thou canst best perform that office where thou art.

47. *Earth's sons*] The giants, sons of Ge (Earth): see Q *Nov* 174*n* (p. 43).
48. *sheeny*] having a shiny surface; the first recorded occurrence of the word in *OED*.
50. *that just maid*] Astraea (Justice): see *Elegia IV* 81 *n* p. (57).
53. The line lacks two syllables. John Heskin in the mid-eighteenth century suggested the emendation 'wert thou Mercy' (following *Nativity Ode* 141–4). J. A. Himes, *MLN* xxxv (1920) 441–2 and xxxvi (1921) 414–19, opposes any emendation and reads the line as a reference to Ganymede. The sex of the child ('Her' 72) is against this. H. N. Maclean, *ELH* xxiv (1957) 302–3 takes the 'youth' to be Peace, pointing out that Astraea is linked with Peace and Truth in *Prolusion IV*. Allen 51 suggests 'Virtue'.
54. *white robed*] One of the representations of Truth (*Verità*) in Cesare Ripa's *Iconologia* (Padua 1611) p. 530 is white-robed (*vestita di color bianco*).
57. *golden-winged*] Spenser's 'bright Cherubins' in *Hymn of Heavenly Beauty* 93–4 have 'golden wings'.

XI

Then thou the mother of so sweet a child
Her false imagined loss cease to lament,
And wisely learn to curb thy sorrows wild;
Think what a present thou to God hast sent,
And render him with patience what he lent;
This if thou do he will an offspring give,
That till the world's last end shall make thy name
to live.

8 *Elegia prima ad Carolum Diodatum*

[Elegy I, to Charles Diodati]

Date. April 1626? This elegy was apparently written from London (*9*), early in M.'s Cambridge career, before he had become reconciled to the university (*14–16, 90*), and in the spring (*48*). He matriculated at Cambridge 9 Apr. 1625. In 1626 the Lent Term ended 31 Mar. and the Easter Term began 19 Apr.

Charles Diodati (*c.* 1609–38), to whom the elegy is addressed, was a schoolfellow of M.'s at St Paul's. He matriculated from Trinity College, Oxford 7 Feb. 1623, took his B.A. 10 Dec. 1625 and remained in residence to work for his M.A. which he took 28 Jul. 1628 (Dorian 102, 111 and 118). Two undated Greek letters from Diodati to M. survive (BM Add. MS 5016, ff 5 and 71: printed in French i 98–9 and 104–5). Dorian 112–13 thinks that the second of these may have been written in spring 1626, while Diodati was holidaying in Cheshire, and that this elegy may be a reply to it.

On the evidence of the reference to 'forbidden rooms' and 'exile' (*12, 17–20*), it has sometimes been assumed that M. was temporarily rusticated from Cambridge, but corroboration is lacking (French i 106): M.'s 'exile' is probably merely the university vacation.

Publication. *1645* (*54.* possit]posset) and *1673* (the text followed here).

Modern criticism. R. W. Condee, *PQ* xxvii (1958) 498–502 detects in this elegy a 'cross-comparison' of M. with Ovid: M.'s exile to London is as happy as Ovid's to Tomis was miserable: the Ovid/Homer collocation (*21–3*) is a cross-development of that in *Tristia* I i 47–8: M.'s books in London (*25–6*) balance the booklessness of Tomis, *Tristia* III xiv 37–8: M.'s theatre-visits (*27–46*) are the counterpart of Ovid's regretful memories of Roman theatres, *Tristia* III xii 23–4 and *Ex Ponto* I viii 35: the barren marshy landscape of Cambridge (*11, 13, 89*) recalls Ovid's complaints about Tomis, *Tristia* III x 71–8, xii 13–16; *Ex Ponto* I iii 51–2, II vii 74, III i 11–13, viii 13–16, IV x 61–2.

Tandem, care, tuae mihi pervenere tabellae,
Pertulit et voces nuntia charta tuas,
Pertulit occidua Devae Cestrensis ab ora

Vergivium prono qua petit amne salum.
Multum crede iuvat terras aluisse remotas
Pectus amans nostri, tamque fidele caput,
Quodque mihi lepidum tellus longinqua sodalem
Debet, at unde brevi reddere iussa velit.
Me tenet urbs reflua quam Thamesis alluit unda,
Meque nec invitum patria dulcis habet.
Iam nec arundiferum mihi cura revisere Camum,
Nec dudum vetiti me laris angit amor.
Nuda nec arva placent, umbrasque negantia molles,
Quam male Phoebicolis convenit ille locus!
Nec duri libet usque minas perferre magistri
Caeteraque ingenio non subeunda meo.
Si sit hoc exilium patrios adiisse penates,
Et vacuum curis otia grata sequi,
Non ego vel profugi nomen, sortemve recuso,
Laetus et exilii conditione fruor.
O utinam vates nunquam graviora tulisset
Ille Tomitano flebilis exul agro,
Non tunc Ionio quicquam cessisset Homero
Neve foret victo laus tibi prima Maro.
Tempora nam licet hic placidis dare libera Musis,
Et totum rapiunt me mea vita libri.

¶ 8. *4. Vergivium . . . salum*] A fairly common name for the Irish Sea in the sixteenth and seventeenth centuries, deriving from Ptolemy's Ὠκεανὸς Οὐεργιόνιος (*Geographia* II ii 5 and II iii 2). M. may have found it in Drayton, who uses the form Vergivian in *Polyolbion* i 24 and v 317, or in Camden, who discusses the name in *Britannia* (1586) 490 and suggests a derivation from the Welsh *Mor Iwerydd* or the Irish *fairge* (open sea).
15–16. These lines are frequently associated with the two words inserted by Aubrey into a passage (Darbishire 10) of his MS life of M., which allege that M. was whipped by his tutor William Chappell. The insertion suggests that the information was not, like that contained in the surrounding passage, received by Aubrey from M.'s brother Christopher, but picked up later from some gossip who was, perhaps, merely elaborating imaginatively upon the hint of these lines. However, among the information which Aubrey claims to have received from Christopher is the fact that M. received 'some unkindness' from Chappell, and was afterwards transferred to the tuition of Nathaniel Tovey.
21. vates] Ovid, banished to Tomis on the north-west shore of the Black Sea by Augustus in 8 A.D.
23. Ionio] Of the seven or more cities usually recorded as claiming to be Homer's birthplace Chios and Smyrna are the most commonly mentioned: Smyrna is in Ionia.

Excipit hinc fessum sinuosi pompa theatri,
Et vocat ad plausus garrula scena suos.
Seu catus auditur senior, seu prodigus haeres,
Seu procus, aut posita casside miles adest,
Sive decennali foecundus lite patronus
Detonat inculto barbara verba foro,
Saepe vafer gnato succurrit servus amanti,
Et nasum rigidi fallit ubique patris;
Saepe novos illic virgo mirata calores
Quid sit amor nescit, dum quoque nescit, amat.
Sive cruentatum furiosa Tragoedia sceptrum
Quassat, et effusis crinibus ora rotat,
Et dolet, et specto, iuvat et spectasse dolendo,
Interdum et lacrymis dulcis amaror inest:
Seu puer infelix indelibata reliquit
Gaudia, et abrupto flendus amore cadit,
Seu ferus e tenebris iterat Styga criminis ultor
Conscia funereo pectora torre movens,
Seu maeret Pelopeia domus, seu nobilis Ili,
Aut luit incestos aula Creontis avos.
Sed neque sub tecto semper nec in urbe latemus,
Irrita nec nobis tempora veris eunt.
Nos quoque lucus habet vicina consitus ulmo
Atque suburbani nobilis umbra loci.
Saepius hic blandas spirantia sidera flammas
Virgineos videas praeteriisse choros.

27. sinuosi pompa theatri] Recalls Propertius IV i 15 *sinuosa cavo pendebant vela theatro* (rippling awnings hung over the hollow theatre).
29–36. The stock characters mentioned suggest Roman comedy, not English. Warton took ll. 31–2 as a reference to a Latin play *Ignoramus* by George Ruggle, Fellow of Clare, but there is no evidence that this was acted in London.
36. Cp. Ovid's Hermaphroditus, *Met.* iv 330 *nescit enim, quid amor.*
37–8. Ovid similarly describes *violenta Tragoedia* with her sceptre in *Am.* III i 11–13.
40. dulcis amaror] Catullus lxviii 18 says that love *dulcem curis miscet amaritiem* (mingles sweet bitterness with cares).
45–6. Pelops was father of Atreus and grandfather of Agamemnon. His descendants appear in the *Oresteia* trilogy of Aeschylus, the *Electra* of Sophocles, and the *Orestes, Electra* and two *Iphigenia* plays of Euripides. Euripides' *Hecuba* and *Trojan Women* deal with the house of Ilus founder of Troy. It is Creon, brother of Jocasta, who offers her hand to Oedipus, actually her son: the tragic after-events are seen in Sophocles' two *Oedipus* plays and his *Antigone*, Aeschylus' *Seven against Thebes*, and Euripides' *Phoenician Maidens* and *Suppliants.*

Ah quoties dignae stupui miracula formae
Quae possit senium vel reparare Iovis;
Ah quoties vidi superantia lumina gemmas,
Atque faces quotquot volvit uterque polus;
Collaque bis vivi Pelopis quae brachia vincant,
Quaeque fluit puro nectare tincta via,
Et decus eximium frontis, tremulosque capillos,
Aurea quae fallax retia tendit Amor.
Pellacesque genas, ad quas hyacinthina sordet
Purpura, et ipse tui floris, Adoni, rubor.
Cedite laudatae toties Heroides olim,
Et quaecunque vagum cepit amica Iovem.
Cedite Achaemeniae turrita fronte puellae,
Et quot Susa colunt, Memnoniamque Ninon.
Vos etiam Danaae fasces submittite Nymphae,
Et vos Iliacae, Romuleaeque nurus.
Nec Pompeianas Tarpeia Musa columnas
Iactet, et Ausoniis plena theatra stolis.

57. Pelops was killed by his father Tantalus and served as a feast for the gods. Only Demeter ate any (part of one shoulder), and when Pelops was restored to life the missing part was made good with ivory. Ovid retells the story, *Met.* vi 403–11.

58. via] The Milky Way. Ovid refers to the milk of sheep as *nectar*, *Met.* xv 117.

62. tui floris, Adoni] Ovid, *Met.* x 731–9, tells how Venus caused the anemone to spring from Adonis' blood.

63. The reference is to Ovid's *Heroides.*

65. Achaemeniae turrita fronte puellae] The *Achaimenidai* (from *Achaemenes*, ancestor of the Persian kings) are named by Herodotus (i 125) as the royal clan of the Persians. The *tiara* or felt headdress of the Persians assumed different shapes according to the rank of the wearer: only royalty could wear it upright (see Aeschylus, *Persae* 662), in which case it became a high, sharp-pointed cap. M.'s *turrita* suggests that he associated this with the high headdress worn by women in the seventeenth century (*OED* Tower *sb.*[1] 6 b), which is first mentioned in Sylvester (Du Bartas[2] 1151); perhaps also with the towered crown of Cybele (Ovid, *Fast.* iv 219, vi 321; Virgil, *Aen.* vi 785).

66. Susa . . . Memnoniamque Ninon] Strabo XV iii 2 says that Susa was supposedly founded by Tithonus, Memnon's father, and that its acropolis was called the Memnonium: also that Memnon was buried in Syria, by the river Badas. Perhaps this is why M. calls Nineveh (founded by Ninos, Strabo II i 31) 'Memnonian', since it was the capital city of Syria.

69–70. The 'Tarpeian Muse' is Ovid, who lived near the Tarpeian Rock (*Tristia* I iii 29–30). He recommends Pompey's colonnade and the Roman

Gloria virginibus debetur prima Britannis,
 Extera sat tibi sit foemina posse sequi.
Tuque urbs Dardaniis Londinum structa colonis
 Turrigerum late conspicienda caput,
Tu nimium felix intra tua moenia claudis
 Quicquid formosi pendulus orbis habet.
Non tibi tot caelo scintillant astra sereno
 Endymioneae turba ministra deae,
Quot tibi conspicuae formaque auroque puellae
 Per medias radiant turba videnda vias,
Creditur huc geminis venisse invecta columbis
 Alma pharetrigero milite cincta Venus,
Huic Cnidon, et riguas Simoentis flumine valles,
 Huic Paphon, et roseam posthabitura Cypron.
Ast ego, dum pueri sinit indulgentia caeci,
 Moenia quam subito linquere fausta paro;
Et vitare procul malefidae infamia Circes
 Atria, divini Molyos usus ope.
Stat quoque iuncosas Cami remeare paludes,
 Atque iterum raucae murmur adire Scholae.
Interea fidi parvum cape munus amici,
 Paucaque in alternos verba coacta modos.

At last, dear friend, your letter has reached me. Messenger-like its paper has carried your words to me from the western bank of Chester's river, the Dee, where it flows down towards the Irish Sea.[4] It is, believe me, a great joy to know that distant lands have bred a heart that loves me and a head so true: that a faraway place owes me a charming companion and is, moreover, ready to repay that debt soon, at my request.

I am still in the city which the Thames washes with its tides: still in the delightful place where I was born. Nor am I reluctant to be here. At present I am not anxious to revisit the reedy Cam. I am not pining away for my rooms, recently forbidden to me. Bare fields which offer no gentle shades do

theatres as likely places for meeting girls (*Ars Am.* i 67–8, 89–90; iii 387–8, 394).

73. The earliest record of the theory that the Britons are descended from Brutus and his Trojan fugitives is found in Nennius's eighth-century *Historia Brittonum*. The tradition is traced by G. S. Gordon in *E & S* ix (1924) 9–30.

77–80. M. is mimicking the claim Ovid made for Rome (*Ars Am.* i 59–60).

83–4. Cnidos and Paphos (a town in Cyprus) were both sacred to Venus (see Horace, *Odes* I xxx 1–2, III xxviii 13–15). The Simois rises on Mount Ida where, according to Ovid, Paris awarded the prize for beauty to Venus (*Her.* xvi 53–88).

88. Molyos] In Homer it is the herb Moly (*Od.* x 305) which makes Odysseus proof against the charms of Circe.

92. alternos . . . modos] The alternate hexameters and pentameters of the elegiac couplet, which Ovid refers to in a similar phrase (*Tristia* III vii 10).

not attract me. How badly that place suits the worshippers of Phoebus! I do not like having always to stomach the threats of a stern tutor, and other things which my spirit will not tolerate.[15] If this be exile–to have come home, to live in welcome leisure free from care–then I do not object to the name or fate of an exile, but gladly enjoy my banishment. Ah! If only that poet[21] who was once a tearful exile in the land of Tomis had never had to put up with anything worse than this: then he would have been a match for Ionian Homer,[23] and you, Virgil, outdone, would not enjoy the supreme glory.

For here I can devote my leisure hours to the mild Muses: here books, which are my life, quite carry me away. When I am tired the pageantry of the rounded theatre[27] attracts me, and the play's babbling speeches claim my applause. Sometimes the speaker is a crafty old man,[29] sometimes a spendthrift heir; sometimes a lover appears, or a soldier (minus his helmet). Sometimes a barrister, with pockets well lined by a ten-year-old case, thunders out his barbarous jargon to an ignorant courtroom. Often there is a wily slave who comes to the rescue of some love-struck son, and tricks the stern father at every turn, under the old man's very nose. Often, too, there is a young girl who is surprised by a warmth of feeling she never felt before, and falls in love without knowing what love is.[36]

Sometimes raging Tragedy, with streaming hair and rolling eyes, brandishes her bloody sceptre.[37] It makes me sad to watch, yet watch I do, and find a pleasure in the sadness. Sometimes there is a sweet bitterness even in weeping,[40] as when some poor lad leaves joys untasted and dies, his love snuffed out, a fit subject for tears; or when a fierce avenger of crime returns from the darkness of death, recrosses the Styx, and perturbs conscience-stricken souls with his dismal firebrand; or when the house of Pelops[45] or of noble Ilus mourns, or Creon's[46] palace atones for incestuous ancestors.

But I do not always hide myself away indoors, or stay in the city: the spring does not pass by me unnoticed. A dense elm grove nearby, and a magnificently shady spot just outside the city are my haunts. Here you can often see parties of young girls walking by–stars which breathe forth seductive flames. Ah, how often have I been struck dumb by the miraculous shapeliness of a figure which might well make even old Jove young again! Ah, how often have I seen eyes brighter than jewels, brighter than all the stars which wheel round both the poles; necks which excel twice-living Pelops's shoulders,[57] or that flowing Way which is drenched in pure nectarous milk;[58] a forehead of exceptional loveliness, light-blown hair–a golden net spread by deceitful Cupid, and enticing cheeks beside which the flush of the hyacinth, and even the blushing red of your flower, Adonis,[62] seem dull. Admit defeat, you heroines so often praised:[63] admit defeat, all you girls who have caught the eye of inconstant Jove. Admit defeat, you Achaemenian girls in your turreted hats,[65] and you who live in Susa and Memnonian Nineveh.[66] Surrender, you maidens of Greece and of Troy and of Rome. Let the Tarpeian Muse[69] stop boasting about Pompey's colonnade, or about theatres crowded with the noblewomen of Italy. The first prize goes to the British girls: be content, foreign woman, to take second place! And you, London, a city built by Trojan settlers,[73] a city whose towery head can be seen for miles, you are more than fortunate for you enclose within your walls whatever beauty there is to be found in all this pendent world. The stars which spangle the calm sky above you[77]–those hosts of handmaidens who wait on Endymion's goddess–are fewer in number than the host which can be seen all a-glitter in your streets: girls whose good looks and golden trinkets catch the eye. There is a story that kindly Venus came to this city, drawn by her twin doves and escorted by her quivered soldiery, and that she preferred it to Cnidos,[83] and to the valleys which the Simois waters, and to Paphos and rosy Cyprus.[84]

But for my part I intend to quit this pampered town as quickly as possible, while the blind boy's indulgence permits, and, with the help of divine moly,[88] to leave far behind the infamous halls of faithless Circe. I am to return to the Cam's reedy marshes and face the uproar of the noisy University again. Meanwhile accept this little gift from a loyal friend–one or two words forced into elegiac metre.[92]

9 *In Obitum Praesulis Eliensis*

[On the Death of the Bishop of Ely]

Date. Oct. 1626. Headed *Anno aetatis 17* in *1645* and *1673*. Dr Nicholas Felton, Bishop of Ely, died 5 Oct. 1626. He had been a great friend of Lancelot Andrewes (commemorated in *Elegia III*); like him he was scholar, fellow (1583) and master (1617) of Pembroke College, Cambridge, and one of the translators of the Authorized Version.

Publication. 1645 (2. lumina;]lumina) and *1673* (the text followed here).

Adhuc madentes rore squalebant genae,
  Et sicca nondum lumina;
Adhuc liquentis imbre turgebant salis,
  Quem nuper effudi pius,
Dum maesta charo iusta persolvi rogo
  Wintoniensis praesulis.
Cum centilinguis Fama (proh semper mali
  Cladisque vera nuntia)
Spargit per urbes divitis Britanniae,
  Populosque Neptuno satos,
Cessisse morti, et ferreis sororibus
  Te generis humani decus,
Qui rex sacrorum illa fuisti in insula
  Quae nomen Anguillae tenet.
Tunc inquietum pectus ira protinus
  Ebulliebat fervida,
Tumulis potentem saepe devovens deam:
  Nec vota Naso in Ibida

¶ 9. *10. Neptuno*] See Q *Nov* 27–30*n* (p. 37).
11. sororibus] The fates, Clotho, Lachesis and Atropos.
14. Anguillae] Ely (O.E. Elig) means eel-isle.
18. Ibida] Ovid's *Ibis* is the example usually cited by Renaissance critics of the curse or *dira* as a literary form.

Concepit alto diriora pectore,
Graiusque vates parcius
Turpem Lycambis execratus est dolum,
Sponsamque Neobolen suam.
At ecce diras ipse dum fundo graves,
Et imprecor neci necem,
Audisse tales videor attonitus sonos
Leni, sub aura, flamine:
Caecos furores pone, pone vitream
Bilemque et irritas minas,
Quid temere violas non nocenda numina,
Subitoque ad iras percita.
Non est, ut arbitraris elusus miser,
Mors atra Noctis filia,
Erebove patre creta, sive Erinnye,
Vastove nata sub Chao:
Ast illa caelo missa stellato, Dei
Messes ubique colligit;
Animasque mole carnea reconditas
In lucem et auras evocat:
Ut cum fugaces excitant Horae diem
Themidos Iovisque filiae;
Et sempiterni ducit ad vultus patris;
At iusta raptat impios
Sub regna furvi luctuosa Tartari,
Sedesque subterraneas
Hanc ut vocantem laetus audivi, cito
Foedum reliqui carcerem,

20. *Graiusque vates*] Archilochus of Paros, a Greek iambic and elegiac poet of the seventh or eighth centuries B.C. The story that, when an unsuccessful suitor for the hand of Lycambes' daughter Neobule, he avenged himself with such biting satires that father and daughter hanged themselves, is alluded to by Horace, *Epist.* I xix 23–31. As Starnes and Talbert (239) point out, the story is summarized three times in Stephanus: under *Archilocus, Lycambes* and *Neobule*.

27–8. *vitream Bilemque*] Black bile or melancholy was supposed to look shiny; cp. Persius iii 8: *vitrea bilis*.

32. *Noctis filia*] Hesiod, *Theog.* 758–9, makes Death daughter of Night.

33. *Erebove*] See *Q Nov* 69*n* (p. 39). *Erinnye*] Virgil, *Aen.* vii 447, and Ovid, *Met.* i 241, iv 490 use the name Erinnys to mean a Fury.

37–8. M.'s Christian-Platonic view of death as release from the body is derived partly from Socrates's discussion of it in *Phaedo* 64–8.

39–40. *Horae . . . filiae*] Hesiod, *Theog.* 901 says that the Hours were daughters of Zeus and Themis.

Volatilesque faustus inter milites
  Ad astra sublimis feror:
Vates ut olim raptus ad coelum senex
  Auriga currus ignei,
Non me Bootis terruere lucidi
  Sarraca tarda frigore, aut
Formidolosi Scorpionis brachia,
  Non ensis Orion tuus.
Praetervolavi fulgidi solis globum,
  Longeque sub pedibus deam
Vidi triformem, dum coercebat suos
  Fraenis dracones aureis.
Erraticorum siderum per ordines,
  Per lacteas vehor plagas,
Velocitatem saepe miratus novam,
  Donec nitentes ad fores
Ventum est Olympi, et regiam crystallinam, et
  Stratum smaragdis atrium.
Sed hic tacebo, nam quis effari queat
  Oriundus humano patre
Amoenitates illius loci, mihi
  Sat est in aeternum frui.

My cheeks were still wet, still begrimed with tears, and my eyes, not yet dry, were still swollen with the shower of streaming salt water that I, tender-hearted, had just spilt as I paid my sad respects beside the dear grave of Winchester's bishop; when hundred-tongued Fame–always, alas, a trustworthy messenger where evil and disaster are concerned–spread through rich Britain's cities and among the race of Neptune's descendants[10] the news that you, the glory of humanity, you who reigned over holy men in that

49. Vates] Elijah is whirled up to heaven in a chariot of fire in *2 Kings* ii 11.
51–2. Bootis . . . Sarraca] The constellation of the Bear (cp. Juvenal v 23 *serraca Bootae*). The lateness of its setting is commented on by Homer, *Od.* v 272, and Ovid therefore calls it *tardus*, *Met.* ii 176. It is 'cold' because of its northern situation. The words *tarda* and *sarraca* occur, Starnes and Talbert (241–2) note, in Stephanus, under *Bootes*.
53–4. Scorpionis . . . Orion] It was the constellation of the Scorpion which terrified Phaëthon (Ovid, *Met.* ii 195–200). Ovid, Lucan, Seneca, Manilius and Claudian all give Orion a spear, but he has a sword which 'frightens the stars' in Statius, *Silv.* I i 44–5.
56–8. deam] Hecate, the moon goddess, 'triform' because she was called Luna or Cynthia in heaven, Diana on earth and Proserpina in hell. The attribution of dragons to her derives from Ovid, *Met.* vii. 218–9, where a dragon-drawn chariot descends in answer to Medea's prayer to Hecate.
63–4. Cp. the vision of new Jerusalem in *Rev.* xxi 10–27, in the Vulgate version of which *crystallum* and *smaragdus* both appear.

island which is called Eel Isle,[14] had succumbed to death and to the iron-hearted sisters.[11] At once my anxious heart began to seethe with fierce anger: again and again I cursed that goddess who has power over the tomb. The curses upon Ibis[18] which Ovid gave vent to from the depths of his heart were not more dreadful than mine: more restrained than I was the Greek poet[20] who heaped abuse upon Lycambes' low trickery and upon his fiancée Neobule. But look what happened! While I was pouring forth these terrible curses and calling down death upon Death, I seemed to my amazement to hear, breathed gently beneath the breeze, syllables like these: 'Stop your blind raging, your melancholy,[27] your useless threats. Why are you so rashly violent against powers which cannot be harmed–powers which are quickly moved to anger themselves? Death is not, as you, poor fool, imagine, the dark daughter of Night.[32] She is not the daughter of Erebus[33] or of a Fury, nor was she born in the gulf of Chaos. On the contrary, she is sent down from the starry heavens to gather in God's harvests in every land. Just as the fleeting Hours,[39] daughters of Themis and Jove, rouse up the dawn, so she calls up into the light and the air souls which were buried beneath a mass of flesh:[37] she leads them up until they are before the face of the eternal Father. But since she is just she carries the wicked off towards the mournful realms of dusky Tartarus, and to his dens under ground. Glad when I heard her calling, I swiftly left my loathsome prison and was carried up in blessedness to the stars amidst winged warriors, as once that ancient prophet[49] was snatched up to the sky, riding in a chariot of fire. The Wain[51] of twinkling Boötes, crawling along because of the cold, did not frighten me, nor did the Scorpion's[53] fearful claws, nor, Orion, did your sword. I flew past the blazing globe of the sun and saw, far away beneath my feet, the triform goddess[56] steering her dragon-team[58] with golden reins. I was carried past the courses of the wandering planets, and through the expanses of the Milky Way, often marvelling at my extraordinary speed, until I reached the gleaming gates of Olympus, the palace of crystal[63] and the forecourt paved with emerald. But now I will hold my tongue: for who of mortal seed could describe the bliss of that place? For me it is enough to enjoy it eternally.'

10 *In Obitum Procancellarii Medici*

[On the Death of the Vice-Chancellor, a Doctor]

Date. Oct.–Nov. 1626. The Vice-Chancellor, Dr John Gostlin, died 21 Oct. 1626; he had been appointed Regius Professor of Medicine in 1623.
Publication. *1645* and *1673* (no significant variants). In both editions the poem is headed *Anno aetatis 16*. This is clearly an error: when Dr Gostlin died M. was almost eighteen.

Parere fati discite legibus,
Manusque Parcae iam date supplices,

¶ 10. *2. Parcae*] The goddesses of Fate (Nona, Decuma and Morta).

Qui pendulum telluris orbem
Iäpeti colitis nepotes.
Vos si relicto mors vaga Taenaro
Semel vocarit flebilis, heu morae
Tentantur incassum dolique;
Per tenebras Stygis ire certum est.
Si destinatam pellere dextera
Mortem valeret, non ferus Hercules
Nessi venenatus cruore
Aemathia iacuisset Oeta.
Nec fraude turpi Palladis invidae
Vidisset occisum Ilion Hectora, aut
Quem larva Pelidis peremit
Ense locro, Iove lacrymante.
Si triste fatum verba Hecatëia
Fugare possint, Telegoni parens
Vixisset infamis, potentique
Aegiali soror usa virga.
Numenque trinum fallere si queant

4. Iäpeti ... nepotes] Japetus was father of Prometheus who, as Ovid relates in *Met.* i 80–6, created man out of the earth.

5. Taenaro] There was supposed to be a mouth of hell at Taenarum, a promontory in Laconia: Ovid calls Tartarus 'the Taenarian vale' in *Fast.* iv. 612.

10–12. When the centaur Nessus was killed by Hercules he gave his blood-stained shirt to Deianira, saying that it would revive her husband's failing love. In fact, as Ovid relates in *Met.* ix 101–272, its burning poison drove Hercules to suicide on *Oeta*, the moutain range between Aetolia and Thessaly (M.'s *Aemathia*=Thessalian).

13–14. In *Il.* xxii 224–46 Homer makes Athene disguise herself as Hector's brother, Deïphobus, in order to persuade Hector to fight his fatal combat with Achilles. During the combat she retrieves Achilles's spear for him when he has thrown and missed (xxii 276–7).

15–16. In *Il.* xvi 426–505 Sarpedon is killed by Patroclus, a Locrian, who wears the armour of Achilles, son of Peleus. Zeus weeps because Sarpedon was his son by Laodamia. *Pelidis* is M.'s error for *Pelidae*.

17. Hecatëia] associated with Hecate, who presides over enchantments. Ovid's Circe uses *Hecatëia carmina, Met.* xiv 44.

18. Telegoni parens] Circe; the tradition that she was mother of Telegonus is found in Hesiod, *Theog.* 1011–14. Ovid calls her *Telegoni parens, Ex Ponto* III i 123.

20. Aegiali soror] Medea. Her brother, whom she murdered, is usually called Absyrtus. The alternative name, Aegialeus, is given by Cicero, *De Deorum Natura* iii 48.

21. Numenque trinum] See l. 2*n*.

Artes medentum, ignotaque gramina,
Non gnarus herbarum Machaon
Eurypyli cecidisset hasta.
Laesisset et nec te Philyreie
Sagitta echidnae perlita sanguine,
Nec tela te fulmenque avitum
Caese puer genitricis alvo.
Tuque O alumno maior Apolline,
Gentis togatae cui regimen datum,
Frondosa quem nunc Cirrha luget,
Et mediis Helicon in undis,
Iam praefuisses Palladio gregi
Laetus, superstes, nec sine gloria,
Nec puppe lustrasses Charontis
Horribiles barathri recessus.
At fila rupit Persephone tua

23–4. Machaon was a surgeon, the son of Aesculapius, and one of the Greeks at Troy (*Il.* xi 514, 614). His death at the hand of Eurypylus is not related by Homer but by Quintus Smyrnaeus in his *Posthomerica* vi 390–429, a work which according to Edward Phillips (Darbishire 60) was used by M. in educating his two nephews. Starnes and Talbert (234) think it more likely that M. was indebted to Stephanus, who mentions Eurypylus as Machaon's killer.
25–6. Philyreie] Chiron, the centaur, son of the nymph Philyra and tutor of Aesculapius. Ovid, who calls him *Phillyrides* and *Philyreius heros*, relates how he was killed when one of Hercules' arrows, poisoned with the blood of the Lernean hydra, dropped from its quiver and struck him (*Fast.* v 379–414). Starnes and Talbert (234–5) note that Stephanus's account of the incident also uses the word *perlita* and perhaps suggested it to M.
27–8. te . . . puer] Aesculapius. Ovid, *Met.* ii 596–648, tells how he was cut from the womb of his dead mother, Coronis, by his father, Apollo. He became so expert a physician that he could raise the dead, so Jupiter killed him with a thunderbolt.
29. alumno] The usual meaning of *alumnus* is pupil, and it may be that M. is paying a hyperbolical compliment to Dr Gostlin by pretending that he was Apollo's tutor. However, *alumnus* can also mean, in late Latin, 'nourisher, one who brings up or educates'.
31–2. Cirrha] An ancient town near Delphi which, like Mount Helicon, was sacred to Apollo.
33. Palladio gregi] Cambridge University. Pallas was goddess of wisdom.
37. Persephone] Ovid tells (*Met.* v 385–424 and *Fast.* iv 420–54) how she was carried off by Pluto and made queen of the Underworld. M. gives her her Latin name *Proserpina* 46 and calls her *Aetnaea* (an adj. used by Ovid, *Met.* viii 260 to mean 'Sicilian') because it was from the meadows of Enna in Sicily that Pluto took her.

Irata, cum te viderit artibus
Succoque pollenti tot atris
Faucibus eripuisse mortis.
Colende praeses, membra precor tua
Molli quiescant cespite, et ex tuo
Crescant rosae, calthaeque busto,
Purpureoque hyacinthus ore.
Sit mite de te iudicium Aeaci,
Subrideatque Aetnaea Proserpina,
Interque felices perennis
Elysio spatiere campo.

Learn to obey the laws of fate. Lift up your hands now in prayer to the goddess of destiny,[2] all you sons of Japetus[4] who live on this pendent orb, the earth. If that dismal visitor, Death, once leaves Taenarus[5] and calls you, ah! then all your tricks and turns will do you no good: down you will have to go through the Stygian darkness. If strength of arm could push back death, once fated, then fierce Hercules[10] would not have lain lifeless on Emathian Oeta, poisoned by Nessus' blood: Troy would not have seen Hector cut down by envious Athene's low trickery,[13] nor Sarpedon killed, while Jove wept, by a man disguised as Achilles[15] but wielding a Locrian sword. If the spells of witchcraft[17] could chase sad fate away, Telegonus' ill-famed mother[18] would have survived: so, too, would Aegialeus' sister,[20] by the aid of her powerful wand. If medical skill and recondite drugs could cheat the three goddesses,[21] then Machaon,[23] who knew all about herbs, would not have fallen a prey to Eurypylus' spear; nor would you, son of Philyra,[25] have been wounded by that arrow smeared with the Hydra's blood; and neither your grandfather's weapons nor his thunderbolt would have done you[27] any harm–you who, as a baby, were cut from your mother's womb.

And you, also, greater than your foster-father,[29] Apollo, you to whom the government of our gowned society was given, you for whom leafy Cirrha[31] is now in mourning, and Helicon, too, amidst its streams–you would still be alive, would still be the happy and glorious shepherd of Pallas' flock:[33] you would not have crossed the dreadful deeps of the Underworld in Charon's boat. But Persephone[37] snapped the thread of your life, angry because she saw that you had rescued so many patients from the black jaws of death by your skill and by your potent medicine. I pray, reverend master, that your limbs may rest peacefully in the soft turf: from your grave may roses and marigolds and the crimson-lipped hyacinth spring. May the judgment Aeacus[45] passes upon you be mild, may Aetnean Proserpina smile, and may you walk for ever among the blessed in the Elysian fields.

38–40. Starnes and Talbert (235–6) suggest M. has taken the reason for Dr Gostlin's death—that his cures were emptying the underworld—from Stephanus's account of the death of Aesculapius.

45. Aeaci] Aeacus was made one of the judges in the Underworld. Ovid mentions him in this capacity, *Met.* xiii 25–6: Virgil gives only Minos and Rhadamanthus, *Aen.* vi 432, 566.

11 *Elegia secunda. In Obitum Praeconis Academici Cantabrigiensis*

[Elegy II. On the Death of the University of Cambridge Beadle]

Date. Oct.-Nov. 1626. Richard Ridding, the subject of this elegy, matriculated from St John's in 1587, took his B.A. in 1591 and his M.A. in 1594, and became Esquire Beadle in 1596. As such one of his duties, referred to by M. (*1*), was to carry the mace before the Vice-Chancellor on public occasions. Ridding died between 19 Sept. 1626, when his will was signed, and 28 Nov. 1626, when it was proved. In both *1645* and *1673* the poem is headed *Anno aetatis 17*, which must mean 'At seventeen years of age' not 'In the seventeenth year of his age': M. was almost eighteen in Nov. 1626.
Publication. *1645* (*12.* tuo,]tuo), *1673* (the text followed here).

Te, qui conspicuus baculo fulgente solebas
Palladium toties ore ciere gregem,
Ultima praeconum praeconem te quoque saeva
Mors rapit, officio nec favet ipsa suo.
Candidiora licet fuerint tibi tempora plumis
Sub quibus accipimus delituisse Iovem,
O dignus tamen Haemonio iuvenescere succo,
Dignus in Aesonios vivere posse dies,
Dignus quem Stygiis medica revocaret ab undis
Arte Coronides, saepe rogante dea.
Tu si iussus eras acies accire togatas,
Et celer a Phoebo nuntius ire tuo,
Talis in Iliaca stabat Cyllenius aula
Alipes, aetherea missus ab arce patris.

¶ 11. *2. Palladium . . . gregem*] See *Proc Med* 33*n* (p. 29).
5–6. Ovid, as he grows old, compares the hair of his own temples to the plumage of a swan (*Tristia* IV viii 1). In his *Her.* viii 67–8 Hermione refers to Jove's transformation to a swan and rape of Leda, using the same words (*plumis delituisse Iovem*) as M. here.
7–8. In Ovid, *Met.* vii 251–93, Medea rejuvenates Jason's father, Aeson, with a brew of herbs, juices (*sucos*) and roots gathered in *Haemonia . . . valle* (a vale of Thessaly).
9–10. In *Fast.* vi 743–56 Ovid tells how Coronides (i.e. Aesculapius, who was son of Apollo by Coronis) restored Hippolytus to life, pitying Diana's grief. Starnes and Talbert (233) think M. indebted to the version of the story in Stephanus, which mentions Diana's prayers.
12. Phoebo . . . tuo] The Vice-Chancellor.
13–14. In Homer, *Il.* xxiv 336–467, Mercury (frequently called *Cyllenius*

Talis et Eurybates ante ora furentis Achillei
  Rettulit Atridae iussa severa ducis.
Magna sepulchrorum regina, satelles Averni
  Saeva nimis Musis, Palladi saeva nimis,
Quin illos rapias qui pondus inutile terrae,
  Turba quidem est telis ista petenda tuis.
Vestibus hunc igitur pullis Academia luge,
  Et madeant lachrymis nigra feretra tuis.
Fundat et ipsa modos querebunda Elegëia tristes,
  Personet et totis naenia moesta scholis.

Fierce Death, the last of beadles, shows no favour even to her own profession. She seizes you, a fellow-beadle–you who, resplendent with your glittering mace, used to rouse Pallas' flock[2] so often with your call. Though your brows were whiter than the swan's down[5] beneath which, so the story goes, Jove hid himself, yet you deserved to be made young again with a Haemonian[7] medicine. You deserved to live on, Aeson-like; you deserved to be called back from the waters of Styx,[9] in answer to the insistent prayer of a goddess, by Coronides and his medical skill. If your Apollo[12] ordered you to carry his swift message and call together the gowned assembly, you were like wing-footed Cyllenius,[13] when he was sent from his father's heavenly citadel and stood in the Trojan court. You were like Eurybates[15] when, face to face with furious Achilles, he delivered the uncompromising commands of his chief, Atrides.

Great queen of tombs, accomplice of Avernus,[17] too cruel to the Muses, too cruel to Pallas, why not carry off those who are a useless burden to the earth?[19] There are crowds of them for you to aim your arrows at!

Grieve then, University, for this man, and wear mourning. May his black hearse be wet with your tears. May plaintive Elegy herself pour sorrowful harmonies forth, and may all the schools resound with a song of lamentation.

in Latin poetry because he was born on Mount Cyllene in Arcadia), is sent by his father, Jupiter, to guide Priam to Achilles. He meets Priam not, as M. implies, in the Trojan court, but outside the walls of Troy.

15–16. In Homer, *Il.* i 318–44, Eurybates and Talthybius, the heralds of Agamemnon (son of Atreus, hence called *Atrides* by M.), are sent to Achilles to demand the return of Briseïs. M.'s reference is inaccurate: the heralds were too frightened to say anything, and Achilles guessed why they had come from their silence.

17. satelles Averni] Cp. Horace, *Odes* II xviii 34 where Charon is called *satelles Orci*. Avernus, used poetically to mean the Underworld (as in Ovid *Am.* III ix 27), is a lake near Naples: close to it was located the cave by which Aeneas descended to the nether world (*Aen.* vi 106–7).

19. pondus inutile terrae] The phrase is taken from Achilles' description of himself in *Il.* xviii 104.

12 *In Proditionem Bombardicam*

[On the Gunpowder Plot]

Date. Nov. 1626? There is no evidence to show when M.'s four epigrams on the Gunpowder Plot or his epigram on the inventor of gunpowder were written. Because of their subject-matter they are generally assumed to be contemporary with *Q Nov* (p. 36 below).
Publication. 1645 and *1673* (no significant variants).

Cum simul in regem nuper satrapasque Britannos
    Ausus es infandum perfide Fauxe nefas,
Fallor? an et mitis voluisti ex parte videri,
    Et pensare mala cum pietate scelus;
Scilicet hos alti missurus ad atria caeli,
    Sulphureo curru flammivolisque rotis.
Qualiter ille feris caput inviolabile Parcis
    Liquit Iordanios turbine raptus agros.

Treacherous Fawkes, when, not long ago, you dared to plot that unutterable wickedness against the King and the English nobles, did you–or am I mistaken?–intend to appear, in a way, merciful? Did you intend to make up for your crime by a sort of evil piety? It was, I take it, to the halls of high heaven that you meant to blow them up in their sulphurous chariot with its wheels of whirling flame: you meant to blow them up just as that man[7] whose life the fierce Parcae could not harm was swept up from Jordan's banks in a whirlwind.

13 *In Eandem*

[On the Same]

Date. Nov. 1626? See headnote to previous poem. This epigram must be dated later than Mar. 1625 because of its allusion to James's death.
Publication. 1645 and *1673* (no significant variants).

Siccine tentasti caelo donasse Iacobum
    Quae septemgemino Belua monte lates?
Ni meliora tuum poterit dare munera numen,
    Parce precor donis insidiosa tuis.
Ille quidem sine te consortia serus adivit
    Astra, nec inferni pulveris usus ope.

¶12. *7. ille*] Elijah is swept up from Jordan's banks by a whirlwind, riding in a chariot of fire, in *2 Kings* ii 11.
¶ 13. *2. Belua*] The Protestants commonly identified the seven-headed beast of *Rev.* xiii 1 with the Roman Church.
5. James I died 27 Mar. 1625.

Sic potius foedos in caelum pelle cucullos,
Et quot habet brutos Roma profana deos,
Namque hac aut alia nisi quemque adiuveris arte,
Crede mihi caeli vix bene scandet iter.

So you tried to send James to heaven did you, you skulking Beast on your seven hills?[2] Traitor! Unless your godship can give better gifts do us the favour of keeping your presents to yourself. James has now gone to join the starry brotherhood,[5] at a ripe old age, without the help of you or your infernal gunpowder. Use it instead to blow up to heaven your filthy monks[7] and all the brutish gods in profane Rome. For believe me, unless you give each of them an upward shove by this means or some other, not one will have an easy climb up the heavenly path.

14 *In Eandem*

[On the Same]

Date. Nov. 1626? See headnote to *Prod Bomb* (p. 33).
Publication. *1645* and *1673* (no significant variants: in l. *4* *1673* misprints *corona* for *cornua*).

Purgatorem animae derisit Iacobus ignem,
Et sine quo superum non adeunda domus.
Frenduit hoc trina monstrum Latiale corona
Movit et horrificum cornua dena minax.
Et nec inultus ait temnes mea sacra Britanne,
Supplicium spreta relligione dabis.
Et si stelligeras unquam penetraveris arces,
Non nisi per flammas triste patebit iter.
O quam funesto cecinisti proxima vero,
Verbaque ponderibus vix caritura suis!
Nam prope Tartareo sublime rotatus ab igni
Ibat ad aethereas umbra perusta plagas.

James joked about the purgatorial fire,[1] without which the soul cannot reach the home of the blessed. At this the triple-crowned monster of Latium[3] gnashed its teeth and lowered its ten horns[4] in a horribly menacing way. 'Briton', it said, 'your contempt for what is sacred to me will not go unpunished. You will pay the penalty for scorning religion. And if ever

7–10. Cp. *PL* iii 474–93 (pp. 589–90).
¶ 14. *1.* As W. MacKellar points out in *MLR* xviii (1923) 472–3, James referred to the idea of purgatory as 'trash' in the *Premonition* prefaced to the second edition (1609) of his *Apology for the Oath of Allegiance*.
3. Latiale] Roman (from *Latium*, the part of Italy in which Rome was situated).
4. cornua dena] The beast of *Rev.* xiii 1 has ten horns.

you get inside the starry citadels it will be only after a fearful journey through the flames.' Oh how near your prophetic words came to being deadly truth! How little they lacked of fulfilment! For he was almost whirled up to the heavenly regions by Tartarean fire, a burnt-up ghost.

15 *In Eandem*

[On the Same]

Date. Nov. 1626? See headnote to *Prod Bomb* (p. 33).
Publication. *1645* and *1673* (no significant variants).

Quem modo Roma suis devoverat impia diris,
  Et Styge damnarat Taenarioque sinu,
Hunc vice mutata iam tollere gestit ad astra,
  Et cupit ad superos evehere usque Deos.

Impious Rome once cursed this man with horrid imprecations[1] and condemned him to Styx and the Taenarian gulf.[2] Now, going to the opposite extreme, she longs to raise him to the stars and desires to lift him up to the gods above.

16 *In Inventorem Bombardae*

[On the Inventor of Gunpowder]

Date. Nov. 1626? See headnote to *Prod Bomb* (p. 33).
Publication. *1645* and *1673* (no significant variants).

Iapetionidem laudavit caeca vetustas,
  Qui tulit aethereum solis ab axe facem;
At mihi maior erit, qui lurida creditur arma,
  Et trifidum fulmen surripuisse Iovi.

¶ 15. *1*. When James came to the throne Clement VIII did not excommunicate him (as Pius V had Elizabeth in 1570); indeed he had high hopes of his conversion, and James's relations with Rome were good up to 1605. Perhaps M. is alluding to the anger felt by English Catholics when the king permitted the fines payable by them under the Elizabethan code to be collected in May 1603. It was this anger which led to William Watson's abortive plot to kidnap the king (see D. H. Willson, *King James VI and I* (1956) 218–23).
2. *Taenarioque sinu*] See *Proc Med* 5n (p. 28).
¶ 16. *1*. *Iapetionidem*] Prometheus, son of Japetus. Hesiod, *Theog*. 562–9, relates how when Jupiter, in anger, denied fire to men Prometheus stole it and brought it to earth hidden in a hollow fennel stalk.
4. Drummond has an epigram on the invention of the cannon (*Madrigals and Epigrams* (1616) xviii) in which Jove, on hearing a cannon for the first time, wonders 'What mortall Wight had stollen from him his Thunder'.

In their blindness the ancients praised Japetus's son[1] for bringing down heavenly fire from the sun's axle. But I think this man greater who, we may well believe, has snatched from Jove his ghastly weapons and three-forked thunderbolt.[4]

17 *In Quintum Novembris*

[On the Fifth of November]

Date. Nov.? 1626. The closing lines suggest that the poem was written for an actual celebration of 5 Nov., but this is not certain. The heading *Anno aetatis 17*, which appears in *1645* and *1673*, could mean either 'In the seventeenth year of his age' or 'At seventeen years of age' (i.e. 1625 or 1626). The same heading, however, is used for *Elegia II* and *Elegia III*, and in both these cases it must refer to 1626.
Publication. *1645* (*84.* salaces.]salaces, *86.* Talis]Talis, *92.* artus?]artus *93.* tuorum!]tuorum, *96.* Britanni:]Britanni; *125.* casumque]casuque *143.* praeruptaque]semifractaque *146.* fauces.]fauces, *148.* timor,] Timor, *149.* Manes,]Manes *150.* Exululat]Exululant,) *1673* (the text followed here, but emended in these instances: *13.* unanimes] unamimes *43.* tentamina]tantamina possunt,]possunt.)
Modern criticism. E. K. Rand, *SP* xix (1922) 121–2, considers that 'the little epic on Guy Fawkes, the work of the author's seventeenth year, shows greater poise and firmness than the little epic on the *Gnat* which Virgil wrote at sixteen'. M. Cheek, *SP* liv (1957) 172–84, demonstrates the Virgilian nature of *Q Nov*: the aerial survey and dream visitation are prefigured in Virgil's epic: M.'s *Fama* derives from *Aen.* iv 173–97 with additions from ix 473–5 and xi 139–41: Satan's mission of destruction parallels Allecto's, *Aen.* vii 335–8. The Satan of *Q Nov*, claims Cheek, is the Satan of *PL* in embryo, as is shown by his numbering of his followers (*10*, cp. *PL* i 571), his sighs of envy (*34*, cp. *PL* iv 31), his character as 'artificer of fraud' (*17*, cp. *PL* iv 121) etc. Tillyard 22–3 suggests the influence of Giles Fletcher's *Locustae* (not published until 1627).

Iam pius extrema veniens Iacobus ab arcto
Teucrigenas populos, lateque patentia regna
Albionum tenuit, iamque inviolabile foedus
Sceptra Caledoniis coniunxerat Anglica Scotis:
Pacificusque novo felix divesque sedebat
In solio, occultique doli securus et hostis:
Cum ferus ignifluo regnans Acheronte tyrannus,

¶ 17. *1.* James came from Scotland in 1603. The date finally planned for the blowing up of Parliament by the plotters was 5 Nov. 1605.
2. Teucrigenas populos] See *Elegia I* 73*n* (p. 22).
7. ignifluo . . . Acheronte] Of the infernal rivers in Virgil Phlegethon, not Acheron, was the river of fire (see *Aen.* vi 295–7 and 550–1).

Eumenidum pater, aethereo vagus exul Olympo,
Forte per immensum terrarum erraverat orbem,
Dinumerans sceleris socios, vernasque fideles,
Participes regni post funera moesta futuros;
Hic tempestates medio ciet aere diras,
Illic unanimes odium struit inter amicos,
Armat et invictas in mutua viscera gentes;
Regnaque olivifera vertit florentia pace,
Et quoscunque videt purae virtutis amantes,
Hos cupit adiicere imperio, fraudumque magister
Tentat inaccessum sceleri corrumpere pectus,
Insidiasque locat tacitas, cassesque latentes
Tendit, ut incautos rapiat, seu Caspia tigris
Insequitur trepidam deserta per avia praedam
Nocte sub illuni, et somno nictantibus astris.
Talibus infestat populos Summanus et urbes
Cinctus caeruleae fumanti turbine flammae.
Iamque fluentisonis albentia rupibus arva
Apparent, et terra Deo dilecta marino,
Cui nomen dederat quondam Neptunia proles
Amphitryoniaden qui non dubitavit atrocem
Aequore tranato furiali poscere bello,
Ante expugnatae crudelia saecula Troiae.
At simul hanc opibusque et festa pace beatam
Aspicit, et pingues donis Cerealibus agros,

8. Eumenidum pater] Virgil names Pluto as father of the Furies in *Aen.* vii 327. *exul Olympo*] Echoes *Aen.* viii 319–20 where Saturn is *Olympo . . . exsul.*

10. vernas] Specifically 'slaves by birth'. Though in *De doctrina* I iv (Columbia xiv 129–30) M. denies that any men are predestined to damnation he admits that some men are, by nature and disposition, more alienated from the grace of God than others.

12. medio . . . aere] The theory of the three regions of the air, current in the seventeenth century, is explained by Du Bartas 35–6, who points out that the middle region is characterized by cold and that from it hail comes.

23. Summanus] Pliny II liii 138 says that Summanus was originally a Tuscan deity, taken over by the Romans as the god of nocturnal thunderbolts.

27–30. In the *History of Britain* M. recounts the legend of Albion, a giant son of Neptune, who reigned in England '44 years. Till at length passing over into *Gaul*, in aid of his brother *Lestrygon*, against whom *Hercules* was hasting out of *Spain* into *Italy*, he was there slain in fight' (Columbia x 4). *Amphitryoniaden*] Hercules, whose real father was Jove, but whose mother, Alcmena, was married to Amphitryon.

31–5. Satan's grief and noxious sighs are borrowed from Ovid's description of Envy coming into sight of Athens (*Met.* ii 790–6).

Quodque magis doluit, venerantem numina veri
Sancta Dei populum, tandem suspiria rupit
Tartareos ignes et luridum olentia sulphur.
Qualia Trinacria trux ab Iove clausus in Aetna
Efflat tabifico monstrosus ab ore Tiphoeus.
Ignescunt oculi, stridetque adamantinus ordo
Dentis, ut armorum fragor, ictaque cuspide cuspis.
Atque pererrato solum hoc lacrymabile mundo
Inveni, dixit, gens haec mihi sola rebellis,
Contemtrixque iugi, nostraque potentior arte.
Illa tamen, mea si quicquam tentamina possunt,
Non feret hoc impune diu, non ibit inulta,
Hactenus; et piceis liquido natat aere pennis;
Qua volat, adversi praecursant agmine venti,
Densantur nubes, et crebra tonitrua fulgent.
   Iamque pruinosas velox superaverat alpes,
Et tenet Ausoniae fines, a parte sinistra
Nimbifer Appenninus erat, priscique Sabini,
Dextra veneficiis infamis Hetruria, nec non
Te furtiva Tibris Thetidi videt oscula dantem;
Hinc Mavortigenae consistit in arce Quirini.
Reddiderant dubiam iam sera crepuscula lucem,
Cum circumgreditur totam Tricoronifer urbem,
Panificosque Deos portat, scapulisque virorum
Evehitur, praeeunt submisso poplite reges,

35. *luridum . . . sulphur*] Echoes Ovid, *Met.* xiv 791: *lurida . . . sulphura.*

36–7. Ovid, *Met.* v 346–53, explains how Jove pinned the giant Tiphoeus down by placing the island of Sicily upon him, with Mount Aetna resting upon his head, through which he spouts flame and ash.

38. *Ignescunt oculi*] Cp. *PL* i 193–4 (p. 473).

47. *Densantur*] Cp. *PL* i 226–7 (p. 475).

48. Echoing Lucan i 183: *Iam gelidas Caesar cursu superaverat Alpes.*

51. *veneficiis*] M. apparently uses the word loosely: the inhabitants of Etruria (modern Tuscany) were, as Livy remarks (V i 6), more devoted to the pagan religious rites than any other nation; they were particularly noted for divination and augury.

52. *Thetidi*] M. uses the name of Thetis, a sea nymph, to mean the sea, as does Virgil, *Ecl.* iv 32.

53. *Mavortigenae . . . Quirini*] Romulus, son of Mars, was called Quirinus after his deification (cp. Ovid, *Fast.* i 199 *Martigenam . . . Quirinum*).

54. *dubiam . . . crepuscula lucem*] Echoes Ovid, *Met.* xi 596 *dubiaeque crepuscula lucis.*

56. *Panificosque Deos*] the Host.

Et mendicantum series longissima fratrum;
Cereaque in manibus gestant funalia caeci,
Cimmeriis nati in tenebris, vitamque trahentes.
Templa dein multis subeunt lucentia taedis
(Vesper erat sacer iste Petro)fremitusque canentum
Saepe tholos implet vacuos, et inane locorum.
Qualiter exululat Bromius, Bromiique caterva,
Orgia cantantes in Echionio Aracyntho,
Dum tremit attonitus vitreis Asopus in undis,
Et procul ipse cava responsat rupe Cithaeron.
His igitur tandem solenni more peractis,
Nox senis amplexus Erebi taciturna reliquit,
Praecipitesque impellit equos stimulante flagello,
Captum oculis Typhlonta, Melanchaetemque ferocem,
Atque Acherontaeo prognatam patre Siopen
Torpidam, et hirsutis horrentem Phrica capillis.
Interea regum domitor, Phlegetontius haeres
Ingreditur thalamos (neque enim secretus adulter
Producit steriles molli sine pellice noctes)
At vix compositos somnus claudebat ocellos,
Cum niger umbrarum dominus, rectorque silentum,
Praedatorque hominum falsa sub imagine tectus
Astitit, assumptis micuerunt tempora canis,

60. Cimmeriis . . . tenebris] In *Od.* xi 13–22 Odysseus sails to the land of the Cimmerians who live on the edge of the world in perpetual darkness.
64. Bromius] Literally, 'the noisy one', Bacchus.
65–7. Echionio Aracyntho] Echion, one of the heroes who sprang from the dragon's teeth sown by Cadmus, founded the citadel of Thebes: thus *Echionius* may mean Theban or, since Thebes was chief city of Boeotia, Boeotian. *Aracynthus*: a mountain between Boeotia and Attica. *Asopus*: a river in Boeotia flowing near Mount *Cithaeron*, which is mentioned as the scene of Bacchic orgies by Ovid, *Met.* iii 702, and Virgil, *Aen.* iv 303. Propertius III xv 25–42, names Aracynthus, Asopus and Cithaeron together in the story of Dirce.
69. Nox . . . Erebi] Hesiod, *Theog.* 123–5, tells how Night, sister of Erebus, bore his children Ether and Day.
70–3. Virgil, *Aen.* v 721, mentions Night's chariot and Spenser gives it 'cole blacke steedes' (*F.Q.* I v 20), but M. invents names for them from the Greek words τυφλός, blind; μέλαν, black and χαίτη, long hair; σιωπή, silence; and φρίξ, shuddering.
72–4. Acherontaeo . . . Phlegetontius] See l. 7*n*.
80–5. Cp. Satan's disguise in *PR* i 314–20 and 497–8. In Buchanan's Latin poem *Franciscanus* 19–20 St Francis is *cannabe cinctus* and has *obrasum . . . caput duro velante cucullo*, and the description of a friar in the same poem

Barba sinus promissa tegit, cineracea longo
Syrmate verrit humum vestis, pendetque cucullus
Vertice de raso, et ne quicquam desit ad artes,
Cannabeo lumbos constrinxit fune salaces.
Tarda fenestratis figens vestigia calceis.
Talis uti fama est, vasta Franciscus eremo
Tetra vagabatur solus per lustra ferarum,
Sylvestrique tulit genti pia verba salutis
Impius, atque lupos domuit, Libicosque leones.
    Subdolus at tali Serpens velatus amictu
Solvit in has fallax ora execrantia voces;
Dormis nate? Etiamne tuos sopor opprimit artus?
Immemor O fidei, pecorumque oblite tuorum!
Dum cathedram venerande tuam, diademaque triplex
Ridet Hyperboreo gens barbara nata sub axe,
Dumque pharetrati spernunt tua iura Britanni:
Surge, age, surge piger, Latius quem Caesar adorat,
Cui reserata patet convexi ianua caeli,
Turgentes animos, et fastus frange procaces,
Sacrilegique sciant, tua quid maledictio possit,
Et quid Apostolicae possit custodia clavis;
Et memor Hesperiae disiectam ulciscere classem,
Mersaque Iberorum lato vexilla profundo,
Sanctorumque cruci tot corpora fixa probrosae,

(45–8) includes *longo sub syrmate rasum . . . caput*. The friar who appears to Buchanan in his *Somnium* 5–9 (printed among the *Fratres Fraterrimi*) wears *fenestratus calceus*.

86–9. Among the anecdotes about St Francis of Assisi preserved in the *Fioretti*, one (xvi) records his preaching to the birds (M.'s 'woodland folk') and another (xxi) his taming of the wolf of Gubbio. St Bonaventure's *Life of St Francis* tells how, after his conversion, he left the city and wandered through the woods chanting praises to God (ii 5), how later he spent Lent in the solitudes of Alverna (viii 10), and how he was able to tame wild beasts (viii 11).

92–3. M. recalls Mercury's rousing speeches to Aeneas, *Aen*. iv 267 and 560, and the Dream's to Agamemnon, *Il*. ii 22–34.

95. *Hyperboreo . . . axe*] See *Mansus* 26*n* (p. 262).

97. Echoing the words of Aeneas' Penates, appearing to him in a dream: *surge age* (*Aen*. iii 169).

101. *Apostolicae . . . custodia clavis*] Refers to the Catholic doctrine by which succeeding Popes inherit the keys of the kingdom of heaven given to Peter by Christ, *Matt*. xvi 19.

102–3 Referring to the Spanish Armada of 1588.

104–5. Referring to the persecution of Catholics during Elizabeth's reign.

Thermodoontea nuper regnante puella.
At tu si tenero mavis torpescere lecto
Crescentesque negas hosti contundere vires,
Tyrrhenum implebit numeroso milite pontum,
Signaque Aventino ponet fulgentia colle:
Relliquias veterum franget, flammisque cremabit,
Sacraque calcabit pedibus tua colla profanis,
Cuius gaudebant soleis dare basia reges.
Nec tamen hunc bellis et aperto Marte lacesses,
Irritus ille labor, tu callidus utere fraude,
Quaelibet haereticis disponere retia fas est;
Iamque ad consilium extremis rex magnus ab oris
Patricios vocat, et procerum de stirpe creatos,
Grandaevosque patres trabea, canisque verendos;
Hos tu membratim poteris conspergere in auras,
Atque dare in cineres, nitrati pulveris igne
Aedibus iniecto, qua convenere, sub imis.
Protinus ipse igitur quoscunque habet Anglia fidos
Propositi, factique mone, quisquamne tuorum
Audebit summi non iussa facessere Papae.
Perculsosque metu subito, casumque stupentes
Invadat vel Gallus atrox, vel saevus Iberus.
Saecula sic illic tandem Mariana redibunt,
Tuque in belligeros iterum dominaberis Anglos.
Et nequid timeas, divos divasque secundas
Accipe, quotque tuis celebrantur numina fastis.
Dixit et adscitos ponens malefidus amictus
Fugit ad infandam, regnum illaetabile, Lethen.
  Iam rosea Eoas pandens Tithonia portas
Vestit inauratas redeunti lumine terras;
Maestaque adhuc nigri deplorans funera nati
Irrigat ambrosiis montana cacumina guttis;
Cum somnos pepulit stellatae ianitor aulae
Nocturnos visus, et somnia grata revolvens.

Thermodoontea: Amazonian: the adjective is formed by M. from *Thermodon*, a river at the mouth of which, according to Strabo I iii 7, the Amazons lived.
109. Aventino . . . colle] The Aventine, one of Rome's seven hills, extends from the Palatine to the Coelian Mount.
127. Saecula . . . Mariana] the reign of Mary (1553–58) with its burning of Protestants, as recorded, for example, in Foxe's *Acts and Monuments* XI–XII.
132. Lethe is the river of forgetfulness in the infernal regions.
133–5. Tithonia] Aurora, the dawn, wife of Tithonus. Her son Memnon fought for the Trojans and was killed by Achilles; Ovid, *Met.* xiii 576–622, tells of her inconsolable grief.
136. montana cacumina] The phrase is from Ovid, *Met.* i 310.

Est locus aeterna septus caligine noctis
Vasta ruinosi quondam fundamina tecti,
Nunc torvi spelunca Phoni, Prodotaeque bilinguis
Effera quos uno peperit discordia partu.
Hic inter caementa iacent praeruptaque saxa,
Ossa inhumata virum, et traiecta cadavera ferro;
Hic dolus intortis semper sedet ater ocellis,
Iurgiaque, et stimulis armata calumnia fauces.
Et furor, atque viae moriendi mille videntur
Et timor, exanguisque locum circumvolat horror,
Perpetuoque leves per muta silentia manes,
Exululat tellus et sanguine conscia stagnat.
Ipsi etiam pavidi latitant penetralibus antri
Et Phonos, et Prodotes, nulloque sequente per antrum
Antrum horrens, scopulosum, atrum feralibus umbris
Diffugiunt sontes, et retro lumina vortunt,
Hos pugiles Romae per saecula longa fideles
Evocat antistes Babylonius, atque ita fatur.
Finibus occiduis circumfusum incolit aequor
Gens exosa mihi, prudens natura negavit
Indignam penitus nostro coniungere mundo:
Illuc, sic iubeo, celeri contendite gressu,
Tartareoque leves difflentur pulvere in auras
Et rex et pariter satrapae, scelerata propago
Et quotquot fidei caluere cupidine verae
Consilii socios adhibete, operisque ministros.
Finierat, rigidi cupide paruere gemelli.

139–54. M.'s cave with its personified inhabitants is based on Virgil's description of hell-gate (*Aen.* vi 273–81) and Spenser's imitation of it (*F.Q.* II vii 21–5).

143. praeruptaque] altered from *1645*'s *semifractaque*, which Salmasius in his *Responsio* (1660) had picked on as a false quantity.

146. calumnia] As C. Symmons points out, *CJ* ix (1814) 344, this word is never used in classical Latin poetry: it is found only in prose.

148. Horror similarly flies about in Spenser's Cave of Mammon, *F.Q.* II vii 23.

149. per muta silentia] The phrase is from Ovid, *Met.* vii 184.

156. Babylonius] In English Protestant literature of the sixteenth and seventeenth centuries the Babylon of *Rev.* xiv 8 and xvii 5 is frequently identified with Rome. Coverdale praises Henry VIII, in the epistle prefaced to his translation of the Bible, for 'delyverynge us out of oure olde Babylonycall captivyte'.

158. prudens] In Horace, *Odes* I iii 22, the division of lands by oceans is ascribed to *deus . . . prudens.*

165. paruere] The short first syllable is a false quantity.

Interea longo flectens curvamine coelos
Despicit aetherea dominus qui fulgurat arce,
Vanaque perversae ridet conamina turbae,
Atque sui causam populi volet ipse tueri.
Esse ferunt spatium, qua distat ab Aside terra
Fertilis Europe, et spectat Mareotidas undas;
Hic turris posita est Titanidos ardua Famae
Aerea, lata, sonans, rutilis vicinior astris
Quam superimpositum vel Athos vel Pelion Ossae
Mille fores aditusque patent, totidemque fenestrae,
Amplaque per tenues translucent atria muros;
Excitat hic varios plebs agglomerata susurros;
Qualiter instrepitant circum mulctralia bombis
Agmina muscarum, aut texto per ovilia iunco,
Dum Canis aestivum coeli petit ardua culmen
Ipsa quidem summa sedet ultrix matris in arce,
Auribus innumeris cinctum caput eminet olli,
Queis sonitum exiguum trahit, atque levissima captat
Murmura, ab extremis patuli confinibus orbis.
Nec tot Aristoride servator inique iuvencae
Isidos, immiti volvebas lumina vultu,

166. longo . . . curvamine coelos] Echoes Ovid, *Met.* vi 64: *longum curvamine caelum.*
170–93. The sources for M.'s description of Fame and her tower are Ovid, *Met.* xii 39–63, Virgil, *Aen.* iv 173–88, and possibly Chaucer *House of Fame* iii. The borrowings from Ovid and Virgil are reviewed in Harding 50–3.
171. Mareotidas] Lake Mareotis is in Egypt, near Alexandria. It was Lake Maeotis (the Sea of Azof) which was considered as part of the boundary between Europe and Asia. Both Ovid and Chaucer place Fame's tower at a central point in the world. Thus possibly M., having mentioned Europe and Asia, meant Lake Mareotis to stand for the third continent, Africa (as A. H. Gilbert suggests, *MLN* xxviii (1913) 30), or possibly *Mareotidas* should be emended to *Maeotidas* (as D. T. Starnes argues, *N & Q* cxcvi (1951) 515–12, quoting Lucan iii 271–8 as evidence for the centrality of Lake Maeotis).
172. Titanidos] Virgil's Fame is sister of the Titans Coeus and Enceladus (*Aen.* iv 178–80).
174. Athos] A mountain at the southern tip of the Hagion Oros peninsula in eastern Greece, given first place in Ovid's list of mountains, *Met.* ii 217. *Pelion* and *Ossa* are mountains in Thessaly. When the giants made war on the gods they piled Ossa on Olympus and Pelion on Ossa in an attempt to climb to heaven, as Homer relates, *Od.* xi 313–16 and Ovid, *Met.* i 151–5.
178–80. The simile of the flies and milking pails is from Homer who uses it to describe the Greeks before Troy, *Il.* ii 469–73, and the Greeks and Trojans fighting over Sarpedon's body, xvi 641–3.
185–6. Aristoride . . . Isidos] According to Ovid, *Met.* i 624–31, Argus, son

Lumina non unquam tacito nutantia somno,
Lumina subiectas late spectantia terras.
Istis illa solet loca luce carentia saepe
Perlustrare, etiam radianti impervia soli.
Millenisque loquax auditaque visaque linguis
Cuilibet effundit temeraria, veraque mendax
Nunc minuit, modo confictis sermonibus auget.
Sed tamen a nostro meruisti carmine laudes
Fama, bonum quo non aliud veracius ullum,
Nobis digna cani, nec te memorasse pigebit
Carmine tam longo, servati scilicet Angli
Officiis vaga diva tuis, tibi reddimus aequa.
Te Deus aeternos motu qui temperat ignes,
Fulmine praemisso alloquitur, terraque tremente:
Fama siles? an te latet impia Papistarum
Coniurata cohors in meque meosque Britannos,
Et nova sceptrigero caedes meditata Iacobo:
Nec plura, illa statim sensit mandata Tonantis,
Et satis ante fugax stridentes induit alas,
Induit et variis exilia corpora plumis;
Dextra tubam gestat Temesaeo ex aere sonoram.
Nec mora iam pennis cedentes remigat auras,
Atque parum est cursu celeres praevertere nubes,
Iam ventos, iam solis equos post terga reliquit:
Et primo Angliacas solito de more per urbes
Ambiguas voces, incertaque murmura spargit,
Mox arguta dolos, et detestabile vulgat
Proditionis opus, nec non facta horrida dictu,

of Arestor, had a hundred eyes of which only one pair closed in sleep at any one time, and Juno therefore set him to guard Io, whom Jove had turned into a heifer. M. calls him 'unjust' because he forced Io away from her father, Inachus (*Met.* i 664–5). Io became identified with the Egyptian goddess Isis: Herodotus (ii 41) draws attention to the similarity between the two, and in the *Mythologiae* (1612) Conti has a chapter (VIII xix) *De Ione sive Iside*.

194–8. The plot was discovered because Lord Monteagle received a letter from his brother-in-law Francis Tresham on 26 Oct. 1605, warning him not to attend the opening of Parliament: he immediately informed the Government.

195. Echoing Virgil, *Aen.* iv 174: *Fama, malum qua non aliud velocius ullum.*

207. Temesaeo ex aere] Temese, on the southern tip of Italy, was famous for its copper mines in Homeric times (see *Od.* i 184). Ovid has *Temesaea . . . aera, Met.* vii 207–8 and *Fast.* v 441.

212. Ambiguas voces . . . spargit] Echoes Virgil, *Aen.* ii 98–9: *spargere voces . . . ambiguas.*

Authoresque addit sceleris, nec garrula caecis
Insidiis loca structa silet; stupuere relatis,
Et pariter iuvenes, pariter tremuere puellae,
Effaetique senes pariter, tantaeque ruinae
Sensus ad aetatem subito penetraverat omnem
Attamen interea populi miserescit ab alto
Aethereus pater, et crudelibus obstitit ausis
Papicolum; capti poenas raptantur ad acres;
At pia thura Deo, et grati solvuntur honores;
Compita laeta focis genialibus omnia fumant;
Turba choros iuvenilis agit: quintoque Novembris
Nulla dies toto occurrit celebratior anno.

Now came good King James[1] from the far north and began his reign over that nation which traces its origins to Troy,[2] and over the extensive domains of the English people. Now an inviolable treaty had united the Scots of Caledonia under English rule. James, the peace-bearer, sat on his new throne. Wealth and good fortune were his: he was not worried about any enemy or secret plot. It happened at that time that the fierce tyrant who controls Acheron's[7] flaming currents, the tyrant who is father to the Furies[8] and a wandering exile from heavenly Olympus, had gone roaming over this huge globe. He was counting up his companions in crime, his faithful slaves by birth,[10] who, after their miserable deaths, were going to share his kingdom. Here and there he stirs up frightful storms in the middle air,[12] or sows hatred between close friends. He arms invincible nations for deadly war one against the other, and overturns kingdoms hitherto flourishing under the olive-branch of peace. He is especially eager to add to his empire any lovers of pure virtue that he comes across: a past-master of trickery, he does his best to corrupt the soul which is locked against sin. Silently he sets his traps, and stretches hidden nets to catch the unwary, just as the Caspian tigress stalks her trembling prey through trackless wastes while the stars wink drowsily in the moonless night: just as Summanus,[23] wrapped in a smoking whirlwind of blue flame, falls upon peoples and cities.

Presently white cliffs and rocks with roaring breakers come into view. It is the land dear to the god of the sea; the land which, long ago, Neptune's son[27] gave his name to: that son who, when he had crossed the ocean, did not shrink from challenging Amphitryon's fierce son to fearful combat, before the cruel days of Troy's downfall.[30]

As soon as he catches sight of this island, blessed with wealth and joyful peace,[31] with its fields cram-full of Ceres's gifts and–what pained him even more–its people worshipping the sacred powers of the true God, he breaks into sighs that stink of hellish flames and yellow sulphur;[35] sighs like those which the savage monster Tiphoeus, imprisoned under Sicilian Aetna by Jove,[36] breathes out from his decaying mouth. His eyes flash fire,[38] his rows of teeth, hard as steel, gnash with a noise like the clash of weapons, like spear crashing against spear. 'I have wandered over the whole world', he says, 'and this is the only thing that brings tears to my eyes; this is the only nation I have found which rebels against me, spurns my government and is mightier than my crafts. But if my efforts have any effect, these people

221. *crudelibus obstitit ausis*] The phrase is from Ovid, *Her.* xiv 49.

will not get away with it for long: they will not go unpunished.' His speech finished, he glides through the calm air on wings as black as pitch. Wherever he flies opposing winds rush in a crowd before him, clouds grow dense,[47] and flashes of lightning come thick and fast. He flew swiftly and had soon crossed the frosty Alps[48] and reached the north of Italy. To his left were the cloud-capped Apennines and the ancient Sabine land; to his right, Etruria, notorious for its sorceries.[51] Now he can see the place where you, Tiber, steal kisses from the sea.[52] Presently he alighted on the citadel of Quirinus,[53] son of Mars. The shades of evening had fallen, bringing twilight,[54] and now the wearer of the Triple Crown is making his tour of the city. He is carried shoulder-high, and with him he bears his gods, made of bread.[56] Kings crawl before him on their knees, and there is a long, long procession of beggarly friars. The blind fools carry wax tapers in their hands, for they were all born in Cimmerian[60] darkness and are dragging out their lives in it still. The procession winds its way into churches which are ablaze with innumerable candles (for it was St Peter's Eve), and again and again the wailing of the chanters fills the empty domes and void spaces. They make a noise like Bromius[64] and his mob howling and singing orgiastic songs on Echionian Aracynthus[65] while startled Asopus shudders beneath his glassy waves and even Cithaeron, far, far away, sends back an echo from its hollow cliff.[67]

When the rites had eventually been performed in the time-honoured way, Night silently slipped from old Erebus's embrace[69] and, with her smarting whip, set her team galloping at a headlong pace–blind Typhlon,[71] fierce Melanchaetes, numb Siope, a mare sired by an Acherontean[72] steed, and shaggy Phrix with his bristling mane.[73]

Meanwhile the king-tamer, the heir of Hell,[74] goes into his bridal apartments (for this secret adulterer does not drag out barren nights without the company of a soft whore). But just as slumber was closing his peaceful eyes the dark lord of shadows, the ruler of the silent dead who preys upon men, appeared at his bedside in disguise. His temples gleamed with white hair, put on for the occasion;[80] a long beard covers his chest; his ash-coloured gown sweeps the floor with its trailing hem; a cowl hangs back from his tonsured head, and to complete his crafty disguise he has bound a hempen rope round his lustful loins and tied latticed sandals to his slow old feet.[85] Francis,[86] so the story goes, looked like this when he wandered alone in the desolate wilderness and through the filthy dens of wild animals and (though unredeemed himself), carried the redeeming words of salvation to woodland folk, and tamed the wolves and Libyan lions.[89]

Disguised in this way the crafty, lying serpent opened his foul lips and spoke these words: 'Are you asleep, my son?[92] Are your limbs heavy with slumber? O forgetful of the faith, neglectful of your flocks,[93] while a barbarous nation born beneath the northern sky[95] is laughing at your throne and triple diadem; while the British archers are spurning your rights–you, who should be revered! Get up, come on, get up, sluggard![97] You whom the Holy Roman Emperor worships: you for whom the locked gate of heaven's vault lies open–break their vaunting spirits, their insolent pride, and let these sacrilegious sinners know the power of your curse, the power which control of the Apostolic key gives you.[101] Remember the past! Avenge the scattered Spanish fleet![102] Avenge the Iberian standards overwhelmed in the deep[103] and the bodies of so many saints nailed to the shameful cross[104] during the Amazonian virgin's recent reign.[105] If you choose, instead, to lie like a dolt in your soft bed, and refuse to crush your enemy's growing strength, he will fill the Tyrrhenian Sea with his swarming battalions and plant his glittering standards on the Aventine hill.[109] He will smash your ancient relics and throw them on the fire and trample your holy neck beneath his profane feet – you whose shoes kings were once glad to kiss! But do not challenge him to war or open combat: that would be a waste of time. Be cunning: use trickery – no trap is too base to use against heretics. At the present moment their great king is summoning the ruling classes to parliament from the furthest corners of their country: the heirs of the nobility and their aged fathers, venerable for their robes of state and their white hair. If you explode gunpowder under the foundations of the building in which they are assembled you will be able to tear them limb from limb, scatter them in the air and burn them to cinders. So inform any of the faithful who are still left in England of this plan of action immediately. Will any of your followers dare to ignore the supreme Papal commands? Afterwards let the fierce Frenchman or the cruel Spaniard invade the Britons while they are still panic-stricken, still wondering at the catastrophe. Thus the Marian regime[127] will at last be re-established in that land, and you will have the warlike English under your thumb again. And in case you should be nervous let me tell you that all the gods and goddesses are on your side, all those deities you worship on your various feast-days.'

When he had finished speaking the deceitful creature abandoned his disguise and fled to Lethe,[132] his unspeakable, joyless kingdom.

Now rosy dawn[133] is opening the eastern gates and clothing the gilded earth with returning light and, still weeping for the sad death of her dark-skinned son,[135] is sprinkling the mountain summits[136] with ambrosial drops. The doorkeeper of the starry court has shaken off slumber and rolled away the sweet dreams and visions of night.

There is a place, shut up in eternal darkness and night,[139] which once formed the giant foundations of a now-ruined building. This place has become the cavernous den of fierce-eyed Murder and double-tongued Treachery, savage Discord's twin children. Here among heaps of rubble and jagged rocks lie unburied skeletons, and corpses thrust through with steel. Here Guile, black and cross-eyed, sits for ever: here are Strife and Calumny,[146] armed with fangs. Here is Rage: Fear and a thousand kinds of death are seen, and bloodless Horror[148] flitting around, and wispy ghosts moving unceasingly through the voiceless silences.[149] The conscious earth shrieks and rots with blood. Murder and Treachery themselves cower terrified into the deepest recesses of that cavernous place and, though no one pursues them through the cave – a horrible cave, jagged with rocks and black with deathly shadows – they flee away guiltily, and keep looking back.[154] The Babylonian priest[156] summons these champions of Rome who have been loyal to her for centuries past, and says: 'By the sea which flows round the western horizon there lives a nation which I detest. Prudent Nature[158] refused to join it up with our continent because it was unworthy. Go there with all speed – that is my command – and let the King and all his nobles, the whole wicked brood, be blown to the four winds by hellish powder. Use all those who are fired with enthusiasm for the true faith as your fellow-conspirators and fellow-workers.' When he had finished speaking the cruel pair eagerly obeyed him.[165]

Meanwhile the Lord who sends the lightning from his skyey citadel and bends the heavens in their wide arc[166] looks down and laughs at the vain attempts of the evil mob, intending to defend His people's cause Himself.

There is, men say,[170] an expanse fronting Lake Mareotis,[171] which separates the Asian continent from fertile Europe. Here the high tower of Fame, daughter of the Titaness,[172] is built–brazen, broad, reverberating, and reaching up nearer to the twinkling stars than Athos[174] or Pelion piled upon Ossa. A thousand doors and entrances gape wide, a thousand windows too, and the spacious halls inside gleam through thin walls. The crowd which swarms here sends up a mingled murmur, like swarms of flies[178] humming and buzzing around the milking pails or through the wattled sheepfolds when the Dog Star is climbing the steeps of heaven to its summer height.[180] Fame herself, her mother's avenger, is seated at the very top of her citadel, and lifts her head high. Innumerable ears stick out all round it, and with these she can intercept even the tiniest sounds and catch the faintest whisper from the remotest corners of the wide world. You, Arestor's son,[185] unjust guardian of the heifer Isis, did not have as many eyes rolling in your harsh face as she–eyes which never close in silent sleep, eyes which keep watch, far and wide, over the lands below. With these Fame often scans unlighted places, where even the sun's rays do not penetrate. Then, blabbing with her thousand tongues, the inconsiderate creature pours out all she has heard and seen to anyone she comes across. She is a liar, too: sometimes she speaks less than the truth, and sometimes more, adding her own invented tales.[193]

But still, Fame, you have deserved praise in my song[194] for one good deed, and there was never a deed more truly good.[195] You deserve to be sung about by me, and I shall never regret having commemorated you at such length in my verse. We English, who were plainly saved by your good offices, wandering goddess, render to you your just dues.[198] God who guides the eternal fires in their wheeling hurled down a thunderbolt and then, as the earth still trembled, said: 'Are you silent, Fame? Is this godless mob of Papists hidden from your sight–this mob which has conspired against me and my Englishmen? Is this new kind of murder which has been planned for sceptred James hidden from you?' He said no more, but the Thunderer's commands had an instant effect on Fame who, though swift of flight before, now puts on creaking wings and covers her thin body with parti-coloured feathers. She takes a blaring trumpet of Temesaean brass[207] in her right hand and, without delay, wings her way through the yielding air. Not content to outstrip the rushing clouds, she soon leaves the winds and the sun's horses behind. As usual she first spreads contradictory rumours[212] and vague murmurings through the English cities, and then in a clear voice she makes public the plots and foul working of treason, its deeds horrible to speak of and, lastly, the instigators of the crime. Chattering away, she makes no secret of the places which have been prepared for the performance of this secret treachery. Her reports caused utter amazement. Young men, girls and weak old men all shuddered. People of all ages were suddenly struck to the heart by the sense of so great a disaster.

But meanwhile our Heavenly Father looked down on his people with pity and put a stop to the Papists' cruel venture.[221] They are captured and hurried off to sharp punishments. Pious incense is burned and grateful honours paid to God. There is merrymaking at every crossroads and smoke rises from the festive bonfires: the young people dance in crowds: in all the year there is no day more celebrated than the fifth of November.

18 *Elegia tertia. In Obitum Praesulis Wintoniensis*

[Elegy III. On the Death of the Bishop of Winchester]

Date. Sept.-Dec. 1626. Headed *Anno aetatis 17* in *1645* and *1673*. Lancelot Andrewes, for whom this elegy was written, died 25 Sept. 1626. If Ernst von Mansfeld is one of the leaders mentioned in *9* the poem cannot have been completed until after news of his death (20 Nov. 1626) reached England. In *Prae E* 1–6 M. says that his eyes were hardly dry from weeping for Andrewes when news of Felton's death (6 Oct. 1626) reached him. Douglas Bush, *HLB* ix (1955) 392–6, takes this to mean that the present elegy must have been completed by 5 Oct., and that *9* cannot, therefore, refer to Mansfeld's death, but there is no need to equate the weeping of *Prae E* 1–6 with the composition of this elegy.

M.'s view of Andrewes had changed by 1641 when he devoted half of *Reason of Church Government* v to a refutation of his 'shallow reasonings' in defence of episcopacy (Columbia iii 201–5; Yale i 768–74).

Publication. 1645 (*34.* Phoebus,]Phoebus) and *1673* (the text followed here).

Moestus eram, et tacitus nullo comitante sedebam,
  Haerebantque animo tristia plura meo,
Protinus en subiit funestae cladis imago
  Fecit in Angliaco quam Libitina solo;
Dum procerum ingressa est splendentes marmore turres
  Dira sepulchrali mors metuenda face;
Pulsavitque auro gravidos et iaspide muros,
  Nec metuit satrapum sternere falce greges.
Tunc memini clarique ducis, fratrisque verendi
  Intempestivis ossa cremata rogis.

¶ 18. *4. Libitina*] Goddess of corpses.
6–7. mors ... Pulsavitque] Echoes Horace, *Odes* I iv 13 *Mors ... pulsat.* B. Whitelocke, *Memorials* (1682) 2–3, records that in 1625 over 35,000 people died of the plague in London and its suburbs, 5,000 of them in one week, and that so many people fled from the city that in Westminster the streets were deserted and overgrown with grass.
9–10. ducis] Probably Ernst von Mansfeld, a mercenary general of a marauding army in the early years of the Thirty Years War, who championed the Protestant cause and was appointed general of Frederick V's army in Bohemia in 1621. He visited London in 1624 to raise an army for the relief of Breda, and was hailed as a hero (see John Chamberlain, *Letters* ed. N.E. McClure (Philadelphia 1939) ii 590: 'all the world here running after Mansfeld and wondering at him like an owle'). He was finally defeated by Wallenstein at Dessau, Apr. 1626. *fratrisque*] Probably Christian of

Et memini heroum quos vidit ad aethera raptos,
  Flevit et amissos Belgia tota duces.
At te praecipue luxi dignissime praesul,
  Wintoniaeque olim gloria magna tuae;
Delicui fletu, et tristi sic ore querebar,
  Mors fera Tartareo diva secunda Iovi,
Nonne satis quod sylva tuas persentiat iras,
  Et quod in herbosos ius tibi detur agros,
Quodque afflata tuo marcescant lilia tabo,
  Et crocus, et pulchrae Cypridi sacra rosa,
Nec sinis ut semper fluvio contermina quercus
  Miretur lapsus praetereuntis aquae?
Et tibi succumbit liquido quae plurima coelo
  Evehitur pennis quamlibet augur avis,
Et quae mille nigris errant animalia sylvis,
  Et quod alunt mutum Proteos antra pecus.
Invida, tanta tibi cum sit concessa potestas;
  Quid iuvat humana tingere caede manus?

Brunswick, who allied himself to Frederick's cause early in 1622 and, with Mansfeld, defeated the Spaniards at Fleurus, Aug. 1622. He was defeated by Tilly at Stadtlohn in 1623, but came back into the war on the Protestant side in 1625, along with Christian IV of Denmark. He died 16 Jun. 1626.

11. heroum] Probably those killed in the operations around Breda, which fell to the Catholic general Spinola in May 1625. They included Henry Vere, Earl of Oxford, who died at the Hague after taking part in the unsuccessful assault on Terheiden, and, says John Chamberlain, *Letters* ii 618, 'Sir Thomas Winne, Sir Walter Devreux, Captain Tubbe, Captain Dakers and I know not how many more'.

12. duces] Probably Maurice of Nassau, Prince of Orange, the great adversary of the Catholic armies in the Netherlands, who died 23 Apr. 1625 after failing to relieve Breda, and Johan van Oldenbarneveldt who, as leading statesman of the Netherlands, had worked with Maurice to drive the Spaniards out of Holland during the 1590s, but who quarrelled with Maurice in 1609 over the truce with Spain, and was finally executed in May 1619.

16. Tartareo . . . Iovi] Pluto, ruler of the underworld; cp. Virgil, *Aen.* iv 638 *Iovi Stygio*.

20. Cypridi] Venus, to whom Cyprus was sacred.

21. contermina quercus] The phrase is from Ovid, *Met.* viii 620.

22. praetereuntis aquae] The phrase is from Buchanan, *Elegy ii* 60.

25. nigris . . . sylvis] The phrase is from Horace, *Odes* I xxi 7–8.

26. pecus] Neptune's seals, among which Odysseus and his companions hide (*Od.* iv 388–460) in order to seize their herdsman Proteus.

Nobileque in pectus certas acuisse sagittas,
Semideamque animam sede fugasse sua?
Talia dum lacrymans alto sub pectore volvo,
Roscidus occiduis Hesperus exit aquis,
Et Tartessiaco submerserat aequore currum
Phoebus, ab eoo littore mensus iter.
Nec mora, membra cavo posui refovenda cubili,
Condiderant oculos noxque soporque meos.
Cum mihi visus eram lato spatiarier agro,
Heu nequit ingenium visa referre meum.
Illis punicea radiabant omnia luce,
Ut matutino cum iuga sole rubent.
Ac veluti cum pandit opes Thaumantia proles,
Vestitu nituit multicolore solum.
Non dea tam variis ornavit floribus hortos
Alcinoi, Zephyro Chloris amata levi.
Flumina vernantes lambunt argentea campos,
Ditior Hesperio flavet arena Tago.
Serpit odoriferas per opes levis aura Favoni,
Aura sub innumeris humida nata rosis.
Talis in extremis terrae Gangetidis oris
Luciferi regis fingitur esse domus.

32. *Roscidus . . . Hesperus*] The evening star (an echo of Ovid, *Fast.* ii 314 *Hesperos . . . roscidus*).

33. *Tartessiaco . . . aequore*] M. probably took his adjective from Silius Italicus, *Punica* vi 1 where the Sun pastures his team by the Tartessian ocean (*Tartessiaco . . . aequore*). Herodotus iv 152 tells of a Greek sailing ship from Samos which was driven far to the west through the pillars of Hercules to the ancient port of Tartessus on Spain's Atlantic coast, previously unknown to the Greeks.

41. *Thaumantia proles*] Iris, the rainbow, daughter of Thaumas and Electra.

44. *Chloris*] The Greek name of Flora, Roman goddess of flowers. Ovid tells of her marriage with Zephyrus, *Fast.* v 197–206. *Alcinoi*] The miraculous gardens of Alcinous, king of the Phaeacians, in which trees bear fruit and flowers bloom all the year round, are described by Homer, *Od.* vii 112–32.

46. *Hesperio . . . Tago*] The river Tagus, which flows through Spain and Portugal to Lisbon, was famed for its golden sands.

47. *Favoni*] Favonius ('the favourable one') was a name for the west wind.

49–50. Lucifer ('light-bearer') means here the Sun. Ovid represents Phaëthon as reaching the palace of the Sun after crossing Ethiopia and India (*Met.* i 778–9): India is M.'s *terra Gangetis* (a term he found in Ovid, *Am.* I ii 47). There is no garden in Ovid's description of the Sun's palace (*Met.* ii 1–18), but Claudian has a vivid description of the garden of the Sun (whom he refers to as Lucifer) in *De Consulatu Stilichonis* ii 467–76.

Ipse racemiferis dum densas vitibus umbras
Et pellucentes miror ubique locos,
Ecce mihi subito praesul Wintonius astat,
Sydereum nitido fulsit in ore iubar;
Vestis ad auratos defluxit candida talos,
Infula divinum cinxerat alba caput.
Dumque senex tali incedit venerandus amictu,
Intremuit laeto florea terra sono.
Agmina gemmatis plaudunt caelestia pennis,
Pura triumphali personat aethra tuba.
Quisque novum amplexu comitem cantuque salutat,
Hosque aliquis placido misit ab ore sonos;
Nate veni, et patrii felix cape gaudia regni,
Semper ab hinc duro, nate, labore vaca.
Dixit, et aligerae tetigerunt nablia turmae,
At mihi cum tenebris aurea pulsa quies.
Flebam turbatos Cephaleia pellice somnos,
Talia contingant somnia saepe mihi.

I was sad, and sat alone and silent. A host of sorrows perturbed my thoughts. All at once there arose before me a vision of the dismal carnage which Libitina[4] caused on English soil, when ghastly death[6] with her sepulchral torch–a fearsome sight–made her way into the gleaming marble palaces of the nobility, beat upon the walls massy with jasper and gold, and did not shrink from mowing down troops of princes with her scythe. Then I called to mind that famous general and his well-respected brother in arms,[9] whose bones were burned on untimely pyres,[10] and I remembered the heroes[11] that all Belgia had seen snatched up to the skies–Belgia, who wept for her lost leaders.[12] But I mourned above all for you, worthiest of bishops, once the great glory of your beloved Winchester. I burst into tears and my voice, filled with grief, made this complaint: 'Pitiless Death, goddess second in power only to Tartarean Jove,[16] is it not enough that the woods are made to feel your rage, that you are given power over the grassy fields, that the lilies, the crocus and the rose sacred to lovely Cypris[20] wither at the touch of your putrid breath? Is it not enough to forbid the oak-tree that grows by the river's brim[21] to gaze for ever upon the water flowing by it?[22] The countless birds that glide through the bright sky on their pinions succumb to you, for all their gift of prophecy, and so do the thousand wild beasts that wander through the black forests,[25] and the silent herd[26] that feeds in Proteus' grottoes. Envious Death, when such great power has been granted to you, what pleasure is there in staining your hands with human blood?

59. gemmatis . . . pennis] Ovid includes these in Cupid's equipment, *Rem.* 39.
67. Cephaleia pellice] Aurora, the dawn, whose love for Cephalus is narrated by Ovid, *Met.* vii 700–13.
68. An adaptation of the last line of *Am.* I v where Ovid, having made love to Corinna one sultry noon, exclaims 'May my lot bring many a midday like this!'

Where is the pleasure in sharpening your unerring darts to pierce a noble breast, or in driving a spirit that was half divine out of its body?'

As I weep and ponder these things in my heart of hearts, dewy Hesperus[32] rises from the western sea and Phoebus, after tracing his course from the eastern strand, sinks his chariot beneath the Tartessian ocean.[33] Without delay I stretched out on my hollowed bed to refresh my limbs. Night and sleep had closed my eyes, when it seemed to me that I was strolling over a wide plain–alas! I have not enough talent to describe what I saw. There everything glowed with a rosy light, like mountain tops flushed by the morning sun. The ground shone, tricked out in a thousand colours, as when Thaumas's daughter[41] spreads her riches to the view. Chloris,[44] the goddess beloved by gentle Zephyrus, did not deck the gardens of Alcinous with flowers as various as these. Silver streams wash the blossoming meadows, and their sands gleam more golden than the sands of Hesperian Tagus.[46] Favonius'[47] light breath steals through the rich, scented foliage–dewy breath, born beneath countless roses. Such[49] is the imagined home of royal Lucifer on the farthest shores of the land of Ganges. As I gaze all around me in wonder at the shining spaces and the thick shadows under the clustering vines, suddenly the Bishop of Winchester appears, close by me. A star-like radiance shone from his bright face, a white robe flowed down to his golden feet and his god-like head was encircled by a white band. As the reverend old man walked forward, dressed in this way, the flowery earth quivered with a joyful sound. The heavenly hosts clap their jewelled wings:[59] the pure upper air rings with the blast of a triumphal trumpet. Each spirit embraces his new companion and greets him with a song, and one of them, with peaceful lips, uttered these syllables: 'Come, my son, and receive in happiness the joys of your Father's kingdom; henceforth be free from cruel toil, my son, for ever.'

When he had spoken the winged squadrons touched their harps. But my golden repose was dispelled with the night, and I wept for the sleep which Cephalus' mistress[67] had disturbed.

May I often be lucky enough to have dreams like this![68]

19 *Elegia Quarta*

Ad Thomam Junium praeceptorem suum, apud mercatores Anglicos Hamburgae agentes, Pastoris munere fungentem

[Elegy IV. To Thomas Young, his tutor, at present performing the office of chaplain among the English merchants living in Hamburg]

Date. Mar.–Apr. 1627. Headed *Anno aetatis 18* in *1645* and *1673*, which according to M.'s usual method of dating (see headnote to Q *Nov*, p. 36) should mean that it was written between Dec. 1626 and Dec. 1627. Harris Fletcher, *TLS* (21 Jan. 1926) 44, argues, however, that this elegy should be dated 1625, on the assumption that it is the *Epistolium quoddam numeris metricis elucubratum* mentioned in the first of M.'s *Epistolae Familiares.* But it seems more likely that the date (26 Mar. 1625) given for this letter in the 1674 *Epistolae* is itself incorrect and that both letter and elegy should be dated 1627, the latter probably, thinks W. R. Parker, *MLN* liii (1938) 399–407, between 21 Mar. and 28 Apr.

Thomas Young (1587?–1655) was a Scotsman with strong Puritan leanings. Some time between his arrival in London, in or before 1618, and his departure for Hamburg, which he reached in 1620, he was one of M.'s private tutors. In 1628 he returned to England and was presented to the living of St Peter and St Mary, Stowmarket, where M. visited him. His *Dies Dominica*, a treatise on Sabbath-observance, appeared in 1639. When Hall published his *Humble Remonstrance* (1640), upholding the divine right of episcopacy, an *Answer* was printed, of which Young was part author, his initials, with those of the four other contributors, forming the pseudonym 'Smectymnuus'. In 1641 M. joined this pamphlet war on the side of his old tutor. Young was nominated to the Westminster Assembly in 1643 and made Master of Jesus College, Cambridge in 1644. M.'s relations with him are examined by A. Barker, *MLR* xxxii (1937) 517–26 and Clark 22–32.

Publication. 1645 and *1673* (no significant variants: in *123 1673* misprints *miseri* for *miseris*).

Curre per immensum subito mea littera pontum,
  I, pete Teutonicos laeve per aequor agros,
Segnes rumpe moras, et nil, precor, obstet eunti,
  Et festinantis nil remoretur iter.
Ipse ego Sicanio fraenantem carcere ventos
  Aeolon, et virides sollicitabo deos;
Caeruleamque suis comitatam Dorida nymphis,
  Ut tibi dent placidam per sua regna viam.
At tu, si poteris, celeres tibi sume iugales,
  Vecta quibus Colchis fugit ab ore viri.
Aut queis Triptolemus Scythicas devenit in oras
  Gratus Eleusina missus ab urbe puer.

¶ 19. *1–4.* M.'s initial instructions to his letter are imitated from Ovid, *Tristia* III vii 1–2.

3. Segnes rumpe moras] The phrase is from Virgil, *Georg.* iii 42–3.

5. Sicanio] Sicilian. Lipara, fabled home of Aeolus, god of the winds, is an island thirty miles N.E. of Sicily. Virgil couples the 'Sicanian coast' and 'Aeolian Lipara' in *Aen.* viii 416–17. *fraenantem . . . Aeolon*] Cp. Ovid, *Met.* xiv 224: *Aeolon . . . cohibentem carcere ventos.*

7. Dorida] Doris, wife of Nereus, was mother of the fifty Nereids or sea nymphs.

10. Colchis] The Colchian, i.e. Medea; for her team see *Prae E* 56–8*n* (p. 26).

11–12. Ovid, *Met.* v 642–61, describes how Ceres sent Triptolemus to

Atque ubi Germanas flavere videbis arenas
  Ditis ad Hamburgae moenia flecte gradum,
Dicitur occiso quae ducere nomen ab Hama,
  Cimbrica quem fertur clava dedisse neci.
Vivit ibi antiquae clarus pietatis honore
  Praesul Christicolas pascere doctus oves;
Ille quidem est animae plusquam pars altera nostrae,
  Dimidio vitae vivere cogor ego.
Hei mihi quot pelagi, quot montes interiecti
  Me faciunt alia parte carere mei!
Charior ille mihi quam tu doctissime Graium
  Cliniadi, pronepos qui Telamonis erat.
Quamque Stagirites generoso magnus alumno,
  Quem peperit Libyco Chaonis alma Iovi.
Qualis Amyntorides, qualis Philyreius heros
  Myrmidonum regi, talis et ille mihi.
Primus ego Aonios illo praeeunte recessus
  Lustrabam, et bifidi sacra vireta iugi,
Pieriosque hausi latices, Clioque favente,
  Castalio sparsi laeta ter ora mero.

Scythia in a chariot drawn by dragons. In *Tristia* III viii 1–4 he links, as does M. here, the dragon-teams of Medea and Triptolemus.

15–16. The story of the fight between the Saxon Hama and the Dane Starcaterus is first found in Saxo Grammaticus, *Danish History* vi, and is repeated by the historian Albert Krantz in his *Saxonia* (1520) with the additional information that Hama gave his name to Hamburg. Both Saxo and Krantz say Starcaterus's weapon was a sword. In Stephanus (*s.v. Hamburg*) the derivation from Hama is given and the story of the fight retold, but without specification of weapon. Probably M.'s source was Stephanus, and the *clava* his own invention.

19–20. Horace, *Odes* I iii 8, calls Virgil *animae dimidium meae*.

23–4. doctissime Graium] Socrates, shown as the intimate friend of Alcibiades, son of Clinias, in Plato's *Symposium*. Alcibiades claims descent from Eurysaces, grandson of Telamon, in Plato's *Alcibiades* 121A; Ovid calls him *Cliniades* in *Ibis* 633.

25–6. Stagirites] Aristotle, born at Stageira, was tutor to Alexander the Great, son of Olympias (called *Chaonis* from Chaonia, the district of Epirus where she was born), who was fathered, according to Plutarch, *Alexander* 2–3, by Jupiter Ammon (called 'Libyan Jove' because he had a shrine in the Libyan desert).

27–8. Achilles, king of the Myrmidons, had two tutors: Phoenix, son of Amyntor (called *Amyntorides* by Ovid, *Ibis* 259), and Chiron, son of the nymph Philyra (called *Philyreius heros* by Ovid, *Met.* ii 676).

29–32. The Parnassus range, with its forked mountain sacred to Apollo and the Muses (born on Mount Pierus in Macedonia: Hesiod, *Theog.* 52–3)

Flammeus at signum ter viderat arietis Aethon,
Induxitque auro lanea terga novo,
Bisque novo terram sparsisti Chlori senilem
Gramine, bisque tuas abstulit Auster opes:
Necdum eius licuit mihi lumina pascere vultu,
Aut linguae dulces aure bibisse sonos.
Vade igitur, cursuque Eurum praeverte sonorum,
Quam sit opus monitis res docet, ipsa vides.
Invenies dulci cum coniuge forte sedentem,
Mulcentem gremio pignora chara suo,
Forsitan aut veterum praelarga volumina patrum
Versantem, aut veri biblia sacra Dei.
Caelestive animas saturantem rore tenellas,
Grande salutiferae religionis opus.
Utque solet, multam, sit dicere cura salutem,
Dicere quam decuit, si modo adesset, herum.
Haec quoque paulum oculos in humum defixa modestos,
Verba verecundo sis memor ore loqui:
Haec tibi, si teneris vacat inter praelia Musis
Mittit ab Angliaco littore fida manus.
Accipe sinceram, quamvis sit sera, salutem;

is in Aonia. At its foot is the sacred Castalian spring at which, according to a fragment of Simonides quoted by Plutarch, *Oracles at Delphi* 402, Clio, Muse of History, was the 'holy guardian of lustration'.

33–4. Aethon] Named by Ovid, *Met.* ii 153, as one of the horses of the Sun, which enters Aries at the vernal equinox (approximately 21 Mar.).

35–6. Chloris was the Greek name for Flora, goddess of flowers, whose festival was at the end of April. There had been three vernal equinoxes since M. saw Young, but Chloris had only twice 'spread fresh turf'. The date of composition must therefore be late March or early April. Since Auster, the South Wind (named as a winter wind in Virgil, *Georg.* iv 261) had only twice carried away Chloris's wealth since that meeting, it must have taken place at the end of winter 1624–5.

41–4. M. is imitating Ovid, who tells his letter to Perilla, *Tristia* III vii 3–4: *aut illam invenies dulci cum matre sedentem, / aut inter libros Pieridasque suas.*

49. oculos . . . modestos] Echoes Ovid, *Am.* III vi 67: *oculos in humum deiecta modestos.*

51. praelia] Hamburg was not attacked in the Thirty Years War. However, when Mansfeld (see *Elegia III* 9–10*n*) advanced to his defeat at Dessau (1626) it was from positions about Lübeck, only thirty miles from Hamburg. Dessau itself and Lutter-am-Barenberge (where Christian IV was defeated in August 1626 by Tilly) are both within a hundred and fifty miles of Hamburg.

Fiat et hoc ipso gratior illa tibi.
Sera quidem, sed vera fuit, quam casta recepit
Icaris a lento Penelopeia viro.
Ast ego quid volui manifestum tollere crimen,
Ipse quod ex omni parte levare nequit.
Arguitur tardus merito, noxamque fatetur,
Et pudet officium deseruisse suum.
Tu modo da veniam fasso, veniamque roganti,
Crimina diminui, quae patuere, solent.
Non ferus in pavidos rictus diducit hiantes,
Vulnifico pronos nec rapit ungue leo.
Saepe sarissiferi crudelia pectora Thracis
Supplicis ad moestas delicuere preces.
Extensaeque manus avertunt fulminis ictus,
Placat et iratos hostia parva deos.
Iamque diu scripsisse tibi fuit impetus illi,
Neve moras ultra ducere passus Amor.
Nam vaga Fama refert, heu nuntia vera malorum!
In tibi finitimis bella tumere locis,
Teque tuamque urbem truculento milite cingi,
Et iam Saxonicos arma parasse duces.
Te circum late campos populatur Enyo,
Et sata carne virum iam cruor arva rigat.
Germanisque suum concessit Thracia Martem,
Illuc Odrysios Mars pater egit equos.
Perpetuoque comans iam deflorescit oliva,
Fugit et aerisonam Diva perosa tubam,
Fugit io terris, et iam non ultima virgo

55–6. In Homer, *Od.* xxiii 1–208, Penelope, daughter of Icarius, delays her welcome because she is not convinced that Odysseus has really returned.

61. *da veniam fasso*] The phrase is from Ovid, *Ex Ponto* IV ii 23.

72. *bella*] See l. 51*n*.

73. *milite*] The armies of Tilly and Wallenstein were not disbanded after Lutter-am-Barenberge. They lived on the country, and in the winter of 1626–7 pressure was being put on Hamburg and other Hanse towns to join Wallenstein against Christian.

74. *Saxonicos . . . duces*] Probably the sons of Duke John of Saxe-Weimar, Dukes Frederick, William and Bernard, who had served with Mansfeld against the imperialists, and were shortly to join Gustavus Adolphus.

75. *Enyo*] Goddess of war, called 'sacker of cities' by Homer, *Il.* v 333.

77–8. Odrysia (see *Met.* vi 490) is an Ovidian name for Thrace. Statius locates Mars' temple on Mount Haemus in Thrace, *Theb.* vii 40–63.

80. *Diva*] Eirene, goddess of peace.

81. *virgo*] The virgin Astraea who, according to Ovid, *Met.* i 149–50, was the last of the immortals to leave the earth.

Creditur ad superas iusta volasse domos.
Te tamen interea belli circumsonat horror,
Vivis et ignoto solus inopsque solo;
Et, tibi quam patrii non exhibuere penates
Sede peregrina quaeris egenus opem.
Patria dura parens, et saxis saevior albis
Spumea quae pulsat littoris unda tui,
Siccine te decet innocuos exponere faetus;
Siccine in externam ferrea cogis humum,
Et sinis ut terris quaerant alimenta remotis
Quos tibi prospiciens miserat ipse Deus,
Et qui laeta ferunt de caelo nuntia, quique
Quae via post cineres ducat ad astra, docent?
Digna quidem Stygiis quae vivas clausa tenebris,
Aeternaque animae digna perire fame!
Haud aliter vates terrae Thesbitidis olim
Pressit inassueto devia tesqua pede,
Desertasque Arabum salebras, dum regis Achabi
Effugit atque tuas, Sidoni dira, manus.
Talis et horrisono laceratus membra flagello,
Paulus ab Aemathia pellitur urbe Cilix.
Piscosaeque ipsum Gergessae civis Iesum
Finibus ingratus iussit abire suis.
At tu sume animos, nec spes cadat anxia curis
Nec tua concutiat decolor ossa metus.
Sis etenim quamvis fulgentibus obsitus armis,
Intententque tibi millia tela necem,
At nullis vel inerme latus violabitur armis,
Deque tuo cuspis nulla cruore bibet.
Namque eris ipse Dei radiante sub aegide tutus,
Ille tibi custos, et pugil ille tibi;
Ille Sionaeae qui tot sub moenibus arcis

87–94. M. is referring to the gradual migration of non-conforming ministers to Holland, Germany and New England. Young, however, cannot have been an extreme Puritan as he returned to England in 1628 and held the living of Stowmarket throughout the Laudian regime.

97–100. vates] Elijah who, in *1 Kings* xix 1–18, flees from Ahab and from Jezebel, daughter of Ethbaal King of Sidon.

101–2. In *Acts* xvi 9–40 Paul and Silas are scourged by order of the magistrates of Philippi in Macedonia. M.'s reference is inaccurate: they are not driven out but asked to leave by magistrates who are anxious because they realize they have scourged Roman citizens.

103–4. Cp. *Matt.* viii 28–34.

113–14. In *2 Kings* xix 35–6 the angel of the Lord destroys Sennacherib's army before the walls of Jerusalem.

Assyrios fudit nocte silente viros;
Inque fugam vertit quos in Samaritidas oras
Misit ab antiquis prisca Damascus agris,
Terruit et densas pavido cum rege cohortes,
Aere dum vacuo buccina clara sonat,
Cornea pulvereum dum verberat ungula campum,
Currus arenosam dum quatit actus humum,
Auditurque hinnitus equorum ad bella ruentum,
Et strepitus ferri, murmuraque alta virum.
Et tu (quod superest miseris) sperare memento,
Et tua magnanimo pectore vince mala.
Nec dubites quandoque frui melioribus annis,
Atque iterum patrios posse videre lares.

Make haste, my letter, run across the wide ocean.[1] Off you go! Seek out the lands of Germany over the smooth sea. Put an end to this idle delay![3] Do not let anything prevent your going, I beg you, or check the speed of your journey. I, for my part, will importune Aeolus (who keeps the winds pent up in their Sicanian[5] den), and the green sea-gods and sky-blue Doris[7] (with her attendant nymphs), to grant you an undisturbed passage through their kingdoms. And you, if you can, get hold of that swift team which Medea[10] drove when she ran away from her husband, or the one which drew that nice lad Triptolemus[11] to the shores of Scythia when he was sent from the city of Eleusis. And when you catch sight of the yellow sands on the shore of Germany, make for the walls of Hamburg, a wealthy city which, according to tradition, takes its name from Hama,[15] who is supposed to have been killed by a Danish club. A pastor lives there, well known for the way he esteems the primitive faith and an expert at the job of tending his Christian flock. That man is more to me than one half of my soul:[19] I am forced, now, to live only a half-life. Ah! How many seas and mountains are thrust between us, to keep me apart from the other half of myself! He is dearer to me than you, most learned of the Greeks,[23] were to Alcibiades, Telamon's descendant:[24] dearer than the great Stagirite[25] was to his noble pupil, the son whom that bountiful girl from Chaonia bore to Libyan Jove.[26] To me he is as Amyntor's son[27] and the heroic son of Philyra were to the Myrmidons' king[28] I was the first to wander under his guidance through the Aonian retreats[29] and over the forked mountain's sacred, grassy slopes. There I drank Pieria's waters and, through the goodness of Clio, three times I made my happy mouth wet with Castalian wine.[32] But three times had flaming Aethon[33] looked upon the sign of the ram and gilded his woolly back with fresh gold, and twice, Chloris,[35] you spread fresh turf over the ageing ground, and twice Auster[36] carried your wealth away: and all this time I have not been allowed to feed my eyes upon his face or to drink in at my ears the sweet sound of his voice.

115–22. In *2 Kings* vii 6–7 the Lord makes the Syrian army under King Ben-hadad flee from their camp by causing them to hear the noise of chariots and horses, 'even the noise of a great host'.

119. An attempt to vie with Virgil's famous *quadrupedante putrem sonitu quatit ungula campum*, *Aen.* viii 596.

Be off, then, and outstrip the shrill east wind in your flight; you can see from the state of affairs how necessary it is for me to spur you on. Perhaps you will find him sitting with his sweet wife,[41] fondling on his lap the dear tokens of their love; or perhaps thumbing through the huge tomes of the Church fathers, or the Holy Bible, the word of the true God;[44] or perhaps watering delicate souls with heavenly dew, the great work of redemptive religion. Make it your business to give him a hearty greeting, according to the custom of the country, and say whatever it would become your master to say if only he were there. And remember to speak these words, too, modestly, having first fixed your bashful eyes on the ground for a little while:[49] A devoted hand sends these verses from the shores of England to you–if there is any time for the gentle Muses when you are surrounded by battles.[51] Accept a sincere, though delayed greeting: may it be all the more welcome to you because of the delay. That greeting which chaste Penelope, Icarius's daughter, received from her long-absent husband was late,[55] it is true, but sincere. But stop! Why try to make nothing of what is manifestly a crime–a crime which the culprit himself is quite unable to mitigate? He is justly accused of delay; he confesses the fault and is ashamed to have failed in his duty. Only forgive him,[61] now he has confessed and begs for pardon: sins are always lessened when they are openly acknowledged. If its victims are quivering with terror a wild beast refrains from drawing wide its gaping jaws: the lion does not seize with rending claws those who lie motionless. The cruel hearts of Thracian spearmen have often melted at a suppliant enemy's tearful prayers. Outstretched hands can turn aside the stroke of the thunderbolt, and even a small sacrifice placates the angry gods.

He has felt the urge to write to you for a long time, and Love would not allow him to delay any longer, for wandering Rumour–a trustworthy bearer, alas, of evil tidings–reports that wars are breaking out in the lands which border yours,[72] that you and your city are surrounded by cruel-looking soldiers,[73] and that the Saxon leaders[74] have already prepared their weapons for battle. All around you Enyo[75] is ravaging the fields and blood is soaking into ground sown with human flesh. Thrace[77] has surrendered Mars to the Germans, and father Mars has driven his Odrysian[78] warhorses onto German soil. The olive tree, always leafy, is withering now, and the goddess[80] who detests the blaring trumpet has fled–look! she has fled from the earth –and no one believes any longer that Astraea[81] was the last to fly for safety to mansions in the sky. But you are living among strangers, in poverty and loneliness, while all around you echoes the horrifying noise of war. In your need you seek in a foreign land the sustenance which your ancestral home denied you. O native country, hard-hearted parent,[87] more cruel than the white cliffs of your coastline, battered by foaming waves, is it fitting that you should expose your innocent children in this way? Is this the way you treat them, iron-hearted land, driving them onto foreign soil and allowing them to search for their food on distant shores, when God Himself has sent them to you in His providence; when they bring joyful news to you from heaven and teach the way which leads beyond the grave to the stars?[94] You really deserve to live shut up in hellish darkness and to die of a never-ending hunger of the soul! Once, long ago, the Tishbite prophet[97] sought refuge, in a similar way, from the hands of King Ahab and from your hands, too, beastly woman of Sidon:[100] with unaccustomed foot he trod the remote wastes and rough desert of Arabia. In a similar way Paul,[101] the Cilician, was driven from the Emathian city, his flesh torn by the whining scourge; and the ungrateful citizens of the fishing port of Gergessa ordered Jesus[103] himself to leave their coasts.

But take heart. Do not let anxieties quench your hope, even if they make you uneasy, and do not allow pale fear to send shudders through your limbs. Though you are hedged in by flashing arms, though a thousand swords threaten you with death, no weapon shall harm your weaponless body, no spear-point suck out your blood. For you will be kept safe beneath God's gleaming shield. He will be your preserver, your champion; He who beat down[113] so many Assyrian soldiers one silent night beneath the walls of Zion;[114] He who routed those troops[115] which the age-old city of Damascus sent out from her ancient territories against the frontiers of Samaria, and spread panic among the battalions close-packed around their trembling king, when the clear-noted war-trumpets shrilled through the empty air, and horny hooves beat the dusty plain,[119] and hard-driven chariots shook the sandy earth, and the whinnying of charging cavalry was heard, and the clash of steel and the deep, distant roar of shouting men.[122]

And for your part, remember to hope: hope remains even for the wretched. Triumph over your misfortunes with sheer greatness of spirit. Do not doubt that some day you will enjoy happier times and be able to see your home again.

20 *Naturam non pati senium*

[That Nature does not suffer from old age]

Date. 1627? There is no evidence for dating these verses: they have sometimes been identified as the *leviculas . . . nugas* (trivial jokes) mentioned in M.'s letter to Gill of 2 Jul. 1628 (Columbia xii 8–13; Yale i 313–15), but this description fits *Id Plat* far better than *Natur*, which is serious in tone. Possibly the subject and attitude of *Natur* were suggested by George Hakewill's *Apology of the Power and Providence of God* (1627), a contribution to the debate about the decay of nature–for an account of which see V. Harris, *All Coherence Gone* (Chicago 1949)–which had been reopened by Godfrey Goodman's *Fall of Man* (1616). Hakewill's *Apology* contained the first published account of a famous phlebotomy carried out by Theodore Diodati, Charles's father. It might have been this which attracted M.'s attention to the book and led to *Natur*. But if so the poem would have to be dated in or after 1630, as it was not until Hakewill's second edition, published in that year, that the phlebotomy-account appeared.
Publication. *1645* (*38.* Raptat]Raptat,) and *1673* (the text followed here).

Heu quam perpetuis erroribus acta fatiscit
Avia mens hominum, tenebrisque immersa profundis
Oedipodioniam volvit sub pectore noctem!

¶ 20. *3. Oedipodioniam*] Self-inflicted, like the blindness of Oedipus.

Quae vesana suis metiri facta deorum
Audet, et incisas leges adamante perenni
Assimilare suis, nulloque solubile saeclo
Consilium fati perituris alligat horis.
  Ergone marcescet sulcantibus obsita rugis
Naturae facies, et rerum publica mater
Omniparum contracta uterum sterilescet ab aevo?
Et se fassa senem male certis passibus ibit
Sidereum tremebunda caput? num tetra vetustas
Annorumque aeterna fames, squalorque situsque
Sidera vexabunt? an et insatiabile Tempus
Esuriet caelum, rapietque in viscera patrem?
Heu, potuitne suas imprudens Iupiter arces
Hoc contra munisse nefas, et temporis isto
Exemisse malo, gyrosque dedisse perennes?
Ergo erit ut quandoque sono dilapsa tremendo
Convexi tabulata ruant, atque obvius ictu
Stridat uterque polus, superaque ut Olympius aula
Decidat, horribilisque retecta Gorgone Pallas.
Qualis in Aegaeam proles Iunonia Lemnon
Deturbata sacro cecidit de limine caeli.
Tu quoque Phoebe tui casus imitabere nati
Praecipiti curru, subitaque ferere ruina

5. *incisas . . . perenni*] In Ovid, *Met.* xv 813, Jove tells Venus that fate is *incisa adamante perenni.*

9. *mater*] Ge, Earth, who according to Hesiod, *Theog.* 117–63, brought forth Heaven, and was thus common ancestor of gods and men.

15. *patrem*] E. Reiss, *MLN* lxxii (1957) 410–12, believes that the usual explanation of this line by reference to the confusion of Chronos (Time) with Cronos (the child-devourer in Hesiod) is unsatisfactory because Time is here thought of as devouring his father, not his children. Reiss directs attention to the doctrine expounded by M. in *De doctrina* I vii, that God created all things out of Himself. In this sense Time could be called a child of God, and the situation M. imagines his opponents looking forward to is the destruction of God Himself by Time. This seems rather forced.

19–20. *sono . . . tremendo*] Cp. *2 Peter* iii 10: 'The heavens shall pass away with a great noise'.

22. *Gorgone*] According to Homer, *Il.* v 741–2, Pallas Athene wears the Gorgon Medusa's head on her shield.

23. *proles Iunonia*] Hephaestus, thrown out of heaven by Zeus, as Homer tells, *Il.* i 590–4.

25. *tui . . . nati*] Phaëthon. Ovid, *Met.* ii 19–328, tells how when driving his father's chariot he lost control of its horses and was struck down by Jove with a thunderbolt, lest he should destroy the earth.

Pronus, et extincta fumabit lampade Nereus,
Et dabit attonito feralia sibila ponto.
Tunc etiam aerei divulsis sedibus Haemi
Dissultabit apex, imoque allisa barathro
Terrebunt Stygium deiecta Ceraunia Ditem
In superos quibus usus erat, fraternaque bella.
At pater omnipotens fundatis fortius astris
Consuluit rerum summae, certoque peregit
Pondere fatorum lances, atque ordine summo
Singula perpetuum iussit servare tenorem.
Volvitur hinc lapsu mundi rota prima diurno;
Raptat et ambitos socia vertigine caelos.
Tardior haud solito Saturnus, et acer ut olim
Fulmineum rutilat cristata casside Mavors.
Floridus aeternum Phoebus iuvenile coruscat,
Nec fovet effoetas loca per declivia terras
Devexo temone deus; sed semper amica
Luce potens eadem currit per signa rotarum,
Surgit odoratis pariter formosus ab Indis
Aethereum pecus albenti qui cogit Olympo
Mane vocans, et serus agens in pascua coeli,
Temporis et gemino dispertit regna colore.
Fulget, obitque vices alterno Delia cornu,
Caeruleumque ignem paribus complectitur ulnis.
Nec variant elementa fidem, solitoque fragore
Lurida perculsas iaculantur fulmina rupes.
Nec per inane furit leviori murmure Corus,
Stringit et armiferos aequali horrore Gelonos

27. *Nereus*] The Old Man of the Sea in Hesiod, *Theog.* 233–6 and Homer, *Il.* xviii 141. Ovid, *Met.* ii 268, makes him hide in a cave while Phaëthon's drive is drying up the sea.
29. *Haemi*] A mountain between Thrace and Thessaly: one of those which Ovid mentions as burned by Phaëthon's drive (*Met.* ii 219).
31. *Ceraunia*] The Ceraunian mountains are between Epirus and Thessaly. *Ditem*] Hades, ruler of the lower world and brother of the other Olympian gods whose war against the older gods, the Titans, is described by Hesiod, *Theog.* 617–731. Hesiod mentions rocks but not mountains as ammunition.
37–51. M. adopts the Ptolemaic cosmogony, and the spheres he mentions are given in their Ptolemaic order, reading inwards from the *primum mobile*: Saturn, Mars, Sun, Venus, Moon, Earth.
45–8. The star referred to is Venus, called Hesperus as evening- and Lucifer as morning-star. *odoratis . . . Indis*] Echoes Silius Italicus xvii 647: *odoratis descendens . . . ab Indis.*
49. *Delia*] Diana, the moon-goddess, born on the island of Delos.
53. *Corus*] The north-west wind.

Trux Aquilo, spiratque hyemem, nimbosque volutat.
Utque solet, Siculi diverberat ima Pelori
Rex maris, et rauca circumstrepit aequora concha
Oceani tubicen, nec vasta mole minorem
Aegaeona ferunt dorso Balearica cete.
Sed neque Terra tibi saecli vigor ille vetusti
Priscus abest, servatque suum Narcissus odorem,
Et puer ille suum tenet et puer ille decorem
Phoebe tuusque et Cypri tuus, nec ditior olim
Terra datum sceleri celavit montibus aurum
Conscia, vel sub aquis gemmas. Sic denique in aevum
Ibit cunctarum series iustissima rerum,
Donec flamma orbem populabitur ultima, late
Circumplexa polos, et vasti culmina caeli;
Ingentique rogo flagrabit machina mundi.

Ah! How perpetual are the errors which drive man's restless mind to exhaustion! How deep the darkness which swallows him when he harbours in his soul the blind night of Oedipus![3] In his madness he dares to measure the deeds of Gods by his own, to make those laws which are cut in everlasting adamant[5] of no more account than his own laws, and to link that decree of fate which no age will ever wear away to his own dwindling hours.

Will the face of Nature really wither away and be furrowed all over with wrinkles? Will our common mother[9] really contract her all-producing womb and totter along wagging her starry head? Will loathsome old age, and the

55. *Aquilo*] The north-east wind.

56. *Pelori*] Pelorus is a promontory on the north-east coast of Sicily, the modern Capo di Faro.

58. *tubicen*] Triton, Neptune's son. He and his trumpet are vividly described by Ovid, *Met.* i 330–42.

59. *Aegaeona*] Aegaeon was a name for the hundred-handed giant Briareus, son of Uranus and Ge (Earth). Homer, *Il.* i 403–4 says he was called Briareus by gods, Aegaeon by men. In Ovid, *Met.* ii 9–10, Aegaeon is a sea god who leans on the backs of two whales. It is not clear why M. associates him with the Balearic Islands, unless he is glancing at the huge Catholic power of Spain, another monster, like Aegaeon, overhanging the Balearic Islands as he does his whales.

61. *Narcissus*] Ovid, *Met.* iii 402–510, tells the story of his transformation into a flower.

62–3. *puer*] Hyacinthus, loved by Apollo, accidentally killed by him with a discus, and transformed to a flower, as Ovid tells in *Met.* x 162–219. *Cypri tuus*] Adonis, loved by Venus (called Cypris because Cyprus was sacred to her). When he was killed by the boar Venus, according to Ovid, *Met.* x 728–39, made the anemone spring from his blood.

67–9. M. has biblical authority for prophesying a final conflagration: 2 Peter iii 10.

years' insatiable hunger, and filth and rust really do any damage to the stars? Will ravenous Time gobble up heaven itself and cram his own father into his stomach?[15] Ah, was Jove so improvident? Couldn't he have fortified his own citadels against this evil thing, and exempted them from Time's depredation, and let them go on whirling round for ever? As it is, there will come a day when the floors of the vaulted universe will collapse with a terrifying crash:[19] the poles of the earth will shriek when they feel the shock: the Olympian will fall headlong from his hall in the skies and Pallas, too, will fall–a horrifying sight with her Gorgon shield uncovered[22]–just as Juno's son[23] fell down on the Aegean island of Lemnos when he was flung from heaven's sacred threshold. You, Phoebus, will also share the fate of your son[25] in your rushing chariot: suddenly you will fall head-first: Nereus[27] will belch steam as he quenches your lamp and the astounded sea will hiss horribly. Then even the peak of skyey Haemus[29] will fly to pieces as its foundations are torn apart, and the Ceraunian[31] heights which Stygian Dis once used against the Titans in wars where brothers banded together, will be dashed down and hurled to the depths of the abyss to terrify him.

No! The Almighty Father has taken thought for the universe, and set the stars more firmly in their place. He has poised the scales of destiny with a sure weight and commanded each thing to keep its course for ever in a supremely ordered whole. So the *primum mobile*[37] turns with daily rotation and drags the enclosed spheres round with it. Saturn is no slower than he used to be, and Mars, as swift and keen as ever, flashes lightning from his crested helmet. Phoebus is always bright with the bloom of youth: he does not steer his chariot downhill to warm a worn-out earth, but ever strong with friendly light speeds along the same marks as his chariot wheels left before. The star[45] which gathers the heavenly flock together as the sky whitens, and calls them home as morning breaks, and which drives them out again at evening into the pastures of heaven, dividing the realms of time with two colours, rises as beautiful as ever from the spicy Indies. Delia[49] alternately waxes and wanes, her horns pointing now this way, now that, and as always she clasps the fire of heaven in her arms. The elements, too, remain true to type: yellow lightning strikes and shatters the rocks with a crashing noise as it always did: Corus[53] rages through the empty air with a voice no more gentle than before: wild Aquilo[55] huddles the armed Scythians together, shivering as much as ever, and breathes winter upon them, and tumbles the clouds about overhead. The sea-king batters at the base of Pelorus[56] the Sicilian promontory, as he always did, and the ocean-trumpeter[58] surrounds the seas with the blare of his hollow-sounding shell, and the Balearic whales bear on their backs an Aegaeon[59] no less vast in bulk than before. Nor, Earth, do you lack that primitive strength which you had in bygone ages: Narcissus[61] keeps his fragrance still: that boy of yours, Phoebus,[62] is as beautiful as ever and so, Cypris, is that boy of yours.[63] The earth was no richer in days gone by when, conscious of wrong, she hid beneath her mountains and seas the gold and gems which were destined to foster crime.

In fact, then, the process of the universe will go on for ever, worked out with scrupulous justice, until the last flames[67] destroy the globe, enveloping the poles and the summits of vast heaven, and the frame of the world blazes on one huge funeral pyre.[69]

21 *De Idea Platonica quemadmodum Aristoteles intellexit*

[Of the Platonic Ideal Form as understood by Aristotle]

Date. June 1628? In M.'s letter to Alexander Gill of 2 Jul. 1628 (see headnote to *Natur*, p. 61 above) he refers to some verses he has been writing for the use of a Fellow of his College chosen to act as Respondent in the philosophical disputation at the Cambridge Commencement (which took place 1 Jul. in 1628). The term *leviculas nugas* used to describe these verses fits the semi-serious *Id Plat* better than *Natur*. It is possible that the verses have not survived at all, but M.'s apparent thoroughness in gathering up even his trifling compositions in Latin verse suggests that he would not have omitted from *1645* a poem he had thought worth sending to Gill on the day after its publication. If the *leviculas nugas* are in *1645* at all, they are probably *Id Plat*.

Publication. M. enclosed in his letter to Gill a printed copy (*typis donata*) of the verses: the Respondent's verses were customarily printed and distributed by the beadles at the Commencement ceremony. Of this printing no copies have survived. Also printed in *1645* and *1673* (no significant variants: in *23 1673* misprints *iis* for *diis*, and in *36 induxit* for *induxti*).

Id Plat is a burlesque of Aristotle's criticisms of Plato's doctrine of ideal forms (outlined, for example, in *Republic* x 596–7, *Cratylus* 389, 439–40, *Phaedo* 75–6, *Parmenides* 135 and *Sophist* 246–7). For Aristotle's attack see *Metaphysics* I ix, VII viii. M. speaks as a literal-minded Aristotelian, demanding where the ideal or archetypal form of man is to be found.

Dicite sacrorum praesides nemorum deae,
Tuque O noveni perbeata numinis
Memoria mater, quaeque in immenso procul
Antro recumbis otiosa Aeternitas,
Monumenta servans, et ratas leges Iovis,

¶ 21. *1. deae*] Possibly the Muses, identified in Latin poetry with the Italian Camenae to whom, as Livy I xxi 3 relates, Numa dedicated a grove outside the Porta Capena. Or perhaps Diana (called *nemorum ... custos*, Virgil, *Aen.* ix 405) and her nymphs. MacKellar 303 suggests that M. calls on Diana because, as moon-goddess, she is sometimes identified with Lucina, goddess of childbirth, and should therefore know about the being who served as pattern for the human race.

3. mater] According to Hesiod, *Theog.* 52–3 the Muses were daughters of Zeus and Mnemosyne (Memory).

4–6. M.'s cave of Eternity is based on the cave of Time in Claudian, *De Consulatu Stilichonis* ii 424–8, where Time, an old man, writes immutable laws and fixes the revolutions of the planets.

Caelique fastos atque ephemeridas Deum,
Quis ille primus cuius ex imagine
Natura sollers finxit humanum genus,
Aeternus, incorruptus, aequaevus polo,
Unusque et universus, exemplar Dei?
Haud ille Palladis gemellus innubae
Interna proles insidet menti Iovis;
Sed quamlibet natura sit communior,
Tamen seorsus extat ad morem unius,
Et, mira, certo stringitur spatio loci;
Seu sempiternus ille syderum comes
Caeli pererrat ordines decemplicis,
Citimumve terris incolit Lunae globum:
Sive inter animas corpus adituras sedens
Obliviosas torpet ad Lethes aquas:
Sive in remota forte terrarum plaga
Incedit ingens hominis archetypus gigas,
Et diis tremendus erigit celsum caput
Atlante maior portitore syderum.
Non cui profundum caecitas lumen dedit
Dircaeus augur vidit hunc alto sinu;
Non hunc silenti nocte Pleiones nepos
Vatum sagaci praepes ostendit choro;
Non hunc sacerdos novit Assyrius, licet

9. aequaevus polo] Probably echoing Claudian, *De Bello Gothico* 54 (of Rome) *aequaeva polo*.
11–12. Pallas Athene sprang fully armed from the head of Zeus.
19–20. The doctrine of metempsychosis is outlined by Plato, *Phaedo* 70–2, *Republic* x 617–18. In Virgil, *Aen.* vi 710–15, Aeneas, in the underworld, is thrilled by the sight of souls, destined to go back to the world, thronging on the banks of Lethe to drink the waters of forgetfulness.
24. Atlante] Atlas, according to Hesiod, *Theog.* 507–20, carries the heavens on his head and shoulders.
26. Dircaeus augur] Tiresias, see *Elegia VI* 68*n* (p. 116). Dircaean (from Dirce, a fountain near Thebes in Boeotia) means Boeotian or Theban.
27. Pleiones nepos] This title for Mercury is from Ovid, *Her.* xvi 62: he was son of Maia, one of the Pleiades–the seven daughters of Atlas and Pleione, a sea nymph.
29. sacerdos . . . Assyrius] Probably Hierombalus, priest of the god Ieuo. It was from him, according to a fragment of Porphyry preserved in Eusebius, *Praeparationis Evangelicae* I ix–a work on which M. draws in his outlines for tragedies in the Trinity MS (Columbia xviii 235)–and quoted in Selden 111, that Sanchuniathon drew the material for his *Phoenician*

Longos vetusti commemoret atavos Nini,
Priscumque Belon, inclytumque Osiridem.
Non ille trino gloriosus nomine
Ter magnus Hermes (ut sit arcani sciens)
Talem reliquit Isidis cultoribus.
At tu perenne ruris Academi decus
(Haec monstra si tu primus induxti scholis)
Iam iam poetas urbis exules tuae
Revocabis, ipse fabulator maximus,
Aut institutor ipse migrabis foras.

Tell me, goddesses[1] who keep watch over the sacred groves; tell me, Memory, most blessed mother of the nine Muses;[3] tell me, Eternity,[4] you who lie at ease in some vast cave far away, looking after the records of the past, the unshakeable laws of Jove, the calendars of heaven and the diaries of the gods[6]–tell me, who was that first being in whose image skilful Nature has modelled the human race: that first, eternal, incorrupt, single yet universal being, as old as the heavens,[9] the pattern used by God? He is not twin brother to the virgin Athene:[11] he does not live like an unborn child inside Jove's mind.[12] Although he is by nature common to all, he has a separate existence just like a normal individual and, extraordinarily enough, is confined within definite spatial limits. Perhaps he wanders about eternally[16] through the ten concentric spheres of the heavens, keeping the stars company, or perhaps he lives next door to the earth in the globe of the moon. Perhaps he sits on Lethe's banks among the souls who are waiting to get into human bodies,[19] and dozes off beside the waters of forgetfulness,[20] or perhaps in

History. Eusebius' work contains the only extant portions of a translation made ostensibly from Sanchuniathon by Philo of Byblos.

30. Philo claims that Sanchuniathon lived at or before the time of the Trojan War, in the reign of Queen Semiramis and King Ninus, founders of the Assyrian empire. Of the passages which Eusebius I x quotes from Philo's translations of the *Phoenician History*, the first deals with the origin of life on earth.

31. Priscumque Belon] Selden devotes a chapter (II i) to Bel or Baal, and quotes (105) from Philo's translation of Sanchuniathon a passage asserting that Bel was thought the only god in the sky by the Phoenicians. Sandys 207 mentions '*Belus Priscus*, (reputed a God and honoured with Temples, called *Bel* by the Assyrians, and *Baal* by the Hebrewes)'. *Osiridem*] see *Nativity Ode* 213*n* (p. 111).

33. Hermes] Hermes Trismegistus, identified with the Egyptian Thoth, god of wisdom, to whom the Alexandrian neo-Platonists of the third and fourth centuries A.D. attributed various of their writings. According to Philo (quoted by Eusebius I ix), Sanchuniathon based his *History* on Hermes, the inventor of writing.

34. Isidis] See *Nativity Ode* 211–12*n* (p. 111).

35. Academi decus] Plato, who excluded poets from his ideal state (*Republic* x 595–607).

some faraway land this archetypal man strides along like an enormous giant, taller than star-bearing Atlas,[24] and rears up his towering head to frighten the gods. The visionary Tiresias,[26] whose blindness gave him piercing sight, never saw this man even in the depths of his heart. Pleione's swift-heeled grandson[27] never showed this man to the crowd of prophetic sages in the silence of the night. The Assyrian priest[29] had never heard of this man, although he could remember the remote ancestors of ancient Ninus,[30] primitive Belus,[31] and famous Osiris. Nor did that seer who glories in a triple name, Hermes Trismegistus,[33] although he knew a lot about erudite things, ever leave word to the worshippers of Isis[34] of a man like this. But you, the immortal glory of the Academy,[35] if you are responsible for introducing these monsters into philosophical discussions, must either hurry up and call home the poets whom you exiled from your Republic or else banish yourself from it, although you were its founder, as the greatest fictional writer of them all.

22 *Elegia septima*

[Elegy VII]

Date. Summer? 1628. Headed in *1645*, *Anno aetatis undevigesimo* [In his nineteenth year]. This heading is singular because of its use of the ordinal: M. normally employs arabic figures. Thus it might be correct to take his dating literally in this case and place the elegy between Dec. 1626 and Dec. 1627. It would be more in keeping with M.'s normal practice, however, to take his heading to mean 'When he was nineteen' (i.e. Dec. 1627–Dec. 1628). There is no need to date *Elegia VII* in May, as do Masson i 268, MacKellar 33 and French i 153–7. 1 May (*14*) is merely given as the date of Cupid's visit. The reference to the London summertime, when citizens promenade (*51*) and the concept of M. being torn between two places (*79*) might suggest that *Elegia VII* was written when M. had returned to Cambridge in the summer vacation of 1628: cp. his sixth *Prolusion*, delivered at this time, where he tells how he has just returned from London 'stuffed, I might almost say, to corpulence with all the pleasures in which that place overflows beyond measure' (Columbia xii 204–5; Yale i 266). W. R. Parker (Taylor 119–21), anxious to prove that the *1645* order of printing represents the order of composition, dates *Elegia VII* May 1630 and conjectures that *undevigesimo* is an error for *uno & vigesimo* [twenty-first]. M. uses the ordinal, he explains, to make the date of his coming-of-age conspicuous. E. Sirluck, *JEGP* lx (1961) 783–4, pertinently objects that, if this was M.'s intention in using the ordinal, it is inconceivable that a printer's error such as Parker postulates, would have escaped his notice.

In *1645* M. presumably printed *Elegia VII* after *Elegiae V* and *VI* (both later in date), because he felt that the retraction, *Haec ego mente* . . . (p. 231 below) which he wished to append to *Elegia VII*, would fit more easily at the end of the numbered elegies, rather than inserted into the run.

Publication. *1645* (*8.* tuae:]tuae. *50.* erat,]erat. *59.* misi]misi, *88.* loqui!]loqui;), *1673* (the text followed here).

Nondum blanda tuas leges Amathusia noram,
  Et Paphio vacuum pectus ab igne fuit.
Saepe cupidineas, puerilia tela, sagittas,
  Atque tuum sprevi maxime, numen, Amor.
Tu puer imbelles dixi transfige columbas,
  Conveniunt tenero mollia bella duci.
Aut de passeribus tumidos age, parve, triumphos,
  Haec sunt militiae digna trophaea tuae:
In genus humanum quid inania dirigis arma?
  Non valet in fortes ista pharetra viros.
Non tulit hoc Cyprius, (neque enim deus ullus ad iras
  Promptior) et duplici iam ferus igne calet.
Ver erat, et summae radians per culmina villae
  Attulerat primam lux tibi Maie diem:
At mihi adhuc refugam quaerebant lumina noctem
  Nec matutinum sustinuere iubar.
Astat Amor lecto, pictis Amor impiger alis,
  Prodidit astantem mota pharetra deum:
Prodidit et facies, et dulce minantis ocelli,
  Et quicquid puero, dignum et Amore fuit.
Talis in aeterno iuvenis Sigeius Olympo
  Miscet amatori pocula plena Iovi;
Aut qui formosas pellexit ad oscula nymphas
  Thiodamantaeus Naiade raptus Hylas;
Addideratque iras, sed et has decuisse putares,
  Addideratque truces, nec sine felle minas.
Et miser exemplo sapuisses tutius, inquit,
  Nunc mea quid possit dextera testis eris.

¶ 22. *1–2. Amathusia*] Venus, who had a temple at Amathus in Cyprus, and another at Paphos (hence *Paphio . . . igne*).

11. Cyprius] Not a classical name for Cupid. M. uses it because Venus, Cupid's mother, is frequently called *Cypria* (the Cyprian).

17. pictis . . . alis] Cp. Cupid's *purpureas alas* in Ovid, *Rem.* 701.

21. iuvenis Sigeius] Ganymede, the youth whom, as Ovid relates, *Met.* x 155–61, Jove, in the shape of an eagle, stole away from Mt Ida to be his cup-bearer. *Sigeum* was the name of a promontory in Troas, thus *Sigeius* could be used, by transference, to mean 'Trojan'. In Homer's account of the rape of Ganymede, *Il.* xx 230–5, his father is given as Tros, the eponym of Troy.

24. Hylas] Son of Theodamas, king of the Dryopes, was dragged down to the depths of a fountain by a nymph captivated by his beauty. M. follows Propertius I xx 6 *Theiodamanteo . . . Hylae.*

Inter et expertos vires numerabere nostras,
  Et faciam vero per tua damna fidem.
Ipse ego si nescis strato pythone superbum
  Edomui Phoebum, cessit et ille mihi;
Et quoties meminit Peneidos, ipse fatetur
  Certius et gravius tela nocere mea.
Me nequit adductum curvare peritius arcum,
  Qui post terga solet vincere Parthus eques.
Cydoniusque mihi cedit venator, et ille
  Inscius uxori qui necis author erat.
Est etiam nobis ingens quoque victus Orion,
  Herculeaeque manus, Herculeusque comes.
Iupiter ipse licet sua fulmina torqueat in me,
  Haerebunt lateri spicula nostra Iovis.

31–4. Cp. Ovid, *Met.* i 452–64: 'Now the first love of Phoebus was Daphne, daughter of Peneus, the river god. It was no blind chance that gave this love, but the malicious wrath of Cupid. Delian Apollo, while still exulting over his conquest of the Python, had seen him bending his bow with tight-drawn string, and had said: "What hast thou to do with the arms of men, thou wanton boy?" . . . And to him Venus' son replied: "Thy dart may pierce all things else, Apollo, but mine shall pierce thee."' When in love Apollo admits: 'My arrow is sure of aim, but oh, one arrow, surer than my own, has wounded my heart.' This episode is the basis for the first part of M.'s poem. Apollo's scornful speech is echoed in ll. 5–10, and Apollo's love is snatched from him as is M.'s.
37–8. Cydoniusque . . . venator] The inhabitants of Cydon (modern Canea), a port in Crete, were famous as archers. Virgil, *Aen.* xii 858, couples Parthians and Cydonians. *ille Inscius*] Cephalus who, as Ovid relates, *Met.* vii 835–62, heard a rustling sound in a bush when he was out hunting, flung his javelin at the place, and killed his wife, Procris, who was hiding there.
39. ingens . . . Orion] Orion pursued the Pleiades, the seven daughters of Atlas. Ovid portrays him love-sick, *Ars Amatoria* i 731: 'Pale did Orion wander in Dirce's glades.'
40. Deianira, Hercules' wife, upbraids him in Ovid, *Her.* ix 47 for his *peregrinos . . . amores* and, 53–118, for his subjection to Omphale, who dressed him as a waiting-maid and made him spin for her. M.'s concentration on Hercules' hands is Deianira's: 'Do you not shrink, Alcides, from laying to the polished wool-basket the hand that has triumphed over a thousand toils; do you draw off with stalwart thumb the coarsely spun strands? . . . Ah, how often, while with dour finger you twisted the thread, have your too strong hands crushed the spindle!' *comes*] probably Jason, leader of the Argonauts, of whom Hercules was one. Jason abandoned Medea in favour of Glauce, daughter of Creon, king of Corinth.
42. The loves of Jove were notorious: Ovid lists them, *Met.* vi 103–14.

Caetera quae dubitas melius mea tela docebunt,
Et tua non leviter corda petenda mihi.
Nec te stulte tuae poterunt defendere musae,
Nec tibi Phoebaeus porriget anguis opem.
Dixit, et aurato quatiens mucrone sagittam,
Evolat in tepidos Cypridos ille sinus.
At mihi risuro tonuit ferus ore minaci,
Et mihi de puero non metus ullus erat,
Et modo qua nostri spatiantur in urbe quirites
Et modo villarum proxima rura placent.
Turba frequens, facieque simillima turba dearum
Splendida per medias itque reditque vias.
Auctaque luce dies gemino fulgore coruscat,
Fallor? an et radios hinc quoque Phoebus habet.
Haec ego non fugi spectacula grata severus,
Impetus et quo me fert iuvenilis, agor.
Lumina luminibus male providus obvia misi
Neve oculos potui continuisse meos.
Unam forte aliis supereminuisse notabam,
Principium nostri lux erat illa mali.
Sic Venus optaret mortalibus ipsa videri,
Sic regina deum conspicienda fuit.
Hanc memor obiecit nobis malus ille Cupido,
Solus et hos nobis texuit ante dolos.
Nec procul ipse vafer latuit, multaeque sagittae,
Et facis a tergo grande pependit onus.

46. *anguis*] Symbol of Aesculapius, god of medicine, son of Apollo. Ovid tells how in the form of a snake (*Phoebeius anguis*) he came to Rome to put an end to a plague, *Met.* xv 626–744. Captivated by Daphne, Apollo laments 'The art of medicine is my discovery ... and all the potency o herbs is given unto me. Alas that love is curable by no herbs, and the arts which heal all others cannot heal their lord!' *Met.* i 521–4, see ll. 31–4*n*.
47. *aurato ... mucrone*] In the Daphne story (see ll. 31–4*n*) Ovid gives Cupid golden arrows to kindle love and leaden to repel it, *Met.* i 468–72.
51. Favourite places for promenading in early seventeenth-century London were Lincoln's Inn Fields, Gray's Inn Fields, the Temple Garden and Moorfields. They were frequented on summer evenings: cp. Jonson, *Bartholomew Fair* I ii 5–7: 'Shee would not ha' worne this habit. I challenge all *Cheapside*, to shew such another: *Moorfields*, *Pimlico* path, or the *Exchange*, in a sommer evening.'
52. Possibly M. is referring to the same 'magnificently shady spot just outside the city' which he had mentioned to Diodati in *Elegia I* 50.
61. *aliis*] *supereminueo*, which here governs the dative, always governs the accusative in the Roman poets.

Nec mora, nunc ciliis haesit, nunc virginis ori,
Insilit hinc labiis, insidet inde genis:
Et quascunque agilis partes iaculator oberrat,
Hei mihi, mille locis pectus inerme ferit.
Protinus insoliti subierunt corda furores,
Uror amans intus, flammaque totus eram.
Interea misero quae iam mihi sola placebat,
Ablata est oculis non reditura meis.
Ast ego progredior tacite querebundus, et excors,
Et dubius volui saepe referre pedem.
Findor, et haec remanet, sequitur pars altera votum,
Raptaque tam subito gaudia flere iuvat.
Sic dolet amissum proles Iunonia coelum,
Inter Lemniacos praecipitata focos.
Talis et abreptum solem respexit, ad Orcum
Vectus ab attonitis Amphiaraus equis.
Quid faciam infelix, et luctu victus, amores
Nec licet inceptos ponere, neve sequi.
O utinam spectare semel mihi detur amatos
Vultus, et coram tristia verba loqui!
Forsitan et duro non est adamante creata,
Forte nec ad nostras surdeat illa preces.
Crede mihi nullus sic infeliciter arsit,
Ponar in exemplo primus et unus ego.
Parce precor teneri cum sis deus ales amoris,
Pugnent officio nec tua facta tuo.
Iam tuus O certe est mihi formidabilis arcus,
Nate dea, iaculis nec minus igne potens:
Et tua fumabunt nostris altaria donis,
Solus et in superis tu mihi summus eris.
Deme meos tandem, verum nec deme furores,

81–2. Vulcan (Hephaestus) son of Juno (Hera) was thrown from heaven by Jove (Zeus). Homer, *Il.* i 590–3, makes him relate to his mother how, after falling for a whole day, he landed on the island of Lemnos.

83–4. Orcum] Orcus was a name for the world of the dead. *Amphiaraus*: one of the seven against Thebes: he was swallowed up by the earth along with his chariot and horses. Statius, *Theb.* vii 690–823, has a dramatic account of the event which mentions, as does M., Amphiaraus' backward glance: 'And as he sank he looked back at the heavens and groaned to see the plain meet above him.'

89. Cp. Theocritus iii 39: 'It may be she'll look upon me then, being she's no woman of adamant.'

90. surdeat] An incorrect form; there is no verb *surdeo*.

97. Cp. Lucretius vi 752: *fumant altaria donis.*

Nescio cur, miser est suaviter omnis amans:
Tu modo da facilis, posthaec mea siqua futura est,
Cuspis amaturos figat ut una duos.

I was still ignorant of your laws, seductive Amathusia,[1] and my breast contained no Paphian[2] fire. I often made fun of Cupid's arrows, calling them childish weapons, and above all I scorned your godhead, Love. 'Go and shoot doves, lad; they can't hurt you', I said, 'a tender campaigner like you is only fit for soft wars. Or go and boast about the triumphs you've won over sparrows, little boy: those are the sort of trophies which your warfare deserves. Why do you aim your stupid darts at human beings? Your quiver's no good against grown-up men.' Cupid[11] could not bear this (not one of the gods is more easily irritated than he), and he grew twice as angry as before.

It was spring, and the dawn shining over the gables of the tall farmhouse had brought your first day, May. But my eyes still longed for the vanishing night, and could not bear the bright morning sunshine. Love stood by my bed, agile Love with his brightly coloured wings.[17] His swinging quiver and his face and his sweetly threatening eyes gave him away, and so did all those other signs which distinguish the boy Cupid. This is what the Trojan lad[21] looks like, while he mixes brimming goblets for infatuated Jove on ageless Olympus' top; and this is what Hylas,[24] Theodamas' son, looked like –Hylas, who lured the beautiful nymphs to his kisses and was stolen away by a Naiad. Cupid was angry, unlike them (though you'd have thought anger made him even lovelier), and what is more he was full of fierce and bitter threats: this is what he said: 'You miserable creature, you would have been wiser and safer if you had learned by the example of others. Now you will yourself witness what my right hand can do. You shall be numbered among those who have felt my strength: by your suffering I shall make people believe the truth about me. It was I, in case you don't know it, who tamed proud Phoebus when he had vanquished the Python.[31] Even he yielded to me, and whenever he remembers Daphne he confesses that my arrows are more accurate and more painful than his own.[34] The Parthian horseman, who is trained to win a fight by shooting behind his back, cannot draw his taut bow more skilfully than I. The Cydonian hunter[37] gives me best too, and so does that hunter who hit his own wife and killed her without knowing who it was.[38] Even the giant Orion[39] was conquered by me; so were the hands of Hercules,[40] and Hercules's comrade as well. Even if Jove himself throws his whirling thunderbolts at me, my little arrows will stick in his side.[42] Whatever other doubts you may have will be resolved by my arrows better than by words, and also by your own heart, which must be my target–and I shall not shoot half-heartedly. Your muses will not be able to protect you, you fool, and Apollo's serpent[46] will not provide you with any cure.' When he had finished speaking he shook a gold-tipped arrow[47] at me and then flew away to nestle between the warm breasts of Cypris. But I was inclined to smile at the threats which this furious little lad thundered at me: I had no fear of the boy. Sometimes the city promenades[51] provided me with entertainment, sometimes the countryside near the outlying houses.[52] A whole host of girls, with faces just like goddesses, go to and fro along the walks, resplendently beautiful. And the day is twice as bright as usual because of the light they add to it. Am I mistaken, or is it from them that the sun borrows his beams? I was not puritanical: I did not run away from such delicious sights. I let myself be driven wherever the impulse of youth carried me. Heedlessly I let my eyes meet theirs: I was unable to keep my eyes in check. Then, by chance, I caught sight of one girl who was far more beautiful than all the rest:[61] that day was the beginning of my downfall. Venus herself, when she appeared to mortals, might have chosen to look like this girl: this is what the queen of the gods must have looked like. That wretch Cupid bore me a grudge and threw her in my way: it was he alone who had woven these nets for me in advance. The artful boy was hiding close at hand with a good supply of arrows and a huge load of torches hung behind his back. Losing no time he swung on the girl's eyelashes, then on her mouth, then jumped between her lips, then perched on her cheek–and wherever the nimble archer landed (alas for me!) he hit my defenceless breast in a thousand places. In an instant passions I had never felt before entered my heart–I burned inwardly with love: my whole being was aflame.

Meanwhile the only girl who could give me relief was taken away from me, never to be seen again. But I went on, madly in love, complaining to myself and irresolute, often wanting to retrace my steps. I am torn apart: one half of me stays here, and the other follows my desire and takes pleasure in weeping for joys so suddenly snatched away. So Juno's son[81] wept for the heaven he had lost, after he had been flung down among the houses of Lemnos:[82] so Amphiaraus,[83] carried down to Hades by his panic-stricken horses, looked back at the sun which was being snatched from his eyes.[84] Luckless, overwhelmed with grief, what am I to do? I am powerless either to stop loving, now I have begun, or to follow my love any further. O if only I may be allowed to see those beloved features once again, and to tell the story of my grief in her presence! Perhaps she is not made of unyielding adamant:[89] it is possible that she may not be deaf[90] to my prayers. Believe me, no one has ever fallen in love in such an unlucky way: I may be chronicled as the first and only example! Spare me, I beg you. After all, you are the winged god of tender love, so do not let your actions be at odds with your office. Child of the goddess, you may be sure that I dread your bow now: you are mighty with your arrows, and no less so with your fire. Your altars shall smoke with my offerings,[97] and you alone shall be supreme to me among the gods. Take away my madness, then–but no, do not take it away! I don't know why, but every lover is miserable in a way which is somehow delightful. Only be gracious enough to grant that, if any girl is ever to be mine in the future, one arrow may pierce both our hearts and make them love.

23 At a Vacation Exercise in the College, part Latin, part English

Date. Aug.? 1628. The Latin part of this entertainment consists of an *Oratio* on the theme *Exercitationes nonnunquam ludicras philosophiae studiis non obesse* (That sometimes light-hearted entertainments are not prejudicial to philosophic studies), and a *Prolusio*, full of dirty jokes and personal references to members of the audience. *Oratio* and *Prolusio* were printed together as *Prolusio VI* (Columbia xii 204–47; Yale i 265–86) in the 1674 volume of *Epistolae Familiares* and *Prolusiones*. The heading of the *Oratio–In feriis aestivis Collegii* (In the summer vacation of the College), and the words *Anno aetatis 19* prefixed to *Vacation Exercise* in *1673*, show that the performance was in the summer vacation of 1628, which extended from July until early October.

Publication. First printed in *1673* (which misprints 'daintest' for 'daintiest' in *14* and 'hollowed' for 'hallowed' in *98*): there is a note in the *1673 Errata* to the effect that *Vacation Exercise* is misplaced and 'should have come in' between *Fair Infant* and *Passion*.

Modern criticism. Allen 14–16 points out the remarkable similarity between *Vacation Exercise 29–52* and a passage in *Prolusio III* (Columbia xii 169–71; Yale i 246–7), and derives both from M.'s reading of the *Corpus Hermeticum* xi 20b.

The Latin Speeches ended, the English thus began

Hail native language, that by sinews weak
Didst move my first endeavouring tongue to speak,
And mad'st imperfect words with childish trips,
Half unpronounced, slide through my infant lips,
Driving dumb silence from the portal door,
Where he had mutely sat two years before:
Here I salute thee and thy pardon ask,
That now I use thee in my latter task:
Small loss it is that thence can come unto thee,
I know my tongue but little grace can do thee.
Thou need'st not be ambitious to be first,
Believe me I have thither packed the worst:
And, if it happen as I did forecast,
The daintiest dishes shall be served up last.
I pray thee then deny me not thy aid
For this same small neglect that I have made;
But haste thee straight to do me once a pleasure,
And from thy wardrobe bring thy chiefest treasure;
Not those new-fangled toys, and trimming slight

¶ 23. *1. Hail*] M. greets his native language because he is now turning from the Latin part of the entertainment to the English.
5. Sylvester has 'dumb silence' (Du Bartas 16).
12. thither] into the Latin part.
14. Cp. *Richard II* I iii 68.
18. wardrobe] M. continues the conceit of language as supplier of clothes in 'trimming' (19), 'robes . . . attire' (21), 'naked . . . array' (23–6) and 'clothe' (32).

Which takes our late fantastics with delight,
But cull those richest robes, and gayest attire
Which deepest spirits, and choicest wits desire:
I have some naked thoughts that rove about
And loudly knock to have their passage out;
And weary of their place do only stay
Till thou hast decked them in thy best array;
That so they may without suspect or fears
Fly swiftly to this fair assembly's ears;
Yet I had rather, if I were to choose,
Thy service in some graver subject use,
Such as may make thee search thy coffers round,
Before thou clothe my fancy in fit sound:
Such where the deep transported mind may soar
Above the wheeling poles, and at heaven's door
Look in, and see each blissful deity
How he before the thunderous throne doth lie,
Listening to what unshorn Apollo sings
To the touch of golden wires, while Hebe brings
Immortal nectar to her kingly sire:
Then passing through the spheres of watchful fire,
And misty regions of wide air next under,

20. late fantastics] W. J. Harvey, *N & Q* n.s. iv (1957) 523–4 thinks this refers to M.'s poetic contemporaries at Cambridge like Thomas Randolph, who mingled metaphysical and Jonsonian strains in their verse. M., in opposing 'richest robes' (a style opulent, decorative and probably Spenserian) to a style which delights in 'new-fangled toys' (i.e. 'new turns of wit'–allowing for the literary sense of 'toy', *OED* sb. 3) but has 'slight' trimming (i.e. is comparatively bare), is perhaps glancing at the cult of 'strong lines'.
29–52. See headnote. Du Bartas 166–7 has a similar passage on the soul's flight, probably also deriving from Hermes.
34–5. wheeling poles] As in *PL*, M. represents heaven as above the ten spheres of the Ptolemaic universe: the 'poles' are the extremities of the axis of each sphere in this universe. In Du Bartas 658 Urania tells of her ability to transport human-kind 'above the *Poles*' to see 'All th'enter-course of the *Celestiall Court*'.
37. unshorn] A classical epithet for Apollo, used by Homer, *Il.* xx 39, Ovid, *Tristia* III i 60 and Horace, *Odes* I xxi 2.
38. Hebe] daughter of Zeus and Hera, cup-bearer to the gods, and goddess of youth.
40. watchful fire] Plato, *Timaeus* 38c says that sun, moon and planets were created to guard the numbers of time. Ovid has *vigiles flammas*, *Ars Am.* iii 463.

And hills of snow and lofts of piled thunder,
May tell at length how green-eyed Neptune raves,
In heaven's defiance mustering all his waves;
Then sing of secret things that came to pass
When beldam Nature in her cradle was;
And last of kings and queens and heroes old,
Such as the wise Demodocus once told
In solemn songs at king Alcinous' feast,
While sad Ulysses' soul and all the rest
Are held with his melodious harmony
In willing chains and sweet captivity.
But fie my wandering Muse how thou dost stray!
Expectance calls thee now another way,
Thou knowest it must be now thy only bent
To keep in compass of thy predicament:
Then quick about thy purposed business come,
That to the next I may resign my room.

Then ENS *is represented as Father of the Predicaments his ten Sons, whereof the eldest stood for* SUBSTANCE *with his Canons, which* ENS *thus speaking, explains.*

Good luck befriend thee Son; for at thy birth
The faëry ladies danced upon the hearth;
Thy drowsy nurse hath sworn she did them spy
Come tripping to the room where thou didst lie;

42. Cp. Sylvester (Du Bartas 354): 'Cellars of winde, and Shops of Sulphury Thunder'.

43. green-eyed] The eyes of Proteus in Virgil, *Georg.* iv 451 are 'ablaze with grey-green light'.

48–52. In Homer, *Od.* viii 521–2 Odysseus weeps as he listens to the bard Demodocus sing of the Trojan war at the court of Alcinous, king of the Phaeacians.

52. An echo of Sylvester (Du Bartas[2] 997) 'The willing Chaines of my Captivitie'.

53. Cp. Horace, *Odes* III iii 70: *quo, Musa, tendis?*

59. Son] Towards the end of the Latin *Prolusio* (see headnote) M. as 'father' of the ceremonies gives to his ten 'sons' (fellow-students taking part in the entertainment) names corresponding to the Categories or Predicaments of Aristotle: Substance, Quantity, Quality, Relation, Place, Time, Posture, State, Action and Passivity. The first he addresses is Substance. To Aristotle Primary Substance is exemplified by a visible, individual man (see *Categories* 3b 10), but to M., the Platonist, the visible world is removed from the reality of eternal Forms, which cannot be seen (cp. *Republic* v 474–510). He therefore mocks Aristotle's Substance by declaring it invisible.

And sweetly singing round about thy bed
Strew all their blessings on thy sleeping head.
She heard them give thee this, that thou shouldst still
From eyes of mortals walk invisible,
Yet there is something that doth force my fear,
For once it was my dismal hap to hear
A Sibyl old, bow-bent with crooked age,
That far events full wisely could presage,
And in time's long and dark prospective glass
Foresaw what future days should bring to pass,
Your son, said she, (nor can you it prevent)
Shall subject be to many an accident.
O'er all his brethren he shall reign as king,
Yet every one shall make him underling,
And those that cannot live from him asunder
Ungratefully shall strive to keep him under,
In worth and excellence he shall outgo them,
Yet being above them, he shall be below them;
From others he shall stand in need of nothing,
Yet on his brothers shall depend for clothing.
To find a foe it shall not be his hap,
And peace shall lull him in her flow'ry lap;
Yet shall he live in strife, and at his door
Devouring war shall never cease to roar:
Yea it shall be his natural property
To harbour those that are at enmity.
What power, what force, what mighty spell, if not
Your learned hands, can loose this Gordian knot?

69. Sibyl] prophetess.

71. prospective glass] Magic crystal for foreseeing events.

74. accident] Playing on the senses, 'calamity' and 'one of the nine Categories after Substance'.

75–6. Substance is first of the Categories (hence 'king'), but 'the primary substances most of all merit that name, since they underlie all other things,' Aristotle, *Categories* 2b 15.

77. Cp. 'And were there no primary substance, nought else could so much as exist', *Categories* 2b 5.

83. Cp. 'Substances never have contraries', *Categories* 3b 25.

85–8. Cp. 'But what is most characteristic of substance appears to be this: that, although it remains notwithstanding, numerically one and the same, it is capable of being the recipient of contrary qualifications', *Categories* 4a 10.

90. loose this Gordian knot] untangle Aristotle's theory. The knot was tied by the Phrygian king Gordius: the oracle declared that whoever undid it would rule Asia. Alexander cut it.

The next Quantity *and* Quality, *spake in prose, then* Relation *was called by his name.*

Rivers arise; whether thou be the son,
Of utmost Tweed, or Ouse, or gulfy Dun,
Or Trent, who like some earth-born giant spreads
His thirty arms along the indented meads,
Or sullen Mole that runneth underneath,
Or Severn swift, guilty of maiden's death,
Or rocky Avon, or of sedgy Lea,
Or coaly Tyne, or ancient hallowed Dee,
Or Humber loud that keeps the Scythian's name,
Or Medway smooth, or royal towered Thame.

The rest was prose.

24 *Elegia quinta. In adventum veris*

[Elegy V. On the Coming of Spring]

Date. Spring 1629. Headed *Anno aetatis 20* in *1645*.
Publication. 1645 (*30.* perennis]quotannis *66.* Tenario]Taenario *106.* Litus]Littus *110.* Virgineos]Virgineas) and *1673* (the text followed here, but corrected in these instances: *74.* titulos]ticulos *115.* Navita] Natvia).

91. Rivers] The two sons of Sir John Rivers of Chafford, Kent, were admitted to Christ's College 10 May 1628. One of them plays the part of Relation.
92. gulfy] full of eddies or whirlpools.
93–4. Drayton, *Polyolbion* xii 546–54, affirms that the Trent has thirty tributaries and that its name means 'thirty'. *earth-born giant*] See *Natur* 59*n* (p. 64 above).
92–100. M.'s catalogue of rivers imitates those in Drayton's *Polyolbion* and Spenser, *F.Q.* IV xi 20–47.
95. The subterranean course of the Mole, in Surrey, is described by Drayton, *Polyolbion* xvii 59 and Spenser, *F.Q.* IV xi 32.
96. maiden's] Sabrina's (see *Comus* 825–30*n*, p. 218).
98. coaly] In *Polyolbion* xxix 122–5 Drayton's Tyne boasts of its coal trade. *hallowed*] Drayton refers to the 'hallowed *Dee*' (x 215) and explains (iv 201–4) that it was thought to change its fords, and that this was regarded as a prophetic omen.
99. Scythian's name] Geoffrey of Monmouth relates (*British History* II ii) that the Humber takes its name from the Scythian king, Humber, who was drowned in it after being defeated by Locrine and his brother Camber. M. (*History of Britain*, Columbia x 15), Drayton (*Polyolbion* viii 45–6) and Spenser (*F.Q.* II x 16 and IV xi 38) repeat the story.

The subject is a very common one among neo-Latin poets of the Renaissance. For other examples see *Delitiae CC Italorum Poetarum* (Frankfurt 1608) i 330 [Balbi], 468 [Buonamico], 1118 [Frascatoro], ii 116 [Navagero], 714 [Sannazaro], 990 [Tito Strozi], 1459 [Zanchi]; *Delitiae C Poetarum Gallorum* (Frankfurt 1609) i 505 [Beaucaire], ii 401 [Lect]; Buchanan *Poemata* (Leyden 1628) 315; Joannes Secundus, *Opera* (Leyden 1619) 58.

In se perpetuo Tempus revolubile gyro
   Iam revocat zephyros vere tepente novos.
Induiturque brevem Tellus reparata iuventam,
   Iamque soluta gelu dulce virescit humus.
Fallor? an et nobis redeunt in carmina vires,
   Ingeniumque mihi munere veris adest?
Munere veris adest, iterumque vigescit ab illo
   (Quis putet) atque aliquod iam sibi poscit opus.
Castalis ante oculos, bifidumque cacumen oberrat,
   Et mihi Pyrenen somnia nocte ferunt.
Concitaque arcano fervent mihi pectora motu,
   Et furor, et sonitus me sacer intus agit.
Delius ipse venit, video Peneide lauro
   Implicitos crines, Delius ipse venit.
Iam mihi mens liquidi raptatur in ardua coeli,
   Perque vagas nubes corpore liber eo.
Perque umbras, perque antra feror penetralia vatum,
   Et mihi fana patent interiora Deum.
Intuiturque animus toto quid agatur Olympo,
   Nec fugiunt oculos Tartara caeca meos.
Quid tam grande sonat distento spiritus ore?
   Quid parit haec rabies, quic sacer iste furor?
Ver mihi, quod dedit ingenium, cantabitur illo;
   Profuerint isto reddita dona modo.
Iam Philomela tuos foliis adoperta novellis
   Instituis modulos, dum silet omne nemus.
Urbe ego, tu sylva simul incipiamus utrique,
   Et simul adventum veris uterque canat.

¶ 24. 9. *Castalis . . . cacumen*] Cp. *Elegia IV* 29–32*n* (p. 55).
10. *Pyrenen*] Pirene, a fountain in the citadel of Corinth which sprang from Pegasus' hoof-mark, was sacred to the Muses.
13. *Peneide lauro*] Ovid, *Met.* i 452–559, tells how Apollo loved Daphne, daughter of the river-god Peneus, and how when her lover pursued her she prayed for help to her father and was turned into a laurel. Apollo vowed to wear laurel leaves in his hair from then on.
25–6. *Philomela . . . nemus*] Cp. *Sonnet I* 1–2 (p. 90). The rape of Philomela by Tereus and her transformation into a nightingale are described by Ovid, *Met.* vi 424–674.

Veris io rediere vices, celebremus honores
Veris, et hoc subeat Musa perennis opus.
Iam sol Aethiopas fugiens Tithoniaque arva,
Flectit ad Arctoas aurea lora plagas.
Est breve noctis iter, brevis est mora noctis opacae
Horrida cum tenebris exulat illa suis.
Iamque Lycaonius plaustrum caeleste Bootes
Non longa sequitur fessus ut ante via,
Nunc etiam solitas circum Iovis atria toto
Excubias agitant sydera rara polo.
Nam dolus, et caedes, et vis cum nocte recessit,
Neve Giganteum Dii timuere scelus.
Forte aliquis scopuli recubans in vertice pastor,
Roscida cum primo sole rubescit humus,
Hac, ait, hac certe caruisti nocte puella
Phoebe tua, celeres quae retineret equos.
Laeta suas repetit sylvas, pharetramque resumit
Cynthia, Luciferas ut videt alta rotas,
Et tenues ponens radios gaudere videtur
Officium fieri tam breve fratris ope.
Desere, Phoebus ait, thalamos Aurora seniles,
Quid iuvat effoeto procubuisse toro?
Te manet Aeolides viridi venator in herba,
Surge, tuos ignes altus Hymettus habet.

30. perennis] Salmasius, *Responsio* (1660) 5, picked on the false quantity in 1645 (*quotannis*, with last syllable short) and M. altered the word in *1673*.
31–2. Aethiopas ... Tithoniaque arva ... Arctoas] The Ethiopians here represent the equator and Tithonus' fields the east (Tithonus was husband to Aurora, the dawn-goddess). After the vernal equinox the sun rises north of east. *Arctos* is the constellation of the Bear, hence the adjective *arctous*, northern.
35–6. Lycaonius] northern. An Ovidian adjective (cp. *Tristia* III ii 2) formed from Lycaon, king of Arcadia, whose daughter, Callisto, was changed to a she-bear by Juno and raised to heaven by Jove as the constellation of the Great Bear. *Bootes*, another northern constellation, was called the Bear-keeper and also the Waggoner, since another name for the Great Bear was the Waggon (*plaustrum*). Starnes and Talbert 262 note that in Calepine's *Dictionarium* (1609 edn), *s.v. Bootes*, he is given as the son of Jove by Callisto.
40. Giganteum ... scelus] See *Q Nov* 174*n* (p. 43).
46. Cynthia] The moon-goddess Diana, called Cynthia from Mount Cynthus on the island of Delos where she was born.
49–52. Aurora's husband Tithonus was granted immortality by the gods, but not eternal youth: hence his old age and impotence, and Aurora's love for Cephalus, son of Aeolus (called *Aeolides* by Ovid, *Met.* vii 672), whom

Flava verecundo dea crimen in ore fatetur,
Et matutinos ocyus urget equos.
Exuit invisam Tellus rediviva senectam,
Et cupit amplexus Phoebe subire tuos;
Et cupit, et digna est, quid enim formosius illa,
Pandit ut omniferos luxuriosa sinus,
Atque Arabum spirat messes, et ab ore venusto
Mitia cum Paphiis fundit amoma rosis.
Ecce coronatur sacro frons ardua luco,
Cingit ut Idaeam pinea turris Opim;
Et vario madidos intexit flore capillos,
Floribus et visa est posse placere suis.
Floribus effusos ut erat redimita capillos
Tenario placuit diva Sicana Deo.
Aspice Phoebe tibi faciles hortantur amores,
Mellitasque movent flamina verna preces.
Cinnamea Zephyrus leve plaudit odorifer ala,
Blanditiasque tibi ferre videntur aves.
Nec sine dote tuos temeraria quaerit amores
Terra, nec optatos poscit egena toros,
Alma salutiferum medicos tibi gramen in usus
Praebet, et hinc titulos adiuvat ipsa tuos.
Quod si te pretium, si te fulgentia tangunt
Munera, (muneribus saepe coemptus Amor)
Illa tibi ostentat quascunque sub aequore vasto,
Et superiniectis montibus abdit opes.
Ah quoties cum tu clivoso fessus Olympo
In vespertinas praecipitaris aquas,
Cur te, inquit, cursu languentem Phoebe diurno
Hesperiis recipit caerula mater aquis?

she first saw spreading nets for deer on Mount Hymettus, as Ovid describes, *Met.* vii 700–13.

60. *Paphiis*] Paphian, from Paphos, a city in Cyprus sacred to Venus.

62. *Idaeam . . . Opim*] Cybele, a Phrygian goddess (*Idaeus* means Phrygian, from Ida, a mountain in Phrygia near Troy), was worshipped in Rome as Ops, goddess of plenty. Ida was crowned with pines (Virgil, *Aen.* x 230) and the pine was sacred to Cybele because, as Ovid relates, *Met.* x 103–5, her love, Attis, was turned into a pine. Ovid explains that Cybele wears a turreted crown because she first gave towers to cities (*Fast.* iv 219–21).

65–6. *Tenario . . . Deo*] Pluto, so called because one of the mouths of hell was a cave in the promontory of Taenarus in Laconia. His rape of Proserpina when she was gathering flowers near Enna, a city in Sicily (called *Sicania* by Ovid) is described in *Met.* v 385–408.

74. *titulos . . . tuos*] Phoebus was god of healing and father of Aesculapius.

79. *clivoso . . . Olympo*] Echoes Ovid, *Fast.* iii 415: *clivosum . . . Olympum.*

Quid tibi cum Tethy? Quid cum Tartesside lympha,
 Dia quid immundo perluis ora salo?
Frigora Phoebe mea melius captabis in umbra,
 Huc ades, ardentes imbue rore comas.
Mollior egelida veniet tibi somnus in herba,
 Huc ades, et gremio lumina pone meo.
Quaque iaces circum mulcebit lene susurrans
 Aura per humentes corpora fusa rosas.
Nec me (crede mihi) terrent Semeleia fata,
 Nec Phaetonteo fumidus axis equo;
Cum tu Phoebe tuo sapientius uteris igni,
 Huc ades et gremio lumina pone meo.
Sic Tellus lasciva suos suspirat amores;
 Matris in exemplum caetera turba ruunt.
Nunc etenim toto currit vagus orbe Cupido,
 Languentesque fovet solis ab igne faces.
Insonuere novis lethalia cornua nervis,
 Triste micant ferro tela corusca novo.
Iamque vel invictam tentat superasse Dianam,
 Quaeque sedet sacro Vesta pudica foco.
Ipsa senescentem reparat Venus annua formam,
 Atque iterum tepido creditur orta mari.
Marmoreas iuvenes clamant Hymenaee per urbes,
 Litus io Hymen, et cava saxa sonant.
Cultior ille venit tunicaque decentior apta,
 Puniceum redolet vestis odora crocum.
Egrediturque frequens ad amoeni gaudia veris
 Virgineos auro cincta puella sinus.

83. Tethy] Tethys (the *caerula mater* of l. 82), a sea goddess; Hesiod explains (*Theog.* 337–62) that she was mother of the rivers. The form of the line is Ovidian; see e.g. *Her.* vi 47–8: *Quid mihi cum Minyis, quid cum Dodonide pinu? / quid tibi cum patria, navita Tiphy, mea?*

91. Semeleia fata] Semele was daughter of Cadmus. She was seduced by Jupiter and tricked by the jealous Juno into asking him to come to her in his divine glory: when he did so she was consumed by fire. Ovid tells the story, *Met.* iii 253–315.

92. Phaetonteo . . . equo] See *Natur 25n* (p. 62).

101–2. Diana, the moon goddess, was patroness of virginity. Vesta was goddess of the household; the Vestal virgins were her priestesses.

105–6. Hymen was god of marriage. The refrains of two of Catullus's marriage songs (lxi and lxii) are *io Hymen Hymenaee* and *Hymen o Hymenaee, Hymen ades o Hymenaee!*

108. Puniceum . . . crocum] Hymen's colour was yellow. Ovid introduces him clad in *croceo . . . amictu* (*Met.* x 1–2) and has *punicei . . . croci* (*Fast.* v 318).

Votum est cuique suum, votum est tamen omnibus unum,
Ut sibi quem cupiat, det Cytherea virum.
Nunc quoque septena modulatur arundine pastor,
Et sua quae iungat carmina Phyllis habet.
Navita nocturno placat sua sidera cantu,
Delphinasque leves ad vada summa vocat.
Iupiter ipse alto cum coniuge ludit Olympo,
Convocat et famulos ad sua festa Deos.
Nunc etiam Satyri cum sera crepuscula surgunt,
Pervolitant celeri florea rura choro,
Sylvanusque sua cyparissi fronde revinctus,
Semicaperque Deus, semideusque caper.
Quaeque sub arboribus Dryades latuere vetustis
Per iuga, per solos expatiantur agros.
Per sata luxuriat fruticetaque Maenalius Pan,
Vix Cybele mater, vix sibi tuta Ceres,
Atque aliquam cupidus praedatur Oreada Faunus,

114. Phyllis] A common name for shepherdesses in pastoral, used by Virgil, *Ecl.* iii 78.
116. Pliny IX viii 24–8 holds that dolphins are susceptible to music and can be charmed by singing: he tells several anecdotes to prove the point.
119. sera crepuscula] The phrase is Ovid's, *Met.* i 219.
121. Sylvanusque . . . revinctus] Sylvanus, the Roman god of uncultivated land, was identified with the Greek satyrs. Servius, in his note to Virgil, *Georg.* i 20, tells how Sylvanus loved a boy called Cyparissus, who died of grief at the loss of a pet hind. The god turned the dead boy into a cypress, and wears leaves of this tree in remembrance.
122. An imitation of Ovid, *Ars Am.* ii 24 *semibovemque virum, semivirumque bovem.* F. R. B. Godolphin, *MP* xxxvii (1940) 356, points to the story in Seneca's *Controversiae* II ii 12, of Ovid being asked by his friends to cancel three lines from his poems which they will name. He agrees on condition that he may first name three lines which shall not be cancelled. It turns out that Ovid and his friends have the same three lines in mind, of which *Ars Am.* ii 24 is one. Godolphin calls M.'s line 'the most striking example of wit' in his Latin poems. J. Goode, *TLS* (13 Aug. 1931) 621, quotes from Sannazaro's Latin elegies *semideusque caper, semicaperque Deus.* Ovid has *semicaperque deus, Fast.* iv 752.
123. Dryades] wood nymphs.
125. Maenalius] Maenalus is a mountain in Arcadia, which was sacred to Pan.
126. Cybele] See l. 62*n*. Her daughter *Ceres* was goddess of agriculture.
127. Oreada] An Oread was a mountain nymph. *Faunus*] protecting deity of agriculture and shepherds.

Consulit in trepidos dum sibi nympha pedes,
Iamque latet, latitansque cupit male tecta videri,
Et fugit, et fugiens pervelit ipsa capi.
Dii quoque non dubitant caelo praeponere sylvas,
Et sua quisque sibi numina lucus habet.
Et sua quisque diu sibi numina lucus habeto,
Nec vos arborea dii precor ite domo.
Te referant miseris te Iupiter aurea terris
Saecla, quid ad nimbos aspera tela redis?
Tu saltem lente rapidos age Phoebe iugales
Qua potes, et sensim tempora veris eant.
Brumaque productas tarde ferat hispida noctes,
Ingruat et nostro serior umbra polo.

Time, turning back upon his own tracks in a never-ending circuit, is now calling the fresh zephyrs once again as the spring grows warm. The Earth has recovered and is decking herself in her brief youth, and now that the frost has melted away the ground is growing pleasantly green. Am I imagining things, or are my powers of song coming back as well? Is inspiration here again as a gift from the spring? It *is* here again as a gift from the spring! With the spring it is beginning to bloom again (who would have thought it?) and already it is clamouring for something to do. The Castalian fountain and the forked peak[9] swim before my eyes, and at night my dreams bring Pirene[10] to me. My soul is deeply stirred and glows with its mysterious impulse, and I am driven on by poetic frenzy and the sacred sound which fills my brain. Apollo himself is coming–I can see his hair wreathed in Penean laurel[13]–Apollo himself is coming. Now my mind is whirled up to the heights of the bright, clear sky: freed from my body, I move among the wandering clouds. I am carried through shadows and caves, the secret haunts of the poets, and the innermost sanctuaries of the gods are open to me. I see in my mind's eye what is going on all over Olympus, and the unseen depths of Tartarus do not escape my eyes. What song is my spirit singing so loudly with wide-open mouth? What is being born of this madness, this sacred frenzy? The spring, which gave me inspiration, shall be the theme of the song it inspires: in this way her gifts will be repaid with interest.

You are already beginning your warbling song, Philomela,[25] hidden among the unfolding leaves, while all the grove is silent.[26] I in the city, you in the woods, let us both begin together and both together sing the coming of the spring. Hurrah! the springtime is here again! Let us hymn the praises of spring; let the never-dying[30] Muse take up the task. Now the sun is running away from the Ethiopians[31] and from Tithonus' fields, and is turning his golden reins towards the northern regions.[32] The course of the night is short, short is the night's dark stay; wild night and his darkness are banished. Now Lycaonian Boötes[35] does not plod wearily down a long road behind his skyey waggon, as once he did. Now in the whole sky there

129–30. The nymph's behaviour is based on that of Galatea in Virgil, *Ecl.* iii 65, who runs off to hide from Damoetas in the willows, but hopes to be seen first.

are now only a few stars to patrol and keep the usual watch around Jove's halls. For fraud, murder and violence have gone away with the night, and the gods are not afraid of the giants' wickedness.[40]

Perhaps some shepherd, stretched out on the top of a crag while the dewy earth grows red in the light of the dawn, exclaims: 'You certainly did not have your girl with you tonight, Phoebus, to delay your swift horses!' When from on high Cynthia[46] sees the wheels of the sun's chariot, she goes back joyfully to her woods and takes up her quiver again, and seems to be glad as she lays her weak moonbeams aside that her own job is made so short by her brother's help. 'Come out of that old man's[49] bedroom, Aurora,' shouts Phoebus, 'what's the use of lying in bed with someone who's impotent? Aeolides, the hunter, is waiting for you on the green grass. Get up! The man you love is on high Hymettus.'[52] The golden-haired goddess acknowledges her guilt by her blushing face, and urges on the horses of dawn to greater speed.

The reviving Earth casts off her detested old age and yearns, Phoebus, for your embrances. She yearns for them, and she deserves them too, for what is more beautiful than she as she voluptuously bares her breasts, mother of all things, and breathes out Arabian spice-harvests and pours Paphian[60] roses and mild perfume from her lovely lips. Look! Her high forehead is crowned with a sacred grove, just as Idaean Ops is ringed with a turret of pine-trees;[62] she has twined many-coloured flowers among her dewy hair, and with her flowers she seems fit to attract the Taenarian god[65] as the Sicanian goddess once attracted him when her flowing hair was plaited with flowers. Look, Phoebus, easily won love is calling to you, and the spring breezes bear honied appeals. Fragrant Zephyrus lightly claps his cinnamon-scented wings and the birds seem to carry blandishments to you. The Earth is not so indiscreet as to seek your love without offering a dowry in return: she is no beggar-maid, praying for a desirable match. She is bountiful, and supplies you with health-giving herbs for use in medicine, and so does something on her own account to increase your glory.[74] If money and glittering gifts touch your heart (love is often bought with gifts), she lays before your eyes all the worth she keeps hidden away under the huge ocean and the heaped-up mountains. Ah, how often she cries out when you plunge into the sea at sunset, tired out by heaven's steep path,[79] 'Phoebus, why should the sky-blue mother take you into her western waves when you are exhausted by your daily journey? What have you got to do with Tethys[83] or the waters of Tartessus? Why do you wash your heavenly face in dirty salt water? It will be more pleasant for you to seek coolness in my shades, Phoebus; come here, and bathe your gleaming hair in dew. You will find softer sleep on the cool grass: come here, and lay your eyes against my breast. The breeze, murmuring gently around you where you lie, will soothe our bodies, stretched out on dewy roses. Semele's fate[91] does not frighten me, I assure you, nor does the chariot which Phaëthon's horses[92] caused to smoke. Come here, and lay your eyes against my breast, and you will put your fire to better use.'

This is the way lascivious Earth breathes out her passion, and all the other creatures are quick to follow their mother's example. For now wandering Cupid speeds through the whole world and renews his dying torch in the flames of the sun. His deadly bow twangs with new strings and his bright arrows, freshly tipped, gleam balefully. Now he tries to subdue even the unconquerable Diana,[101] and chaste Vesta[102] as she sits by her holy hearth. Venus herself, having lasted out the year, is restoring her waning beauty, and seems to have risen again from the warm sea. Through marble cities the young men are shouting 'Hymenaeus!'[105]–the sea-shore and the hollow rocks resound with 'Io Hymen!'[106] Hymen arrives, all decked out and very spruce in his traditional costume; his fragrant gown has the scent of tawny saffron.[108] The girls, with their virgin breasts bound about with gold, run out in crowds to the joys of the lovely springtime. Each one has her own prayer, but all their prayers are the same: that Cytherea will give her the man of her desire. And now the shepherd plays on his pipe of seven reeds, and Phyllis[114] has songs of her own to add to his. At night the sailor sings to his stars to make them gentle, and calls up nimble dolphins[116] to the surface of the sea. Jupiter himself frolics on high Olympus with his wife, and summons even the gods who wait on him to his feast. Now, as the evening twilight[119] falls, the satyrs flit through the flowery meadows in a swift band, and with them Sylvanus,[121] a god half-goat, a goat half-god,[122] crowned with leaves from his favourite tree, the cypress. And the Dryads[123] who lay hidden beneath the ancient trees now wander about on hill-tops and through lonely fields. Maenalian[125] Pan skips through grain-fields and thickets, mother Cybele and Ceres[126] are hardly safe from him. Lustful Faunus catches one of the Oreads,[127] but the nymph saves herself on trembling feet: now she hides, but not very well, and even as she hides she hopes to be seen;[129] she runs away, but as she runs she is anxious to be overtaken.[130] The gods, too, unhesitatingly prefer these woods to their heavens, and each grove has its own particular deities.

Long may each grove have its own particular deities: do not leave your homes among the trees, gods, I beseech you. May the golden age bring you back, Jove, to this wretched world! Why go back to your cruel weapons in the clouds? At any rate, Phoebus, drive your swift team as slowly as you can, and let the passing of the springtime be gradual. May rough winter be tardy in bringing us his dreary nights, and may it be late in the day when shadows assail our sky.

25 Sonnet I

Date. Spring 1629? There is no firm evidence for dating, but the similarity between *Sonnet I* 1–2 and *Elegia V* 25–6 suggests nearness in date.
Publication. 1645 and *1673* (no significant variants).
Modern criticism. J. L. Lievsay, *Renaissance Papers* (1959) 36–45, suggests that M., in his repeated references to the nightingale (*Elegia V* 25–8, *Il Penseroso* 55–64, *Comus* 233–5, 566, *PL* iii 37–40, etc.), came to consider this bird–with its associations of chastity (Philomela), opposition to brute force (Tereus), loneliness and nocturnal song–as the symbol of his own poetic voice.

M.'s sonnets: style and versification. M. wrote twenty-three sonnets. The first six (25 'O nightingale', and 27, 28 and 30–32, the Italian sonnets) are love poems and were written in 1629, by which time the vogue of the sonnet in England had been over for thirty years. Most of the other sonnets belong to the period 1642–55. Three of them—77, to Fairfax (1648), 81, to Cromwell (1652) and 82 to Vane (1652)—are addressed to great political figures of M.'s day. Probably Tasso's *Sonneti Eroici* gave M. the idea of celebrating contemporary leaders in sonnets of epic grandeur. However, the tone of these sonnets, like that of the three sonnets to young friends—87, to Edward Lawrence (1653) and 89–90, to Cyriack Skinner (1655)—is markedly Horatian (see the notes to these poems).

In Dec. 1629 M. bought a copy of Giovanni Della Casa's *Rime e Prose* (1563), now in the New York Public Library (French i 205). Marginal notes and text corrections in M.'s hand bear witness to the thoroughness of his reading: he also copied into it another Della Casa sonnet from the 1623 edition. Della Casa, like Bembo, from whose experiments he profited, gave his sonnets a complex and artificial word-order by devices such as inversion, interpolation and suspension of grammar, in order to create the impression of an intricate syntax akin to Latin. By multiplying pauses within the lines–manipulating clauses and sentences to chop across the verse divisions–he made his sonnets sound abrupt, uncompromising and densely meaningful. To allow opportunities for more elongated syntactical intricacies he planned the development of ideas within the sonnet so that it struck through the formal limits of quatrains and tercets and flowed across the octave-sestet boundary, where Petrarch and his followers had always observed a pause. At the same time, beneath this elaborately irregular surface, he retained an effect of inner balance by frequent pairing of adjectives, nouns and verbs, by antithesis and parallelism, and by other duplex structures. M.'s sonnets imitate these techniques, and at times, as Prince (106) remarks, citing 88 *On the late Massacre in Piedmont* (1655), they carry Della Casa's innovations further than any poet had done in Italian. In these later sonnets M. is clearly developing his epic style.

M.'s versification follows the Italian metrical scheme (as opposed to the English or Shakespearean) of two quatrains and two tercets. His quatrains always rhyme abba abba: this was called the 'enclosed order' and was favoured by Petrarch who, however, along with other Italian poets, sometimes used alternate rhymes in his quatrains. The rhyming of M.'s tercets, as in the Italian poets, is much more varied. Most frequently he uses well-established Petrarchan schemes: cdc dcd in seven sonnets, cde cde in five, and cde dce in four. In four sonnets he employs a couplet-ending, which Petrarch never does unless there is a rhyme with the first line of the sestet: cdc dee in 28, 30 and 31 (a scheme preferred by Wyatt, but previously used, as Smart (17–19) notes, by the fourteenth-century Italian poet Fazio degli Uberti, and mentioned in Minturno's *Arte Poetica*); and cdd cee in 81 (a scheme used by Uberti and also by Tasso). In two of the remaining three sonnets M. introduces a couplet in lines 10 and 11: 77, to Fairfax, has tercets rhyming cdd cdc; and 71 'I did but prompt', a sonnet with only three rhymes, has a variant of this, cbb cbc. 87, to Lawrence, introduces a couplet in lines *12* and *13*, rhyming its tercets cdc eed.

O nightingale, that on yon bloomy spray
Warblest at eve, when all the woods are still,
Thou with fresh hope the lover's heart dost fill,
While the jolly hours lead on propitious May,
Thy liquid notes that close the eye of day,
First heard before the shallow cuckoo's bill
Portend success in love; O if Jove's will
Have linked that amorous power to thy soft lay,
Now timely sing, ere the rude bird of hate
Foretell my hopeless doom in some grove nigh:
As thou from year to year hast sung too late
For my relief; yet hadst no reason why,
Whether the Muse, or Love call thee his mate,
Both them I serve, and of their train am I.

26 Song. On May Morning

Date. Spring 1629? There is no firm evidence for dating. *Song. On May Morning* has obvious similarities with *Elegia V* and may, like it, belong to spring 1629. If the order of poems in *1673* is chronologically significant (as the transference of *Vacation Exercise* to a position after *Fair Infant* in the *1673 Errata* implies), it is worth noting that *Song. On May Morning* is placed after the *Winchester Epitaph* (Apr.–May 1631) and before *Shakespeare* (of which the date, '1630', means strictly before 25 Mar. 1631). This suggests May 1631 as a possible date.
Publication. *1645* (*6.* youth]youth, *7.* groves]groves, *8* dale]dale,) and *1673* (the text followed here).

Now the bright morning Star, Day's harbinger,
Comes dancing from the east, and leads with her

¶ 25. *1.* Echoing Bembo, *Rime* (Venice 1564) 45: *O rosignuol, che'n queste verdi fronde. . . .*
4. hours] the Horae, daughters of Jupiter and Themis.
9. bird of hate] the cuckoo. M. probably read of the belief that it is a good omen for a lover to hear the nightingale before the cuckoo, and a bad to hear the cuckoo before the nightingale, in *The Cuckoo and the Nightingale*, printed among Chaucer's works in Speght's edition (1598) 333.
¶ 26. *1. Day's harbinger*] Cp. Shakespeare, *Midsummer Night's Dream* III ii 380 'Aurora's harbinger'; but the exact phrase is found in R. Niccolls, *The Cuckow* (1607) p. 13: 'Daies herbinger, the bloody crested cocke'.
2. dancing from the east] In Spenser's dawn scene *F.Q.* I v 2, Phoebus 'came dauncing forth', and in Niccolls's *Cuckow* p. 12: 'Daies bright king came dauncing out.'

The flowery May, who from her green lap throws
The yellow cowslip, and the pale primrose.
Hail bounteous May that dost inspire
Mirth and youth and warm desire,
Woods and groves are of thy dressing,
Hill and dale doth boast thy blessing.
Thus we salute thee with our early song,
And welcome thee, and wish thee long.

27 Sonnet II

Date. Nov.–Dec. 1629? The Italian sonnets are so closely related in subject that they are probably of similar date. In *1645* and *1673* they are printed as a group before *Sonnet VII* (Dec. 1631). If the proposed interpretation of *Elegia VI* 89–90 (see p. 117) is correct, the Italian sonnets can be dated (probably late) in 1629 (see *RES* n.s. xiv (1963) 383–6).
Publication. *1645* (*3.* Bene]Ben *6.* sui]suoi) *1673* (the text followed here, but corrected in *7* where *1673* misprints a full stop after 'arco').

Donna leggiadra il cui bel nome honora
L'herbosa val di Rheno, e il nobil varco,
Bene è colui d'ogni valore scarco
Qual tuo spirto gentil non innamora,
Che dolcemente mostra si di fuora
De sui atti soavi giamai parco,
E i don', che son d'amor saette ed arco,
La onde l' alta tua virtù s'infiora.
Quando tu vaga parli, o lieta canti
Che mover possa duro alpestre legno,

3. May ... throws] A probable echo of Spenser, *F.Q.* VII vii 34: 'Then came faire May, the fayrest mayd on ground, / Deckt all with dainties of her seasons pryde, / And throwing flowers out of her lap around' and of Shakespeare, *Rich. II* III iii 47 where England has a 'green lap'.
4. pale primrose] Cp. *Winter's Tale* IV iv 122: 'pale primroses'.
¶ 27. *1–2.* Smart 137–44 explains that these lines mean the lady was called Emilia. Emilia (deriving its name from the Via Emilia) was one of the regions into which Augustus divided Italy. In its eastern part is the 'famous ford' (*nobil varco*) of the Rubicon. Smart cites a close verbal parallel in a sonnet by the sixteenth century Italian poet Gandolfo Porrino, where the name disclosed is Lucia: *O, d'ogni riverenza e d'onor degna, / Alma mia luce, il cui bel nome onora / L'aria, la terra, e le campagne infiora, / E di salir al ciel la via c'insegna, / Luce gentil.*
8. La] in her eyes.

Guardi ciascun a gli occhi, ed a gli orecchi
L'entratà, chi di te si truova indegno;
Gratia sola di sù gli vaglia, inanti
Che'l disio amoroso al cuor s'invecchi.

My lady fair, whose lovely name[1] honours the grassy Reno valley and the famous ford,[2] that man must be utterly worthless who does not fall in love with your gentle spirit, which sweetly shows itself (never niggardly in bestowing soft glances or those favours which are the bows and arrows of love) there[3] where your lofty virtue blossoms. When, graceful lady, you speak or sing for joy (singing that might bring gnarled trees down from the mountains), let every man who is unworthy of you guard the approaches to his eyes and ears. Only grace from above can save him from having desire rooted in his heart for ever.

28 Sonnet III

Date. Nov.–Dec. 1629? See headnote to *Sonnet II*.
Publication. *1645* and *1673* (no significant variants).

Qual in colle aspro, al imbrunir di sera
L'avezza giovinetta pastorella
Va bagnando l'herbetta strana e bella
Che mal si spande a disusata spera
Fuor di sua natia alma primavera,
Cosi amor meco insù la lingua snella
Desta il fior novo di strania favella,
Mentre io di te, vezzosamente altera,
Canto, dal mio buon popol non inteso
E'l bel Tamigi cangio col bel Arno.
Amor lo volse, ed io a l'altrui peso
Seppi ch' Amor cosa mai volse indarno.
Deh! foss' il mio cuor lento e'l duro seno
A chi pianta dal ciel si buon terreno.

As on some rugged mountain at dusk a young shepherdess, used to the climate herself, waters an exotic little plant which can hardly spread its leaves in such unfamiliar surroundings, far from the mild springtime which gave it life, so on my nimble tongue love raises up the new flower of a foreign language as I sing to you, charming in your pride, and exchange the beautiful

¶ 28. *10.* M. means that he is changing from English to the Tuscan dialect of Italy. Bembo's *Prose della Volgar Lingua* (1525) had established the Tuscan writers of the fourteenth century as the source of correct literary usage (see Prince 4–13). M. again uses the Arno to represent the Tuscan language in his letter to Benedetto Buonmattei (Columbia xii 34; Yale i 30).

Thames for the beautiful Arno[10] (without my worthy fellow-countrymen understanding me at all). Love willed it, and I knew at other people's expense that Love never willed anything in vain. Ah that my sluggish heart and stony breast were as good a soil for him who sows his seed from heaven!

29 Canzone

Date. Nov.–Dec. 1629? See headnote to *Sonnet II*.
Publication. *1645* and *1673* (no significant variants).

Prince 101, who considers this, from the point of view of the mastery of the medium, the most successful of M.'s Italian poems, remarks: 'That his technical insight was not yet complete may be gathered from his calling a *canzone* a poem which, however accomplished in achieving its desired effect, is not a *canzone*'. It is true that M.'s poem, which has only one stanza, is not a *canzone* in the strict sense in which Dante defined it in the *De Vulgar Eloquentia*, since this needs several stanzas of similar structure and rhyme scheme. But, as Dante admits (II viii), Italian poets frequently used the term more loosely, as M. does here, to cover sonnets, *ballate* and any lyrics written for music.

Ridonsi donne e giovani amorosi
M' accostandosi attorno, e perche scrivi,
Perche tu scrivi in lingua ignota e strana
Verseggiando d'amor, e come t'osi?
Dinne, se la tua speme sia mai vana,
E de pensieri lo miglior t' arrivi;
Cosi mi van burlando, altri rivi
Altri lidi t' aspettan, ed altre onde
Nelle cui verdi sponde
Spuntati ad hor, ad hor a la tua chioma
L'immortal guiderdon d'eterne frondi
Perche alle spalle tue soverchia soma?
  Canzon dirotti, e tu per me rispondi
Dice mia Donna, e'l suo dir, è il mio cuore
Questa è lingua di cui si vanta Amore.

Girls and boys in love press about me, laughing, and say 'Why, O why do you write your love poems in an odd and unknown language? How do you dare to do it? Tell us, then we'll wish that you may never hope in vain, and that your dreams may come true.' They tease me and say 'There are

¶ 29. *7–12.* The boys and girls, like M. in *Sonnet III* 10, refer to languages as rivers. The *altri rivi* are presumably Latin and English, and the *soverchia soma* the difficulty of writing in Italian. His knowledge of that language was evidently imperfect, as Masson (iii 277–8) and others have noticed.

other rivers[7] and river-banks, and other waters for you, rivers by whose grassy brinks the immortal reward, the crown of unfading leaves, is already sprouting for your head. Why take this excessive load[12] upon your shoulders?'

Canzone, I will tell you, and you can answer for me. My lady says–and her word is my heart–'This is the language on which Love prides himself'.

30 Sonnet IV

Date. Nov.–Dec. 1629? See headnote to *Sonnet II*.
Publication. *1645* (*4.* s'impiglia.]s'impiglia,) and *1673* (the text followed here).

Diodati, e te'l dirò con maraviglia,
Quel ritroso io ch'amor spreggiar soléa
E de suoi lacci spesso mi ridéa
Gia caddi, ov'huom dabben talhor s'impiglia.
Ne treccie d'oro, ne guancia vermiglia
M' abbaglian sì, ma sotto nova idea
Pellegrina bellezza che'l cuor bea,
Portamenti alti honesti, e nelle ciglia
Quel sereno fulgor d' amabil nero,
Parole adorne di lingua piu d'una,
E'l cantar che di mezzo l'hemispero
Traviar ben può la faticosa Luna,
E degli occhi suoi auventa si gran fuoco
Che l'incerar gli orecchi mi fia poco.

Diodati, I'll tell you something which absolutely amazes me: I, the coy creature who used to scorn love, I who made a habit of laughing at his snares, have now fallen into his trap (which sometimes does catch a good man). It is not golden tresses or rosy cheeks which have dazzled me like this, but a foreign beauty, modelled on a new idea of loveliness, which fills my heart with joy: a proud, yet modest bearing;[8] and that calm radiance of lovely blackness in her eyes and lashes; her speech which is graced by more than one language, and her singing[11] which might well draw down the labouring moon from mid-air.[12] And such bright fire flashes from her eyes that it would not be much good for me to seal up my ears.[14]

¶ 30. *8. Portamenti alti honesti*] Emilia's mixture of pride and modesty, which fascinates M. (cp. *Sonnet III* 8), is reminiscent of a similar fascination which Petrarch found in Laura (ccxiii 4 *e'n umil donna altà belta divina*). In the same sonnet Petrarch, like M., praises his lady's singing–*e'l cantar che ne l'anima si sente*–and the light of her eyes–*possenti a rischiarar abisso e notti*.
11–12. Cp. Virgil, *Ecl.* viii 69, where Alphesiboeus declares that 'songs can even draw the moon down from heaven'.
14. incerar gli orecchi] In Homer, *Od.* xii Odysseus, on Circe's advice, puts wax in the ears of his crew so that they will not be able to hear the song of the sirens as they row by.

31 Sonnet V

Date. Nov.–Dec. 1629? See headnote to *Sonnet II*.
Publication. *1645* (*1.* occhi,]occhi *2.* fian]sian) and *1673* (the text followed here, but corrected in *12* where *1673* misprints 'e trovar').

Per certo i bei vostr'occhi, Donna mia
Esser non puo che non fian lo mio sole
Si mi percuoton forte, come ei suole
Per l'arene di Libia chi s'invia,
Mentre un caldo vapor (ne sentì pria)
Da quel lato si spinge ove mi duole,
Che forse amanti nelle lor parole
Chiaman sospir; io non so che si sia:
Parte rinchiusa, e turbida si cela
Scosso mi il petto, e poi n'uscendo poco
Quivi d' attorno o s'agghiaccia, o s'ingiela;
Ma quanto a gli occhi giunge a trovar loco
Tutte le notti a me suol far piovose
Finche mia Alba rivien colma di rose.

Believe me, lady, your beautiful eyes cannot help but be my sun: their power beats down upon me just as the sun's does on a traveller in the Libyan desert; and at the same time a hot cloud of steam (a thing I never felt before) gushes from that side of my body[6] where I feel my pain. What this is, I don't know: perhaps in lovers' language it is called 'a sigh'. Part of it gets shut in and hides itself away, shuddering. Then, when it has thoroughly shaken my breast, a little of it escapes, whereupon it freezes or congeals in the air round about. But that part of it which manages to get into my eyes makes every night a rainy one for me, until my Dawn returns with roses in her hair.

32 Sonnet VI

Date. Nov.–Dec. 1629? See headnote to *Sonnet II*.
Publication. *1645* (*8.* se, d'intero]se, e d'intero) and *1673* (the text followed here).

Giovane piano, e semplicetto amante
Poi che fuggir me stesso in dubbio sono,
Madonna a voi del mio cuor l'humil dono

¶ 31. *6. quel lato*] the left, where his heart is.
¶ 32. *2.* The lover's wish to escape from himself and his thoughts is found in Petrarch, ccxxxiv 9–10: *Né pur il mio secreto, e'l mio riposo, / fuggo, ma più me stesso, e'l mio pensero.*

Farò divoto; io certo a prove tante
L'hebbi fedele, intrepido, costante,
De pensieri leggiadro, accorto, e buono;
Quando rugge il gran mondo, e scocca il tuono,
S'arma di se, d' intero diamante,
Tanto del forse, e d' invidia sicuro,
Di timori, e speranze al popol use
Quanto d'ingegno, e d' alto valor vago,
E di cetra sonora, e delle muse:
Sol troverete in tal parte men duro
Ove amor mise l'insanabil ago.

Since I am a young, unassuming and artless lover, and do not know how to escape from myself,[2] I will make you, lady, in my devotion, the humble gift of my heart. I have proved it in many a trial, faithful, brave and constant, graceful, wise and good in its thoughts. When the whole world roars and the lightning flashes[7] my heart arms itself in itself, in perfect adamant, as safe from chance and envy and from vulgar hopes and fears as it is eager for distinction of mind and real worth, for the sounding lyre and for the Muses.[12] You will find it less hard only in that spot where love stuck its incurable sting.

33 The Fifth Ode of Horace, *Lib.* I

Date. Late 1629? Suggested dates for this translation range from 1626 to 1655. The subject, deliberate rejection of love, may, however, indicate a date of composition near to that of *Elegia VI*.

Publication. First printed in *1673* where M. subjoins a Latin text of Horace's ode, differing in three particulars from modern versions (*munditie* for *munditiis* 5, *quoties* for *quotiens* 5, *intentata* for *intemptata* 13) and headed *Horatius ex Pyrrhae illecebris tanquam e naufragio enataverat, cuius amore irretitos, affirmat esse miseros* (Horace, having escaped from Pyrrha's charms, as from a shipwreck, declares that those who are ensnared by her love are in a wretched state). The text below follows *1673*, except in *12* where it substitutes a question mark for a *1673* full stop.

Quis multa gracilis te puer in rosa

Rendered almost word for word without rhyme according to the Latin measure, as near as the language will permit.

What slender youth bedewed with liquid odours
Courts thee on roses in some pleasant cave,
Pyrrha for whom bind'st thou
In wreaths thy golden hair,

7–12. Finley (34) notices the Horatian quality of these lines, comparing *Odes* III iii 1–8 and xxix 53–9.

Plain in thy neatness; O how oft shall he
On faith and changed gods complain: and seas
    Rough with black winds and storms
    Unwonted shall admire:
Who now enjoys thee credulous, all gold,
Who always vacant always amiable
    Hopes thee; of flattering gales
    Unmindful? Hapless they
To whom thou untried seem'st fair. Me in my vowed
Picture the sacred wall declares t' have hung
    My dank and dropping weeds
    To the stern god of sea.

34 On the Morning of Christ's Nativity

Date. 25 Dec. 1629. Headed 'Compos'd 1629' in *1645*. M. tells Diodati (*Elegia VI* 88) that he began the poem before dawn on Christmas Day.
Publication. *1645* (*23.* sweet,]sweet: *55.* hung,]hung; *82.* new enlightened]new-enlightened *143–4.* Orbed in a rainbow; and like glories wearing / Mercy will sit]Th'enamelled arras of the rainbow wearing, / And Mercy set *156.* deep.]deep, *185.* pale,]pale. *193.* drear]drear, *207.* hue;]hue, *210.* blue;]blue, *231.* wave,]wave. *239.* ending:] ending, *241.* car,]car. *242.* attending:]attending.) and *1673* (the text followed here).

¶ 33. *8. shall admire*] Latin *emirabitur*: shall be very surprised at.
9. enjoys . . . gold] enjoys you, believing that you are pure and beautiful: Horace uses Latin *aurea* figuratively.
10–12. Who . . . Unmindful?] Who, unmindful of deceitful (Latin *fallacis*) gales, hopes that you will always be without other lovers (Latin *vacuam*) and lovable.
13–16. Me . . . sea] The sacred wall shows that I, whose picture hangs there, have hung up my sea-clothes as a thank-offering to the sea-god. Horace here returns to the shipwreck/love analogy suggested in ll. 6–8: shipwrecked by his love for Pyrrha, he has escaped through Neptune's help, on the wall of whose temple he has hung up, as a thank-offering, his wet sea-clothes (for this practice see Virgil, *Aen.* xii 766–9), with a votive tablet (*tabula . . . votiva*: M.'s 'vowed Picture'), presumably showing the circumstances of his escape.
16. stern] M.'s addition: Latin *potenti . . . maris deo*, to the god who is master of the sea.

Sources, style, versification. Christian literature before M. contains innumerable examples of nativity poems, in both neo-Latin and the various vernaculars, and the combination of babe-in-the-manger and hymning angels with the flight of the pagan gods and the cessation of oracles was not uncommon. M.'s poem is more distinctive for the elements of the traditional story which it omits than for those it includes (see Tuve[2] and Broadbent, below). However since M.'s interest in Italian poetry towards the end of 1629, and in the development of a particular style through Bembo, Della Casa and Tasso, is well attested (see headnote to *Sonnet I* on *M.'s sonnets: style and versification*, p. 88 above), it seems likely that what appeared to him as inspiration on Christmas morning 1629 (see *Elegia VI* 87–8) was in some part a memory of Tasso's *Nel giorno della Natività* (*Rime* (Venice 1621) viii 63–7). Tasso, like M., contrasts the 'courts of everlasting day' and their 'harmony' with the 'darksome house' to which Christ comes (*mille, e mille / Corone, e fiamme, e lampi / D'angelico splendor l'han fatto adorno. / Mà da le parti lucide, e tranquille, / Di quei celesti campi / Sparsi d'un bel candor, che vince il giorno / E da quell'armonia, che gira intorno, / La rozza turba a contemplare inchina, / . . . E quell'humile albergo, ov'è nascosa . . . ne la notte ombrosa*: thousands and thousands of crowns and flames and lights of angelic splendour adorned him. But from the bright and tranquil regions of those celestial fields, spread with a lovely whiteness that outshines the day, and from that wheeling harmony, he bowed down to look at the rough crowd, . . . And that lowly inn where he was born . . . in the dark night). He also mentions Nature's awe, the world-wide peace, Apollo and the dumb oracles (*Già divien muto Apollo e l'antro, e l'onde, / E gli Dei falsi, e vani / . . . Ne Dafne ne la quercia altrui risponde / Più con accenti humani*: Already Apollo is mute, and cave and fountain, and the false, vain gods . . . No longer do the laurel or oak give replies in human voices), Lybic Hammon (*giace Amon ne la deserta arena*: Ammon lies in the desert sand), Osiris's 'lowings' and the barking Anubis (*E da gli altari suoi dolente fugge / Api, ed Anubi, e più non latra, o mugge*: Apis and Anubis flee lamenting from their altars, and bark and bellow no more), and concludes his *canzone*, as M. concludes his introductory stanzas, by offering his 'humble' (*humil*) poem, comparing it with the 'odours sweet' (*odori*) that the wise men bring. The similarities between M.'s poem and some passages in the *Apotheosis* of Prudentius–the most remarkable of the early-Christian Latin poets–are hardly less striking (see ll. *173–80n*), though there is no definite evidence that Prudentius was a set author at St Paul's (Clark 125).

No exact precedent for M.'s stanza-form in the *Hymn* (a6a6b10c6c6b10 d8d12) has been found, but its pattern and movement, and the idea of using such a stanza for a solemn ode, derive from the tradition of the *canzone*. No doubt, as Prince 60 suggests, M. found the liberties taken with the *canzone* by Spenser in *Epithalamion* and *Prothalamion* instructive–his final alexandrine has a Spenserian ring. It seems likely that Drummond's experiments in Italian verse forms were useful to M. too. Of his predecessors

Drummond was the most widely read in Italian literature, and his madrigal 'To the delightful green' (*Works*, ed. L. E. Kastner (Manchester 1913) i 22) starts with a verse pattern (a6a6b10c6c6b10) identical with that of the *Hymn*, which is more than can be said for Chiabrera's *Per S. Agata* (a7b7c11 a7b7c11d7d11)–see Fletcher, below.

The introductory stanzas are in a form M. had used before in *Fair Infant* –decasyllables with a final alexandrine, rhyming ababbcc. It is a modification of the Spenserian stanza which Phineas Fletcher, who certainly influenced the young M. elsewhere, had used twice in his *Poetical Miscellanies* and again in *Elisa*, but since neither was published until 1633 one cannot be sure that this stanza form was not M.'s own idea too.

Although there is one striking debt to Petrarch (see *32–4n*), the most potent stylistic influences are not Italian but Elizabethan. Forms like 'wont' (*10*) and 'ychained' (*155*) give a Spenserian flavour, and the elaborate prosopopoeias, culminating in the beautiful baroque image of the sun in bed, which Tillyard 36 finds 'grotesque', are reminiscent of Sidney's rhetorical habits in the *Arcadia*. Even when doubtful likenesses have been discarded, five echoes of the *Faerie Queene* and two of the *Shepheards Calender* remain (see notes), contributing to the poem's ringing first line, and becoming particularly distinct in the Elizabethan pastoral scene of Pan and the shepherds (*85–92*). Shakespeare comes close behind with six apparent echoes, three of them from *A Midsummer Night's Dream* which provides the spirits and fays of lines *232–6*, as well as the moonlight for them. Sylvester's translation of Du Bartas, M.'s earliest English literary model (see notes to Nos. 1 and 2, pp. 6–9 above), still accounts for two or three oddly vivid touches, like the 'lep'rous sin' of line *138*; the leading Spenserian, Giles Fletcher, makes one probable donation to the diction (*110*); Chapman's 'burning axletree' (*84*) sticks in M.'s mind, as later in Eliot's; and M.'s mourning wood-nymphs (*188*) may come from Fairfax's translation (1600, second edition 1624) of Tasso's epic–they are not in the original. Sandys's imaginative account of human sacrifice, with its shrieks and searing flesh, and his illustrations of the 'brutish gods of Nile', supply local colour (see notes to *205–10*, *211*, *212* etc.); so does Selden's treatise on comparative religion (republished in the year the poem was written). Classical influence is, by contrast, scant. Possibly *84* recalls the description of the sun's throne in M.'s favourite, Ovid; and the light flooding into Virgil's hell probably accounted for *139–40*. Twice there are faint echoes of Horatian phrases (*136*, *185*). But in the main M. hails his native language and its authors.

Modern criticism. The poem's structure was first attacked by Warton, who called it 'a string of affected conceits' Wilson Knight 64 agrees that 'though it offers a satisfying lyric integrity' it 'remains somewhat fluid in its addition of stanza to stanza: there is no complex inter-knitting, that is, of central action with design'. On the other side Tillyard 37–8 claims that it displays 'architectonic grasp' in that at the beginning M. is hurrying to offer his poem before the wise men arrive, whereas at the end the star over the stable shows that their arrival is imminent. An abler defence of the structure is that of A. Barker, *UTQ* x (1941) 167–81, who points out that the poem has three sections: the first (i–viii) describing the setting of the nativity and characterized by the reduction of light and sound to a minimum; the second (ix–xvii) devoted largely to the angelic choir, and dominated by light, harmony and order (which start to be dissipated in xvi and xvii); and the third (xviii–xxvi) describing the flight of the pagan gods, full of discordant sounds and shadows. Light and order return in xxvii, which thus balances the second section. In the centre of the poem (xiii) the angelic choir and the music of the spheres are placed in close association, transcending the conflict between the pagan and Christian traditions. A. S. P. Woodhouse, *UTQ* xiii (1943) 66–101, endorses Barker's analysis. Allen 24–9 argues that the poem is based on three vital oppositions, each of which is not reconciled but transcended. The first is that between the past (the last hour of the pre-Christian era) and the time of the poem's composition. From this opposition M. evolves the solution of timelessness, by pressing towards the eternal consequences of the incarnation. The second (i–vii) is that between wanton Nature and Nature ashamed, and is resolved by the sending down of Peace (iii). The third is that between the harmony of the Church Militant (viii–xii) and the harmony of the pagan gods (xix–xxviii), which is transcended by M.'s anticipation of the harmony of the Church Triumphant (xiii–xv).

Tuve[2] (37–72) maintains that the poem's real subject is the incarnation, not the nativity. Her main endeavour is to clarify the tradition that lies behind the 'great ancient images' that M. employs. This approach is brilliantly questioned by J. B. Broadbent (Kermode[3] 12–31) who insists that Tuve's delight in the traditional materials makes her overestimate M.'s use of them. M.'s treatment of the nativity is only partially traditional. Though writing about the incarnation he avoids the flesh and fights shy of Christ's fleshly life. The direction he takes – and traditionally need not have taken – is away from the incarnate towards the ideate. Alone, even among classical and patristic authors, he ignores the central naturalness of motherhood. The poem represents 'the conquest by hard-edged right reason of the soft dim liquid allures of passion'.

Both A. S. Cook, *MLR* ii (1907) 121–4, and Tuve[2] 56 attempt to prove the influence of Mantuan. L. Stapleton, *UTQ* xxiii (1954) 217–26, shows that Clement of Alexandria's *Exhortation to the Greeks* presents an analogous pattern of ideas, particularly the connection of the flight of the pagan gods with the coming of the 'new music' (the discovery of the Logos in Christ), and the identification of this music with the principle of harmonious order in the universe.

Fletcher (ii 496–7), following Prince (60), suggests the influence of Italian metrical patterns and compares the stanza form of the *Hymn* with the first strophe of Chiabrera's *Per S. Agata.*

Røstvig[2] (44–58) examines the poem from the viewpoint of neo-Platonic numerical theory, detecting the influence of Francesco Giorgio's *De Harmo-*

nia Mundi (1525), and pointing out that whereas the numbers of the introduction (four stanzas of seven lines) are earthly, those of the *Hymn* (twenty-seven stanzas of eight lines) are expressive of perfection.

I

This is the month, and this the happy morn
Wherein the Son of heaven's eternal King,
Of wedded maid, and virgin mother born,
Our great redemption from above did bring;
For so the holy sages once did sing,
That he our deadly forfeit should release,
And with his Father work us a perpetual peace.

II

That glorious form, that light unsufferable,
And that far-beaming blaze of majesty,
Wherewith he wont at heaven's high council-table,
To sit the midst of trinal unity,
He laid aside; and here with us to be,
Forsook the courts of everlasting day,
And chose with us a darksome house of mortal clay.

III

Say heavenly Muse, shall not thy sacred vein
Afford a present to the infant God?
Hast thou no verse, no hymn, or solemn strain,
To welcome him to this his new abode,
Now while the heaven by the sun's team untrod,
Hath took no print of the approaching light,
And all the spangled host keep watch in squadrons bright?

¶ 34. *1. happy morn*] Cp. Spenser *F.Q.* IV ii 41: 'Borne . . . in one happie morne.'
5. holy sages] Hebrew prophets.
10. wont] was accustomed. Strictly speaking a past participle (O.E. gewunod) but used by M. as the preterite of the vb *won* (to be accustomed). Spenser has 'wonned' (*Shep. Cal.* Feb. 119) and 'did won' (*F.Q.* III ix 21) in this sense.
14. house of mortal clay] Cp. Marston, *Scourge of Villany* viii 194, where the body which the soul leaves is called a 'smoakie house of mortall clay'.
15. heavenly Muse] Urania, originally the Muse of astronomy, but elevated by Du Bartas in *La Muse Chrétienne* (1574) to the position of Muse of Christian poetry. Lily B. Campbell discusses her history, *HLB* viii (1935) 29–70.
21. spangled . . . bright] See *Psalm cxxxvi* 33–4*n* (p. 8). In Spenser, *F.Q.*

IV

See how from far upon the eastern road
The star-led wizards haste with odours sweet,
O run, prevent them with thy humble ode,
And lay it lowly at his blessed feet;
Have thou the honour first, thy Lord to greet,
  And join thy voice unto the angel quire,
From out his secret altar touched with hallowed fire.

The Hymn

I

It was the winter wild,
While the heaven-born-child
  All meanly wrapped in the rude manger lies;
Nature in awe to him
Had doffed her gaudy trim,
  With her great master so to sympathize:
It was no season then for her
To wanton with the sun her lusty paramour.

II

Only with speeches fair
She woos the gentle air
  To hide her guilty front with innocent snow,
And on her naked shame,
Pollute with sinful blame,

II viii 2 the angels 'their bright Squadrons round about us plant' and 'watch', and in Sylvester (Du Bartas 17) 'Heav'ns glorious Hoast in nimble squadrons flyes'.
23. *star-led wizards*] Cp. Spenser, *F.Q.* V Prologue 8: 'Aegyptian wisards old, / Which in Star-read were wont have best insight.'
24. *prevent*] anticipate.
25. *blessed feet*] Cp. Shakespeare, *I Hen. IV* I i 25–7: 'Those blessed feet / Which fourteen hundred years ago were nail'd / For our advantage on the bitter cross'.
28. *From . . . altar*] Qualifies 'fire' (the line is inverted). In *Isa.* vi 6–7 one of the seraphim takes a live coal from the altar and touches the prophet's lips with it.
32–4. Echoing Petrarch, *Sonnet* 3, of the eclipse on Good Friday: *Era il giorno ch'al sol si scoloraro / per la pietà del suo fattore i rai* (It was the day when the rays of the sun darkened in pity for their creator).
35–6. Cp. *Elegia V* 55–95 (pp. 83–4).
41. *Pollute*] polluted. *blame*] The Fall (cp. *PL* x 649–719).

The saintly veil of maiden white to throw,
Confounded, that her maker's eyes
Should look so near upon her foul deformities.

III

But he her fears to cease,
Sent down the meek-eyed Peace,
She crowned with olive green, came softly sliding
Down through the turning sphere
His ready harbinger,
With turtle wing the amorous clouds dividing,
And waving wide her myrtle wand,
She strikes a universal peace through sea and land.

IV

No war, or battle's sound
Was heard the world around
The idle spear and shield were high up hung,
The hooked chariot stood
Unstained with hostile blood,
The trumpet spake not to the armed throng,
And kings sat still with awful eye,
As if they surely knew their sovran Lord was by.

V

But peaceful was the night
Wherein the Prince of Light
His reign of peace upon the earth began:
The winds with wonder whist,

48. *turning sphere*] The Ptolemaic spheres revolving round the earth. Sylvester has 'turning Spheares' (Du Bartas 95).
50. *turtle*] Of a turtle dove, symbol of harmlessness in *Matt.* x 16. *amorous*] Clinging to Peace as if in love with her: cp. Shakespeare, *Antony and Cleopatra* II ii 201 where the water follows the oars 'as amorous of their strokes'.
51. *myrtle*] The tree of Venus, as Virgil says (*Ecl.* vii 62), hence of love.
52–60. Aquinas, *Summa* III xxxv 8, points out that it was fitting for Christ to be born in the *pax Romana*, as this fulfilled the prophecy in *Isa.* ii 4.
56. *hooked*] Cp. the chariots 'armed with hooks' in *2Macc.* xiii 2, taken over by Spenser, *F.Q.* V viii 28.
64. *whist*] silent. Cp. Shakespeare, *Tempest* I ii 379–80: 'and kiss'd / The wild waves whist.'

Smoothly the waters kissed,
  Whispering new joys to the mild ocean,
Who now hath quite forgot to rave,
While birds of calm sit brooding on the charmed wave.

VI

The stars with deep amaze
Stand fixed in steadfast gaze,
  Bending one way their precious influence,
And will not take their flight,
For all the morning light,
  Or Lucifer that often warned them thence;
But in their glimmering orbs did glow,
Until their Lord himself bespake, and bid them go.

VII

And though the shady gloom
Had given day her room,
  The sun himself withheld his wonted speed,
And hid his head for shame,
As his inferior flame,
  The new enlightened world no more should need;
He saw a greater sun appear
Than his bright throne, or burning axle-tree could bear.

68. birds of calm] halcyons (kingfishers). The belief that calm always prevailed during the fourteen midwinter days when they were laying and sitting ('brooding') on their floating nests, is recorded in Aristotle, *Historia Animalium* v 8, and Pliny x 47.
71. influence] The power exerted upon men by the heavenly bodies; cp. *Job* xxxviii 31: 'the sweet influences of the Pleiades.'
74. Lucifer] A name for the morning star (really Venus).
75. in . . . orbs] Cp. Shakespeare, *Midsummer Night's Dream* III ii 61: 'Venus in her glimmering sphere'.
80–4. Echoing Spenser, *Shep. Cal.* Apr. 73–8: 'I sawe Phoebus thrust out his golden hedde, / Upon her to gaze: / But, when he sawe how broade her beames did spredde, / It did him amaze. / He blusht to see another Sunne belowe, / Ne durst againe his fyrye face out showe.'
83. sun] Cp. the prophesied rising of the 'Sun of righteousness' in *Malachi* iv 2.
84. throne] In Ovid, *Met.* ii 24 the throne of the sun gleams with brilliant emeralds. *burning axle-tree*] Echoes Chapman, *Bussy D'Ambois* V iii 151–2: 'Fly where men feel / The burning axletree.'

VIII

The shepherds on the lawn,
Or ere the point of dawn,
Sat simply chatting in a rustic row;
Full little thought they then,
That the mighty Pan
Was kindly come to live with them below;
Perhaps their loves, or else their sheep,
Was all that did their silly thoughts so busy keep.

IX

When such music sweet
Their hearts and ears did greet,
As never was by mortal finger strook,
Divinely-warbled voice
Answering the stringed noise,
As all their souls in blissful rapture took:
The air such pleasure loth to lose,
With thousand echoes still prolongs each heavenly close.

X

Nature that heard such sound
Beneath the hollow round
Of Cynthia's seat, the airy region thrilling,

85–92. I. L. Myhr, *Explicator* iv (1945) 16, sees viii as a link between the images of light (v–vii) and music (ix–xiv) and explains that Pan is an appropriate link because Renaissance tradition associated him with Christ, giver of spiritual light, as well as with music.
88. then] For the sake of rhyme *1645* and *1673* have 'than': the two forms were interchangeable throughout most of the seventeenth century.
89. Pan] Spenser calls Christ 'great Pan' (*Shep. Cal.* May 54), and E.K. s gloss repeats the famous story from Plutarch (*De Defect. Orac.* 418) about the voice which, at the time of the crucifixion, cried that the great Pan was dead. The identification of Christ and Pan arose partly from Christ's role as 'good shepherd' and partly from the idea of Christ as 'All' (the meaning of Greek *pan*).
90. kindly] Both 'according to his nature' (as a shepherd he was coming to live with shepherds) and 'benevolently'.
92. silly] The senses 'foolish' and 'feeble-minded' had developed in the last quarter of the sixteenth century, but M. presumably intends the older sense 'unlearned, unsophisticated', which was still current in poetry.
98. took] captivated.
100. close] The conclusion of a musical phrase; a cadence.
102–3. hollow round . . . seat] The sphere of the moon.
103. region] On the regions of the air see Q *Nov* 12*n* (p. 37).

Now was almost won
To think her part was done,
And that her reign had here its last fulfilling;
She knew such harmony alone
Could hold all heaven and earth in happier union.

XI

At last surrounds their sight
A globe of circular light,
That with long beams the shame-faced night
arrayed,
The helmed cherubim
And sworded seraphim,
Are seen in glittering ranks with wings displayed,
Harping in loud and solemn quire,
With unexpressive notes to heaven's new-born heir.

XII

Such music (as 'tis said)
Before was never made,
But when of old the sons of morning sung,
While the creator great
His constellations set,
And the well-balanced world on hinges hung,
And cast the dark foundations deep,
And bid the welt'ring waves their oozy channel keep.

XIII

Ring out, ye crystal spheres,
Once bless our human ears,
(If ye have power to touch our senses so)
And let your silver chime

110. globe] Latin *globus* can mean 'troop', and 'globe' has this sense in *PL* ii 512 and *PR* iv 581 – a meaning first recorded in Giles Fletcher's *Christ's Triumph* (1610).

116. unexpressive] inexpressible; first used in this sense by Shakespeare, *As You Like It* III ii 10.

119–24. Cp. *Job* xxxviii 4–8: 'Where wast thou when I laid the foundations of the earth . . . When the morning stars sang together, and all the sons of God shouted for joy? Or who shut up the sea with doors?', and *Isa.* xiv 12: 'Lucifer, son of the morning'.

122. hinges] Cp. Spenser, *F.Q.* I xi 21: 'To move the world from off his stedfast henge.'

125–35. The idea that each sphere of the universe produced a note as it revolved (making up M.'s 'ninefold harmony') was Pythagorean in

Move in melodious time;
And let the base of heaven's deep organ blow,
And with your ninefold harmony
Make up full consort to the angelic symphony.

XIV

For if such holy song
Enwrap our fancy long,
Time will run back, and fetch the age of gold,
And speckled vanity
Will sicken soon and die,
And lep'rous sin will melt from earthly mould,
And hell itself will pass away,
And leave her dolorous mansions to the peering day.

XV

Yea Truth, and Justice then
Will down return to men,
Orbed in a rainbow; and like glories wearing
Mercy will sit between,

origin. See *Arcades* 63–72*n* (p. 159 below). *The Music of the Spheres* was the topic of M.'s second *Prolusion* (Columbia xii 149–57; Yale i 234–9), in which he subscribes to the idea that 'Pythagoras alone among mortal men' was able to hear this music. The rest of mankind cannot, he explains, because of the Fall, as a result of which we are 'buried in sin and degraded by brutish desires'. If our souls were pure, our ears would 'be filled with that exquisite music of the stars in their orbits; then would all things turn back to the Age of Gold'.

130. the base] The Earth, which has not, since the Fall, shared in the ninefold harmony. *organ*] This instrument was thought of as including all others, and therefore as representing universal harmony, as L. Spitzer demonstrates, *Traditio* ii (1944) 442–5.

135. As Tuve[2] (60) points out, the Messianic interpretation of Virgil, *Ecl.* iv, common since Constantine's time, made it the *locus classicus* for the idea of the Nativity as the birth of a restorer of Saturn's Golden Age.

136. speckled vanity] Cp. Horace, *Odes* IV v 22: *maculosum . . . nefas.*

138. lep'rous sin] Sylvester (Du Bartas 232) has 'leprosie of Sin'.

139–40. An echo either of Homer, *Il.* xx 62–5, or Virgil, *Aen.* viii 243–6, where the light of day is imagined flooding into hell.

141–4. Cp. *Ps.* lxxxv 10: 'Mercy and truth are met together, righteousness and peace have kissed each other.' For the departure of Astraea (Justice) from the earth see *Elegia IV* 81*n* (p. 57).

Throned in celestial sheen,
With radiant feet the tissued clouds down steering,
And heaven as at some festival,
Will open wide the gates of her high palace hall.

XVI

But wisest fate says no,
This must not yet be so,
The babe lies yet in smiling infancy,
That on the bitter cross
Must redeem our loss;
So both himself and us to glorify:
Yet first to those ychained in sleep,
The wakeful trump of doom must thunder through the deep.

XVII

With such a horrid clang
As on Mount Sinai rang
While the red fire, and smould'ring clouds out brake:
The aged earth aghast
With terror of that blast,
Shall from the surface to the centre shake;
When at the world's last session,
The dreadful judge in middle air shall spread his throne.

XVIII

And then at last our bliss
Full and perfect is,
But now begins; for from this happy day
The old dragon under ground
In straiter limits bound,

146. tissued] Minsheu (1617) defines *tissu* as 'cloth of silke and silver, or of silver and gold woven together'; cp. *Isa.* lii 7: 'How beautiful upon the mountains are the feet of him . . . that publisheth peace.'

149. Cp. *PL* vii 173 where God says 'and what I will is Fate'.

152. bitter cross] See 25*n*.

155. ychained] M.'s retention of the O.E. prefix 'ge-' (M.E. 'y-') is a Spenserian affectation. See E.K.'s gloss to Spenser, *Shep. Cal.* Apr. 155 ('Y is a poeticall addition').

158–9. Cp. *Exod.* xix 16 where God descends upon Sinai with 'thunder and lightnings and a thick cloud . . . and the voice of the trumpet' (Vulgate *clangorque buccinae*).

163–4. M.'s concept of the Last Judgment is drawn from *Matt.* xxiv 30: 'the Son of man coming in the clouds of heaven'.

168. old dragon] Cp. *Rev.* xx 2: 'the dragon, that old serpent, which is the

Not half so far casts his usurped sway,
And wroth to see his kingdom fail,
Swinges the scaly horror of his folded tail.

XIX

The oracles are dumb,
No voice or hideous hum
Runs through the arched roof in words deceiving.
Apollo from his shrine
Can no more divine,
With hollow shriek the steep of Delphos leaving.
No nightly trance, or breathed spell,
Inspires the pale-eyed priest from the prophetic cell.

XX

The lonely mountains o'er,
And the resounding shore,
A voice of weeping heard, and loud lament;
From haunted spring, and dale
Edged with poplar pale,
The parting genius is with sighing sent,
With flower-inwoven tresses torn
The nymphs in twilight shade of tangled thickets mourn.

Devil', and xii 3–4: 'a great red dragon . . . And his tail drew the third part of the stars of heaven'.
172. Swinges . . . tail] Sylvester's lion is depicted 'often swindging, with his sinnewy train' (Du Bartas 155).
173–80. The passage on the cessation of the oracles at the birth of Christ in Prudentius *Apotheosis* 438–43 mentions the silence of the caves at Delphi (M.'s 'Delphos', where Apollo had an oracle on the steep slope of Parnassus), the fanatic priest panting and foaming at the mouth, and the silencing of Hammon in Libya (203). In the same poem Apollo is tormented with pain by the words of exorcism, and shrieks (*heiulat*) (402–3, 412–13); at the heathen sacrifice (460–502) the priest breaks off because he senses that a Christian is present, and he sees Persephone fleeing in dread; his spells (*carmina*) are of no effect; the flames go out and the laurel falls from the flamen's head.
183. Cp. the slaughter of the innocents in *Matt.* ii 18, quoting *Jerem.* xxxi 15: 'In Rama was there a voice heard, lamentation and weeping and great mourning.'
185. poplar pale] Cp. Horace, *Odes* II iii 9: *albaque poplus.*
186. genius] A strictly local deity in classical mythology.
188. Cp. Fairfax's translation of Tasso iii 75, where a wood is felled at Godfrey's command and 'The weeping Nymphes fled from their bowres exilde'.

XXI

In consecrated earth,
And on the holy hearth,
The lars, and lemures moan with midnight plaint,
In urns, and altars round,
A drear and dying sound
Affrights the flamens at their service quaint;
And the chill marble seems to sweat,
While each peculiar power forgoes his wonted seat.

XXII

Peor, and Baalim,
Forsake their temples dim,
With that twice battered god of Palestine,
And mooned Ashtaroth,
Heaven's queen and mother both,
Now sits not girt with tapers' holy shine,
The Libyc Hammon shrinks his horn,
In vain the Tyrian maids their wounded Thammuz mourn.

191. lars, and lemures] Augustine, *City of God* ix 11, denies Apuleius' theory that men's souls become lars (deities presiding over private houses) if good and lemures (goblins) if bad.
194. flamens] priests *quaint*] elaborate.
195. marble . . . sweat] Virgil, *Georg.* i 480, mentions ivory weeping and bronzes sweating among the prodigies seen at the murder of Caesar, as does Ovid, *Met.* xv 792.
197. Peor] Peor was the name of a mountain (*Num.* xxiii 28) and thence of the local deity Baal-Peor, one of the titles under which Baal, the Phoenician sun-god was worshipped (*Num.* xxv 3). Selden has a chapter (I v) on Baal-Peor. *Baalim*] the plural of Baal, stands for other manifestations of Baal, e.g. Baal-Berith, Baal-Zebub. Cp. *Judges* x 6: 'The children of Israel . . . served Baalim and Ashtaroth.' Selden (II i) discusses these manifestations.
199. twice battered god] Dagon, the Philistine god who is twice overturned during the night in *1 Sam.* v 3–4.
200. mooned Ashtaroth] The plural form (standing for her collective manifestations) of Ashtoreth, supreme goddess of the Phoenicians and identical with the Syrian Astarte. Selden II ii attests her supremacy ('Heaven's queen'), discusses her relationship to the moon and her consequent assumption of horns ('mooned'), and proves her right to the title *Mater Deum* ('Heaven's . . . mother').
203. Hammon] One of the manifestations of Jove, worshipped in Libya (at the Siwah oasis) in the form of a ram.
204. Thammuz] Identical with the Greek Adonis, slain, like him, by a boar

XXIII

And sullen Moloch fled,
Hath left in shadows dread,
His burning idol all of blackest hue;
In vain with cymbals' ring,
They call the grisly king,
In dismal dance about the furnace blue;
The brutish gods of Nile as fast,
Isis and Orus, and the dog Anubis haste.

XXIV

Nor is Osiris seen
In Memphian grove, or green,
Trampling the unshowered grass with lowings loud:
Nor can he be at rest
Within his sacred chest,

and mourned annually at his festival at Byblos in Phoenicia ('Tyrian' because Tyre was the principal city of Phoenicia), where the waters of the stream were said to turn red with his blood. Selden devotes a chapter (II x) to him. Cp. *Ezek.* viii 14: 'There sat women weeping for Tammuz.'

205–10. Moloch was an idol worhipped by the Ammonites at Rabbah, their capital. Sandys 186 tells how 'the *Hebrews* sacrificed their children to *Molech*, an Idoll of brasse, having the head of a calfe, the rest of a kingly figure, with armes extended to receive the miserable sacrifice, seared to death with his burning embracements. For the Idoll was hollow within, and filled with fire. And lest their lamentable shrieks should sad the hearts of their parents, the Priests of *Molech* did deafe their eares with the continuall clangs of trumpets and timbrels.' Selden I vi gives these and other details. Cp. *2 Kings* xxiii 10: 'that no man might make his son or his daughter pass through the fire to Molech'.

211. brutish gods of Nile] Sandys 133 in his section on Egypt illustrates several of these, and describes others 'with the heads of sheepe, haukes, dogs etc. . . . cats, beetles, monkies, and such like', quoting Virgil, *Aen.* viii 698: *omnigenum deum monstra et latrator Anubis.*

212. Isis] Egyptian goddess of the earth. Herodotus ii 41 says she is horned like a cow. Sandys 133–4 has an illustration with the caption: 'a lion; under which shape they adored Isis'. *Orus*] Egyptian sun god, son of Isis. *Anubis*] son of Osiris, represented with jackal's or dog's head. Sandys 133–4 illustrates 'Anubis . . . figured with the head of a dog', and adds: 'the dog throughout Egypt was universally worshipped'.

213. Osiris] Chief Egyptian god, worshipped, as Herodotus describes (iii 27–9) in the shape of the Apis, a black bull with a white star on its forehead, (hence his 'lowings'). Cp. Sandys 132 'In this [Memphis] was the Temple of *Apis* (which is the same with *Osiris*)'. Selden I iv discusses Osiris and the Apis in his chapter on the golden calf.

Nought but profoundest hell can be his shroud,
In vain with timbrelled anthems dark
The sable-stoled sorcerers bear his worshipped ark.

XXV

He feels from Juda's land
The dreaded infant's hand,
The rays of Bethlehem blind his dusky eyn;
Nor all the gods beside,
Longer dare abide,
Not Typhon huge ending in snaky twine:
Our babe to show his Godhead true,
Can in his swaddling bands control the damned crew.

XXVI

So when the sun in bed,
Curtained with cloudy red,
Pillows his chin upon an orient wave,
The flocking shadows pale,
Troop to the infernal jail,
Each fettered ghost slips to his several grave,
And the yellow-skirted fays,
Fly after the night-steeds, leaving their moon-loved maze.

220. ark] Cp. Herodotus ii 63: 'The image of the god, in a little wooden gilt casket, is carried . . . from the temple by the priests.'

226. Typhon] The Greek Typhon was a hundred-headed monster, son of Earth and Tartarus, described by Apollodorus, I vi 3. He was serpent below the waist. Zeus killed him with a thunderbolt. The Egyptian Typhon, or Set, was slayer of Osiris, cp. Sandys 103: 'By *Osiris* they prefigured *Nilus*; . . . by *Typhon* the Sea.'

227–8. Hercules who, as D. C. Allen comments, *JEGP* lx (1961) 619–21, was a common type of Christ, strangled snakes in his cradle. Theocritus xxiv 1–63 tells the story. For other Hercules–Christ references see M. Y. Hughes, *Études anglaises* vi (1953) 193–213.

231. Pillows] *OED* has no previous example of the use of 'pillow' as a verb.

233. Troop] Cp. Shakespeare, *Midsummer Night's Dream* III ii 382–3: 'ghosts, wandering here and there, / Troop home to churchyards.'

234. fettered] i.e. to the body, cp. *Comus* 464–74*n* (p. 199).

235. fays] Selden 163 associates the 'fays' with Lucina and Eileithyia, the Roman and Greek goddesses of childbirth. Their flight is particularly significant in this nativity poem and is therefore placed last.

236. night-steeds] Cp. *Q Nov* 70–3*n* (p. 39). *maze*] Cp. Shakespeare, *Midsummer Night's Dream* II i 99: 'the quaint mazes in the wanton green' where the fairies dance their 'moonlight revels' (II i 141).

XXVII

But see the virgin blest,
Hath laid her babe to rest.
Time is our tedious song should here have ending:
Heaven's youngest teemed star,
Hath fixed her polished car,
Her sleeping Lord with handmaid lamp attending:
And all about the courtly stable,
Bright-harnessed angels sit in order serviceable.

35 *Elegia sexta*
[Elegy VI]

Date. Dec. 1629. The composition of *Nativity Ode* (Christmas 1629) is referred to (*79–88*) as recent and (presumably) incomplete. M.'s prose heading shows that *Elegia VI* is a reply to a letter of Diodati's dated 13 Dec.
Publication. *1645* and *1673* (no significant variants: *1673* misprints *13 quereris* as *queretis*, and in *22* it misprints a comma after *modis*).
Modern criticism. Hanford[2] 369–70 views *Elegia VI* as a deliberate self-consecration, bracketing it with M.'s recollection of his decision to dedicate himself to the 'the experience and the practice of all that which is praiseworthy' for his poetry's sake (Columbia iii 303–4; Yale i 890). W. R. Parker, however, *MLN* lv (1940) 216–17, reads the poem as an academic exercise, 'a rhetorical "debate" discussing each side learnedly from a single point of view'. Z. S. Fink, *English Studies* xxi (1939) 164–5, gives instances of the same debate in J. C. Scaliger and others.

Ad Carolum Diodatum ruri commorantem

Qui cum idibus Decemb. scripsisset, et sua carmina excusari postulasset si solito minus essent bona, quod inter lautitias quibus erat ab amicis exceptus, haud satis felicem operam musis dare se posse affirmabat, hunc habuit responsum.

Mitto tibi sanam non pleno ventre salutem,
Qua tu distento forte carere potes.
At tua quid nostram prolectat musa camoenam,
Nec sinit optatas posse sequi tenebras?
Carmine scire velis quam te redamemque colamque,
Crede mihi vix hoc carmine scire queas.
Nam neque noster amor modulis includitur arctis,

240. *youngest teemed*] latest born.
244. *Bright-harnessed*] bright-armoured.
¶ 35. *3. camoenam*] Latin equivalent of the Greek μοῦσα, a muse.

Nec venit ad claudos integer ipse pedes.
Quam bene sollennes epulas, hilaremque Decembrim
Festaque coelifugam quae coluere Deum,
Deliciasque refers, hiberni gaudia ruris,
Haustaque per lepidos Gallica musta focos.
Quid quereris refugam vino dapibusque poesin?
Carmen amat Bacchum, carmina Bacchus amat.
Nec puduit Phoebum virides gestasse corymbos,
Atque hederam lauro praeposuisse suae.
Saepius Aoniis clamavit collibus Euoe
Mista Thyoneo turba novena choro.
Naso Corallaeis mala carmina misit ab agris:
Non illic epulae non sata vitis erat.
Quid nisi vina, rosasque racemiferumque Lyaeum
Cantavit brevibus Teia musa modis?
Pindaricosque inflat numeros Teumesius Euan,
Et redolet sumptum pagina quaeque merum.

8. M.'s joke about the elegiac couplet 'limping', because its second line was a foot shorter than its first, is borrowed from Ovid, *Tristia* III i 11–12.
13–14. Z. S. Fink, *English Studies* xxi (1939) 164–5, points out that Scaliger, in the *Poetics*, distinguishes between 'divinely possessed' poets like Homer and Hesiod, and poets inspired by wine, like Horace, Ennius, Alcaeus and Aristophanes. Later M. contrasts the kind of poem he wants to write with that raised from 'the vapours of wine' (Columbia iii 241; Yale i 820).
15–16. corymbos . . . hederam] Bacchus was traditionally crowned with ivy berries and wreathed with ivy.
17–18. Aoniis . . . collibus] Cp. *Elegia IV* 29–32*n* (p. 55) *Thyoneo*] *Thyoneus* was a name for Bacchus because, according to one tradition, preserved by Cicero, *Nat. Deor.* III xxiii 58, he was son of Nisus and Thyone (Semele). *Euoe*] the shout of the Bacchic revellers.
19–20. Ovid was exiled in A.D. 8 to Tomis on the Black Sea, where he wrote the *Tristia*, the *Ex Ponto* and the *Ibis*. In *Ex Ponto* IV ii 15–22 he admits that the quality of his poems has suffered from his new surroundings, and in I iii 49–52 complains of the absence from Tomis of fruit and the vine. The Coralli were a tribe of Geats from the Danube of whom he saw a good deal at Tomis: he complains, IV ii 37, 'in this place who is there to whom I can read my compositions except the yellow-haired Coralli?'
21. racemiferumque] The same adjective is used of Bacchus by Ovid, *Met.* xv 413.
22. Teia musa] Anacreon, born at Teos on the Aegean. Ovid calls him by the same name, *Tristia* ii 364.
23–6. Teumesius Euan] Boeotian Bacchus (*Teumesius* from *Teumesus*, a mountain in Boeotia, and *Euan* from *Euoe*, the Bacchic revellers' cry). There is a copy of Pindar, possibly M.'s, at Harvard, with the purchase date 15 Nov. 1629 on its flyleaf (French i 204–5): the connection of this volume

Dum gravis everso currus crepat axe supinus,
  Et volat Eleo pulvere fuscus eques.
Quadrimoque madens lyricen Romanus iaccho
  Dulce canit Glyceran, flavicomamque Chloen.
Iam quoque lauta tibi generoso mensa paratu,
  Mentis alit vires, ingeniumque fovet.
Massica foecundam despumant pocula venam,
  Fundis et ex ipso condita metra cado.
Addimus his artes, fusumque per intima Phoebum
  Corda, favent uni Bacchus, Apollo, Ceres.
Scilicet haud mirum tam dulcia carmina per te
  Numine composito tres peperisse deos.
Nunc quoque Thressa tibi caelato barbitos auro
  Insonat arguta molliter icta manu;
Auditurque chelys suspensa tapetia circum,
  Virgineos tremula quae regat arte pedes.
Illa tuas saltem teneant spectacula musas,
  Et revocent, quantum crapula pellit iners.
Crede mihi dum psallit ebur, comitataque plectrum
  Implet odoratos festa chorea tholos,
Percipies tacitum per pectora serpere Phoebum,
  Quale repentinus permeat ossa calor,
Perque puellares oculos digitumque sonantem
  Irruet in totos lapsa Thalia sinus.
Namque elegia levis multorum cura deorum est,
  Et vocat ad numeros quemlibet illa suos;
Liber adest elegis, Eratoque, Ceresque, Venusque,
  Et cum purpurea matre tenellus Amor.
Talibus inde licent convivia larga poetis,
  Saepius et veteri commaduisse mero.

with M. has, however, been questioned by M. Kelley and S. D. Atkins, *Studies in Bibliography* xvii (1964) 77–82. M. is thinking here of *Olymp.* ii–iv, odes in honour of charioteers who took part in the Olympic games held near Elis.

27–8. lyricen Romanus] Horace, who sings the charms of Glycera in *Odes* I xix and woos Chloe (called 'golden-haired', III ix 19) in I xxiii. *Quadrimoque . . . iaccho*] Echoes *Odes* I ix 7–8 *quadrimum . . . merum*.

31. Massica] Mt Massicus was famous for its wine: M. is echoing Horace, *Odes* I i 19: *veteris pocula Massici*.

37. Thressa . . . barbitos] Cp. Ovid, *Am.* II xi 32 *Threiciam . . . lyram*; the lyre is called Thracian because Orpheus was of Thrace.

48. Thalia] One of the muses; Horace, *Odes* IV vi 25, refers to her as the muse of lyric poetry.

51. Erato] The muse of love poetry, according to Ovid, *Ars Am.* ii 16.

53. licent] M.'s construction here has no classical precedent.

At qui bella refert, et adulto sub Iove caelum,
Heroasque pios, semideosque duces,
Et nunc sancta canit superum consulta deorum,
Nunc latrata fero regna profunda cane,
Ille quidem parce Samii pro more magistri
Vivat, et innocuos praebeat herba cibos;
Stet prope fagineo pellucida lympha catillo,
Sobriaque e puro pocula fonte bibat.
Additur huic scelerisque vacans, et casta iuventus,
Et rigidi mores, et sine labe manus.
Qualis veste nitens sacra, et lustralibus undis
Surgis ad infensos augur iture deos.
Hoc ritu vixisse ferunt post rapta sagacem
Lumina Tiresian, Ogygiumque Linon,
Et lare devoto profugum Calchanta, senemque
Orpheon edomitis sola per antra feris;
Sic dapis exiguus, sic rivi potor Homerus
Dulichium vexit per freta longa virum,

55. *adulto . . . Iove*] As opposed to the youthful and amorous Jove.
58. *cane*] The dog is Cerberus, guardian of the underworld.
59. *Samii . . . magistri*] Pythagoras–'the first', as Ovid remarks, *Met.* xv 72–3, 'to decry the placing of animal food upon our tables'. Iamblichus, *Life of Pythagoras* iii, records that the philosopher entirely abstained from wine and animal food.
68. *Tiresian*] Tiresias was a Theban prophet, blinded by Juno and given prophetic powers by Jove. His water-drinking is given prominence by Stephanus (*s.v.* Tiresias): *Author est Strabo lib. 9 Tiresiae monumentum fuisse sub Tilphosso monte Boeotiae, iuxta fontem eiusdem nominis, ubi profugus diem suum obiit, cum iam senex gelidissimam Tilphossae aquam hausisset, ibidemque Thebanos sepulto divinos honores tribuisse* (According to Strabo Book 9 Tiresias' monument was at the foot of Mount Tilphossus in Boeotia, near the fountain of the same name; he took refuge there and, already advanced in age, died from drinking the freezing water of Tilphossa; the Thebans buried him there and honoured him as a god). Actually all Strabo says (IX ii 27) is that the tomb is near Tilphossus. *Ogygiumque Linon*] Linus, son of Apollo and Terpsichore, instructed Orpheus. *Ogygius* means Theban, from Ogyges, mythical founder of Thebes.
69. *Calchanta*] Calchas is a Greek in Homer. It was Guido delle Colonne who first made him a Trojan, substituting him for Homer's Chryses. Thus in Chaucer's *Troilus and Criseyde* i 64–84 Calchas leaves Troy when he foresees its fall. There is some emphasis in Chaucer on his ensuing poverty (iv 85–91), but no mention of his simple mode of life. Guido merely says that Calchas lives *in paupertate et exilio* among the Greeks.
71. M. here is deliberately contradicting Horace, *Epist.* I xix 1–6, who argues that no good poet is ever a water-drinker, and that the way Homer

Et per monstrificam Perseiae Phoebados aulam,
Et vada femineis insidiosa sonis,
Perque tuas rex ime domos, ubi sanguine nigro
Dicitur umbrarum detinuisse greges.
Diis etenim sacer est vates, divumque sacerdos,
Spirat et occultum pectus, et ora Iovem.
At tu si quid agam, scitabere (si modo saltem
Esse putas tanti noscere siquid agam)
Paciferum canimus caelesti semine regem,
Faustaque sacratis saecula pacta libris,
Vagitumque Dei, et stabulantem paupere tecto
Qui suprema suo cum patre regna colit.
Stelliparumque polum, modulantesque aethere turmas,
Et subito elisos ad sua fana deos.
Dona quidem dedimus Christi natalibus illa
Illa sub auroram lux mihi prima tulit.
Te quoque pressa manent patriis meditata cicutis,
Tu mihi, cui recitem, iudicis instar eris.

To Charles Diodati, staying in the country. He had written on 13 Dec. and asked that his poems should be excused if they had been less good than usual. The reason he gave was that the magnificent reception which his friends had given him had prevented him from paying proper attention to the muses. This was the answer he received.

I, with my empty stomach, wish you health which you, with your full one, may need. But why does your muse lure mine[3] out into the open, and not allow her to seek the obscurity which she desires? Perhaps you want my poem to tell you how warmly I return your love, and how I cherish you. You could scarcely learn that from this poem, believe me, because my love cannot be shut up in tight-fitting metres, and being sound refuses to limp[8] along in elegiac couplets. How well you describe the splendid feasts, the December merry-making, the festal days in honour of the God who came down from heaven, and the charms and delights of the winter country-side, with French wines drunk beside friendly fires. But why complain that

writes about wine shows he was not one. *dapis exiguus*] The pseudo-Herodotean life of Homer presents him wandering from town to town and living on alms. Stephanus (*s.v.* Homer) also draws attention to his poverty (*rebusque omnibus egentem*).

72–6. Dulichium ... virum] Ulysses; the island of Dulichium formed part of his kingdom. *Perseiae Phoebados*] Circe, daughter of Phoebus and Perseis, who turned Ulysses' followers into swine (*Od.* x 274–574). *femineis ... sonis*] The sirens' song, described *Od.* xii 184–92. *tuas ... domos*] The descent to the underworld is narrated *Od.* xi, and the libation of 'dark blood' in xi 34–6.

89–90. The poems which await Diodati along with *Nativity Ode* are, argues J. Carey, *RES* n.s. xiv (1963) 383–6, the Italian sonnets. M. was presumably expecting to see Diodati soon: the latter was in Geneva by Apr. 1630, when he was matriculated at the Academy to read theology.

banquet and bottle frighten poetry away?[13] Song loves Bacchus, and Bacchus loves songs.[14] Phoebus was not ashamed to wear green clusters of ivy-berries,[15] or to prize ivy-leaves more than his own laurel.[16] The troop of nine muses has often mingled with Thyoneus's throng and shrieked 'Euoe!' across the Aonian hills.[17] Ovid sent back poems from the land of the Coralli,[19] but they did not have banquets or cultivate the vine there, so the poems were no good.[20] What did the poet from Teos[22] sing about in his neat little verses but wines and roses and Bacchus with bunches and bunches of grapes?[21] It was Teumasian Bacchus who inspired Pindar's odes,[23] and every page smells of the wine he has been drinking–as the heavy chariot crashes over with its axle in the air and the horseman flashes by, black with Olympia's dust.[26] The Roman lute-player[27] was drunk with four-year-old wine when he sang his sweet songs about Glycera and about Chloe with her golden hair.[28] And now a sumptuous table strengthens *your* mind and warms *your* genius with its rich array. Your goblets of Massic[31] wine foam with poetic power, and you pour out the verses which were stored up inside the bottle. Then again, you have artistry, and Phoebus is present in your heart of hearts. Bacchus, Apollo and Ceres are on your side, and only yours. No wonder you are the mouthpiece for such lovely poems: three gods have combined their godheads and speak through you! Now, too, the Thracian lyre,[37] with its gold engraving, plays for you, as a skilled hand softly plucks it. In rooms hung round with tapestry the harp is heard, and its trembling strings direct the feet of the dancing girls. Let these sights, at any rate, catch your muse's attention, and call back whatever powers sluggish drunkenness drives away. Believe me, while the ivory plectrum dances over the strings and the crowd of merry-makers, keeping time with it, fills the perfumed ballroom, you will notice Phoebus creeping silently into your heart, like a sudden warmth flowing through your bones. Girls' eyes and girls' fingers playing will make Thalia[48] dart into your breast and take command of it. For there are a lot of gods who look after light-footed elegy, and she calls anyone she pleases to her tune. Bacchus aids elegies, and so does Erato[51] and Ceres and Venus and tender little Cupid beside his rosy mother. So grand banquets are quite all right[53] for elegiac poets, and they can get drunk on old wine as often as they like. But the poet who writes about wars, and about a heaven ruled over by a Jove who has outgrown his boyhood,[55] about heroes who stick to their duty and princes who are half gods; the poet whose subject is, one minute, the holy counsels of the gods above, and the next, those deep-buried kingdoms where a savage dog[58] barks–let this poet live frugally, like the philosopher from Samos,[59] and let herbs provide his harmless diet. Let a bowl of beech-wood, filled with clear water, stand by him, and may he drink soberly from a pure spring. In addition his youth must be chaste and free from crime, his morals strict and his hand unstained. He must be like you, priest, when, bathed in holy water and gleaming in your sacred vestment, you rise to go and face the angry gods. In this way, so it is said, wise Tiresias[68] lived after the loss of his sight, and Theban Linus, and Calchas,[69] when he had fled from his doomed home, and old Orpheus, when he tamed wild beasts among lonely caves. In this way, sparing of food, and drinking water from the brook, Homer[71] guided Ulysses[72] across great oceans and through Circe's hall, where men were turned to monsters, and over the shallows made treacherous by the sirens' song, and through your dwellings, infernal king, where he detained the troops of ghosts, or so the story goes, with a libation of dark blood.[76] For the poet is sacred to the gods: he is their priest: his innermost heart and his mouth are both full of Jove.

But if you want to know what I am doing–if, that is, you think it worth while to know whether I am doing anything at all–I am writing a poem about the king who was born of heavenly seed, and who brought peace to men. I am writing about the blessed ages promised in Holy Scripture, about the infant cries of God, about the stabling under a poor roof of Him who dwells with His Father in the highest heavens, about the sky's giving birth to a new star, about the hosts who sang in the air, and about the pagan gods suddenly shattered in their own shrines. These are the gifts I have given for Christ's birthday: the first light of the dawn brought them to me.

Some terse little poems which I have composed on your native country's pipes[89] are also waiting for you. You shall be, as it were, my judge, when I recite them to you.[90]

36 The Passion

Date. Mar. 1630? The opening lines clearly refer to the *Nativity Ode*, so the poem must be dated after Christmas 1629. Its subject suggests that it was an Easter poem (Easter day fell on 28 Mar. in 1630). The metre and rhyme scheme are those of the introductory stanzas of the *Nativity Ode*.
Publication. *1645* (*22.* latest]latter *45.* up lock,]up-lock,) *1673* (the text followed here except in *42* where *1673* misprints a comma after 'fit').
Modern criticism. Louis Martz, *The Poetry of Meditation* (New Haven 1954) pp. 167–8, suggests that in this poem M. is trying to employ the uncongenial devices of the Catholic meditation upon a subject which was itself generally unattractive to the Puritans.

I

Erewhile of music, and ethereal mirth,
Wherewith the stage of air and earth did ring,
And joyous news of heavenly infant's birth,
My muse with angels did divide to sing;
But headlong joy is ever on the wing,
    In wintry solstice like the shortened light
Soon swallowed up in dark and long out-living night.

¶ 36. *4. divide*] execute 'divisions', or rapid melodic passages. Elsewhere in M.'s poetry 'divide' means either 'share' or 'separate': it is nowhere else used intransitively, as here.
6. wintry solstice] The day is shortest at the winter solstice (22 Dec.). The line is inverted.

II

For now to sorrow must I tune my song,
And set my harp to notes of saddest woe,
Which on our dearest Lord did seize ere long,
Dangers, and snares, and wrongs, and worse than so,
Which he for us did freely undergo.
  Most perfect hero, tried in heaviest plight
Of labours huge and hard, too hard for human wight.

III

He sovran priest, stooping his regal head
That dropped with odorous oil down his fair eyes,
Poor fleshly tabernacle entered,
His starry front low-roofed beneath the skies;
O what a mask was there, what a disguise!
  Yet more; the stroke of death he must abide,
Then lies him meekly down fast by his brethren's side.

IV

These latest scenes confine my roving verse,
To this horizon is my Phoebus bound,
His godlike acts; and his temptations fierce,
And former sufferings otherwhere are found;
Loud o'er the rest Cremona's trump doth sound;
  Me softer airs befit, and softer strings
Of lute, or viol still, more apt for mournful things.

V

Befriend me night best patroness of grief,
Over the pole thy thickest mantle throw,

14. labours] Suggesting Hercules, see *Nativity Ode* 227–8*n* (p. 112).
15. priest] Christ is called a 'high priest' in *Heb.* ii 17.
16. The name *Christ*, as M. points out in *De doctrina* I v (Columbia xiv 184–5), means 'anointed' in Greek.
17. The body is referred to as a 'tabernacle' in *2 Cor.* v 1 and *2 Pet.* i 13–14.
21. brethren's] Cp. Christ's references to his 'brethren', *Matt.* xii 48–9 and xxv 40; also *Heb.* ii 14–17: 'that through death he might destroy him that had the power of death. . . . Wherefore in all things it behoved him to be made like unto his brethren.'
26. Cremona's trump] The *Christiad*, a Latin poem, largely a pastiche of Virgil, in six books on the life of Christ, written at the instigation of Pope Leo X by Marco Girolamo Vida and published in Cremona, Vida's birthplace, in 1535.
28. still] quiet.
30. pole] sky.

And work my flattered fancy to belief,
That heaven and earth are coloured with my woe;
My sorrows are too dark for day to know:
  The leaves should all be black whereon I write,
And letters where my tears have washed a wannish
    white.

VI

See see the chariot, and those rushing wheels,
That whirled the prophet up at Chebar flood,
My spirit some transporting cherub feels,
To bear me where the towers of Salem stood,
Once glorious towers, now sunk in guiltless blood;
  There doth my soul in holy vision sit
In pensive trance, and anguish, and ecstatic fit.

VII

Mine eye hath found that sad sepulchral rock
That was the casket of heaven's richest store,
And here though grief my feeble hands up lock,
Yet on the softened quarry would I score
My plaining verse as lively as before;
  For sure so well instructed are my tears,
That they would fitly fall in ordered characters.

34–5. Sylvester's *Lachrimae Lachrimarum* (1612), a funeral elegy on Prince Henry, has a title page printed black with the letters left white. M. may, however, have in mind the more common practice of edging the page on which a funeral elegy was printed with a thick band of black, and thus be distinguishing between his page, which should be 'all' black, and the usual page, which is only edged.

36–40. Ezekiel's vision of the chariot of God was 'by the river of Chebar' (i 1). *rushing wheels*] Cp. 'the noise of the wheels . . . and a noise of a great rushing' (iii 13). *whirled . . . up*] Cp. 'the spirit lifted me up' (iii 14). *cherub*] The 'living creatures' which bear the chariot are later identified as cherubim (x 8–22). *Salem*] Jerusalem, to which Ezekiel was sent with the message 'Thou art become guilty in thy blood that thou hast shed' (xxii 4).

43. rock] Sandys 166–7 uses this word frequently in his description of the Holy Sepulchre: 'the naturall rocke . . . hewne into the forme of a Chappell . . . the selfe same rocke . . . a passage through the midst of the rocke . . . a compast roofe of the solid rocke'.

VIII

Or should I thence hurried on viewless wing,
Take up a weeping on the mountains wild,
The gentle neighbourhood of grove and spring
Would soon unbosom all their echoes mild,
And I (for grief is easily beguiled)
Might think the infection of my sorrows loud,
Had got a race of mourners on some pregnant cloud.

This subject the author finding to be above the years he had when he wrote it, and nothing satisfied with what was begun, left it unfinished.

37 On Shakespeare

Date. 1630: added to title in *1645* and *1673*.

Publication. First printed 1632, anonymously, among prefatory material to the Shakespeare Second Folio, headed *An Epitaph on the admirable Dramatic Poet, W. Shakespeare*, with five verbal variants from *1673* (*1.* needs]need *6.* weak]dull *8.* live-long]lasting *10.* heart]part *13.* itself]herself). In one state of the Second Folio–surviving in eight exemplars, listed by R. M. Smith, *The Variant Issues of Shakespeare's Second Folio and M.'s First Published English Poem* (Lehigh University 1928)–there is an additional verbal variant (*4.* star-ypointing]star-ypointed). Printed for the second time,with the same heading as that in the Second Folio, in *Poems: Written by Wil. Shakespeare, Gent* (1640) with M.'s initials and four verbal variants from *1673* (*1.* needs]need *6.* need'st]needs *13.* itself]ourself *15.* dost]doth).

Next printed *1645* (no significant variants from *1673*, but in *9 1645* misprints 'toth' shame' for 'to th' shame'). Next printed 1664 in Shakespeare Third Folio (heading and five verbal variants as in 1632). Next printed *1673* (the text followed here).

Modern criticism. Fletcher ii 506 suggests that M. knew Robert Allot, the bookseller to whom Edward Blount's share in the First Folio was assigned 26 Jun. 1630, and thus wrote *Shakespeare* in 1630 knowing that a second edition of Shakespeare's works was afoot. There were, however, four other booksellers who had shares in the First Folio.

H. W. Garrod, *E & S* xii (1926) 7–23, discusses the textual variants. He also suggests as sources for *Shakespeare* Massinger and Field's *Fatal Dowry*

50. viewless] invisible; cp. *Comus* 92.

51. Cp. *Jer.* ix 10: 'For the mountains will I take up a weeping.'

56. Pindar, *Pyth.* ii 21–48, tells how Ixion, when a guest on Olympus, tried to rape Hera; but she substituted a cloud for herself, on which he begot Centaurus, father of the Centaurs.

II i 69–72 and Thomas Tomkins's *Albumazar* I iv 3–4. To these H. Mutschmann (*Further Studies Concerning the Origin of Paradise Lost* (Tartu 1934) 47–55) adds the verses *To the memory of my beloved, The Author* which Ben Jonson prefixed to the First Folio, and the anonymous epitaph on Stanley ('Ask who lies here . . .') attributed in some seventeenth century MSS to Shakespeare. The Stanley lines were first proposed as a source by F. Townsend (Todd vi 84–5) and the claim is repeated by T. Spencer, *MLN* liii (1938) 366–7.

What needs my Shakespeare for his honoured bones,
The labour of an age in piled stones,
Or that his hallowed relics should be hid
Under a star-ypointing pyramid?
Dear son of memory, great heir of fame,
What need'st thou such weak witness of thy name?
Thou in our wonder and astonishment
Hast built thyself a live-long monument.
For whilst to the shame of slow-endeavouring art,
Thy easy numbers flow, and that each heart
Hath from the leaves of thy unvalued book,
Those Delphic lines with deep impression took,
Then thou our fancy of itself bereaving,
Dost make us marble with too much conceiving;

¶ 37. 4. *star-ypointing*] Cp. Propertius III ii 19: *Pyramidum sumptus ad sidera ducti*, quoted by Sandys 127–9 in his description of the pyramids, some phrases from which may have influenced M. here ('the labours of the *Jewes* . . . No stone so little throughout the whole, as to be drawne by our carriages . . . Twenty years it was a-building'). The retention of the Middle English 'y-' prefix before the past participle was a common feature of the archaistic language of Spenser and his imitators. Spenser never uses this prefix before a present participle: M.'s 'ypointing' is a false archaism.
5. *son of memory*] M. makes Shakespeare brother to the Muses, see *Id Plat* 3*n* (p. 66). Browne (i 226) calls the English poets 'sons of Memory' in a passage where he is regretting that no 'pyramis' whose top should 'seem the stars to kiss' has been built to commemorate Spenser. M. may be alluding to this passage and contrasting the needs of Spenser with those of Shakespeare.
10. *easy numbers*] Cp. the epistle *To the great Variety of Readers* prefaced by Heming and Condell to the First Folio: 'His mind and hand went together: And what he thought, he uttered with that easinesse, that wee have scarse received from him a blot in his papers.'
11. *unvalued*] invaluable.
12. *Delphic lines*] Apollo, god of poetry, had his oracle at Delphi.
14. Cp. for the conceit *Il Penseroso* 42*n* (p. 141).

And so sepulchred in such pomp dost lie,
That kings for such a tomb would wish to die.

38 On the University Carrier

who sickened in the time of his vacancy, being forbid to go to London, by reason of the Plague

Date. Jan. 1631. Thomas Hobson, who died 1 Jan. 1631, aged eighty-six, was a well-known Cambridge figure. According to Steele (*Spectator* 509; 14 Oct. 1712) the expression 'Hobson's choice' originated in his practice, when he hired out hackney horses, of making each customer take the horse which stood nearest the stable door. His death was commemorated in numerous poems, of which some are printed from seventeenth-century MSS and miscellanies by G. Blakemore Evans, *MLQ* iv (1943) 281–90 and ix (1948) 10, 184, and by W. Evans, *PQ* xxvi (1947) 321–7.
Publication. *1645* (2 And]A). Next printed *Wit Restor'd* (1658), a garbled version, of which the textual variants are discussed by W. R. Parker, *MLR* xxxi (1936) 395–402. *1673* (the text followed here).

Here lies old Hobson, Death hath broke his girt,
And here alas, hath laid him in the dirt,
Or else the ways being foul, twenty to one,
He's here stuck in a slough, and overthrown.
'Twas such a shifter, that if truth were known,
Death was half glad when he had got him down;
For he had any time this ten years full,
Dodged with him, betwixt Cambridge and the Bull.
And surely, Death could never have prevailed,
Had not his weekly course of carriage failed;
But lately finding him so long at home,
And thinking now his journey's end was come,
And that he had ta'en up his latest inn,
In the kind office of a chamberlain
Showed him his room where he must lodge that night,
Pulled off his boots, and took away the light:
If any ask for him, it shall be said,
Hobson has supped, and 's newly gone to bed.

¶ 38. *1. girt*] Variant form of 'girth', current in seventeenth century.
5. shifter] trickster.
8. Dodged with him] Dodged about in an attempt to catch him. According to *OED* this is the first occurrence of 'dodge' in this sense. *the Bull*] The Bull Inn in Bishopsgate, Hobson's stopping-place in London.
14. chamberlain] An attendant at an inn in charge of the bedchambers.

39 Another on the Same

Date. Jan. 1631: see headnote to previous poem.
Publication. An incomplete version was printed in *A Banquet of Jests* (1640, reprinted 1657). *1645* (*4.* on]on, *8.* time:]time; *16.* quickened,] quickn'd;). *Wit Restor'd* (1658), a garbled version. *1673* (the text followed here). There is no evidence to connect the printings of 1640, 1657 or 1658 with M. W.R.Parker discusses the textual variants of 1640 and 1658, *MLR* xxxi (1936) 395–402, and suggests that a third Hobson poem which appears in these miscellanies–'Hobson lies here amongst his many betters ...' (Columbia xviii 359, 590–1)–may be by M.

Here lieth one who did most truly prove,
That he could never die while he could move,
So hung his destiny never to rot
While he might still jog on and keep his trot,
Made of sphere-metal, never to decay
Until his revolution was at stay.
Time numbers motion, yet (without a crime
'Gainst old truth) motion numbered out his time:
And like an engine moved with wheel and weight,
His principles being ceased, he ended straight,
Rest that gives all men life, gave him his death,
And too much breathing put him out of breath;
Nor were it contradiction to affirm
Too long vacation hastened on his term.
Merely to drive the time away he sickened,
Fainted, and died, nor would with ale be quickened,
Nay, quoth he, on his swooning bed outstretched,
If I may not carry, sure I'll ne'er be fetched,
But vow though the cross doctors all stood hearers,

¶ 39. *5. sphere-metal*] Aristotle discusses the indestructibility of the substance of which the spheres of the universe are made in *De Coelo* I iii.
7. Time numbers motion] Aristotle calls time the 'number of motion' in *Physics* iv 11–12, and M. quotes from this discussion of the inter-dependence of time and motion in *De doctrina* I xiii (Columbia xv 240).
10. principles] motive forces.
12. breathing] respite.
14. vacation ... term] M. plays on two meanings of 'term': 'University Term', 'limit in time' (i.e. death). There is a similar pun on 'vacation' in the University sense, and in the sense 'freedom from work'.
18. carry ... fetched] A play on the phrase 'fetch and carry', and the seventeenth-century sense of 'fetch', 'to restore to consciousness'.
19. cross doctors] The Doctors of the University who are opposing (*OED* Cross, *a.* 5. a) Hobson's journeys to and fro.

For one carrier put down to make six bearers.
Ease was his chief disease, and to judge right,
He died for heaviness that his cart went light,
His leisure told him that his time was come,
And lack of load, made his life burdensome,
That even to his last breath (there be that say't)
As he were pressed to death, he cried more weight;
But had his doings lasted as they were,
He had been an immortal carrier.
Obedient to the moon he spent his date
In course reciprocal, and had his fate
Linked to the mutual flowing of the seas,
Yet (strange to think) his wain was his increase:
His letters are delivered all and gone,
Only remains this superscription.

40 An Epitaph on the Marchioness of Winchester

Date. Apr.-May 1631. Jane Savage, who had married Lord John St John Paulet, fifth Marquis of Winchester in 1622, died 15 Apr. 1631. Both she and her husband were Roman Catholics. Sir John Pory wrote to Sir Thomas Puckering that she 'had an impostume upon her cheek lanced; the humour fell down into her throat, and quickly despatched her', adding that her death was lamented 'as well in respect of other her virtues, as that she was inclining to become a Protestant' (*Court and Times of Charles I*, ed. T.

20. *put down*] brought into disuse. *bearers*] of coffin.
22. *heaviness*] sadness.
26. *pressed to death*] Cp. *Harrison's Description of England*, ed. F. J. Furnivall (1876) p. 228: 'Such fellons as stand mute, and speake not at their arraignment, are pressed to death by huge weights [laid upon a boord, that lieth over their brest, and a sharpe stone under their backs] and these commonlie hold their peace, thereby to save their goods unto their wives and children, which, if they were condemned, should be confiscated to the prince.' *cried*] implored.
30. *In course reciprocal*] He went backwards and forwards between London and Cambridge as regularly as the ebbing and flowing of the tide.
32. *wain*] Play on 'wain' meaning 'waggon' and 'wane' meaning 'decrease'.
34. *superscription*] Play on two senses of the word – 'the address on a letter' and 'an inscription above a grave'.

Birch (1894) ii 106). No personal connection between M. and the Paulets is known: probably the poem was intended as a contribution to a proposed volume of Cambridge elegies. Numerous poems on Jane's death survive, including elegies by Jonson, Davenant and Strode, and several in BM MS Sloane 1446, which also contains (37v.–38) a version of M.'s elegy which substitutes for *15–24*: 'Seven times had the yearly star / In every sign set up his car, / Since for her they did request / The god that sits at marriage feast, / When first the early Matrons run / To greet her of her lovely son.' W. R. Parker, *MLR* (1949) 547–50, points out that these lines contain one accurate piece of biographical information not in the published version, and suggests that they represent an authentic early draft which was allowed to circulate.

Publication. 1645 (*52.* lease;]lease, *53.* Here,]Here). *1673* (the text followed here, except in *61* where *1673* misprints a full stop after 'glory').

Modern criticism. Sprott 16–20 argues, on metrical grounds, that the first half of *L'Allegro* may have been written earlier; A. Oras, *N & Q* cxcviii (1953) 332–3, opposes this view. M. F. Moloney, *MLN* lxxii (1957) 174–8, traces M.'s handling of the octosyllabic here to the 'funerary art of Jonson, made familiar by the Folio of 1616'.

This rich marble doth inter
The honoured wife of Winchester,
A viscount's daughter, an earl's heir,
Besides what her virtues fair
Added to her noble birth,
More than she could own from earth.
Summers three times eight save one
She had told, alas too soon,
After so short time of breath,
To house with darkness, and with death.
Yet had the number of her days
Been as complete as was her praise,
Nature and fate had had no strife
In giving limit to her life.
Her high birth, and her graces sweet,
Quickly found a lover meet;
The virgin choir for her request
The god that sits at marriage-feast;
He at their invoking came
But with a scarce-well-lighted flame;

¶ 40. *11–14.* I.e. if she had enjoyed as full a measure of life as she has of praise, her death would be perfectly natural.

17. virgin choir] bridesmaids. *request*] invoke.

18. god] Hymen.

20. In Ovid, *Met.* x 6–7, Hymen appears at another ill-fated marriage,

And in his garland as he stood,
Ye might discern a cypress bud.
Once had the early matrons run
To greet her of a lovely son,
And now with second hope she goes,
And calls Lucina to her throes;
But whether by mischance or blame
Atropos for Lucina came;
And with remorseless cruelty,
Spoiled at once both fruit and tree:
The hapless babe before his birth
Had burial, yet not laid in earth,
And the languished mother's womb
Was not long a living tomb.
So have I seen some tender slip
Saved with care from winter's nip,
The pride of her carnation train,
Plucked up by some unheedy swain,
Who only thought to crop the flower
New shot up from vernal shower;
But the fair blossom hangs the head
Sideways as on a dying bed,

that of Orpheus and Eurydice, with a spluttering and smoky torch that will not catch fire properly.

22. *cypress*] Called 'funeral' by Virgil, *Aen.* vi 216, and by Horace, *Epod.* v 18; the tree of mourning in Elizabethan poetry.

23. *early matrons*] midwives.

24. *greet her of*] M. seems to be using 'greet' in a sense otherwise peculiar to Spenser, 'offer congratulations upon'. But Spenser does not use this verb with the preposition 'of' (here equivalent to 'on account of').

24. *son*] Charles, born 1629, created first Duke of Bolton, 1689.

26. *Lucina*] Roman goddess of childbirth.

28. *Atropos*] One of the Parcae, whose function it was to cut the thread of life.

31. Jane, as the Duchess of Buckingham informed her father in a letter written 16 Apr. 1631, 'was delivered before shee died of a deed boye' (*Rutland MSS*, Hist. MSS Com., 12th report, part iv (1888) i 490).

33. *languished*] reduced to languor. Browne i 190 rhymes 'mother's womb' and 'living tomb', and Sylvester (Du Bartas 616) also rhymes 'womb' and 'living Toomb'.

35. *slip*] A cutting taken from a plant. In M.'s simile Jane is this precious cutting which has survived winter (twenty-three years of life) but is plucked by death (the 'swain'), who meant to take only the baby ('the flower / New shot up').

37. *her carnation train*] her retinue of carnations (clove-pinks).

And those pearls of dew she wears,
Prove to be presaging tears
Which the sad morn had let fall
On her hastening funeral.
Gentle lady may thy grave
Peace and quiet ever have;
After this thy travail sore
Sweet rest seize thee evermore,
That to give the world increase,
Shortened hast thy own life's lease;
Here, besides the sorrowing
That thy noble house doth bring,
Here be tears of perfect moan
Wept for thee in Helicon,
And some flowers, and some bays,
For thy hearse to strew the ways,
Sent thee from the banks of Came,
Devoted to thy virtuous name;
Whilst thou bright saint high sit'st in glory,
Next her much like to thee in story,
That fair Syrian shepherdess,
Who after years of barrenness,
The highly favoured Joseph bore
To him that served for her before,
And at her next birth much like thee,
Through pangs fled to felicity,
Far within the bosom bright
Of blazing majesty and light,
There with thee, new welcome saint,
Like fortunes may her soul acquaint,
With thee there clad in radiant sheen,
No marchioness, but now a queen.

56. *Helicon*] A mountain in Boeotia, sacred to the Muses.

59. *Came*] The river Cam, which flows through Cambridge.

63. *shepherdess*] Rachel, Jacob's wife; cp. *Gen.* xxix 9: 'Rachel came with her father's sheep: for she kept them.' *fair*] Cp. *Gen.* xxix 17: 'Rachel was beautiful and well-favoured'.

65. *bore*] Cp. *Gen.* xxx 22–4.

66. *him*] Jacob; cp. *Gen.* xxix 20: 'And Jacob served seven years for Rachel.'

68. *pangs*] Cp. *Gen.* xxxv 17–18: 'She was in hard labour.' Rachel's son lived and 'as her soul was in departing' she called him Ben-oni.

41 L'Allegro

Date. Summer 1631? There is no certain evidence for dating *L'Allegro* or *Il Penseroso*. Bateson 155 would place them in the late summer of 1629, and Fletcher ii 480–3 agrees, but Bateson's argument rests on a questionable interpretation of *Elegia VI* 89–90 (see note to these lines). Tillyard[2] 1–28 contends that the twin poems grew out of the debate about night and day in M.'s first *Prolusion*, and were written for an academic audience at Cambridge in M.'s last long vacation (1631), thus the opening of *L'Allegro* is academic burlesque (a view opposed by Whiting (136–41) who favours a dating in the Horton period). The absence of the poems from the Trinity MS is usually taken to indicate a date earlier than Horton, though Grierson i xix points out that the art of the two poems is akin to that of the descriptive passages in *Comus*, than which they may therefore be later. The various attempts to locate the poems' scenery in Cambridge, Horton, Stanton St John or near London are all suspect (see, for example, A. H. J. Baines, *N & Q* clxxxviii (1945) 68–71, who recognizes it as that of the Chiltern summits, about two hours' ride from Horton). Rather more trustworthy is A. Oras's argument that the prosody is later than that of the *Winchester Epitaph* (*N & Q* cxcviii (1953) 332–3).

Publication. *1645* (*33.* you]ye *53.* horn]horn, *62.* dight,]dight. *104.* And by the]And he by *108.* corn,]corn *122.* prize,]prize), *1673* (the text followed here, except in *3*, where *1673* misprints a full stop after 'forlorn' (see note), in *18*, where it misprints a full stop after 'spring', and in *124*, where it misprints a comma after 'commend').

Metre and style. *L'Allegro* and *Il Penseroso* are metrically almost identical. No precedent has been found in English for such a combination of intricate prelude with couplet continuation. Each poem begins with a prelude of ten lines rhyming *abbacddeec*, with the number of syllables per line, excluding feminine endings, alternately six and ten. This 6/10 pattern of line-lengths presumably derives from the seven and eleven syllable lines of the *canzone*, just as the rhyme scheme reflects the Italian sonnet. See also Fletcher, below. From line *11* onwards both poems are in nominal octosyllabic (iambic) couplets, but vividly diversified with frequent trochaic (seven-syllable) lines (32 per cent of the lines in *L'Allegro* and 16 per cent in *Il Penseroso*) occurring indiscriminately among the octosyllables, which are themselves sometimes trochaic (e.g. *L'Allegro 19–20, 69–70*) and have a scattering of extrametrical final syllables (e.g. *L'Allegro 46, 85–6, 141–2*; *Il Penseroso 21–2, 48–9*). Sprott has noticed that the percentage of catalectic lines in *L'Allegro 11–100* inclusive is 50, but in *101–152* it is only 15.4, and in *Il Penseroso* 16.9. This change in prosody may, he conjectures, mean that M.

Title. John Florio's *Dictionary* (1598) defines *Allegro* as 'joyfull, merie, jocond, sportfull, pleasant, frolike'.

wrote the first two-thirds of *L'Allegro* at an earlier period than the rest of the poem and *Il Penseroso*. He may be right, but the accelerated pace of the catalectic lines is more evidently suited to the subject matter of *L'Allegro*'s daylight scenes than to any others in the two poems, and this seems a likelier explanation for the change.

Stylistically, as the footnotes demonstrate, the principal model in *L'Allegro* is Shakespeare (fourteen echoes, four from *A Midsummer Night's Dream*, eight of the others from the early plays). Spenser and the Spenserians come next in importance (twelve instances, five from Sylvester). The long sentences differentiate the couplets from those of Jonson and his 'sons'. *Il Penseroso* has noticeably fewer literary echoes than *L'Allegro*, Shakespeare contributing only five (three from *Romeo and Juliet*, but none from *A Midsummer Night's Dream*), and Sylvester three. In both poems there are only two or three echoes of classical poetry, in spite of the parade of mythological figures.

Modern criticism. J. B. Leishman, *E & S* n.s. iv (1951) 1–36, thinks that the starting-point for *L'Allegro* and *Il Penseroso* was the song, perhaps by Strode, in Fletcher's *The Nice Valour* ('Hence, all you vain delights ...'), and Strode's reply to it. This suggestion was originally made by Seward (see Beaumont and Fletcher, *Works* (1750) x 336). Leishman also examines the relationship, first indicated by Warton 94, between the twin poems and *The Author's Abstract of Melancholy* prefixed to the third edition of Burton's *Anatomy* (1628). Connections with the *Anatomy* itself are explored by Whiting 136–41 and W. J. Grace, *SP* lii (1955) 578–83. F. M. Padelford, *MLN* xxii (1907) 200, proposes as source for the morning-scene in *L'Allegro* the anonymous narrative lyric 'The sun when he had spread his rays ...', printed in the second edition of Tottel's *Miscellany*. Another possible source for *L'Allegro*, pointed out by Warton (40) and supported by S. Foster Damon, *PMLA* xlii (1927) 873–4, is Marston's *Scourge of Villainy* (*Proëmium in librum primum* 9–11 and xi 3–8). N. C. Carpenter, *N & Q* cci (1956) 289–92, argues that M. was influenced in the musical passages of both poems by Spenser's *Epithalamion*.

L. Babb, *SP* xxxvii (1940) 257–73, distinguishes between two opposed Renaissance attitudes to melancholy: the first, originating in Galenic medicine, viewed it as a source of stupidity, fearfulness and illusions; the second, originating in Aristotle's *Problemata* xxx 1, and adopted by Ficino in *De Studiosorum Sanitate Tuenda*, stressed that all who have become eminent in philosophy, poetry or the arts have been of melancholy temperament. At the beginning of *L'Allegro* M. exorcises the Galenic melancholy: in *Il Penseroso* he celebrates the Aristotelian. Babb's explanation is supplemented by I. Samuel, *N & Q* cciii (1958) 430–1, who traces the distinction between a 'divine' and a 'damned' melancholy through Erasmus' *Encomium Moriae* to Socrates' division of righthanded from lefthanded madness in the *Phaedrus*.

Allen 3–23 distinguishes between *L'Allegro*, which represents 'common experience', and *Il Penseroso*, which represents 'intellectual experience':

the poet must graduate from one to the other, and thus the two poems are the 'rising steps' of M.'s poetic plans. Similarly D. C. Dorian, *MP* xxxi (1933) 175–8, regarded the poems as the 'autobiographical record of an important step in M.'s development–his consideration of the question whether he should suppress either the lighter or the more serious side of his nature, as man and as poet, for the fuller development of the other'. F. M. Darnall, *MLN* xxxi (1916) 56–8, had previously suggested that the poems grew out of the contrast, as M. saw it, between Diodati and himself, and that this might explain the Italian titles. (Darnall's theory is attacked by A. Thaler, *MLN* xxxi (1916) 437–8, and reasserted, *MLN* xxxii (1917) 377–9.)

Cleanth Brooks, in his examination of the light imagery (Brooks and Hardy 131–44), demonstrates that both poems are dominated by half-light, and that this similarity tends to bring the 'patterns of opposites' together. The progressive emphasis, in both poems, on images of sound and music, culminating in the Anglican ritual at the end of *Il Penseroso*, is traced by K. Svendsen, *Explicator* viii (1950) 49.

S. R. Watson, *PMLA* lvii (1942) 404–20, takes the poems as representations of the 'ideal day' theme, traceable from Theocritus, through Horace, *Epod.* ii, to Drayton and the Spenserians. The central personifications of Mirth and Melancholy, as they had figured in the literary environment of the sixteenth and seventeenth centuries, are discussed by Tuve[2] (15–36), who utilizes some of the valuable information about the neo-Platonic theories of melancholy contained in Erwin Panofsky's *Albrecht Dürer* (Princeton 1943) i 157–71.

R. M. Lumiansky, *MLN* lv (1940) 591–4, draws attention to the predominance of the native element in M.'s vocabulary in the poems, and Fletcher ii 485–9 gives reasons for thinking that their versification was influenced by Italian models.

Hence loathed Melancholy
    Of Cerberus, and blackest Midnight born,
In Stygian cave forlorn
    'Mongst horrid shapes, and shrieks, and sights unholy,
Find out some uncouth cell,
    Where brooding Darkness spreads his jealous wings,

¶ 41. *3. cave*] Cerberus' cave on the bank of the Styx is mentioned by Virgil, *Aen.* vi 418. The mythological parentage is M.'s invention, (cp. *Q Nov* 69*n*, p. 39 above.) The 'shrieks' of l. 4 are heard by Aeneas as he passes the cave (vi 426–7) and come from the souls of dead children. They connect ll. 3 and 4, and so call for an emendation of the *1673* full stop after 'forlorn'.
5. uncouth] unfrequented, desolate.

And the night-raven sings;
  There under ebon shades, and low-browed
    rocks,
As ragged as thy locks,
  In dark Cimmerian desert ever dwell.
But come thou goddess fair and free,
In heaven yclept Euphrosyne,
And by men, heart-easing Mirth,
Whom lovely Venus at a birth
With two sister Graces more
To ivy-crowned Bacchus bore;
Or whether (as some sager sing)
The frolic wind that breathes the spring,
Zephyr with Aurora playing,
As he met her once a-Maying,
There on beds of violets blue,
And fresh-blown roses washed in dew,
Filled her with thee a daughter fair,
So buxom, blithe, and debonair.
Haste thee nymph, and bring with thee

7. *night-raven*] The name given, from Anglo-Saxon times on, to a bird heard to croak or cry in the night and supposedly of evil omen: probably an owl or night-heron.
9. *ragged*] The word occurs nowhere else in M.'s poetry. Cp. *Isa.* ii 21, 'ragged rocks', and *Titus Andronicus* II iii 230: 'the ragged entrails of the pit'.
10. *Cimmerian*] See Q *Nov* 60n (p. 39).
11. *fair and free*] A common formula, found in Drayton, *Eclogue* iv 127 and Sylvester (Du Bartas 17).
12. *yclept*] A Spenserian form (*F.Q.* III v 8) not found elsewhere in M's. poetry. *Euphrosyne*] Mirth, whose sisters were Aglaia (Brightness) and Thalia (Bloom). Servius, in his note to *Aen.* i 720, records the tradition which makes Venus and Bacchus parents of the Graces: they were usually considered to be daughters of Zeus and Hera or Eurynome.
16. *ivy-crowned*] See *Elegia VI* 15–16n, p. 114 above.
17. *as some sager sing*] M. seems to have invented this parentage. Aurora appears as companion of Zephyrus in Jonson's *Entertainment at Highgate*, and their song (93–4) has M.'s rhymes, 'a-Maying' and 'playing'.
22. Echoing *Taming of the Shrew* II i 174: 'morning roses newly wash'd with dew'.
24. J. B. Leishman, *E & S* n.s. iv (1951) 30 shows that these three adjectives were habitually connected in the early seventeenth century, and follows Todd v 77 in quoting Randolph's *Aristippus* (1630) 'blithe, buxome and deboneer'. *buxom*] yielding, compliant. *debonair*] of gentle disposition.

Jest and youthful Jollity,
Quips and cranks, and wanton wiles,
Nods, and becks, and wreathed smiles,
Such as hang on Hebe's cheek,
And love to live in dimple sleek;
Sport that wrinkled Care derides,
And Laughter holding both his sides.
Come, and trip it as you go
On the light fantastic toe,
And in thy right hand lead with thee,
The mountain nymph, sweet Liberty;
And if I give thee honour due,
Mirth, admit me of thy crew
To live with her, and live with thee,
In unreproved pleasures free;
To hear the lark begin his flight,
And singing startle the dull night,
From his watch-tower in the skies,
Till the dappled dawn doth rise;
Then to come in spite of sorrow,

27. *Quips*] smart or witty sayings. *cranks*] jokes which depend upon twisting or changing the form or meaning of a word.

28. *becks*] P. B. Tillyard, *TLS* (25 Jul. 1952) 485 draws attention to Burton's translation (III ii 2 iv) of *nutibus* ('with nods') in a passage from Musaeus as 'With becks and nods and smiles', and deduces that, though *OED* interprets M.'s 'becks' here as 'gestures expressive of salutation or respect', they are in fact upward nods–'coming-on' gestures. E. B. C. Jones, *TLS* (8 Aug. 1952) 517, agrees.

29. *Hebe's*] Cp. *Vacation Exercise* 38*n* (p. 77).

31–2. S. R. Watson, *N & Q* clxxx (1941) 258, anticipated by Warton (46) compares Fletcher's *Purple Island* iv 13: 'Sportful laughter . . . Defies . . . wrinkled care.'

33. *trip it*] Echoes *Tempest* IV i 46: 'Each one tripping on his toe.'

34. *fantastic*] According to *OED* M. is here using this word in a new sense: 'making fantastic or extravagantly conceived movements'; cp. Drayton, *Nimphidia* 29, 'light fantastick mayde'.

36. *mountain nymph*] Oread. In associating Liberty with mountainous districts M. may be referring to Greece, Switzerland or Calvin's Geneva, which lies between the Jura and the Alps.

42. *dull night*] Probably echoes *Henry V* IV Prologue 11: 'Piercing the night's dull ear.'

44. *dappled*] Echoes *Much Ado* V iii 25–7: 'the gentle day . . . Dapple the drowsy east with spots of grey'.

45–6. There has been some argument whether it is L'Allegro or the lark that comes to the window and bids good morrow. Adherents of the latter

And at my window bid good morrow,
Through the sweet-briar, or the vine,
Or the twisted eglantine.
While the cock with lively din,
Scatters the rear of darkness thin,
And to the stack, or the barn door,
Stoutly struts his dames before,
Oft list'ning how the hounds and horn
Cheerly rouse the slumb'ring morn,
From the side of some hoar hill,
Through the high wood echoing shrill.
Sometime walking not unseen
By hedgerow elms, on hillocks green,
Right against the eastern gate,
Where the great sun begins his state,
Robed in flames, and amber light,
The clouds in thousand liveries dight,
While the ploughman near at hand,
Whistles o'er the furrowed land,
And the milkmaid singeth blithe,

quote Sylvester (Du Bartas 87) 'cheerfull Birds, chirping him sweet *Good-morrows*, / With Natures Musick do beguile his sorrows', but grammar and the habits of larks make decisively for the former, as B. A. Wright argues, *TLS* (8 Nov. 1934) 775, supported by E. M. W. Tillyard, *TLS* (15 Nov. 1934) 795, and by J. L. Brereton, *MLN* xli (1926) 533, who refers to the custom of bidding good-morrow to the sun, common in Elizabethan and Jacobean drama (see *Cymbeline* III iii 7 and *Volpone* I i 1).

47–8. Sweet-briar and eglantine are names for the same plant (a species of *Rosa rubiginosa*); 'twisted' suggests M. thought eglantine a plant that climbs by its twining stem, like honeysuckle (which, it has been conjectured, he really meant). G. G. Loane, *N & Q* clxxvi (1939) 225, thinks M. was misled by Spenser, *F.Q.* III vi 44 where ivy, caprifole (honeysuckle) and eglantine are combined. But C. A. Knapp, *N & Q* clxxvi (1939) 276, insists that since 'eglantine' derives from Latin *aculentus* ('prickly') M. must have known it was a plant with thorns.

52. Cp. the peacock in Sylvester (Du Bartas 96) 'To woo his Mistress, strowting stately by her.'

55. hoar] H. H. Hoeltje, *PMLA* xlv (1930) 201–3, points out that in seventeenth century England hunting was common in the summer and that 'hoar' has no connection with hoar frost here but is used to designate colour, referring to the mist-covered hills of a dewy summer morning.

59. Echoes *Midsummer Night's Dream* III ii 391: 'the eastern gate, all fiery-red', in Oberon's description of sunrise.

60. state] stately progress.

62. dight] arrayed.

And the mower whets his scythe,
And every shepherd tells his tale
Under the hawthorn in the dale.
Straight mine eye hath caught new pleasures
Whilst the landscape round it measures,
Russet lawns, and fallows grey,
Where the nibbling flocks do stray,
Mountains on whose barren breast
The labouring clouds do often rest:
Meadows trim with daisies pied,
Shallow brooks, and rivers wide.
Towers, and battlements it sees
Bosomed high in tufted trees,
Where perhaps some beauty lies,
The cynosure of neighbouring eyes.
Hard by, a cottage chimney smokes,
From betwixt two aged oaks,
Where Corydon and Thyrsis met,

67. tells his tale] The argument about whether this means 'counts the tally of his sheep' or 'tells his story (of love)' goes back to Warton and beyond. The former seems more likely in a catalogue of early-morning phenomena, but J. W. Rankin, *MLN* xxvii (1912) 230, argues that in *Nativity Ode* 85–92 the shepherds in the early morning are 'simply chatting'. J. M. Hart, *MLN* xxviii (1913) 159–60, replies that the shepherds are abnormal there because biblical. Cp. *III Henry VI* II v 42–3: 'Gives not the hawthorn-bush a sweeter shade / To shepherds looking on their silly sheep.'
71–2. Bateson 159 calls this couplet 'a masterpiece of concentrated observation. The sheep have broken through the temporary fence round the parish's fallow field, no doubt because the common pastures are "russet", the short-rooted grass having been "burned", as farmers say, in the hot dry weather. "Russet" is decidedly not the epithet one would have expected for "lawns" . . . nor is "grey" what one would have expected for "fallows". M. must have had his eye on a real field. Most fallows after the summer ploughing are brown, but this field, perhaps because the subsoil was chalk, was grey.'
72. nibbling] Cp. *Tempest* IV i 62: 'nibbling sheep'.
73–4. The 'barren' mountains are contrasted with the 'labouring' clouds (bringing forth rain), cp. *Passion* 56*n* (p. 122).
75. pied] variegated, echoing *Love's Labour's Lost* V ii 882: 'daisies pied'.
78. tufted] Sylvester uses the same adjective to describe plane trees (Du Bartas 555).
80. cynosure] The constellation of the Lesser Bear, containing the Pole Star, hence, as here, an object of special attention.
83–8. The names M. chooses for his rustics are common in Renaissance pastoral.

Are at their savoury dinner set
Of herbs, and other country messes,
Which the neat-handed Phillis dresses;
And then in haste her bower she leaves,
With Thestylis to bind the sheaves;
Or if the earlier season lead
To the tanned haycock in the mead,
Sometimes with secure delight
The upland hamlets will invite,
When the merry bells ring round,
And the jocund rebecks sound
To many a youth, and many a maid,
Dancing in the chequered shade;
And young and old come forth to play
On a sunshine holiday,
Till the livelong daylight fail,
Then to the spicy nut-brown ale,
With stories told of many a feat,
How Faëry Mab the junkets eat,
She was pinched, and pulled she said,
And by the friar's lantern led
Tells how the drudging goblin sweat,

85. Sylvester also rhymes 'messes' and 'dresses' (Du Bartas 218).

91. secure] carefree (the Latin meaning).

94. rebecks] fiddles.

96. chequered shade] Echoes *Titus Andronicus* II iii 14–15: 'The green leaves . . . make a chequer'd shadow on the ground.'

102. Mab] The subject of Mercutio's famous speech (*Romeo and Juliet* I iv 54–95); her fondness for 'junkets' (i.e. cream cheeses, or other preparations of cream) may be deduced from Jonson, *Entertainment at Althorp* 47, 53–4 where she runs 'about the creame-bowles sweet' and 'doth nightly rob the dayrie'.

103. It is Mab in Jonson's *Entertainment at Althorp* 58–9 'that pinches countrey wenches, / If they rub not cleane their benches', and this habit of fairies is noted both by Drayton, *Nimphidia* 65–6, and Browne i 61.

104. friar's] Perhaps a reference to the house-spirit Friar Rush, but M. is probably influenced by the apparent identification of 'Robin good-fellow' and 'the Frier' in Samuel Harsnet's *Declaration of Popish Impostures* 134, where the 'bowle of curds, & creame' is 'duly set' as in l. 106. Robin Goodfellow tells how he leads travellers astray disguised as a fire in *Midsummer Night's Dream* III i 11–12.

105. drudging goblin] Robin Goodfellow is called 'Hobgoblin' in *Midsummer Night's Dream* II i 40, and in Jonson's *Love Restored* 58–9 he 'riddles for the countrey maides, and does all their other drudgerie'.

To earn his cream-bowl duly set,
When in one night, ere glimpse of morn,
His shadowy flail hath threshed the corn,
That ten day-labourers could not end;
Then lies him down the lubber fiend.
And stretched out all the chimney's length,
Basks at the fire his hairy strength;
And crop-full out of doors he flings,
Ere the first cock his matin rings.
Thus done the tales, to bed they creep,
By whispering winds soon lulled asleep.
Towered cities please us then,
And the busy hum of men,
Where throngs of knights and barons bold,
In weeds of peace high triumphs hold,
With store of ladies, whose bright eyes
Rain influence, and judge the prize,
Of wit, or arms, while both contend
To win her grace, whom all commend.
There let Hymen oft appear
In saffron robe, with taper clear,
And pomp, and feast, and revelry,
With mask, and antique pageantry,
Such sights as youthful poets dream
On summer eves by haunted stream.
Then to the well-trod stage anon,
If Jonson's learned sock be on,
Or sweetest Shakespeare fancy's child,
Warble his native wood-notes wild,
And ever against eating cares,

106. *cream-bowl*] Cp. Burton I ii 1 ii: 'Hobgoblins, and Robin Goodfellows that would . . . grind corn for a mess of milk, cut wood, or do any manner of drudgery work.'

110. *lubber*] Robin Goodfellow is called 'lob of spirits' in *Midsummer Night's Dream* II i 16.

111. *chimney*] fireplace.

120. Echoing *Troilus and Cressida* III iii 239: 'great Hector in his weeds of peace'.

122. *Rain influence*] The eyes are star-like; 'influence' in astrology was the flowing from the stars of an etherial fluid which affected the destiny of men.

132. *sock*] low-heeled slipper, mark of the comic actor on the Greek and Roman stage. The tragic actor wore buskins.

133. *fancy's child*] Echoes *Love's Labour's Lost* I i 171: 'child of fancy.'

135. *eating cares*] A translation of Horace, *Odes* II xi 18: *curas edaces.*

Lap me in soft Lydian airs,
Married to immortal verse
Such as the meeting soul may pierce
In notes, with many a winding bout
Of linked sweetness long drawn out,
With wanton heed, and giddy cunning,
The melting voice through mazes running;
Untwisting all the chains that tie
The hidden soul of harmony.
That Orpheus' self may heave his head
From golden slumber on a bed
Of heaped Elysian flowers, and hear
Such strains as would have won the ear
Of Pluto, to have quite set free
His half-regained Eurydice.
These delights, if thou canst give,
Mirth with thee, I mean to live.

42 Il Penseroso

Date. Summer 1631? See headnote to previous poem.
Publication. *1645* (*21.* offended,]offended. *170.* spell]spell,), *1673* (the text

136. Lydian airs] Plato, *Republic* iii 398–9, condemns the 'lax' Lydian mode, though as James Hutton points out, *EM* ii (1951) 45–6, Cassiodorus, in his letter to Boethius (*Variae* ii 40), speaks of it approvingly as providing 'relaxation and delight, being invented against excessive cares and worries'. Plato's attitude survived in the English Renaissance, e.g. Guilpin, *Skialetheia* Satyre Preludium 1–2: 'Fie on these *Lydian* tunes which blunt our sprights / And turne our gallants to *Hermaphrodites*.'
139. bout] circuit, orbit. Nan C. Carpenter, *UTQ* xxii (1953) 354–67, suggests that in ll. 139–44 M. has in mind the Italian aria as it was developing in the early seventeenth century. She points out that his father associated for some years with a London colony of Italian musicians, headed by Ferrabosco and Coperario.
145–50. Virgil, *Georg.* iv 453–527 and Ovid, *Met.* x 11–63 both have the story. Virgil's is the earliest surviving version in which Orpheus looks back at his wife as he is leading her from the underworld and loses her. See C. M. Bowra, *CQ* new ser. ii (1952) 113–22.
146. Cp. Dekker, *Patient Grissil* IV ii 99: 'Golden slumbers kisse your eyes.'
151–2. Echoing the conclusion of Marlowe's popular lyric ('Come live with me and be my love'): 'If these delights thy mind may move, / Then live with me, and be my love.'
Title. M.'s *Penseroso* ('pensive') is not the modern spelling, but W. H. David, *N & Q* 7th ser. viii (1889) 326, justifies it by reference to a French-Italian dictionary published by Chouet at Geneva in 1644.

followed here, except in *49*, where *1673* misprints a semi-colon after 'Leisure', and in *81*, *88*, *143* and *156*, where it misprints full stops after 'mirth', 'unsphere', 'sing' and 'pale').

For modern criticism see headnote to previous poem.

Hence vain deluding Joys,
The brood of Folly without father bred,
How little you bestead,
Or fill the fixed mind with all your toys;
Dwell in some idle brain,
And fancies fond with gaudy shapes possess,
As thick and numberless
As the gay motes that people the sunbeams,
Or likest hovering dreams
The fickle pensioners of Morpheus' train.
But hail thou goddess, sage and holy,
Hail divinest Melancholy,
Whose saintly visage is too bright
To hit the sense of human sight;
And therefore to our weaker view,
O'erlaid with black staid wisdom's hue.
Black, but such as in esteem,
Prince Memnon's sister might beseem,

¶ 42. *1–2.* Perhaps an echo of Sylvester (Du Bartas[2] 1084): 'Hence, hence false Pleasures, momentary Joyes; / Mock us no more with your illuding Toyes.'

2. brood of Folly] The same phrase occurs in Jonson, *Love Freed from Ignorance* 274.

3. bestead] help.

6–10. Cp. Sylvester's description of the Cave of Sleep (Du Bartas 396) where Morpheus sleeps and 'fantastick', 'gawdy' swarms of dreams hover like 'Th' unnumbred Moats which in the Sun do play'.

10. pensioners] members of royal bodyguard. *Morpheus*] son of Sleep and god of dreams.

14. hit] suit, fit.

16. black] Melancholy is black bile, and the type of melancholy caused by the influence of Saturn (l. 24) was traditionally associated with a black face as Z. S. Fink, *PQ* xix (1940) 309–13, points out, referring to the same idea in Burton I iii 1 iii and I iii 2 iii.

18. Memnon's sister] called Himera by Dictys Cretensis, *Ephemeris Belli Troiani* vi, as E. Venables, *N & Q* 8th ser. i (1892) 149–50, notes. M. Day, *MLR* xii (1917) 496–7, adds that her beauty is commented on by Guido delle Colonne, *Historia Destructionis Troiae* viii.

Or that starred Ethiop queen that strove
To set her beauty's praise above
The sea-nymphs, and their powers offended,
Yet thou art higher far descended,
Thee bright-haired Vesta long of yore,
To solitary Saturn bore;
His daughter she (in Saturn's reign,
Such mixture was not held a stain)
Oft in glimmering bowers, and glades
He met her, and in secret shades
Of woody Ida's inmost grove,
Whilst yet there was no fear of Jove.
Come pensive nun, devout and pure,
Sober, steadfast, and demure,
All in a robe of darkest grain,
Flowing with majestic train,
And sable stole of cypress lawn,
Over thy decent shoulders drawn.
Come, but keep thy wonted state,
With even step, and musing gait,
And looks commercing with the skies,
Thy rapt soul sitting in thine eyes:
There held in holy passion still,
Forget thyself to marble, till
With a sad leaden downward cast,

19. queen] Cassiopea who, as Hyginus, *Astronomica* II x records, was changed into a constellation because she claimed to be more beautiful than the Nereids. D. T. Starnes (Taylor[2] 44–5) points out that Hyginus' account of the matter, as opposed to the more usual classical version which makes her boast not her own beauty but that of her daughter Andromeda, is given in Conti and in Stephanus.

23. Vesta's motherhood is M.'s invention: she was virgin daughter of Saturn, goddess of flocks and herds and of the household; cp. Hesiod, *Theog.* 454.

25–6. It was common for both classical and Renaissance authors to present the Golden Age, when Saturn reigned on Mount Ida, as a time of sexual licence. See Propertius III xiii 25–46, Tibullus II iii 69–74.

33. grain] dye.

35. cypress] dark, gloomy. See *Winchester Epitaph* 22n, p. 128 above. *lawn*] fine linen.

42. Cp. *Shakespeare* 14 (p. 123). A possible source for both is Thomas Tomkins's *Albumazar* I iv 4: 'Marvel thyself to Marble.' The idea originates in the Niobe legend, employed in an epitaph by Browne ii 294: 'Some kind woman . . . / Reading this, like Niobe / Shall turn marble, and become / Both her mourner and her tomb.'

43. sad] serious.

Thou fix them on the earth as fast.
And join with thee calm Peace, and Quiet,
Spare Fast, that oft with gods doth diet,
And hears the Muses in a ring,
Ay round about Jove's altar sing.
And add to these retired Leisure,
That in trim gardens takes his pleasure;
But first, and chiefest, with thee bring,
Him that yon soars on golden wing,
Guiding the fiery-wheeled throne,
The cherub Contemplation,
And the mute Silence hist along,
'Less Philomel will deign a song,
In her sweetest, saddest plight,
Smoothing the rugged brow of night,
While Cynthia checks her dragon yoke,
Gently o'er the accustomed oak;
Sweet bird that shunn'st the noise of folly,
Most musical, most melancholy!
Thee chauntress oft the woods among,
I woo to hear thy even-song;
And missing thee, I walk unseen
On the dry smooth-shaven green,
To behold the wandering moon,
Riding near her highest noon,
Like one that had been led astray
Through the heaven's wide pathless way;

47–8. M.'s second *Prolusion* (Columbia xii 154–5, Yale i 237) alludes to the dance of the Muses around Jove's altar, as described by Hesiod, *Theog.* 1–10.

53. See *Passion* 36–40*n* (p. 121).

54. cherub Contemplation] C. B. Mount, *N & Q* 7th ser. ii (1886) 323–4, notes that in the pseudo-Dionysian *Celestial Hierarchy* VII i 31–7 the cherubim are distinguished by their 'faculty of seeing God, and of contemplating the beauty of the Supreme Being'.

55. hist] First recorded occurrence of the word in the sense 'summon with the exclamation "hist!"'

56. Philomel] See *Sonnet I* headnote (p. 88).

57. plight] state of mind.

58. brow] Cp. *Romeo and Juliet* III ii 20: 'black-brow'd night'.

59. Cynthia] The moon. *dragon*] See *Prae E* 56–8*n* (p. 26).

62. Most musical] M. refers in the seventh *Prolusion* (Columbia xii 283, Yale i 303–4) to Aristotle, *Hist. Nat.* IV ix 536b, where the nightingale is said to teach her chicks music.

66. smooth-shaven] Echoes Sylvester (Du Bartas 539), 'new-shav'n Fields', which comes eight lines after a reference to the nightingale.

And oft, as if her head she bowed,
Stooping through a fleecy cloud.
Oft on a plat of rising ground,
I hear the far-off curfew sound,
Over some wide-watered shore,
Swinging slow with sullen roar;
Or if the air will not permit,
Some still removed place will fit,
Where glowing embers through the room
Teach light to counterfeit a gloom,
Far from all resort of mirth,
Save the cricket on the hearth,
Or the bellman's drowsy charm,
To bless the doors from nightly harm:
Or let my lamp at midnight hour,
Be seen in some high lonely tower,
Where I may oft outwatch the Bear,
With thrice great Hermes, or unsphere
The spirit of Plato to unfold
What worlds, or what vast regions hold
The immortal mind that hath forsook
Her mansion in this fleshly nook:
And of those demons that are found
In fire, air, flood, or under ground,
Whose power hath a true consent
With planet, or with element.
Sometime let gorgeous Tragedy
In sceptred pall come sweeping by,
Presenting Thebes, or Pelops' line,
Or the tale of Troy divine.
Or what (though rare) of later age,
Ennobled hath the buskined stage.

73. plat] plot.

76. sullen] Cp. *II Henry IV* I i 102: 'sullen bell'.

83–4. For an example of the kind of 'charm' recited by bellmen see Herrick 121 *The Bell-man.*

87. outwatch the Bear] the Bear, symbolizing perfection in Hermes (Allen 13), never sets. 'Outwatch' is first used in Jonson vii 709, by a melancholy student.

88. Hermes] See *Id Plat* 33*n*, p. 68 above.

93. demons] E. C. Baldwin, *MLN* xxxiii (1918) 184–5, points out that these element-inhabiting spirits are found in Hermes.

98. pall] robe. Pall (*palla*) and sceptre occur in Ovid's description of tragedy, *Am.* III i 11–13.

99–100. See *Elegia I* 45–6*n*, p. 20 above.

102. buskined] See *L'Allegro* 132*n*, p. 138 above.

But, O sad virgin, that thy power
Might raise Musaeus from his bower,
Or bid the soul of Orpheus sing
Such notes as warbled to the string,
Drew iron tears down Pluto's cheek,
And made hell grant what love did seek.
Or call up him that left half-told
The story of Cambuscan bold,
Of Camball, and of Algarsife,
And who had Canace to wife,
That owned the virtuous ring and glass,
And of the wondrous horse of brass,
On which the Tartar king did ride;
And if aught else, great bards beside,
In sage and solemn tunes have sung,
Of tourneys and of trophies hung;
Of forests, and enchantments drear,
Where more is meant than meets the ear,
Thus Night oft see me in thy pale career,
Till civil-suited Morn appear,
Not tricked and frounced as she was wont,
With the Attic boy to hunt,
But kerchieft in a comely cloud,
While rocking winds are piping loud,

104. Musaeus] Mythical seer and priest, pupil of Orpheus and founder of priestly poetry in Attica.
105–8. See *L'Allegro* 145–50*n* (p. 139).
109. him] Chaucer: the 'story' is the unfinished *Squire's Tale*. F. W. Emerson, *MLN* xlvii (1932) 153–4, suggests that M. derived the forms 'Cambuscan' and 'Cabmall' (as opposed to the Chaucerian 'Cambynskan' and 'Camballo') from his father's friend John Lane's continuation of the *Squire's Tale* (written in 1615).
113. virtuous] endowed with magical power. Allen 12 suggests that M. refers to the *Squire's Tale* here because he saw ring, glass and brass horse as symbols of intellectual power.
116–20. Referring probably to 'our sage and serious Poet *Spencer*' (Columbia iv 311, Yale ii 516) and perhaps to Ariosto and Tasso as well, whose epics had been allegorized by Renaissance critics.
120. Cp. Seneca, *Epist.* cxiv 1: *In quibus plus intelligendum esset quam audiendum* (in which more was to be understood than heard).
122. civil-suited] Echoes *Romeo and Juliet* III ii 10–11: 'Come, civil night, / Thou sober-suited matron.'
123. tricked and frounced] decked out and with curled hair.
124. Attic boy] See *Elegia V* 49–52*n* (p. 82).

Or ushered with a shower still,
When the gust hath blown his fill,
Ending on the rustling leaves,
With minute drops from off the eaves.
And when the sun begins to fling
His flaring beams, me goddess bring
To arched walks of twilight groves,
And shadows brown that Sylvan loves
Of pine, or monumental oak,
Where the rude axe with heaved stroke,
Was never heard the nymphs to daunt,
Or fright them from their hallowed haunt.
There in close covert by some brook,
Where no profaner eye may look,
Hide me from day's garish eye,
While the bee with honied thigh,
That at her flowery work doth sing,
And the waters murmuring
With such consort as they keep,
Entice the dewy-feathered Sleep;
And let some strange mysterious dream,
Wave at his wings in airy stream,
Of lively portraiture displayed,
Softly on my eyelids laid.
And as I wake, sweet music breathe
Above, about, or underneath,

127. still] quiet.
130. minute] Falling at intervals of a minute; M. is first to use the word in this sense.
131. fling] Probably echoing Drayton, *Muses' Elizium* i 1–2: 'When Phoebus with a face of mirth / Had flung abroad his beams'; cp. also Beaumont and Fletcher, *Maid's Tragedy* I i: 'the day that flings his light'.
132. flaring beams] Marlowe uses the same phrase, *Hero and Leander* ii 332.
134. Sylvan] The Roman wood god.
141. garish eye] Echoes *Romeo and Juliet* III ii 25: 'the garish sun'.
142–4. Echoing Drayton, *The Owl* 117–21: 'the small brookes . . . murmuring. / Each *Bee* with Honey on her laden thye.'
145. consort] musical harmony.
148. his] Sleep's: cp. the address to 'Phant'sie' in Jonson's *Vision of Delight* 45–54: 'Spread thy purple wings; / Now all thy figures are allow'd, / and various shapes of things; / Create of ayrie formes, a streame; / . . . And though it be a waking dreame; / Yet let it like an odour rise / . . . And fall like sleep upon their eies, / or musick in their eare.'
152. M. is probably remembering the magic music in Shakespeare's

Sent by some spirit to mortals good,
Or the unseen genius of the wood.
But let my due feet never fail,
To walk the studious cloister's pale,
And love the high embowed roof,
With antique pillars' massy proof,
And storied windows richly dight,
Casting a dim religious light.
There let the pealing organ blow,
To the full-voiced choir below,
In service high, and anthems clear,
As may with sweetness, through mine ear,
Dissolve me into ecstasies,
And bring all heaven before mine eyes.
And may at last my weary age
Find out the peaceful hermitage,
The hairy gown and mossy cell,
Where I may sit and rightly spell
Of every star that heaven doth shew,
And every herb that sips the dew;
Till old experience do attain
To something like prophetic strain.
These pleasures Melancholy give,
And I with thee will choose to live.

43 Sonnet VII

Date. Dec. 1631. In the Trinity MS after *Solemn Music* and before *Time* there are two drafts in M.'s hand of an undated letter to an unnamed friend, perhaps Thomas Young, (Columbia xii 320–25, Yale i 319–21). The first draft contains this sonnet as an example of 'my nightward thoughts some while since'. M.'s twenty-third year ended 9 Dec. 1631. W. R. Parker, *RES* xi (1935) 276–9, argues from M.'s method of dating some of his Latin

Tempest, particularly I ii 390: 'Where should this music be? i' th' air or th' earth?'

154. genius] See *Arcades 26n* (p. 157).

156. pale] enclosure.

157. embowed] arched.

158. massy] made of great blocks of masonry *proof*] impenetrability.

159. storied] ornamented with scenes from (biblical) history.

165–6. See *Solemn Music 5n* (p. 163).

170–1. spell Of] find out about.

175–6. See *L'Allegro* 151–2n (p. 139).

poems (see headnote to *Q Nov*) that 'my three and twentieth year' should be interpreted 'the year in which I was twenty-three': he thus dates *Sonnet VII* on or soon after 9 Dec. 1632. For objections to Parker's re-dating see E. Sirluck, *JEGP* lx (1961) 781–4.

Publication. 1645 (*11.* mean]mean,) and *1673* (the text followed here, except in *2* where *1673* misprints 'Soln' for 'Stol'n'). The Trinity MS draft has no verbal variants but is, with the exception of a comma after 'me' (*12*), entirely unpunctuated.

Modern criticism. R. M. Smith, *MLN* lx (1945) 394–8, suggests that the octave may have been influenced by a passage in a Latin verse letter from Spenser to Gabriel Harvey, published in 1580.

P. M. Withim, *Bucknell Review* vi (1957) 29–34, offers a prosodic analysis, noting how the cdedce rhyme scheme in the sestet (also used by M. in 27, 32 and 70) throws special weight on 'heaven' (*12*). By concentrating on prosody Withim evades the question of the sestet's meaning. Three alternative explanations are given by K. Svendsen, *Explicator* vii (1949) 53, who would paraphrase *13–14* 'All that matters is whether I have grace to use my ripeness in accordance with the will of God as one ever in His sight'. D. C. Dorian, *Explicator* viii (1949) 10, suggests a quasi-substantive use of 'ever' (*14*) and paraphrases 'All time is, if I have grace to use it so, as eternity in God's sight'. A. S. P. Woodhouse, *UTQ* xiii (1943) 96, proposes the substitution of a colon for the first comma in *13*, and paraphrases 'All [that matters] is: whether I have grace to use it so, as ever [conscious of being] in my great taskmaster's [enjoining] eye'. Since the Trinity MS draft has not even a comma at this point, Woodhouse's proposal seems dubious.

How soon hath time the subtle thief of youth,
Stol'n on his wing my three and twentieth year!
My hasting days fly on with full career,
But my late spring no bud or blossom sheweth.
Perhaps my semblance might deceive the truth,
That I to manhood am arrived so near,
And inward ripeness doth much less appear,
That some more timely-happy spirits endueth.
Yet be it less or more, or soon or slow,

¶ 43. *5. semblance*] appearance. Cp. M.'s statement in the *Defensio Secunda* (Columbia viii 60–1): 'Though [I am] turned of forty, there is scarcely anyone who would not think me younger by nearly ten years.'

8. more timely-happy spirits] Smart 54 suggests Thomas Randolph, M.'s contemporary at Cambridge and already well known as a wit, as one of these.

9–12. L. Campbell, *Classical Review* viii (1894) 349, was the first to point out the apparent debt to Pindar, *Nem.* iv 41–3: 'But, whatsoever excellence

It shall be still in strictest measure even,
To that same lot, however mean or high,
Toward which time leads me, and the will of heaven;
All is, if I have grace to use it so,
As ever in my great task-master's eye.

44 *Ad Patrem*

[To My Father]

Date. 1632? The date is much disputed and there is no firm evidence. Tradition has assigned *Ad Patrem* to the early Horton years (see e.g. Masson i 296) on grounds of its similarity to the letter to an unknown friend (cp. *Sonnet VII* headnote, p. 146). But Grierson I xxii believes that the publication of *Comus* lies behind the conflict felt in *Ad Patrem*, which he dates 1637–8. J. T. Shawcross, *N & Q* cciv (1959) 358–9, agrees. Shawcross suggests that the order of poems in *1645* was dictated by typographical convenience: he contradicts W. R. Parker's claim (Taylor^2 125–8) that the *1645* order represents chronology, and that *Ad Patrem* should thus be dated after the performance of *Comus* (29 Sept. 1634) and before the Greek *Psalm cxiv* (Nov. 1634). E. Sirluck, *JEGP* lx (1961) 784–5, accepts Grierson's dating, as does Tillyard (384) who connects lines *82–4* with a passage in M.'s letter to Diodati dated 23 Sept. 1637 (Columbia xii 23–9, Yale i 325–8). Harris Fletcher (Scott 199–205) feels that *Ad Patrem* may well have been written as late as 1640. H. A. Barnett, *MLN* lxxiii (1958) 82–3, takes *38–40* literally and concludes that the star positions indicate a date in spring (Mar.-Apr.). D. Bush, *MP* lxi (1964) 204–8, questions the linking of *Ad Patrem* with *Comus* and repeats some of the reasons offered by A. S. P. Woodhouse, *UTQ* xiii (1943) 88–92, for dating *Ad Patrem* in M.'s last Cambridge year (1631–2): Bush comments on the present tenses in *71–6*: 'If he were writing *circa* 1637, or even *circa* 1634, it would be hard to imagine his using present tenses about an attitude his father must have taken before or soon after he left Cambridge.' This, and Bush's other reasons for an early date are convincing, but his suggestion that the *secessibus* of *74* are Cambridge seems dubious, since *Abductum* (*75*) must surely imply that M.'s father is himself in the 'seclusion' referred to, which can therefore only be Horton, to which M. probably moved in the summer of 1632 (French i 272–3).

Publication. *1645* (*8.* possunt]possint *13.* ista,]ista) *1673* (the text followed here).

Lord Destiny assigned me, well I know that the lapse of time will bring it to its appointed perfection.'

10. still] always.

10–11. even, To] level with.

Modern criticism. M. Little, *JEGP* xlix (1950) 354–51, claims that there is a note of banter in M.'s *apologia* which links it with Alexander Gill's *In Natalem Mei Parentis.* The *Familiar Letters* show that M. and Gill were in the habit of exchanging verses, so probably M. saw Gill's poem before its publication (1632): the subject is uncommon in neo-Latin verse, and it may well have been Gill's poem which suggested *Ad Patrem.*

Nunc mea Pierios cupiam per pectora fontes
Irriguas torquere vias, totumque per ora
Volvere laxatum gemino de vertice rivum;
Ut tenues oblita sonos audacibus alis
Surgat in officium venerandi Musa parentis.
Hoc utcunque tibi gratum pater optime carmen
Exiguum meditatur opus, nec novimus ipsi
Aptius a nobis quae possunt munera donis
Respondere tuis, quamvis nec maxima possint
Respondere tuis, nedum ut par gratia donis
Esse queat, vacuis quae redditur arida verbis.
Sed tamen haec nostros ostendit pagina census,
Et quod habemus opum charta numeravimus ista,
Quae mihi sunt nullae, nisi quas dedit aurea Clio
Quas mihi semoto somni peperere sub antro,
Et nemoris laureta sacri Parnassides umbrae.
  Nec tu vatis opus divinum despice carmen,
Quo nihil aethereos ortus, et semina caeli,
Nil magis humanam commendat origine mentem,
Sancta Prometheae retinens vestigia flammae.
Carmen amant superi, tremebundaque Tartara carmen
Ima ciere valet, divosque ligare profundos,
Et triplici duros Manes adamante coercet.
Carmine sepositi retegunt arcana futuri
Phoebades, et tremulae pallentes ora Sibyllae;

¶ 44. *1. Pierios*] on Pierus, see *Elegia IV* 29–32*n*, p. 55 above.
14. Clio] J. T. Shawcross, *N & Q* ccvi (1961) 178–9, thinks Clio, in this passage 'the personification of man's individual history', but cites no classical precedent. It seems more likely that she is named as guardian of lustration. See *Elegia IV* 29–32*n*, p. 55 above.
20. Prometheae . . . flammae] Prometheus stole fire from heaven and brought it to man, as Hesiod relates, *Theog.* 565. Conti 317–18 explains that Prometheus, whose name means 'the forethinker', symbolizes reason or prudence.
21–3. See *L'Allegro* 145–50*n*.
25. Phoebades] Priestesses of Apollo, whose temple at Delphi contained a famous oracle. *Sibyllae*] Prophetesses; it is the Cumaean sibyl who escorts Aeneas to the underworld in *Aen.* vi.

Carmina sacrificus sollennes pangit ad aras
Aurea seu sternit motantem cornua taurum;
Seu cum fata sagax fumantibus abdita fibris
Consulit, et tepidis Parcam scrutatur in extis.
Nos etiam patrium tunc cum repetemus Olympum,
Aeternaeque morae stabunt immobilis aevi,
Ibimus auratis per caeli templa coronis,
Dulcia suaviloquo sociantes carmina plectro,
Astra quibus, geminique poli convexa sonabunt.
Spiritus et rapidos qui circinat igneus orbes,
Nunc quoque sydereis intercinit ipse choreis
Immortale melos, et inenarrabile carmen;
Torrida dum rutilus compescit sibila serpens,
Demissoque ferox gladio mansuescit Orion;
Stellarum nec sentit onus Maurusius Atlas.
Carmina regales epulas ornare solebant,
Cum nondum luxus, vastaeque immensa vorago
Nota gulae, et modico spumabat coena Lyaeo.
Tum de more sedens festa ad convivia vates
Aesculea intonsos redimitus ab arbore crines,
Heroumque actus, imitandaque gesta canebat,
Et chaos, et positi late fundamina mundi,
Reptantesque deos, et alentes numina glandes,
Et nondum Aetneo quaesitum fulmen ab antro.

32–3. Cp. *Rev.* iv 4: 'They had on their heads crowns of gold', and v 8 'having every one of them harps.'

35–7. M.'s spirit, released from his body by learning, sings amid the starry choir. The theory of this release is derived from Cicero's *Somnium Scipionis* and Macrobius' commentary on it, as John Carey points out, *RES* n.s. xv (1964) 180–4.

38. serpens] The constellation of the Serpent, between the Greater and Lesser Bear.

39. Orion] See *Prae E* 53–4*n* (p. 26).

40. Maurusius] in Mauritania (the modern Fez and Morocco). *Atlas*] See *Id Plat* 24*n* (p. 67).

43. Lyaeo] Bacchus, god of wine, was also called Lyaeus ('the Relaxer').

48. Tillyard (*Seventeenth-Century Studies presented to Sir Herbert Grierson* (Oxford 1938) 219) takes this as a reference to the infancy of the Olympian gods as described by Hesiod. Hesiod, however, mentions neither crawling nor acorns. A closer parallel is Ovid's description of the creation, where the gods are said to inhabit first the 'floor' of heaven (*Met.* i 73), and where acorns (*Met.* i 106) are included in the diet of the first, golden age, when Saturn reigned.

49. Jupiter, who succeeded Saturn, was armed with thunderbolts forged in a cave under Etna by the Cyclopes, as Virgil describes (*Georg.* iv 170–5).

Denique quid vocis modulamen inane iuvabit,
Verborum sensusque vacans, numerique loquacis?
Silvestres decet iste choros, non Orphea cantus,
Qui tenuit fluvios et quercubus addidit aures
Carmine, non cithara, simulachraque functa canendo
Compulit in lacrymas; habet has a carmine laudes.
   Nec tu perge precor sacras contemnere Musas,
Nec vanas inopesque puta, quarum ipse peritus
Munere, mille sonos numeros componis ad aptos,
Millibus et vocem modulis variare canoram
Doctus, Arionii merito sis nominis haeres.
Nunc tibi quid mirum, si me genuisse poetam
Contigerit, charo si tam prope sanguine iuncti
Cognatas artes, studiumque affine sequamur:
Ipse volens Phoebus se dispertire duobus,
Altera dona mihi, dedit altera dona parenti,
Dividuumque Deum genitorque puerque tenemus.
   Tu tamen ut simules teneras odisse camoenas,
Non odisse reor, neque enim, pater, ire iubebas
Qua via lata patet, qua pronior area lucri,
Certaque condendi fulget spes aurea nummi:
Nec rapis ad leges, male custoditaque gentis
Iura, nec insulsis damnas clamoribus aures.
Sed magis excultam cupiens ditescere mentem,
Me procul urbano strepitu, secessibus altis
Abductum Aoniae iucunda per otia ripae
Phoebaeo lateri comitem sinis ire beatum.
Officium chari taceo commune parentis,
Me poscunt maiora, tuo pater optime sumptu
Cum mihi Romuleae patuit facundia linguae,
Et Latii veneres, et quae Iovis ora decebant
Grandia magniloquis elata vocabula Graiis,

52–5. Orpheus makes oak trees listen to his song in Virgil (*Georg.* iv 510). During his visit to the underworld, as described by Ovid, he walked among ghosts (*Met.* x 14 *simulacraque functa*) and made them weep (x 41).

60. Arionii] Herodotus i 23–4 tells how Arion, a famous lyre-player, so charmed a dolphin with his music that it rescued him from the waves when he was thrown overboard. M.'s father was a musician of some repute.

64. Phoebus] God of poetry and music.

67. camoenas] See *Elegia VI* 3*n* (p. 113).

71. Ovid refers to his own unwillingness to follow the legal profession, *Am.* I xv 5–6.

75. Aoniae . . . ripae] See *Elegia IV* 29–32*n* (p. 55).

79. Romuleae . . . facundia linguae] Echoes Ovid, *Ex Ponto* I ii 67: *Romanae facundia . . . linguae.*

Addere suasisti quos iactat Gallia flores,
Et quam degeneri novus Italus ore loquelam
Fundit, barbaricos testatus voce tumultus,
Quaeque Palaestinus loquitur mysteria vates.
Denique quicquid habet caelum, subiectaque coelo
Terra parens, terraeque et coelo interfluus aer,
Quicquid et unda tegit, pontique agitabile marmor,
Per te nosse licet, per te, si nosse libebit.
Dimotaque venit spectanda scientia nube,
Nudaque conspicuos inclinat ad oscula vultus,
Ni fugisse velim, ni sit libasse molestum.
I nunc, confer opes quisquis malesanus avitas
Austriaci gazas, Peruanaque regna praeoptas.
Quae potuit maiora pater tribuisse, vel ipse
Iupiter, excepto, donasset ut omnia, coelo?
Non potiora dedit, quamvis et tuta fuissent,
Publica qui iuveni commisit lumina nato
Atque Hyperionios currus, et fraena diei,
Et circum undantem radiata luce tiaram.
Ergo ego iam doctae pars quamlibet ima catervae
Victrices hederas inter, laurosque sedebo,
Iamque nec obscurus populo miscebor inerti,
Vitabuntque oculos vestigia nostra profanos.
Este procul vigiles curae, procul este querelae,
Invidiaeque acies transverso tortilis hirquo,
Saeva nec anguiferos extende Calumnia rictus;
In me triste nihil faedissima turba potestis,
Nec vestri sum iuris ego; securaque tutus
Pectora, vipereo gradiar sublimis ab ictu.
At tibi, chare pater, postquam non aequa merenti
Posse referre datur, nec dona rependere factis,

85. *Palaestinus . . . vates*] A Hebrew prophet.
93. Echoing Ovid, *Her.* xii 204: *i nunc . . . confer opes.*
94. *Peruanaque regna*] Peru was conquered by Spain in the 1530s and mercilessly exploited for its gold during the sixteenth and seventeenth centuries.
97–100. See *Natur* 25*n* (p. 62).
98. *Publica . . . lumina*] Ovid's name for the sun in his story of Phaëthon, *Met.* ii 35.
99. *Hyperionios*] Belonging to Hyperion, father of the sun.
102. *hederas*] Horace calls the ivy 'the reward of poets' brows', *Odes* I i 29, and Virgil, *Ecl.* viii 13, envisages his poet's ivy mingling with the laurel about the brows of the victorious Pollio.
106. *transverso . . . hirquo*] Echoes Virgil, *Ecl.* iii 8: *transversa tuentibus hircis.*
107. *Calumnia*] See Q *Nov* 146*n* (p. 42).

Sit memorasse satis, repetitaque numera grato
Percensere animo, fidaeque reponere menti.
Et vos, O nostri, iuvenilia carmina, lusus,
Si modo perpetuos sperare audebitis annos,
Et domini superesse rogo, lucemque tueri,
Nec spisso rapient oblivia nigra sub Orco,
Forsitan has laudes, decantatumque parentis
Nomen, ad exemplum, sero servabitis aevo.

Now I should like the Pierian[1] fountains to divert their watery channels through my heart; I should like every drop of that stream which trickles out from the twin peak to pour between my lips, so that my Muse, forgetting her trivial songs, may soar on fearless wings to do her duty and honour my father. Whether you approve or not, best of fathers, she is now engaged on this poem–this little offering–and I do not know what I may give you that can more fittingly repay your gifts to me. In fact, though, even my greatest gifts could never repay yours, much less could that barren thanks which is paid in empty words make up for the things you have given me. Still, this page shows you what I do possess: I have counted out my wealth upon this sheet of paper, and that wealth is only what golden Clio[14] has provided–the fruit of dreams dreamt in a cavern far away, fruit of the laurel groves in a sacred wood, of the shady groves on Parnassus.

Do not despise divine poetry, the poet's creation. Nothing shows our celestial beginnings, our heavenly seed, more clearly: nothing better graces by its origin our human intellect, for poetry still retains some blessed trace of the Promethean fire.[20] The gods love poetry: poetry has power to stir the quivering depths of Tartarus[21] and to bind the deities of hell: it grips the heartless ghosts in a threefold band of steel.[23] With poetry the priestesses of Apollo and the trembling, pale-lipped sybils[25] reveal the secrets of the distant future. The sacrificing priest who stands before the ceremonial altar utters poetry as he strikes down the bull, its gilded horns tossing, or when, skilled in prophecy, he reads the hidden lines of destiny in the steaming entrails and searches for fate in the beast's hot guts. And we, when we return to Olympus, our first home, and when the eternal ages of changeless time stand still, shall walk through the temples of heaven crowned with gold[32] and wedding our sweet songs to the smooth-voiced strings,[33] and the stars and the vaults of both the hemispheres will make their music in reply. My fiery spirit which whirls round the hurtling spheres is already singing, as it flies among the starry choirs, a deathless melody, an indescribable song. The glittering serpent[38] checks his scorching hisses at the sound, savage Orion[39] grows calm and lets fall his sword, and Mauretanian Atlas[40] no longer feels the weight of the stars.

Songs were the usual ornaments of royal banquets in the days when luxury and the great maw of insatiable gluttony were still things of the future, and when the table foamed with wine,[43] but only in moderation. Then it was customary for the bard to have a place at the happy feast, his flowing locks crowned with a garland of oak leaves, and he sang of the deeds of heroes, of their exploits and good example, of chaos and of the wide

118. Orco] See *Elegia VII* 83*n* (p. 73).

foundations on which the earth was laid, of gods who crawled about and lived on acorns,[48] and of the thunderbolt not yet brought from its cave under Etna.[49] And after all, what use is the voice if it merely hums an inane tune, without words, meaning or the rhythm of speech? That kind of song is good enough for the woodland choristers, but not for Orpheus[52] who with his singing, not his lute, held streams spellbound and gave ears to the oak-trees and moved lifeless phantoms to tears. It is to his singing that he owes his reputation.[55]

I beg you, stop scorning the sacred Muses: don't think them worthless or unprofitable. It is their gift which has made you able to fit a thousand notes to apt rhythms and skilful in adjusting your tuneful voice to a thousand melodies–may you deservedly inherit Arion's fame.[60] No wonder, then, that you should have the good luck to beget me, a poet, or that we who are so closely related by ties of affection and blood should cultivate sister arts and have kindred interests. Phoebus,[64] wishing to share himself between the two of us, gave one lot of gifts to me and the other to my father, with the result that father and son have each one half of a god. But although you pretend to hate the dainty Muses,[67] I do not believe that you hate them really. For, father, you did not tell me to go where the road lies broad and open, where the ground is more favourable for fortune-hunters, and where the golden hope of making piles of money shines bright and clear. You do not force me to enter the legal profession[71] or study our nation's ill-preserved statutes: you do not condemn my ears to that absurd clamour. Instead you have taken me far away from the din of the city into this deep seclusion, with the intention of enriching my already cultivated mind still further, and you allow me to walk by Phoebus's side, happy to be his companion, amidst the leisurely delights of the Aonian spring.[75]

I will not mention the kindnesses which a loving father usually bestows upon his son: there are more considerable things which demand my attention. Best of fathers, when the eloquence of the Roman tongue[79] had been made accessible to me, at your expense, the beauties of Latin and the high-sounding words of the sublime Greeks, words which graced the mighty lips of Jove himself, then you persuaded me to add to my stock those flowers which are the boast of France, and that language which the modern Italian pours from his degenerate mouth (his speech makes him a living proof of the barbarian invasions), and also those mysteries which the prophet of Palestine[85] utters. Should I choose to do so, in fact, I have the chance, thanks to you, of knowing about everything that exists–in the sky, or on mother earth beneath the sky, or in the air that streams between them, or hidden beneath the waves, beneath the heaving marbly surface of the ocean. The mists clear, and science comes into view. Naked, she bends her bright face for my kisses–if I do not choose to run away, if I do not find it irksome to taste her kisses.

Go on, then, pile up your wealth,[93] all you who have an unhealthy hankering for the royal heirlooms of Austria or the realms of Peru.[94] What greater treasures could have been given by a father, or by Jove himself for that matter, even if he had given everything, unless he had included heaven as well? That father[97] who trusted his young son with the universal light[98] of the world and the chariot of Hyperion,[99] with the reins of day and the diadem which radiates waves of light, gave (even had those gifts been safe) no better gifts than my father's.[100] Therefore I, who already have a place, though a very low one, in the ranks of the learned, shall one day sit among those who wear the ivy[102] and the laurels of victory. Now I shall no longer mix with the brainless mob: my steps will shun the sight of common eyes. Away with you, sleep-destroying worries, away with you, complaints, and the squinting eye of envy with its crooked goatish look.[106] Do not stretch your snaky jaws at me, cruel calumny.[107] Your whole filthy gang can do me no harm: I am not within your power. I shall stride on in safety with an unwounded heart, lifted high above your viperous sting.

As for you, dear father, since I am powerless to repay you as you deserve, or to do anything that can requite your gifts, let it suffice that I have recorded them, that I count up your repeated favours with a feeling of gratitude, and store them safely away in my memory.

And you, my youthful poems, my pastimes, if only you are bold enough to hope for immortality, to hope that you will survive your master's funeral pyre and keep your eyes upon the light, then perhaps, if dark oblivion does not after all plunge you down beneath the dense crowds of the underworld,[118] you may preserve this eulogy and my father's name, which has been the subject of my verse, as an example for a far-off age.

45 Note on Ariosto

Date. 1632? Before the preface of his copy of Harington's translation of the *Orlando Furioso*, M. wrote an elegiac couplet, of which the first line is cut away, and this second line cancelled. Columbia xviii 605 dates the line 'about 1642', presumably because elsewhere in the Harington volume M. wrote *Questo libro due volte ho letto, Sept 21. 1642.* ('I have read this book twice'): but the substance of the line makes a date nearer to the renunciation of the legal profession in *Ad Patrem* preferable.

Tu mihi iure tuo Iustiniane vale. J.M.

Farewell, Justinian, with your law book.

46 Arcades

Date. Summer (reference to thick foliage *88–9*) 1633? There is no certainty about the date. The first item in the Trinity MS as it now survives is a draft of *Arcades* (for variant readings see notes) which, according to J. T. Shawcross, *N & Q* cciv (1959) 359–64, is a transcript made after the first performance.

¶ 45. *1. Iustiniane*] Justinian I (A.D. 483–565), Emperor, and codifier of the Roman law.

¶ 46. *Title. Arcades*] Inhabitants of Arcady (Arcadia). In *Trin. MS Arcades* is first headed 'Part of a masque'; this is cancelled and 'Arcades / Part of an Entertainment' substituted.

Alice, Dowager Countess of Derby, was about seventy-two in 1633, and died Jan. 1636. She had long been honoured by poets: Spenser dedicated his *Tears of the Muses* (1591) to her and she was the 'sweet Amaryllis' of his *Colin Clout's Come Home Again.* Marston wrote an *Entertainment* (1607) for her. In 1609 John Davies of Hereford dedicated his *Holy Rood* to her and the same year she played Zenobia in Jonson's *Masque of Queens.* She married her second husband, Sir Thomas Egerton, Lord Keeper, in 1600: a year later they bought Harefield (twelve miles north of Horton). Her second daughter married Sir Thomas's son, Sir John, who became Earl of Bridgewater in 1617. *Comus* was written for him, and probably *Arcades* as well. M.'s connection with the Egertons was through Henry Lawes, who had taught music to the Earl's children since 1626 or earlier (Evans 62). C. G. Osgood, *JEGP* iv (1902) 370–8, argues from the tone of Lawes's epistle prefixed to *Comus* that M. and the Egertons were not personally acquainted, but the Lawes connection makes it probable that the actors of *Arcades* included those of *Comus.*

French (i 226) dates *Arcades* 1631, but the great scandal of that year was the trial and execution (14 May) of the Dowager Countess's son-in-law, the Earl of Castlehaven, for unnatural practices and for causing his wife to be ravished. 1631 is thus a very unlikely date.

Publication. 1645 (*91.* sits]sits, *97.* banks,]banks.) *1673* (the text followed here except in *46* where *1673* prints a full stop after 'grove' and *47* where it prints a semi-colon after 'quaint').

Modern criticism. J. M. Wallace, *JEGP* lviii (1959) 627–36, sees the theme of *Arcades* as a pilgrimage from profane to religious, from classical south to Christian north. The central symbol is the Countess, personifying heavenly wisdom. The Queen of Sheba's amazement at the wisdom of Solomon (*1 Kings* x 6–7) is recalled in *8–13*: the Countess is Solomon's female counterpart. She is connected with Latona (*20*) because Latona was (according to Diodorus Siculus ii 47) born on the isle of the Hyperboreans (commonly identified with Britain), and was regarded by the mythographers Conti and Sandys as a personification of that goodness and innocence which hope to arrive at celestial beauty. Cybele (*21*) was 'admired for her intelligence' (Diodorus Siculus iii 58).

Part of an entertainment presented to the Countess Dowager of Derby at Harefield, by some noble persons of her family, who appear on the scene in pastoral habit, moving toward the seat of state, with this song.

I. SONG

Look nymphs, and shepherds look,
What sudden blaze of majesty
Is that which we from hence descry
Too divine to be mistook:
    This this is she
To whom our vows and wishes bend,

Here our solemn search hath end.

Fame that her high worth to raise,
Seemed erst so lavish and profuse,
We may justly now accuse
Of detraction from her praise,
  Less than half we find expressed,
  Envy bid conceal the rest.

Mark what radiant state she spreads,
In circle round her shining throne,
Shooting her beams like silver threads,
This this is she alone,
  Sitting like a goddess bright,
  In the centre of her light.

Might she the wise Latona be,
Or the towered Cybele,
Mother of a hundred gods;
Juno dares not give her odds;
  Who had thought this clime had held
  A deity so unparalleled?

As they come forward, the Genius of the Wood appears, and turning toward them, speaks.

Gen. Stay gentle swains, for though in this disguise,
I see bright honour sparkle through your eyes,
Of famous Arcady ye are, and sprung
Of that renowned flood, so often sung,

10–11. *We may ... Of*] In *Trin. MS* inserted beside a previous version 'Now seems guilty of abuse / And ...'

12. *we find*] In *Trin. MS* inserted beside previous version 'she hath'.

17. Perhaps a memory of Jonson, *Entertainment at Althorp* 113–7: 'This is shee / This is shee, / In whose world of grace / Every season, person, place, / That receive her, happy be.'

18. *Sitting*] *Trin. MS*: *seated* 'sitting'.

20. *Latona*] Mother of Apollo and Diana.

21–2. Virgil, *Aen.* vi 785–7, calls Cybele mother of a hundred gods and describes her towered crown.

23. *Juno*] Cancelled in *Trin. MS* and 'Ceres' substituted, but 'Juno' restored later. *give her odds*] offer to contest with her on terms which favour the Countess.

24. *had thought*] *Trin. MS*: *would have* 'had' thought.

26. Evans 64–5 suggests that the Genius (protecting local deity) was played by Lawes, and that *Il Penseroso* 154 refers to him. *gentle*] well-born.

28. *Arcady*] Arcadia, 'famous' as the home of pastoral singers in Theocritus and Virgil, *Ecl.* x 31–6, and more recently because of Sidney's *Arcadia*

Divine Alpheus, who by secret sluice,
Stole under seas to meet his Arethuse;
And ye the breathing roses of the wood,
Fair silver-buskined nymphs as great and good,
I know this quest of yours, and free intent
Was all in honour and devotion meant
To the great mistress of yon princely shrine,
Whom with low reverence I adore as mine,
And with all helpful service will comply
To further this night's glad solemnity;
And lead ye where ye may more near behold
What shallow-searching Fame hath left untold;
Which I full oft amidst these shades alone
Have sat to wonder at, and gaze upon:
For know by lot from Jove I am the power
Of this fair wood, and live in oaken bower,
To nurse the saplings tall, and curl the grove
With ringlets quaint, and wanton windings wove.
And all my plants I save from nightly ill,
Of noisome winds, and blasting vapours chill.
And from the boughs brush off the evil dew,
And heal the harms of thwarting thunder blue,
Or what the cross dire-looking planet smites,
Or hurtful worm with cankered venom bites.

(1590) with its 'shepheards boy piping, as though he should never be old' (I ii). *ye*] *Trin. MS*: you.

30–1. Alpheus] An Arcadian river. Ovid, *Met.* v 574–641 tells how the nymph Arethusa bathed in its waters and, when pursued by the amorous river-god, was herself transformed to a river which passed under the Adriatic to Sicily, still pursued by Alpheus. *secret*] hidden *sluice*] channel.

32. breathing] emitting fragrance.

40. ye . . . ye] *Trin. MS*: you . . . you.

41. What shallow-searching] *Trin. MS*: *Those virtues which dull* 'What shallow-searching'.

46. curl] Drayton, *Polyolbion* vii 109 and Browne i 126 have groves with 'curled heads', and in Sylvester (Du Bartas 38) winds 'curl' the locks of trees.

47. With] *Trin. MS*: In. *quaint*] ingeniously contrived. *wove*] woven.

50. boughs] *Trin. MS*: *leaves* 'boughs'. *evil dew*] mildew; cp. *Tempest* I ii 321: 'As wicked dew as e'er my mother brush'd'.

51. thwarting] crossing with a streak; cp. *Julius Ceasar* I iii 50: 'the cross blue lightning'.

52. planet] Saturn, the malign planet.

53. worm . . . cankered] Cankerworm was a name given to caterpillars and insect larvae which destroyed leaves and buds.

When evening grey doth rise, I fetch my round
Over the mount, and all this hallowed ground,
And early ere the odorous breath of morn
Awakes the slumbering leaves, or tasselled horn
Shakes the high thicket, haste I all about,
Number my ranks, and visit every sprout
With puissant words, and murmurs made to bless,
But else in deep of night when drowsiness
Hath locked up mortal sense, then listen I
To the celestial sirens' harmony,
That sit upon the nine enfolded spheres,
And sing to those that hold the vital shears,
And turn the adamantine spindle round,
On which the fate of gods and men is wound.
Such sweet compulsion doth in music lie,
To lull the daughters of Necessity,
And keep unsteady Nature to her law,
And the low world in measured motion draw
After the heavenly tune, which none can hear
Of human mould with gross unpurged ear;

59. *ranks*] of trees. As. C. G. Osgood, *JEGP* iv (1902) 370–8 points out there was an avenue of elms at Harefield called The Queen's Walk in memory of Queen Elizabeth's visit to the house in 1602. In *Trin. MS* the present form of the line is substituted for the earlier 'And number all my ranks, and every sprout'.
60. *puissant . . . bless*] powerful magic charms and blessings.
62. *Hath . . . sense*] *Trin. MS*: *Hath chained mortality* 'Hath locked up mortal *eyes*' 'sense'.
63–72. M. is paraphrasing Plato, *Republic* x 616–7. In Plato the spindle of Necessity has a shaft of adamant (steel) upon which are threaded the eight concentric whorls of the universe. On the rim of each whorl stands a siren who utters a single note, and the notes together produce a harmony. The end of the spindle rests on the knees of Necessity, and at equal distance round sit her daughters, the three Fates, Lachesis, Clotho and Atropos, who turn the spindle with their hands. Strictly speaking the 'vital shears' (the shears which cut the thread of life) were held by Atropos only.
64. *nine*] M. makes Plato's eight spheres nine, following Dante who relates the nine spheres to the nine orders of angels, *Paradiso* xxviii 25–78. As J. Hutton points out, *EM* ii (1951) 23–5, the same relation is found in Ficino and Gafori.
72–3. In *Prolusion II* (Columbia xii 148–57, Yale i 234–9) M. again refers to the Pythagorean doctrine that the music of the spheres is unheard only because human ears are unworthy to hear it. He perhaps recalls *Merchant of Venice* v i 64–5 'But whilst this muddy vesture of decay / Doth grossly

And yet such music worthiest were to blaze
The peerless height of her immortal praise,
Whose lustre leads us, and for her most fit,
If my inferior hand or voice could hit
Inimitable sounds, yet as we go,
Whate'er the skill of lesser gods can show,
I will assay, her worth to celebrate,
And so attend ye toward her glittering state;
Where ye may all that are of noble stem
Approach, and kiss her sacred vesture's hem.

II. SONG

O'er the smooth enamelled green
Where no print of step hath been,
Follow me as I sing,
And touch the warbled string.
Under the shady roof
Of branching elm star-proof.
Follow me,
I will bring you where she sits
Clad in splendour as befits
Her deity.
Such a rural queen
All Arcadia hath not seen.

III. SONG

Nymphs and shepherds dance no more
By sandy Ladon's lilied banks,

close it in, we cannot hear it', and *Midsummer Night's Dream* III i 159 'I will purge thy mortal grossness so'.

74. *blaze*] proclaim.

84. *enamelled*] beautified with various colours (this meaning developed early in the seventeenth century).

89. *elm*] See 59*n*. *star-proof*] Cp. Virgil's gloomy elm at the entrance to the underworld, *Aen.* vi. 282–3, also Statius, *Theb.* x 85: *nulli penetrabilis astro*; and Spenser, *F.Q.* I i 7: 'Not perceable with power of any starre.'

91. *you*] *Trin. MS*: ye.

97. *Ladon*] a river in Arcadia, flowing into the Alpheus; 'sandy' is from Ovid, *Met.* i 702: *arenosi . . . Ladonis*.

On old Lycaeus or Cyllene hoar,
Trip no more in twilight ranks,
Though Erymanth your loss deplore,
A better soil shall give ye thanks.
From the stony Maenalus,
Bring your flocks, and live with us,
Here ye shall have greater grace,
To serve the Lady of this place.
Though Syrinx your Pan's mistress were,
Yet Syrinx well might wait on her.
Such a rural queen
All Arcadia hath not seen.

47 At a Solemn Music

Date. 1633? There is no firm evidence for dating. The Trinity MS has two heavily corrected preliminary drafts, followed by a separate draft of *17–28*, followed by a fair copy of the whole (these four drafts are referred to in the notes as (*a*), (*b*), (*c*) and (*d*) respectively). The drafts begin on the reverse of the leaf containing the end of *Arcades. Solemn Music* can therefore be dated after, probably soon after, *Arcades* (itself not precisely dateable). The drafts are followed by the first draft of the letter to a friend (see headnote to *Sonnet VII* p. 146 above) which is undated but perhaps as late as 1633 (W. R. Parker, *RES* xi (1935) 278–9). *Time* and *Circumcision* do not appear until after the second draft of this letter: they appear, however, as fair copies, so no conclusions about their date of composition relative to that of *Solemn Music* can be drawn from this position. In *1645 Time* and *Circumcision* precede *Solemn Music*, but it cannot be proved that the order of poems in *1645* is strictly chronological.

Publication. 1645 (*6.* concent,]content,) *1673* (the text followed here).

Modern criticism. The history of the idea of world harmony (*musica mundana*),

98–102. Lycaeus ... Cyllene ... Erymanth ... Maenalus] mountains in Arcadia; Virgil, *Georg.* i 16–7, mentions the first and last as haunts of Pan. Starnes and Talbert (292–3) note that these names, along with 'Ladon' and 'Pan', are included in Stephanus *s.v. Arcadia.* 'Hoar' (snow-covered) was perhaps suggested by Virgil, *Aen.* viii 139: 'Cyllene's frozen peak'.

106. Syrinx] Arcadian nymph, pursued by Pan; she fled to the river Ladon and was turned into a reed. In *Trin. MS* ll. 106–7 appear as a later insertion: Todd v 181 takes them as a complimentary allusion to Jonson, *Entertainment at Althorp* 20–1: 'And the dame hath Syrinx grace! / O that Pan were now in place', where the 'dame' was Queen Anne, whom the Countess's father, Lord Spencer of Althorp, was entertaining.

with which *Solemn Music* is concerned, and of the related harmony of man (*musica humana*), is traced by L. Spitzer, *Traditio* ii (1944) 409–64 and iii (1945) 307–64. The second of these articles contains a detailed analysis of the poem, showing that it can be divided into three sections (Graeco-Roman, Jewish and Christian), according to the technical terms and concepts used. John Hollander relates the poem to contemporary ideas about music in *The Untuning of the Sky* (Princeton 1961) pp. 324–31.

Versification in M.'s 'canzone poems'. A. Oras, *N & Q* cxcvii (1952) 314–5, suggested that the model for the stanza form of *Circumcision* (*a*10*b*10*c*10*b*10*a*10*c*10*c*10*d*7*d*7*c*10*e*10*f*7*f*4*e*6) was Tasso's *canzone* to the Virgin of Loreto. Tasso's rhyme scheme, however, differs slightly from M.'s (his first six lines rhyme *abcabc*). As Prince 62 demonstrates, M.'s actual model was Petrarch's *canzone* to the Blessed Virgin (*Vergine bella, che di Sol vestita*). M.'s only modification to the scheme of this poem is to make two separate lines out of the two sections into which Petrarch's last line falls. Even this modification, which is merely typographical, was an afterthought (see *13–14n* and *27–28n*). Petrarch's *canzone* is 137 lines long: M. stops after 28, and does not again attempt the exact repetition of a complex stanza, which is the basis of the *canzone*. In the internal architecture of his stanza he swerves from his Petrarchan model, ignoring the syntactical break at the end of *6* which in Petrarch marks off the *fronte* from the *coda* (M.'s first stanza is a single sentence). For this, however, he had ample precedent in sixteenth-century Italian poetry.

Time and *Solemn Music* (which may have been written either before or after *Circumcision*) adopt the less taxing form of the madrigal–a single, unrepeated stanza of the *canzone* type. Tasso and his Italian followers had used this for epigrammatic effects. Previous to M., Drummond of Hawthornden was the only English poet to imitate their madrigals closely. Both M.'s madrigals are less intricately rhymed and make heavier use of the couplet-rhyme (over half of *Solemn Music* is decasyllabic couplets) than would be usual in Italian, but M. avoids the regularity of couplets by diversifying his syntax and its relation to the line. His closing alexandrine inserts a Spenserian flavour into each poem.

Blest pair of sirens, pledges of heaven's joy,
Sphere-borne harmonious sisters, Voice, and Verse,
Wed your divine sounds, and mixed power employ

¶ 47. *1–2. sirens*] See *Arcades* 63–72*n*, p. 159 above. *pledges*] Earthly music is a pledge or assurance of heavenly bliss because it makes us recollect the divine music. James Hutton, *EM* ii (1951) 1–63, indicates the currency of this idea among Renaissance neo-Platonists. *Sphere-borne*] carried on spheres. *sisters*] Cp. Marino, *Adone* vii 1: *Musica e Poesia son due sorelle.*

3. Trin. MS (*a*): [. . .]vine power and joint force employ. (*b*): *Mix your choice chords, and happiest sounds employ* (deleted, present version inserted).

Dead things with inbreathed sense able to pierce,
And to our high-raised phantasy present,
That undisturbed song of pure concent,
Ay sung before the sapphire-coloured throne
To him that sits thereon
With saintly shout, and solemn jubilee,
Where the bright seraphim in burning row
Their loud uplifted angel trumpets blow,
And the cherubic host in thousand choirs
Touch their immortal harps of golden wires,

4. *Dead things*] Alluding to the myth of Orpheus, whose music could attract trees, streams and rocks.
5. *high-raised phantasy*] Phantasy was thought of in the seventeenth century as intermediate between sense and reason (see *PL* v 100–13, p. 680 below). The idea that music could produce an ecstasy, separating soul from body, was common. It can be traced to the Church Fathers, such as Basil and Chrysostom, and to the neo-Platonists and neo-Pythagoreans, Iamblichus, Porphyry and Plotinus. M. here asks for only the 'phantasy', not the soul, to be 'raised', but see *Nativity Ode* 98 and *Il Penseroso* 165–6 (pp. 105 and 146 above). For a discussion of the whole subject see G. L. Finney, *Journal of the History of Ideas* viii (1947) 153–86. Between 4 and 5 *Trin. MS* (*a*) inserts: [. . .]whilst your `equal' raptures tempered sweet/[. . .]happy spousal meet/[. . .]th a while/[. . .]home-bred `woes' beguile. *Trin. MS* (*b*): And *whilst* `as' your equal raptures tempered sweet/In high mysterious *holy* `happy' spousal meet/Snatch us from earth a while/Us of ourselves and *home-bred* `native' woes beguile. *high-raised phantasy present*] *Trin. MS* (*a*): [. . .]*fancies then* `phantasy' present. *Trin. MS* (*b*): *high* `up' *up-raised* `high-raised' phantasy present.
6. *concent*] harmony, concord. Each of the *Trin. MS* drafts reads 'concent'. In a Bodleian copy of *1645* (8° M168 Art) a hand possibly M.'s has altered 'content' to 'concent'.
7. *Trin. MS* (*a*): [. . .]*ounds* [. . .]ay surrounds the *sovereign* `sapphire-coloured' throne. *sapphire-coloured*] Cp. *Ezek.* i 26: 'the likeness of a throne, as the appearance of a sapphire stone'.
9. *Trin. MS* (*a*): [. . .]vers a[. . .] and solemn cry. (Not deleted; present version inserted).
10. *Trin. MS* (*a*): [. . .]e the ser[. . .] princely row. (*b*): Where the bright seraphim in *tripled* `burning' row.
11. *Trin. MS* (*a*): [. . .]*ire loud unsa*[. . .]*trumpets blow* `Loud symphony of `silver' trumpets blow'. (*b*): `Their' *high-lifted* loud `uplifted' *arch*-angel trumpets blow.
12. *Trin. MS* (*a*): And *the* youthf[. . .]ubim `heaven's henchmen' sweet-winged squires.
13. *Trin. MS* (*a*): In ten thous[. . .]es.

With those just spirits that wear victorious palms,
Hymns devout and holy psalms
Singing everlastingly;
That we on earth with undiscording voice
May rightly answer that melodious noise;
As once we did, till disproportioned sin
Jarred against nature's chime, and with harsh din
Broke the fair music that all creatures made
To their great Lord, whose love their motion swayed
In perfect diapason, whilst they stood
In first obedience, and their state of good.

14. *Trin. MS* (*a*): With those just[...] that 'bear' wear the *fresh green* 'blooming' 'victorious' palms. (*b*): With those just spirits that wear the blooming 'blooming or victorious' palms. *palms*] Cp. *Rev.* vii 9: 'a great multitude . . . clothed with white robes, and palms in their hands'.
15. *Trin. MS* (*a*): *In* hymns d[...] and sacred psalms. (*b*) Hymns devout and sacred 'holy' psalms.
16–17. *Trin. MS* (*a*) and (*b*) insert two lines between 16 and 17. *Trin. MS* (*a*): 'While' *that* all the f[...]e of 'whilst the whole frame of' 'while *then* all the starry' heaven and arches blue / Resound and echo Hallelu. (*b*): *While all the starry rounds and arches blue / Resound and echo Hallelu.*
17. *Trin. MS* (*a*): That we *below may learn with* 'with undiscording' heart and voice. (*b*): That we 'on earth' with undiscording *heart and* voice.
18. *May rightly answer*] *Trin. MS* (*a*): 'May' Rightly *to* answer.
19. *Trin. MS* (*a*) and (*b*) omit ll. 19–25 and read instead, (*a*): By leaving out those harsh chromatic jars / Of sin that all our music mars / And in our lives and in our song. (*b*): By leaving out those harsh *chromatic* 'ill-sounding' jars / Of clamorous sin that all our music mars / And in our lives and in our song. *Trin. MS* (*c*): As once we could 'did' till disproportioned sin. (*d*): As once we *could* 'did' till disproportioned sin.
19–24. Cp. Du Bartas 256, where it is explained that the 'hidden love' which still exists between 'steel and Load-stone' or '*Elm* and the *Vine*', 'Is but a spark or shadow of that Love / Which at the first in every thing did move, / When as th' Earths *Muses* with harmonious sound / To Heav'ns sweet *Musick* humbly did resound. / But *Adam*, being chief of all the strings / Of this large Lute, o're-retched, quickly brings / All out of tune.' The idea that the singing of the heavenly host was audible to human ears till the fall is found in Dante, *Purgatorio* xxix 22–30; M. refers to it again, *PL* iv 680–8 and vii 561 (pp. 652 and 808 below).
20. *Trin. MS* (*c*): *Drowned* 'Jarred against' nature's chime and with *tumultuous* 'harsh' din. *nature's chime*] Echoing Jonson, *Underwoods* lxxv 26–7: 'The Month of youth, which calls all Creatures forth / To doe their Offices in Natures Chime.'
23. *diapason*] concord, harmony: literally, the concord through all the notes of the musical scale.

O may we soon again renew that song,
And keep in tune with heaven, till God ere long
To his celestial consort us unite,
To live with him, and sing in endless morn of light.

48 On Time

Date. 1633? There is no certain evidence for dating. For *Time*'s position in the Trinity MS and *1645* see headnote to *Solemn Music*, p. 161 above. Fletcher ii 174, 417–23 dates *Time* 1627–8 on the grounds that its metrics reflect the influence of Pindar and its content that of M.'s study of physics, begun some time during the academic year 1626–7. These reasons are clearly insufficient in themselves, and the appearance of even a fair copy of *Time* in the Trinity MS suggests a date later than Fletcher's.

In MS the poem was originally headed '[. . .] set on a clock case'. Later this was deleted and 'On Time' substituted.

Publication. *1645* (*10.* all]all,) *1673* (the text followed here).

Fly envious Time, till thou run out thy race,
Call on the lazy leaden-stepping hours,
Whose speed is but the heavy plummet's pace;
And glut thyself with what thy womb devours,
Which is no more than what is false and vain,
And merely mortal dross,
So little is our loss,
So little is thy gain.
For when as each thing bad thou hast entombed,
And last of all thy greedy self consumed,

25. Trin. MS (*c*): O may we soon ˋagainˊ renew that song.
26. And keep] *Trin. MS* (*a*) and (*b*): May keep.
27. consort] a company of musicians.
28. Trin. MS (*a*): To live and sing with him in ever-endless ˋever-gloriousˊ ˋunclipsedˊ ˋwhere day dwells without nightˊ ˋin endless morn ˋcloudless birthˊ ofˊ ˋin never-partingˊ light. (*b*), (*c*) and (*d*): To live and sing with him in endless morn of light.
¶ 48. *2. leaden-stepping*] Controlled by the movement of the lead plummet and moving in regular jerks or steps as the result of the functioning of the clock's escapement.
3. plummet] Commonly used in the seventeenth century, as here, to mean the weight of a clock.

Then long eternity shall greet our bliss
With an individual kiss;
And joy shall overtake us as a flood,
When every thing that is sincerely good
And perfectly divine,
With truth, and peace, and love shall ever shine
About the supreme throne
Of him, to whose happy-making sight alone,
When once our heavenly-guided soul shall climb,
Then all this earthy grossness quit,
Attired with stars, we shall for ever sit,
  Triumphing over Death, and Chance, and thee
  O Time.

49 Upon the Circumcision

Date. 1633? There is no certain evidence for dating. The feast of the Circumcision is 1 Jan., which may be relevant. For position in the Trinity MS and *1645* see headnote to *Solemn Music* and *Time* (pp. 161 and 165 above).
Publication. *1645*, *1673* (no significant variants).

Ye flaming powers and winged warriors bright,
That erst with music, and triumphant song
First heard by happy watchful shepherds' ear,

12. individual] Usually explained as 'inseparable', a common seventeenth-century meaning, i.e. a kiss in which the lips meet and can never again divide. But O. B. Hardinson Jr, *Texas Studies in Lit. and Lang.* iii (1961) 107–22, argues that the word means 'peculiar to a particular person', 'not collective', and that it thus represents M.'s contribution to the controversy, still active in the seventeenth century, over the Averroists' denial of personal immortality–a denial countered by St Thomas in the *De Unitate Intellectus Contra Averroistas Parisienses*. M.'s argument in *De doctrina* i 33 (Columbia xvi 352) that each man will rise from the dead with the same identity as he had in life supports Hardison's thesis.
14. sincerely] purely.
18. happy-making sight] an anglicization of the term 'beatific vision'. Bodleian MS Ashmole 36,37 f. 22r. has a version of *Time* in a seventeenth-century hand which omits ll. 18–22 and reads instead 'Of him whose happy-making sight alone / Shall heap our days with everlasting store / When death and chance and thou, O time, shall be no more'.
¶ 49. *1. powers*] the sixth order of angels in the pseudo-Dionysian nine. M. seems, however, to use the word loosely: it was the seraphim that were 'flaming'. *winged warriors*] Cp. Tasso, *Ger. Lib.* IX lx 1: *guerrieri alati*.
2. erst] formerly.

So sweetly sung your joy the clouds along
Through the soft silence of the listening night;
Now mourn, and if sad share with us to bear
Your fiery essence can distil no tear,
Burn in your sighs, and borrow
Seas wept from our deep sorrow,
He who with all heaven's heraldry whilere
Entered the world, now bleeds to give us ease;
Alas, how soon our sin
    Sore doth begin
        His infancy to seize!
O more exceeding love or law more just?
Just law indeed, but more exceeding love!
For we by rightful doom remediless
Were lost in death, till he that dwelt above
High-throned in secret bliss, for us frail dust
Emptied his glory, even to nakedness;
And that great covenant which we still transgress
Entirely satisfied,
And the full wrath beside
Of vengeful justice bore for our excess,
And seals obedience first with wounding smart
This day, but O ere long
Huge pangs and strong
        Will pierce more near his heart.

6–9. If the angels cannot weep, M. advises them to burn and so, like the sun, draw up water (seas of tears) from the earth.
10. heraldry] heraldic pomp (the first recorded instance of the word in this sense). *whilere*] some time ago.
13–14. These two lines are first written as one in *Trin. MS* and then re-written as two in the margin.
15–16. For the rhetorical pattern, cp. Virgil, *Ecl.* viii 49–50: *Crudelis mater magis, an puer improbus ille? / improbus ille puer: crudelis tu quoque, mater.*
17. doom] judgment.
19. secret] hidden.
20. Emptied his glory] Cp. *Philipp.* ii 7: 'made himself of no reputation', where the Vulgate reads *semetipsum exinanivit*, and M. in *De doctrina* I xvi gives *ipse sese inanivit* (Columbia xv 302).
21. covenant] the Mosaic law; cp. *Matt.* v 17: 'Think not that I am come to destroy the law . . . I am not come to destroy, but to fulfil.' M. argues the point in *De doctrina* I xvi (Columbia xv 316).
27–8. These two lines were first written as one in *Trin. MS*, and then re-written as two in the margin.
28. Will] *Trin. MS*(margin): *Shall* Will.

50 A Masque presented at Ludlow Castle, 1634 [Comus]

Date. 1634. First acted 29 Sept. 1634. The Earl of Bridgewater had been made President of the Council of Wales 26 June 1631, and Lord Lieutenant of Wales and the counties on the Welsh border 8 Jul. 1631. His youngest daughter Alice, aged fifteen, played the Lady, and his only surviving sons John, aged eleven, and Thomas, aged nine, were the Elder and Younger Brothers. The boys had acted in Thomas Carew's *Coelum Britannicum* on 18 Feb. 1634. Portraits of the children are reproduced in Lady Alix Egerton's edition of *Comus* (1910). Henry Lawes, their music teacher, wrote the music for *Coelum Britannicum* and for *Comus*, and played the Attendant Spirit. BM Add. MS 11518 has five songs from *Comus*, with music (reproduced Fletcher³ i 341–4), in a hand which (see French i 283) may be Lawes's. The Church MS (described by Evans 235f.) has the same songs in a hand apparently that of Lawes. The Bridgewater MS of *Comus* (referred to below as *Bridg*.), preserved at Bridgewater House, was once thought to be in Lawes's hand, but D. H. Stevens, *MP* xxiv (1927) 315–20, has demonstrated that it is the work of a professional scrivener. Fascimiles of the text of *Comus* as it appears in *Bridg*., the Trinity MS, the anonymous first edition (*1637*), *1645* and *1673*, will be found in Fletcher³ i 56, 193, 265, 301 and 399. C. S. Lewis's study of the surviving versions, *RES* viii (1932) 170–6, shows that the uncorrected state of the Trinity MS preceded *Bridg*. (a poor copy made without M.'s supervision), that various changes were made in the Trinity MS after *Bridg*. had been copied, that *1637* was based on the Trinity MS at an early stage of correction, and that M.'s tendency in revision was to delete technical terms and colloquialisms and increase the gnomic element at the expense of the dramatic. J. S. Diekhoff, *PMLA* lii (1937) 705–27, has demonstrated that even the uncorrected state of the Trinity MS is not the original draft of *Comus* but a later transcript. He makes a detailed examination, *PMLA* lv (1940) 748–72, of the alterations made by M. in the process of composition, which supplements the less minute study by L. E. Lockwood, *MLN* xxv (1910) 201–5. He also attempts to show, *PMLA* li (1936) 757–98, that the punctuation of *Comus* in *1645* (which differs little from that in *1673*) is frequently, though not consistently, rhetorical and prosodic. J. T. Shawcross, *Bibliog. Soc. of America Papers* liv (1960) 38–56 and 293–4, argues convincingly that *Bridg*. was probably not transcribed until autumn or winter 1637–8 and was derived from a copy of the Trinity MS text during its development into the version which survives; that *1637* (which may have been published early in 1638) was set from a revised intermediate copy (between the Trinity MS and *Bridg*.) with some corrections from the Trinity MS; and that the copy used for *1645* derived from a corrected *1637*.

Publication. *1637* is the first edition of *Comus*. It does not bear M.'s name. The text is preceded by a letter from Henry Lawes to John, Viscount Brackley (the Elder Brother), which makes it clear that Lawes is responsible for publishing. The reason he gives is that 'the often copying of it hath tired my pen to give my several friends satisfaction'. The title-page motto, from Virgil, *Ecl.* ii–*Eheu quid volui misero mihi! floribus austrum/ Perditus* ('Alas, what harm did I mean to my wretched self when I let the south wind blow upon my flowers?') – implies that M. (if M. chose it) had qualms about publishing. The publisher is not named on the title-page, but was probably John Raworth, whose widow Ruth printed *1645*. Probably not more than fifteen copies of this edition now survive (the Bodleian has two and the British Museum three).

1637 is generally more lightly punctuated than *1645* or *1673*. Compared with the text printed here it omits 181 commas, one semicolon, one full stop and one question mark; prints comma for semicolon 10 times, for question mark 5 times, for colon 4 times and for full stop 4 times; semicolon for colon twice and for full stop once. On the other hand, heavier punctuation in *1637*, though rare, is not unexampled. It adds 29 commas, prints semicolon for comma 5 times, full stop for comma (*918*), for semicolon (*553*), question mark for comma (*753*), and inserts one full stop (at the end of *967*). In *20* *1637* misprints 'my' for 'by'. Otherwise its verbal variants are: *43.* you]ye *73.* is]in *167–8. as 1645* *194.* stole]stol'n *213.* hovering]flittering *251.* it]she *389.* a]an *436.* Hath]Has *471.* Lingering]Hovering *512.* ye]you *537.* To]T' *579.* further]farther *604.* forms]bugs *607.* to a foul death]and cleave his scalp *608.* Cursed as his life]Down to the hips *780.* contemptuous]reproachful *955.* grow]are.

1645 was the next edition. (It has the following variants from the text printed here: *43.* you]ye *127.* report,]report. *146.* ground.]ground, *167–8.* And . . . aside]Whom thrift keeps up about his country gear, / But here she comes, I fairly step aside / And hearken, if I may, her business here. (*see footnote*) *347.* yet]yet, *354.* fears,]fears. *473.* sensuality] sensualty *485.* again, again,]again again *512.* vain]vain, *535.* bowers,]bowers. *549.* dissonance]dissonance, *553.* sleep;]sleep. *660.* statue,]statue; *763.* abundance]abundance, *781.* chastity;] chastity, *828.* The]She *855.* virgin]virgin, *922.* line]line, *970.* truth,]truth. *996.* mortals]mortals,). The text followed here is *1673*, except in *86*, *93*, *165* and *970* where *1673* prints full stops after 'song', 'fold', 'dust' and 'truth' (in the last of these instances it has the support of *1645*, see above. I have substituted a comma because the full stop may obscure the sense for a modern reader); and in *546*, *555* and *926*, where *1673* misprints 'meditate upon' for 'meditate', 'stream' for 'steam' and 'tumbled' for 'tumble'.

Genre and style. *Comus* was not put before the public under that title until 1738 when John Dalton (1709–63) adapted it for the eighteenth-century stage. In *1637*, *1645* and *1673* its title is *A Masque presented at Ludlow Castle, 1634*. The seventeenth-century masque developed in various directions (notably towards opera and towards a morality-type drama) so that generalization about it is misleading. But it is safe to say that pageantry and dancing play a smaller part in *Comus* than in most masques. Browne's *Inner Temple Masque* and Jonson's *Pleasure Reconciled to Virtue* are its closest relations in the masque form. The association of Circe with the sirens (classically unprecedented) and the anti-masque of monsters are found in Browne, and his description of Circe's power resembles Comus's speech on the reversal of natural order ('she that by charms can make / The scaled fish to leave the briny lake, / And on the seas walk as on land she were; / She that can pull the pale moon from her sphere, / And at mid-day the world's all-glorious eye / Muffle with clouds in long obscurity' 33–8). In Jonson's masque the figure of Comus first appeared on the stage. Both masques, however, are brief and frivolous compared with M.'s work. *Comus*'s most important affinity with court masques is undoubtedly the personal relationship existing in it and them between actors and members of the audience, resulting in an intimate atmosphere and a minute awareness of the relationships between real and assumed characters. These finer points are now lost irrevocably.

The attempts of Welsford and Haun (see below) to ally *Comus* generically with moral entertainments like Nabbes' *Microcosmus* and Ford and Dekker's *Sun's Darling* cannot survive an impartial reading of those works. They are latterday morality plays mixing low comic relief with stereotyped encounters between an everyman figure and allegorical representations of his attributes.

The Attendant Spirit's first speech, it has often been pointed out, resembles a Euripidean prologue, and there is one passage of stichomythia (*276–90*), but the structural debt to Greek drama does not extend beyond this.

Comus is, then, not a masque nor a moral entertainment (in the early seventeenth-century sense) so much as a Platonic pastoral drama. It derives its ethics largely from Plato's *Phaedo* (its fanciful cosmology is also affected by this work but more extensively by Plutarch's *Moralia*, see footnotes). Its pastoral dramatics stem from Tasso's *Aminta* (see Praz, below) and Guarini's *Pastor Fido*, not directly but by way of Fletcher's *Faithful Shepherdess*. This play prefigures the Lady in its chaste heroines, Clorin and Amoret, and Comus in its lascivious enchanter, the Sullen Shepherd, who, in his encounter with the priest (V i) also uses naturalistic arguments ('Hath not our Mother Nature for her store / And great increase, said it is good and just, / And wills that every living creature must / Beget his like?'), and who, when he meets Amoret benighted in the wood (III i) gives false news of her lost companion and is thanked by her ('Thanks, gentle shepherd') in a way which recalls *Comus 290–329*. Clorin's speech about the protective power of chastity (I i) is close to the Elder Brother's (*420–37*). Fletcher's Satyr, commissioned by Pan to patrol the wood ('Here I must stay / To see what mortals lose their way' III i) prefigures M.'s Attendant Spirit, and the God of the River who can cure the wounded Amoret only because she is a virgin (III i) is a prototype of Sabrina and talks, like her, in heptasyllables ('If thou be'st a virgin pure / I can give a present cure'). These parallels, and the constant struggle between chastity and vice in Fletcher's play, make it the most important single 'source'.

Shakespeare is M.'s stylistic master in *Comus*. Several speeches read like Shakespeare-pastiche (e.g. *325–9* and *596–8*, recalling, on the one hand, Hermione's tone in the *Winter's Tale* trial scene and, on the other, that of the lovers in *Antony and Cleopatra*), and there are thirty-two indisputable echoes, coming from fourteen of the plays and from *Lucrece*. The plays most drawn on are *Midsummer Night's Dream* (5 echoes), *Measure for Measure* and *Tempest* (4), and *Hamlet* and *Macbeth* (3). 'Votarist' (*188*), 'mountaineer' (*425*) and 'throng' (in a transitive sense) (*712*) are words first used by Shakespeare. Sylvester (10 echoes) and Jonson (7) are the other notable English influences. There are seven remarkably close echoes of Virgil and three of Horace. Surprisingly Spenser contributes only one or two phrases, but his effect on the vocabulary is considerable. Words like 'mickle' (*31*) betray an intermittent desire to give the diction Spenserian colour. 'Finny' (*115*), 'single' (in the sense 'absolute') (*203*), 'shroud' (meaning 'seek shelter') (*315*), 'shagged' (*428*) and 'surprisal' (*617*), are Spenserian in origin. 'Swinked' (*292*) is a pseudo-archaism of Spenserian type. M.'s verbal originality in *Comus* derives largely from imitation of Spenser's methods of coinage–adding prefixes ('un-', 'in-' etc.) and suffixes ('-n', '-y' etc.) to existing adjectives, nouns and, occasionally, verbs: 'unprincipled' (*366*), 'unenchanted' (*394*), 'ill-greeting' (*405*), 'unblenched' (*429*), 'imbrutes' (*467*), 'immanacled' (*664*), 'cateress' (*763*), 'azurn' (*892*), 'cedarn' (*989*), 'jocundry' and 'shroudy', both in cancelled passages in the Trinity MS; producing new participial forms: 'swilled' (*177*); coupling: 'love-lorn' (*233*) 'home-felt' (*261*), 'over-exquisite' (*358*); and giving new senses to current forms: 'blear' (in transferred use) (*155*), 'rife' (loud sounding) (*202*), 'siding' (taking side of a person) (*211*), 'mantling' (in transferred use) (*293*), 'unmuffle' (intransitive) (*330*), 'stoop' (bend neck or head) (*332*), 'rule' (shaft of light) (*339*), 'plumes' (preens) (*337*), 'unowned' (lost) (*406*), 'unharboured' (affording no shelter) (*422*), 'embodies' (takes on material character) (*467*), 'brow' (verb) (*531*), 'stabled' (put into stable) (*533*), 'budge' (adjective) (*706*), 'fence' (art of fencing) (*790*).

Modern criticism. In addition to the works specified above, Peele's *Old Wives' Tale* is sometimes mentioned as a 'source'. Arthos 1–15 reviews the case for it. R. H. Singleton, *PMLA* lviii (1943) 949–57, draws attention to the marked resemblances between the description and conception of Comus in M. and in the neo-Latin prose *Comus* (1608) of Erycius Puteanus (Hendrik van der Putten), Professor of Classical Literature at Louvain, which was reprinted at Oxford in 1634. There is less to be said for G. L. Finney's theory, *SP* xxxvii (1940) 482–500, that the form to which *Comus* belongs is the *dramma per musica*, and that it is to a large extent based on *La Catena d'Adone* (1626) by Tronsarelli. Mario Praz claims, on slender evidence, that Tasso's *Aminta* is the real model for *Comus* (*Seventeenth Century Studies Presented to Sir Herbert Grierson* (Oxford 1938) p. 202), and J. M. Major, *Shakespeare*

Quarterly x (1959) 177–83, thinks *The Tempest* influential. A large number of apparent borrowings from Shakespeare, especially *Romeo and Juliet*, are noted by E. Seaton, *E & S* xxxi (1945) 68–80. J. Arthos, *Anglia* lxxix (1961) 204–13, traces elements of the Sabrina episode to Virgil's description of the nymph Cyrene and her sisters in *Georg.* iv, and to Porphyry's neo-Platonic allegorization, in the *De antro nympharum*, of the cave of the nymphs in Homer, *Od.* xiii.

G. F. Sensabaugh, *SP* xli (1944) 238–49, views *Comus* as a reassertion of the genuine Platonic doctrine of love, in opposition to the debased court Platonism encouraged by Henrietta Maria; while for Hanford³ 81 M.'s masque is a reply to the libertine philosophy of Randolph's *Muse's Looking Glass.*

The doctrine of chastity or virginity in *Comus* has occasioned much controversy. Tillyard 373–83 concludes that, at the time he wrote *Comus*, M. 'intended his celibacy to last his life'. In a later study, (Tillyard³ 82–99: a revised version of *E & S* xxviii (1942) 22–37), he suggests that M.'s own ideal changed between 1634 and 1637, and that in the 1637 *Comus* it is represented neither by the Lady (who derives from Spenser's Belphoebe and Phineas Fletcher's Parthenia, and stands for virginity), nor by Comus (who stands for licence). Rather the ideal of *Comus* in its final version is marriage, and this is revealed, as Tillyard sees it, in *998–1010* (lines added some time between the first draft of the Trinity MS and *1637*). W. Haller, *JELH* xiii (1946) 79–97, also feels that virginity cannot be the ideal of *Comus*, because Puritan teaching about sex presented Christian marriage as the ideal: Haller assumes M.'s conformity with the usual Puritan religious and moral training. K. Muir, *Penguin New Writing* xxiv (1945) 141–3, rejects Tillyard's claim that M.'s ideal changed between 1634 and 1637, and holds that *1637* merely makes more explicit what had been M.'s meaning all along: that the views attributed to the Lady are one-sided and exaggerated. J. C. Maxwell, *Cambridge Journal* i (1948) 376–80, denies that there is any suggestion that the Lady's virtue is narrow or one-sided, and maintains that there is no contradiction between her speeches and the doctrine of the Attendant Spirit's last speech. It is merely that the main action displays the negative aspect of virtue, resistance to temptation, while the last speech emphasises the positive aspect, ascent. A. E. Dyson, *E & S* n.s. viii (1955) 89–114, agrees with Maxwell. Before the appearance of Tillyard's second study A. S. P. Woodhouse had argued, *UTQ* xi (1941) 46–71, that M. did set a marked value on the Christian concept of virginity at the time of writing *Comus*, but that the poem's meaning has two levels, one referring to the 'order of nature', the other to the 'order of grace', and that what virginity represents on the level of grace is represented on the level of nature by temperance and continence. C. Clarke, *Wind and Rain* vi (1949) 103–7, correctly objects that interpretations like those of Maxwell and Woodhouse ignore the Sabrina episode, in which 'the transition from a restrictive state of virtue to a positive one is worked out concretely in the poetry'. In reply Woodhouse, *UTQ* xix (1950) 218–23, reasserts his former view of *Comus*, but agrees that

Sabrina is introduced 'to transform chastity into a positive virtue, a principle of action, not in nature, but in grace'. When Sabrina sprinkles water, it represents a new infusion of divine grace, as *937* implies.

More individual judgments of *Comus* are those of D. C. Allen, *JELH* xvi (1949) 104–19, who considers that M. failed to reconcile the discordant elements of masque and drama, and of Circe myth and Sabrina story; R. H. Bowers, *SAMLA* 72–9, who believes that *Comus* is chiefly about the emotional problems of adolescence, that its moral conflict is limned in unsubtle black and white because youth regards life's choices in this way, and that the watchful guardian and the happy outcome emphasize that we are concerned with the world not merely of children but of privileged children; and D. Wilkinson, *E in C* x (1960) 32–43, who points out that, whereas on its first night *Comus* was the enactment of a family ritual, at later, public performances one might hope for something to compensate for private dramatic tensions, but in fact Comus and the Lady fail to engage: he is 'nominally' overwhelmed in an undramatic manner, and her rejection is merely 'nasty assertiveness', implying basic insecurity.

The labyrinthine and musical imagery is examined by Wilson Knight 65–7. In interpreting the rescue scene he suggests that 'mental inhibition is shadowed by the frozen paralysis during resistance imposed by Comus. The reversal of Comus's rod is needed to unbind the spell: which suggests a redirection of the same instinct. But the rod is lost; instinct sunk in repression.' A similar close attention to language and image leads Brooks and Hardy 188–237 to the conclusion that the susceptible Lady and the naïvely self-confident Elder Brother are treated ironically, and that 'haemony' (*637*) symbolizes virtue in a state of awareness of its own imperfection, as opposed to the virtue of the Elder Brother. This and other imaginative readings of *Comus* are rejected by R. M. Adams, *MP* li (1953) 18–32, who offers instead 'the simple beauties of obvious commonplaces set in musical language'. The light and dark imagery, made more complex by the fact that Circe is the Sun's daughter (*51*), is discussed by Tuve[2] 112–61, who regards the Circe myth as the 'hinge' of the masque. As she and others have pointed out (see especially M. Hughes, *Journal of the Hist. of Ideas* iv (1943) 381–99), Conti VI vi allegorizes Circe as lust (*libido*), the conflict between her and Ulysses as that between nature and reason, and moly as *divina clementia*. Tuve takes both haemony and water in *Comus* as symbols of grace, and thinks that M. kept primarily to the traditional purport of the Circe story, as recorded by Conti. This, however, does not make *Comus* 'pagan'–the Circe story had been Christianized before M. took it over. On the other hand J. Arthos, *Studies in the Renaissance* vi (1959) 261–74, sees *Comus* as an attempt to maintain the dignity of philosophy and non-Christian virtue. He explains M.'s association of 'chastity with temperance, prudence, wisdom, the power of contemplation, and the power of a special virtue over nature' by supposing that M. is using 'chastity' as a translation of Plato's σωφροσύνη in the *Charmides* and of Ficino's *temperantia* in his commentary on that work, which Arthos believes to be one of the sources of *Comus*. M. not only substitutes chastity for charity in the list of the three Christian theological virtues but also, says Arthos, secularizes faith and hope, which in the *De vita coelitus comparanda* Ficino names as the necessary prerequisites of effective magic. Another neo-Platonic interpretation is offered by S. Jane, *PMLA* lxxiv (1959) 533–43. He takes Jove (*20*) as the World Soul, and also divine providence, and Neptune (*18*) as natural providence. The action takes place in the realm of natural providence (of which both Comus and Sabrina are ministers) and represents the descent of the soul from heaven, its struggles against the demands of the flesh, and its victorious return. The human soul is represented jointly by the Lady (Reason) and Sabrina (a natural power of the soul, the *mens*, which preserves a memory of divinity). Haemony stands for Christian philosophical knowledge, the Elder Brother for idealism and the Younger Brother for patience. Chastity is one of the seven ways listed by Ficino in which the turning point in the soul's journey, the rejection of the flesh, can be accomplished before physical death.

The genre to which *Comus* belongs is discussed by E. Welsford, *The Court Masque* (Cambridge 1927) pp. 215–16, 315–16, who categorizes it as a moral entertainment like Nabbes' *Microcosmus* and Shirley's *Honoria and Mammon*. She also lists the similarities between *Comus* and Jonson's *Pleasure Reconciled to Virtue* and elaborates upon the differences between *Comus* and the normal court masque. Her conclusions are largely corroborated by E. Haun (Curry 221–39), who adds Ford and Dekker's *Sun's Darling*, Nabbes' *Spring's Glory* and Heywood's *Queen's Masque* to her examples of works in the same genre as *Comus*, and who compares *Bridg.* and the Trinity MS in order to demonstrate that *Comus* originally contained much more music than has come down to us: 'There is every reason to assume that *Comus* was continuous music from the invocation of Sabrina until the end of the masque, with only one interval of speech of nineteen lines.'

THE PERSONS

The Attendant Spirit, afterwards in the habit of Thyrsis.
Comus, with his crew.
The Lady.
1. Brother.
2. Brother.
Sabrina the Nymph.

The chief persons which presented, were
The Lord Brackley,
Mr. Thomas Egerton his brother,
The Lady Alice Egerton.

The first scene discovers a wild wood.
The Attendant Spirit descends or enters.

Before the starry threshold of Jove's court
My mansion is, where those immortal shapes
Of bright aerial spirits live ensphered
In regions mild of calm and serene air,

¶ 50. *Stage direction. The Attendant ... enters*] In *Trin. MS* this direction reads 'A guardian spirit, or daemon', and in *Bridg.* 'Then a guardian spirit or daemon descends or enters'.
1. Bridg. inserts before l. 1 the lines which appear in the printed texts as 975–98, but with the following variations: *975.* To the ocean]From the heavens *978.* fields]field *983–6. omitted* *987.* That there]There *994–5 Bridg. inserts between these lines* Yellow, watchet, green and blue *995.* with Elysian dew]oft with manna dew *996. omitted* *998.* young Adonis]many a cherub.
1–6. As B. A. Wright remarks, *TLS* (27 Oct. 1945) 367 and 511, the Spirit's 'mansion' (dwelling-place) is what Socrates calls the true surface of the earth. Socrates explains (*Phaedo* 109–111) that the earth 'has many hollows of very various forms and sizes, into which the water and mist and air have run together'. What men call earth is actually one of these hollows, 'but the earth itself is pure, and is situated in the pure heaven in which the stars are.... We do not perceive that we live in the hollows, but think we live on the upper surface of the earth.... By reason of feebleness and sluggishness we are unable to attain to the upper surface of the air.... People there have no diseases, and live much longer than we, and in sight and hearing and wisdom, and all such things, are as much superior to us as air [ἀήρ, hence M.'s 'aerial' (3)] is purer than water.' Apparently combined with this in M.'s mind is what Plutarch says in the *Moralia* about 'daemons': they are the souls of those who have 'done with the contests of life, and by prowess of soul become daemons' (593D): they aid those souls on earth which strive towards virtue (593F–594A): they live on the moon, just outside the earth's shadow (591B–C, 942F): theirs is an intermediary state–they await the separation of soul and mind, when mind will finally return to the sun (944E)–this is why M.'s daemon dwells *before* the threshold of Jove's court: they can descend from the moon to the earth 'as warders against misdeeds and chastisers of them' (944D): the earth below appears to them as an 'abyss' from which are heard 'innumerable roars and groans of animals, the wailing of innumerable babes, the mingled lamentations of men and women' (590F).
3. ensphered] placed in a celestial sphere. In Cicero's *Somnium Scipionis* the souls of the just dwell in the Milky Way, in the sphere of the fixed stars (cp. 'the pure heaven in which the stars are' in the previous note, and *Il Penseroso* 88–9 'unsphere / The spirit of Plato').
4–5. Between these lines *Trin. MS* inserts, and later deletes: Amidst the `*gardens*' Hesperian gardens, ON WHOSE BANKS `*where the banks*' / Bedewed with nectar and celestial songs / Eternal roses GROW, `*yield*' `*blow*' `*bloss'm*' `grow' and hyacinth / And fruits of golden rind, on whose fair tree / The scaly-harnessed *watchful* dragons `ever' keeps / His *never charmed* `unenchant-

Above the smoke and stir of this dim spot,
Which men call earth, and, with low-thoughted care
Confined, and pestered in this pinfold here,
Strive to keep up a frail, and feverish being
Unmindful of the crown that virtue gives
After this mortal change, to her true servants
Amongst the enthron'd gods on sainted seats.
Yet some there be that by due steps aspire
To lay their just hands on that golden key
That opes the palace of eternity:
To such my errand is, and but for such,
I would not soil these pure ambrosial weeds,
With the rank vapours of this sin-worn mould.

ed′ eye, and round the verge / And sacred limits of this *happy* ‵*blissful*′ ‵blissful′ isle / The jealous Ocean that old river winds / His far-extended arms, till with steep fall / Half his waste flood the wide Atlantic fills / And half the slow unfathomed ‵*pool of Styx*′ Stygian pool / *I doubt me gentle mortals these may seem / Strange distances to hear and unknown climes* / ‵But soft I was not sent to court your wonder / With distant worlds and strange removed climes′ / Yet thence I come and oft from thence behold.

5. Trin. MS: ‵Above′ The smoke and stir of this dim *narrow* spot.

7. pestered] 'crowded together' or 'with movements obstructed, like hobbled animals'. *pinfold*] a pound for confining stray horses and cattle (see l. 776*n*).

7–8. Trin. MS: ‵2.′ Strive to keep up a frail and feverish being / *Beyond the written date of mortal change* / ‵1.′ Confined and pestered in this pinfold here. (M.'s inserted numerals indicate that he wishes the order of the lines to be reversed).

10. mortal change] Brooks and Hardy 189 comment: 'The phrase "mortal change", for *death*, implies also that *change* is the rule of mortal existence'.

11. Cp. *Rev.* iv 4: 'And round about the throne were four and twenty seats: and upon the seats I saw four and twenty elders sitting, clothed in white raiment; and they had on their heads crowns of gold.'

12. by] *Bridg.*: with.

13. golden key] Cp. *Lycidas* 111 'The golden opes', and *Matt.* xvi 19: 'And I will give unto thee the keys of the kingdom of heaven'; also Jonson, *Hymenaei* 896–8, describing Truth: 'Her right hand holds a sunne with burning rayes, / Her left a curious bunch of golden kayes, / With which heaven gates she locketh, and displayes.'

14. opes] *Trin. MS*: shews ‵opes′.

16. ambrosial] immortal, hence, belonging to paradise, as here. *weeds*] clothes.

17. vapours] Cp. 'into which the water and mist and air have run together', ll. 1–6*n*, above. *sin-worn*] either 'worn out by sin' or, with reference to the first sense of 'mould', 'worn, as a garment, by or among sin'.

But to my task. Neptune besides the sway
Of every salt flood, and each ebbing stream,
Took in by lot 'twixt high, and nether Jove,
Imperial rule of all the sea-girt isles
That like to rich, and various gems inlay
The unadorned bosom of the deep,
Which he to grace his tributary gods
By course commits to several government,
And gives them leave to wear their sapphire crowns,
And wield their little tridents, but this isle
The greatest, and the best of all the main
He quarters to his blue-haired deities,
And all this tract that fronts the falling sun
A noble peer of mickle trust, and power
Has in his charge, with tempered awe to guide

mould] either 'earth, as the material of the human body' or 'the world, the earth'.

18. *Trin. MS*: But to my *business now* \`task.' Neptune *whose sway* \`besides the sway'.

20. *Took in*] annexed; perhaps M. is recalling Sylvester (Du Bartas 1003): 'Both upper Joves and neathers diverse Thrones'. In Homer, *Il.* xv 187–93, Poseidon tells how he and his two brothers drew lots for territories: he drew the sea, Zeus the heavens, Hades ('nether Jove') the underworld.

21. *Trin. MS*: \`Imperial' *The* rule *and title* of *each* \`all the' sea-girt isles. *sea-girt isles*] Echoes Jonson, *Underwoods* lxvii 33: 'sea-girt Isle'.

22. *Trin. MS*: That like to rich *gems inlay* \`and various gems inlay'. Echoing *Rich. II* II i 46: 'This precious stone set in the silver sea'.

24. *grace*] confer honour upon. *tributary*] paying tribute. For a catalogue of the river-gods who follow Neptune, see Spenser, *F.Q.* IV xi 11–47.

25. *By course*] duly. *several*] assigned distributively to a number of individuals.

28. *the main*] *Trin. MS*: *his empire* \`the main'.

29. *quarters*] assigns. *blue-haired deities*] Jonson, *Masque of Blackness* 32, introduces six Tritons, 'their upper parts humane, save that their haires were blue, as partaking of the sea-colour'. Jonson's marginal note refers to Ovid, *Met.* i 333 *caeruleum Tritona*. Cp. also Phineas Fletcher, *Sicelides* II vi: 'blue-beard Neptune'.

30. *this tract*] Wales and the Marches. H. Spencer, *MLN* xxiii (1908) 30, traces the line to Aeschylus, *Suppliants* 254–5: 'I rule all the region . . . on the side toward the setting sun.'

31. *peer*] the Earl of Bridgewater. *mickle*] great. One of the words Spenser employs to give his poetry an archaic ring. He uses it twenty-seven times.

32. *tempered*] free from extremes. *awe*] power to inspire fear or reverence.

An old, and haughty nation proud in arms:
Where his fair offspring nursed in princely lore,
Are coming to attend their father's state,
And new-entrusted sceptre, but their way
Lies through the perplexed paths of this drear wood,
The nodding horror of whose shady brows
Threats the forlorn and wandering passenger.
And here their tender age might suffer peril,
But that by quick command from sovran Jove
I was despatched for their defence, and guard;
And listen why, for I will tell you now
What never yet was heard in tale or song
From old, or modern bard in hall, or bower.
 Bacchus that first from out the purple grape,
Crushed the sweet poison of misused wine
After the Tuscan mariners transformed
Coasting the Tyrrhene shore, as the winds listed,
On Circe's island fell (who knows not Circe
The daughter of the Sun? Whose charmed cup
Whoever tasted, lost his upright shape,

33. *nation*] the Welsh. *proud in arms*] Echoes Virgil, *Aen.* i 21: *populum . . . belloque superbum.*

37. *perplexed*] entangled. *wood*] A symbol for the temptations of life in Dante, *Inferno* i 1–3 and Spenser, *F.Q.* I i 7–10. J. C. Maxwell, *N & Q* cciv (1959) 364, traces this line to Virgil, *Aen.* ix 391–2: *perplexum iter . . . fallacis silvae.*

44. *never yet was heard*] Echoing Horace, *Odes* III i 2–3: *carmina non prius audita.*

45. *From*] *Trin. MS*: *By* `From'.

46. *grape*] *Bridg.*: grapes.

47. *sweet poison*] Echoes *King John* I i 213: 'Sweet, sweet, sweet poison for the age's tooth.'

48. *After . . . transformed*] After the Tuscan (Italian) sailors had been transformed. The incident is described by Ovid, *Met.* iii 650–91: Bacchus, kidnapped by pirates, changes them to dolphins and their ship to an arbour of ivy.

49. *Tyrrhene*] The Tyrrhenian Sea lies between Italy and Corsica and Sardinia. *listed*] chose.

50–1. *Circe's island*] Cp. Homer, *Od.* x 135–8: 'We came to the isle of Aeaea, where dwelt fair-tressed Circe . . . sprung from Helius, who gives light to mortals'; also Browne, *Inner Temple Masque* 32: 'mighty Circe daughter to the Sun'. *who knows not Circe*] the figure is common in Spenser; cp. *Shep. Cal.* August 141: 'Of Rosalend (who knowes not Rosalend?)' and *F.Q.* VI x 16: 'Poore Colin Clout, (who knowes not Colin Clout?)'.

And downward fell into a grovelling swine)
This nymph that gazed upon his clustering locks,
With ivy berries wreathed, and his blithe youth,
Had by him, ere he parted thence, a son
Much like his father, but his mother more,
Whom therefore she brought up and Comus named,
Who ripe, and frolic of his full-grown age,
Roving the Celtic, and Iberian fields,
At last betakes him to this ominous wood,
And in thick shelter of black shades embowered,
Excels his mother at her mighty art,
Offering to every weary traveller,
His orient liquor in a crystal glass,
To quench the drought of Phoebus, which as they taste
(For most do taste through fond intemperate thirst)
Soon as the potion works, their human countenance,
The express resemblance of the gods, is changed

55. *ivy berries*] See *Elegia VI* 15–6*n* (p. 114).
58. *Whom*] *Trin. MS*: Which 'Whom' *Bridg.*: Which. *Comus named*] *Trin. MS*: *named him* Comus 'named'.

The parentage given for Comus is M.'s invention: the name corresponds to the Gk noun κῶμος (revelry). Comus is described in Philostratus, *Imagines* i 2, as a youth crowned with roses, and with a torch in his hand, standing, but falling into a drunken sleep. He appears as 'the god of cheere, or the belly' in Jonson's *Pleasure Reconciled to Virtue*, and, as R. C. Fox, *N & Q* ccvii (1962) 52–3, points out, in Jonson's *Poetaster* III iv 115–6 his name appears between those of Bacchus and Priapus. As Whiting 172 observes, Burton III ii 3 names Comus and Hymen together as loving 'masks and all such merriments above measure'. Massinger, *City Madam* IV ii has 'the god of pleasure . . . Comus'.

59. *frolic*] gay.
60. *Celtic, and Iberian fields*] France and Spain.
62. *shelter*] *Trin. MS*: *covert* 'shelter'. *shades*] *Trin. MS*: shade.
63. *mighty*] *Trin. MS*: *potent* '*mighty*'.
65. *orient*] shining, lustrous. *Trin. MS*: orient *like* liquor.
66. *drought of Phoebus*] thirst caused by the sun.
67. *fond*] foolish. *Trin. MS*: *weak* 'fond'.
68–75. E. G. Ainsworth, *MLN* xlvi (1931) 91–2, thinks that M. is following Ariosto's description of the rout of monsters outside Alcina's bower, *Orlando Furioso* vi 60–6, because the disfigurement is only from the neck upwards, and because the monsters are not aware of it: in Homer, *Od.* x 239–40, Ulysses' men are changed to swine, but their minds remain as before. In Browne's *Inner Temple Masque*, as in Ariosto, only the heads are changed. *potion*] *Trin. MS*: potions.
69. *express resemblance*] Cp. *Gen.* i. 27: 'So God created man in his own

Into some brutish form of wolf, or bear,
Or ounce, or tiger, hog, or bearded goat,
All other parts remaining as they were,
And they, so perfect is their misery,
Not once perceive their foul disfigurement,
But boast themselves more comely than before
And all their friends, and native home forget
To roll with pleasure in a sensual sty.
Therefore when any favoured of high Jove,
Chances to pass through this advent'rous glade,
Swift as the sparkle of a glancing star,
I shoot from heaven to give him safe convoy,
As now I do: but first I must put off
These my sky-robes spun out of Iris' woof,
And take the weeds and likeness of a swain,
That to the service of this house belongs,
Who with his soft pipe, and smooth-dittied song,
Well knows to still the wild winds when they roar,
And hush the waving woods, nor of less faith,
And in this office of his mountain watch,

image', and *Heb.* i 3: 'the express image of his person.' *of the*] *Trin. MS*: *of* o'the.

71. ounce] lynx.

72. they were] *Trin. MS*: *before* `they were′.

75–6. Cp. Homer, *Od.* ix 94–7: 'Whoever ate of the honey-sweet fruit of the lotus, had no longer any wish to bring back word or to return, but there they were fain to abide among the Lotus-eaters, feeding on the lotus, and forgetful of their homeward way.' Plutarch, *Moralia* 985D–992E has a dialogue in which Gryllus, one of Ulysses' companions transformed into a hog by Circe, converses with Ulysses and refuses to be turned back to human shape. This Gryllus appears in Spenser, *F.Q.* II xii 86–7 and Browne, *Inner Temple Masque* 193–216.

J. S. Diekhoff, *PQ* xx (1941) 603–4, remarks that the *1645* and *1673* punctuation allows two senses to emerge: they boast that not only 'themselves' but also 'all their friends' are 'more comely', and also they 'forget' all their friends.

79. advent'rous] *Trin. MS*: adventu`′′rous.

83. sky-robes] *Bridg.*: sky-webs *Iris' woof*] the woven fabric of the rainbow. The Attendant Spirit, called 'daemon' in *Trin. MS* and *Bridg.*, has neo-Platonic origins. Psellus, *De operatione daemonum* xviii, says that daemons' bodies are ductile and can take any form, as can clouds, and that they are also capable, like air or like water, of taking various colours.

86–8. A compliment to Lawes as a musician, equating him with Orpheus.

88. nor of less faith] no less loyal (than skilful as a musician).

Likeliest, and nearest to the present aid
Of this occasion. But I hear the tread
Of hateful steps, I must be viewless now.

Comus enters with a charming-rod in one hand, his glass in the other, with him a rout of monsters, headed like sundry sorts of wild beasts, but otherwise like men and women, their apparel glistering, they come in making a riotous and unruly noise, with torches in their hands.

Comus. The star that bids the shepherd fold,
Now the top of heaven doth hold,
And the gilded car of day,
His glowing axle doth allay
In the steep Atlantic stream,
And the slope sun his upward beam
Shoots against the dusky pole,

90. Trin. MS: Nearest and likeliest to *give* ‵the′ present *aid* ‵*chance*′ ‵aid′.
92. hateful] *Trin. MS*: *virgin* ‵hateful′. *viewless*] invisible. The word is first recorded in *Measure for Measure* III i 124.
Stage direction. Comus enters . . . hands] *Trin. MS*: *Exit* goes out. / Comus enters ‵with a charming rod and GLASS of liquor′ with his rout all headed like some wild beasts their / garments some like men's and some like women's they *begin* ‵come on in′ a wild and / *humorous* ‵antic′ fashion / intrant κωμάζοντες. *Bridg.* stage direction reads as *1673*, with following variants: l. 1. his glass]and a glass of liquor ll. 2–3. headed . . . women]like men and women but headed like wild beasts.
93. star] Hesperus, the evening star; cp. *Measure for Measure* IV ii 218: 'Look, th' unfolding star calls up the shepherd', and, as P. C. Ghosh, *TLS* (19 Feb. 1931) 135, notes, Virgil, *Ecl.* vi 85–6: 'Vesper gave the word to fold the flocks.'
95–6. gilded car . . . glowing axle] M. probably recalls the description of the sun's chariot ('car') in Ovid, *Met.* ii 107–10: 'Its axle was of gold, the pole of gold; its wheels had golden tyres, and a ring of silver spokes', and ii 230: 'He feels the chariot growing white-hot beneath his feet'. *allay*] cool.
97. steep] flowing precipitously. The Greeks imagined the Ocean as a river encircling the earth. As their geographical knowledge extended the name was applied to the outer sea, especially the Atlantic. Athenaeus, *Deipnosophistae* xi 469D–470D, cites several authorities, including Mimnermus and Aeschylus, in support of the belief that the sun travelled back over the waves of the Ocean in a golden bed, bowl or cauldron from the place of its setting to that of its rising. *Atlantic*] *Trin. MS*: *Tartessian* ‵Atlantic′.
98. slope] sloping, descending.
99. dusky] *Trin. MS*: *northern* ‵dusky′ *Bridg.*: northern. *pole*] sky (Latin *polus*, the heavens).

Pacing toward the other goal
Of his chamber in the east.
Meanwhile, welcome joy, and feast,
Midnight shout, and revelry,
Tipsy dance, and jollity.
Braid your locks with rosy twine
Dropping odours, dropping wine.
Rigour now is gone to bed,
And Advice with scrupulous head,
Strict Age, and sour Severity,
With their grave saws in slumber lie.
We that are of purer fire
Imitate the starry quire,
Who in their nightly watchful spheres,
Lead in swift round the months and years.
The sounds, and seas with all their finny drove
Now to the moon in wavering morris move,
And on the tawny sands and shelves,
Trip the pert fairies and the dapper elves;
By dimpled brook, and fountain-brim,
The wood-nymphs decked with daisies trim,
Their merry wakes and pastimes keep:
What hath night to do with sleep?
Night hath better sweets to prove,
Venus now wakes, and wakens Love.

101. chamber] Cp. *Ps.* xix 4–5: 'the sun, which is as a bridegroom coming out of his chamber'.
108. And Advice with] *Trin. MS*: And *nice* [*Cus* ?]*tom* `Advice' with *her*. Advice is personified in *Rape of Lucrece* 907.
110. saws] maxims.
111–4. The idea of the universe as a great dance had been popularized by Sir John Davies's *Orchestra* (1596). Plato, *Tim.* 40 describes the stars and planets 'circling as in a dance'. *We . . . purer fire*] Echoes Randolph ii 609: 'But we whose souls are made of purer fire, / Have other aims.' *watchful spheres*] See *Vacation Exercise* 40n (p. 77). *Lead in*] *Trin. MS*: Lead *with* `in'.
115. sounds] straits. *finny drove*] As E. S. Le Comte, *N & Q* clxxxiv (1943) 17–8, points out, the phrase is taken from Spenser, *F.Q.* III viii 29, who coined the adjective 'finny'.
116. morris] morris (i.e. Moorish) dance.
117. tawny] *Trin. MS*: *yellow* `tawny' (a change perhaps made to avoid too obvious a reminiscence of *Tempest* I ii 376, where Ariel sings of dancing on the 'yellow sands'). *shelves*] sandbanks.
121. wakes] revels.
123. hath] *Bridg.*: has.

Come let us our rites begin,
'Tis only daylight that makes sin
Which these dun shades will ne'er report,
Hail goddess of nocturnal sport
Dark-veiled Cotytto, to whom the secret flame
Of midnight torches burns; mysterious dame
That ne'er art called, but when the dragon womb
Of Stygian darkness spits her thickest gloom,
And makes one blot of all the air,
Stay thy cloudy ebon chair,
Wherein thou rid'st with Hecat', and befriend
Us thy vowed priests, till utmost end
Of all thy dues be done, and none left out,
Ere the blabbing eastern scout,
The nice Morn on th' Indian steep
From her cabined loophole peep,
And to the tell-tale sun descry
Our concealed solemnity.

129. Cotytto] A Thracian goddess whose licentious rites were held secretly at night. Stephanus (*s.v. Cotytto*) calls her *dea impudentiae* and refers to her *nocturna sacra* and the lascivious dances of her priests. Cp. Juvenal ii 91–2, which Stephanus quotes.

130. burns] *Bridg.*: burn.

131. dragon] See *Prae E* 56–8*n*, p. 26 above.

133. Trin. MS: *And makes a blot of nature* *And throws a blot on*' \And makes one blot of' all the air.

134–7. Trin. MS: Stay thy *polished* \cloudy' ebon chair / *And favour our close revelry* *jocundry*' \Wherein thou rid'st with Hecate and befriend / Us thy vowed priests till utmost end' / *Till* \Of' all thy dues be done and *nought* \none' left out. (This is the first occurrence of 'jocundry' cited in *OED*).

135. Hecat'] Hecate, goddess of sorcery, invoked by witches.

138. blabbing] Echoes II *Henry VI* IV i 1: 'The gaudy, blabbing and remorseful day'.

139. nice] affectedly modest. The morn (Aurora) was not really modest, but had carried off Cephalus against his will, as Ovid describes, *Met.* vii 700–13. *steep*] mountain slope; cp. *Midsummer Night's Dream* II i 69: 'the furthest steep of India'.

140. cabined loophole] tiny window: Comus envisages a tiny part of the rising sun peeping above the horizon. 'Loophole' meant particularly 'port-hole', thus there is play on 'cabined' (cramped or confined).

141. tell-tale] Echoes Shakespeare, *Lucrece* 806: 'tell-tale Day'. *descry*] reveal.

142. solemnity] celebration.

Come, knit hands, and beat the ground,
In a light fantastic round.

The Measure.

Break off, break off, I feel the different pace,
Of some chaste footing near about this ground.
Run to your shrouds, within these brakes and trees,
Our number may affright: some virgin sure
(For so I can distinguish by mine art)
Benighted in these woods. Now to my charms,
And to my wily trains, I shall ere long
Be well stocked with as fair a herd as grazed
About my mother Circe. Thus I hurl
My dazzling spells into the spongy air,
Of power to cheat the eye with blear illusion,
And give it false presentments, lest the place
And my quaint habits breed astonishment,
And put the damsel to suspicious flight,
Which must not be, for that's against my course;
I under fair pretence of friendly ends,
And well-placed words of glozing courtesy
Baited with reasons not unplausible

144. Trin. MS: *With* 'In' a light *and frolic* fantastic round *round*] a ring-dance: cp. the 'round' which Titania's fairies dance in the moonlight in *Midsummer Night's Dream* II i 140.
Stage direction. The Measure] In the seventeenth century 'measure' could denote either a tune or a dance. *Trin. MS* and *Bridg.* add 'in a wild rude and wanton antic'.
145. feel] *Trin. MS*: *hear* feel.
147. shrouds] hiding places.
147–8. Trin. MS: *Some virgin sure benighted in these woods / For so I can distinguish by mine art /* Run to your shrouds within these brakes and trees–They all scatter / Our number may affright. Some virgin sure. *Bridg.* reads as *1673* but, like *Trin. MS*, adds the direction 'they all scatter' to l. 147.
150. charms] *Trin. MS*: *trains* charms.
151. trains] allurements. *Trin. MS*: *mother's charms* wily trains.
154. dazzling] *Trin. MS*: *powdered* 'dazzling' (cp. 'magic dust' l. 165–Comus evidently threw some kind of glittering powder into the air). *spongy*] absorbent (i.e. absorbing his spells).
155. with blear illusion] *Trin. MS*: with *sleight* '*blind*' 'blear' illusion. 'Blear' means 'dim, misty', and was originally applied only to the eyes. This is the first recorded usage of the word in a transferred sense.
156. presentments] appearances. *lest*] *Trin. MS*: *else* 'lest'.
157. quaint habits] unfamiliar dress.
161. glozing] flattering. *Bridg.*: glowing.

Wind me into the easy-hearted man,
And hug him into snares. When once her eye
Hath met the virtue of this magic dust,
I shall appear some harmless villager
And hearken, if I may her business hear.
But here she comes, I fairly step aside.

The Lady enters.

Lady. This way the noise was, if mine ear be true,
My best guide now, methought it was the sound
Of riot, and ill-managed merriment,
Such as the jocund flute, or gamesome pipe
Stirs up among the loose unlettered hinds,
When for their teeming flocks, and granges full,
In wanton dance they praise the bounteous Pan,
And thank the gods amiss. I should be loth
To meet the rudeness, and swilled insolence
Of such late wassailers; yet O where else

163. Wind me into] insinuate myself into the confidence of.
164. snares] *Trin. MS*: *nets* ˋsnaresˊ.
165. virtue] power, efficacy.
166–8. As will be seen from the headnote, *1637* and *1645* have a line between ll. 166 and 167 which *1673* omits, and print ll. 167 and 168 in the reverse order. In *1673* l.167 was originally printed 'And hearken, if I may, her business here', but the *Errata* corrected the punctuation, and the spelling of 'here', to make the line read as in the present text. This attention paid to l. 167 in the *1673 Errata* makes it unlikely that the differences between *1637* and *1645* on the one hand, and *1673* on the other, can at this point be attributed merely to the printer. Perhaps the rhyme of 'gear' and 'here' in *1637* and *1645* offended M.'s ear, and made him decide to change the passage. *Trin. MS* and *Bridg.* read with *1645*, except that *Trin. MS* inserts 'thirst' as a marginal alternative to 'thrift' in the line later omitted.
168. fairly] softly.
169. mine] *Trin. MS*: my.
170. My best guide] *Trin. MS*: My ˋbestˊ guide.
173. loose] dissolute. *hinds*] farm workers. *Hero and Leander* ii 218 has 'illit'rate hinds'.
174. Trin. MS: ˋ*When* ˋ*That*ˊ ˋ*When*ˊ for their teeming flocks, and *garners* ˋgrangesˊ full'. *teeming*] breeding offspring.
175. they praise] *Trin. MS*: THEY PRAISE ˋ*adore*ˊ. *Pan*] god of woods and shepherds.
177. swilled] To 'swill' is to fill with drink: *OED* records this as the only occurrence of the participial adjective.
178. wassailers] revellers.

Shall I inform my unacquainted feet
In the blind mazes of this tangled wood?
My brothers when they saw me wearied out
With this long way, resolving here to lodge
Under the spreading favour of these pines,
Stepped as they said to the next thicket-side
To bring me berries, or such cooling fruit
As the kind hospitable woods provide.
They left me then, when the grey-hooded Even
Like a sad votarist in palmer's weed
Rose from the hindmost wheels of Phoebus' wain.
But where they are, and why they came not back,
Is now the labour of my thoughts, 'tis likeliest
They had engaged their wand'ring steps too far,
And envious darkness, ere they could return,
Had stole them from me, else O thievish Night
Why shouldst thou, but for some felonious end,
In thy dark lantern thus close up the stars,
That Nature hung in heaven, and filled their lamps
With everlasting oil, to give due light
To the misled and lonely traveller?
This is the place, as well as I may guess,
Whence even now the tumult of loud mirth
Was rife, and perfect in my listening ear,
Yet nought but single darkness do I find.

179. In *Trin. MS* this line is a later insertion.
180. *Trin. MS*: In the blind *alleys* 'mazes' of *these* 'this' *arched* 'tangled' wood.
187–9. *Bridg.* omits.
188. *votarist*] one who has taken a vow (of pilgrimage): the word is first used by Shakespeare, *Measure for Measure* I iv 5. *palmer*] a pilgrim who had visited the Holy Land, and carried a branch of palm as a sign of this.
189. *wain*] *Trin. MS*: *chair* 'wain'.
192. *wand'ring*] *Trin. MS*: *youthly* 'wand'ring'.
193. *And envious*] *Trin. MS*: *To the soon-parting light* and envious.
194. *stole*] *Trin. MS*: stol'n.
194–224. *Else . . . grove*] *Bridg.* omits.
196. *dark lantern*] A lantern with a slide or arrangement by which the light can be concealed. M.'s use here antedates the first occurrence in *OED* (1650).
197–8. Cp. *Macbeth* II i 4–5: 'there's husbandry in heaven, / Their candles are all out.'
198. *due*] *Trin. MS*: *their* 'due'.
202. *rife*] loud-sounding (the first occurrence in this sense in *OED*). *perfect*] heard distinctly.
203. *single*] absolute–a sense first found in Spenser, *F.Q.* II x 21.

What might this be? A thousand fantasies
Begin to throng into my memory
Of calling shapes, and beckoning shadows dire,
And airy tongues, that syllable men's names
On sands, and shores, and desert wildernesses.
These thoughts may startle well, but not astound
The virtuous mind, that ever walks attended
By a strong siding champion Conscience. . . .
O welcome pure-eyed Faith, white-handed Hope,
Thou hovering angel girt with golden wings,
And thou unblemished form of Chastity,
I see ye visibly, and now believe
That he, the Supreme Good, t' whom all things ill
Are but as slavish officers of vengeance,
Would send a glistering guardian if need were
To keep my life and honour unassailed.
Was I deceived, or did a sable cloud
Turn forth her silver lining on the night?
I did not err, there does a sable cloud
Turn forth her silver lining on the night,
And casts a gleam over this tufted grove.
I cannot hallo to my brothers, but
Such noise as I can make to be heard farthest
I'll venture, for my new-enlivened spirits
Prompt me; and they perhaps are not far off.

207. airy tongues] Echoes *Romeo and Juliet* II i 163 'airy tongue'. *that . . . names*] *Trin. MS*: *that lure night-wanderers* \`that syllable men's names'. Perhaps M. recalls Purchas iii 75: 'They say that there [in the Desert of Lop] dwell many spirits which cause great and mervailous Illusions to Travellers to make them perish. For if any stay behind that he cannot see his company, he shall be called by name, and so going out of the way is lost.'

211. siding] the first recorded use of the word in the sense 'taking the side of a person'.

213. hovering] *Trin. MS*: *flittering* \`hovering'. Diekhoff 723 and Shawcross[2] 42 think 'flittering' the better reading.

214. unblemished] *Trin. MS*: *unspotted* \`unblemished'.

215. Trin. MS: I see ye visibly, *and while I see ye / This dusky hollow is a paradise / And heaven gates o'er my head* \`and' now *I* believe.

216. That he, the] *Trin. MS*: That \`He' the.

218. guardian] *Trin. MS*: *cherub* \`guardian'.

220–3. Imitating Ovid, *Fasti* v 549: *Fallor, an arma sonant? non fallimur, arma sonabant* (Am I deceived, or is that the sound of arms? I am not deceived, it is the sound of arms).

SONG

Sweet Echo, sweetest nymph that liv'st unseen
    Within thy airy shell
  By slow Meander's margent green,
And in the violet-embroidered vale
  Where the love-lorn nightingale
Nightly to thee her sad song mourneth well.
Canst thou not tell me of a gentle pair
  That likest thy Narcissus are?
    O if thou have
  Hid them in some flowery cave,
    Tell me but where
  Sweet queen of parley, daughter of the sphere.
  So mayst thou be translated to the skies,
And give resounding grace to all heaven's harmonies.

Comus. Can any mortal mixture of earth's mould
Breathe such divine enchanting ravishment?
Sure something holy lodges in that breast,
And with these raptures moves the vocal air
To testify his hidden residence;
How sweetly did they float upon the wings
Of silence, through the empty-vaulted night

229–42. The 'echo scene', in which the echo catches up and twists the ends of the speaker's sentences, had been common in Elizabethan and Jacobean drama (e.g. Browne, *Inner Temple Masque* 267–79, Jonson, *Cynthia's Revels* I ii, Webster, *Duchess of Malfi* V iii). The Lady's loneliness is enhanced because, unusually, no echo replies.

230. airy shell] *Trin. MS*: airy shell ˋcellˊ. The 'shell' is the vault of the sky (cp. 'daughter of the sphere', l. 241, where 'sphere' seems to mean 'the apparent outward limit of space, viewed from the earth'). Starnes and Talbert 249 quote from Stephanus *Echo, Nympha, nullo oculo viso . . . Amicam . . . Moderatoris omnium corporum coelestium, ex quibus ipsa componitur atque temperatur.*

231. By slow] *Trin. MS*: By ˋslowˊ.

233. love-lorn] The first recorded occurrence. In later usage it comes to mean 'forsaken by one's love', but as Philomela (the nightingale) was raped by her brother-in-law Tereus, M. presumably uses the term to mean 'lost or ruined through love'.

240. parley] speech.

242. And . . . grace] *Trin. MS*: *And hold a counterpoint* ˋAnd give resounding graceˊ. *Bridg.*: And hold a counterpoint. This is the only alexandrine in *Comus*, mimicking the lengthening of heaven's song by echo.

242–3. Trin. MS inserts: Comus *enters* ˋlooks in and speaksˊ.

247. his] i.e. that of the 'something holy'.

At every fall smoothing the raven down
Of darkness till it smiled: I have oft heard
My mother Circe with the Sirens three,
Amidst the flowery-kirtled Naiades
Culling their potent herbs, and baleful drugs,
Who as they sung, would take the prisoned soul,
And lap it in Elysium, Scylla wept,
And chid her barking waves into attention,
And fell Charybdis murmured soft applause:
Yet they in pleasing slumber lulled the sense,
And in sweet madness robbed it of itself,
But such a sacred, and home-felt delight,
Such sober certainty of waking bliss
I never heard till now. I'll speak to her
And she shall be my queen. Hail foreign wonder
Whom certain these rough shades did never breed
Unless the goddess that in rural shrine

250. *fall*] cadence.
251. For the conception of darkness as a bird, see *L'Allegro* 6. *it*] darkness. *Trin. MS* and *Bridg.*: she.
252–3. *Circe ... Sirens three*] In Homer, *Od.* xii 37–72, it is Circe who tells Ulysses of the Sirens, but Browne, *Inner Temple Masque* 1–96, like M., represents the Sirens as Circe's attendants. In Homer and Browne there are only two Sirens. *Naiades*] freshwater nymphs: in Homer, *Od.* x 348–51, the maidens who wait on Circe are 'children of the springs and groves and of the sacred rivers that flow forth to the sea'.
253–4. *Trin. MS*: '`Sitting'` amidst the flowery-kirtled Naiade`e's / Culling their *potent* `*powerful*' `*mighty*' `potent' herbs and baleful drugs'.
254. *potent herbs*] Echoes Virgil, *Aen.* vii 19, where it is with *potentibus herbis* that Circe transforms men.
255. *as*] *Bridg.*: when.
256. *wept*] *Trin. MS*: *would weep* `wept'.
256–8. Apparently suggested by Silius Italicus xiv 476, where, at the pipe-playing of Daphnis 'Scylla's dogs were silent, black Charybdis stood still'. *barking waves*] Echoes Virgil, *Aen.* vii 588: *latrantibus undis*. *fell Charybdis*] Both Sandys 248 and Sylvester (Du Bartas 273) have this phrase.
257. *And child*] *Trin. MS*: *And* `And' chide`*ing*'.
261. *home-felt*] felt intimately. This is the first recorded occurrence of the word.
264–6. *Hail .... goddess*] Echoes *Tempest* I ii 22–6, where Ferdinand first meets Miranda, 'Most sure, the goddess / On whom these airs attend! ... O you wonder!'
265. *Whom certain these*] *Trin. MS*: Whom `certain' these.
266. *Unless .... goddess*] unless (you are) the goddess.

Dwell'st here with Pan, or Sylvan, by blest song
Forbidding every bleak unkindly fog
To touch the prosperous growth of this tall wood.
Lady. Nay gentle shepherd ill is lost that praise
That is addressed to unattending ears,
Not any boast of skill, but extreme shift
How to regain my severed company
Compelled me to awake the courteous Echo
To give me answer from her mossy couch.
Comus. What chance good lady hath bereft you thus?
Lady. Dim darkness, and this leafy labyrinth.
Comus. Could that divide you from near-ushering guides?
Lady. They left me weary on a grassy turf.
Comus. By falsehood, or discourtesy, or why?
Lady. To seek i' the valley some cool friendly spring.
Comus. And left your fair side all unguarded lady?
Lady. They were but twain, and purposed quick return.
Comus. Perhaps forestalling night prevented them.
Lady. How easy my misfortune is to hit!
Comus. Imports their loss, beside the present need?
Lady. No less than if I should my brothers lose.
Comus. Were they of manly prime, or youthful bloom?
Lady. As smooth as Hebe's their unrazored lips.
Comus. Two such I saw, what time the laboured ox
In his loose traces from the furrow came,
And the swinked hedger at his supper sat;

267. Dwell'st] *Trin. MS*: *Liv'st* `Dwell'st'. *Pan . . . Sylvan*] See l. 175*n* and *Il Penseroso* 134*n* (p. 145). Virgil also mentions the two gods together, *Ecl.* x 24–6.

269. prosperous] *Trin. MS*: *prospering* `prosperous'. *Bridg.*: prospering.

272. shift] expedient necessitated by stress of circumstances.

276–89. An imitation of the dialogue in alternate lines of verse (stichomythia) common in Greek drama.

277. Dim darkness] Echoes Shakespeare, *Lucrece* 118 'dim darkness'.

278. near-ushering guides] *Trin. MS*: *their* `near' ushering *hands* `guides'.

279. weary] *Trin. MS*: wearied.

281. some cool] *Trin. MS*: some `cool'.

285. hit] guess.

286. Imports their loss] Is their loss of importance?

289. Hebe's] See *Vacation Exercise* 38*n* (p. 77).

290–1. Two such] *Trin. MS*: Such two. Homer, *Il.* xvi 779, calls evening 'the time for the unyoking of oxen', and at evening in Virgil, *Ecl.* ii 66: 'The bullocks drag home by the yoke the hanging plough.'

292. swinked] wearied. This is the first occurrence of the word in *OED;*

I saw them under a green mantling vine
That crawls along the side of yon small hill,
Plucking ripe clusters from the tender shoots,
Their port was more than human, as they stood;
I took it for a faëry vision
Of some gay creatures of the element
That in the colours of the rainbow live
And play i' the plighted clouds. I was awe-struck,
And as I passed, I worshipped; if those you seek
It were a journey like the path to heaven,
To help you find them.
Lady. Gentle villager
What readiest way would bring me to that place?
Comus. Due west it rises from this shrubby point.
Lady. To find out that, good shepherd, I suppose,
In such a scant allowance of star-light,
Would overtask the best land-pilot's art,
Without the sure guess of well-practised feet.
Comus. I know each lane, and every alley green
Dingle, or bushy dell of this wild wood,
And every bosky bourn from side to side
My daily walks and ancient neighbourhood,
And if your stray attendance be yet lodged,
Or shroud within these limits, I shall know

M. has coined an archaistic past-participial adjective (O.E. *swincan*, to labour).

293. saw them] *Trin. MS* and *Bridg.*: saw'em. *mantling*] the first recorded usage of the word in the sense 'spreading and covering': previously it had been applied only to liquids, meaning 'gathering a coating of scum'.

296. port] bearing. An echo of Euripides, *Iphigenia in Tauris* 260–74, where the herdsman tells how one of his companions mistook Pylades and Orestes for gods.

298. element] sky.

299. colours] *Bridg.*: coolness.

300. plighted] folded. In the *History of England* (Columbia x 69) M. has 'she [Boadecea] wore a plighted Garment of divers colours'.

303. them] *Trin. MS*: them *out.*

309. the sure guess] *Trin. MS*: ˋtheˊ sure *steerage of* guess.

311. Dingle] hollow between hills. *wild*] *Trin. MS*: wide ˋwildˊ. *Bridg.*: wide. Diekhoff 723 and Shawcross[2] 42 prefer 'wide'.

312. bosky bourn] bushy stream.

314. attendance] attendants.

315. Or shroud within these limits] *Trin. MS*: ˋOr shroudˋ*ed*ˊˊ ˋwithinˊ *Within* these *shroudy* limits. (This is the only occurrence of 'shroudy' re-

Ere morrow wake, or the low-roosted lark
From her thatched pallet rouse, if otherwise
I can conduct you lady to a low
But loyal cottage, where you may be safe
Till further quest.
Lady. Shepherd I take thy word,
And trust thy honest-offered courtesy,
Which oft is sooner found in lowly sheds
With smoky rafters, than in tap'stry halls
And courts of princes, where it first was named,
And yet is most pretended: in a place
Less warranted than this, or less secure
I cannot be, that I should fear to change it,
Eye me blest Providence, and square my trial
To my proportioned strength. Shepherd lead on. . . .

The two Brothers.

Eld. Bro. Unmuffle ye faint stars, and thou fair moon
That wont'st to love the traveller's benison,
Stoop thy pale visage through an amber cloud,
And disinherit Chaos, that reigns here

corded in *OED*). 'Shroud', meaning 'seek shelter', is a Spenserianism, first recorded in *Shep. Cal.* February 122.
316. *Ere . . . wake*] *Trin. MS*: *Ere the lark rouse* 'Ere morrow wake'. *-roosted*] *Bridg.*: -rooster.
317. *pallet*] bed of straw.
320. *quest*] *Trin. MS*: quest *be made*.
321–5. Cp. Ariosto, *Orlando Furioso* xiv 62, which Harington xiv 52 translates: 'As curtesie oft times in simple bowres / Is found as great as in the stately towres'; also Spenser, *F.Q.* VI, which is full of types of rural courtesy like the savage man (VI v) and Pastorella, Sir Calidore's own lady: the graces dance around Colin Clout in a pastoral setting, and it is they who bestow courtesy (VI x 23).
323. *With*] *Trin. MS*: *And* 'With'.
324. *where . . . named*] 'courtesy' derives from 'court'.
325. *yet . . . pretended*] *Trin. MS*: *is pretended yet* yet is most pretended.
326. *or . . . secure*] *Trin. MS*: *I cannot be* or less secure.
328. *square*] adjust. *my trial*] *Trin. MS*: *this* 'my' trial.
330. *Unmuffle*] remove a muffling–the first recorded intransitive use of 'unmuffle'. Echoes Sylvester (Du Bartas 251): 'While nights black muffler hoodeth up the skies', (614) 'A sable ayr so muffles-up the Sky'.
331. *wont'st*] are accustomed to. *benison*] blessing.
332. *Stoop*] *OED* records this as the first usage in the sense 'bend the head, face or neck'.
333. *disinherit*] dispossess.

In double night of darkness, and of shades;
Or if your influence be quite dammed up
With black usurping mists, some gentle taper
Though a rush-candle from the wicker hole
Of some clay habitation visit us
With thy long levelled rule of streaming light,
And thou shalt be our star of Arcady,
Or Tyrian Cynosure.
Sec. Bro. Or if our eyes
Be barred that happiness, might we but hear
The folded flocks penned in their wattled cotes,
Or sound of pastoral reed with oaten stops,
Or whistle from the lodge, or village cock
Count the night-watches to his feathery dames,
'Twould be some solace yet some little cheering
In this close dungeon of innumerous boughs.
But O that hapless virgin our lost sister
Where may she wander now, whither betake her
From the chill dew, amongst rude burs and thistles?
Perhaps some cold bank is her bolster now
Or 'gainst the rugged bark of some broad elm
Leans her unpillowed head fraught with sad fears,

337. *wicker hole*] window covered in wickerwork.
339. *thy*] *Trin. MS*: *a* ‵thy′. *rule*] the first recorded usage in the sense 'shaft or beam of light'. In Euripides, *Suppliants* 650, a ray of the sun is called a 'clear rule'.
340–1. *Cynosure*] constellation of the Lesser Bear, or the Pole Star, at the tip of its tail. 'Tyrian', because the Phoenicians steered by the Lesser Bear, the Greeks by the Greater. 'Star of Arcady', because Arcas, who was stellified as Arcturus, was the son of Callisto, daughter of Lycaon, king of Arcadia. M. may have known the story from Hyginus or, more probably, think Starnes and Talbert 244, from the summary of his version in Stephanus.
343. *in their*] *Trin. MS*: in ‵their′.
344. *pastoral reed with oaten stops*] shepherd's pipe: the 'stops' were the finger-holes. Cp. Spenser, *Shep. Cal.* January 72 'oaten pype', and October 8 'Oten reedes' (glossed there *Avena* by E. K.–a word Virgil uses, *Ecl.* i 2, for the shepherd's pipe).
348. *In . . . close*] *Trin. MS*: In ‵this′ *lone* ‵*sad*′ ‵close′. *Bridg.*: In this lone. *innumerous*] innumerable.
350. *she wander*] *Trin. MS*: she ‵wander′.
351. *amongst . . . thistles*] *Trin. MS*: *in this dead solitude* ‵*surrounding wild*′ ‵*perhaps some cold hard bank*′ ‵amongst rude burs and thistles′.
354. *Trin. MS*: *She* leans her *thoughtful head musing at our unkindness* ‵unpillowed head fraught with sad fears′.

What if in wild amazement, and affright,
Or while we speak within the direful grasp
Of savage hunger, or of savage heat?
Eld Bro. Peace brother, be not over-exquisite
To cast the fashion of uncertain evils;
For grant they be so, while they rest unknown,
What need a man forestall his date of grief,
And run to meet what he would most avoid?
Or if they be but false alarms of fear,
How bitter is such self-delusion!
I do not think my sister so to seek,
Or so unprincipled in virtue's book,
And the sweet peace that goodness bosoms ever,
As that the single want of light and noise
(Not being in danger, as I trust she is not)
Could stir the constant mood of her calm thoughts,
And put them into misbecoming plight.
Virtue could see to do what Virtue would
By her own radiant light, though sun and moon
Were in the flat sea sunk. And Wisdom's self

355. *What if*] *Trin. MS*: *Or else* \`What if'. *Bridg.*: Or else.
356–64. *Trin. MS* and *Bridg.* omit. *Trin. MS* has instead three deleted lines '*So fares as did forsaken Proserpine / When the big \`rolling' wallowing flakes of pitchy clouds / And darkness wound her in. 1 Bro.: Peace brother peace*', and a marginal note '[r]ead the [pa]per over [a]gainst [i]nstead of [. . .]'–but the paper referred to is lost. *Bridg.* has the same three lines as *Trin. MS*, but undeleted, and with 'wallowing' omitted from the second.
358. *over-exquisite*] A Miltonic coinage, 'too careful, too subtle'.
359. *cast*] calculate, forecast.
360. *so*] i.e. evils.
365. *so to seek*] so wanting (in a requisite quality).
366. *unprincipled*] not instructed or grounded (the first recorded occurrence of the word).
367. *bosoms*] carries enclosed in its bosom (the first recorded use of 'bosom' in this figurative sense is in *L'Allegro* 78).
368. *single*] mere.
369. *trust*] *Bridg.*: hope.
370. *constant*] *Trin. MS*: *steady* constant.
371. *misbecoming*] unbecoming.
372. Echoing Jonson, *Pleasure Reconciled to Virtue* 339–422: 'She, she it is, in darkness shines, / 'Tis she that still herself refines, / By her owne light, to everie eye, / More seene, more knowne, when Vice stands by.' Also Spenser, *F.Q.* I i 12: 'Vertue gives her selfe light through darknesse for to wade.'

Oft seeks to sweet retired solitude,
Where with her best nurse Contemplation
She plumes her feathers, and lets grow her wings
That in the various bustle of resort
Were all to-ruffled, and sometimes impaired.
He that has light within his own clear breast
May sit i' the centre, and enjoy bright day,
But he that hides a dark soul, and foul thoughts
Benighted walks under the midday sun;
Himself is his own dungeon.
Sec. Bro. 'Tis most true
That musing Meditation most affects
The pensive secrecy of desert cell,
Far from the cheerful haunt of men, and herds,
And sits as safe as in a senate-house,
For who would rob a hermit of his weeds,
His few books, or his beads, or maple dish,
Or do his grey hairs any violence?
But Beauty like the fair Hesperian tree

375. *Oft seeks to*] often resorts to. *Trin. MS*: *Oft seeks to solitary sweet retire* Oft seeks to.
377. *plumes*] preens or dresses (*OED* does not record this sense until 1821).
378. *resort*] concourse of people.
379. *to-ruffled*] 'to–' is an intensive prefix.
380. *his own*] *Trin. MS*: his `own'.
381. *centre*] of the earth.
383–4. *Benighted . . . dungeon*] *Trin. MS* and *Bridg.*: Walks in black vapours, though the noontide brand/Blaze in the summer solstice. (In *Trin. MS* these lines are deleted and the present version inserted.)
385. *affects*] loves.
387. *and*] *Trin. MS*: *or* `and'. *Bridg.*: or.
389. *a*] *Bridg.*: an. *weeds*] *Trin. MS*: *beads* `*gown*' `*beads*' `weeds'.
390. *His . . . beads*] *Trin. MS*: His `few' books, `or' his *hairy gown* `beads'. *beads*] rosary.
392. *Hesperian tree*] The tree which bore golden apples, given by Ge to Hera as a wedding-present, and guarded by the Hesperides (daughters of Hesperus) and by the dragon, Ladon, which Hercules had to kill as one of his labours. The Younger Brother's sentiment recalls *As You Like It* I iii 107: 'Beauty provoketh thieves sooner than gold.' M. was clearly recalling also Jonson, *Every Man in His Humour* (1601) III i 16–23: 'Who will not judge him worthy to be robd, / That sets his doores wide open to a theefe, / And shewes the felon, where his treasure lyes? / Againe, what earthy spirit but will attempt / To taste the fruite of beauties golden tree, / When leaden sleepe seales up the dragons eyes? / Oh beauty is a Project of some power, / Chiefely when oportunitie attends her.'

Laden with blooming gold, had need the guard
Of dragon-watch with unenchanted eye,
To save her blossoms, and defend her fruit
From the rash hand of bold Incontinence.
You may as well spread out the unsunned heaps
Of miser's treasure by an outlaw's den,
And tell me it is safe, as bid me hope
Danger will wink on opportunity,
And let a single helpless maiden pass
Uninjured in this wild surrounding waste.
Of night, or loneliness it recks me not,
I fear the dread events that dog them both,
Lest some ill-greeting touch attempt the person
Of our unowned sister.
Eld. Bro. I do not, brother,
Infer, as if I thought my sister's state
Secure without all doubt, or controversy:
Yet where an equal poise of hope and fear
Does arbitrate the event, my nature is
That I incline to hope, rather than fear,

394. unenchanted] The first recorded occurrence of the word.
398. treasure] *Bridg.*: treasures.
399. hope] *Trin. MS*: *think* hope.
400. wink on] *Bridg.*: wink at.
401. And let] *Bridg.*: And she.
402. in . . . waste] *Trin. MS*: *th* in this *vast and hideous wild* wide surrounding waste. (Diekhoff 723 and Shawcross[2] 42 prefer 'wide' to the 'wild' of the printed editions).
403. it recks me not] I do not mind (whether night or loneliness is in question).
405. ill-greeting] A Miltonic coinage.
406. unowned] No other occurrence of the word in the sense 'lost' is recorded: usually it meant 'not possessed as property'.
407. Infer] draw a conclusion or inference.
408. or controversy] *Trin. MS* and *Bridg.*: or question, no.
408–9. Between these lines *Trin. MS* inserts: *Beshrew me but I would* I could be willing though now i'th'dark to try / A tough *passado* `encounter' with the shaggiest ruffian / That lurks by hedge or lane of this dead circuit / To have her by my side, though I were sure / She might be free from peril where she is. *Bridg.* inserts the same lines in their corrected state.
409. Yet] *Trin. MS* and *Bridg.*: But. *equal poise*] Echoes *Measure for Measure* II iv 69: 'equal poise of sin and charity'. *hope and fear*] *Trin. MS*: hope*s* and fear*s*.
410. arbitrate] judge of (the only instance of the word in this sense recorded in *OED*). *event*] outcome.

And gladly banish squint suspicion.
My sister is not so defenceless left
As you imagine, she has a hidden strength
Which you remember not.
Sec. Bro. What hidden strength,
Unless the strength of heaven, if you mean that?
Eld. Bro. I mean that too, but yet a hidden strength
Which if heaven gave it, may be termed her own:
'Tis chastity, my brother, chastity:
She that has that, is clad in complete steel,
And like a quivered nymph with arrows keen
May trace huge forests, and unharboured heaths,
Infamous hills, and sandy perilous wilds,
Where through the sacred rays of chastity,
No savage fierce, bandit, or mountaineer
Will dare to soil her virgin purity,
Yea there, where very desolation dwells
By grots, and caverns shagged with horrid shades,
She may pass on with unblenched majesty,
Be it not done in pride, or in presumption.

412. *gladly banish*] *Trin. MS* has the two words in this order, but M. has subjoined numerals to indicate that the order should be reversed. *squint suspicion*] Cp. Spenser, *F.Q.* III xii 15, where Suspect is 'Under his eiebrowes looking still askaunce'.
414. *imagine, she*] *Trin. MS* and *Bridg.*: imagine brother she.
420. *complete steel*] Echoes *Hamlet* I iv 52: 'complete steel'.
421. *Trin. MS*: *And may* (*`up' on any needful accident / Be it not `done' in pride or `in' wilful tempting*) *`presumption)'* [the present version of l. 421 is inserted after deletion].
422. *May trace*] *Trin. MS*: *Walk through* `May trace'. Echoes Shakespeare, *Midsummer Night's Dream* II i 25: 'trace the forests'. *unharboured*] affording no shelter (the first recorded use of the word in this sense).
423. *Infamous hills*] Echoes Horace, *Odes* II iii 20: *infames scopulos*.
424. *rays*] *Trin. MS*: *awe* `rays'.
425. *mountaineer*] mountain dweller. Shakespeare invented the word and always uses it to mean a villanous or monstrous being.
426. *Will*] *Trin. MS*: *Shall* `Will'.
427. *there, where*] *Trin. MS* and *Bridg.*: even where.
428. *shagged*] A Spenserianism, first recorded *F.Q.* V ix 10.
428–9. Between these lines *Trin. MS* and *Bridg.* insert: And yawning dens where glaring monsters house [*Trin. MS* later deletes].
429. *unblenched*] undismayed (the first recorded occurrence of the word).

Some say no evil thing that walks by night
In fog, or fire, by lake, or moorish fen,
Blue meagre hag, or stubborn unlaid ghost,
That breaks his magic chains at curfew time,
No goblin, or swart faëry of the mine,
Hath hurtful power o'er true virginity.
Do ye believe me yet, or shall I call
Antiquity from the old schools of Greece
To testify the arms of chastity?
Hence had the huntress Dian her dread bow
Fair silver-shafted queen for ever chaste,
Wherewith she tamed the brinded lioness
And spotted mountain pard, but set at nought
The frivolous bolt of Cupid, gods and men
Feared her stern frown, and she was queen o' the
woods.
What was that snaky-headed Gorgon shield
That wise Minerva wore, unconquered virgin,
Wherewith she freezed her foes to congealed stone?
But rigid looks of chaste austerity,

431–6. M. recalls Fletcher, *Faithful Shepherdess* I i 114–20: 'Yet I have heard (my mother told it me) / And now I do believe it, if I keep / My virgin flower uncropt, pure, chaste, and fair, / No Goblin, Wood-god, Fairy, Elfe, or Fiend, / Satyr or other power that haunts the Groves, / Shall hurt my body, or by vain illusion / Draw me to wander after idle fires.'
431. Some say] *Trin. MS*: *Some say* `*Nay more*' `Some say'. *Bridg.*: Nay more. Echoing *Hamlet* I i 120–3: 'Some say . . . no spirit dare stir abroad.'
432. fire] *ignis fatuus.* *moorish*] boggy. *Trin. MS*: moory.
433. meagre] *Trin. MS*: *wrinkled* `meagre'. *stubborn*] refusing to be exorcised. *unlaid ghost*] Cp. *Cymbeline* IV ii 278: 'Ghost unlaid'.
436. Hath hurtful power o'er] *Trin. MS*: Has `hurtful' power ov`''er. *Bridg.*: Has hurtful power o'er.
438. schools of Greece] The Greek philosophers.
441. silver-shafted] *Bridg.*: silver shafter. (In *Trin. MS* the whole line is a marginal insertion).
442. brinded] tawny, striped with darker colour.
443. pard] panther.
447. That] *Bridg.*: The. *unconquered*] *Trin. MS*: *eternal* `*unvanquished*' `unconquered'. In Homer, Minerva carries the Gorgon Medusa's head on her shield, and this is explained by Conti IV v: *Gorgonis caput in pectore gestabat, quia nemo contra solis claritatem aut contra sapientiam aciem oculorum intendere impune potest* (She wore the Gorgon's head on her breast, because no one can turn his eyes against the light of the sun or against wisdom and remain unharmed).

And noble grace that dashed brute violence
With sudden adoration, and blank awe.
So dear to heaven is saintly chastity,
That when a soul is found sincerely so,
A thousand liveried angels lackey her,
Driving far off each thing of sin and guilt,
And in clear dream, and solemn vision
Tell her of things that no gross ear can hear,
Till oft converse with heavenly habitants
Begin to cast a beam on the outward shape,
The unpolluted temple of the mind,
And turns it by degrees to the soul's essence,
Till all be made immortal: but when lust
By unchaste looks, loose gestures, and foul talk,
But most by lewd and lavish act of sin,

451. and blank awe] *Trin. MS*: '*of her pureness*' '*of bright rays*' and blank awe.
453. a . . . so] *Trin. MS*: *it finds* a soul 'is found' sincerely so.
455. In *Trin. MS* the whole line is a marginal insertion.
457. gross ear] See *Arcades* 72–3*n* (p. 159).
458–62. The doctrine of the transformation of flesh into spirit is developed in Raphael's speech to Adam, *PL* v 497–500. Cp. *Hermetica* x 6 'He who has apprehended the beauty of the Good can apprehend nothing else . . . he forgets all bodily sensation and all bodily movements, and is still. But the beauty of the Good bathes his mind in light, and takes all his soul up to itself, and draws it forth from the body, and changes the whole man into eternal substance'; also Fulke Greville, *Alaham* Prologue 58–69 (the speaker is a ghost from hell): 'My first charge is, the ruine of mine owne: / Hell keeping knowledge still of earthlinesse, / None coming there but spirits overgrowne, / And more embodied into wickednesse, / The bodie by the spirit living ever, / The spirit in the body joying never: / In heaven perchance no such affections be; / Those angell-soules in flesh imprisoned, / Like strangers living in mortalitie, / Still more and more themselves enspirited, / Refining nature to Eternity; / By being maids in Earths adulterous bed.'
459. Begin] *Trin. MS*: Begins. *Bridg.*: Begins.
460. temple] Cp. 1 *Cor.* iii 16: 'ye are the temple of God, and . . . the Spirit of God dwelleth in you'; and *John* ii 21: 'the temple of his body'.
464. But] *Trin. MS* and *Bridg.*: And. *by . . . lavish*] *Trin. MS*: by *the lascivious* 'lewd and lavish'.
464–74. Cp. Plato, *Phaedo* 81: 'If when it [the soul] departs from the body it is defiled and impure, because it was always with the body, and cared for it and loved it . . . so that it thought nothing was true except the corporeal, which one can touch and see and drink and eat and employ in the pleasures of love . . . it will be interpenetrated with the corporeal which intercourse and communion with the body have made part of its nature . . . And such

Lets in defilement to the inward parts,
The soul grows clotted by contagion,
Embodies, and imbrutes, till she quite lose
The divine property of her first being.
Such are those thick and gloomy shadows damp
Oft seen in charnel-vaults, and sepulchres
Lingering, and sitting by a new-made grave,
As loth to leave the body that it loved,
And linked itself by carnal sensuality
To a degenerate and degraded state.
Sec. Bro. How charming is divine philosophy!
Not harsh, and crabbed as dull fools suppose,
But musical as is Apollo's lute,
And a perpetual feast of nectared sweets,
Where no crude surfeit reigns.
Eld. Bro. List, list, I hear
Some far-off hallo break the silent air.
Sec. Bro. Methought so too; what should it be?
Eld. Bro. For certain
Either some one like us night-foundered here,
Or else some neighbour woodman, or at worst,
Some roving robber calling to his fellows.

a soul is weighed down by this and is dragged back into the visible world, through fear of the invisible and of the other world, and so, as they say, it flits about the monuments and the tombs, where shadowy shapes of souls have been seen, figures of those souls which were not set free in purity but retain something of the visible; and this is why they are seen.'

467. *Embodies*] takes on a material character (the first recorded occurrence of the word in this sense). *imbrutes*] becomes bestial (the first recorded occurrence of the word). *quite lose*] In *Trin. MS* M. subjoins numerals to these two words, indicating that their order should be reversed.

470. *sepulchres*] *Trin. MS*: *monume* sepulchres.

471. *Lingering*] *Trin. MS* and *Bridg.*: Hovering.

473. *sensuality*] *Trin. MS*: sensualty.

475. At the end of this line *Trin. MS* has deleted stage direction: *Hallo within.*

477. Echoing *Love's Labour's Lost* IV iii 339–40: 'Sweet and musical / As bright Apollo's lute.'

479. *crude*] indigestible. *List . . . hear*] *Trin. MS*: List *bro.* list, *me thought* 'I heard'.

480. At the end of this line *Trin. MS* has the stage direction: 'Hallo far off'.

482. *night-foundered*] sunk in night.

484. *Some . . . robber*] *Trin. MS*: Some *curled* 'hedge' *man of the sword* '*some roving robber*'.

Sec. Bro. Heaven keep my sister, again, again, and near,
Best draw, and stand upon our guard.
Eld. Bro. I'll hallo,
If he be friendly he comes well, if not,
Defence is a good cause, and heaven be for us.

The Attendant Spirit habited like a shepherd.

That hallo I should know, what are you? speak;
Come not too near, you fall on iron stakes else.
Spir. What voice is that, my young Lord? speak again.
Sec. Bro. O brother, 'tis my father shepherd sure.
Eld. Bro. Thyrsis? Whose artful strains have oft delayed
The huddling brook to hear his madrigal,
And sweetened every musk-rose of the dale,
How cam'st thou here good swain? hath any ram
Slipped from the fold, or young kid lost his dam,
Or straggling wether the pent flock forsook?
How couldst thou find this dark sequestered nook?
Spir. O my loved master's heir, and his next joy,
I came not here on such a trivial toy
As a strayed ewe, or to pursue the stealth
Of pilfering wolf, not all the fleecy wealth
That doth enrich these downs, is worth a thought
To this my errand, and the care it brought.
But O my virgin Lady, where is she?
How chance she is not in your company?

485. *again, again*] *Trin. MS*: *yet* again, again.
488. *Trin. MS*: *Had best look to* *He may chance scratch*/ *his forehead, here be brambles* *a just Defence is a*/ \Defence is a good cause, and Heaven be for us/.
490. *iron*] *Trin. MS*: *pointed* \iron/.
492. *father*] *Trin. MS* and *Bridg.*: father's.
493. *Thyrsis*] the pastoral singer in Theocritus i, and the losing contestant in the singing-match in Virgil, *Ecl.* vii.
494. *huddling*] The waters in front stop to listen, and those behind 'huddle' up against them.
495. *dale*] *Trin. MS*: *valley* dale.
496. *swain*] *Trin. MS* and *Bridg.*: shepherd.
497. *Slipped . . . fold*] *Trin. MS*: *Leapt o'er the pen* \Slipped from his fold/.
498. *wether the*] *Trin. MS*: wether *hath* the.
500. *next*] nearest.
506. J. F. Bense, *Englische Studien* xlvi (1913) 333–5, complains that the Attendant Spirit has no reason for asking this question: as he goes on to explain, he knows perfectly well where the Lady is (ll. 561–79). Nor is it clear what 'fears' (l. 510) are confirmed by the brothers' words. He has already seen the Lady's danger, and heard her speak about her brothers.

Eld. Bro. To tell thee sadly shepherd, without blame,
Or our neglect, we lost her as we came.
Spir. Ay me unhappy then my fears are true.
Eld. Bro. What fears good Thyrsis? Prithee briefly shew.
Spir. I'll tell ye, 'tis not vain or fabulous,
(Though so esteemed by shallow ignorance)
What the sage poets taught by the heavenly Muse,
Storied of old in high immortal verse
Of dire chimeras and enchanted isles,
And rifted rocks whose entrance leads to hell,
For such there be, but unbelief is blind.
Within the navel of this hideous wood,
Immured in cypress shades a sorcerer dwells
Of Bacchus, and of Circe born, great Comus,
Deep skilled in all his mother's witcheries,
And here to every thirsty wanderer,
By sly enticement gives his baneful cup,
With many murmurs mixed, whose pleasing poison
The visage quite transforms of him that drinks,
And the inglorious likeness of a beast
Fixes instead, unmoulding reason's mintage
Charactered in the face; this have I learnt
Tending my flocks hard by i' the hilly crofts,
That brow this bottom glade, whence night by night
He and his monstrous rout are heard to howl
Like stabled wolves, or tigers at their prey,

508. sadly] seriously.
511. good Thyrsis] *Trin. MS*: good *shep.* 'Thyrsis'.
512. ye] *Trin. MS* and *Bridg.*: you.
512–7. As D. C. Allen points out, *JEGP* lx (1961) 617, these lines recommend the allegorical interpretation of pagan literature in Christian terms: this should help to define the reader's attitude towards the Attendant Spirit's last speech.
516. chimeras] monsters part lion, part goat and part dragon.
518. In *Trin. MS* the whole line is a marginal insertion.
519. navel] centre.
522. Deep skilled] *Trin. MS*: *Inured* 'Deep *learnt*' 'skilled'.
530. hilly crofts] *Trin. MS*: *pastured lawns* 'hilly crofts'. *OED* suggests that M.'s use of 'crofts' (fields) here may be influenced by Dutch *knoft* (high and dry land).
531. brow] form a brow to (the first recorded use of 'brow' as verb).
533. stabled] *OED* cites this as first usage of the word in sense 'put into a stable'. M. may recall Virgil, *Ecl.* iii 80 *Triste lupus stabulis* (Baneful to folds

Plate 1 Milton aged 10. Oils, probably by Cornelius Janssen

Plate 2 Milton aged 21. Oils, by an unknown artist. Acquired in 1961 by the National Portrait Gallery and identified as the so-called Onslow portrait, formerly assumed lost; see David Piper, *Catalogue of Seventeenth-Century Portraits in the National Portrait Gallery, 1625–1714*

Doing abhorred rites to Hecate
In their obscured haunts of inmost bowers,
Yet have they many baits, and guileful spells
To inveigle and invite the unwary sense
Of them that pass unweeting by the way.
This evening late by then the chewing flocks
Had ta'en their supper on the savoury herb
Of knot-grass dew-besprent, and were in fold,
I sat me down to watch upon a bank
With ivy canopied, and interwove
With flaunting honeysuckle, and began
Wrapt in a pleasing fit of melancholy
To meditate my rural minstrelsy,
Till fancy had her fill, but ere a close
The wonted roar was up amidst the woods,
And filled the air with barbarous dissonance
At which I ceased, and listened them a while,
Till an unusual stop of sudden silence
Gave respite to the drowsy frighted steeds
That draw the litter of close-curtained sleep;
At last a soft and solemn-breathing sound

is the wolf). But in *PL* xi 747–8 'sea-monsters whelped / And stabled', the word seems to mean simply 'in their lairs'.
534. *Hecate*] See l. 135*n*.
538. *unweeting*] unheeding.
541. *knot-grass*] *polygonum aviculare*, a weed with numerous creeping stems and small pink flowers.
542–4. Echoing *Midsummer Night's Dream* II i 249–51: 'I know a bank where the wild thyme blows, / Where oxlips and the nodding violet grows; / Quite over-canopied with lush woodbine.'
544. *flaunting*] *Trin. MS*: *suckling* ˋ*blowing*ˊ ˋ*flaunting*ˊ ˋ*blowing*ˊ ˋflauntingˊ.
545–6. These lines are written in the reverse order in *Trin. MS*, but marginal numerals inserted by M. indicate that they should be read in the present order.
546. *meditate ... minstrelsy*] play my shepherd's pipe: see *Lycidas* 66*n*, p. 244 below.
547. *a close*] *Trin. MS*: *the* ˋaˊ close. A 'close' is the conclusion of a musical phrase.
551. *unusual stop*] i.e. at l. 145.
552. *frighted*] *Trin. MS*: flighted.
553. *close-curtained sleep*] Echoes *Macbeth* II i 51, 'curtained sleep', and *Romeo and Juliet* III ii 5, 'Spread thy close curtain . . . night.'
554. *soft*] *Trin. MS*: *soft* ˋ*still*ˊ ˋ*sweet*ˊ ˋsoftˊ. *Bridg.*: sweet.
554–9. Echoing *Antony and Cleopatra* II ii 217–23: 'A strange invisible perfume hits the sense / . . . The city cast / Her people out upon her; and

Rose like a steam of rich distilled perfumes,
And stole upon the air, that even Silence
Was took ere she was ware, and wished she might
Deny her nature, and be never more
Still to be so displaced. I was all ear,
And took in strains that might create a soul
Under the ribs of death, but O ere long
Too well I did perceive it was the voice
Of my most honoured Lady, your dear sister.
Amazed I stood, harrowed with grief and fear,
And O poor hapless nightingale thought I,
How sweet thou sing'st, how near the deadly snare!
Then down the lawns I ran with headlong haste
Through paths, and turnings often trod by day,
Till guided by mine ear I found the place
Where that damned wizard hid in sly disguise
(For so by certain signs I knew) had met
Already, ere my best speed could prevent,
The aidless innocent Lady his wished prey,
Who gently asked if he had seen such two,
Supposing him some neighbour villager;
Longer I durst not stay, but soon I guessed
Ye were the two she meant, with that I sprung
Into swift flight, till I had found you here,
But further know I not.
Sec. Bro. O night and shades,
How are ye joined with hell in triple knot
Against the unarmed weakness of one virgin

Antony, / . . . did sit alone, / Whistling to the air; which but for vacancy, / Had gone to gaze on Cleopatra too, / And made a gap in nature.'

555. *Trin. MS*: Rose like *the* 'a' *soft* steam of '*slow*' 'rich' distill'd perfumes. *Bridg.*: Rose like the soft steam of distill'd perfumes.

557. *took*] charmed.

559. *be so displaced*] *Trin. MS*: be 'so' displaced.

562. *did*] *Trin. MS* and *Bridg.*: might.

571. *knew*] *Bridg.*: know.

573. *aidless*] *Trin. MS*: *helpless* 'aidless'.

573–4. *prey, / Who gently*] *Trin. MS*: prey *who took him / Who gen* Who gently.

576. J. F. Bense, *Englische Studien* xlvi (1913) 333–5, complains that the Attendant Spirit's behaviour is unaccountable. He had the magic herb with him, and should surely have rescued the Lady immediately, rather than leaving her to find the brothers.

577. *with that*] *Trin. MS*: *and* with that.

580. *ye*] *Bridg.*: you.

Alone, and helpless! Is this the confidence
You gave me brother?
Eld. Bro. Yes, and keep it still,
Lean on it safely, not a period
Shall be unsaid for me: against the threats
Of malice or of sorcery, or that power
Which erring men call chance, this I hold firm,
Virtue may be assailed, but never hurt,
Surprised by unjust force, but not enthralled,
Yea even that which mischief meant most harm
Shall in the happy trial prove most glory.
But evil on itself shall back recoil,
And mix no more with goodness, when at last
Gathered like scum, and settled to itself
It shall be in eternal restless change
Self-fed, and self-consum'd, if this fail,
The pillared firmament is rottenness,
And earth's base built on stubble. But come let's on
Against the opposing will and arm of heaven
May never this just sword be lifted up,
But for that damned magician, let him be girt
With all the grisly legions that troop
Under the sooty flag of Acheron,
Harpies and hydras, or all the monstrous forms
'Twixt Africa and Ind, I'll find him out,
And force him to restore his purchase back,
Or drag him by the curls, to a foul death,

584. *period*] sentence.
585. *for me*] as far as I am concerned.
593. *And mix*] *Trin. MS*: *Till all to place* and mix.
595–6. Cp. Sin in *PL* ii 798–800, gnawed by whelps from her own womb.
597. *pillared firmament*] Cp. *Job* xxvi 11: 'the pillars of heaven'.
603. *sooty flag*] Echoes Phineas Fletcher, *Locusts* ii 39: 'All hell run out, and sooty flags display, / A foul deformed rout.' *Acheron*] See Q *Nov 7n* (p. 36).
604–5. *Harpies and hydras*] Echoes Sylvester (Du Bartas 261): 'Hydraes and Harpies'. Harpies were birds with women's faces, and the hydra was the nine-headed serpent killed by Hercules near the Lernean Lake. *forms*] *Trin. MS* and *Bridg.*: bugs. *'Twixt Africa and Ind*] Perhaps echoing Fairfax's translation of Tasso, *Jerusalem Delivered* xv 51: 'All monsters which hot Afric doth forthsend, / 'Twixt Nilus, Atlas, and the southern cape.'
606. *restore . . . back*] *Trin. MS*: *release his new got prey* restore his purchase back. *purchase*] booty.
607. *curls*] In Jonson, *Pleasure Reconciled to Virtue* 8, Comus has 'his haire curld'. *to . . . death*] *Trin. MS* and *Bridg.*: and cleave his scalp.

Cursed as his life.
Spir. Alas good venturous youth,
I love thy courage yet, and bold emprise,
But here thy sword can do thee little stead,
Far other arms, and other weapons must
Be those that quell the might of hellish charms,
He with his bare wand can unthread thy joints,
And crumble all thy sinews.
Eld. Bro. Why prithee shepherd
How durst thou then thyself approach so near
As to make this relation?
Spir. Care and utmost shifts
How to secure the Lady from surprisal,
Brought to my mind a certain shepherd lad
Of small regard to see to, yet well skilled
In every virtuous plant and healing herb
That spreads her verdant leaf to the morning ray,
He loved me well, and oft would beg me sing,
Which when I did, he on the tender grass
Would sit, and hearken even to ecstasy,
And in requital ope his leathern scrip,
And show me simples of a thousand names
Telling their strange and vigorous faculties;
Amongst the rest a small unsightly root,
But of divine effect, he culled me out;
The leaf was darkish, and had prickles on it,
But in another country, as he said,
Bore a bright golden flower, but not in this soil:

608. Cursed . . . life] *Trin. MS*: Down to the *hips lowest* hips. *Bridg.*: Down to the hips.
609. emprise] chivalric enterprise.
610. sword . . . stead] *Trin. MS*: *swo steel* `sword' can do thee LITTLE STEAD *small avail.*
613. unthread] *Trin. MS*: *unquilt* `unthread'.
614. all thy] *Trin. MS*: *every* `all thy'.
615. then thyself approach] *Bridg.*: then approach.
617. surprisal] surprise, a Spenserian coinage (*Virgil's Gnat* 536).
618. shepherd lad] Variously identified with Diodati (Masson iii 229), M. himself (J. H. Hanford, *TLS* (3 Nov. 1932) 815) and Nathaniel Weld (B. G. Hall, *TLS* (12 Oct. 1933) 691).
619. to see to] to look at.
620. virtuous] See *Il Penseroso* 113*n*, p. 144 above.
625. scrip] bag.
626. simples] medicinal herbs. *names*] *Trin. MS*: *hues* names.
631–6. Bridg. omits.

Unknown, and like esteemed, and the dull swain
Treads on it daily with his clouted shoon,
And yet more med'cinal is it than that moly
That Hermes once to wise Ulysses gave;
He called it haemony, and gave it me,

633–4. S. Elledge, *MLN* lviii (1943) 551–3, compares a fragment possibly by Sappho, preserved in Demetrius, *De Elocutione* (one of the rhetorics recommended by M. in *Of Education*): 'Like the hyacinth-flower, that shepherd folk 'mid the mountains tread underfoot, and low on the earth her bloom dark-splendid is shed.' Cp. Marvell, 'Appleton House', 357–60.
634. clouted] studded with broad-headed nails. Echoing *II Hen. VI* IV ii 182: 'clouted shoon'.
635–6. These lines are inserted in the margin of *Trin. MS. med'cinal . . . once*] *Trin. MS*: med'cinal ⸌is it⸍ than that *ancient* moly / *That* Which *Mercury* ⸌Hermes once⸍. *moly*] Plant with black root and white flower given to Ulysses (*Od.* x 302–6) to make him proof against the charms of Circe. According to Pliny xxv 27 some 'Greek authorities have painted its blossom yellow'. R. M. Adams, *MP* li (1953) 24, lists several authorities, including Sandys[3] 479–81, for the allegorical association of moly with prudence and temperance. In Browne, *Inner Temple Masque* 128, Circe uses moly as a charm to banish sleep from Ulysses. S. R. Watson, *N & Q* clxxvi (1939) 244, points out that Drayton (i 130 and iii 290) has two references to moly in his pastoral verse.
637. haemony] The name may be derived from *Haemonia* (Thessaly), the land of magic herbs (see *Elegia II* 7–8*n*, p. 31 above). It is used to mean 'Thessaly' by Spenser, *Astrophel* 3, and this leads S. R. Watson, *N & Q* clxxviii (1940) 260–1, to conjecture that 'haemony' in *Comus* represents pastoral, as opposed to epic poetry. Or the word may be connected with Gk. αἷμα (blood): Coleridge, *Letters* ed. E. L. Griggs (Oxford 1956) ii 866–7, derived it from αἷμα–οἶνος (blood-wine), and suggested that it represented redemption by the Cross. Similarly E. S. Le Comte, *PQ* xxi (1942) 283–98, favouring a derivation from αἱμώνιος (blood-red), conjectures that 'haemony' is connected with the account of moly given by Eustathius in his commentary on the *Odyssey* (namely, that moly sprung from the blood of Pikolous, struck dead by the sun when trying to ravish Circe). He interprets 'haemony' as grace, and associates it with 'rhamnus', a plant mentioned as an antidote against enchantment in Fletcher, *Faithful Shepherdess* II ii 15–8, one type of which is called Christ's Thorn and is mentioned in Gerard's *Herbal* as the material of the Crown of Thorns. R. M. Adams, *MP* li (1953) 24–5, points out rightly the tenuousness of Le Comte's reasoning, but T. P. Harrison, *PQ* xxii (1943) 251–4, takes up the 'rhamnus' suggestion, and argues that M. transferred to the fanciful 'haemony' the attributes of the real 'rhamnus' as described not in Gerard but in Lyte's *New Herbal* (1578). A further allegorical interpretation is put forward by J. H. Hanford, *TLS* (3 Nov. 1932) 815, who understands 'haemony' as

And bade me keep it as of sovran use
'Gainst all enchantments, mildew blast, or damp
Or ghastly Furies' apparition;
I pursed it up, but little reckoning made,
Till now that this extremity compelled,
But now I find it true; for by this means
I knew the foul enchanter though disguised,
Entered the very lime-twigs of his spells,
And yet came off: if you have this about you
(As I will give you when we go) you may
Boldly assault the necromancer's hall;
Where if he be, with dauntless hardihood,
And brandished blade rush on him, break his glass,
And shed the luscious liquor on the ground,
But seize his wand, though he and his cursed crew
Fierce sign of battle make, and menace high,
Or like the sons of Vulcan vomit smoke,
Yet will they soon retire, if he but shrink.
Eld. Bro. Thyrsis lead on apace, I'll follow thee,
And some good angel bear a shield before us.

a symbol for the Platonic doctrine of virtue, and the reference to 'another country' as contrasting the creative mind of England and N. Europe with that of Greece and Italy. Some similarity between M.'s description of 'haemony' and Virgil's of *amellus* (*Georg.* iv 271–8) is suggested by J. Arthos, *N & Q* ccvi (1961) 172.

640. ghastly Furies] Echoes Sylvester (Du Bartas 254): 'ghastly Furies'.

645. lime-twigs] Twigs smeared with bird-lime for catching birds.

647. when . . . go] *Trin. MS*: *as we go* ‵*when on the way*′ ‵when we go′.

648. the necromancer's] *Trin. MS*: *his* ‵the′ necroman*tic*‵cer's′.

649. dauntless hardihood] *Trin. MS*: *sudden violence* ‵dauntless hardihood′.

650. brandished blade] Cp. *Od.* x 294–5, where Hermes advises Ulysses to spring upon Circe with drawn sword.

651. shed] *Trin. MS*: *pour* ‵shed′. *liquor*] *Trin. MS*: *potion* ‵liquor′. M. recalls Spenser, *F.Q.* II xii 57, where Guyon breaks the cup of Excess 'And with the liquor stained all the lond'.

652. But] *Trin. MS*: *And* ‵But′. *cursed crew*] Echoing Sylvester (Du Bartas 17): 'cursed crew'.

654. sons of Vulcan] Echoes Virgil, *Aen.* viii 252–3, where Cacus, a son of Vulcan *fumum . . . evomit.*

655. will they] *Trin. MS*: they will (but M. has subjoined numerals indicating that the order of the words should be reversed).

656. I'll] *Trin. MS* and *Bridg.*: I.

657. And . . . us] *Trin. MS*: *And good Heaven cast his best regard upon us* ‵And some good angel bear a shield before us′.

The scene changes to a stately palace, set out with all manner of deliciousness: soft music, tables spread with all dainties. Comus appears with his rabble, and the Lady set in an enchanted chair, to whom he offers his glass, which she puts by, and goes about to rise.

Comus. Nay lady sit; if I but wave this wand,
Your nerves are all chained up in alabaster,
And you a statue, or as Daphne was
Root-bound, that fled Apollo,
Lady. Fool do not boast,
Thou canst not touch the freedom of my mind
With all thy charms, although this corporal rind
Thou hast immanacled, while heaven sees good.
Comus. Why are you vexed Lady? why do you frown?
Here dwell no frowns, nor anger, from these gates
Sorrow flies far: see, here be all the pleasures
That fancy can beget on youthful thoughts,
When the fresh blood grows lively, and returns
Brisk as the April buds in primrose season.
And first behold this cordial julep here
That flames, and dances in his crystal bounds
With spirits of balm, and fragrant syrups mixed.
Not that Nepenthes which the wife of Thone,

659. Recalling *Tempest* I ii 484–5, where Prospero with his wand charms Ferdinand: 'Thy nerves are in their infancy again, / And have no vigour in them.'
660. or as] *Trin. MS*: *fixed*, \`or' as. *Daphne*] her transformation into a laurel is described by Ovid, *Met.* i 545–52.
661. do not boast] *Trin. MS*: *thou art over proud* \`do not boast'.
661–5. Fool . . . Lady?] The Lady's speech and the first five words of Comus's reply are inserted in the margin in *Trin. MS*. Originally Comus's speech continued uninterrupted: '. . . that fled Apollo. Why do you frown?' See l. 754*n*.
662–4. Cp. Cicero, *De Finibus* III xxii (of the wise man): 'rightly will he be called unconquerable, for though his body be thrown into fetters, no bondage can enchain his soul.'
664. immanacled] The first recorded occurrence of the verb 'immanacle'.
668. Trin. MS: That *youth and fancy* fancy can BEGET \`*invent*' on youthful thoughts.
669. fresh] *Trin. MS*: *brisk* \`fresh'.
670–704. In *Trin. MS* these lines are inserted on a pasted leaf. Comus's speech originally continued uninterrupted: '. . . in primrose season. / O foolishness of men!' See l. 754*n*.
671. julep] sweet drink.
674–5. In Homer, *Od* iv 219–32, Helen puts into Menelaus' drink a drug

In Egypt gave to Jove-born Helena
Is of such power to stir up joy as this,
To life so friendly, or so cool to thirst.
Why should you be so cruel to yourself,
And to those dainty limbs which Nature lent
For gentle usage, and soft delicacy?
But you invert the covenants of her trust,
And harshly deal like an ill borrower
With that which you received on other terms,
Scorning the unexempt condition
By which all mortal frailty must subsist,
Refreshment after toil, ease after pain,
That have been tired all day without repast,
And timely rest have wanted, but fair virgin
This will restore all soon.
Lady. 'Twill not false traitor,
'Twill not restore the truth and honesty
That thou hast banished from thy tongue with lies,
Was this the cottage, and the safe abode
Thou told'st me of? What grim aspects are these,
These ugly-headed monsters? Mercy guard me!
Hence with thy brewed enchantments, foul deceiver,
Hast thou betrayed my credulous innocence
With vizored falsehood, and base forgery,
And wouldst thou seek again to trap me here
With liquorish baits fit to ensnare a brute?

which dispels grief (νηπενθές), which she had been given by Polydamna, an Egyptian woman, the wife of Thon. In *Trin. MS* the Greek word is written in the margin.

678–87. On the pasted sheet in *Trin. MS* l. 677 is followed by two lines: '*Poor lady thou hast need of some refreshing* / That *hast* \`have' been tried all day without repast.' After the deletion of the first of these lines, the present 678–86 are inserted in the margin. *Bridg.* omits ll. 678–86 and has instead the two original *Trin. MS* lines in their uncorrected state (i.e. reading 'hast' in the second).

687. That have] Refers back to 'you' (l. 681).

688. And] *Bridg.*: A. *have*] *Trin. MS*: *hast* \`have'. *but*] *Trin. MS*: *here* \`but'. *Bridg.*: here.

695. brewed . . . deceiver] *Trin. MS*: *hell-brewed opiate foul* \`*brewed*' brewed enchantments foul deceiver.

696–9. Bridg. omits.

697. vizored] having the face covered with visor or mask. *forgery*] *Trin. MS*: forgeries.

699. liquorish] pleasant to the taste. The word could also mean 'lustful', and it retains some of that meaning here.

Were it a draught for Juno when she banquets,
I would not taste thy treasonous offer; none
But such as are good men can give good things,
And that which is not good, is not delicious
To a well-governed and wise appetite.
Comus. O foolishness of men! that lend their ears
To those budge doctors of the Stoic fur,
And fetch their precepts from the Cynic tub,
Praising the lean and sallow Abstinence.
Wherefore did Nature pour her bounties forth,

700–1. Echoing Jonson, *Forrest* ix 7–8: 'But might I of Jove's Nectar sup, / I would not change for thine.'
701–2. Cp. Euripides, *Medea* 618: 'A bad man's gifts convey no benefit.'
706. *budge*] First use of word as adjective recorded in *OED*: meaning possibly 'solemn in demeanour, pompous'. There is probably some reference intended to the fur 'budge' (lamb's skin with wool dressed outwards) used in academic gowns. *Stoic fur*] *Trin. MS*: Stoic *gown* ˋfurˊ. The Stoic school of philosophy was founded by Zeno at the end of the fourth century B.C., taking its name from the N. Stoa of the Athenian agora. Zeno began as a Cynic, and his system grew out of that of the Cynics. Among Roman Stoics, Seneca and Epictetus are the most important. Seneca regards the body as a mere husk or prison of the soul: only with its departure does the soul's true life begin. Epictetus advises renunciation of the world: in his great maxim 'bear and forbear', the last element is a command to refrain from the external advantages of nature. C. W. Broadribb, *TLS* (8 May 1937) 364, replies to Landor's objection ('It is the first time that Cynic or Stoic ever put on fur'), with the information that there is an illustration in Erasmus, *Encomium Moriae*, showing a Stoic philosopher wearing fur.
707. *Cynic*] This school of philosophers derived their name from the Gk *κυών* (dog), and took a dog as their badge. The chief Cynics were Antisthenes, Crates and Diogenes: of these the first laid down the principles of the school, concentrating on the development of the individual will, and regarding the ordinary pleasures of life as harmful, because they interrupted the operation of the will. He claimed that the highest end of life was self-knowledge, and that for this disrepute and poverty were advantageous, because they drove a man back upon himself and increased his self-control. *tub*] Diogenes Laertius vi 23 recounts that when a friend failed to get a cottage for Diogenes, the philosopher 'took for his abode the tub in the Metroön'.
708. *sallow*] *Bridg.*: shallow.
709–35. A large number of parallels to Comus's arguments have been cited, including Seneca, *Hippolytus* 435–82, Pettie, *Petite Pallace* (ed. I. Gollancz (1908) i 82–4), Sidney, *Arcadia* (1590) iii 10, Gabriel Harvey, *Letter Book* (ed. E. J. Scott (1884) 86–7), Warner, *Albion's England* v 24 (quoted by D.

With such a full and unwithdrawing hand,
Covering the earth with odours, fruits, and flocks,
Thronging the seas with spawn innumerable,
But all to please, and sate the curious taste?
And set to work millions of spinning worms,
That in their green shops weave the smooth-haired silk
To deck her sons, and that no corner might
Be vacant of her plenty, in her own loins
She hutched the all-worshipped ore, and precious gems
To store her children with; if all the world
Should in a pet of temperance feed on pulse,
Drink the clear stream, and nothing wear but frieze,
The all-giver would be unthanked, would be
    unpraised,
Not half his riches known, and yet despised,
And we should serve him as a grudging master,

Bush, *PMLA* xliv (1929) 726), Marlowe, *Hero and Leander* i 199–310, Shakespeare, *Venus and Adonis* 163–74, Daniel, *Complaint of Rosamond* 246–52, 260–73, 512–32 (the Marlowe, Shakespeare and Daniel parallels are noted by H. Schaus, *UTSE* xxv (1946) 129–41), Drayton, *Heroical Epistles* 'John to Matilda' 51–8, 119–56, Spenser, *F.Q.* II vi 15–17 (an imitation of Tasso, *Jerusalem Delivered* xiv 62–4), Brandon, *The Virtuous Octavia* 891–932, Donne, *Confined Love*, Heywood, *Troia Britannica* ii 53–4 and Randolph, *Muse's Looking Glass* II iii (G. C. Moore Smith, *TLS* (19 Jan. 1922) 44, suggests this parallel, noting that, though the play was not printed till 1638, it was probably acted at Cambridge where M. and Randolph were contemporaries).

711. fruits, and flocks] *Trin. MS*: *and with* fruits, 'and flocks'.

712. Thronging] *Trin. MS*: *Cramming* 'Thronging'. 'Throng' in a trans. sense ('fill a place with a large number of objects') is first found in *Coriolanus* III iii 36. Cp. Lucretius's praise of Venus as a cosmic force, *quae mare . . . concelebras* (who throngest the sea), *De Rerum Natura* i 3–4, and Ovid's imitation of it, *Fasti* iv 106: *innumeris piscibus implet aquas* (she fills the waters with innumerable fish). Ovid goes on to discuss allurements to love.

713. Trin. MS: *The fields with cattle and the air with fowl* [the present line is inserted after deletion].

715. shops] workshops.

716. To deck] *Trin. MS*: *To deck* 'To *adorn*' 'deck'.

718. hutched] laid up as in a hutch (i.e. coffer).

720. pulse] *Trin. MS*: *pulse* '*vetches*' 'pulse'. Cp. *Daniel* i 12–16, where Daniel and his companions at the court of Nebuchadnezzar insist on eating pulse (i.e. beans, peas, etc.) and drinking water.

721. frieze] coarse woollen cloth.

As a penurious niggard of his wealth,
And live like Nature's bastards, not her sons,
Who would be quite surcharged with her own weight,
And strangled with her waste fertility;
The earth cumbered, and the winged air darked with
plumes,
The herds would over-multitude their lords,
The sea o'erfraught would swell, and the unsought
diamonds
Would so emblaze the forehead of the deep,
And so bestud with stars, that they below
Would grow inured to light, and come at last
To gaze upon the sun with shameless brows.
List Lady be not coy, and be not cozened
With that same vaunted name virginity,
Beauty is Nature's coin, must not be hoarded,
But must be current, and the good thereof
Consists in mutual and partaken bliss,

725. In *Trin. MS* this line is a marginal insertion.
726. *And live like*] *Trin. MS*: ˋAndˊ livˋeˊ*ing as* ˋ*for*ˊ ˋlikeˊ.
729. In *Trin. MS* this line is a marginal insertion.
731. *Trin. MS*: *The sea o'erfraught* The o'er ˋseaˊ o'erfraught would *heave her waters up* ˋswellˊ / *Above the shore* and th'unsought diamonds.
731–5. H. F. Robins, *MLQ* xii (1951) 422–8, explains 'the deep' (l. 732) as 'the central part of the earth'. The 'forehead' or top of the deep, is that part of the inside of the earth's globe which lies nearest the surface. This is envisaged as studded with diamonds, and therefore appearing to those in the centre of the earth like a sky studded with stars. 'They below' (l. 733) are the evil, hell-dwelling spirits, demons and monsters of classical mythology (see *Comus* 601–5, and *PL* ii 624–8). The belief, found in Pliny, that precious stones reproduced themselves like animals, is relayed in later 'encyclopaedias' of science like John Maplet's *A Greene Forest* (1567), which M. is known to have read.
732–3. *Trin. MS*: *Would so bestud the centre with their starlight / Were they not taken thence* that they below [after deletion, the present version of the lines is inserted]. *Bridg.*: Would so emblaze with stars, that they below [732 omitted].
733. *bestud*] M. probably recalls Sylvester (Du Bartas 187), who calls stars 'the gilt studs of the Firmament'.
734. *light*] *Trin. MS*: *day* ˋlightˊ.
736. *and be*] *Trin. MS*: NOR ˋ*and*ˊ ˋnorˊ be.
736–43. Comus's advice owes something to the *carpe diem* tradition, stemming from Horace and Ausonius and popular with neo-Latin and vernacular poets on the continent in the sixteenth and seventeenth centuries.

Unsavoury in the enjoyment of itself
If you let slip time, like a neglected rose
It withers on the stalk with languished head.
Beauty is Nature's brag, and must be shown
In courts, at feasts, and high solemnities
Where most may wonder at the workmanship;
It is for homely features to keep home,
They had their name thence; coarse complexions
And cheeks of sorry grain will serve to ply
The sampler, and to tease the housewife's wool.
What need a vermeil-tinctured lip for that
Love-darting eyes, or tresses like the morn?
There was another meaning in these gifts,
Think what, and be advised, you are but young yet.
Lady. I had not thought to have unlocked my lips
In this unhallowed air, but that this juggler
Would think to charm my judgement, as mine eyes
Obtruding false rules pranked in reason's garb.

Some previous examples are collected by F. Bruser, *SP* xliv (1947) 625–44.
736–54. Bridg. omits.
742–3. Echoing *Midsummer Night's Dream* I i 76–8: 'Earthlier-happy is the rose distill'd / Than that ... withering on the virgin thorn.' This seems closer to M. than Spenser's famous translation from Tasso (*F.Q.* II xii 75), which he may also have had in mind.
743. with ... head] *Trin. MS*: *and fades away* ˋwith languished headˊ.
744. brag] show, display.
745. and high] *Trin. MS*: on high.
748. name ... complexions] *Trin. MS*: name ˋ*from*ˊ thence, coarse *beetle brows* complexions.
749. grain] colour.
750. sampler, and] *Trin. MS*: sample, or. *tease*] comb, in preparation for spinning.
752. Love-darting eyes] Echoes Sylvester (Du Bartas 499): 'love-darting Eyn'.
754. Trin. MS: Think what, *and look upon this cordial julep* ˋand be advised, you are but young yetˊ. Between l. 754 and l. 755 *Trin. MS* inserts what are now ll. 672–7, followed by the two lines 'Poor lady ... repast' (see ll. 678–87*n*), followed by an early form of ll. 688–9 (l. 688. but ... virgin] *Trin. MS*: *here sweet Lady* ˋfair virginˊ. l. 689. 'Twill not] *Trin. MS*: Stand back), followed by ll. 662–4, followed by l. 692 and an early and much corrected form of ll. 693–6, followed by 'if thou give me it / I throw it on the ground' (a threat by the Lady nowhere included in the final version), followed by an early form of ll. 700–2. The whole passage is then heavily deleted. Clearly M. went on to insert its various parts in the places where they now appear (see notes to ll. 670–704 and 661–5).

I hate when vice can bolt her arguments,
And virtue has no tongue to check her pride:
Imposter do not charge most innocent Nature,
As if she would her children should be riotous
With her abundance she good cateress
Means her provision only to the good
That live according to her sober laws,
And holy dictate of spare temperance:
If every just man that now pines with want
Had but a moderate and beseeming share
Of that which lewdly-pampered Luxury
Now heaps upon some few with vast excess,
Nature's full blessings would be well-dispensed
In unsuperfluous even proportion,
And she no whit encumbered with her store,
And then the giver would be better thanked,
His praise due paid, for swinish gluttony
Ne'er looks to heaven amidst his gorgeous feast,
But with besotted base ingratitude
Crams, and blasphemes his feeder. Shall I go on?
Or have I said enough? To him that dares
Arm his profane tongue with contemptuous words
Against the sun-clad power of chastity;
Fain would I something say, yet to what end?
Thou hast nor ear, nor soul to apprehend
The sublime notion, and high mystery

759. bolt] sift, so as to make the thing sifted appear fine and pure.
762. would] *Trin. MS*: *meant* \`would'.
763. cateress] The first recorded instance of the word.
764. Means] *Trin. MS*: *Intends* \`Means'.
767–73. Cp. *King Lear* IV i 70–4: 'Let the superfluous and lust-dieted man / That slaves your ordinance, that will not see / Because he doth not feel, feel your power quickly; / So distribution should undo excess, / And each man have enough.'
771. blessings] *Bridg.*: blessing.
775–6. Cp. Plato, *Republic* 586A, of those who 'have no experience of wisdom and virtue': 'With eyes ever bent upon the earth and heads bowed down over the tables they feast like cattle, grazing and copulating.'
777. besotted] *Trin. MS*: *a* \`be'sott*ish*\`ed'.
778–805. Shall . . . strongly] *Trin. MS* and *Bridg.* omit.
781. sun-clad] Cp. *Rev.* xii 1: 'a woman clothed with the sun', and Petrarch, *Canzone* viii 1 (to the Virgin Mary): *Vergine bella, che di sol vestita* . . . (see note on *Versification in M.'s 'canzone poems'* p. 162 above).
784. mystery] Cp. M. in the *Apology* (Columbia iii 306, Yale i 892): 'having had the docrine of holy Scripture unfolding those chaste and high mysteries

That must be uttered to unfold the sage
And serious doctrine of virginity,
And thou art worthy that thou shouldst not know
More happiness than this thy present lot.
Enjoy your dear wit, and gay rhetoric
That hath so well been taught her dazzling fence,
Thou art not fit to hear thyself convinced;
Yet should I try, the uncontrolled worth
Of this pure cause would kindle my rapt spirits
To such a flame of sacred vehemence,
That dumb things would be moved to sympathize,
And the brute Earth would lend her nerves, and
    shake,
Till all thy magic structures reared so high,
Were shattered into heaps o'er thy false head.
Comus. She fables not, I feel that I do fear
Her words set off by some superior power;
And though not mortal, yet a cold shuddering dew
Dips me all o'er, as when the wrath of Jove
Speaks thunder, and the chains of Erebus
To some of Saturn's crew. I must dissemble,
And try her yet more strongly. Come, no more,
This is mere moral babble, and direct
Against the canon laws of our foundation;

with timeliest care infus'd, that *the body is for the Lord and the Lord for the body.*'

785–6. sage / And serious] Cp. 'our sage and serious Poet *Spencer*' (Columbia iv 311, Yale ii 516).

789. rhetoric] Perhaps echoing Marlowe, *Hero and Leander* i 338: 'Who taught thee rhetoric to deceive a maid?'

790. fence] art of fencing (the first instance of the word in this sense cited in *OED*).

792. uncontrolled] uncontrollable.

796. brute Earth] Echoes Horace, *Odes* I xxxiv 9–12: *bruta tellus . . . concutitur.*   *nerves*] sinews.

799. She fables not] Echoes *I Hen. VI* IV ii 42: 'He fables not; I hear the enemy.'

802–4. Cronos (Saturn) was defeated in battle and deposed by his son Zeus (Jove), who used thunderbolts as weapons, and who then imprisoned the losers in Tartarus.   *Erebus*] primeval Darkness, son of Chaos, according to Hesiod.

805. no more] *Trin. MS*: *y'are too moral* \`no more'.

806–9. Trin. MS: *This is mere moral stuff* \`*Your moral stuff*' *the very* \`*tilted*' *lees / And settlings of a melancholy blood.* (After deletion the present ll. 806–9 are inserted in the margin.)

I must not suffer this, yet 'tis but the lees
And settlings of a melancholy blood;
But this will cure all straight, one sip of this
Will bathe the drooping spirits in delight
Beyond the bliss of dreams. Be wise, and taste....

The Brothers rush in with swords drawn, wrest his glass out of his hand, and break it against the ground; his rout make sign of resistance but are all driven in. The Attendant Spirit comes in.

Spir. What, have you let the false enchanter scape?
O ye mistook, ye should have snatched his wand
And bound him fast; without his rod reversed,
And backward mutters of dissevering power,
We cannot free the Lady that sits here
In stony fetters fixed, and motionless;
Yet stay, be not disturbed, now I bethink me,
Some other means I have which may be used,
Which once of Meliboeus old I learnt
The soothest shepherd that e'er piped on plains.

808–9. lees ... blood] Cp. Nashe, *Terrors of Night* (*Works* ed. R. B. McKerrow (1904–10) i 354–7): 'The grossest part of our blood is the melancholy humour, which ... sinketh downe to the bottome like the lees of wine, and that corrupteth all the blood, and is the causer of lunacie', and Sylvester (Du Bartas 26): 'The pure red part, amid the Mass of Blood, / The Sanguine Aire commands: the clutted mud, / Sunk down in Lees, Earths Melancholy showes.' *settlings*] *Bridg.*: settling.
812–3. Trin. MS stage direction reads: 'The brothers rush in strike his glass down the *monsters* shapes make as though they would resist but are all driven in. Daemon enter with them.' *Bridg.* stage direction is the same as the printed version except that for 'glass' *Bridg.* reads 'glass of liquor' and for 'The Attendant Spirit comes in', 'the Demon is to come in with the brothers'.
813. you let] *Bridg.*: ye left. *scape*] *Trin. MS*: *pass* `scape'.
815. rod] *Trin. MS*: *art* `rod'. *reversed*] Echoes Sandys[3] 462, where Ovid, *Met.* xiv 300 is translated 'her rod reverst', and 481, where it is explained 'as Circe's rod, waved over their heads from the right side to the left: presents those false and sinister persuasions of pleasure, which so much deforms them: so the reversion thereof, by discipline, and a view of their owne deformity, restores them to their former beauties'. Cp. also Spenser, *F.Q.* III xii 36, where, compelled by Britomart, Busirane 'gan streight to overlooke / Those cursed leaves, his charmes backe to reverse'.
817. sits] *Trin. MS*: *remains* `sits'.
820. Some ... which] *Trin. MS*: *There is another way* `Some other means I have' that. *Bridg.*: Some other means I have that.
821. Meliboeus] Tityrus and Meliboeus are the characters in Virgil, *Ecl.* i.

There is a gentle nymph not far from hence,
That with moist curb sways the smooth Severn stream,
Sabrina is her name, a virgin pure,
Whilom she was the daughter of Locrine,
That had the sceptre from his father Brute.
The guiltless damsel flying the mad pursuit
Of her enraged stepdame Guendolen,
Commended her fair innocence to the flood
That stayed her flight with his cross-flowing course,
The water-nymphs that in the bottom played,
Held up their pearled wrists and took her in,
Bearing her straight to aged Nereus' hall,
Who piteous of her woes, reared her lank head,
And gave her to his daughters to imbathe
In nectared lavers strewed with asphodel,
And through the porch and inlet of each sense

Tityrus is Spenser's name for Chaucer (*Shep. Cal.* February 92), and probably as J. F. Bense, *Neophilologus* i (1916) 62–4, suggests, Meliboeus is M.'s name for Spenser, who tells the story of Sabrina *F.Q.* II x.
825. pure] *Trin. MS*: *goddess chaste* pure.
825–30. R. Blenner-Hasset, *MLN* lxiv (1949) 315–8, notes that, in Geoffrey of Monmouth, Guendolen is not Sabrina's 'stepdame': she is the first wife of Locrine (son of Brutus, the Trojan founder of Britain), and Locrine leaves her for Astrild, by whom he became Sabrina's father. Guendolen defeats Locrine and has both Astrild and her daughter drowned: M.'s implication that Sabrina threw herself into the river finds no support in Geoffrey. M.'s account of the story in his *History of Britain* (Columbia x 15–6) does not, however, deviate from Geoffrey's, nor does Spenser's (*F.Q.* II x 17–9), except that in Spenser Astrild (Estrild) is killed outright and only Sabrina thrown into the river. Drayton, *Polyolbion* vi 130–78, also follows Geoffrey.
827. That] *Bridg.*: Who.
830. flood] *Trin. MS*: *flood* \`*stream*' \`flood'.
833. pearled . . . took] *Trin. MS*: *white* \`pearled' wrists *to receive* \`*and carry*' \`*take*' \`took'. The nymphs in Jonson, *Masque of Blackness* 76–8 wear 'on front, eare, neck, and wrists . . . ornament . . . of the most choise and orient pearle', and Drayton, *Polyolbion* v 16–7, personifying the Severn as Sabrina, says 'And where she meant to goe / The path was strew'd with Pearle.'
834. Bearing . . . straight] *Trin. MS*: *And bore* \`Bearing' her \`straight'.
836. daughters] Cp. the nymphs who dress Marinell's wound, Spenser, *F.Q.* III iv 40: 'They pourd in soveraine balme and Nectar good.'
837. lavers] basins. *asphodel*] the immortal flower which covers the meadows of the Elysian fields in Homer, *Od.* xi 539.
838. porch] Echoes *Hamlet* I v 63–4: 'And in the porches of mine ears did pour / The leperous distilment.'

Dropped in ambrosial oils till she revived,
And underwent a quick immortal change
Made goddess of the river; still she retains
Her maiden gentleness, and oft at eve
Visits the herds along the twilight meadows,
Helping all urchin blasts, and ill-luck signs
That the shrewd meddling elf delights to make,
Which she with precious vialed liquors heals.
For which the shepherds at their festivals
Carol her goodness loud in rustic lays,
And throw sweet garland wreaths into her stream
Of pansies, pinks, and gaudy daffodils.
And, as the old swain said, she can unlock
The clasping charm, and thaw the numbing spell,
If she be right invoked in warbled song,
For maidenhood she loves, and will be swift
To aid a virgin such as was herself
In hard-besetting need, this will I try,
And add the power of some adjuring verse.

839. ambrosial oils] Cp. Homer, *Il.* xxiii 186–7, where Aphrodite anoints Hector's body with 'oil, rose-sweet, ambrosial', to protect it.

840–1. L. Bradner, *Musae Anglicanae* (New York 1940) pp. 38–9, thinks that Sabrina's metamorphosis into a goddess was suggested to M. by Giles Fletcher, *De literis antiquae Britanniae* (1633).

844. urchin blasts] A 'blast' is a sudden infection, and since 'urchin' can mean 'a roguish or mischievous youngster', the meaning here may be 'mischievous': but Scot, *Discovery of Witchcraft* vii 15, gives 'urchins' in a catalogue with 'spirits, witches ... elves, hags, fairies' and other 'bugs'. Cp. *Tempest* II ii 3–5: 'spirits ... urchin-shows.'

845. make] *Trin. MS*: *leave* \`makes'.

845–6. Trin. MS inserts between these lines: 'And often takes our cattle with strange pinches'.

846. Bridg. omits.

848. rustic] *Trin. MS*: *lovely* \`rustic'.

850. Trin. MS: Of pansies *and of* \`pinks and' *bonny* \`gaudy' daffodils.

851. old swain] Meliboeus.

852. Trin. MS: *Each* \`The' clasping charm and *secret holding spell* \`*melt each*' \`thaw the' numbing spell.

856. In ... need] *Trin. MS*: *In honoured virtue's cause* \`In hard distressed need'.

857. power ... adjuring] *Trin. MS*: *power* \`*call*' \`power' of some *strong* \`adjuring'.

SONG

Sabrina fair
  Listen where thou art sitting
Under the glassy, cool, translucent wave,
  In twisted braids of lilies knitting
The loose train of thy amber-dropping hair,
  Listen for dear honour's sake,
  Goddess of the silver lake,
    Listen and save.
Listen and appear to us
In name of great Oceanus,
By the earth-shaking Neptune's mace,
And Tethys' grave majestic pace,
By hoary Nereus' wrinkled look,
And the Carpathian wizard's hook,
By scaly Triton's winding shell,
And old soothsaying Glaucus' spell,
By Leucothea's lovely hands,

859. where . . . sitting] *Trin. MS*: *virgin* where thou *sitt'st* 'art sitting'.
862. amber-dropping] dropping ambergris: cp. Sylvester (Du Bartas[2] 1204): 'Locks like streames of liquid Amber.' E. M. Clark *SP* lvi (1959) 626–42 notes Sabrina's 'lockes of amber' in Wither, *Epithalamia*.
866. Trin. MS: inserts stage direction: 'To be said', and *Bridg.*: 'The verse to sing or not'.
867. Oceanus] See l. 97*n*.
868. earth-shaking] Homer, *Il.* ix 183 describes Poseidon as 'the god that holds the earth and shakes it'.
868–73. In *Trin. MS* these lines are a marginal insertion.
869. Tethys] wife of Oceanus: Hesiod, *Theog.* 368, calls her πότνια (queenly, reverend).
870. Nereus] father of Nereids (sea nymphs): Virgil, *Georg.* iv 392 calls him *grandaevus*. *Bridg.* gives 'El. bro.' (Elder Brother) as speaker at beginning of l. 870, '2. bro.' (Second Brother) at l. 872, 'El. bro.' at l. 874, '2. bro.' at l. 876, 'El. bro.' at l. 878 and 'De.' (Daemon) at l. 882.
871. Carpathian wizard] Proteus: according to Virgil, *Georg.* iv 387 he lives in the Carpathian sea, and is a *vates* (seer). He has a 'hook' (shepherd's crook) because he is the shepherd of Poseidon's seals in *Od.* iv 411–3: he could change his shape and was 'skilled in wizard arts', *Od.* iv 460.
872. Triton] Ovid, *Met.* i. 330–8, depicts him as Neptune's herald, blowing through a huge conch-shell.
873. soothsaying Glaucus] Echoes Spenser, *F.Q.* IV xi 13: 'Glaucus, that wise southsayes understood.' Glaucus tells Scylla of his metamorphosis from mortal to sea god and of his reception by Oceanus and Tethys in Ovid, *Met.* xiii 917–65.
874. Leucothea] 'The bright goddess', rises 'from the deep like a sea-mew on

And her son that rules the strands,
By Thetis' tinsel-slippered feet,
And the songs of Sirens sweet,
By dead Parthenope's dear tomb,
And fair Ligea's golden comb,
Wherewith she sits on diamond rocks
Sleeking her soft alluring locks,
By all the nymphs that nightly dance
Upon thy streams with wily glance,
Rise, rise, and heave thy rosy head
From thy coral-paven bed,
And bridle in thy headlong wave,
Till thou our summons answered have.
Listen and save.

Sabrina rises, attended by water-nymphs, and sings.

By the rushy-fringed bank,
Where grows the willow and the osier dank,
My sliding chariot stays,
Thick set with agate, and the azurn sheen
Of turkis blue, and emerald green
That in the channel strays,

the wing' and gives Odysseus a veil which saves him when 'earth-shaking' Poseidon shatters his raft. When he gets ashore he throws the veil back into the water, and Leucothea receives it in her hands, *Od.* v 333–462.

875. *her son*] Melicertes. Sailors, safe in port, 'pay their vows on the shore' to him in Virgil, *Georg.* i 436–7.

876. *Thetis*] One of the Nereids: wife of Peleus and mother of Achilles. Homer, *Il.* xviii 127, calls her 'silver-footed'.

878. *Parthenope*] One of the sirens. Strabo I ii 13 refers to her monument near Naples.

878–81. In *Trin. MS* these lines are deleted.

879. *Ligea*] The other siren: her name means 'shrill-voiced'. Her 'shining tresses float over her snowy neck' in Virgil, *Georg.* iv 336.

882. *that*] *Bridg.*: of.

882–3. In *Trin. MS* these lines are a marginal insertion.

885. *coral-paven*] *Trin. MS*: coral-pave*d* `n'.

891. 'As an immortal she is, of course, fragile to the point of weightlessness. Thus her " sliding chariot" is simply the water, and "stays", waits for her, beside the bank, only in the paradoxical sense that there is always the flowing water there. The jewels that adorn it are only the names of gems applied to the colours of the water' (Brooks and Hardy 225).

892. *azurn*] azure: a Miltonic coinage (*OED* records no other example). *Bridg.*: azur'd.

894. *Trin. MS*: *That my rich wheels inlays.* [After deletion, present version substituted].

Whilst from off the waters fleet
Thus I set my printless feet
O'er the cowslip's velvet head,
    That bends not as I tread,
Gentle swain at thy request
        I am here.
Spir. Goddess dear
We implore thy powerful hand
To undo the charmed band
Of true virgin here distressed,
Through the force, and through the wile
Of unblessed enchanter vile.
Sabr. Shepherd 'tis my office best
To help ensnared chastity;
Brightest Lady look on me,
Thus I sprinkle on thy breast
Drops that from my fountain pure,
I have kept of precious cure,
Thrice upon thy finger's tip,
Thrice upon thy rubied lip,
Next this marble venomed seat
Smeared with gums of glutinous heat
I touch with chaste palms moist and cold,
Now the spell hath lost his hold;
And I must haste ere morning hour
To wait in Amphitrite's bower.

Sabrina descends, and the Lady rises out of her seat.

Spir. Virgin, daughter of Locrine,
Sprung of old Anchises' line

896. set] *Bridg.*: rest. *printless feet*] Echoes *Tempest* V i 34: 'printless foot'.

897. velvet] *Bridg.* omits.

898. bends not] *Trin. MS*: bends \`not´. M. recalls Virgil's Camilla, *Aen.* vii 808–11: 'She might have sped over the topmost blades of unmown corn, nor in her course bruised the tender ears.'

899. request] *Trin. MS*: *behe* request.

903. charmed] *Trin. MS*: *mag* charmed.

906. enchanter] *Bridg.*: enchanters.

909. Brightest] *Trin. MS*: *Virtuous* \`Brightest´.

910. thy] *Bridg.*: this.

916. glutinous] sticky, gluey.

920. Trin. MS: To wait *o*\`i´n Amphitrite\`'s´ *in her* bower. Amphitrite was wife to Neptune.

922. Anchises' line] The legendary Trojan kings of Britain descended from

May thy brimmed waves for this
Their full tribute never miss
From a thousand petty rills,
That tumble down the snowy hills;
Summer drouth, or singed air
Never scorch thy tresses fair,
Nor wet October's torrent flood
Thy molten crystal fill with mud,
May thy billows roll ashore
The beryl, and the golden ore,
May thy lofty head be crowned
With many a tower and terrace round,
And here and there thy banks upon
With groves of myrrh, and cinnamon.
Come Lady while heaven lends us grace,
Let us fly this cursed place,
Lest the sorcerer us entice
With some other new device.
Not a waste or needless sound
Till we come to holier ground,
I shall be your faithful guide
Through this gloomy covert wide,
And not many furlongs thence
Is your father's residence,
Where this night are met in state
Many a friend to gratulate
His wish'd presence, and beside
All the swains that there abide,
With jigs, and rural dance resort,
We shall catch them at their sport,
And our sudden coming there
Will double all their mirth and cheer;

Anchises, father of Aeneas (Anchises–Aeneas–Ascanius–Silvius–Brutus–Locrine).

923. brimmed] *Trin. MS*: *crystal* \`brimmed'.

926. the] *Trin. MS*: *from* \`the'.

936. Trin. MS and *Bridg.* insert stage-direction: 'Song ends'.

937. Come Lady] *Bridg.*: El. bro.: Come *Lady* \`sister'.

943. Bridg. inserts speaker at beginning of line: 'De.' (Daemon).

947. met] *Trin. MS*: *come* \`met'.

950. there] *Trin. MS* and *Bridg.*: near.

952. their] *Bridg.*: this.

Come let us haste, the stars grow high,
But night sits monarch yet in the mid sky.

The scene changes, presenting Ludlow Town and the President's Castle; then come in Country Dancers, after them the Attendant Spirit, with the two Brothers and the Lady.

SONG

Spir. Back, shepherds, back, enough your play,
Till next sunshine holiday,
Here be without duck or nod
Other trippings to be trod
Of lighter toes, and such court guise
As Mercury did first devise
With the mincing Dryades
On the lawns, and on the leas.

This second song presents them to their father and mother.

Noble Lord, and Lady bright,
I have brought ye new delight,
Here behold so goodly grown
Three fair branches of your own,
Heaven hath timely tried their youth,
Their faith, their patience, and their truth,

955. *Bridg.* inserts speaker at beginning of line: 'El. bro.' *grow*] *Trin. MS*: *are* ˋgrowˊ. *Bridg.*: are.
956. *sits*] *Trin. MS*: *reigns* sits.
956–7. In *Trin. MS* stage direction reads: 'Exeunt / The scene changes and then is presented Ludlow town / and the president's castle then enter country dances and such / like gambols etc. / *After* ˋAtˊ those sports the Daemon with the 2. bro. and the Lady enter / the Daemon sings'. In *Bridg.* 'The scene changes then is presented Ludlow town / and the President's Castle, then come in Country / dances, and the like etc., towards the end of these / sports the demon with the 2 brothers and the / lady come in. The spirit sings.'
958. *sunshine holiday*] Cp. *L'Allegro* 98.
961. *Trin. MS*: Of *speedier* ˋ*nimbler*ˊ ˋof lighterˊ toe*ing*ˋsˊ, and *courtly* ˋsuch neatˊ guise Of lighter toes, and such court guise.
962. *Trin. MS*: *Such* as *Hermes* ˋMercuryˊ did ˋfirstˊ devise. Cp. Jonson *Pan's Anniversary* 176–8: 'The best of Leaders, Pan, / That leads the Naiads, and the Dryads forth; / And to their daunces more then Hermes can.'
963. *Dryades*] wood nymphs.
969. *timely*] early.
970. *patience*] *Trin. MS*: *patience* ˋ*temperance*ˊ patience.

And sent them here through hard assays
With a crown of deathless praise,
To triumph in victorious dance
O'er sensual folly, and intemperance.

The dances ended, the Spirit epiloguizes.

Spir. To the ocean now I fly,
And those happy climes that lie
Where day never shuts his eye,
Up in the broad fields of the sky:
There I suck the liquid air
All amidst the gardens fair

972. With] *Trin. MS*: *To* \`With'. *praise*] *Trin. MS*: *bays* \`praise'.
974–5. In *Trin. MS* the stage direction reads: 'They dance. The dances all ended / the Daemon sings. or says'. The last two words seem to be a later insertion. *Bridg.* has the same stage direction, but with no point after 'sings'.
975–8. See ll. 1–6*n*, and l. 97*n*. The daemon flies to the 'moon' (l. 1016)–his dwelling place, according to Plutarch–where day does not 'shut his eye' because, except at times of eclipse, it is 'beyond the range of the earth's shadow' (*Moralia* 942F). The 'ocean' is not only that of the old cosmology (see ll. 980–1*n*) but also that which in Timarchus' vision 'drifts round smoothly and evenly in a circle' with 'islands illuminated by one another with soft fire' (590C-D)–this ocean is the celestial sphere; the islands, stars and planets.
975–1010. Bridg. omits (but see l. 1*n*).
975–1022. Trin. MS has two versions of these lines. The first, referred to in the following notes as *Trin. MS* (*a*), is crossed through and the second, referred to as *Trin. MS* (*b*), is substituted on a separate sheet.
978. Cp. Virgil, *Aen.* vi 887 *aeris in campis latis.* *broad*] *Trin. MS* (*a*): *plain* \`broad'.
978–9. Trin. MS (*a*) inserts: *Far beyond the earth's end / Where the welkin clear* \`*low*' *doth bend.*
979. liquid] clear, bright: cp. ll. 1–6*n*.
980–1. According to Plutarch, *Moralia* 944C, 'the Elysian plain is the part of the moon which is turned towards Heaven', and as D. T. Starnes points out, *UTSE* xxxi (1952) 44, the identification of Elysium with the Gardens of Hesperus, though not made in antiquity, is suggested in Stephanus and Conti (cp. 'Elysian dew' 995). J. Arthos, *MLN* lxxvi (1961) 321–4, adds that Ficino, *In decimum dialogum de Iusto*, distinguishes between two Elysian fields: one corresponding to Plato's 'true earth' (see ll. 1–6*n*), the other to the eighth sphere.

Hesiod, *Theog.* 215, says that the Hesperides 'tend the fair golden apples beyond glorious Okeanos'. R. Eisler, *TLS* (14 Sep. 1945) 451, notes that the *Scholia Basiliensa* (1542, reprinted in the Heinsius edition of Hesiod, 1603) explain these golden apples as the stars which Herakles, the rising sun,

Of Hesperus, and his daughters three
That sing about the golden tree:
Along the crisped shades and bowers
Revels the spruce and jocund Spring,
The Graces, and the rosy-bosomed Hours,
Thither all their bounties bring,
That there eternal summer dwells,
And west winds, with musky wing
About the cedarn alleys fling
Nard, and cassia's balmy smells.
Iris there with humid bow,
Waters the odorous banks that blow
Flowers of more mingled hue
Than her purfled scarf can shew,
And drenches with Elysian dew
(List mortals if your ears be true)

plucks in that he makes them disappear. Perhaps it was this idea which suggested to M. the fusion of the Gardens of Hesperus, which were according to Pliny islands surrounded by ocean, with the less earthbound Elysian plain of Plutarch: Stephanus and Conti would then provide corroboration. Starnes and Talbert 312–13 have demonstrated that many of M.'s details–the 'liquid air', the fragrant west wind, the flowers, especially hyacinths and roses, and the presence of Venus–strongly suggest his recollection of Conti's chapter on the Elysian fields.

981. Trin. MS (a): Of *Atlas* ˋHesperusˊ and his DAUGHTERS ˋ*nieces*ˊ three.

982. Trin. MS (b): *Where grows the right-born gold upon his native tree* [after deletion the present version, already present in *Trin. MS (a)*, is substitued].

983. crisped] curled.

983–7. Along . . . That] *Trin. MS (a)* omits.

985. Hours] See *Prae E* 39–40*n* (p. 25).

988. musky] smelling of musk.

989. cedarn] *Trin. MS (a)*: *myrtle* ˋcedarnˊ (no previous occurrence of 'cedarn' is recorded in *OED*).

990. Trin. MS (a): *Balm* ˋNardˊ, and cassia's *fragrant* ˋbalmyˊ smells. *Nard*] spikenard, an aromatic plant. *cassia*] a bark resembling cinnamon, but less aromatic.

991. Iris] the rainbow. *humid*] *Trin. MS (a)*: *garnished* ˋ*garish*ˊ ˋhumidˊ.

994. purfled] *Trin. MS (a)*: *watchet* ˋpurfledˊ. By the seventeenth century 'purfled', which meant originally 'having a decorated border', could mean 'variegated'.

994–5. Between these lines *Trin. MS (a)* and *(b)* insert: Yellow, watchet, green and blue [in *(b)* this is later deleted].

995. with . . . dew] *Trin. MS (a)*: oft with manna dew. *Trin. MS (b)*: with *Sabaean* ˋElysianˊ dew. *Elysian*] See ll. 980–1*n*.

996. This warning that the following lines are not to be taken as mere

Beds of hyacinth, and roses,
Where young Adonis oft reposes,
Waxing well of his deep wound
1000 In slumber soft, and on the ground
Sadly sits the Assyrian queen;
But far above in spangled sheen

mythological decoration is a marginal insertion in *Trin. MS* (*b*), omitted from *Trin. MS* (*a*).
998. young . . . oft] *Trin. MS* (*a*): many a cherub soft.
998–1001. Venus and Adonis are types of natural love. Conti v 16 identifies Adonis (the author and nourisher of all seeds) with the sun (as does the Orphic *Hymn to Adonis*, from which Conti quotes), and the boar with winter. Sandys 209 repeats these identifications, and identifies Venus with the earth which mourns for the sun's absence and is 'recreated againe by his approach, and procreative vertue'. Spenser's Garden of Adonis, where the wounded Adonis lies, is on earth (*F.Q.* III vi 29), and is 'the first seminarie / Of all things that are borne to live and die' (III vi 30). But M.'s Venus and Adonis lie in the Elysian fields of the moon (see ll. 980–1*n*): there, as daemons, they are in a transitional state (see ll. 1–6*n*.): they await the separation of soul and mind, when mind will finally return to its source, the sun 'through which shines forth manifest the desirable and fair and divine', Plutach, *Moralia* 943E. This sun is to be distinguished from that of mere earthly fruitfulness, which Adonis represents. Plutarch 945A points out that the separation of mind and soul, and final release of the mind, is quickly achieved by 'temperate' and philosophical souls, but those which have been very attached to earthly pursuits have to wait on the moon for a long time before release is attained. Their state is not 'blessed or divine' until this 'second death' (942F). Thus Adonis, as a type of earthly love, takes time to recover from his 'wound'.
999–1011. Waxing . . . But] *Trin. MS* (*a*) omits.
1001. Assyrian queen] Venus: Pausanias I xiv 6 says she was first worshipped by the Assyrians.
1002. spangled sheen] Echoes *Midsummer Night's Dream*, II i 29: 'spangled starlight sheen'.
1002–4. Spenser's Cupid and Psyche play in the Garden of Adonis (on earth), and have a daughter, Pleasure (*F.Q.* III vi 50). In Apuleius, *Met.* vi 23–4, however, Jove has Psyche brought up to heaven by Mercury, makes her immortal with a draught of ambrosia, and holds a great wedding feast for her and Cupid, at which the Hours deck the place with roses and the Graces throw balm around (cp. ll. 985, 990). In due time Psyche has a child, *Voluptas*. Boccaccio, *Gen. Deor.* v 22, paraphrases Apuleius and develops the allegory: Psyche, he explains, represents the soul, and joined to her is that which preserves the rational element (pure Love). She passes through trials and 'at length she regains the enjoyment of divine bliss and contemplation and is joined to her lover for ever . . . from this love is born

Celestial Cupid her famed son advanced,
Holds his dear Psyche sweet entranced
After her wandering labours long,
Till free consent the gods among
Make her his eternal bride,
And from her fair unspotted side
Two blissful twins are to be born,
Youth and Joy; so Jove hath sworn.
  But now my task is smoothly done,
I can fly, or I can run
Quickly to the green earth's end,
Where the bowed welkin slow doth bend,
And from thence can soar as soon
To the corners of the moon.
  Mortals that would follow me,
Love Virtue, she alone is free,
She can teach ye how to climb

Pleasure, which is eternal bliss and joy'. M.'s allegory is near to Boccaccio's: Psyche has attained that release which Venus and Adonis still await.
1003. Celestial Cupid] Cp. *Dam* 191*n*, p. 277 below. In so far as he represents Christ he is the 'son' of Venus (earth) in that he is Son of Man. *advanced*] raised, elevated.
1007. eternal bride] Cp. *Rev.* xxi 9: 'I will shew thee the bride, the Lamb's wife.'
1010. Youth and Joy] not Pleasure (see ll. 1002–4*n*); perhaps there is a reference to *Rev.* xxi 1: 'a new Heaven and a new Earth'; and xxi 4: 'God shall wipe away all tears from their eyes; and there shall be no more death, neither sorrow, nor crying.' Thus Youth (newness) and Joy will be produced. M. concludes the first book of his *De doctrina* (Columbia xvi 379) with a citation of these texts and the comment: 'Our glorification will be accompanied by the renovation of heaven and earth, and of all things therein adapted to our service or delight.'
1011. But now] *Trin. MS* (*a*) and *Bridg.*: Now. *task . . . done*] *Trin. MS* (*a*): *message well* ˋ*business*ˊ ˋtaskˊ is ˋsmoothlyˊ done.
1012–3. Cp. *Midsummer Night's Dream* IV i 102–3: 'We the globe can compass soon, / Swifter than the wandering moon.'
1013. green earth's] *Trin. MS* (*a*): *earth's* green ˋearth'sˊ *Bridg.*: earth's green.
1014. bowed welkin] the curved vault of the sky.
1016. corners of the moon] Echoes *Macbeth* III v 24: 'Upon the corner of the moon.' 'Corner' means 'horn' (Latin *cornu*).
1017–8. Cp. Plutarch, *Moralia* 942F: 'To this point [the moon] rises no one who is evil or unclean.'
1019. ye] *Bridg.*: you.
1019–20. sphery chime] the music of the spheres: see *Ad Pat* 35–7*n* (p. 150).

Higher than the sphery chime;
Or if Virtue feeble were,
Heaven itself would stoop to her.

51 Psalm cxiv

Date. Nov. 1634. In a Latin letter to Alexander Gill dated 4 Dec. 1634, M. says that he is sending in return for some verses of Gill's 'what is not really mine, but belongs just as much to the truly divine poet. Last week I adapted this song (*hanc Oden*) of his to the rule of Greek heroic verse. I did so with no deliberate intention certainly, but acted upon some sudden impulse. I wrote it before daybreak, while I was still practically in bed' (Columbia xii 14–17, Yale i 321–2). If, as seems likely, this 'song' is *Psalm cxiv* it must have been written at the end of Nov. 1634. In the letter to Gill M., apologising for any shortcomings, explains 'this is the first and only thing I have composed in Greek since I left your school'.
Publication. *1645* and *1673* (no significant variants: *1673* misprints in the following instances: *2. Αἰγύπτιον*]*Αἰγυπτον* *15. σκαρθμοῖσιν*] *σκαφμοῖσιν* *16. σφριγόωντες*]*σφριγόωντης* *18. μητέρι*]*μητήρι*). Sometimes in *1645*, and often in *1673*, accents and breathings are misplaced or missing. The present text silently supplies and corrects these. Columbia i 590 conjectures that 'the confusion of *1673* resulted when it was attempted to move the breathings and accents to the beginnings of some of the capital letters, which had been after those letters in *1645*, and to correct the otherwise badly printed Greek text of *1645*. The printer was evidently worse confused than ever by the corrections, and the result an even worse version than the uncorrected copy'.

Ἰσραὴλ ὅτε παῖδες, ὅτ' ἀγλαὰ φῦλ' Ἰακώβου
Αἰγύπτιον λίπε δῆμον, ἀπεχθέα, βαρβαρόφωνον,
Δὴ τότε μοῦνον ἔην ὅσιον γένος υἷες Ἰούδα.
Ἐν δὲ θεὸς λαοῖσι μέγα κρείων βασίλευεν.

1021–2. Perhaps echoing Marlowe, *Hero and Leander* i 365–6: 'hands so pure, so innocent . . . might have made Heaven stoop'; cp. Plutarch, *Moralia* 593F–594A: 'But when in the course of countless births a soul has stoutly and resolutely sustained a long series of struggles, and as her cycle draws to a close, she approaches the upper world, bathed in sweat, in imminent peril and straining every nerve to reach the shore, God holds it no sin for her daemon to go to her rescue, but lets whoever will lend aid.' M. wrote these two lines in Camillo Cardoyn's album when he was at Geneva 10 Jun. 1639 (French i 419).
1022. stoop] *Trin. MS* (*a*): *bow* \`stoop'.

Εἶδε καὶ ἐντροπάδην φύγαδ' ἐῤῥώησε θάλασσα
Κύματι εἰλυμένη ῥοθίῳ, ὁ δ' ἄρ' ἐστυφελίχθη
Ἱρὸς Ἰορδάνης ποτὶ ἀργυροειδέα πηγήν.
Ἐκ δ' ὄρεα σκαρθμοῖσιν ἀπειρέσια κλονέοντο,
Ὡς κριοὶ σφριγόωντες ἐϋτραφερῷ ἐν ἀλωῇ.
Βαιότεραι δ' ἅμα πᾶσαι ἀνασκίρτησαν ἐρίπναι,
Οἷα παραὶ σύριγγι φίλῃ ὑπὸ μητέρι ἄρνες.
Τίπτε σύγ' αἰνὰ θάλασσα πέλωρ φύγαδ' ἐῤῥώησας;
Κύματι εἰλυμένη ῥοθίῳ; τί δ' ἄρ' ἐστυφελίχθης
Ἱρὸς Ἰορδάνη ποτὶ ἀργυροειδέα πηγήν;
Τίπτ' ὄρεα σκαρθμοῖσιν ἀπειρέσια κλονέεσθε
Ὡς κριοὶ σφριγόωντες ἐϋτραφερῷ ἐν ἀλωῇ;
Βαιότεραι τί δ' ἄρ' ὔμμες ἀνασκιρτήσατ' ἐρίπναι,
Οἷα παραὶ σύριγγι φίλῃ ὑπὸ μητέρι ἄρνες,
Σείεο γαῖα τρέουσα θεὸν μεγάλ' ἐκτυπέοντα
Γαῖα θεὸν τρείουσ' ὕπατον σέβας Ἰσσακίδαο
Ὅς τε καὶ ἐκ σπιλάδων ποταμοὺς χέε μορμύροντας,
Κρήνην τ' ἀέναον πέτρης ἀπὸ δακρυοέσσης.

When the children of Israel, when the glorious tribes of Jacob left the land of Egypt, hateful, barbarous in speech, then indeed were the sons of Judah the one devout race; and God ruled in great might among the peoples. The sea saw, and rushed in headlong flight, wrapped in surging waves; and holy Jordan was thrust back towards its silvery source. The topless mountains came forth and tumbled together, leaping like lusty rams in a rich pasture. And all the smaller crags skipped with them, like lambs beneath their dear mother at the sound of the pipe. Why, O huge sea, did you rush terribly in flight, wrapped in surging waves? And why, holy Jordan, were you thrust back towards your silvery source? Why, topless mountains, did you tumble together leaping, like lusty rams in a rich pasture? And why, you smaller

¶ 51. 5. *ἐντροπάδην*] not found in surviving Gk literature. M. was probably thinking of *προτροπάδην* ('headlong'). *ἐῤῥώησε*] there is no such form: M. presumably confused *ἠρώησε* and *ἐρρώσατο* (both = 'rushed').
9. *ἐϋτραφερῷ ἐν ἀλωῇ*] M. evidently means 'in rich pasture'; but *ἀλωή* should be cultivated ground (vineyard, orchard, garden), or a threshing-floor, and there is no such word as *ἐϋτραφερός*. Apparently a half-memory of Hesiod's *ἐϋτροχάλῳ ἐν ἀλωῇ* ('on a rounded threshing-floor') confused with *εὐτραφής* ('thriving, nourishing') and perhaps with *τραφερός* (used by Theocritus as 'well-fed, fat').
12. *πέλωρ*] A noun ('monster'), used by M. as if it were the adjective *πελώριος*, *πέλωρος* ('monstrous, huge').
19. *μεγάλ' ἐκτυπέοντα*] An error for *μεγάλα κτυπέοντα*. The participle has *κτ-* not *ἐκτ-*; M. wrote *ἐκτ-* under the influence of the indicative form *μεγάλ' ἔκτυπε* ('thundered loudly'), three times in Homer.

crags, did you skip like lambs beneath their dear mother at the sound of the pipe? Shake, earth, in fear of God who thunders loud; shake, earth, in fear of the high majesty revered of the son of Isaac; who pours forth sounding torrents from the crags, and an everflowing spring from a weeping rock.

52 *Haec ego mente . . .*

[A postscript to his love poems]

Date. 1635? These verses were appended to *Elegia VII* in *1645* (see headnote to that poem, p. 69 above). They must therefore be post-1628. There is no other evidence for dating. It is possible that they were composed as early as *Elegia VI*. Bateson 161 argues that the force of *olim* (*1*) puts them at least as late as 1635: he views them as 'perhaps the most repellent product of that social vacuum to which M. consigned himself in the reaction against Cambridge'. Or it may be that M. did not write this retraction until he was preparing to publish *1645* (entered on *Stationers' Register* 6 Oct. 1645): the present tenses of the closing lines would come oddly from a married man, however.
Publication. *1645*, *1673* (no significant variants: in *10* *1673* misprints *ipse* for *ipsa*).

Haec ego mente olim laeva, studioque supino
  Nequitiae posui vana trophaea meae.
Scilicet abreptum sic me malus impulit error,
  Indocilisque aetas prava magistra fuit.
Donec Socraticos umbrosa Academia rivos
  Praebuit, admissum dedocuitque iugum.
Protinus extinctis ex illo tempore flammis,
  Cincta rigent multo pectora nostra gelu.
Unde suis frigus metuit puer ipse sagittis,
  Et Diomedeam vim timet ipsa Venus.

These lines are the trifling memorials of my levity which, with a warped mind and a base spirit, I once raised. This, in fact, is how mischievous error seduced me and drove me on: my ignorant youth was a vicious teacher, until the shady Academy offered me its Socratic streams,[5] and taught me to

¶ 52. *5.* Cp. *Apology* (1642): 'Thus from the Laureat fraternity of Poets, riper yeares, and the ceaselesse round of study and reading led me to the shady spaces of philosophy, but chiefly to the divine volumes of *Plato*' (Columbia iii 305, Yale i 891).
10. In Homer, *Il.* v 330–51 Diomedes chases Venus, who is trying to protect Aeneas, and wounds her in the wrist.

unloose the yoke to which I had submitted. From that moment onward the flames were quenched. My heart is frozen solid, packed around with thick ice; so that even the boy himself is afraid to let the frost get at his arrows, and Venus fears the strength of a Diomedes.[10]

53 Lycidas

Date. Nov. 1637. Edward King, a Fellow of Christ's, was drowned 10 Aug. 1637. In the Trinity MS *Lycidas* is headed 'Novemb: 1637'. A volume of memorial verses by King's Cambridge acquaintances appeared in 1638, of which the first part is entitled *Justa Eduardo King naufrago, ab Amicis moerentibus amoris & μνείας χάριν* (Obsequies for Edward King, lost at sea, written by his sorrowful friends in love and remembrance) and contains twenty-three pieces of Greek and Latin verse: the second part, *Obsequies to the memory of Mr Edward King*, contains thirteen English poems, of which M.'s (signed J.M.) is the last and longest. The motto for the volume, from Petronius, reads *Si recte calculum ponas, ubique naufragium est* (If you reckon rightly, shipwreck is everywhere). The Latin preface explains that King's ship struck a rock not far from the British coast and that, while other passengers endeavoured to save their lives, King knelt in prayer on the deck and went down with the ship. According to Edward Phillips 'a particular friendship and intimacy' existed between M. and King (Darbishire 54).
Publication. In *Obsequies to the memory of Mr Edward King* (1638). This text differs from *1645* and *1673* chiefly in its placing of commas. It omits commas after 'rude' (*4*), 'dear' (*6*), 'wind' (*13*), 'well' (*15*), 'turn' (*21*), 'mute' (*32*), 'heel' (*34*), 'caves' (*39*), 'willows' (*42*), 'green' (*42*), 'seen' (*43*), 'flowers' (*47*), 'bards' (*53*), 'Druids' (*53*) (as *1645*, see below), 'roar' (*61*), 'eyes' (*81*), 'brine' (*98*), 'sake' (*114*), 'intrude' (*115*), 'list' (*123*), 'past'

¶ 53. *Title.* The name Lycidas appears in Theocritus vii (where he is 'best of pipers') and xxvii, Bion ii and vi and Virgil, *Ecl.* vii and ix. E. A. Strathmann, *MLN* lii (1937) 398–400 points out that in Bathurst's translation of the *Shepheardes Calender* Piers, the Protestant pastor of the May eclogue, is called Lycidas. E. E. Duncan-Jones, *N & Q* cci (1956) 249, suggests that in choosing the name M. was influenced by Lucan, *Pharsalia* iii 638–9, *Mersus foret ille profundo / sed prohibent socii* (He would sink in the sea, but his friends prevent it) which refers to a character called Lycidas. There is another Lycidas, significantly described as not widely known (*vix urbe sua, vix colle propinquo / cognitus*: known hardly by his own city, hardly by the neighbouring hill) among the shepherds who bring gifts to Mary and her child in Sannazaro, *De Partu Virginis* iii 185–93.

(*132*), 'use' (*136*), 'winds' (*137*), 'shores' (*154*), 'ore' (*170*), 'high' (*172*), 'above' (*178*), 'troops' (*179*), 'shore' (*183*) and 'woods' (*193*); and inserts commas after 'more' (*1*), 'passes' (*21*), 'herself' (*59*) (as *1645*, see below), 'raise' (*70*), 'lives' (*81*), 'wings' (*93*), 'bark' (*100*), 'Return' (*132*), 'return' (*133*), 'low' (*136*), 'violet' (*145*), 'Hebrides' (*156*) (as *1645*, see below), 'shepherds' (*165*), 'societies' (*179*), 'Now' (*181*) and 'Lycidas' (*181*). The only other regular punctuation-variant is the printing of a semi-colon where the later editions have a comma: after 'spring' (*16*), 'lies' (*80*), 'reeds' (*86*), 'story' (*95*), 'strayed' (*97*), 'more' (*165*), 'song' (*176*) and 'grey' (*187*). The other variants from the present text are: *no headnote* *9*. Young Lycidas,](Young Lycidas!) peer:]peer. *15. no indentation in one surviving state of 1638, represented by British Museum copy 1077 d. 51* *17*. string.]string: *18*. excuse,]excuse. *24*. flock;]flock, rill.] rill; *25. no indentation* *26*. opening]glimmering *30*. star that rose, at evening, bright]ev'n star bright *31*. westering]burnisht *33*. flute,]flute: *36*. Damaetas]Dametas *39*. shepherd]shepherds *50. no indentation* *51*. loved]lord (*corrected to* lov'd *in the Cambridge University Library copy* (*CUL*) *and British Museum copy C. 21. c. 42* (*BM*) *in a hand probably M.'s*) *53*. your]the (*corrected to* your *in CUL and BM*) *59*. son]son? *64. no indentation* *66*. strictly]stridly muse,]muse? *67*. use]do (*corrected to* use *in CUL and BM*) *69*. Or with]Hid in Neaera's]Neera's *73*. when]where *76*. life.]life; *77*. ears;]ears. *82*. Jove;]Jove: *85. no indentation* *87*. mood:]mood. *90*. plea,]plea. *94*. promontory;]promontory: *99*. played.]played: *103. no indentation* Camus, reverend sire,]Chamus (reverend sire) *107*. Ah;]Ah! *114*. Enow]Enough *118*. guest;]guest. *129*. nothing]little said,]said. *131*. smite no] smites no *153*. surmise.]surmise; *157*. whelming] humming (*corrected to* whelming *in CUL and BM*) *163*. ruth.]ruth, *167*. floor,]floor: *177. omitted, but written in the margin of CUL and BM* *192*. blue:]blue, .Next printed *1645* (*8*. prime,]prime *30*. bright,]bright *36*. Damaetas]Damoetas *53*. Druids,]Druids *59*. herself]herself, *107*. Ah;]Ah! *113*. thee,]thee swain,]swain. *118*. guest;]guest. *142*. dies,]dies. *156*. Hebrides]Hebrides,) and *1673* (the text followed here except in *65* where *1673* misprints 'end' for 'tend', and in *142* and *173* where *1673* prints a full stop after 'dies' and omits the semi-colon after 'waves').

Versification and style. Lycidas is made up of eleven verse paragraphs of varying length and differing rhyme pattern. It includes ten unrhymed lines (*1, 13, 15, 22, 39, 51, 82, 91, 118, 161*) and has thirteen six-syllable lines mingled with its decasyllables, each of which rhymes with the decasyllable immediately before it. The paragraph-lengths run: 14, 10, 12, 13, 14, 21, 18, 29, 33, 21, 8. It will be seen that only twice does a paragraph exceed its predecessor by more than three or four lines. In the first instance the reply of Phoebus (*76–84*) and in the second the denunciation of the clergy by St Peter (*113–31*) is responsible for the elongation. These two preliminary resolutions are thus thrown into relief.

Though the structure of *Lycidas* cannot be exactly paralleled in Italian literature, it is clearly an extension of M.'s experimentation with Italian verse forms in *Time* and *Solemn Music* (see p. 162 above). Prince 71–81 has drawn attention to the similarities with the *canzone*: the mixture of long and short lines, the conclusion of each paragraph with a couplet (as recommended by Dante in the *De Vulgari Eloquentia*), and the *ottava rima* of the final paragraph corresponding to the *commiato* of the *canzone*. He considers that M.'s adaptation of *canzone* features was influenced by the irregularly rhymed passages of lyric and dialogue in Tasso's *Aminta* and Guarini's *Pastor Fido;* also that *Lycidas* shares the technical aims of sixteenth-century Italian pastoral verse (as represented by the eclogues of Sannazaro and Berardino Rota), in attempting to evolve a poetic diction equivalent to that of Virgil, and to combine the tradition of the *canzone* with that of the classical eclogue. *Lycidas* has ten echoes of Virgil's *Eclogues*, ranging from scraps of phrasing to major associations of ideas (see footnotes). Though the *Lycidas* verse paragraph does not, like the *canzone* stanza, have a key line (*chiave*) which links the stanza's two halves by both introducing a new set of rhymes and rhyming with the last line of the first half, M. does use the *chiave* principle at several points (e.g. *17*, *108*, *136*) where a line which looks backwards for its rhyme looks forward, from the viewpoint of meaning, to a new set of ideas.

M.'s Spenserian pastoralism in *Lycidas* contrasts markedly with the 'metaphysical' diction and imagery of the other contributors to the 1638 volume. All but one of the poem's seven or eight echoes of Spenser are from the *Shepheardes Calender*. M. gives pastoral colour by dialect words like 'rathe' (used twice in the *Calender*) and 'scrannel' (not recorded in literature before), and by the colloquial, rustic-sounding 'daffadillies' (akin to the *Calender*'s 'daffadowndillies'). The 'quills' and the 'oaten' shepherd's pipe are both *Calender* properties. 'Guerdon'–a word found nowhere else in M.'s poetry–is used twenty-three times by Spenser, who was also the first to use 'pledge' (*10*) in the sense 'child'. M.'s own coinages are 'inwrought' (*105*) and 'freaked' (*144*).

Modern criticism. M. Lloyd, *N & Q* n.s. v (1958) 432–4, has suggested that the *Justa Eduardo King* volume was intended as a unified work within a flexible, comprehensive design, and that M.'s poem is a summary and interpretation of themes already stated in the volume.

Tillyard 80–5 claims that King is only the nominal 'subject' of *Lycidas*: fundamentally the poem concerns M. himself. Mindful of the similarity between King's career and his own, he writes in fear of premature death. The 'real subject' is the resolving of that fear (and of his bitter scorn of the clergy) into an exalted state of mental calm. Similarly Tuve[2] 73–111 views *Lycidas* as 'the most poignant and controlled statement in English poetry of the acceptance of that in the human condition which seems to man unacceptable'. To Daiches 73–92 the subject is neither King nor M. but 'man in his creative capacity, as Christian humanist poet-priest'.

John Crowe Ransom, in an important seminal article, *AR* i (1933) 179–203, regards Renaissance poetry as ideally anonymous, form and content

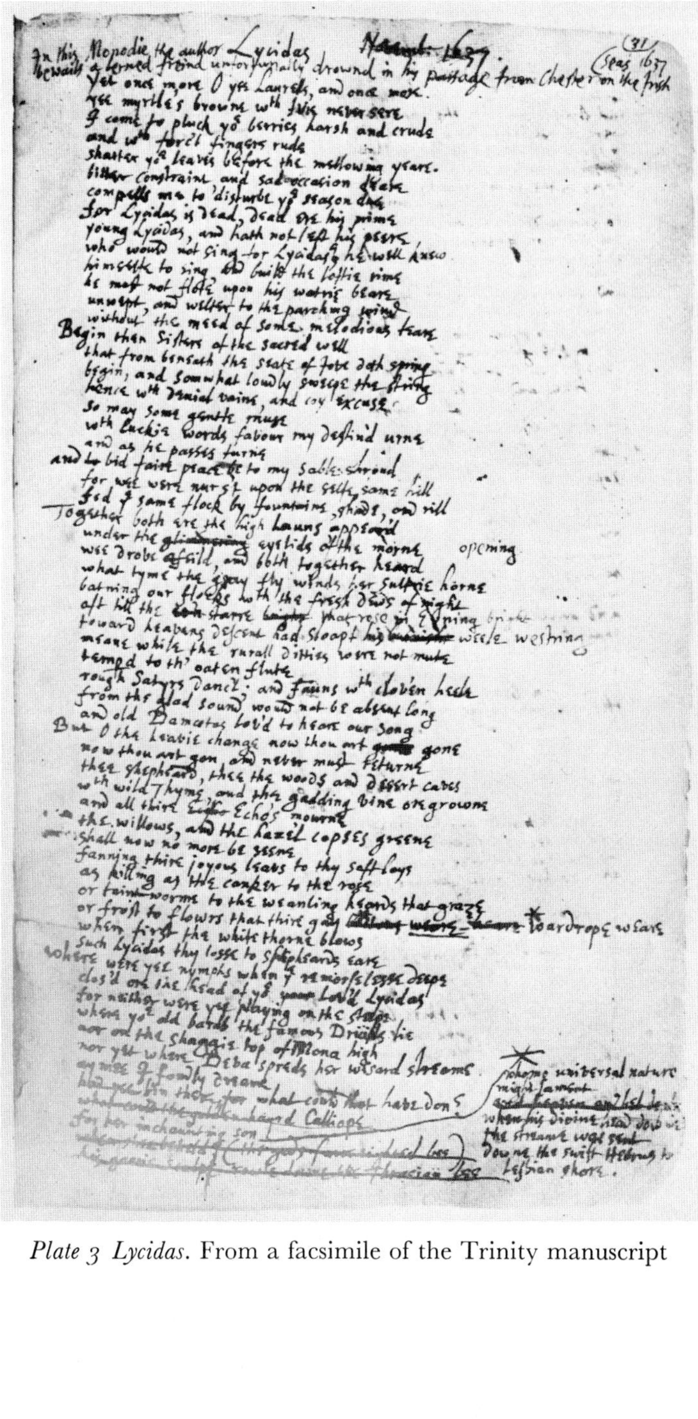

Plate 3 Lycidas. From a facsimile of the Trinity manuscript

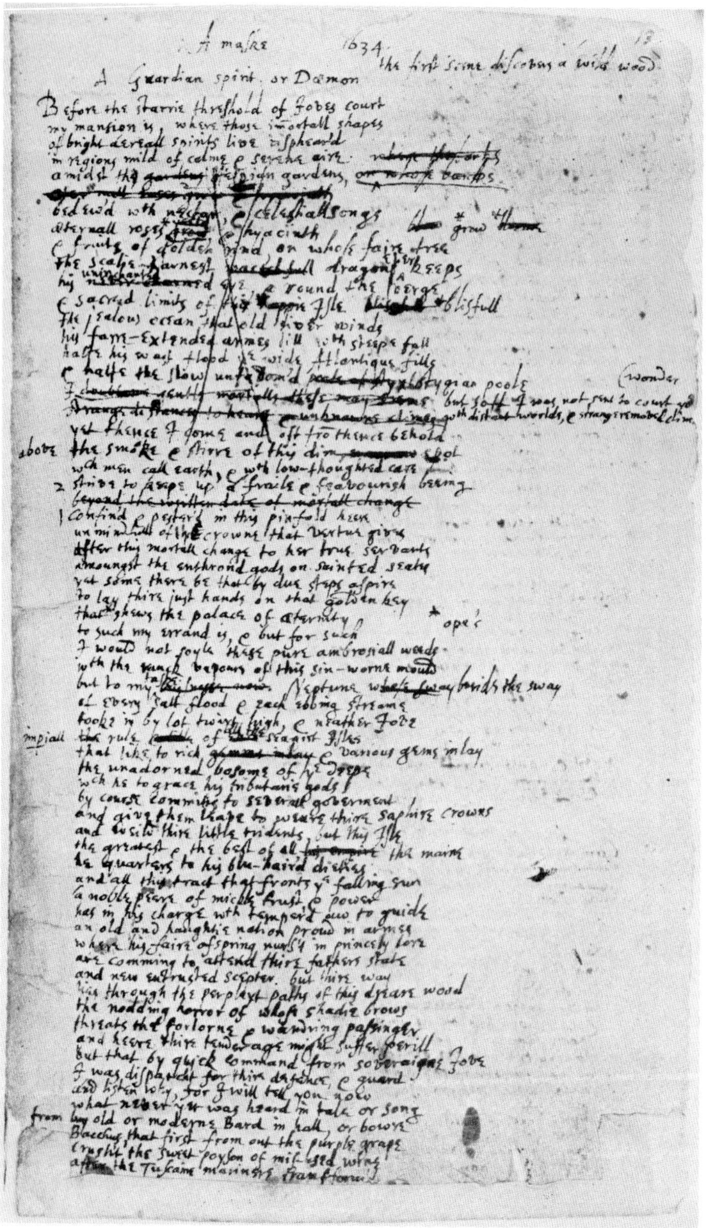
A maske 1634. 13
the first Scene discovers a wild wood.
A Guardian spirit, or Dæmon
Before the starrie threshold of Joves court
my mansion is, where those imortall shapes
of bright aereall spirits live insphear'd
in regions mild of calme & serene aire
amidst th' Hesperian gardens, on whose bancks
bedew'd with nectar, & celestiall songs
æternall roses grow & hyacinth
& fruits of golden rind, on whose faire tree
the scalie-harnest dragon ever keeps
his unenchanted eye, around the verge
& sacred limits of this blissfull Isle
the jealous ocean that old river winds
his farre-extended armes till with steepe fall
halfe his wast flood ye wide Atlantique fills
& halfe the slow unfadom'd Stygian poole
yet thence I come and oft fro thence behold
above the smoke & stirre of this dim spot
wch men call earth, & wth low-thoughted care
strive to keepe up a fraile & feavourish being
confin'd & pester'd in this pinfold heere
unmindfull of the crowne that vertue gives
after this mortall change to her true servants
amongst the enthron'd gods on sainted seats
yet some there be that by due steps aspire
to lay thire just hands on that golden key
that opes the palace of æternity
to such my errand is, & but for such
I would not soyle these pure ambrosiall weeds
with the rank vapours of this sin-worne mould
but to my task. Neptune besides the sway
of every salt flood & each ebbing streame
tooke in by lot twixt high & neather Jove
imperiall rule of all the sea-girt Iles
that like to rich & various gems inlay
the unadorned bosome of ye deepe
wch he to grace his tributarie gods
by course commits to severall goverment
and gives them leave to weare thire saphire crowns
and wield thire little tridents, but this Ile
the greatest & the best of all the maine
he quarters to his blu-haird deities
and all this tract that fronts ye falling sun
a noble peere of mickle trust & power
has in his charge wth temper'd awe to guide
an old and haughtie nation proud in armes
where his faire ofspring nurs't in princely lore
are comming to attend thire fathers state
and new entrusted scepter, but thire way
lies through the perplext paths of this dreare wood
the nodding horror of whose shadie brows
threats the forlorne & wandring passinger
and heere thire tender age might suffer perill
but that by quick command from soveraigne Jove
I was dispatcht for thire defence & guard
and listen why, for I will tell you now
what never yet was heard in tale or song
from old or moderne Bard in hall, or bowre
Bacchus that first from out the purple grape
crusht the sweet poyson of mis-used wine
after the Tuscane mariners transform'd

Plate 4 Comus, From a facsimile of the Trinity manuscript

being both traditional. Because M. was young and 'insubordinate' the 'anonymity' of *Lycidas* is disturbed (*a*) metrically, in that although M. derived his form from the Italian *canzone* he did not keep each verse paragraph the same in structure and length, and introduced ten unrhymed lines 'as a gesture of his rebellion against the formalism of his art': (*b*) stylistically, in that M. departs from the Virgilian grand style in the St Peter passage, where he shows a M. 'who is angry, violent, and perhaps a little bit obscene'; and (*c*) from the viewpoint of 'the logic of composition', in that M. starts his elegy as monologue but then breaks into narrative (*76*), and 'the narrative breaks the monologue several times more, presenting action sometimes in the present tense, sometimes in the past'. M. C. Battestin, *College English* xvii (1956) 223–8, disposes of Ransom's metrical argument by referring to Prince's demonstration that M.'s technical liberties were not unprecedented but modelled upon the efforts which Tasso and Guarini had made to liberate lyric poetry from strict *canzone* patterns: also that authoritative precedent for M.'s rhymeless lines may be found as early as Dante (Prince 71–88). Less satisfactory is Battestin's explanation of M.'s shifts of tense in terms of the Latin practice of alternating between narrative past and historic present. The contradictory tenses are an important part of *Lycidas* as Nelson 64–76 and 138–52 maintains: they strengthen the impression of the poem as performance and ceremony, and dramaticality is further enhanced by the rhetorical situation, so that *Lycidas* may be viewed as 'one of the most nearly complete fulfilments of peculiarly baroque tendencies in style'.

J. E. Hardy, *KR* vii (1945) 99–113, sees *Lycidas* as concerning itself with the expression of the problem of the relationship between two world-views, pagan and Christian, as exemplified in the dual connotational meanings of the word 'shepherd'. The resolution of this problem, Hardy considers, depends on the expression of the conviction that the double meaning of the word represents a bond of necessary kinship between the poetic and the religious experiences, just as poet and preacher are combined in King. Brett 39–50 argues, however, that *Lycidas* represents not a mingling of pagan and sacred, but a conflict between them. M. is torn between the rival claims of Renaissance humanism and deepening Protestant conviction: the former shows itself in the poem's pastoralism, the latter in the three passages (*56–7*, *76–84* and *108–31*) where M. breaks from the pastoral mood. In *193* M. bids farewell to the pastoral tradition and all that it symbolizes. The division which M. Lloyd, *EC* xi (1961) 390–402, considers basic to *Lycidas* is not that between pagan and sacred, however, but that between the self-absorbed world and the world of the good shepherd. The theme is the duty, judgment and salvation of the religious teacher, and poetry, as well as preaching, is elevated to be the shepherd's medium. The self-absorbed world has 'blind' shepherds (*119*) and is ruled by a 'blind' fury (*75*) with 'shears' like those at the 'shearers' feast' where the rapacious shepherds 'scramble' (*117*). But from the viewpoint of the poem's other world, Lloyd argues, the shearers' feast is, as in *1 Sam.* xxv, an occasion for rejoicing:

it may command a 'worthy bidden guest' (*118*)–the words echo Matthew's account of the nuptial feast that represents man's admission to the kingdom of heaven. A view nearer to Brett's is developed by A. S. P. Woodhouse (Norwood 261–78) who takes the pattern of *Lycidas* to be dependent on the contrast between the unreal Arcadian world of the pastoral and the concerns of the real 'extra-aesthetic' life which break in upon it. Similarly J. S. Lawry, *PMLA* lxxvii (1962) 27–32, approaching *Lycidas* as dialectic, draws attention to the opposition beween the initial 'ideal' pastoral world (thesis) and the 'actual' world, represented by the two 'digressions' (antithesis). From their encounter there arises a third statement, one of mystic certainty (synthesis).

The earliest studies seriously to explore the structure of *Lycidas* by concentration upon myth and image were those of C. W. Mayerson, *PMLA* lxiv (1949) 189–207, and R. P. Adams, *PMLA* lxiv (1949) 183–88. Miss Mayerson emphasizes the importance of the Orpheus image (*56–63*). For M.'s readers Orpheus was a type of the poet-prophet, a harmonizing and civilizing influence: the mythographers interpreted the legend of his death as an allegory of the destruction of human wisdom and art by barbarism, and their reappearance in succeeding cycles of culture. He was also associated with Christ. The Renaissance view of Orpheus is further inspected by D. P. Walker, *Journal of the Warburg and Courtauld Institutes* xvi (1953) 100–20, who points out that to the neo-Platonists Orpheus was the source of all Greek theology, through whom Pythagoras and hence Plato had learned that the structure of all things is based on numerical proportions. It was believed that the Jewish revelation, made to Moses, had filtered through to the Egyptians: Orpheus had read the Pentateuch in Egypt, and thus a line could be traced from Moses, through Hermes Trismegistus and the *Orphica* to Plato: Platonism and Christianity could thus be reconciled, since they originated in the same revelation, and M.'s readers might well regard Orpheus as no more pagan than Moses or the Old Testament. R. P. Adams' study concerns itself with the death-and-rebirth pattern more widely than Miss Mayerson's: this pattern is inherent in the imagery of hyacinth (*106*), rose (*45*) and violet (*145*)–flowers which sprung from the blood of Hyacinthus, Adonis and Attis–and particularly in the images of water, the prime source of fertility in all ancient cults as M. knew from Selden's *De Dis Syris*, Lucian's *De Dea Syrea* and Plutarch's *Of Osiris*. Fifty of *Lycidas*'s 193 lines are concerned with water, often treating it as a fertility symbol (*24*, *29*, *137*, *140*) or as a symbol of death and rebirth, as in the references to Alpheus and Arethusa (*132–3*) and to Orpheus (*58*). M. goes to some lengths to show that water, the principle of life, was not responsible for the death of Lycidas (*89–99*): the blame is put on the man-made ship, built in defiance of the powers of nature (*101*). Commenting on Adams' article E. R. Marks, *Explicator* ix (1951) 44, distinguishes between the poem's treatment of salt water, which is destructive, and fresh water, which nourishes life. The same distinction is made in Brooks and Hardy 169–86: 'The streams and fountains which run throughout the poem flow with life-giving water . . . whereas the seas flow chaotically, without pattern . . .

It is ironical, of course, that the streams all have for their destination the sea . . . the lives of men, too, with their purposes and meanings, spill themselves finally into the sea of oblivion.' The water imagery is further inspected by W. Shumaker, *PMLA* lxvi (1951) 485–94, along with that of vegetation. Shumaker notes that the catalogue of flowers which 'sad embroidery' wear picks up and utilizes many preceding references to a blight that has been placed on vegetative nature by King's death: with 'remarkable consistency' M. makes 'every mention of vegetation in the first 132 lines of the elegy suggest a sympathetic frustration in nature to balance the human frustrations about which the poem is built.' The connection of the flower passage with what precedes it is rather differently viewed by Allen 41–70, who illustrates the poem's movement from death to life by pointing out that whereas in the first half the flowers are colourless and the waters becalmed or almost motionless, in the second the waters race and thunder and the flowers flash into brightness. The most whole-hearted discussion of *Lycidas* as a reworking of literary archetypes is that by Northrop Frye (Patrides 200–11), who takes the Adonis myth as the shaping principle: like Adonis, Lycidas is associated with the cyclical rhythms of nature, particularly the daily cycle of the sun across the sky, the yearly cycle of the seasons, and the cycle of water flowing from wells and fountains through rivers to the sea.

The interpretations of Tillyard, Ransom, Hardy, Adams and Frye are viewed sceptically by M. H. Abrams (Patrides 212–31), in a study which reasserts the importance of the poem's surface meaning, laying particular emphasis on the persona, the pastoral elegist who speaks the poem: 'that the rise, evolution and resolution of the troubled thought of the elegist is the key to the structure of *Lycidas*, M. made as emphatic as he could. He forced it on our attention by the startling device of ending the elegy, in a passage set off as a stanza in *ottava rima*, not with Lycidas, but with the elegist himself.'

The best of the source studies is still J. H. Hanford's, *PMLA* xxv (1910) 403–47, which examines as forerunners of *Lycidas* Theocritus i, the *Lament for Bion*, Virgil's *Ecl.* x, Petrarch's *Ecl.* vi and vii, which introduce ecclesiastical satire into pastoral, Castiglione's *Alcon* and Sannazaro's first piscatory eclogue where, as in *Lycidas*, the subject meets death by drowning, and where the lament is spoken by a character named Lycidas. In English Hanford selects as likely influences Spenser's *Shepheardes Calender* and *Astrophel*. Hanford sees M. as original in introducing into the pastoral lament ecclesiastical satire and references to his own poetic career. Sir J. E. Sandys, *TRSL* xxxii (1914) 233–64, repeats several of Hanford's suggestions and adds Amalteo's first eclogue (entitled *Lycidas*) to the possible sources. F. R. B. Godolphin, *MLN* xlix (1934) 162–6, adds Propertius' elegy on the drowning of Paetus (III vii), and W. B. Austin, *SP* xliv (1947) 41–55, discovers general similarities between several passages in *Lycidas* and two Latin elegies by Giles Fletcher on Clere and Walter Haddon. Details like Panope (*101*) and the dolphins (*164*) lead T. B. Stroup (*SAMLA* 100–13) to associate

Lycidas with the Marinell-Florimell story as told by Spenser (*F.Q.* III iv, viii, IV xi–xii). G. Finney, *HLQ* xv (1952) 325–50, argues that the early seventeenth-century Italian musical drama, particularly Striggio's libretto *La favola d'Orfeo*, set by Monteverdi, should be placed among the influences that went to form *Lycidas*.

The vocabulary of M.'s elegy is examined by G. C. Taylor, *N & Q* clxxviii (1940) 56–7, who estimates that only forty-six of its 1,500 words entered the language after 1500, and that eighty per cent of the total are Anglo-Saxon in derivation; also by Josephine Miles (Patrides 95–100), who analyses *Lycidas* in terms of its repeated use of certain words, commenting on the high proportion of these that refer to the natural world, and concluding that the poem's essential motion is from low to high and past to future, with 'fresh', 'high', 'new', 'pure' and 'sacred' as the especial value terms.

The rhyme schemes of the verse paragraphs are scrutinized by Ants Oras, *MP* lii (1954) 12–22, who demonstrates that within each paragraph the complexity of rhyme arrangement first increases and then decreases, so that the design of each paragraph mirrors the broader architectonics of the whole poem. On the evidence of the Trinity MS Oras reconstructs the process by which M. added complexity to the rhyme structure of paragraph nine–in its final form the highest point in rhyme organization reached in *Lycidas*. He shows that the poem's rhyme structure has been largely influenced by the Italian madrigal, especially the madrigals of Bembo, and those which go to make up Tasso's *Il Rogo di Corinna*.

The nature of the 'engine' (*130–1*) has been much disputed. As the *OED* shows 'engine' could mean 'a machine or instrument used in warfare', and in *Pilgrim's Progress* one of the 'engines' Christian sees at the Palace Beautiful is the sword of God. M.'s 'engine' has thus been identified with the two-edged sword which issues from God's mouth in *Rev.* i 16 and xix 15. This interpretation is favoured by L. Howard, *HLQ* xv (1952) 173–84, who points out that the sword of *Rev.* was habitually taken to refer to the word of God; M. presumably identifies this with the power of the Protestant Reformation, substituting the authority of the Bible for that of the church. Supporting Howard J. M. Steadman, *N & Q* cci (1956) 249–50, notes that a two-handed broadsword was used to symbolize the word of God as active in the Reformation in the device of the Geneva printer, John Gerard; T. B. Stroup points to the same symbolic use of the sword device in Phineas Fletcher's *Locusts* (1627). Whiting[2] 29–58 also seconds Howard's suggestion, and thinks that the 'keys' (l. *110*) and the 'engine' are aspects of the same thing. E. S. Le Comte, *SP* xlvii (1950) 589–606, likewise insists that the 'engine' is the biblical sword of God, but identifies it with that manifestation of God's sword which Savonarola saw in his vision and which is referred to in his sermon denouncing the corrupt clergy. E. L. Marilla, *PMLA* lxvii (1952) 1181–4, agrees with Le Comte and suggests that in *131*, as in *Animadversions* (Columbia iii 148, Yale 707) there is evidence that M. shared the conviction that the Protestant movement was rapidly ushering in the Kingdom of Christ on earth. M. Kelley, *N & Q* clxxxi (1941) 273, argues that it is the sword of Michael which is referred to (as in *PL* vi 250–3): M. C. Treip, *N & Q* cciv (1959) 364–6, agrees. R. E. Hughes, *N & Q* cc (1955) 58–9, favours the 'two-edged sword' of *Ps.* cxlix 6. Others have thought that M.'s 'engine' is the axe that is laid to the root of the tree in *Matt.* iii 10, which M. in *Of Reformation* (Columbia iii 47, Yale i 582) identifies with the Protestant movement; or the sheep-hook (l. *120*) which had an iron spud at one end and could be used as a weapon: C. W. Brodribb, *TLS* (June 5 1943) 271, favours this interpretation, supported by L. W. Coolidge, *PQ* xxix (1950) 444–5, who refers to the bishop striking down hardened transgressors with his sheep-hook in *Piers Plowman* viii 94–7. J. M. French, *MLN* lxviii (1953) 229–31, identifies the 'engine' with the 'keys' (l. *110*) (reading 'smite' in a figurative sense): W. A. Turner, *JEGP* xlix (1950) 562–565, prefers to think of it as the lock on St Peter's door. D. A. Stauffer, *MLR* xxxi (1936) 57–60, reads it as the two nations, England and Scotland, recently united. Less likely suggested 'engines' are the executioner's axe, which was to behead Laud, the two houses of Parliament, the 'abhorred shears' (l. *75*), and the iron flail of Spenser's Talus in *F.Q.* v (C. G. Osgood, *RES* i (1925) 339–41). H. F. Robbins, *RES* n. s. v (1954) 25–36, interprets 'engine' as 'agent', and thinks the agent in question is the Son of God, as depicted in *Matt.* xxv 31–46: the phrase 'at the doors' occurs in *Matt.* xxiv 33 meaning 'in the immediate future'. M.'s 'But' (l. *130*) has sometimes been taken as adversative only to the preceding words 'and nothing said': this reading makes the 'engine' a further item in the list of evils under prelacy–perhaps Spain and France, the double threat of Catholicism. W. J. Grace, *SP* lii (1955) 583–9, strongly urges this interpretation: he associates M.'s 'engine' with a passage from Burton and concludes that the twin superstitious appeals of the devil and the Roman Catholic church–hope and fear–are referred to. The *1645* and *1673* headnote ('And by occasion . . . height'), which must refer to the 'engine' couplet, is a serious obstacle to this theory.

In this monody the author bewails a learned friend, unfortunately drowned in his passage from Chester on the Irish Seas, 1637. And by occasion foretells the ruin of our corrupted clergy then in their height.

Yet once more, O ye laurels, and once more
Ye myrtles brown, with ivy never sere,

Headnote. Trin. MS omits 'And by occasion . . . height'.
1–2. Yet once more] D. S. Berkeley, *N & Q* ccvi (1961) 178, thinks that these words are meant to echo *Heb.* xii 26–7 where they are used as a formula signifying God's separation of things transitory from things eternal. *laurels . . . myrtles . . . ivy*] The conjunction is discussed by J. B. Trapp *Journal of the Warburg and Courtauld Institutes* xxi (1958) 227–55, who suggests that it derives from a conflation of Virgil, *Ecl.* viii 12–3 and ii 54. He points out that the crown which Albertino Mussato received from his fellow-citizens at Padua in 1315 mingled the three foliages, and M. may have known

I come to pluck your berries harsh and crude,
And with forced fingers rude,
Shatter your leaves before the mellowing year.
Bitter constraint, and sad occasion dear,
Compels me to disturb your season due:
For Lycidas is dead, dead ere his prime,
Young Lycidas, and hath not left his peer:
Who would not sing for Lycidas? he knew
Himself to sing, and build the lofty rhyme.
He must not float upon his watery bier
Unwept, and welter to the parching wind,

of this ceremony from Mussato's own works. He almost certainly knew Petrarch's *Oration* delivered at his crowning (with ivy, bay and myrtle) in 1341, and of the account of this coronation ascribed to Senuccio dei Bene in which the reasons for the foliages are given (ivy, because Bacchus crowned the first poet with it; bay, the tree of victory; and myrtle, Venus' tree, because poets are abnormally amorous). The crown of three foliages appears in later editions of Ripa's *Iconologia* (after 1630), in the image of *Accademia*. In Horace, *Odes* I i 29 the ivy-crown, usually associated with Bacchus, is mentioned as the reward of learning. *brown*] Horace, *Odes* I xxv 18 calls myrtle 'brown'. *never sere*] evergreen–the adjective applies to all three plants.

1–14. K. Rinehart, *N & Q* cxcviii (1953) 103, refers to the rhyme scheme of these lines as that of a 'broken sonnet' and suggests that M. adopts this form to show that he is 'forcing' himself poetically.

4–5. Trin. MS has two drafts of ll. 1–14, of which one is on a separate sheet, and reads here: *Before the mellowing year* \`And with forced fingers rude' / *And crop your young* \`Shatter your leaves before the mellowing year'.

6. dear] heartfelt. The word can also mean 'dire' and Brooks and Hardy 170 think the effect of the ambiguity is to emphasize the inescapable, fatal character of the poet's obligation to Lycidas.

8. ere his prime] King was twenty-five.

10. Who would not sing] Cp. Virgil, *Ecl.* x 3: *neget quis carmina Gallo? he knew*] *Trin. MS* has 'he well knew', and 'well' is inserted in a hand probably M.'s in the Cambridge University Library copy of *1638*. J. S. Diekhoff, *PQ* xvi (1937) 408–10, argues against and Shawcross (330) for the inclusion of 'well'.

10–11. he . . . sing] Masson[2] i 648–9 lists ten extant sets of Latin verses by King, nine of them contributed to volumes of encomiastic occasional poetry dedicated to various members of the Royal family by scholars of the University, and one prefixed to Peter Hausted's *Senile Odium* (1633).

11. build] Imitates the Latin use of *condo* as in Horace, *Epist.* I iii 24: *condis amabile carmen* (you build charming poetry). R. Y. Tyrrell, *CR* ix (1895) 11–12 compares Pindar's use of *τέκτονες* (*Pyth.* iii 113).

13. welter] be tossed or tumbled about. In the seventeenth century the

Without the meed of some melodious tear.
Begin then, sisters of the sacred well,
That from beneath the seat of Jove doth spring,
Begin, and somewhat loudly sweep the string.
Hence with denial vain, and coy excuse,
So may some gentle muse
With lucky words favour my destined urn,
And as he passes turn,
And bid fair peace be to my sable shroud.
For we were nursed upon the self-same hill,
Fed the same flock; by fountain, shade, and rill.
Together both, ere the high lawns appeared
Under the opening eye-lids of the morn,
We drove a-field, and both together heard

word retained its sense 'writhe, wriggle', thus the idea of King suffering a terrible death comes into the line. *parching*] drying.

14. tear] Collections of elegiac verse were often entitled *Lacrymae* (Tears): thus 'tear' means 'elegy'.

15. sisters] The muses. *well*] Aganippe, on Mount Helicon, where there was an altar to Jove. At the beginning of Hesiod's *Theogony* the muses 'haunt the high and holy mount of Helicon and dance with soft feet around the violet spring and the altar of the mighty son of Kronos'.

19–22. muse] G. M. Gathorne-Hardy, *TLS* (18 Jan. 1934) 44, suggests that this is one of the nine sisters, not a future poet; that 'my destined urn' means 'the memorial (this poem) I am now preparing for Lycidas'; and that 'he' means Lycidas himself, who 'passes' in the funeral procession. This rather strained reading was produced in reply to J. A. S. Barrett, *TLS* (11 Jan. 1934) 28, who pointed out that 'urn' and 'shroud' were incompatible, the one implying cremation, the other burial. *sable*] black. M. is the first to apply this epithet to a shroud: shrouds are normally white or grey. It is true that Sylvester (Du Bartas[2] 991) has the conjunction 'sable Shrowd', but there the 'Shrowd' is being worn by a living woman, and means not 'winding-sheet' but 'clothing'.

20. lucky] G. O. Marshall, *Explicator* xvii (1959) 66, takes this to mean not 'well-omened' (the *OED* explanation) but 'having an unstudied or unsought felicity' (a literary sense not recorded by the *OED* until 1700). The muse, Marshall explains, is to favour M.'s urn in the pastoral strain in which the 'uncouth swain' is favouring the urn of Lycidas.

22. And] Substituted in *Trin. MS* for 'to'.

25. lawns] Open spaces between woods, glades. 'Lawn' does not mean 'a piece of closely-mown grass' until the 1730s. The countryside round Cambridge is more realistically described in *Elegia I* 11–14.

26. opening] In *Trin. MS* substituted for 'glimmering'. Cp. *Job* xli 18, and Middleton, *Game at Chess* I i 79 'the opening eyelids of the morn'.

27. a-field] *1645* and *1673* omit hyphen. *1638* has it, and in a scrap of proof

What time the grey-fly winds her sultry horn,
Battening our flocks with the fresh dews of night,
Oft till the star that rose, at evening, bright,
Toward heaven's descent had sloped his westering
wheel.
Meanwhile the rural ditties were not mute,
Tempered to the oaten flute,
Rough satyrs danced, and fauns with cloven heel,
From the glad sound would not be absent long,
And old Damaetas loved to hear our song.

from an earlier state of *1638* (23–35) now in Cambridge University Library, the hyphen is inserted in a hand possibly M.'s. *Trin. MS*: afield. In the same scrap of proof the correcting hand hyphenates 'eye-lids' (l. 26) and places a full-stop after 'wheel' (l. 31). *1638*, *1645* and *1673* have both these corrections.

28. grey-fly] The name seems to have been used to designate various kinds of insect, including the dung-beetle and the may-fly. *sultry*] presumably indicates that 'What time' (Latin *quo tempore*) is midday.

29. Battening] fattening.

30. star] Hesperus, the evening star. *Trin. MS* has 'Oft till the ev'n star bright' (the 1638 reading) corrected to 'Oft till the star that rose in evening bright'. Shawcross 330 argues that 'in' should be retained instead of 'at'.

31. westering] In *Trin. MS* substituted for 'burnished'.

33. oaten] Cp. 'Oten reeds' in Spenser, *Shep. Cal.* October 8, which E. K. glosses *Avena*, referring to Virgil, *Ecl.* i 2, *tenui . . . avena* ('on slender reed', i.e. on the shepherd's pipe).

34. fauns] There are dancing fauns in Virgil, *Ecl.* vi 27–8.

36. Damaetas] *Trin. MS* has 'Damoetas'. There is a Dametas in Sidney's *Arcadia* who is a loutish clown. This fact led Jerram (56) to suggest that the name was adopted by M. as an insulting reference to his tutor Chappell. F. Pyle, *Hermathena* lxxi (1948) 83–92, makes the same suggestion and, taking the 'fauns' and 'satyrs' to be Cambridge undergraduates, thinks that the 'song' must be *Vacation Exercise*. E. S. De Beer, *N & Q* cxciv (1949) 336–7, agreeing that there is an allusion to the Dametas of the *Arcadia*, interprets it as meaning simply that M. and King could please even an unlearned audience. M. H. Nicolson, *MLN* xli (1926) 293–300, does not think the reference derogatory: she argues that M.'s Damaetas is not Chappell but Joseph Mead, another and popular fellow of Christ's. The whole question is reviewed by H. Fletcher, *JEGP* lx (1961) 250–7. He associates the name Δαμόιτας with the verb δαμάζω (to tame) and concludes that a tutor is meant. The Damoetas of Theocritus vi is clearly young: so, too, in Virgil, *Ecl.* iii and v. Only in *Ecl.* ii 37 do we have an old, indeed dying Damoetas. It seems that Mead did not like poetry, so he will not do as a candidate. Fletcher favours Chappell, who was interested in poetry, especially neo-Latin poetry: he suggests also, as possibilities,

But O the heavy change, now thou art gone,
Now thou art gone, and never must return!
Thee shepherd, thee the woods, and desert caves,
With wild thyme and the gadding vine o'ergrown,
And all their echoes mourn.
The willows, and the hazel copses green,
Shall now no more be seen,
Fanning their joyous leaves to thy soft lays.
As killing as the canker to the rose,
Or taint-worm to the weanling herds that graze,
Or frost to flowers, that their gay wardrobe wear,
When first the white-thorn blows;
Such, Lycidas, thy loss to shepherd's ear.
Where were ye nymphs when the remorseless deep
Closed o'er the head of your loved Lycidas?
For neither were ye playing on the steep,
Where your old bards, the famous Druids, lie,

Michael Honeywood, a fellow of Christ's since 1618, and Abraham Wheelock (1593–1653), first Professor of Arabic. Both have verses which appear in collections along with King's, and Honeywood contributed to the *Justa Eduardo King*.

39–44. Cp. *Lament for Bion* 1–7, 27–35 where the orchards and groves wail for Bion, the trees cast their fruit on the ground and the flowers wither, and Echo mourns among her rocks. Similarly in Ovid, *Met.* xi 44–8 the birds, beasts, rocks, trees and rivers weep for Orpheus.

40. gadding] wandering, straggling.

45. canker] See *Arcades* 53*n* (p. 158).

46. taint-worm] Bateson 159 identifies this as 'the intestinal worm that the modern farmer calls "husk", which is normally only fatal, as M. correctly says, to newly weaned calves when they start grazing'.

47. wardrobe wear] *Trin. MS*: *buttons* \`wardrobe' *wear* \`*bear*' \`wear'.

48–9. Echoing Shakespeare, *Midsummer Night's Dream* I i 184–5: 'More tuneable than lark to shepherd's ear, / When wheat is green, when hawthorn buds appear.'

50–5. Similarly in Theocritus i 66–9 Thyrsis asks the nymphs where they were when Daphnis was dying, for they were not by Anapus or on Etna. Virgil imitates this passage in *Ecl.* x 9–12.

51. loved] In *Trin. MS* substituted for 'youn[g]'.

52–4. steep] The slope of a mountain: M. distinguishes between the slopes and the 'top' of Mona (Anglesey): the nymphs were in neither place. Mona and Anglesey are identified and named as the home of the Druids by Drayton, *Polyolbion* ix 415–29, 436: Selden's note to 417 helps to explain M.'s 'shaggy', since it describes Anglesey as 'well stored with thicke Woods, and religious Groves, in so much that it was called Inis-Dowil [the Dark Isle]'.

Nor on the shaggy top of Mona high,
Nor yet where Deva spreads her wizard stream:
Ay me, I fondly dream!
Had ye been there . . . for what could that have done?
What could the muse herself that Orpheus bore,
The muse herself for her enchanting son
Whom universal nature did lament,
When by the rout that made the hideous roar,
His gory visage down the stream was sent,
Down the swift Hebrus to the Lesbian shore.
  Alas! What boots it with uncessant care
To tend the homely slighted shepherd's trade,
And strictly meditate the thankless muse,
Were it not better done as others use,

55. Deva] The Dee. See *Vacation Exercise* 98*n* (p. 80).
57. In *Trin. MS* 'Had ye' and 'for' are deleted.
58–63. muse] Calliope. The first version of the lines in *Trin. MS* reads: 'What could the golden-haired Calliope / For her enchanting son / When she beheld (the gods far-sighted be) / His gory scalp roll down the Thracian lea'. The last two lines are cancelled and 'Whom universal nature might lament / And heaven and hell deplore / When his divine head down the stream was sent / Down the swift Hebrus to the Lesbian shore' inserted. The present version is then substituted on a separate leaf, but with 'might lament' (corrected to 'did lament') and 'divine visage' (corrected to 'gory visage'). D. S. Berkeley, *N & Q* cciii (1958) 335–6, suggests reasons for the successive changes, pointing out that the epithet 'golden-haired' belonged also to Dionysus, and hence might be associated with the Bacchantes, enemies to Calliope: also that '(the gods far-sighted be)', a parenthesis reminiscent of Spenser's pastoral speech, runs counter to meaning: if gods are 'far-sighted' why are the nymphs, Hippotades and even Neptune ignorant of the causes of Lycidas's death? Cp. *Greek Anthol.* vii 8, on the death of Orpheus: 'Thy mother Calliope . . . bewailed thee. Why sigh we for our dead sons, when not even the gods have power to protect their children from death?'
61–3. Ovid. *Met.* xi 1–55, relates how Orpheus was torn to pieces by the Thracian women and how his severed head floated down the Hebrus and was carried across to the island of Lesbos. The story is also in Virgil, *Georg.* iv 454–527. *swift*] Echoes Virgil, *Aen.* i 317: *volucrem . . . Hebrum.*
64–84. L. S. Friedland, *MLN* xxvii (1912) 246–50, finds similarities between this question and Phoebus' reply and passages in Spenser's *Ruins of Time.*
64. boots] profits, avails.
66. meditate] M.'s use of the word imitates Virgil's *musam meditaris* (*Ecl.* i 2) and *meditabor . . . musam* (*Ecl.* vi 8).
67–8. Cp. Virgil, *Ecl.* ii 14–15: *Nonne fuit satius tristis Amaryllidis iras / atque superba pati fastidia* (Was it not better to put up with Amaryllis' sullen rage

To sport with Amaryllis in the shade,
Or with the tangles of Neaera's hair?
Fame is the spur that the clear spirit doth raise
(That last infirmity of noble mind)
To scorn delights, and live laborious days;
But the fair guerdon when we hope to find,
And think to burst out into sudden blaze,
Comes the blind Fury with th' abhorred shears,
And slits the thin-spun life. But not the praise,
Phoebus replied, and touched my trembling ears;
Fame is no plant that grows on mortal soil,
Nor in the glistering foil
Set off to the world, nor in broad rumour lies,
But lives and spreads aloft by those pure eyes,
And perfect witness of all-judging Jove;

and scornful disdain?) In *Ecl.* i Tityrus, reclining 'in the shade', makes the woods echo with the name of Amaryllis: she appears again in *Ecl.* iii and ix. Virgil borrowed her from Theocritus iii and iv.

69. Or with] P. Maas, *RES* xix (1943) 397–8, prefers the reading of *Trin. MS* (before correction) and of *1638*, 'Hid in'. *Neaera's*] Neaera appears in Virgil, *Ecl.* iii 3, and among the elegies of Tibullus are six addressed to her by Lygdamus of which III ii 11–12 refers to her tangled hair. Horace writes of her in *Epode* xv and in *Odes* III xiv 21 her hair is about to be fastened in a knot. Joannes Secundus addresses his *Basia* to Neaera, as R. J. Schoeck points out, *N & Q* cci (1956) 190–1, and *Basium* viii develops the image of tangled hair. Buchanan also uses the name in his Latin poetry: in the last of his elegies and in *Epigram* 44 he refers to the chains of her hair.

70. Cp. Spenser, *Tears of the Muses* 404: 'Due praise that is the spur of dooing well.'

71. H. MacL. Currie, *N & Q* cciii (1958) 106–7 suggests that Silius Italicus, *Punica* vi 332–3 *fax mentis honestae / gloria* (fame, the torch of a noble mind), may have contributed to this line, but a nearer parallel is Tacitus, *Hist.* iv 6: *Etiam sapientibus cupido gloriae novissima exuitur* (even with wise men the desire for glory is the last to be abandoned).

75. Fury] Atropos was one of the Fates, not a Fury. See *Winchester Epitaph* 28*n* and *Arcades* 63–72*n*, pp. 128 and 159 above.

77. Echoing Virgil, *Ecl.* vi 3–4: *Cynthius aurem / vellit et admonuit* (the Cynthian plucked my ear and warned me).

78–84. Phoebus' reply is paralleled by a passage in M.'s seventh Prolusion, as Allen 66 points out, (Columbia xii 278–81, Yale i 302). Daiches 84 comments: 'The pat aphoristic nature of that final couplet could not possibly be a solution to such a complex poem as *Lycidas*. There is almost a note of irony in the copy-book lesson. It is a deliberately false climax.'

79. foil] The thin leaf of gold or silver placed under a precious stone to increase its brilliancy.

As he pronounces lastly on each deed,
Of so much fame in heaven expect thy meed.
O fountain Arethuse, and thou honoured flood,
Smooth-sliding Mincius, crowned with vocal reeds,
That strain I heard was of a higher mood:
But now my oat proceeds,
And listens to the herald of the sea
That came in Neptune's plea,
He asked the waves, and asked the felon winds,
What hard mishap hath doomed this gentle swain?
And questioned every gust of rugged wings
That blows from off each beaked promontory;
They knew not of his story,
And sage Hippotades their answer brings,
That not a blast was from his dungeon strayed,
The air was calm, and on the level brine,
Sleek Panope with all her sisters played.
It was that fatal and perfidious bark

85–6. The invocation signals the return to pastoral after the 'higher mood' of Phoebus' speech. The Arethuse (see *Arcades* 30–1n, p. 158 above) represents Sicilian, and the Mincius (Virgil's native river) Roman pastoral. Virgil refers to the sedges and reeds of Mincius in *Ecl.* vii 12–3, *Georg.* iii 14–5, and *Aen.* x 205–6, and in the second of these passages describes its course 'wandering in slow windings'. D. C. Allen, *MLN* lxxi (1956) 172–3, points out that Fulgentius in the *Mitologiae* allegorizes the Alpheus-Arethuse myth, interpreting Arethuse as the nobility of justice (*nobilitas Aequitatis*) and Alpheus as the light of truth (*vertitatis lux*). The unpolluted passage of Alpheus' waters through the ocean illustrates the incorruptibility of truth. Sandys repeats this interpretation in his commentary on the *Metamorphoses.* *honoured*] *Trin. MS*: *smooth* `*famed*' `honoured'. *Smooth-sliding*] In *Trin. MS* substituted for 'soft-sliding'. Sylvester has 'smooth-sliding floods' (Du Bartas 218).

89 herald] Triton.

90. in Neptune's plea] to defend Neptune against the charge of responsibility for King's death.

91. felon] savage, wild. T. P. Harrison, *UTSE* xv (1935) 22, points out that de Baïf, in *Eclogue* xv, has *de vents felons* in close association with Neptune and his waves.

96. Hippotades] A Homeric and Ovidian name for Aeolus, god of winds, son of Hippotes. Virgil represents him as imprisoning the winds in a vast cavern, *Aen.* i 52–63. As D. T. Starnes remarks (Taylor² 42–3) Aeolus is called *vir sapiens* in Conti (hence, perhaps, M.'s 'sage').

99. Panope] One of the fifty Nereids (sea nymphs), mentioned by Virgil, *Aen.* v 240.

100. bark] M. Lloyd, *MLN* lxxv (1960) 103–8, suggests that the 'bark'

Built in the eclipse, and rigged with curses dark,
That sunk so low that sacred head of thine.
  Next Camus, reverend sire, went footing slow,
His mantle hairy, and his bonnet sedge,
Inwrought with figures dim, and on the edge
Like to that sanguine flower inscribed with woe.
Ah; who hath reft (quoth he) my dearest pledge?
Last came, and last did go,
The pilot of the Galilean lake,
Two massy keys he bore of metals twain,

is the human body, subject to death ('fatal'), and built in the eclipse man has endured since Adam's fall; also that the 'mount' (161) is not only St Michael's Mount but also the mount of Paradise from which Michael drove man 'without remorse' (*PL* xi 105)–now he is asked to 'melt with ruth'.

101. eclipse] Eclipses were considered evil omens; the witches' cauldron in *Macbeth* IV i 27–8 contains 'slips of yew / Sliver'd in the moon's eclipse'.

103. Camus] The river Cam, representing Cambridge University. J. M. Morse, *N & Q* cciii (1958) 211, suggests that M. is slyly aware of the derivation of 'pedant' from Italian *pedare* 'to foot it', in Florio's *World of Words*.

104. hairy] Refers to the fur of the academic gown. *sedge*] A name applied to various rush-like or flag-like plants, growing near water. It is a common adornment of river-gods in masques, as in Jonson, *King's Entertainment* 101–7, where Tamesis wears bracelets of willow and sedge and a crown of sedge and reed. Jonson cites Virgil, *Aen.* viii 31–4, which M. probably recalled here.

105. Inwrought] The first recorded appearance of the word; in *Trin. MS* substituted for 'scrawled o'er'. The leaf of the flag has dusky streaks in the middle and is serrated at the edge.

106. flower] The hyacinth. Theocritus x 28 speaks of the 'lettered' hyacinth, and *Lament for Bion* 6 mentions its 'writing'. Its letters were *AI* ('Alas'), marked on its leaves because it sprung from the blood of Apollo's beloved Hyacinthus. Ovid retells the story, *Met.* x 214–6: 'Phoebus . . . inscribed his grieving words upon the leaves, and the flower bore the marks AI AI, letters of lamentation.'

107. pledge] child (in that a child is a token of its parents' love); the word is first used in this sense by Spenser, *F.Q.* I x 4.

109. pilot] R. E. Hone, *SP* lvi (1959) 55–61, argues that this figure is not St Peter, but Christ, who is described as a bishop in *1 Pet.* ii 25, and by M. in *Animadversions* (Columbia iii 157, Yale i 715–6), who carries keys, *Rev.* i 18, and who saves the disciples' boat from shipwreck, *John* vi 15–21. The keys which Christ gives to St Peter (*Matt.* xvi 19) seem to fit the description here, however, better than those in *Rev.* i 18. Peter denounces false teachers in *2 Pet.* ii.

(The golden opes, the iron shuts amain)
He shook his mitred locks, and stern bespake,
How well could I have spared for thee, young swain,
Enow of such as for their bellies' sake,
Creep and intrude, and climb into the fold?
Of other care they little reckoning make,
Than how to scramble at the shearers' feast,
And shove away the worthy bidden guest;
Blind mouths! that scarce themselves know how to hold
A sheep-hook, or have learned aught else the least
That to the faithful herdman's art belongs!
What recks it them? What need they? They are sped;
And when they list, their lean and flashy songs
Grate on their scrannel pipes of wretched straw,

111. amain] with force, vehemently.

113–31. G. R. Coffman, *JELH* iii (1936) 101–13, finds some resemblances between M.'s handling of the parable from *John* x 1–28 and that in Bernard of Morlais's *De Contemptu Mundi*, available in four editions by 1637. E. L. Brooks, *N & Q* cci (1956) 67–8, indicates similarities between the 'pilot's' speech and Ezek. xxxiv, and K. McKenzie, *Italica* xx (1943) 121–6, compares Beatrice's denunciation of presumptuous preachers in *Paradiso* xxix 70–126. J. M. Steadman, *N & Q* (1958) 141–2, considers that M. may also have been familiar with a scene which takes place between St Peter and the condemned clergy in *La rappresentazione del dì del giudizio*.

114. Enow] enough.

115. Creep] Echoes the discussion of false shepherds in Spenser, *Shep. Cal.* May 126: 'There crept in Wolves.' *climb*] Cp. *John* x 1: 'He that entereth not by the door into the sheepfold, but climbeth up some other way.'

119. Blind mouths] Ruskin, *Sesame and Lilies* i 22 comments: 'A "Bishop" means "a person who sees". A "Pastor" means "a person who feeds". The most unbishoply character a man can have is therefore to be blind. The most unpastoral is, instead of feeding, to want to be fed–to be a Mouth.' J. A. Himes, *MLN* xxxv (1920) 441, suggests rather that M. is translating the term τυφλόστομος which the geographer Strabo (IV i 8) applies to the mouth of a river choked with mud and sand. Thus M.'s term would imply shallowness and impeded utterance. R. J. Kane, *MLN* lxviii (1953) 239–40, also gives the Strabo reference.

121. herdman's] Shawcross 330 argues for the retention of the *Trin. MS* reading 'herdsman's'.

122. What . . . them?] What business is it of theirs? *sped*] satisfied.

123. list] choose, please. The construction seems to be 'When they choose to grate out their songs the sheep [attracted by the sound] look up'. The *1638* omission of the comma after 'list' makes the connection of 'list' and 'grate' clearer. *flashy*] watery, insipid.

124. scrannel] The first recorded appearance of the word; *OED* suggests

The hungry sheep look up, and are not fed,
But swoll'n with wind, and the rank mist they draw,
Rot inwardly, and foul contagion spread:
Besides what the grim wolf with privy paw
Daily devours apace, and nothing said,
But that two-handed engine at the door,
Stands ready to smite once, and smite no more.
  Return Alpheus, the dread voice is past,
That shrunk thy streams; return Sicilian muse,
And call the vales, and bid them hither cast
Their bells, and flowrets of a thousand hues.
Ye valleys low where the mild whispers use,
Of shades and wanton winds, and gushing brooks,
On whose fresh lap the swart star sparely looks,

connection with a dialect word meaning 'thin'. Cp. Virgil, *Ecl.* iii 27 *stridenti miserum stipula disperdere carmen* (to murder a rotten tune on a harsh-sounding straw).

125–7. E. S. Le Comte, *MLN* lxix (1954) 403–4, shows that M.'s description of sheep-rot is closely modelled on one in Petrarch, *Eclogue* ix, where Petrarch is recalling the Black Death; he suggests M. has the plague in mind. Cp. also Dante, *Paradiso* xxix 106–7: *Si che le pecorelle, che non sanno, / Tornan dal pasco pasciute di vento* (So that the sheep, without knowledge, come back from pasture fed on wind). Northrop Frye considers M.'s description of the sheep as 'picking up' the image of Lycidas' body weltering to the parching wind in l. 13.

128. wolf] The Roman Catholic Church, particularly, as E. S. Le Comte, *SP* xlvii (1950) 606, points out, the Jesuits; the arms of their founder, St Ignatius Loyola, included two grey wolves. Webster describes a Jesuit as 'a gray Woolfe' (*Overburian Characters*, ed. W. J. Paylor (Oxford 1936) p. 75). M. is referring to the proselytism carried on by the Catholic party in England.

129. nothing said] *Trin. MS* corrects to 'little said': Shawcross 330 argues for the retention of this reading.

130–1. See headnote.

132. On this transition Tuve[2] 103 comments: 'Pastoral has its way of reasserting a fundamental and harmonious sympathy, and of proclaiming that not decay and death but life and creativity and love is the universal principle.' And Brooks and Hardy 182: 'The dread voice has been endowed with something of the effect of blazing light–a hot sun inimical to the cool shadows of mythology and the flowers of pastoral poetry.'

136. use] go frequently, haunt.

137. gushing] In *Trin. MS* substituted for 'goshing'.

138. fresh lap] Echoes Shakespeare, *Midsummer Night's Dream* II i 108: 'the fresh lap of the crimson rose'. *swart star*] The Dog-star, Sirius: the Dog-days (the days around the heliacal rising of Sirius) are notorious

Throw hither all your quaint enamelled eyes,
That on the green turf suck the honied showers,
And purple all the ground with vernal flowers.
Bring the rathe primrose that forsaken dies,
The tufted crow-toe, and pale jessamine,
The white pink, and the pansy freaked with jet,
The glowing violet

for heat: 'swart' (darkened by heat) is transferred from effect to cause. *sparely*] *Trin. MS*: *sparely* ˋ*faintly*ˊ ˋsparelyˊ.

139. Throw] In *Trin. MS* substituted for 'Bring'. *enamelled*] See *Arcades* 84*n* p. 160 above.

139–40. Brooks and Hardy 181 suggest that these sucking eyes balance the 'blind mouths' (l. 119). Even the flowers, by contrast with the worthless shepherds, have the kind of spiritual life and awareness we attribute to the seeing eye.

142. rathe] early, a dialect word with pastoral colour for M. because used by Spenser in *Shep. Cal.* July 78 and December 98.

142–50. This flower passage is an afterthought. In the *Trin. MS* draft l. 141 is followed immediately by l. 151, but on a separate sheet there are inserted two versions of ll. 142–50, of which the earlier reads: 'Bring the rathe primrose that unwedded dies / Colouring the pale cheek of unenjoyed love / And that sad flower that strove / To write his own woes on the vermeil grain / Next add Narcissus that still weeps in vain / The woodbine and the pansy freaked with jet / The glowing violet / The cowslip wan that hangs his pensive head / And every bud that sorrow's livery wears / Let daffadillies fill their cups with tears / Bid amaranthus all his beauty shed / To strew the laureate hearse etc.' The second version is, in its corrected state, the same as *1645* and *1673*, except for 'beauties' (l. 149): in its uncorrected state l. 146 read 'The musk-rose and the garish columbine' and l. 148 'And every flower that sad escutcheon bears', and ll. 149–50 were inverted. H. H. Adams, *MLN* lxv (1950) 468–72, thinks that the changes M. made in his draft of the flower-passage were intended partly to conceal his debt to *Winter's Tale* IV iv 113–132, and partly to remove erotic elements which would be out of place in a funeral elegy. W. L. Thompson, *N & Q* cxcvii (1952) 97–9, suggests that M.'s passage is more indebted to Jonson, *Pan's Anniversary* 11–38 than to *Winter's Tale*. Spenser, *Shep. Cal.* April 136–44 is also frequently compared.

143. crow-toe] A popular name for the wild hyacinth. *jessamine*] jasmine, a climbing shrub with fragrant white flowers.

144. freaked] A coinage. There was a noun 'freak' meaning 'capricious humour, whim, vagary', but M. was the first to use the word as a verb. J. F. Killeen, *N & Q* ccvii (1962) 70–3, thinks that M. had in mind the use of the past participle passive of Latin *ludere* (i.e. *lusus*), in the sense 'adorned'. The 'jet' is a sign of mourning.

The musk-rose, and the well-attired woodbine,
With cowslips wan that hang the pensive head,
And every flower that sad embroidery wears:
Bid amaranthus all his beauty shed,
And daffadillies fill their cups with tears,
To strew the laureate hearse where Lycid lies.
For so to interpose a little ease,
Let our frail thoughts dally with false surmise.
Ay me! Whilst thee the shores, and sounding seas
Wash far away, where'er thy bones are hurled,
Whether beyond the stormy Hebrides
Where thou perhaps under the whelming tide
Visit'st the bottom of the monstrous world;
Or whether thou to our moist vows denied,

146. woodbine] The herbals identify this with the honeysuckle, but in Shakespeare, *Midsummer Night's Dream* IV i 47 it is distinguished from the honeysuckle and seems to be equated with convolvulus or bindweed.
147. wan] pale.
149. amaranthus] The immortal flower of Paradise (see *PL* iii 353–7), linked with a poet's death by Spenser, *F.Q.* III vi 45. *beauty*] In *Trin. MS* the cancelled version of the flower-passage reads 'beauty' but the final version reads 'beauties': Shawcross 330 argues for the retention of this reading.
150. daffadillies] Cp. Spenser, *Shep. Cal.* April 140 'Daffadowndillies'. G. S. Fraser comments (Kermode[3] 35) 'Spenser's "daffadowndillies" is matched by M.'s "daffadillies", where Shakespeare, Ben Jonson and Herrick all write of "daffodils".'
153. frail] In *Trin. MS* substituted for cancelled 'sad'. *false surmise*] The surmise is false because King's body is missing, so there is no chance of strewing his hearse. But also, as Brooks and Hardy 183 point out, because the flowers are not really wearing 'sad embroidery' for Lycidas: the cups of the daffodils are not filled with tears for him. Nature is neutral: it does not participate in grief for the dead man. From this viewpoint the function of the flower passage 'in the full context of the poem, is ironic'.
154. shores] In *Trin. MS* M. first wrote 'floods' (a more logical subject for 'wash'), then altered to 'shores', which gives an impression of land and sea in league, the land rejecting the body, the sea tossing it.
157. whelming] *Trin. MS* has 'humming', the 1638 reading, and in the BM and Cambridge University copies of *Justa Eduardo King* 'humming' is starred and 'whelming' written in the margin in a hand probably M.'s. 'Humming' recalls *Pericles* III i 64, 'humming water must o'erwhelm thy corpse', of which the 'o'erwhelm' perhaps suggested 'whelming'.
158. Visit'st] Tuve[2] 96 comments: 'the irony of the intimate communication in "visit'st" is less grim than piteous'. *monstrous world*] The world of sea-monsters.
159. moist vows] tearful prayers.

Sleep'st by the fable of Bellerus old,
Where the great vision of the guarded mount
Looks toward Namancos and Bayona's hold;
Look homeward angel now, and melt with ruth.
And, O ye dolphins, waft the hapless youth.
Weep no more, woeful shepherds weep no more,
For Lycidas your sorrow is not dead,
Sunk though he be beneath the watery floor,

160. Bellerus] In *Trin. MS* M. first wrote 'Corineus' (one of the legendary warriors who, as M. notes in the *History of Britain*, came to Britain with Brutus, Aeneas' great-grandson, and ruled over Cornwall). 'Bellerus' seems to be an eponymous hero invented by M. to explain the name *Bellerium* (the Latin name for Land's End), found on Ortelius's map of Britain.

161. vision of the guarded mount] The chapter on Cornwall in Camden's *Britannia* relates that the monks who had cells on St Michael's Mount said that St Michael himself had appeared there.

162. Namancos] Nemancos is an ancient name for a district in N.W. Spain, one of the subdivisions of the archbishopric of Santiago de Compostella. The name, as A. S. Cook points out, *MLR* ii (1907) 124–8, was misspelt 'Namancos' on Ojea's map of Galicia, first published in the 1606 Ortelius, and subsequent maps, including those in the editions of *Mercator's Atlas* in and after 1613, perpetuated this error. *Bayona*] A fortress town about fifty miles south of Cape Finisterre. The two names represent the threat of Spanish Catholicism, against which St Michael guards England.

163. angel] Michael. As L. H. Kendall Jr points out, *N & Q* cxcviii (1953) 145, 'melt with ruth' is found in Chaucer, *Troilus* i 84 and Spenser, *F.Q.* III vii 9.

164. waft] convey safely by water. T. O. Mabbott, *Explicator* v (1947) 26, argues that the usual interpretation of this line as a reference to Arion who, unlike Lycidas, was not drowned but saved, is unsatisfactory. He proposes Palaemon (the 'son' of *Comus* 876) who according to Pausanias II i 3, was drowned and buried at Corinth and whose body was brought to land by a dolphin: he became a patron of mariners, like Lycidas. Tuve[2] 96 insists, however, that the reference should include 'the love and rescuing pity which had long been thought of as the beauty of Arion's story' and which 'are like in character to the saving heavenly Love that walked the waves'. M. Lloyd, *MLN* lxxv (1960) 106–7, also maintains that the Arion reference should be kept, because the Arion myth emphasizes the dolphin's love of music, and so this allusion looks back to and completes the Orpheus allusion. Lloyd adds that in the myth of Icadius, preserved in a note by Servius to *Aen.* iii 332, Apollo appears in the form of a dolphin to save Icadius from shipwreck and waft him to Parnassus.

So sinks the day-star in the ocean bed,
And yet anon repairs his drooping head,
And tricks his beams, and with new spangled ore,
Flames in the forehead of the morning sky:
So Lycidas sunk low, but mounted high,
Through the dear might of him that walked the waves;
Where other groves, and other streams along,
With nectar pure his oozy locks he laves,
And hears the unexpressive nuptial song,
In the blest kingdoms meek of joy and love.
There entertain him all the saints above,
In solemn troops, and sweet societies
That sing, and singing in their glory move,
And wipe the tears for ever from his eyes.
Now Lycidas the shepherds weep no more;
Henceforth thou art the genius of the shore,
In thy large recompense, and shalt be good
To all that wander in that perilous flood.
Thus sang the uncouth swain to the oaks and rills,
While the still morn went out with sandals grey,

168. day-star] The sun. R. Y. Tyrrell, *CR* ix (1895) 11–2, compares Pindar, *Isth.* iv 40–1 (of Fame): 'She was fallen on sleep; but now she is roused again with beaming form, like the star of morning, a sight to see amid the other stars.'

170. tricks] trims. *ore*] Presumably meaning 'gold'. *OED* gives 1639 for the first use of 'ore' in the sense 'precious metal'. M. is probably influenced by *Hamlet* IV i 25–7: 'like some ore / Among a mineral of metals base, / Shows itself pure.'

173. him] Christ, who walks on the sea in *Matt.* xiv 25–6.

174. groves . . . streams] Cp. *Rev.* xxii 2: 'the tree of life, which bare twelve manner of fruits'; and *Rev.* vii 17: 'living fountains of waters'.

175. nectar] The brooks in Eden run with nectar, *PL* iv 240. *oozy*] slimy from contact with the sea. Cp. *Nativity Ode* 124 'the welt'ring waves their oozy channel keep', the only other place M. uses the word in his poetry.

176. And hears] In *Trin. MS* substituted for 'Listening'. *unexpressive*] See *Nativity Ode* 116*n* p. 106 above. *nuptial*] Pertaining to the 'marriage of the Lamb', *Rev.* xix 7.

181. Cp. *Rev.* vii 17: 'God shall wipe away all tears from their eyes', also *Rev.* xxi 4.

183. genius] Local protective deity. In Virgil, *Ecl.* v 64–5, the dead Daphnis is imagined as a god, being good to his worshippers.

186. uncouth] unknown. The meaning 'uncomely, awkward' was, however, developing during the seventeenth century.

He touched the tender stops of various quills,
With eager thought warbling his Doric lay:
And now the sun had stretched out all the hills,
And now was dropped into the western bay;
At last he rose, and twitched his mantle blue:
Tomorrow to fresh woods, and pastures new.

54 Fix here . . .

Date. Apr. 1638? These two lines are jotted down in M.'s hand on the back of a letter to him from Lawes which enclosed his passport, and which was written probably in Apr. 1638, just before M. went abroad. (For text of letter see Columbia xii 325–6, Yale i 339).
Publication. First printed in Horwood xvi, with *overdaled* for *overdated* in l. *1*. *Overdated* (antiquated, out of date) is not recorded in *OED* until 1641, when M. himself uses it in *Of Reformation*.

Fix here ye overdated spheres
That wing the restless foot of time.

55 *Ad Leonoram Romae canentem*

[To Leonora singing at Rome]

Date. Oct.–Nov. 1638 or Jan.–Feb. 1639. It is not certain on which of M.'s two visits to Rome he heard Leonora Baroni sing. Her mother, Adriana

188. stops] The finger-holes in the pipes. *quills*] The hollow reeds of the shepherd's pipe, for which Spenser uses the same word, *Shep. Cal.* June 67: 'homely shepheards quill'.
189. Doric] Theocritus, Moschus and Bion wrote in the Doric dialect. In *Lament for Bion* 18, Bion is called the Doric Orpheus.
190. The meaning is presumably that the setting sun had stretched out or elongated the shadows of the hills. Cp. Virgil, *Ecl.* i 83 *maioresque cadunt altis de montibus umbrae* (and longer shadows fall from the mountain heights).
191. Brooks and Hardy 186 comment that, when contrasted with the two lines on the rising sun (ll. 170–1) the effect of this line is not to deny the radiant vision of promise, but only to place it in a realistic perspective; 'we are simply reminded that the vision is one of hope, not yet fulfilled, that the elegy has been composed and delivered in a real world in which suns rise and set'.
192. blue] R. C. Fox, *Explicator* ix (1951) 54, notes that though shepherds usually wear grey in the pastoral, blue is the traditional symbol of hope. In Spenser, *F.Q.* I x 14, Speranza (Hope) wears blue.
193. S. R. Watson, *N & Q* clxxx (1941) 258, compares Phineas Fletcher,

Baroni, had also been a famous musician (contemporary poets celebrated her in the *Teatro della gloria d'Adriana* of 1623): Leonora was born in Mantua *c.* 1610, and was a fine singer and theorbo-player. A volume of *Applausi Poetici alle Glorie della Signora Leonora Baroni* (Rome 1639) was collected by Costazuti. It used to be assumed that M. heard Leonora at the entertainment in the palace of Cardinal Barberini, described in his letter to Lukas Holste of 30 Mar. 1639 (Columbia xii 40). But J. S. Smart, *MLR* viii (1913) 91–2, and G. L. Finney, *PMLA* lviii (1943) 658, point out that the Barberini entertainment was not a concert but an opera, Rospigliosi's *Chi sofre, speri*, presented in Feb. 1639, and that women were not allowed to sing in the performances at the Palazzo Barberini. Wherever M. heard Leonora, it was not here.
Publication. 1645 and *1673* (no significant variants).

Angelus unicuique suus (sic credite gentes)
  Obtigit aethereis ales ab ordinibus.
Quid mirum? Leonora tibi si gloria maior,
  Nam tua praesentem vox sonat ipsa Deum.
Aut Deus, aut vacui certe mens tertia coeli
  Per tua secreto guttura serpit agens;
Serpit agens, facilisque docet mortalia corda
  Sensim immortali assuescere posse sono.
Quod si cuncta quidem Deus est, per cunctaque fusus,
  In te una loquitur, caetera mutus habet.

A winged angel from the heavenly ranks–believe me, you nations–has been allotted to each particular individual. It is no wonder if you have a greater privilege, Leonora. And in fact the sound of your voice makes it clear that God is present, or, if not God, at any rate a third mind[5] which has left heaven and creeps warbling along, hidden within your throat. Warbling he creeps and graciously teaches mortal hearts how to grow accustomed, little by little, to immortal sound. If God is all things, and omnipresent, nevertheless he speaks in you alone, and possesses all other creatures in silence.

Purple Island vi 77: 'Tomorrow shall ye feast in pastures new', and Mantuan, *Eclogue* ix: *Candide, coge pecus melioraque pascere quaere* (Candidus, drive the herd and seek better pasture).

¶. 55. *5. mens tertia*] Perhaps a reference to the mysterious and variously interpreted passage in the (almost certainly spurious) second *Epistle* of Plato (312E): 'Related to the King of All are all things, and for his sake they are, and of all things fair he is the cause. And related to the Second are the second things; and related to the Third, the third.' Ficino (*Commentary on the Symposium* II iv) and others explain the 'Third' as the World-Soul.

56 *Ad eandem*

[To the same]

Date. See headnote to previous poem.
Publication. *1645* and *1673* (no significant variants).

Altera Torquatum cepit Leonora poetam,
 Cuius ab insano cessit amore furens.
Ah miser ille tuo quanto felicius aevo
 Perditus, et propter te Leonora foret!
Et te Pieria sensisset voce canentem
 Aurea maternae fila movere lyrae,
Quamvis Dircaeo torsisset lumina Pentheo
 Saevior, aut totus desipuisset iners,
Tu tamen errantes caeca vertigine sensus
 Voce eadem poteras composuisse tua;
Et poteras aegro spirans sub corde quietem
 Flexanimo cantu restituisse sibi.

The poet Torquato[1] fell in love with another Leonora, and his mad love for her drove him out of his mind. Ah, poor man, how much more fortunate for him had he been your contemporary and lost his reason on your account, Leonora! How much more fortunate had he heard you singing with your Pierian[5] voice, and heard the golden strings of your mother's harp vibrating. Even if he had rolled his eyes more savagely than Dircaean Pentheus,[7] or even if he had been utterly dull and witless, you could have calmed his reeling senses with your voice; you could have made him himself again, breathing peace into his sick heart with your soul-soothing song.

57 *Ad eandem*

[To the same]

Date. See headnote to *Leon* (p. 254).
Publication. *1645* and *1673* (no significant variants).

¶ 56. *1. Torquatum*] Tasso, whose madness and consequent imprisonment (1579–86) in the Ospedale d'Sant'Anna by his patron, Alphonso, Duke of Ferrara, was sometimes connected with his alleged love for Alphonso's sister, Leonora d'Este, to whom he wrote poems. He was also supposed to have been in love with Leonora Santivale, Countess of Scandiano.
5. Pieria] See *Elegia IV* 29–32*n* (p. 55).
7. Dircaeo . . . Pentheo] Dirce was a fountain near Thebes, thus 'Dircaean' means 'Theban'. Pentheus, King of Thebes, scorned the Bacchic orgies and was therefore torn to pieces by the Bacchantes. His rage, and the effect it had on his eyes, is described by Ovid, *Met.* iii 577–8.

Credula quid liquidam sirena Neapoli iactas,
Claraque Parthenopes fana Achelöiados,
Littoreamque tua defunctam naiada ripa
Corpora Chalcidico sacra dedisse rogo?
Illa quidem vivitque, et amoena Tibridis unda
Mutavit rauci murmura Pausilipi.
Illic Romulidum studiis ornata secundis,
Atque homines cantu detinet atque deos.

Why, credulous Naples, do you boast of your clear-voiced siren and of the famous shrine of Acheloüs' daughter Parthenope?[2] Why do you boast that when she died upon your shore you placed her, a Naiad of the sands, on a Neapolitan[4] pyre? The fact is, she is still alive, and has changed the booming of hoarse Posillipo[6] for the gentle waters of the Tiber. There, enthusiastically applauded by Roman audiences, her singing holds both men and gods spellbound.

58 *Ad Salsillum poetam Romanum aegrotantem. Scazontes.*

[Scazons addressed to Salzilli, a Roman poet, when he was ill.]

Date. Late 1638 or 1639. M. visited Rome Oct.–Nov. 1638 and Jan.–Feb. 1639. It is implied (*10*) that *Salsill* was written not long after his arrival in Italy. Giovanni Salzilli wrote four flattering lines of Latin verse preferring M. to Homer, Virgil and Tasso: these, along with other commendatory verses, M. later printed before his Latin poems in *1645*. Masson (i 309) discovered a volume called *Poesie de' Signori Accademici Fantastici* (Rome 1637) to which Salzilli is one of the 51 contributors. Nothing more is known of him.
Publication. 1645 (5. lectum,]lectum.) *1673.*

¶ 57. 2. *Parthenopes ... Achelöiados*] See *Comus* 879*n* (p. 221). The sirens were daughters of the river-god Acheloüs and Terpsichore.
4. *Chalcidico*] Neapolitan, because Greek colonists from the island of Euboea, of which the chief town is Chalcis, settled at Naples. Virgil, *Aen.* vi 17, applies the adjective to Naples.
6. *Pausilipi*] Mount Posillipo, N.W. of Naples, is pierced by a tunnel through which the newer Via Antiniana, dating from the time of Agrippa, passes: *murmura* presumably refers to the rumble of traffic in the tunnel.
¶ 58. *Title. Scazontes*] Iambic trimeters with spondees or trochees taking the place of the final iambs, (from Gk σκάζειν, to limp). C. Symmons, *CJ* ix (1814) 342, notes that M.'s scazons admit spondees and even anapaests in the fifth foot. The Greeks sometimes used a spondee in this position, but the Latins always an iamb.

O musa gressum quae volens trahis claudum,
Vulcanioque tarda gaudes incessu,
Nec sentis illud in loco minus gratum,
Quam cum decentes flava Dëiope suras
Alternat aureum ante Iunonis lectum,
Adesdum et haec s'is verba pauca Salsillo
Refer, camoena nostra cui tantum est cordi,
Quamque ille magnis praetulit immerito divis.
Haec ergo alumnus ille Londini Milto,
Diebus hisce qui suum linquens nidum
Polique tractum, (pessimus ubi ventorum,
Insanientis impotensque pulmonis
Pernix anhela sub Iove exercet flabra)
Venit feraces Itali soli ad glebas,
Visum superba cognitas urbes fama
Virosque doctaeque indolem iuventutis,
Tibi optat idem hic fausta multa Salsille,
Habitumque fesso corpori penitus sanum;
Cui nunc profunda bilis infestat renes,
Praecordiisque fixa damnosum spirat.
Nec id pepercit impia quod tu Romano
Tam cultus ore Lesbium condis melos.
O dulce divum munus, O salus Hebes
Germana! Tuque Phoebe morborum terror
Pythone caeso, sive tu magis Paean
Libenter audis, hic tuus sacerdos est.
Querceta Fauni, vosque rore vinoso
Colles benigni, mitis Evandri sedes,
Siquid salubre vallibus frondet vestris,

2. *Vulcanioque . . . incessu*] For the cause of Vulcan's lameness see *Elegia VII* 81–2*n*, p. 73 above.

4. *Dëiope*] Deiopea, in Juno's opinion the loveliest of the nymphs, is promised by her to Aeolus as a reward for destroying Aeneas' fleet (Virgil, *Aen.* i 71–5).

22. *Lesbium . . . melos*] Alcaeus and Sappho were natives of Lesbos. This regularly iambic line, among scanzons, may be M.'s compliment to Salzilli's smoothness, or an error (M. again makes *melos* a spondee on p. 325, l. 8).

23. *Hebes*] See *Vacation Exercise* 38*n* (p. 77).

25. *Pythone caeso*] See *Elegia VII* 31–4*n* (p. 71). *Paean*] an appellation of Apollo, as god of healing. For the construction cp. Horace, *Sat.* II vi 20: *seu Iane libentius audis.*

27. *Fauni*] Faunus, as Virgil relates (*Aen.* vii 45–8), was father of Latinus. It is in a grove 'black with the shade of holm-oaks' that, according to Ovid, *Fast.* iii 295, Numa speaks with him.

28. *Colles*] The hills of Rome. *Evandri sedes*] In Roman legend Evander

Levamen aegro ferte certatim vati.
Sic ille charis redditus rursum musis
Vicina dulci prata mulcebit cantu.
Ipse inter atros emirabitur lucos
Numa, ubi beatum degit otium aeternum,
Suam reclivis semper Aegeriam spectans.
Tumidusque et ipse Tibris hinc delinitus
Spei favebit annuae colonorum:
Nec in sepulchris ibit obsessum reges
Nimium sinistro laxus irruens loro:
Sed fraena melius temperabit undarum,
Adusque curvi salsa regna Portumni.

My muse, you trail a lame foot deliberately: you enjoy imitating Vulcan's walk as you hobble along. This seems to you just as delightful, in its right place, as blonde Deiopea[4] with her trim ankles skipping before Juno's golden couch. Come along now, if you please, and take these few words to Salzilli. My poetry is so dear to him that he prefers it, quite undeservedly, to that of mighty and godlike poets. Young Milton, London-born-and-bred, sends this message, then: Milton, who recently left his nest and his own little bit of sky (where the worst of winds, powerless to control its madly heaving lungs, puffs its panting gusts helter-skelter beneath the heavens), and came to see Italy's fertile soil, its cities–the theme of vaunting fame–its peoples, and the genius of its young intellectuals. This same Milton wishes you every good fortune, Salzilli, and a complete return to health for your tired body. At present an overflow of bile is upsetting your liver and, lodged in your stomach, exhales disease. The disrespectful stuff has shown you no mercy, even though you are such a cultured man, and even though your Roman lips can frame original Greek lyrics![22]

is an Arcadian, son of Carmentis, who founded a colony of his countrymen on the banks of the Tiber at the place where Rome was later to stand.

33–5. Numa Pompilius, second of the legendary kings of Rome, forsook city life and, according to Plutarch, *Numa* iv, 'determined to live for the most part in country places, and to wander alone, passing his days in the groves of the gods'. It was in these groves, Plutarch adds, that he was said to consort with his goddess-love, Egeria. Ovid, *Met.* xv 487–8, tells how at Numa's death Egeria 'fled from the city and hid herself away in the dense forests of the Arician vale'.

38–9. Horace, *Odes* I ii 13–20, recalls how the Tiber overflowed its left bank and flooded the *monumenta regis* (i.e. the Regia, the official residence of the Pontifex Maximus). The building to which M. is probably referring, and to which he may have thought Horace was, is the Mausoleum of Augustus in the Campus Martius, where Augustus and many of the emperors were interred.

41. Portumni] Portumnus was properly god of harbours but, as Harding (56) points out, he was commonly referred to in the Renaissance as god of the sea; *curvus* is used of the sea by Ovid, *Met.* xi 505.

Sweet gift of the gods, health, sister of Hebe,[23] and you, Phoebus (or Paean, if you would rather be called by that name), the terror of all diseases since your slaying of Python,[25] this man Salzilli is your priest. You oak-groves of Faunus,[27] you hills[28] generously hung with juicy grapes, Evander's mellow home, if any health-giving plant sprouts in your valleys, bring it eagerly to cure your sick poet. Then, restored to his dear muses once more, he will soothe the meadows all around with his sweet song. Numa[33] himself will be filled with wonder as he lies at ease among those dark groves where he spends his blessed eternity of rest gazing for ever upon his dear Egeria.[35] Even the flood-swollen Tiber, charmed by the song, will be kind to the farmers' yearly hopes. He will not go rushing along with his left rein held too loosely, to besiege kings in their tombs,[38] but will keep a better grip on the reins of his waters till they come to the salt kingdom of hump-backed Portumnus.[41]

59 *Mansus*
[Manso]

Date. Jan. 1639? After his first stay in Rome M. travelled to Naples Nov.–Dec. 1638. 'Here', he writes (Columbia viii 123–5) 'I was introduced . . . to John Baptista Manso, Marquis of Villa, a man of the first rank and authority, to whom the illustrious Italian poet, Torquato Tasso, addressed his book on friendship. By him I was treated, while I stayed there, with all the warmth of friendship: for he conducted me himself over the city and the viceregent's court, and more than once came to visit me at my own lodgings. On my leaving Naples he gravely apologized for showing me no more attention, alleging that although it was what he wished above all things, it was not in his power in that city, because I had not thought proper to be more guarded on the point of religion.' Manso (1560?–1645) founded the Accademia degli Oziosi, which met at his villa, and befriended Tasso, who seems to have stayed with him in 1588, 1592 and 1594, on the last occasion completing his *Gerusalemme Conquistata*: their friendship must have begun before 1586 when Tasso's *Il Manso*, to which M.'s headnote refers, was published. After Tasso's death (1595) Manso befriended Giambattista Marino. Manso's own works include two sets of dialogues on love and beauty (1608 and 1618), a volume of poems (1635) and a *Life of Tasso* (1619): M. prints a Latin couplet by him as part of the prefatory material of the 1645 *Poemata*: *Ut mens, forma, decor, facies, mos, si pietas sic / Non Anglus, verum hercle Angelus ipse fores* (If your religious persuasions were equal to your mind, your handsome figure, your fame, your face and your manners, then–good heavens!–you would be an angel, not an Englishman).
Publication. 1645, 1673 (no significant variants: in *27 1673* misprints *longinguam* for *longinquam*).

Joannes Baptista Mansus Marchio Villensis vir ingenii laude, tum literarum studio, nec non et bellica virtute apud Italos clarus in primis est. Ad quem Torquati Tassi dialogus extat de Amicitia scriptus; erat enim Tassi amicissimus; ab quo etiam inter Campaniae principes celebratur, in illo poemate cui titulus Gerusalemme conquistata, lib 20.

Fra cavalier magnanimi, e cortesi
Risplende il Manso———

Is authorem Neapoli commorantem summa benevolentia prosecutus est, multaque ei detulit humanitatis officia. Ad hunc itaque hospes ille antequam ab ea urbe discederet, ut ne ingratum se ostenderet, hoc carmen misit.

Haec quoque Manse tuae meditantur carmina laudi
Pierides, tibi Manse choro notissime Phoebi,
Quandoquidem ille alium haud aequo est dignatus
honore,
Post Galli cineres, et Mecaenatis Hetrusci.
Tu quoque si nostrae tantum valet aura Camoenae,
Victrices hederas inter, laurosque sedebis.
Te pridem magno felix concordia Tasso
Iunxit, et aeternis inscripsit nomina chartis.
Mox tibi dulciloquum non inscia Musa Marinum
Tradidit, ille tuum dici se gaudet alumnum,
Dum canit Assyrios divum prolixus amores;
Mollis et Ausonias stupefecit carmine nymphas.
Ille itidem moriens tibi soli debita vates
Ossa tibi soli, supremaque vota reliquit.
Nec manes pietas tua chara fefellit amici,
Vidimus arridentem operoso ex aere poetam.
Nec satis hoc visum est in utrumque, et nec pia cessant
Officia in tumulo, cupis integros rapere Orco,
Qua potes, atque avidas Parcarum eludere leges:
Amborum genus, et varia sub sorte peractam
Describis vitam, moresque, et dona Minervae;
Aemulus illius Mycalen qui natus ad altam
Rettulit Aeolii vitam facundus Homeri.

¶ 59. 2. *Pierides*] The Muses: see *Elegia IV* 29–32*n* (p. 55).
4. *Galli*] Cornelius Gallus, the elegiac poet (d. 27 B.C.), admired by Ovid and friend of Virgil who commemorates him, *Ecl.* vi 64–73. *Mecaenatis*] Maecenas (d. 8 B.C.) was the most famous of the Roman patrons of letters.
11. Marino's long poem *L'Adone* (1623) is a version of the Venus and Adonis story. *Assyrios*] See *Nativity Ode* 200 and 204*nn* (p. 110).
18. *Orco*] See *Elegia VII* 83*n* (p. 73).
19. *Parcarum*] See *Proc Med* 2*n* (p. 27).
20. *Amborum*] Manso's life of Marino is not extant.
21. *Minervae*] Minerva was goddess of wisdom.
22–3. *illius*] Herodotus, born at Halicarnassus. *Mycalen*] The promontory of Mycale in Ionia is on the coast not far north of Halicarnassus. *Aeolii*] Aeolis was a country in Asia Minor, north of Ionia. The first chapter of the *Life of Homer* which used to be attributed to Herodotus tells how Homer was

Ergo ego te Clius et magni nomine Phoebi
Manse pater, iubeo longum salvere per aevum
Missus Hyperboreo iuvenis peregrinus ab axe.
Nec tu longinquam bonus aspernabere musam,
Quae nuper gelida vix enutrita sub Arcto
Imprudens Italas ausa est volitare per urbes.
Nos etiam in nostro modulantes flumine cygnos
Credimus obscuras noctis sensisse per umbras,
Qua Thamesis late puris argenteus urnis
Oceani glaucos perfundit gurgite crines.
Quin et in has quondam pervenit Tityrus oras.
Sed neque nos genus incultum, nec inutile Phoebo,
Quo plaga septeno mundi sulcata Trione
Brumalem patitur longa sub nocte Booten.
Nos etiam colimus Phoebum, nos munera Phoebo
Flaventes spicas, et lutea mala canistris,

conceived in the town of Cyme in Aeolis, but born near Smyrna on the bank of the river Meles.

24. Clius] See *Ad Pat* 14*n* (p. 149). Phoebus is invoked because Manso has befriended poets, Clio, because he has written accounts of their lives.

26. Hyperboreo . . . ab axe] Diodorus Siculus II xlvii 1 places the island of the Hyperboreans in the northern ocean, beyond the land of the Celts.

30–4. cygnos] swans (i.e. poets), cp. Jonson viii 392 (of Shakespeare): 'Sweet Swan of *Avon*! what a sight it were / To see thee in our waters yet appeare,/ And make those flights upon the bankes of *Thames*, / That did so take *Eliza*, and our *James*!' Spenser was born in London and uses the Thames-swan symbol in *Prothalamion*. That M. had him in mind is confirmed by the name Tityrus (for Chaucer), used in *Shep. Cal.* February 102. Chaucer visited Italy 1372 and 1378.

36–7. septeno . . . Trione] The constellation of Ursa Major was compared to a waggon with oxen yoked to it: it has seven prominent stars. *Booten*] See *Elegia V* 35–6*n* (p. 82).

38. Nos . . . Phoebum] Diodorus Siculus II xlvii 2–3 tells of the legend that Leto was born on the island of the Hyperboreans, 'and for that reason Apollo is honoured among them above all other gods; and the inhabitants are looked upon as priests of Apollo'. In his notes to *Polyolbion* viii and ix (Drayton iv 156, 194–5), Selden sets out his reasons for thinking that the ancient British god Belin, the Druids' god of healing, is to be identified with Apollo.

38–48. Herodotus iv 33–5 records how the Hyperboreans brought offerings wrapped in wheat-straw to Apollo and Artemis at Delos: the first Hyperboreans to arrive were the maidens Arge and Opis, who 'came with the gods themselves, and received honours of their own from the Delians. For the women collected gifts for them, calling them by their names in the hymn made for them by Olen, a man of Lycia; it was from Delos that the islanders and Ionians learnt to sing hymns to Opis and Arge.' In Callimachus, *Hymn*

Halantemque crocum (perhibet nisi vana vetustas)
Misimus, et lectas Druidum de gente choreas.
(Gens Druides antiqua sacris operata deorum
Heroum laudes imitandaque gesta canebant)
Hinc quoties festo cingunt altaria cantu
Delo in herbosa Graiae de more puellae
Carminibus laetis memorant Corineida Loxo,
Fatidicamque Upin, cum flavicoma Hecaerge
Nuda Caledonio variatas pectora fuco.
Fortunate senex, ergo quacunque per orbem
Torquati decus, et nomen celebrabitur ingens,
Claraque perpetui succrescet fama Marini,
Tu quoque in ora frequens venies plausumque virorum,
Et parili carpes iter immortale volatu.
Dicetur tum sponte tuos habitasse penates
Cynthius, et famulas venisse ad limina musas:
At non sponte domum tamen idem, et regis adivit
Rura Pheretiadae coelo fugitivus Apollo;
Ille licet magnum Alciden susceperat hospes;
Tantum ubi clamosos placuit vitare bubulcos,
Nobile mansueti cessit Chironis in antrum,
Irriguos inter saltus frondosaque tecta

iv 283–99, the Hyperborean maidens Upis, Loxo and Hecaerge, 'and those who were then the best of the young men', bring 'cornstalks and holy sheaves of corn-ears' to Delos. M. stains the maidens with woad because Caesar, *Bell. Gall.* v 14 says all Britons dye themselves in this way. He makes one of them daughter to Corineus who, according to Drayton iv 13–4, came to Britain with Brutus and defeated the giant Gogmagog at wrestling so that Brutus gave him Cornwall ('of *Corin*, *Cornwall* call'd').

42–3. Druidical rites are described by Selden (Drayton iv 193–4). Caesar, *Bell. Gall.* vi 14 says Druids are concerned with divine worship and all ritual matters, and refers to their strict poetic training.

55. Cynthius] Apollo, so called from his birthplace, Mount Cynthus on Delos.

56–7. Apollo, banished from heaven for killing the Cyclopes, served as herdsman to Admetus, king of the Pherae in Thessaly and son of Pheres (hence *Pheretiades*). Euripides in a beautiful chorus, *Alcestis* 568–86, describes the music Apollo made while Admetus' guest.

58. Apollo granted Admetus that he should not die, when the time came for his death, if a substitute could be found. His wife Alcestis offered herself and died in his stead. In accordance with the laws of hospitality Admetus concealed her death from his guest, Hercules, but the latter discovered the truth, set upon Thanatos (Death) and rescued Alcestis.

60–6. Chironis] See *Proc Med* 25–6n (p. 29). Homer, *Il.* xi 832 calls him 'the most righteous of the Centaurs'. Apollo's visits are M.'s invention, but as

Peneium prope rivum: ibi saepe sub ilice nigra
Ad citharae strepitum blanda prece victus amici
Exilii duros lenibat voce labores.
Tum neque ripa suo, barathro nec fixa sub imo,
Saxa stetere loco, nutat Trachinia rupes,
Nec sentit solitas, immania pondera, silvas,
Emotaeque suis properant de collibus orni,
Mulcenturque novo maculosi carmine lynces.
Diis dilecte senex, te Iupiter aequus oportet
Nascentem, et miti lustrarit lumine Phoebus,
Atlantisque nepos; neque enim nisi charus ab ortu
Diis superis poterit magno favisse poetae.
Hinc longaeva tibi lento sub flore senectus
Vernat, et Aesonios lucratur vivida fusos,
Nondum deciduos servans tibi frontis honores,
Ingeniumque vigens, et adultum mentis acumen.
O mihi si mea sors talem concedat amicum
Phoebaeos decorasse viros qui tam bene norit,
Si quando indigenas revocabo in carmina reges,
Arturumque etiam sub terris bella moventem;
Aut dicam invictae sociali foedere mensae,

Apollodorus II v 4 relates, Chiron's home was Mount Pelion (until he was driven from it by the Lapiths) and this is about ten miles from Pherae. The Peneus, though a Thessalian river, is not near Pelion, however, and Oeta ('the Trachinian cliff'–so called because the town of Trachis stood on its slopes) is sixty miles south-west of Pelion.

72. nepos] Mercury, son of Maia, god of eloquence.

75. Aesonios] See *Elegia II* 7–8*n* (p. 31). *fusos*] spindles, see *Arcades* 63–72*n* (p. 159).

78–93. W. R. Parker, *MLN* lxxii (1957) 488, suggests that these lines imply that M. already knew of Diodati's death when he wrote *Mansus*.

80–4. See *Dam* 162–71 (p. 275). Arthur was not among the twenty-eight subjects from British history set down by M. in *Trin. MS* as possible epic subjects. P. F. Jones, *PMLA* xlii (1927) 901–9, argues that M. dropped the idea of an Arthuriad partly because of doubts about the truth of the Arthurian story: cp. *History of Britain* (Columbia x 127–8): 'But who *Arthur* was, and whether ever any such reign'd in *Britain*, hath bin doubted heertofore, and may again with good reason.'

81. etiam sub terris bella moventem] The descent to the underworld seems to be one of the earliest components of the Arthurian cycle. It is recorded in the Welsh *Spoils of Annwfn* (*Book of Taliesin* xxx), which describes the expedition undertaken by Arthur and his men to a fortress representing the Celtic Hades, which is conceived of as a twilit underworld, with the purpose of carrying off the magic cauldron of the Otherworld.

Magnanimos heroas, et (O modo spiritus ad sit)
Frangam Saxonicas Britonum sub Marte phalanges.
Tandem ubi non tacitae permensus tempora vitae,
Annorumque satur cineri sua iura relinquam,
Ille mihi lecto madidis astaret ocellis,
Astanti sat erit si dicam sim tibi curae;
Ille meos artus liventi morte solutos
Curaret parva componi molliter urna.
Forsitan et nostros ducat de marmore vultus,
Nectens aut Paphia myrti aut Parnasside lauri
Fronde comas, at ego secura pace quiescam.
Tum quoque, si qua fides, si praemia certa bonorum,
Ipse ego caelicolum semotus in aethera divum,
Quo labor et mens pura vehunt, atque ignea virtus
Secreti haec aliqua mundi de parte videbo
(Quantum fata sinunt) et tota mente serenum
Ridens purpureo suffundar lumine vultus
Et simul aethereo plaudam mihi laetus Olympo.

Giovanni Battista Manso, Marquis of Villa, is one of the most famous gentlemen of Italy, not only because of his reputation for intellectual ability but also because of his devotion to literature and his courage in war. The dialogue *On Friendship* which Torquato Tasso dedicated to him is still extant. He was a close friend of Tasso, and is given honourable mention among the princes of Italy in the *Jerusalem Conquered* xx:

Among magnanimous and courteous knights
Shines Manso . . .

While the author was staying in Naples the Marquis looked after him in an extremely thoughtful way and did him many kind services. Accordingly he sent the Marquis this poem, before his visit to the city came to an end, in order not to appear ungrateful.

Manso, the Muses[2] are singing this song, too, in your praise, yes, yours, Manso, Phoebus' choir knows all about you, because since Gallus[4] and Etruscan Maecenas died Phoebus has thought hardly anyone so worthy of honour as you. If my Muses have breath enough you, like Gallus and Maecenas, will get a seat among the victorious wreaths of laurel and ivy.

Great Tasso and you were once joined by a happy friendship which has written your names on the pages of eternity. Not long afterwards the Muse–who knew what she was doing–entrusted her sweet-voiced Marino to your care. He was glad to be called your foster-child while he was writing his long poem about the love of the Assyrian god and goddess[11]—smooth versifier, his song struck the girls of Italy dumb with admiration. So when he died

83. *ad sit*] for *adsit*.
84. The various defeats of the invading Saxons by Arthur and his British army are described at length in Geoffrey of Monmouth's *History*.
92. *Paphia*] Paphos, a city in Cyprus, had a famous temple of Venus, to whom the myrtle was sacred (cp. Ovid, *Ars Am.* iii 181 *Paphias myrtos*). *Parnasside lauri*] See *Elegia IV* 29–32*n* and *Elegia V* 13*n* (pp. 55 and 81).

he left his body, as was right, to you alone, and to you alone confided his last wishes. And your loving devotion did not fail your friend's spirit: I have seen the poet's features smiling at me from an exquisite bronze. But it did not seem to you that you had done enough for either poet: your devotion and generosity did not end at the grave. You are eager to snatch them unharmed from the jaws of death,[18] if it lies in your power, and to cheat the laws of the devouring Fates.[19] So you are writing an account of their[20] lineage, of the various ups and downs of their lives, of the personalities and of their intellectual gifts.[21] Thus you rival that eloquent biographer[22] of Aeolian Homer who was born near high Mycale.[23] Therefore, father Manso, I, a young stranger sent from Hyperborean skies,[26] wish you a long and healthy life in the name of Clio[24] and of great Phoebus. You, in your goodness, will not be scornful of a Muse from a far-off land who, though poorly nourished beneath the frozen Bear, has recently been rash enough to venture a flight through the cities of Italy. I think that I, too, have heard swans[30] on my native river singing among the night's dark shadows, where the silver Thames pours her green tresses from shining urns and spreads them wide among the swirling currents of the ocean. Why, our Tityrus, too, once visited your land.[34]

But we who have to put up with wintry Boötes for long nights on end, in that region of the world which is furrowed by his seven-starred wagon,[36] are neither an uncultured race, nor useless to Phoebus.[38] We worship Phoebus too: we have sent him gifts–golden ears of grain, and flame-coloured apples in baskets, and the fragrant crocus (if ancient tradition is not a mere fairy-tale) and choirs chosen from the Druid race. The Druids,[42] an ancient race, were well practised in the rituals of the gods and used to sing the praises of heroes and their exemplary exploits.[43] So now whenever Grecian girls stand and sing round the altars on grassy Delos, as they usually do on holidays, their happy songs commemorate Corineus' daughter Loxo, and prophetic Upis, and golden-haired Hecaerge–girls whose bare breasts were stained with woad.[48]

Lucky old man! Wherever in the world the glory and great name of Torquato are honoured, wherever the fame of deathless Marino shines and flourishes, your name and your praises, too, will be on everyone's lips, and you will fly on your way to immortality side by side with them. Men will say that, of his own free will, Apollo[55] dwelt in your house, and that the Muses came like servants to your doors. Yet[56] that same Apollo, when he was a fugitive from heaven, came unwillingly to King Admetus' farm,[57] although Admetus had been host to mighty Hercules.[58] When he wanted to get away from the bawling ploughmen Apollo could, at any rate, retreat to gentle Chiron's[60] famous cave, among the moist woodland pastures and leafy shades beside the river Peneus. There often, beneath a dark oak tree, he would yield to his friend's flattering persuasion and, singing to the music of his lute, would soothe the hardships of exile. Then neither the river banks, nor the boulders lodged in the quarry's depths stayed in their places: the Trachinian cliff[66] nodded to the tune, and no longer felt its huge and familiar burden of forest trees; the mountain ashes were moved and came hurrying down their slopes, and spotted lynxes grew tame as they listened to the strange music.

Old man, dear to the gods, Jupiter must have been favourable when you were born, and Phoebus and the grandson[72] of Atlas must have looked at you with kindly eyes: for unless he is dear to the heavenly gods from his birth, a man does not have the chance to befriend a great poet. That is why your old age is green and spring-like, with lingering flowers; that is why it is vigorous and has a thread of life as long as Aeson's,[75] keeping your handsome features still intact, your intellect active and your wit keen and mature. O may it be my good luck to find such a friend,[78] who knows so well how to honour Phoebus's followers, if ever I bring back to life in my songs the kings of my native land[80] and Arthur, who set wars raging even under the earth,[81] or tell of the great-hearted heroes of the round table, which their fellowship made invincible, and–if only the inspiration would come[83]–smash the Saxon phalanxes beneath the impact of the British charge.[84] Then at last, when I had lived out a life in which poetry was not dumb, when I had reached a ripe old age and paid my last debt to the grave, then that friend would stand by my bed with tears in his eyes, and it would be enough for me to say to him as he stood there, 'Look after me'. He would see to it that when my limbs were blue and heavy with death they were laid gently in a little urn. Perhaps he might have my features carved in marble, binding my hair with a wreath of Paphian myrtle[92] or of Parnassian laurel: and I shall rest safe and at peace.[93] Then, too, if one can be sure of anything, and if rewards do really lie in store for the righteous, I myself, far away in the ethereal home of the heavenly gods, the region to which perseverance and a pure mind and ardent virtue carry a man, shall watch this earth and its affairs–as much, that is, as the Fates permit–from some corner of that far-off world, and, with all my soul calmly smiling, a bright red blush will spread over my face, and I shall joyfully applaud myself on ethereal Olympus.

60 *Epitaphium Damonis*

[Damon's Epitaph]

Date. Autumn 1639. M.'s headnote and *15–17* imply composition shortly after his return to England. J. T. Shawcross, *MLN* lxxi (1956) 322–4, suggests Oct.–Nov. on grounds that *58–61* sound like the English weather of these months. Diodati died in London and was buried 27 Aug. 1638: there is some doubt about when M. heard of his death. Shawcross argues that it was in Apr. 1639, while M. was in Florence: he believes that *9–13* refer to Italian crops (in the Arno valley each year there are two wheat harvests–Mar. and Aug.–thus by Apr. 1639 two harvests would have passed since Diodati's death). However W. R. Parker, *MLN* lxxii (1957) 486–8, points out that *9–13* say nothing of M.'s ignorance of Diodati's death: they mean only that

¶ 60. *Title*] A. S. P. Woodhouse (Norwood 265–6) suggests that the choice of the name Damon may be intended to recall the friendship of Damon and Pythias who were, significantly, votaries of the discipline of Pythagoras which M., in *Elegia VI* adopts as a symbol of the virtue and purity essential to the poet of heroic themes.

M. was in Florence in Apr. 1639. Parker maintains that M. heard the news in Naples in Dec. 1638 or Jan. 1639, and that it caused him to cancel his intended journey to Sicily and Greece.

Publication. An apparently unique copy of a previously unknown anonymous undated edition of *Dam* was discovered by L. Bradner, *TLS* (18 Aug. 1932) 581, in the British Museum (C. 57. d. 48). Bradner dates this 'probably 1640'. It has no verbal variants but is much more lightly punctuated than *1645* or *1673*. Compared with the present text it omits commas after 'querelis' (*5*), 'Fluminaque' (*6*), 'recessus' (*6*), 'umbras' (*11*), 'aurea' (*23*), 'agmen' (*24*), 'comes' (*38*), 'umbra' (*52*), 'risus' (*55*), 'oberro' (*58*), 'umbrae' (*59*), 'astrum' (*78*), 'severi' (*84*), 'verba' (*91*), 'iuvenci' (*94*), 'volitet' (*102*), 'discors' (*107*), 'sodale' (*118*), 'eram' (*129*), 'myrtos' (*131*), 'retardat' (*147*), 'Inogeniae' (*163*), 'arma' (*167*), 'lauri' (*180*), 'Mansus' (*181*), 'dedit' (*183*), 'silvae' (*186*), 'Amor' (*191*), 'pharetrae' (*191*), 'perennes' (*205*) and 'beatis' (*218*); full stops after 'ulmo' (*49*), 'magistrum' (*67*), 'plumbo' (*80*), 'silvae' (*160*), 'agni' (*161*) and 'undis' (*178*); semi-colons after 'pyropo' (*192*), 'arcum' (*204*), and 'hymenaeos' (*217*); the colon after 'carmen' (*3*); the exclamation-mark after 'mihi' (*19*) and the question-mark after 'herbis' (*40*). Its other variants are: *12.* Thyrsis;]Thyrsis, *19.* coelo,]coelo? *20.* Damon;]Damon! *30.* illi]illi, *42.* lupos]lupos, *53.* nymphae.] nymphae, *66.* iuvant;]iuvant, *90.* fluenti;]fluenti, *98.* onagri;]onagri, *107.* Gens homines]Gens, homines, *132.* Menalcam.]Menalcam, *135.* Fiscellae;]Fiscellae, (*as 1645, see below*) *153.* Ah](Ah *154.* magistro.]magistro.) *214.* honores;]honores, . Next printed *1645* (*127.* Damon.]Damon, *135.* Fiscellae;]Fiscellae,) and *1673* (the text followed here except in *8* where *1673* misprints 'perrerans' and in *57* where it omits the usual comma after 'vacat').

Modern criticism. T. P. Harrison, *PMLA* l (1935) 480–93, cites a number of parallels between *Dam* and Castiglione's *Alcon*, and W. A. Montgomery (Read 207–20) compares *Dam* with the pastoral laments of Theocritus, Bion, Moschus and Virgil. Ralph W. Condee, *SP* lxii (1965) 577–94, defends the poem's structure against Tillyard 99–100 who suspects it stretches to 219 lines only because M. felt it ought to be longer than *Lycidas*. Condee reads *Dam* as a progressive and deliberate abandonment of pastoralism: the refrain reflects 'the restlessness of a deeply emotional poem within its pastoral garments'. Eventually (*210*) Diodati's pastoral disguise is cast aside and 'the ecstatic hymn which the poem has at last become soars beyond the conventional pastoralism'.

Argumentum

Thyrsis et Damon eiusdem viciniae pastores, eadem studia sequuti a pueritia amici erant, ut qui plurimum. Thyrsis animi causa profectus peregre de obitu Damonis nuncium accepit. Domum postea reversus et rem ita esse comperto, se, suamque solitudinem hoc carmine deplorat. Damonis autem sub persona hic intelligitur Carolus Deodatus ex urbe Hetruriae Luca paterno genere oriundus, caetera Anglus; ingenio, doctrina, clarissimisque caeteris virtutibus, dum viveret, iuvenis egregius.

Himerides nymphae (nam vos et Daphnin et Hylan,
Et plorata diu meministis fata Bionis)
Dicite Sicelicum Thamesina per oppida carmen:
Quas miser effudit voces, quae murmura Thyrsis,
Et quibus assiduis exercuit antra querelis,
Fluminaque, fontesque vagos, nemorumque recessus,
Dum sibi praereptum queritur Damona, neque altam
Luctibus exemit noctem loca sola pererrans.
Et iam bis viridi surgebat culmus arista,
Et totidem flavas numerabant horrea messes,
Ex quo summa dies tulerat Damona sub umbras,
Nec dum aderat Thyrsis; pastorem scilicet illum
Dulcis amor musae Thusca retinebat in urbe.
Ast ubi mens expleta domum, pecorisque relicti
Cura vocat, simul assueta seditque sub ulmo,
Tum vero amissum tum denique sentit amicum,
Coepit et immensum sic exonerare dolorem.
   Ite domum impasti, domino iam non vacat, agni.
Hei mihi! quae terris, quae dicam numina coelo,
Postquam te immiti rapuerunt funere Damon;
Siccine nos linquis, tua sic sine nomine virtus
Ibit, et obscuris numero sociabitur umbris?
At non ille, animas virga qui dividit aurea,
Ista velit, dignumque tui te ducat in agmen,

1. Himerides] The Himera is a Sicilian river, mentioned by Theocritus, v 124 and vii 75: the nymphs of Himera represent the 'Sicilian muses' of pastoral poetry who inspired Theocritus and Moschus (see *Lycidas* 133). *Daphnin*] Daphnis was a shepherd-boy of Ida, changed to stone by a jealous nymph, and mourned in Theocritus i. *Hylan*] See *Elegia VII* 24*n*; here a false quantity – the first syllable of *Hylas* is short.
2. Bionis] Moschus iii is a lament for the pastoral poet Bion.
3. Echoing Virgil, *Georg.* ii 176: *Ascraeumque cano Romana per oppida carmen.*
4. Thyrsis] The name of Theocritus' shepherd in the lament for Daphnis, taken over by Virgil in *Ecl.* vii, here represents M.
13. Thusca . . . in urbe] In Florence. M. was there Aug.–Sept. 1638 and Mar.–Apr. 1639.
18. M.'s refrain is a modification of the last line of Virgil's last eclogue: *Ite domum saturae, venit Hesperus, ite capellae* (Go home, my full-fed goats, the evening-star comes, go home). It occurs seventeen times: in Theocritus i the refrain occurs nineteen times, and in Moschus iii, thirteen. Brett 48–9 argues that M.'s refrain, like the last line of *Lycidas*, represents a farewell to the pastoral tradition and all that it symbolizes: he is now to turn to epic (ll. 168–71).
23. ille] Mercury. Virgil, *Aen.* iv 242–3, refers to his *virga* 'with which he calls pale ghosts from Orcus, and sends others down to gloomy Tartarus'.

Ignavumque procul pecus arceat omne silentum.
Ite domum impasti, domino iam non vacat, agni.
Quicquid erit, certe nisi me lupus ante videbit,
Indeplorato non comminuere sepulchro,
Constabitque tuus tibi honos, longumque vigebit
Inter pastores: illi tibi vota secundo
Solvere post Daphnin, post Daphnin dicere laudes
Gaudebunt, dum rura Pales, dum Faunus amabit:
Si quid id est, priscamque fidem coluisse, piumque,
Palladiasque artes, sociumque habuisse canorum.
Ite domum impasti, domino iam non vacat, agni.
Haec tibi certa manent, tibi erunt haec praemia Damon,
At mihi quid tandem fiet modo? quis mihi fidus
Haerebit lateri comes, ut tu saepe solebas
Frigoribus duris, et per loca foeta pruinis,
Aut rapido sub sole, siti morientibus herbis?
Sive opus in magnos fuit eminus ire leones
Aut avidos terrere lupos praesepibus altis;
Quis fando sopire diem, cantuque solebit?
Ite domum impasti, domino iam non vacat, agni.
Pectora cui credam? quis me lenire docebit
Mordaces curas, quis longam fallere noctem
Dulcibus alloquiis, grato cum sibilat igni
Molle pyrum, et nucibus strepitat focus, at malus auster
Miscet cuncta foris, et desuper intonat ulmo.
Ite domum impasti, domino iam non vacat, agni.
Aut aestate, dies medio dum vertitur axe,

27. There was a superstition that if a man was seen by a wolf before he saw it, he was struck dumb: cp. Virgil, *Ecl.* ix 53–4: 'Even voice itself now fails Moeris; wolves have seen Moeris first.'

31. *Daphnin*] See l. 1*n*.

32. *Pales*] Roman goddess, protectress of flocks. *Faunus*] See *Elegia V* 127*n* p. 85 above. The form of M.'s line mimics Virgil, *Ecl.* v 76–80 'long as the boar loves the mountain ridges, as the fish the streams; long as the bees feed on thyme and the cicalas on dew, so long shall thy honour and name and glories abide'.

34. *Palladiasque artes*] See *Proc Med* 33*n* (p. 29).

46. *Mordaces curas*] See *L'Allegro* 135*n* (p. 138); Lucan ii 681 has *curis . . . mordacibus.*

47. *Dulcibus alloquiis*] Horace uses the same phrase, *Epod.* xiii 18, when telling his friends to pass the winter merrily.

48. *pyrum*] R. W. Condee (see headnote) replies to Keightley's objection that one roasts crab-apples, not pears, by producing a mention of roast pears in Gervase Markham, *The English House-Wife* (1631) 136.

Cum Pan aesculea somnum capit abditus umbra,
Et repetunt sub aquis sibi nota sedilia nymphae.
Pastoresque latent, stertit sub sepe colonus,
Quis mihi blanditiasque tuas, quis tum mihi risus,
Cecropiosque sales referet, cultosque lepores?
    Ite domum impasti, domino iam non vacat, agni.
At iam solus agros, iam pascua solus oberro,
Sicubi ramosae densantur vallibus umbrae,
Hic serum expecto, supra caput imber et Eurus
Triste sonant, fractaeque agitata crepuscula silvae.
    Ite domum impasti, domino iam non vacat, agni.
Heu quam culta mihi prius arva procacibus herbis
Involvuntur, et ipsa situ seges alta fatiscit!
Innuba neglecto marcescit et uva racemo,
Nec myrteta iuvant; ovium quoque taedet, at illae
Moerent, inque suum convertunt ora magistrum.
    Ite domum impasti, domino iam non vacat, agni.
Tityrus ad corylos vocat, Alphesiboeus ad ornos,
Ad salices Aegon, ad flumina pulcher Amyntas,
Hic gelidi fontes, hic illita gramina musco,
Hic Zephyri, hic placidas interstrepit arbutus undas;
Ista canunt surdo, frutices ego nactus abibam.
    Ite domum impasti, domino iam non vacat, agni.
Mopsus ad haec, nam me redeuntem forte notarat
(Et callebat avium linguas, et sydera Mopsus)
Thyrsi quid hoc? dixit, quae te coquit improba bilis?

52. In Theocritus i 15–7 the goatherd refuses to pipe at noon for fear of waking Pan from his midday sleep.

56. *Cecropiosque sales*] Cecrops was first king of Attica and founder of the citadel of Athens; Attic wit was renowned.

65. *Innuba*] The Latin poets speak of the vine as 'wedded' to elm or poplar. Horace calls trees without vines 'celibate' or 'widowed', *Odes* II xv 4, IV v 30.

69–70. *Tityrus*] One of the shepherds in Virgil, *Ecl.* i: used as a general name for 'shepherd' in *Ecl.* viii 55. *Alphesiboeus*] The name means, in Greek, 'bringer-in of oxen': one of the rival singers in *Ecl.* viii. *Aegon*] The owner of a flock in *Ecl.* iii 2. *Amyntas*] The beloved of the shepherd Menalcas in *Ecl.* iii.

71. In Virgil, *Ecl.* x 42–3, Gallus sings to the loved one who has deserted him 'Here are cool springs, Lycoris, here soft meadows, here woodland'. Virgil is imitating Theocritus v 33–4: 'There's cool water falling yonder, and here's grass and a greenbed, and the locusts at their prattling.'

75. *Mopsus*] A *Mopso* is mentioned in Tasso's *Aminta* I ii 459, *ch'intende il parlar de gli augelli* (who understands the language of birds).

76. *avium*] M. contracts the word, incorrectly, into a disyllable.

Aut te perdit amor, aut te male fascinat astrum,
Saturni grave saepe fuit pastoribus astrum,
Intimaque obliquo figit praecordia plumbo.
  Ite domum impasti, domino iam non vacat, agni.
Mirantur nymphae, et quid te Thyrsi futurum est?
Quid tibi vis? aiunt, non haec solet esse iuventae
Nubila frons, oculique truces, vultusque severi,
Illa choros, lususque leves, et semper amorem
Iure petit, bis ille miser qui serus amavit.
  Ite domum impasti, domino iam non vacat, agni.
Venit Hyas, Dryopeque, et filia Baucidis Aegle
Docta modos, citharaeque sciens, sed perdita fastu,
Venit Idumanii Chloris vicina fluenti;
Nil me blanditiae, nil me solantia verba,
Nil me, si quid adest, movet, aut spes ulla futuri.
  Ite domum impasti, domino iam non vacat, agni.
Hei mihi quam similes ludunt per prata iuvenci,
Omnes unanimi secum sibi lege sodales,
Nec magis hunc alio quisquam secernit amicum
De grege, sic densi veniunt ad pabula thoes,
Inque vicem hirsuti paribus iunguntur onagri;
Lex eadem pelagi, deserto in littore Proteus
Agmina phocarum numerat, vilisque volucrum

79–80. Saturni . . . astrum] In astrology those born under Saturn were of melancholy temperament. *obliquo . . . plumbo*] Cp. Spenser, *F.Q.* II ix 52: 'oblique Saturne'; the metal associated with Saturn in alchemy was lead. Horace, *Odes* II xvii 22–3, talks of 'baleful Saturn', and Propertius IV i 84 of 'Saturn that brings woe to one and all'.

86. Echoing Guarini, *Pastor Fido* I i 132–6: *Che se t'assale alla canuta etate / Amorosa talento, / Avrai doppio tormento, / E di quel che, potendo, non volesti, / E di quel che, volendo, non potrai* (For if amorous desire assails you when you are greyhaired, you will suffer the double torment of him who, when he can, does not want to, and of him who, when he wants to, can't).

88–9, Hyas] Ovid, *Fast.* v 169–82, tells how Hyas, a beautiful young hunter, son of Atlas and Aethra, was killed by a lioness. *Dryopeque*] 'The most beautiful of all the Oechalian maids', changed, as Ovid describes, *Met.* ix 330–93, into a lotus-tree. She was mother of Amphissos by Apollo. *Baucidis*] In Ovid, *Met.* viii 631–724 'pious old Baucis' and her husband Philemon, entertain Jupiter and Mercury. Ovid gives her no daughters. *Aegle*] 'Loveliest of the Naiads' in Virgil, *Ecl.* vi 21. Horace's Chloe, *Odes* III ix 10, is *docta modos et citharae sciens.* Presumably M.'s classical names here stand for real people, mutual acquaintances of himself and Diodati.

90. Idumanii . . . fluenti] In the chapter on Essex in his *Britannia* Camden identifies Ptolemy's *Idumanum aestuarium* as Blackwater Bay.

99. Proteus] See *Elegia III 26n* (p. 50).

Passer habet semper quicum sit, et omnia circum
Farra libens volitet, sero sua tecta revisens,
Quem si fors letho obiecit, seu milvus adunco
Fata tulit rostro, seu stravit arundine fossor,
Protinus ille alium socio petit inde volatu.
Nos durum genus, et diris exercita fatis
Gens homines aliena animis, et pectore discors,
Vix sibi quisque parem de millibus invenit unum,
Aut si sors dederit tandem non aspera votis,
Illum inopina dies qua non speraveris hora
Surripit, aeternum linquens in saecula damnum.
  Ite domum impasti, domino iam non vacat, agni.
Heu quis me ignotas traxit vagus error in oras
Ire per aereas rupes, Alpemque nivosam!
Ecquid erat tanti Romam vidisse sepultam?
Quamvis illa foret, qualem dum viseret olim,
Tityrus ipse suas et oves et rura reliquit;
Ut te tam dulci possem caruisse sodale,
Possem tot maria alta, tot interponere montes,
Tot sylvas, tot saxa tibi, fluviosque sonantes.
Ah certe extremum licuisset tangere dextram,
Et bene compositos placide morientis ocellos,
Et dixisse vale, nostri memor ibis ad astra.
  Ite domum impasti, domino iam non vacat, agni.
Quamquam etiam vestri nunquam meminisse pigebit
Pastores Thusci, musis operata iuventus,
Hic charis, atque lepos; et Thuscus tu quoque Damon.
Antiqua genus unde petis Lucumonis ab urbe.
O ego quantus eram, gelidi cum stratus ad Arni
Murmura, populeumque nemus, qua mollior herba,
Carpere nunc violas, nunc summas carpere myrtos,
Et potui Lycidae certantem audire Menalcam.

117. *Tityrus*] In Virgil, *Ecl.* i 26, Meliboeus asks Tityrus (i.e. Virgil, who went to Rome and appealed successfully to Octavian against the confiscation of his farm), *Et quae tanta fuit Romam tibi causa videndi* (And what was the great occasion of your seeing Rome?)

127–8. 'In the sixteenth century, the Diodatis were already honoured as one of the oldest patrician families in the flourishing little north-Italian republic of Lucca. Their earlier history has been traced to Coreglia, a small town about twenty miles north of Lucca' (Dorian 5). M. made an excursion to Lucca on his second visit to Florence.

128. *Lucumonis*] *lucumo* (inspired person) was an appellation of the Etruscan princes and priests.

129. *Arni*] Florence stands on the Arno.

132–7. *Lycidae* ... *Menalcam*] In Theocritus vii Lycidas and Simichidas

Ipse etiam tentare ausus sum, nec puto multum
Displicui, nam sunt et apud me munera vestra
Fiscellae; calathique et cerea vincla cicutae,
Quin et nostra suas docuerunt nomina fagos
Et Datis, et Francinus, erant et vocibus ambo
Et studiis noti, Lydorum sanguinis ambo.
Ite domum impasti, domino iam non vacat, agni
Haec mihi tum laeto dictabat roscida luna,
Dum solus teneros claudebam cratibus hoedos.
Ah quoties dixi, cum te cinis ater habebat,
Nunc canit, aut lepori nunc tendit retia Damon,
Vimina nunc texit, varios sibi quod sit in usus;
Et quae tum facili sperabam mente futura
Arripui voto levis, et praesentia finxi,
Heus bone numquid agis? nisi te quid forte retardat,
Imus? et arguta paulum recubamus in umbra,
Aut ad aquas Colni, aut ubi iugera Cassibelauni?

engage in a singing match, and in viii Daphnis the neatherd and Menalcas the shepherd do the same. M. is referring to the poetical contests at the academies in Florence where, as he relates, 'the manner is that every one must give some proof of his wit and reading' (Columbia iii 235, Yale i 809). Friends in Florence mentioned by M. include Jacopo Gaddi, Carlo Dati, Pietro Frescobaldi, Agostino Coltellini, Benedetto Bonmattei, Valerio Chimentelli and Antonio Francini (Columbia viii 122). Gaddi had founded an academy of his own, the *Svogliati* ('Disgusted'), and Coltellini had founded the *Apatisti* ('Apathetics'). On 16 Sep. 1638 M. read 'a very learned Latin poem in hexameters' to the *Svogliati* (French i 389), and on 17 Mar. 1639 he read 'some noble Latin verses' and on 24 Mar. 'various Latin poems' to the same academy (French i 408–9). He attended again on 31 Mar. (French i 414). M. recalls that the poems he read 'met with acceptance above what was lookt for' and that some of them 'were receiv'd with written encomiums' (Columbia iii 236, Yale i 809–10). Dati–born 1619: best known for his *Lives of the Old Painters* (1667)–and Francini both wrote encomia which were later printed in the 1645 *Poemata*: these are probably the *munera* of 134, given pastoral disguise in 135. One of M.'s letters to Dati, and two of Dati's to M. survive (Columbia xii 296–314, Yale ii 762–75).

138. Lydorum] Herodotus i 94 tells how the Lydians migrated from Asia Minor to N. Italy.

140. roscida luna] The phrase is Virgil's, *Georg.* iii 337.

142. cinis ater habebat] The phrase is Virgil's, *Aen.* iv 633.

149. Colni] The Colne, a tributary of the Thames, flows near Horton. *iugera Cassibelauni*] Caesar, *Bell. Gall.* v 11, mentions a British chief Cassivellaunus and says that his territory 'is divided from the maritime states by the river called Thames, about eighty miles from the sea'. M. repeats this information in the *History of Britain* (Columbia x 44). The Thames forms the

Tu mihi percurres medicos, tua gramina, succos,
Helleborumque, humilesque crocos, foliumque
hyacinthi,
Quasque habet ista palus herbas, artesque medentum,
Ah pereant herbae, pereant artesque medentum
Gramina, postquam ipsi nil profecere magistro.
Ipse etiam, nam nescio quid mihi grande sonabat
Fistula, ab undecima iam lux est altera nocte,
Et tum forte novis admoram labra cicutis,
Dissiluere tamen rupta compage, nec ultra
Ferre graves potuere sonos, dubito quoque ne sim
Turgidulus, tamen et referam, vos cedite silvae.
Ite domum impasti, domino iam non vacat, agni.
Ipse ego Dardanias Rutupina per aequora puppes
Dicam, et Pandrasidos regnum vetus Inogeniae,
Brennumque Arviragumque duces, priscumque
Belinum,

southern boundary of Buckinghamshire, thus Cassivellaunus' territory would include Horton.

153–60. Dorian 180–1 comments: 'These lines, with what one critic [i.e. Visiak 91] has aptly called "the effect of an emotional breaking-point", just achieve that almost impossible concord between a genuine outcry of grief and coherent artistic expression.'

160. vos cedite silvae] In Virgil, *Ecl.* x 63, Gallus bids farewell to pastoral life with the words *concedite silvae*.

162. On M.'s projected British epic see *Mansus* 80–4*n* p. 264 above. On the Trojans in Britain see *Elegia I* 73*n* (p. 22). *Rutupina*] In his chapter on Kent in the *Britannia* Camden identifies Ptolemy's *Rhutupiae* at the mouth of the Wantsum as Richborow.

163. Inogeniae] According to Geoffrey of Monmouth I ix–xi, Ignoge (Imogen) was given to the Trojan Brutus as wife by her father Pandrasus after Brutus had defeated him. Spenser calls her 'fayre Inogene of Italy' (*F.Q.* II x 13). M. tells the story in the *History of Britain* (Columbia x 7–11).

164. Brennumque . . . Belinum] Geoffrey of Monmouth III i–ix and Spenser, *F.Q.* II x 40, tell how Brennus and Belinus, sons of Dunwallo Molmutius, king of Britain, marched victorious through Gaul and finally captured Rome. M. relates that 'by these two all *Gallia* was overrun, the story tells; and what they did in *Italy*, and at *Rome*, if these be they, and not the *Gauls*, who took that City, the Roman Authors can best relate' (Columbia x 25). The reference is to the sack of Rome in 390 B.C. *Arviragumque*] Geoffrey IV xiii–xvi and Spenser, *F.Q.* II x 52, make Arviragus son to King Cymbeline and brother of Guiderius, who was killed in battle after refusing to pay tribute to the Romans. Arviragus submitted to the Roman general Claudius and married his daughter Genuissa, but later revolted against Rome. In the *History of Britain* M. names Cymbeline's sons Togodumnus and Caractacus,

Et tandem Armoricos Britonum sub lege colonos;
Tum gravidam Arturo fatali fraude Iogernen
Mendaces vultus, assumptaque Gorlois arma,
Merlini dolus. O mihi tum si vita supersit,
Tu procul annosa pendebis fistula pinu
Multum oblita mihi, aut patriis mutata camoenis
Brittonicum strides, quid enim? omnia non licet uni
Non sperasse uni licet omnia, mi satis ampla
Merces, et mihi grande decus (sim ignotus in aevum
Tum licet, externo penitusque inglorius orbi)
Si me flava comas legat Usa, et potor Alauni,
Vorticibusque frequens Abra, et nemus omne Treantae,
Et Thamesis meus ante omnes, et fusca metallis

and adds: 'The Monmouth Writer names these two Sones of *Cunobeline*, *Guiderius*, and *Arviragus*; that *Guiderius* beeing slaine in fight, *Arviragus* to conceale it, put on his Brothers Habillements, and in his person held up the Battel to a Victorie; the rest, as of *Hamo* the *Roman Captaine*, *Genuissa* the Emperors Daughter, and such like stuff, is too palpably untrue to be worth rehersing in the midst of Truth' (Columbia x 56).

165. According to William of Malmsbury I i, Constantine founded a colony on the W. coast of Gaul with a force of veteran British soldiers. In the *History of Britain* (Columbia x 118–9) M. tells how some of the inhabitants of Kent, fleeing from Picts, Scots and Saxons, reached '*Armorica*, peopl'd, as som think, with *Britans* long before; either by guift of *Constantine* the *Great*, or else of *Maximus* to those *British* Forces which had serv'd them in Forein Wars . . . But the antient Chronicles of those Provinces attest thir coming thether to be then first when they fled the *Saxons*, and indeed the name of *Britain* in *France* is not read till after that time. Yet how a sort of fugitives who had quitted without stroke thir own Country, should so soon win another, appears not; unless joyn'd to som party of thir own settl'd there before.'

166–8. Geoffrey of Monmouth VIII xix tells how Uther Pendragon, through Merlin's magic, appeared to Igraine (*Igerna*) in the form of her dead husband, Gorlois, King of Cornwall, and had by her a son, Arthur.

169. fistula] The shepherd's pipe; M. is renouncing pastoral verse and echoing Virgil, *Ecl.* vii 24 *pendebit fistula pinu*.

175. Usa] The Ouse. *potor Alauni*] Camden, in the *Britannia*, mentions a river 'Alaun' in Hampshire, near Christ Church, where Stour and Avon join and enter the sea, and a river 'Alne' (Ptolemy's *Alaunus*) in Northumberland.

176. Vorticibusque frequens Abra] In his chapter on the East Riding Camden says that the Ouse 'being very broad, swift and noisy, pours out his stream into the frith of salt water Abus–for that is what Ptolemy calls that arm of the sea which we name Humber. . . . It rises as high as the ocean at every flood tide, and when the same tide ebbs it brings its own stream and the current of the sea together most forcibly and with a mighty noise.'

Tamara, et extremis me discant Orcades undis.
Ite domum impasti, domino iam non vacat, agni.
Haec tibi servabam lenta sub cortice lauri,
Haec, et plura simul, tum quae mihi pocula Mansus,
Mansus Chalcidicae non ultima gloria ripae
Bina dedit, mirum artis opus, mirandus et ipse,
Et circum gemino caelaverat argumento:
In medio rubri maris unda, et odoriferum ver
Littora longa Arabum, et sudantes balsama silvae,
Has inter Phoenix divina avis, unica terris
Caeruleum fulgens diversicoloribus alis
Auroram vitreis surgentem respicit undis.
Parte alia polus omnipatens, et magnus Olympus,
Quis putet? hic quoque Amor, pictaeque in nube pharetrae,

178. Tamara] The Tamar flows between Cornwall and Devonshire: the tin and other metals of Cornwall explain *fusca metallis*. *Orcades*] the Orkneys.

181–97. Mansus] See *Mansus* headnote (p. 260). M. De Filippis, *PMLA* li (1936) 745–56, takes these 'cups' to be two of Manso's books, the *Erocallia* (twelve Platonic dialogues about love and beauty), and the *Poesie Nomiche*, which include an Italian translation of Claudian's *Phoenix*. D. C. Dorian, *PMLA* liv (1939) 612–3, supports this suggestion, pointing out that Pindar, *Olymp.* vii 1–10, refers to a poem as a cup, thus affording M. classical precedent. For the inclusion of an elaborate description of a cup in a pastoral lament M. had to look only to Theocritus i 29–56 (a passage imitated by Virgil, *Ecl.* iii 36–48). A. S. P. Woodhouse (Norwood 270) explains that whereas the figures on Theocritus' bowl represent the life and loves of earth, those on M.'s bowls represent the life and love of heaven, and a promise of resurrection. The fragrant spring betokens the symbolic promise of renewal; the waters of the Red Sea suggest divine protection; Arabia, with trees dropping balm, stands for divine healing (the heavenly completion of Diodati's fallible earthly art); the phoenix and the rising dawn beyond the waters symbolize resurrection.

182. Chalcidicae] See *Leon III* 4*n* (p. 257).

185–9. Hartwell 123–32 suggests that these lines show the influence of a Latin poem *De Ave Phoenice* ascribed to Lactantius. R. Gottfried, *SP* xxx (1933) 497–503, thinks, however, that M.'s source was Tasso's *La Fenice* which combines details from pseudo-Lactantius with others from Claudian's *Phoenix*.

191. Amor] Cp. the 'Celestial Cupid' of *Comus* 1004, and Plato's distinction in the *Symposium* 180–5 between the common and heavenly Aphrodite. Those who are inspired by the offspring of the heavenly Aphrodite turn in love to the male, and are interested rather in mind than body: 'This is the Love that belongs to the Heavenly Goddess, heavenly itself and precious to

Arma corusca faces, et spicula tincta pyropo;
Nec tenues animas, pectusque ignobile vulgi
Hinc ferit, at circum flammantia lumina torquens
Semper in erectum spargit sua tela per orbes
Impiger, et pronos nunquam collimat ad ictus,
Hinc mentes ardere sacrae, formaeque deorum.
  Tu quoque in his, nec me fallit spes lubrica Damon,
Tu quoque in his certe es, nam quo tua dulcis abiret
Sanctaque simplicitas, nam quo tua candida virtus?
Nec te Lethaeo fas quaesivisse sub Orco,
Nec tibi conveniunt lacrymae, nec flebimus ultra,
Ite procul lacrymae, purum colit aethera Damon,
Aethera purus habet, pluvium pede reppulit arcum;
Heroumque animas inter, divosque perennes,
Aethereos haurit latices et gaudia potat
Ore sacro. Quin tu coeli post iura recepta
Dexter ades, placidusque fave quicunque vocaris,
Seu tu noster eris Damon, sive aequior audis
Diodotus, quo te divino nomine cuncti
Coelicolae norint, sylvisque vocabere Damon.
Quod tibi purpureus pudor, et sine labe iuventus
Grata fuit, quod nulla tori libata voluptas,
En etiam tibi virginei servantur honores;
Ipse caput nitidum cinctus rutilante corona,
Letaque frondentis gestans umbracula palmae

both public and private life: for this compels lover and beloved alike to feel a zealous concern for their own virtue.' Ficino in his *Commentary on the Symposium* II vii says that the Love which is paired with the heavenly Aphrodite 'is stimulated to know the beauty of God', and (VI vii) is 'an imitation of the angelic contemplation'. M.'s description also recalls Spenser, *Hymn of Heavenly Love* 1–4: 'Love, lift me up upon thy golden wings, / From this base world unto thy heaven's hight / Where I may see those admirable things / Which there thou workest by thy soveraine might.'

193. ignobile vulgi] The phrase is Virgil's, *Aen.* i 149.

194. flammantia lumina torquens] The phrase is taken from Virgil's description of the water-snake, *Georg.* iii 433.

201. Lethaeo . . . Orco] See *Q Nov* 132*n* and *Elegia VII* 83*n* (pp. 41 and 73).

210. divino nomine] Diodati means 'God-given'.

212–3. purpureus pudor] The phrase is Ovid's, *Am.* I iii 14. *quod . . . voluptas*] Cp. *Rev.* xiv 4: 'These are they which were not defiled with women.'

215. corona] Cp. *1 Pet.* v 4: 'And when the chief Shepherd shall appear, ye shall receive a crown of glory that fadeth not away.'

216. palmae] Cp. *Rev.* vii 9: 'A great multitude . . . stood before the throne, and before the Lamb, clothed with white robes, and palms in their hands.'

Aeternum perages immortales hymenaeos;
Cantus ubi, choreisque furit lyra mista beatis,
Festa Sionaeo bacchantur et orgia thyrso.

Thyrsis and Damon, shepherds of the same neighbourhood, had cultivated the same interests and been the closest possible friends from childhood on. Thyrsis, while travelling abroad for pleasure, received news of Damon's death. Later, when he had returned home and found that this news was true, he bewailed his lot and his loneliness in this poem. 'Damon' here represents Charles Diodati, who was descended on his father's side from the Tuscan city of Lucca, but who was, in every other respect, English. He was, while he lived, a young man extraordinarily endowed with talents, learning and other gifts of a most exemplary kind.

Nymphs of Himera,[1] you keep fresh the memory of Daphnis and Hylas and of Bion's[2] sad fate, long lamented. Now sing your Sicilian air through Thames-side towns.[3] Sing of the cries and moans which poor Thyrsis[4] uttered; his ceaseless laments, which shattered the peace of the caves and the streams, of the wandering rills and the woodland dells, when he wept for Damon, who was snatched from him before his time. Through lonely fields he wandered, filling even the depths of the night with his cries of grief. Already the stalk had twice thrust upwards with its green beard of grain, and the granaries had counted in two yellow harvests, since Damon's last day had swept him down among the shades–yet still Thyrsis was missing: the sweet love of the muse detained him in a Tuscan city.[13] But when he had seen enough abroad, and anxiety for the flock he had left behind called him home, he sat down beneath the old familiar elm tree and then, then at last, he felt the loss of his friend and began to ease his huge burden of pain with these words: 'Go home unfed, lambs, your shepherd has no time for you now.'[18] Ah, what powers in earth or heaven can I call divine, Damon, now that they have clutched you with rigid death? Is this the way you leave me? Must your virtue vanish without trace and mingle with the nameless dead? But no! I pray that he[23] who divides the ghostly ranks with his golden wand may not let that happen: may he guide you to companions who are worthy of you, and keep back the worthless mob whose names are heard no more. 'Go home unfed, lambs, your shepherd has no time for you now.' Whatever happens, one thing is certain: unless a wolf sees me first[27] you will not crumble to dust in the grave unlamented. Your fame will outlive you: it will live on the lips of shepherds for long years to come. It will be their delight to make their vows to you, as second only to Daphnis,[31] and to sing your praises, as second only to the praises of Daphnis, as long as Pales[32] or Faunus continue to love the countryside–this shall be so, unless it is of no avail that a man should have kept the faith of his fathers, observed justice, cultivated the arts of Pallas,[34] and had a poet for his friend. 'Go home unfed, lambs, your shepherd has no time for you now.' You can count on these things, Damon, these will be your reward. But what is to become of me? What loyal comrade will stay by my side, as you often used to do, through

217. hymenaeos] Cp. *Rev.* xix 7: 'Let us be glad and rejoice . . . for the marriage of the Lamb is come.'
219. thyrso] The *thyrsus* was a staff entwined with ivy and vines carried by Bacchus and the Bacchantes.

the hard winter weather, in fields stiff with frost, or under the fierce sun when plants were dying of thirst, whether our job was to stalk the fully grown lions, or to scare the hungry wolves away from our high sheepfolds? Who now will soothe the daylight hours with talk and with song? 'Go home unfed, lambs, your shepherd has no time for you now.' To whom shall I open my heart? Who will teach me to calm eating cares[46] or to beguile the long night with pleasant chatter[47] while soft pears hiss before the cheery blaze and the hearth crackles with nuts, and while the cruel south wind throws everything into confusion out of doors and thunders through the tops of the elms. 'Go home unfed, lambs, your shepherd has no time for you now.' Or in summertime, at high noon, when Pan is asleep,[52] hidden away in the shade of an oak tree, and the nymphs dive down again to their haunts beneath the water, and the shepherds shelter from the sun, and the farm labourer snores under the hedge, who will bring back again for me the charms of your talk, who will bring back your laughter, your flashes of Attic wit[56] and your cultured jokes? 'Go home unfed, lambs, your shepherd has no time for you now.' But now I wander all alone through fields and pastures. I wait for evening in valleys where the shadows of branches are thick and black: over my head the rain and the southeast wind make mournful sounds in the restless twilight of the windswept wood. 'Go home unfed, lambs, your shepherd has no time for you now.' Alas how choked with gadding weeds are my once trim fields! Even the tall grain is spongy with mildew; the unpropped vine rots,[65] its clusters of grapes neglected, and the myrtle groves are joyless. I am even tired of my sheep, and they turn to their shepherd with reproachful eyes. 'Go home unfed, lambs, your shepherd has no time for you now.' Tityrus[69] is calling me to the hazels, Alphesiboeus to the ash-trees, Aegon to the willows, lovely Amyntas[70] to the streams: 'Here are cool fountains! Here is turf covered with moss! Here are soft breezes! Here the wild strawberry tree mingles its murmurs with the mild streams.'[71] They sing to deaf ears. I managed to reach the thickets and escape from them. 'Go home unfed, lambs, your shepherd has no time for you now.' Mopsus,[75] too–Mopsus who knows about the stars and the language of birds[76]–called out, when he happened to see me running away: 'What's the matter, Thyrsis? What melancholy fit is tormenting you? Either love is making you pine away or some malign star has bewitched you. Saturn's star[79] has often been a bane to shepherds: he pierces their heart of hearts with his slanting leaden shaft.'[80] 'Go home unfed, lambs, your shepherd has no time for you now.' The nymphs are amazed and cry 'What will become of you, Thyrsis? What do you mean by all this? Young brows are not usually clouded like yours; young eyes are not usually grim, nor young features so stern. By rights youth should wish for dances and gaiety and games and love, always love. Twice wretched is the man who loves when he is old.'[86] 'Go home unfed, lambs, your shepherd has no time for you now.' Along comes Hyas[88] and Dryope and Baucis's daughter Aegle (a clever musician, good on the lute, but her conceit lets her down),[89] along comes Chloris, who lives by the Idumanean river.[90] No charms, no comforting words, nothing which they can do, no hopes of the future mean anything to me. 'Go home unfed, lambs, your shepherd has no time for you now.' Ah, how like one another are the young bulls which gambol through the meadows! They are all friends together, all of one mind. Not one of them singles out another from the herd as his particular friend. It's the same with wolves, they hunt their food in packs; and the shaggy wild asses mate together by turn. The law of the sea is the same: on the deserted shore Proteus[99] counts his seals in packs. The sparrow, the humblest of birds, always has a companion with whom he flits gaily round every stack of corn, and returns late to his own nest. And if by chance death carries off his mate, if a hook-billed kite cuts short its days or a peasant brings it to earth with his arrow, he goes off and looks for another, there and then, to keep him company as he flies about. But we men are a hard race: a race harassed by cruel fates. Our minds are unfriendly, our hearts discordant. It is hard for a man to find one kindred spirit among thousands of his fellows; and if at last, softened by our prayers, fate grants one, there comes the unexpected day, the unlooked-for hour, which snatches him away, leaving an eternal emptiness. 'Go home unfed, lambs, your shepherd has no time for you now.' Alas, what wanderlust drove me to foreign shores, across the skyey summits of the snow-clad Alps? Was it so very important for me to see buried Rome? Would it have been, even if the city had looked as it once did when Tityrus[117] himself left his flocks and fields to see it? Was it important enough to justify my leaving so sweet a companion and setting between us so many mountains and forests, so many rocks and roaring rivers? Ah, I could at least have held your dying hand and gently closed your lids in peaceful death, and said 'Goodbye! Remember me as you fly up to the stars.' 'Go home unfed, lambs, your shepherd has no time for you now.' And yet I shall never be regretful when I remember you, shepherds of Tuscany, young men formed by the muses: grace and charm dwell with you. You too, Damon, were a Tuscan,[127] descended from the ancient city of Lucca.[128] O how grand I felt, lying by the cool, murmuring Arno,[129] in the shade of a poplar grove, on the soft turf, where I was able to pluck violets and myrtle-tips, and listen to Menalcas and Lycidas[132] having a singing match. I was even bold enough to compete myself, and I don't think I can have been too unpopular, for I still have your gifts, rush baskets and wicker baskets and pipes fastened together with wax. What is more, Dati and Francini,[137] famous poets and scholars both, and both of Lydian[138] blood, made their native beech trees resound with my name. 'Go home unfed, lambs, your shepherd has no time for you now.' These were the sounds which the dewy moon[140] would repeat to me while, happy and solitary, I penned my tender kids in the wattled folds. Ah, how often I used to say (when in reality the black ashes of death had claimed you),[142] 'Now Damon is singing, or laying nets to catch a hare, or making baskets of osiers to serve his various needs.' All unsuspecting, I was quick to seize upon the scenes which I hoped for so longingly in the future, and to imagine them as present: 'Hallo there! What are you up to? If there's nothing else you have to do let's go and lie down a bit in the chequered shade beside the streams of Colne[149] or among the acres of Cassivellaunus. Then, as I listen, you can run through your list of healing potions and herbs–hellebore, humble crocus, hyacinth leaf–all the plants of the fenland, and all the skills of medicine.' O confound herbs and plants and medical skills:[153] they were not able to save their master! And I–for my pipe was sounding some lofty strain, I know not what, eleven nights and a day ago, and I had by chance set my lips to a new set of pipes, when their fastening broke and they fell apart: they could bear the grave notes no longer–I am afraid that I am being swollen-headed, but still, I will tell of that strain. Give place, woods.[160]

'Go home unfed, lambs, your shepherd has no time for you now.' I shall tell of Trojan keels ploughing the sea off the Kentish coast,[162] and of the ancient kingdom of Inogene,[163] daughter of Pandrasus, of the chieftains Brenus and Arviragus and of old Belinus,[164] and of the settlers in Brittany, subject at last to British law.[165] Then I shall tell of Igraine,[166] pregnant with Arthur as a result of fatal deception: I shall tell of the lying features which misled her, and of the borrowing of Gorlois's armour, Merlin's trick.[168] O, if I have any time left to live, you, my pastoral pipe,[169] will hang far away on the branch of some old pine tree, utterly forgotten by me, or else, transformed by my native muses, you will whistle a British tune. But after all, one man cannot do everything, or even hope to do everything. I shall have ample reward, and shall think it great glory, although I be for ever unknown and utterly without fame in the world outside, if only yellow-haired Usa[175] reads my poems, and he who drinks from the Alan, and Humber, full of whirling eddies,[176] and every grove of Trent, and above all my native Thames and the Tamar,[178] stained with metals, and if the Orkneys among their distant waves will learn my song. 'Go home unfed, lambs, your shepherd has no time for you now.' I was keeping these things for you, wrapped in tough laurel bark, these, and more as well. And I was keeping also the two cups[181] which Manso gave me–Manso, not the least glory of the Neapolitan[182] shore. They are a marvellous work of art, and he a marvellous man. Around them he had placed an engraving with a double subject. In the middle are the waves of the Red Sea,[185] and the spicy-smelling spring, the long shores of Arabia, and forests dripping with balsam. Among these the phoenix, the divine bird, the only one on earth, gleams green and blue with parti-coloured wings, and watches Aurora rising from the glassy waves.[189] Another part of the design shows the boundless sky and great Olympus, and here–who would have thought it?–is Cupid[191] with his brightly coloured quivers ringed by a cloud, his glittering arms, his torches and his bronze-coloured arrows. From that height he does not hit trivial spirits or the base hearts of the rabble[193] but, peering all round him with flaming eyes[194] he always releases his darts upwards among the heavenly spheres with tireless aim, and never aims downwards. These shafts kindle holy minds and the forms of the gods themselves.[197] You, too, are among the gods–no deceitful hope beguiles me, Damon–you are among them without doubt, for where else could your sweet and holy simplicity and your snow-white virtue have gone? It would be wrong to look for you in Lethean Orcus.[201] Nothing is here for tears. I shall weep no more. Away with you, tears. Damon dwells now in the pure ether: pure himself, his home is the ether. He spurns the rainbow with his foot, and among the souls of heroes, among the eternal gods, he drinks the draughts of heaven and drains its joys with his holy lips.

Now that you have received your dues in heaven, be present at my side and gently favour me, whatever name you may now bear, whether you are Damon–the name I have given you–or whether you prefer Diodati, the divine name[210] by which all the hosts of heaven will know you, though the woods still call you Damon.

Because the blush of modesty[212] and a youth without stain were your choice, and because you never tasted the delight of the marriage bed,[213] see–virginal honours are reserved for you! Your radiant head circled with a gleaming crown,[215] the joyful, shady branches of leafy palm[216] in your hands, you will take part for ever in the immortal marriage-rite,[217] where singing is heard and the lyre rages in the midst of the ecstatic dances, and where the festal orgies rave in Bacchic frenzy under the thyrsus[219] of Zion.

61 Translations from 'Of Reformation'

Date. Jan.–May 1641. *Of Reformation* was written during the early months of 1641, and published before the end of May.
(i) From Dante, *Inf.* xix 115–7: *Ahi, Costantin, di quanto mal fu matre, / Non la tua conversion, ma quella dote / Che da te prese il primo ricco patre!*
(ii) From Petrarch cxxxix 9–13: *Fondata in casta et umil povertate, / contr' a' tuoi fondatori alzi le corna, / putta sfacciata: e dove hai poste spene? / Ne gli adùlteri tuoi? ne le mal nate / richezze tante? Or Constantin non torna.*
(iii) From Ariosto, *Orlando Furioso* XXXIV lxxiii: *Non stette il duca a ricercare il tutto: / che là non era asceso a quello effetto. / Da l' apostolo santo fu condutto / in un vallon fra due montagne istretto, / ove mirabilmente era ridutto / ciò che si perde o per nostro difetto, / o per colpa di tempo o di Fortuna: / ciò che si perde qui, là si raguna.* The translation M. quotes is Harington's. Though he owned a copy of the 1591 edition of this, he is here apparently quoting from memory, since he makes two minor changes (*And* for Harington's *But* 1, and *Into* for *Unto* 2).
(iv) From Ariosto, *Orlando Furioso* XXXIV lxxx: *Di varii fiori ad un gran monte passa / ch'ebbe già buno odore, or putia forte. / Questo era il dono (se però dir lece) / che Constantino al buon Silvestro fece.* Here M. owes little to Harington, who translates: 'Then by a fayre green mountain he did passe, / That once smelt sweet, but now it stinks perdye. / This was the gift (be't said without offence) / That *Constantin* gave *Silvester* long since.'

(i) Ah Constantine, of how much ill was cause
Not thy conversion, but those rich domains
That the first wealthy Pope received of thee.

(ii) Founded in chaste and humble poverty,
'Gainst them that raised thee dost thou lift thy horn,
Impudent whore, where hast thou placed thy hope?
In thy adulterers, or thy ill-got wealth?
Another Constantine comes not in haste.

(iii) And to be short, at last his guide him brings
Into a goodly valley, where he sees
A mighty mass of things strangely confused,
Things that on earth were lost, or were abused.

(iv) Then passed he to a flowery mountain green,
Which once smelt sweet, now stinks as odiously;
This was that gift (if you the truth will have)
That Constantine to good Sylvestro gave.

62 Translation from 'Reason of Church-Government'

Date. 4 Aug. 1641 to 1 Jan. 1642 (the dates of composition of *Reason of Church-Government*).

The Greek line Ἐμοῦ θανόντος γαῖα μιχθήτω πυρί, probably from a lost play of Euripides (*Bellerophon*), was a favourite saying of Tiberius according to Dio, *Roman History* lviii 23: when someone quoted it to Nero, Suetonius relates, he corrected it to Ἐμοῦ ζῶντος ('When I live . . .') (*Nero* 38). Cicero alludes to the line (*De Finibus* III xix 64) as if it were too familiar to quote. Jonson has it, and the Dio reference, in *Sejanus* II 330.

When I die, let the earth be rolled in flames.

63 Translations from 'Apology for Smectymnuus'

Date. Apr. 1642.

(i) From Horace, *Sat.* I i 24–6: *Quamquam ridentem dicere verum / quid vetat? ut pueris olim dant crustula blandi / doctores, elementa velint ut discere prima.*
(ii) *Ibid.* I x 14–5: *Ridiculum acri / fortius et melius magnas plerumque secat res.*
(iii) From Sophocles, *Electra* 624–5 (Electra talking to Clytemnestra): σύ τοι λέγεις νιν, οὐκ ἐγώ. σὺ γὰρ ποιεῖς / τοὔργον· τὰ δ' ἔργα τοὺς λόγους εὑρίσκεται.

(i) Laughing to teach the truth
What hinders? as some teachers give to boys
Junkets and knacks, that they may learn apace.

(ii) Jesting decides great things
Stronglier, and better oft than earnest can.

(iii) 'Tis you that say it, not I, you do the deeds,
And your ungodly deeds find me the words.

64 Sonnet VIII. When the assault was intended to the City

Date. Nov. ? 1642. In the Trinity MS there is a fair copy in the hand of an amanuensis headed 'On his door when the City expected an assault'. This is crossed through, and 'When ˋtheˊ assault was intended to the City' substituted in M.'s hand, with the date '1642', later deleted. In the printed editions the heading is merely VIII.

After Edgehill (23 Oct. 1642) Essex withdrew to Warwick, leaving the road to London undefended. The advance of the Royalist army caused panic in the capital; on 12 Nov. a Parliamentary force was defeated at Brentford. The city was hastily defended with earthworks and the trained bands were called out and reinforced with the remainder of Essex's army. Thus on 13 Nov. an army of 24,000 was drawn up on Turnham Green to face the Royalists: Charles, however, ordered a retreat. At the time M. was living in Aldersgate Street, educating his two young nephews: his wife had left him.

Publication. *1645* (*3.* If deed of honour did thee ever] If ever deed of honour did thee), *1673* (the text followed here).

Captain or colonel, or knight in arms,
  Whose chance on these defenceless doors may seize,
  If deed of honour did thee ever please,
  Guard them, and him within protect from harms,
He can requite thee, for he knows the charms
  That call fame on such gentle acts as these,
  And he can spread thy name o'er lands and seas,
  Whatever clime the sun's bright circle warms.
Lift not thy spear against the muses' bower,
  The great Emathian conqueror bid spare
  The house of Pindarus, when temple and tower
Went to the ground: and the repeated air
  Of sad Electra's poet had the power
  To save the Athenian walls from ruin bare.

¶ 64. *1. colonel*] Trisyllabic, as often in the seventeenth century.
3. If . . . ever] *Trin. MS*: If ever deed of honour did thee.
10. Emathian conqueror] Alexander; Emathia was a district of Macedon, of which his father was king (Ovid calls him *dux Emathius*, *Tristia* III v 39). Plutarch, *Alexander* 11 and Pliny vii 29 recount that when his army sacked Thebes (335 B.C.) he spared the house once occupied by Pindar, and showed mercy to the poet's descendants.
10–14. Finley 38 compares Horace's frequent practice of ending an ode with two or three examples (e.g. IV vii and viii).
12–13. Plutarch, *Lysander* 15, describes how, when the Spartans with their allies the Thebans and Corinthians had defeated Athens (404 B.C.), Erianthus, a Theban, proposed that Athens should be razed to the ground; but a man from Phocis was heard singing the first chorus from Euripides' *Electra*, 'Electra, Agamemnon's child, I come / Unto thy desert home . . .'), upon which all the hearers were melted with compassion and refused to destroy a city which had produced such great men.

65 Sonnet X. To the Lady Margaret Ley

Date. 1642? There is no certain evidence for dating. According to Edward Phillips (Darbishire 64): 'Our Author, now as it were a single man again [i.e. after his wife's return home in or around July 1642], made it his chief diversion now and then in an Evening to visit the Lady Margaret Lee . . . This Lady being a Woman of great Wit and Ingenuity, had a particular Honour for him, and took much delight in his Company, as likewise her Husband Captain Hobson . . . ; and what esteem he at the same time had for Her, appears by a Sonnet he made in praise of her.' She and her husband, who fought on the Parliamentarian side in the Civil War, lived in Aldersgate Street, and were thus near neighbours of M.

Sonnet X is printed as the last of the ten sonnets in *1645*, so presumably it was written before 6 Oct. 1645, when *1645* was entered in the Stationers' Register. No evidence for dating can be drawn from its position in the Trinity MS, since it is there in fair copy. It is headed 'To the Lady Margaret Ley'.

Publication. 1645 (*3.* fee.]fee, *10.* you,]you) *1673* (the text followed here).

Daughter to that good Earl, once President
  Of England's Council, and her Treasury,
  Who lived in both, unstained with gold or fee.
  And left them both, more in himself content,
Till the sad breaking of that Parliament

¶ 65. *1–2. Earl . . . Treasury*] James Ley (1550–1629), who became Lord Chief Justice in 1622 and was created Earl of Marlborough in 1626 by Charles I. He retired from the Bench in Dec. 1624 to become Lord High Treasurer. Resigning this post in 1628, he was made President of the Council. Finley 53 calls this opening Horatian in that it achieves its poetic effect out of the description of a man's official life: he compares Horace, *Odes* II i 13–6.

3. Sir James Whitelocke, *Liber Famelicus* (Camden Society, 1858) p. 108 says that Ley was crafty, deceitful, underhand and 'an old dissembler . . . wont to be called Vulpone, and I think he as well deserveth it now as ever'. He borrowed money from certain judges when Lord Chief Justice and then, when Lord High Treasurer, attempted to pay these judges their salaries but to withold those of others. The attempt was 'verye honestly' thwarted, says Whitelocke, by Sir Robert Pye.

4. left them] Ley retired from the Presidentship of the Council 14 Dec. 1628.

5–6. Ley died 14 Mar. 1629. On 2 Mar. Charles had directed that Parliament should be adjourned, but the speaker was held down in his chair while Sir John Eliot read out three resolutions calling the country's attention to the

Broke him, as that dishonest victory
At Chaeronea, fatal to liberty
Killed with report that old man eloquent,
Though later born, than to have known the days
Wherein your father flourished, yet by you,
Madam, methinks I see him living yet;
So well your words his noble virtues praise,
That all both judge you to relate them true,
And to possess them, honoured Margaret.

66 Sonnet IX

Date. 1643? In the Trinity MS a working copy of this sonnet follows a fair copy of *Sonnet VIII* (Nov.? 1642). There is no other evidence for dating it, except the presence of the poem in *1645*. The identity of the 'Lady' is not known: some have been tempted to identify her with the 'Lady' of *Comus* (who did not marry until 1652, and who was twenty-four in 1643) but there is no evidence that M. saw her after 1634.

Publication. *1645* (*5.* Mary and with Ruth,]Mary, and the Ruth, *9.* fixed]fixed,) *1673* (the text followed here).

Lady, that in the prime of earliest youth,
Wisely hath shunned the broad way and the green,
And with those few art eminently seen,
That labour up the hill of heavenly truth,

King's misdemeanours. Two days later Eliot and eight other members were sent to the Tower; Parliament was dissolved on 10 Mar.. M. implies that this open breach between Charles and the Parliamentary leaders hastened Ley's end.

6. dishonest] shameful.

7. Chaeronea] Here in 338 B.C. Philip of Macedon defeated the Athenians and Thebans, thus gaining control of the Greek city states.

8. old man] Isocrates. Dionysius of Halicarnassus, in a short biography included in his *Commentaries on the Ancient Orators*, says that Isocrates lived ninety-eight years and died a few days after Chaeronea, for he had vowed that he would not survive the good of Athens. Stephanus repeats this information (*s.v.* Isocrates).

¶ 66. *2. hath*] *Trin. MS*: hast. *broad way*] Cp. *Matt.* vii 13: 'Broad is the way, that leadeth to destruction.'

4. hill . . . truth] Cp. Donne, *Sat.* iii 79–81: 'On a huge hill, / Cragged, and steep, Truth stands, and hee that will / Reach her, about must, and about must goe.' But the hill of truth was a commonplace.

The better part with Mary and with Ruth,
Chosen thou hast, and they that overween,
And at thy growing virtues fret their spleen,
No anger find in thee, but pity and ruth.
Thy care is fixed and zealously attends
To fill thy odorous lamp with deeds of light,
And hope that reaps not shame. Therefore be sure
Thou, when the bridegroom with his feastful friends
Passes to bliss at the mid-hour of night,
Hast gained thy entrance, virgin wise and pure.

67 Translation from title-page of 'Areopagitica'

Date. Nov. 1644.

The translation is of Euripides, *Supplices* 438–41 *τοὐλεύθερον δ' ἐκεῖνο· τίς θέλει πόλει/χρηστόν τι βούλευμ' εἰς μέσον φέρειν ἔχων;/καὶ ταῦθ' ὁ χρῄζων λαμπρός ἐσθ', ὁ μὴ θέλων / σιγᾷ. τί τούτων ἔστ' ἰσαίτερον πόλει;*

This is true liberty when freeborn men
Having to advise the public may speak free,
Which he who can, and will, deserves high praise,
Who neither can nor will, may hold his peace;
What can be juster in a state than this?

68 Translation from 'Tetrachordon'

Date. Feb. 1645. *Tetrachordon* was published 4 Mar.

The translation is of Horace, *Epist*. I xvi 40–5: *Vir bonus est quis? / 'qui consulta patrum, qui leges iuraque servat, / quo multae magnaeque secantur iudice*

5. *Mary . . . Ruth*] Mary sat at Jesus' feet, while Martha was 'cumbered about much serving'. Christ's reply, when Martha complained, was 'one thing is needful: and Mary hath chosen that good part', *Luke* x 39–42. Ruth, unlike Orpah, refused to go off and find a husband, and did not follow 'young men', *Ruth* i 14–7, iii 10.

7. *growing virtues*] *Trin. MS*: *blooming* `*prospering*' virtues `growing virtues'.

11–14. Cp. *Rom*. v 5, 'hope maketh not ashamed', and the parable of the ten virgins, *Matt*. xxv 1–13.

13. *Trin. MS*: *Opens the door of bliss, that hour of night* `Passes to bliss at the mid-*watch* hour' [of] night'.

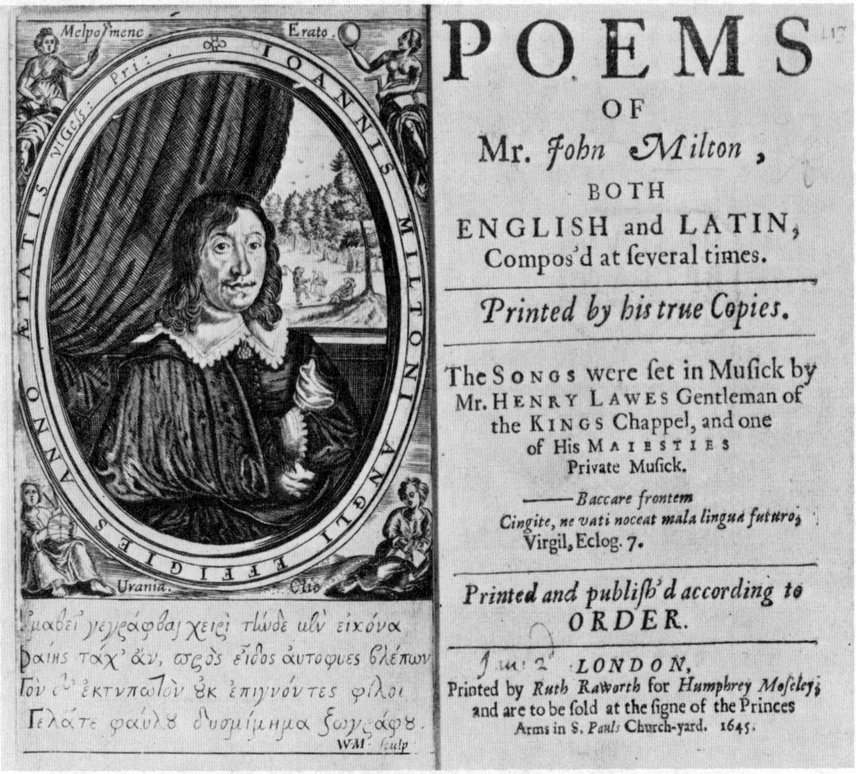
Melpomene
Erato
IOANNIS MILTONI ANGLI EFFIGIES ANNO ÆTATIS VIGESS: PRI:
Urania
Clio
Ἀμαθεῖ γεγράφθαι χειρὶ τήνδε μὲν εἰκόνα
Φαίης τάχ᾽ ἄν, πρὸς εἶδος αὐτοφυὲς βλέπων·
Τὸν δ᾽ ἐκτυπωτὸν οὐκ ἐπιγνόντες φίλοι
Γελᾶτε φαύλου δυσμίμημα ζωγράφου.
WM sculp

POEMS

OF

Mr. *John Milton*,

BOTH

ENGLISH and LATIN,

Compos'd at ſeveral times.

Printed by his true Copies.

The SONGS were ſet in Muſick by
Mr. HENRY LAWES Gentleman of
the KINGS Chappel, and one
of His MAIESTIES
Private Muſick.

——*Baccare frontem*
Cingite, ne vati noceat mala lingua futuro;
Virgil, Eclog. 7.

Printed and publiſh'd according to
ORDER.

LONDON,
Printed by *Ruth Raworth* for *Humphrey Moſeley*;
and are to be ſold at the ſigne of the Princes
Arms in S. *Pauls* Church-yard. 1645.

Title page of *Poems &c.*, first edition, 1645

POEMS, &c.

UPON

Several Occasions.

BY

Mr. *JOHN MILTON*:

Both ENGLISH and LATIN, &c.
Composed at several times.

With a small Tractate of

EDUCATION

To Mr. HARTLIB.

LONDON,
Printed for *Tho. Dring* at the *White Lion*
next *Chancery Lane* End, in
Fleet-street. 1673.

Title page of *Poems &c.*, second edition, 1673

lites, / quo res sponsore et quo causae teste tenentur.' / sed videt hunc omnis domus et vicinia tota / introrsum turpem, speciosum pelle decora.

Whom do we count a good man, whom but he
Who keeps the laws and statutes of the senate,
Who judges in great suits and controversies,
Whose witness and opinion wins the cause;
But his own house, and the whole neighbourhood
Sees his foul inside through his whited skin.

69 *In Effigiei eius Sculptor*

[On the Engraver of his Portrait]

Date. 1645. The portrait which prefaced *1645* was an engraving by William Marshall. These lines were engraved under it, and it seems likely that M. played a practical joke on Marshall in causing him to engrave a condemnation of his own skill in language of which he was ignorant. The portrait of M. is labelled *Anno Aetatis Vigess: Pri:* (At the age of twenty-one), and it has therefore been assumed that Marshall was working from the so-called Onslow portrait of M. at twenty-one, now in the National Portrait Gallery. The two portraits are, though, quite dissimilar: Marshall's is plainly of an older man, in spite of its label. Referring to the Marshall portrait M. later claimed that he 'consented, at the instance and from the importunity of the bookseller [Humphrey Moseley], to employ an unskilful engraver, because at that period of the war there was no other to be found in the city' (Columbia ix 125). Masson[2] iii 457 thinks that M. may have had a grudge against Marshall because he was the engraver of the caricatures of Anabaptists and other sectarians in Daniel Featley's *Dippers Dipt* (1645)–in *Tetrachordon* M. says he does not commend Featley's 'marshalling' (Columbia iv 69, Yale ii 583).

Marshall, who limited himself entirely to book illustration, was the most prolific of the early English engravers. Two of his best known works are the portrait of Donne at the age of eighteen (printed in Donne's *Poems* 1635) and the emblematical frontispiece to the *Eikon Basilike* (1648).

Publication. *1645*, *1673* (no significant variants. The portrait was omitted from *1673*, and the epigram on Marshall printed with the other Greek poems).

'Αμαθεῖ γεγράφθαι χειρὶ τήνδε μὲν εἰκόνα
Φαίης τάχ' ἄν, πρὸς εἶδος αὐτοφυὲς βλέπων·
Τὸν δ' ἐκτυπωτὸν οὐκ ἐπιγνόντες φίλοι
Γελᾶτε φαύλου δυσμίμημα ζωγράφου.

¶ 69. *4. δυσμίμημα*] The word involves a false quantity, and is also an improper formation (though paralleled by δυσχείρωμα in Sophocles, *Ant.*

You would say, perhaps, that this picture was drawn by an ignorant hand, when you looked at the form that nature made. Since you do not recognize the man portrayed, my friends, laugh at this rotten picture of a rotten artist.

70 Sonnet XIII. To Mr H. Lawes, on his Airs

Date. 9 Feb. 1646. The Trinity MS has three drafts: (*a*), headed '13 / To my friend Mr Hen. Lawes Feb. 9 1645', heavily corrected (see notes) and later crossed through, and (*b*), headed '13 / To Mr Hen. Lawes on the publishing of his Airs', are in M.'s hand. Draft (*c*), headed '13 / To Mr H*en*. Law`e's on *the publishing of* his Airs', is a fair copy in another hand.

On M's friendship with Lawes see Evans. Lawes had been a member of the King's Music, and his sympathies were Royalist. His brother William fell fighting for the King at Chester (1645). The 1648 *Choice Psalmes*, which Lawes published to commemorate William, and which contained examples of the latter's work, was dedicated to Charles I, then a prisoner. *Sonnet XIII* was first printed in this volume (headed 'To my Friend Mr Henry Lawes').

The heading of Trinity MS (*b*) looks like a later insertion, since the first of Lawes's three volumes of *Airs and Dialogues* did not appear until 1653.

Publication. Choice Psalmes 1648 (*4*. long;]long, *6*. wan;]wan: *7*. man,] man *10*. choir]choir, *11*. hymn,]hymn *13*. sing]sing,) *1673* (the text followed here, except in *9* where *1673* misprints 'send' for 'lend')

Harry whose tuneful and well-measured song
  First taught our English music how to span
  Words with just note and accent, not to scan
  With Midas' ears, committing short and long;
Thy worth and skill exempts thee from the throng,

126). T. O. Mabbott, *Explicator* viii (1950) 58, points out that δυσμίμημα ζωγράφου may mean a bad picture by or of an artist: he thinks this ambiguity intentional, the idea being that the picture represents the man who made it, not the supposed subject.

¶ 70. *3. Trin. MS* (*a*): *Words with just notes, which till then used `when most were wont' to scan `when most were wont to scan' `words with just note and accent, not to scan'* `words with just note and accent, not to scan'.

4. Midas] As a punishment for preferring the music of Pan to that of Apollo he was, as Ovid relates, *Met.* xi 146–79, given ass's ears. *committing*] *Trin. MS* (*a*): *committing* `misjoining'. The verb 'commit' meaning 'engage (parties) as opponents' is here, according to *OED*, used figuratively for the first time. Waller (*Poems* ed. G. Thorn Drury (1893) i 19–20) also praises Lawes's music for not obscuring the meaning of the verse he is setting.

5. worth] *Trin. MS* (*a*): *worth `wit'* `worth'. *exempts . . . throng*] Horace is similarly exempted, *Odes* I i 32.

With praise enough for envy to look wan;
To after age thou shalt be writ the man,
That with smooth air couldst humour best our tongue.
Thou honour'st verse, and verse must lend her wing
To honour thee, the priest of Phoebus' choir
That tun'st their happiest lines in hymn, or story.
Dante shall give fame leave to set thee higher
Than his Casella, whom he wooed to sing
Met in the milder shades of Purgatory.

71 Sonnet XII. On the Detraction which followed upon my Writing Certain Treatises

Date. 1646. There are two versions of this sonnet in the Trinity MS (referred to as *Trin. MS* (*a*) and (*b*) below). *Trin. MS* (*a*) is not a fair copy (it contains two alterations: see notes) and it appears after and on the same page as a rough draft and a fair copy of *Sonnet XIII*, of which the rough draft is dated 9 Feb.

6. *Trin. MS* (*a*): *And gives thee praise above* the pipe of Pan.
7. *the*] *Trin. MS* (*a*): a.
8. *Trin. MS* (*a*): That didst reform thy art, the chief among (*b*): That with smooth air*s couldst* cou'dst humour best our tongue.
11. *story*] *Choice Psalmes* has a marginal note: 'The story of Ariadne set by him in music.' William Cartwright's *Complaint of Ariadne* was set by Lawes and printed in his first book of *Airs*.
12. *Trin. MS* (*a*): ˋDante shall giveˊ Fame *by the Tuscan's* leave *shall* ˋtoˊ set thee higher.
12–14. In *Purgatorio* ii 76–119 Dante meets the shade of Casella, a Florentine musician who had been his friend, on the threshold of Purgatory. In life Casella had set some of Dante's canzoni to music, and when Dante now asks the shade to sing it complies with the canzone *Amor che nella mente mi ragiona*.
13. *Trin. MS* (*a*): Than *old* ˋhisˊ *Casell'* ˋCasellaˊ whom *Dante* ˋheˊ wonˋoedˊ to sing.
14. *milder*] *Trin. MS* (*a*): *mildest* ˋmilderˊ. Masson iii 289 takes this to mean that the shades of Purgatory are 'milder' than those of Hell, but J. S. Diekhoff, *MLN* lii (1937) 409–10, draws attention to the first reading in *Trin. MS* (*a*) – what is referred to is the mildness of the threshold of Purgatory, where the meeting occurs, by comparison with other parts of Purgatory.

1645 [i.e. 1646]. Therefore *Sonnet XII* must be dated after 9 Feb. 1646. Both versions are headed with the figure 11 [altered later to 12 in *Trin. MS* (*b*)], and with the title given above [later deleted in *Trin. MS* (*a*)]. *Trin. MS* (*b*) is followed by a version of *Sonnet XI* (headed 12), but this order is reversed in *1673* where *XI* precedes *XII*.

The position of *Trin. MS* (*a*) relative to *Sonnet XIII* was used, as above, to date *Sonnet XII* by J. H. Hanford, *MP* xviii (1921) 144–5. Previously D. H. Stevens, *MP* xvii (1919) 27–8 had suggested a date in the autumn of 1644, and more recently J. T. Shawcross, *N & Q* viii (1961) 179–80 has favoured Sep. 1645.

The *Treatises* referred to in the title are the divorce tracts, which appeared as follows: (i) *The Doctrine and Discipline of Divorce* (anonymous) 1 Aug. 1643. Second edition (bearing M.'s name) 2 Feb. 1644. Third and fourth editions 1645. (ii) *The Judgment of Martin Bucer* (entered 15 Jul. 1644: M.'s name appears at end of address to Parliament, in which he asserts that, on the appearance of *Doctrine and Discipline*, 'some of the clergie began to inveigh and exclaim on what I was credibly inform'd they had not read' (Columbia iv 12, Yale ii 434). On 24 Aug. 1644 (French ii 106–8) the Stationers presented a petition to Parliament in which complaint was made against 'the Pamphlet... concerning Divorce', and in Sep. 1644 William Prynne's *Twelve Considerable Serious Questions* hoped for the suppression of the same pamphlet. In Dec. M. was summoned to the House of Lords for examination (French ii 116) but, according to John Phillips (Darbishire 24) 'soon dismiss'd'). (iii) *Tetrachordon* (4 Mar. 1645: bears M.'s name: not licensed or registered. In the address to Parliament M. vindicates himself from the attacks of two ministers, Herbert Palmer, who called for the suppresssion of *Doctrine and Discipline* in a sermon preached before Parliament 13 Aug. 1644 (French ii 106) and Dr Daniel Featley who attacked the same work in *The Dippers Dipt*, 1645) (iv) *Colasterion* (4 Mar. 1645: bears M.'s initials: unlicensed and unregistered. The title means, in Greek, 'instrument of correction'. A reply to the anonymous *Answer to The Doctrine and Discipline of Divorce*, Nov. 1644 (reprinted in Parker 170–216). In Nov. 1645 (French ii 132–3) Robert Baillie attacked M.'s divorce views in *A Dissuasive from the Errors of the Time*, and in Feb. 1646 (French ii 143) Thomas Edwards did the same in *Gangraena*. Other and later attacks than those mentioned here are listed by Parker 73–84).

Publication. 1673.

Modern criticism. N. H. Henry, *MLN* lxvi (1951) 509–13, thinks that *Sonnet XII* is directed not so much against the Presbyterians who rejected M.'s divorce proposals as against the 'lunatic fringe' of the Independents who embraced them in an embarrassing way (e.g. the Mrs Attaway, mentioned in Edwards's *Gangraena*, who left her husband after reading M. on divorce and became 'the mistress of all the she-preachers of Coleman Street').

I did but prompt the age to quit their clogs
  By the known rules of ancient liberty,

When straight a barbarous noise environs me
Of owls and cuckoos, asses, apes and dogs.
As when those hinds that were transformed to frogs
Railed at Latona's twin-born progeny
Which after held the sun and moon in fee.
But this is got by casting pearl to hogs;
That bawl for freedom in their senseless mood,
And still revolt when truth would set them free.
Licence they mean when they cry liberty;
For who loves that, must first be wise and good;
But from that mark how far they rove we see
For all this waste of wealth, and loss of blood.

72 On the New Forcers of Conscience under the Long Parliament

Date. Aug. 1646? By an ordinance of Jan. 1645 Parliament adopted the Directory for Public Worship in place of the Book of Common Prayer (the 'liturgy' of *2*), but not until 28 Aug. 1646 did Parliament draw up the rules of ordination by the Classical Presbyteries. D. H. Stevens, *MP* xvii (1919) 30, thinks that the poem must be dated after this, but before 4 Jun. 1647, when Charles was captured by the army. J. H. Hanford, *MP* xviii (1921) 145, agrees, but feels that a date just before the final realization of the 'just fears' of M. and the Independents on 28 Aug. is also possible.

Trin. MS has a corrected draft in the hand of an amanuensis with a note requiring that the poem should be inserted after *Sonnet XI* (1647?) and before *Fairfax* (Aug. 1648?).

¶ 71. *4. cuckoos*] *Trin MS* (*a*): buzzards.
5–7. Ovid. *Met.* vi 317–81, narrates how when Latona, with her baby twins Apollo and Diana, later deities of sun and moon, wanted to drink at a pool, some Lycian peasants stirred up the water to make it muddy, whereupon Jove turned them to frogs. W. R. Parker, *Explicator* viii (1949) 3, thinks that M. introduced the fable of the 'twin-born progeny' because he had in mind the reception given to his own 'twins', *Tetrachordon* and *Colasterion*, which were published on the same day, 4 Mar. 1645.
10. still . . . free] *Trin. MS* (*a*): *hate the truth whereby they should be free* 'still revolt when truth would set them free' (*b*): still revolt when truth would *make* 'set' them free. Cp. *John* viii 32: 'And the truth shall make you free.'
11. Smart 68–9 points out that the distinction between licence and liberty was common in Roman authors. Finley cites Plato, *Rep.* viii 560E. M. has the distinction in his letter to Parliament prefaced to the *Doctrine and Discipline* (Columbia iii 370, Yale ii 225) and in the *History of Britain* (Columbia x 104).
13. rove] To shoot an arrow away from the 'mark' (target).

Publication. 1673.
Modern criticism. Smart 127 points out that this is an example of the *sonetto caudato* ('tailed sonnet')–a form popular with Italian satirists, particularly those of the school of Berni. M.'s sonnet has two 'tails', each of a half-line and a couplet.

Because you have thrown off your prelate lord,
 And with stiff vows renounced his liturgy
 To seize the widowed whore plurality
 From them whose sin ye envied, not abhorred,
Dare ye for this adjure the civil sword
 To force our consciences that Christ set free,
 And ride us with a classic hierarchy
 Taught ye by mere A. S. and Rutherford?

¶ 72. 1. *thrown . . . lord*] Episcopacy was formally abolished in England by a decree of the Long Parliament, Sep. 1646, but Parliament's ordinance of June 1643 summoning the Assembly of Divines made it quite clear that episcopacy was condemned since one purpose of the Assembly was to decide what should replace it.
3. *widowed*] *Trin. MS*: *vacant* 'widowed'. *plurality*] The practice of holding more than one living. In his *History of Britain* (Columbia x 322), M. complains that members of the Westminster Assembly were quick 'to seise into thir hands or not unwillinglie to accept (besides one sometimes two or more of the best Livings) collegiat master-ships in the universities, rich lectures in the cittie. . . . By which meanes those great rebukers of nonresidence among so many distant cures were not asham'd to be seen so quicklie pluralists and nonresidents themselves.'
5. *adjure*] charge, entreat. M., always opposed to the interference of the civil power in religious matters, complains of the Westminster Assembly's attempt to impose Presbyterianism by force, 'while they taught compulsion without convincement (which not long before they so much complain'd of as executed unchristianlie against themselves) thir intents were cleere to be no other then to have set up a spiritual tyrannie by a secular power' (Columbia x 322).
6. *our*] *Trin. MS*: *the* 'our'.
7. *classic*] Parliament resolved that the English parishes or congregations were to be grouped in Presbyteries or 'Classes' after the Scottish pattern.
8. *A.S.*] Dr Adam Stewart, Scottish Presbyterian controversialist and Professor of Philosophy at Leyden. When the five leading Independents in the Assembly (Goodwin, Simpson, Nye, Burroughs and Bridge) put their case in the *Apologetical Narration* 1644, Stewart's *Some Observations* (signed A. S.) was one of several replies. *Rutherford*] Samuel Rutherford (1600–61), one of the four Scottish divines on the Assembly and Professor of Divinity at St Andrew's. His pamphlets included *A Plea for Presbytery* 1642 and *The Due Right of Presbyteries* 1645.

Men whose life, learning, faith and pure intent
Would have been held in high esteem with Paul
Must now be named and printed heretics
By shallow Edwards and Scotch What-d'ye-call:
But we do hope to find out all your tricks,
Your plots and packing worse than those of Trent,
That so the Parliament
May with their wholesome and preventive shears
Clip your phylacteries, though baulk your ears,
And succour our just fears

9. *Men*] Smart 129 thinks these are the five authors of the *Apologetical Narration.*

12. *shallow*] *Trin. MS*: *hare-brained* 'shallow'. *Edwards*] Thomas Edwards. His *Antapologia*, advocating strict Presbyterianism, was a reply to the *Apologetical Narration*, and his *Gangraena: or a Catalogue of many . . . Heresies . . . of this Time* 1646 included a denunciation of M.'s views on divorce (quoted Parker 76–7). *What-d'ye-call*] probably Robert Baillie, Professor of Divinity at Glasgow. His *Dissuasive from the Errors of the Time* 1645 attacked M.'s divorce-writings: 'I doe not know certainely whither this man professeth Independency (albeit all the Hereticks here, whereof ever I heard, avow themselves Independents)' (quoted Parker 75).

14. *packing*] *Trin. MS*: packings. *OED* defines the word as 'the corrupt constitution or manipulation of a deliberative body', but gives no example before 1653. M. is referring to the overwhelming Presbyterian predominance in the Assembly. *Trent*] the Council of Trent (1545–63) reformulated the doctrines of the Roman Catholic church after the Reformation.

17. *Trin. MS*: *Crop ye as close as marginal P----'s ears* 'Clip your phylacteries, though baulk your ears'. The first version alludes to the cropping of William Prynne's ears in 1634 because passages in his attack on the stage, *Histriomastix*, were taken to refer to the King and Queen. In 1637 he was sentenced to lose the rest of his ears and to be branded for an attack on Wren, Bishop of Norwich. He wrote several pamphlets against Independency and attacked M.'s divorce-views in *Twelve Considerable Serious Questions* 1644. *phylacteries*] a phylactery is a small leather box containing four scriptural texts (*Deut.* vi 4–9; xi 13–21; *Exod.* xiii 1–10, 11–16), worn by Jews during morning prayer as a mark of obedience to their literal interpretation. Christ in *Matt.* xxiii 5 uses the phrase 'make broad their phylacteries' in the sense 'vaunt their own righteousness'; thus 'phylactery' in English comes to mean 'an ostentatious or hypocritical display of piety'–first used by M. thus in 1641 (Yale i 897) antedating *OED*'s citing of *Tetrachordon* (Yale ii 582). *baulk*] miss. D. C. Dorian, *MLN* lvi (1941) 62–4, detects the implication that the Presbyterians will be lucky if they escape a far severer punishment than ear-clipping–their own exclusion from the clergy, because the Mosaic qualifications for the priesthood excluded any man with a physical blemish (*Lev.* xxi 17–23).

When they shall read this clearly in your charge
New *Presbyter* is but old *Priest* writ large.

73 Sonnet XIV

Date. Dec. 1646. The Trinity MS has three drafts: (*a*) a working copy later struck through, headed 'On the religious memory of Mrs Catharine Thom`a'son my Christian friend deceased *16* Decem. 1646' (it was Smart 81 who first noticed the inserted 'a' and thus identified the subject of the sonnet. The deleted *16* are the first two numerals of the year [1646], which M. crossed through in order to insert, first, the month. Mrs Thomason was buried 12 Dec. 1646); (*b*), a second draft, also in M.'s hand, headed '14'; and (*c*) a fair copy made by an amanuensis. Mrs Thomason was the wife of George Thomason, a bookseller whose magnificent collection of civil war pamphlets is now in the British Museum. Several of M.'s treatises contained in it are marked *Ex dono authoris.* Smart 79 suggests that Thomason is the intimate friend (*mihi familiarissimo*) to whom M. entrusted his letter to Carlo Dati in Florence (Columbia xii 52, Yale ii 765) in Apr. 1647. Very little is known of Mrs Thomason. She had nine children, and the mention of her library in her husband's will (Smart 81) indicates scholarly leanings.
Publication. 1673.
Modern criticism. R. L. Ramsay, *SP* xv (1918) 123–58, claims that this sonnet, in its first Trinity MS draft, reads like a condensed version of *Everyman* and is the most detailed example of M.'s use of the medieval allegory.

When faith and love which parted from thee never,
Had ripened thy just soul to dwell with God,
Meekly thou didst resign this earthy load
Of death, called life; which us from life doth sever.
Thy works and alms and all thy good endeavour
Stayed not behind, nor in the grave were trod;

19. they] *Trin. MS*: *you* `they'.
20. 'Priest' is etymologically a contracted form of Latin *presbyter* (an elder); thus 'priest' 'writ large' (expanded) would be 'presbyter'. 'Priest' is found in Old English, but 'presbyter' is a late sixteenth century word. *writ large*] *Trin. MS*: writ *at* large.
¶ 73. *1. which*] *Trin. MS* (*a*): that.
3. load] *Trin. MS* (*a*): *clod* `load'.
4. death . . . doth] *Trin. MS* (*a*): *flesh and sin* `death, called life' which *man* `us' from *heav'n* `life' doth.
5. and all] *Trin. MS* (*a*): `and' all. Cp. *Acts* x 4: 'Thy prayers and thine alms are come up for a memorial before God.'
6. Trin. MS (*a*): *Straight followed thee the path that saints have trod* `Stayed not behind, nor in the grave were trod'.

But as faith pointed with her golden rod,
Followed thee up to joy and bliss for ever.
Love led them on, and faith who knew them best
Thy handmaids, clad them o'er with purple beams
And azure wings, that up they flew so dressed,
And speak the truth of thee on glorious themes
Before the judge, who thenceforth bid thee rest
And drink thy fill of pure immortal streams.

74 *Ad Joannem Rousium Oxoniensis Academiae Bibliothecarium*

De libro Poematum amisso, quem ille sibi denuo mitti postulabat, ut cum aliis nostris in Bibliotheca publica reponeret, Ode

[To John Rouse, Librarian of Oxford University. An Ode on a lost Book of Poems. He requested that a second copy of it should be sent, so that he could place it in the public library with my other books]

Date. 23 Jan. 1647. This date is given in the *1673* heading. Bodleian MS Lat. Misc. f15 is a fair copy of this ode, possibly in M.'s hand, but if so 'in a most formal, set hand, unlike anything we possess today known to have been written by M.' (Fletcher[3] i 458). The Bodleian MS is pasted to the verso of the Latin title-page of a copy of *1645* which may be the substitute copy sent to Rouse by M. There is no evidence that Rouse (1574–1652), who became Bodley's librarian in 1620, was a personal friend of M.'s. M. sent him copies of the eleven prose pamphlets of 1641–44, and these are now bound in one volume in Bodley (4°F.56) bearing, in M.'s hand, a list of the books sent and a presentation inscription which says that Rouse had requested the pamphlets should be sent. On 30 Dec. 1645 Rouse caused something of a stir by

7. *Trin. MS* (*a*): *Still as* \`*when*' *they journeyed from this dark abode* \`But as Faith pointed with her golden rod'.
8. *Trin. MS* (*a*): *Up to the realm of peace and joy for ever* \`Followed thee up to joy and bliss for ever'. Cp. *Rev.* xiv 13: 'Blessed are the dead which die in the Lord . . . their works do follow them.'
9. *Trin. MS* (*a*): Faith *who led on* \`showed' the way, and *knew* \`she who saw' them best (*b*): *Faith* \`*Love*' *showed* \`Love led' the\`m' *way* \`on', and *she* \`Faith' who *saw* \`knew' them best.
11. *that*] *Trin. MS* (*a*): *thence* \`that'.
12. *speak . . . on*] *Trin. MS* (*a*) and (*b*): spake the truth of thee in (*c*): spake the truth of \`thee' on. H. J. C. Grierson, *TLS* (15 Jan. 1925) 40, prefers 'in glorious' (*Trin. MS* (*a*) and (*b*) reading) to 'on glorious', and suggests that 'themes' is being used in a musical sense (meaning 'strains').

refusing to allow Charles I to borrow the *Histoire Universelle du Sieur d'Aubigné* from the Bodleian (which is not a lending library) although the request was countersigned by Fell, the Vice-Chancellor. In 1643 Rouse contributed £50 to a loan to Charles, but he was a lukewarm Royalist: see E. Craster, *Bodleian Library Record* v (1954–6) 130–46.

Publication. 1673.

Modern criticism. From the viewpoint of versification the ode is a daring experiment, and was sharply censured by nineteenth-century critics like Landor (*Imaginary Conversations* (1883) iv 105–6)–'on no occasion has any Latin poet so jumbled together the old metres'–and Symmons (*Life of M.* (1806) 230), who called it 'a wild chaos of verses and no verses heaped together confusedly and licentiously'. W. R. Parker, *PQ* xxviii (1949) 145–66, points out that it is only paralleled by the choruses of *Samson Agonistes* and notes that M. uses the same terms to describe each (see p. 345 below).

Strophe 1.

Gemelle cultu simplici gaudens liber,
Fronde licet gemina,
Munditieque nitens non operosa,
Quam manus attulit
Iuvenilis olim,
Sedula tamen haud nimii poetae;
Dum vagus Ausonias nunc per umbras
Nunc Britannica per vireta lusit
Insons populi, barbitoque devius
Indulsit patrio, mox itidem pectine Daunio
Longinquum intonuit melos
Vicinis, et humum vix tetigit pede;

Antistrophe.

Quis, te, parve liber, quis te fratribus
Subduxit reliquis dolo?
Cum tu missus ab urbe,
Docto iugiter obsecrante amico,
Illustre tendebas iter
Thamesis ad incunabula
Caerulei patris,
Fontes ubi limpidi

¶ 74. *1. Gemelle . . . liber*] *1645* formed a 'twin' volume since it contained the English poems and then the Latin, each with separate pagination and title-page (*Fronde . . . gemina*).

10. Daunio] Daunia was the name given in classical times to a part of Apulia: M. presumably means merely 'Italian,' referring to the Latin poems.

Aonidum, thyasusque sacer
Orbi notus per immensos
Temporum lapsus redeunte coelo,
Celeberque futurus in aevum;

Strophe 2.

Modo quis deus, aut editus deo
Pristinam gentis miseratus indolem
(Si satis noxas luimus priores
Mollique luxu degener otium)
Tollat nefandos civium tumultus,
Almaque revocet studia sanctus
Et relegatas sine sede musas
Iam pene totis finibus Angligenum;
Immundasque volucres
Unguibus imminentes
Figat Apollinea pharetra,
Phineamque abigat pestem procul amne Pegaseo.

Antistrophe.

Quin tu, libelle, nuntii licet mala
Fide, vel oscitantia
Semel erraveris agmine fratrum,
Seu quis te teneat specus,
Seu qua te latebra, forsan unde vili
Callo tereris institoris insulsi,
Laetare felix, en iterum tibi
Spes nova fulget posse profundam
Fugere Lethen, vehique superam
In Iovis aulam remige penna;

21. *Aonidum*] See *Elegia IV* 29–32*n* (p. 55).
25–36. Cp. Horace's similar appeal to an unnamed god or hero, *Odes* I ii 25–52, and castigation of civil war, 21–4.
29–31. The Civil War had broken out in 1642; Oxford was the Royalist headquarters.
33–6. The *volucres* are the harpies, called *Phineam . . . pestem* because Apollonius of Rhodes, *Argon.* ii 187–93, tells how they were sent by Zeus to punish the prophet-king Phineus by defiling him and snatching away his food. The Argonauts, not Apollo, delivered Phineus from the harpies, but M. looks to Apollo because he is a monster-slayer (see *Elegia VII* 31–4*n*, p. 71) and god of poetry. The 'river of Pegasus' is the Thames, on which Oxford stands: Pegasus, the winged horse of the Muses, caused the fountain Hippocrene to flow from Mount Helicon with a blow of his hoof.
45. *Lethen*] See Q *Nov* 132*n* (p. 41).

Strophe 3.

Nam te Roüsius sui
Optat peculi, numeroque iusto
Sibi pollicitum queritur abesse,
Rogatque venias ille cuius inclyta
Sunt data virum monumenta curae:
Teque adytis etiam sacris
Voluit reponi quibus et ipse praesidet

Aeternorum operum custos fidelis,
Quaestorque gazae nobilioris,
Quam cui praefuit Iön
Clarus Erechtheides
Opulenta dei per templa parentis
Fulvosque tripodas, donaque Delphica
Iön Actaea genitus Creusa.

Antistrophe.

Ergo tu visere lucos
Musarum ibis amoenos,
Diamque Phoebi rursus ibis in domum
Oxonia quam valle colit
Delo posthabita,
Bifidoque Parnassi iugo:
Ibis honestus,
Postquam egregiam tu quoque sortem
Nactus abis, dextri prece sollicitatus amici.
Illic legeris inter alta nomina
Authorum, Graiae simul et Latinae
Antiqua gentis lumina, et verum decus.

Epodos.

Vos tandem haud vacui mei labores,
Quicquid hoc sterile fudit ingenium,

56–60. Ion was son of Apollo by Creusa, daughter of Erechtheus, king of Athens. His early history is told by Euripides, *Ion* 1–81: he was exposed in a cave by his mother, but carried to Delphi by Hermes and later made guardian of the treasuries of the sanctuary of Apollo there. The treasuries at Delphi border the sacred way which winds up the hillside to the temple of Apollo. Famous among the thank-offerings there was a golden tripod erected, out of the booty of Plataea, on a bronze column formed of three serpents intertwined. *Actaea*] Actaean (from *Acte*, the old name for Attica) means Attic or Athenian.

65–6. Delos is an island shrine in the Cyclades, the birthplace of Apollo and Diana. *Parnassi*] See *Elegia IV* 29–32*n* (p. 55).

Iam sero placidam sperare iubeo
Perfunctam invidia requiem, sedesque beatas
Quas bonus Hermes
Et tutela dabit solers Roüsi,
Quo neque lingua procax vulgi penetrabit,
atque longe
Turba legentum prava facesset;
At ultimi nepotes,
Et cordatior aetas
Iudicia rebus aequiora forsitan
Adhibebit integro sinu.
Tum livore sepulto,
Si quid meremur sana posteritas sciet
Roüsio favente.

Ode tribus constat Strophis, totidemque Antistrophis una demum epodo clausis, quas, tametsi omnes nec versuum numero, nec certis ubique colis exacte respondeant, ita tamen secuimus, commode legendi potius, quam ad antiquos concinendi modos rationem spectantes. Alioquin hoc genus rectius fortasse dici monostrophicum debuerat. Metra partim sunt κατὰ σχέσιν, partim ἀπολελυμένα. Phaleucia quae sunt, spondaeum tertio loco bis admittunt, quod idem in secundo loco Catullus ad libitum fecit.

Strophe 1 Twin-born book,[1] rejoicing in a single cover but with a double title-page, bright with that unlaboured neatness which a boyish hand once gave you–an earnest, but not too poetic hand–while he wandered in play through the shades of Italy or the green fields of England, roaming about, untainted by the crowd, in unfrequented places, giving himself up to the music of his native lute; or, presently, thundering out to the bystanders a song from far away, strumming a Daunian[10] string, his feet hardly touching the ground;
Antistrophe Who was it, little book, who was it that craftily took you from your brothers when, in reply to my learned friend's ceaseless entreaties, you had been sent from the city and were making that lovely journey to the birthplace of deep-blue Father Thames, where the clear springs of the Aonides[21] are found and the sacred Bacchic dance, known to all the world through the vast tracts of the vanished years and revolving seasons, and famous for all time?
Strophe 2 But what god[25] or god-begotten man will be moved to pity by the native talents which our race has displayed throughout history and–if we have done enough penance for our past evils, and for the degenerate idleness of our womanish luxury–will put an end to this damnable civil war and its skirmishes,[29] restore with his holy power our life-giving pursuits, recall the homeless Muses[31]–banished now from almost every corner of England, transfix with arrows from Apollo's quiver the foul birds[33] who

94. Phaleucia] The regular Phaleucian line consists of a spondee, a dactyl and three trochees.

hover over us with threatening claws, and drive Phineus' bane far from the river of Pegasus? 36

Antistrophe But, little book, though through the messenger's dishonesty or negligence you have wandered on this one occasion from the company of your brothers; though now you lie in some ditch or on some hidden shelf from which, perhaps, you are taken and thumbed over by a block-headed bookseller with calloused, grimy hands–cheer up, lucky little book! See, here is a gleam of hope for you–hope that you will be able to escape from the depths of Lethe 45 and, beating your wings, soar to the high courts of Jove.

Strophe 3 For Rouse wants you to be a part of his collection. He complains that, though you were promised to him, you are missing from the list, and he asks that you should come to him–Rouse, to whose care are entrusted the glorious monuments of illustrious men–he wants you to have a place in those holy sanctuaries over which he presides in person, faithful guardian of immortal works, custodian of a treasure richer than that which far-famed Ion 56 watched over–Ion of Erechtheus's line, Actaean Creusa's son–in the sumptuous temple of his father, Apollo, with its golden tripods and its Delphic treasuries. 60

Antistrophe So you will go and feast your eyes on the lovely glades of the Muses, you will go again to that divine home of Phoebus in the Vale of Oxford–that home which he prefers to Delos 65 or forked Parnassus. 66 You will go in honour, when you leave my side, for you have been remarkably lucky: you have received a pressing invitation from a friend who wishes you well. There you will be read among authors whose great names were of old the guiding lights and are now the true glory of the Greek and Latin race.

Epode. So, my labours, you have not been in vain, as it turns out: not in vain, the tricklings of my sluggish genius. Now at last I can tell you to look forward to peace and rest, all envy past, and to the happy home which kind Hermes and Rouse with his expert guardianship will provide: a home to which the insolent clamourings of the rabble will never penetrate, far away from the vulgar mob of readers. But perhaps the children of the future, in some distant and wiser age, will see things in a fairer light and with unprejudiced hearts. Then, when spite and malice are buried in the past, posterity with its balanced judgment will know–thanks to Rouse–what, if anything, I have deserved.

This ode consists of three strophes and three antistrophes with a concluding epode. Though the strophes and antistrophes do not exactly correspond either in the number of their lines or in the distribution of their particular metrical units, nevertheless I have cut the poem up in this way in order to make it easier to read, rather than with a view to imitating any ancient method of versification. It would perhaps be more correct, in other respects, to call this kind of composition monostrophic. The metres are partly determined by correlation, partly free. In the Phaleucian 93 lines I have twice admitted a spondee in the third foot: Catullus does so quite freely in the second foot.

75 Sonnet XI

Date. 1647? J. H. Hanford, *MP* xviii (1921) 144–5, argues for a date in 1647 or later on the evidence of the position of *Sonnet XI* in the Trinity MS. This, he claims, would fit the meaning of ll. *3–4* better than an earlier date.

The Trinity MS has two versions: a working draft (*a*) and a fair copy (*b*). The latter follows the fair copy of *Sonnet XII*, but in *1673* this order is reversed (see headnote to *Sonnet XII* p. 293 above).
Publication. 1673.

A book was writ of late called *Tetrachordon*;
And woven close, both matter, form and style;
The subject new: it walked the town awhile,
Numbering good intellects; now seldom pored on.
Cries the stall-reader, Bless us! what a word on
A title-page is this! And some in file
Stand spelling false, while one might walk to Mile-
End Green. Why is it harder sirs than Gordon,
Colkitto, or Macdonnel, or Galasp?

¶75. *1. A . . . writ*] *Trin. MS* (*a*): *I writ a book* ‵A book was writ′. For details of *Tetrachordon*'s publication, see headnote to *Sonnet XII* (p. 293). The name means 'four-stringed', and is a reference, as M.'s title-page explains, to 'The four chief places in Scripture, which treat of Marriage, or nullities in Marriage' (i.e. *Gen.* i 27–8 compared with ii 18, 23–4; *Deut.* xxiv 1–2; *Matt.* v 31–2 compared with *Matt.* xix 3–11; *1 Cor.* vii 10–6).
2. woven] *Trin. MS* (*a*): *weav'd it* ‵wov'n′.
3. The . . . walked] *Trin. MS* (*a*): *It went off well about* ‵The subject new; it walked′. Finley 71–2 compares Horace, *Epist.* I xx, where Horace addresses his book as if it were a prostitute gadding about.
4. Numbering] *OED* gives this as the first instance of the vb *number* in the sense 'to have (so many things or persons)'. *intellects; now*] *Trin. MS* (*a*): *wits; but* ‵intellects′ now *is.*
7. spelling false] misinterpreting.
7–8. Mile-End Green] Mile-End was at the first mile stone on the Roman road which left the city at Aldgate: to 'walk to Mile-End Green' is to walk to the outskirts of the city.
8. Gordon] There were several Gordons among Montrose's men: the most famous was George, Lord Gordon, eldest son of the Marquis of Huntly.
9. Colkitto, or Macdonnel] Montrose's lieutenant was called Alexander Macdonald. His father was Coll Keitache (a name abbreviated to Colkitto in the lowlands, and sometimes applied to the son). *Galasp*] George Gillespie, one of the leaders of the Scottish Covenant, and a member of the Westminster Assembly.

Those rugged names to our like mouths grow sleek
That would have made Quintilian stare and gasp.
Thy age, like ours, O soul of Sir John Cheke,
Hated not learning worse than toad or asp;
When thou taught'st Cambridge, and King
Edward Greek.

76 Psalms lxxx-lxxxviii

Date. Apr. 1648. This date heads M.'s translations in *1673*.
Publication. *1673*.
Modern criticism. Masson i 243 believed that M. was prompted to translate these psalms in 1648 by the current controversy over the metrical psalter – the Commons preferred the version of Francis Rous (1641, revised 1646) and the Lords that of William Barton (1644). M.'s metre, accordingly, is Common Measure, like Rous's except that Rous rhymes second and fourth lines, M. first and third.

E. C. Baldwin, *MP* xvii (1919) 457–63, criticising the translations from the viewpoint of the original Hebrew, concluded that M.'s heading implied

10. rugged] *Trin. MS* (*a*): *barbarous* ˋ*rough-hewn*' ˋrugged'. *like*] 'rugged' also. W. F. Smith, *N & Q* ii (1916) 7, connects this line with the English proverb 'Like lips like lettuce' and its Latin equivalent *similes habent labra latuces* which Jerome interprets (*Ad Chromatium*) in the light of the anecdote about M. Crassus (Cicero, *De Finibus* v 92) – that he laughed only once in his life, and that was when he saw an ass eating thistles instead of lettuces because they matched his mouth better.
11. Quintilian] In his discussion of 'barbarisms' *Quintilian* I v 8 includes the use of foreign words, and cites examples.
12. Sir John Cheke] Cheke (1514–57) was the first Professor of Greek at Cambridge, and one of the most famous English humanists: tutor to Edward VI. Masson iii 283 took 'like ours' to mean 'your age did not hate learning *as ours does*'. Smart 73–4, however, paraphrases 'Many men in that age (which has been thought so propitious to such studies), *hated not learning worse than toad or asp*–but as much as they hated either'. In support of this interpretation he quotes from Cheke's *De Pronuntiatione Graecae* (1555) some remarks about general opposition to the growth of Greek studies. H. Schultz, *MLN* lxix (1954) 495–7, agrees with Smart, adding that in 1641 Langbaine's reissue of Cheke's *The True Subject* set the latter's learning off against a background of contemporary obscurantism. J. M. French, *MLN* lxx (1955) 404–5, favours Masson's reading, calling attention to *Tetrachordon* itself, where M. refers to the reign of Edward VI as 'on record for the purest and sincerest that ever shon yet on the reformation of this Iland' (Columbia iv 231, Yale ii 716).

a more literal rendering than he had attained, and that his knowledge of Hebrew was deficient. Baldwin found M.'s versions overlong, and pointed to the frequent use of synonyms, the tendency to substitute the vaguely generic for the concrete (e.g. lxxxi *43–4* means literally 'Open thy mouth wide and I will fill it'), and the weak conventionality of many of the words – especially the adjectives – M. italicizes as insertions (e.g. lxxx *5*, *36*, *53* etc.). Moreover there are more insertions than the italics would suggest (e.g. lxxxvii *21–4* contain nine words with no equivalent in the Hebrew, and in lxxxv *14* 'and us restore' is not in the original). Baldwin thought the Vulgate responsible for some of M.'s errors (e.g. lxxxiii *49* 'wheel' should be 'that which is blown along by the wind' (i.e. dust or chaff), but the Vulgate has *rotam*).

M. H. Studley, *PQ* iv (1925) 364–72, attempting a defence against Baldwin, suggests that M. was following the traditional phraseology of English metrical translations (which were very numerous) rather than the Hebrew: this might explain his tendency to expansion and generalization of the concrete (e.g. at lxxxi *43–4*, which Baldwin specifies, George Wither's translation (1632) reads 'And will thy largest asking give'). M. chose lxxx–lxxxviii, thinks Studley, because these psalms express the need of the church for God's guidance: his translations thus parallel his controversial pamphlets.

H. F. Fletcher, *M.'s Semitic Studies* (Chicago 1926) pp. 97–110, agrees that M. often depended upon previous metrical renderings – not, however, because his Hebrew was deficient, but because of his difficulty in writing strict Common Measure. Fletcher demonstrates his point by a detailed comparison of lxxxii with the Hebrew original: e.g. at lxxxii *2* the Hebrew has 'assembly of God': M. realizes his 'kings and lordly states' are not there, and so italicizes: but Tremellius had *magistratus*, the Great Bible (1539) 'prynces', the A.V. 'the mighty', Buchanan's Latin metrical version (1566) 'reges', and Sternhold and Hopkins 'men of might'. M. is following a tradition of translation.

Comparison of M.'s versions with earlier ones has been taken furthest by W. B. Hunter Jr, *PQ* xxviii (1949) 125–44 and xl (1961) 485–93, who finds that about half the lines in these nine psalms can be matched from other psalters: quatrains in which no parallels can be found are rare (e.g. lxxx 10–11; lxxxi 4–5, 7, 9, 15; lxxxii 1–2, 4). Psalters which most frequently parallel M. are: Sternhold and Hopkins (1562), Ainsworth (1612), Dod (1620), the so-called 'King James' version' (1636), the *Bay Psalm Book* (1640), Barton (1644), Westminster (i.e. Rous) (1646), and Boyd (1648). Because of his expansions M.'s versions are usually much longer than those in other psalters, except Sternhold and Hopkins.

Developing Masson's point (above) Hunter observes that the Westminster Assembly appointed a committee to revise Rous's version in Jul. 1647, that this committee was reconstituted in Apr. 1648 (the month of M.'s translations), and that for the purposes of committee-work the psalms were divided into four sections, of which the third began at lxxx (M.'s starting-point).

M.'s notes (included in the footnotes below) supply the original Heb., or a literal translation of it, at points where his own translation expands or paraphrases.

Nine of the Psalms done into metre, wherein all but what is in a different character, are the very words of the text, translated from the original.

PSALM lxxx

1 Thou shepherd that dost Israel *keep*
Give ear *in time of need*,
Who leadest like a flock of sheep
Thy loved Joseph's seed,
That sitt'st between the Cherubs *bright*
Between their wings outspread
Shine forth, *and from thy cloud give light*,
And on our foes thy dread
2 In Ephraim's view and Benjamin's,
And in Manasseh's sight
Awake thy strength, come, and *be seen*
To save us *by thy might*.
3 Turn us again, *thy grace divine*
To us O God *vouchsafe*;
Cause thou thy face on us to shine
And then we shall be safe.
4 Lord God of Hosts, how long wilt thou,
How long wilt thou declare
Thy smoking wrath, *and angry brow*
Against thy people's prayer.
5 Thou feed'st them with the bread of tears,
Their bread with tears they eat,
And mak'st them largely drink the tears
Wherewith their cheeks are wet.
6 A strife thou mak'st us *and a prey*
To every neighbour foe,
Among themselves they laugh, they play,
And flouts at us they throw
7 Return us, *and thy grace divine*,
O God of Hosts *vouchsafe*

¶ 76. lxxx *6*. M.'s insertion alludes to the ark of the covenant, which had two golden cherubs kneeling, with their wings meeting above (*Exod*. xxv 18–22).

lxxx *11*. *Awake*] '*Gnorera*' (M.): lit. 'arouse'.

lxxx *18–19*. *declare / Thy smoking wrath*] '*Gnashanta*' (M.): lit. 'smoke'.

lxxx *23*. *largely*] '*Shalish*' (M.): lit. 'third of a measure'.

lxxx 27–8. *laugh . . . play . . . flouts . . . throw*] '*Jilnagu*' (M.): lit. 'mock'.

Cause thou thy face on us to shine,
And then we shall be safe.
8 A vine from Egypt thou hast brought,
Thy free love made it thine,
And drov'st out nations *proud and haught*
To plant this *lovely* vine.
9 Thou didst prepare for it a place
And root it deep and fast
That it *began to grow apace,*
And filled the land *at last.*
10 With her *green* shade *that* covered *all,*
The hills were *overspread*
Her boughs as *high as* cedars tall
Advanced their lofty head.
11 Her branches *on the western side*
Down to the sea she sent,
And *upward* to that river *wide*
Her other branches *went.*
12 Why hast thou laid her hedges low
And broken down her fence,
That all may pluck her, as they go,
With rudest violence?
13 The *tusked* boar out of the wood
Upturns it by the roots,
Wild beasts there browse, and make their food
Her grapes and tender shoots.
14 Return now, God of Hosts, look down
From heaven, thy seat divine,
Behold *us, but without a frown,*
And visit this *thy* vine.
15 Visit this vine, which thy right hand
Hath set, and planted *long,*
And the young branch, that for thyself
Thou hast made firm and strong.
16 But now it is consumed with fire,
And cut *with axes* down,
They perish at thy dreadful ire,
At thy rebuke and frown.
17 Upon the man of thy right hand
Let thy *good* hand be *laid,*
Upon the Son of Man, whom thou
Strong for thyself hast made.
18 So shall we not go back from thee
To ways of sin and shame,

lxxx *35. proud and haught*] Echoing *Rich. III* II iii 28: 'haught and proud'.

Quicken us thou, then *gladly* we
Shall call upon thy name.
Return us, *and thy grace divine*
Lord God of Hosts *vouchsafe*,
Cause thou thy face on us to shine,
And then we shall be safe.

PSALM lxxxi

1 To God our strength sing loud, *and clear*
Sing loud to God *our King*,
To Jacob's God, *that all may hear*
Loud acclamations ring.
2 Prepare a hymn, prepare a song
The timbrel hither bring
The *cheerful* psaltery bring along
And harp *with* pleasant *string*,
3 Blow, *as is wont*, in the new moon
With trumpets' *lofty sound*,
The appointed time, the day whereon
Our solemn feast *comes round*.
4 This was a statute *given of old*
For Israel *to observe*
A law of Jacob's God, *to hold*
From whence they might not swerve.
5 This he a testimony ordained
In Joseph, *not to change*,
When as he passed through Egypt land;
The tongue I heard, was strange.
6 From burden, *and from slavish toil*
I set his shoulder free;
His hands from pots, *and miry soil*
Delivered were *by me*.
7 When trouble did thee sore assail,
On me then didst thou call,
And I to free thee *did not fail*,
And led thee out of thrall.
I answered thee in thunder deep
With clouds encompassed round:
I tried thee at the water *steep*
Of Meriba *renowned*.
8 Hear O my people, *hearken well*,
I testify to thee
Thou ancient flock of Israel,
If thou wilt list to me,

lxxxi 29. *in thunder deep*] '*Besether ragnam*' (M.): lit. 'in the secret of thunder'.

9 Throughout the land of thy abode
No alien god shall be
Nor shalt thou to a foreign god
In honour bend thy knee.
10 I am the Lord thy God which brought
Thee out of Egypt land
Ask large enough, and I, *besought*,
Will grant thy full demand.
11 And yet my people would not *hear*,
Nor hearken to my voice;
And Israel *whom I loved so dear*
Misliked me for his choice.
12 Then did I leave them to their will
And to their wandering mind;
Their own conceits they followed still
Their own devices blind.
13 O that my people would *be wise*
To serve me *all their days*,
And O that Israel would *advise*
To walk my *righteous* ways.
14 Then would I soon bring down their foes
That now so proudly rise,
And turn my hand against *all those*
That are their enemies.
15 Who hate the Lord should *then be fain*
To bow to him and bend,
But *they, his people, should remain*,
Their time should have no end.
16 And we would feed them *from the shock*
With flour of finest wheat,
And satisfy them from the rock
With honey *for their meat*.

PSALM lxxxii

1 God in the great assembly stands
Of kings and lordly states,
Among the gods on both his hands
He judges and debates.
2 How long will ye pervert the right
With judgment false and wrong

lxxxii *1. great assembly*] '*Bagnadath-el*' (M.): lit. 'assembly of God'.
lxxxii *3. Among . . . on both his hands*] '*Bekerev*' (M.): lit. 'in the midst of'.
lxxxii *5–6. pervert the right / With judgment false and wrong*] '*Tishphetu gnavel*' (M.): lit. 'judge falsely'.

Favouring the wicked *by your might*
Who thence grow bold and strong.
3 Regard the weak and fatherless
Despatch the poor man's cause,
And raise the man in deep distress
By just and equal laws.
4 Defend the poor and desolate,
And rescue from the hands
Of wicked men the low estate
Of him *that help demands.*
5 They know not nor will understand,
In darkness they walk on
The earth's foundations all are moved
And out of order gone.
6 I said that ye were gods, yea all
The sons of God most high
7 But ye shall die like men, and fall
As other princes *die.*
8 Rise God, judge thou the earth *in might,*
This *wicked* earth redress,
For thou art he who shalt by right
The nations all possess.

PSALM lxxxiii

1 Be not thou silent *now at length*
O God hold not thy peace,
Sit not thou still O God of *strength*
We cry and do not cease.
2 For lo thy *furious* foes *now* swell
And storm outrageously,

lxxxii *9–10. Regard the weak . . . / Despatch the poor man's cause*] '*Shiphtu-dal*' (M.): lit. 'judge the poor'.
lxxxii *11–12. raise . . . / By just and equal laws*] '*Hatzdiku*' (M.): lit. 'justify'.
lxxxii *19–20. are moved / And out of order gone*] '*Jimmotu*' (M.): lit. 'slip'.
lxxxii *24. As other*] E. C. Baldwin, *MP* xvii (1919) 101, points out that M. has here mistaken the Hebrew word meaning 'one' for the closely similar word meaning 'other'. But H. F. Fletcher (see headnote) produces several previous translations which make a similar mistake (e.g. Tremellius: *sicut unus aliorum principum*; Geneva Bible: 'like others'; Bishops' Bible: 'as others do'; Diodati's Italian version–to which M. refers in *Tetrachordon*: *come qualunque altro de' principi*).
lxxxii. *25–6. judge . . . redress*] '*Shophta*' (M.): lit. 'judge'.
lxxxiii *5–6. swell . . . storm outrageously*] '*Jehemajun*' (M.): lit. 'are in tumult'.

And they that hate thee *proud and fell*
Exalt their heads full high.
3 Against thy people they contrive
Their plots and counsels deep,
Them to ensnare they chiefly strive
Whom thou dost hide and keep.
4 Come let us cut them off say they,
Till they no nation be
That Israel's name for ever may
Be lost in memory.
5 For they consult with all their might,
And all as one in mind
Themselves against thee they unite
And in firm union bind.
6 The tents of Edom, and the brood
Of *scornful* Ishmael,
Moab, with them of Hagar's blood
That in the desert dwell,
7 Gebal and Ammon *there conspire,*
And *hateful* Amalek,
The Philistims, and they of Tyre
Whose bounds the sea doth check.
8 With them *great* Ashur also bands
And doth confirm the knot
All these have lent their armed hands
To aid the sons of Lot.
9 Do to them as to Midian *bold*
That wasted all the coast
To Sisera, and as *is told*
Thou didst to Jabin's *host,*
When at the brook of Kishon *old*
They were repulsed and slain,
10 At Endor quite cut off, and rolled
As dung upon the plain.

lxxxiii *9–10. contrive / Their plots and counsels deep*] '*Jagnarimu Sod*' (M.): lit. 'devise cunning counsel'.
xxxiii *11. to ensnare . . . chiefly strive*] '*Jithjagnatsu gnal*' (M.): lit. 'conspire against'.
lxxxiii *11–12. Them . . . / Whom thou dost hide and keep*] '*Tsephuneca*' (M.): lit. 'stored-up things'.
lxxxiii *17. with all their might*] '*Lev jachdau*' (M.): lit. 'with heart together'.
lxxxiii *22. scornful*] Cp. *Gen.* xxi 9: 'mocking'.
lxxxiii *24.* Cp. *Gen.* xxi 20: 'He grew, and dwelt in the wilderness'.
lxxxiii *26. hateful*] Cp. *Deut.* xxv 17–19.
lxxxiii *28.* Cp. *Ezek.* xxvii 4: 'Thy borders are in the midst of the seas'.
lxxxiii *37. old*] Cp. *Judges* v 21: 'that ancient river, the river Kishon'.

11 As Zeb and Oreb evil sped
So let their princes speed
As Zeba, and Zalmunna *bled*
So let their princes *bleed*.
12 *For they amidst their pride* have said
By right now shall we seize
God's houses, and *will now invade*
Their stately palaces.
13 My God, O make them as a wheel
No quiet let them find,
Giddy and *restless* let *them reel*
Like stubble from the wind.
14 As *when* an *aged* wood takes fire
Which on a sudden strays,
The *greedy* flame runs higher and higher
Till all the mountains blaze,
15 So with thy whirlwind them pursue,
And with thy tempest chase;
16 And till they yield thee honour due;
Lord fill with shame their face.
17 Ashamed and troubled let them be,
Troubled and shamed for ever,
Ever confounded, and so die
With shame, *and 'scape it never*.
18 Then shall they know that thou whose name
Jehovah is alone,
Art the Most High, *and thou the same*
O'er all the earth *art One*.

PSALM lxxxiv

1 How lovely are thy dwellings fair!
O Lord of Hosts, how dear
The *pleasant* tabernacles are!
Where thou dost dwell so near.
2 My soul doth long and almost die
Thy courts O Lord to see,
My heart and flesh aloud do cry,
O living God, for thee.
3 There even the sparrow *freed from wrong*
Hath found a house of *rest*,

lxxxiii *47–48. God's houses . . . / Their stately palaces*] '*Neoth Elohim bears both*' (M.): meaning that the single Heb. expression can be translated by either of these English phrases. *Neoth* strictly means 'pastures', hence 'dwellings'.
lxxxiii *59. they yield thee honour*] '*They seek thy Name* Heb.' (M.).

The swallow there, to lay her young
Hath built her *brooding* nest,
Even *by* thy altars Lord of Hosts
They find their safe abode,
And home they fly from round the coasts
Toward thee, my King, my God.
4 Happy, who in thy house reside
Where thee they ever praise,
5 Happy, whose strength in thee doth bide,
And in their hearts thy ways.
6 They pass through Baca's *thirsty* vale,
That dry and barren ground
As through a fruitful wat'ry dale
Where springs and showers abound.
7 They journey on from strength to strength
With joy and gladsome cheer
Till all before *our* God *at length*
In Sion do appear.
8 Lord God of Hosts hear *now* my prayer
O Jacob's God give ear,
9 Thou God our shield look on the face
Of thy anointed *dear.*
10 For one day in thy courts *to be*
Is better, *and more blest*
Than *in the joys of vanity,*
A thousand days *at best.*
I in the temple of my God
Had rather keep a door,
Than dwell in tents, *and rich abode*
With sin *for evermore.*
11 For God the Lord both sun and shield
Gives grace and glory *bright,*
No good from them shall be withheld
Whose ways are just and right.
12 Lord *God* of Hosts *that reign'st on high,*
That man is *truly* blest,
Who *only* on thee doth rely,
And in thee only rest.

PSALM lxxxv

1 Thy land to favour graciously
Thou hast not Lord been slack,
Thou hast from *hard* captivity
Returned Jacob back.
2 The iniquity thou didst forgive
That wrought thy people woe,

And all their sin, *that did thee grieve*
Hast hid *where none shall know.*
3 Thine anger all thou hadst removed,
And *calmly* didst return
From thy fierce wrath which we had proved
Far worse than fire to burn.
4 God of our saving health and peace,
Turn us, and us restore,
Thine indignation cause to cease
Toward us, *and chide no more.*
5 Wilt thou be angry without end,
For ever angry thus
Wilt thou thy frowning ire extend
From age to age on us?
6 Wilt thou not turn, and *hear our voice*
And us again revive,
That so thy people may rejoice
By thee preserved alive.
7 Cause us to see thy goodness Lord,
To us thy mercy shew
Thy saving health to us afford
And life in us renew.
8 *And now* what God the Lord will speak
I will *go straight and* hear,
For to his people he speaks peace
And to his saints *full dear,*
To his dear saints he will speak peace,
But let them never more
Return to folly, *but surcease*
To trespass as before.
9 Surely to such as do him fear
Salvation is at hand
And glory shall *ere long appear*
To dwell within our land.
10 Mercy and Truth *that long were missed*
Now *joyfully* are met
Sweet Peace and Righteousness have kissed
And hand in hand are set.
11 Truth from the earth *like to a flower*
Shall bud and blossom *then,*
And Justice from her heavenly bower
Look down *on mortal men.*

lxxxv *11. thy fierce wrath*] 'Heb. *The burning heat of thy wrath*' (M.).
lxxxv *21–2. turn, and . . . us again revive*] 'Heb. *Turn to quicken us*' (M.).

12 The Lord will also then bestow
Whatever thing is good
Our land shall forth in plenty throw
Her fruits *to be our food.*
13 Before him Righteousness shall go
His royal harbinger,
Then will he come, and not be slow
His footsteps cannot err.

PSALM lxxxvi

1 Thy *gracious* ear, O Lord, incline,
O hear me *I thee pray,*
For I am poor, and almost pine
With need, *and sad decay.*
2 Preserve my soul, for I have trod
Thy ways, and love the just,
Save thou thy servant O my God
Who *still* in thee doth trust.
3 Pity me Lord for daily thee
I call; 4 O make rejoice
Thy servant's soul; for Lord to thee
I lift my soul *and voice,*
5 For thou art good, thou Lord art prone
To pardon, thou to all
Art full of mercy, thou *alone*
To them that on thee call.
6 Unto my supplication Lord
Give ear, and to the cry
Of my *incessant* prayers afford
Thy hearing graciously.
7 I in the day of my distress
Will call on thee *for aid;*
For thou wilt *grant* me *free access*
And answer, *what I prayed.*

lxxxv *54–5.* E. C. Baldwin, MP xvii (1919) 101, comments that M. has not realized that 'Righteousness', a masculine noun, is the subject of the verb in the second half of the parallelism as well as in the first.
lxxxv *55–6. Then will he come, and not be slow / His footsteps cannot err.*] 'Heb. *He will set his steps to the way*' (M.).
lxxxvi 5–6. *I have trod / Thy ways, and love the just*] 'Heb. *I am good, loving, a doer of good and holy things*' (M.). The Heb. term, which M. expands, can be literally translated in any one of the three ways he suggests in his note.

8 Like thee among the gods is none
O Lord, nor any works
Of all that other gods have done
Like to thy *glorious* works.
9 The nations all whom thou hast made
Shall come, *and all shall frame*
To bow them low before thee Lord,
And glorify thy name.
10 For great thou art, and wonders great
By thy strong hand are done,
Thou *in thy everlasting seat*
Remainest God alone.
11 Teach me O Lord thy way *most right*,
I in thy truth will bide,
To fear thy name my heart unite
So shall it never slide
12 Thee will I praise O Lord my God
Thee honour, and adore
With my whole heart, and blaze abroad
Thy name for evermore.
13 For great thy mercy is toward me,
And thou hast freed my soul
Even from the lowest hell set free
From deepest darkness foul.
14 O God the proud against me rise
And violent men are met
To seek my life, and in their eyes
No fear of thee have set.
15 But thou Lord art the God most mild
Readiest thy grace to shew,
Slow to be angry, and *art styled*
Most merciful, most true.
16 O turn to me *thy face at length*,
And me have mercy on,
Unto thy servant give thy strength,
And save thy handmaid's son.
17 Some sign of good to me afford,
And let my foes *then* see
And be ashamed, because thou Lord
Dost help and comfort me.

PSALM lxxxvii

1 Among the holy mountains *high*
Is his foundation fast,
There seated in his sanctuary,
His temple there is placed.

2 Sion's *fair* gates the Lord loves more
Than all the dwellings *fair*
Of Jacob's *land, though there be store,*
And all within his care.
3 City of God, most glorious things
Of thee *abroad* are spoke;
4 I mention Egypt, *where proud kings*
Did our forefathers yoke,
I mention Babel to my friends,
Philistia *full of scorn,*
And Tyre with Ethiop's *utmost ends,*
Lo this man there was born:
5 But *twice that praise shall in our ear*
Be said of Sion *last*
This and this man was born in her,
High God shall fix her fast.
6 The Lord shall write it in a scroll
That ne'er shall be out-worn
When he the nations doth enrol
That this man there was born.
7 Both they who sing, and they who dance
With sacred songs are there,
In thee *fresh brooks, and soft streams glance*
And all my fountains *clear.*

PSALM lxxxviii

1 Lord God that dost me save and keep,
All day to thee I cry;
And all night long, before thee *weep*
Before thee *prostrate lie.*
2 Into thy presence let my prayer
With sighs devout ascend
And to my cries, that *ceaseless are,*
Thine ear with favour bend.
3 For cloyed with woes and trouble store
Surcharged my soul doth lie,
My life *at death's uncheerful door*
Unto the grave draws nigh.
4 Reckoned I am with them that pass
Down to the *dismal* pit
I am a man, but weak alas
And for that name unfit.
5 From life discharged and parted quite
Among the dead *to sleep,*

lxxxviii 15. *a man, but weak . . . And for that name unfit*] 'Heb. *A man without manly strength*' (M.).

And like the slain *in bloody fight*
That in the grave lie *deep*.
Whom thou rememberest no more,
Dost never more regard,
Them from thy hand delivered o'er
Death's hideous house hath barred.
6 Thou in the lowest pit *profound*
Hast set me *all forlorn*,
Where thickest darkness *hovers round*,
In horrid deeps *to mourn*.
7 Thy wrath *from which no shelter saves*
Full sore doth press on me;
Thou break'st upon me all thy waves,
And all thy waves break me.
8 Thou dost my friends from me estrange,
And mak'st me odious,
Me to them odious, *for they change*,
And I here pent up thus.
9 Through sorrow, and affliction great
Mine eye grows dim and dead,
Lord all the day I thee entreat,
My hands to thee I spread.
10 Wilt thou do wonders on the dead,
Shall the deceased arise
And praise thee *from their loathsome bed*
With pale and hollow eyes?
11 Shall they thy loving-kindness tell
On whom the grave *hath hold*,
Or they *who* in perdition *dwell*
Thy faithfulness *unfold*?
12 In darkness can thy mighty *hand*
Or wondrous acts be known,
Thy justice in the *gloomy* land
Of *dark* oblivion?
13 But I to thee O Lord do cry
Ere yet my life be spent,
And *up to thee* my prayer *doth hie*
Each morn, and thee prevent.
14 Why wilt thou Lord my soul forsake,
And hide thy face from me,
15 That am already bruised, and shake

lxxxviii *31–2. Thou break'st upon me all thy waves, / And all thy waves break me*] '*The* Heb. *bears both*' (M.). M.'s note suggests that either line would be a correct translation of the Heb. In fact, only the first would.

lxxxviii *59. shake*] 'Heb. *Prae Concussione*' (M.). The meaning of the Heb.

With terror sent from thee;
Bruised, and afflicted and *so low*
As ready to expire,
While I thy terrors undergo
Astonished with thine ire.
16 Thy fierce wrath over me doth flow
Thy threat'nings cut me through.
17 All day they round about me go,
Like waves they me pursue.
18 Lover and friend thou hast removed
And severed from me far.
They *fly me now* whom I have loved,
And as in darkness are.

77 On the Lord General Fairfax at the siege of Colchester

Date. Aug. 1648. After defeating the Kentish Royalists at Maidstone (2 Jun. 1648) Fairfax laid siege to Colchester (13 Jun.). The town fell on 27 Aug. Of the Royalist leaders Sir Charles Lucas and Sir George Lisle were immediately shot after trial by court-martial, and the Earl of Norwich and Lord Capel were left to the mercy of Parliament; Capel was subsequently executed. The military career of Sir Thomas Fairfax up to 1648 had been a brilliant one. In Jan. 1643 he recaptured Leeds, and in May took Wakefield. With Cromwell he was victorious at Winceby in Oct., and in Jan. 1644 he defeated Lord Byron at Nantwich. In Mar. he returned to Yorkshire and was victorious at Selby: at Marston Moor (Jul.) he commanded the Parliamentarian right wing. In Jan. 1645 he was made Commander-in-chief of the New Model Army, and on 14 Jun. inflicted a crippling defeat on the King at Naseby, where he behaved with reckless courage and captured a Royalist standard with his own hands. He went on to recapture Leicester, defeat Goring at Langport (10 Jul.), and take Bridgwater (24 Jul.) and Bristol (10 Sep.). In the campaign of 1646 he defeated Hopton at Torrington and took Exeter (9 Apr.) and Oxford (20 Jun.). M.'s hope that Fairfax might take over the management of peacetime affairs was not realised: after the execution of the King, of which he disapproved, he resigned his Commandership (25 Jun. 1650) and retired to his seat, Nun Appleton, Yorkshire. M. includes a long eulogy of him in the *Defensio Secunda* (Columbia viii 216–19).
Publication. Fairfax was never printed by M. It first appeared in the *Letters of State* edited by Edward Phillips in 1694. Phillips' text (Fletcher[3] i 372)

is disputed. M. brings out one of the meanings of the Heb. root, 'shaking' (Lat. *concussio*). Another meaning is 'boyhood', hence the A.V. translation 'from my youth up'.

differs in several respects from the fair copy in M.'s hand in the *Trin. MS* (which the present text follows): *1694* verbal variants are indicated in the notes. *Modern criticism.* Finley considers this and M.'s other sonnets of the period, particularly *Cromwell* and *Vane*, eminently Horatian in tone and spirit. He compares ll. *3–4* with Horace's repeated enumerations of foreign peoples (e.g. *Odes* I xxxv 9–12, II xx 13–20), and l. *7* with Horace's hydra reference (IV iv 61–2).

Fairfax, whose name in arms through Europe rings
Filling each mouth with envy, or with praise,
And all her jealous monarchs with amaze,
And rumours loud, that daunt remotest kings,
Thy firm unshaken virtue ever brings
Victory home, though new rebellions raise
Their hydra heads, and the false North displays
Her broken league, to imp their serpent wings,
O yet a nobler task awaits thy hand;
For what can war, but endless war still breed,

¶ 77. *2. Filling each mouth*] *1694*: And fills all mouths.
4. that] *1694*: which.
5. virtue] *1694*: valour. M. is using 'virtue' in the Latin sense, meaning 'courage'.
6. though] *1694*: while.
6–7. new rebellions . . . heads] The hydra had nine heads: it was one of Hercules' labours to destroy it, and he did so with the aid of Iolaus who held a lighted torch to the stump when Hercules cut a head off, to stop it growing again. The rebellions are hydra-headed in that they break out in several regions: there were Royalist risings in S. Wales and Kent, and the Scots invaded from the north.
7. false North] The Scots, having come to an understanding with Charles, invaded England in violation of the Solemn League and Covenant. They were defeated by Cromwell at Preston (17 Aug. 1648). Smart 84 takes the present tense ('displays') as an indication that *Fairfax* was written before this date.
8. imp] When a falcon had broken wing-feathers its flight was impaired, and new feathers were therefore fixed to the stumps of the old to remedy the loss: this process was called 'imping'. *their*] *1694*: her. J. T. Shawcross, *N & Q* cc (1955) 195–6, wishes to read 'her', claiming that in *Trin. MS* 'her' has been altered to 'their' by some hand other than M.'s. The 'e' and the 'r' of the word, however, seem too far apart to allow this theory.
10. war, but endless] *1694*: war, but acts of. Shawcross (see note to l. 8) claims that the reading should be 'wars but endless'. What appears to be a comma after 'war' in *Trin. MS* is in fact, he says, the bottom part of an 's', of which the top part is still visible on the end of the 'r'. He is unable, however, to

Till truth, and right from violence be freed,
And public faith cleared from the shameful brand
Of public fraud. In vain doth valour bleed
While avarice, and rapine share the land.

78 Translation from 'Tenure of Kings and Magistrates'

Date. Feb. 1649. The pamphlet appeared 13 Feb., a fortnight after Charles' execution, which it defended. The translation is from Seneca, *Hercules Furens* 922–4 *victima haud ulla amplior / potest magisque opima mactari Iovi / quam rex iniquus.*

There can be slain
No sacrifice to God more acceptable
Than an unjust and wicked king.

79 Translations from 'The History of Britain'

Date. Feb.–Mar. 1649. M. says in *Defensio Secunda* (Columbia viii 136–8) that before he was appointed Secretary for Foreign Tongues (13 Mar. 1649) he had finished four books of his *History*. He seems to imply, in the same place, that he began the *History* only after writing *Tenure of Kings and Magistrates* (published 13 Feb. 1649). He had, of course, been collecting material

produce another example of 'r' and 's' joined in M.'s hand where the top of the 's' resembles the mark at the end of the 'r' in 'war' to which he refers.
11. truth, and right] *1694*: injured truth.
12. cleared . . . shameful] *1694*: be rescued from the.
13–4. The financial chaos under the Long Parliament (with Royalist estates changing hands at bargain prices) is denounced by M. in *History of Britain* (Columbia x 319–20): 'Straite every one betooke himself, setting the commonwealth behinde and his private ends before, to doe as his own profit

for some time. French ii 214 quotes from Samuel Hartlib's notebook for 1648: 'Milton is . . . writing a Univ. History of Engl.'
Publication. 1670.
(i) and (ii) are from Geoffrey of Monmouth, *History* I xi [Brutus' prayer to Diana] *Diva potens nemorum, terror silvestribus apris: / Cui licet amfractus ire per aethereos, / Infernasque domos: terrestria iura resolve, / Et dic quas terras nos habitare velis? / Dic certam sedem qua te venerabor in aevum, / Qua tibi virgineis templa dicabo choris?* [and Diana's reply] *Brute sub occasum solis trans Gallica regna / Insula in Oceano est undique clausa mari: / Insula in Oceano est habitata gigantibus olim, / Nunc deserta quidem: gentibus apta tuis. / Hanc pete, namque tibi sedes erit illa perennis: / Sic fiet natis altera Troia tuis: / Sic de prole tua reges nascentur: et ipsis / Totius terrae subditus orbis erit.*
(iii) In the *Flores Historiarum*, under A.D. 821, the story is told of the murder of young Kenelm. The location of his body, it is said, was announced miraculously by a dove which appeared over the altar of St Peter's in Rome carrying a message *In clenc cu beche Kenelm cunebearn lith under thorne haudes bereafed.* This the *Flores* translates into Latin as *In pastura vaccarum Kenelmus regis filius iacet sub spina, capite privatus,* and a couplet version is added (which M. here translates) attributed in the margin to Abbot John de Cella *In clenc sub spina iacet in convalle bovina, / Vertice privatus, Kenelmus rege creatus.*

(i) Goddess of shades, and huntress, who at will
Walk'st on the rolling sphere, and through the deep,
On thy third reign the earth look now, and tell
What land, what seat of rest thou bidd'st me seek,
What certain seat, where I may worship thee
For ay, with temples vowed, and virgin choirs.

(ii) Brutus far to the west, in the ocean wide
Beyond the realm of Gaul, a land there lies,
Sea-girt it lies, where giants dwelt of old,
Now void, it fits thy people; thither bend
Thy course, there shalt thou find a lasting seat,
There to thy sons another Troy shall rise,
And kings be born of thee, whose dreaded might
Shall awe the world, and conquer nations bold.

(iii) Low in a mead of kine under a thorn,
Of head bereft li'th poor Kenelm king-born.

or ambition led him. Then was justice delai'd & soone after deny'd, spite and favour determin'd all . . . ev'ry where wrong & oppression, foule and dishonest things commited daylie . . . Some who had bin call'd from shops & warehouses without other merit to sit in supreme councels & committies, as thir breeding was, fell to hucster the common-wealth.'

80 Epigram from *Defensio Pro Populo Anglicano*

Date. 1650. M.'s *Defensio* was entered in the Stationers' Register 31 Dec. 1650. It was a reply to the *Defensio Regia Pro Carolo I*, published in Holland (1649), which the English Royalists had employed Claude de Saumaise (1588–1653), one of the greatest classical scholars of the seventeenth century, to write. In his *Defensio* (Columbia vii 428–9) M. mocks at Saumaise's misuse of English terms in the *Defensio Regia*, and adds this epigram (an adaptation of Persius, *Prologue* 8–14 'Who was it that made the parrot so glib with his "Good morning"?...'), with the words and phrases which are copied exactly from Persius italicized.
Publication. 24 Feb. 1651.

Quis expedivit Salmasio suam Hundredam,
Picamque *docuit verba nostra conari?*
Magister artis venter, et Iacobei
Centum, exulantis viscera marsupii regis.
Quod si dolosi spes refulserit nummi,
Ipse Antichristi qui modo primatum Papae
Minatus uno est dissipare sufflatu,
Cantabit ultro Cardinalitium *melos*.

Who was it made Saumaise so glib with his 'hundreda',[1] and taught that magpie to try our words? His stomach was his schoolmaster–that, and the hundred Jacobuses[3] which were the vitals of the exiled king's purse. If hope of turning a dishonest penny so much as glimmers he–who[6] recently threatened to shatter the supremacy of the Pope, the Antichrist, with a single puff[7]–will willingly sing the Cardinals' tune.

81 To the Lord General Cromwell

Date. May 1652. The sonnet appears in the Trinity MS in the hand of an amanuensis, headed 'To the Lord General Cromwell, May 1652. / On the

¶ 80 *1. Hundredam*] In *Defensio Regia* 204, Saumaise (*Salmasius*) gives the plural of 'Hundred' as 'Hundreda', a mistake not corrected in the *Errata*.
3–4. Iacobei / Centum] Charles II met the expenses of printing the *Defensio Regia*, and paid Saumaise £100. 'Jacobus' was a slang name for a coin first struck in 1603 and called officially the sovereign (worth 20s. originally and about 24s. by mid-seventeenth century).
6–7. Saumaise was a Protestant. His first publication (1608) was an edition of a work by a fourteenth-century bishop of Thessalonica, Nilus Cabasilas,

proposals of certain ministers 'at the Committee' for Propagation of the Gospel'. This committee, of which Cromwell was a member, had been appointed 10 Feb. 1652, to consider questions like the payment of ministers and limits of toleration. On 18 Feb. 1652 John Owen (formerly Cromwell's chaplain) and other Independent ministers laid certain proposals before it. They advocated an established church with clergy paid for by the state: dissenters were to be allowed freedom of worship so long as they did not promulgate doctrines contrary to fifteen fundamental tenets. Cromwell, however, was in favour of unlimited liberty of dissent. M. urges him away from establishment altogether: this would entail the union of civil and religious power ('secular chains'), which he always opposed, and a stipendiary clergy ('hireling wolves'). On 29 Apr. Parliament had resolved that the tithe system should be continued until the committee had evolved some other means of providing for the clergy: this resolve seemed to take it for granted that the clergy should be stipendiary, hence M.'s alarm. The text printed here follows the Trinity MS.
Publication. First printed in Phillips's *Letters of State* (1694) in a mangled form (see notes for *1694* readings, and headnote to *Fairfax*, p. 321).

Cromwell, our chief of men, who through a cloud
 Not of war only, but detractions rude,
 Guided by faith and matchless fortitude
 To peace and truth thy glorious way hast ploughed,
And on the neck of crowned fortune proud
 Hast reared God's trophies and his work pursued,
 While Darwen stream with blood of Scots imbrued,
 And Dunbar field resounds thy praises loud,

against the primacy of the Pope. This was republished in 1645 with an accompanying treatise by Saumaise himself, *De Primatu Papae*.
¶ 81. *1. who . . . cloud*] *1694*: that . . . crowd. M.'s 'cloud' echoes Virgil, *Aen.* x 809 *nubem belli*. Finley 48–9 compares this opening with Horace's addresses to Augustus (*Odes* IV v 1, 5; xiv 6).
2. detractions] *1694*: distractions.
5. crowned fortune] Refers to Charles I and to his successor whose army Cromwell defeated at Worcester after he had been crowned king in Scotland, 1 Jan. 1651.
5–6. And . . . pursued] *1694*: And fought God's battles, and his work pursued.
7. Darwen stream] *1694*: Darwent streams. The Darwen, in Lancashire, joins the Ribble near Preston where, 17–19 Aug. 1648, Cromwell, joining Lambert, routed the invading Scottish army under the Duke of Hamilton, destroying almost half of it.
7–9. Finley 60–1 comments on the Horatian quality of this list of victories, and compares *Odes* II ix 19–24.
8. Dunbar field] *Trin. MS*: *Dunbar field* 'Worcester's laureate wreath' [this

And Worcester's laureate wreath; yet much remains
To conquer still; peace hath her victories
No less renowned than war, new foes arise
Threatening to bind our souls with secular chains:
Help us to save free conscience from the paw
Of hireling wolves whose gospel is their maw.

82 To Sir Henry Vane the Younger

Date. Jun.–Jul. 1652. In George Sikes's *Life and Death of Sir Henry Vane* (1662) 93–4, M.'s sonnet is printed (reproduced Fletcher[3] i 368) together with the information that it was sent to Vane by M. 3 Jul. 1652.

In the Trinity MS the sonnet appears in the hand of an amanuensis, headed 'To Sir Henry Vane the Younger' (this title is crossed through and the figure '17' inserted above). Vane (1613–62), called 'the younger' because his father did not die until 1655, emigrated to New England in 1635 and became Governor of Massachusetts. Returning to England (1637) he became Treasurer of the Navy (1639): the successful issue of the Dutch war was largely due to his efficient administration. Elected a member of the Council of State (Feb. 1649), he was appointed (13 Mar.) to the committee to consider relations with other European powers; M., as secretary to this committee, learnt to respect his skill as a statesman. Vane, like M., was utterly opposed to an established church. He broke with Cromwell (1653) over the dissolution

correction is obviously erroneous: see next line]. At Dunbar, 3 Sep. 1650, Cromwell, after being virtually surrounded, routed the Scottish army under Leslie: 3,000 Scots fell and 10,000 were taken. *resounds*] *1694*: resound.
9. Worcester's . . . wreath] *Trin. MS*: *twenty battles more* `Worcester's laureate wreath' [this is obviously the correction for which that in 8 was an error]. At Worcester, 3 Sep. 1651, Cromwell virtually annihilated Charles II's Royalist Scottish army.
10–11. peace . . . war] Cp. Cicero, *De Officiis* I xxii 74: *Cum plerique arbitrentur res bellicas maiores esse quam urbanas vere autem si volumus iudicare, multae res extiterunt urbanae maiores clarioresque quam bellicae* (Most people think that the achievements of war are more important than those of peace... but there have been many instances of achievement in peace more important and no less renowned than in war), and M. in *Defensio Secunda*, addressing his countrymen (Columbia viii 240–1): 'If, after putting an end to war, you neglect the arts of peace; if war be your peace and liberty, war alone your virtue, your highest glory, you will find, believe me, that your greatest enemy is peace itself; peace itself will be by far your hardest warfare.'
11. renowned than] *1694*: than those of.

of the Long Parliament. Although he did not approve of the King's execution he was excluded from the Act of Indemnity and executed 14 Jan. 1662.

Publication. 1662 in Sikes's *Life* (see above): this is the text followed here. 1694 in Phillips's *Letters of State* (see headnote to *Fairfax*, p. 321); the Phillips text is very poor.

Vane, young in years, but in sage counsel old,
Than whom a better senator ne'er held
The helm of Rome, when gowns not arms repelled
The fierce Epirot and the African bold.
Whether to settle peace or to unfold
The drift of hollow states, hard to be spelled,
Then to advise how war may best, upheld,
Move by her two main nerves, iron and gold
In all her equipage: besides to know
Both spiritual power and civil, what each means,

¶ 82. *1. young in years*] Echoes Sylvester (Du Bartas 424): 'Isaac, in yeers yong, but in wisdom growen.' *counsel*] *Trin. MS*: counsel*s*.

3–4. gowns not arms] Cicero, *De Officiis* I xxii 77, quotes the dictum *cedant arma togae* when arguing in favour of civic rather than military virtues. The firmness of the senators in the face of constant defeat, and their refusal to allow the Romans captured by Hannibal at Cannae to be ransomed is described by Livy XXII lx–lxi 4–5. *Epirot*] Pyrrhus, King of Epirus. *African*] Hannibal.

6. drift] *Trin. MS*: drift*s*. *hollow*] a punning reference to Holland, 'hollow' because much of it is below sea-level, but also, implies M., 'hollow' in a moral sense. Ill-feeling between Holland and England was brought to a head 19 May 1652, when shots were exchanged between the English fleet under Blake and the Dutch fleet under Tromp in the Downs. The Dutch ambassadors remained in London, ostensibly to continue friendly relations but actually, it was believed in some quarters, for purposes of espionage. Vane was appointed (4 Jun.) to the committee to prepare an answer to the Dutch ambassadors. This answer, though not ruling out further negotiations, accused the Dutch of attempting to destroy the English fleet by surprise. The Dutch ambassadors withdrew, and war became inevitable.

8. by] *Trin. MS*: *on* 'on' 'by'. *nerves . . . gold*] Machiavelli, *Discourses* ii 10, argues that money is not the sinew of war (*Dico pertanto, non l'oro, come grida la comune opinione, essere il nervo della guerra*), but that iron is (*la guerra si faceva col ferro e non con l'oro*). M. notes this twice in his Commonplace Book (Columbia xviii 160, 212, Yale i 414–5, 498): Maurice Kelley, *Studies in Bibliography* iv (1951–2) 123–7, dates these Machiavelli notes between Nov. 1651 and Feb. 1652.

10. Trin. MS: *What power the Church and what the civil means* 'Both spiritual power and civil, what *it means* each means'.

10–11. Refers to Vane's support of disestablishment (see headnote).

What severs each, thou hast learned, which few
have done.
The bounds of either sword to thee we owe;
Therefore on thy firm hand Religion leans
In peace, and reckons thee her eldest son.

83 Sonnet XVI

Date. 1652? There is some doubt about the exact date. French iii 201 thinks 1652 likely, shortly after M. became totally blind (i.e. about 28 Feb., according to French). L. Kemp's theory, *Hopkins Review* vi (1952) 80–3, that the poem's subject is not blindness but loss of inspiration, and that it should be dated 1642, is ably countered by M. Kelley, *XVIIth-Century News* xi (1953) 29. Kelley himself, *MP* liv (1956) 20–5, favours mid or late 1655, on the evidence of the order of the later sonnets in *1673*, which he takes as chronological. W. R. Parker, *PMLA* lxxiii (1958) 196–200, questions this assumption. He argues that M. considered himself blind for all practical purposes in Nov. 1651, when he was forty-two years old. Since his father lived to be at least eighty-four (when, according to Aubrey, he could read without spectacles), 'Ere half my days' (*2*) may be a reference to M.'s age as compared with his father's. Parker thus dates the sonnet late 1651. Another explanation of 'Ere half my days' is offered by D. C. Dorian, *Explicator* x (1951) 16, who interprets 'days' as 'working days'–at forty-two M. was perhaps less than halfway through a working life. J. T. Shawcross, *N & Q* iv (1957) 442–6, dates Oct.–Nov. 1655, on the grounds that 'half my days is estimated with reference to *Isa.* lxv 20 ('an hundred years old'): this verse, however, is taken from a prophecy about the new Jerusalem, and relates to a future, not an actual state of affairs.
Publication. 1673
Modern criticism. J. L. Potter, *N & Q* iv (1957) 447, refers to Barnabe Barnes, *Divine Century of Spiritual Sonnets* (1595) xxvi and xxxviii to show that M. was not the first sonnetteer to use the parable of the talents (*Matt.* xxv 14–30) as a conceit.

11. Trin. MS: Thou *teachest best, which few have ever done* \`hast learnt well, a praise which few have won' \`What severs each thou' hast learnt, which few have do[ne]'.
12. either sword] i.e. civil and spiritual sword. In *Observations on the Articles of Peace* (Columbia vi 262) M. remarks that to extirpate 'Heresy, Schism, and prophaness' 'can be no work of the Civil sword, but of the spirituall, which is the Word of God'.
13. firm] *Trin. MS*: *right* \`firm'.

When I consider how my light is spent,
Ere half my days, in this dark world and wide,
And that one talent which is death to hide,
Lodged with me useless, though my soul more bent
To serve therewith my maker, and present
My true account, lest he returning chide,
Doth God exact day-labour, light denied,
I fondly ask; but Patience to prevent
That murmur, soon replies, God doth not need
Either man's work or his own gifts, who best
Bear his mild yoke, they serve him best, his state
Is kingly. Thousands at his bidding speed
And post o'er land and ocean without rest:
They also serve who only stand and wait.

84 Samson Agonistes

Date. 1647–53? Forceful reasons for abandoning the traditional dating (1666–70) are advanced by W. R. Parker, *PQ* xxviii (1949) 145–66 and *N & Q* v (1958) 201–2. Edward Phillips, who was in close contact with M.

9–10. M. repeats this sentiment in *De Doctrina* (Columbia xvii 20–22) quoting *Job* xxii 2.

11. mild yoke] Cp. *Matt.* xi 30: 'My yoke is easy.'

12–3. Cp. *Ps.* lxviii 17: 'The chariots of God are twenty thousand, even thousands of angels', and *Zech.* i 10: 'These are they whom the Lord hath sent to walk to and fro through the earth.'

14. H. F. Robins, *RES* n. s. vii (1956) 360–6, reiterates the conclusion of Sir Herbert Grierson, *Poems of John Donne* (Oxford 1912) ii 5, that 'They' are the four highest orders of angels who, according to pseudo-Dionysius and Aquinas do not act as messengers like the inferior orders ('thousands' l. 12), but stand about God's throne, waiting on him and passing on to the inferior orders the secrets of the divine mysteries. F. Pyle, *RES* n.s. ix (1958) 376–87, notes however that in *De doctrina* M. does not regard any angels as reserved for exclusive service in heaven, and in *PL* Cherub and Seraph are not confined to God's presence. Pyle agrees with Smart 109–10, that 'They' are devout men on earth, who obey such frequent biblical injunctions as *Ps.* xxxvii 14, 'Wait on the Lord' (cp. the parable in *Luke* xii 35–40 about 'men that wait for their Lord'). J. L. Jackson and W. E. Weese, *MLN* lxxii (1957) 91–3, associate the use of 'stand' with that in *Ephes.* vi 14, where the word means 'take up a position against the enemy'. R. A. Haug, *N & Q* clxxxiii (1942) 224–5, thinks the source for the idea *1 Sam.* xxx 24, where David allots an equal share of booty to those who pursue and to those who wait behind.

¶ 84. *Title. Samson*] In both Blount's *Glossographia* (1656) and Edward Phillips's *New World of Words* (1658) the name is said to mean 'there the

during the last years of his life, affirms that *PR* was written entirely between 1667 and 1670, which he considers 'a wonderful short space considering the sublimeness of it' (Darbishire 75). If he believed *SA* had also been written in that period, it is highly unlikely that Phillips would not have thought it worth comment. He says, however, that when *SA* was written 'cannot certainly be concluded' (Darbishire 75).

M.'s note added to late issues of the first edition of *PL* in 1668 attacks rhyme as 'the invention of a barbarous age, to set off wretched matter and lame metre' rejected 'long since' by 'our best English tragedies'. Yet about one-eleventh of *SA* is rhymed. M. could not, when writing it, have felt about rhyme as he did in 1668.

Parker thinks that *SA* was begun 1646–7 (Phillips was resident in M.'s house until about 1646, so ought to have known about the composition of *SA* if it was going on then), and taken up again 1652–3. The Trinity MS contains clear evidence of amanuenses preparing M.'s poems for publication, and these preparations seem to belong to 1653. In 1653, *1645* was still in print, so the only reason for a new edition could be the addition of a new work of some size, and *SA* seems the only possibility. The audacious metrical experiments of *SA*'s choruses are matched only by those of the Latin ode to Rouse (1647), and M. uses precisely the same terms to explain the versification of the two works (see pp. 303 and 345). Further, the experience of approaching and of new blindness reflects in the psalm translations of Apr. 1648 and Aug. 1653 and, in similar tones, in *SA*. Samson's great speeches on blindness do not seem to be those of a man resigned to a long-lived-with disability. This last point, however, is less telling than Parker's others, since it smacks of that autobiographical interpretation which he elsewhere distrusts. Fanciful identifications (M. is Samson; Salmasius, Harapha; Mary Powell, Dalila etc.) have often been undertaken by critics attempting to date *SA*, but there is little to be said for them. By depicting himself as a character punished with blindness for loss of virtue, M. would be taking the side of the Royalist satirists and pamphleteers. Early biographers and critics seem unaware of any autobiographical or topical elements.

second time'. If M. believed in this (incorrect) etymology it would be a possible starting-point for his idea of a second encounter with Dalila. No such encounter occurs in *Judges*, where he resists her three times by lying, then falls (xvi 6–17). *Agonistes*] In Greek the word can mean a contestant in the games (Samson is a contestant at the Philistines' games, though unopposed, *SA* 1628) or a champion. Phillips's *New World of Words* (1658 and 1663) defines 'agonize' as 'play the champion' (cp. *SA* 705, 1152, 1751). Krouse 110–16 connects the term *agonistes* with the exertion of mind and spirit called for in the Platonic ethic (ἀγών came to mean 'spiritual struggle', and ἀγωνιστής, 'a fully educated person, ready to take his place in the ἀγών of life'), and in the Christian tradition (Theodoret uses ἀγωνιστής to mean 'saint' or 'martyr'; Christ's atonement was looked upon as an ἀγών–Augustine wrote a treatise called *De Agone Christiano*).

E. Sirluck's attempt, *JEGP* lx (1961) 749–85, to counter Parker's theory leaves it in the main unimpaired: so does A. S. P. Woodhouse's ill-supported plea for a date between the Restoration (May 1660) and the spring of 1661, *Trans. of the Royal Soc. of Canada* xliii (1949) 157–75. Ants Oras's statistical analysis of the blank verse of *Comus*, *PL*, *PR* and *SA* (*SAMLA* 128–197) is designed to support the traditional chronology, but much of his evidence goes against it (e.g. the relative percentages of terminal and medial strong pauses are exactly the same in *Comus* and *SA;* the percentage of run-on lines in *SA* is nearer to that in *Comus* than to that in *PL* or *PR;* the relative percentages of feminine and masculine pauses in *SA* are nearer to those in *Comus* than to those in *PL* or *PR;* the frequency of feminine line-endings in *SA* is nearer to that in *Comus* than to that in *PL* or *PR*).

Publication. The volume containing *PR* and *SA* (*1671*) was licensed 2 Jul. 1670 by Thomas Tomkyns, and entered in the Stationers' Register 10 Sep. 1670. The volume was advertised in the 1670 Michaelmas Term catalogue. All known title-pages, however, have the date 1671. Parker suggests that the delay in appearance was due to the time taken by the blind M. supervising proof-reading. There are two slightly different states of some pages in *1671*; see notes to *306*, *548*, *1033*, *1078*, *1086*, *1093*, *1337* and *1340*.

Modern criticism. Criticism of *SA* has centred round two major questions: its structure and its spirit. The second of these, leading to discussions about whether the play is 'Hellenic', 'Hebraic' or 'Christian', has also motivated examination of its sources, its claims to 'tragic' stature, its differences from or similarities to previous Samson literature, and its 'meaning'.

Argument over the structure of *SA* began with Johnson's declaration (*Rambler* 139) that 'the poem . . . has a beginning and an end . . . but it must be allowed to want a middle, since nothing passes between the first act and the last, that either hastens or delays the death of Samson'. J. W. Tupper, *PMLA* xxxv (1920) 375–89, sides with Johnson: the Dalila and Harapha episodes are 'mere padding'. P. F. Baum, *PMLA* xxxvi (1921) 354–71, in reply, makes the obvious point that 'dramatic action includes not only visible acts but also the invisible mental changes which underlie and mould actual events'. From this viewpoint the central episodes of *SA* are necessary to the action, though they do not follow one another, as Aristotle required, in probable or necessary sequence. It is this last fact which mars the play for E. C. Knowlton, *MLN* xxxvii (1922) 333–9: as he sees it, tragic action 'depends for its value structurally and spiritually upon the principle of causality': not only are the Dalila and Harapha episodes themselves without proper cause, but they do not cause the death of Samson. The catastrophe, however, is not the death of Samson but his victory-through-death, as W. C. Curry insists, *Sewanee Review* xxxii (1924) 336–52, and the spiritual development necessary for this is a direct result of the central episodes. Dalila is still attractive to Samson (*952–3*, *1003–7*), thus her appearance gives him a chance to redeem himself by resisting precisely that temptation to which he formerly succumbed. After this it is necessary that he should be roused from lethargy, and the behaviour of Harapha is calculated to have that effect. An alternative reply to Johnson is framed by M. E. Grenander, *UTQ* xxiv (1955) 377–89, who points out that the play's action begins long before the play itself, with Samson's initial victory over the Philistines: viewed thus the action has a beginning, middle and end, as Aristotle required. Another aspect of *SA*'s structure–its symmetry–is studied by W. R. Parker, *MLN* l (1935) 355–60, who draws attention to the similarity in length between successive speeches and episodes, and between *prologos* and *kommos*.

The argument about whether *SA* is 'Hellenic' or 'Hebraic' in spirit was begun by R. C. Jebb, *Proc. of the Brit. Acad.* iii (1907–8) 341–8. In spite of its Greek form, and in spite of the fact that, as a drama of inward action, it can find a parallel in the *Prometheus Bound* of Aeschylus, *SA* seems to Jebb to have the spirit of the Hebrew prophets. Samson is a tribal champion: Jehovah and Dagon, tribal Gods. The issue of the drama is that Jehovah has prevailed over Dagon, Israel over Philistia. It is Hebraism which thus contrasts God and his servants with idols and their servants: Hellenism contrasts man with fate. Jebb's case is strongly attacked by W. R. Parker *E & S* xx (1934) 21–44. Greek tragedy, Parker argues, is serious, thoughtful, didactic, religious and sublime: so is *SA*. It is dominated by fate: so is *SA*, where Samson's fate is decreed before his birth (*38–9*), and where dramatic irony (which implies a fatalistic philosophy of life) runs through the entire action. *SA* is Sophoclean rather than Aeschylean in that it displays unmerited suffering: Parker feels that Samson suffers more than he deserves: despite the final chorus, human passions and wrongs are seen to be more real than the divine scheme into which they are supposed to fit. Parker's reply to Jebb later became the basis for his book (Parker[2]) which also reprints and expands previous articles on the play's tragic irony, *Études Anglaises* i (1937) 314–20; its *kommos* (which, Parker considers, extends from *1660* to the end of the play, and resembles that in Aeschylus' *Suppliants*), *SP* xxxii (1935) 240–4; and its alleged misogyny, which Parker denies, *PQ* xvi (1937) 139–44. He includes two chapters (168–85) on *SA*'s debt to the *Oedipus at Colonus* and the *Prometheus Bound*, maintaining that W. Brewer, *PMLA* xlii (1927) 910–20, was mistaken in asserting that M. took his plot 'almost entirely' from these two plays: the debt, Parker believes, is more miscellaneous. Comparison with the *Oedipus at Colonus* had been made before Brewer by P. H. Epps, *SP* xiii (1916) 190–6, and Sir Maurice Bowra has returned to it in his study of *SA*, *Inspiration and Poetry* (1955) 112–29. The extent of M.'s knowledge of Aeschylus has been questioned by J. C. Maxwell, *RES* n.s. iii (1952) 366–71: though the structure of the *Prometheus Bound* almost certainly influenced that of *SA*, there are no convincing verbal parallels between M. and Aeschylus at all. The influence of the third Greek tragic dramatist, Euripides, has been studied by P. W. Timberlake (Parrott 315–40): the litigious element, the sententiousness, and the treatment of the messenger, making for suspense, all smack of Euripides, quite apart from verbal similarities (e.g. *SA 1–2*, *Phoenician Maidens* 834–5; *SA 115–6*, *Orestes* 140; *SA 1034*f., *Hippolytus* 616f. and *Orestes* 604–5).

Claims that *SA* is neither 'Hellenic' nor 'Hebraic' but Christian have been made by several critics. T. S. K. Scott-Craig, *Renaissance News* v (1952) 45–53, sees it as 'a poem on the spiritual agony of Christ': 'the celebration of the agony of Samson is a surrogate for the unbloody sacrifice of the Mass', and the catastrophe, with Samson's prayer and destruction of the theatre, is a typological version of Christ's passion, with the prayer in Gethsemane followed by physical accompaniments of the crucifixion like the rending of the temple veil and the earthquake. In support of Scott-Craig it can be said that, as Krouse has made clear (41, 51, 69), the conception of Samson as a figure of Christ was the main current in the Samson tradition of the Middle Ages and the Renaissance. It originated, apparently, in Ambrose, and received its fullest treatment in Augustine's *Sermo de Samsone*: the most ingenious of the scholastic writers in finding parallels between Samson and Christ was Rupert of St Heribert (d. 1135). As late as 1640, Thomas Hayne in his *General View of the Holy Scriptures* prints an elaborate tabular analysis of the parallels between the two figures. However it must be stressed that, in view of this tradition, it is all the more striking that M. should refrain from making any explicit comparison between his protagonist and Christ. Krouse's insistence that the temptations of M.'s Samson are equivalent to the temptations of Christ in the wilderness as schematized by Protestant theologians (Manoa representing temptation by necessity; Dalila, temptation by fraud; Harapha, temptation by violence), cannot be said to convince. Scott-Craig's view is shared by M. M. Ross, *Poetry and Dogma* (New Brunswick 1954) pp. 12–3. A less extreme Christianization is offered by Allen 82–94, who reads the play as an 'analysis of the problem of Christian despair': the episode with Manoa shows Samson resisting the enticement to sloth, while that with Harapha, which to Allen is the hinge of the tragedy, enables him to subdue his apathy.

If *SA* is Christian, can it also be 'tragic'? P. F. Baum, *PMLA* xxxvi (1921) 354–71, thinks not: tragic force is diminished by the play's insistence on a beneficent divine providence–'with this belief there can be no properly tragic catastrophe'. Bowra (see above) agrees–'since all is best, there is nothing to regret'–and so does Miss Ellis-Fermor, *Frontiers of Drama* (1945) 17–33–'by justifying the ways of God to man he leaves no room for tragic ecstasy and substitutes an ecstasy of another kind'. W. C. Curry, *Sewanee Review* (1924) xxxii 336–52, on the other hand, thinks that a belief in beneficent divine providence is not incompatible with tragedy but only with Greek tragedy, and J. H. Hanford, *Studies in Shakespeare, Milton and Donne* (New York 1925) pp. 167–89, maintains that 'all is best' does not represent our feeling at the end of the drama: in spite of M.'s Christianity, a keen sense of the reality of suffering, and a habitual stoicism remain. A. S. P. Woodhouse, *UTQ* xxviii (1959) 205–22, finds the drama, though Christian, also 'tragic' in that M. makes 'the way of repentance and restoration, the way back to God, also the way that leads inevitably to the catastrophe, and has thus achieved at a stroke the only kind of irony that is at once compatible with a Christian outlook and as potent as any to be found in tragedy anywhere'.

One objection to the view of *SA* as a Christian work is that it condones and centres upon an act of vengeance (Kenneth Burke, *Hudson Review* i (1948) 151–67, calls it 'a wonder-working spell by a cantankerous old fighter-priest who would slay the enemy in effigy'). This difficulty is examined by K. Fell, *English Studies* xxxiv (1953) 145–55, who finds that, in spite of its mature concentration on purgation and dedication, the play fails to transcend the limitations inherent in its vengeful ending–an integral part of its primitive story, which is an ancient solar myth of Syrian origin. That the ending is indeed morally disgusting does not seem to be realised by E. L. Marilla, *Studia Neophilologica* xxix (1957) 67–76; to him the moral of *SA*–a moral of which he approves–is that man must 'unreservedly commit himself, without regard for possible costs in personal sacrifice, to upholding the ideals that are entrusted to him as a spiritual being'. A hardly less objectionable moral (from the viewpoint of the slaughtered Philistines) is drawn by J. D. Ebbs, *MLQ* xxii (1961) 377–89: M. teaches that 'a just and glorious end awaits those who are repentant, have patience under trials, and show faith in the ultimate manifestation of God's will'.

One interpretation which falls outside the Hellenic-Hebraic-Christian question is the political. E. M. Clark, *UTSE* vii (1927) 144–54, reads the play as a political allegory of the temporary downfall and ultimate triumph of the Puritan state, and draws attention to M.'s previous allegorization of the Samson story in *Reason of Church Government* (Columbia iii 276–7, Yale i 858–9).

In determining the spirit of *SA* it is clear that its divergence from or agreement with previous handlings of the Samson story will be significant. W. Kirkconnell's mainly irrelevant study of six sixteenth-century treatments of the story, *Trans. of the Royal Soc. of Canada* xliii (1949) 73–85, is far too narrow in scope, but Krouse allows the play to be seen in its full cultural context. The elevated nature of M.'s Samson, when compared with the Samson of *Judges*, which E. M. Clark, *UTSE* viii (1928) 88–99, had previously commented on, Krouse proves to be not so much the achievement of M. as of the historical tradition in which he wrote. The history of the Christian conception of Samson helps to explain why M. saw a tragic hero in the biblical figure who seems an often undignified tribal hero. Tradition had drawn attention away from the earlier, less dignified part of his life: Josephus had seen his fall as the result of *hubris*, and to Gregory the Great he had exemplified *hamartia*. The Renaissance minimized the physical aspects of his fall and magnified the spiritual: the idea of his repentance and mental anguish (not recorded in the Bible) was so prevalent by the late-sixteenth century that Nashe coined the verb 'sampsown' meaning 'to cast down in dejection and anguished thought'. Similarly the supernatural nature of Samson's strength and his status as God's champion are ideas which M. takes over from tradition rather than from *Judges*, where the state of affairs is more doubtful.

Search for possible sources outside Greek tragedy has produced very little. R. Galland, *Revue Anglo-Américaine* xiii (1936) 326–33, finds some dubious 'parallels' between *SA* and the anonymous English translation (1642) of Buchanan's *Baptistes*, and A. Gossman, *Renaissance News* xiii (1960) 11–15, suggests two classical analogues for Manoa's ransom attempt–that of Crito in Plato's *Crito* and that of Priam in *Il.* xxiv 484–502. Prince 145–68, analysing the verse of the choruses, finds no precise parallels in Italian verse, but some similar features in the choruses and lyrical passages of Tasso's *Aminta*, Guarini's *Pastor Fido* and Andreini's *L'Adamo*. Frank Kermode on the other hand, *Durham Univ. Journal* xiv (1952) 59–63, suggests that in the lyric portions of *SA* M. is following up his rejection of the Greek ode in *PR*, and imitating Hebrew lyric measures and rhymes as he understood them.

The source and nature of M.'s Harapha figure has been the topic of some debate. D. C. Boughner, *JELH* xi (1944) 297–306, finds him a comic figure: his ancestors, Boughner believes, are the mock-chivalric cowardly braggarts with their farcical employment of the code of honour, of the sixteenth- and early seventeenth-century Italian stage, who pass into English drama in such characters as Jonson's Bobadill and Shakespeare's Don Armado. J. M. Steadman, *JEGP* lx (1961) 786–95, is dubious: to him, the primary source of M.'s giant is not Renaissance comedy but the description of his son, Goliath, in *1 Sam.* xvii. G. R. Waggoner, *PQ* xxxix (1960) 82–92, suggests that the Harapha episode is primarily chivalric rather than comic: like the entries in M.'s Commonplace Book under the heading 'Of Duels', it displays an interest in single combat and in the conventions of the duel perhaps stimulated by M.'s reading of his friend John Selden's *Duello* (1610). E. Wright, *N & Q* vii (1960) 222–4, finds a similar chivalric flavour elsewhere in *SA* (e.g. in the details of armour, *131–4*, as well as *1119–21*, and in the mention of lists, *462–3*).

Style and imagery. The Elizabethan influences so marked in M.'s other attempt at drama, *Comus*, are severely excised from *SA*, which has only half-a-dozen echoes of Shakespeare, one of Sylvester and none of Spenser. More in evidence are Euripides and Sophocles, who are repeatedly recalled both by M.'s phrasing and by his situations (see footnotes).

Most of M.'s stylistic mannerisms in *SA* can be illustrated from Samson's first speech (*1–114*). Modern readers are likely to be struck first by the insistent disturbances of English word order, (e.g. 'Who this high gift of strength committed to me, / In what part lodged, how easily bereft me, / Under the seal of silence could not keep' (*47–9*), where the imitation of the Latin initial copulative relative is followed by an inverted construction in which the object and the indirect questions connected with it precede the verb which, as often in Latin, occupies the final position). A common displacement of normal word order in *SA* is the promotion of adverbs or adverbial phrases or clauses to the start of a clause, sentence or, sometimes, speech: e.g. 'A little onward lend' (*1*), 'Daily in the common prison else enjoined' (*6*), 'Scarce half I seem to live' (*79*). Notable instances from later in the drama are 'With cause this hope relieves thee' (*472*), 'All otherwise to me my thoughts portend' (*590*, also *594*), Dalila's first words (*732–3*), and Samson's first reasoned reply to her (*819*). This adverbial promotion can become elaborate, e.g. 'Wherever fountain or fresh current flowed / Against the eastern ray, translucent, pure / With touch ethereal of heaven's fiery rod / I drank' (*547–50*).

The objects of verbs are similarly up-graded to leading positions: e.g. 'Immeasurable strength they might behold' (*206*), 'The first I saw at Timna' (*219*), 'That fault I take not on me' (*241*), 'His pardon I impore' (*521*). Sometimes both adverb and object take precedence: e.g. 'unwillingly this rest / Their superstition yields me' (*14–15*), 'Me easily indeed mine may neglect' (*291*), and Samson's last words, reported by the messenger, 'Hitherto, Lords, what your commands imposed / I have performed' (*1640–1*).

SA is full of questions: all the characters ask them, so does the chorus. There are six in Samson's first speech; seven in Manoa's first speech after his entrance (*340–71*). The catastrophe is signalled through Manoa's two questions 'What noise or shout was that? It tore the sky' (*1472*), and 'O what noise?' (*1508*). Speakers frequently answer their own questions and meet their own objections (a figure known as *anthypophora*): e.g. in Samson's first speech, 'Yet stay, let me not . . .' (*43*) and 'But peace, I must not ...' (*60*). Besides the interrogative, the imperative mood is prominent: 'lend' (*1*), 'leave' (*11*), 'ask' (*40*), 'stay' (*43*) etc. There are twenty-seven speeches with an imperative in the opening line.

M.'s habit of using a word in its original Latin rather than its developed English sense is fairly widely exemplified: Samson's first speech has 'popular noise' (*16*) ('popular' already had its modern sense at the beginning of the seventeenth century), 'Annulled' meaning 'reduced to nothing' (*72*), and 'obvious' meaning 'exposed' (*95*) (the modern senses, 'cancelled, declared invalid' and 'palpable', were already current when M. wrote).

The speeches gain internal vigour not only from their knotty and unaccustomed syntax but also from the persistent use of rhetorical figures involving repetition. Immediate repetition of a word (*epizeuxis*) is rare, e.g. 'dark, dark, dark' (*80*), 'No, no, of my condition take no care' (*928*), but repetition with intervening words (*ploce*) constantly occurs, e.g. in Samson's first speech, 'strength . . . strength' (*36*), 'the vilest . . . the vilest' (*73–4*), 'dark . . . dark' (*80–1*), 'life . . . life' (*90–1*). Moments of tension, introspective or argumentative, are screwed tighter by heightening the density of this, as of other figures. When Samson engages in dispute with Dalila he uses 'weakness' and 'love' four times each in ten lines (*829–38*), matching Dalila's four uses of each word in the previous speech (*766–818*). A closer patterning is supplied when this figure approaches *antimetabole* (repetition with inversion), as in *423–5* 'occasion . . . foes / foes . . . occasion', *462–3*, *686* etc.; *anaphora* (repetition of initial words or phrases), as in *361*, *394–5*, *445–6*, *449*, *487*, *493*, *890*, etc.; and *anadiplosis* (starting a line with the last word of the line before), as in *17–18*, *247–8*, *376–7*, *878–9* etc. *Traductio* (the repetition of a word in a different grammatical form) starts in the first speech, 'deliver . . . deliverer' (*39–40*), 'affliction . . . afflict' (*113–4*), and is heavily used right through to the conclusion when, with *ploce*, it welds together the brief speeches of Manoa and the chorus (*1508–22*), bridges the two semi-choruses, 'blindness . . . blind' (*1686–7*), and lends an air of finality to Manoa's summing-up, 'heroicly hath finished / A life heroic' (*1709–10*). Figures which depend upon the juxtaposition of two elements are called upon to emphasise contrasts like that between Samson's past and present, his blindness and the light which surrounds him, and the uncertain relationship between Dalila's inner and outer selves: e.g. *antithesis*, 'In power of others, never in my own' (*78*), also *195*, *234*, *270–1*, *305*, *338–9*, *689* etc.; *oxymoron*, 'dark in light' (*75*), also *100*, *307* etc.; *zeugma*, 'O'ercome with importunity and tears' (*51*), 'With doubtful feet and wavering resolution' (*732*). Bitter or sardonic word-play sharpens Samson's own speeches even when he is at his most dejected: e.g. 'a *moving* grave' (*102*), 'my *accomplished* snare' (*230*), 'My *capital* secret '(*394*), 'food / *Consume* me' (*574–5*) etc.

A way of building up swift climax of sound or stress which *SA* constantly avails itself of is the listing of adjectives or nouns, or even verbs and adverbs, either with conjunctions (*polysyndeton*) or without (*asyndeton*). Samson's first speech, for example, has 'Betrayed, captived, and both my eyes put out' (*33*), 'vast, unwieldly, burdensome, / Proudly secure, yet liable to fall' (*54–5*), 'chains, / Dungeon, or beggary, or decrepit age!' (*68–9*), 'fraud, contempt, abuse and wrong' (*76*). There are fifteen examples in the first 500 lines, and the figure is regularly repeated until the conclusion. After the entrance of the officer (*1308*) his asyndeton, 'With sacrifices, triumph, pomp, and games' (*1312*), is capped by Samson's 'gymnic artists, wrestlers, riders, runners, / Jugglers and dancers, antics, mummers, mimics' (*1324–5*), and Samson's subsequent asyndetic self-justification, 'how vile, contemptible, ridiculous, / What act more execrably unclean, profane?' (*1361–2*), is parried by the chorus's deployment of the same figure, 'Yet with this strength thou serv'st the Philistines, / Idolatrous, uncircumcised, unclean' (*1363–4*).

A remarkable verbal feature of *SA* is the amount of activity delegated to abstract nouns. They carry the weight of the action, either as the subjects or as the objects of the verbs. In Samson's first speech '*chance* / Relieves' (*4–5*), '*superstition* yields' (*14–15*), '*strength*' is 'put to the *labour*' (*36–7*), '*wisdom* bears command' (*57*), '*miseries* . . . ask' (*64–6*); Samson fears to 'call in doubt / Divine *prediction*' (*43–4*), bewails his '*impotence* of mind' (*52*), hesitates to 'quarrel with the *will* / of highest *dispensation*' (*60–1*), hears 'the *tread* of many feet' (*111*) and takes it to be sightseers coming to 'stare / At my *affliction*' (*112–3*). This abstraction might be thought a way of conveying Samson's blindness, if it were not prominent in the speeches of the other characters also, and of the chorus. When the chorus recall, for example, Samson's previous exploits, where solidity might be expected, we find it was 'the *forgery* / Of brazen shield and spear' (*131–2*) that he made useless. Manoa counsels that '*self-preservation* bids' Samson to avoid punishment or leave 'the *execution* . . . to high *disposal*' (*504–6*). Of M.'s dozen or so coinages in *SA* two, 'ramp' (*139*) and 'obstriction' (*312*) are abstract nouns.

If the internal nature of Samson's drama is unobtrusively clarified by the abstract character of many grammatical agents and objects, another result is that the play's sparse imagery is thrown into bolder relief. Ricks 49–56 is disappointed with the metaphors of *SA* because they do not 'live along the line': they are not enlivened by and do not extend tendrils into their immediate context. He instances the counterfeit 'coin' of *189* which suddenly becomes a 'swarm' two lines later. But the base coin is not, from the perspective of the whole work, as lonely as he would have us suppose. Dalila as Danae in the shower of Philistian gold (*388–91*, *831*) keeps it company in Samson's tormented mind. It is only isolated if viewed in isolation from the rest of the work. The rarity of *SA*'s imagery allows it to make connections across areas too large for Ricks's focus. The connections seem at first merely to reinforce the explicit meanings of the play: to add definition to the curve which takes the protagonist from zenith to nadir and back again. But, if allowed, they prove ready to contribute meanings of their own which run counter to the drama's apparent values and threaten to pull the curve out of shape.

The marine imagery–which provides, at Dalila's entrance, the play's one moment of flamboyance, is introduced in the opening speech, where Samson characterizes the Philistines' god, Dagon, as 'their sea-idol' (*13*). The suggestion that the power of the sea is on the side of Samson's enemies becomes more pronounced when he views his present anguish in marine terms–'suffers not / Mine eye to harbour sleep' (*458–9*)–and his past ruin as a shipwreck: he was and is unable to combat the sea's force: 'Who like a foolish pilot have shipwrecked, / My vessel trusted to me from above, / Gloriously rigged; and for a word, a tear' (*198–200*). It is bitterly ironic that a 'tear' of Dalila's–so small a quantity of salt water–should have been enough to wreck Samson's glorious vessel, and the irony lends her later tears, to which both she and the chorus draw Samson's attention (*729*, *735*), a dangerous potency. The temptation which she presents is enhanced, just as the subtler temptation to despair which the chorus, for all their intended 'counsel and consolation', bring, is delicately underlined when Samson hears them 'steering' (*111*) towards him. ('Steer', originally an exclusively nautical word, was still alive with marine associations for the seventeenth century, and M. in *PL* ix 513–5, 'As when a ship . . . steers, and shifts her sail', was the first to use it with ship rather than helmsman as agent). The famous ship-simile which announces Dalila (*714–9*) is, however, the major indication of her power. She is able to control the sea, that element which had overcome Samson, with effortless ease: 'stately', 'trim', decked with streamers and 'courted' by the winds, she moves upon its surface. The simile also connects her with the Philistines, worshippers of the 'sea-idol', and she is, in fact, a Philistine in M., though not in *Judges*. One question, at her entrance, is whether she is still in league with them, or whether love and pity for Samson are behind her return. It is posed, in terms of the predominant image, by the chorus: 'But who is this, what thing of sea or land?' (*710*). The other question is whether Samson will be able to withstand her. That he is still in love with her is clear. He dare not even let her touch him: 'Not for thy life, lest fierce remembrance wake / My sudden rage to tear thee joint by joint'. If he hated her he would hardly warn her against risking her life. Blindness protects him from her physical attractions to some extent, (though as the chorus notice (*720*), she has artfully perfumed herself with ambergris–another link with the sea), but he knows he will not be able to resist the feel of her body: 'other senses', as Dalila is aware, 'want not their delights'. The chorus, too, guess what 'secret sting of amorous remorse' (*1007*) Samson feels. Only if Dalila is still an enticement to Samson will his temptation be the same as that which caused his fall–and it must be so if her reappearance is to be a genuine second chance for him. (To seventeenth-century etymologists his name meant 'There-the-second-time': this may be at the back of his unscriptural second encounter with Dalila in *SA*). It is self-esteem, as the perceptive Manoa tells him, that he has lost–he is 'self-displeased / For self-offence' (*514–5*)–and he is able to regain it by standing firm where before he succumbed. Dalila's entrance is therefore the hinge of the drama. The fanfare of imagery which heralds her is a structural pointer.

Because Samson resists this cardinal temptation, he takes upon himself the power of the sea. Dalila finds him more unappeasable than the sea itself. The 'stately ship of Tarsus' which was 'courted' by the winds, cannot calm the tempest into which Samson is now transformed: 'I see thou art implacable, more deaf / To prayers than winds and seas, yet winds to seas / Are reconciled at length, and sea to shore: / Thy anger, unappeasable, still rages, / Eternal tempest never to be calmed' (*960–4*). In the chorus's opinion, Samson's chances of successful navigation, now that Dalila has been rejected, are improved: 'What pilot so expert but needs must wreck / Embarked with such a steers-mate at the helm?' (*1044–5*) is their comment on her departure: the blame for what has happened is tactfully shifted from the 'foolish pilot' to his mate. But Dalila has seen Samson, in his anger, as a 'tempest', and just as the images of his 'gloriously rigged' vessel and of her ship with its 'tackle trim' and 'streamers waving' tend to draw the two of them into an implied, and disturbing, parallelism, so this tempest image aligns him, unexpectedly, with Harapha, whose blustering entrance as a 'tempest' (*1063*) is next announced. Harapha's tempestuous lack of self-control is less of a threat than Dalila's dangerous mastery. The difference between them is implied in terms of shipping: 'What wind hath blown him hither / I less conjecture than when first I saw / The sumptuous Dalila floating this way' (*1070–2*). Samson is still a tempest when he destroys the Philistines. Just before the noise of the calamity is heard Manoa speaks of his son's locks 'waving' down (*1493*)–a word which clarifies the sea echoes of the earlier 'redundant locks' (*568*)–and, as the messenger relates, it is 'with the force of winds and waters' and 'with burst of thunder' (*1647–51*) that the pillars are tugged down. The destructive and amoral power of the sea which, at the opening of the drama, was specifically associated with the Philistines, has now been transferred to Samson. His last bloody act of vengeance, which the surface voice of the drama invites us to applaud, is condemned, at a deeper level, by the progression of imagery.

Snakes and serpents are not so obtrusively present in the language of *SA* as the sea is. Samson is afraid that, if he pardons Dalila, he will be 'entangled with a poisonous bosom snake' (*763*). At her spiteful leave-taking the chorus recognize her as 'a manifest serpent by her sting / Discovered in the end', and Samson agrees that she is a 'viper' (*997–1001*). The revelation of Dalila as a stinging creature sets her among Samson's torments and disappointments: the 'deadly swarm of hornets' (*19–20*), the 'scorpion's tail' (*360*) and the thoughts 'armed with deadly stings' that 'Mangle my apprehensive tenderest parts' (*623*)–the physical reference stabs excruciatingly at the area of sexual betrayal, as does the 'thorn intestine' (*1037–8*) which is also Dalila. Samson's physical prowess, his tearing of the lion (*128*), draws to itself, like the lion's swarming carcass, both honey and sting: Dalila, the stinging creature, with her 'honied words' (*1066*), and a 'swarm' (*192*) of deceitful friends. But as Samson assumed the power of the sea, so he tells Dalila in his crucial interview with her that he has learned 'adder's wisdom' (*936*), and when he destroys the Philistines he uses snake-like cunning, creeping in below the 'roosts' of their amphitheatre to divert their attention downwards, while striking them from above: 'And as an evening dragon came, / Assailant on the perched roosts, / And nests in order ranged / Of tame villatic fowl; but as an eagle / His cloudless thunder bolted on their heads' (*1692–6*). 'Dragon', especially when coupled with 'fiery' (*1690*), throws a specious glamour over the snake which, when the blind Samson first learned to envy it, was a mere 'worm' (*74*). 'Dragon' sounds better with 'eagle', and the eagle, like the Phoenix (*1699*) belongs to and completes the explicit elevation of Samson which is engineered through the imagery of birds and animals. (Samson, a 'lion' before his fall (*128, 139*), is caught in Dalila's 'snares' (*230, 409, 532, 931*), 'gins' and 'toils' (*933*), becomes a farmyard animal, 'a tame wether' (*538*), in his subjection to her, and is 'Put to the labour of a beast' (*37*) among the 'asses' (*1162*) at the mill. But the first words he speaks to Dalila–'Out, out hyaena' (*748*)–transfer his animal baseness to her, and in the Harapha episode the 'chafed wild boars' and 'ruffled porcupines' (*1138*)–wild and heraldic creatures–show him rapidly regaining his animal nobility. His insistence that the Philistines 'shall not trail me through their streets / Like a wild beast' (*1402–3*) acquires irony from the sequence). But 'dragon' means 'snake' nevertheless (*OED* defines it as 'huge serpent or snake; python'): the eagle and the Phoenix are undercut by the snake in the henroost, which looks much more like the 'serpent' Dalila than they do, but which is Samson.

If Dalila is ship and snake, she is also flower. The chorus describe her, weeping, 'with head declined / Like a fair flower surcharged with dew' (*727–8*). There is a sense in which this image, like that of the ship, emphasizes Dalila's dangerous potentiality, and it does this not only through the attractiveness implied by 'flower' but also through the coolness implied by 'dew'. From the outset Samson's torment is presented as an 'inflammation' (*626*); his griefs are 'sores', 'tumours', 'festered wounds' (*184–6*) which 'ferment and rage', 'Rankle, and fester, and gangrene' (*619–21*). The suggested lenitives are all evocations of coolness–'cooling herb', 'breath of vernal air from snowy alp' (*626–8*), 'Salve', 'balm' (*184–6*), 'The breath of heaven fresh-blowing' (*10*)–and they connect, naturally enough, with Samson's earlier mode of life before his fall and anguish, when he drank 'the cool crystalline stream' from 'fountain or fresh current' (*546–7*). This healing coolness is felt for the last time, pathetically, in the 'lavers pure and cleansing herbs' and the 'shade / Of laurel ever green and branching palm' (*1727–35*) of Manoa's funeral preparations, but it is twice utilized, in the course of the drama, to accentuate the pressure of a particular temptation: once when Samson describes death as the 'balm' (*651*) of all his miseries, and the second time when Dalila stands like a flower 'surcharged with dew'. But the flower image does not only provide this kind of emphasis. Like other images, it narrows the apparent disparity between Dalila and the Philistines on the one hand and Samson on the other. Dalila, 'with head declined', is a flower, perhaps one of the 'flower' (*1654*) of the Philistine nobility upon whose 'heads' (*1652*), declined as they watch him in the arena below, Samson tugs down the roof. In his early exploits, also, it was the 'flower of Palestine' (*144*) that he cut down. But he, too, was in the 'flower' (*938*) of his youth and strength when Dalila destroyed him, and at his death Manoa grieves that the 'first-born bloom of spring' has been 'Nipped with the lagging rear of winter's frost' (*1576–7*). Dalila imagines that her 'tomb' will be 'visited' with 'annual flowers' (*986–7*), and Manoa, mourning his son, prophesies that the virgins will 'Visit his tomb with flowers' (*1742*). A flower is recognizably an apt emblem for Dalila. Its beauty, like hers, is external: her behaviour makes the chorus wonder whether it was because 'outward ornament /Was lavished' on women 'that inward gifts / Were left for haste unfinished' (*1025–7*). What might escape notice, without the flower symbol, is the similarity between this and the externality confessed by Samson (*58–9, 206–8*). This aspect of Milton's Samson, his weak-mindedness, is not emphasized either in *Judges* or in the Christian tradition of Samson literature. It is revealing, in this context, that both Dalila and Samson tend to externalize intellectual or moral debate–internal conflict–through the use of military terminology. To Dalila the persuasive arguments of the Philistine magistrates are 'assaults' and 'sieges' (*845–6*), and Samson apprehends Dalila's enticements as a 'peal' of artillery (*235*), as 'feminine assaults' and 'Tongue-batteries' which 'storm' (*403–5*) the undefended 'gate' (*560*) of his 'fort of silence' (*236*).

The flames among which the Phoenix dies into life (*1699–1707*) mark the termination of a line of fires which have flared all along the course of Samson's career. His birth was foretold by an angel which ascended 'in flames' (*25, 1433*), 'As in a fiery column' (*27*); ropes to him were 'threads / Touched with the flame' (*262*); 'heaven's fiery rod' (*549*) pointed out a fountain for his thirst; his fall is marked by his inability to share the 'blaze' of noon (*80*); as he leaves the stage the chorus call down 'a shield, / Of fire' (*1434–5*) for him. The elevatory force of this fire imagery is, however, sharply questioned when, shortly before the apparently 'extinguished' Samson rouses his own 'fiery virtue' into 'sudden flame' (*1688–92*), he is warned not to add fuel to the 'flame' (*1351*) of the Philistine lords, and himself speaks of the priests and worshippers of Dagon 'fired' with zeal and 'unquenchable' (*1419–22*). An equivalence between the religious fervour of the Philistines and that of the protagonist is momentarily revealed.

In *SA*, then, the imagery does not merely reinforce the drama's triumphant upward arc. On the contrary, it contributes meanings which threaten to invert this arc and bring the weak-minded, vengeful hero to the level of Dalila and the Philistines. In this way it makes a major contribution to the moral maturity of the work.

OF THAT SORT OF DRAMATIC POEM WHICH IS CALLED TRAGEDY

TRAGEDY, as it was anciently composed, hath been ever held the gravest, moralest, and most profitable of all other poems: therefore said by Aristotle to be of power by raising pity and fear, or terror, to purge the mind of those and such-like passions, that is to temper and reduce them to just measure with a kind of delight, stirred up by reading or seeing those passions well imitated. Nor is nature wanting in her own effects to make good his assertion: for so in physic things of melancholic hue and quality are used against melancholy, sour against sour, salt to remove salt humours. Hence philosophers and other gravest writers, as Cicero, Plutarch and others, frequently cite out of tragic poets, both to adorn and illustrate their discourse. The Apostle Paul himself thought it not unworthy to insert a verse of Euripides into the text of Holy Scripture, 1 Cor. xv. 33, and Paraeus

Introduction 1–9. Tragedy . . . humours] P. R. Sellin, *JEGP* lx (1961) 712–30, notes that, although M.'s version of Aristotelian catharsis, with its homoeopathic analogy, has been traced to Minturno, *De Poeta* (1563) and Guarini, *Il Compendio della Poesia Tragicomica* (1601), Minturno conceives of catharsis as the driving out of undesirable passions rather than the reduction of all passions to a norm, as in M.'s account, and Guarini takes Aristotle's τοιούτων παθημάτων, which M. translates 'of those and such-like passions', to refer to pity and fear alone, and goes on to make a distinction, not in M., between good fear and pity and bad. A theory of catharsis nearer to M.'s, though not identical is advanced by Daniel Heinsius, *De Tragoediae Constitutione* (1611), which Sellin thinks M.'s source. However, in Heinsius' theory, as in Guarini's, pity and fear seem the only emotions involved in the tragic catharsis.
Introduction 12–13 verse of Euripides] J. J. Lynch, *N&Q* iii (1956) 477, says that the maxim referred to ('Evil communications corrupt good manners') is from Menander's *Thais*, not Euripides. But in fact the fragment in which it survives is found in editions of both Euripides and Menander.
Introduction 13. Paraeus] David Paraeus (1548–1622), a German Calvinist whose *Commentary on Romans* (1609) was publicly burned by the universities of Oxford and Cambridge. His work *On the Divine Apocalypse* (1618), to which M. here refers, was translated into English by Elias Arnold, 1644. A. C.

commenting on the *Revelation*, divides the whole book as a tragedy, into acts distinguished each by a chorus of heavenly harpings and song between. Heretofore men in highest dignity have laboured not a little to be thought able to compose a tragedy. Of that honour Dionysius the elder was no less ambitious, than before of his attaining to the tyranny. Augustus Caesar also had begun his *Ajax*, but unable to please his own judgement with what he had begun, left it unfinished. Seneca the philosopher is by some thought the author of those tragedies (at least the best of them) that go under that name. Gregory Nazianzen a Father of the Church, thought it not unbeseeming the sanctity of his person to write a tragedy, which he entitled, *Christ Suffering*. This is mentioned to vindicate tragedy from the small esteem, or rather infamy, which in the account of many it undergoes at this day with other common interludes; happening through the poet's error of intermixing comic stuff with tragic sadness and gravity; or introducing trivial and vulgar persons, which by all judicious hath been counted absurd; and brought in without discretion, corruptly to gratify the people. And though ancient tragedy use no prologue, yet using sometimes in case of self-defence, or explanation, that which Martial calls an epistle; in behalf of this tragedy coming forth after the ancient manner, much different from what among us passes for best, thus much beforehand may be *epistled*; that chorus is here introduced after the Greek manner, not ancient only but modern, and still in use among the Italians. In the modelling therefore of this

Cook, *Archiv für das Studium der Neueren Sprachen* cxxix (1912) 74–80, quotes the relevant passages from Paraeus.

Introduction 18. Dionysius] Tyrant of Syracuse (431–367 B.C.). Diodorus Siculus xiv 109 tells how his poems were ridiculed at the Olympic games, and, xv 74, how he died from a debauch following the news that his play had won the prize at the Lenaea at Athens.

Introduction 19. Augustus Caesar . . . Ajax] Suetonius ii 85 says Augustus, dissatisfied with what he had written of the *Ajax*, erased it.

Introduction 21. Seneca] Lucius Annaeus Seneca (3 B.C.–65 A.D.). There are ten tragedies which bear his name (the *Octavia*, also ascribed to him, is certainly later). The doubt as to his authorship of the tragedies is due to a mistake of Sidonius Apollinaris, *Carmen* ix 230–8, who clearly distinguishes between Seneca the philosopher and Seneca the tragedian.

Introduction 22–3. Gregory Nazianzen] Bishop of Constantinople (AD 325?–390?); his *Christus Patiens*, a piece of Byzantine Euripidean pastiche, has also been ascribed to Apollinarius the elder.

Introduction 28. sadness] seriousness.

Introduction 31. prologue] M. uses the term in its modern sense (a preliminary address to the audience), not in Aristotle's sense (the part of a tragedy which precedes the entrance of the chorus).

Introduction 33. Martial (epistle to *Epig.* ii) notes that tragedies and comedies may need epistles since 'they cannot speak for themselves'.

Introduction 37. Italians] Tasso's *Aminta* and Guarini's *Pastor Fido*, for example,

poem, with good reason, the ancients and Italians are rather followed, as of much more authority and fame. The measure of verse used in the chorus is of all sorts, called by the Greeks monostrophic, or rather apolelymenon, without regard had to strophe, antistrophe or epode, which were a kind of stanzas framed only for the music, then used with the chorus that sung; not essential to the poem, and therefore not material; or being divided into stanzas or pauses, they may be called alloeostropha. Division into act and scene referring chiefly to the stage (to which this work never was intended) is here omitted.

It suffices if the whole drama be found not produced beyond the fifth act. Of the style and uniformity, and that commonly called the plot, whether intricate or explicit, which is nothing indeed but such economy, or disposition of the fable as may stand best with verisimilitude and decorum; they only will best judge who are not unacquainted with Aeschylus, Sophocles, and Euripides, the three tragic poets unequalled yet by any, and the best rule to all who endeavour to write tragedy. The circumscription of time wherein the whole drama begins and ends, is according to ancient rule, and best example, within the space of twenty-four hours.

THE ARGUMENT

Samson made captive, blind, and now in the prison at Gaza, there to labour as in a common workhouse, on a festival day, in the general

both have a chorus, as did sixteenth-century Italian tragic drama frequently. M. cites 'the Italian Commentaries of Castelvetro, Tasso, Mazzoni, and others', along with Aristotle and Horace, as authorities in *Of Education* (Columbia iv 286, Yale ii 404).

Introduction 40–1. monostrophic] of one stanza only. *apolelymenon*] Greek 'freed' (i.e. from the restraint of any firm stanza pattern). In Gk drama the strophe was a stanza sung by the chorus as it moved from right to left, the antistrophe, corresponding exactly to the strophe in structure, as it moved in the opposite direction. The concluding epode was sung standing still. M. says that if his choruses do seem at times to divide into stanzas, then they should be called alloeostropha (Greek 'of irregular strophes').

Introduction 49. intricate . . . explicit] Aristotle, *Poetics* 6, divides plots into two classes, simple (ἁπλοῖ) and complex (πεπλεγμένοι). *which is nothing indeed*] i.e. the plot is merely the management ('economy') of the events: the 'putting together of the incidents', as Aristotle calls it.

Introduction 52. Aeschylus] J. C. Maxwell, *RES* n.s. iii (1952) 366–71, points out that Aeschylus was not popular, even among scholars, in the seventeenth century, and that M. is unusual in ranking him with Sophocles and Euripides here.

Introduction 55–6. ancient rule] Aristotle, *Poetics* 5, gives no 'rule'. It was Renaissance criticism that hardened his general statement into the 'unity of time'. *best example*] there are five exceptions among surviving Greek tragedies: Aeschylus' *Persians*, *Agamemnon* and *Eumenides*, Sophocles' *Trachiniae* and Euripides' *Suppliants*.

cessation from labour, comes forth into the open air, to a place nigh, somewhat retired there to sit a while and bemoan his condition. Where he happens at length to be visited by certain friends and equals of his tribe, which make the Chorus, who seek to comfort him what they can; then by his old father Manoa, who endeavours the like, and withal tells him his purpose to procure his liberty by ransom; lastly, that this feast was proclaimed by the Philistines as a day of thanksgiving for their deliverance from the hands of Samson, which yet more troubles him. Manoa then departs to prosecute his endeavour with the Philistian lords for Samson's redemption; who in the meanwhile is visited by other persons; and lastly by a public officer to require his coming to the feast before the lords and people, to play or show his strength in their presence; he at first refuses, dismissing the public officer with absolute denial to come; at length persuaded inwardly that this was from God, he yields to go along with him, who came now the second time with great threatenings to fetch him; the Chorus yet remaining on the place, Manoa returns full of joyful hope, to procure ere long his son's deliverance: in the midst of which discourse an Hebrew comes in haste confusedly at first; and afterwards more distinctly relating the catastrophe, what Samson had done to the Philistines, and by accident to himself; wherewith the tragedy ends.

THE PERSONS

Samson
Manoa, the father of Samson
Dalila his wife
Harapha of Gath
Public Officer
Messenger
Chorus of Danites

The Scene before the Prison in Gaza

Sam. A little onward lend thy guiding hand
To these dark steps, a little further on;
For yonder bank hath choice of sun or shade,
There I am wont to sit, when any chance
Relieves me from my task of servile toil,
Daily in the common prison else enjoined me,

1–2. This opening has been compared to the first scene of the *Oedipus at Colonus*, where Oedipus is led forward by Antigone, and to Euripides, *Phoenician Maidens* 834–5, where Tiresias asks his daughter to lead him on, and says she is as eyes to his 'blind feet'. In Sidney, *Arcadia* II x 3, the blinded king of Paphlagonia complains that there is no one to 'lende me a hande to guide my darke steppes'.

3. choice of sun or shade] 'The opening lines, describing mere physical sensation, also suggest the internal drama to come' (Stein[2] 139).

Where I a prisoner chained, scarce freely draw
The air imprisoned also, close and damp,
Unwholesome draught: but here I feel amends,
The breath of heaven fresh blowing, pure and sweet,
With day-spring born; here leave me to respire.
This day a solemn feast the people hold
To Dagon their sea-idol, and forbid
Laborious works, unwillingly this rest
Their superstition yields me; hence with leave
Retiring from the popular noise, I seek
This unfrequented place to find some ease,
Ease to the body some, none to the mind
From restless thoughts, that like a deadly swarm
Of hornets armed, no sooner found alone,
But rush upon me thronging, and present
Times past, what once I was, and what am now.
O wherefore was my birth from heaven foretold
Twice by an angel, who at last in sight
Of both my parents all in flames ascended
From off the altar, where an offering burned,
As in a fiery column charioting
His godlike presence, and from some great act
Or benefit revealed to Abraham's race?
Why was my breeding ordered and prescribed
As of a person separate to God,
Designed for great exploits; if I must die
Betrayed, captived, and both my eyes put out,
Made of my enemies the scorn and gaze;
To grind in brazen fetters under task

10. Stein[2] 139 takes this line as an early note of the regeneration theme.

11. day-spring] daybreak, cp. *Luke* i 78: 'The day-spring from on high hath visited us.'

13. Dagon] National deity of the Philistines, presented in *PL* i 462–3 as half-man, half-fish (the name is possibly derived from Heb. *Dag*, 'fish'). His chief temples were at Gaza (*Judges* xvi 23) and Ashdod (*1 Sam.* v 1–2).

24. Twice] First to his mother alone, *Judges* xiii 3–5, and later to both parents, xiii 10–20.

27. charioting] Cp. the fiery chariot of Elijah, *2 Kings* i 11, and Josephus, *Antiquities* v 8, who says that the angel ascended from the rock on which Manoa's sacrifice burned 'by means of the smoke, as by a vehicle'.

28. from] The angel ascended 'From off the altar' and 'from' revealing 'some great act / Or benefit'.

31. separate] 'Nazarite' is derived from Heb. *nazar*, 'to separate oneself', and the angel says to Samson's mother, *Judges* xiii 7: 'The child shall be a Nazarite unto God.'

With this heaven-gifted strength? O glorious strength
Put to the labour of a beast, debased
Lower than bond-slave! Promise was that I
Should Israel from Philistian yoke deliver;
Ask for this great deliverer now, and find him
Eyeless in Gaza at the mill with slaves,
Himself in bonds under Philistian yoke;
Yet stay, let me not rashly call in doubt
Divine prediction; what if all foretold
Had been fulfilled but through mine own default,
Whom have I to complain of but myself?
Who this high gift of strength committed to me,
In what part lodged, how easily bereft me,
Under the seal of silence could not keep,
But weakly to a woman must reveal it,
O'ercome with importunity and tears.
O impotence of mind, in body strong!
But what is strength without a double share
Of wisdom, vast, unwieldly, burdensome,
Proudly secure, yet liable to fall
By weakest subtleties, not made to rule,
But to subserve where wisdom bears command.
God, when he gave me strength, to show withal
How slight the gift was, hung it in my hair.
But peace, I must not quarrel with the will
Of highest dispensation, which herein
Haply had ends above my reach to know:
Suffices that to me strength is my bane,
And proves the source of all my miseries;
So many, and so huge, that each apart
Would ask a life to wail, but chief of all,
O loss of sight, of thee I most complain!
Blind among enemies, O worse than chains,
Dungeon, or beggary, or decrepit age!
Light the prime work of God to me is extinct,
And all her various objects of delight
Annulled, which might in part my grief have eased,

38. Promise was] Cp. *Judges* xiii 5: 'He shall begin to deliver Israel out of the hand of the Philistines.'

52. This aspect of M.'s Samson, his weak-mindedness, is not emphasised either in *Judges* or in the Christian tradition of Samson literature (Krouse 100).

53–4. Cp. Horace, *Odes* III iv 65: 'Brute force bereft of wisdom falls to ruin by its own weight.'

66–7. Contrast l. 195.

Inferior to the vilest now become
Of man or worm; the vilest here excel me,
They creep, yet see, I dark in light exposed
To daily fraud, contempt, abuse and wrong,
Within doors, or without, still as a fool,
In power of others, never in my own;
Scarce half I seem to live, dead more than half.
O dark, dark, dark, amid the blaze of noon,
Irrecoverably dark, total eclipse
Without all hope of day!
O first-created beam, and thou great word,
Let there be light, and light was over all;
Why am I thus bereaved thy prime decree?
The sun to me is dark
And silent as the moon,
When she deserts the night
Hid in her vacant interlunar cave.
Since light so necessary is to life,
And almost life itself, if it be true
That light is in the soul,
She all in every part; why was the sight
To such a tender ball as the eye confined?

77. still] always.

79–109. For a rhetorical analysis of this passage see J. B. Broadbent, *MP* lvi (1959) 226–7.

83–4. Cp. *Gen.* i 3.

87–9. silent] The time when the moon is in conjunction with the sun is called, says Pliny xvi 74, either the day of the silent moon (*silentis lunae*) or the interlunar day (*interlunii*). *OED* first records the word 'silent' meaning 'not shining', as applied to the moon, in 1646. Pathetically Samson translates a visual fact, the moon's absence, into the terms of the sense he still retains, hearing. *vacant*] M. thinks of the moon at leisure (Latin *vacare*) resting in a cave.

92–3. A. Williams, *MLN* lxiii (1948) 537–8, refers to the theory that the soul is whole in the whole body and whole in every part of the body – a commonplace deriving from the Fathers. He compares Augustine, *De Trinitate* vi 6: *anima . . . in unoquoque corpore, et in toto tota est, et in qualibet eius parte tota est* (The soul . . . in any body, is both all in the whole, and all in every part).

93–7. T. Spencer and J. Willis, *N & Q* cxcvi (1951) 387, quote a parallel from Arnobius, *Adversus Gentes* ii 59 – a writer to whom M. refers twice elsewhere – *Cur cum esset utilius oculis nos illuminare compluribus ad periculum caecitatis, duorum sumus angustiis applicati?* (Why, since it would be an advantage considering the danger of blindness for us to be enlightened with many eyes, are we tied to the inconvenience of two?)

So obvious and so easy to be quenched,
And not as feeling through all parts diffused,
That she might look at will through every pore?
Then had I not been thus exiled from light;
As in the land of darkness yet in light,
To live a life half dead, a living death,
And buried; but O yet more miserable!
Myself, my sepulchre, a moving grave,
Buried, yet not exempt
By privilege of death and burial
From worst of other evils, pains and wrongs,
But made hereby obnoxious more
To all the miseries of life,
Life in captivity
Among inhuman foes.
But who are these? for with joint pace I hear
The tread of many feet steering this way;
Perhaps my enemies who come to stare
At my affliction, and perhaps to insult,
Their daily practice to afflict me more.
Chor. This, this is he; softly a while,
Let us not break in upon him;
O change beyond report, thought, or belief!
See how he lies at random, carelessly diffused,
With languished head unpropped,
As one past hope, abandoned,
And by himself given over;
In slavish habit, ill-fitted weeds
O'er-worn and soiled;
Or do my eyes misrepresent? Can this be he,
That heroic, that renowned,
Irresistible Samson? whom unarmed
No strength of man, or fiercest wild beast could
withstand;
Who tore the lion, as the lion tears the kid,
Ran on embattled armies clad in iron,
And weaponless himself,

95. obvious] exposed.
106. obnoxious] liable to.
118–9. diffused . . . languished] Echoes Ovid, *Ex Ponto* III iii 8: *fusaque erant toto languida membra toro* (languid limbs diffused over the bed).
128. Cp. *Judges* xiv 6: 'And he rent him [the young lion] as he would have rent a kid.'

Made arms ridiculous, useless the forgery
Of brazen shield and spear, the hammered cuirass,
Chalybean-tempered steel, and frock of mail
Adamantean proof;
But safest he who stood aloof,
When insupportably his foot advanced,
In scorn of their proud arms and warlike tools,
Spurned them to death by troops. The bold Ascalonite
Fled from his lion ramp, old warriors turned
Their plated backs under his heel;
Or grovelling soiled their crested helmets in the dust.
Then with what trivial weapon came to hand,
The jaw of a dead ass, his sword of bone,
A thousand foreskins fell, the flower of Palestine
In Ramath-lechi famous to this day:
Then by main force pulled up, and on his shoulders
bore
The gates of Azza, post, and massy bar
Up to the hill by Hebron, seat of giants old,

131. forgery] The craft of forging metal.
133. Chalybean] Cp. Virgil, *Georg.* i 58: 'the naked Chalybes give us iron'– they were famous metal-workers. Starnes and Talbert 246 quote from Stephanus *Chalybs, fluvius in Hispania, in quo ferrum optime temperatur.*
134. Adamantean] the only recorded instance of the adjective in *OED*; 'adamant' (*adamas*) was the name applied by Latin writers to the hardest known substance–at first steel, later diamond. *proof*] a noun (='proof armour', armour which was considered impenetrable), in apposition to 'frock of mail'.
136. insupportably] irresistibly.
138. Ascalonite] Ascalon is mentioned in *1 Sam.* vi 17 as one of the five main cities of the Philistines. In *Judges* xiv 19, Samson goes down to Ascalon and kills thirty men there.
139. lion] lion-like. *ramp*] act of ramping (the first occurrence of the noun in this sense recorded in *OED*); to 'ramp' is to raise the forepaws in the air.
140. plated] wearing armour.
143. In *Judges* xv 15–6 Samson finds the jawbone of an ass, and kills a thousand men with it.
144. foreskins] uncircumcised Philistines.
145. Ramath-lechi] The marginal note to A.V. *Judges* xv 17 translates 'Ramath-lehi' as meaning 'The lifting up' or 'casting away of the jawbone'.
146–8. This exploit is narrated in *Judges* xvi 3. 'Azza' is a variant form of Gaza.
148. seat of giants] Hebron was the city of Arba, *Josh.* xiv 15, father of Anak, xv 13–4, whose children, the Anakim, were giants, *Num.* xiii 33.

No journey of a sabbath-day, and loaded so;
Like whom the Gentiles feign to bear up heaven.
Which shall I first bewail,
Thy bondage or lost sight,
Prison within prison
Inseparably dark?
Thou art become (O worst imprisonment!)
The dungeon of thyself; thy soul
(Which men enjoying sight oft without cause complain)
Imprisoned now indeed,
In real darkness of the body dwells,
Shut up from outward light
To incorporate with gloomy night;
For inward light alas
Puts forth no visual beam.
O mirror of our fickle state,
Since man on earth unparalleled!
The rarer thy example stands,
By how much from the top of wondrous glory,
Strongest of mortal men,
To lowest pitch of abject fortune thou art fallen.
For him I reckon not in high estate
Whom long descent of birth
Or the sphere of fortune raises;
But thee whose strength, while virtue was her mate,
Might have subdued the earth,
Universally crowned with highest praises.
Sam. I hear the sound of words, their sense the air
Dissolves unjointed ere it reach my ear.
Chor. He speaks, let us draw night. Matchless in might,
The glory late of Israel, now the grief;

150. whom] Atlas.
157. (Which . . . complain)] i.e. men often complain that the soul is imprisoned in the body. *1671* prints 'complain'd', but the *Errata* corrects to 'complain'.
161. incorporate with] combine with.
163. visual beam] beam of eyesight.
165. Since . . . unparalleled!] i.e. O mirror, unparalleled since man was on earth!
166–7. The rarer . . . By how much] The spectacular nature of Samson's fall makes his example proportionately more noteworthy. M.'s construction is based on the Latin use of *eo . . . quo* with a comparative.
170–5. Parker[2] 112 takes these lines as M.'s justification of his disobedience to Aristotle (*Poetics* 13) who said the tragic hero should be 'a personage like Oedipus, Thyestes, or other illustrious men of such families'.

We come thy friends and neighbours not unknown
From Eshtaol and Zora's fruitful vale
To visit or bewail thee, or if better,
Counsel or consolation we may bring,
Salve to thy sores, apt words have power to 'suage
The tumours of a troubled mind,
And are as balm to festered wounds.
Sam. Your coming, friends, revives me, for I learn
Now of my own experience, not by talk,
How counterfeit a coin they are who friends
Bear in their superscription (of the most
I would be understood) in prosperous days
They swarm, but in adverse withdraw their head
Not to be found, though sought. Ye see, O friends,
How many evils have enclosed me round;
Yet that which was the worst now least afflicts me,
Blindness, for had I sight, confused with shame,
How could I once look up, or heave the head,
Who like a foolish pilot have shipwrecked,
My vessel trusted to me from above,
Gloriously rigged; and for a word, a tear,
Fool, have divulged the secret gift of God
To a deceitful woman: tell me friends,
Am I not sung and proverbed for a fool
In every street, do they not say, how well
Are come upon him his deserts? yet why?
Immeasurable strength they might behold
In me, of wisdom nothing more than mean;
This with the other should, at least, have paired,
These two proportioned ill drove me transverse.
Chor. Tax not divine disposal, wisest men
Have erred, and by bad women been deceived;
And shall again, pretend they ne'er so wise.
Deject not then so overmuch thyself,
Who hast of sorrow thy full load besides;

181. Samson was born at Zora, *Judges* xiii 2, and buried between Zora and Eshtaol, xvi 31. These towns lay 'in the valley' and are ascribed to both Judah and Dan (*Josh.* xv 33 and xix 41).
190. superscription] The stamp on a coin.
203. proverbed] Cp. *Ps.* lxix 11: 'I became a proverb to them', and Job xxx 9: 'And now am I their song, yea, I am their byword' (vulg. *proverbium*).
207. mean] average.
209. transverse] sideways, off-course, a nautical term, continuing the ship image of 198–200.

Yet truth to say, I oft have heard men wonder
Why thou shouldst wed Philistian women rather
Than of thine own tribe fairer, or as fair,
At least of thy own nation, and as noble.
Sam. The first I saw at Timna, and she pleased
Me, not my parents, that I sought to wed,
The daughter of an infidel: they knew not
That what I motioned was of God; I knew
From intimate impulse, and therefore urged
The marriage on; that by occasion hence
I might begin Israel's deliverance,
The work to which I was divinely called;
She proving false, the next I took to wife
(O that I never had! fond wish too late.)
Was in the vale of Sorec, Dalila,
That specious monster, my accomplished snare.
I thought it lawful from my former act,
And the same end; still watching to oppress
Israel's oppressors: of what now I suffer
She was not the prime cause, but I myself,

215–8. This is the reply to Samson's question, ll. 203–5.

216. In assuming that Dalila was a Philistine M. follows one stream of exegetical tradition and rejects another, deriving from Cajetan, which suggested that she might have been an Israelite (Krouse 102).

219–26. M. follows the account in *Judges* xiv 1–4 exactly, except in the detail of Samson's 'intimate impulse', which is not in *Judges*–the reason Samson gives there for the match is 'she pleaseth me well'. Krouse 96 points out that Christian tradition had argued from Theodoret onwards that all Samson's apparent waywardness–like his marrying the woman of Timna–was at the instigation of God. In M.'s own age Calvin, Brenz, Bullinger, Paraeus and others had defended Samson on these grounds.

222. motioned] *1671* prints 'mention'd' but the *Errata* corrects to 'motioned'.

227. proving false] In *Judges* xiv 5–20 she extracts from Samson the answer to the riddle he has set the young men of Timna, and tells it to them. Her father then gives her to Samson's 'companion, whom he had used as his friend'. *to wife*] The Samson of *Judges* was not married to Dalila. Krouse 76 comments that the question most discussed in the Renaissance was whether she had been his wife or his concubine: many commentators followed Chrysostom in maintaining that she was his wife. M.'s Samson calls her a 'concubine' (l. 537), but M. makes her Samson's wife from the outset (see list of 'Persons' p. 346 above).

229. Cp. *Judges* xvi 4: 'He loved a woman in the valley of Sorek.' Stein[a] 146 comments: 'The first feeling for Dalila . . . is to be heard in the softened beauty of the line that announces her.'

230. specious] having a deceptively attractive appearance. *accomplished*]

Who vanquished with a peal of words (O weakness!)
Gave up my fort of silence to a woman.
Chor. In seeking just occasion to provoke
The Philistine, thy country's enemy,
Thou never wast remiss, I bear thee witness:
Yet Israel still serves with all his sons.
Sam. That fault I take not on me, but transfer
On Israel's governors, and heads of tribes,
Who seeing those great acts which God had done
Singly by me against their conquerors
Acknowledged not, or not at all considered
Deliverance offered: I on the other side
Used no ambition to commend my deeds,
The deeds themselves, though mute, spoke loud the
doer;
But they persisted deaf, and would not seem
To count them things worth notice, till at length
Their lords the Philistines with gathered powers
Entered Judea seeking me, who then
Safe to the rock of Etham was retired,
Not flying, but forecasting in what place
To set upon them, what advantaged best;
Meanwhile the men of Judah to prevent
The harass of their land, beset me round;
I willingly on some conditions came
Into their hands, and they as gladly yield me

The snare is accomplished in that it has fulfilled its function and caught Samson, and Dalila is accomplished because she has various accomplishments, persuasiveness, for example.

235. peal] The military imagery ('fort') suggests that 'peal' is here an artillery term. A peal of guns was used as a salute or sign of rejoicing: the guns were not weapons of attack when pealing. Samson's disgrace is all the more bitter: he gave up his fort at the mere sound of guns.

242. In *Judges* xv 20, xvi 32 Samson himself rules Israel for twenty years: this does not suit M.'s conception of an unsupported leader.

247. ambition] in the sense of Latin *ambitio*, 'walking about to solicit votes or applause'.

251–5. In *Judges* xv Samson burns the Philistines' standing corn. They, in revenge, burn his wife and her father, 5–6; he smites them 'hip and thigh with a great slaughter' and goes to dwell 'in the top of the rock Etam', 8. 'Then the Philistines went up, and pitched in Judah', 9.

256–7. Cp. *Judges* xv 11–2.

258. on some conditions] *Judges* xv 12: 'Swear unto me, that ye will not fall upon me yourselves.'

259–64. Cp. *Judges* xv 13–6, where the men of Judah bind Samson 'with

To the uncircumcised a welcome prey,
Bound with two cords; but cords to me were threads
Touched with the flame: on their whole host I flew
Unarmed, and with a trivial weapon felled
Their choicest youth; they only lived who fled.
Had Judah that day joined, or one whole tribe,
They had by this possessed the towers of Gath,
And lorded over them whom now they serve;
But what more oft in nations grown corrupt,
And by their vices brought to servitude,
Than to love bondage more than liberty,
Bondage with ease than strenuous liberty;
And to despise, or envy, or suspect
Whom God hath of his special favour raised
As their deliverer; if he aught begin,
How frequent to desert him, and at last
To heap ingratitude on worthiest deeds?
Chor. Thy words to my remembrance bring
How Succoth and the fort of Penuel
Their great deliverer contemned,
The matchless Gideon in pursuit
Of Madian and her vanquished kings;
And how ingrateful Ephraim

two new cords' and hand him over to the Philistines, but 'the cords that were upon his arms became as flax that was burnt with fire, and his bands loosed from off his hands'. He then kills a thousand men with the ass's jawbone.

266. by this] by this time. *Gath*] one of the five great cities of Philistia.

271. Cp. *PL* ii 255–7*n*.

275. frequent] accustomed; a fairly common seventeenth-century sense.

277–89. Gideon] Cp. *Judges* viii 5–9 where Gideon, pursuing 'Zebah and Zalmunna, kings of Midian', asks for bread for his three hundred followers from Succoth and Penuel, but is refused. 'Madian' is the Vulgate form and Sylvester's (Du Bartas 468 'Madian Kings'). *Jephtha*] Cp. *Judges* xi 12–33 and xii 1–6 where the Ephraimites refuse to help Jephtha against the Ammonites, whom he nevertheless first refutes in argument and then defeats in battle. Later the Ephraimites pick a quarrel with Jephtha and his Gileadites, but he takes the passages of the Jordan, and anyone wishing to go over is asked 'Art thou now an Ephraimite?' If any Ephraimite denied his nationality: 'Then said they unto him, Say now Shibboleth: and he said Sibboleth; for he could not frame to pronounce it right. Then they took him, and slew him.' Forty-two thousand Ephraimites were thus killed. The Heb. *shibboleth* means either 'ear of corn' or 'stream in flood'. Krouse 98 comments that Gideon and Jephtha were considered saints like Samson, and for the same reason: they had been mentioned by Paul, *Heb.* xi 32.

Had dealt with Jephtha, who by argument,
Not worse than by his shield and spear
Defended Israel from the Ammonite,
Had not his prowess quelled their pride
In that sore battle when so many died
Without reprieve adjudged to death,
For want of well pronouncing *Shibboleth.*
Sam. Of such examples add me to the roll,
Me easily indeed mine may neglect,
But God's proposed deliverance not so.
Chor. Just are the ways of God,
And justifiable to men;
Unless there be who think not God at all,
If any be, they walk obscure;
For of such doctrine never was there school,
But the heart of the fool,
And no man therein doctor but himself.
Yet more there be who doubt his ways not just,
As to his own edicts, found contradicting,
Then give the reins to wandering thought,
Regardless of his glory's diminution;
Till by their own perplexities involved
They ravel more, still less resolved,
But never find self-satisfying solution.
As if they would confine the interminable,
And tie him to his own prescript,
Who made our laws to bind us, not himself,
And hath full right to exempt
Whom so it pleases him by choice
From national obstriction, without taint
Of sin, or legal debt;
For with his own laws he can best dispense.
He would not else who never wanted means,
Nor in respect of the enemy just cause
To set his people free,
Have prompted this heroic Nazarite,

291. mine] my people.
298. Cp. *Ps.* xiv 1: 'The fool hath said in his heart, There is no God.'
305. ravel] become entangled.
306. There are two different *1671* states of this line. In the first it, as well as l. 307, is indented.
312. obstriction] M.'s coinage. The obligation referred to is *Deut.* vii 3, but seemingly no O.T. prohibition bars marriage with Philistines.
313. legal debt] duty owed to the (Mosaic) law. Like 'national obstriction' 'legal debt' is the object of 'exempt from'.

Against his vow of strictest purity,
To seek in marriage that fallacious bride,
Unclean, unchaste.
Down Reason then, at least vain reasonings down,
Though Reason here aver
That moral verdict quits her of unclean:
Unchaste was subsequent, her stain not his.
But see here comes thy reverend sire
With careful step, locks white as down,
Old Manoa: advise
Forthwith how thou ought'st to receive him.
Sam. Ay me, another inward grief awaked,
With mention of that name renews the assault.
Man. Brethren and men of Dan, for such ye seem,
Though in this uncouth place; if old respect,
As I suppose, towards your once gloried friend,
My son now captive, hither hath informed
Your younger feet, while mine cast back with age
Came lagging after; say if he be here.
Chor. As signal now in low dejected state,
As erst in highest, behold him where he lies.
Man. O miserable change! is this the man,
That invincible Samson, far renowned,
The dread of Israel's foes, who with a strength
Equivalent to angel's walked their streets,
None offering fight; who single combatant
Duelled their armies ranked in proud array,

319. Celibacy was not in the Nazarite vow (*Num.* vi 1–21), and marriage with Gentiles was not impurity until after the reformation of Ezra.
322–5. The chorus first (l. 322) dispose of those who attempt to reason about God's ways (ll. 300–6), and call their 'reasoning' vain. What is more, they go on, even reason must confess that the woman (of Timna) whom God prompted Samson to marry was, at the time, neither morally unclean nor unchaste. She was unclean only in a legal sense, as a Gentile, and her unchastity took place afterwards ('was subsequent'); cp. *Judges* xiv 20: 'Samson's wife was given to his companion.' Thus ll. 323–5 justify Samson's first marriage from a 'reasonable' point of view.
324. quits] acquits.
333. uncouth] unknown.
334. once gloried] The phrase may mean 'friend once boasted of' or 'friend once honoured': *OED* records this as the only instance of the past participle of the verb 'glory'.
338. signal] remarkable.
340. miserable change] The phrase is Shakespeare's, *Antony and Cleopatra* IV xv 51.

Himself an army, now unequal match
To save himself against a coward armed
At one spear's length. O ever-failing trust
In mortal strength! and O what not in man
Deceivable and vain! Nay what thing good
Prayed for, but often proves our woe, our bane?
I prayed for children, and thought barrenness
In wedlock a reproach; I gained a son,
And such a son as all men hailed me happy;
Who would be now a father in my stead?
O wherefore did God grant me my request,
And as a blessing with such pomp adorned?
Why are his gifts desirable, to tempt
Our earnest prayers, then given with solemn hand
As graces, draw a scorpion's tail behind?
For this did the angel twice descend? for this
Ordained thy nurture holy, as of a plant;
Select, and sacred, glorious for a while,
The miracle of men: then in an hour
Ensnared, assaulted, overcome, led bound,
Thy foes' derision, captive, poor, and blind
Into a dungeon thrust, to work with slaves?
Alas methinks whom God hath chosen once
To worthiest deeds, if he through frailty err,
He should not so o'erwhelm, and as a thrall
Subject him to so foul indignities,
Be it but for honour's sake of former deeds.
Sam. Appoint not heavenly disposition, father,
Nothing of all these evils hath befall'n me
But justly; I myself have brought them on,
Sole author I, sole cause: if aught seem vile,
As vile hath been my folly, who have profaned
The mystery of God given me under pledge
Of vow, and have betrayed it to a woman,
A Canaanite, my faithless enemy.
This well I knew, nor was at all surprised,

354. And such] *1671* prints 'Such,' but the *Errata* supplies 'And'.
373. Appoint] *OED* gives meaning as 'arraign'. G. C. Moore Smith, *MLR* iii (1907–8) 74, disagrees, preferring the more common meaning 'prescribe or determine the course of', but E. Weekley, *MLR* iii (1907–8) 373–4, supports *OED*, noting that Fr. *appointer* can mean 'arraign' in legal contexts.
377. profaned] published (Latin *profanus*, 'outside the temple', hence 'public').
380. Canaanite] The Philistines were actually immigrants into Canaan from 'Caphtor' (i.e. Crete? Phoenicia?), *Amos* ix 7.

But warned by oft experience: did not she
Of Timna first betray me, and reveal
The secret wrested from me in her height
Of nuptial love professed, carrying it straight
To them who had corrupted her, my spies,
And rivals? In this other was there found
More faith? who also in her prime of love,
Spousal embraces, vitiated with gold,
Though offered only, by the scent conceived
Her spurious first-born; treason against me?
Thrice she assayed with flattering prayers and sighs,
And amorous reproaches to win from me
My capital secret, in what part my strength
Lay stored, in what part summed, that she might know:
Thrice I deluded her, and turned to sport
Her importunity, each time perceiving
How openly and with what impudence
She purposed to betray me, and (which was worse
Than undissembled hate) with what contempt
She sought to make me traitor to myself;
Yet the fourth time, when mustering all her wiles,
With blandished parleys, feminine assaults,
Tongue-batteries, she surceased not day nor night
To storm me over-watched, and wearied out.
At times when men seek most repose and rest,
I yielded, and unlocked her all my heart,
Who with a grain of manhood well resolved
Might easily have shook off all her snares:
But foul effeminacy held me yoked
Her bond-slave; O indignity, O blot
To honour and religion! servile mind
Rewarded well with servile punishment!

382–7. See l. *227n.*
388–9. Spousal embraces] In apposition to 'prime of love'; 'vitiated' (corrupted) qualifies 'who'.
390. Though offered only] Qualifying 'gold'. Cp. *Judges* xvi 5: 'And we will give thee every one of us eleven hundred pieces of silver.'
392. Thrice] Cp. *Judges* xvi 6–15.
393. amorous reproaches] Cp. *Judges* xvi 15: 'How canst thou say, I love thee, when thine heart is not with me?'
394. capital] A pun: 'most important', and also 'pertaining to the head' (Latin *caput*).
403. blandished] invested with flattery or blandishment (the only occurrence of the word recorded in *OED*).
405. over-watched] kept awake too long.

The base degree to which I now am fall'n,
These rags, this grinding, is not yet so base
As was my former servitude, ignoble,
Unmanly, ignominious, infamous,
True slavery, and that blindness worse than this,
That saw not how degenerately I served.
Man. I cannot praise thy marriage-choices, son,
Rather approved them not; but thou didst plead
Divine impulsion prompting how thou might'st
Find some occasion to infest our foes.
I state not that; this I am sure; our foes
Found soon occasion thereby to make thee
Their captive, and their triumph; thou the sooner
Temptation found'st, or over-potent charms
To violate the sacred trust of silence
Deposited within thee; which to have kept
Tacit, was in thy power; true; and thou bear'st
Enough, and more the burden of that fault;
Bitterly hast thou paid, and still art paying
That rigid score. A worse thing yet remains,
This day the Philistines a popular feast
Here celebrate in Gaza; and proclaim
Great pomp, and sacrifice, and praises loud
To Dagon, as their god who hath delivered
Thee Samson bound and blind into their hands,
Them out of thine, who slew'st them many a slain.
So Dagon shall be magnified, and God,
Besides whom is no god, compared with idols,
Disglorified, blasphemed, and had in scorn
By the idolatrous rout amidst their wine;
Which to have come to pass by means of thee,
Samson, of all thy sufferings think the heaviest,
Of all reproach the most with shame that ever
Could have befall'n thee and thy father's house.
Sam. Father, I do acknowledge and confess
That I this honour, I this pomp have brought
To Dagon, and advanced his praises high
Among the heathen round; to God have brought
Dishonour, obloquy, and oped the mouths

423. *infest*] harass.
424. *state*] *OED* records this as the only instance of the verb in the sense 'assign a value to, have an opinion upon'.
433. *score*] account of a debt.
439. *them*] An imitation of a Latin dative: 'to their loss'.
442. *Disglorified*] deprived of glory.

Of idolists, and atheists; have brought scandal
To Israel, diffidence of God, and doubt
In feeble hearts, propense enough before
To waver, or fall off and join with idols;
Which is my chief affliction, shame and sorrow,
The anguish of my soul, that suffers not
Mine eye to harbour sleep, or thoughts to rest.
This only hope relieves me, that the strife
With me hath end; all the contest is now
'Twixt God and Dagon; Dagon hath presumed,
Me overthrown, to enter lists with God,
His deity comparing and preferring
Before the God of Abraham. He, be sure,
Will not connive, or linger, thus provoked,
But will arise and his great name assert:
Dagon must stoop, and shall ere long receive
Such a discomfit, as shall quite despoil him
Of all these boasted trophies won on me,
And with confusion blank his worshippers.
Man. With cause this hope relieves thee, and these words
I as a prophecy receive: for God,
Nothing more certain, will not long defer
To vindicate the glory of his name
Against all competition, nor will long
Endure it, doubtful whether God be Lord,
Or Dagon. But for thee what shall be done?
Thou must not in the meanwhile here forgot
Lie in this miserable loathsome plight
Neglected. I already have made way
To some Philistian lords, with whom to treat
About thy ransom: well they may by this
Have satisfied their utmost of revenge
By pains and slaveries, worse than death inflicted
On thee, who now no more canst do them harm.

453. idolists] idolators.

455. propense] inclined, disposed.

466. connive] remain dormant. *OED* gives this and *PL* x 624 as the only two instances of the word in this sense.

469. discomfit] defeat.

471. blank] nonplus.

481. In having Manoa sue with the Philistines for the release of his son, M. made an innovation in the story for which there is no warrant either in Scripture or in the Samson tradition (Krouse 99).

Sam. Spare that proposal, father, spare the trouble
Of that solicitation; let me here,
As I deserve, pay on my punishment;
And expiate, if possible, my crime,
Shameful garrulity. To have revealed
Secrets of men, the secrets of a friend,
How heinous had the fact been, how deserving
Contempt, and scorn of all, to be excluded
All friendship, and avoided as blab,
The mark of fool set on his front!
But I God's counsel have not kept, his holy secret
Presumptuously have published, impiously,
Weakly at least, and shamefully: a sin
That Gentiles in their parables condemn
To their abyss and horrid pains confined.
Man. Be penitent and for thy fault contrite,
But act not in thy own affliction, son,
Repent the sin, but if the punishment
Thou canst avoid, self-preservation bids;
Or the execution leave to high disposal,
And let another hand, not thine, exact
Thy penal forfeit from thyself; perhaps
God will relent, and quit thee all his debt;
Who evermore approves and more accepts
(Best pleased with humble and filial submission)
Him who imploring mercy sues for life,
Than who self-rigorous chooses death as due;
Which argues over-just, and self-displeased
For self-offence, more than for God offended.
Reject not then what offered means, who knows
But God hath set before us, to return thee
Home to thy country and his sacred house,
Where thou may'st bring thy off'rings, to avert
His further ire, with prayers and vows renewed.
Sam. His pardon I implore; but as for life,
To what end should I seek it? when in strength

493. fact] deed.

499–501. Alluding to the myth of Tantalus who was placed in Hades for revealing the secrets of the gods.

503–8. Cp. *De doctrina* ii 8 (Columbia xvii 200–1): 'The love of man towards himself consists in loving himself next to God . . . Opposed to this is, first, a perverse hatred of self . . . In this class are to be reckoned those who lay violent hands on themselves.'

509. quit . . . debt] remit all your debt to him ('thee' is a dative).

514. argues over-just] proves a man just to excess.

515. self-offence] offence against oneself.

All mortals I excelled, and great in hopes
With youthful courage and magnanimous thoughts
Of birth from heaven foretold and high exploits,
Full of divine instinct, after some proof
Of acts indeed heroic, far beyond
The sons of Anak, famous now and blazed,
Fearless of danger, like a petty god
I walked about admired of all and dreaded
On hostile ground, none daring my affront.
Then swoll'n with pride into the snare I fell
Of fair fallacious looks, venereal trains,
Softened with pleasure and voluptuous life;
At length to lay my head and hallowed pledge
Of all my strength in the lascivious lap
Of a deceitful concubine who shore me
Like a tame wether, all my precious fleece,
Then turned me out ridiculous, despoiled,
Shaven, and disarmed among my enemies.
Chor. Desire of wine and all delicious drinks,
Which many a famous warrior overturns,
Thou couldst repress, nor did the dancing ruby
Sparkling, out-poured, the flavour, or the smell,
Or taste that cheers the heart of gods and men,
Allure thee from the cool crystalline stream.
Sam. Wherever fountain or fresh current flowed
Against the eastern ray, translucent, pure
With touch ethereal of heaven's fiery rod
I drank, from the clear milky juice allaying

526. instinct] impulse.
528. sons of Anak] See 148*n*. *famous . . . blazed*] Qualifies 'I': 'blazed' means 'published, made famous'.
533. venereal trains] snares of sexual desire.
536. lap] Cp. *Judges* xvi 19: 'She made him sleep upon her knees.'
537. shore] In *Judges* xvi 19 Dalila calls for a man to shave Samson's head: here she apparently does it herself.
541–6. As a Nazarite Samson vowed to abstain from strong drink, *Num.* vi 3.
545. cheers . . . men] Cp. *Judges* ix 13: 'wine, which cheereth God and man'.
548. Against] in the direction of. In *Ezek.* xlvii 8–9 the waters which flow eastward are attributed life-giving powers; cp. Burton, *Anatomy* II ii 1 i: 'Rain water is purest . . . Next to it fountain water that riseth in the east, and runneth eastward.' *pure*] The first state of *1671* has a full stop after this word.
549. fiery rod] Cp. Euripides, *Suppliants* 650, where the sunbeam is called κανὼν σαφής.
550. milky] The same adjective for fresh water is used *PL* v 306. The concept

Thirst, and refreshed; nor envied them the grape
Whose heads that turbulent liquor fills with fumes.
Chor. O madness, to think use of strongest wines
And strongest drinks our chief support of health,
When God with these forbidden made choice to rear
His mighty champion, strong above compare,
Whose drink was only from the liquid brook.
Sam. But what availed this temperance, not complete
Against another object more enticing?
What boots it at one gate to make defence,
And at another to let in the foe
Effeminately vanquished? by which means,
Now blind, disheartened, shamed, dishonoured,
quelled,
To what can I be useful, wherein serve
My nation, and the work from heaven imposed,
But to sit idle on the household hearth,
A burdenous drone; to visitants a gaze,
Or pitied object, these redundant locks
Robustious to no purpose clustering down,
Vain monument of strength; till length of years
And sedentary numbness craze my limbs
To a contemptible old age obscure.
Here rather let me drudge and earn my bread,
Till vermin or the draff of servile food
Consume me, and oft-invocated death
Hasten the welcome end of all my pains.
Man. Wilt thou then serve the Philistines with that gift
Which was expressly given thee to annoy them?
Better at home lie bed-rid, not only idle,
Inglorious, unemployed, with age outworn.

is of earth as mother: cp. Sir John Davies, *Orchestra* lii, where hills are called 'The Earth's great duggs: for every wight is fed / With sweet fresh moisture from them issuing'. Possibly M. recalls *Song of Solomon* v 12: 'doves by the rivers of water, washed with milk', where the last phrase can be translated 'Splashed by the milky water'.

557. *liquid*] transparent (Latin *liquidus*).

560. *What boots it*] of what use is it?

567. *gaze*] object gazed at.

568. *redundant*] abounding to excess (the first instance of the word in this sense recorded in *OED*).

569. *Robustious*] robust, strong (a common seventeenth-century word).

571. *craze*] render decrepit.

574. *draff*] refuse, pig-swill.

578. *annoy*] molest, harm.

But God who caused a fountain at thy prayer
From the dry ground to spring, thy thirst to allay
After the brunt of battle, can as easy
Cause light again within thy eyes to spring,
Wherewith to serve him better than thou hast;
And I persuade me so; why else this strength
Miraculous yet remaining in those locks?
His might continues in thee not for naught,
Nor shall his wondrous gifts be frustrate thus.
Sam. All otherwise to me my thoughts portend,
That these dark orbs no more shall treat with light,
Nor the other light of life continue long,
But yield to double darkness nigh at hand:
So much I feel my genial spirits droop,
My hopes all flat, nature within me seems
In all her functions weary of herself;
My race of glory run, and race of shame,
And I shall shortly be with them that rest.
Man. Believe not these suggestions, which proceed
From anguish of the mind and humours black,
That mingle with thy fancy. I however
Must not omit a father's timely care
To prosecute the means of thy deliverance
By ransom or how else: meanwhile be calm,
And healing words from these thy friends admit.

581–98. M. seems to have remembered the exchange between Jason and Phineus in Apollonius Rhodius, *Argonautica* ii 438–48 'Assuredly there was then, Phineus, some god who cared for thy bitter woe . . . and if too he should bring sight to thine eyes, verily I should rejoice. . . . Thus he spake, but Phineus replied to him with downcast look: "Son of Aeson, that is past recall, nor is there any remedy hereafter, for blasted are my sightless eyes. But instead of that may the god grant me death at once, and after death I shall take my share in perfect bliss".'

581–3. Cp. *Judges* xv 19: 'But God clave an hollow place that was in the jaw [or 'in Lehi'], and there came water thereout.' Some translators take the verse to mean that the water came from the jawbone itself, some that it came from the rock which takes its name from the jawbone. M. accepts the latter explanation, as did Josephus, *Antiquities* v 8: 'God . . . raised him up a plentiful fountain of sweet water at a certain rock.'

594. genial] pertaining to genius or natural disposition.

595. flat] overthrown (*OED* gives this as the first figurative application of the word in this sense).

600. humours black] The black humour was melancholy (black bile).

601. fancy] imagination.

603. prosecute] persist in.

605. healing words] Cp. Euripides, *Hippolytus* 478: λόγοι θελκτήριοι.

Sam. O that torment should not be confined
To the body's wounds and sores
With maladies innumerable
In heart, head, breast, and reins;
But must secret passage find
To the inmost mind,
There exercise all his fierce accidents,
And on her purest spirits prey,
As on entrails, joints, and limbs,
With answerable pains, but more intense,
Though void of corporal sense.
  My griefs not only pain me
As a lingering disease,
But finding no redress, ferment and rage,
Nor less than wounds immedicable
Rankle, and fester, and gangrene,
To black mortification.
Thoughts my tormentors armed with deadly stings
Mangle my apprehensive tenderest parts,
Exasperate, exulcerate, and raise
Dire inflammation which no cooling herb
Or med'cinal liquor can assuage,
Nor breath of vernal air from snowy alp.
Sleep hath forsook and given me o'er
To death's benumbing opium as my only cure.
Thence faintings, swoonings of despair,
And sense of heaven's desertion.
  I was his nursling once and choice delight,
His destined from the womb,
Promised by heavenly message twice descending.
Under his special eye
Abstemious I grew up and thrived amain;
He led me on to mightiest deeds
Above the nerve of mortal arm
Against the uncircumcised, our enemies.

609. *reins*] kidneys.
612. *accidents*] In medical terminology, 'symptoms'.
615. *answerable*] corresponding.
620. *wounds immedicable*] Cp. Ovid, *Met.* x 189: *immedicabile vulnus.*
622. *mortification*] gangrene.
624. *apprehensive*] sensitive.
625. *Exasperate*] increase the fierceness of a disease. *exulcerate*] cause ulcers.
628. *alp*] Used from late sixteenth century to mean any high, snow-capped mountain.
639. *nerve*] muscle.

But now hath cast me off as never known,
And to those cruel enemies,
Whom I by his appointment had provoked,
Left me all helpless with the irreparable loss
Of sight, reserved alive to be repeated
The subject of their cruelty, or scorn.
Nor am I in the list of them that hope;
Hopeless are all my evils, all remediless;
This one prayer yet remains, might I be heard,
No long petition, speedy death,
The close of all my miseries, and the balm.
Chor. Many are the sayings of the wise
In ancient and in modern books enrolled;
Extolling patience as the truest fortitude;
And to the bearing well of all calamities,
All chances incident to man's frail life
Consolatories writ
With studied argument, and much persuasion sought
Lenient of grief and anxious thought,
But with the afflicted in his pangs their sound
Little prevails, or rather seems a tune,
Harsh, and of dissonant mood from his complaint,
Unless he feel within
Some source of consolation from above;
Secret refreshings, that repair his strength,
And fainting spirits uphold.
God of our fathers, what is man!

643. *appointment*] command.
645. *repeated*] spoken of as.
656. Echoing *Timon* V i 203–5: 'With other incident throes / That nature's fragile vessel doth sustain / In life's uncertain voyage.' *1671* prints a full stop after 'life', but the *Errata* deletes it.
657. *Consolatories*] writings containing topics of comfort (the noun is first recorded in *OED* in 1654).
658. *persuasion sought*] persuasion painstakingly constructed.
659. *Lenient of*] tending to soothe (*OED* first records 'lenient' in this sense in 1652, and gives the present instance as the first example of its construction with 'of'). Cp. Horace, *Epist.* I i 34: *sunt verba et voces quibus hunc lenire dolorem / possis* (There are words and sayings with which you may soothe the pain).
660. *with*] *1671* prints 'to' but the *Errata* corrects to 'with'.
667. Cp. *Ps.* viii 4: 'What is man, that thou art mindful of him?'

That thou towards him with hand so various,
Or might I say contrarious,
Temper'st thy providence through his short course,
Not evenly, as thou rul'st
The angelic orders and inferior creatures mute,
Irrational and brute.
Nor do I name of men the common rout,
That wandering loose about
Grow up and perish, as the summer fly,
Heads without name no more remembered,
But such as thou hast solemnly elected,
With gifts and graces eminently adorned
To some great work, thy glory,
And people's safety, which in part they effect:
Yet toward these thus dignified, thou oft
Amidst their height of noon,
Changest thy countenance, and thy hand with no
regard
Of highest favours past
From thee on them, or them to thee of service.
Nor only dost degrade them, or remit
To life obscured, which were a fair dismission,
But throw'st them lower than thou didst exalt them
high,
Unseemly falls in human eye,
Too grievous for the trespass or omission,
Oft leav'st them to the hostile sword
Of heathen and profane, their carcases
To dogs and fowls a prey, or else captived:
Or to the unjust tribunals, under change of times,
And condemnation of the ingrateful multitude.
If these they scape, perhaps in poverty
With sickness and disease thou bow'st them down,
Painful diseases and deformed,
In crude old age;
Though not disordinate, yet causeless suffering
The punishment of dissolute days, in fine,

688. dismission] dismissal.

693–4. Echoing Homer, *Il.* i 4–5 (of the dead in the Trojan war) 'made a spoil for dogs and all manner of birds'.

700. crude] premature.

701–2. Though . . . days] i.e. though they are not themselves immoderate they suffer, without cause, the punishment (illness) which usually follows an intemperate life.

Just or unjust, alike seem miserable,
For oft alike, both come to evil end.
So deal not with this once thy glorious champion,
The image of thy strength, and mighty minister.
What do I beg? how hast thou dealt already?
Behold him in this state calamitous, and turn
His labours, for thou canst, to peaceful end.
But who is this, what thing of sea or land?
Female of sex it seems,
That so bedecked, ornate, and gay,
Comes this way sailing
Like a stately ship
Of Tarsus, bound for th' isles
Of Javan or Gadire
With all her bravery on, and tackle trim,
Sails filled, and streamers waving,
Courted by all the winds that hold them play,
An amber scent of odorous perfume
Her harbinger, a damsel train behind;
Some rich Philistian matron she may seem,
And now at nearer view, no other certain
Than Dalila thy wife.
Sam. My wife, my traitress, let her not come near me.
Chor. Yet on she moves, now stands and eyes thee fixed,
About t' have spoke, but now, with head declined
Like a fair flower surcharged with dew, she weeps
And words addressed seem into tears dissolved,
Wetting the borders of her silken veil:

714. Various 'sources' for the Dalila/ship simile have been suggested. G. M. Young, *TLS* (9 Jan. 1937) 28, traces it to a passage in Harrington's *A Word Concerning a House of Peers* (1659), and R. C. Fox, *N& Q* vi (1959) 370–2, to Vida, *Christiad* 304–34. More sensibly J. G. McManaway, *TLS* (20 Feb. 1937) 131, comments that the comparison of woman and ship is a commonplace of Tudor and Stuart literature. One striking parallel he cites is from Robert Wilkinson, *Merchant Royal* (1607) – a sermon on *Prov.* xxxi 14. Barbara K. Lewalski, *N & Q* vi (1959) 372–3, relates the ship image here to a larger pattern of ship and tempest imagery in the play (see ll. 197–200, 960–64, 1044–5, 1070, 1061–3, 1647–51).
715. Tarsus] The biblical phrase 'ships of Tarshish' (i.e. probably, Tartessus in S. Spain) is found *Isa.* xxiii 1, 14 and *Ps.* xlviii 7.
715–6. isles / Of Javan] Ionian isles. Javan, son of Japhet (*Gen.* x 2) and grandson of Noah was the supposed ancestor of the Ionians. *Gadire*] Cadiz, on the S. coast of Spain.
719. hold them play] keep them moving.
720. amber scent] scent as of ambergris.

But now again she makes address to speak.
Dal. With doubtful feet and wavering resolution
I came, still dreading thy displeasure, Samson,
Which to have merited, without excuse,
I cannot but acknowledge; yet if tears
May expiate (though the fact more evil drew
In the perverse event than I foresaw)
My penance hath not slackened, though my pardon
No way assured. But conjugal affection
Prevailing over fear, and timorous doubt
Hath led me on desirous to behold
Once more thy face, and know of thy estate.
If aught in my ability may serve
To lighten what thou suffer'st, and appease
Thy mind with what amends is in my power,
Though late, yet in some part to recompense
My rash but more unfortunate misdeed.
Sam. Out, out hyaena; these are thy wonted arts,
And arts of every woman false like thee,
To break all faith, all vows, deceive, betray,
Then as repentant to submit, beseech,
And reconcilement move with feigned remorse,
Confess, and promise wonders in her change,
Not truly penitent, but chief to try
Her husband, how far urged his patience bears,
His virtue or weakness which way to assail:
Then with more cautious and instructed skill
Again transgresses, and again submits;
That wisest and best men full oft beguiled
With goodness principled not to reject
The penitent, but ever to forgive,

731. *makes address*] prepares.
732. Parker² 126 compares the following episode with that between Helen and Menelaus in Euripides, *Troades* 895–1059.
736. *fact*] deed (i.e. her betrayal).
737. *perverse event*] unpropitious outcome.
748. *hyaena*] According to Pliny viii 44, the hyaena is believed to contain within itself both sexes, to imitate the human voice and thus lure men out to devour them, and to be the only animal that digs up graves to get at the bodies of the dead. Magicians, he says (xxviii 27), believe it has magical powers and can deprive human beings of their senses. All these attributes help to give point to Samson's abuse. Cp. also Jonson, *Volpone* IV vi 3 'now, thine eies / Vie teares with the hyaena'. M. abuses More with this term in the *Pro Se Defensio* (Columbia ix 124–5) 'Hyaena! or if there be any other

Are drawn to wear out miserable days,
Entangled with a poisonous bosom snake,
If not by quick destruction soon cut off
As I by thee, to ages an example.
Dal. Yet hear me Samson; not that I endeavour
To lessen or extenuate my offence,
But that on the other side, if it be weighed
By itself, with aggravations not surcharged,
Or else with just allowance counterpoised,
I may, if possible, thy pardon find
The easier towards me, or thy hatred less.
First granting, as I do, it was a weakness
In me, but incident to all our sex,
Curiosity, inquisitive, importune
Of secrets, then with like infirmity
To publish them, both common female faults:
Was it not weakness also to make known
For importunity, that is for naught,
Wherein consisted all thy strength and safety?
To what I did thou show'dst me first the way.
But I to enemies revealed, and should not.
Nor shouldst thou have trusted that to woman's frailty
Ere I to thee, thou to thyself wast cruel.
Let weakness then with weakness come to parle
So near related, or the same of kind,
Thine forgive mine; that men may censure thine
The gentler, if severely thou exact not
More strength from me, than in thyself was found.
And what if love, which thou interpret'st hate,
The jealousy of love, powerful of sway
In human hearts, nor less in mine towards thee,
Caused what I did? I saw thee mutable
Of fancy, feared lest one day thou wouldst leave me
As her at Timna, sought by all means therefore
How to endear, and hold thee to me firmest:
No better way I saw than by importuning

brute equally destructive, and equally infamous for the blackness of its guile'.

763. bosom snake] Cp. the proverb 'to nourish a snake (viper) in one's bosom' (Tilley V68).

769. aggravations] exaggerations.

775. importune / Of secrets] irksomely persistent in discovering secrets (the construction with 'of' is not recorded in *OED*).

784. thou . . . cruel] Cp. Shakespeare, *Sonnet* i: 'to thy sweet self too cruel'.

785. parle] parley.

To learn thy secrets, get into my power
Thy key of strength and safety: thou wilt say,
Why then revealed? I was assured by those
Who tempted me, that nothing was designed
Against thee but safe custody, and hold:
That made for me, I knew that liberty
Would draw thee forth to perilous enterprises,
While I at home sat full of cares and fears,
Wailing thy absence in my widowed bed;
Here I should still enjoy thee day and night
Mine and love's prisoner, not the Philistines',
Whole to myself, unhazarded abroad,
Fearless at home of partners in my love.
These reasons in love's law have passed for good,
Though fond and reasonless to some perhaps;
And love hath oft, well meaning, wrought much woe,
Yet always pity or pardon hath obtained.
Be not unlike all others, not austere
As thou art strong, inflexible as steel.
If thou in strength all mortals dost exceed,
In uncompassionate anger do not so.
Sam. How cunningly the sorceress displays
Her own transgressions, to upbraid me mine!
That malice not repentance brought thee hither,
By this appears: I gave, thou say'st, the example,
I led the way; bitter reproach, but true,
I to myself was false ere thou to me,
Such pardon therefore as I give my folly,
Take to thy wicked deed: which when thou seest
Impartial, self-severe, inexorable,
Thou wilt renounce thy seeking, and much rather
Confess it feigned, weakness is thy excuse,
And I believe it, weakness to resist
Philistian gold: if weakness may excuse,
What murderer, what traitor, parricide,
Incestuous, sacrilegious, but may plead it?
All wickedness is weakness: that plea therefore
With God or man will gain thee no remission.
But love constrained thee; call it furious rage
To satisfy thy lust: love seeks to have love;
My love how couldst thou hope, who took'st the way

800–3. In *Judges* xvi 5, the Lords of the Philistines say to Dalila: 'Entice him . . . that we may bind him to afflict [marginal note: 'or *humble*'] him' (A.V.). The Vulgate has *affligere*.
803. made for me] was to my advantage.

To raise in me inexpiable hate,
Knowing, as needs I must, by thee betrayed?
In vain thou striv'st to cover shame with shame,
Or by evasions thy crime uncover'st more.
Dal. Since thou determin'st weakness for no plea
In man or woman, though to thy own condemning,
Hear what assaults I had, what snares besides,
What sieges girt me round, ere I consented;
Which might have awed the best-resolved of men,
The constantest to have yielded without blame.
It was not gold, as to my charge thou lay'st,
That wrought with me: thou know'st the magistrates
And princes of my country came in person,
Solicited, commanded, threatened, urged,
Adjured by all the bonds of civil duty
And of religion, pressed how just it was,
How honourable, how glorious to entrap
A common enemy, who had destroyed
Such numbers of our nation: and the priest
Was not behind, but ever at my ear,
Preaching how meritorious with the gods
It would be to ensnare an irreligious
Dishonourer of Dagon: what had I
To oppose against such powerful arguments?
Only my love of thee held long debate;
And combated in silence all these reasons
With hard contest: at length that grounded maxim
So rife and celebrated in the mouths
Of wisest men; that to the public good
Private respects must yield; with grave authority
Took full possession of me and prevailed;
Virtue, as I thought, truth, duty so enjoining.
Sam. I thought where all thy circling wiles would end;
In feigned religion, smooth hypocrisy.
But had thy love, still odiously pretended,
Been, as it ought, sincere, it would have taught thee
Far other reasonings, brought forth other deeds.
I before all the daughters of my tribe
And of my nation chose thee from among
My enemies, loved thee, as too well thou knew'st,

840. Knowing . . . betrayed] knowing myself to be betrayed.

857. priest] No priest is mentioned in the biblical account.

865. grounded] firmly established.

878–81. loved thee . . . Too well . . . could deny thee nothing] Echoes *Othello* III iii 83: 'I will deny thee nothing'; V ii 345: 'lov'd not wisely, but too well'.

Too well, unbosomed all my secrets to thee,
Not out of levity, but overpowered
By thy request, who could deny thee nothing;
Yet now am judged an enemy. Why then
Didst thou at first receive me for thy husband?
Then, as since then, thy country's foe professed:
Being once a wife, for me thou wast to leave
Parents and country; nor was I their subject,
Nor under their protection but my own,
Thou mine, not theirs: if aught against my life
Thy country sought of thee, it sought unjustly,
Against the law of nature, law of nations,
No more thy country, but an impious crew
Of men conspiring to uphold their state
By worse than hostile deeds, violating the ends
For which our country is a name so dear;
Not therefore to be obeyed. But zeal moved thee;
To please thy gods thou didst it; gods unable
To acquit themselves and prosecute their foes
But by ungodly deeds, the contradiction
Of their own deity, Gods cannot be:
Less therefore to be pleased, obeyed, or feared,
These false pretexts and varnished colours failing,
Bare in thy guilt how foul must thou appear!
Dal. In argument with men a woman ever
Goes by the worse, whatever be her cause.
Sam. For want of words no doubt, or lack of breath,
Witness when I was worried with thy peals.
Dal. I was a fool, too rash, and quite mistaken
In what I thought would have succeeded best.
Let me obtain forgiveness of thee, Samson,
Afford me place to show what recompense
Towards thee I intend for what I have misdone,
Misguided; only what remains past cure
Bear not too sensibly, nor still insist
To afflict thyself in vain: though sight be lost,
Life yet hath many solaces, enjoyed
Where other senses want not their delights

890. Echoes *Troilus and Cressida* II ii 184–5: 'these moral laws / Of nature and of nations'.
897. *acquit themselves*] discharge the duties of their position.
901. *varnished colours*] speciously tricked-out excuses.
906. *peals*] See l. 235*n*.
913. *Bear . . . sensibly*] do not feel too acutely.
916. Dalila slyly reminds Samson of the pleasures of her bed (cp. ll. 806–8).

At home in leisure and domestic ease,
Exempt from many a care and chance to which
Eyesight exposes daily men abroad.
I to the lords will intercede, not doubting
Their favourable ear, that I may fetch thee
From forth this loathsome prison-house, to abide
With me, where my redoubled love and care
With nursing diligence, to me glad office,
May ever tend about thee to old age
With all things grateful cheered, and so supplied,
That what by me thou hast lost thou least shalt miss.
Sam. No, no, of my condition take no care;
It fits not; thou and I long since are twain;
Nor think me so unwary or accursed
To bring my feet again into the snare
Where once I have been caught; I know thy trains
Though dearly to my cost, thy gins, and toils;
Thy fair enchanted cup, and warbling charms
No more on me have power, their force is nulled,
So much of adder's wisdom I have learnt
To fence my ear against thy sorceries.
If in my flower of youth and strength, when all men
Loved, honoured, feared me, thou alone could hate me,
Thy husband, slight me, sell me, and forgo me;
How wouldst thou use me now, blind, and thereby
Deceivable, in most things as a child
Helpless, thence easily contemned, and scorned,
And last neglected? How wouldst thou insult
When I must live uxorious to thy will
In perfect thraldom, how again betray me,
Bearing my words and doings to the lords
To gloss upon, and censuring, frown or smile?
This jail I count the house of liberty
To thine whose doors my feet shall never enter.
Dal. Let me approach at least, and touch thy hand.
Sam. Not for thy life, lest fierce remembrance wake
My sudden rage to tear thee joint by joint.
At distance I forgive thee, go with that;

926. *grateful*] pleasing.

932. *trains*] snares.

934. *cup . . . charms*] Alludes to the Circe story.

936–7. The proverb 'As deaf as an adder' (Tilley A32) originated in *Ps.* lviii 4: 'They are like the deaf adder that stoppeth her ears.'

948. *gloss upon*] comment on.

Bewail thy falsehood, and the pious works
It hath brought forth to make thee memorable
Among illustrious women, faithful wives:
Cherish thy hastened widowhood with the gold
Of matrimonial treason: so farewell.
Dal. I see thou art implacable, more deaf
To prayers than winds and seas, yet winds to seas
Are reconciled at length, and sea to shore:
Thy anger, unappeasable, still rages,
Eternal tempest never to be calmed.
Why do I humble thus myself, and suing
For peace, reap nothing but repulse and hate?
Bid go with evil omen and the brand
Of infamy upon my name denounced?
To mix with thy concernments I desist
Henceforth, nor too much disapprove my own.
Fame if not double-faced is double-mouthed,
And with contrary blast proclaims most deeds,
On both his wings, one black, the other white,
Bears greatest names in his wild aery flight.
My name perhaps among the circumcised
In Dan, in Judah, and the bordering tribes,
To all posterity may stand defamed,
With malediction mentioned, and the blot
Of falsehood most unconjugal traduced.
But in my country where I most desire,
In Ecron, Gaza, Asdod, and in Gath
I shall be named among the famousest
Of women, sung at solemn festivals,
Living and dead recorded, who to save
Her country from a fierce destroyer, chose
Above the faith of wedlock-bands, my tomb
With odours visited and annual flowers.

967. *omen*] prophetic sign. Dalila is referring to Samson's sarcastic remark about her future reputation, ll. 956–7.

971–4. No source has been found for M.'s representation of Fame as male, double-mouthed and with one wing black, one white. In Silius Italicus, *Punica* xv 6–9 *Infamia* flies with black wings (*atris . . . pennis*) and *Victoria* with white (*niveis . . . alis*). In Chaucer's *House of Fame* 1571–82, 1637, Fame employs Aeolus, god of winds, as trumpeter and he has two trumpets, one 'Clere Laude' the other, coloured black, 'Sklaundre'.

976. *Dan*] Samson's tribe.

981. Four of the five chief Philistine cities.

987. *odours*] from burnt spices: cp. *Jerem.* xxxiv 5: 'So shall they burn odours for thee.'

Not less renowned tnan in Mount Ephraim
Jael, who with inhospitable guile
Smote Sisera sleeping through the temples nailed.
Nor shall I count it heinous to enjoy
The public marks of honour and reward
Conferred upon me for the piety
Which to my country I was judged to have shown.
At this whoever envies or repines,
I leave him to his lot, and like my own.
Chor. She's gone, a manifest serpent by her sting
Discovered in the end, till now concealed.
Sam. So let her go, God sent her to debase me,
And aggravate my folly who committed
To such a viper his most sacred trust
Of secrecy, my safety, and my life.
Chor. Yet beauty, though injurious, hath strange power,
After offence returning, to regain
Love once possessed, nor can be easily
Repulsed, without much inward passion felt
And secret sting of amorous remorse.
Sam. Love-quarrels oft in pleasing concord end,
Not wedlock-treachery endangering life.
Chor. It is not virtue, wisdom, valour, wit,
Strength, comeliness of shape, or amplest merit
That woman's love can win or long inherit;
But what it is, hard is to say,
Harder to hit,
(Which way soever men refer it)
Much like thy riddle, Samson, in one day
Or seven, though one should musing sit;

988–90. In *Judges* iv 21 Jael, Heber's wife, kills Sisera the Canaanite general by driving a nail into his temples as he sleeps after taking refuge in her tent from Barak and the Israelites. Jael's praises are sung (v 24) by Barak and by the prophetess Deborah, who lived (iv 5) in Mount Ephraim.
995–6. Cp. Sophocles, *Ajax* 1038–9: 'If there be any in whose mind this wins no favour, let him hold to his own thoughts, as I hold to mine.'
1000. aggravate] add to the gravity of.
1008. Cp. the tag quoted by Chremes in Terence, *Andria* iii: *amantium irae amoris integratio est.*
1012. inherit] hold.
1016–7. riddle] Cp. *Judges* xiv 8–14: Samson, finding that bees have made honey in the carcase of the lion he killed, sets the thirty companions a riddle 'Out of the eater came forth meat, and out of the strong came forth sweetness', and gives them seven days to solve it.

If any of these or all, the Timnian bride
Had not so soon preferred
Thy paranymph, worthless to thee compared,
Successor in thy bed,
Nor both so loosely disallied
Their nuptials, nor this last so treacherously
Had shorn the fatal harvest of thy head.
Is it for that such outward ornament
Was lavished on their sex, that inward gifts
Were left for haste unfinished, judgement scant,
Capacity not raised to apprehend
Or value what is best
In choice, but oftest to affect the wrong?
Or was too much of self-love mixed,
Of constancy no root infixed,
That either they love nothing, or not long?
Whate'er it be, to wisest men and best
Seeming at first all heavenly under virgin veil,
Soft, modest, meek, demure,
Once joined, the contrary she proves, a thorn
Intestine, far within defensive arms
A cleaving mischief, in his way to virtue
Adverse and turbulent, or by her charms
Draws him awry enslaved
With dotage, and his sense depraved
To folly and shameful deeds which ruin ends.
What pilot so expert but needs must wreck
Embarked with such a steers-mate at the helm?

1020. paranymph] groomsman. In *Judges* xiv 20 Samson's wife is 'given to his companion, whom he had used as his friend'. M. takes 'friend' in the technical sense (groomsman), following the Vulgate *pronubus*.

1022. both] both first and second wives. *disallied*] M. seems to have coined the verb 'disally' (cancel by separation) for this line.

1025. for that] because.

1033. nothing,] In its first state *1671* has no comma.

1034–7. Cp. *Doctrine and Discipline of Divorce* (Columbia iii 394, Yale ii 294): 'The sobrest and best govern'd men are least practiz'd in these affairs; and who knowes not that the bashful mutenes of a virgin may oft-times hide all the unlivelines and naturall sloth which is really unfit for conversation.'

1037. thorn] Cp. *2 Cor.* xii 7: 'a thorn in the flesh'.

1038. Intestine] domestic.

1039–40. cleaving] Perhaps a reference to the poisoned shirt sent to Hercules by Deianira. Cp. Euripides, *Orestes* 605–6: 'Women were born to mar the lives of men / Ever, unto their surer overthrow.'

Favoured of heaven who finds
One virtuous rarely found,
That in domestic good combines:
Happy that house! his way to peace is smooth:
But virtue which breaks through all opposition,
And all temptation can remove,
Most shines and most is acceptable above.
Therefore God's universal law
Gave to the man despotic power
Over his female in due awe,
Nor from that right to part an hour,
Smile she or lour:
So shall he least confusion draw
On his whole life, not swayed
By female usurpation, nor dismayed.
But had we best retire, I see a storm?
Sam. Fair days have oft contracted wind and rain.
Chor. But this another kind of tempest brings.
Sam. Be less abstruse, my riddling days are past.
Chor. Look now for no enchanting voice, nor fear
The bait of honeyed words; a rougher tongue
Draws hitherward, I know him by his stride,
The giant Harapha of Gath, his look
Haughty as is his pile high-built and proud.
Comes he in peace? what wind hath blown him hither
I less conjecture than when first I saw
The sumptuous Dalila floating this way:
His habit carries peace, his brow defiance.

1046–9. Cp. *Prov.* xxxi 10–28.
1062. contracted] brought together.
1064. riddling days] See ll. 1016–7*n*.
1068. Harapha] W. R. Parker, *TLS* (2 Jan. 1937) 12, notes that the 1671 edition of Edward Phillips's *New World of Words* is the first to mention 'Harapha', glossing the name as 'a medicine' (a meaning which arises, as J. Leveen, *TLS* (23 Jan. 1937) 60, points out, from Phillips's quite mistaken association of the name with Hebrew *rephu'ah*, 'medicine'), and as 'a Philistim whose sons being gyants were slain by David and his servants' (an allusion to *2 Sam.* xxi, where A. V. translates merely 'the giant' but some commentators take *harapha* as a proper name). H. Loewe, *TLS* (23 Jan. 1937) 60, adds that Hebrew *Rephaim*, 'giants' is a euphemism (from *rapha*, 'to be weak') meaning 'the flabby, powerless ones'–a pointer to the real nature of M.'s Harapha?
1069. pile] can mean 'a mole or pier in the sea' or 'a lofty mass of buildings'; *OED* gives the present instance as the first figurative application of the word in the latter sense.

Sam. Or peace or not, alike to me he comes.
Chor. His fraught we soon shall know, he now arrives.
Har. I come not Samson, to condole thy chance,
As these perhaps, yet wish it had not been,
Though for no friendly intent. I am of Gath,
Men call me Harapha, of stock renowned
As Og or Anak and the Emims old
That Kiriathaim held, thou know'st me now
If thou at all art known. Much I have heard
Of thy prodigious might and feats performed
Incredible to me, in this displeased,
That I was never present on the place
Of those encounters, where we might have tried
Each other's force in camp or listed field:
And now am come to see of whom such noise
Hath walked about, and each limb to survey,
If thy appearance answer loud report.
Sam. The way to know were not to see but taste.
Har. Dost thou already single me; I thought
Gyves and the mill had tamed thee? O that fortune
Had brought me to the field where thou art famed
To have wrought such wonders with an ass's jaw;
I should have forced thee soon wish other arms,

1075. fraught] the cargo of a ship.
1078. Gath,] The first state of *1671* omits the comma.
1080–1. Og] Cp. *Deut.* iii 11: 'Only Og king of Bashan remained of the remnant of the giants.' *Anak*] Cp. *Numb.* xiii 33: 'And there we saw the giants, the sons of Anak . . . and we were in our own sight as grasshoppers.' *Emims . . . Kiriathaim*] Cp. *Deut.* ii 10–11: 'The Emims dwelt therein . . . Which also were accounted giants', and *Gen.* xiv 5: 'the Emims in Shaveh [margin 'the plain of'] Kiriathaim'.
1082. known] possessed of knowledge.
1086. encounters,] The first state of *1671* omits the comma.
1087. camp] open field (Latin *campus*). *listed*] provided with lists for tournament (*OED* gives this instance as the first example of this sense).
1089. The use of the verb 'walk' with subjects like 'report' or 'fame' is common from fourteenth century onwards, though obsolete by end of seventeenth.
1092. single] single out. *OED* gives this as first recorded example of verb 'single' in sense 'separate person from others'.
1093. thee?] The first state of *1671* has semicolon for second state's question mark.
1096. wish] A. H. Gilbert, *MLN* xxix (1914) 161–2, claims that the *1671* reading is 'with', and argues that the line means 'I should have forced you (i.e. taken you prisoner) with my arms (cp. 1119, 1130) which are more

Or left thy carcase where the ass lay thrown:
So had the glory of prowess been recovered
To Palestine, won by a Philistine
From the unforeskinned race, of whom thou bear'st
The highest name for valiant acts, that honour
Certain to have won by mortal duel from thee,
I lose, prevented by thy eyes put out.
Sam. Boast not of what thou wouldst have done, but do
What then thou wouldst, thou seest it in thy hand.
Har. To combat with a blind man I disdain,
And thou hast need much washing to be touched.
Sam. Such usage as your honourable lords
Afford me assassinated and betrayed,
Who durst not with their whole united powers
In fight withstand me single and unarmed,
Nor in the house with chamber ambushes
Close-banded durst attack me, no not sleeping,
Till they had hired a woman with their gold
Breaking her marriage faith to circumvent me.
Therefore without feigned shifts, let be assigned
Some narrow place enclosed, where sight may give thee,
Or rather flight, no great advantage on me;
Then put on all thy gorgeous arms, thy helmet
And brigandine of brass, thy broad habergeon,
Vantbrace and greaves, and gauntlet, add thy spear
A weaver's beam, and seven-times-folded shield,
I only with an oaken staff will meet thee,
And raise such outcries on thy clattered iron,
Which long shall not withhold me from thy head,

effective than a jawbone'. However Fletcher[3] iv 253 gives the *1671* reading as 'wish' in all sixty copies examined (including, incidentally, a copy numbered 30 supplied by Gilbert himself). R. I. McDavid, *PQ* xxxiii (1954) 86–9, has checked all the copies used by Fletcher and finds that all read 'wish'. The first edition to read 'with' is the Tonson edition of 1720: the reading, therefore, has no authority.

1109. assassinated] wounded by treachery.

1113. Close-banded] secretly banded together.

1120–2. brigandine] body armour of metal rings or plates sewn on canvas or leather. *habergeon*] sleeveless coat of mail. *Vantbrace*] armour for the fore-arm. *weaver's beam*] the wooden roller in a loom on which the warp is wound before weaving, and the similar roller on which the cloth is wound as it is woven; cp. *1 Sam.* xvii 7 (of Goliath) 'the staff of his spear was like a weaver's beam'. *shield*] Cp. the shield of Ajax, *Il.* vii 220, made of seven layers of bull's hide.

That in a little time while breath remains thee,
Thou oft shalt wish thyself at Gath to boast
Again in safety what thou wouldst have done
To Samson, but shalt never see Gath more.
Har. Thou durst not thus disparage glorious arms
Which greatest heroes have in battle worn,
Their ornament and safety, had not spells
And black enchantments, some magician's art,
Armed thee or charmed thee strong, which thou from heaven
Feign'dst at thy birth was given thee in thy hair,
Where strength can least abide, though all thy hairs
Were bristles ranged like those that ridge the back
Of chafed wild boars or ruffled porcupines.
Sam. I know no spells, use no forbidden arts;
My trust is in the living God who gave me
At my nativity this strength, diffused
No less through all my sinews, joints and bones,
Than thine, while I preserved these locks unshorn,
The pledge of my unviolated vow.
For proof hereof, if Dagon be thy god,
Go to his temple, invocate his aid
With solemnest devotion, spread before him
How highly it concerns his glory now
To frustrate and dissolve these magic spells,
Which I to be the power of Israel's God
Avow, and challenge Dagon to the test,
Offering to combat thee his champion bold,
With the utmost of his godhead seconded:
Then thou shalt see, or rather to thy sorrow
Soon feel, whose God is strongest, thine or mine.
Har. Presume not on thy God, whate'er he be,
Thee he regards not, owns not, hath cut off
Quite from his people, and delivered up

1132–4. As Krouse 130 notes, Rupert of St Heribert, the only commentator who ever called Samson's sainthood into question, suggested that perhaps he wrought his wondrous feats by magic and by alliance with Satan.

1138. chafed] angered. *ruffled*] with quills sticking out irregularly.

1139. Cp. the oath taken by the parties in a single combat to the effect that they were not aided by magic: Selden, *Duello* (1610) 34: 'that hee was free from all use of Art Magique, that he did not carry with him any hearbe, stone or other kinde of experiment of Witchcraft', and *Antiduello* (1632) 52: 'Sweare . . . that you have . . . no stone no hearbe of vertue; no charme, experiment, or any other inchantment, by whose power you beleeve you may the easier overcome your adversary.'

Into thy enemies' hand, permitted them
To put out both thine eyes, and fettered send thee
Into the common prison, there to grind
Among the slaves and asses thy comrades,
As good for nothing else, no better service
With those thy boisterous locks, no worthy match
For valour to assail, nor by the sword
Of noble warrior, so to stain his honour,
But by the barber's razor best subdued.
Sam. All these indignities, for such they are
From thine, these evils I deserve and more,
Acknowledge them from God inflicted on me
Justly, yet despair not of his final pardon
Whose ear is ever open; and his eye
Gracious to readmit the suppliant;
In confidence whereof I once again
Defy thee to the trial of mortal fight,
By combat to decide whose god is God,
Thine or whom I with Israel's sons adore.
Har. Fair honour that thou dost thy God, in trusting
He will accept thee to defend his cause,
A murderer, a revolter, and a robber.
Sam. Tongue-doughty giant, how dost thou prove me these?
Har. Is not thy nation subject to our lords?
Their magistrates confessed it, when they took thee
As a league-breaker and delivered bound
Into our hands: for hadst thou not committed
Notorious murder on those thirty men
At Ascalon, who never did thee harm,
Then like a robber stripp'dst them of their robes?
The Philistines, when thou hadst broke the league,
Went up with armed powers thee only seeking,
To others did no violence nor spoil.

1169. thine] thy people.

1180. Samson's challenge to single combat is justified by this accusation; cp. Selden, *Duello* (1610) 24: 'Treason . . . Murder, Robery, or such like, have from ancient time . . . beene tryable at the Defendant's pleasure by the Duell.'

1182–5. See ll. 259–64*n*.

1185–8. Cp. *Judges* xiv 19. Samson had wagered 'thirty change of garments' that his 'companions' would not be able to solve his riddle: they extracted the answer from his wife, so he killed thirty men at Ascalon and took their clothes in order to be able to pay the wager.

Sam. Among the daughters of the Philistines
I chose a wife, which argued me no foe;
And in your city held my nuptial feast:
But your ill-meaning politician lords,
Under pretence of bridal friends and guests,
Appointed to await me thirty spies,
Who threatening cruel death constrained the bride
To wring from me and tell to them my secret,
That solved the riddle which I had proposed.
When I perceived all set on enmity,
As on my enemies, wherever chanced,
I used hostility, and took their spoil
To pay my underminers in their coin.
My nation was subjected to your lords.
It was the force of conquest; force with force
Is well ejected when the conquered can.
But I a private person, whom my country
As a league-breaker gave up bound, presumed
Single rebellion and did hostile acts.
I was no private but a person raised
With strength sufficient and command from heaven
To free my country; if their servile minds
Me their deliverer sent would not receive,
But to their masters gave me up for nought,
The unworthier they; whence to this day they serve.
I was to do my part from heaven assigned,
And had performed it if my known offence
Had not disabled me, not all your force:
These shifts refuted, answer thy appellant
Though by his blindness maimed for high attempts,

1195. politician] politic, in a bad sense.
1197. spies] There is nothing in *Judges* to support this claim that the thirty 'companions' were spies. Josephus v 8, however, says: 'now the people of Timnath, out of dread of the young man's strength, gave him during the time of the wedding feast . . . thirty of the most stout of their youth, in pretence to be his companions, but in reality to be a guard upon him, that he might not attempt to give them any disturbance.'
1201–3. Seeing himself surrounded by enemies, he treated them as enemies (with hostility) wherever he came upon them.
1204. pay . . . in their coin] They threatened to kill in order to win a wager: he killed in order to pay it. For the proverb, see Tilley C507. *underminers*] secret assailants.
1208. See l. 242*n*.
1220. appellant] one who challenges another to single combat.

Who now defies thee thrice to single fight,
As a petty enterprise of small enforce.
Har. With thee a man condemned, a slave enrolled,
Due by the law to capital punishment?
To fight with thee no man of arms will deign.
Sam. Cam'st thou for this, vain boaster, to survey me,
To descant on my strength, and give thy verdict?
Come nearer, part not hence so slight informed;
But take good heed my hand survey not thee.
Har. O Baal-zebub! can my ears unused
Hear these dishonours, and not render death?
Sam. No man withholds thee, nothing from thy hand
Fear I incurable; bring up thy van,
My heels are fettered, but my fist is free.
Har. This insolence other kind of answer fits.
Sam. Go baffled coward, lest I run upon thee,
Though in these chains, bulk without spirit vast,
And with one buffet lay thy structure low,
Or swing thee in the air, then dash thee down
To the hazard of thy brains and shattered sides.
Har. By Astaroth ere long thou shalt lament
These braveries in irons loaden on thee.
Chor. His giantship is gone somewhat crestfall'n,
Stalking with less unconscionable strides,
And lower looks, but in a sultry chafe.

1222. thrice] Previously at ll. 1151 and 1175: cp. Selden, *Duello* (1610) 33: 'At the third proclamation, the Esquire appeares mounted.'

1223. enforce] effort.

1224–6. Cp. Vincentio Saviolo, *Practice* (1595) ii ('Of Honour and Honourable Quarrels') sig. Cc3v (under the heading 'Who is not to be admitted to the proof of Arms'): 'They are not to be admitted proofe by armes, who have committed any treason against their Prince or Countrie . . . Likewise, all theeves, robbers, ruffians, taverne hunters, excommunicate persons, hereticks, usurers, and all other persons, not living as a Gentleman or a Souldier.'

1231. Baal-zebub] god of the flies; a Philistine idol, with temple at Ekron, *2 Kings* i 2. *unused*] not used to hearing 'dishonours'.

1234. van] foremost division of a military force; Samson is mockingly grandiloquent.

1237. baffled] Another of the episode's chivalric terms; from the mid-sixteenth century 'baffle' means primarily 'subject to public disgrace' and particularly 'disgrace a perjured knight with infamy'.

1242. Astaroth] See *Nativity Ode* 200n (p. 110).

1244. giantship] Not previously recorded in *OED*.

1245. unconscionable] unreasonably excessive.

Sam. I dread him not, nor all his giant-brood,
Though fame divulge him father of five sons
All of gigantic size, Goliah chief.
Chor. He will directly to the lords, I fear,
And with malicious counsel stir them up
Some way or other yet further to afflict thee.
Sam. He must allege some cause, and offered fight
Will not dare mention, lest a question rise
Whether he durst accept the offer or not,
And that he durst not plain enough appeared.
Much more affliction than already felt
They cannot well impose, nor I sustain;
If they intend advantage of my labours
The work of many hands, which earns my keeping
With no small profit daily to my owners.
But come what will, my deadliest foe will prove
My speediest friend, by death to rid me hence,
The worst that he can give, to me the best.
Yet so it may fall out, because their end
Is hate, not help to me, it may with mine
Draw their own ruin who attempt the deed.
Chor. O how comely it is and how reviving
To the spirits of just men long oppressed!
When God into the hands of their deliverer
Puts invincible might
To quell the mighty of the earth, the oppressor,
The brute and boisterous force of violent men
Hardy and industrious to support
Tyrannic power, but raging to pursue
The righteous and all such as honour truth;
He all their ammunition
And feats of war defeats
With plain heroic magnitude of mind
And celestial vigour armed,
Their armouries and magazines contemns,
Renders them useless, while
With winged expedition
Swift as the lightning glance he executes

1248. divulge] *1671* prints 'divulg'd' but the *Errata* corrects to 'divulge'.
1248–9. Cp *2 Sam*. xxi 16–22 (also l. 1068*n*).
1268. O how comely] Cp. *Ecclesiasticus* xxv 4–5: 'O how comely a thing is judgment . . . O how comely is the wisdom of old men!'
1277. ammunition] military stores and supplies; a more general term in the seventeenth century than now.

His errand on the wicked, who surprised
Lose their defence distracted and amazed.
  But patience is more oft the exercise
Of saints, the trial of their fortitude,
Making them each his own deliverer,
And victor over all
That tyranny or fortune can inflict,
Either of these is in thy lot,
Samson, with might endued
Above the sons of men; but sight bereaved
May chance to number thee with those
Whom patience finally must crown.
This idol's day hath been to thee no day of rest,
  Labouring thy mind
More than the working day thy hands,
And yet perhaps more trouble is behind.
For I descry this way
Some other tending, in his hand
A sceptre or quaint staff he bears,
Comes on amain, speed in his look.
By his habit I discern him now
A public officer, and now at hand.
His message will be short and voluble.
Off. Hebrews, the prisoner Samson here I seek.
Chor. His manacles remark him, there he sits.
Off. Samson, to thee our lords thus bid me say;
This day to Dagon is a solemn feast,
With sacrifices, triumph, pomp, and games;
Thy strength they know surpassing human rate,
And now some public proof thereof require
To honour this great feast, and great assembly;
Rise therefore with all speed and come along,
Where I will see thee heartened and fresh clad
To appear as fits before the illustrious lords.
Sam. Thou know'st I am an Hebrew, therefore tell
    them,
Our law forbids at their religious rites
My presence; for that cause I cannot come.
Off. This answer, be assured, will not content them.

1303. *quaint*] ingeniously contrived.
1307. *voluble*] characterized by readiness of utterance; straightforward.
1309. *remark*] distinguish; a meaning found only in the seventeenth century.
1313. *rate*] 1671 prints 'race' but the *Errata* corrects to 'rate'.
1320. *law forbids*] Cp. *Exod.* xx 4–5, xxiii 24.

Sam. Have they not sword-players, and every sort
Of gymnic artists, wrestlers, riders, runners,
Jugglers and dancers, antics, mummers, mimics,
But they must pick me out with shackles tired,
And over-laboured at their public mill,
To make them sport with blind activity?
Do they not seek occasion of new quarrels
On my refusal to distress me more,
Or make a game of my calamities?
Return the way thou cam'st, I will not come.
Off. Regard thyself, this will offend them highly.
Sam. Myself? my conscience and internal peace.
Can they think me so broken, so debased
With corporal servitude, that my mind ever
Will condescend to such absurd commands?
Although their drudge, to be their fool or jester,
And in my midst of sorrow and heart-grief
To show them feats, and play before their god,
The worst of all indignities, yet on me
Joined with extreme contempt? I will not come.
Off. My message was imposed on me with speed,
Brooks no delay: is this thy resolution?
Sam. So take it with what speed thy message needs.
Off. I am sorry what this stoutness will produce.
Sam. Perhaps thou shalt have cause to sorrow indeed.
Chor. Consider, Samson; matters now are strained
Up to the height, whether to hold or break;
He's gone, and who knows how he may report
Thy words by adding fuel to the flame?
Expect another message more imperious,
More lordly thundering than thou well wilt bear.
Sam. Shall I abuse this consecrated gift
Of strength, again returning with my hair
After my great transgression, so requite
Favour renewed, and add a greater sin

1324. gymnic] A more usual form in the seventeenth century than 'gymnastic'.

1325. antics] clowns.

1333. Regard thyself] have a care for your own interests.

1337. commands?] In its first state *1671* has a full stop instead of a question mark.

1340. feats,] The first state of *1671* omits the comma.

1342. Joined] enjoined. *OED* records no example of this sense after the mid-sixteenth century.

1346. stoutness] pride.

By prostituting holy things to idols;
A Nazarite in place abominable
Vaunting my strength in honour to their Dagon?
Besides, how vile, contemptible, ridiculous,
What act more execrably unclean, profane?
Chor. Yet with this strength thou serv'st the Philistines,
Idolatrous, uncircumcised, unclean.
Sam. Not in their idol-worship, but by labour
Honest and lawful to deserve my food
Of those who have me in their civil power.
Chor. Where the heart joins not, outward acts defile not.
Sam. Where outward force constrains, the sentence holds
But who constrains me to the temple of Dagon,
Not dragging? the Philistian lords command.
Commands are no constraints. If I obey them,
I do it freely; venturing to displease
God for the fear of man, and man prefer,
Set God behind: which in his jealousy
Shall never, unrepented, find forgiveness.
Yet that he may dispense with me or thee
Present in temples at idolatrous rites
For some important cause, thou need'st not doubt.
Chor. How thou wilt here come off surmounts my reach.
Sam. Be of good courage, I begin to feel
Some rousing motions in me which dispose
To something extraordinary my thoughts.
I with this messenger will go along,
Nothing to do, be sure, that may dishonour
Our Law, or stain my vow of Nazarite.
If there be aught of presage in the mind,

1368. Cp. Aristotle, *Ethics* III i 1: 'It is only voluntary actions for which praise and blame are given; those that are involuntary are condoned, and sometimes even pitied.'

1369. sentence] maxim.

1375. jealousy] Cp. *Exod.* xx 5: 'I the Lord thy God am a jealous God.'

1377. dispense with] 'arrange administratively with (a person) so as to grant him relaxation or remission of a penalty incurred by breach of the law' (*OED*).

1380. come off] escape (a sense first recorded by *OED* in *Comus* 646).

1387–9. J. C. Maxwell, *PQ* xxxiii (1954) 90–1, comments that Samson sees his destiny dimly at this point. He does not realize that the day will be both his 'last' and 'remarkable'. M. is perhaps indebted to Sophocles, *Trachiniae*

This day will be remarkable in my life
By some great act, or of my days the last.
Chor. In time thou hast resolved, the man returns.
Off. Samson, this second message from our lords
To thee I am bid say. Art thou our slave,
Our captive, at the public mill our drudge,
And dar'st thou at our sending and command
Dispute thy coming? come without delay;
Or we shall find such engines to assail
And hamper thee, as thou shalt come of force,
Though thou wert firmlier fastened than a rock.
Sam. I could be well content to try their art,
Which to no few of them would prove pernicious.
Yet knowing their advantages too many,
Because they shall not trail me through their streets
Like a wild beast, I am content to go.
Masters' commands come with a power resistless
To such as owe them absolute subjection;
And for a life who will not change his purpose?
(So mutable are all the ways of men)
Yet this be sure, in nothing to comply
Scandalous or forbidden in our Law.
Off. I praise thy resolution, doff these links:
By this compliance thou wilt win the lords
To favour, and perhaps to set thee free.
Sam. Brethren farewell, your company along
I will not wish, lest it perhaps offend them
To see me girt with friends; and how the sight
Of me as of a common enemy,
So dreaded once, may now exasperate them
I know not. Lords are lordliest in their wine;
And the well-feasted priest then soonest fired
With zeal, if aught religion seem concerned:
No less the people on their holy-days
Impetuous, insolent, unquenchable;
Happen what may, of me expect to hear

1169–73, where Heracles realizes that the oracle which foretold release from his labours meant death to him, not final prosperity. M., says Maxwell, 'has transposed the riddling oracle into Christian (or Hebraic) terms by means of the notion of divine inscrutability'.

1404–5. Samson here 'sums up the whole history of his drama by pretending to deny it . . . In the grimly untrue we hear the true' (Stein[2] 190).

1421–2. Cp. Horace, *Ars Poetica* 224: 'The spectator, after the rites had been observed, was drunk and in a lawless mood.'

1423–6. R. F. Flatter, *TLS* (7 Aug. 1948) 443, puts forward the theory that

Nothing dishonourable, impure, unworthy
Our God, our Law, my nation, or myself,
The last of me or no I cannot warrant.
Chor. Go, and the Holy One
Of Israel be thy guide
To what may serve his glory best, and spread his name
Great among the heathen round:
Send thee the angel of thy birth, to stand
Fast by thy side, who from thy father's field
Rode up in flames after his message told
Of thy conception, and be now a shield
Of fire; that spirit that first rushed on thee
In the camp of Dan
Be efficacious in thee now at need.
For never was from heaven imparted
Measure of strength so great to mortal seed,
As in thy wondrous actions hath been seen.
But wherefore comes old Manoa in such haste
With youthful steps? much livelier than erewhile
He seems: supposing here to find his son,
Or of him bringing to us some glad news?
Man. Peace with you brethren; my inducement hither
Was not at present here to find my son,
By order of the lords new parted hence
To come and play before them at their feast.
I heard all as I came, the city rings
And numbers thither flock, I had no will,
Lest I should see him forced to things unseemly.
But that which moved my coming now, was chiefly
To give ye part with me what hope I have
With good success to work his liberty.
Chor. That hope would much rejoice us to partake
With thee; say reverend sire, we thirst to hear.
Man. I have attempted one by one the lords,
Either at home, or through the high street passing,

these lines refer to M.'s intention to have his heterodox *De doctrina* published after his death, and are thus a personal message to his readers. This unlikely view is questioned by F. F. Farnham-Flower and M. Kelley, *TLS* (21 Aug. 1948) 471.

1431–3. See l. 24*n* and l. 27*n*.

1435–6. Cp. *Judges* xiii 25; also xiv 6 'the Spirit of the Lord came mightily upon him' (Vulg. *irruit*, rushed on).

1454. *success*] outcome.

1457. *attempted*] sought to influence.

With supplication prone and father's tears
To accept of ransom for my son their prisoner,
Some much averse I found and wondrous harsh,
Contemptuous, proud, set on revenge and spite;
That part most reverenced Dagon and his priests,
Others more moderate seeming, but their aim
Private reward, for which both god and state
They easily would set to sale, a third
More generous far and civil, who confessed
They had enough revenged, having reduced
Their foe to misery beneath their fears,
The rest was magnanimity to remit,
If some convenient ransom were proposed.
What noise or shout was that? It tore the sky.
Chor. Doubtless the people shouting to behold
Their once great dread, captive, and blind before them,
Or at some proof of strength before them shown.
Man. His ransom, if my whole inheritance
May compass it, shall willingly be paid
And numbered down: much rather I shall choose
To live the poorest in my tribe, than richest,
And he in that calamitous prison left.
No, I am fixed not to part hence without him.
For his redemption all my patrimony,
If need be, I am ready to forgo
And quit: not wanting him, I shall want nothing.
Chor. Fathers are wont to lay up for their sons,
Thou for thy son art bent to lay out all;
Sons wont to nurse their parents in old age,
Thou in old age car'st how to nurse thy son,
Made older than thy age through eyesight lost.
Man. It shall be my delight to tend his eyes,
And view him sitting in the house, ennobled
With all those high exploits by him achieved,
And on his shoulders waving down those locks,
That of a nation armed the strength contained:
And I persuade me God had not permitted
His strength again to grow up with his hair
Garrisoned round about him like a camp
Of faithful soldiery, were not his purpose
To use him further yet in some great service,

1459. *prone*] Manoa implies that he prostrated himself before the lords.
1470. It would, they said, be a magnanimous act to remit the rest of their revenge.
1472. *shout*] Cp. l. 1620.

Not to sit idle with so great a gift
Useless, and thence ridiculous about him.
And since his strength with eyesight was not lost,
God will restore him eyesight to his strength.
Chor. Thy hopes are not ill founded nor seem vain
Of his delivery, and thy joy thereon
Conceived, agreeable to a father's love,
In both which we, as next participate.
Man. I know your friendly minds and—O what noise?
Mercy of heaven what hideous noise was that?
Horribly loud unlike the former shout.
Chor. Noise call you it or universal groan
As if the whole inhabitation perished,
Blood, death, and deathful deeds are in that noise,
Ruin, destruction at the utmost point.
Man. Of ruin indeed methought I heard the noise,
O it continues, they have slain my son.
Chor. Thy son is rather slaying them, that outcry
From slaughter of one foe could not ascend.
Man. Some dismal accident it needs must be;
What shall we do, stay here or run and see?
Chor. Best keep together here, lest running thither
We unawares run into danger's mouth.
This evil on the Philistines is fall'n,
From whom could else a general cry be heard?
The sufferers then will scarce molest us here,
From other hands we need not much to fear.
What if his eyesight (for to Israel's God
Nothing is hard) by miracle restored,
He now be dealing dole among his foes,
And over heaps of slaughtered walk his way?
Man. That were a joy presumptuous to be thought.
Chor. Yet God hath wrought things as incredible
For his people of old; what hinders now?
Man. He can I know, but doubt to think he will;
Yet hope would fain subscribe, and tempts belief.
A little stay will bring some notice hither.

1507. next] In interest and kinship, since, like Samson, they are Danites.

1512. inhabitation] population.

1521–2. Cp. a similarly hesitant chorus in Euripides, *Hippolytus* 782–5.

1529. dealing dole] A pun; 'dole' means 'that which is dealt' and also 'grief, pain'.

1536–7. In *1671* ll. 1527–35 and 1537 were omitted, but supplied in the *Omissa*. Thus in the uncorrected state of *1671* l. 1536 was given to the chorus, not Manoa. In the corrected state the chorus take up and finish what Manoa

Chor. Of good or bad so great, of bad the sooner;
For evil news rides post, while good news baits.
And to our wish I see one hither speeding,
A Hebrew, as I guess, and of our tribe.
Messenger. O whither shall I run, or which way fly
The sight of this so horrid spectacle
Which erst my eyes beheld and yet behold;
For dire imagination still pursues me.
But providence or instinct of nature seems,
Or reason though disturbed, and scarce consulted
To have guided me aright, I know not how,
To thee first reverend Manoa, and to these
My countrymen, whom here I knew remaining,
As at some distance from the place of horror,
So in the sad event too much concerned.
Man. The accident was loud, and here before thee
With rueful cry, yet what it was we hear not,
No preface needs, thou seest we long to know.
Mess. It would burst forth, but I recover breath,
And sense distract, to know well what I utter.
Man. Tell us the sum, the circumstance defer.
Mess. Gaza yet stands, but all her sons are fall'n,
All in a moment overwhelmed and fall'n.
Man. Sad, but thou know'st to Israelites not saddest
The desolation of a hostile city.
Mess. Feed on that first, there may in grief be surfeit.
Man. Relate by whom.
Mess. By Samson.
Man. That still lessens
The sorrow, and converts it nigh to joy.
Mess. Ah Manoa I refrain, too suddenly
To utter what will come at last too soon;
Lest evil tidings with too rude irruption
Hitting thy aged ear should pierce too deep.
Man. Suspense in news is torture, speak them out.

is saying, thus: '(*Manoa*) a little wait will bring some information (*Chorus*) about such a great good or evil as–judging from the noise–has just occurred: and that information will come all the quicker if the occurrence is evil.'
1538. baits] travels slowly (for the proverb see Tilley N147).
1552. here] *1671* prints 'heard' but the *Errata* corrects to 'here'.
1562. Echoes *Two Gentlemen of Verona* III i 220–1 'O, I have fed upon this woe already, / And now excess of it will make me surfeit.'
1567. irruption] bursting in.

Mess. Then take the worst in brief, Samson is dead.
Man. The worst indeed, O all my hope's defeated
To free him hence! but death who sets all free
Hath paid his ransom now and full discharge.
What windy joy this day had I conceived
Hopeful of his delivery, which now proves
Abortive as the first-born bloom of spring
Nipped with the lagging rear of winter's frost.
Yet ere I give the reins to grief, say first,
How died he? death to life is crown or shame.
All by him fell thou say'st, by whom fell he,
What glorious hand gave Samson his death's wound?
Mess. Unwounded of his enemies he fell.
Man. Wearied with slaughter then or how? explain.
Mess. By his own hands.
Man. Self-violence? what cause
Brought him so soon at variance with himself
Among his foes?
Mess. Inevitable cause
At once both to destroy and be destroyed;
The edifice where all were met to see him
Upon their heads and on his own he pulled.
Man. O lastly over-strong against thyself!
A dreadful way thou took'st to thy revenge.
More than enough we know; but while things yet
Are in confusion, give us if thou canst,
Eye-witness of what first or last was done,
Relation more particular and distinct.
Mess. Occasions drew me early to this city,
And as the gates I entered with sun-rise,
The morning trumpets festival proclaimed
Through each high street: little I had dispatched
When all abroad was rumoured that this day
Samson should be brought forth to show the people
Proof of his mighty strength in feats and games;
I sorrowed at his captive state, but minded
Not to be absent at that spectacle.

1570. Cp. the announcement of Orestes's death in Sophocles, *Electra* 673 'In short, Orestes is dead.'
1574. windy] apparent pregnancy turns out to be flatulence.
1576–7. Echoing *Love's Labour's Lost* I i 100–1: 'An envious-sneaping frost, / That bites the first-born infants of the spring.'
1596. Occasions] business.
1599. little . . . dispatched] i.e. I had not done much business.
1605–10. Cp. *Judges* xvi 27, where the building is called a 'house', and has

The building was a spacious theatre,
Half round on two main pillars vaulted high,
With seats where all the lords and each degree
Of sort, might sit in order to behold,
The other side was open, where the throng
On banks and scaffolds under sky might stand;
I among these aloof obscurely stood.
The feast and noon grew high, and sacrifice
Had filled their hearts with mirth, high cheer, and wine,
When to their sports they turned. Immediately
Was Samson as a public servant brought,
In their state livery clad; before him pipes
And timbrels, on each side went armed guards,
Both horse and foot before him and behind
Archers, and slingers, cataphracts and spears.
At sight of him the people with a shout
Rifted the air clamouring their god with praise,
Who had made their dreadful enemy their thrall.
He patient but undaunted where they led him,
Came to the place, and what was set before him
Which without help of eye might be assayed,
To heave, pull, draw, or break, he still performed
All with incredible, stupendious force,
None daring to appear antagonist.
At length for intermission sake they led him
Between the pillars; he his guide requested
(For so from such as nearer stood we heard)

3,000 men and women on the roof. Also Sandys 149: 'On the North-east corner, and summite of the hill [at Gaza], are the ruines of huge arches sunke low in the earth, and other foundations of a stately building. From whence the last Sanziack conveyed marble pillars of an incredible bignesse; enforced to saw them asunder ere they could be removed ... The Jewes do fable this place to have bin the theater of Sampson, pulled down on the head of the Philistims.' Krouse 90 explains that behind M.'s determination to be specific about the details of the building lies a long tradition of rationalistic exegesis which had produced such things as the floor-plan of the temple of Dagon, provided in Arias Montanus, *De Varia Republica* (Antwerp 1592).

1610. banks] benches.

1619. cataphracts] From the Greek word for a 'coat of mail'; *OED* cites this as the first usage of 'cataphract' in the sense 'soldier in full armour'. *spears*] spearsmen.

1627. stupendious] the common form of modern 'stupendous' until the late-seventeenth century

1630–4. Cp. *Judges* xvi 26: 'And Samson said unto the lad that held him by

As over-tired to let him lean a while
With both his arms on those two massy pillars
That to the arched roof gave main support.
He unsuspicious led him; which when Samson
Felt in his arms, with head a while inclined,
And eyes fast fixed he stood, as one who prayed,
Or some great matter in his mind revolved.
At last with head erect thus cried aloud,
Hitherto, lords, what your commands imposed
I have performed, as reason was, obeying,
Not without wonder or delight beheld.
Now of my own accord such other trial
I mean to show you of my strength, yet greater;
As with amaze shall strike all who behold.
This uttered, straining all his nerves he bowed,
As with the force of winds and waters pent,
When mountains tremble, those two massy pillars
With horrible convulsion to and fro
He tugged, he shook, till down they came and drew
The whole roof after them, with burst of thunder
Upon the heads of all who sat beneath,
Lords, ladies, captains, counsellors, or priests,
Their choice nobility and flower, not only
Of this but each Philistian city round
Met from all parts to solemnize this feast.
Samson with these immixed, inevitably
Pulled down the same destruction on himself;
The vulgar only scaped who stood without.
Chor. O dearly-bought revenge, yet glorious!
Living or dying thou hast fulfilled

the hand, Suffer me that I may feel the pillars whereupon the house standeth, that I may lean upon them.'

1637. In Judges xvi 30 Samson prays: 'Let me [Heb. 'my soul'] die with the Philistines.' This speech, as Krouse 51 makes clear, with its suicidal implications, was one of the major obstacles to those who wished to regard Samson as a saint: in the Scholastic period his suicide was excused as the prompting of the Holy Ghost. Sir Herbert Grierson, *Essays and Addresses* (1940) 55–63, refers to a passage in Augustine (*De Civitate Dei* I xxi) which makes this excuse, and remarks that the Dutch dramatist Joost van den Vondel in his *Samson of Heilige Wraeck* (1660), which has sometimes been compared with *SA*, concerns himself neither with the suicide question, which M handles so carefully (cp. ll. 307–14, 1637–9, 1664–5), nor with Samson's inner conflict.

1647–8. winds . . . pent] The theory that the earth is full of pent-up winds which occasionally burst forth is referred to by Ovid, *Met.* xv 296–306, 346.

1659. Not found in the scriptural account (*Judges* xvi 30).

The work for which thou wast foretold
To Israel, and now li'st victorious
Among thy slain self-killed
Not willingly, but tangled in the fold,
Of dire necessity, whose law in death conjoined
Thee with thy slaughtered foes in number more
Than all thy life had slain before.
Semichor. While their hearts were jocund and sublime,
Drunk with idolatry, drunk with wine
And fat regorged of bulls and goats,
Chanting their idol, and preferring
Before our living dread who dwells
In Silo his bright sanctuary:
Among them he a spirit of frenzy sent,
Who hurt their minds,
And urged them on with mad desire
To call in haste for their destroyer;
They only set on sport and play
Unweetingly importuned
Their own destruction to come speedy upon them.
So fond are mortal men
Fallen into wrath divine,
As their own ruin on themselves to invite,
Insensate left, or to sense reprobate,
And with blindness internal struck.
Semichor. But he though blind of sight,
Despised and thought extinguished quite,
With inward eyes illuminated
His fiery virtue roused
From under ashes into sudden flame,

1665–6. fold . . . necessity] A. S. Cook, *MLN* xxi (1906) 78, thinks that, since 'dire necessity' is from Horace, *Odes* III xxiv 6 *dira necessitas*, the *laqueis* of III xxiv 8 may have suggested 'fold'–or possibly Orestes' characterization of the robe in which his father was wound and killed (Aeschylus, *Libation Bearers* 998–1000, Euripides, *Orestes* 25–6). F. Tupper, *MLN* xxii (1907) 46, however, doubts the influence of these Greek phrases on M.
1667–8. Cp. *Judges* xvi 30: 'The dead which he slew at his death were more than they which he slew in his life.'
1669. sublime] exalted in feeling, elated (a sense, says *OED*, found only in M.).
1671. regorged] re-swallowed (a sense not in *OED* before 1700) by ruminants.
1674. Silo] Where the ark remained from the time of Joshua until, *1 Sam.* iv 4, 'the people sent to Shiloh, that they might bring from thence the ark of the covenant.'
1685. Either left senseless, or left to a reprobate sense (cp. *Rom.* i 28: 'God gave them over to a reprobate mind').

And as an evening dragon came,
Assailant on the perched roosts,
And nests in order ranged
Of tame villatic fowl; but as an eagle
His cloudless thunder bolted on their heads.
So virtue given for lost,
Depressed, and overthrown, as seemed,
Like that self-begotten bird
In the Arabian woods embossed,
That no second knows nor third,
And lay erewhile a holocaust,
From out her ashy womb now teemed,
Revives, reflourishes, then vigorous most
When most unactive deemed,
And though her body die, her fame survives,
A secular bird ages of lives.
Man. Come, come, no time for lamentation now,
Nor much more cause, Samson hath quit himself
Like Samson, and heroicly hath finished
A life heroic, on his enemies
Fully revenged, hath left them years of mourning,
And lamentation to the sons of Caphtor
Through all Philistian bounds. To Israel
Honour hath left, and freedom, let but them
Find courage to lay hold on this occasion,
To himself and father's house eternal fame;
And which is best and happiest yet, all this
With God not parted from him, as was feared,
But favouring and assisting to the end.
Nothing is here for tears, nothing to wail
Or knock the breast, no weakness, no contempt,
Dispraise, or blame, nothing but well and fair,
And what may quiet us in a death so noble.

1692. dragon] huge snake or python (a common meaning from thirteenth century onwards).
1695. villatic] farmyard (adj.). M. has coined the word for this line.
1699. bird] The Phoenix; see *Dam* 185–9*n* (p. 277).
1700. embossed] A term used of a hunted animal when it takes shelter in wood or thicket.
1702. holocaust] a thing wholly consumed by fire (*OED* cites this as the first use of the word with reference to anything but a burnt sacrifice).
1707. secular] lasting for ages (a sense which developed at the start of the seventeenth century).
1713. Caphtor] See l. 380*n*.

Let us go find the body where it lies
Soaked in his enemies' blood, and from the stream
With lavers pure, and cleansing herbs wash off
The clotted gore. I with what speed the while
(Gaza is not in plight to say us nay)
Will send for all my kindred, all my friends
To fetch him hence and solemnly attend
With silent obsequy and funeral train
Home to his father's house: there will I build him
A monument, and plant it round with shade
Of laurel ever green, and branching palm,
With all his trophies hung, and acts enrolled
In copious legend, or sweet lyric song,
Thither shall all the valiant youth resort,
And from his memory inflame their breasts
To matchless valour, and adventures high:
The virgins also shall on feastful days
Visit his tomb with flowers, only bewailing
His lot unfortunate in nuptial choice,
From whence captivity and loss of eyes.
Chor. All is best, though we oft doubt,
What the unsearchable dispose
Of highest wisdom brings about,
And ever best found in the close.
Oft he seems to hide his face,
But unexpectedly returns
And to his faithful champion hath in place
Bore witness gloriously; whence Gaza mourns
And all that band them to resist
His uncontrollable intent,
His servants he with new acquist

1727. lavers] wash-basins.
1728. what speed] i.e. what speed I can.
1730–3. Cp. *Judges* xvi 31: 'Then his brethren and all the house of his father came down, and took him, and brought him up, and buried him.'
1745–8. Cp. the closing chorus of Euripides, *Alcestis* 1160–4: 'Manifold things unhoped-for the Gods to accomplishment bring . . . So fell this marvellous thing'. The same chorus is used at the end of *Andromache*, *Bacchae*, *Helen* and (with a different first line: 'All dooms be of Zeus in Olympus; 'tis his to reveal them') *Medea*.
1749. Cp. *Ps*. civ 29: 'Thou hidest thy face, they are troubled' (also xxx 7 and xxvii 9).
1751. in place] at hand.
1755. acquist] acquisition.

Of true experience from this great event
With peace and consolation hath dismissed,
And calm of mind all passion spent.

85 Psalms i-viii

Date. 1653. M. gives the day and month of each translation (except i) in his heading to it.
Publication. 1673.
Modern criticism. M. H. Studley, *PQ* iv (1925) 364–72, remarks that this group of translations reveals M.'s struggle and suffering in the early days of his blindness. In vi *14* he alone of all versifiers of this psalm uses the word 'dark'. Similarly 'mark' (vi *15*) is not found in the other paraphrases, or in the original: M. seems aware of his enemies, on the alert to watch his suffering–the same thing is shown by his inserting 'those / That do observe if I transgress' (v *22–3*). W. B. Hunter Jr, *PQ* xxviii (1949) 125–44, comments on the metrical range of these versions (each is in a different metre, and only the couplets of *Psalm i* had been employed in previous metrical psalters). It is in these translations, thinks Hunter, that we first see M. attaining his mature prosody.

PSALM i

Done into verse, 1653

Bless'd is the man who hath not walked astray
In counsel of the wicked, and i' the way
Of sinners hath not stood, and in the seat
Of scorners hath not sat. But in the great
Jehovah's law is ever his delight,
And in his law he studies day and night.
He shall be as a tree which planted grows
By wat'ry streams, and in his season knows
To yield his fruit, and his leaf shall not fall,
And what he takes in hand shall prosper all.
Not so the wicked, but as chaff which fanned
The wind drives, so the wicked shall not stand
In judgment, or abide their trial then,
Nor sinners in the assembly of just men.
For the Lord knows the upright way of the just,
And the way of bad men to ruin must.

PSALM ii

Done August 8, 1653.—*Terzetti*

Why do the Gentiles tumult, and the nations
Muse a vain thing, the kings of the earth upstand
With power, and princes in their congregations
Lay deep their plots together through each land,

Against the Lord and his Messiah dear
Let us break off, say they, by strength of hand
Their bonds, and cast from us, no more to wear,
Their twisted cords: he who in heaven doth dwell
Shall laugh, the Lord shall scoff them, then severe
Speak to them in his wrath, and in his fell
And fierce ire trouble them; but I saith he
Anointed have my king (though ye rebel)
On Sion my holy hill. A firm decree
I will declare; the Lord to me hath said
Thou art my Son I have begotten thee
This day; ask of me, and the grant is made;
As thy possession I on thee bestow
The heathen, and as thy conquest to be swayed
Earth's utmost bounds: them shalt thou bring full low
With iron sceptre bruised, and them disperse
Like to a potter's vessel shivered so.
And now be wise at length ye kings averse
Be taught ye judges of the earth; with fear
Jehovah serve, and let your joy converse
With trembling; kiss the Son lest he appear
In anger and ye perish in the way
If once his wrath take fire like fuel sere.
Happy all those who have in him their stay.

PSALM iii

August 9, 1653

When he fled from Absalom

Lord how many are my foes
How many those
That in arms against me rise
Many are they
That of my life distrustfully thus say,
No help for him in God there lies.
But thou Lord art my shield my glory,
Thee through my story
The exalter of my head I count
Aloud I cried
Unto Jehovah, he full soon replied
And heard me from his holy mount.
I lay and slept, I waked again,
For my sustain
Was the Lord. Of many millions
The populous rout
I fear not though encamping round about
They pitch against me their pavilions.

Rise Lord, save me my God for thou
Hast smote ere now
On the cheek-bone all my foes,
Of men abhorred
Hast broke the teeth. This help was from the Lord
Thy blessing on thy people flows.

PSALM iv

August 10, 1653

Answer me when I call
God of my righteousness
In straits and in distress
Thou didst me disenthrall
And set at large; now spare,
Now pity me, and hear my earnest prayer.
Great ones how long will ye
My glory have in scorn
How long be thus forborne
Still to love vanity,
To love, to seek, to prize
Things false and vain and nothing else but lies?
Yet know the Lord hath chose
Chose to himself apart
The good and meek of heart
(For whom to choose he knows)
Jehovah from on high
Will hear my voice what time to him I cry.
Be awed, and do not sin,
Speak to your hearts alone,
Upon your beds, each one,
And be at peace within.
Offer the offerings just
Of righteousness and in Jehovah trust.
Many there be that say
Who yet will show us good?
Talking like this world's brood;
But Lord, thus let me pray,
On us lift up the light
Lift up the favour of thy countenance bright.
Into my heart more joy
And gladness thou hast put
Than when a year of glut
Their stores doth over-cloy
And from their plenteous grounds
With vast increase their corn and wine abounds.

In peace at once will I
Both lay me down and sleep
For thou alone dost keep
Me safe where'er I lie
As in a rocky cell
Thou Lord alone in safety mak'st me dwell.

PSALM v

August 12, 1653

Jehovah to my words give ear
My meditation weigh
The voice of my complaining hear
My King and God for unto thee I pray.
Jehovah thou my early voice
Shalt in the morning hear
I' the morning I to thee with choice
Will rank my prayers, and watch till thou appear.
For thou art not a God that takes
In wickedness delight
Evil with thee no biding makes
Fools or mad men stand not within thy sight.
All workers of iniquity
Thou hat'st; and them unblest
Thou wilt destroy that speak a lie
The bloody and guileful man God doth detest.
But I will in thy mercies dear
Thy numerous mercies go
Into thy house; I in thy fear
Will towards thy holy temple worship low.
Lord lead me in thy righteousness
Lead me because of those
That do observe if I transgress
Set thy ways right before, where my step goes.
For in his faltering mouth unstable
No word is firm or sooth
Their inside, troubles miserable;
An open grave their throat, their tongue they smooth.
God, find them guilty, let them fall
By their own counsels quelled;
Push them in their rebellions all
Still on; for against thee they have rebelled;
Then all who trust in thee shall bring
Their joy, while thou from blame
Defend'st them, they shall ever sing,
And shall triumph in thee, who love thy name.

For thou Jehovah wilt be found
To bless the just man still,
As with a shield thou wilt surround
Him with thy lasting favour and goodwill.

PSALM vi

August 13, 1653

Lord in thine anger do not reprehend me
Nor in thy hot displeasure me correct;
Pity me Lord for I am much deject
Am very weak and faint; heal and amend me,
For all my bones, that even with anguish ache,
Are troubled, yea my soul is troubled sore
And thou O Lord how long? Turn Lord, restore
My soul, O save me for thy goodness' sake
For in death no remembrance is of thee;
Who in the grave can celebrate thy praise?
Wearied I am with sighing out my days,
Nightly my couch I make a kind of sea;
My bed I water with my tears; mine eye
Through grief consumes, is waxen old and dark
I' the midst of all mine enemies that mark.
Depart all ye that work iniquity.
Depart from me, for the voice of my weeping
The Lord hath heard, the Lord hath heard my prayer
My supplication with acceptance fair
The Lord will own, and have me in his keeping.
Mine enemies shall all be blank and dashed
With much confusion; then grow red with shame,
They shall return in haste the way they came
And in a moment shall be quite abashed.

PSALM vii

August 14, 1653

Upon the words of Chush the Benjamite against him

Lord my God to thee I fly
Save me and secure me under
Thy protection while I cry,
Lest as a lion (and no wonder)
He haste to tear my soul asunder
Tearing and no rescue nigh.

Lord my God if I have thought
Or done this, if wickedness
Be in my hands, if I have wrought
Ill to him that meant me peace,
Or to him have rendered less,
And not freed my foe for naught;

Let the enemy pursue my soul
And overtake it, let him tread
My life down to the earth and roll
In the dust my glory dead,
In the dust and there outspread
Lodge it with dishonour foul.

Rise Jehovah in thine ire
Rouse thyself amidst the rage
Of my foes that urge like fire;
And wake for me, their fury assuage;
Judgment here thou didst engage
And command which I desire.

So the assemblies of each nation
Will surround thee, seeking right,
Thence to thy glorious habitation
Return on high and in their sight.
Jehovah judgeth most upright
All people from the world's foundation.

Judge me Lord, be judge in this
According to my righteousness
And the innocence which is
Upon me: cause at length to cease
Of evil men the wickedness
And their power that do amiss.

But the just establish fast,
Since thou art the just God that tries
Hearts and reins. On God is cast
My defence, and in him lies
In him who both just and wise
Saves the upright of heart at last.

God is a just judge and severe,
And God is every day offended;
If the unjust will not forbear,
His sword he whets, his bow hath bended
Already, and for him intended
The tools of death, that waits him near.

(His arrows purposely made he
For them that persecute.) Behold
He travails big with vanity,
Trouble he hath conceived of old
As in a womb, and from that mould
Hath at length brought forth a lie.

He digg'd a pit, and delved it deep,
And fell into the pit he made,
His mischief that due course doth keep,
Turns on his head, and his ill trade
Of violence will undelayed
Fall on his crown with ruin steep.

Then will I Jehovah's praise
According to his justice raise
And sing the Name and Deity
Of Jehovah the Most High.

PSALM viii

August 14, 1653

O Jehovah our Lord how wondrous great
And glorious is thy name through all the earth!
So as above the heavens thy praise to set
Out of the tender mouths of latest birth,

Out of the mouths of babes and sucklings thou
Hast founded strength because of all thy foes
To stint the enemy, and slack the avenger's brow
That bends his rage thy providence to oppose.

When I behold thy heavens, thy fingers' art,
The moon and stars which thou so bright hast set,
In the pure firmament, then saith my heart,
O what is man that thou rememberest yet,

And think'st upon him; or of man begot
That him thou visit'st and of him art found?
Scarce to be less than gods, thou mad'st his lot,
With honour and with state thou hast him crowned.

O'er the works of thy hand thou mad'st him lord,
Thou hast put all under his lordly feet,
All flocks and herds, by thy commanding word,
All beasts that in the field or forest meet,

Fowl of the heavens, and fish that through the wet
Sea-paths in shoals do slide. And know no dearth.
O Jehovah our Lord how wondrous great
And glorious is thy name through all the earth.

86 Verses from *Defensio Secunda*

Date. 1653. Saumaise (Salmasius) died in 1653. M. says (Columbia viii 57) that he wrote *Gaudete scombri* . . . in expectation of the reply Saumaise was said to be preparing to the *Defensio Pro Populo Anglicano* (see headnote to the epigram from this work, p. 325). Saumaise's reply was eventually published by his son in 1660, *Ad Iohannem Miltonum Responsio, Opus Posthumum.*

(ii) These lines against Alexander More (1616–70) are an adaptation of Juvenal ii 20–1. The sexual misbehaviour referred to is More's seduction of Saumaise's maid, Bontia, which M. relates at length in the *Defensio Secunda* (Columbia viii 34–8). More, a distinguished Protestant divine, was, in 1652, Professor of Ecclesiastical History at Amsterdam. The *Regii Sanguinis Clamor* (1652) was generally ascribed to him, (its actual author was Pierre du Moulin). Hence he is violently attacked in the *Defensio Secunda.*

Publication. 30 May 1654.

(i) Gaudete scombri, et quicquid est piscium salo,
Qui frigida hieme incolitis algentes freta,
Vestrum misertus ille Salmasius eques
Bonus amicire nuditatem cogitat;
Chartaeque largus apparat papyrinos
Vobis cucullos praeferentes Claudii
Insignia nomenque et decus Salmasii,
Gestetis ut per omne cetarium forum
Equitis clientes, scriniis mungentium
Cubito virorum, et capsulis gratissimos.

(ii) de virtute loquutus
Clunem agitas: ego te ceventem, More, verebor?

(i) Mackerels, rejoice, and briny fish-folk all who spend your winters freezing in the ocean! The good knight Saumaise pities your estate, and plans to clothe your nakedness. Unsparing of paper he is designing overcoats for you, each one blazoned with the insignia, name and honours[7] of Claude Saumaise, so that you may wear them proudly through the length and breadth of the fish-market, true pages of the knight, and be heartily welcome to the chests and coffers of the gentlemen who wipe their noses on their sleeves.

(ii) Having spoken of virtue, you go a-whoring yourself. Shall I stand in awe of you, More, when you yourself are depraved?

87 Sonnet XVII

Date. Winter (see *2–5*) 1653? The sonnet could have been written during any winter from 1651–2 to 1656–7. M. moved from Scotland Yard 17 Dec.

¶ 86. i *7. nomenque et decus*] Echoes Virgil, *Aen.* ii 89: *nomenque decusque.*

1651 to 'a pretty Garden-house . . . opening into St James's Park' where, says Edward Phillips, he lived for eight years and was frequently visited by 'young Laurence (the Son of him that was President of Oliver's Council) to whom there is a Sonnet among the rest, in his Printed Poems' (Darbishire 71–4). Edward Lawrence (b. 1633) became an M.P. Nov. 1656 and died the following year, aged 24. Smart 166–72 discovered four letters from Henry Oldenburg to Edward Lawrence (one dated Apr. 1654, the others undated), and Oldenburg's letters to M. of 28 Dec. 1656 and 27 Jun. 1657 send best wishes to Lawrence (French iv 129–31, 155–7).

Publication. *1673.*

Modern criticism. Finley 51–2, 64–5, reviews the sonnet's Horatian echoes and concludes that it loses 'nothing of Horace's charm, while yet conveying perfectly M.'s more puritan and austere temper'. To have omitted the reference to Christian literature (*8*) would, Finley argues, 'have shown that the classicism was superficial and could not bear the expression of M.'s complete mind'.

Lawrence of virtuous father virtuous son,
  Now that the fields are dank, and ways are mire,
  Where shall we sometimes meet, and by the fire
  Help waste a sullen day; what may be won
From the hard season gaining: time will run
  On smoother, till Favonius reinspire
  The frozen earth; and clothe in fresh attire
  The lily and rose, that neither sowed nor spun.
What neat repast shall feast us, light and choice,
  Of Attic taste, with wine, whence we may rise
  To hear the lute well touched, or artful voice
Warble immortal notes and Tuscan air?
  He who of those delights can judge, and spare
  To interpose them oft, is not unwise.

¶ 87. *1. father*] Henry Lawrence (1600–64) travelled abroad during the civil war but was appointed one of the Council of State 14 Jul. 1653, and Cromwell made him permanent chairman of the Council 16 Jan. 1654. His works include a treatise *Of Baptism* (1646) and *Of Our Communion and War with Angels* (1646). There is an encomium of him by M. in *Defensio Secunda* (Columbia viii 234). The form of the line imitates Horace, *Odes* I xvi 1: *O matre pulchra filia pulchrior.*

6. Favonius] the west wind: M. probably recalls Horace, *Odes* I iv i: *Solvitur acris hiems grata vice veris et Favoni* (Keen winter is melting at the welcome change to spring and Favonius).

8. Cp. *Matt.* vi 28.

9–12. Horace, like M., considers song a fitting accompaniment to simple fare and wine, *Odes* I xvii 17–22, IV xi 1–2, 34–6.

10. Attic taste] marked by simple and refined elegance.

13. spare] The word is ambiguous. Masson iii 294, Smart 115 and L. Aber-

88 Sonnet XV. On the late Massacre in Piedmont

Date. May? 1655. The Vaudois, founded by Peter Valdes in the twelfth century, were looked upon as the first of the Protestant churches. The sect was formally excommunicated in 1215: in the seventeenth century its strongholds were in the Alpine villages on the borders of France and Italy. A treaty with the Duke of Savoy in 1561 granted them the right to reside within certain territorial limits, from which the lower villages, including Torre Pellice and San Giovanni, were excluded. The Vaudois continued to live in these villages until 1655 when an army under the Marquis of Pianezza was sent by Charles Emmanuel II, Duke of Savoy, to expel them. They fled to the hills; Pianezza pursued, and massacred the inhabitants of the upper villages (24 Apr.). Many who tried to escape into France by the pass of St Julian died in the snow, others were butchered. The prisoners taken were hanged at Torre Pellice bridge. The Vaudois themselves estimated their dead at 1,712. Cromwell took up their cause, and M., as Secretary, wrote letters of protest to various European heads-of-state (May 25) and an address to be delivered to the Duke of Savoy by Sir Samuel Morland, a special ambassador (French iv 24–30). Meanwhile the tide turned and the Vaudois won several victories against the Piedmontese troops, and a decisive battle on 12 Jul. A peace treaty, restoring their ancient rights, was signed 18 Aug.
Publication. 1673.

Avenge O Lord thy slaughtered saints, whose bones
Lie scattered on the Alpine mountains cold,
Even them who kept thy truth so pure of old
When all our fathers worshipped stocks and stones,

crombie, *TLS* (11 Apr. 1936) 316, take it to mean 'refrain, forbear': Keightley, *Poems of M.* (1859) i 160, F. Neiman, *PMLA* lxiv (1949) 480–3 and E. Jackson, lxv (1950) 328–9 favour the opposite meaning, 'spare time to, afford'.

¶ 88. *1–2.* Cp. *Luke* xviii 7: 'shall not God avenge his own elect', and *Rev.* vi 9–10: 'the souls of them that were slain for the word of God . . . cried with a loud voice, saying, How long, O Lord, holy and true, dost thou not judge and avenge our blood', and *Ps.* cxli 7: 'Our bones are scattered at the grave's mouth.'

2. Alpine mountains cold] J. Willock, *N & Q* ix (1914) 147, finds this phrase in Fairfax's translation of Tasso (xiii 60).

4. stocks and stones] D. S. Berkeley, *Explicator* xv (1957) 58, suggests a reminiscence of Jeremiah's condemnation (ii 27) of the idolatrous leaders of his people. M. thus links the image worship of pre-Reformation England to the adoration of Baal, Ashtoreth and other idols.

Forget not: in thy book record their groans
Who were thy sheep and in their ancient fold
Slain by the bloody Piedmontese that rolled
Mother with infant down the rocks. Their moans
The vales redoubled to the hills, and they
To heaven. Their martyred blood and ashes sow
O'er all the Italian fields where still doth sway
The triple Tyrant: that from these may grow
A hundredfold, who having learnt thy way
Early may fly the Babylonian woe.

89 Sonnet XVIII

Date. 1655? Cyriack Skinner (b. 1627) was, according to Aubrey and Wood, at one time M.'s pupil (French iv 275). He is mentioned by Edward Phillips (Darbishire 74) as a frequent visitor at the Petty France house to which M. moved Dec. 1651. Andrew Marvell, in a letter to M. of 2 Jun. 1654, says he is 'exceeding glad to thinke that Mr Skyner is got near to you', and a letter of M.'s to Henry Oldenburg of 25 Jun. 1656 sends greetings from Skinner (French iii 385–7, iv 102–4). He did not die until 1700. W. R. Parker, *TLS* (13 Sep. 1957) 547, thinks him the author of the biography of M. which Darbishire 17–34 ascribes to John Phillips, (this view, previously suggested by M. Kelley, *MP* liv (1956) 20–5, is questioned by R. W. Hunt, *TLS* (11 Oct. 1957) 609). What is now page 49 of the Trinity MS contains *5–14* of this sonnet in a hand which Parker believes to be Skinner's own. It is fairly clear that the sheet now numbered 45 and that now numbered 49, both of which are smaller in size than the other sheets in the MS, were once

5. book] Cp. *Rev.* v 1: 'I saw in the right hand of him that sat on the throne a book.'
8. Mother with infant] Cromwell's agent, Sir Samuel Morland, in his account of the massacre (*History of the Evangelical Churches of the Valleys of Piedmont* (1658) 333–84) records that the wife of Giovanni, son of Pol Parise, was hurled down a precipice with her baby in her arms–the baby survived (363); that Jacopo Pecols's wife and son were thrown down the rocks at Tagliaretto (368); and that a woman and her baby were hurled down a precipice in the mountains of Villaro (374).
10–13. As K. Svendsen remarks, *Shakespeare Assoc. Bulletin* xx (1945) 147–55, these lines blend the parable of the sower with the legend of the dragon's teeth.
12. triple Tyrant] the Pope with his three-tiered crown.
14. Babylonian] The Puritans frequently identified Rome with the Babylon of *Revelation.*

the front and back pages respectively of a separate MS booklet which probably contained only sonnets. The first of the two sheets still bears a number 1 in its left margin, and the second of them a number 7. Presumably it was the missing sheet 6 which had the first four lines of this sonnet.
Publication. 1673.

Cyriack, whose grandsire on the royal bench
  Of British Themis, with no mean applause
  Pronounced and in his volumes taught our laws,
  Which others at their bar so often wrench;
Today deep thoughts resolve with me to drench
  In mirth, that after no repenting draws;
  Let Euclid rest and Archimedes pause,
  And what the Swede intend, and what the French.

¶ 89. *1. grandsire*] Skinner's mother was Bridget, daughter of Sir Edward Coke (1552–1634), the most celebrated lawyer of the Elizabethan and Jacobean period, who became Chief Justice of the King's Bench in 1613. He conducted the prosecution in the trials of Essex and Southampton (1600), Raleigh (1603) and the gunpowder plotters (1605). Throughout the early years of the seventeenth century he appeared as a champion of the law, opposing both the King and successive Archbishops of Canterbury in their attempts to gain judicial independence for the ecclesiastical courts. He constantly resisted James's exaggerations of the royal prerogative, and was, as a result, removed from the Chief Justiceship in 1616. After the Parliament of 1620–1 James had Coke and other members of the 'turbulent' party imprisoned. He continued his opposition to the royal prerogative in Charles's Parliaments of 1625 and 1628.
2. Themis] Roman goddess of justice.
3. volumes] Coke's major legal works are the *Reports* and *Institutes*.
5. 'resolve' is an imperative, and 'deep thoughts' the object of 'drench'.
7. Let . . . pause] discontinue, for the time being, your study of mathematics and physics. Cp. Horace, *Odes* III viii 17: *mitte civiles super urbe curas.*
8. Swede] Charles X of Sweden came to the throne in Jun. 1654. After a meeting of a secret committee of the Swedish Parliament (Mar. 1655) he began his Polish adventure (10 Jul.) and won brilliant initial victories but lost two thirds of his army in the winter of 1655–6. *intend, and*] *Trin. MS*: intends and. *French*] Throughout the 1650s the war between France and Spain dragged on. Cardinal Mazarin, who was in charge of French policy, approached Cromwell several times, and finally the Treaty of Westminster (24 Oct. 1655) established friendly relations between England and France and led to the expulsion of the future Charles II and the Duke of York from French dominions. M.'s line echoes Horace, *Odes* II xi 1–4: 'What the warlike Cantabrian is plotting, Quinctius Hirpinus, and the Scythian, divided from us by the intervening Adriatic, cease to enquire'.

To measure life, learn thou betimes, and know
  Toward solid good what leads the nearest way;
  For other things mild heaven a time ordains,
And disapproves that care, though wise in show,
  That with superfluous burden loads the day,
  And when God sends a cheerful hour, refrains.

90 To Mr Cyriack Skinner Upon his Blindness

Date. 1655? A clue is provided by 'this three years' day' (*1*) but it is not clear precisely when M. came to consider himself totally blind. French iii 197–8 thinks that this was 28 Feb. 1652, Parker, *PMLA* lxxiii (1958) 196–200, suggests autumn 1651.

In the Trinity MS this sonnet appears on the sheet now numbered 49, in a hand probably Skinner's (see headnote to *Sonnet XVIII*, p. 412): this is the text followed here.

Publication. First printed 1694 in Edward Phillips's edition of the *Letters of State*: for *1694* verbal variants, see notes.

Cyriack, this three years' day these eyes, though clear
  To outward view, of blemish or of spot;
  Bereft of light their seeing have forgot,
  Nor to their idle orbs doth sight appear
Of sun or moon or star throughout the year,
  Or man or woman. Yet I argue not
  Against heaven's hand or will, nor bate a jot
  Of heart or hope; but still bear up and steer
Right onward. What supports me dost thou ask?
  The conscience, friend, to have lost them overplied
  In liberty's defence, my noble task,
Of which all Europe talks from side to side.
  This thought might lead me through the world's vain mask
  Content though blind, had I no better guide.

¶ 90. *3. light*] *1694*: sight.
4. sight] *1694*: day.
5. Of] *1694*: Or.
7. heaven's] *Trin. MS*: *God's* \`Heaven's'. *a jot*] *1694*: one jot.
8. bear up and] *Trin. MS*: *attend to* \`bear up and'.
9. Right onward] *Trin. MS*: *Uphillward* \`Right onward'.
12. talks] *1694*: rings.
13. the] *1694*: this.
14. better] *1694* : other.

91 Sonnet XIX

Date. 1658? It is disputed whether the sonnet is about M.'s second wife, Katherine Woodcock, whom he married 12 Nov. 1656 and who died 3 Feb. 1658 having borne him a daughter, 19 Oct. 1657, or about his first wife, Mary Powell, who died May 1652, three days after giving birth to a daughter. Mary's candidature was first proposed by W. R. Parker, *RES* xxi (1945) 235–8. Mary died before the end of the period of purification laid down in *Lev.* xii 5: Katherine after it. In the sonnet the wife appears 'as' (like) one 'washed from spot of childbed taint' (5). The description fits Katherine in fact, but if the point of the line is dream-reversal of fact, then it fits Mary and not Katherine. R. M. Frye misses this distinction in his reply to Parker, *N & Q* clxxxix (1945) 239. F. Pyle, *RES* n.s. ii (1951) 152–4, thinks 'whom' (5) is the Blessed Virgin, who survived 'the days of her purification according to the Law of Moses', *Luke* ii 22. Katherine died the day after the Feast of the Purification of the Blessed Virgin. However, even if Pyle is right about 'whom', it might be argued that Mary's name associates her with the Blessed Virgin more surely than Katherine. He is on firmer ground in insisting, *RES* xxv (1949) 57–60, that the figure's 'veiled' (*10*) face fits Katherine, whom M. married after he was blind, better than Mary ('it is typical of M.'s habitual rectitude of mind that even in the dream state he will not endow his visionary figure with a face supplied by guesswork'). Parker, *RES* n.s. ii (1951) 147–52, admits that the veil gains in appropriateness if Katherine is the subject. Another argument for Katherine is advanced by E. S. Le Comte, *N & Q* i (1954) 245–6, who notices the poem's insistence on purity ('washed' *5*, 'Purification' *6*, 'white, pure' *9*) and connects it with the name Katherine (from Greek *katharos*, pure): M., an inveterate etymologist, is perhaps doing what Dante had done with 'Beatrice' and Petrarch with 'Laura'. This carries more conviction than J. T. Shawcross's theory, *N & Q* iii (1956) 202–4, that the purity of the wife's mind (*9*) is only mentioned to contrast with the impurity of her (i.e. Mary's) body, uncleansed from childbirth.

Both C. R. Dahlberg, *N & Q* cxciv (1949) 321, and M. Kelley, *MP* liv (1956) 20–5, remark that the sonnet is written in the Trinity MS in the hand of Jeremy Picard, who also entered the deaths of Katherine and her daughter in M.'s Bible, and that there is no evidence that Picard was M.'s amanuensis earlier than Jan. 1658. Strictly, however, this helps to date only the fair-copy in the Trinity MS, not the poem's composition.

Publication. *1673.*

Methought I saw my late espoused saint
    Brought to me like Alcestis from the grave,

¶ 91. *2. Alcestis*] In Euripides' *Alcestis* she gives her life for her husband Admetus, but Hercules ('Jove's great son') wrestles with death and brings her back from the grave.

Whom Jove's great son to her glad husband gave,
Rescued from death by force though pale and faint.
Mine as whom washed from spot of childbed taint,
Purification in the old Law did save,
And such, as yet once more I trust to have
Full sight of her in heaven without restraint,
Came vested all in white, pure as her mind:
Her face was veiled, yet to my fancied sight,
Love, sweetness, goodness in her person shined
So clear, as in no face with more delight.
But O as to embrace me she inclined
I waked, she fled, and day brought back my night.

92 From the title-page of the second edition of 'The Ready and Easy Way'

Date. Mar.–Apr. 1660. The first edition of *The Ready and Easy Way* was published Mar. 3 1660.

The verse is an adaptation of Juvenal i 15–6: *Et nos / consilium dedimus Sullae, privatus ut altum / dormiret* [I too have given advice to Sulla to sleep soundly in a private station]. Juvenal uses Sulla as a type of ambition. Smart 92 thinks that M.'s Sylla is Cromwell.

Publication. The second edition, of which there is only one extant copy, was probably published Apr. 1660 (French iv 309–10).

et nos
Consilium dedimus Syllae, demus populo nunc.

I too have given advice to Sylla, now let me give it to the people.

6. old Law] Cp. *Lev*. xii 4–8, where it is laid down that, after bearing a female child a woman shall be unclean 'two weeks, as in her separation: and she shall continue in the blood of her purifying threescore and six days' (i.e. during this period 'she shall touch no hallowed thing, nor come into the sanctuary').

13–4. Cp. Odysseus' attempt to clasp his mother's shade, *Od*. xi 204–9, imitated by Virgil, *Aen*. vi 700–2, and Dante, *Purg*. ii 80–1: in each of these, however, there are three attempts; in M. only one. T. B. Stroup, *PQ* xxxix (1960) 125–6, compares *Aen*. ii 789–95, which is also an imitation of the Homeric passage.

Paradise Lost

Edited by
ALASTAIR FOWLER

93 Paradise Lost

INTRODUCTION

Composition

It is very likely that at an early stage of its composition *Paradise Lost* was conceived not as an epic but as a tragedy. Edward Phillips says so in his *Life* (1694); where he quotes *PL* iv 32–41 as having been shown to him several (Aubrey says, fifteen or sixteen) years before the epic was begun, as the 'very beginning' of a tragedy (Darbishire 13, 72f). Moreover, the Trinity College Cambridge MS contains four drafts–written perhaps in 1640–of an outline for a tragedy on Paradise Lost, which bear many suggestive resemblances to the epic. This outline is of such interest that it deserves to be given here in full (spelling is modernized, punctuation unaltered, cancellations omitted):

Draft i

The Persons

Michael.
Heavenly love
Chorus of angels
Lucifer
Adam } with the serpent
Eve }
Conscience
Death
Labour }
Sickness }
Discontent } mutes.
Ignorance }
with others }
Faith
Hope
Charity.

Draft ii

The Persons

Moses
Justice
Mercy
Wisdom
Heavenly love
Hesperus the evening star
Chorus of angels
Lucifer
Adam
Eve
Conscience
Labour }
Sickness }
Discontent }
Ignorance } mutes
Fear }
Death }
Faith
Hope
Charity.

Draft iii

PARADISE LOST

The Persons

Moses προλογίζει recounting how he assumed his true body, that it corrupts not because of his [being] with God in the mount declares the like of Enoch and Eliah, besides the purity of the place that certain pure winds, dews, and clouds preserve it from corruption whence he hastes to the sight of God, tells they cannot see Adam in this state of innocence by reason of their sin

Justice
Mercy
Wisdom } debating what should become of man if he fall

Chorus of angels sing a hymn of the Creation

Act 2

Heavenly love
Evening star
Chorus sing the marriage song and describe Paradise

Act 3

Lucifer contriving Adam's ruin
Chorus fears for Adam and relates Lucifer's rebellion and fall.

Act 4

Adam
Eve } fallen

Conscience cites them to God's examination
Chorus bewails and tells the good Adam hath lost

Act 5

Adam and Eve, driven out of Paradise presented by an angel with

Labour
Grief
Hatred
Envy
War
Famine
Pestilence
Sickness
Discontent
Ignorance
Fear
Death } mutes to whom he gives their names likewise Winter, Heat Tempest &c. entered into the world

Faith
Hope
Charity } comfort him and instruct him

Chorus briefly concludes.

Draft iv

ADAM UNPARADIZED

The angel Gabriel, either descending or entering, showing since this globe was created, his frequency as much on earth, as in heaven, describes Paradise. Next the Chorus showing the reason of his coming to keep his watch in Paradise after Lucifer's rebellion by command from God, and withal expressing his desire to see, and know more concerning this excellent new creature man. The angel Gabriel as by his name signifying a prince of power tracing paradise with a more free office passes by the station of the chorus and desired by them relates what he knew of man as the creation of Eve with their love, and marriage. After this Lucifer appears after his overthrow, bemoans himself, seeks revenge on man the Chorus prepare resistance at his first approach at last after discourse of enmity on either side he departs whereat the chorus sings of the battle, and victory in heaven against him, and his accomplices, as before after the first act was sung a hymn of the creation. Here again may appear Lucifer relating, and insulting in what he had done to the destruction of man. Man next and Eve having by this time been seduced by the serpent appears confusedly covered with leaves conscience in a shape accuses him, Justice cites him to the place whither Jehova called for him in the mean while the chorus entertains the stage, and is informed by some angel the manner of his fall here the chorus bewails Adam's fall. Adam then and Eve return accuse one another but especially Adam lays the blame to his wife, is stubborn in his offence Justice appears reasons with him convinces him the chorus admonisheth Adam, and bids him beware by Lucifer's example of impenitence the angel is sent to banish them out of Paradise but before causes to pass before his eyes in shapes a mask of all the evils of this life and world he is humbled relents, despairs. At last appears Mercy comforts him promises the Messiah, then calls in Faith, Hope, and Charity, instructs him he repents gives God the glory, submits to his penalty the chorus briefly concludes. Compare this with the former draft.

The significance of the drafts is that they prepare us for seeing *Paradise Lost* as in certain respects a tragic work. We should even, perhaps, consider it a tragical epic rather than a pure epic. It is not so much that it has too much dialogue for an ordinary epic; though this may be true of Books ii, iii, viii, and ix. It is more that the characters have always the choice of falling into a tragic role–of becoming, as it were, tragic characters. Satan, who quite often soliloquizes, can be thought of as one who has in fact chosen to be an Elizabethan villain-hero. (A line of thought opened up by Helen Gardner in 'Milton and the Tragedies of Damnation', *E & S* i (1948) and developed by Dennis Burden in *The Logical Epic.*) Milton announces at the beginning of Book ix 'I now must change / Those notes to tragic' (5f); and it is in fact the subsequent portion of the poem that approximates to tragedy most closely. Its action very nearly obeys the Unity of Time; for it is only the visions shown by Michael that take us beyond the 24 hours proper to neo-classic tragedy. There are even fully developed *peripeteias* or discoveries, when events reveal to Adam new meanings in the terms both of God's prohibition against eating the forbidden fruit and of his promise about the seed of Eve. These *peripeteias* are broken up into series of partial discoveries (rather like the ones in *Oedipus Tyrannus*), in such a way as to communicate wonderfully a sense of life's unfathomable capacity to keep disclosing new truths and new ironies. According to the prohibition, for example, Adam is to die on 'the day' he eats the forbidden fruit; and right up to the end of the poem new facets of this word go on emerging (see x 49–53*n*, 773*n*, 1050*n*; xii 588–9*n*).

It might be added that the visions Michael shows to Adam in Book xi are like brief tragedies, some of them with subjects that figure among the 53 Old Testament tragedies projected in the Trinity MS. Not that there is any question of *Paradise Lost* being tragedy imperfectly adapted for epic. But neither will it quite do to speak of tragedy as one of a number of similar formal ingredients–though it is true that epic can embrace many different modes. (This is a fruitful line of thought about *Paradise Lost* in particular, which has pastoral, lyrical, philosophical, historical, and devotional, as well as tragical, passages.) For it is possible to regard the loss of Paradise as the tragedy *par excellence*, the tragedy underlying all tragedies; so that the tragic mode must have a special place among those used. Certainly it is far from being confined to the last books. The whole poem can be seen as tragic, because of our knowledge of the fatal conclusion. Milton so often utilizes this knowledge to produce effects of dramatic irony that the latter becomes almost a permanent property of the style of *Paradise Lost*. At the same time, the tragedy is not tragedy *simpliciter*. And this fact, that the tragic possibilities can be seen, if one so wills it, as outweighed by epic actuality–by the creativity and triumph of Messiah, by the prophecies of Paradise regained–is perhaps the first critical observation to be made about the poem. As epic, it presents a world; but a world that can be viewed either as tragic or (if we can reach Adam's instructed vision) as heroic. Thus Milton's decision to change one form for another may have been in more ways than one an act of faith.

About the order in which the different parts of *Paradise Lost* were composed, we know nothing. A. H. Gilbert's *On the Composition of 'Paradise Lost'* (Chapel Hill 1947) sets out an elaborate theory of six stages of composition (iv 8–31, e.g., belongs to the first, ii 1–520 to the last), and at least merits praise for its rejection of the common false assumption that composition has to be *seriatim*. But the theory is based on a long list of internal discrepancies, only two of which are established at all persuasively (see iv 712*n* and ix 163–7*n*). Nevertheless some have hoped to use it against the position that Milton's power declined during his work on the poem; or even against A. J. A. Waldock's more plausible view that in the later books Milton tries to correct the early blunder of making Satan too magnificent. If Gilbert's speculation can help anyone to see the falsity of these others, it may have served some purpose. It is naive, however, to suppose (as Gilbert does, no less than Waldock) that the author of such a poem as *Paradise Lost* can have failed to revise his work carefully. The question of the order of composition needs fresh consideration; but in the present state of our ignorance we can only regard the poem as composed *in toto* at one moment of time, at least in the only sense that matters critically. This moment was when Milton decided to stop revising and to leave the poem as it is. He became responsible at that moment for the whole text we know: if it has inconsistencies, he allowed them, then, to remain.

Of the time and manner of composition we know a little. Milton seems to have contemplated writing *some* epic from the beginning of his adult life; though at one stage the subject envisaged was the matter of Britain (see *Vacation Exercise*; *Mans*; *Dam*; and *Reason of Church-Government* ii Pref., Yale i 812ff). There are many speculations as to why Milton chose a scriptural theme, but no firm knowledge. It is fairly certain that he took some years over the poem we have; that he mostly composed during the winter, usually in the night or early morning; that he sometimes lay awake unable to write a verse, and at other times was inspired easily 'with a certain *impetus* and *oestro* [frenzy, *furor poeticus*]'; that he dictated in the first part of the day to whatever amanuensis happened to be available; that after dictating perhaps as much as 40 lines he would 'reduce them to half the Number'; and that he had his nephew Edward Phillips in from time to time to correct the orthography and pointing of the last part written, 'a Parcel of Ten, Twenty, or Thirty Verses at a Time' (see *PL* iii 22ff, vii 25ff, and ix 21ff; Aubrey, Edward Phillips, and Richardson in Darbishire 13, 73 and 291). According to Edward Phillips and Aubrey, the poem was written in four or five years, about 1658–63; Thomas Elwood says he saw it complete in 1665.

Printing history

Milton's contract with the printer Samuel Simmons is dated 27 April 67; and *Paradise Lost* was licensed (after some difficulty, according to John Toland) on 20 August of the same year. A MS of the first book (*MS*) has survived, which printers' marks show to be the one actually used in setting up the first edition. It is a final fair copy written by an amanuensis with a somewhat old-fashioned taste in orthography, but corrections in other hands indicate that its punctuation and spelling may have been revised under Milton's directions. The MS is now in the Pierpont Morgan Library, New York. There is a careful edition of it, with a facsimile, by Helen Darbishire (Oxford 1931). An examination of the MS makes one aware of the difficulties under which Milton worked because of his blindness. It reveals a concern about textual accuracy in *minutiae*, but also an inevitable and tantalizing failure to achieve the uniformity that might have made the special orthographic rules invaluable to an interpretative critic. The MS has disappointingly little textual interest, however: the readings peculiar to it are insignificant. Only in its punctuation (which is very light indeed) does it differ much from the first printed edition.

There were two editions of *Paradise Lost* in Milton's lifetime, both printed by Simmons. The first edition, a quarto (*Ed I*), appeared in 1667, 1668, and 1669, in six issues marked by six different title-pages. The title itself reads, with insignificant variants, *Paradise Lost. A poem in ten books.* From the fourth issue onwards the text is accompanied by preliminaries: 'The Printer to the Reader'; the 'Argument' (which stood all together, not distributed through the books); Milton's note on 'The Verse'; and the 'Errata'. In spite of his blindness Milton seems to have supervised the printing of *Ed I* very carefully–so carefully, indeed, that its authority is in general greater than that of *MS*. Corrections were made, as *Ed I* went through the press, for which he himself, or his agent, may have been responsible: these are studied in H. F. Fletcher's facsimile edition, and in Darbishire[2] i 314–22.

The second, octavo edition (*Ed II*) appeared in 1674, under the title

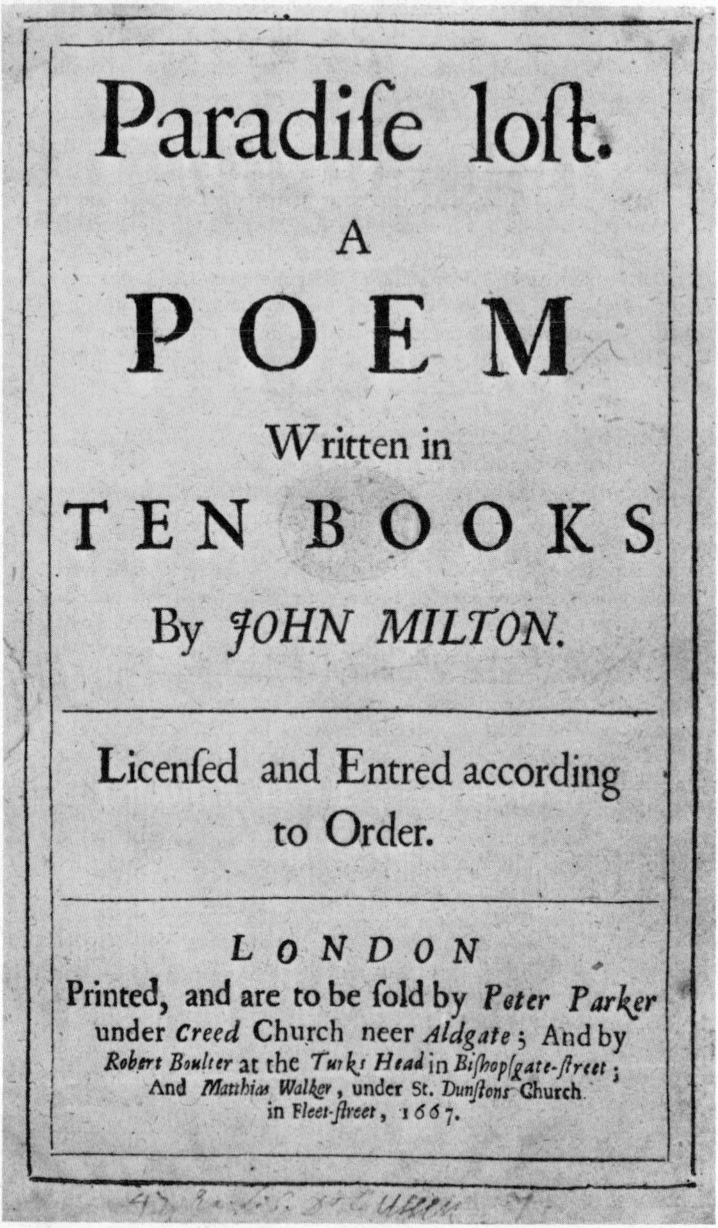

Paradiſe loſt.

A

POEM

Written in

TEN BOOKS

By *JOHN MILTON.*

Licenſed and Entred according to Order.

LONDON

Printed, and are to be ſold by *Peter Parker* under *Creed* Church neer *Aldgate*; And by *Robert Boulter* at the *Turks Head* in *Biſhopſgate-ſtreet*; And *Matthias Walker*, under St. *Dunſtons* Church in *Fleet-ſtreet*, 1667.

Title page of *Paradise Lost*, first edition, 1667

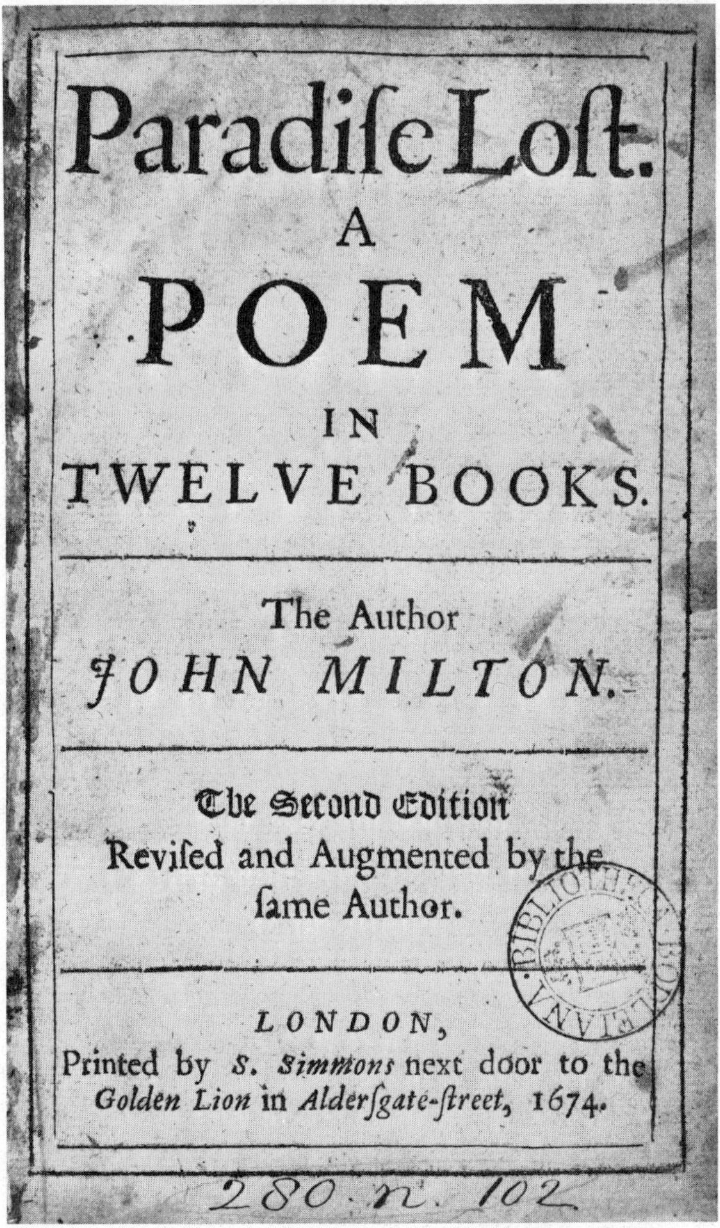
Paradiſe Loſt.
A
POEM
IN
TWELVE BOOKS.

The Author
JOHN MILTON.

The Second Edition
Reviſed and Augmented by the
ſame Author.

LONDON,
Printed by *S. Simmons* next door to the
Golden Lion in *Alderſgate-ſtreet*, 1674.

Title page of *Paradise Lost*, second edition, 1674

Paradise Lost. A poem in twelve books. To the preliminaries are added S[amuel] B[arrow]'s Latin verses 'In Paradisum Amissam summi poetae Johannis Miltoni' and A[ndrew] M[arvell]'s verses 'On Paradise Lost'; while the Argument is now distributed through the books, and the Errata assimilated (or forgotten). The poem itself is redivided into twelve books, by a simple dichotomy of *Ed I* vii and x (which become *Ed II* vii, viii and xi, xii). Minor additions or alterations of up to five lines are also made, at i 504–5, v 636–9, viii 1–4, xi 485–7, 551–2, and xii 1–5. Naturally enough, *Ed II* underwent less correction at the press than *Ed I*. In some cases it follows uncorrected sheets of the latter; and it will occasionally introduce new errors of its own. Nevertheless, on the whole *Ed II* represents an improvement. We may agree with B. A. Wright that its authority is usually to be preferred to that of *Ed I*.

After a slow start, *Ed I* went quickly, selling 1300 copies–a large sale for the period, even if the author only received £10. After Milton's death there were three unimportant editions (1678, 1688, 1691), then a sixth with full-scale commentary by Patrick Hume (1695). Of many subsequent editions the most notable have been Richard Bentley's, an eccentric emendation-list that has been valued for the rebuttals it provoked (1732); Thomas Newton's fine edition incorporating many of Pearce's strong replies to Bentley (1749); J. H. Todd's variorum edition (1809); and A. W. Verity's solid commentary (revised edn 1910). More recently, M. Y. Hughes's is the only considerable annotated edition of the whole poem (New York 1957); though the first two books have been well edited by B. Rajan (1964). Of textual interest are H. C. Beeching's decent text (1900); the Columbia University edition, a reprint of *Ed II* (New York 1931); H. F. Fletcher's photographic facsimile edition of both *Ed I* and *Ed II*, with very elaborate apparatus (Urbana, Ill. 1943–8); Helen Darbishire's synthetic normalized text (Oxford 1952), as well as her reprint of *Ed II* (1961; not to be confused with her 1958 Oxford Standard Authors edition); and B. A. Wright's edition, also with normalized spelling and punctuation (1956). The commentaries from Hume to Todd are shrewdly studied in Ants Oras, *Milton's Editors and Commentators* (Tartu [Yuriev] 1930).

Text

Although the primary purpose of this edition is not textual, the text is in large part freshly prepared. The printed copies followed–apart from supplementation in the case of the corrected sheets of *Ed I*–were BM C 14 a 9 (*Ed I*) and BM 1076 f 20 (*Ed II*). Other copies collated, however, were all within the range of copies already covered by Miss Darbishire. Since orthographic accidentals were to be modernized, and since the texts of *Ed I* and *Ed II* differ very seldom in other respects, the choice of copy-text scarcely mattered. For the sake of consistency and for the evidential value the readings of *Ed II* have been printed throughout, except where they are palpably in error. Unless it is otherwise stated, *Ed I* and *Ed II* agree in punctuation and in all features of their spelling that seem of any interest. Punctuation variants and significant spelling variants are recorded in the notes. The treatment of *MS* readings is similar; except that in this case some insignificant punctuation variants are omitted (the *MS* punctuation is generally lighter overall than that of the printed editions). The present text will be found to differ very little from the received text; but see, e.g., iii 592*n*, vii 588–90*n*, viii 332*n*, ix 394*n*, 944*n*, and x 989–90*n*.

Punctuation

Punctuation is unusually important in Milton's *Paradise Lost*. For the long verse paragraphs to have their full effect must be sustained grammatically and rhythmically beyond the limits of the ordinary syntactic breath, with the sense drawn out in such a way as to require light punctuation. On the other hand Milton's temperament, as well as the particular character of his subject, lead him to make many nice logical discriminations; which calls for somewhat closer, 'slower', pointing. Finally there are countless ambiguities in which more than one chain of discourse has to be left so far as possible open; and this needs very judiciously chosen points or none at all. Reconciling these demands would have been impossible if the pointing rules of the time had not given Milton a certain room for manoeuvre.

In the seventeenth century punctuation was often rhetorical: i.e. it was apt to reflect the physical pauses and stresses of speech directly and simply, rather than to signpost the sentence structure logically or grammatically. B. A. Wright even goes so far as to say that the punctuation of *Paradise Lost* 'is strictly rhetorical inasmuch as it always conforms to the prosody'. But in a good poet such as Milton, prosody is the handmaid of rhetoric, not rhetoric of prosody. Besides, Milton and his intermediaries seem to have paid unusually close attention to the grammatical operation of pointing. The main differences from modern punctuation are as follows:

1. While the full stop is sometimes used like ours (though more seldom), it is also used before comparisons (i 768) and before direct speech (i 272).
2. The colon can be much heavier than ours; so that we often find it where we would have put a full stop. But it also has a great variety of uses, of different rhetorical weights: namely to mark logical divisions, and to introduce alternatives, reasons, concessions, comparisons, defining clauses, afterthoughts, interruptions, and direct speech.
3. The lighter semicolon often separates stages in a narrative sequence or items in a catalogue (ii 959, 961, 963, 965).
4. Exclamation and question marks occasionally seem to us transposed (i 183).
5. The comma is like ours, but may be omitted before a defining relative clause, before a vocative (v 388), before and after an appositional phrase (iv 270), and at one end of a qualifying or parenthetic phrase (ix 1037–9).

The punctuation of *Paradise Lost* will not give much trouble if a fast enough reading pace is kept up to allow the movement of thought on the scale of the paragraph to assert itself and if allowance is made for rhetorical and economical use of the points. Some difficulties will be experienced, however, particularly with the colon and semicolon, which have no exact modern equivalents. It may be some consolation, therefore, to glance at the terrible effect that modernization would have had, if the alternative course had been adopted. It goes without saying that heavy modern pointing must impede the flow of the blank verse. But that is the least of it. Even Verity, who modernizes far more leniently and sporadically than Masson, will render a passage such as

> a flame,
> Which oft, they say, some evil spirit attends
> Hovering and blazing with delusive light . . .
> (ix 637–9)

like this:

> a flame
> (Which oft, they say, some evil spirit attends),
> Hovering and blazing with delusive light. . . .

The old punctuation of these lines allows us to think of the *spirit* hovering and deluding; and this ambiguity may well have been intentional on Milton's part, in view of the superstition that held the *ignis fatuus* to be a spirit. But with modern punctuation the editor opts for a single chain of discourse, allowing other possibilities to be bitten off by a parenthesis whose jaw closes either after *attends* (with only the *flame* hovering) or after *light* (with only the *spirit* hovering). And such passages abound: there is another within a few lines, at ix 650.

Sources and Models

The principal source of *Paradise Lost* is the Bible, with which it has a closer and more intimate relation than with any other work, ancient or modern. Naturally the scriptural allusions in many individual passages have long been editorial stock. But in the present edition it has been possible to add a surprising number of new scriptural parallels, echoes and allusions; in many cases thanks to James H. Sims's *The Bible in Milton's Epics* (Gainesville, Fla. 1962). It is beginning to be understood that the Bible for Milton meant the Bible glossed by commentators. For this reason Milton's modern reader would do well to consult Arnold Williams's *The Common Expositor* (Chapel Hill, N.C. 1948), which gives some indication of the interest and relevance of this neglected body of writing. In preparing the notes that follow, extensive use was made of Willet's *Hexaplus* on *Genesis*, an unoriginal commentary summarising a fairly broad spectrum of contemporary and earlier opinion. An important set of sources intersecting with the last are the Patristic. Sister M. I. Corcoran's *Milton's Paradise with Reference to the Hexaemeral Background* opened this territory as early as 1945, but it shows little sign of becoming a built-up area. Rabbinical sources, on the other hand, have probably been over-exploited, as a result of H. F. Fletcher's *Milton's Rabbinical Readings* (Urbana, Ill. 1930). The same author's series of volumes on *The Intellectual*

Development of John Milton (Urbana, Ill. 1956–) promises to be more balanced, and to contain a great deal of useful information on sources and potential sources; but so far it is not very accurate. Milton's ideas about angels are studied at length in Robert H. West's *Milton and the Angels*, (Athens, Ga. 1955); the sources are found to be numerous and the angelology unsystematic. It is to be suspected that Milton's angels will come still more sharply into focus, however, when they are looked at through the spectacles of the sacred iconographer. The iconographical sources of *Paradise Lost* have not been studied.

Not neglected, but requiring further study, are Milton's classical models–particularly the Homeric epics and Virgil's *Aeneid.* Such articles as Condee's have shown that the study of these models can mean much more than cataloguing verbal and narrative echoes. Milton's allusions to earlier epics are so consistent as to constitute a distinct strand of meaning in the poem: even, sometimes, a kind of critical accompaniment. What still remains to be investigated is the extent to which *Paradise Lost* allegorizes the inherited epic images, in the Neoplatonic manner of a Landino or a Spenser–that is, the extent to which the poem is tertiary rather than secondary epic.

The mention of Spenser gives occasion to remark that *The Faerie Queene* (contrary, perhaps, to expectation) is the most important, even if not the most obvious, vernacular model of *Paradise Lost.* Naturally Milton had studied earlier literary treatments of the Fall, such as the dramas of Grotius (*Adamus exul*, 1601) and Andreini (*L'Adamo*, 1613); and, in the Ninth Book of *Paradise Lost*, at least, they must be considered as main sources and perhaps even as models, in a certain sense. They may be conveniently studied in Watson Kirkconnell's splendid collection of analogues, *The Celestial Cycle* (Toronto 1952). But, from a critical point of view, the study proves on the whole unrewarding. Milton had the taste not to allude to these works in quite the same way that he alluded to Homer and Virgil. The situation is similar with respect to the hexaemeral parts of the poem, with Tasso's *Sette Giornate del Mondo Creato* (1607) as the model with literary worth. But here for once one must allow that Milton's taste erred. The quality of Du Bartas's *Sepmaines*, even in Sylvester's translation, does not seem to us to justify the extensiveness of Milton's allusions to it. Or was it that even in his fit audience there were limitations of taste and learning, within which he had to work?

Language and style

We are fortunate in now having a statistical analysis of Milton's language: R. D. Emma's *Milton's Grammar* (The Hague 1964). Though Emma's samples are too small to support those of his conclusions which concern rare phenomena, many of his results are convincing and of interest to the critic. We learn that Milton was outstandingly modern in his diction and even in his accidence (e.g., the avoidance of obsolescent verb terminals). And it seems that the diction of *Paradise Lost* is characterised by a very high incidence of words qualifying substantives; in spite of the fact that the use of adjectives is restrained compared with, say, Spenser's (Emma 26, 70). There is also a high incidence of conjunctions–nearly double their frequency in T. S. Eliot's poetry (Emma 87*n*, 129f). Both these features correlate with Milton's tendency in *Paradise Lost* to develop fine discriminations, and to introduce qualifications in an oblique or indirect way. The frequency of conjunctions of a coordinating kind has also of course to be seen in relation to the needs of Milton's sentence structure, which is markedly paratactic. But the complicated paratactic structure seems itself to result from a compromise between Milton's desire on the one hand to achieve fluent continuity and energy of movement, on the other to interpose continual corrections and qualifications.

It is to be hoped that this work of Emma's may be the first of a series of more objective and descriptive studies of Milton's style. For a long time, now, the emphasis has been dogmatic and polemical. F. R. Leavis began the present trend, with an essay in *Scrutiny* in 1933, in which he spoke of Milton's verse as monotonously ritualistic, 'not doing as much as its impressive pomp and volume seem to be asserting'; of his grand style as compelling an attitude 'incompatible with sharp, concrete realization'. Three years later T. S. Eliot also attacked Milton, in *Essays and Studies*; though his attack (as he explained in his Henriette Hertz Lecture to the British Academy in 1947) was somehow directed against the influence of Milton's verse without being directed against the verse itself. It is not necessary to accept all of Herbert Howarth's interesting suggestions about private motives for attacking Milton ('Eliot and Milton: the American Aspect', *UTQ* xxx (1961)), but we can hardly help feeling that Eliot's tactical warfare against the Georgians got disastrously out of hand. His influence on subsequent Milton criticism has been bad. And his criticism was bad too: like Leavis's it was dogma, built on unexamined premises and unsupported by demonstration. There have since been several sympathetic accounts of Milton's style; notably in C. S. Lewis, *A Preface to Paradise Lost* (1942), in Arnold Stein, *Answerable Style* (Minneapolis, Minn. 1953), and in Isabel G. MacCaffrey, *Paradise Lost as 'Myth'* (Cambridge, Mass. 1959). What was left of the attack has been routed–surely with finality–by Christopher Ricks in *Milton's Grand Style* (Oxford 1963), which shows how superlatively good Milton's style is, even judged by Leavis's criteria.

Perhaps the most notorious feature of the style of *Paradise Lost* has been its Latinity. An early comment was Jonathan Richardson's: '*Milton's* Language is English, but 'tis *Milton's* English; 'tis Latin, 'tis Greek English; not only the Words, the Phraseology, the Transpositions, but the Ancient Idiom is seen in All he Writes, So that a Learned Foreigner will think *Milton* the Easiest to be Understood of All the English Writers' (Darbishire 313). He adds a comparison of the language of *Paradise Lost* with that of New Testament Greek (colloquial, but affected by 'Oriental Dialects') and with that of Shakespeare. Even this view is a far cry from the contrast between Milton's and Shakespeare's use of English in the essay by Leavis, or from Eliot's emphasis on 'the remoteness of Milton's verse from ordinary speech'.

Now the sentence structure of *Paradise Lost* has nothing overtly neo-classical about it. It is a native English coordinate structure, loose rather than periodic, paratactic rather than syntactic. The verse paragraphs do not keep us waiting, perplexed, for the sense, or force us to traverse a single long syntactic line of subordinated parts. Instead the sense is 'diffused throughout a larger block of words' than is common (Prince 122). Usually there is a series of very temporary stopping-places, from which the thought darts off in unforeseen directions. And it is characteristic that any new phrase may introduce a modification, or show that a syntactic schema earlier applied was wrong or partial. Thus 'Of man's first disobedience, and the fruit [of that disobedience]' passes to 'Of man's first disobedience, and the fruit / Of that forbidden tree . . .' This unexpectedly sustained syntactic breath not only has continuity and force, but also communicates a strong effect of passion, or of thought in process. It is anything but an ordinary sentence structure; but it is not extraordinary in a manner foreign to the genius of English. In a more essential way, of course, the built order and flowing mass of the verse paragraphs are profoundly classical. Classicism in that sense, however, is only a virtue.

If the sentence structure is native, there are nevertheless many individual clauses or phrases that could be described as having a Latin or Greek construction; though information on this point is surprisingly scanty. Lewis (45f) thought Milton's Latin constructions justified by the freedom of word order they secure. But this point ought perhaps to be made another way round. At their best the arrangements of words in *Paradise Lost* have their own poetic reasons. If (subsequently, as it were) they can be made to correspond to Latin constructions, so much the better. Milton naturally preferred his poetic dislocations of conventional English syntax to have the additional value of corresponding to ancient usage. Thus the common omission of the article, and the occasional use of *after* with a past participle (e.g. iii 552 'after heaven seen') produce effects that are first concise, spare and pungent; then Latinate. Latinate constructions, we notice, are commonest in the transitions, where they give a sense of command and artistic detachment (e.g. x 229).

Perhaps the word order of *Paradise Lost* has lent as much support as anything to the charge of unidiomatic remoteness; for about one quarter of its clauses are inverted. We are now coming to understand, however, that the word order of Milton's time was very much freer than that permissible with us (see Emma 140ff). The best recent work on Milton's diction is probably F. T. Prince's *The Italian Element in Milton's Verse* (Oxford 1954), which isolates many of the features we consider most characteristic of *Paradise Lost*, and assigns them their context in contemporary literary practice. (Professor Prince is especially interesting on the disposition of epithets–e.g. the device adjective + noun + *and* + adjective, as in 'sad task and hard' v 564.) But even this fine book requires to be rewritten on a statistical basis, so as to make clear which features of Milton's word order were non-standard. What statistical information there is about Milton's word order is of doubtful value, partly because of the uncertainty with which parameters have been set and partly because of the inadequacy of samples. Emma, e.g., working with a sample of only 140 lines of *Paradise Lost* (and about three times as much of the other poetry) finds the Subject–Object–Verb inversion ('She . . . Her unadorned golden tresses wore', iv 304f) to be the commonest; whereas if one works with a sample of about 1400 lines of *Paradise Lost* it turns out to be comparatively rare. Similarly the Object–Subject–Verb inversion ('the companions of his fall . . . He soon discerns', i 76–8) is more frequent than Emma's figures imply; and the Verb–Subject inversion ('So spake the apostate angel', i 125) much more frequent. Verb–Subject 'inversion', however, can hardly be described as alien to the genius of the language. Not only was it a common alternative in seventeenth-century English, but it was the regular order at an earlier stage. (See R. Quirk and C. L. Wrenn, *An Old English Grammar* (1957) 94; Otto Jespersen, *A Modern English Grammar*, vol. vii (1961) pp. 59, 78f; and–with many examples–E. Mätzner, *Englische Grammatik* (Berlin 1885) pp. 587ff, 627.) For poetic purposes Milton followed one indigenous alternative to an extent that was unusual: that is all we are entitled to say. And it is the same with other forms of inversion. We should never assume them to be simply Italianate or Latinate, until seventeenth-century English colloquial and literary usage has been examined with some care statistically.

In much the same way, the Latinity of Milton's choice of diction has generally been assumed, without recourse to a good English dictionary. An honourable exception is Lalia Phipps Boone, who arrives at the conclusion that Milton's Latinity has been exaggerated, in 'The Language of Book VI, *PL*' in *S.A.M.L.A. Studies in Milton*, ed. J. Max Patrick (Gainesville, Fla. 1953). On closer inspection it turns out that the general assumption is in need of many qualifications. Often what has been taken for imitation of Latin or Greek is really only poetic departure from ordinary usage; often, too, even when the ancient idiom is really present it contributes no more than an Empsonian ambiguity. Hence innumerable ghost Latinisms, which were raised by early editors and superstitiously believed in by their successors.

There is a spectrum of possible Latinity of diction in which four bands may be distinguished:

1. The Latin usage is the primary sense or chain of discourse; and is completely new in English. Milton very seldom innovates so extremely, but *omnific* (vii 217) and *recline* (iv 333, 'they sat recline') are probably instances of this kind of Latinizing coinage.
2. The Latin usage is the primary sense; and occurs in English only or mostly in poetic contexts: i.e. the familiar Augustan 'gradus diction' (viii 263, 'liquid lapse of murmuring streams', where *liquid*, = 'flowing', is poetic diction). *Paradise Lost* has few Latinisms of this kind.
3. The Latin usage is a secondary sense only. The primary sense is an ordinary English usage, but a Latin usage is present in addition, as an allusion or ambiguity (e.g. vii 264f, 'The firmament, expanse of liquid . . . air', which

may well allude to Latin *expansum*, supposed a better translation than *firmamentum* of the Hebrew word in *Gen.* i 6). There are many 'Latinisms' of this type; but they could never be said to weaken the native sinews of anyone's style. Such effects enrich and deepen.

4. The primary sense is an ordinary English usage, occurring in prose contexts, which happens also to be a Latin usage. This, if it were to be considered Latinism at all, would be Latinism at its faintest and least objectionable. Examples of this type naturally occur throughout *Paradise Lost* in great numbers.

By any reasonable criterion the term Latinism should only be applied to forms recognizable in Milton's time as in some way non-standard usage – i.e. Types 1–2, or at most Types 1–3. It follows that most of the supposed Latinisms in *Paradise Lost* are really nothing of the sort. Thus x 155–6, 'to bear rule, which was thy part / And person', which was hailed by Newton as 'a pure Latinism', had been perfectly good English back in Milton's time (*OED* gives six instances in non-technical prose, earlier than 1667, of *person*='role'). And it is the same with vii 93, *absolved*='completed', which is treated as a Latinism even by Ricks (six earlier instances in prose). There are, of course, difficult borderline cases. But this does not excuse us from doing what we can to distinguish the extremes. In some respects we are actually better equipped than Richardson and Dr Johnson to estimate the degree of Latinity of Milton's diction.

If therefore a usage occurs in English, in non-technical non-fiction prose contexts earlier than *Paradise Lost*, it may ordinarily be assumed not to be a Latinism. In such cases only the meaning has been given in the notes, with perhaps an indication of the relevant section in *OED*, where citations of earlier instances will be found. A simple gloss of this type is to be taken to imply that the word has more or less its standard seventeenth-century English sense. Milton would of course know the etymology of many of the words in *Paradise Lost* (though not as many as Verity). But unless he used them in such a way as to draw attention to and exploit the derivation, it is hard to see how that knowledge concerns us. Naturally the interplay between words of Romance and of Anglo-Saxon origin is an important feature of Milton's style, as of most English styles. But that is a matter for the critic, not the editor. In consequence, many 'Latinisms' have been ignored in the notes to the present edition, and the diction of the poem has been allowed to resume its original strongly colloquial character. True, it is only colloquial in a comparative sense; for much of it is in high style rhetorically. But it remains, nevertheless, the most colloquial secondary epic ever written – a fact that ignorant emphasis on its Latinity has done much to obscure.

If the Latinisms in *Paradise Lost* have been overestimated, it is quite the reverse with the ambiguities and ironies. There are far more instances of such effects than any critic has led us to expect. They may almost be said, indeed, to form the general texture of the style. The effects range from what I shall call double syntax, through puns, ironies and *doubles entendres*, to outright radical ambiguities challenging a choice of attitude on the part of the reader. Double syntax occurs when three word groups *a*, *b*, *c* are connected in such a manner that *ab* forms one chain of discourse and *bc* another (to which *a* may or may not belong), e.g. in

> That shepherd, who first taught the chosen seed,
> In the beginning how the heavens and earth
> Rose out of chaos (i 8–10)

In the beginning seems linked with *first taught*, until we find a better connection with *rose*. (Notice how the effect is assisted by the inversion in l. 9, which is as far as possible from existing for its own sake.) Such double syntax has a large role in the drawing out of the sense through the poem's verse paragraphs. The reader is constantly led on by the fluid movement of phrases or even clauses that relate first retrospectively and then prospectively. But this grammatical illusionism is not so emphatic as to constitute full ambiguity. In fact, if its mechanism is noticed at all, the alternatives will usually be dismissed as trivial.

At the other extreme are radical ambiguities which present real alternatives of value. These constitute one of the most characteristic features of Milton's style, giving it much of its surprising sharpness and subtlety. Yet they have often been regarded as mere troublesome cruxes. Thus Miss Darbishire is so annoyed with iv 410, where Adam 'Turned him all ear to hear new utterance flow'–*him* being either Adam or Satan–that she adds a pair of commas in her normalized text, 'to make the sense clear'. But the way in which Adam and Satan share the pronoun *him* can seem positively effective, if the passage is related to others in which Satan takes Adam's place (see e.g. v 40f and *n*). A more typical ambiguity, perhaps, is Satan's soliloquizing address to Adam and Eve: 'League with you I seek, / And mutual amity so strait . . .' (iv 375f). If we are of the devil's gullible party, we shall take *strait* to mean only 'intimate' (*OED* 14); for the pun with *straight* (= 'honest') is almost excluded by the appositional phrase *so close* and by the consequence that follows. But if we have our wits about us we recall that *strait* could also mean 'involving privation'. Similarly, at iii 397f the choice of syntactical connections in

> Back from pursuit thy powers with loud acclaim
> Thee only extolled, Son of thy Father's might,

is related to the choice between Satan's and Raphael's accounts of the expulsion of the rebel angels. In a high proportion of instances, the ambiguities in *Paradise Lost* call for discrimination of this kind on the reader's part.

If discrimination is challenged by the ambiguities, it is almost forced on us by the similes. After all, Milton had lived through a vogue for difficult and witty comparisons; so that we may expect him to engage our attention especially strenuously in this area. At one level, of course, the similes are easy and pleasant: so much so that to earlier generations of critics they were oases where a reader could refresh himself, as one who in his journey bates.

More recently the similes have been studied by James Whaler, in *PMLA* xlvi (1931); by William Empson, in *Some Versions of Pastoral* (1935); by Laurence Lerner, in *EC* iv (1954); and by Christopher Ricks, in *Milton's Grand Style* (Oxford 1963). They have disclosed many beauties, but also many difficulties. The most serious problem is that the comparisons sometimes seem curiously thin, with only slender grounds of resemblance between tenor and vehicle. Consequently the doctrine has been developed that Milton often uses similes 'with a clear sense of the fact that they don't fit exactly' (Ricks 127). Now it is certainly true sometimes that an element of disparity is present–particularly in the similes relating to Satan, whom we may agree with Ricks in regarding as a hideous parody of the good (e.g. i 338–44, discussed Ricks 128f). But it is much more often the case that the comparison is positive but difficult. We may perhaps be invited to discriminate between right and wrong ways of applying the simile, or to catch an allusion and read with the eyes of faith. The typical case is iii 510–25, where Satan, looking up at the entrance to heaven, is compared at some length with Jacob:

> The stairs were such as whereon Jacob saw
> Angels ascending and descending, bands
> Of guardians bright, when he from Esau fled
> To Padan-Aram in the field of Luz,
> Dreaming by night under the open sky,
> And waking cried, *This is the gate of heaven.*

If the only resemblance between Jacob and Satan were that each saw steps leading to heaven's gate it might be right to conclude that the point of the simile lay in the disparity betwen them. But we are meant to see a deeper similarity of situation. Satan, like Jacob, is escaping from retribution and has come to a critical turning-point. He will go on, after his vision of the cosmos, to harden his heart; whereas Jacob was awed and repentant and 'vowed a vow' (*Gen.* xxviii 20f). For the moment, however, the resemblance holds.

It will have been noticed that in the last example an important element on the vehicle side of the comparison–the moral significance of the vision to Jacob–is present only by implication. This type of simile, in which the vehicle is partially suppressed or compressed into allusive form, is common in *Paradise Lost*: a fairly extreme instance is the group of three similes at ix 439–43. The notes that follow achieve some increase in the number of similes whose resonant or allusive character has been recognized. And it is likely that the number will be increased still further as our understanding of the structure of poetic analogy grows. For one of the difficulties with Milton's similes lies in the astonishing complexity and variety of their logical forms. There are comparisons within comparisons; comparisons cast in negative form; comparisons with double or triple vehicles (e.g. ix 670–6); and even a few comparisons that appear to have double tenors (e.g. x 289–93).

What might be called ideological awareness is in evidence not only in the similes of *Paradise Lost* but throughout its style. This is well established with respect to the imagery, and diction in the broader sense. Thus, much recent criticism of the poem has been given over to faithful and sometimes remorseless tracing of how Milton's every use of certain key words is in accordance with strategic considerations of placement, association, sequence, and the like (whether following or preceding the Fall; whether used of God or of Satan; etc.). Parts of Isabel MacCaffrey's and Christopher Ricks's fine books fall into this class of criticism, and so does almost all of Jackson Cope's *The Metaphoric Structure of 'Paradise Lost'* (Baltimore, Md. 1962). This has been a rich vein, and there is little fear of its being bled dry in the near future. For almost any word in the poem could be shown to be a key word: it is a work of that degree of intellectual concentration. And when scepticism has been allowed the relief of expression; when it has been said that in any poem about the Fall words such as *fall* and *rise* are bound to be specially 'significant' (whether without the poet's help, like *beetroot* in a book on beetroot; or with the poet's unconscious help), still real thanks are due to the pursuers of thematic words for repeating the work of the poet so fully. For there are a great many genuine key words in *Paradise Lost*. And the study of them has put it beyond question that Milton chooses and builds his words with an extraordinarily sustained awareness of their ideological and moral implications. It is very characteristic, e.g., that the only time he uses *guiltless* in an innocent amoral sense is immediately before the Fall, at ix 392: 'Guiltless of fire'. (There is a similar ordonnance in the field of character, where the poem's psychology seems less crude when it is understood to be orientated according to a polarity of innocence and guilt–what matters is usually the distinction between states before and after the Fall.) Richardson put it well when he said that 'a Reader of *Milton* must be Always upon Duty; he is Surrounded with Sense, it rises in every Line, every Word is to the Purpose; There are no Lazy Intervals, All has been Consider'd, and Demands, and Merits Observation' (Darbishire 315).

The study of the thematic words in *Paradise Lost* seems to be at its most interesting (as often in the work of Mrs MacCaffrey and Ricks) when it concerns itself with the semantic fields surrounding objects or events literally present in the physical world of the poem. Naturally the important themes, to which Milton would give most attention, gain an expression beyond the merely verbal. Thus the study of the key words becomes at its best a study of key images and objects: of the symbolic organization of the world of the poem. This is especially striking with one of the earliest key words announced in the poem, *fruit*. When Milton's exploitation of the semantic field of *fruit* is reviewed, it is found to account for no small proportion of the poem's content. It extends not only to innumerable concrete and abstract uses of *fruit* itself (as well as of *fruitless* and *fruition*) but also to almost every other reference to vegetable nature. Thus Eve is herself a 'fairest unsupported flower' (ix 432) and Christ's promise is to her seed; the fallen angels lie like leaves in Vallombrosa (i 302); the serpent is a shoot of fraud (ix 89); and under the Covenant mankind proceeds 'as from a second stock [trunk]' (xii 7). But none of these images would have half so much force if it were not for the actual presence of the trees that dominate the physical landscape of the poem. The sacred Biblical Trees of Life and of Knowledge, the emblematic trees and plants of virtue, the ordinary wild natural trees that complete the grotesque surrounding frame–everywhere in Paradise vegetation burgeons luxuriantly. It is natural and inevitable that the universe itself should be thought of as a plant whose 'bright consummate flower' is breathed in heaven (v 481). Mankind is as naturally both part and guardian of a plant; and a plant's desecration must inevitably have cosmic repercussions.

Milton's extraordinary artistic self-awareness and intelligence is nowhere more characteristically manifested than in the command with which he deploys his materials effortlessly to achieve the simultaneous effects in which he delighted. He will in general avoid *sententiae*; then suddenly concentrate them in Book ix, before the fatal separation, having them delivered not *in persona auctoris* but by Adam (ix 232–4, 249, 250, 267f): a disposition that secures their maximum effect, helps to establish the book's newly introduced tragic mode and at the same time illustrates a phase of the development of Adam's moral authority. Or, he will use word order simultaneously for grammatical, rhythmic and spatial-symbolic ends. Thus it has often been noticed how the sentence structure of *Paradise Lost* is moulded partly with a view to sustaining an accompaniment of mimetic effects. Already Jonathan Richardson remarked how at ii 910ff Satan's hesitation on the brink of chaos is mimed. 'Into this wild abyss' is followed not by a plunge but by several lines of description; and when it is repeated, and leads at last to a main verb, the verb we get is unexpectedly diffident:

Into this wild abyss . . .
Into this wild abyss the wary fiend
Stood on the brink of hell and looked a while,
Pondering his voyage. . . .

Such effects have so far proved too elusive for thorough analysis. But there are some interesting pages in Ricks (27ff, 78ff). And it is probably no exaggeration to say that similar uses of syntax could be demonstrated in almost any passage in the poem.

Even more elusive, now, is the rhetorical patterning of Milton's language. This was once a chief glory of the poem, but it is so little to the modern taste that any attempt to cultivate a discriminating appreciation of it would now be uphill work. All we can hope for is to come to a vague recognition of its presence. The identification of all the schemes and tropes would not only be pedantry but useless and ignorant pedantry; for at its best rhetoric depended on a response much more sophisticated than the elementary one of recognition. It was rather a matter of appreciating the significance of an unusual frequency of this scheme, or an aptness to the subject in that, or a surprising departure from the range of figures usual within the prevailing 'style'. An example of which we can be fairly sure comes in the first part of Book vi, where we get a remarkably high concentration of such figures as puns, which were considered low and easily liable to excess. Paradoxically, the frequent 'indecorum' of this passage is appropriate to the subject, the 'wild work' of the angelic war: see vi 498*n*, 578–94*n*, 566*n*, 698–9*n*. Thus, from a rhetorical point of view, the description of the devils' cannon at vi 572–84 is viciously inflated (bomphiologia); while immediately afterwards the diction is at the other extreme of indecorum, when the firing is described in such low terms as *belched*, *embowelled*, *entrails*, *disgorging*, *glut*. A very different example is Eve's lyrical expression of her love at iv 639–56. The major scheme of these verses, a kind of large-scale *epanalepsis* or *enumeratio*, is itself a mimetic repetition rendering Eve's responsiveness to Adam. From its intricate magic circle all schemes are excluded but those of completeness and varied reflection; though at the semantic level this expansive repose is made to rest on Eve's sustained rejection of the world of separation from Adam. The smooth returning flow of *epanalepsis* and *epanodos*, the copiousness of *merismus* within *merismus*, and the exquisite balance of similarity against variety in the poignant negative repetition, put the passage among the most satisfying, from a formal point of view, ever composed in this mode.

On occasion Milton could carry the patterning of his language to astonishing lengths. We find it, for example, even in enumerative passages. He seldom *just* gives a catalogue of names or a list of like items: usually he is simultaneously at work ordering and informing the arrangement with silent meaning. Thus by a neat irony the very catalogue of place-names that T. S. Eliot dismissed as 'a solemn game' has a pattern that shows Milton's creative intellect at its most energetic, shaping almost pure form into a body of thought:

> Of Cambalu, seat of Cathaian khan
> And Samarchand by Oxus, Temir's throne,
> To Paquin of Sinaean kings, and thence
> To Agra and Lahor of great mogul
> Down to the golden Chersonese, or where
> The Persian in Ecbatan sat, or since
> In Hispahan, or where the Russian czar
> In Mosco, or the sultan in Bizance,
> Turchestan-born. . . . (xi 388–96)

The Asian names sound out their exotic grandeur with a power, a magic, that no sensible person will despise (for its particularity lies close to the heart of poetry). But the names do something else besides. By their disposition they tacitly confer upon one of their members, golden Chersonese (Ophir), the sovereignty that accords with its central position. The same pattern is repeated in the vista of African principalities, with 'Sofala thought Ophir' in the central position. Ophir rules, because the gold of Ophir is the gold of Christ's sovereignty (*Is.* xiii 12: 'I will make a man more precious than fine gold; even a man than the golden wedge of Ophir'). And about this centre, various symmetrical patterns are formed (see xi 388–95*n*, 396–407*n*). This may seem to some a strange, even an alien, poetic form; but it is not one that much suggests vague aestheticism.

Prosody

The standard line in *Paradise Lost* has ten syllables, with stresses on those of even number: 'United thoughts and counsels, equal hope' (i 88). Naturally such lines are not in an overwhelming majority; but departures from the norm are subject to certain restrictions. Most scholars agree that the verse is syllabic, not accentual; which is to say that while the number of heavy speech accents a line contains is variable, the number of theoretical syllables is not. (In accentual verse, on the contrary, there is a fixed complement of accents, but the number of unaccented syllables may vary widely.) It is probable, though not certain, that a distinction has to be made, in the verse of *Paradise Lost*, between accent and stress. The line 'Stirred up with envy and revenge, deceived' (i 35) has only four heavy accents; while 'Fallen cherub, to be weak is miserable' (i 157) has only three. But *and*, *to*, and *-able*, though they bear little accent, seem either to have had actual quantitative length, or to have been regarded as bearing 'theoretical' stress. Thus the line always has five *stresses*, but may have fewer than five *accents*.

As for the number of syllables, it is very often greater than ten. But it has to be reducible to a theoretical ten by one or other of the customary procedures that had been imported into English prosody from Italian. By far the most usual of these are elision, synaloepha, and contraction. In the line 'Till, as a signal given, the uplifted spear' (i 347) *given* is contracted to a monosyllable, while *the uplifted* is run together by synaloepha to give *th'uplifted*; so that the syllables theoretically number ten. Synaloepha may or may not involve the complete loss of one of the vowels concerned; in the former case it is often called elision. It can occur within a word ('Of man's first disobed*ie*nce'); also when the vowels are separated by *h*. One exception to the theoretical limit of ten syllables should be mentioned: namely the occasional excess of a final extrametrical syllable. Milton seems to have regarded this variation as a definite licence; and Ernest Sprott plausibly suggests that the licence is introduced mimetically. Thus it is most frequent at the end of Book ix, where Adam is 'estranged in look and altered style' (ix 1132; see Sprott 58f).

A great many other 'rules' governing Milton's prosodic freedom have from time to time been formulated. But they are all either illusory, or merely statistical and not invariable, or trivial, or irrelevant to literary criticism. Who but a prosodist cares how often Milton allowed himself an inverted *n*th foot? Even the famous rule about the fourth syllable always being stressed is probably not a rule at all. As Sprott (102) suggests, the statistical predominance of stressed fourth syllables may only be a consequence of the need to compensate for the inversion in the opening foot of which Milton was so fond.

Robert Bridges's *Milton's Prosody* (revised edn, Oxford 1921) is still worth reading for incidental felicities, but has been replaced by S. E. Sprott's more systematic and sensitive *Milton's Art of Prosody* (Oxford 1953). Both are, up to a point, clear and convincing. But both shy away from the topic of quantity–indeed, from the whole question of what (if anything) decided heavy stress on unaccented syllables. Yet the poetic of, e.g., Alexander Gill (Milton's old headmaster at St Paul's) goes into this subject in some detail. Gill discusses how syllable length is affected by vowel length, internal accent and position; also how these considerations are overriden by rhetorical accent, our grammatical accent (*Logonomia anglica* (revised edn, 1621) 132ff). Thus, in the opening line of *Paradise Lost*, if Milton were following Gill's system (or a system like it), in which prefixes such as *dis–* had to be short whenever position allowed, we would get the scansion: 'Of mán's fírst disobédience, ánd the frúit'– always supposing that the grammatical accents didn't decide the matter otherwise. The inverted second foot here is of some interest; for strong grammatical accent on *first* is in fact by no means inevitable. Obviously this is a matter that calls for early enquiry. Until more is known about the rules governing syllable length, indeed, it is probably vain to bother with more difficult and delicate problems of scansion.

Not that we need be shut out from all appreciation of the prosodic effects in *Paradise Lost.* Fortunately in the majority of lines the grammatical accent–*pace* Albert Cook in *UTQ* xxix (1960)–is strong and dominant. And in some others where this is not the case, the effect Milton intends is nevertheless clear enough: e.g. in 'O'er bog or steep, through straight, rough, dense, or rare,' (ii 948) most readers will agree that the stress and accent gradients from *rough* to *dense* and from, say, *or* to *steep* are different; and that this difference somehow mimes the roughness of the rough patch. Commenting on this line Sprott for once grasps the nettle of quantity, and says the effect is due to the length of *rough* 'because of the labial spirant'. Well, perhaps. But it seems to me that we have to know much more about what Milton meant by 'fit quantity of syllables' before we can explain the *mechanism* of the effect. (We would also have to allow for such other factors as the contrasting extraordinarily smooth liaison in *or rare*, and the interruption of the sequence preposition / noun / conjunction / noun at the terms *rough, dense.*) Nevertheless, the existence of the effect itself is beyond doubt.

Similarly, there is no obstacle to our enjoyment of Milton's skilful variation of caesura position. This variation is almost certainly what is meant, in the Note on the Verse, by 'the sense variously drawn out from one verse into another'.

Numerology

Still more doubtful, at present, is the question of the numerical organization of *Paradise Lost.* The first work on the subject, James Whaler's *Counterpoint and Symbol* (Copenhagen 1956) dealt with elaborate patterns formed by the numbers of beats intervening between breaks in the sense. Numerology based on units so elusive and debatable, even if it existed, could only be a private method of the poet's. And in any case, the symbolisms Whaler assigns to numbers are often arbitrary meanings, without foundation in seventeenth-century arithmology (3, e.g., simply was not the number of justice). It is possible, however, that some of the patterns really exist. Whaler may have stumbled on something quite different from numerology: namely, organic laws governing enjambement in blank verse.

Gunnar Qvarnström's *Dikten och den nya vetenskapen. Det astronautiska motivet* (Lund 1961) (now in a modified English version: *Poetry and Numbers*, Scripta minora Regiae Societatis Humaniorum Litterarum Lundensis (1964–5)) more convincingly argues for the existence of a line-count numerology governing the length of speeches throughout the poem. Qvarnström (93) draws attention, e.g., to Christ's two speeches at the very centre of the poem (vi 723–45, 801–23), both of them 23 lines long. Between the speeches Christ ascends his chariot to drive the rebel angels from heaven. Now in the number symbolism of the time 23 sometimes signified the fulness of Christ's redemption, sometimes vengeance upon the heathen (see Bongo 442, Fowler 247*n*). Qvarnström's most impressive result is that in *Ed I* the numerological centre of the whole poem by line-count falls between vi 761 and 762, i.e., precisely where Christ ascends his triumphal chariot:

He in celestial panoply all armed
761 Of radiant urim, work divinely wrought,
762 Ascended, at his right hand victory
Sat, eagle-winged. . . .

It would be hard to exaggerate the importance of this observation, which lends point to a whole series of other symmetries about the midpoint of the poem (see, e.g., vi 761*n* and viii 249*n*). Some of these symmetries have been independently studied (though not from a numerological point of view) by J. R. Watson in 'Divine providence and the structure of *Paradise Lost*', *EC* xiv (1964) 148–55, an excellent article which nevertheless fails to notice the centre of the symmetry in the triumphal chariot of Christ. Watson speaks of a tension between the poem's dramatic effects–especially the apparent climax in Bk ix–and its enclosing symmetrical pattern. He rightly sees in this an analogy with the characteristic contrasting movements of Baroque architecture.

There is the difficulty, of course, that the additions made in *Ed II* have the net effect of moving the centre point 4½ lines later, to vi 766. (It may be relevant that the lines are numbered in the margin–sometimes erratically–in *Ed I*, but not numbered in *Ed II*.) This is partly offset, however, by the simultaneous reordering of the book division; which as Mrs MacCaffrey 57*n* remarks makes the poem more obviously symmetrical about its midpoint:

Ed I Book	(1667) Lines	*Ed II* Book	(1674) Lines	
i	798	i	798	
ii	1055	ii	1055	
iii	742	iii	742	
iv	1015	iv	1015	
v	904	v	907	(3 lines added at 636–9)
vi	912	vi	912	
vii	1290	vii	640	
		viii	653	(3 lines added at 1–4)
viii	1189	ix	1189	
ix	1104	x	1104	
x	1541	xi	901	(3 lines added at 485–7 and 1 at 551–2)
		xii	649	(5 lines added at 1–5)
	10550		10565	

There is no external evidence as to why Milton made the change. Whaler (165) suggests that he wanted to draw attention to the poem's number symbolism without forgoing conformity to the Virgilian twelve-book pattern. (In the Pythagorean system, Ten was the divine tetractys, the fountain of number from which all created being arises.) Barker, however, thinks that the change is essentially one from a dramatic structure–with five two-book acts–to an epic structure. In any case, the extreme length of *Ed I* Bk x (=*Ed II* xi and xii) certainly suggests that the subsequent division was planned from the start. The same conclusion might be drawn from vii 21, 'Half yet remains unsung', which in *Ed I* came in the seventh of ten books.

In *Ed II*, 'Half yet remains' is not only true, but also a useful structural signpost. For the two six-book halves of the poem match one another formally with some precision. Thus, each is divided by renewed invocations of the Muse into two parts bearing the octave proportion of harmony, 1 : 2, the proportion that according to Pico della Mirandola ought to exist between reason and concupiscence in the well-tempered soul; i.e., each half consists of two followed by four books: 2/4//2/4 (see ix 1–47*n* below, and Fowler 281*n*). Cutting across this division in the Baroque manner is a more emphatic upward movement to a double centre in Bks vi and vii (both editions). The first and more important of these centres is where Messiah, the *Sol iustitiae*, ascends his triumphal throne; the second is the 'crowned' central day of creation, when his image the sun is set to rule the day (see below, p. 445). In *Ed II*, which has more obvious symmetry, the point of bisection of twelve books falls between the two 'centres'. Moreover, as we work inwards from the outside books we find a series of connections between the matter of the first half and the answering matter in corresponding books of the second half. A few examples must suffice. The outermost two books in each case are concerned with the consequences of a fall:

i–ii portray the evil consequences of the fall of the angels, xi–xii the mixed consequences of the Fall of man. Next comes a divine council of deliberation on man's fall, and Christ's offer of mediation (iii); this is answered by a council of judgment, and by Christ's descent to judge and clothe fallen man (x). Similarly, in iii Satan enters the universe, in x he leaves it. Bk iv has the first temptation, which is answered in ix by the second. Then in the centre four books v–viii we have the 'episode' of Raphael, elevating Christ first in war then in creation.

A subsidiary pattern in *Ed II* is the correspondence between hell and chaos at the beginning of the first half, and the chaotic war of the angels at the end of the first half. In the same way the second half is flanked by pairs of books setting out the Mirror of Nature (vii–viii) and the Mirror of History (xi–xii).

In *Ed I*, 'Half yet remains unsung' refers to the line-count, not to the book-division. But there too the invocations have their significance. They mark the inceptions of groups of 2, 4, 1, and 3 books. Just as the book-totals of these four parts denote the tetractys in its expanded form (1, 2, 3, 4), so the total number of books in the whole of *Ed I* denotes the tetractys in its summed form (10 = 1 + 2 + 3 + 4).

Numerology may prove an even more useful tool to the interpretative critic of *Paradise Lost* when more is known about the particular sources of number symbolism on which Milton drew. Some steps have already been taken in this direction by Maren-Sofie Røstvig ('The Hidden Sense' in *Norwegian Studies in English* ix (Oslo 1963)).

Chronology

Newton thought Milton 'not very exact in the computation of time' (see his note to *PL* xi 135): a judgment that seems to have discouraged critics from bothering with the time scheme of the poem. (Even Grant McColley, who gives much interesting information about patristic ideas as to the timing of the Fall relative to the Creation, largely ignores the chronological indications in *Paradise Lost* itself.) With more justice Ricks 19 speaks of 'characteristic pedantry about the passage of time'. Milton does in fact take pains to arrange precise indications of the passage of time; dwelling fondly on *chronologiae* and giving long-drawn-out descriptions of sunset and sunrise (e.g. the especially elaborate nightfall at iv 352–633). But the indication of time is with him by no means an end in itself. For important thematic ideas are set out formally and structurally through the medium of the poem's chronology. These ideas will be better understood when work in progress by Qvarnström and Miss Röstvig is published. The present account agrees with theirs in the main, though not in all details.

Current confusion about the temporal scheme of *Paradise Lost* arises in part from a false conception of what Milton meant by 'day'. It is assumed that he meant a 24-hour period beginning and ending at midnight. Milton's fit audience, however, would be familiar with several different ways of reckoning days–from sunrise or noon or sunset, for example (see Riccioli i 31ff). It is clear, especially from Raphael's narration, that in *Paradise Lost* Milton in general follows the Biblical practice of reckoning the day from evening to evening (e.g. v 227, vii 260, 338). The Biblical 'evening' was itself a term of debated meaning (see Willet 4 on *Gen.* i 4); but that Milton agreed with St Jerome in reckoning evening from sunset is certain from vii 582f: 'Evening arose in Eden, for the sun / Was set'. Time is thus divided ordinally or calendrically into Biblical days consisting each of an evening followed by a morning. On the other hand, *duration* of time may be reckoned in 24-hour periods, also called days, beginning at any point (e.g. vi 871). The resultant ambiguity is exploited when Adam waits for judgment to descend on 'the day' he ate the forbidden fruit (see x 773*n*).

With this in mind it is not very difficult to determine the main lines of the poem's chronology:

EVENING AND MORNING	EVENT	INDICATION IN TEXT
1	First exaltation of Christ	v 582f, 618
2–4	War in heaven	v 642, vi 406, 524, 684–6, 748
4–13	Rebel angels' 9-day pursuit through chaos	vi 871
13–22	Rebel angels' 9-day stupor in hell	i 50
14–20	The creation	vi 715f, vii 131ff
17	Creation of sun and moon	vii 386
19	Creation of man	vii 550
22	Rebel angels' awakening; building of Pandaemonium (1 hour); council; Satan's departure	i 697
23	Satan's observation of the universe (midnight); his conversation with Uriel (noon)	iii 555–61, iv 564
24	First temptation of Eve; Satan's expulsion (midnight); Raphael's visit (noon to sunset)	iv 1015, v 311, viii 630
24–31	Satan's 7-day encompassing of earth	ix 58–67
32	Satan's reentry (midnight); the Fall (noon); Messiah's judgement of man (late afternoon)	ix 739, x 92f
33	Michael's visit (sunrise to noon); the Expulsion of man (noon)	xi 184, xii 589

NOTES: (*a*) Additional time could be interposed if one were to speculate about what happens outside the poem (e.g. while Satan 'long . . . wandered' on the surface of the universe, iii 499). But I think Milton means us only to reckon days necessarily expended in the action actually presented.
(*b*) The duration assigned to Satan's journey to earth finds some additional confirmation in the time Raphael took to fly to hell gate (viii 229–46).

(*c*) The critical chronology of the events assigned to Days 32–3 is established in more detail in the notes. See x 49–53*n*, 92–102*n*, 328–9*n*, 342*n*, 1050*n*, and especially 773*n*.
(*d*) It seems reasonable to assume that Messiah went straight on to create after driving the rebel angels down to hell. This would put the week of creation on Days 14–20, and the creation of man on Day 19, as shown in the accompanying Table. Raphael's finding the gate of hell barred on the 6th day of creation (viii 240) would tally with this scheme; for the gate was barred from the 13th to the 22nd. Some, it is true, infer from the sounds of torment Raphael heard on this occasion that the devils had risen from their stupor; which would fix the creation of man on the opening day of the poem, Day 22. But the sounds Raphael heard are chronologically irrelevant, since they may be explained as the noise of Sin and her hell hounds at the gate (ii 862), and since in any case devils were believed to undergo torment during their sleep (viii 242–4*n*). Moreover, such passages as v 3, 31, and especially iv 449–50 ('That day I oft remember, when from sleep / I first awaked', spoken on Day 23), seem to rule out a creation of man on the 22nd.

From the above analyses, several numerological patterns emerge. (It is very natural that Milton should have organized his poem in this way; for speculation about the number symbolism underlying the sequence of the days of creation had long been a prominent element in the hexaemeral tradition.) We note that in *Ed I* the action of the first 3 books takes place off the earth and ends with an account of creation; while the first-order action of the remaining 7 books (iv–x; *Ed II* iv–xii) is almost exclusively terrestrial. If we recall that 7 was the number of the world and of the week of creation, it may well seem significant that in *Ed I* the centre book of these terrestrial 7 is Bk vii (*Ed II* vii–viii); and that the content of that book is an account of the creation and a discussion of the 7 planetary spheres. In the course of the hexaemeron itself, moreover, the central day of the week, which is also the central day of the poem's whole action, is said to be 'crowned' (vii 386), i.e., to occupy the central position of sovereignty. On that day (Day 17) is created the sun, whose centrality is suggested by Raphael in the central line of a long paragraph in the dialogue on astromony. The simplest diagram of the poem's action would be:

FALL OF THE ANGELS	CREATION	FALL OF MAN
13 days	7 days	13 days

In both editions, the direct action of the poem occupies 11 days, i.e., Days 23–33. There is an obvious number symbolism in this, since 11 signified sin–transgressing the 10 of the Decalogue. (See St Augustine, *Civ. Dei* xv 20; Hopper 87, 101, 152; Fowler 54; Qvarnström 90.) Less obviously, the 11 days of action directly represented are in a ratio of 11 :22 or 1 :2 with the remaining days of retrospectively narrated action. Now the ratio 1 :2, the octave proportion, signified the ideal relation between the reason and the concupiscible faculty. (See Pico della Mirandola, *Conclusiones secundum mathematicam Pythagorae* in *Opera omnia* (Basel 1573) i 79; Fowler 281*n*. The same ratio is used in *Paradise Lost* for the proportions of the universe: see i 73–4*n*.) Thus the form of the action repeats, but also repairs, man's first concupiscence. A similar symbolism governs the detailed arrangement of the 11 days of direct action. Satan's briefly recounted week of miscreation is framed or contained by the remaining 4 days–

Bks i–iv	*Bk ix 48–66*	*Bks ix–xii*
	week of miscreation	
23rd, 24th	25th–31st	32nd, 33rd

–so that the 7 of mutability is ordered and raised by the 4 of concord and virtue, the holy tetractys.

Finally, there is significance in the ordinal numbers denoting certain days of the action. For example, the first day, the only unfallen 'undivided' day, the only day without a preceding night, is appropriately denoted by the monad. The sole event that takes place on this unique day is the generation of God's only Son, under whose reign the angels are to abide 'United as one individual soul'. Again, it is on the day denoted by the evil and rebellious dyad that war breaks out in heaven. The Fall itself and the judgment of man take place on Day 32: appropriately, since 32 was a number symbolizing pleasure, whose Pythagorean name was Justice (Bongo 486). The last day of the poem's action, when Adam is shown visions of the Fall's consequences and of the redemptive history, and when he himself leaves Paradise to enter that history, is denoted by 33. This number, the number of man's earthly suffering and of the life of Christ, was a very familiar symbol, which had already been used as the numerological basis of Dante's *Divina commedia*.

We conclude that the prominence given to the succession of day and night is entirely justified on thematic grounds. Seen with the eyes of faith, that succession sets out the divine nature, our covenant with whom must be as sure 'as the days of heaven' (xii 344–7*n*). It is not only Adam who discovers, in the peripeteias of x–xii, that God's judgment is numerically sure. The reader, too, learns to say with the Psalmist 'teach us to number our days'. For the whole form of the poem is designed to lead us up to the mount of God, where a cave is alternately inhabited by light and darkness (vi 4–12) to image his transcendence over time, as over good and evil. Isabel MacCaffrey puts it well when she speaks of the alternation of day and night in heaven as 'an elaborate kind of changelessness'. The imagery is in keeping with a seventeenth-century fashion for philosophical optics and astronomical mysticism. But it would be a mistake to think of it as the result of easy or impersonal choices on Milton's part. It is more like a confession of his faith in the justice of the God who had made darkness succeed light for him so unnaturally.

Milton's Universe

If the God of *Paradise Lost* can be said to contain and yet transcend light and darkness and the time they divide, the same is true of his relation to physical space. In an obvious way he is 'high throned above all height' (iii 58); more mysteriously, the spatial universe is imagined throughout as his Son's *vehicle*. The central image of the poem, physically, is that of a triumphal chariot, formed by cherubs, on which is carried the throne of Christ (see vi 749–59*n*). Ranged around this centre are ten thousand stellar beings, all praising and acknowledging his transcendent sovereignty. For the stars lighting the heavens are identified–sometimes metaphorically (v 700–16), sometimes almost literally (iii 622ff)–with angels. Their revolutions are a sacred *choresis*, a 'starry dance' (iii 580), that 'resembles nearest' the 'mystical dance' of the angels 'about the sacred hill' (v 619–22). Thus the poem's world can be regarded as expanding and developing the terrific idea concentrated in its central image, the *machina mundi* enthroning Christ. Like the universe imagined in Plato's *Timaeus* it is a living creature, a being animate throughout. It has motion; it engages in continual metabolic exchanges (v 414ff); and it exhales, transpiring fragrance and spirit up to God in prayer. This world with its celestial canopy was not of course one whose fabric Milton cut out of whole cloth. It is patched together from Neoplatonic pieces, or from worn canonicals handed down by medieval Christian Platonists. But the way in which the world is imaged, in passionate fullness of detail, is original. Instinct as it is with life, Milton's cosmos, however orderly, has always something of life's capacity to surprise.

This quality of unexpectedness is nowhere more striking than in the panoramic vistas, on which Mrs MacCaffrey has written so well. Whenever you move your eye over one of these vistas, or follow out any of the poem's innumerable flights through space, or trace out its chartings of the movements of heavenly bodies, you are constantly astonished by the power of spatial realization and by the sustained inventiveness with which natural phenomena are imaged more fully than ever before. Milton was the first Englishman, for example, to describe a sunset in detail. Everything we see in his poem tells us that Miss M. M. Mahood (*Poetry and Humanism* (1950) pp. 199–201) is right and T. S. Eliot ('A Note on the Verse of John Milton,' *Essays and Studies* (1936)) wrong: Milton had a strong spatial imagination. The surprise, then, is first at the unexpected sharpness of the perspectives. The space opened up has not only the amplitude of Poussin's space but also the dramatic force of the Mannerists' or Piranesi's.

And then a further surprise comes, when we notice to what extent each of Milton's perspectives is a 'legitimate construction': an exact reproduction, correct in every geographical or astronomical detail, of the actual world as it appears from a unique point of view. (This strong indication of a single distinctive physical standpoint can perhaps be regarded as a formal correlate of the poem's ideological engagement, of its constant discrimination between theological 'points of view'.) This is not just a matter of neatness or prosaic thoroughness. The details of Milton's astronomy are always significant, and almost always in more ways than one. Thus, when Satan leaves earth after the Fall 'Betwixt the Centaur and the Scorpion steering / His zenith, while the sun in Aries rose:' (x 328–9), we may at first be inclined to see only a magnificent visual image. Between the Centaur and the Scorpion stretches a starry serpent, the constellation Anguis. But then the details assert themselves, and the lines can be seen as a *chronographia*. A point between Sagittarius and Scorpio will be 120°–150° from Aries, so that, if the zenith at Paradise is such a point, it must there be between 2.00 and 4.00 am. This has a crucial significance for the chronology of the day of judgment after the Fall, the day whose termination is repeatedly delayed (see x 773*n*). But even this does not exhaust the content of the image. For there is also a dramatic irony, if we remember that the sun will not rise always in Aries. This sole occasion on which the sun's position in the *thema coeli* of creation is explicitly stated occurs almost immediately before it is displaced as a result of the Fall (x 668ff).

It would be inappropriate here to attempt an account of the Ptolemaic, Copernican and other planetary systems available to Milton. For that the reader must be referred to the Introduction to D. J. Price, ed., *The Equatorie of the Planetis* (Cambridge 1955); F. R. Johnson, *Astronomical Thought in Renaissance England* (Baltimore, Md. 1937); J. L. E. Dreyer, *A History of Astronomy from Thales to Kepler* (1953); or P. Duhem, *Le Système du Monde* (Paris 1913). There are also numerous articles and books on Milton's astronomy, such as A. H. Gilbert's in *SP* xix (1922), *SP* xx (1923) and *PMLA* xxxviii (1923); G. McColley's in *MLN* xlvii (1932), *SP* xxxiv (1937) and *PMLA* lii (1937); Marjorie Nicolson's in *ELH* ii (1935) and *SP* xxxii (1935); her *The Breaking of the Circle* (Evanston 1950); and Chs ii–iii of Kester Svendsen's *Milton and Science* (Cambridge, Mass. 1956). The theory that Milton was a Ptolemaist who rejected the new science of his day, like the theory that he was a Copernican who cynically used the Ptolemaic universe for poetic purposes, has now been abandoned. McColley's articles, in particular, have shown that there was a wide choice of planetary systems available to Milton, and that he alludes to many of these in his poem. The universe of *Paradise Lost* is a more subtly considered one than could have been devised by anyone with a naive belief in the exclusive truth of a scientific model. Not only does it combine elements of several systems but it even sometimes contrives (as at iv 592–7) to be geocentric and heliocentric simultaneously. Always it avoids unambiguous resolution of such uncertainties as the order of proximity of the planets to the earth.

This is not the result of a disinclination to risk backing a theory that might promptly be invalidated by some new Galileo; though this was a real consideration at a time when planetary systems were ten-a-penny. It is rather that Milton is using astronomical controversy as a symbol of all enquiry into knowledge hidden beyond the verge of man's capacities and limitations. The heliocentric and geocentric alternatives have to be kept open so that the seventeenth-century Adam of the poem may be only just at the point of beginning, with Raphael's help, to realize the inadequacies of the Ptolemaic system. Milton would want to relate the Fall to actual processes of cultural development, actual exchanges of new knowledge for simpler happiness. At such junctures, orientation and moral awareness matter as much as the capacity to choose the next scientific model. But there is also, one suspects, a deeper and less complicated reason for the carefully sustained uncertainty about the order of the planets (an uncertainty that in 1667 must almost have had a historical flavour). It goes without saying that Milton is trying to render something of the elusiveness and mystery of nature herself, who is not always as committed as we would wish her to be. The world of *Paradise Lost* is also, however, an attempt to render a visionary and perfected nature. She will not fit the girdling circles of Ptolemy, or Copernicus, or Galileo, or Brahe, because these were all devised, new and old alike, to describe our own fallen world.

By contrast, the universe of *Paradise Lost* is an ideal universe. For, in a remarkably original way, Milton has constructed a complete imaginary astronomy, based on a premise that does not hold for the existing world. The premise is that the ecliptic and equatorial planes coincide. The astronomical implications of this axiom are worked out with an almost science-fictional inventiveness: see, e.g., iii 555–61, iv 209–16, 354f, v 18–25, x 328f below. (Milton seems to have believed, like Plato and St Augustine, that creation has to be by number and measure.) Thus a world is generated that is beautifully simple and symmetrical–and exhilaratingly easy for a reader to imagine. It is one where day and night are always equal, where the sun remains always in the same sign, and where the positions of the constellations at any given time can easily be determined without recourse to an astrolabe. There are no variations in the declination of the sun, no equinoctial points, no precession and no distinction between sidereal, natural and civil days. The loss of this simple world is from one point of view a physical expression of the consequences of the Fall. The prelapsarian stasis of the Golden Age passes, then, into oblique movement; the sun starts his seasonal and precessional journeys; a new Platonic Great Year, a cycle of decay, sets in (v 583, x 651–706). But the original coincidence of ecliptic and equatorial does not exist just to provide, in its passing, another symbol of the Fall–any more than it is an aetiological myth to explain away bad weather. Rather is it part of Milton's offering of a purified integral pristine world, a macrocosmic setting for his righteous Adam. Like the removal of hell outside the universe, the rectifying of the zodiac allows a revaluation of nature and an aspiration towards unflawed beauty. Milton's golden world is just in its division of light and darkness where ours, in the short run, is not: it remains always constant where ours decays: it has a clockwork regularity, emblematic of its temperance, where ours is inordinate and mutable. But all the same it is the most naturalistic golden world to be found in the whole epic tradition.

Milton was the last great poet to work within a Christian world-picture frame, interpreting nature as endowed in all her features with significance. After him the capacity (or the wish) to give literary expression to such a reverence for nature was almost entirely lost, and when it was recovered, more than a century later, the sensibility had assumed a much altered form. Nevertheless it is right to think of Milton as a nature poet; and to attend to the tradition that extends from him through James Thomson to the Romantic poets, especially Wordsworth and Shelley.

Milton's God

When Johnson said that 'the want of human interest is always felt' in *Paradise Lost*, he betrayed his blindness to the metaphorical activity of the poem, whereby angels, devils, and even Sin and Death–not to say the divine persons–all convey insights into the psychology of man. Nor do Adam and Eve themselves simply portray before the Fall all that is virtuous, after it all that is not. For, without being quite naturalistic in his portrayal of character, Milton is nevertheless very well able to render stages of transition from innocence to experience. And there is besides something elusive about prelapsarian psychology and morality that has interested critics during the last two decades. For example, there is uncertainty about the point at which temptation begins, and at which the Fall becomes inevitable. The tendency to regard these points as lying earlier than Bk ix is exemplified in Millicent Bell's 'The Fallacy of the Fall in *Paradise Lost*', *PMLA* lxviii (1953), which reaches the extreme view that prelapsarian man was pretty much like the passionate, sinful, post-lapsarian man we are familiar with. There is something to be said for this view. At least, such passages as viii 530ff and 588ff show clearly enough that Johnson was wrong to say that 'human passions did not enter the world before the Fall'. The evidences of temptation, however, do not go back before Eve's dream. And the doctrine that the Fall was gradual was after all quite a familiar and venerable one. (Burden quotes, in this connection, William Ames's popular work *The Marrow of Sacred Divinity* (1642) 56: 'man was a sinner before he had finished that outward act of eating'; while Broadbent (197) quotes St Augustine: 'our first parents fell into open disobedience because already they were secretly corrupted'.) Certainly to conclude, as Mrs Bell does, that Milton is interested in showing the effects rather than the causes of the Fall, seems quite without warrant.

It would be more obedient to the main movement of the poem to say that Milton is throughout concerned with the causes of evil *as the term cause was then understood*; and that he pushes this enquiry as far back, and as deeply, as he can. For the action moves from the already fallen society of the devils, sunk in darkness and falsehood, up through confusion, to the clarity of heaven; then back through a universe with Satan already in it, back through a Fall, to the creation of a pristine universe. In iii we are taken to an ultimate point of origin: the mind of God, who not only foresees that evil is inevitably bound up with the freedom of created spirits but also carefully avoids doing anything to curtail that freedom. But however sceptical the enquiry may at times become, however difficult the ground it invades, the end is unquestionably intended to be justification: 'Evil into the mind of God . . . / May come and go, so unapproved, and leave / No spot or blame behind . . .' (v 117–9). For we should not for a moment assume that Milton was preoccupied by causation in our own sense of the term; far less that his artistic purpose was to set out a single naturalistic series of cause–effect relations leading up to and 'explaining' the Fall.

There is also some uncertainty about the motives of Adam and Eve at the time of the Fall itself. A. J. A. Waldock in *Paradise Lost and its Critics* (Cambridge 1947) and William Empson in *Milton's God* both try to exonerate Eve and lay blame instead on Adam or Raphael or God. But anyone who has been sensitive to the painfulness of Adam's experience of moral dilemma–of the difficulty of a world fast losing its simplicity–will think it a shallow response merely to blame Adam for allowing Eve to go off to work by herself. Book ix is presented by Milton as tragic; it is tragic action, therefore, and tragic moral predicaments that we should expect to find portrayed there. Adam makes himself in a sense responsible for the Fall by giving Eve permission to go. Yet he could hardly, without degrading her, have acted differently at that time–an inevitability that distantly echoes the inevitability of God's supra-tragic decision in Bk iii. As for Eve, at the separation she is 'sinless' (as she still is at ix 659); but she is sufficiently influenced by her dream for the epithet to be no longer superfluous. Of course Eve's motives, even in her fall, are often lofty. That she would act from motives that seem high to wretches like ourselves is only to be expected. And in any case it would hardly have justified God to show only his dealings with low people; for that would have left a way open for the objection that his unfairness to noble souls remained unjustified. Nevertheless, to pretend that Eve was not wrong to eat the fruit is to loosen the moral nexus of the whole poem. Cowley might think that 'Less hard 'tis not to err ourselves than know / If our forefathers erred or no' ('Reason')–but Milton was of a different temper.

A contrary tendency, which seems in the long run much more promising, is observable in J. S. Diekhoff, *Milton's 'Paradise Lost': A Commentary on the Argument* (New York 1964); Leon Howard, '"The Invention" of Milton's "Great Argument": A Study of the Logic of "God's Ways to Men"', *HLQ* ix (1945); J. Steadman, 'Heroic Virtue and the Divine Image in *Paradise Lost*', *JWI* xxii (1959) and 'Man's First Disobedience', *JHI* xxi (1960); and Dennis Burden, *The Logical Epic* (1967).

All of these show, in their different ways, a new respect for the logical structure of *Paradise* Lost. When the poem is approached by this admittedly arduous route it takes on an authentic, challenging aspect. Details of the action no longer seem confusingly ambiguous attempts at naturalism, but work together to unfold the logical 'causes' of the fallen world, and the nature of true virtue. No longer the pawns of controversial critics, the most trivial events show moving reasons of their own for being precisely what they are. Some belong to an elaborate portrayal of the various stages of repentance (e.g. x 1073*n*, 1088–92*n*); others constitute graded exercises in moral discrimination (e.g. the different accounts of the size of Satan's army, and of the pursuit of the devils after the war in heaven). Others again have to be taken with their counterparts for their function to be appreciated. Thus, the portrayals of Paradise before and after the Fall are in minutely organized opposition, and so are those of heaven and hell. It would hardly be exaggeration to say that everything in heaven has its devilish counterpart. There is an infernal Creation, an infernal Trinity, even a Satanic travesty of the Incarnation.

When once the fruits of this kind of criticism have been tasted, and the extent to which *Paradise Lost* is organized around 'that right Porphyrian tree which did true Logic shew' has been glimpsed, there can never be uncertainty about Milton's overall artistic intention. Questions about whether Satan is the hero of the poem come to seem childish, or else excessively concerned with one phase of the poem's argument. It is not just that we come to be sure of Milton's moral intention, his intention to justify the ways of God, but that we come to see this intention as worked out in the structure of *Paradise Lost* and in the details of its action. Almost throughout its extent, the poem is found to be theologically informed to a remarkable degree. This should not much surprise any student of the period. Anyone who has read the notes Cowley appended to his *Davideis* knows that quite minute physical particulars could at any time involve a seventeenth-century poet in exegetical controversy. Milton is so involved very frequently indeed in *Paradise Lost*, and invariably he takes up a position that has good Scriptural or patristic authority. This point finds confirmation of a sort in the many close parallels with the *De doctrina Christiana*; some of which are carefully listed by Maurice Kelley in *This Great Argument* (Princeton 1941).

But if Milton's conscious intentions are broadly speaking unambiguous, this need not be true of his unconscious intentions. Indeed, several critics besides Waldock have argued that what Milton actually performs in *Paradise Lost* is something radically different from what he intends and professes to perform. The most brilliant work in this tradition is *Milton's God*, which sets out the theory of a contradiction between intention and performance in an unusually subtle form. Empson imagines a Milton who grappled consciously with the most difficult theological problems, and searched sincerely for ways to present God in the best light possible. Unfortunately God was too nasty for this to work, so that contradictions kept creeping into the poem, and it ended up better (and more antitheistic) than Milton ever knew. Empson's book contains much with which we can agree, or at least sympathize. It is true, for example, that Milton focuses penetratingly on some awkward or weak parts of the doctrine of the Fall. And it is in a sense wonderful that he could go on being a Christian after expressing some of the objections to belief raised in the poem. But the fact remains that, after allowing these objections their say, he came to a Christian conclusion; whereas *Milton's God* is propaganda in the interest of a different conclusion. The points made in that work deserve separate consideration at the relevant places in the notes. Here we can only speculate whether Milton may not have been even more conscious of the complexities of the God of *Paradise Lost* than Empson gives him credit for being. Not that he would have understood them at all in the terms of our quaint opinions wide. But he could have formulated his awareness of the objections to belief well enough theologically. For such topics as God's responsibility for evil were discussed in the seventeenth century with a hardihood that would shock many a liberal theologian of our own day. It is hard for us to imagine – yet it seems to have been the case – that Milton could seriously be concerned about what the world is really like, and still be able most of the time to conduct the enquiry in the classic terms of theology. Indeed, what makes *Paradise Lost* perhaps the most serious epic ever written is largely the refusal to take the character of the divine protagonist for granted. But, for that very reason, if the poem leaves us at the end in any doubt about God's justice and love, then it has failed in its communication, not merely in one respect, but altogether.

Critics often call the portrayal of God in *Paradise Lost* a failure, without adequately considering how ludicrous it would be to call any such portrayal a complete success, or even a good likeness. For it would not be a wholly extra-literary judgment to say that Milton was bound to overreach himself, from the time when he decided to introduce a divine character. Nevertheless, it should be the business of the critic not to deplore the attempt but rather to weigh performance against possibility by the standards proper to literature. If this is done, a somewhat different verdict from Waldock's may be arrived at. The sacred conversations, for example, seem to me better than has ever been allowed. Stylistically, almost all the passages concerned are vigorous and intelligent. Indeed, the effects of poetic syntax, whereby the timelessness of God's thoughts and his reflective relationship with Messiah are rendered, must rank among Milton's finest (see iii 125*n*, 261*n*). The high level of abstraction: the sustained abstention from imagery, except the very simplest and least sensuous: the calm freedom from unresolved emotional expressions: all these qualities now arouse distaste in readers whose formal demands are at once narrow and sensational. But Milton's fit audience would see the aptness of these qualities in speeches that are not intended to be merely human.

For, in spite of all that Waldock says to the contrary, it is not the human impression left by the God of *Paradise Lost* that matters. He is not human, though he is personal: he is not a character, though he thinks and speaks. He sees the world of events, and also the world in which agents are themselves events – 'His own works and their works at once to view' (iii 59); and his mere looking upon them confers bliss. The conception of such a divine point of view deserves to be admired as a feat of imagination, at the same time as we acknowledge the inevitability of its failure. Even the comprehensible difficulties in the way of this achievement were staggering. Milton had not only to assimilate and condense a vast mass of theological erudition but also to transcend it, incorporating the whole tradition in personal terms in the speeches of a consistent being. On top of this he must add his own contribution; for he was himself a theologian. It would perhaps be enough to defend the position that Milton in the face of these difficulties has managed to convey the impression of a distinct divine person – one with a presence so strong that we come to detect his unseen hand in the earthly events and visions, and to hear echoes of his subtleties in the poem's dramatic ironies. But we can say more than this. For Milton's God can be taken seriously both as a theological and as an imaginative construct, in a way that almost no other in our literature can.

From a literary point of view what should be noticed is not so much the direct representation of God, which has already received disproportionate attention, as the indirect. I refer to the formal symbolism–if a category of presentation may be distinguished, complementary to Ian Watt's formal realism (*The Rise of the Novel* (1957) pp 32f)–whereby Milton makes God and Messiah the only agents in the poem who have full consciousness of what they are doing. Only they participate in the dramatic ironies, only they express themselves in interior monologues that are not self-dramatising. On a smaller scale, the indirect presentation of God's attributes is accomplished in such formal dispositions as the order in which, during the first divine exchanges, traditional theological doctrines are introduced. By dealing with Predestination to salvation before even Atonement, for example, Milton implies that his God's thought is 'mercy first and last' (iii 134; see 173–202*n*).

The question whether the God of *Paradise Lost* obeys the rules of classical theology is declining in interest; so that his personal qualities (as distinct both from the doctrinal and from the human) can be better appreciated. As it happens, however, the poem is also coming more and more to be seen as substantially orthodox in its theology. Its account of creation, for example, in which Denis Saurat saw a *recherché* heresy of divine 'withdrawal', is now understood to be Christian-Platonic theistic materialism; see R. J. Z. Werblowski in *JWI* xviii (1955); A. S. P. Woodhouse in *PQ* xxviii (1949); and W. C. Curry, Milton's *Ontology, Cosmogony, and Physics* (Lexington, Ky. 1957). It is the same with the christology. Milton has been thought Arian, yet *Paradise Lost* accords the Son as supreme a transcendence as any poem in the language. William B. Hunter ('Milton's Arianism Reconsidered', *Harvard Theological Review* lii (1959) 9–35; cp. C. A. Patrides in *JEGP* lxiv (1965)) is probably right in his view that Milton is Subordinationist rather than Arian. The 'Arianism' is perhaps to be seen as an attempt–characteristic of his time–to get beyond the scholasticism of Trinitarian theology to the pure doctrine of the ante-Nicene Fathers. Even if H. F. Robins does not quite convince us of the rightness of concentrating exclusively on Milton's debt to Origen, his *If This Be Heresy: A Study of Milton and Origen* (Urbana, Ill. 1963) remains the best study so far of the theology of *Paradise Lost*. It is clear that Milton was not content with the amalgam of Christianity and Platonism inherited from the Middle Ages, but preferred to attempt a fresh synthesis in the manner of the early Fathers. The *De doctrina* shows that this attempt could involve him in controversy. But *Paradise Lost* expresses rather the impulse behind the controvery: namely, a desire to understand the Trinity as a rational description of the activity of a living and creative God. Thus at the divine level the action of the poem moves from scenes in which Father and Son appear together (iii, v) to others in which the Son emerges separately in the creation and judgment of the universe (vii, x).

Though Milton was not so religious a man as Dante, he has succeeded, by honesty and faith, in constructing an image of deity no less marvellous than that of the *Divina Commedia*. Milton's God is surprising enough to be a universal father figure; enigmatic enough to be the subject of interminable scholastic debates; sublime enough to be awe-inspiring; remote enough from our wishes to be partly true. And certainly there is no divine image in English literature half so interesting.

THE PRINTER TO THE READER

Added in 1668 to the remaining copies of *Ed I*: the text is that of the slightly revised form used in the fifth issue and in some copies of the fourth.

Courteous reader, there was no argument at first intended to the book, but for the satisfaction of many that have desired it, I have procured it, and withal a reason of that which stumbled many others, why the poem rhymes not.

S. Simmons

ON *PARADISE LOST*

Added in *Ed II*. The text is that of 1674: there are no significant variants in the text printed in the 1681 edn of Marvell's *Miscellaneous Poems* and followed by Margoliouth. Lines 18–26 have been taken to refer to Dryden's opera *The Fall of Angels and Man in Innocence*, which was licensed 17 April 1674 but apparently never performed. (Aubrey says that Dryden 'went to him to have leave to putt his Paradise Lost into a drama in rhymne. Mr. Milton received him civilly, and told him he would give him leave to tagge his verses'.) Line 47 certainly refers to Dryden, who was satirized in Buckingham's *Rehearsal* (1672) under the character of Bayes. Lines 51f allude with gentle irony to a passage in the immediately following Note on 'The Verse': 'modern poets, carried away by custom, but much to their . . . constraint to express many things otherwise, and for the most part worse then else they would have expressed them.'

When I beheld the poet blind, yet bold,
In slender book his vast design unfold,
Messiah crowned, God's reconciled decree,
Rebelling angels, the forbidden tree,
Heaven, hell, earth, chaos, all; the argument
Held me a while misdoubting his intent,
That he would ruin (for I saw him strong)
The sacred truths to fable and old song
(So Sampson groped the Temple's post in spite)
The world o'erwhelming to revenge his sight.
Yet as I read, soon growing less severe,
I liked his project, the success did fear;
Through that wide field how he his way should find

O'er which lame faith leads understanding blind;
Lest he perplexed the things he would explain,
And what was easy he should render vain.
Or if a work so infinite he spanned,
Jealous I was that some less skilful hand
(Such as disquiet always what is well,
And by ill imitating would excell)
Might hence presume the whole creation's day
To change in scenes, and show it in a play.
Pardon me, mighty poet, nor despise
My causeless, yet not impious, surmise.
But I am now convinced, and none will dare
Within thy labours to pretend a share.
Thou hast not missed one thought that could be fit,
And all that was improper dost omit:
So that no room is here for writers left,
But to detect their ignorance or theft.
That majesty which through thy work doth reign
Draws the devout, deterring the profane.
And things divine thou treatest of in such state
As them preserves, and thee, inviolate.
At once delight and horror on us seize,
Thou singest with so much gravity and ease;
And above human flight dost soar aloft
With plume so strong, so equal, and so soft.
The bird named from that Paradise you sing
So never flags, but always keeps on wing.
Where couldst thou words of such a compass find?
Whence furnish such a vast expense of mind?
Just heaven thee like Tiresias to requite
Rewards with prophecy thy loss of sight.
Well mightest thou scorn thy readers to allure
With tinkling rhyme, of thy own sense secure;
While the town-Bayes writes all the while and spells,
And like a pack-horse tires without his bells:
Their fancies like our bushy-points appear,
The poets tag them, we for fashion wear.
I too transported by the mode offend,
And while I meant to praise thee must commend.
Thy verse created like thy theme sublime,
In number, weight, and measure, needs not rhyme.

A[ndrew]. M[arvell].

THE VERSE

Added in *Ed II*. For explanations of the meanings of the technical terms used, see Sprott 39ff, and Introd., 'Prosody', above.

The measure is English heroic verse without rhyme, as that of Homer in Greek, and of Virgil in Latin; rhyme being no necessary adjunct or true ornament of poem or good verse, in longer works especially, but the invention of a barbarous age, to set off wretched matter and lame metre; graced indeed since by the use of some famous modern poets, carried away by custom, but much to their own vexation, hindrance, and constraint to express many things otherwise, and for the most part worse than else they would have expressed them. Not without cause therefore some both Italian and Spanish poets of prime note have rejected rhyme both in longer and shorter works, as have also long since our best English tragedies, as a thing of it self, to all judicious ears, trivial and of no true musical delight; which consists only in apt numbers, fit quantity of syllables, and the sense variously drawn out from one verse into another, not in the jingling sound of like endings, a fault avoided by the learned ancients both in poetry and all good oratory. This neglect then of rhyme so little is to be taken for a defect, though it may seem so perhaps to vulgar readers, that it rather is to be esteemed an example set, the first in English, of ancient liberty recovered to heroic poem from the troublesome and modern bondage of rhyming.

Paradise Lost

BOOK I

The Argument

This first book proposes, first in brief, the whole subject, man's disobedience, and the loss thereupon of Paradise wherein he was placed: then touches the prime cause of his fall, the serpent, or rather Satan in the serpent; who revolting from God, and drawing to his side many legions of angels, was by the command of God driven out of heaven with all his crew into the great deep. Which action passed over, the poem hastes into the midst of things, presenting Satan with his angels now fallen into hell, described here, not in the centre[1] (for heaven and earth may be supposed as yet not made,[2]

¶ 94. i *Argument*[1]. *described here, not in the centre*] The obvious meaning is that hell is here described not at the centre of the earth, but at another situation. As MacCaffrey 54 implies, however, there is a secondary sense in which M., still discussing his *in medias res* narrative method, is telling us that we shall not find hell at the centre of *PL*. On the symbolic importance of the mid-point of the poem, which is occupied by Christ in his triumphal chariot, see vi 749–59*n*. M. displaces hell from the centre of the earth for theological reasons: namely, that when hell was formed the earth was not yet cursed; and that the earth is to be destroyed at the last (*De doctrina* i 33, Columbia xvi 372–4). Cp. Cowley's note 11 to *Davideis* i: 'making *Hell* to be in the *Center* of the Earth, it is far from infinitely large, or deep; yet, on my conscience, where e're it be, it is not so strait, as that *Crowding* and sweating should be one of the *Torments* of it, as is pleasantly fancied by *Bellarmin*.'
i *Argument*[2]. *yet not made*] Earth was not yet made when Satan and his angels

certainly not yet accursed) but in a place of utter[3] darkness, fitliest called Chaos: here Satan with his angels lying on the burning lake, thunderstruck and astonished, after a certain space recovers, as from confusion, calls up him who next in order and dignity lay by him; they confer of their miserable fall. Satan awakens all his legions, who lay till then in the same manner confounded; they rise, their numbers, array of battle, their chief leaders named, according to the idols known afterwards in Canaan and the countries adjoining. To these Satan directs his speech, comforts them with hope yet of regaining heaven, but tells them lastly of a new world and new kind of creature to be created, according to an ancient prophecy or report in heaven; for that angels were long before this visible creation, was the opinion of many ancient Fathers.[4] To find out the truth of this prophecy, and what to determine thereon he refers to a full council. What his associates thence attempt.[5] Pandemonium the palace of Satan rises, suddenly built out of the deep: the infernal peers there sit in council.

Of man's first disobedience, and the fruit
Of that forbidden tree, whose mortal taste
Brought death into the world, and all our woe,

fell into hell; but it is made *now*: see Introduction, 'Chronology', pp. 443–45 above.

i *Argument*[3]. *utter*] Either 'outer' or 'utter.'

i *Argument*[4]. *De doctrina* i 7 (Columbia xv 33–5): 'Many at least of the Greek, and some of the Latin Fathers, are of opinion that angels, as being spirits, must have existed long before the material world; and it seems even probable, that the apostasy which caused the expulsion of so many thousands from Heaven, took place before the foundations of this world were laid.' In M.'s own day, however, the commoner belief was that the angels were created at the same time with the world.

i *Argument*[5]. *What his associates thence attempt*] The building of Pandaemonium, as the next sentence explains.

i *1–49*. Rhetorically, the *invocatio*, consisting of an address to the Muse; 1–26 is also the *principium* that states the whole scope of the poem's action. M.'s particular overlapping arrangement of the opening parts traditional in epic combines the Virgilian and Homeric plans; so that, without the interruption of direct allusion, *PL* is silently related to its three principal analogues. A metaphorical comparison is set up between Adam and Achilles, Odysseus and Aeneas, and between the loss of Paradise and the loss of Troy (Condee). On the placing of the poem's four invocations, see ix 1–47*n* below.

i *1–13*. As Sims 11 points out, the widely separated persons and events referred to in these lines have a typological or figural connection that M. assumes his readers will grasp: 'the disobedience of Adam in Eden, the receiving of the Law by Moses on Sinai, and the placing of the Ark of the Covenant in the Temple on '*Sion* Hill' are not causally connected as a horizontal chain of events, but the divine scheme of salvation as seen by centuries of Christians seeking to align the Old Testament with the New had vertically

With loss of Eden, till one greater man
Restore us, and regain the blissful seat,
Sing heavenly Muse, that on the secret top

connected these events as successive stages in God's plan for man's redemption.' See, however, Lewis 40f for the view that the true function of the opening 'is to give us the sensation *that some great thing is now about to begin*'.

i *1–5*. The sequence *disobedience–loss of Eden–regain the blissful seat* corresponds to the sequence in Virgil's *principium*, from the fall of Troy through a journey to the founding of Rome. See Arthur Barker in *PQ* xxviii (1949) 17f, MacCaffrey 83f.

i *1–2*. This definition of the first sin follows exactly that given in Calvin's Catechism, in its familiar Ursinian form: see Fletcher ii 95f. Daiches (56f) finds in the alliterative connection between *first*, *fruit* and *forbidden* an 'acoustical' allusion to the oblation of firstfruits, prescribed in *Lev.* xxiii. More obviously, the metrical pause between the lines invites us to connect *fruit* with *disobedience*–'disobedience and its organic consequences'–until *Of* (2) shows that the grammatical link is with the words that follow. Such double syntactical or lexical sequences are ubiquitous in *PL*, but will not be noticed below unless some special difficulty is involved. The *taste* of the fruit is *mortal* in a derivative sense: 'deadly', 'death-bringing' (Latin *mortalis*). On the strict logical structure of these lines, and on M.'s concern with the *causes* of the Fall, see Howard, especially 152.

i *3*. *all our woe*] A key phrase in *PL*; see MacCaffrey 84.

i *4–5*. *loss of Eden*] By a synecdoche, the whole is put for the part; Eden is not lost, though Paradise is. The *greater man* is Christ, in Pauline theology the second Adam (see especially *Rom.* v 19). M.'s repetition of *man* is mainly intended to make this point, though it also glances at Virgil's *virumque* (*Aen.* i 1) and Homer's ἄνδρα (*Od.* i 1). Virgil sings one man, but M. will sing two: setting the supernatural Christ over against the natural man, he deliberately departs from pagan epic tradition. There were, however, precedents for having two heroes; see Spenser's Letter to Raleigh on Tasso's practice in this respect. *Restore*] Both 'replace in a state of grace; free from the effects of sin' (*OED* 4 a) and 'make amends for' (*OED* 2). In the latter sense, *Restore* is followed by an ethic dative (Emma 54*n*).

i *6–22*. The *heavenly Muse*, later addressed as *Urania* (vii 1), is here apparently identified as the divine Logos, the second person of the Trinity, who inspires both the prophetic vision of a Moses on Mount *Oreb* and the sacerdotal wisdom and Temple ritual of *Sion hill*, but who is not confined to these localities (ll. 17f). M. is signifying his readiness to assume either the prophetic or the priestly role, as the Spirit wills (Daiches[2] 61). M.'s opening was particularly bold in view of contemporary attacks on invocation. Davenant, e.g., condemned the invoking of the Holy Ghost in poetry as 'saucy familiarity with a true God'; see Broadbent 67, also ll. 17–22*n* below.

i *6–8*. The form of this allusion, with its casual assumption of common

Of Oreb, or of Sinai, didst inspire
That shepherd, who first taught the chosen seed,
In the beginning how the heavens and earth
Rose out of chaos: or if Sion hill
Delight thee more, and Siloa's brook that flowed
Fast by the oracle of God; I thence
Invoke thy aid to my adventurous song,
That with no middle flight intends to soar

ground with the reader, resembles Dante's periphrastic references to historical personages. As *shepherd* of Jethro's flock, Moses was granted the vision of the burning bush on Mount Horeb (*Exod.* iii: for euphony, the Vulgate form, *Oreb*, is preferred); as pastor, he received the Law, either on Mount Horeb (*Deut.* iv 10) or on its lower part, Mount Sinai (*Exod.* xix 20). The *top* is *secret* because set apart (Latin *secretus*) and concealed by storm clouds (*Exod.* xix; cp. *PL* xii 227–9).

i *7. MS* omits both commas.

i *8. the chosen seed*] The children of Israel, whom Moses, the *first* (note the emphatic repetition of this word, in ll. 1, 19, 27, 28, 33) Jewish writer, taught about the *beginning* of the world in *Genesis*, the principal source of the mythos of *PL*. Cp. Gabriel Harvey, *Marginalia*, ed. Smith (Stratford-upon-Avon 1913) 209, where the Pentateuch is called the root and fountain of all books in the world. Moses should not be regarded merely as M.'s authority, but as his original. For the reference is no mere literary artifice: M. believed himself 'possessed', in the Platonic sense, by Moses; as his successor, he was similarly animated by divine afflatus (Hanford 414f).

i *9. In the beginning*, the opening words of the Bible, are mimetically moved earlier by the inversion.

i *10. Sion hill*] The sanctuary, a place of ceremonial song, but also (*Is.* ii 3) of oracular pronouncements.

i *11. Siloa*] A spring immediately west of Mount Zion and beside Calvary, often used as a symbol of the operation of the Holy Ghost 'in gentle mild manner' (Lancelot Andrewes, *Sermons*, Libr. of Anglo-Cath. Theol., iii (1841) 267f) or in a manner not obvious (e.g. Calvin's Comm. on *Is.* viii 6). But M. may have in mind the curative and purificatory pool of Siloam ('which is by interpretation, Sent': *John* ix 7). If so, an analogy would seem to be implied between the poet, and the blind disciple given sight and insight by Jesus and sent to wash in the pool (*John* ix 1–11, 30–9; see Paul Lauter, *N & Q* cciii (1958) 204f). As *PL* iii 26–32 shows, M. intends, in the brook flowing beside the Temple Mount, a complete sacred counterpart to the brook frequented by the pagan Muses: Aganippe, that 'from beneath the seat of Jove doth spring' (*Lycidas* 16, following Hesiod). *Sion* and *Siloa* are again Vulgate forms.

i *13. adventurous*] 'adventrous' in *MS* and the early edns; probably pronounced as a trisyllable. See *Comus* 79*n*.

Above the Aonian mount, while it pursues
Things unattempted yet in prose or rhyme.
And chiefly thou O Spirit, that dost prefer
Before all temples the upright heart and pure,
Instruct me, for thou know'st; thou from the first
Wast present, and with mighty wings outspread
Dove-like sat'st brooding on the vast abyss

i *15*. *the Aonian mount*] Helicon, sacred to the Muses. M. believes his source of inspiration and the matter he *pursues* (i.e. treats: Latin *sequor*) to be higher than any possible in the pagan world. Appropriately, he makes the Biblical mountains–sources of inspiration–more numerous than the classical (Daiches[2] 63). The spelling in *MS* and the early edns indicates the synaloepha: th'Aonian. *MS* has semicolon after *mount.*

i *16*. Ironically translating Ariosto's boast in *Orl. Fur.* i 2: *Cosa non detta in prosa mai, né in rima*; cp. ix 27–47 below. On the claim to novelty as a traditional opening topic, see Curtius 85f. *unattempted*] 'Unattempted even in the Bible? . . . "unattempted in English literature"?' asks Daiches[2] 63.

i *17–22*. If not before, surely now it is the Holy Spirit who is addressed; in spite of M.'s argument in *De doctrina* i 6 (Columbia xiv 392–4), that invocation of the Holy Spirit as a separate person has no Biblical foundation. Unlocalised and operating inwardly, the Spirit provides the impulse of every creative act, divine or human. The analogy M. implies between creation and poetic making is examined by Cormican (178f), who finds it to be developed in a Metaphysical manner; and by Daiches ([2] 66f), who traces its theological content. An unnoticed analogue is Sylvester's Du Bartas 9f: 'As a good Wit . . . on his Book still muses: / . . . Or, as a Hen that fain would hatch a Brood / . . . Even in such sort seemed the Spirit Eternall / To brood upon this Gulf.' In visual art of the period, chaos was often depicted as an egg-shaped mass. *temples*] Cp. the Pauline idea of the body as the 'temple of the Holy Ghost' (*1 Cor.* vi 19). St Paul also regarded the Spirit as the only instructor about the things of God (Sims 17). *Dove-like*] Identifying the Spirit present at the creation with the Spirit in the form of a dove that descended on Jesus at the beginning of his ministry (*John* i 32). *brooding*] rendering the Heb. word in *Gen.* i 2 that is translated in A.V. as 'moved', but in St Basil and other patristic authors as *incubabat* (brooded). *brooding . . . madest it pregnant*] Not a mixed metaphor, but a deliberate allusion to the Hermetic doctrine that God is both masculine and feminine. Cp. Nicolas Cusanus, *De docta ignorantia* i 25; tr. G. Heron, ed. D. J. B. Hawkins (1954) 57. *vast*] In addition to the primary sense ('large') there is a Latinizing secondary sense, 'waste, deserted, unformed' (Lat. *vastus*).

i *17*. *MS* has no point after *Spirit.*

i *18*. *MS* has no point after *pure.*

i *19*. Cp. Homer, *Il.* ii 484: 'Tell me, Muses . . . since you are goddesses and are present and know all things.'

And madest it pregnant: what in me is dark
Illumine, what is low raise and support;
That to the highth of this great argument
I may assert eternal providence,
And justify the ways of God to men.
  Say first, for heaven hides nothing from thy view
Nor the deep tract of hell, say first what cause
Moved our grand parents in that happy state,
Favoured of heaven so highly, to fall off
From their creator, and transgress his will
For one restraint, lords of the world besides?
Who first seduced them to that foul revolt?
The infernal serpent; he it was, whose guile
Stirred up with envy and revenge, deceived
The mother of mankind, what time his pride

i *22–6.* Both in sense and in rhetorical form, this prayer of invocation echoes the celebrated 'Golden Sequence', *Veni sancte Spiritus*: '*Veni, lumen cordium.* / ... *Lava quod est sordidum,* / ... *Rege quod est devium.*' *argument*] subject, theme. *justify* does not mean merely 'demonstrate logically' but has its Biblical meaning and implies spiritual rather than rational understanding (Cormican 175). *to men*] The plural contrasts with the generalising singular of *man* (1): the Fall is universal, but M. writes for the elect, a 'fit audience ... though few' (Daiches² 57).

i *25. eternal*] th'eternal *Ed I*; corr. in 1668 *Errata. MS* originally had 'th'eternal', and the deletion of *th'* seems to have been ignored by the *Ed I* printer.

i *27–49.* Rhetorically the *initium*, introducing the first scene and giving the cause of the action. With l. 28, cp. the *initium* of Virgil's *Aen.* (i 8: '*Musa mihi causas memor*); and with 33 cp. Homer's question about the source of discord between Achilles and Agamemnon (*Il.* i 8). M.'s formulaic method assists the involvement of 'a whole segment of western culture', and counterpoints the deeds of classical heroes with those of Adam (Condee 507). The counterpoint emerges here as a strong contrast, for in Virgil it is the cause of divine wrath that seems inexplicable.

i *28–31. cause*] M. turns at once to the instrumental cause of the Fall (Howard 159).

i *29. grand*] Implies not only titular greatness, but also inclusiveness or generality of parentage–a meaning that now survives only in the phrase 'grand total'.

i *32.* i.e. because of a single restraint; even though their autonomy in all other respects was unrestricted.

i *34. The infernal serpent*] 'That old serpent, called the Devil, and Satan' (*Rev.* xii 9) both because Satan entered the body of a serpent to tempt Eve, and because his nature is guileful and dangerous to man. See also x 506–47, where the devils are metamorphosed into serpents.

i *36–7. MS* has colon, altered to semicolon, after *mankind*, and semicolon

Had cast him out from heaven, with all his host
Of rebel angels, by whose aid aspiring
To set himself in glory above his peers,
He trusted to have equalled the most high,
If he opposed; and with ambitious aim
Against the throne and monarchy of God
Raised impious war in heaven and battle proud
With vain attempt. Him the almighty power
Hurled headlong flaming from the ethereal sky
With hideous ruin and combustion down
To bottomless perdition, there to dwell
In adamantine chains and penal fire,

after *heaven.* *what time*] Usually compared with Lat. *quo tempore*–needlessly, since the phrase was perfectly idiomatic English; see *OED* s.v. *What* C II 10. Cp. *Comus* 291, *Lycidas* 28.

i *38. aspiring*] The first of the poem's comparatively rare feminine line-endings. The only other certain instances in Bk i are at ll. 98, 102 and 606. On the theory underlying M.'s practice in this respect, see Prince 135.

i *39.* Satan's crime was not his aspiring *above his peers*–he was already 'high above' them (v 812)–but aspiring *To set himself in* [divine] *glory*.

i *40–8.* Numerous verbal echoes relate these lines to the Biblical accounts of the fall and binding of Lucifer, in *2 Pet.* ii 4, *Jude* 6, *Rev.* xx 1–2, and *Is.* xiv 12–15: 'Thou hast said . . . I will exalt my throne above the stars of God . . . I will be like the most High. Yet thou shalt be brought down to hell.'

i *40.* The construction with a past infinitive was standard English.

i *42. MS* has comma after *God.*

i *43. impious war*] Perhaps has a secondary Latinate sense; *bellum impium* means internecine war.

i *44. With vain attempt*] 'The typically Miltonic half-line of derision' (Broadbent 69). Cp. ll. 746f below.

i *44–5. Him . . . Hurled*] Object–subject–verb inversions constitute one of the two types of inversion commonest in *PL*, according to Emma (143ff). But larger samples than his show this to be the only common form of inversion. (Subject–object–verb inversions, Emma's other common type, are in fact rare.)

i *45.* Characteristically mingling a Biblical allusion (to *Luke* x 18, 'I beheld Satan as lightning fall from heaven') with a classical (to Homer, *Il.* i 591, Hephaistos 'hurled from the ethereal threshold').

i *46. ruin*] falling, downfall. Not a Latinism, except etymologically. *combustion*] M. may intend an ambiguity; in astronomical contexts the word meant 'obscuration of a planet due to near conjunction with the sun'.

i *48.* Cp. *Jude* 6 and *2 Pet.* ii 4; 'God spared not the angels that sinned, but . . . delivered them into chains of darkness.' The *adamantine* chains, however, perhaps also allude to Aeschylus, *Prom.* 6. *MS* omits comma after *fire.*

Who durst defy the omnipotent to arms.
Nine times the space that measures day and night
To mortal men, he with his horrid crew
Lay vanquished, rolling in the fiery gulf
Confounded though immortal: but his doom
Reserved him to more wrath; for now the thought
Both of lost happiness and lasting pain
Torments him; round he throws his baleful eyes
That witnessed huge affliction and dismay
Mixed with obdurate pride and steadfast hate:
At once as far as angels' ken he views
The dismal situation waste and wild,

i *49*. The elliptic *Who* (=He who) is common in Spenser, Shakespeare and Donne (see Emma 57). It is not a Latinism. Empson 37 brings out the implication that 'though Milton believes God to be omnipotent, Satan dared to hope he could be defeated'. Note how M. gives an early signal to prepare the reader to recognize this as one of the many things about which Satan deludes himself.

i *50–83*. In rhetorical terminology, the *exordium*, which supplies the setting and stage directions of the opening scene (Condee 507f). The nine days during which the devils *Lay vanquished* (Days 13–22) immediately follow the nine days of their fall from Heaven (Days 4–13; see vi 871, also Introduction, 'Chronology', pp. 443–46 above. The choice of this particular time interval points up the analogy between the fall of the devils and the fall of the defeated Titans (also lasting nine days: see Hesiod, *Theog.* 664–735). Throughout, M. makes extensive use of this mythological parallel; it was important to him, since it justified treating the brief Biblical references to a war in heaven as more than allegory.

i *55*. The fallen angels became vulnerable to pain when their natures were 'impaired' by sin (vi 327 and 691).

i *56*. *MS* has comma after *him*. *baleful*] 'full of evil'; but also 'full of suffering'. On the change of tense, see MacCaffrey 43; also Broadbent 69f: 'the tenses shift imperceptibly into an immediate Hell.'

i *57*. *witnessed*] bore witness to.

i *58*. *obdurate*] Stressed on the second syllable.

i *59*. *Angels' ken*] the field of vision of angels (*OED* 2). As was common seventeenth-century orthographical practice, however, the apostrophe is omitted in *MS*, *Ed I* and *Ed II*, so that *Angels ken* is also a possible reading. Both uses of *ken* (i.e., as noun or as verb) can be matched in *PL* (e.g. xi 379 and 396).

i *60*. *MS* has no stop after *wild*. It is usually said that the sense demands a colon. This is not so, however, if 'flamed' (l. 62) is understood as a past participle='aflame' (see *OED* s.v. *Flamed* 1). *dismal*] A stronger word than it has since become: 'dreadful' or 'sinister', rather than merely 'gloomy'. Emma 73 finds the epithet–noun–epithet scheme infrequent in M. But this

A dungeon horrible, on all sides round
As one great furnace flamed, yet from those flames
No light, but rather darkness visible
Served only to discover sights of woe,
Regions of sorrow, doleful shades, where peace
And rest can never dwell, hope never comes

extraordinary conclusion may be the result of taking an inadequate sample, or of underestimating the rarity of the scheme in the corpus of literature at large. Until we have rank-ordered rhetorical tables, one can only record the guess that this will in fact be found to be a favourite device of M.'s. Cp. ll. 69, 180, 304f; and for a discussion of earlier uses of the device by the Italian poets, see Prince 112–9.

i *61. dungeon horrible*] M. customarily avoided inversion of the normal noun-adjective order; see Emma (69f), who finds an incidence of only 4·7 per cent of the adjectives in his poetry. On the symbolic nature of M.'s hell, see Joseph E. Duncan in *HLQ* xx (1957); Merritt Y. Hughes in *MP* liv (1956); Ernest Schanzer in *UTQ* xxiv (1955); and Broadbent Ch. ii.

i *62–4.* Oddly censured by T. S. Eliot as 'difficult to imagine'; but of course the passage is not intended merely as physical description. Cp. the account of the land of the dead in *Job* x 22: 'the light is as darkness'; and see Ann Gossman *N & Q* ccvi (1961) 182 on Plutarch's affirmative answer to the question 'Whether darkness can be visible to us'. The paradoxes M. alludes to would be familiar to his contemporaries, for they were the subject of much theological speculation. Thus, the notion of flames without light had its classic statement in St Basil's *Homil. in Ps. xxviii*, where we are told that God separates the brightness of fire from its burning power, in such a way that the brightness works to the joy of the blessed, the burning to the torture of the damned; cp. Herrick 387, 'The fire of Hell this strange condition hath' / To burn, not shine (as learned *Basil* saith.)'; and see further Hughes 183 and John M. Steadman, 'John Collop and the flames without light', *N & Q* cc (1955) 382–3. Discussing the paradox of *sights of woe* visible in darkness, Edgar F. Daniels ('Thomas Adams and "Darkness Visible"("Paradise Lost", I, 62–3)', *N & Q* cciv (1959)) finds authority in Adams for the idea of a special visory power granted to devils. But a more obvious source is Aquinas *Summa theol.* Supple. xcvii 4, where it is debated whether the damned have any light and can see, and where the Basilian passage is cited. Among literary analogues to M.'s description, the best known is the O.E. *Genesis B*, 333: 'þæt wæs leohtes leas | and wæs liges full'. Broadbent 71 notes that i and ii 'are full of paradoxical expressions–antithesis, antimetabole, oxymoron, etc.' This is the case with almost all those parts of the poem where the devils appear. See vi 498*n* on the extravagant rhetoric used to portray the angelic war.

i *66.* Cp. Dante, *Inf.* iii 9, 'All hope abandon, you who enter here'; also Euripides, *Troades* 681, 'to me even hope, that remains to all mortals, never comes'.

That comes to all; but torture without end
Still urges, and a fiery deluge, fed
With ever-burning sulphur unconsumed:
Such place eternal justice had prepared
For these rebellious, here their prison ordained
In utter darkness, and their portion set
As far removed from God and light of heaven
As from the centre thrice to the utmost pole.
O how unlike the place from whence they fell!
There the companions of his fall, o'erwhelmed
With floods and whirlwinds of tempestuous fire,
He soon discerns, and weltering by his side
One next himself in power, and next in crime,
Long after known in Palestine, and named
Beelzebub. To whom the arch-enemy,

i *68. urges*] presses.
i *69. sulphur*] The sulphurousness of the *deluge* goes back at least to Statius, who speaks of Cocytus' *sulfureas undas* (*Theb.* i 91).
i *71. those*] these *MS*. *prison*] In *MS* an apostrophe over the *o* indicates elision, by a convention common at the time.
i *72. utter*] Both 'outer' and 'utter'.
i *73–4.* See iv 20–3*n*. For the association of heaven with the celestial pole, see Cicero, *De nat.* ii 40f, rendering Aratus, *Phainomena*. Whereas Homer simply places Hades as far below earth as heaven is above it (*Il.* viii 16), and Virgil places Tartarus 'twice' as far below (*Aen.* vi 577), M. gives a more intricate formulation: a 'typically "geometrical" statement of relationships', as MacCaffrey 78 calls it. By so doing, he draws attention to the numerical proportion, heaven–earth: earth–hell : : 1 : 2, i.e., earth divides the interval between heaven and hell in the proportion that Neoplatonists believed should be maintained between reason and concupiscence: the harmonious diapason. See, e.g., Pico della Mirandola, *Conclusiones*, 'secundum mathematicam Pythagorae', *Opera omnia* (Basel 1573) i 79. For the view that 'thrice' is merely an intensive, see B. A. Wright in *RES* xxi (1945) 43.
i *76. MS* omits comma after *fall*.
i *79. MS* omits comma after *power*.
i *81. Beelzebub*] Hebrew 'Lord of the flies'; *Matt.* xii 24, 'the prince of the devils'; cp. *Mark* iii 22, *Luke* xi 15, etc. Although M. would know that Beelzebub's name had an anthropological background in the cults of deliverers from insect pests (see John Selden, *De dis Syris* ii 6), his portrayal of the devil seems rather to be based on an allegorization invented by St Jerome and cited by Valeriano in his discussion of the fly as a symbol of pertinacity. Beelzebub is god of flies 'because he never ceases to infest the human race in every way, and to lay now this snare, now that, for our destruction' (Valeriano 320). It is in keeping with his pertinacious malignity

And thence in heaven called Satan, with bold words
Breaking the horrid silence thus began.
   If thou beest he; but O how fallen! how changed
From him, who in the happy realms of light
Clothed with transcendent brightness didst outshine
Myriads though bright: if he whom mutual league,
United thoughts and counsels, equal hope
And hazard in the glorious enterprise,
Joined with me once, now misery hath joined
In equal ruin: into what pit thou seest
From what highth fallen, so much the stronger proved
He with his thunder: and till then who knew
The force of those dire arms? Yet not for those,

towards mankind that Beelzebub should be made the spokesman of Satan's plan to ruin the 'new race' (ii 345–76). *arch-enemy,*] *MS* omits comma.
i *82. Satan*] Hebrew, 'enemy'. After his rebellion, Satan's 'former name' (according to patristic tradition, Lucifer) was no longer used (v 658).
i *84.* Rhetorically, the *ianua narrandi* or opening of the action proper. Satan's exclamation echoes Aeneas' at the appearance of Hector's ghost during the fall of Troy: *ei mihi, qualis erat! quantum mutatus ab illo / Hectore* (*Aen.* ii 274). But cp. also *Is.* xiv 12: 'How art thou fallen from heaven, O Lucifer.' The 41-line speech beginning here, the first speech in the book, exactly balances the last, which also is spoken by Satan and also consists of 41 lines (i 622–62). For the numerological significance of speech-lengths in *PL*, see Introduction, 'Numerology', p. 441 above. *he;*] he? *MS*, question mark altered to comma. *fallen!*] *MS* no point.
i *85. him,*] *MS* omits comma.
i *86. didst*] The break in grammatical concord reflects Satan's doubt whether Beelzebub is present and so whether second-person forms are appropriate. In *PL*, such incomplete grammar usually implies agitation in the speaker.
i *87. If he*] Ellipsis for 'If thou beest he' as in l. 84. For the closeness of Beelzebub's alliance with Satan, see v 673–96.
i *88–9. MS* comma after *hope* is transferred to the end of the line following in *Ed I* and *Ed II*, probably correctly.
i *91–2. into what . . . From what*] Possibly imitating the Greek construction οἷος . . . οἷος. Cp. v 543 and *PR* ii 30.
i *94–8.* Perhaps echoing Aeschylus, *Prom.* 987–96, or Dante, *Inferno* xiv 52–60, the boast of Capaneus (one of the Violent against God) that all Jove's thunderbolts will never crush his spirit. *fixed mind*] Cp. *Il Penseroso* 4 and Spenser, *F.Q.* IV vii 16: 'nothing could [Aemylia's] fixed mind remove'. *high disdain*] A common phrase in Elizabethan poetic diction, rendering the Italian *alto sdegno*, and not necessarily implying adverse criticism of the aristocratic sentiment. So Satan intends it here; but M. means it to betray the speaker's contemptuous pride, as 'fixed' does his rigidity.
i *94. MS* and *Ed I* omit comma.

Nor what the potent victor in his rage
Can else inflict, do I repent or change,
Though changed in outward lustre, that fixed mind
And high disdain, from sense of injured merit,
That with the mightiest raised me to contend,
And to the fierce contention brought along
Innumerable force of spirits armed
That durst dislike his reign, and me preferring,
His utmost power with adverse power opposed
In dubious battle on the plains of heaven,
And shook his throne. What though the field be lost?
All is not lost; the unconquerable will,
And study of revenge, immortal hate,
And courage never to submit or yield:
And what is else not to be overcome?
That glory never shall his wrath or might
Extort from me. To bow and sue for grace
With suppliant knee, and deify his power,

i *96*. *MS* and *Ed I* omit comma after *inflict*.

i *97*. *Though . . . lustre*] A parenthesis, so that *MS* comma after *lustre* at first seems preferable to *Ed I* and *Ed II* semicolon. But semicolon dividing a verb from its object was common seventeenth-century rhetorical punctuation.

i *98–9*. Contrast iii 309–11; Satan conceives 'merit' in terms of might, but Christ's merit consists in being good. See vi 820*n*.

i *105*. *shook his throne*] Untrue, as we learn at vi 834. 'In fact it is the Son's chariot rather than Satan's armies which shake heaven to its foundations (vi 710–2)' (Rajan[2] 12). Cp. Cowley, *Davideis* i, *n* 15, 'it were improper for a *Devil* to make a whole speech without some lies in it; such are those precendent exaltations of the *Devils* power, which are most of them false, but not *All*.' Throughout the present passage Satan sees himself as the hero of the sort of Satanic or pagan epic that the devils show a taste for at ii 549ff (Burden 64). Empson 44 defends the difficult position that Satan's argument is false, yet his defiant belief in it somehow creditable.

i *105–6*. Enlarging on the speech of Satan in Fairfax's translation of Tasso *Gerusalemme liberata* iv 15: 'We lost the field, yet lost we not our heart.'

i *106–10*. The question mark after l. 109 shows the primary chain of discourse to be 'what else is it, not to be overcome?' But in a secondary chain *And what is else* corresponds to the Latin construction *Et si quid sit:* 'And if there is anything else (besides *will . . . study of revenge . . . hate . . . courage*) that is not to be overcome.' *That glory*] Either 'the glory of overcoming me' or 'my glory of *will*, etc.'

i *107*. *study*] pursuit of.

i *112*. *MS* and *Ed I* omit comma after *power*.

Who from the terror of this arm so late
Doubted his empire, that were low indeed,
That were an ignominy and shame beneath
This downfall; since by fate the strength of gods
And this empyreal substance cannot fail,
Since through experience of this great event
In arms not worse, in foresight much advanced,
We may with more successful hope resolve
To wage by force or guile eternal war
Irreconcilable, to our grand foe,
Who now triumphs, and in the excess of joy
Sole reigning holds the tyranny of heaven.
So spake the apostate angel, though in pain,
Vaunting aloud, but racked with deep despair:

i *114*. *Doubted*] feared for. *MS* has semicolon after *empire*.
i *115*. *ignominy*] Possibly pronounced 'ignomy', as it was often spelled. But the word has four syllables at vi 383, and may have here, if we assume synaloepha or coalescence between *-y* and *and*.
i *116–7*. Implying not only that as angels they are immortal (which M. himself believed, on the basis of *Luke* xx 36: see *De doctrina* i 7 (Columbia xv 34), but also that the continuance of their strength (another quality of angels: see *Ps.* ciii 20 and *De doctrina* i 7) is assured *by fate*, in accordance with which, Satan thinks, he was self-begotten in his own 'puissance' (v 864). Contrast Moloch's and Belial's doubts at ii 92–100 and 142–54. Throughout, the devils acknowledge the ultimate power of fate; yet like the Stoics of *PR* iv 317 they avoid the identification of it with the will of God that is stated at vii 137. *gods*] As used by God the Father in iii 341, this is merely another term for angels; but as Satan uses it here, and as it is used in his temptations of Eve (v 70–81); ix 708–18), it is more ambiguous, implying the pagan illusion of a pantheon. Cp. v 853–64, where Satan asserts that the angels are uncreated. *MS* has full stop after *downfall*. *empyreal substance*] Contrast Raphael's 'intelligential substances' (v 408); Satan's phrase obscures the fact that the qualities of the substance depend on continuing rationality.
i *122*. *foe*] Note how the devils studiously avoid naming God directly; cp. ll. 95, 131.
i *123*. *triumphs*] Stressed on the second syllable.
i *124*. *tyranny*] An obvious instance of devilish partiality, exposed in advance by 'monarchy of God' in l. 42 and 'joy' in l. 123. Less obvious is Beelzebub's careful choice of *perpetual* rather than 'eternal' in l. 131.
i *126*. Empson (31) tries to excuse Satan's despair by saying it is not despair in the religious sense, but the feeling of a defeated general. But it is hard to imagine any sense in which fighting against God is not a religious experience.

And him thus answered soon his bold compeer.
O prince, O chief of many throned powers,
That led the embattled seraphim to war
Under thy conduct, and in dreadful deeds
Fearless, endangered heaven's perpetual king;
And put to proof his high supremacy,
Whether upheld by strength, or chance, or fate,
Too well I see and rue the dire event,
That with sad overthrow and foul defeat
Hath lost us heaven, and all this mighty host
In horrible destruction laid thus low,
As far as gods and heavenly essences
Can perish: for the mind and spirit remains
Invincible, and vigour soon returns,
Though all our glory extinct, and happy state
Here swallowed up in endless misery.
But what if he our conqueror, (whom I now
Of force believe almighty, since no less

i *127*. *MS* colon after *compeer* is probably an error, for M. regularly uses period before direct speech.

i *128–9*. *throned powers*] Obliquely evokes thrones and powers–orders, like the seraphim, in Dionysius' angelic hierarchies. But the direct meaning is less specific: 'exalted and powerful beings'. The seraphim are mentioned as one of the offices or degrees that distinguish the angels, in *De doctrina* i 7 (Columbia xv 36f). See also 324*n*, ii 512*n*. Seraphim receive mention at i 539, 794; ii 750; iii 381, 667; v 277, 749, 804, 875, 896; vi 249, 579, 604, 841; vii 113, 198.

i *131*. *endangered . . . king*] As Empson 38 hints, this verges on paradox. *MS* has semicolon after *Fearless*. For the medieval and Renaissance concept of a metaphysical perpetuity or continuity of kingship, consult Ernst H. Kantorowicz, *The King's Two Bodies: A Study in Mediaeval Political Theology* (Princeton 1957) chs vi, vii. But there is an allusion also to Boethius' distinction between *aeternus* and *perpetuus* in *De consolatione* v, Prose 6: 'If we would apply proper epithets to those subjects, we can say, following Plato, that God is eternal, but the universe is continual.'

i *133*. The main powers recognized in the devils' ideology. All the explanations of God's supremacy miss the mark: the loyal angels were unable to win by *strength*; and, as Raphael tells Adam at v 534, God never exacts obedience by destiny (*fate*). God's power rests on a quality that does not occur to Beelzebub: goodness. *MS* has semicolon after *fate*.

i *141*. *extinct*] 'put out, as a Flame, or any thing that burns and shines' (Patrick Hume, *cit*. Ricks 61).

i *144*. Empson 38 notes that as Beelzebub uses it *almighty* means only 'able to defeat any opposing combination in battle'. From the defeat of the devils

Than such could have o'erpowered such force as ours)
Have left us this our spirit and strength entire
Strongly to suffer and support our pains,
That we may so suffice his vengeful ire,
Or do him mightier service as his thralls
By right of war, whate'er his business be
Here in the heart of hell to work in fire,
Or do his errands in the gloomy deep;
What can it then avail though yet we feel
Strength undiminished, or eternal being
To undergo eternal punishment?
Whereto with speedy words the arch-fiend replied.
  Fallen cherub, to be weak is miserable
Doing or suffering: but of this be sure,
To do aught good never will be our task,
But ever to do ill our sole delight,

Beelzebub concludes that the supremacy of heaven's king is upheld by *strength* (l. 133), not *chance*. See ll. 116–7*n* and ii 232–3*n*. *Of force*] perforce.
i *148. suffice*] satisfy (*OED* 5); not a Latinism.
i *149–52.* 'The evil angels are reserved for punishment. They are sometimes, however, permitted to wander throughout the whole earth, the air, and heaven itself, to execute the judgments of God' (*De doctrina* i 9; Columbia xv 106–9).
i *154–5.* i.e., 'being that is eternal, merely so that our punishment may also be eternal'. A secondary connection between *avail* (153) and *To undergo* is not out of the question, *pace* Verity.
i *156. the Fiend*] *MS* corr. to 'th'Arch-fiend' by a different hand.
i *157. cherub*] The cherubim were the second order of the angels, who excelled in knowledge. See l. 128–9*n* and vi 102*n*.
i *158. Doing or suffering*] Some will choose to hear an echo of Livy ii 12: *Et facere et pati fortia Romanum est*, the famous words of Mutius Scaevola when he demonstrated Roman fortitude by voluntarily burning his right hand, and thus frightened the Etruscan Porsenna into withdrawing his army. But the phrase also recalls Horace, *Odes* III xxiv 43, where it is covetousness that impels men 'to do and to suffer' anything, and to desert the path of virtue. In any case the idiom was not uncommon, both in Latin and in English. Cp. *PL* ii 199. Broadbent 76–8 gives an account of the theological process whereby in this passage Satan's heart is hardened into a demonic nihilism.
i *159–68.* This fundamental disobedience and disorientation makes Satan's heroic virtue into the corresponding excess of vice (Steadman 94). 163–5 looks forward to xii 470–8 and Adam's wonder at the astonishing reversal whereby God will turn the Fall into an occasion for good. For 'the inmost counsel of God was the Fortunate Fall of man' (Empson 39).

As being the contrary to his high will
Whom we resist. If then his providence
Out of our evil seek to bring forth good,
Our labour must be to pervert that end,
And out of good still to find means of evil;
Which oft-times may succeed, so as perhaps
Shall grieve him, if I fail not, and disturb
His inmost counsels from their destined aim.
But see the angry victor hath recalled
His ministers of vengeance and pursuit
Back to the gates of heaven: the sulphurous hail
Shot after us in storm, o'erblown hath laid
The fiery surge, that from the precipice
Of heaven received us falling, and the thunder,
Winged with red lightning and impetuous rage,
Perhaps hath spent his shafts, and ceases now
To bellow through the vast and boundless deep.
Let us not slip the occasion, whether scorn,
Or satiate fury yield it from our foe.
Seest thou yon dreary plain, forlorn and wild,
The seat of desolation, void of light,
Save what the glimmering of these livid flames
Casts pale and dreadful? Thither let us tend
From off the tossing of these fiery waves,

i *167. if I fail not*] unless I am mistaken; err (*OED* s.v. *Fail* III 11). Not a Latinism.

i *169–71.* Although Messiah was 'sole victor' at the expulsion (vi 880), it is just possible that he subsequently sent loyal detachments in pursuit of the falling rebels. At least, Chaos confirms Satan's account in this respect, at ii 997–8 (*q.v.*). Raphael, however, omits any mention of an immediate pursuit. This could be due to modesty on his part, or oversight on M.'s. But if the discrepancy is intentional it presumably means that Satan is reluctant to admit that Christ won singlehanded. Or is M. more subtly implying that to encounter Messiah's power is not to have his kingship irresistibly proved, but only to be 'thunderstruck' (vi 858); so that memory is confused and the problem of belief remains? At any rate, as Empson (43) perceives, 'the rebels are as if emerging from a drug, and remember nothing of the intervening period' between the war and their release from chains.

i *172. laid*] caused to subside.

i *173. The fiery*] This fiery *MS*.

i *178. MS* has colon after *occasion*.

i *181–3.* See ll. 62–4*n*. *livid*] Cp. the address of the damned Oedipus to the Styx, which he 'sees' with sightless eyes: *umbrifero Styx livida fundo* (Statius, *Theb.* i 57). *MS* erroneously has exclamation mark after *dreadful*.

There rest, if any rest can harbour there,
And reassembling our afflicted powers,
Consult how we may henceforth most offend
Our enemy, our own loss how repair,
How overcome this dire calamity,
What reinforcement we may gain from hope,
If not what resolution from despair.
  Thus Satan talking to his nearest mate
With head uplift above the wave, and eyes
That sparkling blazed, his other parts besides
Prone on the flood, extended long and large
Lay floating many a rood, in bulk as huge
As whom the fables name of monstrous size,
Titanian, or Earth-born, that warred on Jove,

i *185*. The allusion to *Richard II* V i 5–6, 'Here let us rest, if this rebellious Earth / Have any resting for her true king's queen', is particularly appropriate, since Earth was rebellious because mother of the Giants, the 'Earth-born' of l. 198 below.
i *186–7*. *afflicted*] downcast. *offend*] strike at so as to hurt; harm, injure (*OED* II 6).
i *191*. *If not*] This may be elliptical ('If we may not gain such reinforcement'), or it may imply that for Satan despair is preferable to hope (cp. vi 787–8)– '. . . from hope if not . . . from despair'. The comma after *not* which would have singled out the first line of meaning is not found in *MS*, *Ed I*, or *Ed II*.
i *193–5*. Anticipating Satan's later metamorphosis into a serpent, these lines are modelled on Virgil's description of the sea-serpents swimming towards Laocoon; cp. esp. *pectora quorum inter fluctus arrecta iubaeque / sanguineae superant undas*; *pars cetera pontum / pone legit* and *ardentisque oculos suffecti* (*Aen.* ii 206–8, 210). Burden 56 notes that in the last glimpse we have of Satan he is again a sea-serpent. For the periodic conversion of devils to serpent form see x 556*n*.
i *196*. So Virgil makes the body of the Giant Tityos cover an area of nine *iugera*, as he lies suffering the tortures of Tartarus (*Aen.* vi 596); while Spenser's 'old Dragon', a descendant of the dragon of *Revelation*, 'with his largenesse measured much land' (*F.Q.* I xi 8).
i *197–200*. According to most accounts, the serpent-legged *Briareos* was a Titan, the serpent-headed *Typhon* (=Typhoeus) a Giant; though often the two races were confused. Each was a son of Earth; each fought against Jupiter; and each was eventually confined beneath Aetna (in this connecttion, note the comparison of the 'dry land' of hell to the shattered side of Aetna, at ll. 232–7). Typhon was so powerful that when he first made war on the Olympians they had to resort to metamorphoses to escape (Ovid, *Met.* v 325–31 and 346–58); thus M.'s choice of simile prepares for the devils' assumption of new shapes at ll. 392–521 below. The main force of the simile, however, is to continue the rebel angel / Giant analogy (see ll. 50–83*n*).

Briareos or Typhon, whom the den
By ancient Tarsus held, or that sea-beast
Leviathan, which God of all his works
Created hugest that swim the ocean stream:
Him haply slumbering on the Norway foam
The pilot of some small night-foundered skiff,
Deeming some island, oft, as seamen tell,
With fixed anchor in his scaly rind
Moors by his side under the lea, while night
Invests the sea, and wished morn delays:

Here the analogy is not only a matter of size: Conti and others had interpreted the myth of Typhon's attack on Jupiter allegorically, taking it to mean that 'there is no religion, no humanity, no justice, where the fury of ambition rears itself' (*Mythologiae* vi 22). At *Nativity Ode* 226 M. conflates this snaky Typhon with the Typhon of Egyptian mythology, an important deity representing the cosmic principle of divisive evil (see Plutarch, *De Iside*); and in *Areopagitica* he interprets the Egyptian Typhon as a type of those who dismember truth (Yale ii 549). *den / By ancient Tarsus*] The Biblical Tarsus was the capital of Cilicia, and both Pindar and Aeschylus describe Typhon's habitat as a Cilician cave or 'den' (*Pyth.* i 17; *Prom.* 351–4).

i *200–8. Leviathan*] The monster of *Job* xli, identified in Isaiah's prophecy of judgment as 'the crooked serpent' (*Is.* xxvii 1), but also sometimes thought of as a whale. The anecdote of the illusory island is from the *Physiologus*, where the moral drawn is that the devil is similarly deceitful (see J. H. Pitman, 'Milton and the Physiologus', *MLN* xl (1925) 439). It was a familiar story, which was not only repeated in Renaissance encyclopaedias, but even achieved the currency of visual representation. At Hardwick House, e.g., there is an emblematic mural showing a ship anchored to a whale, with the legend *Nusquam tuta fides* (see Freeman 92). On the traditional comparison of Satan to a whale-island Ricks (6) cites James Whaler in *PMLA* xlvi (1931) 1050; Svendsen 33–5; and D. M. Hill in *N & Q* cci (1956) 158. Other refs. will be found in White 197f; E. G. Millar, ed., *A Thirteenth Century Bestiary* (Oxford 1958) 38f and Pl. 76; and Jurgis Baltrušaitis, *Réveils et Prodiges* (Paris 1960) 130f and Fig. 20A. T. S. Eliot (*Proc. of the Brit. Acad.* xxxiii (1947) 74) thought the simile an extraneous digression; but it illustrates the delusiveness of Satan and the danger of trusting his false appearance of greatness in the early books of the poem.

i *202. ocean stream*] A Homeric phrase (ῥόος ὠκεάνοιο).

i *203. foam*] Bentley thought this an unhappily inadequate support for a whale; but Ricks 16 defends the synecdoche, on the ground that M. intends a mysterious, sinister effect. Cp. ll. 226f below.

i *204. night-foundered*] sunk in night, benighted; as in *Comus* 483.

i *208. Invests*] wraps, covers; but also 'night beleaguers, and morn is slow to raise the siege'.

So stretched out huge in length the arch-fiend lay
Chained on the burning lake, nor ever thence
Had risen or heaved his head, but that the will
And high permission of all-ruling heaven
Left him at large to his own dark designs,
That with reiterated crimes he might
Heap on himself damnation, while he sought
Evil to others, and enraged might see
How all his malice served but to bring forth
Infinite goodness, grace and mercy shown
On man by him seduced, but on himself
Treble confusion, wrath and vengeance poured.
Forthwith upright he rears from off the pool
His mighty stature; on each hand the flames
Driven backward slope their pointing spires, and rolled
In billows, leave i' the midst a horrid vale.
Then with expanded wings he steers his flight
Aloft, incumbent on the dusky air
That felt unusual weight, till on dry land
He lights, if it were land that ever burned
With solid, as the lake with liquid fire;

i *209–13*. See *De doctrina* i 9 (Columbia xv 108f): the 'proper place' of the devils is the pit, 'from which they cannot escape without permission'. In *De doctrina* i 8 M. explains why God is blameless, even though he permits, and even tempts, the wicked to sin. Lewis 66 cites St Augustine on God's exploitation of evil wills: *voluntatum malarum iustissimus ordinator*. Empson 42f dwells on the horror of God's leading Satan into evil; but it is wayward to take the first part of the sentence without the second. God's purpose is not that Satan should damn himself, but that grace should be shown to man (in spite of all Satan's malice, which only redounds on himself). *heaved*] raised.

i *217–20*. Cp. 163–5 and xii 470–8; also *De doctrina* i 8 (Columbia xv 72–5): 'The will being already in a state of perversion, he [God] influences it in such a manner, that out of its own wickedness it either operates good for others, or punishment for itself.'

i *224*. *horrid*] bristling (with *spires*).

i *226–7*. *incumbent*] 'pressing with his weight', then a common use of the word. The conceit of the air oppressed by Satan's weight recalls Spenser, *F.Q.* I xi 18, where the burden is a similar one: the old dragon.

i *229–30*. Darbishire[2] i 285 prefers the punctuation of *MS* (comma after *fire*, semicolon after *hue*), since it throws the volcano simile 'into relation with the whole phenomenon of the fiery liquid–solid land of Hell, while the punctuation of the first edition [and one might add, the second also] relates it erroneously to the one aspect of colour'. But 'hue' means far more

And such appeared in hue, as when the force
Of subterranean wind transports a hill
Torn from Pelorus, or the shattered side
Of thundering Aetna, whose combustible
And fuelled entrails thence conceiving fire,
Sublimed with mineral fury, aid the winds,
And leave a singed bottom all involved
With stench and smoke: such resting found the sole
Of unblessed feet. Him followed his next mate,
Both glorying to have scaped the Stygian flood
As gods, and by their own recovered strength,
Not by the sufferance of supernal power.
  Is this the region, this the soil, the clime,
Said then the lost archangel, this the seat
That we must change for heaven, this mournful gloom
For that celestial light? Be it so, since he

than colour. It was a complex word in the seventeenth century, referring to both surface appearance and texture.

i *230–7.* For a full exposition of the seismological theory that attributed earthquakes and volcanoes to the action of imprisoned winds swelling the body of the earth, see Gabriel Harvey's 'Discourse, of the Earthquake' (Spenser, *The Prose Works*, ed. R. B. Gottfried (Baltimore, Md. 1949), pp. 449–59). The same anthropomorphic notion underlies Virgil's and Ovid's descriptions of Aetna, the main sources of the present passage: *Aen.* iii 571–7 (note esp. *viscera montis*; cp. M.'s image of *entrails*) and *Met.* xv 297–306, 340–55 (note the mention of combustible material 'containing the seeds of flame'). The passage continues the Typhon allusion of 199, for, according to one theory, Typhon symbolised the power of volcanoes (see Conti, *Mythologiae* vi 22). See further in vi 195–8*n* below. It may be relevant that Raban Maur interprets the 'great mountain burning with fire' of *Rev.* viii 8 as the devil himself (Migne cxi 365).

i *232–3. Pelorus*] Cape Faro, the north-eastern promontory of Sicily, near Aetna. The allusion is to Virgil, *Aen.* iii 570ff, a description of the uptorn entrails of the volcano, with a version of the myth that the Giant Enceladus lies beneath the mountain.

i *235. Sublimed*] converted directly from solid to vapour by volcanic heat in such a way as to resolidify on cooling. *mineral fury*] disorder of minerals, or subterranean disorder.

i *236. involved*] wreathed.

i *239. Stygian flood*] the 'gulf' of l. 52. The epithet perhaps also implies darkness, as in *Elegia iv* 95 *Stygiis . . . tenebris.*

i *240–1.* This is illusion, as ll. 210–20 has enabled us to recognize.

i *244. change for*] have instead of.

Who now is sovereign can dispose and bid
What shall be right: furthest from him is best
Whom reason hath equalled, force hath made supreme
Above his equals. Farewell happy fields
Where joy for ever dwells: hail horrors, hail
Infernal world, and thou profoundest hell
Receive thy new possessor: one who brings
A mind not to be changed by place or time.
The mind is its own place, and in itself
Can make a heaven of hell, a hell of heaven.
What matter where, if I be still the same,
And what I should be, all but less than he
Whom thunder hath made greater? Here at least
We shall be free; the almighty hath not built
Here for his envy, will not drive us hence:
Here we may reign secure, and in my choice
To reign is worth ambition though in hell:
Better to reign in hell, than serve in heaven.

i *246. sovereign*] M. customarily used the Italianate spelling 'sovran', in his later poetry–possibly to ensure a disyllabic reading.

i *255.* The view that heaven and hell are states of mind was held by Amaury de Bene, a medieval heretic often cited in seventeenth-century accounts of atheism; it is to be distinguished from the Ubiquism of Marlowe's Mephistophilis in *Doctor Faustus* l. 316 (D. C. Allen, *MLN* lxxi (1956) 325). As MacCaffrey 70f points out, this passage has a strong irony that has generally been missed. Satan's specious denial of the effects of the fall of the angels is belied by his shock at the change in Beelzebub (84 above), and almost verbally contradicted at iv 75ff, 'Which way I fly is hell'.

i *257. all but less than*] The confusion of the idioms 'all but equal to' and 'only less than' reflects Satan's self-deception about his status.

i *258.* In Satan's view it is only God's power that makes him greater. See vi 820–3*n*.

i *259.* As Empson 40 notes, Satan is here speaking with an ironic tone, sneering at the metaphysical sense of 'almighty'.

i *262. worth ambition*] worth striving for (Latin *ambitio*). Satan refers, not merely to a mental state, but to an active effort that is the price of power (B. A. Wright, *N & Q* cciii (1958) 200).

i *263.* An almost proverbial commonplace: cp. *Ps.* lxxxiv 10; Homer, *Od.* xi 488 (better a living swain than king of the dead); Aeschylus, *Prom.* 965; Plutarch, *Life of Julius Caesar* xi 2 ('I would rather be first here[in a miserable barbarian village]than second in Rome'); Serafino della Salandra, *Adamo caduto* ii 1; and Phineas Fletcher, *The Purple Island* vii 10: 'In heav'n they scorn'd to serve, so now in hell they reigne.' And contrast *PL* vi 183–4, where Abdiel, who prefers to serve in heaven, points out that hell is a prison, not a kingdom.

But wherefore let we then our faithful friends,
The associates and copartners of our loss
Lie thus astonished on the oblivious pool,
And call them not to share with us their part
In this unhappy mansion, or once more
With rallied arms to try what may be yet
Regained in heaven, or what more lost in hell?
So Satan spake, and him Beelzebub
Thus answered. Leader of those armies bright,
Which but the omnipotent none could have foiled,
If once they hear that voice, their liveliest pledge
Of hope in fears and dangers, heard so oft
In worst extremes, and on the perilous edge
Of battle when it raged, in all assaults
Their surest signal, they will soon resume
New courage and revive, though now they lie
Grovelling and prostrate on yon lake of fire,
As we erewhile, astounded and amazed,
No wonder, fallen such a pernicious highth.
He scarce had ceased when the superior fiend
Was moving toward the shore; his ponderous shield
Ethereal temper, massy, large, and round,
Behind him cast; the broad circumference

i *266. oblivious pool*] the pool attended by oblivion; the 'forgetful lake' of ii 74. Unlike the river Lethe of the classical underworld and of M.'s hell (ii 583–614), with which Merritt Hughes wrongly identifies it, this pool lacks the power to wash out memory and woe completely. In ii 606–14 the devils are tortured by their inability to drink from the Lethe: a torture they would be oblivious to, if they had already drunk. *astonished*] stunned; dismayed; stupefied.

i *268. MS* has semicolon after *mansion*.

i *276. edge*] critical position; also 'front line', rendering the related Latin word *acies* (though not necessarily felt as a Latinism – *OED* cites Coverdale). cp. vi 108.

i *282. fallen . . . highth*] As often in *PL*, the preposition is by an ellipsis omitted.

i *284. Was moving*] Poetic syntax, rendering Satan's haste by the use of a continuative tense, where some such phrase as 'started to move', describing the inception of the movement, would have been more ordinary. A similar graphic use of the imperfect tense is common in Latin and Greek.

i *285. Ethereal temper*] tempered in celestial fire; cp. ii 139 and 813. Syntactically elusive, the phrase is an ellipsis for 'Ethereal in its temper' or 'Of ethereal temper'.

i *286–91.* Homer compares Achilles' shield to the moon in *Il.* xix 373, but

Hung on his shoulders like the moon, whose orb
Through optic glass the Tuscan artist views
At evening from the top of Fesole,
Or in Valdarno, to descry new lands,
Rivers or mountains in her spotty globe.
His spear, to equal which the tallest pine
Hewn on Norwegian hills, to be the mast
Of some great ammiral, were but a wand,

there the comparison is one of brightness, not of size. Cp. also the shield of the proud Radigund in Spenser, *F.Q.* V v 3, 'that shined wide, / As the faire Moone in her most full aspect'. In *Areopagitica* M. mentions having visited Galileo, the *Tuscan artist*–i.e., scientist–who first studied the moon with a telescope powerful enough to resolve its surface features. At the time Galileo had been placed under house arrest by the Inquisition, near Florence, which is in the 'Valdarno' or Valley of the Arno, overlooked by the hills of *Fesole* or Fiesole (Latin *Faesulae*). (The apparently supererogatory geographical details may be M.'s indulgence of fond memories; or they may be intended to supply terrestrial counterparts to the lunar *Rivers or mountains* of l. 291.) For a review of the controversy as to whether M. did actually visit Galileo, see Yale ii 538*n*; and for his fascination with Galileo's researches–which is reflected also in iii 588–90 and v 261–3–see Grant McColley in *PMLA* lii (1937) 728–62, and Nicolson[2]. The mountainous formation of the moon's surface was described in Galileo's *Siderius nuncius* (Venice 1610). In his reference to the telescope M. as it were lays in advance the evidential basis for the world in which the action of this 'first modern cosmic poem' (Nicolson[4] 81) is to take place. As Cope (50ff) argues, however, space in *PL* is much more than topical scientific reality: it is also 'the aesthetic shape of the myth'. And in any case it is possible that Galileo is introduced here as the representative of 'a culture quite different from, and implicitly superior to, the military heroism' of Satan (Broadbent 72). *optic glass*] telescope (not poetic diction).

i *292–4*. The comparison of a weapon to a mast was common; e.g. the club of Polyphemus (Homer, *Od.* ix 322) and the lances of Tancredi and Argante (Tasso, *Gerus. lib.* vi 40 and–in Fairfax's translation only–iii 17). But the comparison to a tree suggests more particularly the rude weapon that was a conventional attribute of the lawless Wild Man: cp. the 'lopped pine' of Polyphemus in Virgil, *Aen.* iii 659 and the 'snaggy Oke' of the proud Orgoglio in Spenser, *F.Q.* I vii 10; and see Richard Bernheimer, *Wild Men in the Middle Ages: A Study in Art, Sentiment and Demonology* (Cambridge, Mass. 1952). A famous engraving by Melchior Lorch (illus. Cohn, Fig. 2) shows Satan-Antichrist with a roughly lopped tree. *equal*] compare with. *Norwegian*] Ships' masts were commonly made from imported Norwegian fir. *ammiral*] flagship; a spelling current in M.'s time.

He walked with to support uneasy steps
Over the burning marl, not like those steps
On heaven's azure, and the torrid clime
Smote on him sore besides, vaulted with fire;
Natheless he so endured, till on the beach
Of that inflamed sea, he stood and called
His legions, angel forms, who lay entranced
Thick as autumnal leaves that strew the brooks
In Vallombrosa, where the Etrurian shades
High overarched imbower; or scattered sedge
Afloat, when with fierce winds Orion armed
Hath vexed the Red Sea coast, whose waves o'erthrew
Busiris and his Memphian chivalry,

i *296. marl*] rich clay soil, but probably used here as a sensuously rich synonym for 'ground'.

i *297. MS* semicolon after *azure.*

i *299. Natheless*] nevertheless. Perhaps already archaic-poetic.

i *302–4.* Cp. *Is.* xxxiv 4: 'And all the host of heaven shall be dissolved, and the heavens shall be rolled together as a scroll: and all their host shall fall down, as the leaf falleth off from the vine, and as a falling fig from the fig tree.' Fallen leaves were an enduring simile for the numberless dead: see Homer, *Il.* vi 146, Virgil, *Aen.* vi 309–10 ('multitudinous as the leaves of the forest that in the first frost of autumn fall away and drop') and Dante, *Inf.* iii 112–5. But M. adds the concrete precision of an actual locality, again near Florence. If he visited *Vallombrosa* he would know that (as its name partly suggests) it was shaded by extensive deciduous woods. The use of *shades*, by metonymy, for foliage or woods is a characteristic of M.'s diction (B. A. Wright, *N & Q* cciii (1958) 205–8). Broadbent 86 notes the correspondence between the 'Etrurian shades / High overarched' and hell's fiery vault. MacCaffrey 124ff explores the implication that Satan's legions are morally unfruitful and withering.

i *304–6.* The acronychal rising of Orion's belt was anciently supposed to mark the season of storms (see Pliny xviii 223; Virgil, *Aen.* i 535; and Riccioli i 473). But the point of the simile depends on Orion's force as a Biblical symbol. Commentators on *Job* ix 9 and *Amos* v 8 interpreted the creation of Orion as a symbol of God's power to raise tempests and floods to execute his judgments (Riccioli i 408). Thus M.'s transition to the Egyptians overwhelmed by God's judgment in ll. 306–11 is a natural one. *sedge*] The Hebrew name for the Red Sea was 'Sea of Sedge'. *armed*] Cp. Virgil, *Aen.* iii 517, *armatumque auro . . . Oriona.* *vexed*] tossed about.

i *306–11.* Contrary to his promise, the Pharaoh with his *Memphian* (i.e. Egyptian; a favourite word in Sylvester's Du Bartas) charioteers pursued the Israelites–who had been in captivity in *Goshen*–across the Red Sea. The Israelites passed over safely; but the Egyptians' *chariot wheels* were broken (*Exod.* xiv 25), and the rising sea engulfed them and cast their corpses on the

While with perfidious hatred they pursued
The sojourners of Goshen, who beheld
From the safe shore their floating carcasses
And broken chariot wheels, so thick bestrewn
Abject and lost lay these, covering the flood,
Under amazement of their hideous change.
He called so loud, that all the hollow deep
Of hell resounded. Princes, potentates,
Warriors, the flower of heaven, once yours, now lost,
If such astonishment as this can seize
Eternal spirits; or have ye chosen this place
After the toil of battle to repose
Your wearied virtue, for the ease you find
To slumber here, as in the vales of heaven?
Or in this abject posture have ye sworn
To adore the conqueror? who now beholds
Cherub and seraph rolling in the flood
With scattered arms and ensigns, till anon

shore (*ibid.* 30). Traditionally, the Pharaoh was interpreted as a type of the Devil (Rabanus Maurus, in Migne cxi 51). The mythical tyrant *Busiris* was commonly identified with the Pharaoh of *Exod.* i (see, e.g., George Sandys[2] 321, commenting on Ovid, *Met.* ix 183 and citing Reinerus Reineccius: 'Busiris . . . is held to be that king of Aegipt who so grievously oppressed the Israelites: and the author of that inhumane Edict of drowning their male-children; whence arose the tradition of his sacrificing strangers'); but naming the later Pharaoh of Exod. xiv Busiris was less usual, and shows, according to D. C. Allen, *MLN* lxv (1950) 115, that M. had learned from the *Chronicle* of Carion, as rewritten by Melancthon, that 'there were many kings with the same name, Busirises'. Perhaps, however, M. simply conflates the two Pharaohs, in the interests of dramatic concentration; as he may be thought to do also at xii 165–96.

i *311. MS* has full stop after *wheels*, as in seven other places before 'So' or 'As' beginning a simile.

i *313. amazement*] consternation, stupefaction.

i *314. deep*] In view of iv 76, many will prefer the *MS* reading 'deeps'.

i *317. astonishment*] mental prostration; cp. 313*n*. Note the double lines of discourse: 'If indeed you are the flower of heaven, when such astonishment can seize you' and 'Heaven lost indeed, if you are susceptible to such astonishment'.

i *318. MS* colon after *spirits* may be preferable.

i *320. virtue*] strength, power, courage.

i *322.* Alluding to the conspirators' oath sworn by the rebel angels; see ii 693.

i *324. seraph*] See i 128–9*n*. The singular form may be M.'s own coinage; earlier only *seraphim* was used, the form with the Hebrew plural inflection.

His swift pursuers from heaven gates discern
The advantage, and descending tread us down
Thus drooping, or with linked thunderbolts
Transfix us to the bottom of this gulf.
Awake, arise, or be for ever fallen.
  They heard, and were abashed, and up they sprung
Upon the wing, as when men wont to watch
On duty, sleeping found by whom they dread,
Rouse and bestir themselves ere well awake.
Nor did they not perceive the evil plight
In which they were, or the fierce pains not feel;
Yet to their general's voice they soon obeyed
Innumerable. As when the potent rod
Of Amram's son in Egypt's evil day
Waved round the coast, up called a pitchy cloud
Of locusts, warping on the eastern wind,
That o'er the realm of impious Pharaoh hung
Like night, and darkened all the land of Nile:
So numberless were those bad angels seen
Hovering on wing under the cope of hell
'Twixt upper, nether, and surrounding fires;
Till, as a signal given, the uplifted spear
Of their great sultan waving to direct
Their course, in even balance down they light
On the firm brimstone, and fill all the plain;
A multitude, like which the populous north

i *328. linked thunderbolts*] The weapon used by Jupiter and Minerva against the rebel Giants.

i *332. MS* has semicolon after *wing*.

i *335. nor did they not*] Simulating the Latin idiom *neque non*.

i *337*. M.'s use of the somewhat unusual construction 'obey to' may be meant to recall *Rom.* vi 16 (its sole occurrence in A.V.), and thus to imply that Satan's followers are 'servants . . . of sin unto death'.

i *338–44. Amram's son*] Moses, who used his *rod* to bring down on the Egyptians a plague of locusts that 'covered the . . . earth, so that the land was darkened' (*Exod.* x 12–15; cp. *PL* xii 185–8). M.'s comparison of devils to locusts is based on allegorisations of this passage and of *Rev.* ix 3 (e.g. Raban Maur's, Migne cxi 257), which had become so familiar that Phineas Fletcher could allude to them in the title of his poem *Locustae.* Callot used the locust schema–on which see E. H. Gombrich, *Art and Illusion* (1962) 68f–for some of the devils in his engraving *The Temptation of St Anthony* (1617). *warping*] floating or turning through the air.

i *345. cope*] canopy, as in iv 992 and vi 215.

i *351–5.* Completing the series of three similes (arranged in ascending order of cosmic degree), whereby M. successively compares the numerousness of

Poured never from her frozen loins, to pass
Rhene or the Danaw, when her barbarous sons
Came like a deluge on the south, and spread
Beneath Gibralter to the Lybian sands.
Forthwith from every squadron and each band
The heads and leaders thither haste where stood
Their great commander; godlike shapes and forms
Excelling human, princely dignities,
And powers that erst in heaven sat on thrones;
Though of their names in heavenly records now
Be no memorial blotted out and razed
By their rebellion, from the books of life.
Nor had they yet among the sons of Eve
Got them new names, till wandering o'er the earth,
Through God's high sufferance for the trial of man,

the fallen angels to that of plants, insects, and human armies. In *Prol v*, M. uses barbarian hordes as a symbol for the multitude of errors that threaten truth. Certain particulars in the present passage, such as the mention of the Rhine and the Danube, may possibly be drawn from the first few sentences in Macchiavelli's *Istorie Fiorentine*. See also v 689*n*. The effect of the series of similes is a complex one: the devils are raised, necromantically; but at the same time the comparisons are all, in one way or another, morally unfavourable.

i *352. frozen loins*] Bentley thought frozen loins unsuitable for generation; but as MacCaffrey 129 notices, the image is deliberately unnatural and infertile.

i *358. godlike*] Frequently used in *PL* as a synonym for 'heroic'; heroic virtue being essentially a reflection of the divine (Steadman 95–6).

i *361–3*. Cp. i 82*n* and v 658–9. *books of life*] The allusion is principally to *Rev*. iii 5 ('He that overcometh . . . I will not blot out his name out of the book of life') and *Exod*. xxxii 32–3. 'The emphasis upon the names has an ironic effect when one remembers that the Biblical overcomers of evil are given new names in Heaven (*Rev*. iii 12), while these fallen angels 'Got them new Names' upon earth through the evil of pagan idolatry" (Sims 13).

i *364–75*. Cp. Hooker, *Laws of Eccles. Pol.* I iv 3: 'These wicked spirits the Heathens honoured instead of Gods, both generally under the name of *Dii inferi*, Gods infernal; and particularly, some in Oracles, some in Idols, some as household Gods, some as Nymphs.' The origins of the doctrine that the fallen angels came to earth and deceived men into worshipping them as gods are traced in Verity 672–4. It was authorized by such texts as *1 Cor*. x 20 and *Deut*. xxxii 17 ('They sacrificed unto devils, not to God'; see Sims 14); but a Platonic influence is more conspicuous in such versions as St Augustine's (*Civ. Dei* vii–x). Broadbent (88f) sees this passage, and indeed the whole catalogue of devils, as a liberal and aggressively Reformist attack on the 'multiplex superstition' of Rome.

By falsities and lies the greatest part
Of mankind they corrupted to forsake
God their creator, and the invisible
Glory of him that made them, to transform
Oft to the image of a brute, adorned
With gay religions full of pomp and gold,
And devils to adore for deities:
Then were they known to men by various names,
And various idols through the heathen world.
Say, Muse, their names then known, who first, who
last,
Roused from the slumber, on that fiery couch,
At their great emperor's call, as next in worth
Came singly where he stood on the bare strand,
While the promiscuous crowd stood yet aloof?
The chief were those who from the pit of hell
Roaming to seek their prey on earth, durst fix
Their seats long after next the seat of God,
Their altars by his altar, gods adored
Among the nations round, and durst abide
Jehovah thundering out of Sion, throned

i *368–71.* Cp. *Rom.* i 23: the Gentiles 'changed the glory of the uncorruptible God into an image made like to corruptible man, and to birds, and four-footed beasts, and creeping things'.

i *370. Ed I* has comma after *him*.

i *372. religions*] rites.

i *376.* Echoing Virgil, *Aen.* xi 664 (*Quem . . . primum, quem postremum*), itself an echo of Homer, *Il.* v 703; while the list of heathen deities that follows (ll. 392–522) is M.'s counterpart to Homer's catalogue of the captains and ships of the Greeks in *Il.* ii 484–877. *then known*] By a kind of prolepsis, M. anticipates the names given to the fallen angels in later ages.

i *377. MS* omits comma after *slumber*.

i *380. MS* has full stop after *aloof*.

i *381–91.* Introducing the first group of angels (ll. 392–506), those who later became the gods of nations in contact with the Israelites, and for whom there is therefore direct Biblical authority. M. imagines their geographical proximity to Jehovah in his sanctuary to be evidence of their special boldness. On the classification of the devils according to the authority for their early existence, see Sims 14. Thammuz-Adonis, e.g., is accorded a prominent place on the strength of Ezekiel's reference to him. *Between the cherubim*] A formulaic description, frequent in the O.T. (e.g. *2 Sam.* vi 2, *Is.* xxxvii 16), that gains fresh point in the present context. Jehovah is so throned in his sanctuary, because images of cherubim flanked the ark in the tabernacle (*Exod.* xxv 18–21).

i *383. MS* has commas after *seats* and *after*.

Between the cherubim; yea, often placed
Within his sanctuary itself their shrines,
Abominations; and with cursed things
His holy rites, and solemn feasts profaned,
And with their darkness durst affront his light.
First Moloch, horrid king besmeared with blood
Of human sacrifice, and parents' tears,
Though for the noise of drums and timbrels loud
Their children's cries unheard, that passed through fire
To his grim idol. Him the Ammonite
Worshipped in Rabba and her watery plain,
In Argob and in Basan, to the stream
Of utmost Arnon. Nor content with such

i *387–91*. M. refers to apostasies of the kings of Judah, such as that of Manasseh, who followed 'the abominations [i.e., unclean practices] of the heathen' and 'built altars for all the host of heaven in . . . the house of the Lord' (*2 Kings* xxi 2–7). *affront*] confront, insult.

i *392–490*. Satan gathers twelve disciples: Moloch, Chemos, Baalim, Ashtaroth, Astoreth, Thammuz, Dagon, Rimmon, Osiris, Isis, Horus, Belial. This travesty of Christ's calling of his disciples may have been suggested to M. by various traditional schemes, such as the Manilian astrological system of twelve Olympian Guardians, or the many attempts to introduce the twelve apostles into the solar zodiac (*EB* vii 13).

i *392–6*. Here and at ii 43, vi 357, M. refers to *Moloch* as *king* because this is the literal meaning of his name. He comes first as the 'strongest and fiercest' (ii 44) of the rebel angels. With the account of his cult, cp. *Nat* 205–10. *passed through fire*] Cp. *2 Kings* xxiii 10: 'that no man might make his son or daughter to pass through fire to Molech'. George Sandys describes the idol of Moloch as hollow, filled with fire; and explains that 'least [the children's] lamentable shreeks should sad the hearts of their parents, the Priests of *Molech* did deafe their eares with the continuall clang of trumpets and timbrels' (*A relation of a journey* (1637) 186); cp. Fuller IV vii 34.

i *397–9*. Though ostensibly magnifying Moloch's empire, these lines look forward to his eventual defeat; for *Rabba*, the Ammonite royal city, is best known for its capture by David after his repentance (*2 Sam.* xii), while the Israelite conquest of the regions of *Argob* and *Basan*, as far as the boundary river *Arnon*, is recalled by Moses as particularly crushing (*Deut.* iii 1–13). *watery plain*] From *2 Sam.* xii 27. *Basan* is the Septuagint and Vulgate form; as usual, M. avoids the *sh* sound.

i *399–403*. Solomon's wives drew him into idolatry (*1 Kings* xi 5–7); but the 'high places that were before Jerusalem . . . on the right hand of the mount of corruption which Solomon . . . had builded for Ashtoreth the abomination of the Zidonians, and for Chemosh the abomination of the Moabites, and for Milcom the abomination of the children of Ammon' were later destroyed by Josiah (*2 Kings* xxiii 13–4; and see l. 418).

Audacious neighbourhood, the wisest heart
Of Solomon he led by fraud to build
His temple right against the temple of God
On that opprobrious hill, and made his grove
The pleasant valley of Hinnom, Tophet thence
And black Gehenna called, the type of hell.
Next Chemos, the obscene dread of Moab's sons,
From Aroar to Nebo, and the wild
Of southmost Abarim; in Hesebon
And Horonaim, Seon's realm, beyond
The flowery dale of Sibma clad with vines,
And Eleale to the Asphaltic Pool.

i *403. opprobrious hill*] The Mount of Olives, because of Solomon's idolatry called 'mount of corruption' (A.V.) or *mons offensionis* (Vulgate). M. approximates even more closely to the Vulgate form at 416 and 443. Throughout the poem, Solomon functions as a type both of Adam and of Christ. Here Solomon's uxoriousness foreshadows Adam's. Cp. vi 833–4*n*, ix 439–43*n*, xi 396–407*n*, xii 332–4*n*.

i *403–5*. To abolish sacrifice to Moloch, Josiah 'defiled Topheth, which is in the valley of the children of Hinnom' (*2 Kings* xxiii 10). Fuller treats Tophet as a synonym for 'the *Valley of* the sons of *Hinnom*', deriving it from *toph*, a drum (an allusion to Moloch's ritual music) (*Pisgah-Sight* IV vii 34). *Gehenna*] 'Valley of Hinnom': not an O.T. form, but used in *Matt.* x 28 as a name for hell. St Jerome explains that because it was a place of sacrifice, known as 'the Graveyard', the Valley of Hinnom became a type of the 'everlasting punishments with which sinners were afflicted' (*Comm. in Matt.*; Migne xxvi 68). The *grove* of Moloch, which is not mentioned in the Bible, also comes from St Jerome. George Sandys remarks that before the grove was hewn down it was 'most delightful' and 'a Paradise' (*Relation* 186).

i *406. Chemos*, 'the abomination of Moab', is associated with the neighbouring god Moloch in *1 Kings* xi 7, and follows naturally therefore in M.'s catalogue.

i *407–11*. Most of these places are named in *Num.* xxxii as the formerly Moabite inheritance assigned by Moses to the tribes of Reuben and Gad (see also Fuller's map in *Pisgah-Sight*). *Aroar*] Aroer *MS* and *Ed I*, as A.V. A town in the extreme north of the territory. *Nebo*] A town in the south, near the *Abarim* mountains. *Num.* xxi 25–30 rejoices at the Israelite capture of *Hesebon* (Heshbon), a Moabite city which had been taken by the Amorite King *Seon* or Sihon. Heshbon, Horonaim, 'the vine of Sibmah', and Elealeh all figure in Isaiah's sad prophecy of the destruction of Moab (*Is.* xv 5, xvi 8f). *Horonaim*] *MS*, *Errata* and *Ed II*; Heronaim *Ed I*. *Asphaltic Pool*] The Dead Sea or *lacus Asphaltites*, so called because of its bituminous scum; the south-west Moabite boundary.

Peor his other name, when he enticed
Israel in Sittim, on their march from Nile,
To do him wanton rites; which cost them woe.
Yet thence his lustful orgies he enlarged
Even to that hill of scandal, by the grove
Of Moloch homicide, lust hard by hate;
Till good Josiah drove them thence to hell.
With these came they, who from the bordering flood
Of old Euphrates to the brook that parts
Egypt from Syrian ground, had general names
Of Baalim and Ashtaroth; those male,
These feminine. For spirits when they please
Can either sex assume, or both; so soft
And uncompounded is their essence pure,

i *412–4. Num.* xxv 1–3 and *Hos.* ix 10.   *woe*] A plague that killed 24,000 (*Num.* xxv 9).

i *415–7. hill of scandal*] See 399–403*n*. The *orgies* (ὄργια, rites) are called lustful on the authority of *Num.* xxv 1, and of the Fathers, especially St Jerome, who identified the Moabite deity Chemosh or Baal-Peor with the Latin Priapus (Migne xxv 896).

i *418. Josiah*] Always a favourite with the Reformers, because of his destruction of idolatrous images; see Broadbent 88.

i *419–21.* An area stretching from the north-east limit of Syria to the south-west limit of Canaan, the river Besor. The Euphrates is *old* because mentioned in *Gen.* ii 14.

i *421–3. Baal*] 'Baal. That is, a lord, being the name general for most idols' (Fuller, *Pisgah-Sight* IV vii 23). The Phoenician and Canaanite sun-gods were collectively called *Baalim* (plural form), each local cult being particularised by a further surname, as Baal-Peor. Similarly the variants of the moon goddess Ashtoreth were *Ashtaroth*. 'Milton proves his control over the devils by sophisticated anthropological manipulation, and invites us to stand back from them without necessity of belief' (Broadbent 88).

i *423–31.* Cp. vi 344–53 and see vi 328–34*n*. In *Anatomy of Melancholy* I ii 1 ii, Burton gathers authorities for and against the view that devils are corporeal; but 'that they can assume other aerial bodies, all manner of shapes at their pleasures, appear in what likeness they will themselves', most angelologists, he reports, 'credibly believe'. Todd and McColley cite various sources and analogues; but R. H. West in *PQ* xxvii (1949) argues that M. is dependent on Michael Psellus. M.'s Satan is later to assume many different forms; see, e.g., his metamorphosis into a young cherub at iii 636. Such instability of form is in Renaissance poetry almost always evil: one thinks in particular of Spenser's Archimago (esp. *F.Q.* I ii 10). The last metamorphosis of the devils in *PL*, however, is punitive and perhaps subordinated to a cyclic pattern (see x 575f).   *dilated*] expanded.

i *425. MS* has semicolon after *pure*.

Not tied or manacled with joint or limb,
Nor founded on the brittle strength of bones,
Like cumbrous flesh; but in what shape they choose
Dilated or condensed, bright or obscure,
Can execute their airy purposes,
And works of love or enmity fulfil.
For those the race of Israel oft forsook
Their living strength, and unfrequented left
His righteous altar, bowing lowly down
To bestial gods; for which their heads as low
Bowed down in battle, sunk before the spear
Of despicable foes. With these in troop
Came Astoreth, whom the Phoenicians called
Astarte, queen of heaven, with crescent horns;
To whose bright image nightly by the moon
Sidonian virgins paid their vows and songs,
In Sion also not unsung, where stood
Her temple on the offensive mountain, built
By that uxorious king, whose heart though large,
Beguiled by fair idolatresses, fell
To idols foul. Thammuz came next behind,

i *432. those*] these *MS.*

i *433.* Cp. *1 Sam.* xv 29: 'Strength of Israel', a formulaic periphrasis for Jehovah.

i *438.* The image of *Astoreth* or *Astarte*, the *Sidonian* (Phoenician) moon-goddess and Venus, was 'the statue of a woman, having on her own head the head of a bull, where the horns erected resembled the crescent moon' (Fuller, *Pisgah-Sight* IV vii 22, drawing on Selden *De Dis Syris* ii 2). Cp. *Nativity Ode* 200, 'mooned Ashtaroth'. *queen of heaven*] from *Jer.* xliv 17–19; cp. *Comus* 1002, 'Assyrian queen'.

i *442–6.* See 399–403*n.* *large*] Alluding to *1 Kings* iv 29: 'God gave Solomon . . . largeness of heart' (i.e., capaciousness of intellect).

i *446. Thammuz* follows appropriately, as the lover of Astarte (Cicero, *De nat. deor.* iii 23). His identification with Adonis was based on St Jerome's commentary on the passage in Ezekiel drawn on by M. in 454–6: 'Then he brought me to the door of the gate of the Lord's house which was toward the north; and, behold, there sat women weeping for Tammuz' (*Ezek.* viii 14). The Syrian festival of Tammuz was celebrated after the summer solstice: the slaying of the young god by a boar was mourned as a symbol of the southward withdrawal of the sun and the death of vegetation (Macrobius, *Saturn.* i 21, Selden ii 11). Each year when the River Adonis became discoloured with red mud it was regarded as a renewed sign of the god's wound (Conti, *Mytholog.* v 26). Literary treatments of this myth and popular accounts of the cult (such as Fuller's and Sandys's) had made the story of Tammuz very familiar: see Fuller IV vii 43: 'the poets are almost hoarse

Whose annual wound in Lebanon allured
The Syrian damsels to lament his fate
In amorous ditties all a summer's day,
While smooth Adonis from his native rock
Ran purple to the sea, supposed with blood
Of Thammuz yearly wounded: the love-tale
Infected Sion's daughters with like heat,
Whose wanton passions in the sacred porch
Ezekiel saw, when by the vision led
His eye surveyed the dark idolatries
Of alienated Judah. Next came one
Who mourned in earnest, when the captive ark
Maimed his brute image, head and hands lopped off
In his own temple, on the groundsel edge,
Where he fell flat, and shamed his worshippers:
Dagon his name, sea monster, upward man
And downward fish: yet had his temple high
Reared in Azotus, dreaded through the coast
Of Palestine, in Gath and Ascalon
And Accaron and Gaza's frontier bounds.
Him followed Rimmon, whose delightful seat
Was fair Damascus, on the fertile banks
Of Abbana and Pharphar, lucid streams.
He also against the house of God was bold:

with singing the sad elegies. . . .' For other mentions by M., see *Nativity Ode* 204, *Mans* 11.

i *455. Ezekiel*] Ezechiel *MS*.

i *457–63.* When the Philistines put the ark of the Lord, which they had captured, into the temple of Dagon, 'on the morrow morning, behold, Dagon was fallen upon his face to the ground . . . and the head of Dagon and both the palms of his hands were cut off upon the threshold' (*1 Sam.* v 4). *groundsel*] threshold. The name *Dagon* was sometimes referred to the Hebrew word for 'corn'; but M. prefers to follow Selden's authority (*De dis Syris* ii 3) in deriving it from Heb. *dag*, 'fish', and in representing the god as half fish. Cp. Fuller, *Pisgah-Sight* II x 32: 'Upwards man-like he ascended, / Downwards like a fish he ended.'

i *464–6. Azotus, Ascalon, Accaron*] Vulgate forms (A.V. Ashdod, Askelon, Ekron) current in the seventeenth century. Divine vengeance on these Philistine cities is prophesied in *Zeph.* ii 4. *MS* has semicolon after *Azotus*.

i *467–71.* When Elisha told Naaman that his leprosy would be cured if he washed in the Jordan, the Syrian was at first angry (*2 Kings* v 12: 'Are not Abana and Pharpar, rivers of Damascus, better than all the waters of Israel?'), but then humbled himself and was cured. On Naaman as a type of the regenerate sinner, see Tuve 198.

A leper once he lost and gained a king,
Ahaz his sottish conqueror, whom he drew
God's altar to disparage and displace
For one of Syrian mode, whereon to burn
His odious offerings, and adore the gods
Whom he had vanquished. After these appeared
A crew who under names of old renown,
Osiris, Isis, Orus and their train
With monstrous shapes and sorceries abused
Fanatic Egypt and her priests, to seek
Their wandering gods disguised in brutish forms
Rather than human. Nor did Israel scape
The infection when their borrowed gold composed
The calf in Oreb: and the rebel king
Doubled that sin in Bethel and in Dan,
Likening his maker to the grazed ox,
Jehovah, who in one night when he passed
From Egypt marching, equalled with one stroke
Both her first born and all her bleating gods.
Belial came last, than whom a spirit more lewd

i *471–6.* After successfully engineering the overthrow of Damascus by the Assyrians, the *sottish* (foolish) King Ahaz became interested in the cult of Rimmon, and had an altar of the Syrian type put in the temple of the Lord (*2 Kings* xvi 9–17).

i *476–506.* Gods 'whose Scriptural authority is not so clear' (Sims 14).

i *477–82.* Cp. the flight of 'the brutish gods of Nile' in *Nativity Ode* 211–28. *wandering gods*] M. alludes to the myth–highly appropriate to this context–of the Olympian gods fleeing from the Giant Typhoeus into Egypt, and hiding in bestial forms (Ovid, *Met.* v 319–31) afterwards worshipped by the Egyptians. *abused*] deceived.

i *482–4.* Perhaps the most familiar of all Israelite apostasies was their worship of 'a calf in Horeb' (*Ps.* cvi 19) made by Aaron while Moses was away receiving the tables of the Law (*Exod.* xxxii). The calf is identified by Fuller as the golden ox image of the Egyptian deity Apis (*Pisgah-Sight* IV vii 20).

i *484–5. rebel king*] Jeroboam, who led the revolt of the ten tribes of Israel against Rehoboam, Solomon's successor; he 'doubled' Aaron's sin, since he made 'two calves of gold', placing one in Bethel and the other in Dan (*1 Kings* xii 28–9).

i *486.* 'Thus they changed their glory into the similitude of an ox that eateth grass' (*Ps.* cvi 20).

i *488–9.* At the passover, Jehovah smote all the Egyptian firstborn, 'both man and beast' (*Exod.* xii 12); presumably this stroke would extend to their sacred animals. Calves could be described as *bleating*, though the main force of the word is in its contemptuousness.

i *490–3.* Of the devils treated at length Belial comes last, both because he

Fell not from heaven, or more gross to love
Vice for itself: to him no temple stood
Or altar smoked; yet who more oft than he
In temples and at altars, when the priest
Turns atheist, as did Ely's sons, who filled
With lust and violence the house of God.
In courts and palaces he also reigns
And in luxurious cities, where the noise
Of riot ascends above their loftiest towers,
And injury and outrage: and when night
Darkens the streets, then wander forth the sons
Of Belial, flown with insolence and wine.
Witness the streets of Sodom, and that night
In Gibeah, when the hospitable door
Exposed a matron to avoid worse rape.
These were the prime in order and in might;
The rest were long to tell, though far renowned,

had no local cult, and because in the poem he is 'timorous and slothful' (ii 117). Properly, 'Belial' is an abstract noun meaning 'iniquity'; though the personification in *2 Cor.* vi 15, and the common Biblical and proverbial phrase 'sons of Belial', encouraged the notion that it was a name. Burton makes Belial prince of the third order of devils, the 'inventors of all mischief' (*Anatomy of Melancholy* I ii 1 ii). Cp. *PR* ii 150–224 where Belial is again portrayed as lustful. Rajan ([2] 35) sees Belial as 'the cavalier type in Puritan eyes–suave, dilettante, dissolute and lacking in courage'.

i *494–6.* The impiety and fornication of *Ely's sons* are described in *1 Sam.* ii 12–24.

i *497–8.* Cp. the similar touch of satire at *PR* ii 183.

i *498–502. flown*] Literally 'swollen, in flood', but in the seventeenth century used metaphorically of people. Cp. James Ussher, *Annals* (1658) vi 250: 'Being somewhat high flowen with wine'.

i *504–5. Gen.* xix helps to account for the *MS* and *Ed I* reading, 'In Gibeah, when hospitable doors / Yielded their matrons to prevent[*MS* avoid] worse rape'. In *Ed II* the allusion is more clearly to Judges xix, where we are told of a Levite lodging in Gibeah, whose concubine was put outside the door and given up to the 'sons of Belial' in order to save him from homosexual rape. She herself was raped to death. Cp. M.'s draft of a tragedy on the burning of Sodom: 'The first Chorus beginning may relate the course of the citty each evening every one with mistresse, or Ganymed, gitterning along the streets, or solacing on the banks of Jordan, or down the stream' (*Trin. MS*; Columbia xviii 234).

i *506–7.* See ll. 381–7*n*.

i *507–21.* Gods, enumerated much more perfunctorily, for whom there is little or no Scriptural authority. The *Ionian* (Greek) people were by some held to be the issue of *Javan* the son of Japhet the son of Noah, on the basis

The Ionian gods, of Javan's issue held
Gods, yet confessed later than Heaven and Earth
Their boasted parents; Titan Heaven's first born
With his enormous brood, and birthright seized
By younger Saturn, he from mightier Jove
His own and Rhea's son like measure found;
So Jove usurping reigned: these first in Creet
And Ida known, thence on the snowy top
Of cold Olympus ruled the middle air
Their highest heaven; or on the Delphian cliff,
Or in Dodona, and through all the bounds
Of Doric land; or who with Saturn old
Fled over Adria to the Hesperian fields,
And o'er the Celtic roamed the utmost isles.
All these and more came flocking; but with looks
Down cast and damp, yet such wherein appeared
Obscure some glimpse of joy, to have found their chief
Not in despair, to have found themselves not lost
In loss itself; which on his countenance cast
Like doubtful hue: but he his wonted pride
Soon recollecting, with high words, that bore

of the Septuagint version of *Gen.* x 1f (also *Is.* lxvi 19). Cp. iv 717 and *SA* 715–6. Hesiod and other ancient authors make *Heaven* (Uranus, Coelus) and *Earth* (Ge, Terra, Thea) the parents of *Saturn* and the other Titans, but the story of *Titan* the eldest child and of his war against *Saturn* (Cronos) is transmitted only by the Christian author Lactantius. Saturn was rescued and enthroned by his son *Jove*, who later banished him, however, so that he had to flee across *Adria* (the Adriatic). *enormous*] monstrous.

i *514–5*. Cp. *Il Penseroso* 29. On Mt *Ida*, in *Creet* (Crete), *Jove* was born and secretly reared.

i *515–6*. 'Snow-capped Olympus' is a Homeric formula (cp. *Il.* i 420, xviii 615). *middle air*] the cold vaporous *media regio*, the second, only, of the three layers into which the Schoolmen divided the atmosphere. See Sylvester's Du Bartas 35, Verity 674–6 and Svendsen 88.

i *517*. *Delphian cliff*] Cp. *Nativity Ode* 178 'steep of Delphos'. Delphi was famed as the site of the Pythian oracle of Apollo, but cults of Ge, Poseidon, and Artemis were also celebrated there.

i *518*. The oracle of Zeus at Dodona in Epirus was thought to be the most ancient in Greece.

i *519–21*. *Doric land* is Greece; *the Hesperian fields* Italy; the *Celtic* fields France; and *the utmost isles* the British Isles (*ultima Thule*: Virgil, *Georg.* i 30), or else Britain, Ireland and Iceland.

i *523*. *damp*] depressed or stupefied; cp. xi 293.

i *528*. recollecting] recovering (*OED* s.v. *Recollect* v.[1]4). Perhaps ironic, in view of the common use of the word in devotional contexts, to mean

Semblance of worth, not substance, gently raised
Their fainting courage, and dispelled their fears.
Then straight commands that at the warlike sound
Of trumpets loud and clarions be upreared
His mighty standard; that proud honour claimed
Azazel as his right, a cherub tall:
Who forthwith from the glittering staff unfurled
The imperial ensign, which full high advanced
Shone like a meteor streaming to the wind
With gems and golden lustre rich imblazed,
Seraphic arms and trophies: all the while
Sonorous metal blowing martial sounds:
At which the universal host upsent

'concentrating the mind in mystical contemplation' (*OED* s.v. *Recollect* v.[2] 4).

i *529.* M. sometimes signposts an obvious moral intention; here this is occasioned, no doubt, by Satan's attractive tenderness towards his troops.

i *530. fainting*] Darbishire prefers *MS* and *Ed I* 'fainted': 'The context supports *fainted*: the collapse is over, their courage is not fainting, it begins to revive.' But 'fainting' could mean 'drooping, feeble'; and is stylistically preferable, in such close proximity to two preterites in *-ed*.

i *531–53.* Eisenstein 58f draws attention to the 'audio-visual distribution of images' in this passage.

i *532. clarions*] shrill narrow-tubed trumpets.

i *533–4. Azazel* figures as one of the chief of the fallen angels who are the object of God's avenging wrath in the apocryphal apocalypse *The Book of Enoch* (see esp. Chs viii, x, xiii, liv, lv, and lxix; Charles ii 192–4, 196, 220–1, 233). For the healing of the earth he is bound and cast into the same wilderness where the scapegoat was led (*Enoch* x 4–8; see also *Lev.* xvi, where the word *azazel* is again associated with the scapegoat). *Enoch* was not directly accessible in the seventeenth century; but cabbalistic tradition made Azazel one of the four standard-bearers in Satan's army. M. could have learned this from Reuchlin or Archangelus of Borgo Nuovo, or Fludd; see West 155f (we need not, however, imitate West's contortions to avoid the natural conclusion, that M. was interested in cabbalistic ideas).

i *537. meteor*] comet; appropriate not only visually, but also because it is ominous to man.

i *538. imblazed*] adorned with heraldic devices.

i *539.* Contrast the 'ensigns high advanced' in heaven, which are emblazoned with 'holy memorials, acts of zeal and love' (v 593; see Rajan 47). The ancient Roman practice in triumphal processions of carrying memorials of battles had been revived in the secular processions of the Renaissance. See, e.g., *The Triumph of Maximilian I*, ed. S. Appelbaum (New York 1964) 10ff.

i *541. upsent*] sent or discharged upwards (first instance in *OED*).

A shout that tore hell's concave, and beyond
Frighted the reign of Chaos and old Night.
All in a moment through the gloom were seen
Ten thousand banners rise into the air
With orient colours waving: with them rose
A forest huge of spears: and thronging helms
Appeared, and serried shields in thick array
Of depth immeasurable: anon they move
In perfect phalanx to the Dorian mood
Of flutes and soft recorders; such as raised
To highth of noblest temper heroes old
Arming to battle, and in stead of rage
Deliberate valour breathed, firm and unmoved
With dread of death to flight or foul retreat,
Nor wanting power to mitigate and swage,

i *542. concave*] A common term for the vault of heaven.

i *543. reign*] realm (*OED* 2; not a Latinism). See ii 894–909 and 959–70, where Chaos and Night are portrayed as rulers of the region of unformed matter between heaven and hell.

i *546. orient*] brilliant, resplendent; also, perhaps, 'rising': on the vertical movement throughout this passage (*raised* 529, *upreared* 532, *high advanced* 536, *upsent* 541, *rise* 545, *rose* 546, *raised* 551), which belong to a repeated pattern of ascents and falls, see Allen 108 and Cope 97–9.

i *550. phalanx*] A square battle formation common in M.'s time. Cp. the 'quadrate' of faithful angels at vi 62; also *Reason of Church-Government* i 6 (Yale i 789): 'as those smaller squares in battell unite in one great cube, the main phalanx, an embleme of truth and stedfastnesse'. On the cube as an iconographical symbol of virtue and stability, see Tervarent cols. 136f; there is a good example in Achille Bocchi's beautiful emblem book *Symbolicae quaestiones* (Bologna 1555). On the meanings of the square and the quadrate (Virtue, Justice, etc.) see Fowler, App. i. Note that at vi 552–5 the devils' square is a deceptive and hollow one.

i *550–61.* A parody of the 'instrumental harmony that breathed / Heroic ardour' into the loyal angels (vi 65–6); though M. allows the devils to use the best *mood* (mode) for encouraging calm and heroic firmness–the Doric mode, contrasted in this respect with the soft and indolent Ionian and Lydian modes, in Plato, *Republic*, iii 398–9. On 'grave and Dorick' music see *Areopagitica* (Yale ii 523) and *Lycidas* 189; and on the assuaging effect of music, *Of Education* (Yale ii 410–1).

i *551–2.* Unlike the Romans, who used trumpets, the Spartans went into battle, as many ancient authors remark, to the sound of flutes. The evocation of noble courage is one of several 'consciously designed to suggest the idea of heroic virtue' in the fallen angels (Steadman 91).

i *555. MS* has semicolon after *retreat.*

i *556. swage*] assuage.

With solemn touches, troubled thoughts, and chase
Anguish and doubt and fear and sorrow and pain
From mortal or immortal minds. Thus they
Breathing united force with fixed thought
Moved on in silence to soft pipes that charmed
Their painful steps o'er the burnt soil; and now
Advanced in view, they stand, a horrid front
Of dreadful length and dazzling arms, in guise
Of warriors old with ordered spear and shield,
Awaiting what command their mighty chief
Had to impose: he through the armed files
Darts his experienced eye, and soon traverse
The whole battalion views, their order due,
Their visages and stature as of gods,
Their number last he sums. And now his heart
Distends with pride, and hardening in his strength
Glories: for never since created man,
Met such embodied force, as named with these
Could merit more than that small infantry
Warred on by cranes: though all the Giant brood

i *560–1.* At vi 64 the loyal angels also 'moved on / In silence'; cp. Homer, *Il.* iii 8: 'The Achaians marched in silence breathing courage.'
i *563. horrid*] bristling (with spears). A poetic word, perhaps felt as a Latinism, though it had been used by Spenser (*F.Q.* I vii 31), Burton (I ii 3 xiv), and Evelyn (27 June 1654).
i *568. traverse*] across.
i *569. MS* has semicolon after *views*, and so has at least one copy of *Ed I*.
i *573. since created man*] since man was created; a Latin construction.
i *574. embodied*] united into one body.
i *575. small infantry*] The Pygmies (see l. 780), whose smallness tradition much exaggerated. The image may have been suggested by Homer's simile (*Il.* iii 5) in the passage M. used for 561. Addison suspected *infantry* to be a pun; probably with justice (*Spectator* No. 297; 9 Feb. 1712). The same pun is perpetrated by Jonson; see *Time Vindicated* 176ff.
i *576–90.* To amplify the heroic stature of the angels, and *a fortiori* of their leader, M. dismisses only to mention a series of armies that had been thought worthy of epic treatment. Successively he evokes the 'matter of Rome the great', the 'matter of Britain' and the 'matter of France'–all pygmy arguments compared with his own.
i *576–7.* See 197–200*n*. Ovid (*Met.* x 151) and Statius (*Theb.* vi 358) and others locate the warfare of the Giants with the Olympian gods on the Phlegraean plains. The combat was supposed to have been begun at Phlegra in Macedonia (Pallene) and renewed at Phlegra in Italy, near Cumae. See 713–7*n* below.

Of Phlegra with the heroic race were joined
That fought at Thebes and Ilium, on each side
Mixed with auxiliar gods; and what resounds
In fable or romance of Uther's son
Begirt with British and Armoric knights;
And all who since, baptized or infidel
Jousted in Aspramont or Montalban,
Damasco, or Marocco, or Trebisond,
Or whom Biserta sent from Afric shore
When Charlemain with all his peerage fell
By Fontarabbia. Thus far these beyond

i *577–9*. Two of the principal ancient epic cycles centred on the strife of the Theban brothers and on the siege of Troy. Conventionally, the gods assisted their mortal protégés in battle–as they do, e.g., in Homer's *Iliad* and Statius' *Thebaid*.

i *579–87*. Omitted by Bentley as 'Romantic Trash'.

i *580–1*. *Uther's son*] King Arthur. M. once projected an Arthurian epic (see *Mans* 81, *Dam* 165–70 and Hanford[2] 179–81); though in *PR* ii 359–61 such fables are represented as a temptation. *Armoric*] from Brittany.

i *582*. The diction is Ariostan; cp. *Orlando Furioso* xviii 56: *Non men de le 'nfedel le battezzate*.

i *583*. *Aspramont*] A castle near Nice. M. may have in mind Andrea da Barberino's popular romance *Aspromonte* (but see also Ariosto, *Orlando Furioso* xvii 14). *Montalban*] The castle of Rinaldo, which figures in Luigi Pulci's *Morgante Maggiore*, Boiardo's *Orlando Innamorato* and Ariosto's *Orlando Furioso*. All these romances are concerned with chivalric wars between Christians and Saracens.

i *584*. Ariosto describes jousting of *baptized* and *infidel* at *Damasco* (Damascus) in *Orlando Furioso* xvii. The splendid Byzantine city of Trebizond was known for its tournaments, both from Bessarion's *Encomion Trapezountos* (fifteenth century) and from Giovanni Ambrosio Marini's widely popular romance, the *Caloandro Fedele* (1640).

i *585*. In *Orlando Innamorato* ii, Boiardo tells how the Saracens gathered at Bizerta in Tunis for their invasion of Spain.

i *586–7*. M. would know late versions of the Charlemagne legend, such as Barberino's *Reali di Francia* (*c*. 1400). Charlemagne's whole rearguard, led by Roland, one of the twelve peers or paladins, was massacred at Roncesvalles, about forty miles from *Fontarabbia* (mod. Fuenterrabia). One Spanish author, Mariana, put the defeat at Fontarabbia itself; but there was no version in which Charlemagne fell. Is it pure coincidence that, when the royalist rising of August 1659 failed, Fuenterrabia was where Charles went, to seek support from both French and Spanish? M. may have seen a symbolic contrast between this treating with friend and foe, and the uncompromising chivalry of the greater Charles.

Compare of mortal prowess, yet observed
Their dread commander: he above the rest
In shape and gesture proudly eminent
Stood like a tower; his form had yet not lost
All her original brightness, nor appeared
Less than archangel ruined, and the excess
Of glory obscured: as when the sun new risen
Looks through the horizontal misty air
Shorn of his beams, or from behind the moon
In dim eclipse disastrous twilight sheds
On half the nations, and with fear of change
Perplexes monarchs. Darkened so, yet shone
Above them all the archangel: but his face
Deep scars of thunder had intrenched, and care
Sat on his faded cheek, but under brows
Of dauntless courage, and considerate pride
Waiting revenge; cruel his eye, but cast
Signs of remorse and passion to behold
The fellows of his crime, the followers rather
(Far other once beheld in bliss) condemned
For ever now to have their lot in pain,
Millions of spirits for his fault amerced
Of heaven, and from eternal splendours flung
For his revolt, yet faithful how they stood,

i *588. observed*] honoured.

i *591.* 'Satan's stature is self-reductive if we recall that, as we earlier found it on the lips of George Fox the Quaker, the "Tower" is a traditional epithet for Christ' (Cope 98, and see 39). 'Good and bad angels have the same Nature. . . . If no good (that is, no being) remained to be perverted, Satan would cease to exist' (Lewis 66).

i *596–9.* The comparison is ironically double-edged; for the ominous solar eclipse presages not only disaster for creation, but also the doom of the Godlike ruler for whom the sun was a traditional symbol. (Thus Charles II's Licenser for the Press is said by Toland (Darbishire[3] x) to have regarded these lines as politically subversive.) See Broadbent[2] 166f, where a parallel is found with the *shorn* Samson; also Svendsen 69f, MacCaffrey 173f and Cope 98f. Cp. the solar eclipse at xi 183f, 203–7, an early sign of the changes produced in nature by man's fall.

i *603. courage*] valour *MS.* Darbishire plausibly suggests that the change was made in the interests of melopoeia–to get in another hard consonant. *considerate*] deliberate.

i *609. amerced*] punished by deprivation. The slightly unusual construction may have been resorted to for the sake of the ambiguity: 'deprived of heaven' and 'punished by God'.

i *611. yet . . . stood*] Goes with 'behold' (l. 605).

Their glory withered. As when heaven's fire
Hath scathed the forest oaks, or mountain pines,
With singed top their stately growth though bare
Stands on the blasted heath. He now prepared
To speak; whereat their doubled ranks they bend
From wing to wing, and half enclose him round
With all his peers: attention held them mute.
Thrice he essayed, and thrice in spite of scorn,
Tears such as angels weep, burst forth: at last
Words interwove with sighs found out their way.
O myriads of immortal spirits, O powers
Matchless, but with the almighty, and that strife
Was not inglorious, though the event was dire,
As this place testifies, and this dire change
Hateful to utter: but what power of mind
Foreseeing or presaging, from the depth
Of knowledge past or present, could have feared,
How such united force of gods, how such
As stood like these, could ever know repulse?
For who can yet believe, though after loss,
That all these puissant legions, whose exile
Hath emptied heaven, shall fail to re-ascend
Self-raised, and repossess their native seat?
For me be witness all the host of heaven,

i *620*. Probably meant to recall the famous tears of the proud Persian King Xerxes, on reflecting that the vast army he was reviewing would some day all be dead; see x 307–11*n* below. The hardening of Satan's heart is not yet complete. There has been a good deal of discussion as to whether the present passage is sublime or matter-of-fact (Davie[2] 81f, Rajan[2] 44). Peter is probably right in thinking that M. means to imply that angels are corporeal and therefore capable of weeping. But the line would nevertheless have had a strong shocking effect. Contrast Marvell, 'Eyes and Tears' 48: 'only humane Eyes can weep'. On the other hand, there was a strong iconographical traditon of angels *mourning*; see, e.g., Réau II ii 491.

i *623–4. almighty*] Satan 'cannot intend the metaphysical sense of the word', because he congratulates his followers on 'having stood against him for a time' (Empson 41). However, the not inglorious strife was hardly with the almighty himself: see vi 423–8*n*. *event*] result.

i *628. MS* has no point after *feared*.

i *632–3*. A rhetorical exaggeration: see ii 692*n*. *exile*] Stressed on the second syllable.

i *634. seat?*] *MS* has no point, *Ed I* full stop.

i *635. MS* and *Ed I* have comma after *me*.

If counsels different, or danger shunned
By me, have lost our hopes. But he who reigns
Monarch in heaven, till then as one secure
Sat on his throne, upheld by old repute,
Consent or custom, and his regal state
Put forth at full, but still his strength concealed,
Which tempted our attempt, and wrought our fall.
Henceforth his might we know, and know our own
So as not either to provoke, or dread
New war, provoked; our better part remains
To work in close design, by fraud or guile
What force effected not: that he no less
At length from us may find, who overcomes
By force, hath overcome but half his foe.
Space may produce new worlds; whereof so rife
There went a fame in heaven that he ere long
Intended to create, and therein plant
A generation, whom his choice regard
Should favour equal to the sons of heaven:
Thither, if but to pry, shall be perhaps
Our first eruption, thither or elsewhere:
For this infernal pit shall never hold
Celestial spirits in bondage, nor the abyss
Long under darkness cover. But these thoughts
Full counsel must mature: peace is despaired,

i *636. different*] differing; see B. A. Wright, *N & Q* cciii (1958) 205. Florence M. Stewart, *N & Q* clxvi (1934) 79, argues for the sense 'procrastinating, deferring'.

i *641–2.* In Empson's arraignment of M.'s God, one of the principal accusations is the one implied in these lines: that Satan was deliberately deceived into thinking that a rebellion might come off (see, e.g., Empson 47). But if God *had* displayed his strength earlier, no doubt that would have been intimidation. The error here lies in accepting Satan's reduction of life to power politics.

i *646. close*] secret.

i *650. Space may produce*] 'The first hint to the reader (not of course to the rebels) of Satan's doubt whether God can really create anything' (Empson 48).

i *651. MS* has comma after *heaven*. For other mentions of the *fame* or rumour, see ii 345–53, 830–5, and x 481–2. Cp. Dryden, *Aeneis* i 27f, where Juno has heard an 'ancient Rumour . . . Long cited by the People of the Sky' that Rome will displace Carthage. Throughout *PL* Rome corresponds to mankind as Carthage to the fallen angels.

i *656. MS* has semicolon after *eruption*.

For who can think submission? War then, war
Open or understood must be resolved.
He spake: and to confirm his words, out flew
Millions of flaming swords, drawn from the thighs
Of mighty cherubim; the sudden blaze
Far round illumined hell; highly they raged
Against the highest, and fierce with grasped arms
Clashed on their sounding shields the din of war,
Hurling defiance toward the vault of heaven.
There stood a hill not far whose grisly top
Belched fire and rolling smoke; the rest entire
Shone with a glossy scurf, undoubted sign
That in his womb was hid metallic ore,
The work of sulphur. Thither winged with speed
A numerous brigade hastened. As when bands
Of pioneers with spade and pickaxe armed
Forerun the royal camp, to trench a field,
Or cast a rampart. Mammon led them on,
Mammon, the least erected spirit that fell

i *661–2.* According to Broadbent 73f Satan began the speech in his tragic hero role, but now in the peroration reverts to 'extraordinary epical crudity'.
i *666–7.* With the play on *highly* (proudly, overbearingly) and *highest*, cp. 642 ('tempted our attempt'), etc. In *PL* such puns often have a sardonic flavour. They were in the fashion of seventeenth-century poetic wit, but were not generally appreciated by M.'s eighteenth-century editors: see Empson[2] 157–9.
i *670–90.* Broadbent 73 suggests that the traditional physiognomy of the fiend is in M.'s hell displaced on to the landscape. And it is a dead or corrupt body imaged as scurf, belching, ransacked womb, bowels, entrails, and ribs (cp. *ibid.* 84f).
i *670–5.* Cp. the mining of the materials of war in vi 507–15.
i *674. sulphur*] Regarded, because of its active nature, as the father of metals; see Caron 161.
i *675. brigade*] Stressed on the first syllable.
i *678.* In *Matt.* vi 24 and *Luke* xvi 13, 'Mammon' is an abstract noun meaning wealth, but later it was used as the name of 'the prince of this world' (*John* xii 31). Medieval and Renaissance tradition often associated Mammon with Plutus, the Greek god of riches, and so, by confusion, with Pluto. M. had a special admiration for Spenser's account of the Cave of Mammon in *F.Q.* II vii, where the god presides, as here, over the mining of gold (see Yale ii 516, also i 719). Burton makes Mammon prince of the lowest order of devils (*Anat. of Mel.* I ii I ii).
i *679–84.* Mammon is the reverse of the Senecan ideal of the astral contemplative, who despised terrestrial things, and 'wandering among the heavens enjoyed laughing at the pavements of the rich' (*divitum pavimenta*);

From heaven, for even in heaven his looks and thoughts
Were always downward bent, admiring more
The riches of heaven's pavement, trodden gold,
Than aught divine or holy else enjoyed
In vision beatific: by him first
Men also, and by his suggestion taught,
Ransacked the centre, and with impious hands
Rifled the bowels of their mother earth
For treasures better hid. Soon had his crew
Opened into the hill a spacious wound
And digged out ribs of gold. Let none admire
That riches grow in hell; that soil may best
Deserve the precious bane. And here let those
Who boast in mortal things, and wondering tell

see John M. Steadman in *N & Q* ccv (1960) 220. With the emphasis on Mammon's limited vision, cp. *Animadversions* (Yale i 697): 'a pearle [cataract] in your eye, Mammons Praestriction'.
i *679. erected*] uplifted.
i *682. gold*] In *Rev.* xxi 21 the street of the City of God is described as 'pure gold'.
i *684. vision beatific*] The Scholastic term for the mystical sight of heaven's glories: the 'Sabbath's sight' that every Christian longed to share with the angels. Cp. iii 61–2, v 613 ('blessed vision'), *Time* 18 ('happy-making sight'), and *Of Reformation* (Yale i 616).
i *684–92.* Ovid, *Met.* i 125–42 is the *locus classicus* for the commonplace that the impious age began when men first delved into the bowels of the earth for the wealth hid amidst 'Stygian shades'; cp. also Spenser, *F.Q.* II vii 17 and Sidney, *Arcadia* (1590), ed. Feuillerat (Cambridge 1939) 135. But M.'s version is nearest, especially in the oxymoron *precious bane*, to Boethius' in *De consolat.* II metre v: 'the anguysschous love of havynge brenneth in folk more cruely than the fyer of the mountaigne of Ethna that ay brenneth [cp. M.'s hill belching smoke, 670f]. Allas! what was he that first dalf up the gobbettes or the weyghtes of gold covered undir erthe and the precyous stones that wolden han be hydd? He dalf up precious periles' (Chaucer's transl.). Cp. vi 470–520. *ribs*] veins of ore (a common usage then), but also carrying on the anatomical image. Empson[2] 175f salutes as 'profound' Pearce's comment that the phrase 'alludes to the formation of Eve viii 463 he *Open'd my Left, and took from thence a Rib:– wide was the wound*' (cp. Ricks 141f). The observation is certainly a sensitive one, and could be shown to be just by tracing Eve's role as universal mother, as well as the connections between this figure and the concept *mother Earth* (687). Nevertheless, the allusion is not necessary to the primary sense of the passage. It main concern is with the aggression underlying the many human activities represented in the devils' mining and land development operation.
i *690. admire*] wonder; not a Latinism.

Of Babel, and the works of Memphian kings
Learn how their greatest monuments of fame,
And strength and art are easily outdone
By spirits reprobate, and in an hour
What in an age they with incessant toil
And hands innumerable scarce perform.
Nigh on the plain in many cells prepared,
That underneath had veins of liquid fire
Sluiced from the lake, a second multitude
With wondrous art founded the massy ore,
Severing each kind, and scummed the bullion dross:
A third as soon had formed within the ground
A various mould, and from the boiling cells
By strange conveyance filled each hollow nook,
As in an organ from one blast of wind
To many a row of pipes the sound-board breathes.
Anon out of the earth a fabric huge

i *694. Babel*] The Tower of Babel, built by the ambitious Nimrod (xii 38–62). The *works of Memphian* (Egyptian) *kings* are probably the Pyramids, which ancient and modern authors alike regarded as memorials of vanity (see Rajan[2] 48).

i *702. Sluiced*] led through sluices.

i *703. founded*] (*MS, Ed I*) melted. Preferable to the easier *Ed II* reading 'found out', though that is defended by B. A. Wright in *TLS*, 9 Aug. 1934, 553. As Darbishire[2] i 289 points out, the 'ribs of gold' have already been discovered and dug out by the first gang.

i *707. MS* has colon after *nook* (as often before comparisons).

i *708–9.* Cp. xi 560ff, where the arts of music and metal-working are again associated, and the skills of the fallen angels rediscovered by man. The connection depends on the fact that Jubal the inventor of music, and his half-brother Tubalcain the inventor of metal-working, were both descendants of Cain (*Gen.* iv). See xi 556–73*n* below.

709. *row of*] hundred *MS*, corr. to 'row of'. *pipes*] pipe *MS*, corr. to 'pipes'.

i *710–2.* Pandaemonium rises to music, as Thebes to the sound of Amphion's lyre, since in the Renaissance it was believed that musical proportions governed the forms of architecture (see Wittkower *passim*). It rises *like an exhalation* because an exhalation can become a meteor or a comet or lightning, and so is ominous for man (Svendsen 87); but also because it 'suggests the insubstantial, elusive, mystifying, the edifice a façade for the ugly discomforts of Hell' (Broadbent 101f). Several scholars have suggested that 'the palace rises like the machinery of a masque–artificial, temporary, illusory' (*ibid.*) In view of ll. 728–30 below, we are probably meant to see the rising of Pandaemonium as a grotesque travesty of the rising of earth out of

Rose like an exhalation, with the sound
Of dulcet symphonies and voices sweet,
Built like a temple, where pilasters round
Were set, and Doric pillars overlaid
With golden architrave; nor did there want
Cornice or frieze, with bossy sculptures graven,
The roof was fretted gold. Not Babilon,

chaos at the Creation. The whole passage should be compared with Marvell's attempt at a similar theme (with Cromwell as Amphion) in *The First Anniversary of the Government under O.C.* (1655) 49–74.
i *712. MS* has colon after *sweet.*
i *713–7.* There is an ironic allusion to Ovid's description of the Palace of the Sun built by Mulciber (*Met.* ii 1–4); but the main point is simply that Pandaemonium has a classical design, complete in every respect, like that of the ancient (but still surviving) gilt-roofed Pantheon, the most admired building of M.'s time. Note that the *pillars,* like the music of l. 550, are Doric. Cp. also l. 682: 'the *roof* of Pandaemonium is made of the same material as the *pavement* of Heaven' (Rajan 47). Marjorie Nicolson suggests in 'Milton's Hell and the Phlegraean Fields', *UTQ* vii (1938) that M. may have had in mind as a model the Forum Vulcani near Naples. The features in common include a volcanic landscape, abundance of pitch and the exploitation of mineral resources. Miss R. W. Smith (*MP* xxix (1931) 187–98) makes the interesting suggestion that Pandaemonium may be modelled on St Peter's at Rome. The pilasters, the carved roof, the gilding, the brazen doors and the adjacent council chamber: all these details fit. Even the bee simile is appropriate, for bees appeared in the arms of the Barberini Pope Urban viii. The *Doric pillars* (l. 714), however, would appear to be an insuperable obstacle to this interpretation. Unless, that is, M.'s allusion extends to Alexander vii, Pope from 1655 to 1667, who was famous for his patronage of Bernini's colonnade in the piazza of St Peter's, the gigantic columns of which are modified Doric. *pilasters*] properly square engaged columns; so that 'pilasters round' may have been felt to have the effect of a momentary oxymoron, until the continuation showed that *round* could be taken as an adverb. Similarly *overlaid / With golden* makes us think of gilding (*OED* s.v. *Overlay* 2) until *architrave* shows that the reference is to the superimposed spanning entablature (*OED* s.v. *Overlay* 1 and perhaps 1 b). The *frieze* is the member of the entablature above the architrave, and the *cornice* is the member above the frieze. *bossy*] projecting in relief. *fretted*] adorned with carved work in decorative, perhaps interlaced, patterns in relief.
i *717–22.* In traditional Biblical exegesis *Babylon,* a place of proud iniquity, was often a figure of Antichrist or of hell (see e.g., Raban Maur, in Migne cxii 872). *Alcairo*] Memphis (modern Cairo), the most splendid city of heathen Egypt. *Belus*] Bel, the Babylonian Baal, whose temple is described by Herodotus; see 421–3*n* and *Jer.* li 44: 'I will punish Bel in Babylon.' *Serapis*] an Egyptian deity, often identified with Apis;

Nor great Alcairo such magnificence
Equalled in all their glories, to enshrine
Belus or Serapis their gods, or seat
Their kings, when Egypt with Assyria strove
In wealth and luxury. The ascending pile
Stood fixed her stately highth, and straight the doors
Opening their brazen folds discover wide
Within, her ample spaces, o'er the smooth
And level pavement: from the arched roof
Pendent by subtle magic many a row
Of starry lamps and blazing cressets fed
With naphtha and asphaltus yielded light
As from a sky. The hasty multitude
Admiring entered, and the work some praise
And some the architect: his hand was known
In heaven by many a towered structure high,
Where sceptred angels held their residence,
And sat as princes, whom the supreme king
Exalted to such power, and gave to rule,
Each in his hierarchy, the orders bright.
Nor was his name unheard or unadored
In ancient Greece; and in Ausonian land

see 482–4*n*. Broadbent (101f) draws attention to the irony underlying the magnificence of Pandaemonium. For M., like George Sandys, regarded the exotic wonders named in this passage as '"barbarous monuments of prodigality and vain-glory". . . . The oriental similes place the building as a citadel of barbaric despotism.'

i *728–9*. The solid pieces of *asphaltus* (asphalt, pitch) would go in the *cressets* or iron baskets, the *naphtha*, an oily constituent of asphalt, in the lamps. For the significance of the choice of this material, see x 296–8 below. Broadbent 102 condemns the devils for the superficiality of this attempt to escape hell by constructing a heaven with lamps that shine *As from a sky*. On chronological grounds this is of course in a sense unfair; for the devils' roof cannot imitate a sky they have never seen. But the moral point may stand: the correspondence is a formal one, non-naturalistic and unmotivated. The printer italicizes *naphtha* and *asphaltus*, either in error or as technical terms.

i *733*. On the rhetorical scheme, see l. 69*n*.

i *735*. *supreme*] Stressed on the first syllable.

i *737*. See ll. 128–9*n*.

i *738–40*. The Greek god Hephaistos, in Latin *Mulciber* or Vulcan, presided over all arts, such as metal-working, that required the use of fire. He built all the palaces of the gods (see ll. 713–7*n*). *Ausonian land*] The old Greek name for Italy.

Men called him Mulciber; and how he fell
From heaven, they fabled, thrown by angry Jove
Sheer o'er the crystal battlements; from morn
To noon he fell, from noon to dewy eve,
A summer's day; and with the setting sun
Dropped from the zenith like a falling star,
On Lemnos the Aegaean isle: thus they relate,
Erring; for he with this rebellious rout
Fell long before; nor aught availed him now
To have built in heaven high towers; nor did he scape
By all his engines, but was headlong sent
With his industrious crew to build in hell.
Mean while the winged heralds by command
Of sovereign power, with awful ceremony
And trumpet's sound throughout the host proclaim
A solemn council forthwith to be held
At Pandaemonium, the high capital
Of Satan and his peers: their summons called
From every band and squared regiment
By place or choice the worthiest; they anon
With hundreds and with thousands trooping came
Attended: all access was thronged, the gates

i *740–8.* Terence Spencer ('John Milton: the Great Rival', *The Listener* lxx (1963) 123f) notes M.'s sophisticated wit in first magnificently emulating Homer's description of the daylong fall of Hephaistos (*Il.* i 591–5), then deflating it in the casual but commanding dismissal of ll. 746–8. The devastating position of *Erring* is possibly in imitation of Lucretius' similar use of *errat* (i 393). Cp. *Elegia VII* 81f; and the academic exercise *Natram non pati senium* 23f, where the story of Vulcan's fall is treated as a myth of cosmic destruction.

i *756.* The name *Pandaemonium* is formed from Gk. *πᾶν*, 'all' and *δαιμόνιον* 'demon, evil spirit' (N.T.); or, more classically, from *δαίμων* with the termination *-ιον* added to mean 'assembly' – cp. *Παναθήναιον*. Hughes compares Henry More's *Pandaemoniothen*, the mundane dominion of the devils, in *Psychozoia* I iii 23. *capital*] *MS* at first 'Capitoll', later corr. in a different hand to 'Capitall'. *Ed I* and *Ed II* have 'Capital'. As Theobald and Darbishire recognize, the original reading had the virtue of precision. The Roman Capitol was a place of assembly for debates of peace or war; while at the level of verbal propriety M.'s 'high capitol' with its roof of 'fretted gold' (l. 717) recalls Virgil's *Capitolia . . . alta* (*Aen.* vi 836) *aurea nunc* (viii 348). But Adams 88 seems right in his view that M. meant this only as a secondary allusion, and that the correct reading is 'capital'.

i *758. squared*] See 550*n.* *band and*] and band *Ed I*, corr. in *Errata.*

i *760. hundreds*] hundreds *MS* and *Ed I*, corr. in *Errata* to 'hunderds'.

And porches wide, but chief the spacious hall
(Though like a covered field, where champions bold
Wont ride in armed, and at the soldan's chair
Defied the best of paynim chivalry
To mortal combat or career with lance)
Thick swarmed, both on the ground and in the air,
Brushed with the hiss of rustling wings. As bees
In spring time, when the sun with Taurus rides,
Pour forth their populous youth about the hive
In clusters; they among fresh dews and flowers
Fly to and fro, or on the smoothed plank,
The suburb of their straw-built citadel,
New rubbed with balm, expatiate and confer
Their state affairs. So thick the airy crowd
Swarmed and were straitened; till the signal given,
Behold a wonder! they but now who seemed

i *763 covered field*] like a field, only covered. Perhaps punning also on French *champ clos* ('closed lists': the area prepared for a duel or judicial combat, as distinct from the ordinary 'listed field' of *SA* 1087). Cp. Dryden, *Aeneis* xii 1034, where Turnus and Aeneas fight in 'clos'd Field'.

i *766*. The two varieties of chivalric encounter, combat *a l'outrance* and the less dangerous exhibition joust. 'Milton makes chivalry almost peculiar to hell, and to earth as hell's satellite' (Broadbent 96).

i *768–75*. In Homer, *Il*. ii 87–90 the Achaians going to a council, in Virgil *Aen*. i 430–6 the busy Carthaginians, are compared to bees. But as the last phrase shows M. also glances at Virgil's mock-epic account of the ideal social organization of the hive (*Georg*. iv 149–227). D. P. Harding notes that at *Georg*. iv 170ff there is a comparison of the bees to labouring Cyclopes at Aetna (*JEGP* lx (1961)). For an elaborate discussion of the simile, with citation of many analogues, see James Whaler in *PMLA* xlvii (1932) 545ff. In the *First Defence* M. found it necessary to rebut Salmasius' argument that the loyalty of bees to their monarchs sets an example to mankind. Miss R. W. Smith notes that the bee was Pope Urban viii's emblem, and that his followers were nicknamed 'bees'; see ll. 713–7*n*. But Urban viii, founder of the new St Peter's, had died in 1644.

i *769. Taurus*] In M.'s time the sun entered the second sign of the zodiac in mid-April, according to the Julian calendar. Perhaps this chronographia is proleptic of the sun's movement from Aries into Taurus after the Fall (x 673).

i *774. expatiate*] walk about at large without restraint, roam (*OED* 1); not a Latinism – the literal sense continued in use until the nineteenth century.

i *777–92*. For the possibility that 'this is another of Milton's mockeries of the falsely epical, all the more convincing than French and Augustan mockery for occurring in a genuine epic', see Broadbent (105f), who cites Voltaire's comment that the metamorphosis 'heightens the ridicule of the whole

In bigness to surpass Earth's giant sons
Now less than smallest dwarfs, in narrow room
Throng numberless, like that pygmean race
Beyond the Indian mount, or faerie elves,
Whose midnight revels, by a forest side
Or fountain some belated peasant sees,
Or dreams he sees, while overhead the moon
Sits arbitress, and nearer to the earth
Wheels her pale course, they on their mirth and dance
Intent, with jocund music charm his ear;
At once with joy and fear his heart rebounds.
Thus incorporeal spirits to smallest forms
Reduced their shapes immense, and were at large,
Though without number still amidst the hall
Of that infernal court. But far within
And in their own dimensions like themselves
The great seraphic lords and cherubim

Contrivance to an unexpressible Degree. Methinks the true Criterion for discerning what is really ridiculous in an *Epick* Poem, is to examine if the same Thing would not fit exactly the Mock Heroick .... no-thing is so adapted to that ludicrous way of writing, as the Metamorphosis of the Devils into Dwarfs' (*Voltaire's Essay on Epic Poetry*, ed. Florence D. White (Albany, N.Y. 1915) 137).

i *778. giant sons*] giant-sons *MS*.

i *780–1.* Cp. 575*n*. Pliny located the land of the Pygmies in the mountains beyond the source of the Ganges (*Nat. hist.* vii 26); and *extra Imaum* (see iii 421 below) was a common phrase on seventeenth-century maps.

i *781–7.* Echoing *Midsummer Night's Dream* II i 28f and 141. *the moon / Sits arbitress* because the moon-goddess was queen of faery: cp. Horace, *Epodes* v 49–52: 'O witnesses (*arbitrae*) not unloyal to my purposes, Night and Diana, who rulest the silence when mystic rites are performed.' On faery mythology in the Renaissance, consult I. E. Rathborne, *The Meaning of Spenser's Fairyland* (New York 1937) and K. M. Briggs, *Pale Hecate's Team* (1962).

i *783–4. sees, / Or dreams he sees*] Alluding to *Aen.* vi 451–4, Virgil's comparison of Dido's shade to the fleeting moon. The function of the simile as a device to magnify the scale of Pandaemonium is discussed in Lewis 41. Rajan[2] 53f compares 573ff above: 'The angels are giants in their potentiality for destruction; they are equally pygmies in the presence of righteousness.'

i *783. MS* has comma after *fountain.*

i *786. MS* has colon after *course.*

i *789–90.* The 'superbly contemptuous pun' is discussed in Ricks 15.

In close recess and secret conclave sat
A thousand demi-gods on golden seats,
Frequent and full. After short silence then
And summons read, the great consult began.

THE END OF THE FIRST BOOK

Paradise Lost

BOOK II

The Argument

The consultation begun, Satan debates whether another battle be to be hazarded for the recovery of heaven: some advise it, others dissuade: a third proposal is preferred, mentioned before by Satan, to search the truth of that prophecy or tradition in heaven concerning another world, and another kind of creature equal or not much inferior to themselves, about this time to be created: their doubt who shall[1] be sent on this difficult search: Satan their chief undertakes alone the voyage, is honoured and applauded. The council thus ended, the rest betake them several ways and to several employments, as their inclinations lead them, to entertain the time till Satan return. He passes on his journey to hell gates, finds them shut, and who sat there to guard them, by whom at length they are opened, and discover to him the great gulf between hell and heaven, with what difficulty he passes through, directed by Chaos, the power of that place, to the sight of this new world which he sought.

High on a throne of a royal state, which far
Outshone the wealth of Ormus and of Ind,

i *795. close*] secret. *conclave*] Could refer to any assembly in secret session, but had already the specifically ecclesiastical meaning on which M.'s satire here depends.

i *797. Frequent*] crowded; not a Latinism. The phrase used here, *Frequent and full*, was particularly idiomatic; see *OED* s.v. *Frequent* 1 for examples.

i *798. consult*] consultation.

ii *Argument[1] shall*] should *Ed I, 1669 issue.*

ii *1–4.* Cp. Spenser's description of the bright throne of the Phaethon-like Lucifera, embodiment of pride: 'High above all a cloth of State was spred, / And a rich throne, as bright as sunny day' (*F.Q.* I iv 8). Satan has already been portrayed as an eastern tyrant at i 348.

Or where the gorgeous East with richest hand
Showers on her kings barbaric pearl and gold,
Satan exalted sat, by merit raised
To that bad eminence; and from despair
Thus high uplifted beyond hope, aspires
Beyond thus high, insatiate to pursue
Vain war with heaven, and by success untaught
His proud imaginations thus displayed,
   Powers and dominions, deities of heaven,
For since no deep within her gulf can hold
Immortal vigour, though oppressed and fallen,
I give not heaven for lost. From this descent
Celestial virtues rising, will appear
More glorious and more dread than from no fall,
And trust themselves to fear no second fate:
Me though just right, and the fixed laws of heaven
Did first create your leader, next free choice,
With what besides, in counsel or in fight,
Hath been achieved of merit, yet this loss
Thus far at least recovered, hath much more
Established in a safe unenvied throne
Yielded with full consent. The happier state

ii *2. Ormus* (modern Ormuz), an island town in the Persian gulf, was famous as a jewel market.
ii *3. gorgeous east*] Cp. Shakespeare's account of a different sort of idolatry, in *Love's Labour's Lost* IV iii 218ff: 'Who sees the heavenly Rosaline, / That, like a rude and savage man of Inde, / At the first opening of the gorgeous east, / Bows not his vassal head, and strooken blind, / Kisses the base ground with obedient breast?'
ii *4. barbaric*] Italicized as a proper name in the early edns, perhaps through confusion with 'Barbarian' (= native of Barbary). Cp. Virgil, *Aen.* ii 504: *barbarico postes auro spoliisque superbi.* Also Euripides, *Iph. in Aul.* 74, where Paris' clothing is described as 'gleaming with gold, barbaric bravery'.
ii 5. Cp. 20f. On Satan's eminence through *merit*, see i 98*n* and vi 820*n*. There is an implicit parallel and contrast with the Messiah's throne (vi (758–72), to which he too is exalted by merit (vi 43).
ii *9. success*] the result. So in l. 123; the modern sense is commoner in the later books and in *PR*.
ii *11. powers and dominions*] Two of the angelic orders mentioned by St Paul in *Col.* i 16; see i 128–9*n*. On the description of angels as 'gods' or *deities*, see i 116–7*n*.
ii *14–16.* In 'a kind of parody of the *felix culpa*', Satan's words 'describe what happens to man, but only through God's grace' (MacCaffrey 65).
ii *15. virtues*] Perhaps a pun, in that the virtues are another of the angelic orders.

In heaven, which follows dignity, might draw
Envy from each inferior; but who here
Will envy whom the highest place exposes
Foremost to stand against the thunderer's aim
Your bulwark, and condemns to greatest share
Of endless pain? Where there is then no good
For which to strive, no strife can grow up there
From faction; for none sure will claim in hell
Precedence, none, whose portion is so small
Of present pain, that with ambitious mind
Will covet more. With this advantage then
To union, and firm faith, and firm accord,
More than can be in heaven, we now return
To claim our just inheritance of old,
Surer to prosper than prosperity
Could have assured us; and by what best way,
Whether of open war or covert guile,
We now debate: who can advise, may speak.
He ceased, and next him Moloc, sceptred king
Stood up, the strongest and the fiercest spirit
That fought in heaven; now fiercer by despair:
His trust was with the eternal to be deemed
Equal in strength, and rather than be less
Cared not to be at all; with that care lost
Went all his fear: of God, or hell, or worse
He recked not, and these words thereafter spake.
My sentence is for open war: of wiles,
More unexpert, I boast not: them let those
Contrive who need, or when they need, not now.
For while they sit contriving, shall the rest,

ii *28. thunderer's*] Cp. i 93, and see i 122*n* and i 258*n*. By identifying him with thunder, the attribute of Jupiter, Satan reduces God to a mere Olympian tyrant.
ii *30–8*. Empson 48 finds it a noble paradox in the high Roman manner that Satan should praise the benefits of hell. While this is no doubt part of the meaning, the desperate irrationality seems also a symptom of self-delusion: note, e.g., how 32f is belied by ll. 471–3 below.
ii *43*. On *Moloc*, see i 392*n* and vi 357ff. *sceptred*] in the Homeric councils, kings are described formulaically as 'sceptred'; see *Il.* ii 86, *Od.* ii 231.
ii *50. thereafter*] accordingly.
ii *51. sentence*] opinion.
ii *52–6*. Eliot and Leavis find an inconsistency between *millions . . . stand* and *sit lingering*; not noticing that *stand* is present, *sit* future. Moloch is being contemptuous: 'the superb upward thrust of *sit, stand, ascend* is razed by the deliberate bathos of *sit* again' (Ricks 13). *unexpert*] inexperienced.

Millions that stand in arms, and longing wait
The signal to ascend, sit lingering here
Heaven's fugitives, and for their dwelling place
Accept this dark opprobrious den of shame,
The prison of his tyranny who reigns
By our delay? No, let us rather choose
Armed with hell flames and fury all at once
O'er heaven's high towers to force resistless way,
Turning our tortures into horrid arms
Against the torturer; when to meet the noise
Of his almighty engine he shall hear
Infernal thunder, and for lightning see
Black fire and horror shot with equal rage
Among his angels; and his throne itself
Mixed with Tartarean sulphur, and strange fire,
His own invented torments. But perhaps
The way seems difficult and steep to scale
With upright wing against a higher foe.
Let such bethink them, if the sleepy drench
Of that forgetful lake benumb not still,
That in our proper motion we ascend
Up to our native seat: descent and fall
To us is adverse. Who but felt of late
When the fierce foe hung on our broken rear
Insulting, and pursued us through the deep,
With what compulsion and laborious flight
We sunk thus low? The ascent is easy then;

ii *61. hell flames and fury*] The violent yoking of concrete and abstract words (a kind of zeugma) is one of the most characteristic figures of M.'s style; cp. l. 67.
ii *65. engine*] machine of war. Used at vi 484, 586 of artillery, but probably here referring to the Messiah's chariot with its 'whirlwind sound' (vi 749), or perhaps to his thunder (vi 764).
ii *69.* In the Renaissance manner, M. identifies the Christian hell with the classical underworld, in which Tartarus was the place of the guilty. *strange fire*] Cp. *Lev.* x 1–2: 'Nadab and Abihu, the sons of Aaron ... offered strange fire before the Lord, which he commanded them not. And there went out fire from the Lord, and devoured them.'
ii *73–4.* See note on the 'oblivious pool' of i 266. *drench*] 'soporific drink'; though Moloch may also intend the bad half-pun (*drench*, verb= soak).
ii *79. Insulting*] Both 'making assaults' and 'exulting'.
ii *81. ascent is easy*] Given the lie through the allusion to Virgil, *Aen.* vi 126–9: *facilis descensus Averno: / ... / sed revocare gradum superasque evadere ad*

The event is feared; should we again provoke
Our stronger, some worse way his wrath may find
To our destruction: if there be in hell
Fear to be worse destroyed: what can be worse
Than to dwell here, driven out from bliss, condemned
In this abhorred deep to utter woe;
Where pain of unextinguishable fire
Must exercise us without hope of end
The vassals of his anger, when the scourge
Inexorably, and the torturing hour
Call us to penance? More destroyed than thus
We should be quite abolished and expire.
What fear we then? what doubt we to incense
His utmost ire? which to the highth enraged,
Will either quite consume us, and reduce
To nothing this essential, happier far
Than miserable to have eternal being:
Or if our substance be indeed divine,
And cannot cease to be, we are at worst
On this side nothing; and by proof we feel
Our power sufficient to disturb his heaven,
And with perpetual inroads to alarm,
Though inaccessible, his fatal throne:
Which if not victory is yet revenge.
   He ended frowning, and his look denounced
Desperate revenge, and battle dangerous
To less than gods. On the other side up rose

auras, / hoc opus, hic labor est (B. A. Wright in *N & Q* cciii (1958) 208f). See i 633 and vi 856–77.

ii *82. event*] outcome.

ii *87. utter*] Primarily 'extreme; out-and-out' (*OED* a. II 4); but also indicating the verb, 'express' (*OED* v.[1] II 6 b), and perhaps even the word *outer*, as in i 72 above.

ii *89. exercise*] subject to ascetic discipline; afflict (*OED* 3 and 4 b); not a Latinism nor (as Highet and Rajan maintain) an un-English use of the word.

ii *90. vassals*] slaves; cp. Spenser, *Tears of the Muses* 126: 'vassals of Gods wrath, and slaves of sin'. But there is also a half-suppressed allusion to *Rom.* ix 22: 'What if God, willing to shew his wrath, and to make his power known, endured with much longsuffering the vessels of wrath fitted to destruction . . . ?'

ii *97. essential*] essence (adj. for noun).

ii *100–1.* i.e., already we are in the worst condition possible, short of being nothing, being annihilated. *proof*] practical experience.

ii *104. fatal*] Both 'destructive' and 'destined'; see i 116–7*n*.

Belial, in act more graceful and humane;
A fairer person lost not heaven; he seemed
For dignity composed and high exploit:
But all was false and hollow; though his tongue
Dropt manna, and could make the worse appear
The better reason, to perplex and dash
Maturest counsels: for his thoughts were low;
To vice industrious, but to nobler deeds
Timorous and slothful, yet he pleased the ear,
And with persuasive accent thus began.
I should be much for open war, O peers,
As not behind in hate; if what was urged
Main reason to persuade immediate war,
Did not dissuade me most, and seem to cast
Ominous conjecture on the whole success:
When he who most excels in fact of arms,
In what he counsels and in what excels
Mistrustful, grounds his courage on despair
And utter dissolution, as the scope
Of all his aim, after some dire revenge.
First, what revenge? The towers of heaven are filled
With armed watch, that render all access

ii *109–17. Belial*] See i 490*n* and, for his witty jests during the war in heaven, vi 620–7. Starting, perhaps, from the tradition transmitted by Reginald Scot (*The discoverie of witchcraft* (1584) xv 2: 'This Beliall . . . taketh the forme of a beautifull angell . . . he speaketh faire'), M. has constructed a 'character' in the seventeenth-century Theophrastian manner. See E. E. Stoll, 'Belial as an Example', *MLN* xlviii (1933) 419–27. *humane*] courteous, elegant.
ii *110–18.* Fletcher[2] 263 attempts to relate Belial's dialectically brilliant but empty speech to the travesties of disputation delivered by the Prevaricators at Cambridge Commencements. The relationship is not, however, very close. Empson 52 characterises Belial as a sober lawyer, in spite of the explicit warning in the present lines, which should have saved him from being gulled by appearances. M. is satirising the 'hollow', yet persuasively negative, reactionary. But l. 113f presents something of a problem: By what criterion, exactly, are Belial's reasons here *worse*?
ii *113–4. make . . . reason*] This was the claim of the Greek Sophists, and one of the charges against Socrates (Plato, *Apology* 18 B). *reason*] argument.
ii *124. fact*] feat, deed.
ii *127. scope*] target.
ii *129.* Not only does Belial answer Moloch point by point, but he even takes up particular phrases, as here (cp. l. 62). For the opposition of Belial and Moloch M. had a model in the contrast between two Saracen ambassadors, the smooth rhetorician Aletes and the fierce Argantes, in Tasso, *Gerus. Lib.* ii 58–90.

Impregnable; oft on the bordering deep
Encamp their legions, or with obscure wing
Scout far and wide into the realm of night,
Scorning surprise. Or could we break our way
By force, and at our heels all hell should rise
With blackest insurrection, to confound
Heaven's purest light, yet our great enemy,
All incorruptible would on his throne
Sit unpolluted, and the ethereal mould
Incapable of stain would soon expel
Her mischief, and purge off the baser fire
Victorious. Thus repulsed, our final hope
Is flat despair: we must exasperate
The almighty victor to spend all his rage,
And that must end us, that must be our cure,
To be no more; sad cure; for who would lose,
Though full of pain, this intellectual being,
Those thoughts that wander through eternity,
To perish rather, swallowed up and lost
In the wide womb of uncreated night,
Devoid of sense and motion? and who knows,
Let this be good, whether our angry foe
Can give it, or will ever? How he can
Is doubtful; that he never will is sure.
Will he, so wise, let loose at once his ire,

ii *132. obscure*] Stressed on the first syllable.

ii *138–42.* Criticising Moloch's proposal to mix God's throne with sulphur (ll. 68–9) and shoot 'black fire' among his angels. This *baser fire* Belial contrasts with the *ethereal* fire of the throne, or perhaps of the angels (whose substance is called 'empyreal' at i 177). See *Dan.* vii 9: 'his throne was like the fiery flame' and *Ps.* civ 4: 'Who maketh his angels spirits; his ministers a flaming fire'. God, who is also a 'consuming fire' (*Deut.* iv 24) is described as 'incorruptible' in the *De doctrina* (Columbia xiv 47), on the basis of *Rom.* i 23.

ii *143. flat*] absolute; coloured perhaps by the meaning 'dull'.

ii *146–51.* Cp. Claudio's fear that death will make 'this sensible warm motion to become / A kneaded clod' (*Measure for Measure* III i 120f). Several Senecan passages describe the soul's power to range through heaven: see *De consolat.* xi 4f, and cp. i 679–84*n* above. *wander*] Something of a key word in *PL* (see, e.g., i 365, xi 779, xii 648), often subsidiarily implies 'err' (cp. Latin *erro*). So in *Areopagitica* (Yale ii 527f): 'God . . . gives us minds that wander beyond all limit and satiety.' Belial is sensitive and intellectual; but the idea that he is like M. himself should be scouted.

Belike through impotence, or unaware,
To give his enemies their wish, and end
Them in his anger, whom his anger saves
To punish endless? Wherefore cease we then?
Say they who counsel war, we are decreed,
Reserved and destined to eternal woe;
Whatever doing, what can we suffer more,
What can we suffer worse? Is this then worst,
Thus sitting, thus consulting, thus in arms?
What when we fled amain, pursued and struck
With heaven's afflicting thunder, and besought
The deep to shelter us? This hell then seemed
A refuge from those wounds: or when we lay
Chained on the burning lake? That sure was worse.
What if the breath that kindled those grim fires
Awaked should blow them into sevenfold rage
And plunge us in the flames? or from above
Should intermitted vengeance arm again
His red right hand to plague us? what if all

ii *156. Belike*] no doubt. *impotence*] weakness of mind, lack of restraint, passion.
ii *159–61.* The endlessness of the devils' punishments was a commonplace. See, e.g., Sir T. Browne, *Christian Morals* ii 13 'evil Spirits, as undying Substances, are unseparable from their calamities . . . bound up with immortality can never get out of themselves' and *Religio medici* i 51; also *De doctrina* i 9 (Columbia xv 107) 'The evil angels are reserved for punishment.'
ii *160. they who*] Belial prefers to couch his reference to Moloch in a courteously impersonal form.
ii *165. What when*] 'What about when . . .' *amain*] at full speed. *struck*] M.'s spelling 'strook' records a common seventeenth-century form and the pronunciation he probably preferred; see the rhyme with 'took' at *Nativity Ode* 95.
ii *166. afflicting*] striking down.
ii *168–9.* See i 48*n* and 209–13*n*.
ii *170–86.* On the relentlessness with which Belial's argument drives on to a deliberately delayed conclusion, see Ricks 30.
ii *170.* Cp. *Is.* xxx 33: 'Tophet is ordained of old . . . the pile thereof is fire and much wood; the breath of the Lord, like a stream of brimstone, doth kindle it.' For Tophet as a type of hell, see i 403–5*n*.
ii *174–84.* Corresponding in general to classical accounts of the fate of the Giants, expecially Typhon: see i 197–200*n*, and Aeschylus, *Prometheus vinctus* 353–68.
ii *174. red right hand*] Horace, *Odes* I ii 1–4, recalling the horrors of civil war writes: 'Enough . . . hath the Father smiting with the bolt from his red right hand (*rubente dextera*) . . . struck panic into Rome'.

Her stores were opened, and this firmament
Of hell should spout her cataracts of fire,
Impendent horrors, threatening hideous fall
One day upon our heads; while we perhaps
Designing or exhorting glorious war,
Caught in a fiery tempest shall be hurled
Each on his rock transfixed, the sport and prey
Of racking whirlwinds, or for ever sunk
Under yon boiling ocean, wrapped in chains;
There to converse with everlasting groans,
Unrespited, unpitied, unreprieved,
Ages of hopeless end; this would be worse.
War therefore, open or concealed, alike
My voice dissuades; for what can force or guile
With him, or who deceive his mind, whose eye
Views all things at one view? He from heaven's highth
All these our motions vain, sees and derides;

ii *176. cataracts*] Perhaps here 'flood-gates', the sense in which *cataractae* is used in Vulgate *Gen.* vii 11–as in Tremellius' Protestant version–in the account of the Flood: Cp. *King Lear* III ii 2: 'You cataracts and hurricanoes, spout.'

ii *180–1.* Cp. Virgil, *Aen.* i 44f: to punish the frenzy of Ajax, Pallas 'caught him in a whirlwind and impaled him on a spiky crag'.

ii *181–2.* Cp. the sufferings of the dead in Virgil, *Aen.* vi 740f: 'hung stretched out to the empty winds'; and in *Measure for Measure* III i 124: 'imprisoned in the viewless winds'. *racking*] both 'torturing' and 'driving'.

ii *184. converse with*] A pun ('dwell with' and 'talk by means of').

ii *185.* M. is fond of this scheme, in which asyndeton (omission of grammatical connections) is combined with similarity or sameness of prefix; cp. iii 231, v 899 and *SA* 1422. He could have learned it from the Greek tragedians (e.g. Sophocles, *Antigone* 1071); from Spenser (*F.Q.* VII vii 46: 'Unbodied, unsoul'd, unheard, unseen'); or from Shakespeare (*Hamlet* I v 77: 'Unhousel'd, disappointed, unanel'd').

ii *187.* Exactly opposed to the conclusion of Satan's earlier speech, i 661–2.

ii *188–90.* Cp. *De doctrina* (Columbia xiv 57): 'So extensive is the prescience of God, that he knows beforehand the thoughts and actions of free agents as yet unborn, and many ages before those thoughts or actions have their origin.' Satan at least seems not to have believed God to be omniscient before the rebellion (see esp. v 682f); but perhaps the devils have been convinced by recent events (Empson 51f). On the synoptic character of the creator's vision, see iii *77n.*

ii *190–1. Ps.* ii 4: 'He that sitteth in the heavens shall laugh: the Lord shall have them in derision.' M. did not believe in a detached impassible God, but in one who displays a whole range of emotions. See *De doctrina* (Columbia xiv 33–5) and Kelley 194. *motions*] schemes.

Not more almighty to resist our might
Than wise to frustrate all our plots and wiles.
Shall we then live thus vile, the race of heaven
Thus trampled, thus expelled to suffer here
Chains and these torments? Better these than worse
By my advice; since fate inevitable
Subdues us, and omnipotent decree,
The victor's will. To suffer, as to do,
Our strength is equal, nor the law unjust
That so ordains: this was at first resolved,
If we were wise, against so great a foe
Contending, and so doubtful what might fall.
I laugh, when those who at the spear are bold
And venturous, if that fail them, shrink and fear
What yet they know must follow, to endure
Exile, or ignominy, or bonds, or pain,
The sentence of their conqueror: this is now
Our doom; which if we can sustain and bear,
Our supreme foe in time may much remit
His anger, and perhaps thus far removed,
Not mind us not offending, satisfied
With what is punished; whence these raging fires
Will slacken, if his breath stir not their flames.
Our purer essence then will overcome
Their noxious vapour, or enured not feel,

ii *199*. *To suffer, as to do*] The affirmation of Mucius Scaevola; see i 158*n*.

ii *200*. *law*] Not necessarily admitting that God's law is just: 'drawing as usual upon the classics for the thoughts of devils, Milton has him say that they have been defeated by . . . some kind of law of Nature which may be prior to God' (Empson 51). But perhaps the timorous Belial, fearing renewal of the pains of the fall (cp. Lewis 102), and really believing that he is overheard by God (189f), is unwilling to commit himself. He would like to trim a safe course between good and evil.

ii *207*. *ignominy*] Fcr pronunciation see i 115*n*.

ii *210*. *supreme*] Often stressed on the first syllable, as here probably.

ii *211*. See i 73–4*n*.

ii *213–6*. St Augustine, *Civ. Dei* xxi 10, explains how devils suffer the everlasting fire–either through passible aery bodies, or through natures specially adapted so that they can feel pain without being destroyed.

ii *215–6*. Empson 51 argues that Belial's description of the incorruptibility of the rebel angels and of God and the good angels (ii 138–41) by the same chemical metaphors means that he thinks of them as two comparable groups who 'should arrange co-existence'. But Belial only says that the devils' essence will overcome the vapour if God ceases to stir the flames, i.e., their incorruptibility is dependent on his will.

Or changed at length, and to the place conformed
In temper and in nature, will receive
Familiar the fierce heat, and void of pain;
This horror will grow mild, this darkness light,
Besides what hope the never-ending flight
Of future days may bring, what chance, what change
Worth waiting, since our present lot appears
For happy though but ill, for ill not worst,
If we procure not to ourselves more woe.
Thus Belial with words clothed in reason's garb
Counselled ignoble ease, and peaceful sloth,
Not peace: and after him thus Mammon spake.
Either to disenthrone the king of heaven
We war, if war be best, or to regain
Our own right lost: him to unthrone we then
May hope when everlasting fate shall yield
To fickle chance, and Chaos judge the strife:

ii *217–9*. A point taken up by Mammon at ll. 274–8. *temper*] temperament, the mixture or adjustment of humours. Thus the phrase means 'adjusted psychologically and physically to the new environment'.
ii *220*. *light*] 'easy to bear', and 'illumination'. Bentley argued that only the first sense can apply, in view of the parallelism between *horror . . . mild* and *darkness* (in a moderate degree). But 'both . . . senses are present, and the combination allows Belial to suggest high hopes without obvious absurdity' (Empson[2] 159). If *light* is taken as 'luminous', the effect is oxymoron rather than hyperbole. Note the rhyme between l. 220 and l. 221 – perhaps meant as a suitably jingling accompaniment to Belial's cheerful fantasy. The absurdity of the stoicism is far from obvious: I think we are meant to recognize not only the irrationality and self-contradiction of Belial's wish but also the fact that in a grim sense it has already been granted (cp. the 'darkness visible' of i 63).
ii *221*. *never-ending*] Compound adjectives are rare in *PL*; see Emma 70f.
ii *224*. *for happy*] as far as happiness is concerned.
ii *226*. Cp. *Comus* 759: 'false rules pranked in reason's garb'.
ii *228*. *Mammon's* character has been given at i 678–84.
ii *232–3*. Both Bentley's interpretation (strife between *fate* and *chance*) and Pearce's (strife between *the king of heaven* and the devils) are possible, but the former is preferable. If providence – which the devils call fate – yielded to chance, the result would be chaotic; so that the adjudication is appropriately by *Chaos*. There may also be an allusion to the Empedoclean notion of a universal Strife. M.'s devils on the whole concede more than Tasso's Satan, who claims to have been overthrown only by chance (*Gerus. Lib.* iv 15); see 551, i 116–7*n*, 133, and 144*n*. *Ed I* has comma after *hope*. The early edns give *Chaos* italics and initial capital, but *fate* and *chance* an initial capital only.

The former vain to hope argues as vain
The latter: for what place can be for us
Within heaven's bound, unless heaven's lord supreme
We overpower? Suppose he should relent
And publish grace to all, on promise made
Of new subjection; with what eyes could we
Stand in his presence humble, and receive
Strict laws imposed, to celebrate his throne
With warbled hymns, and to his Godhead sing
Forced hallelujahs; while he lordly sits
Our envied sovereign, and his altar breathes
Ambrosial odours and ambrosial flowers,
Our servile offerings? This must be our task
In heaven, this our delight; how wearisome
Eternity so spent in worship paid
To whom we hate. Let us not then pursue
By force impossible, by leave obtained
Unacceptable, though in heaven, our state
Of splendid vassalage, but rather seek
Our own good from ourselves, and from our own
Live to ourselves, though in this vast recess,
Free, and to none accountable, preferring

ii *243*. The word *hallelujah* (Heb. 'praise Jehovah') occurred in so many psalms that it came to mean a song of praise to God. Cp. and contrast vi 744, where Messiah promises that once the rebellious angels are expelled, the remnant will sing 'unfeigned hallelujahs'.

ii *245*. *Ambrosial*] fragrant and perfumed; immortal. Ambrosia was the fabled food, or drink, of the gods. It was, however, also identified by the herbalist with certain specific plants: see, e.g., Gerard, *Herball* (1597) p. 950: 'The fragrant smell that this kinde of *Ambrosia* or Oke of Cappadocia [sometimes 'Oak of Jerusalem'] yeeldeth, hath mooved the Poets to suppose that this herbe was meate and foode for the gods.'

ii *247*. *Ed II*, probably wrongly, omits comma after *heaven*.

ii *249*. *pursue*] seek to attain to. The interposition of the compressed phrases floating between the verb and its distant object *state* (e.g., either 'pursue by force' or 'pursue what is by force impossible to obtain') may be meant to mime the difficulty of access.

ii *254*. *Live to ourselves*] Echoing Horace's isolationist resolve 'let me live to myself for what remains of life' (*Epodes* I xviii 107f), but omitting the sober continuation 'if the gods will that anything remain'.

ii *255–7*. In *SA* 271 Samson condemns those who are fonder of 'bondage with ease than strenuous liberty'. The antithesis is from M.'s favourite Roman historian, Sallust, who puts it in the mouth of Aemilius Lepidus, an opponent of the dictator Sulla. But cp. also Jesus' words in *Matt.* xi 28–30: 'Come unto me. . . . For my yoke is easy.'

Hard liberty before the easy yoke
Of servile pomp. Our greatness will appear
Then most conspicuous, when great things of small,
Useful of hurtful, prosperous of adverse
We can create, and in what place so e'er
Thrive under evil, and work ease out of pain
Through labour and endurance. This deep world
Of darkness do we dread? How oft amidst
Thick clouds and dark doth heaven's all-ruling sire
Choose to reside, his glory unobscured,
And with the majesty of darkness round
Covers his throne; from whence deep thunders roar
Mustering their rage, and heaven resembles hell?
As he our darkness, cannot we his light
Imitate when we please? This desert soil
Wants not her hidden lustre, gems and gold;
Nor want we skill or art, from whence to raise
Magnificence; and what can heaven show more?
Our torments also may in length of time
Become our elements, these piercing fires
As soft as now severe, our temper changed
Into their temper; which must needs remove

ii *258–61*. Explicitly here, implicitly in ll. 252–7 and elsewhere, Mammon keeps up a juxtaposition of contraries which indicates his confused values and his hopes of an impossible compromise. Both Adam (xii 561–9) and Mammon recognize that if great things are to be accomplished from small beginnings, patience is needed. But to this Adam joins obedience, Mammon *liberty* (l. 256); see Mindele C. Treip, *N& Q* cciii (1958) 209f.

ii *264–5*. Ironically, the words come from 'unfeigned hallelujahs', *Ps.* xviii 11–13, 'He made darkness his secret place; his pavilion round about him were dark waters and thick clouds of the skies. . . . The Lord also thundered in the heavens', and xcvii 2, 'Clouds and darkness are round about him: righteousness and judgment are the habitation of his throne'. Cp. also 2 *Chron.* v 13–vi 1.

ii *275*. Possibly referring to the belief that the fallen angels inhabit one or another of the four *elements*: 'being dispersed, some in the air, some on the earth, some in the water, some amongst the minerals, dens, and caves, that are under the earth' (Hooker, *Laws of Eccles. Pol.* I iv 3; cp. *Il Penseroso* 93–6: 'Daemons that are found / In fire, air, flood, or under ground' and have a 'true consent . . . with element'). But the point of the line more probably lies in the allusion (M.'s not Mammon's) to an idea of St Augustine's, that the devils are bound to tormenting fires as if to bodies (*Civ. Dei* xxi 10).

The sensible of pain. All things invite
To peaceful counsels, and the settled state
Of order, how in safety best we may
Compose our present evils, with regard
Of what we are and where, dismissing quite
All thoughts of war: ye have what I advise.
He scarce had finished, when such murmur filled
The assembly, as when hollow rocks retain
The sound of blustering winds, which all night long
Had roused the sea, now with hoarse cadence lull
Seafaring men o'erwatched, whose bark by chance
Or pinnace anchors in a craggy bay
After the tempest: such applause was heard
As Mammon ended, and his sentence pleased,
Advising peace: for such another field
They dreaded worse than hell: so much the fear
Of thunder and the sword of Michael
Wrought still within them; and no less desire
To found this nether empire, which might rise
By policy, and long process of time,
In emulation opposite to heaven.
Which when Beelzebub perceived, than whom,
Satan except, none higher sat, with grave
Aspect he rose, and in his rising seemed
A pillar of state; deep on his front engraven
Deliberation sat and public care;
And princely counsel in his face yet shone,

ii *278. The sensible of pain*] the part of pain apprehended through the senses; see J. C. Maxwell in *RES*, n.s., v (1954) 268.

ii *281. Compose*] order, adjust.

ii *282. where*] *Ed I.* Since Mammon is exhorting the devils to accept and to exploit their present situation, *Ed II* 'were', which would make him direct their attention elsewhere, is obviously an error.

ii *291. sentence*] opinion.

ii *294.* In the war in Heaven, Michael's two-handed sword felled 'squadrons at once' and wounded even Satan (see vi 250ff and 320ff). *Michael* is here a trisyllable; cp. vi 411, but contrast xi 453.

ii *297. policy*] statesmanship; often in a bad sense, implying Machiavellian strategems. The earlier history of the word is traced in M. Praz, 'Machiavelli and the Elizabethans', *Proc. of the Brit. Acad.* xiii (1928) *process*] stressed on the second syllable.

ii *299. Beelzebub*] Satan's closest associate; see i 81*n* and v 671*n*.

ii *301. Aspect*] Stressed on the second syllable.

ii *302. front*] forehead (*OED* I 1) or face (*OED* I 2). Neither sense would have been felt as a Latinism.

Majestic though in ruin: sage he stood
With Atlantean shoulders fit to bear
The weight of mightiest monarchies; his look
Drew audience and attention still as night
Or summer's noontide air, while thus he spake.
   Thrones and imperial powers, offspring of heaven
Ethereal virtues; or these titles now
Must we renounce, and changing style be called
Princes of hell? For so the popular vote
Inclines, here to continue, and build up here
A growing empire; doubtless; while we dream,
And know not that the king of heaven hath doomed
This place our dungeon, not our safe retreat
Beyond his potent arm, to live exempt
From heaven's high jurisdiction, in new league
Banded against his throne, but to remain
In strictest bondage, though thus far removed,
Under the inevitable curb, reserved
His captive multitude: for he, be sure
In highth or depth, still first and last will reign
Sole king, and of his kingdom lose no part
By our revolt, but over hell extend
His empire, and with iron sceptre rule
Us here, as with his golden those in heaven.
What sit we then projecting peace and war?

ii *306.* Statesmen burdened by affairs of state were commonly compared to Atlas (see, e.g., *Antony and Cleopatra* I v 23 and Spenser, Sonnet to Lord Burleigh prefaced to *F.Q.*); but in the present context *Atlantean* functions as one of a large set of allusions to the Titans. Atlas was forced by Jupiter to carry the heavens on his shoulders specifically as a punishment for his part in the rebellion.

ii *310–2.* On the angelic orders, see i 128–9*n* and ii 11*n*. *style*] ceremonial title.

ii *321.* Answering Belial's argument at ll. 211f.

ii *324.* Contrast v 165, where Adam and Eve in their morning hymn joyfully call on all creatures 'to extol / Him first, him last'. Both speakers anticipate *Rev.* i 11 (cp. xxi 6, xxii 13): 'I am Alpha and Omega, the first and the last.'

ii *327–8.* *Beelzebub* perhaps only intends the gold and iron sceptres that were traditionally symbolic of merciful equity and rigorous justice. But the specific allusion to *Ps.* ii 9 ('Thou shalt break them with a rod of iron') makes the reader realise that Abdiel's warning of v 886–8 is coming true, and that God will ultimately destroy evil. See Sims 16.

ii *329.* *What*] Why; idiomatic and colloquial: see *OED* III 19.

War hath determined us, and foiled with loss
Irreparable; terms of peace yet none
Vouchsafed or sought; for what peace will be given
To us enslaved, but custody severe,
And stripes, and arbitrary punishment
Inflicted? And what peace can we return,
But to our power hostility and hate,
Untamed reluctance, and revenge though slow,
Yet ever plotting how the conqueror least
May reap his conquest, and may least rejoice
In doing what we most in suffering feel?
Nor will occasion want, nor shall we need
With dangerous expedition to invade
Heaven, whose high walls fear no assault or siege,
Or ambush from the deep. What if we find
Some easier enterprise? There is a place
(If ancient and prophetic fame in heaven
Err not) another world, the happy seat
Of some new race called Man, about this time
To be created like to us, though less
In power and excellence, but favoured more
Of him who rules above; so was his will

ii *330. determined*] finished (as in vi 318). But the context also activates a subsidiary meaning, 'war has given us a settled aim'.
ii *332. Vouchsafed*] M.'s spelling, 'Voutsaf't', indicates the seventeenth-century pronunciation he preferred.
ii *336. to our power*] to the limit of our power.
ii *337. reluctance*] resistance, not just 'unwillingness' (*OED* 1).
ii *346–52.* Clarifying the obscure passage at i 651ff about a rumour of a new race. The creation of man was the subject of a public oath by God, but the time of the creation was the subject of a rumour only ('it is not for you to know the times or seasons', *Acts* i 7). Beelzebub's use of the foreordinance to persuade the devils that God means to supplant them is dramatic irony; for the devils' spite makes this lie come true. To prevent their being supplanted they agree to the corruption of man, which in turn occasions Christ's incarnation and the elevation of manhood. On the other hand (so complex is the manner of God's foreknowledge), at iii 678–80 Uriel evidently thinks of man as created to fill the vacancies in heaven; as Raphael does at vii 150–61. God's 'foreknowledge prevents the two stories from being inconsistent; he would have known throughout all past time that he was going to want to spite [the devils]' (Empson 56). The Biblical authority for the relative status of man and angel was *Ps.* viii 5: 'thou hast made him a little lower than the angels, and hast crowned him with glory and honour' – developed and applied to Jesus in *Heb.* ii 6–9.

Pronounced among the gods, and by an oath,
That shook heaven's whole circumference, confirmed.
Thither let us bend all our thoughts, to learn
What creatures there inhabit, of what mould,
Or substance, how endued, and what their power,
And where their weakness, how attempted best,
By force or subtlety: though heaven be shut,
And heaven's high arbitrator sit secure
In his own strength, this place may lie exposed
The utmost border of his kingdom, left
To their defence who hold it: here perhaps
Some advantageous act may be achieved
By sudden onset, either with hell fire
To waste his whole creation, or possess
All as our own, and drive as we were driven,
The puny habitants, or if not drive,

ii *352–3*. Editors have treated this heaven-shaking oath as an instance of M.'s obedience to epic formula (e.g. Homer, *Il.* i 530, Virgil, *Aen.* ix 106 *totum nutu tremefecit Olympum*). In fact the thought is much nearer to *Is.* xiii 12–3: 'I will make a man more precious than fine gold; even a man than the golden wedge of Ophir. Therefore I will shake the Heavens' (a key verse in *PL*: see xi 396–407, vi 832f). Cp. *Heb.* vi 17, 'God, willing . . . to shew . . . the immutability of his counsel, confirmed it by an oath', and *Heb.* xii 26, 'Whose voice then shook the earth: but now he hath promised, saying, Yet once more I shake not the earth only, but also heaven'; also *Gen.* xxii 16 and *Is.* xlv 23. *gods*] See i 116–7*n* and iii 341*n*.
ii *356*. *endued*] gifted. The *substance* of man is of the greatest practical importance to the devils, for it is the Material Cause of the Fall. See Howard 161–3.
ii *357*. *attempt*] Both 'try to entice or seduce' and 'attack, overthrow, rape'. Each meaning is further developed in ll. 366–8 below.
ii *359*. *arbitrator*] arbiter, judge, sole controller. Yet another of the many antonomasias by which the devils desperately attempt 'to assert Dualistic equality with [their] Creator' (Broadbent 130). Cp. 'conqueror' (l. 338 above), 'king of heaven' (l. 316), 'heaven's all-ruling sire' (l. 264), 'heaven's lord' (l. 236), 'supreme foe' (l. 210), etc. *God* is always avoided.
ii *360*. To encourage the war-weary devils, Beelzebub here minimises the danger; but later (ll. 410–3) he maximises it, to ensure the choice of a sufficiently meritorious explorer.
ii *367*. *puny*] weak; but also, as Hume and Newton noted, 'born since us' (the original meaning, from Fr. *puis né*). That men are puny 'superbly compresses Beelzebub's contemptuous reasons for hating them (new favourites) *and* his reasons for revenge: they are weak' (Ricks 66). *drive*] put to flight. Hughes compares Joseph Beaumont, *Psyche* (1648) i 24: 'Was't not enough, against the righteous Law / Of Primogeniture, to

Seduce them to our party, that their God
May prove their foe, and with repenting hand
Abolish his own works. This would surpass
Common revenge, and interrupt his joy
In our confusion, and our joy upraise
In his disturbance; when his darling sons
Hurled headlong to partake with us, shall curse
Their frail original, and faded bliss,
Faded so soon. Advise if this be worth
Attempting, or to sit in darkness here
Hatching vain empires. Thus Beelzebub
Pleaded his devilish counsel, first devised
By Satan, and in part proposed: for whence,
But from the author of all ill could spring,
So deep a malice, to confound the race
Of mankind in one root, and earth with hell
To mingle and involve, done all to spite
The great creator? But their spite still serves
His glory to augment. The bold design

throw Us down / From that bright home, which all the world do's know / Was by confest inheritance our own: / But, to our shame, Man, that vile worm, must dwell / In our fair Orbs, and Heav'n with Vermin fill.'

ii *369–70*. Cp. *Gen.* vi 7: 'And the Lord said, I will destroy man whom I have created from the face of the earth; both man, and beast . . . for it repenteth me that I have made them.'

ii *374. partake with us*] share in our condition; also, 'take sides with us'.

ii *375. original*] originals *Ed I*. Either reading is feasible. The *Ed II* reading could mean 'origin, derivation' or 'parentage' or 'author, progenitor' (*OED* s.v. *Original* sb. 1, 2); 'originals' could have only the last sense.

ii *376–8*. For the devils, this is merely sarcasm directed against Mammon; but, for the reader, the allusion in *sit in darkness* to *Ps.* cvii 10f ('Such as sit in darkness and in the shadow of death, being bound in affliction and iron; Because they rebelled against the words of God') may suggest 'the ultimate fate of all rebels against God' (Sims 16). *Advise*] consider.

ii *383. one root*] Adam, the root of the genealogical tree of man. The Biblical horticultural metaphor, which runs throughout *PL* (e.g. iii 288, ix 89, 645) was very extensively used by the Reformers in their discussions of the doctrine of Original Sin. Rajan cites the Westminster Confession: Adam and Eve 'being the root of all mankind, the guilt of this sin was imputed, and the same death in sin and corrupted nature conveyed, to all their posterity'.

ii *384. involve*] entangle in trouble, implicate; perhaps also 'envelop'. On the inextricable mingling of good and evil in the fallen world, see *Areopagitica* (Yale ii 514): 'Good and evill we know in the field of this World grow up together almost inseparably; and the knowledge of good is . . . involv'd and interwoven with the knowledge of evill.'

Pleased highly those infernal states, and joy
Sparkled in all their eyes; with full assent
They vote: whereat his speech he thus renews.
   Well have ye judged, well ended long debate,
Synod of gods, and like to what ye are,
Great things resolved, which from the lowest deep
Will once more lift us up in spite of fate,
Nearer our ancient seat; perhaps in view
Of those bright confines, whence with neighbouring
      arms
And opportune excursion we may chance
Re-enter heaven; or else in some mild zone
Dwell not unvisited of heaven's fair light
Secure, and at the brightening orient beam
Purge off this gloom; the soft delicious air,
To heal the scar of these corrosive fires
Shall breathe her balm. But first whom shall we send
In search of this new world, whom shall we find
Sufficient? Who shall tempt with wandering feet
The dark unbottomed infinite abyss
And through the palpable obscure find out
His uncouth way, or spread his airy flight
Upborne with indefatigable wings
Over the vast abrupt, ere he arrive

ii *387. states*] estates of the realm, people of rank and authority.
ii *391. synod*] A carefully chosen term, since it could be used of the conjuntion of stars as well as the meeting of councillors. We are not long allowed to forget that the devils were once 'sons of the morning'; see v 700–14*n*.
ii *400. Purge . . . gloom*] In one sense the meaning is psychological ('clear away this depression'); in another, it develops the same catachresis as 'palpable obscure' at l. 406–the darkness is so thick that the devils think of washing it off.
ii *402. breathe*] *Ed I* wrongly has 'breath'.
ii *404. tempt*] try (*OED* I 3) or 'venture upon' (*OED* I 2 c, first instance); perhaps aphetic for *attempt*.
ii *405. unbottomed*] Points to the primary meaning of *abyss* (Greek *ἄβυσσος* bottomless); cp. *Rev*. xx 3, where the A.V. translation is 'bottomless pit'. The repeated delay of the noun may mime the infinite regression of the chasm.
ii *406. palpable obscure*] Cp. xii 188, 'Palpable darkness'; the allusion is to *Exod*. x 21: 'The Lord said unto Moses, Stretch out thine hand toward heaven, that there may be darkness over the land of Egypt, even darkness which may be felt [Vulgate *palpari queant*, Tremellius *palpet*].'
ii *407. uncouth*] unknown, and so unfrequented.
ii *409. abrupt*] The adjective (precipitous, broken off) is here used as a noun,

The happy isle; what strength, what art can then
Suffice, or what evasion bear him safe
Through the strict sentries and stations thick
Of angels watching round? Here he had need
All circumspection, and we now no less
Choice in our suffrage; for on whom we send,
The weight of all and our last hope relies.
   This said, he sat; and expectation held
His look suspense, awaiting who appeared
To second, or oppose, or undertake
The perilous attempt: but all sat mute,
Pondering the danger with deep thoughts; and each
In other's countenance read his own dismay
Astonished: none among the choice and prime
Of those heaven-warring champions could be found
So hardy as to proffer or accept
Alone the dreadful voyage; till at last
Satan, whom now transcendent glory raised
Above his fellows, with monarchal pride
Conscious of highest worth, unmoved thus spake.

and refers to the *abyss* between hell and heaven. *arrive*] arrive at, reach (*OED* I 3).

ii *410*. Metaphors and similes in which Satan is a voyager or trader, and earth an island, are extremely common in *PL*. Cp. ll. 426, 636–42, 919, 1011, 1042–4, in this book alone; and see iv 159–66*n*. *happy isle*] Hints at the Fortunate Isles, or Isles of the Blessed (Happy), from the antique descriptions of which M. is to draw much of his imagery for Paradise. The suggestion is taken up more firmly near the end of Satan's voyage: see iii 568–9*n*.

ii *411*. *evasion*] subterfuge, evasive action.

ii *412*. *sentries*] A trisyllable, spelt 'senteries'–a not unusual seventeenth-century form. *stations*] guard posts.

ii *414*. *we*] *Ed I* and *Ed II*. But a famous *erratum* in *Ed I*–'Lib. 2. v. 414 for *we* read *wee*'–has wrongly been taken, since Richardson, as evidence that M. meant to distinguish emphatic and unemphatic forms of the pronoun. See Preface, p. xii.

ii *415*. *Choice . . . suffrage*] discrimination in our vote (to elect him).

ii *418*. *suspense*] attentive; in a state of suspense, waiting for the issue (*OED* a. 1, 2).

ii *423*. *Astonished*] dismayed. *prime*] first in rank or importance.

ii *425*. Reflecting the irresolution of the devils, *proffer* hesitates between two incomplete meanings: 'offer the voyage (to Satan)' and 'offer (to go on) the voyage, volunteer'.

ii *427*. Contrasting with Messiah's 'meek' offering of himself at iii 227ff where sovereignty is objectively present, but conferred by the Father.

O progeny of heaven, empyreal thrones,
With reason hath deep silence and demur
Seized us, though undismayed: long is the way
And hard, that out of hell leads up to light;
Our prison strong, this huge convex of fire,
Outrageous to devour, immures us round
Ninefold, and gates of burning adamant
Barred over us prohibit all egress.
These passed, if any pass, the void profound
Of unessential night receives him next
Wide gaping, and with utter loss of being
Threatens him, plunged in that abortive gulf.
If thence he scape into whatever world,
Or unknown region, what remains him less
Than unknown dangers and as hard escape.
But I should ill become this throne, O peers,
And this imperial sovereignty, adorned
With splendour, armed with power, if aught proposed
And judged of public moment, in the shape
Of difficulty or danger could deter
Me from attempting. Wherefore do I assume
These royalties, and not refuse to reign,

ii *430–66*. Cp. Satan's speech, in a similar situation, in *PR* i 44–105.
ii *432–3*. See l. 81*n* and iii 20f. Cp. Virgil, *Aen*. vi 126–9, the Sibyl's warning to Aeneas before his descent into the world of the dead: 'easy is the descent to Avernus . . . but to recall your steps and pass out to the upper air, this is the task, this the toil'; and Dante, *Inf*. xxxiv 95: 'the way is long and the road is hard'. Rajan contrasts the 'smooth, easy' bridge built by Sin and Death at x 282ff below.
ii *434*. *convex*] vault; both a poetic and a scientific word.
ii *436*. Virgil's underworld is *immured* by the *ninefold* Styx (*Aen*. vi 439), and his Tartarus has a gate with pillars of *adamant* (*Aen*. vi 552).
ii *439*. *unessential*] without substance or being; cp. l. 150, 'uncreated night'.
ii *441*. *abortive*] A strong and difficult word. The gulf itself can hardly be 'aborted' or 'born prematurely', while, if it is abortion-causing in the sense of 'frustrating' (Hughes), this is weak beside the threat of l. 440, 'utter loss of being'. Perhaps Satan thinks of the gulf as a miscarrying womb (cp. l.150, 'wide womb of uncreated night') from which the traveller may never be born, or which may render him as if unborn. A rather arcane pun may also be intended (Latin *aborior* = set, disappear; used of heavenly bodies such as, e.g., Lucifer).
ii *444*. The fourth (1688) and subsequent edns have question mark after *escape*. But Satan may well be meant to amplify the dangers before him with an affirmatory rather than an interrogative tone.

Refusing to accept as great a share
Of hazard as of honour, due alike
To him who reigns, and so much to him due
Of hazard more, as he above the rest
High honoured sits? Go therefore mighty powers,
Terror of heaven, though fallen; intend at home,
While here shall be our home, what best may ease
The present misery, and render hell
More tolerable; if there be cure or charm
To respite or deceive, or slack the pain
Of this ill mansion: intermit no watch
Against a wakeful foe, while I abroad
Through all the coasts of dark destruction seek
Deliverance for us all: this enterprise
None shall partake with me. Thus saying rose
The monarch, and prevented all reply,
Prudent, lest from his resolution raised
Others among the chief might offer now
(Certain to be refused) what erst they feared;
And so refused might in opinion stand
His rivals, winning cheap the high repute
Which he through hazard huge must earn. But they
Dreaded not more the adventure than his voice
Forbidding; and at once with him they rose;
Their rising all at once was as the sound
Of thunder heard remote. Towards him they bend
With awful reverence prone; and as a god
Extol him equal to the highest in heaven:
Nor failed they to express how much they praised,
That for the general safety he despised

ii *452. Refusing*] 'if I refuse'; the speech is unfortunately open however to an exactly contrary interpretation–'refusing as I do'.
ii *457. intend*] consider, concentrate on; not a Latin sense.
ii *461. respite*] rest, relieve. *deceive*] beguile away.
ii *467.* See i 348 and iv 393: Satan is 'a blend of oriental despot and Machiavellian prince' (Lewis 65).
ii *468. raised*] encouraged.
ii *477.* Rajan points out that just as the adoption of the scheme to ruin mankind is accompanied by thunder, so is the completion of the original sin at ix 1002.
ii *478. awful*] respectful, reverent. *prone*] grovelling. Contrast the loyal angel's obeisance at iii 349f.
ii *479. highest*] 'the highest of the gods (angels) in heaven' and 'the highest, in heaven: God'. The second meaning belongs to the detailed parallel between Satan's self-sacrifice and Messiah's.

His own: for neither do the spirits damned
Lose all their virtue; lest bad men should boast
Their specious deeds on earth, which glory excites,
Or close ambition varnished o'er with zeal.
Thus they their doubtful consultations dark
Ended rejoicing in their matchless chief:
As when from mountain tops the dusky clouds
Ascending, while the north wind sleeps, o'erspread
Heaven's cheerful face, the louring element
Scowls o'er the darkened landscape snow, or shower;
If chance the radiant sun with farewell sweet
Extend his evening beam, the fields revive,
The birds their notes renew, and bleating herds
Attest their joy, that hill and valley rings.
O shame to men! Devil with devil damned
Firm concord holds, men only disagree
Of creatures rational, though under hope
Of heavenly grace: and God proclaiming peace,
Yet live in hatred, enmity, and strife
Among themselves, and levy cruel wars,
Wasting the earth, each other to destroy:
As if (which might induce us to accord)
Man had not hellish foes enow besides,
That day and night for his destruction wait.
The Stygian council thus dissolved; and forth

ii *483. lest . . . boast*] so that men ought not to boast; cp. *Eph.* ii 8f: 'by grace are ye saved. . . . Not of works, lest any man should boast.'
ii *485. close*] secret.
ii *488–95.* 'The volcanoes of Book i are charmed into pastoral hills' (Broadbent 121) by the deceiving elf of the devils' imagination. The north wind is appropriate to Satan (see v 689*n*).
ii *490. element*] sky.
ii *491. scowls*] The transitive use is discussed as an instance of expressive syntax by Ricks (81). *landscape*] Early edns have the variant spelling 'lantskip', but there seems to have been no phonetic difference between the two forms.
ii *492. If chance*] if it chance that.
ii *494. bleating*] Used of goats or calves, as well as of sheep.
ii *496–502.* 'The lines state an orthodox doctrine that is found in Antonio Rusca's *De Inferno et Statu Daemonum* (Milan 1621), pp. 505–7. . . . The devils avoid civil strife and maintain orders and ranks among themselves so as to tempt mankind most efficiently' (Hughes).
ii *503. accord*] agree.
ii *504. enow*] enough.

In order came the grand infernal peers,
Midst came their mighty paramount, and seemed
Alone the antagonist of heaven, nor less
Than hell's dread emperor with pomp supreme,
And God-like imitated state; him round
A globe of fiery seraphim enclosed
With bright emblazonry, and horrent arms.
Then of their session ended they bid cry
With trumpets' regal sound the great result:
Toward the four winds four speedy cherubim
Put to their mouths the sounding alchemy
By herald's voice explained: the hollow abyss
Heard far and wide, and all the host of hell
With deafening shout returned them loud acclaim.
Thence more at ease their minds and somewhat raised
By false presumptuous hope, the ranged powers
Disband, and wandering, each his several way
Pursues, as inclination or sad choice
Leads him perplexed, where he may likeliest find
Truce to his restless thoughts, and entertain

ii *507*. A heavier stop seems to be required after *peers*.

ii *508*. *midst*] This adverbial use is peculiar to M. *OED* suggests it may be a contracted form of 'middest'. *paramount*] lord paramount, ruler.

ii *510–20*. Broadbent (113) sees in these lines a portrayal of the English mob's easy gullibility and of their passion (which M. detested) for the regalia of monarchy.

ii *512*. *globe*] compact body (often of soldiers). The word had been used of angels by Giles Fletcher: 'A globe of winged angels, swift as thought' (*Christs triumph after death* 13). *fiery*] the word *seraphim* was connected with the Heb. root *saraph*, to burn. Cp. Spenser, *Hymn to Heavenly Beauty* 94f: 'Those eternall burning Seraphins, / Which from their faces dart out fierie light'. John Norris of Bemerton asks: 'What is it that makes the Seraphin burn and flame above the rest of the Angelical Orders?' (*Practical discourses* (1691) 298). See also i 129*n*.

ii *513*. *imblazonry*] heraldic devices. *horrent*] bristling; first instance in *OED*; perhaps a Latinizing coinage based on *horrens*; but cp. M.E. *horrend*= dreadful, also *horrendous*.

ii *515*. *result*] resolution, outcome of the *session*. Note M.'s use, in the passage, of terms appropriate to an earthly parliament.

ii *517*. *alchemy*] alloy, brass (alchemy gold, imitation gold).

ii *521*. *raised*] encouraged.

ii *522*. *ranged powers*] armies drawn up in ranks.

ii *526*. *entertain*] while away.

The irksome hours, till this great chief return.
Part on the plain, or in the air sublime
Upon the wing, or in swift race contend,
As at the Olympian games or Pythian fields;
Part curb their fiery steeds, or shun the goal
With rapid wheels, or fronted brigades form.
As when to warn proud cities war appears
Waged in the troubled sky, and armies rush
To battle in the clouds, before each van
Prick forth the airy knights, and couch their spears
Till thickest legions close; with feats of arms
From either end of heaven the welkin burns.
Others with vast Typhoean rage more fell
Rend up both rocks and hills, and ride the air
In whirlwind; hell scarce holds the wild uproar.
As when Alcides from Oechalia crowned

ii *527. this*] his *Ed I* – perhaps preferably, since it does not abandon the point of view of the individual devil.
ii *528–69.* Epic models include the sports of the Myrmidons during Achilles' absence from the war (Homer, *Il.* ii 774ff); the Greek funeral games of *Il.* xxiii and the Trojan of *Aen.* v; and – closest of all – the amusements of the blessed dead in Virgil's Elysium (*Aen.* vi 642–59).
ii *528. sublime*] uplifted, high (archaic).
ii *530.* The Pythian games at Delphi were next in importance after the Olympian.
ii *531–2.* Imitating Horace's image of the turning posts shunned by chariot-wheels (*Od.* I i 4–5: *metaque fervidis / evitata rotis.* *fronted*] opposed, face to face. *brigades*] Stressed on the first syllable. With the 'aggressive war-games' (Broadbent 118) of the devils contrast the 'unarmed' games of the good angels (iv 552 below).
ii *533–8.* Among portents of the burning of the Temple at Jerusalem, Josephus mentions chariots and troops of soldiers in their armour . . . running about among the clouds, and surrounding of cities (*De bellis* VI v 3).
ii *539. Typhoean rage*] See i 197–200*n*.
ii *541. whirlwind*] Brings out a mild pun in *Typhoean*, for 'typhon', besides being a name, was an English word meaning 'whirlwind'. Cp. the storm made by Satan in *PR* iv 409–19, though here the emphasis is on the whirlwind as a torment of the damned: see i 77, ii 180–2 and vi 749*n*. For the throwing of hills as a symbol of rebellion, see vi 639–66*n*.
ii *542–6. Alcides* (Hercules) returning *victor ab Oechalia* (Ovid, *Met.* ix 136) put on a ritual robe which had inadvertently been soaked by his wife in corrosive poison. Mad with pain, he blamed his friend Lichas, who had brought the robe, and hurled him far into the *Euboic* (Euboean) sea. Throughout M. follows Ovid rather than Seneca (*Hercules furens*) or Sophocles (*Trachiniae*). The rhythmic and syntactic organization of the passage,

With conquest, felt the envenomed robe, and tore
Through pain up by the roots Thessalian pines,
And Lichas from the top of Oeta threw
Into the Euboic sea. Others more mild,
Retreated in a silent valley, sing
With notes angelical to many a harp
Their own heroic deeds and hapless fall
By doom of battle; and complain that fate
Free virtue should enthral to force or chance.
Their song was partial, but the harmony
(What could it less when spirits immortal sing?)
Suspended hell, and took with ravishment
The thronging audience. In discourse more sweet
(For eloquence the soul, song charms the sense,)
Others apart sat on a hill retired,
In thoughts more elevate, and reasoned high
Of providence, foreknowledge, will and fate,

attacked in Davie 67, is defended in Ricks 43–5, where the separation of *tore* from *up*, e.g., is noticed as an effect mimetic of violent effort. On the uprooting of trees as a symbol of lawless wildness, see i 292–4*n*. M.'s use of torn hills and uprooted trees as images of reversion to chaos is traced in MacCaffrey 88f. *Oechalia*] Oealia *Ed I* misprint.

ii *545 Oeta*] See *Proc Med* 10–12*n*.

ii *546–69*. Burden 58ff argues that M., not content to write divine poetry, must also construct a refutation of ordinary, merely charming, poetry. The rejected secular poetry has its place in hell, and is shown to have definite satanic characteristics. Thus the satanic epic hero is not free, but subjected by fate to chance. We notice the close correlation between satanic literature and 'perplexed' satanic philosophy. For M., unideological literature is an impossibility. According to Webster's *Displaying of witchcraft* (1677) 215–41, it is the devils' custom 'to sing melodiously' and 'with their impure mouths' to 'meditate and talk of holy scriptures' (Schultz 86).

ii *551–2. partial*] perhaps 'in parts'; but primarily 'prejudiced' (since they sang their own version of the Fall, in which virtue is on their side, force or chance on God's, and the ultimate power is fate). See 232–3*n*.

ii *554. Suspended*] held the attention of. The parenthesis delaying the verb 'suspends as it were the event' (Newton). It would be better still if the syntactical effect echoed a 'play on *suspend*–suspension as a technical harmonic term' (Ricks 79), but this term does not seem to have been used before about 1800. *took*] charmed.

ii *557–69*. Cp. the Castle of Wisdom in Dante's Limbo (*Inf.* iv).

ii *557–8. retired*] In thought as well as on the hill (Ricks 88).

ii *559–61*. Eighteenth-century critics noticed a mimetic intricacy in the rhetorical patterning of these lines. The devils, lacking the resources of Scriptural authority, are lost among these labyrinthine preoccupations of

Fixed fate, free will, foreknowledge absolute,
And found no end, in wandering mazes lost.
Of good and evil much they argued then,
Of happiness and final misery,
Passion and apathy, and glory and shame,
Vain wisdom all, and false philosophy:
Yet with a pleasing sorcery could charm
Pain for a while or anguish, and excite
Fallacious hope, or arm the obdured breast
With stubborn patience as with triple steel.
Another part in squadrons and gross bands,
On bold adventure to discover wide
That dismal world, if any clime perhaps
Might yield them easier habitation, bend
Four ways their flying march, along the banks
Of four infernal rivers that disgorge
Into the burning lake their baleful streams;
Abhorred Styx the flood of deadly hate,

medieval and Reformation scholasticism. Dialectic itself is one of the results of the Fall: the devils have 'lost the power of intuitive reasoning which differentiates [angels] from men' (Rajan[2] 83, citing v 486–90). *mazes*] Rajan contrasts the regular 'mazes intricate' of the loyal angels' dance at v 622, and compares Adam's attempt to escape from recognition of his guilt 'through mazes' of evasion and error at x 830. The heavenly maze is a cosmic labyrinth like the ones on medieval cathedral floors; whereas that of hell is a Labyrinth of Error.

ii *564–9*. Directed especially against Stoicism, the most formidable ethical challenge to Christianity. *apathy*] complete freedom from passion; a Stoic ideal, contrasted with true *patience* in *De doctrina* ii 10 (and see also *PR* iv 300–18). Henry More (*Immortality of the soul* III ix 2) held that '*Stoicks*, *Epicureans*, and whatever other sects and humors are on the Earth, may in likelihood be met with there' (i.e. among aerial spirits).

ii *568*. *obdured*] hardened, made callous.

ii *569*. *stubborn patience*] contrast the 'true patience' of xi 361.

ii *570*. *gross*] large, or compact.

ii *575–81*. This description of the four rivers of hell takes its broad outline from Virgil's (esp. *Aen.* vi), Dante's (e.g. *Inf.* xiv), and Spenser's (e.g. *F.Q.* II vii 56f). M. adds the detail of confluence in the 'burning lake' (for which see i 210 and *Rev.* xix 20), perhaps to provide a counterpart to the common source of the four rivers of Paradise (iv 223–33 and *Gen.* ii 10). The epithet or description attached to each river translates its Greek name (e.g. *Στύξ*, hateful). These etymologies were familiar ones, easily accessible in dictionaries such as Calepinus'. The rivers had often been allegorised, notably by Cristoforo Landino (*Opera* (Basel 1596) 3038, 3044), but M. does not seem to pursue this possibility very far. *baleful*] evil, painful, sorrowful.

Sad Acheron of sorrow, black and deep;
Cocytus, named of lamentation loud
Heard on the rueful stream; fierce Phlegethon
Whose waves of torrent fire inflame with rage.
Far off from these a slow and silent stream,
Lethe the river of oblivion rolls
Her watery labyrinth, whereof who drinks,
Forthwith his former state and being forgets,
Forgets both joy and grief, pleasure and pain.
Beyond this flood a frozen continent
Lies dark and wild, beat with perpetual storms
Of whirlwind and dire hail, which on firm land
Thaws not, but gathers heap, and ruin seems
Of ancient pile; all else deep snow and ice,
A gulf profound as that Serbonian bog
Betwixt Damiata and Mount Casius old,
Where armies whole have sunk: the parching air
Burns frore, and cold performs the effect of fire.
Thither by harpy-footed Furies haled,

ii *583*. *Lethe*] Not the 'forgetful lake' of 74 above; see i *266n*.

ii *592–4*. *Serbonian bog*] Serbonis, a lake bordered by quicksands on the Egyptian coast; Diodorus Siculus (I xxx 5–7) and Sandys (*A relation of a journey* (1637) 137) speak of it devouring 'whole armies'. *Damiata* (mod. Damietta, east of the Nile) and Mt *Casius* were both names that often occurred in the Italian epics; and Dante made Damiata a symbol of mankind's early, eastern past (*Inf.* xiv 104). M. probably introduces the Serbonian lake because, according to one tradition, Typhon after his unsuccessful rebellion against heaven lay overwhelmed beneath its waters. The name is a bad omen for Satan's enterprise.

ii *594–5*. *parching*] drying, withering; as in xii 636 and *Lycidas* 13. *frore*] frozen, intensely cold. The idea that hell's torments include cold as well as heat goes back to O.T. apocryphal writings (e.g. II *Enoch* x 2–3, Charles ii 435: 'frost and ice, thirst and shivering'), and had become well established in medieval tradition. See Vulgate *Job* xxiv 19; Dante, *Inf.* iii 87 and xxxii; St Thomas Aquinas, *Summa Theol.* Supple. xcvii 1; and, among later writers, Shakespeare, *Measure for Measure* III i 121–2; and Giles Fletcher, *Christs victorie on Earth* 22.

ii *596*. Dante had introduced Virgil's claw-handed Harpies (*Aen.* iii 211–8) into his hell (*Inf.* xiii 10); and M. combines them with the *Furies* or Eumenides, daughters of Acheron and Night, and agencies of divine vengeance. In Homer, the Harpies snatch souls off to death and to the ministrations of the Erinyes or Furies: see *Od.* xx 77 and Jane Harrison, *Prolegomena to the Study of Greek Religion* (New York 1957) 176–83. *haled*] obviously preferable to 'hailed'; though the spelling of the early edns, 'hail'd', could indicate either word.

At certain revolutions all the damned
Are brought: and feel by turns the bitter change
Of fierce extremes, extremes by change more fierce,
From beds of raging fire to starve in ice
Their soft ethereal warmth, and there to pine
Immovable, infixed, and frozen round,
Periods of time, thence hurried back to fire.
They ferry over this Lethean sound
Both to and fro, their sorrow to augment,
And wish and struggle, as they pass, to reach
The tempting stream, with one small drop to lose
In sweet forgetfulness all pain and woe,
All in one moment, and so near the brink;
But fate withstands, and to oppose the attempt
Medusa with Gorgonian terror guards
The ford, and of itself the water flies
All taste of living wight, as once it fled
The lip of Tantalus. Thus roving on
In confused march forlorn, the adventurous bands
With shuddering horror pale, and eyes aghast
Viewed first their lamentable lot, and found
No rest: through many a dark and dreary vale
They passed, and many a region dolorous,
O'er many a frozen, many a fiery alp,
Rocks, caves, lakes, fens, bogs, dens, and shades of death,
A universe of death, which God by curse

ii *600. starve*] die lingeringly from cold.

ii *603–10.* Virgil's Lethe is drunk by those who, after the completion of *certain revolutions* or *periods of time*, have become purified (*Aen.* vi 745–51), but M.'s devils, unrepentant, only cross the river for another term of suffering.

ii *607. lose*] *Ed I* and *Ed II* 'loose' could indicate either 'lose' or 'loose'. 'Loose' is just possible, in the sense 'do away with' (*OED* 7).

ii *608.* On the reverberations in the word *woe*, which echoes i 3 and anticipates x 754, see MacCaffrey 85.

ii *611. Medusa*] One of the Gorgons; Odysseus during his visit to the dead is terrified of meeting her petrifying glance (*Od.* xi 634).

ii *614.* In Homer's hell *Tantalus* is tormented by thirst, standing in a pool that recedes whenever he tries to drink (*Od.* xi 582–92). According to one theory, he was so punished because he gave the food of the gods to mortal men (see Conti, *Mytholog.* vi 18); according to another, he was a type of ambition.

ii *617–8.* Echoing *Matt.* xii 43.

Created evil, for evil only good,
Where all life dies, death lives, and nature breeds,
Perverse, all monstrous, all prodigious things,
Abominable, inutterable, and worse
Than fables yet have feigned, or fear conceived,
Gorgons and Hydras, and Chimeras dire.
Mean while the adversary of God and man,
Satan with thoughts inflamed of highest design,
Puts on swift wings, and towards the gates of hell
Explores his solitary flight; some times
He scours the right hand coast, some times the left,
Now shaves with level wing the deep, then soars
Up to the fiery concave towering high.
As when far off at sea a fleet descried
Hangs in the clouds, by equinoctial winds
Close sailing from Bengala, or the isles
Of Ternate and Tidore, whence merchants bring

ii *624. nature*] *Ed I* no initial capital. The degree of personification is uncertain.

ii *628.* Virgil's and Tasso's hells have similar shadowy horrors: see *Aen.* vi 287–9; *Gerus. Lib.* iv 5. The *Hydra* was many-headed; the *Gorgons* had serpents for hair; and the *Chimaera*, a composite monster, breathed flame. The last two are treated as the pains of a guilty conscience in *Prol i* (Yale i 231).

ii *631. towards*] toward *Ed I.*

ii *632. Explores*] puts to the proof; a Latinism (see Elizabeth Holmes in *Essays and Studies* x (1924) 106), though the construction probably also depends on the English idiom 'to fond one's flight' (make trial of one's powers). See *OED* s.v. *Flight* sb.[1] 1 b.

ii *635. towering*] 'rising aloft' is probably meant. But the spelling in *Ed I* and *Ed II*, 'touring', does not distinguish 'towering' from 'touring' (turning, making a circuitous journey).

ii *636–41.* In M.'s time there was increased trade with *Bengala* (Bengal) and *Ternate* and *Tidore* (two of the 'spice islands' or Moluccas). The spice-ships would cross the *Ethiopian* sea (the ancient name for the Indian Ocean) before rounding the Cape of Good Hope. The simile is a good example of M.'s power in maintaining multiple correspondences between tenor and vehicle: 'the ships ply nightly because Satan was in the darkness visible of Hell; are far off so that they hang like a mirage and seem flying like Satan . . . and are going towards the Pole because Satan (from inside) is going towards the top of the concave wall of Hell' (Empson[2] 171). They carry *spicy drugs* because Satan is going to barter for Eve's innocence the fragrant fruit of the forbidden tree.

ii *638. Close sailing*] sailing close to the wind.

Their spicy drugs: they on the trading flood
Through the wide Ethiopian to the Cape
Ply stemming nightly toward the pole. So seemed
Far off the flying fiend: at last appear
Hell bounds high reaching to the horrid roof,
And thrice threefold the gates; three folds were brass,
Three iron, three of adamantine rock,
Impenetrable, impaled with circling fire,
Yet unconsumed. Before the gates there sat
On either side a formidable shape;
The one seemed woman to the waist, and fair,
But ended foul in many a scaly fold
Voluminous and vast, a serpent armed

ii *640. trading*] 'carrying in the way of trade' (*OED* 8); or perhaps an extension by analogy with such phrases as 'trading path' and 'trading course'. Some editors take *trading flood*='sea where the Trade Winds blow'.
ii *642. Ply*] beat up against the wind, work to windward (*OED* v.[2] II 6). *stemming*] A pun between 'making headway against water or wind' (*OED* v.[3] 1) and–in the tenor discourse–'mounting upwards' (*OED* v.[4] 1). Note that the former word was often applied figuratively in the sense 'defying'.
ii *645–6.* See l. 436*n*.
ii *647. impaled*] enclosed.
ii *649.* 'Sin and Death are shadowy and temporary figures because they are, ultimately, unreal–figments of the "evil imagination"' (Broadbent 128f).
ii *650–66.* M.'s personified Sin incorporates several iconographical motifs, noted below. The nearest analogues are probably Spenser's Errour, who is half serpent and half woman, has a 'mortal sting', and swallows her young (*F.Q.* I i 14f), and Phineas Fletcher's Hamartia (*The Purple Island* xii 27–31), a monster who at first 'fair and lovely seems': 'A woman seem'd she in her upper part; / To which she could such lying glosse impart, / That thousands she had slain with her deceiving art. // The rest (though hid) in serpents form arayd, / With iron scales, like to a plaited mail: / Over her back her knotty tail displaid, / Along the empty aire did lofty sail: / The end was pointed with a double sting, / Which with such dreaded might she wont to fling, / That nought could help the wound, but bloud of heav'nly King.'
ii *650–3.* The serpent of sin that tempted Adam and Eve was traditionally portrayed as having a woman's head or bust: see Didron ii 139f.
ii *652. voluminous*] consisting of many convolutions (*OED* 1). Rajan[2] 90 defends the word against Davie[2] 78 by saying that Sin is voluminous because its 'consequences are involved'. But it is worth noting that Valeriano, discussing a not dissimilar serpent of sin in *Hieroglyphica* xiv 25, interprets the coils as 'the multiplication of pleasure by supply of variety' (Valeriano 176). M. probably only means us to notice that Sin presents three phases or

With mortal sting: about her middle round
A cry of hell hounds never ceasing barked
With wide Cerberian mouths full loud, and rung
A hideous peal: yet, when they list, would creep,
If aught disturbed their noise, into her womb,
And kennel there, yet there still barked and howled,
Within unseen. Far less abhorred than these
Vexed Scylla bathing in the sea that parts
Calabria from the hoarse Trinacrian shore:
Nor uglier follow the Night-hag, when called
In secret, riding through the air she comes
Lured with the smell of infant blood, to dance
With Lapland witches, while the labouring moon

aspects: the specious front of temptation, the foul involvement and the mortal consequence.
ii *653. mortal*] death-dealing; see *1 Cor.* xv 56: 'The sting of death is sin.'
ii *653–9.* John Illo (*N & Q* ccv (1960) 425f) notes that neither Scylla nor Errour rewhelps her young. He compares instead Du Bartas's untameable chiurca, or opposum, who does (i 6; p. 152). More relevant, it seems, are certain emblems of Opinion and of Error, such as Beza's *Icones* (Geneva 1580) Embl. xxxii. There is a whole *cry* (pack) of hounds, because one sin engenders many consequences, sometimes hidden. Cerberus was the many-headed dog who guarded Hades.
ii *655. Cerberian*] Cerberean *Ed I.*
ii *659–61.* Circe, jealous of the nymph Scylla, changed her lower parts into a knot of 'gaping dogs' heads, such as a Cerberus might have' (Ovid. *Met.* xiv 50–74). Later Scylla was again transformed, into a dangerous rock between *Trinacria* (Sicily) and Calabria. Finally, in the medieval moralized Ovid, she became a symbol of lust or of sin. See l. 746*n* and J. F. Gilliam in *PQ* xxix (1950) 346.
ii *662. Night-hag*] Hecate, whose charms were used by Circe in her spell against Scylla. M. may allude here to the hellish yeth hounds which according to popular superstition followed the queen of darkness across the sky in pursuit of the souls of the damned. On the lore of Hecate generally, see K. M. Briggs, *Pale Hecate's Team* (1962). *called*] summoned by rites.
ii *664–6.* Jonson cites many authorities to the effect that witches' 'killing of infants is common, both for confection of theyr oyntment . . . as also out of a lust to doe murder' (*The Masque of Queenes* 176*n*; ed. Herford and Simpson vii 291–2).
ii *665. Lapland*] Renowned as a centre of witchcraft: see, e.g., *The Comedy of Errors* IV iii 11 ('Lapland sorcerers'). In allowing witches power over the moon, M. leaves the main direction of the best contemporary thought, and follows superstition, for the sake of another poetic 'iteration of physical and moral disorder' (Svendsen 75). The superstition was ancient; see Horace, *Epodes* v 46. *labouring*] troubled, suffering a defect; secondarily alluding

Eclipses at their charms. The other shape,
If shape it might be called that shape had none
Distinguishable in member, joint, or limb,
Or substance might be called that shadow seemed,
For each seemed either; black it stood as night,
Fierce as ten Furies, terrible as hell,
And shook a dreadful dart; what seemed his head
The likeness of a kingly crown had on.
Satan was now at hand, and from his seat
The monster moving onward came as fast
With horrid strides, hell trembled as he strode.
The undaunted fiend what this might be admired,
Admired, not feared; God and his Son except,
Created thing nought valued he nor shunned;
And with disdainful look thus first began.
   Whence and what art thou, execrable shape,
That darest, though grim and terrible, advance
Thy miscreated front athwart my way
To yonder gates? Through them I mean to pass,
That be assured, without leave asked of thee:
Retire, or taste thy folly, and learn by proof,

to Lat. *laborare*, poet., = to be eclipsed. Cp. John Wilkins, *The Discovery of a World in the Moone* (1638) 12: 'the supposed labour of the Moone in her eclipses'.

ii *666–73*. With this prosopopeia or personified description of Death, cp. Spenser's, which is similarly negative: 'Unbodied, unsoul'd, unheard, unseene' (*F.Q.* VII vii 46). The *dreadful dart* was a traditional attribute of Death, signifying his sharpness and suddenness (Hawes, *Pastime of Pleasure* 5383f: 'But whan I thoughte longest to endure / Dethe with his darte a rest me sodaynly'); see Tervarent, s.v. *Flèche*, col. 187. So was the *kingly crown*, on the basis of *Rev.* vi 2, where 'a crown was given' to the first of the riders of the apocalypse, 'and he went forth conquering'; see Didron ii 168–9. Coleridge noted the powerful indeterminateness of the phrase *what seemed his head.* Emma 41 remarks that M.'s choice of masculine gender for the personification of Death was probably guided less by linguistic considerations than by literary precedent 'from the biblical Angel of Death to the Greek cherub, twin of Sleep, and the Continental grotesque, the skeleton in the Dance of Death and the Renaissance Triumphs of Death'.

ii *677–8. admired*] wondered. *Admired, not feared*] 'The distinction . . . has all the distracting inertness of a footnote' (Davie[2] 76); 'the calm of supreme courage' (Ricks 46). But, as Rajan[2] 92 points out, 'to "value" evil is to learn to shun it'. Satan's is not the calm of admirable courage, but of nihilism: when God and his Son are *except* (past participle, *OED* A 3 b: 'excluded'), no basis for value remains.

ii *686. taste*] put to the proof. *proof*] experience.

Hell-born, not to contend with spirits of heaven.
To whom the goblin full of wrath replied,
Art thou that traitor angel, art thou he,
Who first broke peace in heaven and faith, till then
Unbroken, and in proud rebellious arms
Drew after him the third part of heaven's sons
Conjured against the highest, for which both thou
And they outcast from God, are here condemned
To waste eternal days in woe and pain?
And reckonest thou thyself with spirits of heaven,
Hell-doomed, and breathest defiance here and scorn
Where I reign king, and to enrage thee more,
Thy king and lord? Back to thy punishment,
False fugitive, and to thy speed add wings,
Lest with a whip of scorpions I pursue
Thy lingering, or with one stroke of this dart
Strange horror seize thee, and pangs unfelt before.
So spake the grisly terror, and in shape,
So speaking and so threatening, grew tenfold
More dreadful and deform: on the other side
Incensed with indignation Satan stood
Unterrified, and like a comet burned,

ii *688. replied,*] The usual punctuation before direct speech in *PL* is a full stop, so that the comma is probably an error. *goblin*] evil spirit.
ii *692.* Satan boasts that nearly half of the angels belong to his party (i 633, ix 141), but Death, Raphael (v 710) and Satan himself while in heaven (vi 156; unless this is due to Raphael's editing) reckon only a third. This estimate agrees with *Rev.* xii 4: 'And his [the dragon's] tail drew the third part of the stars of heaven, and did cast them to the earth.'
ii *693. Conjured*] sworn together in conspiracy (*OED* I 1 b; not a Latinism); secondarily 'bewitched; conveyed away by magic' (*OED* III 5 b, 7, 8). Stressed as an iamb.
ii *697. Hell-doomed*] Scornfully echoing Satan's 'Hell-born' (687).
ii *701.* The allusion to *1 Kings* xii 11 ('my father hath chastised you with whips, but I will chastise you with scorpions') implies that Satan would have done better to accept God's governance.
ii *707–11.* Cp. Tasso's description of Argantes: 'As when a comet far and wide descried, / In scorn of Phoebus midst bright heaven doth shine, / And tidings sad of death and mischief brings / To mighty lords, to monarchs, and to kings: / So shone the Pagan in bright armour clad' (*Gerus. Lib.* vii 52f, tr. Fairfax), which imitates Virgil's comparison of Aeneas to a comet, at *Aen.* x 272. For a variety of contemporary views about the significance and influence of comets, see Svendsen 91f and 266. H. H. Turner plausibly identifies the comet referred to here as the comet of 1618, a specially magnificent one with a tail of 104°, which appeared in *Ophiuchus*. Evelyn in his

That fires the length of Ophiucus huge
In the Arctic sky, and from his horrid hair
Shakes pestilence and war. Each at the head
Levelled his deadly aim; their fatal hands
No second stroke intend, and such a frown
Each cast at the other, as when two black clouds
With heaven's artillery fraught, come rattling on
Over the Caspian, then stand front to front
Hovering a space, till winds the signal blow
To join their dark encounter in mid air:
So frowned the mighty combatants, that hell
Grew darker at their frown, so matched they stood;
For never but once more was either like
To meet so great a foe: and now great deeds
Had been achieved, whereof all hell had rung,
Had not the snaky sorceress that sat
Fast by hell gate, and kept the fatal key,
Risen, and with hideous outcry rushed between.

Diary held it responsible for the Thirty Years' War. See G.F. Chambers, *The Story of the Comets* (Oxford 1909) 211f. But Ophiuchus (Serpent Bearer) is also chosen to allude to Satan's later transformation into a serpent (cp. the very similar astronomical allusion at x 328f).

ii *710. Arctic*] not only because comets were traditionally associated with the north, nor because that is Satan's place (see v 689*n* below, and Svendsen 91) but also because the Serpent held by Ophiuchus is described by Ovid as lying 'nearest the icy pole' (*quaeque polo posita est glaciali proxima Serpens, Met.* ii 173). The relations of tenor and vehicle are multiple; the dominant suggestions, however, seem to be of transient brightness, and of ominousness, together with the identification of Satan as the cosmic serpent. *horrid hair*] Wittily replete with aptness: 'horrid' means both 'bristling' and 'dreadful', while 'hair' alludes to the derivative meaning of comet (Greek ἀστὴρ κομήτης, 'long-haired star').

ii *714–9.* M.'s onomatopoeic lines perhaps emulate a simile of Boiardo's, which compares the shock of the encounter between Orlando and Agricane to that between two thunderclouds (*Orl. Innam.* I xvi 10). The *Caspian* of the poets was always stormy; thus Tasso's Argantes rages 'as when clouds together crushed and bruised, / Pour down a tempest by the Caspian shore' (*Gerus. Lib.* vi 38, tr. Fairfax; cp. Horace, *Odes* II ix 2 and Spenser, *F.Q.* II vii 14).

ii *718. mid air*] See i 515–16*n*. The middle of the three regions of air was the one in which storms arose; see Svendsen 93f.

ii *721–2.* When Christ destroys 'him that had the power of death, that is, the devil' (*Heb.* ii 14), as well as 'the last enemy . . . death' (*1 Cor.* xv 26); as Sin herself prophesies at l. 734.

O Father, what intends thy hand, she cried,
Against thy only son? What fury, O son,
Possesses thee to bend that mortal dart
Against thy father's head? and know'st for whom;
For him who sits above and laughs the while
At thee ordained his drudge, to execute
What e'er his wrath, which he calls justice, bids,
His wrath which one day will destroy ye both.
She spake, and at her words the hellish pest
Forbore, then these to her Satan returned:
So strange thy outcry, and thy words so strange
Thou interposest, that my sudden hand
Prevented spares to tell thee yet by deeds
What it intends; till first I know of thee,
What thing thou art, thus double-formed, and why
In this infernal vale first met thou call'st
Me father, and that phantasm call'st my son?
I know thee not, nor ever saw till now
Sight more detestable than him and thee.
To whom thus the portress of hell gate replied;
Hast thou forgot me then, and do I seem
Now in thine eye so foul, once deemed so fair
In heaven, when at the assembly, and in sight
Of all the seraphim with thee combined
In bold conspiracy against heaven's king,
All on a sudden miserable pain

ii *727–8*. The allegory whereby Sin is daughter of Satan and mother of Death is from St Basil's *Hexaemeron*; see John M. Steadman, 'Grosseteste on the Genealogy of Sin and Death', *N & Q* cciv (1959) 367f and 'Milton and St Basil: the Genesis of Sin and Death', *MLN* lxxiii (1958) 83f. The Scriptural authority is *James* i 15: 'Then when lust hath conceived, it bringeth forth sin: and sin, when it is finished, bringeth forth death.' Similar genealogies had been traced by Gower (*Mirour de l'Omme*); by Andreini (*Adamo caduto*); and by Phineas Fletcher, whose Hamartia is daughter of Eve by Satan (*The Purple Island* xii 29).
ii *746*. See ll. 774–7. Since Cerberus guarded the gate of Hades, Sin's 'Cerberean mouths' (l. 655) are appropriate to her function as portress. Empson 117f argues that God's choice of Sin and Death as guardians of the gate shows that he 'always intended them to let Satan out'. But Sin's office is an allegorical statement of the idea that access to hell is by sinning, so that it is difficult to think of any other guardian who could have been chosen to fill it.
ii *752–61*. See 727–8*n*. The circumstances of Sin's birth recall the ancient myth about Athene springing fully-formed from the head of Zeus. It is thus presented as a parody of God's generation of the Son, since Minerva's

Surprised thee, dim thine eyes, and dizzy swum
In darkness, while thy head flames thick and fast
Threw forth, till on the left side opening wide,
Likest to thee in shape and countenance bright,
Then shining heavenly fair, a goddess armed
Out of thy head I sprung: amazement seized
All the host of heaven; back they recoiled afraid
At first, and called me Sin, and for a sign
Portentous held me; but familiar grown,
I pleased, and with attractive graces won
The most averse, thee chiefly, who full oft
Thy self in me thy perfect image viewing
Becamest enamoured, and such joy thou took'st
With me in secret, that my womb conceived
A growing burden. Mean while war arose,
And fields were fought in heaven; wherein remained
(For what could else) to our almighty foe
Clear victory, to our part loss and rout
Through all the empyrean: down they fell
Driven headlong from the pitch of heaven, down
Into this deep, and in the general fall
I also; at which time this powerful key
Into my hand was given, with charge to keep
These gates for ever shut, which none can pass
Without my opening. Pensive here I sat
Alone, but long I sat not, till my womb

birth had traditionally been allegorised by theologians in that sense (see, e.g., the *Observationum libellus*, attached to Conti's *Mythologiae*, s.v. *Pallas*). The mention of pain (l. 752) at first seems to conflict with vi 327 and 432, where we are told that Satan 'first knew pain' during the war in heaven (see Empson 54). But M. is being subtle, not casual. Raphael would naturally be ignorant of Satan's feelings during the inception of his sin at the rebel council, while it is part of the change in Satan that he himself should have forgotten and should not even recognize his sin for what it is. He has certainly forgotten now (ii 744); why, then, should he not already have forgotten at vi 432?

ii *761–7*. From this passage Empson 58f concludes that, to allow time for the gestation of Death, there must have been more than one conference of the rebel angels; their theological opinions can thus be regarded as deeply and rationally considered. But this is to assume that the embryology of Death resembles that of man: an assumption hardly encouraged by the mode of his mother's birth (following immediately on Satan's first overt act of disobedience), or indeed of his own (ll. 783–5).

ii *764*. Continuing the parody of divine generation: cp. iii 138ff.

ii *772*. *pitch*] apex, summit, height, slope.

Pregnant by thee, and now excessive grown
Prodigious motion felt and rueful throes.
At last this odious offspring whom thou seest
Thine own begotten, breaking violent way
Tore through my entrails, that with fear and pain
Distorted, all my nether shape thus grew
Transformed: but he my inbred enemy
Forth issued, brandishing his fatal dart
Made to destroy: I fled, and cried out Death;
Hell trembled at the hideous name, and sighed
From all her caves, and back resounded Death.
I fled, but he pursued (though more, it seems,
Inflamed with lust than rage) and swifter far,
Me overtook his mother all dismayed,
And in embraces forcible and foul
Ingendering with me, of that rape begot
These yelling monsters that with ceaseless cry
Surround me, as thou sawest, hourly conceived
And hourly born, with sorrow infinite
To me, for when they list into the womb
That bred them they return, and howl and gnaw
My bowels, their repast; then bursting forth
Afresh with conscious terrors vex me round,
That rest or intermission none I find.
Before mine eyes in opposition sits
Grim Death my son and foe, who sets them on,
And me his parent would full soon devour
For want of other prey, but that he knows
His end with mine involved; and knows that I
Should prove a bitter morsel, and his bane,
When ever that shall be; so fate pronounced.
But thou, O Father, I forewarn thee, shun
His deadly arrow; neither vainly hope
To be invulnerable in those bright arms,
Though tempered heavenly, for that mortal dint,
Save he who reigns above, none can resist.
She finished, and the subtle fiend his lore

ii *799–802.* See ll. 650–66*n* and 653–9*n*. Here Sin's offspring are presented in a new aspect, and appear to symbolize the pangs of guilt or fear.

ii *801. conscious terrors*] terrors of guilty knowledge. *vex*] harass, irritate, afflict, worry (in both its physical and its abstract senses).

ii *806–9.* See ll. 721–2*n*. Like all those of hell, Sin regards fate as the supreme power; see i 116–17*n*.

ii *813. dint*] stroke given with a weapon; or thunder-clap (*OED* 1 b).

ii *815. lore*] lesson. See ix 695*n*.

Soon learned, now milder, and thus answered smooth.
Dear Daughter, since thou claim'st me for thy sire,
And my fair son here show'st me, the dear pledge
Of dalliance had with thee in heaven, and joys
Then sweet, now sad to mention, through dire change
Befallen us unforeseen, unthought of, know
I come no enemy, but to set free
From out this dark and dismal house of pain,
Both him and thee, and all the heavenly host
Of spirits that in our just pretences armed
Fell with us from on high: from them I go
This uncouth errand sole, and one for all
My self expose, with lonely steps to tread
The unfounded deep, and through the void immense
To search with wandering quest a place foretold
Should be, and, by concurring signs, ere now
Created vast and round, a place of bliss
In the purlieus of heaven, and therein placed
A race of upstart creatures, to supply
Perhaps our vacant room, though more removed,
Lest heaven surcharged with potent multitude
Might hap to move new broils: be this or aught
Than this more secret now designed, I haste
To know, and this once known, shall soon return,

ii *823. house*] Used of the place of the dead in *Job* xxx 23; cp. also Tasso, *Gerus. Lib.* ix 59, where hell is called 'the house of grief and pain' (tr. Fairfax).

ii *825. pretences*] pretensions, claims to dignity. There may be an Empsonian ambiguity, due to the modern sense, already equally well-established in M.'s time.

ii *827. uncouth*] strange, as in l. 407; here another obsolete meaning–'shocking', 'repellent'–adds a grim overtone.

ii *829. unfounded*] bottomless, uncreated.

ii *830–5.* On the implications of the prophecy, see ii 346–52*n*. Empson 57 suggests that *signs* ought perhaps to be taken very literally, since God certainly gives 'signs' at iv 997 and elsewhere.

ii *836. surcharged*] having an excess of inhabitants. Rajan draws attention to Satan's insinuation that God is a tyrant always having to be on guard against rebellion.

ii *839–44.* A promise later amply fulfilled, when Satan hands over his 'new kingdom' of earth to be administered by their 'joint power' (x 397–407). Empson 67 denies that Satan's promise to Sin and Death is evidence that he feels malice towards mankind at this stage: it is just a lie, 'the only way to make them let him pass'. But M. tells us that Beelzebub's counsel, which Empson admits to be malicious, was 'devised / By Satan' (ll. 379f). Satan's

And bring ye to the place where thou and Death
Shall dwell at ease, and up and down unseen
Wing silently the buxom air, embalmed
With odours; there ye shall be fed and filled
Immeasurably, all things shall be your prey.
He ceased, for both seemed highly pleased, and Death
Grinned horrible a ghastly smile, to hear
His famine should be filled, and blessed his maw
Destined to that good hour: no less rejoiced
His mother bad, and thus bespake her sire.
The key of this infernal pit by due,
And by command of heaven's all-powerful king
I keep, by him forbidden to unlock
These adamantine gates; against all force
Death ready stands to interpose his dart,
Fearless to be o'ermatched by living might.
But what owe I to his commands above
Who hates me, and hath hither thrust me down
Into this gloom of Tartarus profound,
To sit in hateful office here confined,
Inhabitant of heaven, and heavenly-born,
Here in perpetual agony and pain,
With terrors and with clamours compassed round
Of mine own brood, that on my bowels feed:
Thou art my father, thou my author, thou
My being gavest me; whom should I obey
But thee, whom follow? Thou wilt bring me soon
To that new world of light and bliss, among
The gods who live at ease, where I shall reign
At thy right hand voluptuous, as beseems
Thy daughter and thy darling, without end.

present promise is not so much a lie as an improvisation. He has just been reminded about Sin, and taught about Death; now for the first time he has an inkling of their possibilities.

ii *842. buxom*] unresisting (poet.). *embalmed*] balmy, though the more usual meaning, 'rendered resistent to decay' is present as a sinister overtone– the whole earth is a body, frailly preserved against corruption.

ii *847. famine*] hunger.

ii *869–70.* Parodying the Nicene creed ('on the right hand of the Father... [Christ] whose kingdom shall have no end'). In Sin's fantasy she enjoys glory like Christ's (cp. iii 62–4); for, as Rajan (47, 50) and others have noticed, Satan, Sin and Death form a complete anti-Trinity. Even the doctrine of the procession of the Holy Ghost from the Father through the Son has its counterpart, in the begetting of Death by Satan on his own daughter. See also ll. 752–61*n*; and, on trinities of evil generally, Didron ii 21–2.

Thus saying, from her side the fatal key,
Sad instrument of all our woe, she took;
And towards the gate rolling her bestial train,
Forthwith the huge portcullis high updrew,
Which but her self, not all the Stygian powers
Could once have moved; then in the key-hole turns
The intricate wards, and every bolt and bar
Of massy iron or solid rock with ease
Unfastens: on a sudden open fly
With impetuous recoil and jarring sound
The infernal doors, and on their hinges grate
Harsh thunder, that the lowest bottom shook
Of Erebus. She opened, but to shut
Excelled her power; the gates wide open stood,
That with extended wings a bannered host

ii *872. instrument*] The word may stand in apposition to *she* as well as to *key*; for it could mean 'a person made use of by another, for the accomplishment of a purpose'. This possibility is important in view of Empson's theory that Satan is duping Sin (ll. 839–44*n*). Burden 25 holds that since Sin lets Satan out, she is responsible for his leaving hell, and, in the sense that she is *Satan's* disobedient sin, this must be so. But it seems simpler to take the passage as generalized allegory: by helping Satan, Sin is as usual providing the means by which man may enter the world of woe. As an image, the key is an antitype of the key of eternal life that opens the gates of death in more conventional allegories. The fact that in *PL* it is Sin, not Christ, who opens the gates, may be yet another expression of the *felix culpa* theme. Sin's key is *fatal* because it leads not only to man's fall and death, but also to his redemption and eternal life (cp. ll. 807–9). In view of the earlier comparison with the Night-hag (l. 662), it may be of interest that the key was an attribute of Hecate.

ii *877. wards*] the incisions in a key's bit, corresponding to the wards projecting on the inside of the lock; not 'tumblers' (as Rajan).

ii *879–83*. Contrast the gates of heaven (vii 205–7), which open harmoniously, 'on golden hinges moving'. 'Both gates give access to chaos but the son makes his journey into the abyss to create, Satan in order to destroy' (Rajan[2] 100).

ii *881. grate*] great *Ed I* corr. in *Errata*. The opinion that 'the correction shows M.'s dislike of the pun inadvertently contributed by the printer' (Rajan[2] 100 following Adams 86) rests on the false assumption that the *Errata* list was authorial.

ii *883*. In *Prol i* (Yale i 223) M. cites Hesiod's line 'From Chaos sprang Erebus and black Night'. Erebus was often used to refer to hell itself–as in Virgil, *Georg.* iv 471, where the shades of the dead are 'startled from the lowest realms of Erebus' by the song of Orpheus.

Under spread ensigns marching might pass through
With horse and chariots ranked in loose array;
So wide they stood, and like a furnace mouth
Cast forth redounding smoke and ruddy flame.
Before their eyes in sudden view appear
The secrets of the hoary deep, a dark
Illimitable ocean without bound,
Without dimension, where length, breadth, and highth,
And time and place are lost; where eldest Night
And Chaos, ancestors of Nature, hold
Eternal anarchy, amidst the noise
Of endless wars, and by confusion stand.
For Hot, Cold, Moist, and Dry, four champions fierce
Strive here for mastery, and to battle bring
Their embryon atoms; they around the flag
Of each his faction, in their several clans,
Light-armed or heavy, sharp, smooth, swift or slow,

ii *889. redounding*] surging, issuing, overflowing.
ii *891. secrets*] 'secret places' or 'secret processes'. Suggesting also objects of forbidden knowledge: Satan is now out of bounds.
ii *892.* On the accentuation *wìthout*, see B. A. Wright, 'Stressing of the preposition "without" in the verse of "Paradise Lost,"' *N & Q* cciii (1958) 202f; and cp. iv 256, iv 656, etc.
ii *894. Night*] The early edns omit italics here, by error; in general, allegorical characters' names are treated as proper nouns.
ii *895–903.* In works such as Hesiod's *Theogony* and Boccaccio's *De genealogiis*, Chaos and Night were made *ancestors* of the more determinate powers of nature. M.'s description of the strife between contrary qualities that preceded the emergence of the cosmos is close to Ovid's account of the primeval chaos where 'cold things strove with hot, moist with dry, soft with hard, weightless with heavy' (*Met.* i 19f); though the development of the military metaphor in *PL* is much more forceful. Backed by the authority of Philo and the Church Fathers (e.g. St Augustine, *Conf.* XII xxix 40), even the most orthodox Reformers managed to reconcile the Platonic and Ovidian chaos with the doctrine of creation *e nihilo*: see, e.g., the preface to Golding's transl. of the *Metamorphoses*; Du Bartas 8f; Spenser's creative Garden of Adonis with its 'huge eternall Chaos' (*F.Q.* III vi 36); and the same author's vision of Empedoclean Strife restrained by Concord (*F.Q.* IV x 35). Sandys ([2] 19) thought Ovid's account of creation 'so consonant. to the truth, as doubtlesse he had either seene the Books of Moses, or receaved that doctrine by tradition', but he balked a little at the seeming 'eternitie of his Chaos'. See Ellrodt 79 (citing St Augustine's *De Genesi*), Svendsen 50 and Taylor 67f.
ii *899. mastery*] Spelt *Maistrie*, though this does not indicate a dissyllable There is synaloepha with *and*.

Swarm populous, unnumbered as the sands
Of Barca or Cyrene's torrid soil,
Levied to side with warring winds, and poise
Their lighter wings. To whom these most adhere,
He rules a moment; Chaos umpire sits,
And by decision more embroils the fray
By which he reigns: next him high arbiter
Chance governs all. Into this wild abyss,
The womb of nature and perhaps her grave,
Of neither sea, nor shore, nor air, nor fire,
But all these in their pregnant causes mixed
Confusedly, and which thus must ever fight,
Unless the almighty maker them ordain
His dark materials to create more worlds,
Into this wild abyss the wary fiend
Stood on the brink of hell and looked a while,
Pondering his voyage; for no narrow frith
He had to cross. Nor was his ear less pealed

ii *904. Barca*] Well known from the mention in Virgil, *Aen.* iv 42; an ancient city of Cyrenaica, of which *Cyrene* was the capital.
ii *905–6.* The atoms are *levied*–both 'enlisted' and 'raised'–to balance, or provide ballast for, the wings of the winds. The physical raising of the army is a Latinizing pun, alluding to *levare.*
ii *906. To whom . . . adhere*] i.e., to whom most of these adhere; the one with a numerical majority.
ii *907–10.* See ll. 232–3*n*.
ii *911.* Cp. Spenser, *F.Q.* III vi 36, where chaos is 'the wide wombe of the world', and Lucretius, *De rerum nat.* v 259 *omniparens eadem rerum commune sepulcrum.* Lucretius refers to earth, not to the abyss; but the context, a demonstration of the material mortality of the world, is distilled into M.'s one echoing line. *perhaps*] As usual, M. avoids committing himself to any particular cosmological theory.
ii *912–4.* Note that M.'s chaos is a confusion not of elements but of their component qualities. For the relation of this concept to the theories of the ancient atomists see Chambers 60.
ii *917–8. Stood . . . and looked*] 'standing looked', as often in *PL* (cp. v 368–9). But Bentley's stupid objection that *Into this wild abyss* cannot relate to *Stood* is a critical *felix culpa*, since it directs our attention to a fine passage of mimetic syntax. The lack of any continuation at all after the first 'Into this wild abyss' (l. 910), and the lack of the expected verb of motion after the second, render the repeated hesitations of the wary fiend: when we are fully prepared for him to leap or plunge, he stands.
ii *919. frith*] Metathetic form of 'firth'.
ii *920. pealed*] stormed, dinned.

With noises loud and ruinous (to compare
Great things with small) than when Bellona storms,
With all her battering engines bent to raze
Some capital city; or less than if this frame
Of heaven were falling, and these elements
In mutiny had from her axle torn
The steadfast earth. At last his sail-broad vans
He spreads for flight, and in the surging smoke
Uplifted spurns the ground, thence many a league
As in a cloudy chair ascending rides
Audacious, but that seat soon failing, meets
A vast vacuity: all unawares
Fluttering his pennons vain plumb down he drops
Ten thousand fathom deep, and to this hour
Down had been falling, had not by ill chance
The strong rebuff of some tumultuous cloud
Instinct with fire and nitre hurried him
As many miles aloft: that fury stayed,
Quenched in a boggy Syrtis, neither sea,

ii *921–2.* Here and at vi 310f, x 306, and *PR* iv 563f, M. uses a formula put in currency by Virgil (e.g. *Georg.* iv 176). *ruinous*] falling, crashing. *Bellona*] the goddess of war, here a metonymy for war itself.

ii *924. Ed I* has comma after *city*.

ii *927. vans*] wings (poet.; lit. 'fans'). *sail-broad*] An enhancing suggestion recalling the persistent comparisons of Satan to a voyager; see ll. 410*n*, 636–41*n* above.

ii *933. pennons*] plumes, wings. In this sense a Latinism, translating *pennae*; first instance in *OED*.

ii *934. fathom*] Spelt 'fadom'.

ii *935.* Note that the temptation and Fall of man is made to depend not only on evil will, but on contingency. The threat to integrity comes *via* the realm of the chaotic and fortuitous. Although Rajan ridicules this idea, it seems to have been taken seriously by M., who frequently returns to it. See, e.g., iv 530, ix 85, 421, 423.

ii *936–8.* Thunder and lightning were commonly explained as effects of the ignition of vapours: according to one theory, of a mixture of hot sulphurous and cold nitrous vapours, as in gun-powder (cp. vi 512). See Svendsen 101, 269f, and E. H. Duncan in *PQ* xxx (1951) 442f. *Instinct*] 'inflamed, impelled' (*OED* 2); not 'charged with' (a recent use only).

ii *939.* The Syrtes were two huge and proverbially dangerous shifting sandbanks off the North African shore. M. echoes Lucan's description: *Syrtes vel primam mundo natura figuram / Cum daret, in dubio pelagi terraeque reliquit* (*Pharsalia* ix 303f). In *Argonaut.* iv 1235ff Syrtis is elaborately described by Apollonius Rhodius as a misty featureless wasteland stretching to the dim horizon. There is a brief mention in *Acts* xxvii 17 (Greek and Vulgate).

Nor good dry land: nigh foundered on he fares,
Treading the crude consistence, half on foot,
Half flying; behoves him now both oar and sail.
As when a gryphon through the wilderness
With winged course o'er hill or moory dale,
Pursues the Arimaspian, who by stealth
Had from his wakeful custody purloined
The guarded gold: so eagerly the fiend
O'er bog or steep, through straight, rough, dense, or rare,
With head, hands, wings or feet pursues his way,
And swims or sinks, or wades, or creeps, or flies:
At length a universal hubbub wild
Of stunning sounds and voices all confused
Borne through the hollow dark assaults his ear
With loudest vehemence: thither he plies,
Undaunted to meet there what ever power
Or spirit of the nethermost abyss
Might in that noise reside, of whom to ask
Which way the nearest coast of darkness lies

ii *941.* Spenser's dragon of evil is similarly described as 'halfe flying, and halfe footing in his hast' (*F.Q.* I xi 8).

ii *943–7.* The legend of 'gold-guarding griffins' in Scythia, from whom the one-eyed Arimaspi steal, was often retold out of Herodotus (iii 116) and Pliny (*Nat. hist.* vii 10). The griffin (a composite monster: half eagle, half lion) is appropriate here partly because it was subdued by the sun god Apollo (Valeriano 279), as Satan will be by Christ. The gold-guarding griffin is associated with Satan in an allegory of Raban Maur's (Migne cxi 342). The country of the griffin (the inhospitable Scythia) symbolizes, we are told, those who are without the warmth of the Holy Spirit, and who are Satan's subjects. The gold jealously guarded is the gold of Ophir, King David's gold, which was often allegorized as Wisdom or Righteousness (*sensus tropologicus*), or as Christ's sovereignty (*sensus allegoricus*). The gold of Ophir reappears later in the poem: see xi 396–407*n*.

ii *948–50.* Here 'verse-filling asyndeton' (see Curtius 285) imitates the hectic confusion of sense-data that a journey through chaos would occasion. The lines are also *versus rapportati*: cp. vii 502f and see Curtius 286f. For a further discussion of l. 948 see Introduction, 'Prosody', p. 440.

ii *948. straight*] The *Ed I* and *Ed II* spelling 'strait' could indicate either 'strait' or 'straight'; but only the latter will give the antithesis with *rough* that is required to match the one between *dense* and *rare*.

ii *953. borne*] the *Ed I* and *Ed II* spelling 'born', does not distinguish between 'borne' and 'born'; but the former word clearly gives the primary sense.

ii *954. vehemence*] force, intensity; perhaps also derivatively implying mindlessness (see viii 526*n*, ix Argument).

Bordering on light; when straight behold the throne
Of Chaos, and his dark pavilion spread
Wide on the wasteful deep; with him enthroned
Sat sable-vested Night, eldest of things,
The consort of his reign; and by them stood
Orcus and Ades, and the dreaded name
Of Demogorgon; Rumour next and Chance,
And Tumult and Confusion all embroiled,
And Discord with a thousand various mouths.
To whom Satan turning boldly, thus. Ye powers
And spirits of this nethermost abyss,
Chaos and ancient Night, I come no spy,

ii *959–67*. In general, this court of personifications resembles Virgil's halls of Pluto (*Aen.* vi 268–81), though the only member common to both is Discord. Cp. Spenser's house of the Fates, 'Downe in the bottome of the deepe Abysse, / Where Demogorgon in dull darkenesse pent / . . . / The hideous Chaos keepes' (*F.Q.* IV ii 47). Like Spenser's, M.'s Demogorgon is from Boccaccio's *De genealogiis deorum*, where he comes first of all the dark gods. Among his brood are Night, Tartarus, Erebus, the serpent Python, Litigium (cf. M.'s Tumult and Discord) and Fama (M.'s Rumour). In *Prol i* (Yale i 222), M. supposes 'Demogorgon, the ancestor of all the gods . . . to be identical with the Chaos of the ancients'; see Fletcher ii 433–4.
ii *961. wasteful*] desolate, excessive, limitless. 'An epithet peculiarly suited to Chaos, at once an inferno of fruitlessly warring elements, and the source of all fertility, when God commands': MacCaffrey 105, where a persistent strand of imagery is shown to run through M.'s many uses of the word.
ii *962–7. Ed I* fails to italicize *Night, Rumour, Chance, Tumult, Confusion* and *Discord* as proper names.
ii *962. Night*] For the interesting view that M.'s Night is a personification of prime matter, see Chambers 75f. It may be because she is unformed dark and 'unapparent' that Night is not described.
ii *964–5. name / Of Demogorgon*] the divine nature of Demogorgon; alluding also to Statius' mention of 'the name whose knowing and whose speaking' the ghosts dread (*Theb.* iv 514) – identified by the scholiast as Demogorgon. *Orcus* and *Ades* are both names of the classical god of hell.
ii *965. Chance*] see 909f.
ii *966.* Broadbent 133 objects to *Confusion* being personified here, when the term has occurred as an ordinary substantive so recently (l. 897 above, cp. l. 966 below). And it is the same with *Tumult* (l. 1040). But this is to criticize not M.'s performance but a whole form of discourse: what the rhetoricians called 'mixed allegory'.
ii *967. a thousand various mouths*] Cp. Spenser, *F.Q.* IV i 27, where Ate, 'mother of debate', has a divided tongue. The presence of *Rumour* (l. 965), if not of *Tumult* (l. 966), shows that chaos gives rise to social and moral forms, as well as physical.

With purpose to explore or to disturb
The secrets of your realm, but by constraint
Wandering this darksome desert, as my way
Lies through your spacious empire up to light,
Alone, and without guide, half lost, I seek
What readiest path leads where your gloomy bounds
Confine with heaven; or if some other place
From your dominion won, the ethereal king
Possesses lately, thither to arrive
I travel this profound, direct my course;
Directed no mean recompense it brings
To your behoof, if I that region lost,
All usurpation thence expelled, reduce
To her original darkness and your sway
(Which is my present journey) and once more
Erect the standard there of ancient Night.
Yours be the advantage all, mine the revenge.
  Thus Satan; and him thus the anarch old
With faltering speech and visage incomposed
Answered. I know thee, stranger, who thou art,
That mighty leading angel, who of late
Made head against heaven's king, though overthrown.
I saw and heard, for such a numerous host

ii *972. secrets*] See l. 891*n*: 'secret places or processes'.
ii *973. Ed II* comma after *way* is clearly wrong.
ii *977. Confine with*] border on.
ii *980.* Editors generally insert a semicolon after *profound*; but M. may have wanted to keep the double syntax (with *direct* as verb or adjective) that the comma makes possible.
ii *983–5.* Empson (67) is probably right in thinking that Satan here misleads Chaos and Night in order to get past them. Reduction of creation to its *original darkness* was only one of the alternative plans provisionally adopted at the infernal council; another was that the devils should take possession of it themselves (ii 364–6 and 397–402).
ii *988. anarch*] Chaos, ruler or anti-ruler of the 'eternal anarchy' (l. 896); the word is perhaps M.'s coinage, on the analogy of 'mon-arch' from 'monarchy', etc.
ii *989. incomposed*] discomposed, disordered.
ii *990.* Another contrast between Satan and Christ: these are the words addressed by a devil to Jesus in *Luke* iv 34.
ii *993–7.* Confirmed in part by Raphael's account of the same events at vi 867–74. In his mention of *bands / Pursuing*, however, Chaos' account of the expulsion agrees with Satan's (see i 169–71*n*). One must expect Chaos to be confused. The sequence of the various reports of the expulsion, and the spatial locations of their delivery, are probably significant. In hell, Satan's

Fled not in silence through the frighted deep
With ruin upon ruin, rout on rout,
Confusion worse confounded; and heaven gates
Poured out by millions her victorious bands
Pursuing. I upon my frontiers here
Keep residence; if all I can will serve,
That little which is left so to defend,
Encroached on still through our intestine broils
Weakening the sceptre of old Night: first hell
Your dungeon stretching far and wide beneath;
Now lately heaven and earth, another world
Hung o'er my realm, linked in a golden chain
To that side heaven from whence your legions fell:
If that way be your walk, you have not far;
So much the nearer danger; go and speed;
Havoc and spoil and ruin are my gain.
He ceased; and Satan stayed not to reply,
But glad that now his sea should find a shore,
With fresh alacrity and force renewed
Springs upward like a pyramid of fire

hold on the facts is inferior to Chaos'. The latter's report is merely chaotic; Satan's is consistently perverted.

ii *1000. Ed I* omits comma after *defend.* *so*] in this way; by keeping residence.

ii *1001. our*] Pearce's conjecture 'your' is probably right. The intestine broils of the angels weakened Night's sceptre, because indirectly they led to the 'encroachment' of creation. See Adams 98f.

ii *1002. Ed I* fails to italicize *Night*.

ii *1004. heaven*] the sky of earth.

ii *1005. golden chain*] See l. 1051*n*.

ii *1006. heaven*] the empyrean.

ii *1007. walk*] 'As a believer in the providence of God, Milton could not possibly have believed in the huge success-story of Satan fighting his way to Paradise'; thus Chaos 'jeers at the heroic piece of space-travel' (Empson 118). It is true that Satan later greatly exaggerates the difficulties of his journey (x 477–9*n*), but the present passage hardly prepares us for that. Far from jeering, Chaos is most respectful (see esp. 991f). *walk* may rather be chosen for its religious overtones ('manner of behaviour', 'course of conduct'; cp. *Ps.* lxxxvi 11), and in any case need not imply a very easy journey. M. explicitly states that Satan moved with difficulty, at l. 1021f. *not far*] the proximity of the world to chaos amplifies the fragility and delicacy of its created order.

ii *1013. pyramid*] Often denoted an elongated spire-like or pillar-like form: see the many examples of this use gathered in L. Hotson, *Mr W. H.* (1964)

Into the wild expanse, and through the shock
Of fighting elements, on all sides round
Environed wins his way; harder beset
And more endangered, than when Argo passed
Through Bosporus, betwixt the jostling rocks:
Or when Ulysses on the larboard shunned
Charybdis, and by the other whirlpool steered.
So he with difficulty and labour hard
Moved on, with difficulty and labour he;
But he once past, soon after when man fell,
Strange alteration! Sin and Death amain
Following his track, such was the will of heaven,
Paved after him a broad and beaten way
Over the dark abyss, whose boiling gulf
Tamely endured a bridge of wondrous length
From hell continued reaching the utmost orb
Of this frail world; by which the spirits perverse
With easy intercourse pass to and fro
To tempt or punish mortals, except whom
God and good angels guard by special grace.

86. Anciently derived from πῦρ ('fire'), the root meaning was taken to be 'flame-shape', so that M.'s use of the word here constitutes a half-pun. For the symbolic meaning of the pyramid in *PL*, see v 758–*9n*.

ii *1017–8*. When Jason and the Argonauts sailed through the *Bosporus* (Straits of Constantinople) *en route* to Colchis, their boat, the *Argo*, narrowly escaped destruction between the Symplegades–the clashing or *jostling rocks*. See Apollonius Rhodius, *Argonaut*. ii 317, 552–611. *jostling*] M.'s spelling 'justling' represents a common variant pronunciation. The comparison is said to be apt because 'The *Argo* in Greek mythology was the first ocean going ship and Satan the first to cross chaos of his own will' (Rajan² 108). But this is perhaps to underestimate the aptness. The Argonauts were not the first to pass through the rocks: they were preceded by a dove, just as Satan had been preceded by Messiah and by the creative spirit of God, who 'Dove-like sat'st brooding on the vast abyss'.

ii *1019–20*. Homer tells how Odysseus followed Circe's advice in avoiding *Charybdis* and sailing close by Scylla (*the other whirlpool*), in his passage through the Straits of Messina between Sicily and Italy (*Od*. xii). Sailing before a south wind, he would have Charybdis on his *larboard* (port) side–not his starboard, as Bentley had it (Pearce weakly agreeing).

ii *1024–30*. Death's construction of the bridge is described at x 293–305.

ii *1024*. *amain*] without delay.

ii *1033*. See *De doctrina* i 9 (Columbia xv 101), where M. states that the ministry of angels 'relates especially to believers'; citing *Heb*. i 14, *Ps*. xxxiv 7, etc.

But now at last the sacred influence
Of light appears, and from the walls of heaven
Shoots far into the bosom of dim Night
A glimmering dawn; here nature first begins
Her farthest verge, and Chaos to retire
As from her outmost works a broken foe
With tumult less and with less hostile din,
That Satan with less toil, and now with ease
Wafts on the calmer wave by dubious light
And like a weather-beaten vessel holds
Gladly the port, though shrouds and tackle torn;
Or in the emptier waste, resembling air,
Weighs his spread wings, at leisure to behold
Far off the empyreal heaven, extended wide
In circuit, undetermined square or round,
With opal towers and battlements adorned
Of living sapphire, once his native seat;
And fast by hanging in a golden chain

ii *1034*] *the sacred influence / Of light*] Cp. ix 107*n*.

ii *1037. nature*] the agency of creation, who begins her work with light (cp. iii 1ff).

ii *1038. farthest*] spelt 'fardest'.

ii *1039. broken*] broked *Ed II*, almost certainly an error.

ii *1042. dubious light*] Echoes a phrase in Seneca's account of the passage of Hercules out of hell (*Hercules furens* 668).

ii *1043. holds*] remains in (*OED* I 7 d, citing Gavin Douglas, 'haldand the deip see'); perhaps secondarily 'reaches' (a Latinism, cp. *tenere*, to hold, reach).

ii *1048*. So wide that it was impossible to tell whether the boundary was rectilinear or curved. See also x 381*n*.

ii *1049–50*. In *Rev.* xxi 19 one of the foundations of the wall of the heavenly city is said to be of sapphire. *living*] native, unshaped; the city, like Jehovah's altar, is built not 'of hewn stone: for if thou lift up thy tool upon it, thou hast polluted it' (*Exod.* xx 25; see Tuve 183).

ii *1051*. Homer's Zeus asserts his transcendence by claiming that if a golden chain were lowered from Heaven, he could draw up by it all the other gods, together with the earth and the sea, and hang them from a pinnacle of Olympus (*Il.* viii 18–27). In *Prol ii* (Yale i 236) M. interprets this chain as 'the universal concord and sweet union of all things which Pythagoras poetically figures as harmony'; thus accepting a philosophical and literary tradition that runs from Plato (*Theaetetus* 153D), through Boethius (*De consolat.* iv prose 6 and metre 6: 'the bond of love'), Chaucer (*Knight's Tale* I (A) 2987–93: 'the faire cheyne of love') and Spenser (*F.Q.* II vii 46). The philosophical history of the idea is treated at length in Lovejoy 63 *et passim*, Emil Wolff, *Die goldene Kette* (Hamburg 1947) and in Ludwig Edelstein, 'The

This pendant world, in bigness as a star
Of smallest magnitude close by the moon.
Thither full fraught with mischievous revenge,
Accursed, and in a cursed hour he hies.

THE END OF THE SECOND BOOK

Paradise Lost

BOOK III

The Argument

God sitting on his throne sees Satan flying towards this world, then newly created; shows him to the Son who sat at his right hand; foretells the success of Satan in perverting mankind; clears his own justice and wisdom from all imputation, having created man free and able enough to have withstood his tempter; yet declares his purpose of grace towards him, in regard he fell not of his own malice, as did Satan, but by him seduced. The Son of God renders praise to his Father for the manifestation of his gracious purpose towards man; but God again declares, that grace cannot be extended toward man without the satisfaction of divine justice; man hath offended the majesty of God by aspiring to Godhead, and therefore with all his progeny devoted to death must die, unless some one can be found sufficient to answer for his offence, and undergo his punishment. The Son of God freely offers himself a ransom for man: the Father accepts him, ordains his incarnation, pro-

Golden Chain of Homer', *Studies in Intellectual History* (Baltimore, Md. 1953) pp. 48–67. Coming as it does immediately after the poem's principal treatment of chaos, the chain of Concord (or, as it was sometimes interpreted, the chain of Necessity) has the effect of binding and ordering. It is a necessary image, as it were, before we can pass to the worlds of order that follow. According to the cabbalists and alchemical philosophers the chain was a symbol (like Jacob's ladder) of the *scala naturae*; see iii 516–17*n*, v 469–90*n*, 483*n*.

ii *1052–3. This pendant world*] the whole created universe, which compared with heaven seems tiny. Our own world will not be visible until Satan has penetrated the 'firm opacous globe' of iii 418. 'Pendant' may mean 'in the balance, undecided' as well as 'hanging'. The simile echoes Dante, *Par.* xxviii 19–21.

ii *1054. fraught with*] destined to produce; but continuing also the mercantile or maritime images of ll. 636–42, 1043–4, etc.

nounces his exaltation above all names in heaven and earth; commands all the angels to adore him; they obey, and hymning to their harps in full choir, celebrate the Father and the Son. Mean while Satan alights upon the bare convex of this world's outermost orb; where wandering he first finds a place since called the Limbo of Vanity; what persons and things fly up thither; thence comes to the gate of heaven, described ascending by stairs, and the waters above the firmament that flow about it: his passage thence to the orb of the sun; he finds there Uriel the regent of that orb, but first changes himself into the shape of a meaner angel; and pretending a zealous desire to behold the new creation and man whom God had placed here, inquires of him the place of his habitation, and is directed; alights first on Mount Niphates.

Hail, holy Light, offspring of heaven first-born,
Or of the eternal co-eternal beam
May I express thee unblamed? since God is light,

iii *1–55*. A fresh exordium, as the *mise en scène* changes from hell and chaos to heaven (ll. 13–21; see vii 1–39*n*), and a ceremonial approach to the divine presence is required. With the new invocation, cp. that in Bk i, to the heavenly Muse and the Spirit, and that in Bk vii, to Urania; this is the most personal, yet also the richest in theological, philosophical, and artistic implications, which keep the autobiographical element firmly in proportion. There has been an extended controversy about the nature of the Light addressed in the invocation. The positions include (*a*) Sewell's, that the Light is the Son of God, like the 'living Light' of Dante, *Par.* xiii 55; (*b*) that M. 'was speaking of light in the physical sense', as ll. 21–4 indicate (Kelley 92–4); and (*c*) that the Light is both physical and divine: that M. followed the Platonic system, in which Light is not only the principal image of God, but also the divine emanation itself (cp. M.'s *effluence*), which breaks into separate beams to produce the various splendours of created things (Williams 54 and Allen 101). It is obvious from l. 2 and ll. 51–5 that more than a merely physical light (in the modern sense) is involved. And it is difficult to imagine that M. could have been uninfluenced by a central Christian tradition that extended from medieval versions of pseudo-Dionysius' mysticism of light (on which see Otto von Simson, *The Gothic Cathedral* (New York 1956) pp. 50–5), through Renaissance Neoplatonic developments (see, e.g., Ficino's *De sole* and *De lumine*, and his commentary on Dionysius' *De divinis nominibus*), to the philosophy of the Cambridge Platonists. But it would appear that, in his tentative address to 'that immortall light' which 'from th' eternall Truth . . . doth proceed' (Spenser, *An Hymne of Heavenly Beautie* 169–75), M. has deliberately eschewed, as far as he can, any presumptuous commitment to particular human systems of truth. On the placement of the four invocations of *PL*, see ix 1–47*n*; also Introduction, 'Numerology' (p. 442f).

iii *1–12*. The whole opening passage should be compared with Drummond of Hawthornden's 'An Hymn of the Fairest Fair', esp. ll. 125–30 and 137–42: 'O most holy One! / Unprocreate Father, ever-procreate Son, / Ghost

And never but in unapproached light
Dwelt from eternity, dwelt then in thee,
Bright effluence of bright essence increate.

breath'd from both, you were, are, aye shall be, / Most blessed, three in one, and one in three, / Incomprehensible by reachless height, / And unperceived by excessive light. . . . so the spring, / The well-head, and the stream which they forth bring, / Are but one selfsame essence, nor in aught / Do differ, save in order, and our thought / No chime of time discerns in them to fall, / But three distinctly bide one essence all.'

iii *1–8*. M. proposes three images or forms of address, *offspring*, *beam*, and *stream*, each of which associates the divine Light or Wisdom with a different aspect of deity. The passage as a whole recalls the address of the Wisdom of God by 3 x 7 names in *Wisdom* vii (Charles i 547). Cp. also the opening of Tasso's *Le sette giornate del mondo creato*: 'Father of heaven, and you of the Father eternal / Eternal Son, and uncreated offspring, / Of mind unchangeable the only child: / Image divine, to your divine example / Equal; and pure light of ardent light: / And you who breathe from both, and from both shine, / Or of doubled light the Spirit kindled / Who are pure holy light, from holy flame, / Like lucid stream within a fountain clear / And true image still of image true'.

iii *1*. Either 'Light the Son of God', or, as Kelley and others interpret the line, 'Light the first creation' (cp. vii 243–4, 'Light . . . first of things'). In the New Testament Christ is several times referred to as the firstborn; see, e.g., *Col.* i 15 and 18. *Ed I* fails to give *Light* an initial capital.

iii *2*. 'Or, Light the beam of the eternal, equally eternal with him.' Sewell regards 1f as a hesitation between Arian and Trinitarian formulations–between the view that the Son, the Word or Light of God, is begotten in time, and the view that he is co-eternal with the Father. But M.'s line of thought may be quite different, and more speculative; see Broadbent 141 on Fludd's question whether 'light is increate or created by an increate light'.

iii *3*. Presumably the blame could attach only to using the second name, *co-eternal beam;* it is this name which is justified by the implicit appeal to Scriptural authority that follows (3–6). *express*] represent symbolically, image. *God is Light*] From *1 John* i 5.

iii *4–5*. God 'only hath immortality, dwelling in the light which no man can approach unto' (*1 Tim.* vi 16). See vii 243–9*nn* for M.'s distinction between visible and invisible light.

iii *6*. *effluence*] effulgence, radiance; cp. *Wisdom* vii 25f, where the divine Sapience is said to be 'a clear effluence of the glory of the Almighty; / Therefore can nothing defiled find entrance into her. / For she is an effulgence from everlasting light' (Charles i 547). *essence increate*] the uncreated divine essence. In the physics and metaphysics of M.'s time, light was regarded as an 'accident' (quality), not a body or substance; see Fletcher ii 191.

Or hear'st thou rather pure ethereal stream,
Whose fountain who shall tell? Before the sun,
Before the heavens thou wert, and at the voice
Of God, as with a mantle didst invest
The rising world of waters dark and deep,
Won from the void and formless infinite.
Thee I revisit now with bolder wing,
Escaped the Stygian pool, though long detained
In that obscure sojourn, while in my flight
Through utter and through middle darkness borne
With other notes than to the Orphean lyre
I sung of Chaos and eternal Night,
Taught by the heavenly Muse to venture down
The dark descent, and up to reascend,
Though hard and rare: thee I revisit safe,
And feel thy sovereign vital lamp; but thou
Revisit'st not these eyes, that roll in vain

iii *7. hear'st thou rather*] do you prefer to be called; a Latinism: first instance in *OED*.
iii *8.* 'Where is the way where light dwelleth?' *Job* xxxviii 19; cp. Dante's vision of a river of light, which symbolizes grace poured forth upon creation (*Par.* xxx 61–73).
iii *9–12.* Cp. vii 233–52, and *Gen.* i 1–5. *invest*] cover, wrap. In *Ps.* civ 2 God covers himself 'with light as with a garment'. *void*] not of matter (see vii 233); M. refers to chaos.
iii *13–16.* The *Stygian pool* and the *utter* (outer) darkness is hell, the *middle darkness* chaos. The structural connections between the present ascent and the corresponding descent in vii 12–16, 21–5, are discussed in MacCaffrey 58. Cp. Dante's prayer in *Par.* xxxii 22–4, where he speaks of having ascended from the 'deepest pool of the universe'.
iii *17–21.* Alluding to the 'generally-sung fable of Orpheus, whom they faigne to have recovered his Euridice from Hell with his Musick, that is, Truth and Equity from darkenesse of Barbarisme and Ignorance with his profound and excellent Doctrines; but, that in the thicke caliginous way to the upper-earth, she was lost againe' (Henry Reynolds, *Mythomystes*, in *Critical Essays of the Seventeenth Century*, ed. J. E. Spingarn (Oxford, 1908) i 158–9). The allusion is especially apt in view of the common ground between the Orphic cosmogony and the account of the court of Chaos at the end of the last book.
iii *17. other notes*] Because M., unlike Orpheus, claims not to have lost his Eurydice.
iii *19. the heavenly Muse*] Urania; see vii 1.
iii *20–1.* On the Virgilian echo, see ii 432–3*n*.
iii *23.* Certainly now referring to physical light. But there is no change of address: the celestial light of Truth or Wisdom was thought of as purer and

To find thy piercing ray, and find no dawn;
So thick a drop serene hath quenched their orbs,
Or dim suffusion veiled. Yet not the more
Cease I to wander where the Muses haunt
Clear spring, or shady grove, or sunny hill,
Smit with the love of sacred song; but chief
Thee Sion and the flowery brooks beneath
That wash thy hallowed feet, and warbling flow,
Nightly I visit: nor sometimes forget
Those other two equalled with me in fate,
So were I equalled with them in renown,
Blind Thamyris, and blind Maeonides,
And Tiresias and Phineus prophets old.

brighter, but not categorically different from physical light. See Spenser, *An Hymne of Heavenly Beautie* 169–71, where the 'immortall light' of Truth 'is many thousand times more bright, more cleare, / More excellent, more glorious, more divine' than that of the sun. *roll*] spelt *rowle*.

iii *25. drop serene*] Literally translating *gutta serena*, the medical term for the form of blindness from which M. suffered.

iii *26. suffusion*] cataract (medical term); *dim suffusion* perhaps translates *suffusio nigra*.

iii *29.* An allusion to Virgil's prayer that 'smitten with a great love' of the Muses (*ingenti percussus amore*), he may be shown by them the secrets of nature (*Georg.* ii 475–89).

iii *30.* Among all the 'places' of *sacred song* M. chiefly visits Sion: i.e., he loves Hebrew poetry best. See i 10–11*n*, and cp. *PR* iv 347: 'Sion's songs, to all true tastes excelling'.

iii *32.* M. was often inspired to compose during the night; see vii *29n. nor . . . forget*] often remember.

iii *34. So were I equalled*] would that I were similarly equalled.

iii *35–6. Thamyris*] A Thracian poet mentioned in Homer, *Il.* ii 594–600, who fell in love with the Muses and challenged them to a contest in which the loser was to give the winner whatever he wanted. The Muses having won took Thamyris' eyes and his lyre (sometimes, his ability to sing), so that it became proverbial to say of those who attempted what was beyond their talents, '*Thamyras insanit*' (*Dictionarium historicum ac poeticum* (Lyons 1579)). No prophetic compositions of Thamyris' survived, so that M. may mean that he pondered on the myth of his fate as a blinded bard. (Or perhaps M. feels a reasonable trepidation in case the portrayal of heaven may be beyond *his* talents?) *Maeonides*] Homer's surname; 'blind Homer' would have been infelicitous, for Calepinus and others derived that name from a Greek word for eyes. The contrast between his outward blindness and inner vision was a commonplace. Pico–who like other Renaissance philosophers sought a mystical connection between blindness and initiation–cites both Homer and Tiresias as examples: 'many who were rap-

Then feed on thoughts, that voluntary move
Harmonious numbers; as the wakeful bird
Sings darkling, and in shadiest covert hid
Tunes her nocturnal note. Thus with the year
Seasons return, but not to me returns
Day, or the sweet approach of even or morn,
Or sight of vernal bloom, or summer's rose,
Or flocks, or herds, or human face divine;
But cloud in stead, and ever-during dark
Surrounds me, from the cheerful ways of men
Cut off, and for the book of knowledge fair
Presented with a universal blank
Of nature's works to me expunged and razed,
And wisdom at one entrance quite shut out.

tured to the vision of spiritual beauty, were by the same cause blinded in their corporal eyes'; see Wind 61. In his Latin poem *De Idea Platonica* (p. 67), M. refers to *Tiresias* as 'the Dircaean augur, whose very blindness gave him boundless light' (*profundum lumen*). The Thracian king *Phineus* lost his sight, according to one account, because he had become too good a prophet and was publishing the counsels of the gods (Hyginus, *Fab.* xix). In the *Second Defence* M. quotes Apollonius Rhodius to similar effect, but only to refute this explanation. 'Recompensed with far more excelling gifts', Phineus' loss of sight (like M.'s own, it is implied) 'is not to be considered as the punishment for any crime' (Columbia viii 63ff).

iii *37–8*. The double syntax is noticed in Davie[2] 73. *move* seems intransitive until *Harmonious numbers* reveals it as transitive: 'This flicker of hesitation about whether the thoughts move only themselves, or something else, makes us see that the numbers aren't really "something else" but are the very thoughts themselves, seen under a new aspect.'

iii *38. numbers*] rhythmic measure. *wakeful bird*] the nightingale. Is it coincidence that the soul of Thamyris passed into a nightingale (Plato, *Rep.* 620 A)?

iii *39. darkling*] in the dark; not yet a specially poetic word.

iii *47. the book of knowledge*] The Book of Nature; cp. viii 67, 'the book of God'. For the history of the commonplace, see Curtius 319–26; among many other examples he cites this from Quarles: 'The world's a book in folio, printed all / With God's great works in letters capital: / Each creature is a page; and each effect / A fair character, void of all defect.' The mention is appropriate here, in the invocation that begins the part of the poem in which the Book or Mirror of Nature itself will appear. See Introduction, 'Numerology'.

iii *48. blank*] spelt 'blanc' (but M. did not distinguish orthographically different senses of 'blank', as Grierson argued). The primary sense is 'blank page' (cp. *OED* 5–7), carrying on the metaphor of the previous line. But 'void' may be a secondary meaning (*OED* 6 b).

So much the rather thou celestial Light
Shine inward, and the mind through all her powers
Irradiate, there plant eyes, all mist from thence
Purge and disperse, that I may see and tell
Of things invisible to mortal sight.
 Now had the almighty Father from above,
From the pure empyrean where he sits
High throned above all highth, bent down his eye,
His own works and their works at once to view:
About him all the sanctities of heaven
Stood thick as stars, and from his sight received
Beatitude past utterance; on his right
The radiant image of his glory sat,
His only Son; on earth he first beheld
Our two first parents, yet the only two
Of mankind, in the happy garden placed,
Reaping immortal fruits of joy and love,
Uninterrupted joy, unrivalled love
In blissful solitude; he then surveyed

iii *51–5*. On external blindness as an opportunity for inner illumination, see 35–6*n* and esp. Wind 61. *all mist . . . purge*] Cp. Beelzebub's hope that the devils may somewhere 'purge off this gloom' at heaven's 'orient beam' (ii 399f). See also M.'s similar prayer at i 22–6.
iii *59*. Beginning the first of the poem's comprehensive panoramic views of creation. This one has its obvious counterpart later in the book, in Satan's 'sudden view / Of all this world at once' (ll. 542f) – the view of one planning not man's salvation but his destruction. More distantly, there is a resonance with vi 673, where we learn that God eternally sits 'consulting on the sum of things'. *their works*] The works performed by creatures who are themselves the works of God.
iii *60*. *sanctities*] gods; by a metonymy they are represented by one of their qualities, holiness.
iii *61–2*. On the supreme happiness of the beatific vision of the faithful in heaven, see i 684*n* and *De doctrina* i 33 (Columbia xvi 375): 'perfect happiness, arising chiefly from the divine vision'.
iii *63*. In *De doctrina* i 5 (Columbia xiv 193), M. admires the 'sublimity and copiousness' with which 'the generation of the divine nature is described' in *Heb*. i 2f: 'His Son . . . Who being the brightness of his glory, and the express image of his person . . . when he had by himself purged our sins, sat down on the right hand of the Majesty on high.'
iii *69–73*. On the change in perspective, whereby Satan is now reduced in scale to a 'small night-bird', see MacCaffrey 60. *on this side night*] 'Translates what is for us a temporal unit into a physical area, as it would look if we could escape the limits of earthly knowledge' (*ibid*.; but see iv 555*n*). *sublime*] aloft. *stoop*] 'descend from aloft' (esp. of bird of

Hell and the gulf between, and Satan there
Coasting the wall of heaven on this side night
In the dun air sublime, and ready now
To stoop with wearied wings, and willing feet,
On the bare outside of this world, that seemed
Firm land imbosomed without firmament,
Uncertain which, in ocean or in air.
Him God beholding from his prospect high,
Wherein past, present, future he beholds,
Thus to his only Son foreseeing spake.
Only begotten Son, seest thou what rage
Transports our adversary, whom no bounds
Prescribed, no bars of hell, nor all the chains
Heaped on him there, nor yet the main abyss
Wide interrupt can hold; so bent he seems
On desperate revenge, that shall redound
Upon his own rebellious head. And now
Through all restraint broke loose he wings his way
Not far off heaven, in the precincts of light,
Directly towards the new created world,
And man there placed, with purpose to assay

prey); perhaps also suggesting the human posture of weariness, as well as metaphorical stooping or degradation. The close juxtaposition of this bird image with that of ll. 38–40 is provocative. *dun air*] perhaps imitates the common Italian description of murkiness as *aer bruno*.

iii *74. world*] universe, not earth; see ii 1052–3*n*.

iii *75. firmament*] The firmament or atmosphere (see vii 261–7), being inside the shell of the universe that Satan stands on, is invisible to him.

iii *76.* 'It being difficult to see whether the surrounding matrix was liquid or gaseous.' In chaos the usual categories are confused; cp. ii 939f.

iii *77.* On the spatial quality of God's simultaneous vision, see MacCaffrey 53f. *prospect*] look-out point (*OED* I 1 b).

iii *80–6.* 'The only consistent view after the firm statement [at i 209f, where Satan's release is permitted by God; cp. also the more recent statement to the same effect, at ii 1025] is that this is the first of God's grisly jokes' (Empson 119). Grisly or not, the passage is certainly sardonic–a tone set by the opening pun on *Transports.* On the syntax Ricks 60 comments: 'The crucial verb *can hold* flies triumphantly free, at the very end of its clause, from the grip of the previous twenty-two words of heaped chains.'

iii *83–4.* Cp. ii 405–9. *interrupt*] breached; not a Latinism. *wide*] Formerly as often adverbial as adjectival.

iii *88. precincts*] Often applied to the ground immediately surrounding a place of worship.

iii *90. assay*] test, try. Notice that the phrase *with . . . assay* can relate not only to *wings* (with Satan as subject) but also to *placed* (with God as subject).

If him by force he can destroy, or worse,
By some false guile pervert; and shall pervert
For man will hearken to his glozing lies,
And easily transgress the sole command,
Sole pledge of his obedience: so will fall,
He and his faithless progeny: whose fault?
Whose but his own? Ingrate, he had of me
All he could have; I made him just and right,
Sufficient to have stood, though free to fall.
Such I created all the ethereal powers
And spirits, both them who stood and them who failed;
Freely they stood who stood, and fell who fell.
Not free, what proof could they have given sincere
Of true allegiance, constant faith or love,
Where only what they needs must do, appeared,
Not what they would? What praise could they receive?

The ambiguity expresses the character of providence: viewed in one way the purposefulness is all Satan's, in another, all God's.
iii *94–5. the sole command*] i.e. not to taste the fruit of the forbidden tree. *sole pledge*] Cp. iv 428 ('the sign of our obedience'), v 551, and viii 329; also *De doctrina* i 10 (Columbia xv 115): 'The tree of knowledge of good and evil was not a sacrament, as it is generally called; for a sacrament is a thing to be used, not abstained from: but a pledge, as it were, and memorial of obedience.' The emphasis accords with that of the main Christian tradition, as St Augustine, e.g., expresses it: the Fall was a lapse from 'obedience, the mother and guardian of all the other virtues'; the command being a single one was 'easy to observe; and so short to remember' (*Civ. Dei* xiv 12). See Lewis 67f. Burden 126 notes that the fruit is never mentioned in iii; since *sub specie aeternitatis* it is seen to exist solely as a test of obedience.
iii *96*. The epithet *faithless* is transferred from *He* to *progeny*, just as Adam's guilt and its consequences pass on to his descendants. They are involved with him in the original sin of breaking faith with God, because 'he either stood or fell for the whole human race' (*De doctrina* i 11: Columbia xv 183); cf. 209 below.
iii *98–9. Sufficient*] Referring to the doctrine of Sufficient Grace, then common ground for almost all Christians; see Corcoran 104f.
iii *100–2*. Satan later (iv 63–72) admits what is stated here and at v 525–43: that the angels, like Adam and Eve, had the power to 'persevere', to remain faithful. The equilibrium, then, was such that the fall of the rebel angels depended solely on their own free will.
iii *103–6*. See *De doctrina* i 4 (Columbia xiv 141): if free will 'be not admitted, whatever worship or love we render to God is entirely vain and of no value; the acceptableness of duties done under a law of necessity . . . is annihilated altogether, inasmuch as freedom can no longer be attributed to that will over which some fixed decree is inevitably suspended'.

What pleasure I from such obedience paid,
When will and reason (reason also is choice)
Useless and vain, of freedom both despoiled,
Made passive both, had served necessity,
Not me. They therefore as to right belonged,
So were created, nor can justly accuse
Their maker, or their making, or their fate,
As if predestination overruled
Their will, disposed by absolute decree
Or high foreknowledge; they themselves decreed
Their own revolt, not I: if I foreknew,
Foreknowledge had no influence on their fault,
Which had no less proved certain unforeknown.
So without least impulse or shadow of fate,
Or aught by me immutably foreseen,
They trespass, authors to themselves in all
Both what they judge and what they choose; for so
I formed them free, and free they must remain,
Till they enthrall themselves: I else must change

iii *108*. M. probably alludes here to Aristotle's analysis of choice in *Nic. Ethics* 1112^a (though see also *Commonplace Book* (Yale i 363)); as he does in *Areopagitica* (Yale ii 527): those are foolish who 'complain of divin Providence for suffering Adam to transgresse, foolish tongues! when God gave him reason, he gave him freedom to choose, for reason is but choosing; he had bin else a meer artificiall Adam.'
iii *110*. God disassociates himself from Necessity or Fate, which has become the devils' idea of the supreme power.
iii *113–23*. *De doctrina* i 4 shows that M. believed in a liberal version of the doctrine of Predestination, but that he carefully defined predestination and foreknowledge in such a way as to exclude 'necessity' or determinism. See, e.g., Columbia xiv 85: 'Future events which God has foreseen, will happen certainly . . . because the divine prescience cannot be deceived, but they will not happen necessarily, because prescience can have no influence on the object foreknown, inasmuch as it is only an intransitive action.'
iii *120*. As the use of the logical term *impulse* signalizes, M. is here explicitly allowing God to exonerate himself from responsibility for the 'more proximate' efficient causes of the Fall (Howard 158).
iii *125–8*. The predicament of God is similarly appreciated in *De doctrina* i 3 (Columbia xiv 77): 'God is not mutable, so long as he decrees nothing absolutely which could happen otherwise through the liberty assigned to man; he would indeed be mutable, neither would his counsel stand, if he were to obstruct by another decree that liberty which he had already decreed, or were to darken it with the least shadow of necessity.'
iii *125*. Apparently now referring once again to Adam and Eve, though there has been no signposting of the abandonment of 'ethereal powers' (l. 100)

Their nature, and revoke the high decree
Unchangeable, eternal, which ordained
Their freedom, they themselves ordained their fall.
The first sort by their own suggestion fell,
Self-tempted, self-depraved: man falls deceived
By the other first: man therefore shall find grace,
The other none: in mercy and justice both,
Through heaven and earth, so shall my glory excel,
But mercy first and last shall brightest shine.
Thus while God spake, ambrosial fragrance filled
All heaven, and in the blessed spirits elect
Sense of new joy ineffable diffused:
Beyond compare the Son of God was seen

as a subject. This grammatical fluidity allows the Fall (undetermined whether angelic or human) to be now future (l. 125), now present (ll. 122f and 130), now past (ll. 116, 118f, and 128); thus rendering God's single 'prospect high, / Wherein past, present, future he beholds'.

iii *129. suggestion*] temptation. *sort*] species. Some have found here a contradiction of v 694–6 and 703–10, where Raphael implies that the rebel angels were tempted into their Fall by Satan. But here M. simply means that the angelic species fell by intramural temptation, from within their own kind; whereas the human species will fall by temptation from without, from the *other* (sort, species). The theory that a deliberate disparity is intended between the two accounts of the angels' Fall leans heavily on the existence of separate theological traditions on this point in the seventeenth century (see E. F. Daniels, 'Milton's fallen angels–self corrupted or seduced?', *N & Q* ccv (1960) 447–50). Even if the theory were right, we need not infer that God is being portrayed as harsh. *De doctrina* i 9 shows that M. held God's more disparaging account to be true, and Raphael would naturally be partial in judging his own kind.

iii *135. ambrosial*] See ii 245*n*.

iii *136. spirits elect*] the 'elect angels' of *1 Tim.* v 21–explained in *De doctrina* i 9 as angels 'who have not revolted'; for M. rejected the view that 'the good angels are now upheld, not so much by their own strength, as by the grace of God', and that because of their own election they have a 'delighted interest . . . in the mystery of man's salvation'. Instead he thought that 'the good angels are upheld by their own strength no less than man himself was before his fall;–that they are called *elect*, in the sense of beloved, or excellent;–that it is not from any interest of their own, but from their love to mankind, that they desire to look into the mystery of our salvation' (Columbia xv 97–9).

iii *138–42.* Ricks 140 contrasts 'the passions and pains which scar Adam and Eve and Satan', who are 'defaced' (ix 901) by sin. In the present passage 'it is not likely to be an accident that "Grace" there so plangently echoes "face", nor that the rhyme is proffered by the magnificent chiasmus of the

Most glorious, in him all his Father shone
Substantially expressed, and in his face
Divine compassion visibly appeared,
Love without end, and without measure grace,
Which uttering thus he to his Father spake.
O Father, gracious was that word which closed
Thy sovereign sentence, that man should find grace;
For which both heaven and earth shall high extol
Thy praises, with the innumerable sound
Of hymns and sacred songs, wherewith thy throne
Encompassed shall resound thee ever blessed.
For should man finally be lost, should man
Thy creature late so loved, thy youngest son

last line'. Rhyme and chiasmus were both schemes used, often, to express likeness or correspondence.

iii *139–40*. Taken by Sewell as evidence that *PL* iii represents an earlier, more orthodox, stage in the development of M.'s christological opinions than *De doctrina* i 5, which denies the Son to be co-essential with the Father (Columbia xiv 187). But *Substantially expressed* may mean only that 'God imparted to the Son as much as he pleased of the divine nature, nay of the divine substance itself, care being taken not to confound the substance with the whole essence' (*De doctrina* i 5, Columbia xiv 193, glossing *Heb.* i 2f, the same text that underlies the present passage); in which case the phrase need not conflict with M.'s later Arianism (Kelley 29f). At the same time, the emphasis laid in *all his Father* shows that M. is here avoiding theological controversy and seeking–as far as his own position will allow–a generally acceptable catholic statement of the Biblical doctrine of divine generation.

iii *140*. *expressed*] In one chain of discourse perhaps not a past participle but an intransitive preterite (*OED* II 8 b); then *all his Father* would be the subject of three parallel verbs–*shone*, *expressed* and *appeared*. The uncertainty as to the subject of *appeared* would not be a trivial ambiguity; for it would render the fulness of the Father's expression in the Son's compassion.

iii *142*. The Son of God, Adam, and Satan are all described as gloriously heroic, but each manifests heroic excess or preeminence in a characteristically different quality. With the Son it is grace 'without measure'; with Adam, 'exceeding love' (ix 961); with Satan, merit (ii 427–9) (Steadman 92).

iii *144*. Broadbent 148f thinks that 'the Son's rhetoric is more flexible'. It is true that the Father speaks more with the closed hand of logic, the Son with the open hand of rhetoric, and that the latter often gives a lyrical expansion of a theme stated by the former. But what is more striking is the faithfulness with which the Son's speeches reflect the Father's–a correlate, at the formal level, of his obedience in imaging the divine will.

iii *145*. *sovereign*] spelt 'sovran'.

iii *147–9*. *sound . . . resound*] The repetition, which Bentley disliked, is of course mimetic.

Fall circumvented thus by fraud, though joined
With his own folly? That be from thee far,
That far be from thee, Father, who art judge
Of all things made, and judgest only right.
Or shall the adversary thus obtain
His end, and frustrate thine, shall he fulfil
His malice, and thy goodness bring to nought,
Or proud return though to his heavier doom,
Yet with revenge accomplished and to hell
Draw after him the whole race of mankind,
By him corrupted? Or wilt thou thy self
Abolish thy creation, and unmake,
For him, what for thy glory thou hast made?
So should thy goodness and thy greatness both
Be questioned and blasphemed without defence.
  To whom the great creator thus replied.
O Son, in whom my soul hath chief delight,
Son of my bosom, Son who art alone
My word, my wisdom, and effectual might,
All hast thou spoken as my thoughts are, all
As my eternal purpose hath decreed:
Man shall not quite be lost, but saved who will,

iii *152–3*. 'Even if man's own folly did contribute (together with fraud) to his circumvention.'

iii *153–4*. Cp. *Gen.* xviii 25: 'That be far from thee to do after this manner, to slay the righteous with the wicked: and that the righteous should be as the wicked, that be far from thee.'

iii *156*. *adversary*] The literal meaning of *Satan*; see i 82*n*.

iii *163*. At ii 367–70 Beelzebub considers the possibility that if the devils seduce rather than attack mankind, God may be forced to 'abolish his own works'.

iii *166*. *blasphemed*] defamed.

iii *168–9*. Echoing *Mark* i 11, the words out of the heavens at Jesus' baptism: 'Thou art my beloved Son, in whom I am well pleased' (cp. *Is.* xlii 1): also *John* i 18: 'the only begotten Son, which is in the bosom of the Father'.

iii *170*. Steadman finds an echo of *Aen.* i 664 (*nate, meae vires, mea magna potentia*)–words of Venus to her son which had been transferred to the Christian God of love, speaking at the baptism of Christ, in Proba's *Centones Virgiliani ad Testimonium Veteris et Novi Testamenti* (alluded to by St Jerome: see 'Milton, Virgil, and St Jerome ("Paradise Lost", iii 168–170)', *N & Q* cciv (1959)). Cp. also, however, *1 Cor.* i 24: 'Christ the power of God'. The Son is God's *effectual* might, because he is the Word or Logos by whom God's creative will is made effective (*John* i 1–3).

iii *173–202*. In *De doctrina* i 4, M. undeniably sets out an Arminian position, explicitly opposed to the Calvinist, on such doctrines as Predestination,

Yet not of will in him, but grace in me
Freely vouchsafed; once more I will renew
His lapsed powers, though forfeit and enthralled
By sin to foul exorbitant desires;
Upheld by me, yet once more he shall stand
On even ground against his mortal foe,
By me upheld, that he may know how frail
His fallen condition is, and to me owe
All his deliverance, and to none but me.
Some I have chosen of peculiar grace
Elect above the rest; so is my will:

Election and Reprobation, and he could be regarded as doing something similar here (Kelley 15–18); e.g., his God seems to make salvation depend on man's will to avail himself of grace–or on *prayer, repentance, and obedience* (l. 191); whereas Calvinists regarded man as totally incapable of contributing in any way to his own salvation (Calvin, *Institutes* III xxii 1–3). By the logic of M.'s day, however, he would not be taken to mean that repentance was a link in a causal chain leading to salvation, but only that it was one of a set of parallel causes. In itself the notice of the 'helping cause' man's will (l. 173) as well as the 'instrumental cause' God's grace (l. 174) was uncontroversial, and might well have been acceptable to Calvinist readers (Howard 168). But, in emphasis at least, the succeeding passage is less conventional. While predestinarian theologians usually made a radical separation between the secret and the revealed wills of God, M. here asserts their unity: God's secret will is free only for good. And throughout (*pace* Empson 120) the Calvinist *impasse* of a capricious deity, at once offering redemption and predestinating reprobation, is strenuously avoided (see further Schultz 129–31). The ordonnance exemplifies this strikingly: M. makes God speak about Predestination first, long before getting round to Atonement (ll. 203–16); thus revealing his eagerness (as it were) to save man. 'The ultimate purpose of predestination is salvation . . . God could never have predestinated reprobation' (*De doctrina* i 4; Columbia xiv 99).

iii *175. vouchsafed*] spelt 'voutsafed'.

iii *176. lapsed*] decayed; fallen into sin; forfeited (like *forfeit*, legal terminology) (*OED* I 2, 1 b, 3). The theological meaning of the noun 'lapse' (='the Fall') is also relevant. The legal diction here and throughout ll. 204–24 is appropriate to the Anselmic theory of the Atonement that M. mainly relies on (see ll. 210–12*n*). The forfeit of man's powers over the passions is described in similar legal or political imagery, after it has actually taken place (ix 1127–31, xii 88–90; see Lewis 68).

iii *179. mortal*] Both 'implacable' and 'death-dealing'; cp. i 1–2*n*.

iii *180–1. Ps.* xxxix 4: 'Lord, make me to know . . . how frail I am.'

iii *184.* By the term *elect* M. usually means no more than 'whoever believes and continues in the faith' (*De doctrina* i 4; Columbia xiv 125). See also *ibid.* 117: 'Believers are the same as the elect.'

The rest shall hear me call, and oft be warned
Their sinful state, and to appease betimes
The incensed Deity, while offered grace
Invites; for I will clear their senses dark,
What may suffice, and soften stony hearts
To pray, repent, and bring obedience due.
To prayer, repentance, and obedience due,
Though but endeavoured with sincere intent,
Mine ear shall not be slow, mine eye not shut.
And I will place within them as a guide
My umpire conscience, whom if they will hear,
Light after light well used they shall attain,
And to the end persisting, safe arrive.
This my long sufferance and my day of grace
They who neglect and scorn, shall never taste;
But hard be hardened, blind be blinded more,
That they may stumble on, and deeper fall;
And none but such from mercy I exclude.
But yet all is not done; man disobeying,
Disloyal breaks his fealty, and sins
Against the high supremacy of heaven,
Affecting Godhead, and so losing all,
To expiate his treason hath nought left,
But to destruction sacred and devote,

iii *193.* The fulfilment of this promise begins at xi 1–47, when God receives the prayer and repentance of Adam and Eve.

iii *194–5.* To be distinguished from the Comforter, sent to *guide* only God's 'own' (xii 486–90). The notion of conscience or reason as an arbitrator between God and man was very important to M. In a sense the whole poem depends on it: only if reason is the court of appeal for both, can there be any question of justifying to man the ways of God.

iii *197–200.* Cp. *Heb.* iii 13f: 'Exhort one another daily, while it is called To day; lest any of you be hardened through . . . sin. For we are made partakers of Christ, if we hold the beginning of our confidence stedfast unto the end.' M. defends God's hardening of sinners' hearts in *De doctrina* i 8 (Columbia xv 81): 'As God's instigating the sinner does not render him the author of sin, so neither does his hardening the heart or blinding the understanding involve that consequence; inasmuch as he does not produce these effects by infusing an evil disposition, but on the contrary by employing such just and kind methods, as ought rather to soften the hearts of sinners than harden them.'

iii *206.* At ix 708–17 Satan tempts Eve with the promise that she and Adam will 'be as gods'. *Affecting*] seeking, aiming at.

iii *208.* *sacred*] dedicated, accursed. *devote*] consigned to destruction (*OED* s.v. *Devoted* 3).

He with his whole posterity must die,
Die he or justice must; unless for him
Some other able, and as willing, pay
The rigid satisfaction, death for death.
Say heavenly powers, where shall we find such love,
Which of ye will be mortal to redeem
Man's mortal crime, and just the unjust to save,
Dwells in all heaven charity so dear?
He asked, but all the heavenly choir stood mute,
And silence was in heaven: on man's behalf
Patron or intercessor none appeared,
Much less that durst upon his own head draw
The deadly forfeiture, and ransom set.
And now without redemption all mankind
Must have been lost, adjudged to death and hell
By doom severe, had not the Son of God,
In whom the fulness dwells of love divine,
His dearest mediation thus renewed.

iii *210–12.* Note that the death of man is here regarded by God not as a punishment, but as a *satisfaction* for the treason. See *De doctrina* i 16 (Columbia xv 315–17): 'The satisfaction of Christ is the complete reparation made by him . . . by the fulfilment of the Law, and payment of the required price for all mankind.' In general M. takes for granted the 'Satisfaction theory' of the Atonement, which had been widely accepted ever since St Anselm first expounded it. Occasionally, however, as at ll. 221–3, he alludes to the earlier 'ransom theory' of St Irenaeus, St Augustine, and others. *as willing*] as willing as he is able.
iii *214–15. will be mortal*] (i.e., is willing to be subject to death) corresponds to 'willing' at l. 211, as *just*– i.e., righteous, perfectly obedient within the human context, capable of offering worthy satisfaction–corresponds to 'able' in the same line. Cp. *1 Pet.* iii 18: 'Christ also hath once suffered for sins, the just for the unjust.' For the pun on 'mortal' see 179*n*; with the play on *just*, cp. l. 252, and i 642.
iii *216. charity*] compassionate love, *caritas*.
iii *217–26.* So at the hellish council (ii 418–26) 'all sat mute', since none of the devils dared undertake the expedition against man. 'Satan alone was fit to undertake the one [work], as the Son of God the other' (Newton). The passage impressed Dryden enough to inspire a sustained imitation in *The Hind and the Panther* ii 499–514.
iii *218.* Cp. *Rev.* viii 1: when the seventh seal was opened 'there was silence in heaven'.
iii *219. Patron*] advocate.
iii *221. ransom set*] put down the ransom price (i.e. by giving his own life).
iii *224. doom*] judgment.
iii *225. Col.* ii 9: 'In him dwelleth all the fulness of the Godhead bodily.'

Father, thy word is past, man shall find grace;
And shall Grace not find means, that finds her way,
The speediest of thy winged messengers,
To visit all thy creatures, and to all
Comes unprevented, unimplored, unsought,
Happy for man, so coming; he her aid
Can never seek, once dead in sins and lost;
Atonement for himself or offering meet,
Indebted and undone, hath none to bring:
Behold me then, me for him, life for life
I offer, on me let thine anger fall;
Account me man; I for his sake will leave
Thy bosom, and this glory next to thee
Freely put off, and for him lastly die
Well pleased, on me let Death wreak all his rage;
Under his gloomy power I shall not long
Lie vanquished; thou hast given me to possess
Life in my self for ever, by thee I live,
Though now to Death I yield, and am his due

iii *227. thy word is past*] Not merely 'thy speech is uttered', but 'thy word of honour is pledged'.
iii *231. unprevented*] unanticipated, therefore not even prayed for. Cp. the Collect 'Prevent us, O Lord, in all our doings'; and contrast *Ps.* lxxxviii 13: 'in the morning shall my prayer prevent thee'. The line alludes to the doctrine of divine Prevenience–the priority of God's love to man's response. On the rhetorical scheme, see ii 185*n*.
iii *232–5*. Developing the idea introduced at l. 207. *Happy*] fortunate.
iii *233*. *Eph.* ii 4f: 'God . . . for his great love . . . even when we were dead in sins, hath quickened us.'
iii *236–8*. The dramatic repetition of the pronoun occurs again in a related passage, vi 812–8, where the Son is an instrument, not of grace to mankind, but of revenge on the rebel angels. Cp. x 738–40, and see x 832*n*. But M. may also intend an echo of Nisus' guilt-accepting cry at *Aen.* ix 427–8: *Me, me, adsum, qui feci, in me convertit ferrum, / O Rutuli! mea fraus omnis.*
iii *240. lastly die*] As a 'description of the career of the Son' the phrase is puzzling (Empson 127). But is it intended to be such a description? Perhaps rather it mentions the third and last–in logical rather than in chronological order–of the diminishments accepted by Christ at the Incarnation.
iii *243–4*. Cp. *John* v 26: 'As the Father hath life in himself: so hath he given to the Son to have life in himself.'
iii *245–9*. Kelley thinks that M. is here 'tersely' presenting the Mortalist doctrine, according to which death is suffered not only by the body but also by the soul. Thus 'even the soul of Christ was for a short time subject unto death', and *All that of me can die* means 'the whole man . . . body, soul, and spirit' (Kelley 32). Admittedly *De doctrina* i 13 shows that M. embraced

All that of me can die, yet that debt paid,
Thou wilt not leave me in the loathsome grave
His prey, nor suffer my unspotted soul
For ever with corruption there to dwell;
But I shall rise victorious, and subdue
My vanquisher, spoiled of his vaunted spoil;
Death his death's wound shall then receive, and stoop
Inglorious, of his mortal sting disarmed.
I through the ample air in triumph high
Shall lead hell captive maugre hell, and show
The powers of darkness bound. Thou at the sight
Pleased, out of heaven shalt look down and smile,
While by thee raised I ruin all my foes,
Death last, and with his carcass glut the grave:
Then with the multitude of my redeemed
Shall enter heaven long absent, and return,

the so-called Mortalist 'heresy'; but the doctrine could only be extracted from the present passage by force. 'Milton is not splitting theological hairs; he is dealing with the justice of Christ's incarnation and crucifixion' (Hughes).
iii *248–59*. As is usual with the poem's divine utterances, this speech is a carefully interwoven tissue of Scriptural allusions (Sims 18–19).
iii *248–9*. Cp. *Ps.* xvi 10, where David, the type of Christ, prophesies: 'Thou wilt not leave my soul in hell; neither wilt thou suffer thine Holy One to see corruption.'
iii *251–3*. Cp. *Col.* ii 15, 'having spoiled principalities and powers'. The image of death's sting, used also by Michael in his prophecy of Christ's victory at xii 432, is from *1 Cor.* xv 55–6: 'O death, where is thy sting? O grave, where is thy victory? The sting of death is sin; and the strength of sin is the law.' *Death his death's wound* is often taken to be no more than a verbal play. But the meaning is exact: death is fatally wounded at this stage, but not 'killed' until the second coming of Christ (l. 259).
iii *255*. Cp. *Ps.* lxviii 18, applied to Christ in *Eph.* iv 8: 'When he ascended up on high, he led captivity captive.' *maugre*] in spite of.
iii *256*. Cp. again *Col.* ii 15: 'Having spoiled principalities and powers, he made a shew of them openly, triumphing over them in it.' Also *Col.* i 13, 'power of darkness'.
iii *259*. *Death last*] Alludes to *1 Cor.* xv 26: 'The last enemy that shall be destroyed is death.' Cp. Sin's prophecy at ii 734.
iii *261*. A difficult line, because the Son speaks of only one absence: he conflates his first with his second coming. Since he thinks of his reentry into heaven 'with the multitude of [his] redeemed' as taking place after his final ruin of Death (ll. 259–61), it seems that he envisages being away throughout what we would call history, and perhaps also during the millenium speculated on by Michael at xii 461–5. There are at least three possible lines of interpretation: (1) The Son does not have complete foreknowledge, and

Father, to see thy face, wherein no cloud
Of anger shall remain, but peace assured,
And reconcilement; wrath shall be no more
Thenceforth, but in thy presence joy entire.
His words here ended, but his meek aspect
Silent yet spake, and breathed immortal love
To mortal men, above which only shone
Filial obedience: as a sacrifice
Glad to be offered, he attends the will
Of his great Father. Admiration seized
All heaven, what this might mean, and whither tend
Wondering; but soon the almighty thus replied:
O thou in heaven and earth the only peace
Found out for mankind under wrath, O thou
My sole complacence! well thou know'st how dear,
To me are all my works, nor man the least
Though last created, that for him I spare
Thee from my bosom and right hand, to save,
By losing thee awhile, the whole race lost.
Thou therefore whom thou only canst redeem,
Their nature also to thy nature join;
And be thy self man among men on earth,
Made flesh, when time shall be, of virgin seed,

underestimates the complexity of the task before him (Empson 127). He imagines, reasonably but mistakenly, that one mission will be enough. (2) The Son offers 'a longer mission than the Father decided to require of him' (Empson 129). Similarly the crucifixion is not mentioned for the sublime reason that it is thought a 'trivial sacrifice'. (3) M. is here presenting a supratemporal vision (like Donne's in 'At the round earths imagin'd corners, blow'), so that we should not look for detailed chronological sequence. The important thing, *sub specie aeternitatis*, is simply that heaven has to be left at all. M.'s occasional use of a timeless present is in accord with this third interpretation: see l. 301*n*.

iii *267–9*. Note that the Son's obedience is superior to his charity; as indeed it must be, according to M.'s hierarchy of the virtues. Messiah is the only heroically obedient person in the poem (see vi 820–3*n*, ix 31–2*n*, vii 602–7*n*, and Steadman 93). *attends*] awaits.

iii *271*. *Admiration*] Either in its modern sense; or in its older sense, 'wonder'; or in both.

iii *276*. *complacence*] source of complacence, satisfaction. See ll. 210–12*n*. Comma after *dear* is almost certainly an error.

iii *277–8*. Cp. *King Lear* I i 85: to Lear, Cordelia is 'Although our last, not least'.

iii *283–4*. Echoing *John* i 14: 'The Word was made flesh.'

By wondrous birth: be thou in Adam's room
The head of all mankind, though Adam's son.
As in him perish all men, so in thee
As from a second root shall be restored,
As many as are restored, without thee none.
His crime makes guilty all his sons, thy merit
Imputed shall absolve them who renounce
Their own both righteous and unrighteous deeds,
And live in thee transplanted, and from thee
Receive new life. So man, as is most just,
Shall satisfy for man, be judged and die,
And dying rise, and rising with him raise
His brethren, ransomed with his own dear life.
So heavenly love shall outdo hellish hate
Giving to death, and dying to redeem,

iii *285–6.* Cp. *1 Cor.* xi 3: 'The head of every man is Christ.' *room*] place.
iii *287.* Cp. *1 Cor.* xv 22: 'As in Adam all die, even so in Christ shall all be made alive.'
iii *290–4.* The general course of the argument follows that of *Rom.* v 17–19.
iii *290–2.* The source is ultimately *Rom.* iv 5–8 (e.g. 6: 'the blessedness of the man, unto whom God imputeth righteousness without works'), but the doctrine of Imputed Righteousness had in M.'s day come to be a very familiar topic for theological debate. For a simple statement, see *De doctrina* i 22 (Columbia xvi 27): 'As therefore our sins are imputed to Christ, so the merits or righteousness of Christ are imputed to us through faith.' *both righteous and unrighteous*] This is no pleonasm for it implies the whole conciliatory position with respect to Justification that M. takes up in *De doctrina* (see *ibid.*). If one simply renounced dependence on *righteous* deeds, one would be justified by faith alone; but for the 'living faith'–faith issuing in works–that M. believes necessary, one has to renounce (in a different sense) *unrighteous* deeds.
iii *293.* *transplanted*] Continues the horticultural image begun in 'seed' (l. 284) and 'second root' (l. 288), which has its Scriptural authority in such passages as *Rom.* vi 16–24. See also *De doctrina* i 21, 'Of being ingrafted in Christ, and its effects': 'Believers are said to be ingrafted in Christ when they are planted in Christ by God the Father, that is, are made partakers of Christ' (Columbia xvi 3–5). The first of the effects of ingrafting is 'newness of life'. The horticultural imagery (appropriate to the occupation of Adam and Eve) runs throughout *PL*: see, e.g., ii 383*n*.
iii *295–6.* Note M.'s finesse on the *climax* scheme.
iii *299.* *Giving to*] Often interpreted as 'yielding to, submitting'; but it may mean 'giving (Christ) up to'–describing the Father's part in the Atonement, as the second half of the line describes the Son's. *redeem*] Cp. *Matt.* xx 28, and see 210–12*n*.

So dearly to redeem what hellish hate
So easily destroyed, and still destroys
In those who, when they may, accept not grace.
Nor shalt thou by descending to assume
Man's nature, lessen or degrade thine own.
Because thou hast, though throned in highest bliss
Equal to God, and equally enjoying
Godlike fruition, quitted all to save
A world from utter loss, and hast been found
By merit more than birthright Son of God,
Found worthiest to be so by being good,
Far more than great or high; because in thee
Love hath abounded more than glory abounds,
Therefore thy humiliation shall exalt
With thee thy manhood also to this throne,
Here shalt thou sit incarnate, here shalt reign
Both God and man, Son both of God and man,

iii *301*. Note the tenses: while not altogether inconsistent with the main verbs in the prophetic future, *destroyed* and *destroys* could easily be taken to imply that the Fall has already occurred. The overall effect is of a timeless meditation, or of a comprehensive vision that enfolds many different temporal perspectives. 'The fall is spoken of as a thing past; perhaps because all things, even future ones, are present to the divine Mind' (Pearce). Cp. ll. 151, 181, 287, and see 261*n*.

iii *305–20*. 'The best moment of God in the poem . . . because he is envisaging his abdication'–the Son could not be rewarded by exaltation to the throne he already occupies (l. 305), and must therefore be destined for the Father's throne (Empson 137). But there is no question of reward: rather does Christ's exaltation restore and make manifest the Godhead he already enjoyed. See *De doctrina* i 16 (Columbia xv 315).

iii *306*. *Equal to God*] This seems at first a Trinitarian formulation; but as M. shows in *De doctrina* i 5, the text to which the passage alludes–*Phil.* ii 6–can be seen as having quite a different implication: 'Co-equality with the Father . . . rather refutes than proves his unity of essence; since equality cannot exist but between two or more essences' (Columbia xiv 343). As at iii 243f, M. prefers a wording that on the one hand is Biblical, on the other open to Arian interpretation.

iii *307*. The oddness of diction signalizes a punning allusion to Adam's contrasting behaviour: Christ is ready to renounce *Godlike fruition* for man, but man will not renounce the fruit that makes him Godlike (cp., e.g., ix 717). *quitted*] Another pun, since it meant 'redeemed, remitted' as well as 'left'.

iii *312*. See iii 267–9*n*.

Anointed universal king, all power
I give thee, reign for ever, and assume
Thy merits; under thee as head supreme
Thrones, princedoms, powers, dominions I reduce:
All knees to thee shall bow, of them that bide
In heaven, or earth, or under earth in hell,
When thou attended gloriously from heaven
Shalt in the sky appear, and from thee send
The summoning archangels to proclaim
Thy dread tribunal: forthwith from all winds
The living, and forthwith the cited dead
Of all past ages to the general doom
Shall hasten, such a peal shall rouse their sleep.
Then all thy saints assembled, thou shalt judge
Bad men and angels, they arraigned shall sink
Beneath thy sentence; hell her numbers full,
Thenceforth shall be for ever shut. Mean while
The world shall burn, and from her ashes spring

iii *317–18*. Cp. *Matt.* xxviii 18: 'All power is given unto me'–in the *De doctrina* a proof text showing that Christ and the Father are not of the same essence (Columbia xiv 305 and 343).

iii *318–19*. *assume / Thy merits*] Renders even more concise Horace's valedictory to his Muse: *sume superbiam / quaesitam meritis* (*Odes* III xxx 14f. On the tense of *give*, see 301*n*. *head supreme*] See *Eph.* iv 15.

iii *320*. Alluding to *Col.* i 16. Cp. *PL* v 840, a similar roll-call by Satan in his 'rabble-rousing speech. . . . No doubt this was the standard form in Heaven, but the effect is to make the reader compare the two offers' (Empson 138). *princedoms*] principalities.

iii *321–2*. Cp. *Phil* ii 10: 'At the name of Jesus every knee should bow, of things in heaven, and things in earth, and things under the earth.' Some scent an inconsistency here; supposing that M. has fallen back to the old notion of a hell 'at the centre', discarded in Bk i Argument. There is no reason, however, why if the universe is below heaven (ii 1051) hell should not be still farther below.

iii *324–9*. The imagery of this vision of judgment is drawn from Revelation, from *Matt.* xxiv 30f, and from *1 Cor.* xv 51f. Cp. *Nativity Ode* 115f: 'To those ychained in sleep, / The wakeful trump of doom must thunder.'

iii *326–7*. *from all winds*] from all four points of the compass–perhaps combining the angels and winds of *Rev.* vii 1 with the resurrecting wind of *Ezek.* xxxvii 9 ('Come from the four winds, O breath, and breathe upon those slain, that they may live'). *cited*] summoned. *doom*] judgment.

iii *330*. *saints*] elect; a common usage in the seventeenth century.

iii *334–5*. Like xi 900f and xii 546–51, these lines are based on *2 Pet.* iii 12f, a prophecy of 'the day of God, wherein the heavens being on fire shall be dissolved, and the elements shall melt with fervent heat', but when the

New heaven and earth, wherein the just shall dwell,
And after all their tribulations long
See golden days, fruitful of golden deeds,
With joy and love triumphing, and fair truth.
Then thou thy regal sceptre shalt lay by,
For regal sceptre then no more shall need,
God shall be all in all. But all ye gods,
Adore him, who to compass all this dies,
Adore the Son, and honour him as me.
No sooner had the almighty ceased, but all

elect will 'look for new heavens and a new earth, wherein dwelleth righteousness'. In *De doctrina* i 33, M. dismisses as of no importance the question whether this final conflagration means 'the destruction of the substance of the world itself, or only a change in the nature of its constituent parts'. In both Old and New Testament apocryphal literature, however, the operation of the destroying and refining fire was sometimes dwelt on. *Ed I* has no comma after *dwell*.

iii *337*. A network of allusions introducing the key word 'fruit' runs throughout the poem (MacCaffrey 83–6). The present passage refers back most immediately to the first glimpse of Adam and Eve–'in the happy garden placed, / Reaping immortal fruits of joy and love' (66f). But cp. also xi 20–2 and xii 550f.

iii *339–43*. Some think that M. is here expressing the view that God means to abdicate and become an immanent or Cambridge Platonist sort of deity (see Empson 130–5). On the frequent use of *all* in *PL*, see Empson[3] 101–4. The present instance may be important theologically; though the frequency is actually no more prominent than in the source, *1 Cor.* xv 28: 'When all things shall be subdued unto him, then shall the Son also himself be subject unto him that put all things under him, that God may be all in all.' *need*] be needful. *gods*] angels; see i 116–17*n* and cp. *Ps.* xcvii 7: 'Worship him, all ye gods.' In *De doctrina* i 5 (Columbia xiv 245) M. notes that 'the name of God is not unfrequently ascribed . . . even to angels and men.' But here the deliberate–and unique–concession of the name by God himself contrasts with Satan's presumptuous taking of it for granted. See T. H. Banks, 'The Meaning of "Gods" in *Paradise Lost*', *MLN*, liv (1939) 450–4.

iii *343*. *John* v 23: 'All men should honour the Son, even as they honour the Father.'

iii *344–415*. The songs of the angels occupy 72 lines because 72 was the mystic number of Christ's disciples. There were also 72 names of angels; see Bongo 557.

iii *344–9*. The unusually sustained syntactic breath of the word group in absolute construction (*angels . . . uttering joy*) makes the main verb that follows resoundingly emphatic. On the grammar of the sentence see Empson[2] 160. Adams 106, however, takes *The multitude of angels* as the subject, and *heaven* as the object, of the verb *rung*.

The multitude of angels with a shout
Loud as from numbers without number, sweet
As from blest voices, uttering joy, heaven rung
With jubilee, and loud hosannas filled
The eternal regions: lowly reverent
Towards either throne they bow, and to the ground
With solemn adoration down they cast
Their crowns inwove with amarant and gold,
Immortal amarant, a flower which once
In Paradise, fast by the tree of life
Began to bloom, but soon for man's offence
To heaven removed where first it grew, there grows,
And flowers aloft shading the fount of life,
And where the river of bliss through midst of heaven

iii *346*. Contrasting with the 'deafening shout' with which the infernal council ends (ii 520).

iii *348*. *jubilee*] jubilation, shouting; but also 'the year of remission or emancipation'. The Hebrew jubilee – a type of the Atonement – was a ritual occasion occurring every fifty natural years, when slaves were freed and property reverted to its first owner.

iii *350–71*. Most of the details of heaven – the thrones, the crowns of gold cast down before them, the jasper (l. 363), the harps – are from Revelation. But others (like the river) combine pagan and Christian visions of bliss.

iii *350–2*. Cp. *Rev.* iv, where the twenty-four elders with 'crowns of gold' 'cast their crowns before the throne'. The crowns are *inwove with amarant* on the strength of *1 Pet.* v 4: 'Ye shall receive a crown of glory that fadeth not away' (Greek ἀμαράντινον).

iii *353–7*. *amarant*] 'unwithering'; a purple flower that, as Hume and Newton noted, was for Clement of Alexandria a 'symbol of immortality'. 'The fair crown of amaranth is laid up for those who have lived well. This flower the earth is not able to bear' (*Paedagogus* ii 8; ed. A. Roberts and J. Donaldson (Edinburgh 1867) i 237). But this is only half the story; for M. well knew – if only from the Clementine chapter just cited – that floral crowns were distinctively pagan, and the amarantine crown an ancient symbol of untroubled tranquility and health (see, e.g., Valeriano 690). Like Clement himself, M. is deliberately comparing a pagan religious symbol with a Christian one very like it. Cp. xi 78 and *Lycidas* 149.

iii *357–9*. Among many Scriptural passages that use river imagery to describe the joy of the believer, the closest is perhaps *Ps.* xxxvi 8f: 'Thou shalt make them drink of the river of thy pleasures. For with thee is the fountain of life.' Cp. also *Rev.* xxii 1. The blissful rivers of heaven contrast with the 'baleful streams' of hell at ii 575–81. The Fountain of Life emblem is developed as a symbol of heavenly bliss in the poem attributed to Raleigh 'The passionate mans Pilgrimage'.

Rolls o'er Elisian flowers her amber stream;
With these that never fade the spirits elect
Bind their resplendent locks inwreathed with beams,
Now in loose garlands thick thrown off, the bright
Pavement that like a sea of jasper shone
Impurpled with celestial roses smiled.
Then crowned again their golden harps they took,
Harps ever tuned, that glittering by their side
Like quivers hung, and with preamble sweet
Of charming symphony they introduce
Their sacred song, and waken raptures high;
No voice exempt, no voice but well could join
Melodious part, such concord is in heaven.
  Thee Father first they sung omnipotent,
Immutable, immortal, infinite,

iii *359*. The river is probably said to roll *o'er* the flowers because the amarant renewed its life when it was moistened. Contrary to expectation, *Rolls* is not a Latinism, since it had been used for centuries in the sense 'undulates, flows' (*OED* II 11 b, 16). But some allusion may have been felt to Virgil, *Aen.* vi 656–9, the description of spirits chanting in chorus beside the Eridanus, in the Elysian fields. For *amber* as a standard of purity or clarity, see Callimachus, *Hymns* vi 29 and Virgil, *Georg.* iii 522.
iii *363–4*. The New Jerusalem shines with light 'like a jasper stone, clear as crystal' (*Rev.* xxi 11); at *Rev.* iv 3 the throned deity himself is compared to a jasper. As so often, M.'s descriptive passages give veiled expression to a Baroque mysticism almost as intense as Crashaw's. With this beatific vision of heaven's pavement, contrast Mammon's concentration on its riches (i 679–84*n*) and the horror of hell's 'burning marl' (i 296).
iii *366–7*. Ancient quivers designed to contain both bow and arrows were harp-shaped.
iii *367*. *preamble*] prelude; *OED* gives no other example but this of the use of the word in a musical context.
iii *370*. *exempt*] debarred.
iii *372*. So in *Rev.* xix 6 the voice of a multitude is heard saying: 'Alleluia: for the Lord God omnipotent reigneth.' Contrast the song of the rebel angels, which is about 'their own heroic deeds' (ii 549). While the hymn is in *melodious parts*, the song is 'partial'. Note also that the mid-point of Bk. iii falls between ll. 371 and 372. Thus the second half begins with the angels' hymn to God the fountain of light, just as its first half began with the poet's. On the substantive relation between the two hymns, see ll. 410–15*n*.
iii *373–4*. Cp. the doxology in *1 Tim.* i 17 'unto the King eternal, immortal, invisible'. But l. 373 is transplanted in its entirety from Sylvester's Du Bartas (2): 'God all in all . . . / Immutable, immortall, infinite, / Incomprehensible, all spirit, all light / All Majesty, all-self-Omnipotent / Invisible, impassive, excellent.'

Eternal king; thee author of all being,
Fountain of light, thy self invisible
Amidst the glorious brightness where thou sit'st
Throned inaccessible, but when thou shadest
The full blaze of thy beams, and through a cloud
Drawn round about thee like a radiant shrine,
Dark with excessive bright thy skirts appear,
Yet dazzle heaven, that brightest seraphim
Approach not, but with both wings veil their eyes.
Thee next they sang of all creation first,
Begotten Son, divine similitude,
In whose conspicuous countenance, without cloud
Made visible, the almighty Father shines,
Whom else no creature can behold; on thee

iii *375–82.* Cp. v 599. In content, though not in expression, resembling *1 Tim.* vi 16 (God dwells in light that no man can approach); *Exod.* xxiv 16f (God speaks out of a cloud on Mt Sinai, yet his glory looks like fire) and xxxiii 18–23 (God promises Moses a glimpse of his 'back parts' only: to see his face would be fatal); and *Is.* vi 1f (Isaiah sees God enthroned among seraphim, who cover their faces with their wings). *Fountain of light*] Cp. l. 8. *but when*] i.e., except when. *Dark with excessive bright*] Perhaps suggested by a similar oxymoron in Drummond's 'An Hymn of the Fairest Fair' (ed. Ward ii 41), where the Trinity is 'unperceived by excessive light' (l. 130) and 'angels dazzled are' (l. 144). Among other probable models are Tasso, *Gerus. Lib.* ix 57 and Spenser, *An Hymne of Heavenly Beautie*, 118f, 176–9.

iii *383. first*] Could be regarded as theologically tendentious. In *Rev.* iii 14 Christ is 'the beginning of the creation of God', and in *Col.* i 15–17 he is 'the firstborn of every creature. For by him were all things created. . . . And he is before all things.' But *De doctrina* i 7 interprets these texts in an Arian sense. Though M. believed that Christ 'is termed first born, not only in respect of dignity, but also of time', *first* carried for him the further implication of *primus inter pares*. Christ was himself created, 'the first of the whole creation' (*De doctrina* i 5; Columbia xiv 181). The point is a fine one, however, since M. also believed in the divinity and preexistence of Christ, and his agency in subsequent creation.

iii *384. Begotten Son*] Cp. *John* iii 16: 'God so loved the world, that he gave his only begotten Son.'

iii *385–7.* See *John* i 18 and xiv 9. For a full appreciation of the paradox, contrast ll. 387–81. In himself, the Father is invisible even when hidden (*through a cloud*); but in the Son he is visible even when not hidden (*without cloud*). *conspicuous*] clearly visible; eminent.

iii *387–9.* Cp. vi 680–2. *spirit*] There seems no reason to join Kelley (109) in doubting that the Holy Spirit is here intended. The allusion is to *John* iii 34: 'God giveth not the Spirit by measure unto him.'

Impressed the effulgence of his glory abides,
Transfused on thee his ample Spirit rests.
He heaven of heavens and all the powers therein
By thee created, and by thee threw down
The aspiring dominations: thou that day
Thy Father's dreadful thunder didst not spare,
Nor stop thy flaming chariot wheels, that shook
Heaven's everlasting frame, while o'er the necks
Thou drovest of warring angels disarrayed.
Back from pursuit thy powers with loud acclaim
Thee only extolled, Son of thy Father's might,
To execute fierce vengeance on his foes,
Not so on man; him through their malice fallen,
Father of mercy and grace, thou didst not doom
So strictly, but much more to pity incline:
No sooner did thy dear and only Son
Perceive thee purposed not to doom frail man
So strictly, but much more to pity inclined,
He to appease thy wrath, and end the strife
Of mercy and justice in thy face discerned,
Regardless of the bliss wherein he sat
Second to thee, offered himself to die

iii *390*. Cp. the *Te Deum*: 'To thee all Angels cry aloud: the heavens and all the powers therein.'
iii *392–9*. The victory briefly recalled here is narrated more fully at vi 824–92. *dominations*] One of the orders of heavenly beings, named as having been created by Christ's agency in *Col.* i 16.
iii *397–8*. The devils would say that *back from pursuit* qualifies *powers;* since they salve their dignity by pretending that the good angels joined with Messiah in the pursuit. See i 169–71*n* and vi 880f.
iii *400*. This distinction was explained earlier, at ll. 129–32.
iii *401*. Alluding to *2 Cor.* i 3: 'Father of mercies, and the God of all comfort'. *doom*] judge.
iii *405–6*. Most editors say that *but* or *than* has to be supplied before *He*. If, however, *much more to pity inclined* refers to the Son, the *but* immediately preceding is available for the main clause. True, the repetition of l. 402 almost unchanged in l. 405 leads us to expect that the Father is again the subject. But isn't this just the point?–The syntax is miming the Son's 'divine similitude' to the Father.
iii *407. mercy and justice*] On the basis of *Ps.* lxxxv 10, God's deliberations over man's destiny had often been portrayed as a debate between four personified attributes: Mercy and Justice, Truth and Peace. See Hope Traver, *The Four Daughters of God* (Philadelphia, Pa. 1907).

For man's offence. O unexampled love,
Love nowhere to be found less than divine!
Hail, Son of God, saviour of men, thy name
Shall be the copious matter of my song
Henceforth, and never shall my harp thy praise
Forget, nor from thy Father's praise disjoin.
Thus they in heaven, above the starry sphere,
Their happy hours in joy and hymning spent.
Mean while upon the firm opacous globe
Of this round world, whose first convex divides
The luminous inferior orbs, enclosed
From Chaos and the inroad of darkness old,
Satan alighted walks: a globe far off
It seemed, now seems a boundless continent
Dark, waste, and wild, under the frown of Night
Starless exposed, and ever-threatening storms
Of Chaos blustering round, inclement sky;
Save on that side which from the wall of heaven
Though distant far some small reflection gains
Of glimmering air less vexed with tempest loud:
Here walked the fiend at large in spacious field.
As when a vulture on Imaus bred,

iii *410–15*. A continuation of the hymn; though the use of the singular (*my song . . . my harp*) allows M. to add an overtone of allusion to his own art, which participates in the concord of the heavenly chorus. See *372n*. In ancient hymns, the promise to resume the god's praises was a common feature: cp., e.g., Callimachus, *Hymns* iii 137. Broadbent (157) notices that *Hail Son of God* 'brings the episode in a circle from "Hail holy light"', the opening line of the book, also spoken by the poet in his own person.
iii *412*. Echoing the concluding words of Virgil's hymn to Hercules at *Aen.* viii 301.
iii *416–21*. *starry sphere*] Either, the sphere of the fixed stars; or, more loosely, the stars and planets together, as at v 620. The stars are enclosed within the *primum mobile* or *first convex* (sphere), the 'bare outside' that Satan was ready to alight on at 74. Both heaven and chaos lie outside that opaque (*opacous*) shell; see ll. 481–3*n* and ii 1052–3*n*.
iii *416–17*. The preceding passage is to be contrasted with the account of how the devils 'entertain / The irksome hours' (ii 522–628).
iii *423*. Cp. Astolfo's amazement at the moon's size, when he climbs onto it in *Orl. Fur.* xxxiv 71.
iii *424–6*. In *Ed I* and *Ed II Chaos* is treated as a proper name, *Night* is not.
iii *429*. *vexed*] tossed about.
iii *431–41*. As is often the case with M.'s longer similes, many different

Whose snowy ridge the roving Tartar bounds,
Dislodging from a region scarce of prey
To gorge the flesh of lambs or yeanling kids
On hills where flocks are fed, flies toward the springs
Of Ganges or Hydaspes, Indian streams;
But in his way lights on the barren plains
Of Sericana, where Chineses drive
With sails and wind their cany wagons light:
So on this windy sea of land, the fiend
Walked up and down alone bent on his prey,

points of correspondence are involved. Thus, the *vulture* is like Satan in respect of rapacity, distant knowledge of his prey, and mode of locomotion; while the lambs and *yeanling* (new born) *kids* are like mankind in respect of innocence, and division into redeemed sheep and reprobate goats (*Matt.* xxv). One journey is from *snowy Imaus*, which notably failed to bound *the roving Tartar* Genghis Khan, to the rivers of India; the other from the 'frozen continent' (ii 587) of Tartarus, which did not keep Satan from roving, to Eden with its rivers (Huntley[2] 107f, Lerner 302). More subtly, the *barren plains of Sericana* correspond to the *primum mobile* not merely because both are stopping-places, but also because in both the elements are confused. (The Chinese use sails, the means of propulsion for ships, on their land vehicles; and the *primum mobile* is a *sea of land.*) This emphasis on confusion of the elements perhaps implies that Satan's entry into our world is an inroad of chaos (cp. 420f). Note that, as often in *PL*, evil comes here from the north; cf. v 689 and see *n.* *Ganges*] For the identification of the Ganges with the Pison of *Gen.* ii, see e.g. Calepinus' *Dictionary*: at this point the tenor and vehicle of the simile coincide.

iii *431*. So at x 273–81, when Death scents his prey and leaves hell for earth, he is compared to a flock of vultures. Maps such as Mercator's *Tartaria* showed *Imaus* as a mountain range extending from modern Afghanistan to the Frozen (Arctic) Ocean, so that a vulture flying to the Ganges would pass Sericana (N.W. China). Some phrases of the simile can probably be traced to dictionary entries under 'Tartaria', 'Scythia' and 'Imaus' (see Starnes 322).

iii *436*. Idiosyncratic diction: cp. 36, i 469. *Hydaspes*] the Chelum or Jhelum River in the Punjab; eastern boundary of Alexander's conquests.

iii *438–9*. The Chinese landships described by the traveller Mendoza in his *Historie of the Great and Mightie Kingdome of China* (tr. Parke, 1588) aroused great interest in Europe. Grotius himself rode in one of the copies constructed by the Dutch scientist Stevin and celebrated in De Gheyn's famous print (see Huntley).

iii *440–1*. Cp. Job i 7: 'Whence comest thou? Then Satan answered the Lord, and said, From going to and fro in the earth, and from walking up and down in it.'

Alone, for other creature in this place
Living or lifeless to be found was none,
None yet, but store hereafter from the earth
Up hither like aerial vapours flew
Of all things transitory and vain, when sin
With vanity had filled the works of men:
Both all things vain, and all who in vain things
Built their fond hopes of glory or lasting fame,
Or happiness in this or the other life;
All who have their reward on earth, the fruits
Of painful superstition and blind zeal,
Nought seeking but the praise of men, here find
Fit retribution, empty as their deeds;
All the unaccomplished works of nature's hand,
Abortive, monstrous, or unkindly mixed,
Dissolved on earth, fleet hither, and in vain,
Till final dissolution, wander here,

iii *444–97*. In *Orl. Fur.* xxxiv 73 ff., a passage from which M. quotes in *Of Reformation*, Ariosto tells how Astolfo searches for his lost wits in a Limbo of Vanity on the moon. Ariosto's limbo is more lightly and casually portrayed than M.'s; it is filled with 'The precious time that fools misspend in play, / The vain attempts that never take effect, / The vows that sinners make and never pay, / The counsels wise that careless men neglect' (xxxiv 75; tr. Harington). But it offered a precedent for antiprelatic satire with a science fiction *mise en scène*, in its lunar mountain symbolizing the Constantine Donation, 'which once smelt sweet, now stinks as odiously' (xxxiv 80; M.'s own tr.–see Yale i 560). Addison refused to impose on himself by seeing any possibility in the passage (*Spectator* No. 297); while Bentley denied it to M. altogether. M., however, no doubt meant it to be incredible, when he based it on Ariosto's burlesque. There is also a limbo of fools in the sixteenth-century satire *Julius exclusus*; see Broadbent 163.
iii *447*. Images of unnatural sexuality begin to be mingled with the images of vacuity; see, e.g., ll. 456, 463, 474. In perverse parody of God's creative generation in the void, a corrupt nature is now being conceived. See Huntley[2] 110–12, where allusions are discovered to the monstrous birth of Sin, and to the supposed hermaphroditism of vultures.
iii *452*. *painful*] laborious, diligent, careful.
iii *454*. The fitness of the retribution partly depends on the etymology of *vanity* (Lat. *vanus*, empty).
iii *455–8*. See 447*n*. The *unkindly mixed* (unnaturally conceived) works correspond to the first group of fools, the Giants (ll. 463–5); the *monstrous* to the Babel-builders (ll. 466–8); and the *abortive* (prematurely born) to the *embryos* etc. of ll. 474–80, and the suicides of ll. 469–73, who in their 'painful superstition' begin their life after death prematurely.

Not in the neighbouring moon, as some have dreamed;
Those argent fields more likely habitants,
Translated saints, or middle spirits hold
Betwixt the angelical and human kind:
Hither of ill-joined sons and daughters born
First from the ancient world those Giants came
With many a vain exploit, though then renowned:
The builders next of Babel on the plain
Of Sennaar, and still with vain design
New Babels, had they wherewithal, would build·
Others came single; he who to be deemed
A god, leaped fondly into Aetna flames,
Empedocles, and he who to enjoy
Plato's Elysium, leaped into the sea,

iii *459. some*] i.e. Ariosto. Bruno, Cardan, Henry More and others speculatively peopled the moon, but with less abstract inhabitants. Schultz (16) thinks it was the frivolity of such pluralist speculations that occasioned their introduction here, as an illustration of vain curiosity. If so, then M. also confesses the vanity of his own work; for he offers an alternative speculation on his own account in ll. 460–2. See ll. 565–71*n*.

iii *461. Translated saints*] Probably such as Enoch (*Gen.* v 24) and Elijah (*2 Kings* ii). On 'Old Testament Sainthood' see C. A. Huttar, in *N & Q* ccix (1964) 86–8.

iii *463–5*. The first group of fools are the Giants, 'mighty men . . . of renown', born of the misunion of 'sons of God' with 'daughters of men' (*Gen.* vi 4). See xi 621–2*n*.

iii *466–8*. At xii 45–7 the builders of Babel are said to have formed their *vain design* out of a desire for fame. *Sennaar*, the Septuagint and Vulg. form, is preferred to the *Shinar* of A. V. *Gen.* xi 2. *New Babels* suggests the New Babylon of anti-Papist propaganda: see Cohn, Index s.v. *Babylon*. Schultz (127) notes that Giants were also a common symbol of Antichrist.

iii *469–73*. *Empedocles* and *Cleombrotus* were not associated by classical writers, but occur together in Lactantius' ch. on 'Pythagoreans and Stoics who, Believing in the Immortality of the Soul, Foolishly Persuade a Voluntary Death' (*Divinae Institutiones* iii 18). Cleombrotus drowned himself after an unwise reading of Plato's *Phaedo* (Lactantius, Migne vi 408; from Callimachus, *Epigrams* xxv), while Empedocles' motive was to conceal his own mortality (see, e.g., Horace, *De arte poetica* 464–6). Empedocles was also an inhabitant of Dante's more dignified *Limbo patrum* (*Inf.* iv 138). See Horrell 417–24, where it is argued that M. placed suicides in limbo on the strength of Virgil's account of the regions of Hades nearest the threshold (*Aen.* vi 426–39: 'those sad souls who in innocence wrought their own death'). *single*: punning between 'individual' and 'celibate'.

Cleombrotus, and many more too long,
Embryos and idiots, eremites and friars
White, black and gray, with all their trumpery.
Here pilgrims roam, that strayed so far to seek
In Golgotha him dead, who lives in heaven;
And they who to be sure of Paradise
Dying put on the weeds of Dominic,
Or in Franciscan think to pass disguised;
They pass the planets seven, and pass the fixed,

iii *473. too long*] Bentley thought this 'deficiently expressed'; but it is surely a deliberate anacolouthon miming impatient negligence. Cp. *PR* ii 189.
iii *474–5.* M. here satirizes a Catholic tradition which consigned *idiots*, cretins and unbaptized infants to a much debated *limbo infantum*. The Franciscans maintained that this limbo was situated above the Earth, in a region of light. *White*, etc.] The mendicant orders were quite usually specified by robe colour. Thus, 'white friar' meant Carmelite, 'black friar' Dominican and 'grey friar' Franciscan. The contemptuous juxtaposition of all three colours, however, ridicules the importance assigned to external trappings, and prepares for ll. 479f. *eremites*] hermits; referring to the fourth of the four main orders: the Austin friars or Order of Friars Hermits.
iii *476–7. Golgotha*] The hill where Christ was crucified and buried (*John* xix 17 and 41). M. represents palmers as repeating the error of the disciples, before they learned of the resurrection (*Luke* xxiv 5f: 'Why seek ye the living among the dead? He is not here, but is risen').
iii *479–80.* Preparing for Satan's assumption of disguise in ll. 634 ff. Cp. *Inf.* xxvii 67–84, where Dante tells how Guido da Montefeltro hoped to get into heaven by virtue of Franciscan weeds, but found to his cost that absolution without repentance is vain. The practice was not uncommon: see Horrell 419 and Huizinga 184.
iii *481–3.* In order of proximity to earth, the spheres passed are: the seven planetary spheres; the eighth sphere, containing the *fixed* stars; the ninth, *crystalline sphere*; and the tenth sphere, the *first moved* or *primum mobile. balance*] A punning reference both to the sign Libra, the Scales, and to the 'libration' or balance-like movement of the Firmament in relation to the Crystalline. This trepidation of the sphere of the fixed stars, together with the Alfonsine calendrical precession, composed equinoctial precession in the modern sense. Libra measures or *weighs* trepidation, because the first point in the sign (as distinct from the constellation) Libra is the equinoctial point, the point of reference for the measurement. On the 'foolishness' of the speculative and much-discussed theory of trepidation, see Dreyer 279. The medieval state of the theory is lucidly explained in Price 104–6, while Renaissance developments are discussed in Fletcher ii 317–18 and Svendsen 54–7. Copernicus still believed that an irregular trepidation accounted for equinoctial precession (see Johnson 110f, Dreyer 329f and Rosen 45f), but the theory was exploded by Brahe, who showed the irregularities to be

And that crystalline sphere whose balance weighs
The trepidation talked, and that first moved;
And now Saint Peter at heaven's wicket seems
To wait them with his keys, and now at foot
Of heaven's ascent they lift their feet, when lo
A violent cross wind from either coast
Blows them transverse ten thousand leagues awry
Into the devious air; then might ye see
Cowls, hoods and habits with their wearers tossed
And fluttered into rags, then relics, beads,
Indulgences, dispenses, pardons, bulls,
The sport of winds: all these upwhirled aloft
Fly o'er the backside of the world far off
Into a limbo large and broad, since called
The Paradise of Fools, to few unknown
Long after, now unpeopled, and untrod;
All this dark globe the fiend found as he passed,
And long he wandered, till at last a gleam
Of dawning light turned thitherward in haste
His travelled steps; far distant he descries,
Ascending by degrees magnificent
Up to the wall of heaven a structure high,
At top whereof, but far more rich appeared

observational. On the importance of the Balance symbol in *PL*, see below, iv 997–1004*n*.

iii *482*. *crystalline*] Stressed on the second syllable.

iii *484*. *wicket*] A 'low' word underlining the satire on the Romanist doctrine that St Peter controls the keys of heaven: a doctrine based on an allegorization of *Matt.* xvi 19 which Protestants thought to be foolish. ll. 505–22 is meant to show that in reality heaven's gate is not such as a man could ever control. Cp. *Lycidas* 110f.

iii *490–3*. W. J. Grace, *SP* lii (1955), finds several echoes of *Anat. of Melan.* III iv 1 ii, where, e.g., Burton speaks of false prophets deluding the silly multitude who 'are apt to be carried about by the blast of every wind'.

iii *492*. *dispenses*] dispensations. A dispensation was an exemption from a solemn obligation, by licence of an ecclesiastical dignitary, especially the Pope. *pardons*] absolutions.

iii *493*. In Virgil, *Aen.* vi 74f it is the Sibyl's pronouncements that are *ludibria ventis*. On the association of winds with limbo, see Horrell 416.

iii *494*. *backside*] the dark hemisphere of the *primum mobile*, furthest from heaven and the 'glimmering air' of ll. 428f and 499.

iii *495*. *limbo*] fringe region.

iii *496*. Then as now, 'fool's paradise' was a proverbial idiom.

iii *501*. *travelled*] experienced in travel; but cp. also Ital. *travagliato*, tired.

iii *502*. *degrees*] steps.

The work as of a kingly palace gate
With frontispiece of diamond and gold
Embellished, thick with sparkling orient gems
The portal shone, inimitable on earth
By model, or by shading pencil drawn.
The stairs were such as whereon Jacob saw
Angels ascending and descending, bands
Of guardians bright, when he from Esau fled
To Padan-Aram in the field of Luz,
Dreaming by night under the open sky,
And waking cried, *This is the gate of heaven.*

iii *506–7. frontispiece*] Either a decorated entrance or (more probably) a pediment over the gate. Cp. the gem-studded New Jerusalem of *Tob.* xiii 16, as well as Ovid's description of the portico of the sun's palace, carved by Mulciber (*Met.* ii 1–19). *orient*] 'brilliant, lustrous, resplendent' (a term applied to gems, especially pearls); perhaps also 'like the rising sun'. In *Rev.* xxi 21 'the twelve gates' of the New Jerusalem 'were twelve pearls'.
iii *508.* In fact Jacob's Ladder had for long been a standard subject in sacred iconography (see Didron ii 271, 350). There is even a portrayal of it–certainly no exception to M.'s generalisation–in Fuller, *Pisgah-sight*, map to II xii.
iii *510–15.* The unregenerate Jacob was terrified by the vision of a ladder reaching to heaven, just after he had cheated Esau out of his father's blessing (*Gen.* xxvii–xxviii). The experience awed him into belief and a vow to the Lord. Jacob's ladder was often interpreted as a symbol of ascesis through contemplation–the sense in which the image is used in *Para.* xxi. (At the ladder's foot Dante is overwhelmed by a terrible cry of execration at the corruption of the Church.) Here it implies that entrance to heaven is by repentance and devotion and meditation on created nature (see 516–17*n*), not by Peter's keys. The relevance of the simile to Satan's situation is usually missed. Satan like Jacob has fled retribution and is at a parting of the ways where he could still repent. And there is also a counterpart to Jacob's vision; for Satan is about to contemplate 'all this world at once' (ll. 542f). The simile is by no means one in which tenor and vehicle are dissimilar (as Ricks 127f holds); though it is true that Satan will go on to choose deeper damnation, Jacob to repent.
iii *511. Angels . . . descending*] The formula used in *Gen.* xxviii and *John* i 51.
iii *513.* We would put comma after *Padan-Aram*, not after *Luz*. Jacob was fleeing to Paddan-Aram (Syria); it was Bethel, where he stopped and dreamed, that 'was called Luz at the first' (*Gen.* xxviii 19). Comma after *Luz* may be error; but the early edns often have an apparently unnecessary comma at the end of a line.
iii *515.* Following the punctuation of *Ed I. Ed II* omits full stop after *heaven.* Cp. *Gen.* xxviii 17: 'And he was afraid, and said, How dreadful is this place! this is none other but the house of God, and this is the gate of heaven.'

Each stair mysteriously was meant, nor stood
There always, but drawn up to heaven sometimes
Viewless, and underneath a bright sea flowed
Of jasper, or of liquid pearl, whereon
Who after came from earth, sailing arrived,
Wafted by angels, or flew o'er the lake
Rapt in a chariot drawn by fiery steeds.
The stairs were then let down, whether to dare
The fiend by easy ascent, or aggravate
His sad exclusion from the doors of bliss.
Direct against which opened from beneath,
Just o'er the blissful seat of Paradise,
A passage down to the earth, a passage wide,
Wider by far than that of after-times
Over Mount Sion, and, though that were large,
Over the Promised Land to God so dear,
By which, to visit oft those happy tribes,
On high behests his angels to and fro
Passed frequent, and his eye with choice regard
From Paneas the fount of Jordan's flood

iii *516–17*. Jacob's ladder had been identified with Homer's golden chain linking the universe to Jupiter (see ii 1051*n*) in Jean Bodin, *Heptaplomeres*, ed. Noack (Paris 1857) 23. Each could be interpreted as a hierarchical *scala naturae* or generative sequence, extending 'from the supreme God even to the bottomest dregs of the universe' (Macrobius, *In somn. Scip.* I xiv 15). In view of ll. 595–612 below, it is of interest that Jacob's ladder was sometimes also used as a symbol for the alchemist's ascesis of purification; see, e.g., Caron 20. *stair*] step, degree. *mysteriously*] as an arcane mystery; symbolically.
iii *518–19*. *sea*] The 'water above the firmament', outside the universe and flowing around the gate of heaven: see iii Argument; vii 271*n*, 619*n*; also *Rev*. iv 6 ('a sea of glass'). *jasper*] see 363–4*n*.
iii *521–2*. The beggar Lazarus was carried off by angels when he died (*Luke* xvi 22), and Elijah by a 'chariot of fire, and horses of fire' (*2 Kings* ii 11: cp. *PR* ii 16f); but the mention of *sailing* more specifically recalls Dante's fine image of a swift angel-powered craft, in *Purg*. ii. Cp. *Prae E* 47–50.
iii *523–5*. Or perhaps to tempt the reader to fall into the satanic point of view ironically reflected in these conjectures?
iii *530*. For Zion as a holy place, see i 10–11*nn* and 386, and iii 30f.
iii *534*. *eye*] An additional subject of *Passed*. *choice*] careful, accurate.
iii *535–7*. *Paneas*] A later Greek name for Dan; not the city of Dan, but the spring of the same name, 'the easternmost fountain of Jordan' (Fuller, *Pisgah-sight* IV i 12). *Beersaba*] A.V. Beersheba (for M.'s preference for Septuag. and Vulg. 's' see i 397–9*n*); the southern limit of Canaan, as Dan

To Beersaba, where the Holy Land
Borders on Aegypt and the Arabian shore;
So wide the opening seemed, where bounds were set
To darkness, such as bound the ocean wave.
Satan from hence now on the lower stair
That scaled by steps of gold to heaven gate
Looks down with wonder at the sudden view
Of all this world at once. As when a scout
Through dark and desert ways with peril gone
All night; at last by break of cheerful dawn
Obtains the brow of some high-climbing hill,
Which to his eye discovers unaware
The goodly prospect of some foreign land
First-seen, or some renowned metropolis
With glistering spires and pinnacles adorned,
Which now the rising sun gilds with his beams.
Such wonder seized, though after heaven seen,
The spirit malign, but much more envy seized,
At sight of all this world beheld so fair.
Round he surveys, and well might, where he stood

was the northern. 'From Dan even to Beersheba' is a common formula: see, e.g., *Judges* xx 1.

iii *538–9.* The darkness meant is of course that of chaos; though the many links with the preceding line (*borders* with *bounds*, *ocean wave* with *shore*) adumbrate a secondary, metaphorical sense: the darkness of pagan ignorance, bounded by the borders of the Holy Land. Cp. *Job* xxviii 3: 'He setteth an end to darkness.'

iii *542–51.* 'An image that exactly conveys the effect produced by the poem itself, a solid and intricate thing that can be seen as a whole' (MacCaffrey 50). On the moral significance of panoramic visions in *PL* as images of order, see *ibid.* 68. The description of heaven's gate that precedes this panoptic vision of the universe is based on Ovid's description of the sun's palace portico, which was itself a symbol of cosmos (see Heninger 315). Regarded as *scala naturae*, the cosmos leads up to heaven.

iii *546. Obtains*] reaches, occupies.

iii *552. though . . . seen*] even after having seen heaven's wonders. The same Latin construction that is imitated at i 573.

iii *555–61.* It requires some effort to grasp the details of Satan's astronomically sophisticated vantage-point, as he stands at the passage through the *primum mobile* (l. 540). Since the celestial poles mark for him points of extreme separation on the interior of the shell of the universe (ll. 560f), it follows that he is situated on the celestial equator, which before the Fall was also the ecliptic (see x 668ff). Next, since *the fleecy star* Aries is receding *Beyond the horizon*, i.e., setting behind the earth, Satan is apparently in the portion of the ecliptic exactly opposite, namely Libra. *from . . . Libra* he

So high above the circling canopy
Of night's extended shade; from eastern point
Of Libra to the fleecy star that bears

looks west to Aries along the 'length' of the universe, which is lying, as it were, on its side. (The north and south poles are the extreme points of *breadth.*) Now, it was commonly believed that the world was created at the vernal equinox (e.g. Dante, *Inf.* i 38f; for the authorities, see below, iv 268*n*; also Riccioli ii 232), so that the sun would now be in Aries. (This is explicitly confirmed at x 329: 'the sun in Aries rose'.) Hence Satan, in the opposite sign Libra, stands *above the circling canopy / Of night's extended shade* in a very precise sense. The sun is on the other side of earth, and Satan is just *above* the Earth's apparently circular shadow. Since Satan is also at the moment *just o'er* Paradise (l. 527), it follows that there it is now the critical hour of midnight–the same hour as that of his more cautious return at ix 58.

This elaborate topographia establishes an association between Satan and the portion of the firmament designated by Libra: an association that is of some importance throughout the poem. Not only is Libra opposite the sun (cp. Satan's avoidance of the sun, by keeping to the dark side of the earth, in ix 63–6), but it also contains the head of the Serpent constellation (Anguis). For the poem's most prominent piece of Serpent and Scales imagery, see iv 997–1015; for other appearances of the cosmic Serpent, ii 709, x 328. Note that Satan's entering the universe at the head of the serpent and leaving it at the tail has a correlate in the portrayal of Satan's character, which is at first alluring, then disgusting. According to a tradition that went back to Bede (see Williams 116) the serpent had the face of an attractive virgin.

iii *556–7. canopy*] Usually an image for the whole sky; cp. *Hamlet* II ii 318–21: 'this most excellent canopy, the air . . . this brave o'erhanging firmament, this majestical roof fretted with golden fire'. Here it means the part of the heavens in the shadow of earth. It is midnight at Eden directly beneath, and from Satan's point of view earth is almost entirely dark and casts a conical shadow up towards his feet. The effect of foreshortening, however, is to flatten this long cone and make it look circular. Note, however, that the *canopy* or baldachin over a throne (*OED* s.v. *Canopy* 1) was often conical in shape. *circling*] A pun: the shade encircles or forms a circle round Satan; but it also revolves in a circular orbit. (Note that the shade revolves irrespectively of whether the system followed is geocentric or heliocentric; in the former case the motion will be diurnal, in the latter annual.) Dramatic perspective such as this, based on a sophisticated optics, was often a feature of Baroque visual art.

iii *557–8. Libra* is *eastern* because longitude on the celestial sphere was measured from west to east from the vernal equinoctial point in Aries. Strictly speaking this is a dramatic irony or prolepsis; for there is no vernal equinoctial point until after the Fall, when the ecliptic plane is inclined with respect to the equatorial (see x 651–706*n*, 668–80*n*).

iii *558–9.* Aries and Andromeda are immediately adjacent constellations,

Andromeda far off Atlantic seas
Beyond the horizon; then from pole to pole
He views in breadth, and without longer pause
Down right into the world's first region throws
His flight precipitant, and winds with ease
Through the pure marble air his oblique way
Amongst innumerable stars, that shone
Stars distant, but nigh hand seemed other worlds,
Or other worlds they seemed, or happy isles,
Like those Hesperian gardens famed of old,

which would go behind the earth together. (Note that in the prelapsarian universe constellations and signs need not be distinguished.) Qvarnström suggests that Andromeda may be singled out for mention because the mythological Andromeda was threatened by a dragon.

iii *560–1.* The poles referred to are celestial, not terrestrial (as Empson[2] 155 apparently takes them to be); just as *world's* in l. 562 refers to the universe as a whole. Turning the universe on its side, as M. does when he makes the polar axis measure *breadth*, is a tour de force of imagination. The Biblical authority is Job xxxviii 18, 'Hast thou perceived the breadth of the earth?'

iii *562–7.* Cp. Raphael's similar descent 'between worlds and worlds' in v 266–70.

iii *562. the world's first region*] Not one of the three regions of the earth's atmosphere (see i 515–16*n*) that lay below the fiery element, but a fourth layer, fatal to mortals, reaching up to the Firmament and beyond. See Svendsen 88, and cp. xii 76f below.

iii *564. marble*] 'smooth as marble' (a Latinism; cp., e.g., Virgil, *Aen.* vi 729, *marmoreo ... aequore*); perhaps also 'sparkling, glistening, gleaming' (cp. Gk μαρμάρεος). Cp. Shakespeare, Othello III iii 461, 'by yond marble heaven' (though there the image may be one of permanence).

iii *565–71.* M. introduces the idea of life on other worlds on a great many occasions: cp. ll. 459, 670; v 263; vii 621; viii 140–58 and 175. There was an extensive seventeenth-century literature concerning plurality of worlds, and most astronomers accepted the more limited idea of a plurality of inhabited globes within the solar system. See Nicolson[2]; Rajan 153; Lovejoy 108–42 *passim*; and Bernard Le Bovier de Fontenelle, *Entretiens sur la pluralité des mondes*, ed. R. Shackleton (Oxford 1955). 'Satan's voyage through Chaos is one of the great "cosmic voyages" of a period that sent imaginary mariners to the moon and planets in search of other worlds and other men' (Nicolson[3] 165). The space-travel element is complicated, however, by an allusion to the 'true earth' of *Phaedo* 114B–C, which is placed in the 'broad fields of the sky' among the *Hesperian gardens* in *Comus* 977ff.

iii *568–9.* The gardens where the Hesperides (Atlantides) unsuccessfully guarded apples entrusted to them by Jupiter were by Hesiod located beyond the ocean (cp. l. 559, 'far off Atlantic seas'). M. perhaps glances at the

Fortunate fields, and groves and flowery vales,
Thrice happy isles, but who dwelt happy there
He stayed not to inquire: above them all
The golden sun in splendour likest heaven
Allured his eye: thither his course he bends
Through the calm firmament; but up or down
By centre, or eccentric, hard to tell,
Or longitude, where the great luminary
Aloof the vulgar constellations thick,
That from his lordly eye keep distance due,
Dispenses light from far; they as they move

much-discussed question whether inhabitants of other planets were 'infected with Adam's sin' (John Wilkins, *cit.* Lovejoy 109); though the proleptic allusion to our own Fall might sufficiently account for the passage.
iii *570. happy isles*] Recalling the Isles of the Blessed of Greek myth, where favoured mortals passed without dying. Cp. viii 631f.
iii *571–3.* The sun is *above* the stars in splendour, but below many of them, of course, in space.
iii *573–6.* A difficult passage, probably because it combines cosmological alternatives with alternatives in respect of Satan's route. He can either take a collision course across the universe, travelling in a centric (*centre*) orbit such as the central meridian, or an *eccentric* orbit; or he can pursue the sun round the ecliptic, through a western *longitude*. What makes the course *hard to tell* is presumably uncertainty as to the proper terms for a description: M. scrupulously avoids accepting any single astronomical model as authoritative. For a similar avoidance, see iv 592–7. Here the sun or the earth may be at the centre of the universe; or neither. For M. would be familiar with current speculations whether the universe had any centre, or whether the stars are scattered 'without any system or common centre . . . like so many islands in an immense sea' (Bacon 683; see Lovejoy 109, and cp. 567 above).
iii *575. centre*] centric, a circle or orbit with the earth (or sun) at its centre; as distinct from an *eccentric*, a circle with the earth (sun) not at its centre. Cp. viii 83: 'the sphere / With centric and eccentric scribbled o'er'. Eccentric orbits were postulated, to account for inequalities in the motions of the sun and planets, both by Ptolemaic and Copernican astronomers.
iii *576. longitude*] Not a line of longitude, but a distance (measured by degrees of arc) along the ecliptic (*OED* s.v. *Longitude* 4).
iii *577. Aloof*] apart from.
iii *578.* For the eye of heaven as an Orphic description of the sun, see Fowler 74; for a common symbolic interpretation of the image–God's omnipresence–see Wind 179f, 186f.
iii *579–81.* The cosmic dance is a favourite idea of M.'s; cp. v 178, vii 374, viii 125 and *Comus* 112. At v 617ff and ix 103 a correspondence between the cosmic and the celestial dance is asserted (see Rajan 151, Spaeth 43–5 and

Their starry dance in numbers that compute
Days, months, and years, towards his all-cheering lamp
Turn swift their various motions, or are turned
By his magnetic beam, that gently warms
The universe, and to each inward part
With gentle penetration, though unseen,
Shoots invisible virtue even to the deep:
So wondrously was set his station bright.
There lands the fiend, a spot like which perhaps
Astronomer in the sun's lucent orb
Through his glazed optic tube yet never saw.
The place he found beyond expression bright,
Compared with aught on earth, metal or stone;

158f). Treated elaborately in Sir John Davies's *Orchestra* (1596), the notion goes back ultimately to the 'choric dances' of the stars in Plato, *Timaeus* 40 C. The generation of the day, the month and the year is described in an earlier passage of the same dialogue: God created the planets 'for the determining and preserving of the numbers of time' (*Tim.* 38C). Cp. also *Gen.* i 14: 'And God said, Let there be lights in the firmament of the heaven to divide the day from the night; and let them be for signs, and for seasons, and for days, and years'.

iii *580. starry*] sarry *Ed I* is almost certainly an error, though the form did occur as an old variant of 'savoury' ('spiritually delightful and edifying'). *numbers*] rhythms.

iii *583–6.* The influence or *virtue* of the sun was supposed to penetrate even under the earth's surface; see v 301–3, vi 472–83*n*, and Svendsen 67. Kepler's theory that the planets are driven round by the sun's *magnetic* force was 'the first serious attempt to interpret the mechanism of the solar system' (Dreyer 397).

iii *586.* Probably to be scanned with *even* as a stressed monosyllable.

iii *588–90.* To appreciate the simile one needs to know that the spots on the sun were thought by some to impair its perfection and incorruptibility (see Riccioli i 97). The first descriptions of the spots had been published by Fabricius and then Galileo (*Letters on the Solar Spots* (Rome 1613)).

iii *590. optic tube*] Not poetic diction.

iii *591.* On the description of the sun that follows, Broadbent 165–8 comments that it accomplishes 'the contrast with Hell and Paradise that Heaven only suggested'. He finds M.'s sun poetry out of place, even if magnificently, in a poem where God the source of celestial light is also presented. But the Neoplatonic cult of the sun had long been assimilated to the Christian mysticism of light. Within the tradition of Christian Platonism to which *PL* belongs it is natural for dignity and splendour to be attributed to so important an image of emanation as the sun.

iii *592. metal*] medal *Eds I* and *II.* The case for retaining the original reading would be that the brightest stones on earth were cut precious stones, so

Not all parts like, but all alike informed
With radiant light, as glowing iron with fire;
If metal, part seemed gold, part silver clear;
If stone, carbuncle most or chrysolite,
Ruby or topaz, to the twelve that shone
In Aaron's breastplate, and a stone besides

that the other member of the pair may be presumed an artifact too. There is also the apt resemblance between the sun's disk and a bright burnished medal. The antithesis of ll. 595f, however, seems to count decisively in favour of emending.

iii *594–605*. In Scripture, Aaron's twelve jewels simply represent the twelve tribes of Israel. M.'s numerology, however, also mimes the alchemic process. For he names one chemic stone (l. 600), two stages in the *magnum opus* (ll. 603f), three metals (ll. 594f) and four stones (ll. 596f); thus representing the 1, 2, 3, 4 of the *tetractys* in its triangular form. As the fountain of nature, the creative *tetractys* was often identified with the method and goal of the alchemist's (and the regenerate Christian's) ascesis; see, e.g., Caron 91, 138, and the title-page to Dee's *Monas hieroglyphica* (Antwerp 1564, tr. and ed. C. H. Josten in *Ambix* xii (1964) 84–221).

iii *594*. *With*] Which *Ed I*, wrongly.

iii *596–8*. In *Exod.* xxviii 15–20 Aaron's foursquare 'breastplate of judgment' is described as having four rows of stones, of which the first row 'shall be a sardius [marginal gloss: 'ruby'], a topaz, and a carbuncle'. *Chrysolite*] Replaces diamond (not beryl, as Newton and Verity have it) in the fourth row, in the Vulgate version. *to the twelve*] i.e., 'etc., until the twelve are completed'. All the stones named were associated with the sun in contemporary mineralogical theory, and were supposed to shine even in the dark; see Duncan, Svendsen 29f, Broadbent 165; also George F. Kunz, *The Curious Lore of Precious Stones* (New York 1938) 143–75, 347. Mystical interpretations gained support from the fact that the same stones occur in the walls of the New Jerusalem (see *Rev.* xxi 19f).

Aaron was traditionally the type of the true priest, who had 'put on' Christ, and so wore 'light and perfections on the breast' (see Tuve 154): a holy disguise that contrasts ironically with Satan's disguise as a young cherub. Aaron's vestments had recently been elaborately interpreted by Henry More in his *Conjectura cabbalistica* (1662) 120f as a symbol of the universe.

iii *598–601*. *a stone besides*] The 'urim' contained in Aaron's breastplate (*Exod.* xxviii 30). It was *imagined . . . oft . . . elsewhere* because it was identified by many alchemical theorists (such as Joachim Tancke) with the philosophers' stone itself. The (lunar) thummim could transform base metals to silver, but the (solar) urim could transform them to gold (see Qvarnström, and cp. l. 595 above). In the Christian alchemical tradition, the philosopher's stone was regarded as a symbol of Christ's regenerating grace; see, e.g., Benlowes, *Theophila* (1652) i 90 ('grace . . . the chemic-stone') and ix 66.

Imagined rather oft than elsewhere seen,
That stone, or like to that which here below
Philosophers in vain so long have sought,
In vain, though by their powerful art they bind
Volatile Hermes, and call up unbound
In various shapes old Proteus from the sea,
Drained through a limbeck to his native form.
What wonder then if fields and regions here
Breathe forth elixir pure, and rivers run
Potable gold, when with one virtuous touch

iii *601–5.* The principal meaning is that alchemists have sought the philosopher's stone in vain, however capable they may be of the intermediate stage of making 'philosophic mercury'. The Proteus of mythology was anciently interpreted as matter, because of his ability to assume a variety of forms (see Wind, Index s.v. *Proteus*). Here, however, the reference is specifically to the primal matter of creation: cp. v 472f, 'first matter ... Indued with various forms'. In alchemy, prime matter or philosophic mercury was the essence or soul or ordinary *volatile* mercury, made by binding it (removing the volatile principle air) and by freeing it from the liquid principle. But the *native* or prime matter had then to be acted upon by the philosopher's stone to produce the qualities desired (see *EB* i 521; Caron 156, 162).

The passage can be applied to Satan in a variety of ways. (1) Satan is like the alchemists, in that his deceptions fail to accomplish more than a partial purification. Grace (the philosopher's stone) eludes him; yet without it he can only imitate his native unfallen brightness externally (cp. Svendsen 126f). (2) Satan is like the volant deceptive Mercury, god of disguises. In the purification of man's soul, the first step must be the binding of Satan. (One of mercury's alchemical names was the serpent. Note, too, that some astronomers thought sun-spots were caused by the planet Mercury.) (3) Satan is like Proteus in that he is *unbound* from the sea of fire, suffers the metamorphoses of passion, and is a wily, experienced politician (Conti, *Mytholog.* viii 8 *ad fin.*).

iii *603. Volatile*] Spelt *Volatil*; stressed on the second syllable. *limbeck*] the alembic or retort in which the mercury was distilled.

iii *606. here*] Primarily, 'here in the sun'; though secondarily it may be said of terrestrial rivers that one touch of sunshine turns them to gold. The ambiguity runs from l. 606 to l. 610.

iii *607–8. elixir*] Any medium, such as the philosopher's stone, that would transmute base metals to gold. The 'elixir of long life', or *potable* [liquid] *gold,* was closely identified with the goal of the alchemists. According to Bernard of Treviso it was a 'reduction of the philosopher's stone to mercurial water' (Caron 168; see also Svendsen 125).

iii *608–12. arch-chemic*] Because it was believed that the sun's influence penetrated beneath the earth, and there, by an extremely slow process,

The arch-chemic sun so far from us remote
Produces with terrestrial humour mixed
Here in the dark so many precious things
Of colour glorious and effect so rare?
Here matter new to gaze the devil met
Undazzled, far and wide his eye commands,
For sight no obstacle found here, nor shade,
But all sunshine, as when his beams at noon
Culminate from the equator, as they now
Shot upward still direct, whence no way round
Shadow from body opaque can fall, and the air,
No where so clear, sharpened his visual ray
To objects distant far, whereby he soon
Saw within ken a glorious angel stand,
The same whom John saw also in the sun:
His back was turned, but not his brightness hid;
Of beaming sunny rays, a golden tiar
Circled his head, nor less his locks behind
Illustrious on his shoulders fledge with wings

generated precious stones. Cp. ll. 583–6, vi 447–81, and *Comus* 732–6; and see Harry F. Robins, 'The Key to a Problem in Milton's *Comus*', *MLQ* xii (1951) 422–8. *humour*] moisture; see Dryden's note to *Annus Mirabilis* st. 3: 'Precious Stones at first are Dew, condens'd and harden'd by the warmth of the Sun.'

iii *613. gaze*] The transitive use was more or less confined to poetic contexts.

iii *616–17.* A heavenly body is said to *culminate* when it reaches the highest, meridian point of its apparent orbit. In the world as we know it, the sun can culminate at the celestial equator only when it is at one of the equinoctial points, where the ecliptic and the equator intersect. But before the sun went astray from his true 'equinoctial road' at the Fall (x 668–91), equator and ecliptic coincided; so that the disappearance of shadows was then a daily occurrence. Elsewhere in *PL* noon symbolizes the time of divine judgment (see ix 739*n*). Here, however, the continual noon on the solar surface also expresses the sun's power over matter. For the Proteus of legend–unlike the Proteus of 604 above–could not be called up at will, but had to be caught when he emerged at noon (Homer, *Od.* iv). Thus, on the sun the prime matter is continually available for creation.

iii *620. visual ray*] M. is probably utilizing the ancient theory of optics according to which rays emanated from the eye onto the object seen. Cp. *SA* 162f: 'inward light, alas, / Puts forth no visual beam.'

iii *623. Rev.* xix 17: 'I saw an angel standing in the sun.'

iii *625. tiar*] crown (poet.)

iii *627. illustrious*] lustrous, shining. *fledge*] fledged, feathered.

Lay waving round; on some great charge employed
He seemed, or fixed in cogitation deep.
Glad was the spirit impure as now in hope
To find who might direct his wandering flight
To Paradise the happy seat of man,
His journey's end and our beginning woe.
But first he casts to change his proper shape,
Which else might work him danger or delay:
And now a stripling cherub he appears,
Not of the prime, yet such as in his face
Youth smiled celestial, and to every limb
Suitable grace diffused, so well he feigned;
Under a coronet his flowing hair
In curls on either cheek played, wings he wore
Of many a coloured plume sprinkled with gold,
His habit fit for speed succinct, and held

iii *630*. *Ed II* and some copies of *Ed I* with uncorrected sheet have no point after *impure*; other copies of *Ed I* with corrected sheet have semicolon.

iii *634*. Discussing Satan's 'protean habit' of metamorphosis, Broadbent 106 remarks that 'all fluctuations of shape, changes of nature . . . are presented as evil, symptoms of the Fall itself.' Spenser had similarly expressed the multiplicity of evil in the metamorphoses of his Archimago; see Fowler 8. The immediate allusion is to *2 Cor.* xi 13f: 'such are false apostles, deceitful workers, transforming themselves into the apostles of Christ. And no marvel; for Satan himself is transformed into an angel of light.' *casts*] resolves.

iii *636–7*. Empson (59–61) finds the idea of a *stripling cherub* difficult, in view of our feeling (Satan's feeling?) that the angels are self-begot. He supposes that Satan has assumed the role of a newly promoted angel, to avoid suspicion: an ordinary angel would not be bothered to inspect the new creation 'but Uriel finds it natural for a promoted proletarian to be a busybody'. But M. more probably put 'stripling' merely because of the common iconographical representation of the cherub as a winged child. Satan's reason for preferring this particular disguise would be that the order of cherubim was supposed to excel in knowledge; so that in asking questions he is pursuing his proper vocation. *Not of the prime*] 'not yet of the prime of life'; or, 'not one of the chief cherubim'.

iii *637–42*. Cp. Spenser's description of a young angel, in *F.Q.* II viii 5: 'a faire young man, / Of wondrous beautie, and of freshest yeares . . . / His snowy front curled with golden heares, / Like *Phoebus* face adornd with sunny rayes, / Divinely shone, and two sharpe winged sheares, / Decked with diverse plumes, like painted Jayes, / Were fixed at his backe, to cut his ayerie wayes.'

iii *643*. 'His clothing girt up' would be a possible sense. But M.'s angels are not normally clothed, so that the phrase probably means 'a uniform

Before his decent steps a silver wand.
He drew not nigh unheard, the angel bright,
Ere he drew nigh, his radiant visage turned,
Admonished by his ear, and straight was known
The archangel Uriel, one of the seven
Who in God's presence, nearest to his throne
Stand ready at command, and are his eyes
That run through all the heavens, or down to the earth
Bear his swift errands over moist and dry,
O'er sea and land: him Satan thus accosts.
Uriel, for thou of those seven spirits that stand
In sight of God's high throne, gloriously bright,
The first art wont his great authentic will

suitable and prepared for speed'. Wings (l. 641) were a distinctive mark of the cherub order.

iii *644. decent*] graceful, as well as 'in accordance with propriety'.

iii *648–61.* In *Zech.* iv a visionary seven-branched candlestick is interpreted as 'the eyes of the Lord, which run to and fro through the whole earth' (cp. *Rev.* v 6). The seven principal angels are mentioned also in *Tob.* xii 15; *Rev.* viii 2; and *Rev.* i 4: 'Grace be unto you, and peace, from him which is, and which was, and which is to come; and from the seven Spirits which are before his throne.'

iii *648. Uriel*] 'Light of God'. The name is not Biblical, though it occurs in the apocryphal *2 Esdras.* But in Jewish and cabbalistic tradition Uriel was prominent (together with Michael, Gabriel and Raphael) as one of the great archangels who rule the four corners of the world. As the angel of the south, Uriel 'rules in the power of the Meridian Sunne' (Henry More, *cit.* West 208). While the general notion of angels or 'intelligences' guiding the spheres is a very familiar one, there has been much speculation as to M.'s authority for assigning Uriel to the sun. It has been suggested, e.g., that he drew on esoteric rabbinical lore. No doubt the system was originally esoteric; but Uriel had been assigned to Sol in a textbook as standard as Valeriano's *Hieroglyphica*: 'Greek theology calls Michael's power in God *Venus*; Gabriel it calls *Mars*; and Raphael *Jupiter*, to whom especially the throne of judgment was ascribed. Sol, the fourth, having both feminine and masculine power, the manifest origin of all generation, is named in Hebrew both *Uriel* and *Adonis*' (549). The context, an important one for the interpretation of *PL*, is an account of the cosmic chariot of God; see l. 656*n*, iv 549–50*n*, vi 749–59*n*, vii 197ff.

iii *653. Ed II* and some copies of *Ed I* with uncorrected sheet have semicolon after *accosts*, erroneously. Other copies of *Ed I* with corrected sheet have full stop.

iii *656.* Uriel was *first* of the angels in a very special sense. The chariot which Solomon constructed in *Song* iii 9f was interpreted as a type of the New

Interpreter through highest heaven to bring,
Where all his sons thy embassy attend;
And here art likeliest by supreme decree
Like honour to obtain, and as his eye
To visit oft this new creation round;
Unspeakable desire to see, and know
All these his wondrous works, but chiefly man,
His chief delight and favour, him for whom
All these his works so wondrous he ordained,
Hath brought me from the choirs of cherubim
Alone thus wandering. Brightest seraph tell
In which of all these shining orbs hath man
His fixed seat, or fixed seat hath none,
But all these shining orbs his choice to dwell;
That I may find him, and with secret gaze,
Or open admiration him behold
On whom the great creator hath bestowed
Worlds, and on whom hath all these graces poured;
That both in him and all things, as is meet,
The universal maker we may praise;
Who justly hath driven out his rebel foes
To deepest hell, and to repair that loss
Created this new happy race of men
To serve him better: wise are all his ways.

Covenant, which Christ established to carry believers to heaven. Now the angels were not only related to this symbolic chariot as its parts (l. 648*n*), but their names were also associated with the Heb. word for chariot, *argaman*, in the following manner: *Prima litera fit Uriel, per* A *enim illi scribunt. Sequenti* R, *Raphael. Tertia* G, *Gabriel. Quarta* M, *Michael* (Valeriano 549). Thus Uriel, the first good angel to appear in the poem, is also the first in the chariot of God. But the lines could also be read in simpler senses. As the 'sharpest-sighted spirit' (l. 691), Uriel would naturally have most insight as the interpreter of God's will; while his charge the sun had an obvious primacy among the planets.

iii *658*. 'Satan when disguised as a good angel gets a cosy piety into his speech chiefly by packing it with *all's*' (Empson[3] 103). *sons*] angels; cp. *Job* ii 1. *attend*] await.

iii *664*. *favour*] object of favour; first post-medieval instance in *OED*, in this sense.

iii *668–70*. As Broadbent 165 notes, Satan here echoes M.'s own antimetabole of ll. 565–7.

iii *670*. The form of Satan's question shows that he would like to know whether any of creation is out of bounds to man.

iii *671–2*. Satan echoes the words of Herod enquiring after the whereabouts of the second Adam (*Matt.* ii 8).

So spake the false dissembler unperceived;
For neither man nor angel can discern
Hypocrisy, the only evil that walks
Invisible, except to God alone,
By his permissive will, through heaven and earth:
And oft though wisdom wake, suspicion sleeps
At wisdom's gate, and to simplicity
Resigns her charge, while goodness thinks no ill
Where no ill seems: which now for once beguiled
Uriel, though regent of the sun, and held
The sharpest sighted spirit of all in heaven;
Who to the fradulent impostor foul
In his uprightness answer thus returned.
Fair angel, thy desire which tends to know
The works of God, thereby to glorify
The great work-master, leads to no excess
That reaches blame, but rather merits praise
The more it seems excess, that led thee hither
From thy empyreal mansion thus alone,
To witness with thine eyes what some perhaps
Contented with report hear only in heaven:
For wonderful indeed are all his works,
Pleasant to know, and worthiest to be all
Had in remembrance always with delight;

iii *681. unperceived*] undetected, not seen through.
iii *682.* Cp. ll. 705–7*n* below. M. is always careful to avoid angelolatry, and perhaps for this reason he makes his good angels often unsuccessful, even unheroic.
iii *685. permissive will*] Distinguished from God's positive will, which permits only good. See i 209–13*n*.
iii *694–6.* The conditions for blamelessness in a desire for knowledge are (1) that it shall be knowledge of the right things (God's works); and (2) that it shall be sought for the right reason (to glorify God). In view of (2), the clash between Uriel's permissiveness and the prohibition of iv 515 is only apparent.
iii *696–8.* It was a doctrine of Renaissance Neoplatonism 'that no extreme in the contemplation of God and his works could violate Aristotle's principle' of the virtuous mean (Hughes). Cp. Wind 53 on Ficino's doctrine of divine love: 'Only by looking towards the Beyond as the true goal of ecstasy can man become balanced in the present.'
iii *699. empyreal*] Stressed on the second syllable. *mansion*] dwelling place.
iii *702–4.* Cp. *Ps.* cxi 2, 4: 'The works of the Lord are great, sought out of all them that have pleasure therein. . . . He hath made his wonderful works to be remembered.'

But what created mind can comprehend
Their number, or the wisdom infinite
That brought them forth, but hid their causes deep.
I saw when at his word the formless mass,
This world's material mould, came to a heap:
Confusion heard his voice, and wild uproar
Stood ruled, stood vast infinitude confined;
Till at his second bidding darkness fled,
Light shone, and order from disorder sprung:
Swift to their several quarters hasted then
The cumbrous elements, earth, flood, air, fire,
And this ethereal quintessence of heaven

iii *705–7*. As Burden 110 notes, this implies that God keeps some knowledge secret even from the angels, and so makes it more reasonable that a similar reservation should be made in the case of man. In *De doctrina* i 9 (Columbia xv 107) the limitations of the angels' knowledge are indeed emphasised: 'The good angels do not look into all the secret things of God, as the Papists pretend. . . . there is much . . . of which they are ignorant.' Even Christ 'knows not all things absolutely; there being some secret purposes, the knowledge of which the Father has reserved to himself alone' (*ibid.* i 5; Columbia xiv 317).
iii *706–7*. Cp. *Prov.* iii 19 ('The Lord by wisdom hath founded the earth'), and see *Prov.* viii, where Wisdom's part in creation as the master-workman is described at length. The present passage prepares for Raphael's account of creation by the Word of God, in *PL* vii. On the relation between the Word and the Lady Wisdom of Proverbs, see Claude Chavasse, *The Bride of Christ* (1939), 45–8.
iii *708–15*. Uriel's excited reminiscence of creation is couched in traditional Christian-Platonic terms. According to this system, creation was not from the void, but from primal matter, whose initial chaos was ordered by the separation out of the four elements in interlocking layers (see, e.g., Plato, *Timaeus* 30A and 32B–C; Ovid, *Met.* i; Macrobius, *In somn. Scip.* I vi 23–40). From the time of Philo, the Platonic cosmology had been syncretized with that of *Genesis*, as it is here (with the *second bidding* of l. 712, cp. *Gen.* i 3).
iii *708*. Like Raphael, Uriel was one of the angels who witnessed creation (vii 197–205).
iii *709*. *mould*] substance. Cp. vii 356.
iii *710*. *Confusion*] Already personified, as one of Chaos' courtiers, at ii 966.
iii *716*. *ethereal quintessence*] Cp. vii 243f, 'light ethereal . . . quintessence'. Unlike the four cumbrous elements, the fifth element ether had no weight, and consequently formed a heaven above the atmosphere (see Ovid, *Met.* i 23, Macrobius, *In somn. Scip.* I xxii 5). The fullest contemporary treatment of light as a quasi-element was that of Bartholomew Keckermann: see Fletcher ii 191. *this*] The demonstrative is in order because the sun on

Flew upward, spirited with various forms,
That rolled orbicular, and turned to stars
Numberless, as thou seest, and how they move;
Each had his place appointed, each his course,
The rest in circuit walls this universe.
Look downward on that globe whose hither side
With light from hence, though but reflected, shines;
That place is earth the seat of man, that light
His day, which else as the other hemisphere
Night would invade, but there the neighbouring moon
(So call that opposite fair star) her aid
Timely interposes, and her monthly round
Still ending, still renewing, through mid heaven;
With borrowed light her countenance triform
Hence fills and empties to enlighten the earth,
And in her pale dominion checks the night.
That spot to which I point is Paradise,

which Uriel stands is composed of ether; see ll. 718–19*n.* *quintessence*] Stressed on the first and third syllables, as was usual in the seventeenth century.

iii *717.* 'Each several soul [God] assigned to one star ... setting them each as it were in a chariot' (Plato, *Timaeus* 41E).

iii *718–19.* The doctrine that the ether is especially adapted to circular or *orbicular* motion, and that it is the substance of the stars, is Aristotelian (*De caelo* 270b).

iii *721.* The remaining quintessence fills the celestial spaces above the atmosphere, forming a sphere that encloses the universe; see Lucretius, *De rerum nat.* v 470.

iii *724–32.* Were it not for the sun's light, this hemisphere would be invaded like the other. But there, though Night may *invade*, the moon's dominion prevents her from conquering–a dramatic irony on Satan's invasion. In *Mythologiae* iii 15 Conti gathers a great variety of reasons why the lunar goddess should have been described by the ancients as *triformis* (she is Luna, Diana and Hecate; she is Juno, Diana and Proserpina; she rules in heaven, earth and hell; etc.). The only explanation strictly relevant here, however, is that which traces the epithet to the moon's phases. Cp. *Prae E* 56f; Jonson, *The Masque of Queenes* 273f ('*three-formed Starre* ... to Whose triple Name'); and Shakespeare, *A Midsummer Night's Dream* V ii 14 ('triple Hecate's team').

iii *729.* Some copies of *Ed I* have comma after *heaven*, no comma after *renewing*; perhaps correctly.

iii *731.* *Hence*] from the sun here.

iii *733.* Since Eden is now visible from the sun, it follows that Satan's journey from the *primum mobile* has occupied at least the latter half of Eden's

Adam's abode, those lofty shades his bower.
Thy way thou canst not miss, me mine requires.
Thus said, he turned, and Satan bowing low,
As to superior spirits is wont in heaven,
Where honour due and reverence none neglects,
Took leave, and toward the coast of earth beneath,
Down from the ecliptic, sped with hoped success,
Throws his steep flight in many an airy wheel,
Nor stayed, till on Niphates' top he lights.

THE END OF THE THIRD BOOK

Paradise Lost

BOOK IV

The Argument

Satan now in prospect of Eden, and nigh the place where he must now attempt the bold enterprise which he undertook alone against God and man, falls into many doubts with himself, and many passions, fear, envy, and despair; but at length confirms himself in evil, journeys on to Paradise, whose outward prospect and situation is described, overleaps the bounds, sits in the shape of a cormorant on the tree of life, as the highest in the garden to look about him. The garden described; Satan's first sight of Adam and Eve; his wonder at their excellent form and happy state, but with resolution to work their

night. See ll. 556–7*n*. We subsequently learn that the journey took twelve hours; see iv Argument, 564 and Introduction, 'Chronology'.
iii *739. coast*] side.
iii *740. ecliptic*] Not, here, the apparent orbit of the sun round the celestial sphere, but its actual path. See ll. 616–17*n*. *sped with hoped success*] Seems to refute the theory (Empson 61) that Uriel's account of creation convinced Satan of his own creatureliness, and so threw him into the despair he expresses in his Niphates speech. Unless, of course, the shock of the discovery was delayed.
iii *741. in*] some copies *Ed I*, *Errata* and *Ed II*; other copies *Ed I* have 'with'.
iii *742.* It was from the *Niphates*, a mountain on the borders of Armenia and Assyria (see iv 126), that the Tigris took its origin; see Strabo, Geog. XI xii 4. And at ix 71 below Tigris is the name given to the river of Paradise before it divides. There is no evidence for the interesting speculation that Niphates may be the same mountain from which Adam later contemplates the world, or on which Christ is tempted (xi 376–84).

fall; overhears their discourse, thence gathers that the tree of knowledge was forbidden them to eat of, under penalty of death; and thereon intends to found his temptation, by seducing them to transgress: then leaves them a while to know farther of their state by some other means. Mean while, Uriel descending on a sunbeam warns Gabriel, who had in charge the gate of Paradise, that some evil spirit had escaped the deep, and passed at noon by his sphere in the shape of a good angel down to Paradise, discovered after by his furious gestures in the mount. Gabriel promises to find him ere morning. Night coming on, Adam and Eve, discourse of going to their rest: their bower described; their evening worship. Gabriel drawing forth his bands of night-watch to walk the round of Paradise, appoints two strong angels to Adam's bower, lest the evil spirit should be there doing some harm to Adam or Eve sleeping; there they find him at the ear of Eve, tempting her in a dream, and bring him, though unwilling, to Gabriel; by whom questioned, he scornfully answers, prepares resistance, but hindered by a sign from heaven, flies out of Paradise.

O for that warning voice, which he who saw
The Apocalypse, heard cry in heaven aloud,
Then when the dragon, put to second rout,
Came furious down to be revenged on men,
Woe to the inhabitants on earth! that now,
While time was, our first parents had been warned
The coming of their secret foe, and scaped
Haply so scaped his mortal snare; for now
Satan, now first inflamed with rage, came down,
The tempter ere the accuser of mankind,
To wreak on innocent frail man his loss
Of that first battle, and his flight to hell;

iv *1–12.* The Revelation or *Apocalypse* of St John relates a vision of a second battle in heaven between Michael and *the dragon*, Satan. Then there was 'a loud voice saying in heaven Now is come salvation, and strength, and the kingdom of our God, and the power of his Christ: for the accuser of our brethren is cast down, which accused them before our God day and night.... Woe to the inhabiters of the earth and of the sea! for the devil is come down unto you, having great wrath, because he knoweth that he hath but a short time' (*Rev.* xii 7–12). M. wishes for the voice prophesying apocalyptic afflictions 'in order to raise the horror and attention of his reader' (Newton). M.'s wishing 'that Adam and Eve could have been warned by himself... shows he felt there was something inadequate about the warning of Raphael' (Empson 61f). Empson's inference is wrong, because Raphael's warning mission has yet to take place. The present passage may be regarded as a lead-in to the warnings both of Uriel and of Raphael.
iv *6. While time was*] Echoes *Rev.* xii 12 ('but a short time'); thus implying an analogy between the end of the prelapsarian world and the end of M.'s own world. *first-parents*] *Ed I* omits hyphen.
iv *11. wreak*] avenge.

Yet not rejoicing in his speed, though bold,
Far off and fearless, nor with cause to boast,
Begins his dire attempt, which nigh the birth
Now rolling, boils in his tumultuous breast,
And like a devilish engine back recoils
Upon himself; horror and doubt distract
His troubled thoughts, and from the bottom stir
The hell within him, for within him hell
He brings, and round about him, nor from hell
One step no more than from himself can fly
By change of place: now conscience wakes despair
That slumbered, wakes the bitter memory
Of what he was, what is, and what must be
Worse; of worse deeds worse sufferings must ensue.
Sometimes towards Eden which now in his view
Lay pleasant, his grieved look he fixes sad,
Sometimes towards heaven and the full-blazing sun,

iv *13–19*. Empson 61–3 attributes Satan's *horror and doubt* to the overwhelming effect of the information he received from Uriel about the creativity of God; see iii 740*n*. But M.'s own explanation is to be preferred: that the imminence of the actual aggression–*nigh the birth*–causes him to shrink in horror. *rolling*] moving on (*OED Roll* vb.[2] 14: used of time, and especially of cyclic periods). *devilish engine*] the cannon devised by Satan in the war in heaven (vi 469–500); but playing also on *engine*='plot' (*OED* 3; cp. i 750 above). Like all devilish plots this one is redounding to the confusion of the plotter.
iv *20–3*. See i 255*n*, and cp. *Doctrine and Discipline* ii 3 (Yale ii 294): 'To banish for ever into a locall hell, whether in the aire or in the center, or in that uttermost and bottomlesse gulph of Chaos, deeper from holy blisse then the worlds diameter multiply'd, [the pagan authors] thought not a punishing so proper and proportionat for God to inflict, as to punish sinne with sinne.' Also Sir Thomas Browne, *Religio Medici* i 51: 'men speake too popularly who place it in those flaming mountains, which to grosser apprehensions represent Hell. The heart of man is the place the devill dwels in; I feele sometimes a Hell within my selfe', and Marlowe, *Doctor Faustus* (1616) ed. Greg, ll. 513–5: 'Hell hath no limits, nor is circumscrib'd, / In one selfe place: but where we are is hell, / And where hell is there must we ever be.'
iv *24*. Bentley objected to the notion of remembering the future; but it is clear that M. primarily means 'recollect' (cp. *memento mori*). The passage seems also, however, to echo St Augustine's deep meditation on time in *Confess.* xi 28, so that M. may imply that Satan *can* only remember–there is for him, as we say, no future.
iv *25*. Cp. *SA* 22: 'what once I was, and what am now'.
iv *27–8*. The etymological meaning of *Eden* was well known in the seventeenth century to be 'pleasure, delight'.

Which now sat high in his meridian tower:
Then much revolving, thus in sighs began.
  O thou that with surpassing glory crowned,
Look'st from thy sole dominion like the God
Of this new world; at whose sight all the stars
Hide their diminished heads; to thee I call,

iv *30. meridian tower*] The tower image is Virgilian: *Igneus aetherias iam Sol penetrarat in arces* (*Culex* 42). Noon, when the sun crosses the *meridian*, is throughout *PL* a critical time of judgment. The basis of the association is ultimately *Mal.* iv 1f: 'The day cometh, that shall burn as an oven. . . . But unto you that fear my name shall the Sun of righteousness arise.' This *Sol iustitiae* metaphor was sometimes given an astronomical development, whereby the central position of the sun at noon was specified: 'As the sun, when in the centre of his orbit, that is to say, at the midday point, is hottest, so shall Christ be when He shall appear in the centre of heaven and earth, that is to say, in Judgment' (Pierre Bersuire, *Dictionarium seu repertorium morale* (Nuremberg 1489), iii 194^{r}, *cit.* Panofsky 262). As Panofsky notes, this analogy depends on an 'equation of the astrological notion, *medium coeli*, with the theological notion, *medium coeli et terrae*, presumed to be the seat of the Judge'. The point is of thematic importance, in view of M.'s structural positioning of Christ the Sun of righteousness at the numerological centre of the whole poem (see vi 762*n*). For other instances of a symbolic noon, see iii 616–17*n*, ix 739*n*; and for Spenser's use of the image, see Fowler 67, 70. The present moment is critical for Satan, because he is on the point of beginning his 'dire attempt'.
iv *31. revolving*] pondering; as in *PR* i 185–'Musing and much revolving in his breast, / How best the mighty work he might begin'.
iv *32–41*. According to Edward Phillips, this passage was shown to him and some others 'several Years before the Poem was begun', when M. intended to write a tragedy on the Fall. The lines were 'designed for the very beginning of the said Tragedy' (Darbishire 72f and see Introduction, 'Composition'). A resemblance to the opening of Aeschylus' *Prometheus vinctus* is sometimes discovered, but consists in little more than that both have an address to the sun. The whole speech (ll. 32–113) is intensely dramatic. It presents an interior duologue between Satan's better and worse selves, that should be compared with the repartee of good and evil angels in Marlowe's *Doctor Faustus*. At the same time, the self-dramatising of despair is for M. itself satanic. 'The characters of *Paradise Lost* do not soliloquise until they have fallen' (Broadbent 80).
iv *33*. The Orphic and Platonic doctrine that the sun is a divine image had been elaborated by Neoplatonists into a full-scale solar theology. See, e.g., Plato, *Rep.* 508; Dionysius, *De divin. nom.*; and Ficino, *De Sole* and *Epist.* vi, *Orphica comparatio Solis ad Deum* (966, 825).

But with no friendly voice, and add thy name
O sun, to tell thee how I hate thy beams
That bring to my remembrance from what state
I fell, how glorious once above thy sphere;
Till pride and worse ambition threw me down
Warring in heaven against heaven's matchless king:
Ah wherefore! He deserved no such return
From me, whom he created what I was
In that bright eminence, and with his good
Upbraided none; nor was his service hard.
What could be less than to afford him praise,
The easiest recompense, and pay him thanks,
How due! Yet all his good proved ill in me,
And wrought but malice; lifted up so high
I sdeigned subjection, and thought one step higher
Would set me highest, and in a moment quit
The debt immense of endless gratitude,
So burdensome still paying, still to owe;
Forgetful what from him I still received,

iv *37*. 'Every one that doeth evil hateth the light' (*John* iii 20).
iv *38–9*. 'Remember therefore from whence thou art fallen, and repent' (*Rev.* ii 5).
iv *41*. *matchless king*] Edward Phillips gives the phrase as 'Glorious King', which may represent an earlier version. See ll. 32–41*n*.
iv *42–3*. The *volte face* from Satan's earlier attitude to God is so complete that some have attributed it to a change in the poet's intention, others to his use of old material. Empson 64f refutes the view that this first private speech by Satan admits his earlier public ones to have been full of lies–but only to the satisfaction of those whose values are as sophisticated as Satan's own. Earlier readers seem not to have been at all surprised by the change in attitude. They would expect the first offender to be remorseful, after he had had time for solitary reflection. When remorse led not to repentance but to hardened persistence, they would recognize that a new phase in damnation had been reached: see ll. 110–12*n*.
iv *43*. An important admission. During the rebellion in heaven Satan believed–or pretended–that the angels were 'self-begot, self-raised / By [their] own quickening power' (v 860f). See iii 740*n*.
iv *45*. Cp. *Jas.* i 5: 'If any of you lack wisdom, let him ask of God, that giveth to all men liberally, and upbraideth not; and it shall be given him.' The context is precepts about how to behave under temptation.
iv *50*. *sdeigned*] disdained (mainly poet.). Originally imitating Ital. *sdegnare*, a word with aristocratic associations: see Fowler 110.
iv *53–4*. *still*] always.

And understood not that a grateful mind
By owing owes not, but still pays, at once
Indebted and discharged; what burden then?
O had his powerful destiny ordained
Me some inferior angel, I had stood
Then happy; no unbounded hope had raised
Ambition. Yet why not? Some other power
As great might have aspired, and me though mean
Drawn to his part; but other powers as great
Fell not, but stand unshaken, from within
Or from without, to all temptations armed.
Hadst thou the same free will and power to stand?
Thou hadst: whom hast thou then or what to accuse,
But heaven's free love dealt equally to all?
Be then his love accursed, since love or hate,
To me alike, it deals eternal woe.
Nay cursed be thou; since against his thy will
Chose freely what it now so justly rues.
Me miserable! Which way shall I fly
Infinite wrath, and infinite despair?
Which way I fly is hell; my self am hell;
And in the lowest deep a lower deep
Still threatening to devour me opens wide,
To which the hell I suffer seems a heaven.
O then at last relent: is there no place

iv *55–7*. Simply by owning an obligation gratefully, one ceases to owe it; cp. Cicero, *Pro Plancio* xxviii 68: 'In a moral debt, when a man pays he keeps, and when he keeps, he pays by the very act of keeping.' Just as Cicero plays on two senses of *habere*, so M. plays on *owe* (*OED* I 1 c, = acknowledge as one's own; and II 2, = be under obligation to repay).
iv *59*. *stood*] Combining 'remained' (*OED Stood* 15 e) with 'stood firm and not fallen' (*OED* 9 b; cp. l. 64 below).
iv *66–70*. God the Father has explained that predestination did not over-rule the freedom of the angels' wills, and that his love desired a free response from them (see iii 100–2*n* and cp. v 535–40). This divine love can be represented as ultimately responsible for Satan's fall, since it occasioned the freedom of his will.
iv *74*. *Me miserable*] A similar exclamatory use of 'me' was common in Elizabethan dramatic contexts (*OED* 7 a, citing also Greene, *Menaphon*: 'Ay me unhappie'. M. secondarily imitates the Lat. idiom *me miserum*, but the primary point is that Satan's diction is theatrical.
iv *75*. See ll. 20–3*n* and i 255*n*; and cp. *Comus* 384: 'Himself is his own dungeon.'
iv *79–80*. Esau having sold his birthright, 'when he would have inherited the blessing . . . was rejected: for he found no place of repentance' (*Heb.*

Left for repentance, none for pardon left?
None left but by submission; and that word
Disdain forbids me, and my dread of shame
Among the spirits beneath, whom I seduced
With other promises and other vaunts
Than to submit, boasting I could subdue
The omnipotent. Ay me, they little know
How dearly I abide that boast so vain,
Under what torments inwardly I groan;
While they adore me on the throne of hell,
With diadem and sceptre high advanced
The lower still I fall, only supreme
In misery; such joy ambition finds.
But say I could repent and could obtain
By act of grace my former state; how soon
Would highth recall high thoughts, how soon unsay
What feigned submission swore; ease would recant
Vows made in pain, as violent and void.
For never can true reconcilement grow
Where wounds of deadly hate have pierced so deep:

xii 17). The A.V. marg. gloss explains the last phrase as meaning 'way to change his mind'.
iv *82.* Not a confession by the better Satan, but a justification by the worse; since *Disdain* carries the force of Ital. *sdegno*–'scorn, indignation; contempt for what is base and unbecoming to the self-respect of an angel and a gentleman'. See l. 50*n*. *Disdain* is italicized as a proper name in the early edns.
iv *84. other . . . other*] The scheme, a special form of ploce, was a favourite with M.; cp., e.g., x 861f ('With other echo late I taught your shades / To answer, and resound far other song'), *Comus* 612f, and *Lycidas* 174. It occurs in Dante, *Inf.* iii 91f: *Per altra via, per altri porti / verrai a piaggia, non qui, per passare.* ('You must pass over by other roads, by other ferries: not here.')
iv *88.* Some copies *Ed I* have colon after *groan.*
iv *89. adore*] Empson 76f imagines Satan as sneering apologetically at the word: 'he has at times accepted for himself what he had disapproved of giving to the Son. But this would be hard to avoid, and to worry about it only proves that he is a deeply conscientious republican.' But 'adore' is sufficiently explained as an amplification of the contrast between outward supremacy and inward torment. Satan says that his advancement is made hollow by his misery, not that it is excessive. Apparently either his remorse or his political education is insufficient for qualms about the class structure of hell.
iv *94. By act of grace*] by concession of favour, not of right (*OED Grace* II 6). The phrase was often used in political contexts, in the special sense 'free pardon by formal act of Parliament' (*OED* II 15 b).

Which would but lead me to a worse relapse
And heavier fall: so should I purchase dear
Short intermission bought with double smart.
This knows my punisher; therefore as far
From granting he, as I from begging peace:
All hope excluded thus, behold in stead
Of us outcast, exiled, his new delight,
Mankind created, and for him this world.
So farewell hope, and with hope farewell fear,
Farewell remorse: all good to me is lost;
Evil be thou my good; by thee at least
Divided empire with heaven's king I hold
By thee, and more than half perhaps will raign;
As man ere long, and this new world shall know.
  Thus while he spake, each passion dimmed his face
Thrice changed with pale, ire, envy and despair,
Which marred his borrowed visage, and betrayed
Him counterfeit, if any eye beheld.

iv *100*. Some copies of *Ed I* have comma after *relapse*.

iv *110–12*. The hardening of Satan's heart (see iii 200) and his despairing nihilism are analysed in Broadbent 76–8. *by thee . . . By thee*] Curiously doubled–perhaps to render the divisive, dyadic character of the evil addressed.

iv *110*. By ix 122f the more painful converse has been experienced: 'all good to me becomes / Bane'. See i 159–68*n*, and cp. *Is.* v 20: 'Woe unto them that call evil good, and good evil.'

iv *111*. *Divided*] shared; but alluding also to the number symbolism whereby Satan's rule is dyadic and divisive.

iv *112–13*. i.e., if in addition to ruling hell Satan succeeds in conquering the world. The idea is further developed at x 372–82. *raign*] the transitive use of 'reign' was obsolete; so that 'raign' (an aphetic form of arraign) is the word primarily indicated; 'reign', however, is clearly present as an ambiguity–indeed, most editors treat it as belonging to the primary chain of discourse.

iv *115–17*. i.e., each of the three passions named caused *pale* (paleness, pallor). Since he is disguised as a cherub (iii 636), Satan's face ought to be of the appropriate colour; and cherubim were conventionally red. See, e.g., Randle Cotgrave, *A dictionarie of the French and English tongues* (1611), s.v. *Cherubin*: '*Rouge comme un Cherubin,*' Red-faced, Cherubin-faced, having a fierie facies like a Cherubin.' M. puns visually on red the cherubic colour, and red the ordinary ruddiness of a sanguine human complexion unaffected by passion.

iv *115*. *ire, envy and despair*] Note that the Argument has 'fear, envy, and despair'.

For heavenly minds from such distempers foul
Are ever clear. Whereof he soon aware,
Each perturbation smoothed with outward calm,
Artificer of fraud; and was the first
That practised falsehood under saintly show,
Deep malice to conceal, couched with revenge:
Yet not enough had practised to deceive
Uriel once warned; whose eye pursued him down
The way he went, and on the Assyrian mount
Saw him disfigured, more than could befall
Spirit of happy sort: his gestures fierce
He marked and mad demeanour, then alone,
As he supposed, all unobserved, unseen.
So on he fares, and to the border comes,
Of Eden, where delicious Paradise,

iv *118. distempers*] disorders of the mind, due to disturbances of the proper temper or proportion of the humours.
iv *121. Artificer*] inventor; cp. the alternative formula 'father of lies'.
iv *123. couched*] hidden, laid in concealment (*OED* III 13); perhaps also–in view of l. 120–with the overtone 'quelled, suppressed' (*OED* II 10). *with* introduces a further complication, for *couched with* meant 'inlaid with, set with' (*OED* I 4). The intricacy of the line is mimetic.
iv *124–30.* Cp. Uriel's report to Gabriel, 364–72 below.
iv *124. enough*] *Ed I* and *Ed II* have the variant form 'anough'.
iv *125. warned*] made aware; i.e., Satan had only been able to deceive Uriel temporarily, by catching him unawares (see iii 624 and 629: 'fixed in cogitation'). Or perhaps 'it only means that Uriel after being asked the way by this character felt enough curiosity to follow his later movements' (Empson 66). But Gilbert (40) finds a discrepancy here, which he puts down to inadequate assimilation of an early tragedy.
iv *126. the Assyrian mount*] Niphates; see iii 742*n*.
iv *127.* According to Henry More, *The immortality of the soul* III x 5, spirits find it quite difficult to hide their true natures: 'Nor may the various Transfiguration of their shapes conceal their persons, no more then the disguises that are used by fraudulent men.'
iv *131.* Lewis 47 comments on the gradualness of the approach to Paradise.
iv *132–59.* Starnes and Talbert (310–15) argue that M. in part built his image of Paradise out of material quarried from Stephanus' entry on the Hesperides and Conti's description of the Elysian fields. It may be misleading, however, to cite particular sources for the details of M.'s Paradise; for it really assimilates and refines upon the whole European tradition of paradises, gardens, pleasances, fortunate isles, and lands of the blessed as subjects for conventional description.
iv *132. Paradise* is the garden situated within the land of *Eden*: see ll. 209–

Now nearer, crowns with her enclosure green,
As with a rural mound the champaign head
Of a steep wilderness, whose hairy sides
With thicket overgrown, grotesque and wild,
Access denied; and over head up grew
Insuperable highth of loftiest shade,

10*n*; also i 4–5*n*. *delicious Paradise* renders the *deliciarum paradisum* of the Fathers (see Corcoran 20*n*).

iv *134*. *champaign*] unenclosed (contrast the *enclosure*, l. 133, of Paradise itself); also open, level, free from trees.

iv *135*. *hairy sides*] Cp. 134, *head*: 'The Freudian idea that the happy garden is an image of the human body would not have frightened Milton in the least' (Lewis 47). In Spenser's Garden of Adonis there is a myrtle-clad mount with a similar anatomical significance (*F.Q.* III vi 43; see Ellrodt 88*n*, Fowler 135f). In Dante, *Purg.* xxviii 91–102 Paradise is located on the summit of the purgatorial mountain, to ensure that it will be free from the effects of atmospheric change; cp. Ariosto, *Orl. Fur.* xxxiv 48, where the hill of Paradise 'nigh touched the circle of the moon'. The elevated Paradise goes back to *Ezek.* xxviii 13f: 'Thou hast been in Eden the garden of God . . . thou wast upon the holy mountain of God'; but in its more exaggerated expression shades off into the supraterrestrial garden ridiculed by Heylyn (*Cosmographie* (1652) iii 147; see also iii 565–71*n* above, and Hanford 408f). As an *enclosed* garden it recalls the *hortus conclusus* of *The Song of Solomon* iv 12, which in medieval religious iconography was one of the principal symbols of Mary, the second Eve.

iv *136*. 'In most exquisite pictures they use to blaze and portraict not onely the daintie lineaments of beautye, but also rounde about it to shadow the rude thickets and craggy clifts, that by the basenesse of such parts, more excellency may accrew to the principall' (E.K., Epistle to Harvey, before Spenser's *Shepheardes Calender*). *grotesque*] (*Ed II* gottesque) romantic, picturesque. Originally used with reference to an antique style of ornament consisting of fantastically interwoven foliage. It often took the form of extravagant, excessive, or even monstrous and diabolic forms: see André Chastel, 'La Renaissance fantaisiste' in *L'Oeil* xxi (1956) 34–41; Arnold von Salis, *Antike und Renaissance* (Bâle 1947). Curtius has labelled the pleasance within a wild wood 'the specialized Tempe motif'.

iv *138–43*. Recalling many famous *loci amoeni*–especially perhaps Spenser's Mt Acidale, which was 'plaste in an open plaine, / That round about was bordered with a wood / Of matchlesse hight, that seem'd th'earth to disdaine, / In which all trees of honour stately stood / And did all winter as in sommer bud' (*F.Q.* VI x 6); and the home of his Belphoebe, 'in a pleasant glade, / With mountaines round about environed, / And mighty woods, which did the valley shade, / And like a stately Theatre it made, / Spreading it selfe into a spatious plaine' (*F.Q.* III v 39). Cp. also the 'second paradise'

Cedar, and pine, and fir, and branching palm,
A sylvan scene, and as the ranks ascend
Shade above shade, a woody theatre
Of stateliest view. Yet higher than their tops
The verdurous wall of Paradise up sprung:
Which to our general sire gave prospect large
Into his nether empire neighbouring round.
And higher than that wall a circling row
Of goodliest trees loaden with fairest fruit,
Blossoms and fruits at once of golden hue
Appeared, with gay enamelled colours mixed:
On which the sun more glad impressed his beams
Than in fair evening cloud, or humid bow,

surrounding Spenser's Temple of Venus: 'No tree, that is of count, in greene-wood growes, / From lowest Juniper to Ceder tall . . . / But there was planted' (*F.Q.* IV x 22). According to a persistent tradition based on *Gen.* ii 5 ('every plant of the field') and exemplified in Dante, *Purg.* xxviii, all plant life was represented in Paradise. On the climbing serialism of the description, see Lewis 48. For the tree catalogue commonplace, cp. 693–701 and *Comus* 999ff, and see Curtius 195; the only unconventional tree in M.'s list is the palm, which is possibly to be accounted for by *Ps.* xcii 12: 'The righteous shall flourish like the palm tree: he shall grow like a cedar in Lebanon.' Cp. also Du Bartas 189, where the palm is an emblem of chastity or marital loyalty: let the adulteress, he says, 'Blush (at the least) at Palm-Trees loyaltie, / Which never bears, unless her Male be by'. *sylvan scene*] Echoes Virgil, *Aen.* i 164, *silvis scaena coruscis.*

iv *148. at once*] at the same time. The simultaneous concurrence of all stages of growth was a well-established feature of earthly paradises: cp., e.g., Homer *Od.* vii 122–32; Ariosto, *Orl. Fur.* xxxiv 49; Tasso, *Gerus. Lib.* xvi 10f ('ere the fruit drop off, the blossom comes, / This springs, that falls, that ripeneth and this blooms. // The leaves upon the self-same bough did hide / Beside the young the old and ripened fig'); and Spenser, *F.Q.* III vi 42 ('There is continuall spring, and harvest there / Continuall, both meeting at one time'). Usually the Golden Age stasis is left unexplained, but in *PL* the absence of seasons is traced to astronomical causes, at x 651–706. For M. the motif would be associated with the exegetical controversies over *Gen.* i 12, which has God commanding the earth to bring forth simultaneously 'the bud of the herb' (Vulg. *herbam virentem*) and trees bearing fruit. Willet (9) tried to solve the problem by supposing that the first bearing of fruit was supernatural and that 'in the beginning, trees did beare fruit in the yeare more then once'–as the tree of life does in *Rev.* xxii 2.

iv *149. enamelled*] fresh, lustrous, bright; variegated. With no suggestion of hardness.

iv *151. humid bow*] rainbow; cp. *Comus* 992: 'Iris there with humid bow, / Waters the odorous banks.'

When God hath showered the earth; so lovely seemed
That landscape: and of pure now purer air
Meets his approach, and to the heart inspires
Vernal delight and joy, able to drive
All sadness but despair: now gentle gales
Fanning their odoriferous wings dispense
Native perfumes, and whisper whence they stole
Those balmy spoils. As when to them who sail

iv *153*. Cp. Stephanus, *Dictionarium*, s.v. *Elysium*: *Hunc locum alii inferorum foelicitatibus plenum, alii fortunatas insulas, alii circa lunarem circulum esse dicunt, ubi iam aer purior est*. See xii 76–8*n* below. Contrary to the common assumption, the use of *of* to express transformation from a former condition was not Latinate; see *OED* s.v. *Of* VII 20 b, where examples from English authors as venerable as Bede are cited. *landscape*] lantskip *Ed I* and *Ed II*: see ii 491*n*.
iv *156–8*. Cp. Conti's description of the Elysian fields: *atque ventos plurimum suaves et odoriferos leniter spirare*. The echo is not so clear as it may seem, however, for *odoriferous* was a familiar word in M.'s day. The idea of perfumes stolen by the wind was a commonplace.
iv *156*. *gale*] In the eighteenth century the use of 'gale' in the sense 'gentle breeze' was to become conventional poetic diction. But in M.'s time and before, the ordinary (and in particular the nautical) meaning of 'gale' was very near to Mod. Eng. 'wind'. Thus Capt. John Smith gives the ascending series 'a calme, a brese, a fresh gaile, a pleasant gayle, a stiffe gayle' *An accidence or the path-way to experience, necessary for all young sea-men* (1626) 17).
iv *158*. *perfumes*] Stressed on the second syllable.
v *159–66*. Resuming at the end of Satan's journey to Eden the comparison made near its beginning (see ii 636–41*n*). *Cape of Hope*] Cape of Good Hope. R. I. S. Jones sees an implication that Satan is now past hope. Cp. l. 108, 'farewell hope'. *Mozambic*] (Stressed on the second syllable.) The Portuguese province of Mozambique, between which and Madagascar the trade route lay. *Sabean*] of Saba or Sheba (now Yemen). M. draws on the description of *Arabie the blest–Arabia felix*–in Diodorus Siculus III xlvi 4. Balsam and cassia grow along the shore, and inland thick forests of frankincense and cinnamon: 'A divine thing and beyond the power of words to describe seems the fragrance which greets the nostrils and stirs the senses of everyone. Indeed, even though those who sail along this coast may be far from the land, that does not deprive them of a portion of the enjoyment . . . When the wind is blowing off shore, one finds that the sweet odours exhaled by the myrrh-bearing and other aromatic trees penetrate to the near-by parts of the sea.' It may be relevant that Diodorus qualifies this impression of a country blessed with every advantage, by telling how it is infested with poisonous serpents (III xlvii 1f). Cp. *Elegia V* 59, and *PR* ii 364.

Beyond the Cape of Hope, and now are past
Mozambic, off at sea north-east winds blow
Sabean odours from the spicy shore
Of Arabie the blest, with such delay
Well pleased they slack their course, and many a league
Cheered with the grateful smell old Ocean smiles.
So entertained those odorous sweets the fiend
Who came their bane, though with them better pleased
Than Asmodeus with the fishy fume,
That drove him, though enamoured, from the spouse

Since the mariners are sailing N.E., they must *slack their course* when they meet N.E. winds.
iv *166–71. Tobit's son*] The apocryphal book *Tobit* relates the story of Tobit's son Tobias, who was sent into Media on an errand, and there married Raguel's daughter Sara. Sara had previously been given to seven men, but all were killed by the jealous spirit *Asmodeus* before their marriages could be consummated. By the advice of Raphael, however, Tobias succeeded where the others had failed; for he burned the heart and liver of a fish, and made smoke: 'the which smell when the evil spirit had smelled, he fled into the utmost parts of Egypt, and the angel bound him' (*Tob.* viii 3). Lewis (42) thinks that M. introduces the simile 'to make us feel the full obscenity of Satan's presence in Eden by bringing a sudden stink of fish across the sweet smell of the flowers' and finds 'the pretence of logical connection . . . too strained'. But the connections seem close enough, once the typology of the *Tobit* episode is recalled. Tobias directly compares himself to Adam at *Tob.* viii 6, and like M.'s Adam is instructed by Raphael (see *Tob.* vi, and *PL* v 221–3, where the parallel is drawn explicitly); while the binding of Asmodeus foreshadows the binding of Satan by the new Adam, Christ (see *PL* xii 454). M.'s simile is designed to amplify the inappropriateness of the welcome Satan receives in Eden. *Though* he lacks Asmodeus' excuse of infatuation, Satan gets no worse treatment: indeed, he is met with sweet perfumes, even *though* they please him. *with a vengeance*] The odd coupling of this intensive phrase with the unemphatic *sent* alerts one to the sardonic pun–Tobias's success was vengeance, typologically, for Adam's failure. The story of Tobias provided several subjects that were very popular with seventeenth-century artists–e.g., Rembrandt's *The Angel Raphael departing from Tobit and his family* (Louvre); Elsheimer's *Tobias and the Angel* (Nat. Gall.); and Santi's *Landscape with Tobias and the Angel* (Imola, Pinacoteca Civica).
iv *168. Asmodeus*' part in the war in heaven is related at vi 365; cp. also *PR* ii 151f, where he is 'the fleshliest incubus'. According to a Scholastic tradition transmitted by Cornelius Agrippa, Heywood, Burton and others, there were nine orders of devils, of which Asmodeus led the fourth, the 'malicious revenging devils' (*Anat. of Melan.* I ii 1 ii).

Of Tobit's son, and with a vengeance sent
From Media post to Aegypt, there fast bound.
  Now to the ascent of that steep savage hill
Satan had journeyed on, pensive and slow;
But further way found none, so thick entwined,
As one continued brake, the undergrowth
Of shrubs and tangling bushes had perplexed
All path of man or beast that passed that way:
One gate there only was, and that looked east
On the other side: which when the arch-felon saw
Due entrance he disdained, and in contempt,
At one slight bound high over leaped all bound
Of hill or highest wall, and sheer within
Lights on his feet. As when a prowling wolf,
Whom hunger drives to seek new haunt for prey,
Watching where shepherds pen their flocks at eve
In hurdled cotes amid the field secure,
Leaps o'er the fence with ease into the fold:
Or as a thief bent to unhoard the cash
Of some rich burgher, whose substantial doors,
Cross-barred and bolted fast, fear no assault,
In at the window climbs, or o'er the tiles;
So clomb this first grand thief into God's fold:

iv *172. savage*] wild, rugged.
iv *176. had perplexed*] (Conditional) 'would have perplexed (tangled, interwoven)'–i.e. would, if there had been any passing.
iv *178.* On the eastern gate, see ll. 542–50*n*.
iv *181.* The subdued pun or paronomasia is I think simply an instance of M.'s re-enlivening awareness of language–a not particularly successful instance. There is no comic implication, despite Tillyard[3] 71–5.
iv *183–7.* Cp. *Lycidas* 115, and see *John* x 1: 'He that entereth not by the door into the sheepfold, but climbeth up some other way, the same is a thief and a robber.' *cotes*] shelters. *secure*] over-confident.
iv *188–91.* There is just possibly an allusion here to the vision of judgment in *Joel* ii 3–9: 'The land is as the garden of Eden before them . . . they shall climb up upon the houses; they shall enter in at the windows like a thief.'
iv *188. unhoard*] take out of hoard. *OED* gives no example earlier than this.
iv *192–3.* Returning to the simile of ll. 183–7, whose vehicle thus becomes the tenor of the intervening comparison. For the application of the Johannine parable to contemporary ecclesiastical conditions, cp. xii 507ff and *Cromwell* 11–14: 'new foes arise / Threatening to bind our souls with secular chains: / Help us to save free conscience from the paw / Of hireling wolves whose gospel is their maw.' In the debate on church government M. was against a salaried ministry and he wrote a tract in this sense, *Considerations Touching the Likeliest Means to Remove*

So since into his church lewd hirelings climb.
Thence up he flew, and on the tree of life
The middle tree and highest there that grew,
Sat like a cormorant; yet not true life
Thereby regained, but sat devising death
To them who lived; nor on the virtue thought
Of that life-giving plant, but only used
For prospect, what well used had been the pledge
Of immortality. So little knows
Any, but God alone, to value right
The good before him, but perverts best things
To worst abuse, or to their meanest use.
Beneath him with new wonder now he views
To all delight of human sense exposed

Hirelings out of the Church (1659) (Yale vii). *lewd*] wicked, vile; or more probably 'untrained, ignorant'–M. thought ministers ought to support themselves (as many Sectarians in fact did) by learning a trade or profession.
iv *195*. On the siting of the tree of life, see ll. 217–21*n*.
iv *196*. The image of the *cormorant* really continues the invective of l. 193. Anyone guilty of greedy rapaciousness might be called a cormorant, but the term was especially often used of 'hireling' clergy: cp. Nashe, *Anatomie of Absurditie*: 'The cormorants of our age, who ... have alwaies their mouthes open to aske, and ... gape after Colledge living' (ed. McKerrow i 36). The immortal fruit of the *tree of life* is the reward promised the faithful believer, in the New Jerusalem (*Rev.* ii 7, xxii 14): the cormorant is made to sit on it, because hirelings want a corner in immortality. The image has also, however, a broader meaning, and like other of the forms taken by Satan foreshadows judgment. See *Is.* xxxiv 11: in the day of the Lord's vengeance Edom will lie waste: 'The cormorant and the bittern shall possess it.' But it should not be thought that the bird had for M. a purely literary existence. Indeed, we know that he must often have at least heard its cry; for just across the road from his house in Petty France the king's cormorants were kept in St James's Park.
iv *196–201*. It is asked how Satan could ever have *used* the tree *well*. The answer is that if he had thought on the *virtue* (secret property) of the tree, and had been obedient, he might have *true life ... regained*. For M. considered the tree of life as 'not ... so much a sacrament, as a symbol of eternal life, or rather perhaps the nutriment by which that life is sustained'–a positive complement, as it were, to the tree of knowledge, which was also 'a pledge ... and memorial of obedience' (*De doctrina* i 10; Columbia xv 115). M.'s position is like that of Andrew Willet, who in his *Hexapla in Genesin* (1608) 28 and 55 fixed in popular form the Augustinian view that the tree of life was not effectual but significative: 'a signe of true immortalitie, which hee should receive of God, if he continue in obedience.' See *Gen.* ii 9 and iii 22.

In narrow room nature's whole wealth, yea more,
A heaven on earth, for blissful Paradise
Of God the garden was, by him in the east
Of Eden planted; Eden stretched her line
From Auran eastward to the royal towers
Of great Seleucia, built by Grecian kings,
Or where the sons of Eden long before
Dwelt in Telassar: in this pleasant soil
His far more pleasant garden God ordained;
Out of the fertile ground he caused to grow
All trees of noblest kind for sight, smell, taste;
And all amid them stood the tree of life,
High eminent, blooming ambrosial fruit

iv *207–8.* A tradition, based on *Gen.* ii 5 and 9, that creation was instantaneous and that Paradise comprehended the potentiality of all future life, is traced by Ellrodt (75–81) from Augustine's *De Genesi* to Spenser's Garden of Adonis, 'the first seminarie / Of all things, that are borne to live and die' (*F.Q.* III vi 30). See also ll. 138–43*n* above. For the idea of Paradise as a shadow of heaven, see v 574*n*.

iv *209–16.* See *Gen.* ii 8: 'The Lord God planted a garden eastward in Eden; and there he put the man whom he had formed.' For summary accounts of the furious controversy about the location of Paradise, see Willet and Heylyn iii 127. Among those who believed in a local terrestrial Paradise, as many placed it S. of modern Persia, in Chaldea, at the fertile confluence of the Tigris and the Euphrates, as N., at the source of these rivers, near Mt Niphates. M. contrives to include both views. (He neatly succeeds, also, in accommodating yet another competing theory–going back to St Bonaventura–that Eden was 'under the Equinoctiall' (Willet 27), by making the ecliptic and the equator coincide before the Fall: see x 651–706*n* below.) *Auran* (Vulg. *Auran*, A.V. *Hauran*), an eastern boundary of the land of Israel in *Ezek.* xlvii 16–8, possibly confused with Haran–a name associated with Eden at *Ezek.* xxvii 23, and in *Gen.* xi 31–xii 4 a place Abraham is commanded by the Lord to leave. *Great Seleucia* was built by Alexander's general Seleucus Nicator as a seat of government for his Syrian empire; Heylyn (iii 129) notes that it was sometimes confused with Babylon. It is situated on the Tigris, not E. but S.E. from Auran. The mention of *Telassar* is another dramatic irony, for it prophesies war in Eden. The allusion is to *2 Kings* xix 11f or *Is.* xxxvii 11f, where Telassar is an instance of lands destroyed utterly: 'them which my fathers have destroyed, as Gozan, and Haran, and Rezeph, and the children of Eden which were in Telassar'.

iv *217.* See ll. 138–43*n*, and cp. Spenser's description of Mt Acidale 'in which all trees of honour stately stood' (*F.Q.* VI x 6).

iv *217–21.* See *Gen.* ii 9: 'And out of the ground made the Lord God to grow every tree that is pleasant to the sight, and good for food; the tree of life also in the midst of the garden, and the tree of knowledge of good and

Of vegetable gold; and next to life
Our death the tree of knowledge grew fast by,
Knowledge of good bought dear by knowing ill.
Southward through Eden went a river large,
Nor changed his course, but through the shaggy hill
Passed underneath ingulfed, for God had thrown

evil.' *fruit of ... gold*] Recalls the Hesperidean fruit (Ovid, *Met.* iv 637f) which was gathered by Hercules in spite of its dragon sentinel. *blooming*] (Trans.; rare) causing to flourish. *ambrosial*: see ii 245*n*. *vegetable gold*] This strange phrase has more to it than the mere paradox of attributing life and growth to a mineral substance. 'Vegetable stone' and 'potable gold' (see iii 608*n*) were both varieties of the philosophers' stone that preserved health (*OED* s.v. *Vegetable* a. 1 d), so that M. seems here to be imagining that there is alchemical significance in God's anxiety lest the fruit of the tree of life prove an elixir to the fallen Adam (*Gen.* iii 22). Both the tree of life and the Hesperian fruit gathered by Atalanta as she ran were often used to symbolize the alchemical *Magnum Opus*; as, e.g., in Michael Maier's emblematic *Atalanta fugiens*. For Fludd's attempt to achieve the vegetable stone, and his partial success in producing a humor 'like aurum potabile', see C. H. Josten, 'Robert Fludd's "Philosophical Key" and His Alchemical Experiment on Wheat', *Ambix* xi (1963) 1–23, esp. 19.

iv *220–2*. While the other trees are splendidly described the tree of knowledge is not, so as to avoid any suggestion of provocativeness on the part of God (Burden 126ff).

iv *222*. Cp. *De doctrina* i 10, Columbia xv 115: 'It was called the tree of knowledge of good and evil from the event; for since Adam tasted it, we not only know evil, but we know good only by means of evil'; also *Areopagitica* (Yale ii 514): 'It was from out the rinde of one apple tasted, that the knowledge of good and evill as two twins cleaving together leapt forth into the World. And perhaps this is that doom which Adam fell into of knowing good and evill, that is to say of knowing good by evill.'

iv *223–32*. The fertility of Paradise (see ll. 215–7) is explained in *Gen.* ii 5f as not due to rain: 'But there went up a mist from the earth, and watered the whole face of the ground.' This passage was a well-known crux (see Willet 26f); St Jerome's Vulgate version, e.g., had a fountain instead of a mist: *Sed fons ascendebat e terra, irrigans universam superficiem terrae.* Dante had used the detail in his earthly paradise (*Purg.* xxviii 121ff), where it is emphasised that the moisture, being independent of rainfall, does not fluctuate in abundance, 'but comes from a stable and certain source'. Dante also had two divisions of the main stream, Lethe and Eunoe; these were allegorical in character, however: one removed memory of sins, the other restored memory of good deeds. The principal model for M.'s description is Philo, *Quaest. in Gen.* i 12, where the difficulty of finding any location for Paradise that meets the requirements of *Gen.* ii 10–14 is overcome by the speculation that 'perhaps Paradise is in some distant place far from our inhabited world,

That mountain as his garden mould high raised
Upon the rapid current, which through veins
Of porous earth with kindly thirst up drawn,
Rose a fresh fountain, and with many a rill
Watered the garden; thence united fell
Down the steep glade, and met the nether flood,
Which from his darksome passage now appears,
And now divided into four main streams,
Runs diverse, wandering many a famous realm
And country whereof here needs no account,
But rather to tell how, if art could tell,

and has a river flowing under the earth, which waters many great veins so that these rising send water to other recipient veins, and so become diffused. And as these are forced by the rush of water, the force which is in them makes its way out to the surface, both in the Armenian mountains and elsewhere.' Note that M. agrees with Philo and many later exegetes in the view that the real source of the four rivers is not in Paradise, but that they have their origin in a river flowing *through Eden* and into (or under) the garden itself; cp. *Gen.* ii 10: 'A river went out of Eden to water the garden.' Lewis (49) notes the suggestion of a human body in words such as *shaggy*; *veins*; *thirst*; cf. 135*n* above. *kindly thirst*] natural thirst. The phrase at first suggests capillary attraction, especially in view of *porous earth* (l. 228); but this force would be insufficient to produce the fountain and rills of ll. 229–31. Either the pressure of the head of water behind the *rapid current* l. 227) causes the fountain, or else the passage is based on a misconception. Certain branches of hydromechanics had been carried to a considerable height of sophistication in M.'s time, thanks to the work of Galileo's pupils Castelli and Torricelli, but accurate observations of capillary action were not made until 1709 (Hawksbee). The point is worth examining, because M. usually makes strenuous efforts to work out the literal implications of Genesis with all the rigour he is capable of.

iv *233–5*. *Gen.* ii 10: 'And a river went out of Eden to water the garden; and from thence it was parted, and became into four heads.' Some commentators took *Gen.* ii 5 to mean that the whole earth was watered from Paradise; and in any case the account in *Gen.* ii 11–14, of lands watered by the four distributaries Pison, Gihon, Hiddekel and Euphrates, mentioned three *famous realms*–Havilah, Ethiopia, and Assyria. According to a tradition that went back to St Ambrose and in part to Philo (see Fowler[2]) the four rivers were allegorized as the four cardinal virtues, the single source as the fountain of grace on which these depend. On M.'s use of the Tigris (Hiddekel), see ix 71*n*. His decision that geographical description of the four streams is unnecessary extricates him from a thorny choice between at least eight competing theories about their identity and location (see Willet 29).

How from that sapphire fount the crisped brooks,
Rolling on orient pearl and sands of gold,
With mazy error under pendant shades
Ran nectar, visiting each plant, and fed
Flowers worthy of Paradise which not nice art

iv *237–8. orient*] lustrous; a term specially applied to pearls. M.'s introduction of pearls into the river of Paradise has little to do with his reading of travel books. It is authorized by *Gen.* ii 11f, the account of the first of the four distributaries, Pison, 'which compasseth . . . Havilah, where there is gold; And the gold of that land is good: there is bdellium and the onyx stone.' According to Eugubinus and Oleaster, bdellium was 'a kind of Margarite or pearle' (Willet 30). While Vulg., Tremellius and A.V. have bdellium and onyx, Philo, who follows the Septuagint version, takes the stones to be 'ruby and greenstone' (ὁ ἄνθραξ καὶ ὁ λίθος ὁ πράσινος: *Leg. alleg.* i 66). Greenstone he interprets as a symbol of 'the man who exercises good sense', and identifies with the sapphire in Aaron's breastplate (*Leg. alleg.* i 79–81; see iii 594–605*n* above, also ii 1049–50*n*). Thus M.'s *sapphire fount* would appear to be more than an image of natural beauty: to symbolize, indeed, the wisdom underlying all the virtues. Delicate as it is, this touch seems to imply a more or less moralized landscape. Cp. also *Ezek.* xxviii 13–15: 'Thou hast been in Eden the garden of God; every precious stone was thy covering, the sardius, topaz, and the diamond, the beryl, the onyx, and the jasper, the sapphire, the emerald, and the carbuncle, and gold. . . . Thou wast perfect in thy ways from the day that thou wast created, till iniquity was found in thee.'
iv *237. crisped*] curled into short wavy folds; cp. Ben Jonson's description of a land of perpetual spring in *The Vision of Delight* 186f: 'The Rivers runne as smoothed by his [Zephyr's] hand; / Onely their heads are crisped by his stroake.'
iv *239. error*] devious wandering course. One of the most resonant key words in the poem; discussed in Stein 66f. Here 'the evil meaning is consciously and ominously excluded. Rather than the meaning being simply "wandering", it is "wandering (not error)". Certainly the word is a reminder of the Fall, in that it takes us back to a time when there were no infected words because there were no infected actions' (Ricks 110). Similarly the *pendant* shades are not merely convenient hanging trees but also a proleptic suggestion of the horrid shadows that impend. See viii 653*n* below.
iv *240.* Ovid's *saturnia regna* has rivers of nectar (*Met.* i 111). Cp. also M.'s 'river of bliss' in heaven, that 'rolls o'er Elysian flowers' (iii 358f). At this time the amarant (iii 352–6) still grew in Paradise. See ix 70*n*, 71–5*n*; xi 278–9*n*. Cp. Dante *Purg.* xxviii 144.
iv *241–2.* As Burden 44ff notes, man's commission in *Gen.* i 28 is to 'subdue' the earth. This was a difficult notion, which in the poem is at first given the most innocent explanation possible: namely, that the earth has to be subdued only in the sense that art will be needed to put profuse nature in order.

In beds and curious knots, but nature boon
Poured forth profuse on hill and dale and plain,
Both where the morning sun first warmly smote
The open field, and where the unpierced shade
Embrowned the noontide bowers: thus was this place,
A happy rural seat of various view;
Groves whose rich trees wept odorous gums and balm,
Others whose fruit burnished with golden rind
Hung amiable, Hesperian fables true,

iv *242. knots*] flower-beds laid out in intricate regular designs (often labyrinths). See e.g., Henry Peacham, *The compleat gentleman* (1634) p. 241: 'Here are the goodliest walkes in Europe, for the trees themselves are placed in curious knots, as we use to set our herbes in gardens.' In M.'s time such formal, artificial arrangements could already seem insipid. *boon*] bounteous, benign.

iv *246. Embrowned*] darkened, made dusky (poet., probably imitating the common Ital. use of *imbrunire* to describe any effect of shading; M.'s spelling is 'Imbrowned'). No earlier example in *OED*. In M.'s time shadows were in fact for some reason regularly painted brown.

iv *246–7. thus*] such (*seat* is in apposition to *place*). *happy rural seat*] 'is almost laughably the England of Penshurst, Cooper's Hill and Appleton House' (Broadbent 184). M. mingles glimpses of preserved or recovered beauty seen in many different directions: why should it be more laughable to see them in the countryside than in books?

iv *248–9*. In Diodorus' account of *Arabia felix* (see ll. 159–66*n*) the balsam (balm) and other trees producing aromatic resins figure prominently. Cp. also *Othello* V ii 349f: 'Drop tears as fast as the Arabian trees / Their med'cinable gum.' *rich*] Newton thought an antithesis on the basis of commercial value was implied, between the trees producing aromatics (which fetched a great price) and those bearing mere fruit. But Hesperian fruit would not be cheap. *golden rind*] With this and other particulars of the description, cp. the deleted passage at the opening of *Comus* in *Trin. MS*: 'fruits of golden rind, on whose fair tree / The scaly harnessed dragon ever keeps / His unenchanted eye'. See Empson[2] 186f for the view that the nostalgia for a lost Eden is attached here to the trees; also that 'the same Nature produced the *balm* of healing and the fatal *fruit*; they cannot convey to Adam either its knowledge or the knowledge that it is to be avoided'. M. would hardly have agreed, however, that the trees 'by their own nature foretell the necessity of the Fall'. He seems to imply quite a different thought–that Nature's balm precedes the 'wound' of Nature in the same way that Election to salvation precedes the Fall.

iv *250. amiable*] desirable, lovely. *Hesperian fables*] See ll. 217–21*n* and iii 568–9*n*.

If true, here only, and of delicious taste:
Betwixt them lawns, or level downs, and flocks
Grazing the tender herb, were interposed,
Or palmy hillock, or the flowery lap
Of some irriguous valley spread her store,
Flowers of all hue, and without thorn the rose:
Another side, umbrageous grots and caves
Of cool recess, o'er which the mantling vine
Lays forth her purple grape, and gently creeps
Luxuriant; mean while murmuring waters fall
Down the slope hills, dispersed, or in a lake,
That to the fringed bank with myrtle crowned,
Her crystal mirror holds, unite their streams.

iv *251. and . . . taste*] The Hesperian apples themselves were not for eating, however.
iv *255. irriguous*] irrigated, well-watered.
iv *256.* Cp. Herrick, 'The Rose': 'Before Mans fall, the Rose was born / (S. *Ambrose* sayes) without the Thorn.' Starting from the curse pronounced on Adam in *Gen.* iii 18–'Thorns also and thistles shall it bring forth to thee'– St Basil (*Hexaemeron* v 45) and St Ambrose (*Hexaemeron* iii 11; Migne xiv 188) went on to infer a thornless rose: *Surrexerat ante floribus immista terrenis sine spinis rosa.* See G. W. Whiting, in *RES* n.s. x (1959) 60–2. The thornless rose was used to symbolize the whole sinless state of man before the Fall; or (as Valeriano 686) the state of grace.
iv *257. umbrageous*] shady.
iv *258. mantling vine*] Recalls the climbing vines of Diodorus' Nysa (iii 68). Cp. *Comus* 294.
iv *262.* That the *myrtle* is intended as Venus' tree is made clear by the immediately succeeding image of the mirror, another of her iconographical attributes (see Tervarent 274). Venus is present not only in her capacity as goddess of gardens, but also as the form-giver, presiding over the generative cycle unfolded in the Graces and the Hours. Paradises were commonly portrayed as gardens of Venus; see, e.g., Spenser, *F.Q.* III vi and IV x. The vine at 258–60 falls in with the same complex of associations; see Ovid, *Ars am.* i 244 (*Venus in vinis, ignis in igne fuit*), also Euripides, *Bacch.* 773, and Dodd's note there, on the theory (not confined to the Peripatetics) that wine contains *pneuma*, the stuff of life.
iv *263–6.* The harmony of bird song, rustling leaves and *murmuring waters* (l. 260) was a usual feature of gardens of Venus; cp., e.g., Tasso's garden of Armida (*Gerus. Lib.* xvi 12) and Spenser's Bower of Bliss (*F.Q.* II xii 70f). Separately, the items of the description were both natural and conventional. They had their places among the 'charms of landscape' listed by the rhetoricians (see Curtius 197). *apply*] 'join' or 'practise'. *airs*] The primary meaning is 'breezes'; but an obvious secondary chain of discourse runs through *choir . . . airs* (melodies) . . . *attune*, as was noticed by Patrick Hume

The birds their choir apply; airs, vernal airs,
Breathing the smell of field and grove, attune
The trembling leaves, while universal Pan
Knit with the Graces and the Hours in dance
Led on the eternal spring. Not that fair field

in 1695, and later by Empson ([2] 157). For a full account of the needless controversies the passage has occasioned, see Ricks 104–6.

iv *266–8*. The part played by the Graces in mythological poems on spring is discussed in Wind 101ff. Ovid (*Fasti* v 193–222) tells how Chloris–Flora, ravished by Zephyrus, brings forth the flowers of spring, which are then gathered by the Seasons (*Hours*) and the Graces. The present passage may be regarded as a more idealized treatment of the same subject that M. had earlier handled in *Elegia V* (cp. also *Comus* 986). *universal Pan*] Renaissance mythographers cited *Homeric Hymns* xix 47 as authority for interpreting Pan as a symbol of 'universal nature' (see, e.g., Conti, *Mytholog.* v 6 and Valeriano 730D, and cp. Gk. πᾶν, all). *knit with the Graces*] Because the triadic pattern of their dance was thought by Neoplatonists to express the movement underlying all natural generation (see Wind 109).

iv *268–85*. The dismissive comparisons with other gardens recall a similar list in Spenser, *F.Q.* II xii 52: 'More sweet and holesome, then the pleasaunt hill / Of *Rhodope*, on which the Nimphe, that bore / A gyaunt babe, her selfe for griefe did kill; / Or the Thessalian *Tempe*, where of yore / Faire *Daphne Phoebus* hart with love did gore; / Or *Ida*, where the Gods lov'd to repaire, / When ever they their heavenly bowres forlore; / Or sweet *Parnasse*, the haunt of Muses faire; / Or *Eden* selfe, if ought with *Eden* mote compaire.' M. mentions four streams–*Orontes*; *the inspired Castalian spring*; *Triton*; and *Nilus*–corresponding to, and as it were replacing, the four undescribed rivers of Paradise (235). Indeed, the two sets have a member in common: the Nile, which was almost invariably identified with Gihon, the second Biblical river (see, e.g., Valeriano 255, and the discussion in Fowler[2] 292). Note also that the first comparison introduces a lunar deity, the second solar and lunar deities together (ll. 272–4*n*) and the third a solar deity; while the fourth comparison refers to the equinoctial line, and thus to the just balancing of the domains of sun and moon, day and night. For Adam as sun god, see l. 303*n*.

iv *268–72*. The rape of Proserpina by *Dis* (Pluto) the king of hell was located in *Enna* by Ovid (*Fasti* iv 420ff). The search for her made the world barren, and even when she was found she was restored to Ceres, and fruitfulness to the world, only for half the year. She might have been recovered unconditionally had she not 'eaten seven graines of a Pomegrannet (a fatall liquorishnesse, which retaines her in Hell; as the Apple thrust Evah out of Paradice, whereunto it is held to have a relation)' (Sandys, *Ovid's Metamorphosis* 195).

iv *268*. The view that the world was created in March had the authority of Eusebius, Cyrillus, Athanasius, Gregory of Nazianzus, John of Damascus,

Of Enna, where Proserpine gathering flowers
Her self a fairer flower by gloomy Dis
Was gathered, which cost Ceres all that pain
To seek her through the world; nor that sweet grove
Of Daphne by Orontes, and the inspired
Castalian spring, might with this Paradise
Of Eden strive; nor that Nyseian isle
Girt with the river Triton, where old Cham,
Whom Gentiles Ammon call and Libyan Jove,
Hid Amalthea and her florid son
Young Bacchus from his stepdame Rhea's eye;
Nor where Abassin kings their issue guard,

Ambrose and Bede. It was supported by typological argument ('Christ was crucified the same day that Adam was created'); by appeal to tradition (when Moses instituted the custom of reckoning Nisan–March / April–the 'first' month, he was returning to primitive usage; see *Exod.* xii 2); and by numerical calculations based on literalistic applications of Scripture. See Willet 9f, and Riccioli ii 232; also iii 555–61*n* above.

iv *270. Herself a fairer flower*] Cp. ix 432, describing Eve: 'Herself, though fairest unsupported flower'. See also Empson[2] 173: 'Proserpina, like Eve, was captured by the king of Hell, but she then became queen of it, became Sin, then, on Milton's scheme; Eve, we are to remember, becomes an ally of Satan when she tempts Adam to eat with her.'

iv *272–4.* There was a beautiful grove called *Daphne* beside the River *Orontes*, near Antioch. It had an Apolline oracle (hence *inspired*) and a stream named after the famous *Castalian spring* of Parnassus. Daphne was there changed to a laurel after pursuit by one of Belial's crew: cp. *PR* ii 187.

iv *274. Ed I* has no comma after *spring*.

iv *275–9.* Diodorus' description of Nysa has been used more than once in the preceding description, and the island is now referred to directly. Diodorus relates (iii 67–70) how Ammon, King of Libya, had an illicit affair with a maiden Amaltheia, who gave birth to a marvellous son Dionysus (*Bacchus*). To protect mother and child from the jealousy of his wife Rhea (Uranus' daughter), Ammon hid them on Nysa, an island near mod. Tunis. The identifications of Ammon with the Libyan Jupiter (who appeared under the form of a ram which later became the constellation Aries) and with Noah's son Ham (Vulg. Cham) were widely accepted: see Sandys[2] 191, Starnes 237. *florid*] ruddy-complexioned – a distinctive feature of Bacchus.

iv *280–5.* Heylyn describes Mt *Amara* as 'a dayes journey high; the Rock so smooth and even . . . that no wall can be more evenly polished'. The summit, he says, is compassed with a high wall, within which are gardens and palaces where 'the younger sons of the *Emperour* are continually inclosed, to avoid sedition: they enjoy there whatsoever is fit for delight or *Princely* education' (iv 64). The province Amara to the west 'stretcheth

Mount Amara, though this by some supposed
True Paradise under the Ethiop line
By Nilus' head, enclosed with shining rock,
A whole day's journey high, but wide remote
From this Assyrian garden, where the fiend
Saw undelighted all delight, all kind
Of living creatures new to sight and strange:
Two of far nobler shape erect and tall,
Godlike erect, with native honour clad
In naked majesty seemed lords of all,
And worthy seemed, for in their looks divine

towards the Nile'; and it was blessed with 'such ravishing pleasures of all sorts, that some have taken (but mistaken) it for the place of *Paradise*'. Like most of the geographers of the time, Heylyn thought Amara 'not much distant from the *AEquator*, if not plainly under it'. M.'s emphasis on the situation of Amara under the *Ethiop line* (equator) (l. 282) makes explicit the notion of an equinoctial Paradise enjoying *eternal spring* (l. 268) that has been ironically latent in the previous comparisons. Proserpina's division of her time between the superior and inferior hemispheres was often interpreted as a seasonal myth. See Sandys[2] 197: 'The seede, which is Proserpina, while the Sun is on the south of the Aequinoctiall, lies hid in the earth, which is Pluto: but when he travells through the Northerne signes, it shouteth [shooteth] up, and growes to maturity; and then Proserpina is said to be above with Ceres.'

iv *285*. J. C. Maxwell points out that the present episode alludes to Homer's account of Hermes' arrival at the isle of Calypso (*Od.* v 51–76). Common elements include caves, vine, fourfold fountain and the comparison of the supernatural visitor to a cormorant. Satan's reaction, however, contrasts with Hermes', which is one of wonder and delight.

iv *288*. The notion of man's distinctive upright stance is developed at vii 506–11.

iv *289*. *Godlike*] To evoke his perfect human figure, M. appeals to 'innumerable remembered versions' of the pagan gods in his readers' imaginations (MacCaffrey 98). *native honour*] A striking oxymoron; for the Golden Age was more usually portrayed as free from the restraints and falsities of honour. See, e.g., the First Chorus of Tasso's *Aminta*. M.'s ideal of natural honour–contrasted with fallen *honour dishonourable* (l. 314)–had been anticipated more than once; as, e.g., in Guarini's moralization of Tasso (*Pastor Fido* iv 9: *onor felice, verace onor*). But M. seems to go beyond Guarini, and to entertain the conception of an honour like that of a Noble Savage–'primitive honour', in Conrad's phrase.

iv *291–3*. See *Gen.* i 27: 'God created man in his own image.' Steadman (98) shows that Adam and Eve here manifest the divine image in a very precise way; for the virtues enumerated are the standard ones attributed to God, by writers as diverse as St Gregory and Calvin. But see also MacCaffrey

The image of their glorious maker shone,
Truth, wisdom, sanctitude severe and pure,
Severe but in true filial freedom placed;
Whence true authority in men; though both
Not equal, as their sex not equal seemed;
For contemplation he and valour formed,
For softness she and sweet attractive grace,
He for God only, she for God in him:
His fair large front and eye sublime declared
Absolute rule; and hyacinthine locks
Round from his parted forelock manly hung
Clustering, but not beneath his shoulders broad:

98, on M.'s 'habit of naming qualities and attaching them to the central figures'; in the world of M.'s vision, the qualities are substantial.

iv *295*. *Whence*] i.e., from the divine image; the authority is symbolic. *authority*] autority *Ed I* and *Ed II*.

iv *299*. The thought corresponds to that of *1 Cor.* xi 3: 'The head of every man is Christ; and the head of the woman is the man; and the head of Christ is God.'

iv *300*. *front*] forehead. *sublime*] uplifted.

iv *301–8*. The hair-length proper for each sex follows directly from the statement of their hierarchic relation; for, according to St Paul, 'a man indeed ought not to cover his head, forasmuch as he is the image and glory of God: but the woman is the glory of the man. . . . if a woman have long hair, it is a glory to her: for her hair is given her for a covering' (*1 Cor.* xi 7, 15; cp. the A.V. marginal gloss on 10, which explains that the covering is a 'sign that she is under the power of her husband'). *hyacinthine locks*] When Athene 'shed grace about his head and shoulders', Odysseus' hair flowed 'like the hyacinth flower' (Homer, *Od*, vi 231). If a colour were implied, it might be either blue, the colour of the hyacinth flower or gem (i.e., the sapphire: cp. l. 237*n*), or just possibly tawny (the hyacinth of heraldry, near to the colour of M.'s own hair), or black (Eustathius' gloss on the Homeric passage), or very dark brown (Suidas' gloss); in fact, almost any colour at all. But it is just as likely that a shape is meant (the idealized treatment accorded to hair in antique sculpture ?), or an allusion to the beautiful youth Hyacinthus, beloved of Apollo but doomed to die. The elaborateness of the present passage lends some support to the theory that M. had a special sexual interest in hair. (In this connection cp. 496f, *Lycidas* 69, 175.) *wanton*] luxuriant; unrestrained.

iv *303*. *clustering*] So Apollo's hair is described in Apollonius Rhodius, *Argonaut.* ii 678. Adam's hair hangs clustering like bunches of grapes, Eve's like the more ancillary *vine . . . tendrils* (l. 307). The fact that Adam has been given no beard is due to the influence of visual art. Adam was usually portrayed beardless, because he had so often been represented as an Apollo. See, e.g., Panofsky 249–65 and Cartari 37.

She as a veil down to the slender waist
Her unadorned golden tresses wore
Dishevelled, but in wanton ringlets waved
As the vine curls her tendrils, which implied
Subjection, but required with gentle sway,
And by her yielded, by him best received,
Yielded with coy submission, modest pride,
And sweet reluctant amorous delay.
Nor those mysterious parts were then concealed,
Then was not guilty shame, dishonest shame
Of nature's works, honour dishonourable,
Sin-bred, how have ye troubled all mankind
With shows instead, mere shows of seeming pure,
And banished from man's life his happiest life,
Simplicity and spotless innocence.
So passed they naked on, nor shunned the sight
Of God or angel, for they thought no ill:
So hand in hand they passed, the loveliest pair
That ever since in love's embraces met,
Adam the goodliest man of men since born
His sons, the fairest of her daughters Eve.
Under a tuft of shade that on a green
Stood whispering soft, by a fresh fountain side
They sat them down, and after no more toil
Of their sweet gardening labour than sufficed

iv *308–11.* M. 'foreshadows the means by which Satan will manage to separate them' (Sims 25). *coy*] quiet, modest. Cp. *Ars amatoria* ii 717f: *non est veneris properanda voluptas, / Sed sensim tarda prolicienda mora.*
iv *313–15.* Cp. Tasso's and Guarini's attacks on false honour, cited in l. 289*n*.
iv *313.* *shame, dishonest shame*] Bentley's full stop after the first 'shame' obscures the gradual swell from cool appositional phrases into angry anacolouthon and apostrophe.
iv *321.* Cp. xii 648. At their entrance, as at their final exit, Adam and Eve go *hand in hand.*
iv *323–4.* 'Their children spring eternally from a syntactical union' (Broadbent 190). But M.'s syntax here is the syntax of ordinary prose, and would not have been noticed as having any special pattern. Cp., e.g., Browne, *Pseudodoxia* i 1 (ed. Keynes p. 18): 'As some affirm, [Adam] was the wisest of all men since.'
iv *328.* Burden 41ff comments on M.'s originality in achieving a variation of the usual Golden Age pastoral occupation. Instead of being shepherds his Adam and Eve are gardeners, engaged in light and pleasant, though necessary, work. Gardening had in M.'s time become a fashionable highbrow activity; as the existence of such books as Evelyn's *Sylva* testifies.

To recommend cool zephyr, and made ease
More easy, wholesome thirst and appetite
More grateful, to their supper fruits they fell,
Nectarine fruits which the compliant boughs
Yielded them, sidelong as they sat recline
On the soft downy bank damasked with flowers:
The savoury pulp they chew, and in the rind
Still as they thirsted scoop the brimming stream;
Nor gentle purpose, nor endearing smiles
Wanted, nor youthful dalliance as beseems
Fair couple, linked in happy nuptial league,
Alone as they. About them frisking played
All beasts of the earth, since wild, and of all chase

But, as Broadbent 177 hints, the gardening should probably be regarded as an emblem of moral or even of political activity (like the gardening in *Richard II* III iv, which symbolizes maintenance of order in the commonwealth).

iv *329. zephyr*] 'The frolic wind that breathes the spring' (*L'Allegro* 18); the west wind. In Neoplatonic mythology, the enlivening touch of Zephyr begins the initial phase in the generative progression (see Wind 103, 113). From the time of Ovid (in his account of the Golden Age, *Met.* i 107f), Zephyr had figured in most poetic visions of eternal spring; but he received particularly elaborate treatment in Jonson's masque *The Vision of Delight*. See also v 16*n* below.

iv *330. easy*] luxurious, comfortable.

iv *332. Nectarine*] sweet as nectar (though the variety of peach called nectarine was known at least as early as 1616). *compliant*] pliant (by false etymology from Lat. *plicare*); *OED*'s earliest instance in this sense; perhaps a genuine Latinism.

iv *333. recline*] recumbent, reclining (Lat. *reclinis*); the only instance of this Latinising coinage listed in *OED*.

iv *334. downy*] feathery; or soft as down.

iv *335. savoury*] appetizing, fragrant. Note that the word often meant 'spiritually edifying'.

iv *337. gentle purpose*] polite (i.e., not coarse) conversation; as in Shakespeare, *Much Ado* III i 11f: 'There will she hide her, / To listen our purpose.'

iv *338. Wanted*] lacked; or were lacking. *dalliance*] not 'conversation' (which would be pleonastic after *purpose*) but 'caressing'.

iv *340–52.* The idyllic scene of Adam and Eve surrounded by the animals was a familiar one, from countless visual representations. Among fine examples are Cranach's painting *The Garden of Eden* (Vienna, Kunsthistorisches Museum), Dürer's engraving *The Fall of Man* (Bartsch 1) and Goltzius' Windsor Castle ink drawing (No. 4758); among popular examples, the frontispiece to 'Eden' in Sylvester's 1613 Du Bartas. Contrast the scene of enmity at x 710–14.

In wood or wilderness, forest or den;
Sporting the lion ramped, and in his paw
Dandled the kid; bears, tigers, ounces, pards,
Gambolled before them, the unwieldly elephant
To make them mirth used all his might, and wreathed
His lithe proboscis; close the serpent sly
Insinuating, wove with Gordian twine
His braided train, and of his fatal guile
Gave proof unheeded; others on the grass
Couched, and now filled with pasture gazing sat,
Or bedward ruminating: for the sun
Declined was hasting now with prone career
To the Ocean Isles, and in the ascending scale
Of heaven the stars that usher evening rose:
When Satan still in gaze, as first he stood,
Scarce thus at length failed speech recovered sad.
O hell! What do mine eyes with grief behold,

iv *344. ounces*] properly 'lynxes'; but in the seventeenth century applied loosely to various feline beasts.
iv *348. Insinuating*] penetrating by sinuous ways. *Gordian twine*] coil, convolution, as difficult to undo as the Gordian knot, which it took the hero Alexander to cut (cp. ix 499, where the serpent's folds are a 'surging maze'). But 'twine' could also mean 'division, separation, disunion' (*OED* sb.[2]; cp. Sylvester's Du Bartas 586, 'Th'Unity dwels in God, i'th' Fiend the Twine'): an allusion, perhaps, to the division made by Satan between Adam and Eve. In *Civ. Dei* xiv 11 St Augustine says that Satan chose the serpent for his instrument because it was 'a creature slippery, pliable, wreathed in knots, and fit for his work'.
iv *350. proof unheeded*] Burden 53 argues that the serpent's guile is openly demonstrated so that man may have no excuse. But the phrase may only be meant to point the irony that no one is paying any attention to the creature who will have the most momentous importance; 'proof' need only have been chosen for the sake of the context it suggests: the serpent's very movements are dialectical.
iv *352. Bedward ruminating*] chewing the cud before going to rest.
iv *354–5. Ocean Isles*] the Azores, beneath which the sun has set in l. 592. *ascending scale*] A serious pun. Since the sun is in Aries (iii 555–61*n*, x 329*n*), the *stars that usher evening* rise in Libra, the Scales, the portion of the sky exactly opposite. But *scale of heaven* implies also the balancing of light and darkness that originally determined the visual representation of the equinoctial sign (see Eisler 100, Fowler 195*n*). For the culmination of the constellation Libra at midnight, six hours after the time of the present passage, see ll. 1014f; and for the equinoctial theme elsewhere in *PL*, see ll. 280–5*n*, ix 50f, x 651–706*n*.

Into our room of bliss thus high advanced
Creatures of other mould, earth-born perhaps,
Not spirits, yet to heavenly spirits bright
Little inferior; whom my thoughts pursue
With wonder, and could love, so lively shines
In them divine resemblance, and such grace
The hand that formed them on their shape hath poured.
Ah gentle pair, ye little think how nigh
Your change approaches, when all these delights
Will vanish and deliver ye to woe,
More woe, the more your taste is now of joy;
Happy, but for so happy ill secured
Long to continue, and this high seat your heaven
Ill fenced for heaven to keep out such a foe
As now is entered; yet no purposed foe
To you whom I could pity thus forlorn
Though I unpitied: league with you I seek,
And mutual amity so strait, so close,
That I with you must dwell, or you with me
Henceforth; my dwelling haply may not please
Like this fair Paradise, your sense, yet such

iv *359. room*] place. Cp. vii 189f, where God is praised by the loyal angels for bringing 'a better race' into the 'vacant room' of the rebels.
iv *361–2.* Cp. *Heb.* ii 7 and *Ps* viii 5: 'Thou hast made him a little lower than the angels, and hast crowned him with glory and honour.'
iv *370–4.* Satan's pity is by no means to his credit. He is unable to act as firmly as Michael, because he knows himself to be in the wrong. As Burden 36 notes, the implied accusation of God for making man too frail is false. Man is 'sufficient to have stood'–as indeed Satan's fear of approaching Adam shows (ix 483ff).
iv *370.* i.e., 'not so well secured as one would expect in the case of such happy creatures'. *Ed I* (catchword only) has semicolon after *Happy*.
iv *372. for heaven*] considering it is your heaven.
iv *375–7.* 'Perverting the "happy nuptial league" of Adam and Eve in the previous paragraph' (Broadbent 171). *strait*] intimate (*OED* 14); but also with the sinister overtone 'involving privation' (*OED* 6 b). The *Ed I* and *Ed II* spelling 'streight' allows a play with *straight*= honest; but this must be considered very secondary in view of the continuation *so close.*
iv *377.* Rajan 100 finds this line characteristic, in its 'tiredness', of Satan's later speeches. It may seem differently, however, to readers who appreciate the villainous implication of the sequence *I with you* (i.e., temptation and sin, the inner hell): *you with me* (damnation, the external hell).

Accept your maker's work; he gave it me,
Which I as freely give; hell shall unfold,
To entertain you two, her widest gates,
And send forth all her kings; there will be room,
Not like these narrow limits, to receive
Your numerous offspring; if no better place,
Thank him who puts me loth to this revenge
On you who wrong me not for him who wronged.
And should I at your harmless innocence
Melt, as I do, yet public reason just,
Honour and empire with revenge enlarged,
By conquering this new world, compels me now
To do what else though damned I should abhor.
So spake the fiend, and with necessity,
The tyrant's plea, excused his devilish deeds.

iv *380–1*. The blasphemous echo of *Matt.* x 8 ('freely ye have received, freely give') redounds to Satan's discredit, especially in view of the more distant resonance with *Rom.* viii 32 ('He that spared not his own Son, but delivered him up for us all, how shall he not with him also freely give us all things?').
iv *381–5*. Cp. Isaiah's prophecy of the fall of Babylon (*Is.* xiv 9): 'Hell from beneath is moved for thee to meet thee at thy coming: it stirreth up the dead for thee, even all the chief ones of the earth; it hath raised up from their thrones all the kings of the nations.' Empson is deeply committed to the view that Satan is sincere in offering high honour in hell, and that 'the irony of his offer belongs only to the God who made Hell' (Empson 68f; cp. Empson[2] 168, Empson[3] 103). One may agree that Satan does not sustain the irony of 375f or of the understatement *may not please* (l. 378), and that 385f is in a certain narrow sense 'sincere'. If high honour is accompanied with woe and opposed to joy (ll. 367–9), however, it is hard to see how it could be offered other than maliciously, to harm God's image in Adam and Eve–out of *revenge*, in fact, as Satan himself admits at 386f. Besides, the offer of *room* (l. 383) is belied in advance by the sinister *so strait, so close* (l. 376).
iv *389. public reason*] 'Reason of state, a perversion of the Ciceronian principle (*Laws* III iii 8) that the good of the people is the supreme law. . . . Henry Parker approved its use by Parliament and condemned the Royalists for too frequent appeals to it. . . . In *Adamo caduto* V ii, Serafino della Salandra has Satan tell the devils that they are going to corrupt mankind by inventing *ragione di stato*' (Hughes). Satan is here cast in the role of a contemporary Machiavellian politician, excusing the evil means he resorts to by appeals to such values as 'the common weal', 'the good of the state', 'policy' and *necessity* (l. 393). Cp. Dalila's excuse that she had finally been persuaded to betray Samson by 'that grounded maxim / So rife and celebrated in the mouths / Of wisest men; that to the public good / Private respects must yield' (*SA* 865–8).

Then from his lofty stand on that high tree
Down he alights among the sportful herd
Of those four-footed kinds, himself now one,
Now other, as their shape served best his end
Nearer to view his prey, and unespied
To mark what of their state he more might learn
By word or action marked: about them round
A lion now he stalks with fiery glare,
Then as a tiger, who by chance hath spied
In some purlieu two gentle fawns at play,
Straight couches close, then rising changes oft
His couchant watch, as one who chose his ground
Whence rushing he might surest seize them both
Griped in each paw: when Adam first of men
To first of women Eve thus moving speech,
Turned him all ear to hear new utterance flow.
    Sole partner and sole part of all these joys,

iv *400.* Satan's overhearing the prohibition was not a common motif in hexaemeral literature; though McColley notes an instance in the *Paradise* of Moses bar Cepha, and Hughes another in Salandra's *Adamo caduto*.

iv *401–2.* In accordance with *1 Pet.* v 8: 'Be sober, be vigilant; because your adversary the devil, as a roaring lion, walketh about, seeking whom he may devour.' Burden 49f notes that the real animals are tame and gentle before the Fall, but that Satan assumes their later, postlapsarian forms.

iv *402–8.* Similarly in Du Bartas 239: 'Our freedoms felon, fountain of our sorrow, / Thinks now the beauty of a Horse to borrow; / Anon to creep into a Haifers side; / Then in a Cock, or in a Dog to hide; / Then in a nimble Hart himself to shroud; / Then in the starr'd plumes of a Peacock proud', before deciding that the serpent is best suited to his purpose. This is contrary to a strong tradition, going back to St Augustine, that Satan was not allowed to make use of any other beast but the serpent.

iv *404. purlieu*] land on the fringe of a forest. The more specific sense–land disafforested, but still subject to the provisions of the forest laws–does not seem to apply.

iv *405. Straight*] at once; but punning with 'Strait', 'tightly' (*OED* s.v. *Strait* adv. 1). *Ed I* and *Ed II* 'Strait' could indicate either word, and made the play more obvious.

iv *410.* It soon becomes clear, from the length of the succeeding speech by Adam, that *him* must refer not to the speaker (with *Turned* reflexive), but to the eavesdropper. The momentary uncertainty, however, is enough to give the impression that Satan has insinuated himself into Adam's grammatical place. *all ear*] Imitates a Lat. idiom, and is perhaps the earliest instance in English.

iv *411. Sole partner and sole part*] The first *sole* means 'only', the second

Dearer thy self than all; needs must the power
That made us, and for us this ample world
Be infinitely good, and of his good
As liberal and free as infinite,
That raised us from the dust and placed us here
In all this happiness, who at his hand
Have nothing merited, nor can perform
Aught whereof he hath need, he who requires
From us no other service than to keep
This one, this easy charge, of all the trees
In Paradise that bear delicious fruit
So various, not to taste that only tree
Of knowledge, planted by the tree of life,
So near grows death to life, what e'er death is,
Some dreadful thing no doubt; for well thou know'st
God hath pronounced it death to taste that tree,
The only sign of our obedience left
Among so many signs of power and rule
Conferred upon us, and dominion given
Over all other creatures that possess
Earth, air, and sea. Then let us not think hard
One easy prohibition, who enjoy
Free leave so large to all things else, and choice
Unlimited of manifold delights:
But let us ever praise him, and extol
His bounty, following our delightful task
To prune these growing plants, and tend these flowers,
Which were it toilsome, yet with thee were sweet.
  To whom thus Eve replied. O thou for whom

'unrivalled' (*OED* 5 c); Eve is the only sharer in Adam's joys, and also herself the chief part of them. Newton wanted a comma after *part*, on which to base his less obvious but more interesting interpretation–'the only one of the joys which is a *part* of me' (cp. l. 487).

iv *421–4*. See *Gen.* ii 16f: 'The Lord God commanded the man, saying, Of every tree of the garden thou mayest freely eat: But of the tree of the knowledge of good and evil, thou shalt not eat of it: for in the day that thou eatest thereof thou shalt surely die.'

iv *428*. Cp. iii 95: 'Sole pledge of his obedience'; and see *n*.

iv *430–2*. See *Gen.* i 28: 'God said unto them . . . have dominion over the fish of the sea, and over the fowl of the air, and over every living thing that moveth upon the earth.'

iv *433*. *easy*] easy to keep; involving no effort; not constraining or oppressive.

iv *440*. *for whom*] See *1 Cor.* xi 9: 'Neither was the man created for the woman; but the woman for the man.' And cp. l. 299.

And from whom I was formed flesh of thy flesh,
And without whom am to no end, my guide
And head, what thou hast said is just and right.
For we to him indeed all praises owe,
And daily thanks, I chiefly who enjoy
So far the happier lot, enjoying thee
Pre-eminent by so much odds, while thou
Like consort to thyself canst nowhere find.
That day I oft remember, when from sleep
I first awaked, and found myself reposed
Under a shade of flowers, much wondering where
And what I was, whence thither brought, and how.
Not distant far from thence a murmuring sound
Of waters issued from a cave and spread
Into a liquid plain, then stood unmoved
Pure as the expanse of heaven; I thither went
With unexperienced thought, and laid me down

iv *441*. See *Gen.* ii 23: 'Adam said, This is now bone of my bones, and flesh of my flesh: she shall be called Woman, because she was taken out of Man.'
iv *443*. *head*] see *1 Cor.* xi 3: 'The head of every man is Christ; and the head of the woman is the man; and the head of Christ is God.'
iv *447*. *odds*] difference, superiority, advantage; usually construed as singular, in the seventeenth century.
iv *449–50*. At viii 253f Adam uses the same comparison to describe his experience immediately after his creation. *reposed*] placed.
iv *449*. *That day*] Clearly implies that Adam and Eve have been created for two days at least, so that we must reject the theory advanced in McColley (16f *et passim*) that this is the very day of their creation. The impression that they have been in Paradise for some days is confirmed by many other passages (see, e.g, ll. 610–20, 639ff, 681ff, 710ff, v 31, v 145); though it is of course possible that M. meant us to assume that man was created with a readymade understanding of seasonal change. See Introduction, 'Chronology' (p. 444).
iv *451*. *of*] Preferable to *Ed I* 'on', which sounds too brisk coming so soon after *Under*.
iv *453–6*. 'Milton insists on the indistinguishable commingling [of *lake* and *sky*, l. 459] not only by the explicit comparisons, but also by the syntactical mingling in a "sound . . . spread into a liquid Plain"' (Ricks 101). Notice, though, that *issued, spread* and *stood* could just possibly all be transitive past participles describing *waters*. (For the trans. use of *issue*, see *OED* II 7.) The landscape is probably meant to be philosophically significant; for the water and the cave recall a Homeric image interpreted by Porphyry as a symbol of the descent of the soul (*De antro nympharum*, discussed in Henry More, *Conjectura Cabbalistica*, Defence i 6). See Homer, *Il.* v 872, 'low Hyle's [Matter's] watery plain'.

On the green bank, to look into the clear
Smooth lake, that to me seemed another sky.
As I bent down to look, just opposite,
A shape within the watery gleam appeared
Bending to look on me, I started back,
It started back, but pleased I soon returned,
Pleased it returned as soon with answering looks
Of sympathy and love; there I had fixed
Mine eyes till now, and pined with vain desire,
Had not a voice thus warned me, What thou seest,
What there thou seest fair creature is thyself,
With thee it came and goes: but follow me,
And I will bring thee where no shadow stays
Thy coming, and thy soft embraces, he
Whose image thou art, him thou shall enjoy
Inseparably thine, to him shalt bear
Multitudes like thyself, and thence be called
Mother of human race: what could I do,
But follow straight, invisibly thus led?

iv *460–71.* Alluding to Ovid's story of the proud youth Narcissus, who was punished for his scornfulness by being made to fall in love with his own reflection in a pool, and to pine with vain desire (*Met.* iii 402–36). Thus the passage has considerable ironic force; for we know that Eve is to fall into precisely this error of seeking an end in herself or desiring an ideal self, until like Narcissus she 'loves an unsubstantial hope and thinks that substance which is only shadow' (*Met.* iii 417). Hence the divine warning that her true desire must be for the substantial Adam (l. 470). Bush cites a Christian tradition that 'some of the newly created angels looked up to God, others fell in love with themselves': see Donne, *Sermons*, ed. Potter and Simpson, iii 254.

iv *465. Ed I* has comma after *love*.

iv *470. stays*] waits for.

iv *471. embraces*] In early edns, 'imbraces'.

iv *473. Inseparably*] Literally true before the Fall, when Sin and Death had not yet entered the world.

iv *474–5.* See *Gen.* iii 20: 'And Adam called his wife's name Eve; because she was the mother of all living.' (A.V. marginal gloss on *Eve*: 'Chavah, or, living'.) The commentators made much of the fact that this name was given only after the Fall (before, she was called simply 'woman': see *Gen.* ii 23, and Willet 54), so that M. may be deliberately correcting the conventional chronology, to enhance the status of sexuality and motherhood. See ll. 741ff for a similar piece of ideology, and on Eve's name see also xi 168f.

iv *476. straight*] immediately; *Ed I* and *Ed II* spelling 'strait' could also indicate 'closely'.

Till I espied thee, fair indeed and tall,
Under a platan, yet methought less fair,
Less winning soft, less amiably mild,
Than that smooth watery image; back I turned,
Thou following cried'st aloud, Return fair Eve,
Whom fly'st thou? Whom thou fly'st, of him thou art,
His flesh, his bone; to give thee being I lent
Out of my side to thee, nearest my heart
Substantial life, to have thee by my side
Henceforth an individual solace dear;
Part of my soul I seek thee, and thee claim
My other half: with that thy gentle hand
Seized mine, I yielded, and from that time see
How beauty is excelled by manly grace
And wisdom, which alone is truly fair.
So spake our general mother, and with eyes
Of conjugal attraction unreproved,

iv *478–80*. Burden 84f suggests that the point of the incident lies in Eve's freedom to choose. She goes with Adam not because there is no one else but because at l. 489 she freely chooses to love him rather than her own image. Similarly, her initial reluctance emphasises her freedom to have rejected him.
iv *478*. Adam is *Under a platan* (plane tree) because the plane was a symbol of Christ 'his head' (see Raban Maur, Migne cix 931; and cp. 299*n*, 443*n*). The basis of this well-known allegory was *Ecclus*. xxiv 14–16: 'I . . . grew up as a plane tree [Vulg. and Tremellius *platanus*] by the water. . . . my branches are the branches of honour and grace.' This association seems more probable than those which made the platan tree a symbol of erotic love (see Todd K. Bender, 'The Platan Tree in Donne, Horace and Theocritus', *TLS* (12 Aug. 1965) p. 704).
iv *483*. *Gen*. ii 23: 'Adam said, This is now bone of my bones, and flesh of my flesh.'
iv *484*. *nearest my heart*] 'It is . . . a superfluous question, out of what side of Adam Eva was taken, whether out of the right or left: it is resolved by most, out of the left, because Adams heart lay there: but these are frivolous and needelesse matters' (Willet 38, on *Gen*. ii 21f).
iv *486*. *individual*] inseparable; cp. Shakespeare, *Timon* I ii 6: 'Where ere thou go'st I still will folowe thee / An individuall mate.'
iv *487*. Horace consoling Maecenas in his illness calls him *meae . . . partem animae* (*Odes* II xvii 5).
iv *493*. *unreproved*] irreproachable, innocent. A Latin use of the past participle (e.g. *invictus*, unconquered, unconquerable) that M. was fond of imitating. Cp. 'unremoved' in l. 987, 'unreproved' in *L'Allegro* 40, 'unenchanted' in *Comus* 395, etc. Here, however, the immediate model may be Spenser, *F.Q.* II vii 16: 'The antique world, in his first flowring youth, /

And meek surrender, half embracing leaned
On our first father, half her swelling breast
Naked met his under the flowing gold
Of her loose tresses hid: he in delight
Both of her beauty and submissive charms
Smiled with superior love, as Jupiter
On Juno smiles, when he impregns the clouds
That shed May flowers; and pressed her matron lip
With kisses pure: aside the devil turned
For envy, yet with jealous leer malign
Eyed them askance, and to himself thus plained.
Sight hateful, sight tormenting! Thus these two
Imparadised in one another's arms
The happier Eden, shall enjoy their fill
Of bliss on bliss, while I to hell am thrust,
Where neither joy nor love, but fierce desire,
Among our other torments not the least,
Still unfulfilled with pain of longing pines;
Yet let me not forget what I have gained

Found no defect in his Creatours grace, / But with glad thankes, and unreproved truth, / The gifts of soveraigne bountie did embrace: / Like Angels life was then mens happy cace.'

iv *499–501.* In the physical application of mythology, Jupiter was often the *aether* and Juno the air, source of rain-storms. And 'from the air growing ardent, animals and plants are born' (Conti, *Mytholog.* x, s.v. *Iuno*; p. 1021). Cp. also Virgil, *Georg.* ii 325–7: 'Then Heaven, the Father almighty, comes down in fruitful showers into the lap of his joyous spouse, and his might, with her mighty frame commingling, nurtures all growths.' *impregns*] impregnates, makes pregnant. *matron*] implying that the kisses are lawful; cp. Lucretia's 'matron cheeks' in Ovid, *Fasti* ii 828. Cp. viii 514.

iv *502. the devil*] Cp. 'the fiend' (l. 393): 'Satan's dimensions are reduced so effectively that we hardly notice how, in the process, his titles lose their lustre, how the "Archfiend" of the first book becomes "the Fiend" or the "arch-fellon" and how for the first time he begins to be "the Devil"' (Rajan 99).

iv *503.* From what Raphael tells him, Adam later imagines that conjugal love is likely to excite Satan's envy more than any other human bliss (ix 263f).

iv *506. Imparadised*] A very romantic and poetic word, here used bitterly.

iv *509–10.* Empson 68 rightly rejects Lewis's characterization of Satan as a peeping Tom, on the grounds that his jealousy is open: 'God has recently cut him off from his own corresponding pleasures.'

iv *511. pines*] torments, troubles (trans.).

From their own mouths; all is not theirs it seems:
One fatal tree there stands of knowledge called,
Forbidden them to taste: knowledge forbidden?
Suspicious, reasonless. Why should their Lord
Envy them that? Can it be sin to know,
Can it be death? And do they only stand
By ignorance, is that their happy state,
The proof of their obedience and their faith?
O fair foundation laid whereon to build
Their ruin! Hence I will excite their minds
With more desire to know, and to reject
Envious commands, invented with design
To keep them low whom knowledge might exalt
Equal with gods; aspiring to be such,
They taste and die: what likelier can ensue?
But first with narrow search I must walk round
This garden, and no corner leave unspied;
A chance but chance may lead where I may meet
Some wandering spirit of heaven, by fountain side,

iv *513.* The knowledge of devils being 'spurious, erroneous, fallacious' and limited, Satan is really dependent on eavesdropping for information. See Schultz 86, where Webster's *Displaying of Witchcraft* is cited to the effect that if a man remains silent, Satan cannot know his mind.
iv *515–22.* Far from being 'genuinely indignant' (Empson 69) Satan is here exhilarated, because he has just thought of the basis of a scheme for the destruction of mankind. Enthusiastically he begins to rough out the speech with which he *will excite* (l. 522) Eve's mind. Thus *Equal with gods* (l. 526) corresponds to–though it is improved upon in–ix 547 'goddess among gods'. True, as Empson 32 rightly remarks, Satan could only invent these arguments if he half believed them. But for M. what mattered would be what was just, not what Satan contrived to half-believe. And the injustice of Satan's argument is heavily underlined: as, e.g., in the irony that God not only intended Adam and Eve to be *equal with gods,* if they were obedient (v 499–501), but even to exalt manhood to the throne of God himself, when they were disobedient, fallen and redeemed (iii 303–17). Broadbent 151 characterizes Satan's rhetoric in the present passage as 'forensic, flickering through ploce and traductio and erotema with suspicious speed; pragmatic, lacking the ceremoniousness that in places gives to what the Father (and especially Adam) says an aesthetic value.'
iv *523. Gen.* iii 4f: 'The serpent said unto the woman . . . God doth know that in the day ye eat thereof, then your eyes shall be opened, and ye shall be as gods, knowing good and evil.'
iv *530. chance but chance*] 'It is only a chance; but chance *may* lead.' Satan's jaunty jingle perhaps imitates the Lat. idiom *forte fortuna.* For a possible theological implication, see ii 935*n.*

Or in thick shade retired, from him to draw
What further would be learned. Live while ye may,
Yet happy pair; enjoy, till I return,
Short pleasures, for long woes are to succeed.
So saying, his proud step he scornful turned,
But with sly circumspection, and began
Through wood, through waste, o'er hill, o'er dale his roam.
Mean while in utmost longitude, where heaven
With earth and ocean meets, the setting sun
Slowly descended, and with right aspect
Against the eastern gate of Paradise

iv *533–4.* As Broadbent 190 observes, the *carpe diem* sentiment in which the more fleshly Renaissance paradises were so often bathed (e.g. Spenser, *F.Q.* II xii 74f; Tasso, *Gerus. Lib.* xvi 15) is here channelled exclusively into Satan's mouth.

iv *538. roam*] the act of roaming. Earliest instance in *OED*.

iv *539. utmost longitude*] the farthest west. See iii 573–6*nn*.

iv *541. Slowly*] Editors have cavilled at 'Slowly' (in view, e.g., of 352f, 'the Sun / Declined was hasting now with prone career'); but M., further advanced in the study of astronomy, allowed for the refractive effect of the earth's atmosphere during the ultimate phase of the sunset. This effect produces an apparent deceleration of the sun's descent; see Riccioli ii 581, Problem 33, *Tempus Apparens Ortus et Occasus Limborum Solis definire*. *right aspect*] direct view. Assuming that the gate is more or less vertical (547f), the rays of the setting sun will be at *right* angles with it.

iv *542.* In *Gen.* iii 24 the guard of cherubim that excludes Adam and Eve from Paradise is placed 'at the east of the garden'. Since the gate is so high, even the setting sun's horizontal rays illuminate it, after passing over the 'insuperable height' of the western 'verdurous wall' (l. 143).

iv *542–50.* A complex and highly condensed description. Among possible sources may be mentioned Purchas's and Heylyn's paradise of Mt Amara, which has smooth overhanging rock and a single 'ascending place, a faire gate' (see above, ll. 280–5*n*); and the marble 'crag of immense height' above the cave where Bacchus was hidden (Diodorus iii 69; see ll. 275–9*n* above). But earlier readers would also be quick to recognize the iconographical features of the description, in which five motifs may be distinguished. (1) The rock ascending *to the clouds* is a supraterrestrial Paradise 'in the air, under the circle of the Moon' (Heylyn iii 127; see 135*n*). (2) The way to its *entrance high* is an arduous Path of Virtue (see Wind 79). (3) Its *pillars* are Pillars of Virtue (see Tervarent 107). (4) The *craggy cliff* that overhangs symbolizes impending divine punishment (see Wind[2] 18), so that it proleptically foreshadows the Expulsion, in which the gate is to play a prominent part (xii 641–4). (5) the mention of *alablaster* directs attention to the receptacle in which the ointment of faith was kept uncorrupted (Vulg. *John*

Levelled his evening rays: it was a rock
Of alablaster, piled up to the clouds,
Conspicuous far, winding with one ascent
Accessible from earth, one entrance high;
The rest was craggy cliff, that overhung
Still as it rose, impossible to climb.
Betwixt these rocky pillars Gabriel sat
Chief of the angelic guards, awaiting night;
About him exercised heroic games
The unarmed youth of heaven, but nigh at hand
Celestial armoury, shields, helms, and spears,
Hung high with diamond flaming, and with gold.
Thither came Uriel, gliding through the even
On a sun beam, swift as a shooting star

xii 3, *nardus pisticus*; cp. *Matt.* xxvi 7, and see Raban Maur, Migne cvii 1101f). Allegorically, then, the receptacle of Paradise must be the true Church–as indeed M. has indicated at 193: 'So since into his Church lewd hirelings climb.' The gate itself, however, is Christ; see *John* x 7 ('I am the door of the sheep'), and cp. Giles Fletcher, *Christs victorie* ii 13, where Christ's legs are 'as two white marble pillars that uphold / Gods holy place'. Corcoran (20) notes that Heylyn's description of Meroe (*Cosmographie* iv 62f) includes an alabaster gate. Meroe was according to Josephus the capital of the Queen of Sheba.

iv *544. alablaster*] alabaster (a common seventeenth-century spelling): a specially white variety of marble, variegated with other colours; carbonate of lime, used by the ancients for holding and preserving unguents.

iv *549–50. Gabriel*] 'Strength of God', one of the four archangels ruling the corners of the world, and one of the angels of the cosmic chariot (see iii 648*n*). In the Bible (*Dan.* viii, ix; *Luke* i) he is a peaceful ambassador, rather than a warrior. But M. followed a Jewish and cabbalistic tradition that identified Gabriel with Mars (Valeriano 549). In making him guardian of Paradise he followed another tradition, which presumably went back ultimately to *Enoch* xx 7: 'Gabriel, one of the holy angels, who is over Paradise and the serpents and the Cherubim' (Charles ii 201). This verse does not seem to have occurred, however, in the parts of *Enoch* accessible to M.

iv *552. unarmed*] Contrast the more aggressive games of the devils (ii 532–8).

iv *555.* Bentley objects to Satan's gliding through a period of time; Pearce compares l. 557 (see also iii 71), interpreting *even* as the part of the celestial hemisphere where it was evening; and at last Empson (^{2}157f) sees the pun: 'the angel is sliding, choosing a safe gradient, down a nearly *even* sunbeam'. For a further implication, see l. 590f below. Broadbent 87 contrasts the easy movement of the good angels with the laboured, swarming, or zombie movement of the devils.

iv *556–60. thwarts*] crosses (often in a nautical context, and thus appropriate diction here); also 'obstructs'–i.e., interrupts the victory of darkness over

In autumn thwarts the night, when vapours fired
Impress the air, and shows the mariner
From what point of his compass to beware
Impetuous winds: he thus began in haste.
  Gabriel, to thee thy course by lot hath given
Charge and strict watch that to this happy place
No evil thing approach or enter in;
This day at highth of noon came to my sphere
A spirit, zealous, as he seemed, to know
More of the almighty's works, and chiefly man
God's latest image: I described his way
Bent all on speed, and marked his airy gait;
But in the mount that lies from Eden north,
Where he first lighted, soon discerned his looks
Alien from heaven, with passions foul obscured:
Mine eye pursued him still, but under shade
Lost sight of him; one of the banished crew
I fear, hath ventured from the deep, to raise
New troubles; him thy care must be to find.

light. Uriel's arrival is like the *shooting star* not only in visual respects, but also because he brings a warning to the *mariner* (Gabriel) and so temporarily *thwarts* the powers of darkness. Homer (*Il.* iv 75–9) similarly compares the descent of Minerva to that of a shooting star 'portent to mariners'.

iv *556. swift*] Yet Uriel has taken some considerable time over a journey that Satan accomplished almost instantaneously (see ll. 30 and 564). Perhaps the inference to be drawn is that Uriel had to wait until sunset, when a sun god's mythological task is completed for the day, before leaving his post.

iv *557–8.* This piece of meteorology goes back at least to Seneca. Shooting stars were thought to be caused by exhalations from the earth that failed to ascend beyond a certain point, were ignited through repulsion by the surrounding air, and then slid away. Or the stars were a sign of storm because in falling they were thrust down by winds, which began earliest in the upper atmosphere. See Svendsen 89f.

iv *561.* Modelled on the Hebrew temple service, in which the distribution of offices was by lot. See especially *1 Chron.* xxvi 13: 'they cast lots . . . for every gate'. Cp. v 655*n*.

iv *564.* Note that M.'s universe is throughout on 'Paradise Time': the term *noon* can have no meaning unless a particular horizon is specified. Cp. Argument.

iv *567.* God's first *image* being Christ, and the intervening images the angels, heaven and the products of the first five days of mundane creation; see iii 63, 384, etc. *described*] descried; a common seventeenth-century confusion: see *OED* s.v *Describe* 7.

iv *572. shade*] trees; as often in *PL* (cp. i 302–4, and see Wright 207).

To whom the winged warrior thus returned:
Uriel, no wonder if thy perfect sight,
Amid the sun's bright circle where thou sit'st,
See far and wide: in at this gate none pass
The vigilance here placed, but such as come
Well known from heaven; and since meridian hour
No creature thence: if spirit of other sort,
So minded, have o'erleaped these earthy bounds
On purpose, hard thou know'st it to exclude
Spiritual substance with corporeal bar.
But if within the circuit of these walks,
In whatsoever shape he lurk, of whom
Thou tell'st, by morrow dawning I shall know.
So promised he, and Uriel to his charge
Returned on that bright beam, whose point now raised
Bore him slope downward to the sun now fallen
Beneath the Azores; whether the bright orb,

iv *577*. *Uriel*] 'Light of God', one of God's 'eyes'; see iii 648–61*n*.
iv *580*. *vigilance*] guard, watch; probably a metonymy, putting an attribute of the guard for the guard itself.
iv *585*. See i 423–31*n*, vi 344–53.
iv *586*. *Ed I* has no comma after *walks*.
iv *590–1*. Since the sun has now set, its rays incline 'upwards' (regarded Ptolemaically) from the plane of the horizon. The ingenious routing, which allows Uriel to come and go without having to ascend, disgusted Addison. But the detail is no mere prettiness; for it emphasises the balancing of the hemispheres of light and dark at sunset, and so prepares for the important scales image of ll. 997ff. (Note the pun in *beam*–sunbeam, balance beam–and cp. the 'scale of heaven' at 354f, a passage linked to the present one by its mention of the 'Ocean Isles'.) Moreover, the numerological pattern demands that prominence be given to the precise moment of sunset: see l. 777*n*.
iv *592–7*. Cp. iii 573–6*n*. The appearance of sunset can be regarded as caused either by orbital motion of the sun about the earth, or by the earth's rotation (a lesser movement). M.'s avoidance of the choice between the two models, Ptolemaic and post-Copernican, is rendered by a dizzying series of verbal and syntactical ambiguities: e.g., 'whether the *primum mobile* (*prime orb*= first sphere) had rolled there carrying the sun with it, or the turning earth had left him'; and 'whether the sun (*prime orb*=principal planet) had rolled there, or etc.' *rolled*] May also be trans., with 'him' as the understood object. *whether*] The early edns spelled 'whither', thus allowing a further chain of discourse, which does not persist, however, beyond *thither*. *Diurnal*] occupying one day (in the performance of the action). In the Ptolemaic system the *primum mobile* revolved about the earth, carrying the sun with it, in approximately one solar day; see Price 106. *Incredible how*

Incredible how swift, had thither rolled
Diurnal, or this less voluble earth
By shorter flight to the east, had left him there
Arraying with reflected purple and gold
The clouds that on his western throne attend:
Now came still evening on, and twilight grey
Had in her sober livery all things clad;
Silence accompanied, for beast and bird,
They to their grassy couch, these to their nests
Were slunk, all but the wakeful nightingale;
She all night long her amorous descant sung;
Silence was pleased: now glowed the firmament
With living sapphires: Hesperus that led
The starry host, rode brightest, till the moon
Rising in clouded majesty, at length
Apparent queen unveiled her peerless light,

swift] An argument in favour of the Copernican system was that it avoided the enormous velocities implied by the Ptolemaic. According to Copernicus', Kepler's and later estimates, the velocity of the earth's diurnal motion had only to be about 0·06 German miles per second, as against 70 Ger. m.p.s. for the velocity of solar diurnal motion. And even the velocity of terrestrial annual motion was estimated at only 12.3 Ger. m.p.s. See Riccioli i 126f, and cp. viii 25–38 below, where Adam puts this argument to Raphael. *voluble*] 'capable of ready rotation on its axis'; possibly stressed on the second syllable.

iv *598*. Cp. *Comus* 188f: 'the gray-hooded Even / Like a sad votarist in palmer's weed'.

iv *600–3*. *Silence accompanied*] 'Silence associated with them' (*OED* II 5, intrans., absol.); but also, possibly, 'silence accompanied musically (by the nightingale)'. The second sense is supported by *descant*, but not demanded by it; when used of a bird it could mean simply a melodious warbled song, without necessarily implying polyphony.

iv *604*. Cp. *Comus* 557–60, where Silence, surprised and captivated by the Lady's song, wishes to be forever displaced by it. Also *Il Penseroso* 51–6: 'with thee bring . . . mute silence . . . 'Less Philomel will deign a song.'

iv *605*. *sapphires*] See ll. 237–8*n* and ii 1049–50*n*. *Hesperus*] Cp. xi 588f ('the evening star / Love's harbinger') and ix 49ff ('Hesperus, whose office is to bring / Twilight upon the earth, short arbiter / Twixt day and night').

iv *608*. *Apparent queen*] manifest queen; but also playing on 'heir-apparent' (often shortened to 'apparent'). While the moon was clouded (l. 607) her majesty was only presumptive; now, like her light, she is *peerless*, her succession unchallenged. The effect of the queen's sudden disrobing is heightened by the elaborate images of clothing at ll. 596–9.

And o'er the dark her silver mantle threw.
When Adam thus to Eve: Fair consort, the hour
Of night, and all things now retired to rest
Mind us of like repose, since God hath set
Labour and rest, as day and night to men
Successive, and the timely dew of sleep
Now falling with soft slumbrous weight inclines
Our eyelids; other creatures all day long
Rove idle unemployed, and less need rest;
Man hath his daily work of body or mind
Appointed, which declares his dignity,
And the regard of heaven on all his ways;
While other animals unactive range,
And of their doings God takes no account.
To morrow ere fresh morning streak the east
With first approach of light, we must be risen,
And at our pleasant labour, to reform
Yon flowery arbours, yonder alleys green,
Our walk at noon, with branches overgrown,
That mock our scant manuring, and require
More hands than ours to lop their wanton growth:
Those blossoms also, and those dropping gums,
That lie bestrewn unsightly and unsmooth,
Ask riddance, if we mean to tread with ease;
Mean while, as nature wills, night bids us rest.
To whom thus Eve with perfect beauty adorned.

iv *614–15*. Cp. Spenser, *F.Q.* I i 36, 'the sad humour loading their eye liddes, / As messenger of *Morpheus* on them cast / Sweet slombring deaw'; *Richard III* IV i 83, 'the golden dew of sleep'; and *Julius Caesar* II i 230, 'the honey-heavy dew of slumber'.

iv *618–19*. The Augustinian Adam, and indeed the medieval Adam generally, lived a purely contemplative life before the Fall. But Protestants tended to advance the prelapsarian status of the active life. See, e.g., l. 625*n*.

iv *620*. *regard*] attention, care.

iv *625*. Cp. ll. 327f. 'Though man should not have toyled or wearied himselfe with any labour in Paradise, for that was laid upon him as a punishment afterward . . . yet it is evident that hee should have exercised himselfe in some honest labour, even in Paradise . . . his charge was . . . to dresse the garden . . . in which kind of husbandrie many even now doe take a delight, and hold it rather to be a recreation, then any wearines unto them' (Willet 33, on *Gen.* ii 15).

iv *627*. *walk*] walks *Ed I*.

iv *628*. *manuring*] cultivating, training. *wanton*] luxuriant, unrestrained.

iv *631*. *bestrewn*] spelt 'bestrowne'.

iv *632*. *Ask*] need, call for, demand.

My author and disposer, what thou bid'st
Unargued I obey; so God ordains,
God is thy law, thou mine: to know no more
Is woman's happiest knowledge and her praise.
With thee conversing I forget all time,
All seasons and their change, all please alike.
Sweet is the breath of morn, her rising sweet,
With charm of earliest birds; pleasant the sun
When first on this delightful land he spreads
His orient beams, on herb, tree, fruit, and flower,
Glistering with dew; fragrant the fertile earth
After soft showers; and sweet the coming on
Of grateful evening mild, then silent night
With this her solemn bird and this fair moon,
And these the gems of heaven, her starry train:

iv *635. author*] origin (see viii 465ff); prompter, mover, initiator (*OED* 1 d). The forms of address used by Adam and Eve before the Fall have a magnificence, appropriate to their dignity, that is afterwards lost. Marjorie Barstow notices the abandonment of courteous titles after the Fall in 'Milton's use of the forms of epic address', *MLN* xxxi (1916) 120f. The prelapsarian titles are as much Biblical, however, as epic – e.g., the second Adam is called 'author of life' in *Acts* iii 15 (A.V. marg.) and 'author and finisher of faith' in *Heb.* xii 2.

iv *639–56.* A rhetorically magnificent passage, exploiting to the full the possibilities of such circular or completive figures as epanalepsis (l. 641), epanodos and merismus (the division of l. 640 into the individual items of ll. 641–9) and irmus (the extreme periodicity of ll. 650–6). MacCaffrey (77) compares xii 617f ('thou to me / Art all things under heaven, all places thou'); for Eve 'Adam *is* Eden', and in their communion the constancy of Paradise reaches its culmination. The repetition of ll. 641–9 in ll. 650–6 'enacts a timeless recurrence' and renders the 'changing sameness' of time in Eden. In this connection it is particularly interesting to note the circularity of the self-subsistent 16-line passage 641–56, *Sweet is . . . is sweet*, with its large scale epanalepsis. Numerologically, 16 divided in this way, into portions of 9 and 7, symbolizes virtue harmoniously adjusting the mutable to the heavenly, *anima* to *mens*, soul to mind (see Fowler 269–88 on Spenser's use of a similar symbolism in the Castle of Alma). Note that the 9-line spiritual portion refers to Paradise with Adam, the mutable 7-line portion to Paradise without Adam. In the latter portion each item in the former suffers alteration; though this alteration is as yet hypothetical and held in check by negation.

iv *640. seasons*] time of day; as in viii 69. Not 'seasons of the year', since it is still eternal spring.

iv *642. charm*] song.

iv *648. solemn bird*] Cp. 'solemn nightingale' in vii 435.

But neither breath of morn when she ascends
With charm of earliest birds, nor rising sun
On this delightful land, nor herb, fruit, flower,
Glistering with dew, nor fragrance after showers,
Nor grateful evening mild, nor silent night
With this her solemn bird, nor walk by moon,
Or glittering starlight without thee is sweet.
But wherefore all night long shine these, for whom
This glorious sight, when sleep hath shut all eyes?
To whom our general ancestor replied.
Daughter of God and man, accomplished Eve,
Those have their course to finish, round the earth,
By morrow evening, and from land to land
In order, though to nations yet unborn,
Ministering light prepared, they set and rise;
Lest total darkness should by night regain

iv *652–3.* Note how *herb . . . dew*, merismus at ll. 644f, is now varied to an independent enumeratio. The passage is full of such theme-and-variation effects, which enact Eve's responsiveness to Adam, and perhaps (proleptically) the effect of her independence. See ll. 639–56*n* above.
iv *656.* On the accentuation *wíthout*, see ii 892*n*: it implies strong emphasis.
iv *657–8.* A good question, in a way; for, although Adam gives partial answers in the speech that follows, his doubts have been aroused, and he himself addresses a very similar enquiry to Raphael at viii 15ff. Note, however, at what a disadvantage M. puts the question in the present context. Eve's preceding song of love is magnificent and sophisticated, but coming after it her intellectual query sounds perfunctory, casually abrupt in rhythm, shallow.
iv *660.* See l. 635*n*. *Daughter of God* is dramatic irony, for one of the most familiar titles of Mary the second Eve is 'Mother of God' (the usual Eng. translation of the title *Theotokos*: the subject of bitter controversy in the fifth century, but a commonplace of later Marian devotion). *accomplished*] An epithet of address in actual use; cp. Shakespeare, *Twelfth Night* III i 96: 'Most excellent accomplished lady'.
iv *661–73.* Cp. the account of the stars' function at vii 340–52; common to both passages are the duties of illumination, and restraint of Night. Svendsen 76f traces these notions, as also that of the stars' *various influence*, to encyclopaedias such as the *De proprietatibus rerum* of Bartholomew of England. But it is misleading to give particular sources for ideas so generally held.
iv *661. Those*] Perhaps 'These' was intended—*o* for *e* was an easy error.
iv *664. light prepared*] Echoes *Ps.* lxxiv; see ll. 724–5*n*.
iv *665.* Cp. iii 725–32, where Uriel explains that Night has invaded the nocturnal hemisphere, but that the moon's 'pale dominion checks the night' and prevents a return to the 'original darkness' (ii 984) of chaos.

Her old possession, and extinguish life
In nature and all things, which these soft fires
Not only enlighten, but with kindly heat
Of various influence foment and warm,
Temper or nourish, or in part shed down
Their stellar virtue on all kinds that grow
On earth, made hereby apter to receive
Perfection from the sun's more potent ray.
These then, though unbeheld in deep of night,
Shine not in vain, nor think, though men were none,
That heaven would want spectators, God want praise;
Millions of spiritual creatures walk the earth
Unseen, both when we wake, and when we sleep:
All these with ceaseless praise his works behold
Both day and night: how often from the steep
Of echoing hill or thicket have we heard
Celestial voices to the midnight air,
Sole, or responsive each to other's note
Singing their great creator: oft in bands
While they keep watch, or nightly rounding walk
With heavenly touch of instrumental sounds
In full harmonic number joined, their songs
Divide the night, and lift our thoughts to heaven.

iv *668–73*. See Caxton 147f., *cit.* Svendsen 77: though the sun is more virtuous than the other stars, 'yet somtyme they restrayne his heetes and after they enlarge them, after that they be fer or nygh, as he otherwhile hath nede'. In Neoplatonic astrology, Sol was said to accomplish the generation of new life by acting through each of the other planets in turn; their function was only to modulate his influence, or to select from his complete spectrum of virtues. See, e.g., Ficino, *In Timaeum* xx (*Opera omnia* 1468). After the Fall the influence of the stars becomes less *kindly* (benign; natural): see x 660 ff.

iv *675*. The first comma may be in error for a heavier point.

iv *681–4*. Cp. Lucretius, *De rerum nat.* iv 586ff, where the music heard is that of Pan's pipe (often interpreted allegorically as the music of the spheres).

iv *682–3*. Cp. the angels' skill in polyphony at iii 370f. Socrates Scholasticus tells how Ignatius 'saw a vision of angels praising the Holy Trinity in responsive hymns', and how this vision was the source of antiphonal music in the Church (*Ecclesiasticae historiae autores* (Paris 1544) fol. 258v); a tradition referred to by M. in his *Commonplace Book* (Yale i 383).

iv *688*. *Divide the night*] mark the watches of the night by giving the signal for a change of guard (Lat. *dividere noctem*). In view of the context, perhaps there is also a play on the musical sense of *divide* (*OED* 11 a, perform with 'divisions'–florid melodic passages or descants).

Thus talking hand in hand alone they passed
On to their blissful bower; it was a place
Chosen by the sovereign planter, when he framed
All things to man's delightful use; the roof
Of thickest covert was inwoven shade
Laurel and myrtle, and what higher grew
Of firm and fragrant leaf; on either side
Acanthus, and each odorous bushy shrub
Fenced up the verdant wall; each beauteous flower,

iv *690–703.* In the description of Paradise in Bk iv Art and Nature cooperate: 'The more artificial nature's works appear, the more they "illustrate" the immanence of God. ... When the terms of art predominate ... the reference is usually to the Bower of Adam and Eve which has been deliberately made for them by God' (Broadbent 179f). This equilibrium of Art and Nature is delicate and unstable, however; it is liable to slip into excess or artificiality, 'brutalism or sophistication'.

iv *691. planter*] See *Gen.* ii 8: 'God planted a garden.'

iv *694.* Cp. the arbour of generation within the 'grove of myrtle' in the Garden of Adonis in Spenser, *F.Q.* III vi 43–4, which is certainly sexually, and probably even anatomically, symbolic (see Ellrodt 88*n*, Fowler 137). *laurel and myrtle*] Associated in Virgil, *Ecl.* ii 54 ('You too will I pluck, laurels, and you their neighbour myrtle, for so placed you blend sweet fragrance'); but at this juncture M. must intend more than an elegant allusion. Myrtle later figures prominently in an emblematic context at a critical stage of the action, immediately before the Fall. There it is clearly a symbol of virtue or modesty (see ix 426–31*n*). But here the trees seem rather to symbolize the complementary roles of Apollo and Venus, male and female, *mens* and *anima*, reason and virtue. The force of the passage lies in the suggestion of a comprehensive polarity.

iv *696. acanthus*] Mentioned among the trees and shrubs, so that M. may intend the Egyptian acacia, the evergreen tree that Virgil describes as *semper frondens* (*Ecl.* ii 119), and not the acanthus flower. The Virgilian context, a list of exotic fragrant trees, may account for the introduction of the acanthus here; or perhaps the fact that since ancient times acanthus leaves have been used as a decorative architectural motif (see ll. 690–703*n*, and note *wall ... mosaic ... inlay*). Like the *hyacinth* (l. 701) the acanthus was the result of the metamorphosis of a love of Apollo (cp. Spenser's similar list of metamorphosed lovers in the Garden of Adonis, *F.Q.* III vi 45). *Acanthus* is treated as a proper name in *Ed I* and *Ed II*.

iv *697–701.* Combining the flowers of the Atlantic Isles, with those that sprang up beneath Zeus and Hera to raise them from the soil of Mt Ida (Homer, *Il.* xiv 347–9: crocus, hyacinth). See Conti, *Mytholog.* iii 19 on the Atlantic Isles: *Hi duas esse parvas insulas referebant mari inter se divisas, atque ventos ibi plurimum suaves et odoriferos leniter spirare, tanquam per incredibilem florum varietatem et amoenitatem transeuntes. Nam qualis odor est multis rosis,*

Iris all hues, roses, and jessamine
Reared high their flourished heads between, and
wrought
Mosaic; underfoot the violet,
Crocus, and hyacinth with rich inlay
Broidered the ground, more coloured than with stone
Of costliest emblem: other creature here
Beast, bird, insect, or worm durst enter none;
Such was their awe of man. In shady bower
More sacred and sequestered, though but feigned,
Pan or Silvanus never slept, nor nymph,
Nor Faunus haunted. Here in close recess
With flowers, garlands, and sweet-smelling herbs
Espoused Eve decked first her nuptial bed,
And heavenly choirs the hymenean sung,

violis, hyacinthis, liliis, narcissis, myrtetis, lauris, cyparissis, talis aspirantium ventorum est suavitas.'

iv *698. jessamin*] jasmine.

iv *699. flourished*] flowered, adorned with flowers.

iv *700–3. emblem*] The word could mean any ornament of inlaid work; see, e.g., the contemporary definition by the emblematist George Whitney, *cit.* Freeman 37, 'such figures, or works, as are wrought in plate, or in stones in the pavements, or on the walls, or such like, for the adorning of the place'. But it is difficult to think that the other sense of *emblem* (pictorial symbol) is not also meant to operate here, and to draw attention to the emblematic properties of the flowers (the humility of the *violet*, prudence of the *hyacinth*, amiability of the *jessamin*, etc.). More generally, the bower as a whole is an emblem of true married love. Thus its seclusion and concealment (ll. 693, 704) reflect the privacy and particular belonging of the marital relation.

iv *705–8.* Often *Pan Silvanus* and *Faunus* were confused, for all were represented as half man, half goat. For Pan as Nature, see ll. 266–8*n*; here he is more specifically a symbol of fecundity and a god of *sequestered* places. Silvanus, said by some to be the son of Faunus, was a god of woods, gardens and limits. Faunus himself was a more ambiguous deity. On the one hand he was the Roman Pan, a benignly priapic wood god, *nympharum fugentium amator* (Horace, *Odes* III xviii 1), who *haunted* the forest as an oracle (Virgil, *Aen.* vii 81–4); on the other, the father of satyrs, an emblem of Concupiscence (Alciati (Lyons 1600) Embl. lxxii; Ripa, *Iconologia* (Padua 1611) 315) or even of Satan, tempter of Eve (see Fowler[3] 101f).

iv *705. shady*] shadier *Ed I.*

iv *708. close*] secret.

iv *711. hymenean*] wedding hymn; Hymenaeus or Hymen being the ancient god of marriage. See *Elegia V* 105–8, where youths shout the hymenean chorus 'Io, Hymen'.

What day the genial angel to our sire
Brought her in naked beauty more adorned,
More lovely than Pandora, whom the gods
Endowed with all their gifts, and O too like

iv *712. genial*] nuptial, generative. The role that in poetry of a different mode would be taken by Genius, the deity presiding over generation and marriage (cp. 'Old Genius' the porter of Spenser's Garden of Adonis, *F.Q.* III vi 31f), is here instead taken by the mysterious invisible *genial angel* of ll. 467–76. Gilbert (45) finds a discrepancy between the present passage and viii 484–7, where Eve is guided by her maker; and perhaps he is right. The genial angel is not of course to be confused with Raphael, who on the day of Adam's creation was away on a mission to hell gate (viii 229).

iv *714–19.* Verbal echoes suggest that M. has followed Charles Estienne's version of the myth: 'Pandora . . . is feigned by Hesiod the first woman–made by Vulcan at Jupiter's command–*whom the gods all adorned* with their gifts. . . . hence she was called Pandora, either because she was *endowed with all their gifts*, or because she was endowed with gifts by all. The tradition is that she was afterwards sent with a closed casket to Epimetheus, since Jupiter wanted revenge on the human race for the boldness of Prometheus, who had stolen fire from heaven and taken it . . . down to earth; and that Epimetheus received her and opened the casket, which contained every kind of evil, so that it filled the world with diseases and calamaties' (*cit.* Starnes 270; my itals). Empson's queer smack at M. (Empson[2] 179: 'Not only was Eve not trying to avenge Satan but Pandora was not trying to avenge Prometheus') is beside the point, for it is not Satan who steals the authentic fire of forbidden knowledge. Man is both Prometheus and Epimetheus: so long as he has foresight and wisdom, he enjoys (as here) divine gifts; but when in the *sad event* (result) he is *unwiser*, he comes to resemble Epimetheus, and to experience the consequences of sin. M. had applied the myth in a similar manner in *Doctrine and Discipline* ii 3 (Yale ii 293): '*Plato* and *Chrysippus* with their followers the *Academics* and the *Stoics* who knew not what a consummat and most adorned *Pandora* was bestow'd upon *Adam* to be the nurse and guide of his arbitary happinesse and perseverance, I mean his native innocence and perfection, which might have kept him from being our true *Epimetheus*.' Prometheus and Epimetheus were sons of Iapetus, the Titan son of Coelus and Terra. Starnes and Talbert (260) advance the rash theory that M. invented the 'interesting identification' of Iapetus and Iaphet (Noah's son: *Gen.* ix–x) by conflating two dictionary entries. In fact the identification was an established piece of syncretism, important enough to have a chapter devoted to it in the anonymous *Observationum libellus* appended to Conti's *Mythologiae* ((Lyons 1653) Sig. Kkk iii^r): '*De Iapeto seu Iapheto primogenito Noachi Patriarchae filio extant plurima apud Ethnicos vestigia. Is enim est, quem ipsi Hebraeam vocem ad suae linguae normam ac suavitatem inflectentes, vocant Iapetum priscum. Nam plures postea eodem hoc nomine sunt appellati. Priscus vero iste Iapetus, terrae et coeli filius.*'

In sad event, when to the unwiser son
Of Japhet brought by Hermes, she ensnared
Mankind with her fair looks, to be avenged
On him who had stole Jove's authentic fire.
Thus at their shady lodge arrived, both stood
Both turned, and under open sky adored
The God that made both sky, air, earth and heaven
Which they beheld, the moon's resplendent globe
And starry pole: Thou also madest the night,
Maker omnipotent, and thou the day,
Which we in our appointed work employed
Have finished happy in our mutual help
And mutual love, the crown of all our bliss
Ordained by thee, and this delicious place
For us too large, where thy abundance wants
Partakers, and uncropt falls to the ground.
But thou hast promised from us two a race
To fill the earth, who shall with us extol
Thy goodness infinite, both when we wake,
And when we seek, as now, thy gift of sleep.
This said unanimous, and other rites
Observing none, but adoration pure
Which God likes best, into their inmost bower

Cp. i 507–21*n* above, and see Hesiod, *Theogony* 570ff. For a full history of the theological interpretation of the Pandora myth, see Dora and Erwin Panofsky, *Pandora's Box* (1956). *authentic*] entitled to respect; original.

iv *720. stood*] See xi 1–2*n*. Some copies *Ed I* have comma after *stood*, others period.

iv *722.* The use of *both* to qualify more than two nouns was quite usual in prose in M.'s time (*OED* B 1 b).

iv *724–5.* Cp. *Ps.* lxxiv 16: 'The day is thine, the night also is thine: thou hast prepared the light and the sun.' *pole*] sky (poet.).

iv *729.* Though various other syntactical connections have been proposed and are not impossible, *place* is primarily the object of *madest* (l. 724).

iv *732–3.* Referring to *Gen.* i 28, where, before the Fall, 'God said unto them, Be fruitful, and multiply, and replenish the earth'–a controversial text that could be taken as proof that marriage not only had its 'institution in mans innocencie', but was allowable to all (see Willet 21).

iv *735.* Cp. *Ps.* cxxvii 2: 'It is vain for you to rise up early, to sit up late, to eat the bread of sorrows: for so he giveth his beloved sleep.' But the idea of sleep as a divine gift is almost universal; see, e.g., Homer, *Il.* ix 713 ('they laid themselves down and took the gift of sleep'), Virgil, *Aen.* ii 268f ('rest begins, and by grace of the gods steals gratefully over them').

iv *736–7.* Cp. xii 534 on the inadequacy of 'outward rites and specious forms'.

Handed they went; and eased the putting off
These troublesome disguises which we wear,
Straight side by side were laid, nor turned I ween
Adam from his fair spouse, nor Eve the rites
Mysterious of connubial love refused:
Whatever hypocrites austerely talk
Of purity and place and innocence,
Defaming as impure what God declares
Pure, and commands to some, leaves free to all.

iv *739. Handed*] joined hand in hand.

iv *743. Mysterious*] In *Eph.* v St Paul describes coitus as 'mysterious' in the sense that the state of 'one flesh' is a mystery or symbol of the relations between Christ and the Church. Some think M. is guilty of the generous fault of allowing inconsistencies of plot for the sake of getting in prelapsarian sex. If Adam and Eve share the fertility of Paradise, must they not conceive before the Fall, and thus bear a child free from original sin? But the subtlety of M. and the Biblical commentators has been underestimated. Willet, e.g., was quite capable of believing both that marriage was instituted 'in mans innocencie' (21) and that 'Adam in the state of innocencie should [sc. would] not have gotten so ungratious a sonne, as Caine was' (60). It was possible, we must conclude, to hold that Adam and Eve made love in Paradise without conceiving. But in any case, traditional embryological theories allowed ample opportunity for the subsequent infection of children conceived in innocence.

iv *744–9. 1 Tim.* iv 1–3–an apocalyptic text that Protestants found it useful to apply to the church of Rome–warns that 'in the latter times some shall depart from the faith . . . Speaking lies in hypocrisy; having their consciences seared with a hot iron; Forbidding to marry'. Fervently believing that 'marriage is honourable in itself, and prohibited to no order of men' (*De doctrina* i 10, Columbia xv 155), M. leaves his reader in no doubt that the sexual act was performed in the time of man's *innocence*. To put the first intercourse of Adam and Eve before the Fall was in itself to assume a theological position–one that went back at least to Hugh of St Victor, who believed that 'if we had remained in the state of innocence we should have generated *sine carnis incentivo*' (Lewis[2] 15). Similarly, the preparatory allusion to *Gen.* i 28 (see ll. 732–3*n*) had ideological bearing. For Bellarmine and Pererius held that that verse contained no precept to marry, but only an 'institution of nature'; whereas Protestants found in it 'a libertie graunted to all that will marrie, that thereby mankinde may still be propagated' (Willet 21). See also Williams 88.

iv *745. place*] Explained by l. 759.

iv *747. commands to some*] 'It is good for a man not to touch a woman. Nevertheless, to avoid fornication, let every man have his own wife' (*I Cor.* vii 1f). 'Hence marriage is not a command binding on all, but only on those

Our maker bids increase, who bids abstain
But our destroyer, foe to God and man?
Hail wedded love, mysterious law, true source
Of human offspring, sole propriety
In Paradise of all things common else.
By thee adulterous lust was driven from men
Among the bestial herds to range, by thee
Founded in reason, loyal, just, and pure,
Relations dear, and all the charities
Of father, son, and brother first were known.
Far be it, that I should write thee sin or blame,
Or think thee unbefitting holiest place,
Perpetual fountain of domestic sweets,
Whose bed is undefiled and chaste pronounced,

who are unable to live with chastity out of this state' (*De doctrina* i 10; Columbia xv 155).

iv *750–65*. Many Protestant hexaemeral poems had their panegyrics on married love. Cp. especially Du Bartas 172: 'O blessed Bond! o happy Marriage! / Which doost the match 'twixt Christ and us presage! / O chastest friendship, whose pure flames impart / Two Soules in one, two Hearts into one Hart! / O holy knot, in *Eden* instituted / (Not in this Earth with blood and wrongs polluted. . . .)' On the three ends of marriage (society, procreation, remedy for lust) in seventeenth-century thought, see D. Sherwin Bailey, *The Mystery of Love and Marriage* (1952) pp. 101–4. M., like Hooper, Bucer, Becon, Taylor and the majority of Anglican divines (but unlike Donne, who emphasised remedy), placed society first: 'The *form* of marriage consists in the mutual exercise of benevolence, love, help, and solace between the espoused parties. . . . The end of marriage is nearly the same with the form' (*De doctrina* i 10, Columbia xv 155). Procreation of children he regarded merely as the 'proper fruit' of marriage (*ibid.*). As for remedy, it is only 'since Adam's fall' that 'the provision of a remedy against incontinency has become in some degree a secondary end' (*ibid.*; cp. Jeremy Taylor, *cit.* Bailey 103: avoidance of fornication 'came in by the superfoetation of the evil accidents of the world'). In accordance with the same emphasis, *mutual love* comes first in the present passage (ll. 728, 750, 760), then *increase* (ll. 732, 748), while remedy, appropriately, is ignored (except perhaps in l. 753).

iv *750. mysterious*] See l. 743*n*.

iv *751–2*. i.e., the exclusive relationship and mutual rights of Adam and Eve were the only *propriety* (proprietorship, ownership) in Paradise. The institution of marriage was prelapsarian, but not that of property rights.

iv *756. charities*] affections.

iv *761*. Cp. *Heb.* xiii 4: 'Marriage is honourable in all, and the bed undefiled.'

Present, or past, as saints and patriarchs used.
Here Love his golden shafts employs, here lights
His constant lamp, and waves his purple wings,
Reigns here and revels; not in the bought smile
Of harlots, loveless, joyless, unendeared,
Casual fruition, nor in court amours
Mixed dance, or wanton mask, or midnight ball,
Or serenade, which the starved lover sings
To his proud fair, best quitted with disdain.
These lulled by nightingales embracing slept,
And on their naked limbs the flowery roof
Showered roses, which the morn repaired. Sleep on
Blest pair; and O yet happiest if ye seek

iv *763*. Cupid's *golden shafts* were sharp and gleaming, and kindled love; while those of lead were blunt, and put love to flight (Ovid, *Met.* i 468–71). The symbolism was ubiquitous in Renaissance love poetry and emblem literature (see Tervarent 186f). In the specification of golden arrows for marital love, M. had been preceded by Erasmus (*Coll.* iv).

iv *764*. *constant lamp*] An ironic contrast between love in Paradise and in the fallen world; for a lamp usually symbolized inconstancy of love, particularly woman's inconstancy. See Valeriano, *Hieroglyphica* xlvi 19, *Mulieris amor*: 'Among interpreters of dreams one reads that a burning lamp is the symbol of a woman who has been captivated by love; because their love is very light, inconstant and weak, and like a lamp can be extinguished by the influence of the slightest breeze' (p. 582). Since in the present passage Love himself lights the lamp, it is difficult to see how it can allude to the one Psyche used for her disastrous scrutiny of Cupid. On the other hand, the lamps of the constant virgins expecting the divine bridegroom (*Matt.* xxv 1–13) must surely constitute an allegorical overtone. Love is probably given *purple wings* on the authority of *Rem. amor.* 701, where he has *purpureas . . . alas* (cp. also Cupid's 'winges of purple and blewe' in Spenser, *Shep. Cal.* March 33). Ovid's *purpureas*, however, meant 'shining'; whereas many of M.'s early readers would have taken the hint of *Reigns* (l. 765) and assumed that purple as an emblem of sovereignty was intended. Note also that purple was the distinctive colour of Hymen (see l. 711*n*).

iv *765*. *Reigns . . . revels*] Stealing from Marino's *L'Adone* (ii 114) a tune there devoted to a pagan Love: *Quivi Amor si trastulla, e quindi impera.*

iv *767–8*. Cp. the satire on the sons of Belial at i 497ff and *PR* ii 183; also the attack on the 1633 *Book of Sports* – which seemed to M. to encourage 'gaming, jigging, wassailing, and mixt dancing' – in *Of Reformation* ii (Yale i 589). *masque*] masked ball.

iv *769*. Ironic, for the lover is both *starved* of love and perished with cold. Serenades were sung *in sereno*, on clear cold nights. *serenade*] *Ed I* and *Ed II* have the early form 'serenate'.

iv *773*. *repaired*] made up for (with new roses).

No happier state, and know to know no more.
Now had night measured with her shadowy cone
Half way up hill this vast sublunar vault,
And from their ivory port the cherubim
Forth issuing at the accustomed hour stood armed
To their night watches in warlike parade,
When Gabriel to his next in power thus spake.
Uzziel, half these draw off, and coast the south

iv *775*. Either 'know that it is best not to seek new knowledge (by eating the forbidden fruit)' or 'know (*OED* IV 12) *how to* limit your experience to the state of innocence'.

iv *776–80*. Cp. iii 556–7. The earth's shadow is a cone that appears to circle round it, in diametrical opposition to the sun. When the axis of the cone reaches the meridian, it is midnight; but here it is only *Half way up*, so that the time is nine o'clock (night and day being equal in Paradise, each is of exactly twelve hours' duration). For the Hebrew and Roman practice of dividing the night into four equal watches of three hours each, see, e.g., Riccioli i 36, and St Jerome on *Ps.* xc 4 (Vulg. lxxxix 4). Here the second watch is just beginning. Numerologically, as the content demands, l. 777 exactly marks–'measures'–the *Half way* point between l. 539, when the sun *in utmost longitude* begins its descent beneath the horizon at six o'clock, and l. 1015, the last line of Bk iv, when 'the shades of night' first begin to flee at midnight (ll. 1013–15*n*). The cone of the earth's shadow should be regarded as another form of a thematic shape common in *PL*, the pyramid of pride (see v 758–9*n* below). In *Reason of Church-Government* i 6, M speaks of 'hierarchies acuminating still higher and higher in a cone of Prelaty'. *port*] gate. In ancient legend deceptive dreams issued from a gate of ivory, true dreams from a gate of horn. Since the cherubim are to interrupt a false dream, it is the ivory gate they use.

iv *781*. For Gabriel's office as keeper of Paradise and ruler of cherubim, see l. 549–50*n*.

iv *782–8*. Of the obscure names M. assigns to his cherub guards, *Uzziel* (Strength of God) occurs in the Bible as an ordinary human name (e.g. *Exod.* vi 18) and so does *Zephon* (Searcher of Secrets: *Num.* xxvi 15). But the aptness goes beyond literal meaning; for in Rabbinical tradition Uzziel was one of the seven angels before the throne of God. Though a printed source cannot be specified, it seems very probable that M. knew of this tradition: see West 154f and 206; also his 'The names of Milton's Angels', *SP* xlvii (1950) 211–23, and Fletcher[2] 252–5. The name *Ithuriel* (Discovery of God) is not from the Bible, but it occurs–or at least a form very like it–in the disreputable *Key of Solomon*.

iv *782–4*. Here and at ll. 797f and 974–6 the movements of the angels almost seem to resemble the apparent nightly courses of the constellations (see also ll. 985–7*n*). Uzziel's detachment are (as it were) the stars of the southern

With strictest watch; these other wheel the north,
Our circuit meets full west. As flame they part
Half wheeling to the shield, half to the spear.
From these, two strong and subtle spirits he called
That near him stood, and gave them thus in charge.
  Ithuriel and Zephon, with winged speed
Search through this garden, leave unsearched no nook,
But chiefly where those two fair creatures lodge,
Now laid perhaps asleep secure of harm.
This evening from the sun's decline arrived
Who tells of some infernal spirit seen
Hitherward bent (who could have thought?) escaped
The bars of hell, on errand bad no doubt:
Such where ye find, seize fast, and hither bring.
  So saying, on he led his radiant files,
Dazzling the moon; these to the bower direct
In search of whom they sought: him there they found
Squat like a toad, close at the ear of Eve;
Assaying by his devilish art to reach
The organs of her fancy, and with them forge
Illusions as he list, phantasms and dreams,
Or if, inspiring venom, he might taint
The animal spirits that from pure blood arise

hemisphere, Gabriel's those of the northern. Cp. Marvell, 'Upon Appleton House', st. 40: 'the vigilant *Patroul* / Of Stars walks round about the *Pole*'.

iv *785. shield* for 'left' and *spear* for 'right' were ancient military terms.

iv *786. these*] i.e., the half under his own command, who wheeled to the right.

iv *791. secure*] unapprehensive, careless.

iv *799.* Burden 93 regards the capture of Satan merely as a graphic demonstration that God could have stopped him if he had wanted to. For a partial confirmation of this view see l. 1012*n* below, and for an alternative possibility l. 996*n*.

iv *802–3. organs*] Punning between 'instruments' and a sense nearer to the modern ('functionally adapted parts of the body'). *phantasms*] illusions, deceptive appearances; mental images.

iv *805. Animal spirits*] Spirits in this sense were fine vapours, regarded by some as a medium between body and soul, by others as a separate soul. Natural spirits originated in the liver and circulated venously; while vital spirits were formed in the heart from the natural, and circulated arterially. Animal spirits (Lat. *anima*, soul) were formed from the vital (hence *from pure blood*), ascended to the brain and issued through the nerves to impart motion to the body. Local movement of the animal spirits could also produce imaginative apparitions, and it was through these that angels were thought to affect the human mind. The alternatives before Satan are either

Like gentle breaths from rivers pure, thence raise
At least distempered, discontented thoughts,
Vain hopes, vain aims, inordinate desires
Blown up with high conceits engendering pride.
Him thus intent Ithuriel with his spear
Touched lightly; for no falsehood can endure
Touch of celestial temper, but returns
Of force to its own likeness: up he starts
Discovered and surprised. As when a spark
Lights on a heap of nitrous powder, laid
Fit for the tun some magazine to store
Against a rumoured war, the smutty grain
With sudden blaze diffused, inflames the air:
So started up in his own shape the fiend.
Back stept those two fair angels half amazed

to manipulate the organ of fancy itself; or else to work on the animal spirits, the source of sense-data, which retained past experiences he could mould to his purposes. Contrary to early demonology, the doctrine of M. and his contemporaries was that devils had no access to man's reason, and could only operate through the imagination. See W. B. Hunter, 'Eve's Demonic Dream', *ELH* xiii (1946) 255–65, with extensive documentation ranging from St Thomas to Glanvill.

iv *807. distempered*] vexed, troubled; disordered.

iv *810–13. Ithuriel with his spear*] Burden (100) thinks that a magic spear has to be provided so that Ithuriel can pierce Satan's disguise more effectively than Uriel did at first. But the fact that a toad has dared to enter the nuptial bower – an unnatural occurrence; see l. 704 – is enough to alert the guard. The spear is rather an emblematic expression of their perceptiveness. It is necessary to the story in another way, however: Satan has to be got back into a presentable form for the confrontation that follows.

iv *812. temper*] tempering, temperament. The primary reference is to the spear, which has been tempered in heaven; but the odd diction allows a secondary reference to Ithuriel's own spiritual constitution.

iv *814–19.* Broadbent (110) sees this as an instance of the 'alternating inflation and deflation of the devils begun in Book i, and continued for Satan all through'; the next instance coming not far below, at ll. 986–1015. *nitrous*] mixed with nitre (potassium nitrate or saltpetre, an ingredient in gunpowder) to form an explosive. *Fit for the tun*] In proper condition for casking, ready for use. *Against*] in preparation for. *smutty grain*] Perhaps this sets up a resonance with the next simile, of corn and chaff (ll. 981–5). For earlier mentions of guns or gunpowder in connection with Satan, see ii 937, iv 17; all these passages acquire new significance with Raphael's account of the invention of gunpowder, in vi 469–500. The present simile gains aptness from the fact that gunpowder was commonly called 'serpentine powder'.

So sudden to behold the grisly king;
Yet thus, unmoved with fear, accost him soon.
  Which of those rebel spirits adjudged to hell
Comest thou, escaped thy prison, and transformed,
Why sat'st thou like an enemy in wait
Here watching at the head of these that sleep?
  Know ye not then said Satan, filled with scorn,
Know ye not me? Ye knew me once no mate
For you, there sitting where ye durst not soar;
Not to know me argues your selves unknown,
The lowest of your throng; or if ye know,
Why ask ye, and superfluous begin
Your message, like to end as much in vain?
To whom thus Zephon, answering scorn with scorn.
Think not, revolted spirit, thy shape the same,
Or undiminished brightness, to be known
As when thou stood'st in heaven upright and pure;
That glory then, when thou no more wast good,
Departed from thee, and thou resemblest now
Thy sin and place of doom obscure and foul.
But come, for thou, be sure, shalt give account
To him who sent us, whose charge is to keep
This place inviolable, and these from harm.
  So spake the cherub, and his grave rebuke
Severe in youthful beauty, added grace
Invincible: abashed the devil stood,
And felt how awful goodness is, and saw
Virtue in her shape how lovely, saw, and pined

iv *836*. The construction makes one expect some such inverted form as 'Or [thy] brightness undiminished'; but *undiminished brightness* mimetically resists the grammatical pressure to alter.

iv *840*. *obscure*] dark, dismal; but also answering scorn with scorn by implying remote, lowly.

iv *845*. Cp. Virgil's description of Euryalus, *gratior et pulchro veniens in corpore virtus*. On the significance of angelic age, see iii 636–7*n*. Empson (60) thinks the 'young' angels are those recently promoted to fill the room of the rebel third. Alternatively we may suppose that *youthful* means 'youthful': cherubim enjoy perpetual youth iconographically.

iv *848*. So at ix 457–65 Eve's innocence and 'heavenly form / Angelic' overawe Satan. Underlying both passages is the Platonic notion that virtue can affect a person's outward appearance; cp. Cicero, *De officiis* i 5: *Formam quidem ipsam et quasi faciem honesti vides, quae si oculis cerneretur, mirabiles amores (ut ait Plato) excitaret sapientiae*. The establishment of the idea as one of the principal doctrines of Renaissance love poetry was apparently due to

His loss; but chiefly to find here observed
His lustre visibly impaired; yet seemed
Undaunted. If I must contend, said he,
Best with the best, the sender not the sent,
Or all at once; more glory will be won,
Or less be lost. Thy fear, said Zephon bold,
Will save us trial what the least can do
Single against thee wicked, and thence weak.
The fiend replied not, overcome with rage;
But like a proud steed reined, went haughty on,
Champing his iron curb: to strive or fly
He held it vain; awe from above had quelled
His heart, not else dismayed. Now drew they nigh
The western point, where those half-rounding guards
Just met, and closing stood in squadron joined
Awaiting next command. To whom their chief
Gabriel from the front thus called aloud.
O friends, I hear the tread of nimble feet
Hasting this way, and now by glimpse discern
Ithuriel and Zephon through the shade,
And with them comes a third of regal port,

Dante: see, e.g., *Convivio*, Ode iii 7, 'The soul whom this excellence [blessedness] adorns, / holds it not concealed; / for, from the first when she weds the body, / she shows it forth till death', and cp. Ode ii 4 etc.; consult also Charles Williams, *The Forgiveness of Sins* (1942) 23f. Cp. further *Reason of Church-Government* i 1: 'Discipline is . . . the very visible shape and image of vertue, whereby she is not only seene in the regular gestures and motions of her heavenly paces as she walkes, but also makes the harmony of her voice audible to mortall eares' (Yale i 751f). *pined*] mourned.

iv *858–61*. He allows himself to be arrested by two young angels, and later is ready to fight a whole squadron, because 'it is a point of honour to refuse to fight except with his equals. This is the reason he gives, and Milton does not contradict it while adding that his feelings were more complex' (Empson 60). But doesn't M. contradict Satan's reason? The point of honour is said to be part of his seeming dauntlessness (ll. 850–2), whereas his true feeling is dismay at the visible difference between good and evil–a difference of which he has apparently repressed the full memory. We are explicitly told that Satan *to strive . . . held it vain* because he was awe-struck. Presumably this feeling has passed by the time he defies the whole squadron at l. 987: Satan would be quick to recover self-composure.

iv *862*. See ll. 782–4, where the half-circuits of the cherubim, starting from the E. gate, were arranged. *half-rounding*] No other instance of the use as a verb is given in *OED*.

iv *868*. *shade*] trees; see Wright 207.

But faded splendour wan; who by his gait
And fierce demeanour seems the prince of hell,
Not likely to part hence without contest;
Stand firm, for in his look defiance lours.
He scarce had ended, when those two approached
And brief related whom they brought, where found,
How busied, in what form and posture couched.
To whom with stern regard thus Gabriel spake.
Why hast thou, Satan, broke the bounds prescribed
To thy transgressions, and disturbed the charge
Of others, who approve not to transgress
By thy example, but have power and right
To question thy bold entrance on this place;
Employed it seems to violate sleep, and those
Whose dwelling God hath planted here in bliss?
To whom thus Satan, with contemptuous brow.
Gabriel, thou hadst in heaven the esteem of wise,
And such I held thee; but this question asked
Puts me in doubt. Lives there who loves his pain?
Who would not, finding way, break loose from hell,
Though thither doomed? Thou wouldst thy self, no doubt,
And boldly venture to whatever place
Farthest from pain, where thou might'st hope to change
Torment with ease, and soonest recompense
Dole with delight, which in this place I sought;
To thee no reason; who know'st only good,

iv *870.* Gabriel, one of the principal angels, has no difficulty in recognizing Satan, even by his gait; so that Satan's gibe at l. 830 is evidently well-founded.
iv *872. contest*] Stressed on the second syllable.
iv *879. transgressions*] A pun on the etymological meaning 'transcursions'. As usual, the pun was divided up among M.'s early editors into univocal shares. Bentley would have only 'transcursions', Pearce only 'sins'. *charge*] 'task' (*OED* 12); perhaps also 'ward, person entrusted to the care of another' (*OED* 14)–i.e., Eve.
iv *886. esteem of wise*] reputation of being wise.
iv *887.* For the second time Satan attacks the question he is asked: cp. ll. 832f, also l. 930, where he again criticizes the words of his questioner.
iv *894. Dole*] There is irony here; for, while Gabriel is meant to understand 'grief, distress' (From Lat. *dolium*: *OED* sb.[2] 1) or 'pain, suffering' (*OED* sb.[2] 3; archaic, perhaps influenced by Lat. *dolor*), the word could also mean 'guile, deceit, fraud' (from Gk δόλος: *OED* sb.[3] 1). Cp. *Hamlet* I ii 13: 'In equal scale weighing delight and dole.'

But evil hast not tried: and wilt object
His will who bound us? Let him surer bar
His iron gates, if he intends our stay
In that dark durance: thus much what was asked.
The rest is true, they found me where they say;
But that implies not violence or harm.
Thus he in scorn. The warlike angel moved,
Disdainfully half smiling thus replied.
O loss of one in heaven to judge of wise,
Since Satan fell, whom folly overthrew,
And now returns him from his prison scaped,
Gravely in doubt whether to hold them wise
Or not, who ask what boldness brought him hither
Unlicensed from his bounds in hell prescribed;
So wise he judges it to fly from pain
However, and to scape his punishment.
So judge thou still, presumptuous, till the wrath,
Which thou incurr'st by flying, meet thy flight
Sevenfold, and scourge that wisdom back to hell,
Which taught thee yet no better, that no pain
Can equal anger infinite provoked.
But wherefore thou alone? Wherefore with thee
Came not all hell broke loose? Is pain to them
Less pain, less to be fled, or thou than they
Less hardy to endure? Courageous chief,
The first in flight from pain, hadst thou alleged
To thy deserted host this cause of flight,
Thou surely hadst not come sole fugitive.
To which the fiend thus answered frowning stern.
Not that I less endure, or shrink from pain,
Insulting angel, well thou know'st I stood
Thy fiercest, when in battle to thy aid
The blasting vollied thunder made all speed

iv *896. object*] adduce as a reason against (breaking loose from hell) (*OED* 3 and 4).
iv *899. durance*] forced confinement, imprisonment. *thus much what*] thus much in reply to what.
iv *904. judge of wise*] 'judge of what is wise, judge wisdom'; retorting the rhetorical figure used by Satan at 886.
iv *906. returns*] Either transitive, with 'folly' as subject, or reflexive, with 'Satan' as subject (arch.).
iv *911. However*] howsoever, in any way he can.
iv *926. stood*] put up with, endured (*OED* V 59).
iv *928. The*] *Ed II* 'Thy' is an error, probably due to the proximity of other instances of the word.

And seconded thy else not dreaded spear.
But still thy words at random, as before,
Argue thy inexperience what behoves
From hard assays and ill successes past
A faithful leader, not to hazard all
Through ways of danger by himself untried,
I therefore, I alone first undertook
To wing the desolate abyss, and spy
This new created world, whereof in hell
Fame is not silent, here in hope to find
Better abode, and my afflicted powers
To settle here on earth, or in mid air;
Though for possession put to try once more
What thou and thy gay legions dare against;
Whose easier business were to serve their Lord
High up in heaven, with songs to hymn his throne,
And practised distances to cringe, not fight.
  To whom the warrior angel soon replied.
To say and straight unsay, pretending first
Wise to fly pain, professing next the spy,
Argues no leader but a liar traced,
Satan, and couldst thou faithful add? O name,
A sacred name of faithfulness profaned!
Faithful to whom? To thy rebellious crew?
Army of fiends, fit body to fit head;

iv *928*. According to Raphael's account of the war in heaven, however, Messiah did not put forth all his strength, 'but checked / His thunder in mid volley, for he meant / Not to destroy' (vi 853–5).
iv *930–3*. See l. 887*n*. The sense is 'You are still talking like one ignorant of the duties of a faithful leader after hard engagements and defeats'. *assays*] attacks, efforts.
iv *938*. See i 651–4*n*.
iv *939*. *afflicted*] ruined, outcast. Cp. i 186.
iv *940*. *mid air*] See ii 275*n*; also *Eph*. ii 2: 'The prince of the power of the air, the spirit that now worketh in the children of disobedience.'
iv *942*. *gay*] fine; as often, used ironically (*OED* 6 b); but perhaps also with the contemptuous or envious overtone 'showily dressed' (*OED* 4), in reply to ll. 839f.
iv *945*. Zeugma; since *practised distances* goes with *fight* as well as with *cringe*. Footwork was no less important in combat than in court etiquette. *And*] Dr Johnson's emendation to 'At' is unnecessary.
iv *946*. So *Ed I*. *Ed II* has comma after *angel*, by error.
iv *949*. *traced*] discovered, searched out (*OED* v.[1] II 8). Is *traced*='twisted, interwoven' (*OED* v.[3] 1) a secondary implication?

Was this your discipline and faith engaged,
Your military obedience, to dissolve
Allegiance to the acknowledged power supreme?
And thou sly hypocrite, who now wouldst seem
Patron of liberty, who more than thou
Once fawned, and cringed, and servilely adored
Heaven's awful monarch? Wherefore but in hope
To dispossess him, and thy self to reign?
But mark what I aread thee now, avaunt;
Fly thither whence thou fled'st: if from this hour
Within these hallowed limits thou appear,
Back to the infernal pit I drag thee chained,
And seal thee so, as henceforth not to scorn
The facile gates of hell too slightly barred.
So threatened he, but Satan to no threats
Gave heed, but waxing more in rage replied.
Then when I am thy captive talk of chains,
Proud limitary cherub, but ere then
Far heavier load thyself expect to feel

iv *954. your*] Gabriel addresses the whole *Army of fiends* through their *head* and representative Satan.
iv *957–61.* 'A quaint bit of spite . . . quite enough to prove that God had already produced a very unattractive Heaven before Satan fell' (Empson 111). If M. allowed the inference that servility was general in heaven, he must be thought either to have blundered, or to have half-belonged to the devil's party in the way Empson suggests. But it seems more likely that Gabriel is simply falling in with Satan's choice of words (with *cringed*, cp. 'cringe' l. 945, with *servilely* cp. 'serve' l. 943), as people do in the heat of an argument. Thus he amplifies the effect of his counter-accusation of hypocrisy–'If it's cringing you call it you've cringed too; and without even being sincere, either'. *Patron*] advocate, supporter.
iv *962. aread*] advise.
iv *965–7.* As Empson (112) points out, Gabriel's being content to warn Satan is not weakness: 'he might mean to grant Satan one hour for decision whether to go of his own accord or be dragged in chains; it is a statesmanlike proposal, though no use because Satan decides to fight at once.' Cp. i 45–8 and iii 82; and see *Rev.* xx 1–3: 'An angel . . . having the key of the bottomless pit and a great chain in his hand . . . laid hold on the dragon, that old serpent . . . and bound him a thousand years, And cast him into the bottomless pit, and shut him up, and set a seal upon him, that he should deceive the nations no more, till the thousand years should be fulfilled: and after that he must be loosed a little season.' *facile*] easily moved (*OED* 5 c); perhaps also 'working freely' (*OED* 3).
iv *971. limitary*] stationed on the boundary; sarcastically seizing on Gabriel's word 'limits' (l. 964). For Gabriel as a cherub see ll. 549–50*n*.

From my prevailing arm, though heaven's king
Ride on thy wings, and thou with thy compeers,
Used to the yoke, draw'st his triumphant wheels
In progress through the road of heaven star-paved.
  While thus he spake, the angelic squadron bright
Turned fiery red, sharpening in mooned horns
Their phalanx, and began to hem him round
With ported spears, as thick as when a field

iv *973–6.* Satan refers to the central image of the poem, the cosmic chariot ridden by the Messiah at vi 750ff. See also iii 656*n*. *the road of heaven*] the Milky Way. See vii 577–81*n*.
iv *978. fiery red*] Iconographically the appropriate colour for cherubim in any case (see ll. 115–17 above); but here indicating angry ardour. *mooned*] shaped like the crescent moon. Crescent-shaped formations were classic in warfare, and still often used in M.'s time; cp. Gascoigne, *A hundreth sundrie floures* (1572), 'The Christian crew came on in forme of battayle pight, / And like a cressent cast themselves preparing for to fight', also Dryden, *Annus mirabilis* st. 125. Symbolically, the description is appropriate not only because images of Ceres-Isis anciently had crescent horns to indicate her lunar godhead (Plutarch, *De Iside* 372D–E), but also because Satan is an eclipsing power of darkness, occupying as it were the shadowed part of the imaginary lunar orb.
iv *980–5.* The comparison of an excited army to wind-stirred corn is Homeric; see *Il.* ii 147–50. On the present passage Empson[2] (172) objects: 'If God the sower is the ploughman, then he is anxious; another hint that he is not omnipotent. If the labouring Satan is the ploughman he is only anxious for a moment, and he is the natural ruler or owner of the good angels.' But the *ploughman* (peasant) cannot be Satan, since Satan has his own simile *On the other side* (l. 985). Thus, unless with Ricks (ll. 129f) we pay the simile off as 'beautiful but digressive', the ploughman has to be in some sense 'like' God. This doesn't mean, of course, that he 'is' God in all respects, or that M.'s God is anxious and less than omnipotent. Critics' puzzlement at the simile can be traced to Bentley's introduction of an irrelevant notion, that the ploughman is afraid of a storm. In fact M. never specifies which of the many possible causes of poor crops the ploughman ponders. We are only told of his fear that when threshed the crop may prove chaff, and of his doubt whether it is time to reap. (The Virgilian lines alluded to–*Georg.* i 192, *nequiquam pinguis palea teret area culmos* and 226, *exspectata seges vanis elusit aristis*–refer to the consequences, not of storm damage, but of sowing at the wrong time.) Now *threshing* was a very familiar metaphor for divine judgment (for the iconographical background of the metaphor, see Mâle 31: for its Biblical sources, see *Jer.* li 33, 'Babylon is like a threshingfloor, it is time to thresh her: yet a little while, and the time of her harvest shall come'; *Hab.* iii 12; etc.). Thus M. may mean that God is *careful* that the final judgment, and the final reckoning with Satan, should

Of Ceres ripe for harvest waving bends
Her bearded grove of ears, which way the wind
Sways them; the careful ploughman doubting stands
Lest on the threshing floor his hopeful sheaves
Prove chaff. On the other side Satan alarmed
Collecting all his might dilated stood,
Like Teneriff or Atlas unremoved:
His stature reached the sky, and on his crest
Sat horror plumed; nor wanted in his grasp
What seemed both spear and shield: now dreadful deeds
Might have ensued, nor only Paradise

not be premature. It might even be maintained that the simile, by opening the theme of divine judgment followed up in the Scales image of ll. 997ff, actually contributes to an impression of God's secret transcendence.

iv *980. ported*] held diagonally across the body, in both hands. A military term, denoting the arms-drill position intermediate between 'shouldered' and 'charged' (levelled). It follows that the spears are not pointing towards Satan.

iv *981. Ceres* the goddess of agriculture is by metonymy put for 'corn'; so Virgil, *Georg.* i 297: *at rubicunda Ceres medio succiditur aestu.*

iv *985–7.* On Satan's dilation, see ll. 814–19*n*. The impressive stance is as usual bathetically punctured–here by the grumbling retreat of ll. 1014f. Broadbent 106 compares this metamorphosis with that of the devils into dwarfs in i 777–92, noting the recurrence of the peasant as a 'mundane intensifier of the supernatural change'. He rightly emphasises that such metamorphoses would have a ludicrous mock-epic quality for early readers; see i 777–92*n*. The present simile is double-edged; since Satan sustains the pressure of the angels as *Atlas* sustained the weight of the stars (for the angels as stars, see ll. 782–4*n*), but is also, like Atlas, a rebel against the supreme deity. The comparison with the Titan Atlas has already been made at ii 306. The mountain Atlas is not the Libyan range, but the far western range of Mauretania or Morocco. Because its summit was perpetually hidden by cloud, it was regarded as one of the pillars of Hercules or pillars of the sky. *Teneriff*] A pyramid-shaped mountain on the Canary island of the same name, estimated to be fifteen or even sixty miles high. 'With truth enough most of our *Travellers* and *Geographers* hold it to be the highest in the whole world' (Heylyn iv 88; and see v 758–9*n*). Notice how these Satanic sky-pillars to the west of Paradise are set over against the divine 'rocky pillars' to the east (see ll. 542–50*n*). *unremoved*] perhaps 'unremovable'; see l. 493*n*.

iv *988.* Cp. Homer's description of Strife, sister and friend of Ares the god of war: 'her crest is lowly at first, but afterwards she holds up her head in heaven, and her feet walk on earth' (*Il.* iv 441–3).

In this commotion, but the starry cope
Of heaven perhaps, or all the elements
At least had gone to wrack, disturbed and torn
With violence of this conflict, had not soon
The eternal to prevent such horrid fray
Hung forth in heaven his golden scales, yet seen

iv *992. cope*] sky, firmament, as in i 345, vi 215. The primary notion was 'canopy' (cp. iii 556) or 'vault, covering of vaulted form'; but the metaphor had long been a dead one.

iv *996*. Empson (112f) would rather have had the fray, on the grounds that scenery is unimportant when man's Fall is at stake. But M.'s God would have been reckless and partial if he had ignored the risk to other species inhabiting the *starry cope*. And besides, he is not interested in preventing the Fall by force; he has already explained in iii 90–133 about the degree of latitude to be allowed to Satan, in order that Adam's freedom may have real content. When Empson concludes 'that God was determined to make man fall, and had supplied a guard only for show' he slips into what M. himself in *De doctrina* i 2 calls 'anthropopathy' ('It is better . . . to contemplate the Deity, and to conceive of him, not with reference to human passions . . . forming subtle imaginations respecting him, but after the manner of Scripture': Columbia xiv 33). It is in one sense true that the angelic guard–like everything else that is less than divine–is unnecessary and 'only for show'; Gabriel indeed admits this at l. 1009. Still, they have ambassadorial dignity. And we are allowed to speculate that their interruption of Satan had critical significance, if he was to get in enough suggestion to be able later to tempt Eve, but not so much as to brainwash the freedom of choice out of her.

iv *997–1004*. A culmination in the development of the Balance image-complex, some of whose ramifyings have already been noted (see, e.g., ll. 354–5*n* and iii 555–61*n*; also Fowler ch. xii where similar cosmic Balance imagery in *The Faerie Queene* is discussed). Here the emphasis is on the Balance as a sign of God's predestinating justice. It is not that it shows the *sequel* [consequence] . . . *of fight* to be less advantageous for Satan, as Verity suggests, but that it shows God has decided against there being any fight at all. Homer's Zeus balances fates of death for the Trojans and Achaians in his golden scales at *Il.* viii 68–77, and for Hector and Achilles at *Il.* xxii 208–13 (imitated by Virgil at *Aen.* xii 725–7. Note that the first of these judgments is delivered at the critical hour of noon; see ll. 1013–15*n*). But in Homer the loser's scale sinks down to death, while in M. the inferior consequence rises, being 'found wanting'–an allusion to *Dan.* v 27, where writing on the wall tells Belshazzar 'Thou art weighed in the balances, and art found wanting'. The identification of God's Balance with the constellation Libra is not Homeric, though the idea of Libra as a 'righteous ballance' (Spenser, *F.Q.* V i 11) was certainly ancient; see Fowler 196. The visual effect of the identification is startling. For Satan himself has already been linked with the Serpent constellation, which at midnight (see 1013–5*n*)

Betwixt Astrea and the Scorpion sign,
Wherein all things created first he weighed,
The pendulous round earth with balanced air
In counterpoise, now ponders all events,
Battles and realms: in these he put two weights
The sequel each of parting and of fight;
The latter quick up flew, and kicked the beam;
Which Gabriel spying, thus bespake the fiend.
    Satan, I know thy strength, and thou know'st mine,
Neither our own but given; what folly then
To boast what arms can do, since thine no more
Than heaven permits, nor mine, though doubled now
To trample thee as mire: for proof look up,
And read thy lot in yon celestial sign
Where thou art weighed, and shown how light, how weak,

would lie immediately beneath the beam of Libra. Thus Gabriel's words have, besides their abstract sense, a concrete astronomical reference: the Serpent is 'weighed' (1012) on a cosmic scale. On Satan's identification with the constellation Anguis, the Serpent, see iii 555–61*n*.

iv *998*. Libra is the seventh sign of the zodiac, coming after Virgo and before Scorpio. It is appropriate to call Virgo *Astrea* in the Fallen world, since the just Astraea lived on earth during the Golden Age, but was later driven up to heaven by human wickedness, and is there *yet seen* stellified (see, e.g., Ovid, *Met.* i 149f, Spenser, *F.Q.* V i).

iv *999–1001*. For God's use of a balance in creation, *see* Job xxviii 24f: 'He looketh to the ends of the earth, and seeth under the whole heaven; To make the weight for the winds; and he weigheth the waters by measure'; also *Job* xxxvii 16, *Is.* xl 12. For his subsequent use of it, see *Is.* xl 15 ('nations . . . are counted as the small dust of the balance') *1 Sam.* ii 3 ('by him actions are weighed') and *Prov.* xvi 2 ('the Lord weigheth the spirits'). *ponders*] A pun ('weighs' and 'weighs up') but not a Latinism, for the concrete sense of the English word was still current in M.'s time.

iv *1010*. *trample thee as mire*] Cp. *Isa.* x 6: 'I will send him against an hypocritical nation . . . to tread them down like the mire of the streets.'

iv *1012*. Cp. *Dan.* v 27, 'TEKEL; Thou art weighed in the balances, and art found wanting.' Various attempts have been made to reconcile this line with ll. 1002–4, but it would seem that the weighing is quite differently understood by God, Gabriel and Satan. God, M. tells us, is really pondering the consequences of Satan's 'parting' and of his remaining to 'fight' (l. 1003). The consequence of parting is that Satan will be able to complete the temptation of Eve, thus occasioning the Fall, the Redemption, and eventually the Last Judgment. Against this is balanced the consequence of fight–presumably that Satan will be defeated at once, and that man's faith will remain untested. Since the pondering of this issue may well include question

If thou resist. The fiend looked up and knew
His mounted scale aloft: nor more; but fled
Murmuring, and with him fled the shades of night.

THE END OF THE FOURTH BOOK

about how many souls are to be saved at the last, it is pertinent to recall that in sacred iconography the Weighing of Souls–in a balance held by Michael and sometimes 'mounted' (l. 1014) by devils–had long been established as one of the main events of the Last Judgment (see Mâle 366, 376f). Gabriel, however, unless indeed he deliberately misapplies the omen in an exulting or gibing way, clearly fails to grasp how much it signifies; which is not surprising, in view of the strong probability that as yet he has had no news of the heavenly council on Predestination and the Fall (iii 80–343; iv 581f, 'since meridian hour / No creature thence'). For Gabriel the Balance is simply a sign of judgment upon Satan, who is being weighed and found wanting (the reference is to *Dan.* v 27: see ll. 997–1004*n*). As Pearce put it, 'the scale, in which lay the weight, that was the *sequel* of his *fighting*, by ascending show'd him that he was *light in arms*, and could not obtain victory', while the other scale 'was a sign that his going off quietly would be his wisest and weightiest attempt'. Satan's interpretation may not be different from Gabriel's, if we take *scale* (1014) as 'balance' (*OED* s.v. *Scale* sb.[1] II 4; cf. vi 245 below, 'long time in even scale / The battle hung'). But the more usual sense of *scale*, except in a few set phrases, was 'pan of a balance'; so that Satan may imagine that his destiny is being weighed against Gabriel's, in the Homeric (pagan) manner.

iv *1013–15*. Satan did not begin to flee at daybreak (as is usually said); for at ix 58 we are explicitly informed that he fled 'By night'. We should rather think of him as going immediately after midnight. At midnight the powers of light and darkness are for a moment in equal balance. Then the *shades of night* begin to flee, and they continue to do so during the six hours that intervene before sunrise. The state of the heavens confirms this interpretation for us, and would immediately communicate it to M.'s early readers. For Satan and the angels although on a mountain have to look *up* to see Libra (l. 1010, cp. l. 1014), so that Libra, it is to be assumed, is *hung forth* at or about the zenith. Now when the sun is in Aries, as here (see iii 555–61*n* and x 329*n*), the opposing sign Libra reaches the zenith at midnight. (At sunrise, on the other hand, Libra sets beneath the W. horizon, and Satan would not need to look up to see it.) The zenith is in any case appropriate, since it is the central position of judgment (see l. 30*n*, Panofsky 261f, Fowler 70–2). We recall also the tradition (traced in Mâle 368 to the *Elucidarium* of Honorius of Autun) that Christ the judge will appear at midnight, the same hour that saw the resurrection. For a discussion of M.'s numerological expression of the present midnight hour, see ll. 776–80*n*.

Paradise Lost

BOOK V

The Argument

Morning approached, Eve relates to Adam her troublesome dream; he likes it not, yet comforts her: they come forth to their day labours: their morning hymn at the door of their bower. God to render man inexcusable sends Raphael to admonish him of his obedience, of his free estate, of his enemy near at hand; who he is, and why his enemy, and whatever else may avail[1] Adam to know. Raphael comes down to Paradise, his appearance described, his coming discerned by Adam afar off sitting at the door of his bower; he goes out to meet him, brings him to his lodge, entertains him with the choicest fruits of Paradise got together by Eve; their discourse at table: Raphael performs his message, minds Adam of his state and of his enemy; relates at Adam's request who that enemy is, and how he came to be so, beginning from his first revolt in heaven, and the occasion thereof; how he drew his legions after him to the parts of the north, and there incited them to rebel with him, persuading all but only Abdiel a seraph, who in argument dissuades and opposes him, then forsakes him.

Now Morn her rosy steps in the eastern clime
Advancing, sowed the earth with orient pearl,
When Adam waked, so customed, for his sleep
Was airy light from pure digestion bred,

v *Argument* [1] *whatever else may avail*] It is important that Adam should be allowed the best indirect knowledge of evil, because his innocence was often regarded as one of the formal causes of the original sin (Howard 161–3).
v *1–2. Now Morn*] The morning of the twenty-fourth day of the poem's action; see Introduction, 'Chronology'. *rosy steps*] Cp. vi 2f, 'Morn . . . with rosy hand'; both passages imitate the Homeric description of Eos as ῥοδοδάκτυλος (*Il.* i 477). *orient pearl*] 'Pearl' has been taken to mean dew, which is 'orient' because brilliant and sparkling. But the use of the singular may indicate rather a reference to the lustrous grey rising light Morn throws before her; cp. *Ps.* xcvii 11 ('Light is sown for the righteous') and Lucretius, *De rerum nat.* ii 211 (*lumine conserit arva*). A pun with *orient*='eastern' is secondarily operative.
v *4–7.* Contrast the 'grosser sleep' bred of the 'exhilarating vapour bland' that is developed during digestion of the forbidden fruit (ix 1046–51). After the Fall *vapours*–exhalations rising from the stomach to the brain–came to be thought of as injurious; but this is before, and *bland* has its favourable sense: 'mild, genial, balmy'. Blandness was a characteristic of the sanguine temperament, the temperament Adam and Eve were believed to have had before the Fall; see Klibansky 62, 103ff, *et passim*.

And temperate vapours bland, which the only sound
Of leaves and fuming rills, Aurora's fan,
Lightly dispersed, and the shrill matin song
Of birds on every bough; so much the more
His wonder was to find unwakened Eve
With tresses discomposed, and glowing cheek,
As through unquiet rest: he on his side
Leaning half-raised, with looks of cordial love
Hung over her enamoured, and beheld
Beauty, which whether waking or asleep,
Shot forth peculiar graces; then with voice
Mild, as when Zephyrus on Flora breathes,
Her hand soft touching, whispered thus. Awake
My fairest, my espoused, my latest found,
Heaven's last best gift, my ever new delight,
Awake, the morning shines, and the fresh field
Calls us, we lose the prime, to mark how spring
Our tended plants, how blows the citron grove,

v *5–7*. The *only* (mere) sound of leaves, water and birds was enough to rouse Adam. The *fan* of *Aurora*, the goddess of morning, is the *leaves* not the *rills*: a word order common with M. *dispersed*] A gentler word than 'dispelled', which Bentley substituted.

v *15–17*. Ricks 91 argues that *soft* applies to *hand* as well as to *touching*; but see ix 385–6*n*. *peculiar graces*] graces all its own.

v *16*. Note the integration of unfallen man with his environment: Adam's vapours have had their counterparts in the *fuming rills*; now his whisper has its, in the wind. Zephyrus' sweet breath was supposed to produce flowers, as was that of his wife, the flower-goddess Flora, 'nymph of the blessed fields' (Ovid, *Fasti* v 197). For Zephyrus as the awakener of vegetation, see iv 329*n*; his son by Flora was Carpus (Fruit). Cp. also iv 500f, where Adam is cast in the role of Jupiter, progenitor of 'May flowers'. Eve's association with flowers is symbolic of the frailty of the flesh (see Valeriano 683 on *Imbecillitas humana*), but also of fertility. It is further developed in her Proserpina, Ceres and Pomona roles: see iv 269–71, ix 393–6, 426–32.

v *18–25*. Cp. *Song of Sol.* ii 10–3 and vii 12: 'Rise up, my love, my fair one, and come away. For... the fig tree putteth forth her green figs, and the vines with the tender grape give a good smell.... Let us get up early to the vineyards; let us see if the vine flourish, whether the tender grape appear, and the pomegranates bud forth'; though M. has substituted a different catalogue of natural beauties. *prime*, the first hour of the day, either began at six o'clock throughout the year, or else at the changing time of sunrise. In M.'s Paradise these alternative possibilities coincide, since before the Fall sunrise is always at six o'clock (see x 651–706*n*). In its ecclesiastical sense, prime was one of the Canonical Hours of the Divine Office. The relevance of this sense is shown by ll. 145ff. *blow*] flourish, blossom.

What drops the myrrh, and what the balmy reed,
How nature paints her colours, how the bee
Sits on the bloom extracting liquid sweet.
  Such whispering waked her, but with startled eye
On Adam, whom embracing, thus she spake.
  O sole in whom my thoughts find all repose,
My glory, my perfection, glad I see
Thy face, and morn returned, for I this night,
Such night till this I never passed, have dreamed,
If dreamed, not as I oft am wont, of thee,
Works of day past, or morrow's next design,
But of offence and trouble, which my mind
Knew never till this irksome night; methought
Close at mine ear one called me forth to walk
With gentle voice, I thought it thine; it said,
Why sleep'st thou Eve? Now is the pleasant time,
The cool, the silent, save where silence yields
To the night-warbling bird, that now awake
Tunes sweetest his love-laboured song; now reigns
Full-orbed the moon, and with more pleasing light

v *23. balmy reed*] For the poetic diction, cp. vii 321, 'corny reed'. The balm was a balsam-bearing tree belonging, like the *myrrh*, to the genus Balsamodendron. Both yielded aromatic resins used to soothe pain, heal wounds and prevent corruption; and from the time of Coverdale they had been associated in English translations of *Gen.* xxxvii 25: 'A company of Ishmeelites came from Gilead with their camels bearing spicery and balm and myrrh.' As the earliest balsam known, Balm of Gilead or True Balsam was an object of veneration.

v *34. offence*] In addition to the primary sense 'transgression', this could mean 'occasion of doubt'.

v *38.* Beautiful as it is, the love-song that follows appeals to unreason (notice 'ravishment' at l. 46), and may be compared with the kind of 'serenade' ridiculed by M. in iv 769f. It contrasts with the less exaggerated but more considerate true love displayed in Adam's speech in ll. 95–128 (Burden 130ff).

v *40–1.* Contrary to poetic convention the nightingale is masculine; not so much because it is in fact the cock bird that sings, as because this particular nightingale is correlated with Satan. For the passage is a travesty of *Song of Sol.* ii, where the awakener is likened to a dove. Cp. ll. 18–25 above, where the same text is imitated straight; also l. 48, where the relation between Adam and Satan his supplanter is made explicit. See H. Schultz, 'Satan's Serenade', *PQ* xxvii (1948) 17–26, esp. 24. Schultz plausibly connects the language of the amorous Satan with that of the fashionable Cavalier gallantry of his time.

Shadowy sets off the face of things; in vain,
If none regard, heaven wakes with all his eyes,
Whom to behold but thee, nature's desire,
In whose sight all things joy, with ravishment
Attracted by thy beauty still to gaze.
I rose as at thy call, but found thee not;
To find thee I directed then my walk;
And on, methought, alone I passed through ways
That brought me on a sudden to the tree
Of interdicted knowledge: fair it seemed,
Much fairer to my fancy than by day:
And as I wondering looked, beside it stood
One shaped and winged like one of those from heaven
By us oft seen; his dewy locks distilled
Ambrosia; on that tree he also gazed;
And O fair plant, said he, with fruit surcharged,
Deigns none to ease thy load and taste thy sweet,

v *43–5*. Satan works on the doubt he heard Eve express at iv 657f: 'for whom/ This glorious sight, when sleep hath shut all eyes?' *sets off*] makes conspicuous by contrast; but also 'shows to advantage, enhances'–Satan is already appealing to Eve's vanity.

v *44*. The eyes-of-heaven image was a familiar one: cp. Ariosto, *Orl. Fur.* xiv 99, Tasso, *Gerus. Lib.* xii 22 and Spenser, *F.Q.* III xi 45. Usually the eyes were witnesses to clandestine love; as in Catullus, *Carm.* vii 7f: *aut quam sidera multa, cum tacet nox, / furtivos hominum vident amores.* Here it may also be relevant that Satan was sometimes represented as a many-eyed Argus. *Ed I* has semicolon after *regard*.

v *45–90*. Briefly stating themes to be developed more subtly and in greater detail in the second temptation. Thus v 45–7 corresponds to ix 532–48, and v 67–81 to ix 679–732. Note, however, the great difference between the concluding phases (v 86–90 and ix 782–833): Eve's aerial flight on the former occasion more closely resembles the temptation of Christ. According to Waldock (33), Eve's dream constitutes the first phase in her fall. It is probably true (as Burden 129f suggests) that Satan needs the dream in order to instil into Eve an evil motion. According to Aristotle (*De anima* iii 3) sleep divests the mind of moral responsibility. But M. makes it quite explicit that having evil motions and feeling tempted does not mean being fallen.

v *53*. The real tree, as Burden 128ff emphasises, is not provocative. In dream, however, when judgment and reason are in abeyance, Satan can make its image provoke the desire to taste.

v *55–7*. M. alludes to Virgil's description of Venus leaving Aeneas outside Carthage: 'From her head her ambrosial tresses breathed celestial fragrance' (*Aen.* i 403f.) *Ambrosia*] Probably here referring to the fabled anointing oil of the gods. For other senses of the word, see ii 245*n*. For Satan's disguise as a good angel, see iii 634*n*.

Nor God, nor man; is knowledge so despised?
Or envy, or what reserve forbids to taste?
Forbid who will, none shall from me withhold
Longer thy offered good, why else set here?
This said he paused not, but with venturous arm
He plucked, he tasted; me damp horror chilled
At such bold words vouched with a deed so bold:
But he thus overjoyed, O fruit divine,
Sweet of thy self, but much more sweet thus cropt,
Forbidden here, it seems, as only fit
For gods, yet able to make gods of men:
And why not gods of men, since good, the more
Communicated, more abundant grows,
The author not impaired, but honoured more?
Here, happy creature, fair angelic Eve,
Partake thou also; happy though thou art,
Happier thou mayst be, worthier canst not be:
Taste this, and be henceforth among the gods
Thy self a goddess, not to earth confined,
But sometimes in the air, as we, sometimes

v *60. god*] spirit. See i 116–17*n* and iii 341*n*.

v *61.* Cp. ix 729. *reserve*] limitation, restriction, or knowledge kept secret, on the part of God; but perhaps also inhibition, self-restraint on the part of man.

v *67–8.* Lewis 67f observes that the fruit has intrinsic importance only for the poem's bad characters. Satan assumes that it will communicate knowledge magically.

v *70–81.* Emotive use of the term *god* is even more fully exploited in the second temptation: cp. ix 700–32. The Scriptural authority is *Gen.* iii 5: 'God doth know that in the day ye eat thereof, then your eyes shall be opened, and ye shall be as gods, knowing good and evil.'

v *73.* Empson 155 ingeniously argues that since Satan is despised in heaven at v 665 for the grudging impulse of feeling *impaired* (injured, lowered in rank), Eve 'may naturally conclude that [this feeling] cannot also actuate God; the argument of the mysterious voice is again confirmed'. But is this not to accept the *non sequitur* concealed by Satan's audacious rhetoric? Though God cannot be impaired by the cropping of fruit (nor indeed by anything else), it does not follow that all acts honour him.

v *74. happy*] See viii 282*n* for the ironic implications.

v *79–80.* Pearce noted that 'the words *as we* are so placed between the two sentences, as equally to relate to both'. *in the air*] So at *PR* i 39–42 and ii 117f the devils hold council in 'middle air' (see above i 515–16*n*). The idea stems from *Eph.* ii 2, where Satan is referred to as 'the prince of the powers of the air'. Cp. xii 454, where allusion to the same text is more direct. The doubt implied by the syntax 'whether he could go to Heaven himself

Ascend to heaven, by merit thine, and see
What life the gods live there, and such live thou.
So saying, he drew nigh, and to me held,
Even to my mouth of that same fruit held part
Which he had plucked; the pleasant savoury smell
So quickened appetite, that I, methought,
Could not but taste. Forthwith up to the clouds
With him I flew, and underneath beheld
The earth outstretched immense, a prospect wide
And various: wondering at my flight and change
To this high exaltation; suddenly
My guide was gone, and I, me thought, sunk down,
And fell asleep; but O how glad I waked
To find this but a dream! Thus Eve her night
Related, and thus Adam answered sad.
  Best image of my self and dearer half,
The trouble of thy thoughts this night in sleep
Affects me equally; nor can I like
This uncouth dream, of evil sprung I fear;
Yet evil whence? In thee can harbour none,
Created pure. But know that in the soul

shows a natural embarrassment in the disguised Satan' (Empson[2] 163). See further v 498–500*n*.

v *84–5. savoury smell*] At the second temptation the fruit again smells 'savoury' (ix 740f). This description depends on a serious pun. The primary meaning is that the fruit has an appetizing, fragrant scent (*OED* s.v. *Savoury*, 1). But 'savoury' could also mean 'spiritually edifying, full of spiritual savour' (*OED* 2b; thus literal interpretation is described as 'sometyme savory, sometyme bareyne' in *The myroure of oure Ladye*, EETS (1873) 49). For ungoverned appetite as the immediate cause of the Fall, see ix 740*n*.

v *87.* Angels can fly, but not men; therefore the very means of locomotion here is evil (Burden 117f). For a similar reason, knowledge about other worlds turns out to be forbidden knowledge (viii 121).

v *88.* 'Eve is allowed for a moment to "view all things at one view", like God' (MacCaffrey 61). Cp. iii 543 and see iii 59*n*.

v *89–92.* The unusual punctuation may be intended to express disturbed abruptness in Eve's speech, incoherence in relating a strange experience, or her dramatic rendering of the suddenness of Satan's departure.

v *94. sad*] grave, serious.

v *98. uncouth*] Perhaps 'strange' (*OED* 3), but in view of the continuation more probably 'unpleasant, distasteful, unseemly' (*OED* 4).

v *100–13. fancy*] M. may simply mean 'imagination': Coleridge's distinction between the two faculties was not usually observed at this time. The psychology involved here was common knowledge. Thus in Bar-

Are many lesser faculties that serve
Reason as chief; among these fancy next
Her office holds; of all external things,
Which the five watchful senses represent,
She forms imaginations, airy shapes,
Which reason joining or disjoining, frames
All what we affirm or what deny, and call
Our knowledge or opinion; then retires
Into her private cell when nature rests.

tholomew, 'the *Imaginative* vertue . . . is in the soule as the eye in the body, by beholding to receive the images that are offered unto it by the outward sences . . . Now after that the *Imagination* hath received the images . . . then doth it as it were prepare and digest them, either by joyning them together, or by separating them according as their natures require. They that distinguish *Imagination* from *Fantasie*, attribute this office to *Fantasie*' (*cit.* Svendsen 38). Cp. Burton, *Anatomy of Melancholy* I i 2 vii: 'Phantasy, or imagination . . . is an inner sense which doth more fully examine the species perceived by common sense, of things present or absent. . . . In time of sleep this faculty is free, and many times conceives strange, stupend, absurd shapes . . . it is subject and governed by reason, or at least should be.' Dr Johnson's comment on the present passage–'Adam's discourse of dreams seems not to be the speculation of a new-created being'–betrays ignorance of the Augustinian tradition that man's original righteousness included superhuman intellectual powers. See, e.g., Du Bartas, *Babilon, a part of the seconde weeke. Englished by W. L'Isle* (1595) 44f: 'Adam a man parfitly wise before he sinned ... enriched his language with all maner of ornaments that might be required to make it parfit: So that before his fall he spake more eloquently than any mortall man since . . . from him had we first our Arts and Sciences derived.' And cp. Goulart, *A Learned Summary Upon . . . Bartas*, tr. T. Lodge (1621) 136: 'Adam . . . had a great vivacity of spirit, to meditate and comprehend the nature of things.' On the theology underlying this notion, see Williams 361f.

v *104. represent*] bring before the mind; show.

v *109.* i.e., retires from the warm and dry front ventricle or *cellula phantastica* into the warm and moist middle-brain, the *cellula logistica.* On the psychological system implied here, see Klibansky 68f. A very familiar poetic rendering of the same system is given in the turret of Spenser's Castle of Alma (*F.Q.* II ix 47–58). *cell*] Not wholly metaphorical, for the word was regularly used for 'compartment of the brain'. Thus Burton calls the organ of the Imagination 'the middle cell of the brain' (*Anatomy of Melancholy* I i 2 vii). In Ficino's system, the topographical distribution of faculties within the brain (most usually *imaginatio, ratio* and *memoria*, in that order from front to back) is distinguished from a hierarchical division into *imaginatio, ratio* and *mens* (see Klibansky 265).

Oft in her absence mimic fancy wakes
To imitate her; but misjoining shapes,
Wild work produces oft, and most in dreams,
Ill matching words and deeds long past or late.
Some such resemblances methinks I find
Of our last evening's talk, in this thy dream,
But with addition strange; yet be not sad.
Evil into the mind of god or man
May come and go, so unapproved, and leave
No spot or blame behind: which gives me hope
That what in sleep thou didst abhor to dream,
Waking thou never wilt consent to do.
Be not disheartened then, nor cloud those looks
That wont to be more cheerful and serene
Than when fair morning first smiles on the world,
And let us to our fresh employments rise
Among the groves, the fountains, and the flowers
That open now their choicest bosomed smells
Reserved from night, and kept for thee in store.
So cheered he his fair spouse, and she was cheered,

v *115. our last evening's talk*] their discussion of the prohibition of the Tree of Knowledge (iv 421ff).
v *117–19. god*] Probably 'angel', in view of ll. 59 and 70. But M. (if not Adam) may also intend a reference to the doctrine that God's omniscience extends to evil. Hughes cites St Thomas Aquinas, *Summa theol.* I q 14 a 10: 'God would not know good things perfectly unless he knew evil things.' For an earlier play on different senses of *god*, see i 116f and *n*.
v *119–21.* Adam's speech brings into sharp focus a problem often raised by later books of the poem. Are we to believe, with Tillyard, that Eve, already anxious and troubled, is no longer innocent? Or does her dream only strengthen her resistance, and is Satan unable to do more than put ideas into her head? See Empson 149.
v *121.* Some copies *Ed I* have colon after *do*.
v *124. Than*] spelt 'Then', but probably indicating 'than': otherwise the rhythm would be awkward.
v *127. bosomed*] hidden, confined in the bosom; perhaps comparing the scent of the flowers with breath pent up, to be exhaled as Eve passes. Adam's compliment was a gallantry common in M.'s time. Cp. Marvell, 'Upon Appleton House' st. 38.
v *128.* A grim dramatic irony, for after the Fall 'the heavens and the earth ... are kept in store, reserved unto fire against the day of judgment' (2 *Pet.* iii 7).
v *129.* The diction is that of the A.V. Cp. *Jer.* xx 7.

But silently a gentle tear let fall
From either eye, and wiped them with her hair;
Two other precious drops that ready stood,
Each in their crystal sluice, he ere they fell
Kissed as the gracious signs of sweet remorse
And pious awe, that feared to have offended.
  So all was cleared, and to the field they haste.
But first from under shady arborous roof,
Soon as they forth were come to open sight
Of day-spring, and the sun, who scarce up risen
With wheels yet hovering o'er the ocean brim,
Shot parallel to the earth his dewy ray,
Discovering in wide landscape all the east
Of Paradise and Eden's happy plains,
Lowly they bowed adoring, and began
Their orisons, each morning duly paid

v *130–1.* The allusion to the typical repentant sinner Mary Magdalene (*Luke* vii 38: 'stood at his feet behind him weeping, and began to wash his feet with tears, and did wipe them with the hairs of her head') need not support the view that Eve is already partly fallen. It could imply instead a resemblance between the unfallen and the regenerate.

v *132–3.* Cp. Marvell, 'Eyes and Tears': especially sts. 3f (the preciousness of the tears), 8 (an allusion to the Magdalene), and 11 (the image of a 'double sluice').

v *136. all was cleared*] This slightly unusual expression implies a meteorological metaphor: 'all the trouble cleared up'.

v *137. arborous*] consisting of trees.

v *139. day-spring*] daybreak, dawn. The word was too common for one to be sure of an allusion to *Luke* i 78, 'the dayspring from on high hath visited us'.

v *142.* See ii 491*n*.

v *144.* Contrast xi 1–2. Whereas now Adam and Eve bow *lowly*, after the Fall they stand to pray–but in 'lowliest plight'.

v *145–52.* Often taken as a gibe at the Anglican Church's worship, on the strength of M.'s known antipathy to set liturgical forms (See *De doctrina* ii 4, Columbia xvii 85, and *Eikonoklastes* 16, Yale iii 503–8). But to read the lines in this sense is to diminish them and to ignore the fact that the orisons below are closely modelled on the liturgy. M.'s more positive meaning appears to be that prelapsarian prayers lack neither formal elaboration (*various style*) nor inspired spontaneity (*rapture*). Adam and Eve pray from the heart and 'have words from thir affections' (Yale iii 505). Similarly, it would be wrong to infer from the absence of *lute or harp* that M. dislikes the use of instrumental music in worship: indeed, he allows it even in the worship of the angels (e.g .vii 258 below). *numerous*] measured, rhythmic. *tunable*] tuneful, sweet-sounding.

In various style, for neither various style
Nor holy rapture wanted they to praise
Their maker, in fit strains pronounced or sung
Unmeditated, such prompt eloquence
Flowed from their lips, in prose or numerous verse,
More tuneable than needed lute or harp
To add more sweetness, and they thus began.
These are thy glorious works, parent of good,
Almighty, thine this universal frame,
Thus wondrous fair; thy self how wondrous then!
Unspeakable, who sit'st above these heavens
To us invisible or dimly seen
In these thy lowest works, yet these declare
Thy goodness beyond thought, and power divine:
Speak ye who best can tell, ye sons of light,
Angels, for ye behold him, and with songs
And choral symphonies, day without night,
Circle his throne rejoicing, ye in heaven,
On earth join all ye creatures to extol
Him first, him last, him midst, and without end.
Fairest of stars, last in the train of night,

v *151*. Some copies *Ed I* have comma after *harp*.

v *153–208*. The morning hymn is quasi-liturgical, being based on *Ps*. cxlviii and on the Canticle *Benedicite, omnia opera* (set for Matins in Lent in the 1549 Book of Common Prayer), in which angels, stars, light and darkness, and various meteorological entities are addressed, in the same sequence as here; see ll. 185–201*n* below. M. also echoes *Ps*. xix ('The heavens declare the glory of God; and the firmament sheweth his handywork'), which was set for Monday at Prime, the Office said at sunrise. According to one theory the day of the present passage is in fact Monday; see Introduction, 'Chronology'.

v *153*. Some copies *Ed I* omit comma after *works*.

v *154*. *frame*] Used of heaven, earth, or universe regarded as structures fabricated by God; e.g. Calvin, *Inst*. i 21, tr. T. Norton: 'The knowledge of God . . . in the frame of the world and all the creatures is . . . plainly set forth.'

v *156*. Some copies of *Ed I* have comma after *heavens*.

v *162*. M.'s heaven has twilight, but nothing darker: see ll. 642–6. *symphonies*] concerted or harmonious music in parts.

v *165*. Cp. *Rev*. i 11; also Jonson, *Masque of Augures* 444: 'Jove is that one, whom first, midst, last, you call.'

v *166–70*. The transition from circling angels to circling stars is a smooth one: see iv 782–4*n*. *Fairest of stars*] The planet Venus, which in western elongation rises in the east just before sunrise, and is known as the morning star (Lucifer, Phosphorus). Note that the astronomical events reviewed

If better thou belong not to the dawn,
Sure pledge of day, that crown'st the smiling morn
With thy bright circlet, praise him in thy sphere
While day arises, that sweet hour of prime.
Thou sun, of this great world both eye and soul,

here correspond–though in reverse order–to those of the procession of Evening (iv 593–609; here recalled by the phrase *train of night*). Newton imagined he had caught M. out, on the ground that Venus cannot be both a morning star and an evening star at the same date. But as usual M. proves a better astronomer than his critics have understood. On every occasion when Venus passes from eastern to western elongation during the hours of darkness, it will be the evening star on the evening immediately preceding the conjunction, and the morning star on the morning immediately following. (Conjunctions of Venus occur twice in each synodic period of 584 days.) This was well known in M.'s time and indeed long before. See, e.g., Riccioli i 661: 'Now we report another peculiar appearance of the same planet, most worthy of note, which occurs especially in extreme northern latitudes: namely, that on the same natural day it is seen in the evening a little after the setting of the sun, and is Hesperus, and the following morning it is seen in the morning a little before the rising of the sun, and is then Lucifer; because with the help of the northern latitude these events seem almost to coincide with the perigee of the epicycle' (citing Regiomontanus, Maurolycus *et al.*). According to Kepler, the double phenomenon could persist for as many as three days at a time. For additional evidence that Venus is at or near conjunction, see vii 366*n* below. Adam's calling on the star associated with Satan to praise God seems at first a very bitter dramatic irony. But it should be remembered that in pious tradition the identity of the Evening and Morning Stars was commonly a symbol of Christ's resurrection.

v *170. prime*] See 18–25*n* above. This reference to the first Day Hour immediately precedes the address to the sun, which traces its diurnal *course* in a way reminiscent of the psalm for Monday at Prime: *In sole posuit tabernaculum suum: et ipse tamquam sponsus procedens de thalamo suo: Exsultavit ut gigas ad currendam viam, a summo caelo egressio eius: Et occursus eius usque ad summum eius: nec est qui se abscondat a calore eius* (*Ps.* xix 4–6; Vulg. xviii 1).

v *171*. Renaissance writers were fond of describing the sun as an eye: cf., e.g., Spenser, *F.Q.* I iii 4, 'the great eye of heaven'; Shakespeare, Sonnet 18, 'eye of heaven'; Du Bartas, tr. Sylvester, I iv 551, 'Daies glorious Eye'. The metaphor was regarded as Orphic (Ficino, *De Sole* 6), though in fact it had a wide distribution in ancient authors: see Adams's note to Plato, *Rep.* 508B. It often implied a connection between seeing and understanding, and hence an identification of the sun with the creative word. For the eye as a symbol of divine omniscience, see Wind 186. The sun is *soul* of the world in the sense that it gives life. To many readers, the phrase would recall Orphic and Platonic solar mysticism, in which the animating power

Acknowledge him thy greater, sound his praise
In thy eternal course, both when thou climb'st,
And when high noon hast gained, and when thou
fall'st.
Moon, that now meet'st the orient sun, now fly'st
With the fixed stars, fixed in their orb that flies,
And ye five other wandering fires that move
In mystic dance not without song, resound
His praise, who out of darkness called up light.
Air, and ye elements the eldest birth

of the sun was dwelt upon. See, e.g., Ficino's commentary on Dionysius' *De divinis nominibus*: 'A single sun with a single light generates, nourishes, vivifies, moves, distinguishes and unites the natures of all sensible things.'
v *174*. *noon*] On the symbolic meaning attached to noon elsewhere in *PL*, see iv 30*n*. Here the reference is perhaps to the Church's traditional times of prayer. But M. does not necessarily mean the Canonical Hours (Lauds or Prime at sunrise, Sext at noon, Vespers at sunset; cp. the mention of 'prime' at l. 170). As early as St Cyprian (*De orat. Dom.*) sunrise and sunset had been added to the Apostolic Hours, which included noon.
v *176*. M.'s contemporaries had a reasonably good idea of stellar distances, so that the velocity of the sphere of fixed stars in a Ptolemaic daily revolution about the earth would have seemed to them almost incredible–a suitable marvel to be included in the hymn of Adam and Eve. See Riccioli i 419; also iv 592–7*n* above.
v *177*. Actually only four of the planets (Saturn, Jupiter, Mars, Mercury) remain to be mentioned, since Venus has already appeared at ll. 166–70. If the discrepancy is intentional, it may be designed as a correlate to the real doubt about whether the earth should be counted as a planet: cp. viii 128f, 'six thou seest, and what if seventh to these / The planet Earth'. Alternatively, the point may lie in an allusion to the correspondence between the planets and the *quaternion* (l. 181) of elements and humours. Traditionally Saturn was connected with earth (melancholy), Mars with fire (choler) and Jupiter with air (sanguine), so that Venus–also connected with air–is here *de trop*. However, the division of the planets into two chief luminaries and five others was so routine that M.'s phrase may have slipped in in casual obedience to it. *wandering*] Renders the etymological meaning of 'planet' (Gk πλανήτης): poetic diction.
v *178*. On the dance of the stars, see iii 579–81*n*. *not without*] Good English, but possibly also felt to correspond to the Latin idiom *non sine*, a litotes of which M. was particularly fond. *song*] i.e., the music of the spheres, inaudible now to fallen man's gross hearing (see *Arcades* 61–73).
v *180–2*. *quaternion*] The elements are not only four, but also a form of the *tetractys* or 'quaternion'. Adam here shows familiarity with Macrobius' explanation of the structure of the elements in terms of the Pythagorean theory of symbolic numbers (*In somn. Scip.* I vi 22–41). Macrobius also held

Of nature's womb, that in quaternion run
Perpetual circle, multiform; and mix
And nourish all things, let your ceaseless change
Vary to our great maker still new praise.
Ye mists and exhalations that now rise
From hill or steaming lake, dusky or grey,
Till the sun paint your fleecy skirts with gold,
In honour to the world's great author rise,
Whether to deck with clouds the uncoloured sky,
Or wet the thirsty earth with falling showers,
Rising or falling still advance his praise.
His praise ye winds, that from four quarters blow,
Breathe soft or loud; and wave your tops, ye pines,
With every plant, in sign of worship wave.
Fountains and ye, that warble, as ye flow,
Melodious murmurs, warbling tune his praise.
Join voices all ye living souls, ye birds,
That singing up to heaven gate ascend,
Bear on your wings and in your notes his praise;
Ye that in waters glide, and ye that walk

that the seven planets can be regarded as consisting of a group of three and a group of four; the latter group corresponding to the elements' quaternion or tetrad with two mean terms. For the transformation of the elements into one another, see Cicero, *De nat. deor.* ii 33: 'As there are four sorts of bodies, the continuance of nature is caused by their reciprocal changes; for the water arises from the earth, the air from the water, and the fire from the air; and reversing this order, the air arises from fire, the water from the air, and from the water the earth, the lowest of the four elements, of which all beings are formed. Thus by their continual motions . . . the conjunction of the several parts of the universe is preserved'. Cicero, like Adam, believes that the constitution of the elements is eternal, or at least 'of very long duration' (cp. *Perpetual*).

Air is named separately from the elements either (*a*) because the upper air, above the region of the elements, is meant (cp. iii 562*n*); or (*b*) because air was the element connected with the sanguine humour, and therefore most worthy of mention (sanguine was the uncorrupted specially human humour that prevailed in man before the Fall; see Klibansky 103, 105, 110); or most likely (*c*) in allusion to an obscure passage in Ovid (*Fasti* v 11) where the 'three elements'–excluding air–are mentioned as the entities that emerged after chaos.

v *185–201*. Cp. the Canticle *Benedicite, omnia opera*: 'O ye Winds of God . . . O ye Dews and Frosts . . . O ye Lighnings and Clouds . . . O all ye Green Things upon the Earth . . . O ye Wells, bless ye the Lord: praise him, and magnify him for ever.' See ll. 153–208*n* above.

v *193. breathe*] breath *Ed I*, corr. in *Errata*.

The earth, and stately tread, or lowly creep;
Witness if I be silent, morn or even,
To hill, or valley, fountain, or fresh shade
Made vocal by my song, and taught his praise.
Hail universal Lord, be bounteous still
To give us only good; and if the night
Have gathered aught of evil or concealed,
Disperse it, as now light dispels the dark.
So prayed they innocent, and to their thoughts
Firm peace recovered soon and wonted calm.
On to their morning's rural work they haste
Among sweet dews and flowers; where any row
Of fruit-trees over-woody reached too far
Their pampered boughs, and needed hands to check
Fruitless embraces: or they led the vine

v *205–19*. The concluding words of the hymn recall the Collect for the Eighth Sunday after Trinity: 'O God, whose never-failing providence ordereth all things both in heaven and earth: We humbly beseech thee to put away from us all hurtful things, and to give us those things which be profitable for us. . . .' This allusion gains point when one notices that the Gospel for the same day is *Matt.* vii 15–21, the conclusion of the Sermon on the Mount, which develops at some length a distinction between the fruit of 'good trees' and 'corrupt trees'. The inference would seem to be that the *rural work* of Adam and Eve is of a symbolic nature.

v *206–8*. Modelled, with l. *166*, on the Hymn *Somno refectis*, set in the Breviary for Monday at Matins in summer: *Cedant tenebrae lumini, / Et nox diurno sideri, / Ut culpa, quam nox intulit, / Lucis labascat munere.*

v *213*. *overwoody*] Probably 'excessively bushy'.

v *214*. *pampered*] Primarily 'overindulged'; but a secondary play on Fr. *pampre* ('leafy vine-branch', from Latin *pampinus*), noticed by Newton, may be Miltonic. Some authorities regarded the two words as etymologically related.

v *215–9*. The idea that the elm is wedded to the vine it supports is very ancient: Horace, *Odes* II xv 4 already takes its familiarity for granted. But the moral allegory of mutual dependence and complementary gifts, which ensured the popularity of the image in the Renaissance, seems to go back principally to Ovid, *Met.* xiv 661ff, Vertumnus' persuasion of Pomona to marry. The elm came to be an emblem of firm masculine strength, the vine of fruitfulness and feminine softness, submission and sweetness. Here the implication is that Adam and Eve are reunited after the division of Eve's dream. 'The stereotype rehearses in singularly appropriate sexual symbols an act which has an air of ritual about it' (Svendsen 134). Cp. *Dam* 65, Horace, *Epodes* ii 9, Virgil, *Georg.* ii 367, Tasso, *Gerus. Lib.* iii 75, Spenser, *F.Q.* I i 8 and instances in Bartholomew, Batman and Maplet, *cit.* Svendsen 271*n*. Nowhere is the metaphor given a physically sexual application. See also

To wed her elm; she spoused about him twines
Her marriageable arms, and with her brings
Her dower the adopted clusters, to adorn
His barren leaves. Them thus employed beheld
With pity heaven's high king, and to him called
Raphael, the sociable spirit, that deigned
To travel with Tobias, and secured
His marriage with the seven-times-wedded maid.
Raphael, said he, thou hear'st what stir on earth
Satan from hell scaped through the darksome gulf
Hath raised in Paradise, and how disturbed
This night the human pair, how he designs
In them at once to ruin all mankind.
Go therefore, half this day as friend with friend
Converse with Adam, in what bower or shade
Thou find'st him from the heat of noon retired,
To respite his day-labour with repast,
Or with repose; and such discourse bring on,
As may advise him of his happy state,
Happiness in his power left free to will,
Left to his own free will, his will though free,
Yet mutable; whence warn him to beware
He swerve not too secure: tell him withal
His danger, and from whom, what enemy
Late fallen himself from heaven, is plotting now
The fall of others from like state of bliss;
By violence, no, for that shall be withstood,
But by deceit and lies; this let him know,
Lest wilfully transgressing he pretend
Surprisal, unadmonished, unforewarned.

J. Brown, *PMLA* lxxi (1956) 16f and L. Lerner, *EC* iv (1954) 305 (one 'of the most strikingly sexual passages in *Paradise Lost*').

v *221–3*. See iv 166–71*n*. The name *Raphael*, 'Health of God', is Biblical (e.g. *Tob.* iii 17). Raphael was one of the four archangels who formed God's cosmic chariot (iii 648*n* above); in the cabbalistic fusion of planetary with angelic deities he was sometimes jovial, sometimes solar. Apparently he is the appropriate archangel to choose for a mission that involves marital relations; perhaps because his role is to effect a right psychological adjustment ('*Mixtum ex iis medicina et temperamentum Raphael*': Valeriano 549).

v *229*. So at *Exod.* xxxiii 11 'The Lord spake unto Moses face to face, as a man speaketh unto his friend.'

v *235–7*. For a fuller development of the theology underlying this portrayal of man as 'sufficient to have stood' see iii 96–125 above.

v *237–8*. i.e., 'to be careful not to err through overconfidence' (*secure* = careless).

So spake the eternal Father, and fulfilled
All justice: nor delayed the winged saint
After his charge received; but from among
Thousand celestial ardours, where he stood
Veiled with his gorgeous wings, up springing light
Flew through the midst of heaven; the angelic choirs
On each hand parting, to his speed gave way
Through all the empyreal road; till at the gate
Of heaven arrived, the gate self-opened wide
On golden hinges turning, as by work
Divine the sovereign architect had framed.
From hence, no cloud, or, to obstruct his sight,

v *246–7. fulfilled / All justice*] Scriptural diction; cp. *Matt.* iii 15, 'thus it becometh us to fulfil all righteousness'. The application of *saint* to angel is also a Biblical usage; see *Jude* 14, and *Deut.* xxxiii 2: 'The Lord . . . shined forth from mount Paran, and he came with ten thousands of saints.' To be distinguished is *saints*='the Elect' (e.g. iii 330 above).
v *248. After . . . received*] Imitates a Latin construction; cp. i 573.
v *249. ardours*] Concretely 'flames', figuratively, 'zeals, fervours'. Thyer may have been right in regarding the word as a variant of 'seraphim' (see ii 512*n* above); but *Ps.* civ 4 suggests that any spirit could be regarded as 'a flaming fire'.
v *253. empyreal*] M. always stresses the second syllable of the adjectival form.
v *254–6.* So at *Acts* xii 10 St Peter and an angel 'came unto the iron gate that leadeth unto the city; which opened to them of his own accord'. Cp. also Homer, *Il.* v 749, where the gates of heaven open automatically for Hera. Addison, not appreciating the potential range of technological possibility, felt the need for a stiff, solemn defence of M. against the charge that he allows the marvellous 'to lose sight of the probable'. But only the squarest critics have ever objected to the science-fiction element in poetry. Poetry itself has always abounded with ingenious automata: see, e.g. Homer, *Od.* viii 555ff, Ariosto, *Orl. Fur.* xxx 10f and Spenser, *F.Q.* II vi 5 (self-propelled boats), and Homer, *Il.* xviii 376 (automatic tripods). M. probably had more centrally in view, however, the mystical machinery of *Ezek.* i, to which he makes extensive allusion in the following book. Cp. also vii 203–8.
v *257–61.* The mimetically *interposed* clauses make the syntax difficult. *however . . . sees,* though it secondarily relates to *cloud* or *star*, primarily relates to *Earth*. The point of view is meant to be startling–to Raphael earth might be thought unlike *other shining globes* not because larger, but because smaller. Cp. Eve's fond hope at ix 811–3 that she is invisible from heaven; and see *Job* xxii 13: 'How doth God know? Can he judge through the dark cloud?'
v *257.* Some copies *Ed I* begin a new paragraph at *From*, and omit comma after *cloud*.

Star interposed, however small he sees,
Not unconform to other shining globes,
Earth and the garden of God, with cedars crowned
Above all hills. As when by night the glass
Of Galileo, less assured, observes
Imagined lands and regions in the moon:
Or pilot from amidst the Cyclades
Delos or Samos first appearing kens
A cloudy spot. Down thither prone in flight
He speeds, and through the vast ethereal sky
Sails between worlds and worlds, with steady wing
Now on the polar winds, then with quick fan
Winnows the buxom air; till within soar

v *261–3*. Contrast i 286–91, where there was no question of the lunar surface features being imaginary. *glass / Of Galileo*] telescope.

v *264–6*. The Cyclades, a circular group of islands in the S. Aegean (Gk κύκλος, circle), corresponds in shape to the whole *globe* of Earth. *Delos*] 'Floating once' (x 296), was fixed among the Cyclades to provide a birthplace for Apollo and Diana; the whole island was anciently held in great reverence and elaborate precautions were taken to keep it free from pollution. *Samos*] Not among the Cyclades. It resembles Delos only in that Juno was born there, and married there to Jupiter; so that each island is a mythic analogue to Eden. Raphael's unimpeded vision resembles the pilot's glimpse of *a cloudy spot* in the extremity of the range. Note also that whereas Satan is repeatedly compared to a trader Raphael is compared to a navigator.

v *266–70*. Finely emulating the earthward plunges of Mercury in Virgil, *Aen.* iv 238–58 and of Michael in Tasso, *Gerus. Lib.* ix 60–2. Cp. also the descent of Satan between worlds at iii 562–90 above, where scale is similarly conveyed by an image of telescopic observation. 'The effect is at once to expand our attention toward the significant regions beyond Earth, and to contract it upon small, significant Paradise, as these spoke-like paths converge for their struggle' (MacCaffrey 63). *prone*] downward sloping. *fan*] A poetic word for 'wing' (cp. ii 927 above); *winnows* adds an allusion to the apocalyptic winnowing fan of judgment at *Matt.* iii 12. *buxom*] yielding.

v *270–4*. Every 500 years the legendary *phoenix* used to build a pyre or nest of spices (cp. ll. 292f) on which it yielded up its life; whereupon a new phoenix would grow from the marrow of its bones, and would fly to Heliopolis, the City of the Sun, to deposit its *relics* (Ovid, *Met.* xv 391–407, Pliny, *Nat. hist.* x 2). Starnes and Talbert (272f) show that according to Renaissance dictionaries the names *Heliopolis* and *Egyptian* [i.e. not Boeotian] *Thebes* were interchangeable; also that the phoenix was described as *aquilae magnitudine*. It was *unica semper avis* (Ovid, *Amores* II vi 54; cf. *Dam* 187) because there was never more than one alive at a time. In Christian symbolism

Of towering eagles, to all the fowls he seems
A phoenix, gazed by all, as that sole bird
When to enshrine his relics in the sun's
Bright temple, to Aegyptian Thebes he flies.
At once on the eastern cliff of Paradise
He lights, and to his proper shape returns
A seraph winged; six wings he wore, to shade

the bird was an emblem of the triumph of eternal life over death, as well as of regeneration; while in secular iconography it signified uniqueness, or virtuous constancy (Tervarent 304f); or (since according to Lactantius' *De ave phoenice* it was sexless or hermaphroditic) ideal true love. See Jean Hubay and Maxime Leroy, *Le Mythe du Phénix*, Bibliothèque de la Faculté de Philosophie et Lettres de L'Université de Liège lxxxii (1939); F. J. Kermode, 'On Shakespeare's Learning', Wesleyan Univ. Centre for Advanced Studies Monday Evening Papers 2 (1965); Ripa s.v. *Resurrettione*; and Camerarius' Embl. '*Vita mihi mors est*'. Proverbially 'a faithful friend is like a phoenix' (see Whaler, *PMLA* xlvii (1932) 545). Thus Raphael resembles the phoenix in that he is a friend of man (cp. ix 2); a marriage counsellor (v 221–3); unique among eagle-sized creatures flying in that area; and bound for a consecrated solar shrine (ll. 264–6*n*; iv 268–85*nn*); but principally in that he manifests the virtue of the Elect. M. uses the phoenix myth also at *SA* 1699–1707.

v *271. towering*] The *Ed I* and *Ed II* spelling 'towring' does not distinguish between 'towering' = rising high in flight, and 'touring' = turning, wheeling. Cp. xi 185 and see *n*.

v *275*. The only gate of Paradise is on the eastern side (iv 178). Raphael's entry by the gate contrasts with Satan's climbing like a 'thief into God's fold' (iv 178–92) – a contrast for which foundation has already been laid by the introduction of the story of Tobias and Raphael at iv 170.

v *277–85*. Cp. the seraphim of *Is.* vi 2: 'Each one had six wings; with twain he covered his face, and with twain he covered his feet, and with twain he did fly.' *regal*] Implies that the first pair of wings is purple (cp. xi 241 below); the second is *gold*; while the third is *sky-tinctured*. All these colours together with the description *downy*, seem to have been taken from the elaborate account of the plumage of the phoenix in Pliny; perhaps via Robert Estienne's dictionary (Starnes 273f). *lineaments*] the shape of his body generally. *starry zone*] cp. Michael's belt, which is compared to 'a glistering zodiac' at xi 247. *mail*] A comparison between the overlapping feathers of the wing and the scales of jazerant-work armour. *sky-tinctured grain*] tinctured sky-blue 'in grain'; fast dyed. Implying permanence, but also perhaps richness, of colour. See Cowley, *Davideis* i *n* 60: '*Sacred Blew*. Because of the use of it in the *Curtains* of the *Tabernacle*, the Curtain for the Door, the *Vail*, the *Priests Ephod*, *Breast-Plate*, and briefly all sacred Ornaments. The reason of chusing *Blew*, I suppose to have been in the *Tabernacle* to represent the seat of *God*, that is, the *Heavens*, of which the

His lineaments divine; the pair that clad
Each shoulder broad, came mantling o'er his breast
With regal ornament; the middle pair
Girt like a starry zone his waist, and round
Skirted his loins and thighs with downy gold
And colours dipped in heaven; the third his feet
Shadowed from either heel with feathered mail
Sky-tinctured grain. Like Maia's son he stood,
And shook his plumes, that heavenly fragrance filled
The circuit wide. Straight knew him all the bands
Of angels under watch; and to his state,
And to his message high in honour rise;
For on some message high they guessed him bound.
Their glittering tents he passed, and now is come
Into the blissful field, through groves of myrrh,

Tabernacle was an *Emblem*, Numb. 15.38. The Jews are commanded to make that lace or ribband of *Blew*, wherewith their fringes are bound to their cloaths; and they have now left off the very wearing of Fringes; because, they say, the art is lost of dying that kind of *Blew*, which was the perfectest sky-colour.'

v *285–7. Maia's son*] Mercury, the ambassador of the gods and giver of grace, whose noble stance is similarly focused on in *Hamlet* III iv 58f: 'A station like the herald Mercury / New-lighted on a heaven-kissing hill.' See ll. 266–70*n* above. The shaking of the wings, but not the resultant fragrance, had been anticipated in Fairfax's description of Gabriel's landing on Earth (*Gerus. Lib.* i 14 – in Tasso the wings are only readjusted or smoothed).

v *288. state*] rank or degree.

v *289–90. message*] mission, errand.

v *292–4. blissful field*] Recalls the Elysian fields, home of the blessed, which were described in Renaissance dictionaries as full of the odours of sweet spices, and which have already provided a model for M.'s Paradise (see iv 153*n*, 159–66*n*). Cp. also the fragrant groves and mountains 'full of choice nard and fragrant trees and cinnamon and pepper' in the Garden of Righteousness visited by Enoch and Raphael (*Enoch* xxxii; not accessible to M.). *myrrh*] According to Henry Hawkins (*Partheneia sacra*, 1633, *cit.* Broadbent 183) a prophylactic against devils. *flowering odours*] Bentley, Pearce, Richardson and Ricks (95) treat this phrase as a daring hypallage for 'odorous flowers'; speaking of the 'beautifully [or disgustingly, as the case may be] unexpected substantiality of the scents'. But if there is any hypallage at all here, it is faint in the extreme; for in M.'s time 'odour' was regularly used to mean a 'substance that emits a sweet smell . . . spice . . . odoriferous flower' (*OED* 2). Cp. Prior, 'If wine and music': 'Thy Myrtles strow, thy Odours burn.' *cassia*] a cinnamon-like spice; an ingredient in the holy oil used to anoint the Tabernacle (*Exod.* xxx 24). *nard*] the ointment poured over Jesus' head to anoint him 'to the burying' (*Mark* xiv 3,

And flowering odours, cassia, nard, and balm;
A wilderness of sweets; for nature here
Wantoned as in her prime, and played at will
Her virgin fancies, pouring forth more sweet,
Wild above rule or art; enormous bliss.
Him through the spicy forest onward come
Adam discerned, as in the door he sat
Of his cool bower, while now the mounted sun
Shot down direct his fervid rays to warm
Earth's inmost womb, more warmth than Adam needs;
And Eve within, due at her hour prepared
For dinner savoury fruits, of taste to please
True appetite, and not disrelish thirst
Of nectareous draughts between, from milky stream,

8; cp. iv 542–50*n* above). The association of the two was fairly common: cp. *Comus* l. 991 and Tasso, *Gerus. Lib.* tr. Fairfax xv 53 (Armida's isle of bliss). *balm*] (see l. 23*n* above), prominent during Satan's entry of Paradise (iv 159, 248).

v *294–7. played*] represented or imitated in sport (*OED* III 16 c, citing Lamb: 'the noises of children, playing their own fancies'. *sweet*] sweetly. *above . . . art*] Arts, though intended to repair the Fall, can never quite attain the original level of uncorrupted nature. *enormous*] 'deviating from ordinary rule' (Lat. *norma*); but probably influenced also by the modern meaning 'immense'. Note that the punctuation makes it clear that *enormous bliss* is in apposition to the rest of the sentence, and not the object of *pouring*. *Wantoned*] An ominous word; here it is still innocent; but 'it is not long after the Fall that Adam and Eve become liable to the grimmer meaning [i.e. at ix 1015]' (Ricks 112).

v *299–300*. Adam's entertainment of Raphael is throughout modelled on Abraham's entertainment of three angels in *Gen.* xviii. Here cp. *Gen.* xviii i: 'And the Lord appeared unto him in the plains of Mamre: and he sat in the tent door in the heat of the day.'

v *301. direct*] Since the ecliptic and equatorial planes coincided before the Fall, 'direct' implies that Paradise is situated on the line. See iv 209–16*n*. Some copies *Ed I* have comma after *rays*.

v *302*. For the penetration of the sun's rays beneath the surface of the earth, see iii 608–12*n* above. *needs*] Some copies *Ed I* have *need* and omit semicolon after it.

v *303. due*] duly. After the Fall, by contrast, time's 'measure' falters, and Eve is late (ix 844–56).

v *304. savoury*] appetizing in odour. See ll. 84–5*n* above.

v *306–7. milky*, often applied to the juices of fruits, probably here qualifies *berry* and *grape* as well as *stream*. Used of water, it seems to have meant 'sweet': cp. *SA* 550. The allusion to the Promised Land 'flowing with milk and honey' (*Josh.* v 6) was not so obvious, perhaps, as it seems now.

Berry or grape: to whom thus Adam called.
Haste hither Eve, and worth thy sight behold
Eastward among those trees, what glorious shape
Comes this way moving; seems another morn
Risen on mid-noon; some great behest from heaven
To us perhaps he brings, and will vouchsafe
This day to be our guest. But go with speed,
And what thy stores contain, bring forth and pour
Abundance, fit to honour and receive
Our heavenly stranger; well we may afford
Our givers their own gifts, and large bestow
From large bestowed, where nature multiplies
Her fertile growth, and by disburdening grows
More fruitful, which instructs us not to spare.
To whom thus Eve. Adam, earth's hallowed mould,
Of God inspired, small store will serve, where store,
All seasons, ripe for use hangs on the stalk;
Save what by frugal storing firmness gains
To nourish, and superfluous moist consumes:
But I will haste and from each bough and brake,
Each plant and juiciest gourd will pluck such choice
To entertain our angel guest, as he
Beholding shall confess that here on earth
God hath dispensed his bounties as in heaven.
So saying, with dispatchful looks in haste

v *318–20.* An argument distorted and misapplied as a justification for libertinism in *Comus* 710–29.

v *322.* Picking up Adam's inappropriate choice of word at l. 314, Eve sarcastically plays on *store*='cache' and 'abundance'.

v *321.* See *Gen.* ii 7: 'The Lord God formed man of the dust of the ground.' Eve perhaps shows herself familiar with an etymology later noted by Josephus and repeated in Renaissance dictionaries such as Calepino's, whereby Adam (Hebrew 'Red') was supposed to get his name from the red earth of which he was made.

v *324–5.* They only store food that improves in firmness or dryness by keeping. Thyer thought *superfluous moist* too philosophical for Eve, but it seems quite appropriate for an intelligent woman to have technical knowledge about food storage. Eve was in no position to leave such things to the servants.

v *326–7.* The sources of produce fall into four classes: fruit trees, bushes, small plants like the strawberry and cucurbitaceous climbers like the melon. *gourd*] Perhaps specific enough to constitute an allusion to *Jonah* iv 6–10, where a gourd enjoyed then destroyed by a worm is a type of the corruption of mankind.

v *328. as*] that.

She turns, on hospitable thoughts intent
What choice to choose for delicacy best,
What order, so contrived as not to mix
Tastes, not well joined, inelegant, but bring
Taste after taste upheld with kindliest change,
Bestirs her then, and from each tender stalk
Whatever Earth all-bearing mother yields
In India east or west, or middle shore
In Pontus or the Punic coast, or where
Alcinous reigned, fruit of all kinds, in coat,
Rough, or smooth rined, or bearded husk, or shell
She gathers, tribute large, and on the board
Heaps with unsparing hand; for drink the grape
She crushes, inoffensive must, and meaths

v *335*. Such tastes as, if they were not well joined, would be inelegant. But *inelegant* = 'inelegantly' gives a secondary chain of discourse. The present passage is horribly travestied after the Fall, at ix 1017f. At least one copy of *Ed I* has semicolon after *Tastes*.

v *336*. *upheld*] sustained without impairment. *kindliest*] most natural. At least one copy of *Ed I* has semicolon after *change*.

v *338*. Rendering the ancient titles *Παμμῆτορ γῆ* and *Omniparens*.

v *339–41*. Eden's produce is, first, geographically comprehensive. It includes fruits later to be grown in India and the surrounding islands to the east, in America to the west, and on the coasts of seas in between: namely *Pontus*, the south shore of the Black Sea, Tunis, the *Punic* or Carthaginian south shore of the Mediterranean and (between these north and south limits) Scheria, the Phaeacian island paradise of *Alcinous*. (Notice the Baroque centralised pattern: India–coast–island–coast–India.) Secondly, the places named were anciently famous for their fruit. Thus *Pontus* gave its name to rhubarb and to a variety of hazel-nut; Carthage was famous for its figs; and the gardens of Alcinous are described as perpetually fruitful in Homer, *Od.* vii 113–21. But the passage also contains a grim irony. For Pontus was notorious as a source of poisons (Virgil, *Ecl.* viii 96), and the thing best known about Punic figs was the threat to Rome they symbolized in an anecdote of Plutarch's (*Life of M. Cato* xxvii 1 (352): the elder Cato shook an African fig from his sleeve onto the floor of the Senate, and when it was admired said 'The country that produced it is three days' sailing from Rome.'). Paradise is again compared with the garden of Alcinous at ix 440f below.

v *342*. *smooth rined*] smooth-rinded. *Rough . . . rined*] Distinguishes the two classes of *coat*.

v *344–9*. Note how the catalogue of foods is combined with a progression through the stages of preparing a meal.

v *345*. *must*] the unfermented juice of the grape. Intoxicating wine has to be excluded because its origin was connected with rebellion against God. Thus

From many a berry, and from sweet kernels pressed
She tempers dulcet creams, nor these to hold
Wants her fit vessels pure, then strews the ground
With rose and odours from the shrub unfumed.
Mean while our primitive great sire, to meet
His godlike guest, walks forth, without more train
Accompanied than with his own complete
Perfections, in himself was all his state,
More solemn than the tedious pomp that waits
On princes, when their rich retinue long
Of horses led, and grooms besmeared with gold

the priests of Isis were forbidden to drink it 'for wine they say is blood, / Even the bloud of Gyants, which were slaine, / By thundring Iove in the Phlegrean plaine' and drinking it might 'stirre up old rebellious thought' (Spenser, *F.Q.* V vii 10f, drawing on Plutarch, *De Iside* 353B–C). Moreover, intoxication was a favourite symbol for the disturbance of rational control caused by the Fall. See, e.g., St Bernard *Sermones in Cantica Canticorum* ix 9f on 'the pleasures of the flesh, with which we were formerly enthralled and intoxicated as with wine'. Carnal desires are like wine because the grape 'once pressed has nothing more to yield'. A woman crushing grapes was also a common emblem of Excess. Cp., e.g., Spenser's Dame Excess (*F.Q.* II xii 55f); and a mural at Culross Palace, Fife, with the legend MIHI PONDERA LUXUS'. *meath*] mead; here used poetically to mean simply 'a sweet drink'. Contrast the present passage with ix 793, where the fallen Eve is 'heightened as with wine'.

v *347. tempers*] mixes–though the word has psychological overtones, in that it draws attention to the emblematic value of the foods (see l. 345*n*). *dulcet*] sweet, soothing, bland.

v *348.* Even the utensils seem moralized. Cp., e.g., *1 Thess.* iv 4: 'every one of you should know how to possess his vessel in sanctification and honour'; and *Is.* lxvi 20: 'The children of Israel bring an offering in a clean vessel into the house of the Lord.' The presence of utensils in a Paradise innocent of technological development is explained at iv 335.

v *349. unfumed*] At this holy supper there is no trace of papistical incense–only the natural scent of the shrub. In any case the shrub could not have been fumed, because Adam and Eve are as yet guiltless of fire. See l. 396*n*, ix 387–92*n*, x 1078–81*n*. *odours*] spices, odoriferous flowers; see ll. 292–4*n*.

v *353.* On an alleged absence of 'character' in Adam before the Fall, see Broadbent 191f, where the present passage is discussed. *state*] dignity.

v *355. retinue*] Accented on the second syllable.

v *356. besmeared with gold*] Cp. e.g. Horace, *Odes* IV ix 14f: '*aurum vestibus illitum . . . regalisque cultus.* A note in the Columbia MS reads: 'English Phrases derivd from the Latine tongue &c: A Coat *bedaubd* with Gold &c. Virgil: Per Tunicam squalentem Auro. The words seem to be alike improper;

Dazzles the crowd, and sets them all agape.
Nearer his presence Adam though not awed,
Yet with submiss approach and reverence meek,
As to a superior nature, bowing low,
 Thus said. Native of heaven, for other place
None can than heaven such glorious shape contain;
Since by descending from the thrones above,
Those happy places thou hast deigned a while
To want, and honour these, vouchsafe with us
Two only, who yet by sovereign gift possess
This spacious ground, in yonder shady bower
To rest, and what the garden choicest bears
To sit and taste, till this meridian heat
Be over, and the sun more cool decline.
 Whom thus the angelic virtue answered mild.
Adam, I therefore came, nor art thou such
Created, or such place hast here to dwell,
As may not oft invite, though spirits of heaven
To visit thee; lead on then where thy bower
O'ershades; for these mid-hours, till evening rise
I have at will. So to the silvan lodge
They came, that like Pomona's arbour smiled

but the Latin is thus vindicated by Servius; and from thence our Phrase arises *Squalens*, significat copiam densitatemque auri, in *Squammosum* spolium nitenti. Quicquid igitur nimis inculcatum obsitumque aliqua re erat, ut incuteret videntibus facie nova horrorem id squalere dicebatur. Vid: Macrob: Lib: 6. Cap. 7.' (Columbia xviii 226).

v *358–71* Contrast the opening of the interview with Michael at xi 249ff. With the first words of Adam here, cp. Aeneas' famous greeting of his mother Venus: *O–quam te memorem, virgo? namque haud tibi voltus / mortalis, nec vox hominem sonat; o dea certe!* (Virgil, *Aen.* i 327ff).

v *359*. *submiss*] submissive.

v *365*. *want*] feel the loss of, miss (*OED* 2 f).

v *366*. *sovreign*] spelt 'sov'ran'; see i *246n*.

v *371*. Perhaps only a figurative way of saying 'the angel' (as Homer puts 'Priam's strength' for 'Priam' at *Il.* iii 105). But more likely 'as a seraph or one of the supreme rank in the heavenly hierarchy, Raphael may have the title of any of the inferior orders, of which the *Virtues* were one' (Hughes). At vii 41, similarly, Raphael is an archangel.

v *374*. The ellipsis calls for some such expansion as 'invite guests, even if they are spirits. . . .'

v *378–84*. Burden 71 draws attention to the care with which M. discriminates between the ways in which Eve is like and unlike Pomona, her arbour and Venus. The distinctions drawn amplify the spiritual character of Eve's

With flowerets decked and fragrant smells; but Eve
Undecked, save with her self more lovely fair
Than wood-nymph, or the fairest goddess feigned
Of three that in Mount Ida naked strove,
Stood to entertain her guest from heaven; no veil
She needed, virtue-proof, no thought infirm
Altered her cheek. On whom the angel Hail
Bestowed, the holy salutation used
Long after to blest Marie, second Eve.
Hail mother of mankind, whose fruitful womb

adornment (nakedness symbolized sincere virtue) and her historical reality (not *feigned* or mythological).

v *378–81*. The Roman *wood-nymph Pomona* presided over gardens and especially fruit trees. An analogy between Eve and Pomona is drawn again at ix 394f; but by then the goddess of fruitfulness is imminently threatened and in flight. *undecked . . . herself*] Eve is repeatedly identified with symbolically fair or fragile flowers; cp., e.g., iv 270, and ix 432, 'Eve though fairest unsupported flower'.

v *381–2*. The three goddesses Juno Minerva and Venus all claimed the apple of Strife inscribed TO THE FAIREST, and the mortal Paris, famed for his wisdom, was appointed arbiter. The judgment of Paris was delivered on Mount Ida, where the goddesses appeared before him naked and without ornament. But the simile has also a more ironic application. For Paris' fatal choice of the beauty offered by Venus led to the rape of Helen and eventually to the destruction of Troy, which is for M. a mythic analogue to the Fall of man (see i 1–94*n*). The inference is that, in respect of virtue, Adam is like, but Raphael unlike, Paris. Raphael, indeed, corresponds rather to Mercury, who is commonly present in representations of the Judgment of Paris (see, e.g., the painting by the Paris Master in the Fogg Museum, Harvard). For Raphael's Mercury role in *PL*, see ll. 266–70*n*, 285–7*n*.

v *384*. *virtue-proof*] invulnerable through her virtue. But the expected meaning, on the analogy of other such compounds (e.g. shot-proof), is difficult to exclude, and must have occurred to M–proof against virtue. Proof, then, against Raphael, *the angelic virtue* (l. 371)? *infirm*] frail; Spenser, *Epithalamion* 236f, 'That suffers not one looke to glaunce awry, / Which may let in a little thought unsownd.'

v *385–7*. At the Annunciation, the angel Gabriel, come to tell the Virgin Mary she would conceive a son, to be called Jesus, addressed her with the words 'Hail, thou that art highly favoured, the Lord is with thee: blessed art thou among women' (*Luke* i 28). *second Eve*] Cp. x 183. Just as Christ is the 'last Adam' (*1 Cor*. xv 45; and see i 4–5*n*), so the Virgin was typologically related to Eve.

v *388*. Cp. Michael's greeting at xi 158f: 'Hail to thee, / Eve rightly called, mother of all mankind.' Eve is mother of mankind, as Mary is *Theotokos* or mother of God. The title is based on *Gen*. iii 20: 'Adam called his wife's

Shall fill the world more numerous with thy sons
Than with these various fruits the trees of God
Have heaped this table. Raised of grassy turf
Their table was, and mossy seats had round,
And on her ample square from side to side
All autumn piled, though spring and autumn here
Danced hand in hand. A while discourse they hold;
No fear lest dinner cool; when thus began
Our author. Heavenly stranger, please to taste
These bounties which our nourisher, from whom
All perfect good unmeasured out, descends,
To us for food and for delight hath caused

name Eve; because she was the mother of all living.' The juxtaposition with the immediately preceding *Hail* is curious, in view of the prevailing opinion of the Reformers that it was 'but a fond conceit, to derive *Ave*, the first word of the Angels salutation to Marie of *Eva*, invented because shee repaired what was lost by *Eva*, for the one is a latine word, the other hebrewe' (Willet 54).

v *391. turf*] Because the shaping of wood had not yet begun. For Renaissance theories about the various primitive stages of technological development, see Panofsky² 33–67, 'Early History of Man'.

v *393. square*] A shape emblematic of virtue and particularly of temperance. See, e.g., Achille Bocchi, *Symbolicarum quaestionum libri quinque* (Bologna 1574), Embl. 144; also the discussions in Fowler, s.v. 'Square' and 'Quadrate'. The symbolism was originally Pythagorean (the square is a form of the *tetrad*); but it later became generally familiar. Cp. the expressions 'four-square'; 'square'=honest (*OED* a. II 8); and 'square'=rule (*OED* sb. I 2; e.g. Calvin on *Ps.* i 6, tr. Golding: 'Whose duetye it is to settle the state of the world according to the right squyre'). The moral meaning of *square* is here reinforced by the use of the personal pronoun *her*.

v *394–5.* For the simultaneity of spring and autumn in Paradise, see iv 148*n*. The dance of the Seasons or Horae is the same as the dance of the Graces.

v *396.* Hypersophisticated critics despise the domesticity of this line, and even Empson seems to lack enthusiasm for fruitarian meals (Empson² 153). But we should give M. credit for enriching the traditional fare of primitive man–acorns and water–so plausibly. Nor should we mistake his sophistication for naivety. Fire cannot be used before the Fall, since its discovery was one of the Fall's consequences (see l. 349*n*, ix 387–92*n*, x 1078–81*n*), but instead of accepting this as a disadvantage M. turns it to good effect by pointing to an inconvenience of our own world.

v *397. author*] ancestor.

v *399.* 'Every good gift and every perfect gift is from above, and cometh down from the Father of lights' (*Jas.* i 17).

The earth to yield; unsavoury food perhaps
To spiritual natures; only this I know,
That one celestial Father gives to all.
To whom the angel. Therefore what he gives
(Whose praise be ever sung) to man in part
Spiritual, may of purest spirits be found
No ingrateful food: and food alike those pure
Intelligential substances require,
As doth your rational; and both contain
Within them every lower faculty
Of sense, whereby they hear, see, smell, touch, taste,
Tasting concoct, digest, assimilate,

v *401–3*. Burden 112 notes that this the first of Adam's curious investigations begins (as all true knowledge began and ended) with God. Yet it verges already on forbidden knowledge: questions about the diet of angels are in one way not far from questions about how to become a god by eating. In this connection it is interesting to note that Cowley actually refers to the forbidden fruit of the tree of knowledge as '*Angels* meat' (ed. Waller 45). For the pun in *unsavoury* see ll. 84–5*n* above.

v *407–13*. Bentley's sneer must be included, if only for its elephantine wit: 'If the Devils want *feeding*, our Author made poor Provision for them in his Second Book; where they have nothing to eat but *Hell-fire*; and no danger of their *Dinner cooling*.' Manna is called 'the corn of heaven' and 'angels' food' (cp. l. 633 below) in *Ps*. lxxviii 24f; and on such authority it was believed fairly generally that angels ate *in some sense*. But many authors regarded the eating as merely symbolic; while most made a distinction between merely swallowing (as the angels did) on the one hand, and on the other really digesting (see, e.g., Willet 199 on *Gen*. xviii 8; and Vermigli, *Commonplaces, cit*. Rajan 149). But M. insists on the latter sense (see esp. l. 412), and in so doing rejects the Scholastic view that angels are immaterial. In emphasizing 'the reality of angelic nourishment' he adopts instead the view of Platonic theology, according to which all created spirits are corporeal (Lewis 105f). *No ingrateful*] acceptable; but perhaps also suggesting the recipient's gratitude.

v *408*. *Intelligential substances*] intellectual beings.

v *409*. Cp. *De doctrina* i 7, Columbia xv 25: 'Spirit being the more excellent substance, virtually and essentially contains within itself the inferior one; as the spiritual and rational faculty contains the corporeal, that is, the sentient and vegetative faculty.'

v *411*. The finer senses that nourish the soul (sight and hearing) take precedence of the grosser senses that nourish the body. For this sequence and its philosophical implications, see Frank Kermode, 'The Banquet of Sense', *Bulletin of the John Rylands Libr*. xliv (1961) 78.

v *412*. Physiological theory distinguished three stages of digestion: the 'first concoction' or digestion in the stomach (*concoct*), the 'second con-

And corporeal to incorporeal turn.
For know, whatever was created, needs
To be sustained and fed; of elements
The grosser feeds the purer, earth the sea,
Earth and the sea feed air, the air those fires
Ethereal, and as lowest first the moon;
Whence in her visage round those spots, unpurged
Vapours not yet into her substance turned.
Nor doth the moon no nourishment exhale
From her moist continent to higher orbs.
The sun that light imparts to all, receives
From all his alimental recompense
In humid exhalations, and at even

coction' or conversion to blood (*digest*) and the 'third concoction' or secretion (*assimilate*).

v *414. needs*] Ideologically an important word. Most theologians held that angels did not eat of necessity: see, e.g., Willet 199, on *Gen.* xviii 8. M. is stressing that the angels' corporeality is not assumed.

v *415–8.* On the conversion of the elements, see ll. 180–2*n* above.

v *418–20. lowest*] i.e., of the planetary spheres. *round*] An exact choice of epithet; since the vapours were supposed not to be visible until the moon was full: 'So long as she appeareth by the halfe in sight, [she] never sheweth any spots, because as yet she hath not her full power of light sufficient, to draw humour unto her. For these spots be nothing els but the dregs of the earth, caught up with other moisture among the vapors' (Pliny, *Nat. Hist.*, tr. Holland (1601) ii 7). It seems odd that M. should put in Raphael's mouth an archaic theory about lunar spots that seems to us obviously inferior to Galileo's explanation of them as landscape features–an explanation already used above at i 287–91. But the subject of lunar spots was still highly controversial in M.'s time. For a survey of the different schools of opinion, see Riccioli i 206f.

v *423–6.* Older opinion about the sun's sustenance is gathered in Swan's *Speculum mundi*: 'Cleanthes . . . allowed the matter of the sunne to be fierie, and that it was nourished by humours attracted from the ocean. Also Anaximander and Diogenes, after whom Epicurus, and the Stoics' (*cit.* Svendsen 66). But this alimentary version of the Great Chain of Being was also popular in M.'s own time with mystical and alchemic Platonists such as Robert Fludd (see, e.g., the engraving to his *Utriusque cosmi historia* I v 6). Cp. also the imitation of Anacreon in Cowley 51: 'The busie *Sun* (and one would guess / By's drunken fiery face no less) / Drinks up the *Sea*, and when h'as done, / The *Moon* and *Stars* drink up the *Sun*.' And see Plato, *Tim.* 49C; Cicero, *De nat. deor.* ii 33. The cosmic generalization of eating and drinking into a universal exchange of higher and lower is indispensable to M.'s vision. For the importance of the way an apple is eaten must seem appropriate, if not organically inevitable.

Sups with the ocean: though in heaven the trees
Of life ambrosial fruitage bear, and vines
Yield nectar, though from off the boughs each morn
We brush mellifluous dews, and find the ground
Covered with pearly grain: yet God hath here
Varied his bounty so with new delights,
As may compare with heaven; and to taste
Think not I shall be nice. So down they sat,
And to their viands fell, nor seemingly
The angel, nor in mist, the common gloss
Of theologians, but with keen despatch
Of real hunger, and concoctive heat
To transubstantiate; what redounds, transpires

v *427. ambrosial*] See ii 245*n*. Ambrosia was anciently the food of the gods, as *nectar* the drink. There was dominical authority for *vines* in heaven: 'I will not drink henceforth of this fruit of the vine, until that day when I drink it new with you in my Father's kingdom' (*Matt.* xxvi 29). For the perpetual *fruitage* of the tree of life, see *Rev.* xxii 2.

v *429. mellifluous*] sweet as honey; honey-flowing.

v *430. pearly grain*] manna, the 'corn of heaven' (see ll. 407–13*n* above); Cp. *Exod.* xvi 14: 'And when the dew that lay was gone up, behold, upon the face of the wilderness there lay a small round thing, as small as the hoar frost on the ground.' Iconographically, manna was represented most commonly as scattered pellets, more or less pearl-sized. See, e.g., Dirk Bouts's *The Gathering of the Manna* in St Peter's, Louvain; or Tintoretto's painting of the same subject in S. Giorgio Maggiore, Venice.

v *433. nice*] over-refined, difficult to please.

v *434–8.* See ll. 407–14*nn* above. *seemingly*] Refers to the Docetist theories about angelic appearances, devised to explain away the awkwardly materialistic accounts of angels in the Bible (e.g. at *Gen.* xviii 8, 'they did eat'). The Reformers on the whole rejected such mealy-mouthed evasions: 'We neither think with *Theodoret*, that these angels seemed onely [i.e., only seemed] to have bodies, and so also seemed to eate, but neither in truth' (Willet 199). It is particularly decisive that M. should make Raphael eat, because it was Raphael's explanation to Tobias (*Tob.* xii 19: 'I did neither eat nor drink, but ye did see a vision') that provided the immaterialists with their main proof text. The bases for M.'s conviction about the corporeality of spirits would include the broiled fish and honey eaten by the risen Christ (*Luke* xxiv 39–43).

v *438–9. redounds*] remains in excess. With characteristic imaginative extremism, M. is quite prepared to envisage angels excreting, if their corporeality entails it. *transubstantiate*] The word seems to have a double function here. Most obviously it is an abstract theological term, contrasting sharply with the direct concrete simplicity of *keen . . . hunger*. More subtly,

Through spirits with ease; nor wonder; if by fire
Of sooty coal the empiric alchemist
Can turn, or holds it possible to turn
Metals of drossiest ore to perfect gold
As from the mine. Mean while at table Eve
Ministered naked, and their flowing cups
With pleasant liquors crowned: O innocence
Deserving Paradise! If ever, then,
Then had the sons of God excuse to have been
Enamoured at that sight; but in those hearts
Love unlibidinous reigned, nor jealousy
Was understood, the injured lover's hell.
  Thus when with meats and drinks they had sufficed,
Not burdened nature, sudden mind arose
In Adam, not to let the occasion pass
Given him by this great conference to know
Of things above his world, and of their being
Who dwell in heaven, whose excellence he saw
Transcend his own so far, whose radiant forms
Divine effulgence, whose high power so far
Exceeded human, and his wary speech
Thus to the empyreal minister he framed.

however, it makes the implicit point that Adam and Eve were already enjoying Communion with the gods. If they had been content to wait, this hierarchical mobility would no doubt have increased. For the themes of ascent through eating, and of alimentary interchange between the lower and higher stages of the scale of nature, see ll. 84–5*n* and 423–6*n* above.

v *439–43*. The analogy between physiological and alchemical processes was regarded as very close: several terms (such as *concoction* and *digestion*) were common to both disciplines. In both, 'heat' (l. 437) refined matter and drove off impurities. *empiric alchemist*] i.e., a mere 'puffer' or vulgar practitioner, as distinct from the adept or grand alchemist who worked on a theoretical and often mystical basis. See Caron 69, 78f, 89.

v *445*. *crowned*] filled to the brim; perhaps referring specifically to the meniscus. Cp. Homer, *Il.* i 470 (during a ritual meal in honour of Apollo) and Virgil, *Georg.* ii 528 (*socii cratera coronant*, in honour of Bacchus); though the latter passage properly refers to the wreathing of the cup with a garland.

v *446–50*. *sons of God*] angels; alluding to *Gen.* vi 2: 'The sons of God saw the daughters of men that they were fair; and they took them wives of all which they chose.' Note, however, that M. does not say that the angels ever did take wives of the daughters of men. See xi 621–2*n* below.

v *451–2*. The temperance taken for granted before the Fall has to be made the subject of explicit advice by Michael, at xi 531.

v *459*. As Burden 113 notes, Adam is *wary* because for all he knows it may be the forbidden knowledge for which he is about to ask.

Inhabitant with God, now know I well
Thy favour, in this honour done to man,
Under whose lowly roof thou hast vouchsafed
To enter, and these earthly fruits to taste,
Food not of angels, yet accepted so,
As that more willingly thou couldst not seem
At heaven's high feasts to have fed: yet what compare?
  To whom the winged hierarch replied.
O Adam, one almighty is, from whom
All things proceed, and up to him return,
If not depraved from good, created all
Such to perfection, one first matter all,

v *467. compare*] comparison.

v *468.* It has been said that if angelic digestion appears a far-fetched subject of instruction this may be just the point. M. may want to amplify the wideness of Adam's permitted researches by showing him at work on something really arcane. On the other hand, there is a clear thematic relevance: M. is concerned to place eating in a context of cosmic relations. Raphael changes the subject, imperceptibly but firmly, to more practical matters: how and how much to know. The transition is easy; since for M. knowledge, like eating or sex, is a moral activity which can be engaged in either obediently and in moderation, or to excess.

v *469–90.* Raphael's world picture is characterised by a cyclic movement of emanation and return that marks it as Platonic; just as does the notion of successive degrees of spirituousness. It was an ancient and familiar picture; so much so that it would be pointless to list sources and models. The plant simile was a common enough way of explaining the notion of a scale of being. It is often found in a more detailed form than here, but seldom if ever so passionately expressive. Cp., e.g., Mercator's tree, whose sole trunk is chaos: 'Chaos is the onely truncke of all the Species to be created, having his roote and beginning in the Universall Idea Creatrix, which is in the mind, and divine will' (*Historia Mundi, cit.* Svendsen 115). Another common analogy for the ascent of species was the series of successive purifications of the alchemical Magnum Opus, to which M. alludes in his choice of such bivalent diction as *first matter* and *refined* and *sublimed*. The cosmic tree, identified with the Tree of Life, was itself one of the foremost symbols of theoretical alchemy; see iv 217–21*n* above. Note that the whole model is as dynamic as any evolutionary system of more recent times. The vision of nature as a working, striving organism could to some extent be paralleled in authors ranging from Aristotle to the Cambridge Platonists; but it is also an individual poetic vision, never fully conceptualized even in M.'s own theological work in prose. See W. C. Curry and W. B. Hunter, in *Research Studies of the Univ. of Louisiana* (1941) 173–92.

v *472. first matter*] In *De doctrina* i 7 (Columbia xv 20–7) M. argues strongly against creation *e nihilo*. He holds that God, not nothing, is the material

Indued with various forms, various degrees
Of substance, and in things that live, of life;
But more refined, more spirituous, and pure,
As nearer to him placed or nearer tending
Each in their several active spheres assigned,
Till body up to spirit work, in bounds
Proportioned to each kind. So from the root
Springs lighter the green stalk, from thence the leaves
More airy, last the bright consummate flower
Spirits odorous breathes: flowers and their fruit
Man's nourishment, by gradual scale sublimed
To vital spirits aspire, to animal,
To intellectual, give both life and sense,
Fancy and understanding, whence the soul
Reason receives, and reason is her being,
Discursive, or intuitive; discourse
Is oftest yours, the latter most is ours,
Differing but in degree, of kind the same.
Wonder not then, what God for you saw good
If I refuse not, but convert, as you,
To proper substance; time may come when men
With angels may participate, and find

cause of the world, and that it is framed out of an 'original matter ... intrinsically good, and the chief productive stock of every subsequent good'. For primal matter as a term in alchemy, see iii 601–5*n* above.

v *477–9.* For a moral application of this idea, see *Comus* 459–63. The Pauline notion of change from corruptible to incorruptible (*1 Cor.* xv) had already been combined poetically with the Aristotelian view of nature as growth and the Platonic vision of a return or *remeatio*, in Spenser, *F.Q.* VII vii 58: 'all things ... by their change their being doe dilate: / And turning to themselves at length againe, / Doe worke their owne perfection so by fate'.

v *481. consummate*] completed, perfected, final. *airy*] A good word, since it implies lightness and therefore a tendency upward: cp. Adam's sleep, 'airy light from pure digestion bred' (l. 4 above). Air was the element connected with the sanguine temperament, generally considered the most perfect of the four. On sanguine as the temperament of unfallen man, see Klibansky 105, 110f.

v *483. scale*] i.e., the *scala naturae* or cosmic ladder. *sublimed*] 'raised'; but also in its alchemic sense, 'sublimated'. For the ladder as an alchemical symbol, see iii 516–7*n*. Rajan 150 *n* 9 gives a list of authorities on the *scala naturae*; to which should be added Agrippa of Nettesheim (see Klibansky 352).

v *494. vital spirits*] Extremely fine pure fluids, given off by the blood of the heart, and sustaining life. *animal spirits*] Had their seat in the brain, and controlled sensation and voluntary motion. Cp. iv 805.

No inconvenient diet, nor too light fare:
And from these corporal nutriments perhaps
Your bodies may at last turn all to spirit,
Improved by tract of time, and winged ascend

v *478–90*. The distinction between the *intuitive*, simple, undifferentiated operation of the contemplating intellect (*mens*) and the *discursive* or ratiocinative, piecemeal operation of the intellect working in conjunction with the reason (*ratio*) goes back ultimately to Plato. See, e.g., his dichotomies between pure intellect and opinion, and between understanding and knowledge of shadows, in *Rep.* 533f. It was customary to connect angels with intellect or intelligence only, and to say that they practised only the first kind of reasoning. Cp. the presupposition underlying Ficino, *De immortal. anim.* xiii 2 (*Opera omnia* 290): *Ratio interponitur, vis quaedam verarum propria animarum, per quam in universali conceptu a principiis rerum ad conclusiones temporali successione discurrunt, effectus resolvunt in causas, causas iterum in effectus deducunt, discurrunt etiam conceptu particulari ad discursionis universalis exemplar. Sed in prima ipsa et universali discursione, ratio intellectualis vocanda est, in discursione particulari, ratio cogitatrix et opinatrix. Mens autem illa quae est animae caput, et auriga, suapte natura angelos imitata, non successione, sed momento quod cupit assequitur.*' (The intellect, which is head and charioteer of the soul, by its own nature imitates the angels, and pursues what it desires not successively but in an instant). But M. describes the angels as practising both kinds of reasoning, in *De doctrina* i 9 (Columbia xv 106): the good angels know some things *per revelationem*, others *per eminentem quandam ratiocinationem*. The preoccupation of M.'s contemporaries with the ideal of intuitive knowledge has been called the 'heresy of angelism' by Jacques Maritain (see MacCaffrey 53).

v *493*. *proper*] distinctive, peculiar (*OED* I 2) or suitable (*OED* III 9).

v *496–500*. Cp. ll. 79–80*n* above. God's ambassador and the voice in Eve's dream seem to be saying the same thing, 'that God expects them to manage to get to Heaven, and that what they eat has something to do with it' (Empson 150). The resemblance is reinforced formally by the echo of 'as we'. However, there is no need to infer that this resemblance excuses Eve or convicts God of machiavellianism. On the contrary, it simplifies the issue before man into a direct choice between eating obediently and eating disobediently. Eating is shown to be in itself a neutral act. The idea that, if mankind had not fallen, it would eventually have been raised to the same spiritual level with the angels, was quite orthodox. See, e.g., St Augustine, *Civ. Dei* xiv 10, *cit.* Lewis 66. Cp. also vii 157ff, and the conclusion of *Of Reformation* with its glorious vision of the faithful being rewarded with angelic titles (Yale i 616). Burden 36f notes how important it is that the station ordained for man should be progressive rather than static. Eating the fruit must not be in any way a necessary step to man's full development. *tract*] duration, lapse; *tract of time* was ordinary prose usage (cp. Heylyn iii 127).

Ethereal, as we, or may at choice
Here or in heavenly paradises dwell;
If ye be found obedient, and retain
Unalterably firm his love entire
Whose progeny you are. Mean while enjoy
Your fill what happiness this happy state
Can comprehend, incapable of more.
   To whom the patriarch of mankind replied,
O favourable spirit, propitious guest,
Well hast thou taught the way that might direct
Our knowledge, and the scale of nature set
From centre to circumference, whereon
In contemplation of created things
By steps we may ascend to God. But say,
What meant that caution joined, *If ye be found
Obedient?* Can we want obedience then
To him, or possibly his love desert
Who formed us from the dust, and placed us here
Full to the utmost measure of what bliss
Human desires can seek or apprehend?
   To whom the angel. Son of heaven and earth,

v *501*. Cp. *Is.* i 19: 'If ye be willing and obedient, ye shall eat the good of the land.' But the irony lies in the implied allusion to the verse following: 'But if ye refuse and rebel, ye shall be devoured with the sword: for the mouth of the Lord hath spoken it.'

v *503*. Alluding to St Paul's Mars' Hill sermon on the Unknown God, *Acts* xvii 28: 'For in him we live, and move, and have our being; as certain also of your own poets have said, For we are also his offspring.' St Paul was quoting the astronomical poet Aratus, *Phaenomena* 5. On M.'s marginal comment on the Aratus passage (he notes another version of the idea, in Lucretius, *De rerum nat.* ii 991f), see M. Kelley and S. D. Atkins, 'M.'s Annotations of Aratus', *PMLA* lxx (1955) 1092.

v *504*. *Your fill*] Biblical diction; e.g. *Deut.* xxiii 24, 'When thou comest into thy neighbour's vineyard, then thou mayest eat grapes thy fill at thine own pleasure; but thou shalt not put any in thy vessel.'

v *505*. *incapable*] The primary meaning is that their happy state is 'unable to hold more (happiness)' (*OED* I 1), but in a secondary dramatic irony it is Adam and Eve who are unable to hold their happiness.

v *509–12*. Cp. the symbolic Jacob's ladder used in reverse by Satan in Bk iii; see iii 510–5*n* and 516–7*n*. In the *scale* or ladder of nature Adam refers to the Platonic ascesis from image to universal, up the hierarchic grades of existence. But the alchemical language in the preceding passage (l. 469–90*n* and 472*n*) renders probable the existence of a secondary meaning – an allusion to the (presumptuous?) ladder of alchemic purification.

Attend: that thou art happy, owe to God;
That thou continuest such, owe to thyself,
That is, to thy obedience; therein stand.
This was that caution given thee; be advised.
God made thee perfect, not immutable;
And good he made thee, but to persevere
He left it in thy power, ordained thy will
By nature free, not over-ruled by fate
Inextricable, or strict necessity;
Our voluntary service he requires,
Not our necessitated, such with him
Finds no acceptance, nor can find, for how
Can hearts, not free, be tried whether they serve
Willing or no, who will but what they must
By destiny, and can no other choose?
My self and all the angelic host that stand
In sight of God enthroned, our happy state
Hold, as you yours, while our obedience holds;
On other surety none; freely we serve,
Because we freely love, as in our will
To love or not; in this we stand or fall:
And some are fallen, to disobedience fallen,
And so from heaven to deepest hell; O fall

v *520–43.* Covering similar ground to that covered in God the Father's rejection of determinism and predestination at iii 93–128, but from the standpoint, now, of practical theology. The brevity of the sentences is in accordance with Horace's prescription for the style of precepts: *Quidquid praecipies esto brevis, ut cito dicta / percipiant animi dociles teneantque fideles* (*Ars poet.* 335f).

v *529–34.* Cp. *De doctrina* i 3 (Columbia xiv 141): 'The acceptableness of duties done under a law of necessity is diminished, or rather is annihilated altogether, inasmuch as freedom can no longer be attributed to that will over which some fixed decree is inevitably suspended.' Raphael's emphasis–and the emphasis throughout *PL*–on obedience, may at first seem coldly moralistic. But a study of the passionately committed discussion of free will and predestination in *De doctrina* i 3 soon suggests that obedience is for M. bound up with the value of freedom. Only if God wishes obedience as a sign of faithful love can man's freedom of will have significance.

v *534.* Satan, however, actually prefers to think in terms of destiny; see iv 58.

v *538. Ed I* has period after *serve.*

v *540.* Cp. *De doctrina* i 3 (Columbia xiv 81): 'In assigning the gift of free will God suffered both men and angels to stand or fall at their own uncontrolled choice'.

From what high state of bliss into what woe!
To whom our great progenitor. Thy words
Attentive, and with more delighted ear,
Divine instructor, I have heard, than when
Cherubic songs by night from neighbouring hills
Aerial music send: nor knew I not
To be both will and deed created free;
Yet that we never shall forget to love
Our maker, and obey him whose command
Single, is yet so just, my constant thoughts
Assured me, and still assure: though what thou tell'st
Hath passed in heaven, some doubt within me move,
But more desire to hear, if thou consent,
The full relation, which must needs be strange,
Worthy of sacred silence to be heard;
And we have yet large day, for scarce the sun
Hath finished half his journey, and scarce begins
His other half in the great zone of heaven.
Thus Adam made request, and Raphael
After short pause assenting, thus began.
High matter thou enjoinest me, O prime of men,

v *543*. For the rhetorical scheme see i 91–2*n*.

v *547*. The songs of the cherub guard, which Adam has described at iv 680–8.

v *551–2*. Cp. iv 419ff and 432ff. Obey him who has given only a *single* command (and therefore easy to obey) and also (*yet*: *OED* I 1 a) a *just* command (and therefore right to obey).

v *553*. *Ed I* has no comma after *me*.

v *556*. *relation*] account.

v *557*. *Worthy . . . silence*] Alluding to the songs 'worthy of sacred silence' that Sappho and Alcaeus sing to the wondering shades in Horace, *Odes* II xiii 29f: *utrumque sacro digna silentio / mirantur umbrae dicere*. But the point (as so often with M.'s allusions) lies in the passage immediately following that quoted. The fit audience would know that Horace continued: *sed magis pugnas et exactos tyrannos / densum umeris bibit aure vulgus* (but most the tale of battles and of banished tyrants the crowd, shouldering close, drinks greedily).

v *558*. *large day*] ample day (*OED* s.v. *Large* A II 2). If the more usual sense of the phrase, 'a day and more' (*OED* s.v. *Large* A II 5), is present as a secondary meaning it may express M.'s formal intention. For of course Raphael's narration fills out the time until it becomes in a sense far more than a day. In fact, however, Raphael spends, as he was instructed (l. 229), just six hours with Adam and Eve: see viii 630–2.

v *563*. *prime*] Already used to denote a symbolic time of freshness, perfection

Sad task and hard, for how shall I relate
To human sense the invisible exploits
Of warring spirits; how without remorse
The ruin of so many glorious once
And perfect while they stood; how last unfold
The secrets of another world, perhaps
Not lawful to reveal? Yet for thy good
This is dispensed, and what surmounts the reach
Of human sense, I shall delineate so,
By likening spiritual to corporal forms,

and worship (ll. 18–25*n* and 170*n*); so that when it is now applied to Adam it no longer means simply 'first' or 'best'.

v *563–4.* Raphael's account of the war in heaven continues to the end of Bk vi. It is one of the two long 'episodes' or inset narrations, that conclude the two halves of the poem. (For the other, and its relation to this, see xi 356–8*n*; also Introduction, 'Numerology'.) Such episodes, often relating events that happened before the time of the poem's main action, were usual in epic; and have continued in a modified form in the flash-back of modern fiction. Cp. Odysseus' narration to Alcinous and the Phaeacians in *Od.* ix, a parallel drawn explicitly at l. 341 above. But the sentiment here also recalls that of Aeneas, as he begins his long narration to Dido at *Aen.* ii 3: *infandum, regina, iubes renovare dolorem.* Raphael's narration is *high matter* in a literal as well as metaphorical sense; for he is about to rise above earth to the high central point of the poem spatially, and to tell 'what surmounts the reach of human sense' (ll. 571f; see MacCaffrey 57).

v *566. how without remorse*] Burden thinks Raphael must tell the story without remorse for the same reason that God was pitiless during the events themselves. He is perfectly just, so that there is no occasion for remorse. But Raphael may on the contrary mean that the task is going to be a *sad* one, and that he doesn't know whether he can get through it without feeling more remorse than he can bear. Cp. xi 99.

v *569–70.* Cp. vii 120 and viii 174f. 'It occurs rather often to Raphael that he is not sure how much God will allow him to tell' (Empson 149).

v *572–4.* Hanford 416 argues on the basis of this passage that M. did not intend his poem to be regarded as literal truth, but as a symbolic embodiment of inspired revelation. Cp. Dante's acknowledgment at *Par.* xxiii 55–78 of the difficulty of representing heaven (*figurando il Paradiso*). Just as Dante plays on *figurare* (represent, symbolize), so M.'s lines apply to his own imitation as much as to Raphael's, and challenge the fit reader to demythologize.

v *573. corporal*] Darbishire[2] i 298 emends to *corporeal*, on the ground that M. observed a distinction between *corporeal* (='having a body') and *corporal* (='relating to the body'). But if M. observed the distinction at all, he did so erratically. See, e.g. *Treatise of Civil Power* (Columbia vi 10), 'commuting of corporal for spiritual'; also *Art of Logic* i 7 (Columbia xi 63). *Cor-*

As may express them best, though what if earth
Be but the shadow of heaven, and things therein
Each to other like, more than on earth is thought?
    As yet this world was not, and Chaos wild
Reigned where these heavens now roll, where earth now rests
Upon her centre poised, when on a day
(For time, though in eternity, applied
To motion, measures all things durable
By present, past, and future) on such day
As heaven's great year brings forth, the empyreal host

poral='embodied, material' was common usage at the time (see *OED* s.v. *Corporal* 1 c, 2).

v *574–6*. It was a fundamental doctrine of Platonism that the phenomenal world bears to the heavenly world of Ideas the same relation as shadow to reality. The most extensive discussion of the doctrine in Plato is *Rep*. x. Cp. iv 207f above.

v *578–9*. For the position of earth in the creation, see vii 240–2*n*. *these heavens*] the visible, astronomical heavens.

v *579–82*. Here M. shows himself well aware of the limitations of corporeal language, in describing spiritual and eternal actions. He has to navigate round the Platonic doctrine (*Tim*. 37E–38E) that time, a moveable image of eternity, is generated by the heavenly bodies 'and existed not before the heavens came into being' (*Tim*. 37E). This he does by way of the plausible assumption that there can be motion in eternity–a possibility excluded by Plato himself (*Tim*. 38A). Cp. *De doctrina* i 7 (Columbia xv 35): 'It seems even probable, that the apostasy which caused the expulsion of so many thousands from heaven, took place before the foundations of this world were laid. Certainly there is no sufficient foundation for the common opinion, that motion and time (which is the measure of motion) could not, according to the ratio of priority and subsequence, have existed before this world was made; since Aristotle, who teaches that no ideas of motion and time can be formed except in reference to this world, nevertheless pronounces the world itself to be eternal.'

v *583–6*. Cp. *Job* i 6: 'Now there was a day when the sons of God [i.e., angels] came to present themselves before the Lord, and Satan came also among them.'

v *583*. The *great year* or *annus magnus platonicus* is the cycle completed when all the heavenly bodies simultaneously return to their original positions. The period of the cycle was variously estimated (e.g. by Servius at 12,954 natural years, by Macrobius at 15,000, by Plato himself probably at 36,000), and it was often connected with the equinoctial precessional period. The point of the present passage lies in the fact that the Great Year was also identified with the *Politicus* Cycles of Uniformity and Dissimilarity, the latter of

Of angels by imperial summons called,
Innumerable before the almighty's throne
Forthwith from all the ends of heaven appeared
Under their hierarchs in orders bright
Ten thousand thousand ensigns high advanced,
Standards, and gonfalons twixt van and rear
Stream in the air, and for distinction serve
Of hierarchies, of orders, and degrees;
Or in their glittering tissues bear imblazed
Holy memorials, acts of zeal and love
Recorded eminent. Thus when in orbs
Of circuit inexpressible they stood,
Orb within orb, the Father infinite,

which was in turn identified with the process of deterioration begun with the Fall or the loss of the Golden Age. The *day* Raphael is to describe resembles the day brought forth by the Great Year because the generation of the Son begins a new age, but also because it is the first day of the poem's cycle. See Introduction, 'Chronology'. From another point of view, the day may be seen as preceding the start of the angelic rebellion. The Cycle of Uniformity is at full term, and brings forth the first day of the Cycle of Deterioration. See Adams ii 295–302; and, for Spenser's use of the same idea, Fowler 37f, 193–5.

v *587*. On the *orders* of the angels see i 128–9*b*; and Verity's Appendix, 680–2. A heavy point is needed after *bright*.

v *588*. Cp. Daniel's vision of the judgment of the Ancient of days: 'A fiery stream issued and came forth from before him: thousand thousands ministered unto him, and ten thousand times ten thousand stood before him' (*Dan.* vii 10). The angels are multiple, and therefore unlike the divine Monad from whom they derive their being. But before the Fall their number symbolizes a clear reflection of God; for ten and powers of ten were held to be forms of the monad. On angelic multiplicity and unity see Dante, *Par.* xxix 130–45; and on unity and multitude in *PL* see 610–2*n*; vi 766*n*, 809–10*n*.

v *589*. *gonfalons*] banners fastened to cross-bars; unlike *Standards*, which are fastened to the flagpoles themselves. Gonfalons were very often carried in ecclesiastical processions.

v *593*. Contrast the ensigns of the rebel angels (i 539*n*), which naturally are devoid of *Holy memorials* ('chronicles, commemorations', often in an ecclesiastical sense) and instead have pagan or secular 'arms and trophies'.

v *594–6*. So Dante describes the angels as encircling God the spaceless centre of the universe, in *Par.* xxviii. The *orbs* of the angels merge imperceptibly both with the orbs of astronomical bodies and with 'the orbs / Of his fierce chariot' (the Messiah's cosmic vehicle: vi 828f). For the angels, symbolically considered, are no less than the operations of providence throughout the universe of secondary causes.

By whom in bliss embosomed sat the Son,
Amidst as from a flaming mount, whose top
Brightness had made invisible, thus spake.
Hear all ye angels, progeny of light,
Thrones, dominations, princedoms, virtues, powers,
Hear my decree, which unrevoked shall stand.
This day I have begot whom I declare

v *597*. For the Son in the bosom of the Father, cp. iii 168–9*n*; also iii 239 and 279.

v *598*. *whose top*] whoseop *Ed I*, corr. in *Errata*.

v *599*. For God's 'majesty of darkness' see ii 264–5*n*; and for the description of even the skirts of God as 'dark with excessive bright', iii 375–82*n*.

v *601*. Not the mere sonorous roll-call of titles that it is usually taken to be. The Scriptural passage alluded to, *Col.* i 16, is a proof text for Christ's agency in the creation of the angels: 'By him were all things created, that are in heaven, and that are in earth, visible and invisible, whether they be thrones, or dominions, or principalities, or powers: all things were created by him, and for him.'

v *603–6*. These lines are among the most controversial in the poem; and quite unnecessarily so. The principal allusions are to *Ps.* ii 6f ('Yet have I set my king upon my holy hill of Zion. I will declare the decree . . . Thou art my Son; this day have I begotten thee') and *Heb.* i 5 ('unto which of the angels said he at any time, Thou art my Son, this day have I begotten thee? And again, I will be to him a Father, and he shall be to me a Son?)'. Both texts are treated by M. in *De doctrina* i 5 as relating to the metaphorical generation of the Son (Columbia xv 182–4), and he explains 'begotten' in the first as meaning 'made him a king'. There is therefore no contradiction between the present passage and v 832 (*contra* Empson[2] 167). The *Hebrews* verse refers to 'the exaltation of the Son above the angels', an action by implication distinct from 'unction to the mediatorial office' (Columbia xv 183). The latter 'event' is presumably the one to be correlated with the exaltation of the Messiah (earlier in the poem but chronologically later) at *PL* iii 313ff. There is thus no basis for identifying the exaltations in Bks iii and v–an identification that Empson (99) rightly dislikes, since it 'lets you off attending to the story'. M. seems to have envisaged a series of 'metaphorical generations' and exaltations: see, e.g., vi 760ff and 890–2. The difficulty raised by Kelley (104), that the events of the epic belong to a far earlier era than those of *De doctrina*, is unimportant, since M. believed events in eternity to have sequence but no measure. Nor is there any obtrusive evidence of Arianism in the passage. Empson finds it shocking, however, because it shows arbitrariness in God: 'If the Son had inherently held this position from before the creation of all angels, why has it been officially withheld from him till this day? . . . to give no reason at all for the Exaltation makes it appear a challenge' (102). M., who was always unwilling to think of the freedom of God as conditioned, may well have intended to give just such

My only Son, and on this holy hill
Him have anointed, whom ye now behold
At my right hand; your head I him appoint;
And by my self have sworn to him shall bow
All knees in heaven, and shall confess him Lord:
Under his great vicegerent reign abide
United as one individual soul
For ever happy: him who disobeys
Me disobeys, breaks union, and that day
Cast out from God and blessed vision, falls
Into utter darkness, deep engulfed, his place
Ordained without redemption, without end.

an impression; for in *De doctrina* he takes *Ps.* ii to show 'that however the generation of the Son may have taken place, it arose from no natural necessity, as is generally contended, but was no less owing to the decree and will of the Father than his priesthood or kingly power, or his resuscitation from the dead' (i 5; Columbia xiv 185). Cp. *ibid.* 187: all God's works 'are executed freely according to his own good pleasure'. The tradition that Christ's exaltation was an occasion of the angelic rebellion had some vogue in the seventeenth century; and in Valamarana's *De bello intelligentiarum* (1623) Satan had rebelled because of God's prophecy of the Incarnation. See McColley 33.

v *606–11.* 'The Father's delegation of His powers to the Son is paralleled by Satan's sending Sin and Death to earth as his viceregents' (Rajan 47).

v *606. head*] Cp. *Eph.* iv 15; and *Col.* ii 9f: 'For in him dwelleth all the fulness of the Godhead bodily. And ye are complete in him, which is the head of all principality and power.'

v *607–8.* 'By myself have I sworn, saith the Lord' (*Gen.* xxii 16). Cp. also *Phil.* ii 9–11: 'God also hath highly exalted him, and given him a name which is above every name: That at the name of Jesus every knee should bow, of things in heaven, and things in earth, and things under the earth; And that every tongue should confess that Jesus Christ is Lord.'

v *608.* Some copies *Ed I* have comma after *Lord.*

v *609. vicegerent*] viceregent; the title was applied to kings or priests in their capacity as representatives of God.

v *610–2.* One of the most explicit statements of the contrast between divine unity and evil multitude that underlies so much of the poem's action and imagery. See, e.g., ll. 588*n*, 898–903*n*, i 338ff, vi 767*n* and vi 809–10*n*. For the evil dyad (or principle of division) as a rebellion against the monad, see F.M. Cornford, 'Mysticism and Science in the Pythagorean Tradition', *CQ* xvii (1933) 6; also Hopper 39f. *individual*] indivisible, inseparable.

v *613. blessed vision*] Cp. the 'beatific vision' of i 684.

v *614. utter*] outer.

v *615.* For the variable positioning of stress on *without*, see B. A. Wright's note in *N & Q* cciii (1958) 202f, and cp. ii 892*n*.

So spake the omnipotent, and with his words
All seemed well pleased, all seemed, but were not all.
That day, as other solemn days, they spent
In song and dance about the sacred hill,
Mystical dance, which yonder starry sphere
Of planets and of fixed in all her wheels
Resembles nearest, mazes intricate,
Eccentric, intervolved, yet regular
Then most, when most irregular they seem,
And in their motions harmony divine
So smooths her charming tones, that God's own ear

v *616.* Some copies *Ed I* have no new paragraph.
v *618. solemn days*] holy days, festivals.
v *620–4.* For the notion of the universe as a dance, see l. 178*n* and iii 579–81*n*. Here M.'s intention seems to be a positive presentation of obedience, to offset the negative presentation in Satan's speech, ll. 787–99. See Rajan 63: 'That gaiety, innate yet ceremonial, those turning, pirouetting half rhymes and caesuras, reach to the heart of what discipline can give us.' In *PL* the movement of angels is frequently connected with that of astronomical bodies. See, e.g., iv 782–4*n*. The Biblical authority for the connection would be *Job* xxxviii 7: 'the morning stars sang together, and all the sons of God shouted for joy'. *sphere*] the apparent celestial sphere. *fixed*] fixed stars. The eccentric circles utilised in the astronomical systems of M.'s time (see iii 575*n*) were themselves instances of apparent irregularities embraced within a higher regularity. Cp. Cicero, *Tusc. disp.* V xxiv 69: *quorum vagi motus rata tamen et certa sui cursus spatia definiant*; the context is an account of the wise man's pleasure in astronomy.
v *625–8.* M. devoted the whole Second Prolusion to the 'Music of the Spheres'. Originating with the Pythagoreans, the idea had attained very wide and popular distribution (see Yale i 235*n* and Svendsen 60f), but M.'s use of it here is marked by his usual precision. The Platonists believed that 'the intervals in the corporeal universe, which were filled with sesquitertians, sesquialters, superoctaves, half-tones, and a *leimma*, followed the pattern of the Soul's fabric, and that harmony was thus forthcoming, the proportional intervals of which were interwoven into the fabric of the Soul and were also injected into the corporeal universe which is quickened by the Soul' (Macrobius, *In somn. Scip.* II iii 15, quoting Porphyry). The intervals between the planetary spheres were analysed as musical proportions by astronomers as late as Kepler (see Dreyer 406–8). The *tones* of the spheres are thus not *charming* in the sense 'pleasant', but in the sense 'magical'. Cp. Macrobius, *loc. cit.* 11: 'It is natural for everything that breathes to be captivated by music since the heavenly Soul that animates the universe sprang from music.' *now*] Added in *Ed II*. The *evening* is that of Day 2 of the poem's action, since M. reckons the days from sunset in the Hebrew manner. See Introduction, 'Chronology'. The sequence *evening . . . morn* is thus deliberate.

Listens delighted. Evening now approached
(For we have also our evening and our morn,
We ours for change delectable, not need)
Forthwith from dance to sweet repast they turn
Desirous; all in circles as they stood,
Tables are set, and on a sudden piled
With angels' food, and rubied nectar flows
In pearl, in diamond, and massy gold,
Fruit of delicious vines, the growth of heaven.
On flowers reposed, and with fresh flowerets crowned,
They eat, they drink, and in communion sweet
Quaff immortality and joy, secure
Of surfeit where full measure only bounds
Excess, before the all bounteous king, who showered
With copious hand, rejoicing in their joy.
Now when ambrosial night with clouds exhaled
From that high mount of God, whence light and shade
Spring both, the face of brightest heaven had changed
To grateful twilight (for night comes not there
In darker veil) and roseate dews disposed
All but the unsleeping eyes of God to rest,
Wide over all the plain, and wider far

v *631*. *Ed I* has comma after *desirous*.
v *633*. See ll. 407–13*n*. *Ed I* has colon after *flows*.
v *636–40*. *Ed I* 'They eat, they drink, and with refection sweet / Are filled, before the all bounteous king, who showered'. One effect of the additions is to draw closer the link with Raphael's meal with Adam and Eve (cp. ll. 451f); another is to endow the eating with a spiritual value. *vines*] See 427*n*. *fresh flowerets*] Presumably amarant: see iii 350–7*nn*. *communion sweet*] Cp. the 'fellowships of joy' in which the angels sit at xi 80. *immortality*] on the strength of *John* iv 10 ('living water') or *Ps*. xxxvi 8f: 'Thou shalt make them drink of the river of the pleasures. For with thee is the fountain of life: in thy light shall we see light.'
v *642*. *ambrosial*] fragrant; used of night in Homer, *Il*. ii 57. But see also ii 245*n* above.
v *643*. In *De doctrina* i 7 (Columbia xv 31) M. distinguishes between the visible heaven, and an 'invisible and highest heaven' situated in 'the heaven of the blessed'. The latter was a 'throne and habitation of God' which perhaps existed before creation. Cp. vi 4–12 and vii 584–6 below.
v *645*. Cp. l. 162, and see *Rev*. xxi 25: 'There shall be no night there.'
v *646*. Cp. 'the timely dews of sleep' which Adam feels inclining his eyelids at iv 614.
v *647*. 'Behold, he that keepeth Israel shall neither slumber nor sleep' (*Ps*. cxxi 4).

Than all this globous earth in plain out spread,
(Such are the courts of God) the angelic throng
Dispersed in bands and files their camp extend
By living streams among the trees of life,
Pavilions numberless, and sudden reared,
Celestial tabernacles, where they slept
Fanned with cool winds, save those who in their course
Melodious hymns about the sovereign throne
Alternate all night long: but not so waked
Satan, so call him now, his former name
Is heard no more in heaven; he of the first,
If not the first archangel, great in power,
In favour and pre-eminence, yet fraught
With envy against the Son of God, that day
Honoured by his great Father, and proclaimed
Messiah king anointed, could not bear
Through pride that sight, and thought himself
impaired.
Deep malice thence conceiving and disdain,
Soon as midnight brought on the dusky hour
Friendliest to sleep and silence, he resolved
With all his legions to dislodge, and leave
Unworshipped, unobeyed the throne supreme

v *652. living streams*] See ll. 636–40*n*. The river and the *trees of life* occur together in *Rev*. xxii 1–2.

v *655–7*. Alluding to the alteration of offices in the temple-service (see iv 561*n*. But *course* is also an astronomical term: for the connection between angels and stars see ll. 620–4*n*, 700–14*n* and iv 782–4*n*.

v *658–9*. See i 82*n* and 361–3: after the rebellion the names of the unfaithful were razed from the books of life and they were given the names now current. For Fludd's acceptance of the Scholastic idea that Satan's name before his fall was Lucifer, see West 76.

v *659. in*] omitted in *Ed I* (corr. in *Errata*).

v *660*. It is not certain whether Raphael means that Satan was among the first only of the *order* of archangels, or among the first angels of all orders; l. 812 favours the latter interpretation. At vi 690 we are told that Satan was created the 'equal' of Michael; and, in the first day's fighting, that he met no equal except Michael (vi 246–8).

v *664*. See ll. 603–6*n*. Taken literally, the Hebrew title *Messiah* means 'anointed'.

v *665. impaired*] injured, reduced in status.

v *669. dislodge*] shift his quarters; a military term. Note the secondary transitive meaning 'displace', with *throne* as object.

Contemptuous, and his next subordinate
Awakening, thus to him in secret spake.
   Sleep'st thou companion dear, what sleep can close
Thy eyelids? And remember'st what decree
Of yesterday, so late hath passed the lips
Of heaven's almighty. Thou to me thy thoughts
Was wont, I mine to thee was wont to impart;
Both waking we were one; how then can now
Thy sleep dissent? New laws thou seest imposed;
New laws from him who reigns, new minds may raise
In us who serve, new counsels, to debate
What doubtful may ensue, more in this place
To utter is not safe. Assemble thou
Of all those myriads which we lead the chief;
Tell them that by command, ere yet dim night
Her shadowy cloud withdraws, I am to haste,
And all who under me their banners wave,
Homeward with flying march where we possess
The quarters of the north, there to prepare

v *671. his next subordinate*] Presumably Beelzebub; cp. ii 299f. Some critics try to explain the fact that he is not named in the present book by recourse to the theory that v was written before ii (see, e.g., Empson 99). It is simpler to suppose that M. did not know the name Beelzebub had before his fall; see ll. 658–9*n*.

v *672. in secret*] An explanation of how Raphael could know what Satan said 'in secret' is quickly given, at ll. 682f, so that there is no need to follow Gilbert (63) in speculating whether the angelic wars may originally have been narrated by an omniscient author. On the other hand, M. has no intention of trying for naturalistic verisimilitude. Both he and his Raphael throughout avail themselves of the antique historian's freedom to invent speeches and probable details.

v *673*. Echoing the first words (*Il.* ii 23) of the baneful dream sent by Zeus to Agamemnon–ostensibly to incite the Greeks to a new attack on Troy, but with the ulterior purpose of doing honour to Achilles.

v *681*. Empson (72) thinks we can infer from this line that there had been earlier public debate 'about the claims of God'. But the antitheses count against this inference, or at least imply that any earlier counsels–or councils–were not disloyal.

v *685–93*. Empson (72) regards this lie, no doubt correctly, as 'an ordinary wartime propaganda operation', but is not far from admitting that by his deception Satan attempts to deprive his subordinates of the free option of loyalty.

v *689. north*] See P. Salmon, 'The Site of Lucifer's Throne', *Anglia* lxxxi (1963) 118–23; also F. N. Robinson's note to Chaucer, *Friar's Tale* 1413,

Fit entertainment to receive our king
The great Messiah, and his new commands,
Who speedily through all the hierarchies
Intends to pass triumphant, and give laws.
So spake the false archangel, and infused
Bad influence into the unwary breast
Of his associate; he together calls,
Or several one by one, the regent powers,
Under him regent, tells, as he was taught,
That the most high commanding, now ere night,
Now ere dim night had disencumbered heaven,
The great hierarchal standard was to move;
Tells the suggested cause, and casts between
Ambiguous words and jealousies, to sound

citing Gregory's Commentary on *Job* xvii 24 (Migne lxxvi 26). The traditional association of the north with evil goes back to patristic applications of *Is.* xiv 12–4 to the fall of Satan: 'How art thou fallen from heaven, O Lucifer, son of the morning! . . . For thou hast said in thine heart, I will ascend into heaven, I will exalt my throne above the stars of God: I will sit also upon the mount of the congregation, in the sides of the north.' Cp. *Jer.* i 14, iv 6, vi 1. The localization of Satan adds point to several other passages, such as the simile of the multitude poured from the 'populous north' at i 351ff. Satan's rebellion was similarly placed in the north in Valamarana's *De bello intelligentiarum* (1623).

v *700–14.* The revolt is described in terms of a 'sustained astronomical metaphor', with Satan *ere dim night had disencumbered heaven* leading off a *starry flock*. 'Bentley complained about the leadership of Satan that the Morning Star disappears last of the stars in the morning, so cannot be said to lead them; Pearce smartly replied that a shepherd walks at the back. But the words are *drew after him*, and the inversion acts as part of the conflict of feeling; he leads them only towards night' (Empson[2] 184f). See also ll. 620–4*n*. The passage partly depends on our knowledge of a long-established symbolism whereby the morning star represented both Satan and Christ. As evening star Christ died; as morning star he was resurrected. Satan as morning star mimes the brightness of Christ–a point amplified here by his role as shepherd. Cowley (244) hit on a very similar description of Lucifer, perhaps independently, as he claims in *Davideis* i *n* 3: 'Once *General* of a guilded *Host* of *Sprights*, / Like *Hesper*, leading forth the spangled *Nights*.'

v *701. hierarchal standard*] Cp. 591, 692, etc.; throughout this passage M. plays on 'evocations of degree' (Rajan 63). See ll. 787–802*n*.

v *702. suggested*] Tends to imply 'insinuating or prompting to evil' (*OED* 1 a) *casts*] machinates, schemes.

v *703. jealousies*] suspicions.

v *703–10.* Peter, Burden and others make heavy weather over a fancied

Or taint integrity; but all obeyed
The wonted signal, and superior voice
Of their great potentate; for great indeed
His name, and high was his degree in heaven;
His countenance, as the morning star that guides
The starry flock, allured them, and with lies
Drew after him the third part of heaven's host:
Mean while the eternal eye, whose sight discerns
Abstrusest thoughts, from forth his holy mount
And from within the golden lamps that burn
Nightly before him, saw without their light
Rebellion rising, saw in whom, how spread
Among the sons of morn, what multitudes
Were banded to oppose his high decree;
And smiling to his only Son thus said.

disparity between Raphael's and God's accounts of the Fall of the angels; on which see iii 129*n*.

v *708–9*. Bentley questioned the propriety of Satan's *countenance* telling *lies*, and Pearce felt it necessary to bring rhetorical analogies to M.'s defence. But the point lies in the allusion to *Rev.* xxii 16, where Christ is the true *morning star*: the bright face of 'Lucifer, son of the morning' (*Is.* xiv 12) is itself a mendacious impersonation.

v *710*. On the size of Satan's party, see ii 692*n*.

v *711*. For the eye(s) of God, see iii 648–61*n*; also *Prov.* xv 3 ('The eyes of the Lord are in every place, beholding the evil and the good'); *Ps.* xxxiii 18 and liv 7; etc. A single eye was a common Renaissance emblem of God's unmoving omniscience: see Wind 179ff, 186ff.

v *713–14*. Cp. *Rev.* iv 5: 'There were seven lamps of fire burning before the throne, which are the seven Spirits of God.' Empson[2] 184 is perhaps right in identifying the *lamps* as planets. At least, the present passage is to be related to iii 648ff, where the seven archangelic eyes have more or less this significance (see iii 648*n* and 656*n*). Perhaps we should say, rather, 'intelligences of planets'.

v *713*. Some copies *Ed I* have comma after *within*.

v *716*. *sons of morn*] see ll. 708–9*n*. The angels are called morning stars at *Job* xxxviii 7.

v *718*. *smiling*] Makes us certain that the speech to follow will not be delivered in simple seriousness; so that it is untrue that we begin, as Empson 96 says we do, by taking God's anxiety at its face value, and hence by sharing Satan's disbelief in his omnipotence. Empson finds the joke 'appallingly malignant', on the grounds that God's complacent passivity will drive the rebels 'into real evil'. But it is hard to see how God could have acted earlier without restricting the angels' freedom of choice. For the O.T. idea that God mocks his foes, see *Ps.* ii 4, xxxvii 13 etc. (discussed in Empson 121); and cp. ii 190–1*n* above. Here God's laughter is specifically a manifestation

Son, thou in whom my glory I behold
In full resplendence, heir of all my might,
Nearly it now concerns us to be sure
Of our omnipotence, and with what arms
We mean to hold what anciently we claim
Of deity or empire, such a foe
Is rising, who intends to erect his throne
Equal to ours, throughout the spacious north;
Nor so content, hath in his thought to try
In battle, what our power is, or our right.
Let us advise, and to this hazard draw
With speed what force is left, and all employ
In our defence, lest unawares we lose
This our high place, our sanctuary, our hill.
To whom the Son with calm aspect and clear
Lightning divine, ineffable, serene,
Made answer. Mighty Father, thou thy foes
Justly hast in derision, and secure
Laugh'st at their vain designs and tumults vain,
Matter to me of glory, whom their hate
Illustrates, when they see all regal power
Given me to quell their pride, and in event
Know whether I be dextrous to subdue
Thy rebels, or be found the worst in heaven.

of his omnipotence; M.'s hope of an escape from dualism would rest in the ability of God to remain good-humoured in the face of evil. But in any case, why should God only be forbidden to smile at what is inherently absurd?

v *720*. 'His Son, whom he hath appointed heir of all things, by whom also he made the worlds' (*Heb.* i 2).

v *726*. See l. 689*n* for the north as the region of evil.

v *728*. Some copies *Ed I* omit comma after *battle.*

v *734*. Cp. the angel of the resurrection at *Matt.* xxviii 3, whose 'countenance was like lightning'–a description that alludes to the apocalyptic vision of *Dan.* x 6.

v *736–7*. See l. 718*n*. Cp. especially *Ps.* ii 4: 'He that sitteth in the heavens shall laugh: the Lord shall have them in derision.'

v *739–40*. Cp. Christ's words during a resurrection appearance: 'All power is given unto me in heaven and in earth' (*Matt.* xxviii 18). *Illustrates*] renders illustrious; illumines. *in event*] in result.

v *741*. The Son's wit matches the Father's; for Christ's 'dextrous' (*OED* 1) position 'at the right hand of bliss' (vi 892; cp. *Mark* xvi 19 etc.) is a consequence of his *dextrous* (skilful) defeat of Satan.

So spake the Son, but Satan with his powers
Far was advanced on winged speed, an host
Innumerable as the stars of night,
Or stars of morning, dewdrops, which the sun
Impearls on every leaf and every flower.
Regions they passed, the mighty regencies
Of seraphim and potentates and thrones
In their triple degrees, regions to which
All thy dominion, Adam, is no more
Than what this garden is to all the earth,
And all the sea, from one entire globose
Stretched into longitude; which having passed
At length into the limits of the north
They came, and Satan to his royal seat
High on a hill, far blazing, as a mount
Raised on a mount, with pyramids and towers

v *743. powers*] armies. Not referring to the sixth order of the celestial hierchies; though the vaguer sense 'celestial beings' may be a secondary meaning. Cp. i 128–9*n*.

v *745*. For angels as stars, see ll. 700–14*n* and 620–4*n*.

v *746. stars of morning*] See 708–9*n*. *dew-drops*] Cp. l. 2 and see *Hos*. vi 4–'O Judah, what shall I do unto thee? for your goodness is as a morning cloud, and as the early dew it goeth away.' Dew as an emblem of evanescence was very familiar at the time from its use in Henry King's much-imitated '*Sic vita*' (1657): 'Like to the falling of a Starre; / Or as the flights of Eagles are; / Or silver drops of morning dew; / . . . / Even such is man, whose borrowed light / Is streight call'd in, and paid to night. / . . . / The Dew dries up; the Starre is shot; / The flight is past; and Man forgot.' Some copies *Ed I* omit comma after *morning*.

v *748. regencies*] dominions.

v *749–50. potentates*] powers; see l. 743*n*. *triple degrees*] Because from the time of Dionysius the nine orders of the angels were divided into three groups, or hierarchies, of three, expressing the Trinity. See, e.g., Dante, *Par.* xxviii; and Spenser, *F.Q.* I xii 39: 'many an Angels voice, / Singing before th'eternall majesty, / In their trinall triplicities on hye.'

v *753–4. globose*] sphere; the adj. (cp. vii 357) for the noun. *Stretched into longitude*] in flat projection.

v *755. north*] See l. 689*n*.

v *756*. Empson 77 exonerates Satan from the charge of disloyalty by portraying him as a 'grand aristocrat' owing only loose allegiance to the central government, like a Norman lord. But this analogy would hardly have seemed creditable to M. Chapman's Byron plays remind us how warily the thoughtful republican regarded the ideal of aristocratic autonomy.

v *758–9. pyramids . . . From diamond quarries*] The apparent durability of 'pyramids' and 'diamond' has been undercut by the comparison of the

From diamond quarries hewn, and rocks of gold,
The palace of great Lucifer, (so call
That structure in the dialect of men
Interpreted) which not long after, he
Affecting all equality with God,
In imitation of that mount whereon
Messiah was declared in sight of heaven,
The Mountain of the Congregation called;
For thither he assembled all his train,
Pretending so commanded to consult
About the great reception of their king,
Thither to come, and with calumnious art
Of counterfeited truth thus held their ears.
  Thrones, dominations, princedoms, virtues, powers,
If these magnific titles yet remain

angels to dew drops; see l. 746*n*. The pyramids could be spires or obelisks as well as the squat form the word now denotes: see ii 1013*n* (Satan himself compared to a pyramid), iv 985–7*n*. The symbolism of the shape is clarified by M.'s more explicit use of it in *Reason of Church-Government* i 6 (Yale i 790). There he writes that Prelaty's 'pyramid aspires and sharpens to ambition . . . it is the most dividing, and schismaticall forme that Geometricians know of'.

v *760–6.* Satan aspires in calling his mountain by the same name as God's (see *Is.* xiv 13). But as a result he loses his own original name: *Lucifer* is his name only before the Fall. Cp. l. 658–9*n*, vii 132. *Affecting*] 'aspiring to' or 'assuming a false appearance of'. *that mount*] the 'holy hill' of l. 604.

v *772–802.* In his 1936 essay on M.'s style, T. S. Eliot chose this speech as an example of imprecision; of complication dictated by merely musical demands. Empson 26ff shows the injustice of this attack and convincingly proposes a Satan imprecise on purpose, bent on confusing his hearers. The sudden changes of direction are explained in terms of the theory that the rebels 'already hate God, or hate the recent ukase of God, so much that they do not require completed arguments' (Empson 27f). But it seems more likely that M. intends a brief impression of a speaker who dares not lay out any of his points openly and fully. We need not suppose, though, that Satan's speech was as short as Raphael makes it. It may well have seemed to him imprudent to expose frail Adam to the full power of Satan's oratory.

v *772.* The first line (which imitates the opening of God's speech at the anointing of the Messiah) gives the lie to what follows, since it implicitly admits the Messiah's claim; see l. 601*n*. It is characteristic of the oversophistication of Milton criticism that several critics hold that the speech that follows *has* to be inadequate, because if M. had let it be effective Satan would have seemed to tempt the other angels; with the consequence that God would have seemed unjust for not having mercy on them as on Adam. For an escape from this impasse see iii 129*n*.

Not merely titular, since by decree
Another now hath to himself engrossed
All power, and us eclipsed under the name
Of king anointed, for whom all this haste
Of midnight march, and hurried meeting here,
This only to consult how we may best
With what may be devised of honours new
Receive him coming to receive from us
Knee-tribute yet unpaid, prostration vile,
Too much to one, but double how endured,
To one and to his image now proclaimed?
But what if better counsels might erect
Our minds and teach us to cast off this yoke?
Will ye submit your necks, and choose to bend
The supple knee? Ye will not, if I trust
To know ye right, or if ye know your selves
Natives and sons of heaven possessed before
By none, and if not equal all, yet free,
Equally free; for orders and degrees
Jar not with liberty, but well consist.
Who can in reason then or right assume
Monarchy over such as live by right

v *776*. For the Son's inheritance of all power, see ll. 720 and 739.
v *777*. *king anointed*] See l. 605.
v *783*. Cp. Gabriel's view of Satan's earlier servility (iv 959).
v *787–802*. The appeal to native freedom is 'a perfectly orthodox version of the claim that monarchy is not grounded on the law of Nature' (Rajan 63, citing an analogue in Rutherford's *Lex Rex*). But Satan omits altogether the value of obedience or discipline, which M. regarded as the essential condition of republican freedom. (The Son is exalted insofar as he is prepared to humble himself more than the angels.) See, e.g., *Reason of Church-Government* i (Yale i 751): 'The flourishing and decaying of all civill societies . . . are mov'd to and fro as upon the axle of discipline.' The angelic orders were for M. a supreme example of this discipline: 'The Angels themselves, in whom no disorder is fear'd . . . are distinguisht and quaterniond into their celestiall Princedomes, and Satrapies, according as God himselfe hath writ his imperiall decrees through the great provinces of heav'n. The state also of the blessed in Paradise, though never so perfect, is not therefore left without discipline' (*ibid.* 752). Cp. also *John* viii 33f: 'We be Abraham's seed, and were never in bondage to any man: how sayest thou, Ye shall be made free? Jesus answered them, Verily, verily, I say unto you, Whosoever committeth sin is the servant of sin.'
v *788*. *supple knee*] A proverbial expression. Cp., e.g. Shakespeare, *Richard II* I iv 32f: 'A brace of draymen bid God speed him well, / And had the tribute of his supple knee.'

His equals, if in power and splendour less,
In freedom equal? Or can introduce
Law and edict on us, who without law
Err not, much less for this to be our lord,
And look for adoration to the abuse
Of those imperial titles which assert
Our being ordained to govern, not to serve?
  Thus far his bold discourse without control
Had audience, when among the seraphim
Abdiel, than whom none with more zeal adored
The Deity, and divine commands obeyed,
Stood up, and in a flame of zeal severe
The current of his fury thus opposed.
  O argument blasphemous, false and proud!
Words which no ear ever to hear in heaven
Expected, least of all from thee, ingrate
In place thy self so high above thy peers.
Canst thou with impious obloquy condemn
The just decree of God, pronounced and sworn,
That to his only Son by right endued
With regal sceptre, every soul in heaven
Shall bend the knee, and in that honour due
Confess him rightful king? Unjust thou say'st

v *798. edict*] Stressed on the second syllable.
v *799. for this*] For this purpose of introducing law. But there may also just possibly be an allusion to *Luke* xix 14: 'We will not have this (man) to reign over us.'
v *802.* In Satan's corrupt version of republicanism, 'every angel deserves to have some men as his slaves' (Empson 82).
v *805–7. Abdiel*] 'Servant of God', occurs in the Bible only in a human genealogical context (*1 Chron.* v 15). But the occultists, who were short of names for angels, were accustomed to utilize any obscure names the Bible had to offer. *Abdiel* had been transferred in this way in the sensational *Sepher Raziel.* As Cornelius Agrippa remarked, 'he that is inquisitive' can discover the names of spirits from the names of notable men or places in the Bible (West 152). See Gilbert 123, West 152–4, and cp. iv 782–8*n* above. Abdiel opposes Satan in a *flame of zeal* because the *seraphim* were thought of as especially ardent in their devotion, and were often imagined as flames; see ii 512*n*.
v *809. blasphemous*] Stressed on the second syllable.
v *812.* For Satan's status see l. 660*n*.
v *817.* 'God also hath highly exalted him . . . That at the name of Jesus every knee should bow, of things in heaven, and things in earth, and things under the earth; And that every tongue should confess that Jesus Christ is Lord' (*Phil.* ii 9–11).

Flatly unjust, to bind with laws the free,
And equal over equals to let reign,
One over all with unsucceeded power.
Shalt thou give law to God, shalt thou dispute
With him the points of liberty, who made
Thee what thou art, and formed the powers of heaven
Such as he pleased, and circumscribed their being?
Yet by experience taught we know how good,
And of our good, and of our dignity
How provident he is, how far from thought
To make us less, bent rather to exalt
Our happy state under one head more near
United. But to grant it thee unjust,
That equal over equals monarch reign:
Thy self though great and glorious dost thou count,
Or all angelic nature joined in one,
Equal to him begotten Son, by whom
As by his Word the mighty Father made
All things, even thee, and all the spirits of heaven
By him created in their bright degrees,
Crowned them with glory, and to their glory named

v *821. unsucceeded power*] power never to be succeeded, everlasting power; though at iii 339ff God envisaged a laying aside at least of the 'regal sceptre'.
v *822.* The thought is that of *Rom.* ix 20: 'O man, who art thou that repliest against God? Shall the thing formed say to him that formed it, Why hast thou made me thus?' (Margin 'Or, answerest again, or, disputest with God?').
v *830.* Cp. *Col.* ii 10: 'Ye are complete in him, which is the head of all principality and power.' *one*] Some copies *Ed I* our.
v *832.* See ll. 603–6*n* and 787–802*n*.
v *835–40.* Cp. *Col.* i 16–17: 'For by him [Christ] were all things created, that are in heaven, and that are in earth, visible and invisible, whether they be thrones, or dominions, or principalities, or powers: all things were created by him, and for him: And he is before all things, and by him all things consist.' Abdiel makes explicit the doctrine that was implied in earlier allusions to the same Biblical passage, at ll. 601 and 772. Although M. was Arian to the extent that he did not believe the Son to be generated from all eternity, nevertheless he had no doubt of Christ's agency in creation as the Logos or divine Word. See *De doctrina* i 5 (Columbia xiv 180–2), and iii 170*n* and 383*n* above.
v *839. Crowned . . . glory*] Underlines the affirmation of God's creativity, by alluding to *Ps.* viii 5: 'Thou hast made him a little lower than the angels, and hast crowned him with glory and honour.' Note also that this verse was often regarded as a prophecy of the Incarnation.

Thrones, dominations, princedoms, virtues, powers,
Essential powers, nor by his reign obscured,
But more illustrious made, since he the head
One of our number thus reduced becomes,
His laws our laws, all honour to him done
Returns our own. Cease then this impious rage,
And tempt not these; but hasten to appease
The incensed Father, and the incensed Son,
While pardon may be found in time besought.
  So spake the fervent angel, but his zeal
None seconded, as out of season judged,
Or singular and rash, whereat rejoiced
The apostate, and more haughty thus replied.
That we were formed then say'st thou? And the work
Of secondary hands, by task transferred
From Father to his Son? Strange point and new!
Doctrine which we would know whence learned: who saw
When this creation was? Remember'st thou
Thy making, while the maker gave thee being?
We know no time when we were not as now;
Know none before us, self-begot, self-raised

v *842–5*. Abdiel appears to regard the Messiah's kingship over the angels as a kind of incarnation, involving the setting aside of divinity; just as his human incarnation in Jesus will, at a later stage of the divine emanation.
v *845–8*. Echoing *Ps.* ii 12 and *Is.* lv 6f.
v *853–71*. Rajan 102 draws attention to the tawdriness of Satan here, to his 'jaunty sarcasm and irrelevant puns'.
v *855*. An important line from the narrative point of view. Empson argues that the Son's agency in creation has never been mentioned in the poem before, and that it is Satan's reaction to an unfamiliar argument that brings him to deny his own creation, even his creation by the Father. God himself keeps the doctrine of creation by Christ esoteric, preferring 'to issue a bare challenge' at the coronation of the Messiah (Empson 83). However, the doctrine is known to Abdiel; so that we must conclude either that an angel who chose to be obedient could intuit it, or else that God's speech at the coronation was fuller than Raphael gives it at ll. 600–15.
v *860*. Satan commits the primal sin of wishing to exist 'on his own' (Lewis 65, citing Augustine, *Civ. Dei* xiv 13), and seeks justification in his own ignorance of the state of non-being. (Contrast viii 251, where Adam is wiser about a similar limitation of his experience.) Satan's denial of creation by God is sustained until i 116–17 (*q.v.*), but abandoned in iv 43; unless, indeed, it is all along a public profession only. The standpoint was a traditional one for the devils: see, e.g., *Par.* xxix 49–63, where Dante contrasts the angels

By our own quickening power, when fatal course
Had circled his full orb, the birth mature
Of this our native heaven, ethereal sons.
Our puissance is our own, our own right hand
Shall teach us highest deeds, by proof to try
Who is our equal: then thou shalt behold
Whether by supplication we intend
Address, and to begirt the almighty throne
Beseeching or besieging. This report,
These tidings carry to the anointed king;
And fly, ere evil intercept thy flight.
He said, and as the sound of waters deep
Hoarse murmur echoed to his words applause
Through the infinite host, nor less for that
The flaming seraph fearless, though alone
Encompassed round with foes, thus answered bold.
O alienate from God, O spirit accurst,
Forsaken of all good; I see thy fall
Determined, and thy hapless crew involved
In this perfidious fraud, contagion spread
Both of thy crime and punishment: henceforth
No more be troubled how to quit the yoke
Of God's Messiah; those indulgent laws
Will not be now vouchsafed; other decrees
Against thee are gone forth without recall;
That golden sceptre which thou didst reject
Is now an iron rod to bruise and break
Thy disobedience. Well thou didst advise,
Yet not for thy advice or threats I fly
These wicked tents devoted, lest the wrath

who fell with those who modestly acknowledged their status as creatures and began the dance of the heavens.

v *861–2.* A secularised version of the Great Year that in its true version expresses the will of God: see l. 583*n*.

v *864–5.* Cp. *Ps.* xlv 4: 'Thy right hand shall teach thee terrible things.'

v *872.* Satan has apparently achieved his purpose, for this 'voice of many waters' is the sound of worship (*Rev.* xix 6).

v *875. flaming*] See ll. 805–7*n*.

v *882–3.* Cp. Christ's promise 'my yoke is easy, and my burden is light' (*Matt.* xi 30).

v *886–7.* See ii 327–8*n*.

v *890.* Alluding to Moses' warning to the Israelites not to support Korah's rebellion: 'Depart, I pray you, from the tents of these wicked men, and touch nothing of theirs, lest ye be consumed in all their sins' (*Num.* xvi 26).

Impendent, raging into sudden flame
Distinguish not: for soon expect to feel
His thunder on thy head, devouring fire.
Then who created thee lamenting learn,
When who can uncreate thee thou shalt know.
So spake the seraph Abdiel faithful found,
Among the faithless, faithful only he;
Among innumerable false, unmoved,
Unshaken, unseduced, unterrified
His loyalty he kept, his love, his zeal;
Nor number, nor example with him wrought
To swerve from truth, or change his constant mind
Though single. From amidst them forth he passed,
Long way through hostile scorn, which he sustained
Superior, nor of violence feared aught;
And with retorted scorn his back he turned
On those proud towers to swift destruction doomed.

THE END OF THE FIFTH BOOK

Paradise Lost

BOOK VI

The Argument

Raphael continues to relate how Michael and Gabriel were sent forth to battle against Satan and his angels. The first fight described: Satan and his powers retire under night: he calls a council, invents devilish engines, which in the second day's fight put Michael and his angels to some disorder; but they at length pulling up mountains overwhelm both the force and machines of Satan: yet the tumult not so ending, God on the third day sends Messiah

devoted] doomed; just possibly felt as a Latinism, though there are many seventeenth-century instances. Before *lest*, supply 'but'.
v *893*. 'For our God is a consuming fire' (*Heb*. xii 29).
v *898–903*. Again the confrontation of one and multitude: see ll. 610–12*n*. On the Pythagorean origin of the contrast between the singleness of truth and the multiplicity of falsehood, see Fowler 5–7.
v *899*. For the rhetoric, see ii 185*n*.
v *906*. *retorted*] requited (*OED* I 1 a). But there is also a play between the root sense ('turned back') and *his back he turned*.

his Son, for whom he had reserved the glory of that victory: he in the power of his Father coming to the place, and causing all his legions to stand still on either side, with his chariot and thunder driving into the midst of his enemies, pursues them unable to resist towards the wall of heaven; which opening, they leap down with horror and confusion into the place of punishment prepared for them in the deep: Messiah returns with triumph to his Father.

All night the dreadless angel unpursued
Through heaven's wide champaign held his way, till
morn,
Waked by the circling hours, with rosy hand
Unbarred the gates of light. There is a cave
Within the mount of God, fast by his throne,
Where light and darkness in perpetual round
Lodge and dislodge by turns, which makes through
heaven
Grateful vicissitude, like day and night;
Light issues forth, and at the other door
Obsequious darkness enters, till her hour

vi *1. the dreadless angel*] Abdiel.
vi *2–4.* A very clearly defined motif. Cp. especially Ovid, *Met.* ii 112–14: 'Aurora, who keeps watch in the reddening dawn, has opened wide her purple gates, and her courts glowing with rosy light.' The *hours* are *circling* because they personify the spatial sidereal hours or portions of the firmament that appear to revolve about the earth. Homer put them in charge of the gates of heaven at *Il.* v 749. For their wakefulness, implied here, cp. Spenser, *F.Q.* VII vii 45: 'Then came the *Howres*, faire daughters of high *Jove* / . . . who did them Porters make / Of heavens gate (whence all the gods issued) / Which they did dayly watch, and nightly wake / By even turnes, ne ever did their charge forsake.' The best concise account of the Hours is A. Kent Hieatt's Appendix in *Short Time's Endless Monument* (New York 1960) pp. 111–13.
vi *4–11.* The thought follows on closely from l. 3, for the Hours were often described as moving *by turns* (alternately) and as forming a set of light / dark pairs. Hesiod's abysm, alternately inhabited by Night and by Day (*Theog.* 736–57) is rendered more thematic by its relocation *fast by* God's *throne*. Time is allowed very near to M.'s God: see v 579–82*n*. On the other hand, God's mount clearly *contains* time in its cave; much as Venus the form-giver keeps the boar of darkness and death and chaos imprisoned in a cave beneath the mount in the paradise of *F.Q.* III vi 48. The breath-taking image may, as Burden suggests, be drawn in part from *Rev.* vii 15f and xxii 5, where ordinary light and darkness are excluded from heaven. *dislodge*] move quarters; a military term; cp. v 669. *vicissitude*] change. *obsequious*] dutiful; compliant.

To veil the heaven, though darkness there might well
Seem twilight here; and now went forth the morn
Such as in highest heaven, arrayed in gold
Empyreal, from before her vanished night,
Shot through with orient beams: when all the plain
Covered with thick embattled squadrons bright,
Chariots and flaming arms, and fiery steeds
Reflecting blaze on blaze, first met his view:
War he perceived, war in procinct, and found
Already known what he for news had thought
To have reported: gladly then he mixed
Among those friendly powers who him received
With joy and acclamations loud, that one
That of so many myriads fallen, yet one
Returned not lost: on to the sacred hill
They led him high applauded, and present
Before the seat supreme; from whence a voice
From midst a golden cloud thus mild was heard.
  Servant of God, well done, well hast thou fought
The better fight, who single hast maintained
Against revolted multitudes the cause
Of truth, in word mightier than they in arms;
And for the testimony of truth hast borne
Universal reproach, far worse to bear
Than violence: for this was all thy care
To stand approved in sight of God, though worlds
Judged thee perverse: the easier conquest now
Remains thee, aided by this host of friends,
Back on thy foes more glorious to return
Than scorned thou didst depart, and to subdue
By force, who reason for their law refuse,

vi *11–12.* For the absence of night in heaven, see v 645*n*. The *morn* is that of Day 2; see Introduction, 'Chronology'.
vi *16. embattled*] set in battle array.
vi *19. in procinct*] prepared; not a common phrase, it would probably be felt as an imitation of the Latin *in procinctu*.
vi *29–34.* Cp. *Matt.* xxv 21 ('Well done, thou good and faithful servant'); *1 Tim.* vi 12 ('fight the good fight of faith'); and *Ps.* lxix 7 ('for thy sake I have borne reproach'). *servant of God*] the literal meaning of Abdiel: see v 805*n*.
vi *41–3.* For M.'s sustained contrast between the devils' reliance on *force* or strength and God's on merit or goodness, see Steadman *passim*. *right reason*] upright, true reason; conscience. Originally the phrase was a translation of the Stoic and Scholastic term *recta ratio*. See Robert Hoopes, *Right Reason in the English Renaissance* (Cambridge, Mass. 1962); also xii 80–101*n*.

Right reason for their law, and for their king
Messiah, who by right of merit reigns.
Go Michael of celestial armies prince,
And thou in military prowess next
Gabriel, lead forth to battle these my sons
Invincible, lead forth my armed saints
By thousands and by millions ranged for fight;
Equal in number to that godless crew
Rebellious, them with fire and hostile arms
Fearless assault, and to the brow of heaven
Pursuing drive them out from God and bliss,
Into their place of punishment, the gulf
Of Tartarus, which ready opens wide
His fiery chaos to receive their fall.
  So spake the sovereign voice, and clouds began
To darken all the hill, and smoke to roll
In dusky wreaths, reluctant flames, the sign

vi *44*. See *Dan.* xii 1, and *Rev.* xii 7f: 'And there was war in heaven: Michael and his angels fought against the dragon; and the dragon fought and his angels, And prevailed not; neither was their place any more in heaven.' The commoner Protestant view was that Michael ('Who is like to God?') signifies Christ: see West 125. But in *De doctrina* i 9 (Columbia xv 105) M. argues at some length that 'Christ vanquished the devil, and trampled him under foot singly; Michael, the leader of the angels, is introduced in the capacity of a hostile commander waging war with the prince of the devils, the armies on both sides being drawn out in battle array, and separating after a doubtful conflict.' The same point about Christ's transcendence, and independence of angelic assistance, underlies the plot of *PL* vi.
vi *46*. *Gabriel*] 'Strength of God', see iv 549–50*n*.
vi *49*. 'From the point of view of numbers (easily) the match of the godless crew.' Actually the loyal angels are twice as numerous (see ii 692*n*); but Empson 41 is right to reject Peter's unnecessary speculation that God only allows half the good angels to fight.
vi *54–5*. For the identification of Tartarus with hell, see ii 69*n*. *fiery chaos*] An exact description, since the building of hell 'encroached' on chaos (ii 1002). Presumably hell came into existence at the moment of Satan's fall: see l. 292*n*.
vi *56–60*. Before the issuing of the Ten Commandments, 'there were thunders and lightnings, and a thick cloud upon the mount, and the voice of the trumpet exceeding loud; so that all the people that was in the camp trembled: . . . And mount Sinai was altogether on a smoke, because the Lord descended upon it in fire: and the smoke thereof ascended as the smoke of a furnace, and the whole mount quaked greatly' (*Exod.* xix 16, 18). *reluctant*] writhing; or in its modern sense. *gan*] began to; not the older auxiliary verb 'gan' = 'did'. See xi 73–6*n*.

Of wrath awaked: nor with less dread the loud
Ethereal trumpet from on high gan blow:
At which command the powers militant,
That stood for heaven, in mighty quadrate joined
Of union irresistible, moved on
In silence their bright legions, to the sound
Of instrumental harmony that breathed
Heroic ardour to adventurous deeds
Under their godlike leaders, in the cause
Of God and his Messiah. On they move
Indissolubly firm; nor obvious hill,
Nor straitening vale, nor wood, nor stream divides
Their perfect ranks; for high above the ground
Their march was, and the passive air upbore
Their nimble tread, as when the total kind
Of birds in orderly array on wing
Came summoned over Eden to receive
Their names of thee; so over many a tract
Of heaven they marched, and many a province wide
Tenfold the length of this terrene: at last
Far in the horizon to the north appeared
From skirt to skirt a fiery region, stretched
In battailous aspect, and nearer view
Bristled with upright beams innumerable

vi *62*. Cp. the 'phalanx' of the rebels in hell, which outwardly imitates this virtuous shape; see i 550*n*.
vi *63–8*. Cp. the silent march of the rebel angels, to the music of flutes and recorders played in the Dorian mode (i 549–61).
vi *69*. *Indissolubly*] Stressed on the second syllable. *obvious*] standing in the way.
vi *71–2*. M.'s angels move like the ancient gods, without touching the ground.
vi *73–6*. 'And Adam gave names to all cattle and to the fowl of the air, and to every beast of the field' (*Gen.* ii 20). M. overgoes the famous comparisons of gathering armies to birds in Homer *Il.* ii 459 and Virgil, *Aen.* vii 699, by achieving numerical superiority (*total kind*), but also by maintaining greater propriety. Airborne angels resemble birds more closely than earthbound human armies do; and there is the correspondence of species with orders.
vi *78–86*. Cited as an example of montage in Eisenstein 59.
vi *78*. *terrene*] *OED* gives no earlier instance of this absolute use of the adj. = earth.
vi *79*. *north*] The region of evil; see v 689*n*.
vi *81*. *battailous*] warlike, bellicose. *aspect*] As usual in M., stressed on the second syllable: 'áspect' had been an alternative pronunciation for about half a century.

Of rigid spears, and helmets thronged, and shields
Various, with boastful argument portrayed,
The banded powers of Satan hasting on
With furious expedition; for they weened
That self same day by fight, or by surprise
To win the mount of God, and on his throne
To set the envier of his state, the proud
Aspirer, but their thoughts proved fond and vain
In the mid way: though strange to us it seemed
At first, that angel should with angel war,
And in fierce hosting meet, who wont to meet
So oft in festivals of joy and love
Unanimous, as sons of one great sire
Hymning the eternal Father: but the shout
Of battle now began, and rushing sound
Of onset ended soon each milder thought.
High in the midst exalted as a god
The apostate in his sun-bright chariot sat
Idol of majesty divine, enclosed
With flaming cherubim, and golden shields;
Then lighted from his gorgeous throne, for now
'Twixt host and host but narrow space was left,
A dreadful interval, and front to front
Presented stood in terrible array
Of hideous length: before the cloudy van,
On the rough edge of battle ere it joined,
Satan with vast and haughty strides advanced,
Came towering, armed in adamant and gold;

vi *83.* M.'s very corporeal angels have arms not unlike those of the combatants in Homer, Ariosto, or Spenser. Contrast the conception of Heywood in *The hierarchie of the blessed angells* (1635): 'No Lances, Swords, nor Bombards they had then. . . . Onely spiritual Armes to them were lent.'

vi *84. argument*] Punning between 'motif' and 'subject for debate'. No doubt the rebel *imprese* were provocative. M. possibly alludes to the boastful arms of the Seven against Thebes (Euripides, *Phoen.* 1108–40).

vi *86. expedition*] expeditiousness, celerity.

vi *87. selfsame day*] Biblical diction; cp. *Gen.* vii 13.

vi *91. In the mid way*] See l. 762*n*.

vi *93. hosting*] hostile encounter. *wont*] were used.

vi *100–2.* Satan is particularly an *idol* or false image of *majesty divine* when he is mounted on his triumphal *sun-bright chariot* because Messiah himself rides a cosmic vehicle; see ll. 749–59*n* below. The *cherubim*–always characterised by their brightness–correspond to the 'four cherubic shapes' of the divine chariot.

vi *108. edge of battle*] front line. See i 276*n*.

Abdiel that sight endured not, where he stood
Among the mightiest, bent on highest deeds,
And thus his own undaunted heart explores.
O heaven! That such resemblance of the highest
Should yet remain, where faith and realty
Remain not; wherefore should not strength and might
There fail where virtue fails, or weakest prove
Where boldest; though to sight unconquerable?
His puissance, trusting in the almighty's aid,
I mean to try, whose reason I have tried
Unsound and false; nor is it aught but just,
That he who in debate of truth hath won,
Should win in arms, in both disputes alike
Victor; though brutish that contest and foul,
When reason hath to deal with force, yet so
Most reason is that reason overcome.
So pondering, and from his armed peers
Forth stepping opposite, half way he met
His daring foe, at this prevention more
Incensed, and thus securely him defied.
Proud, art thou met? Thy hope was to have reached
The highth of thy aspiring unopposed,
The throne of God unguarded, and his side
Abandoned at the terror of thy power
Or potent tongue; fool, not to think how vain
Against the omnipotent to rise in arms;

vi *114–26.* A soliloquy in the manner of Homer's thoughtful combatants. Cp. especially Hector's soliloquy, before engaging Achilles, at *Il.* xxii 99–130. *PL* has other allusions that similarly cast Satan in the role of the proud and jealous Achilles: see, e.g., i 286–91*n*, v 673*n*.
vi *115. realty*] reality (*OED* 1 a) or sincerity (*OED* 2) or both.
vi *120. tried*] proved, judged after trial.
vi *124. contest*] Stressed on the second syllable.
vi *122–3.* Empson (54) is right to say that M. was by no means a pacifist; as the passage on Truth and the sword of Justice in *Eikonoklastes* makes sufficiently clear (Yale iii 583f). On the other hand he hated war in itself and despised it as a subject for epic (see ix 27ff below). It has been suggested that the angelic war should be regarded as burlesque rather than serious epic. But this is most unlikely in view of the undoubtedly serious concluding phase, Messiah's victory. M. would not consider this ordinary war, but a spiritual conflict like the one *milites Christiani* fight in; or at least an unquestionably just war. In any case, it is fought solely to amplify the transcendence of Christ.
vi *129. prevention*] frustration, obstruction (*OED* 4).
vi *130. securely*] confidently, without apprehension.

Who out of smallest things could without end
Have raised incessant armies to defeat
Thy folly; or with solitary hand
Reaching beyond all limit at one blow
Unaided could have finished thee, and whelmed
Thy legions under darkness; but thou seest
All are not of thy train; there be who faith
Prefer, and piety to God, though then
To thee not visible, when I alone
Seemed in thy world erroneous to dissent
From all: my sect thou seest, now learn too late
How few sometimes may know, when thousands err.
    Whom the grand foe with scornful eye askance
Thus answered. Ill for thee, but in wished hour
Of my revenge, first sought for thou return'st
From flight, seditious angel, to receive
Thy merited reward, the first assay
Of this right hand provoked, since first that tongue
Inspired with contradiction durst oppose
A third part of the gods, in synod met
Their deities to assert, who while they feel
Vigour divine within them, can allow
Omnipotence to none. But well thou com'st
Before thy fellows, ambitious to win
From me some plume, that thy success may show

vi *137–9*. Echoing *Matt.* xxvi 53 and iii 9: 'And think not to say within yourselves, We have Abraham to our father: for I say unto you, that God is able of these stones to raise up children unto Abraham.'
vi *143*. *there be who*] there are (those) who. Current usage in M.'s time. *faith*] faithfulness.
vi *147*. *sect*] kind of persons. But there is probably also a reference to the contemptuous Royalist practice of classifying all who were not in favour of bishops as 'sectaries'. Cp. *Eikonoklastes*, Pref. (Yale iii 348): 'I never knew that time in *England*, when men of truest Religion were not counted Sectaries. . . . if ignorance and perversness will needs be national and universal, then they who adhere to wisdom and to truth, are not therfore to be blam'd, for beeing so few as to seem a sect or faction.' Contrast, however, the view expressed in *Areopagitica* (Yale ii 566).
vi *153*. *assay*] trial, experiment.
vi *156*. *third*] For the size of the rebel party, see ii 692*n*. *gods*] In Satan's mouth a presumptuous word, meaning more than 'angels': see i 116–7*n*.
vi *161–3*. Satan means that there will be a short pause before he destroys Abdiel, because this is the only chance he will ever have of answering his taunts, and he does not want Abdiel to be able to boast that they went unanswered. The confused threat betrays a lack of confidence in his own

Destruction to the rest: this pause between
(Unanswered lest thou boast) to let thee know;
At first I thought that liberty and heaven
To heavenly souls had been all one; but now
I see that most through sloth had rather serve,
Ministering spirits, trained up in feast and song;
Such hast thou armed, the minstrelsy of heaven,
Servility with freedom to contend,
As both their deeds compared this day shall prove.
To whom in brief thus Abdiel stern replied.
Apostate, still thou err'st, nor end wilt find
Of erring, from the path of truth remote:
Unjustly thou deprav'st it with the name
Of servitude to serve whom God ordains,
Or nature; God and nature bid the same,
When he who rules is worthiest, and excels
Them whom he governs. This is servitude,
To serve the unwise, or him who hath rebelled
Against his worthier, as thine now serve thee,
Thy self not free, but to thy self enthralled;
Yet lewdly dar'st our ministering upbraid.

ability to destroy Abdiel before he can boast again. *plume*] 'feather in your cap'; but there is also a dramatic irony, in which the feather is one of pretentious display by Satan–cp. Shakespeare, *1 Hen. VI* III iii 5–7: 'Let frantic Talbot triumph for a while, / And like a peacock sweep along his tail; / We'll pull his plumes and take away his train.'

vi *167. ministering spirits*] The phrase is used in *Heb.* i 13f to emphasise the low status of the angels compared with Christ: 'To which of the angels said he at any time, Sit on my right hand? . . . Are they not all ministering spirits, sent forth to minister for them who shall be heirs of salvation?'

vi *168. minstrelsy*] minstrels.

vi *169.* Cp. ii 255–7*n*.

vi *174. depravest*] misconstrue, vilify, defame.

vi *175. Ed I* and *Ed II* italicize *servitude.*

vi *176.* Satan's vague invocation of the value of liberty at l. 164 implied an appeal to Natural Law (see v 787–802*n*), and Abdiel makes this explicit in his rebuttal. The agreement of Natural Law with God's Eternal Law was a fundamental doctrine of Christian Humanism: see, e.g., Hooker, *Laws of Eccles. Pol.* I iii 1–4, where nature is 'God's instrument'. Abdiel's argument is that when all is arranged according to 'degree' of excellence, freedom lies in the obedience of taking one's natural place. See Rajan 64f.

vi *181.* Cp. xii 90ff, also *PR* ii 466–9: 'Yet he who reigns within himself, and rules / passions, desires, and fears, is more a king; / Which every wise and vertuous man attains: / And who attains not, ill aspires to rule.'

vi *182. lewdly*] wickedly; or foolishly.

Reign thou in hell thy kingdom, let me serve
In heaven God ever blest, and his divine
Behests obey, worthiest to be obeyed,
Yet chains in hell, not realms expect: mean while
From me returned, as erst thou saidst, from flight,
This greeting on thy impious crest receive.
    So saying, a noble stroke he lifted high,
Which hung not, but so swift with tempest fell
On the proud crest of Satan, that no sight,
Nor motion of swift thought, less could his shield
Such ruin intercept: ten paces huge
He backed recoiled; the tenth on bended knee
His massy spear upstayed; as if on earth
Winds under ground or waters forcing way
Sidelong, had pushed a mountain from his seat
Half sunk with all his pines. Amazement seized
The rebel thrones, but greater rage to see
Thus foiled their mightiest, ours joy filled, and shout,
Presage of victory and fierce desire
Of battle: whereat Michael bid sound

vi *183–6.* Remembered in hell; cp. i 263, 'Better to reign in hell, than serve in heaven', and see *n.*
vi *185.* A heavier point is needed after *obeyed.*
vi *187.* So Ascanius hurls back Numanus' gibe 'twice captured Phrygians', with the accompaniment of a blow, at *Aen.* ix 599 and 635.
vi *193–5.* Whaler 100 plausibly suggests that since ten symbolized divine power and creativity, ten reversed would symbolize destruction. *ruin*] destruction; fall. For Satan's spear see i 292–4*n.*
vi *195–8.* See i 230–7*n.* The image is not only one of destruction and chaos, but also of unnatural and proud rebellion; at least, this was most usually the meaning of the volcano as a symbol. For water as an additional cause of earthquakes and volcanoes, see Svendsen 104; but here the action of the water seems more like erosion. Cp. the fall of the Old Dragon in *F.Q.* I xi 54: 'So downe he fell, as an huge rockie clift, / Whose false foundation waves have washt away, / With dreadfull poyse is from the mayneland rift.' On the association of Satan with *pines,* see i 292–4*n.*
vi *199.* By a synecdoche, *thrones* stands for all the angelic orders. We know from v 772 and vi 102 that there were rebels of at least six different orders. Presumably M. subscribed to the medieval doctrine that 'out of all these orders some certain were lost' (Dante, *Convivio* II vi 95ff).
vi *200.* The *shout* is *Presage* of the final *victory* over Satan; when 'The Lord himself shall descend from heaven with a shout, with the voice of the archangel, and with the trump of God: and the dead in Christ shall rise' (I Thess. iv 16).

The archangel trumpet; through the vast of heaven
It sounded, and the faithful armies rung
Hosanna to the highest: nor stood at gaze
The adverse legions, nor less hideous joined
The horrid shock: now storming fury rose,
And clamour such as heard in heaven till now
Was never, arms on armour clashing brayed
Horrible discord, and the madding wheels
Of brazen chariots raged; dire was the noise
Of conflict; over head the dismal hiss
Of fiery darts in flaming volleys flew,
And flying vaulted either host with fire.
So under fiery cope together rushed
Both battles main, with ruinous assault
And inextinguishable rage; all heaven
Resounded, and had earth been then, all earth
Had to her centre shook. What wonder? When
Millions of fierce encountering angels fought
On either side, the least of whom could wield
These elements, and arm him with the force
Of all their regions: how much more of power
Army against army numberless to raise
Dreadful combustion warring, and disturb,
Though not destroy, their happy native seat;
Had not the eternal king omnipotent
From his strong hold of heaven high overruled
And limited their might; though numbered such
As each divided legion might have seemed

vi *209. brayed*] Often used of thunder, or of any jarring sound. Cp. Blackmore, *Prince Arthur* (1695) viii 375: 'Swords clash with Swords, Bucklers on Bucklers bray.'

vi *213.* It seems that the weapons of M.'s angels are spiritual after all: cp. *Eph.* vi 16, 'the shield of faith, wherewith ye shall be able to quench all the fiery darts of the wicked', and see l. 83*n.*

vi *215. cope*] sky; see iv 992*n.* *So under*] Sounder, *Ed I*, corr. in *Errata.*

vi *216. battles main*] the main bodies of the armies, as distinct from the van or the wings (*OED* s.v. *Battle* II 9).

vi *221–2.* i.e., had the power to wield the four elements of which earth was later to be created.

vi *225. combustion*] confusion, commotion, tumult; a very common seventeenth-century meaning.

vi *229–36.* The three features of the armies' power–numbers, strength and skill–are probably meant to be in ascending order of importance. *numbered such*] so numerous. *yet . . . chief*] yet each single warrior seemed

A numerous host, in strength each armed hand
A legion; led in fight, yet leader seemed
Each warrior single as in chief, expert
When to advance, or stand, or turn the sway
Of battle, open when, and when to close
The ridges of grim war; no thought of flight,
None of retreat, no unbecoming deed
That argued fear; each on himself relied,
As only in his arm the moment lay
Of victory; deeds of eternal fame
Were done, but infinite: for wide was spread
That war and various; sometimes on firm ground
A standing fight, then soaring on main wing
Tormented all the air; all air seemed then
Conflicting fire: long time in even scale
The battle hung; till Satan, who that day
Prodigious power had shown, and met in arms
No equal, ranging through the dire attack
Of fighting seraphim confused, at length

a commander-in-chief. *ridges of grim war*] Perhaps 'ranks'; but see Lewis 135: 'I do not think, with Verity, that Milton has Shakespeare (*Lucrece* 1438 ["To Simois' reedy banks the red blood ran, / Whose waves to imitate the battle sought / With swelling ridges; and their ranks began / To break upon the galled shore"]) in mind. The whole passage is full of Homeric echoes, and the *ridges* reproduce πολέμοιο γέφυραι (*Il.* iv 371, etc.). What *they* were, I do not know.'

vi *231–46.* Eisenstein 60f analyses the montage of this passage and concludes that there is 'an identical number of lines and shots'.

vi *239. moment*] determining influence (*OED* 5); but also beginning the balance image of l. 245–the 'moment of a balance' (*OED* 3 a, comparing Vulg. *momentum staterae*) was a tiny increment, that might yet alter its equilibrium. Cp. x 45–7, also Wyclif's *Is.* xl 15: 'Lo! Jentiles as a drope of a boket, and as a moment of a balaunce ben holden.'

vi *243. on main wing*] fully airborne.

vi *245.* For the balance symbol in *PL*, see iv 999–1012*nn.* *long time*] here and in *De doctrina* i 9 (Columbia xv 104) M. takes the war in heaven to be a protracted one, on slender Biblical authority. For a discussion of contemporary theologians who took a similar view, see Edgar F. Daniels, 'M.'s "doubtful conflict" and the seventeenth-century tradition', *N & Q* ccvi (1961) 430–2.

vi *248. no equal*] For Gilbert (5), evidence that Satan's encounter with Abdiel is a late addition. But Newton may well have been right in his view that Abdiel's advantage was only a temporary one. Of course it is *just* 'That he who in debate of truth hath won, / Should win in arms' also (vi 122f). Often, however, as M. knew as well as anyone, it does not happen that way.

Saw where the sword of Michael smote, and felled
Squadrons at once, with huge two-handed sway
Brandished aloft the horrid edge came down
Wide wasting; such destruction to withstand
He hasted, and opposed the rocky orb
Of tenfold adamant, his ample shield
A vast circumference: at his approach
The great archangel from his warlike toil
Surceased, and glad as hoping here to end
Intestine war in heaven, the arch foe subdued
Or captive dragged in chains, with hostile frown
And visage all inflamed first thus began.
  Author of evil, unknown till thy revolt,
Unnamed in heaven, now plenteous, as thou seest
These acts of hateful strife, hateful to all,
Though heaviest by just measure on thy self
And thy adherents: how hast thou disturbed
Heaven's blessed peace, and into nature brought
Misery, uncreated till the crime
Of thy rebellion? How hast thou instilled
Thy malice into thousands, once upright
And faithful, now proved false. But think not here

vi *250–1*. This passage, together with ll. 318–21, is sometimes used in explanation of the 'two-handed engine' in *Lycidas*: see Mindele C. Treip, in *N & Q* cciv (1959) 364–6, with refs. to earlier material; but also T. B. Stroup, *ibid.* 366f. Michael's sword is also referred to at ii 294 above, and xi 247f; though unauthorized by any Biblical text it was his regular iconographical attribute.

vi *254–5*. For Satan's shield, see i 286–91*n*. In the seventeenth century *adamant* was most often identified with diamond; and this raises something of a problem. For a shield of diamond would most obviously be an emblem either of Fortitude or of constant Faith (cp., e.g., Fido's shield 'of one pure diamond, celestiall fair' in Phineas Fletcher, *Purple Island* xii 24, or Arthur's shield used against the dragon in *F.Q.* V xi 10, or M.'s Zeal armed in complete diamond (ll. 840–1*n*); and see Tervarent 147f). If he means to do more than amplify the hardness of the armour, therefore, M. must intend an irony, or a deceptively pure and bright Satan. *tenfold*] Cp. the 'sevenfold' shield of Guyon in *F.Q.* II viii 32, and the 'seven-times-folded' shield of *SA* 1122. In ancient usage the term was concrete and descriptive, but in Spenser it alluded to the protection afforded by the seven virtues against the seven deadly sins.

vi *259*. *Intestine war*] internal, civil war.

vi *267*. Note that for M. the angels are not supernatural, but part of (celestial) nature.

vi *269*. Perhaps question mark is in error for exclamation mark.

To trouble holy rest; heaven casts thee out
From all her confines. Heaven the seat of bliss
Brooks not the works of violence and war.
Hence then, and evil go with thee along
Thy offspring, to the place of evil, hell,
Thou and thy wicked crew; there mingle broils,
Ere this avenging sword begin thy doom,
Or some more sudden vengeance winged from God
Precipitate thee with augmented pain.
   So spake the prince of angels; to whom thus
The adversary. Nor think thou with wind
Of airy threats to awe whom yet with deeds
Thou canst not. Hast thou turned the least of these
To flight, or if to fall, but that they rise
Unvanquished, easier to transact with me
That thou shouldst hope, imperious, and with threats
To chase me hence? Err not that so shall end
The strife which thou call'st evil, but we style
The strife of glory: which we mean to win,
Or turn this heaven it self into the hell
Thou fablest, here however to dwell free,
If not to reign: mean while thy utmost force,
And join him named Almighty to thy aid,
I fly not, but have sought thee far and nigh.
   They ended parle, and both addressed for fight
Unspeakable; for who, though with the tongue
Of angels, can relate, or to what things
Liken on earth conspicuous, that may lift
Human imagination to such highth
Of Godlike power: for likest Gods they seemed,
Stood they or moved, in stature, motion, arms

vi *275–6.* For Satan's generation of Sin, see ii 743–60.
vi *282. adversary*] The literal meaning of 'Satan'; *Job* i 6, A.V. marg.; also i 82*n* above.
vi *284–8.* i.e., has your failure to defeat my followers decisively by *deeds* made you think it may be easier to deal (*transact*) with me–to negotiate at the summit and frighten me off with words?
vi *288. Err not*] do not imagine erroneously.
vi *289.* Referring to l. 262.
vi *292. fablest*] At l. 276. Hell has been in existence since ll. 54f at least, but perhaps only the loyal angels have heard about it until now. Abdiel mentions it (at l. 183) only after he has rejoined the loyalists.
vi *296. parle*] parley, truce, debate. *addressed*] made ready.
vi *302.* For the godlike movement of the angels, see ll. 71f above.

Fit to decide the empire of great heaven.
Now waved their fiery swords, and in the air
Made horrid circles; two broad suns their shields
Blazed opposite, while expectation stood
In horror; from each hand with speed retired
Where erst was thickest fight, the angelic throng,
And left large field, unsafe within the wind
Of such commotion, such as to set forth
Great things by small, if nature's concord broke,
Among the constellations war were sprung,
Two planets rushing from aspect malign
Of fiercest opposition in mid sky,
Should combat, and their jarring spheres confound.
Together both with next to almighty arm,
Uplifted imminent one stroke they aimed
That might determine, and not need repeat,

vi *303*. It is curiously naive or conceited of Raphael to think that angels could even *seem* fit to decide such a matter.

vi *306–7*. Personifying the apprehension of the angels. Cp. Shakespeare, *Troilus* Prol., and *Henry V* II Prol.: 'For now sits Expectation in the air / And hides a sword from hilts unto the point / With crowns imperial.'

vi *310–11*. For the source see ii 921–2*n*; and for Raphael's metaphoric programme, v 571–6.

vi *310–15*. It is usually said that the syntax of this passage is defective, unless a copulative is added between lines 312 and 313. But no addition is necessary, if we analyse as follows: 'as planets should combat, if, concord broken (*broke*), war were sprung among the constellations.' The dramatic irony here is strong: the reader knows it will not be long before concord is in fact broken by the Fall. Already at x 657–61 the planets are taught 'aspects / . . . Of noxious efficacy'. *aspect . . . opposition*] From the time of Ptolemy, astrologers recognized five definite geometrical relations between the heavenly bodies, called 'aspects'. Of these, two, including 'opposition' (when the bodies occupied diametrically opposite signs 'enclosing two right angles'), were disharmonious and therefore malign in their influence on man: see *Tetrabiblos* i 13. *mid sky*] 'the zenith'; rendering *medium coeli*, a technical term in astronomy. Cp. Ulysses' famous speech on the concord of degree and sovereignty of the sun, which restrain 'the ill aspects of planets evil', as well as 'commotion in the winds', and prevent 'each thing' from meeting 'in mere oppugnancy' (*Troilus* I iii 85–111).

vi *317*. *Uplifted imminent*] For the violence and paradoxicality of diction that critics have found here, see Ricks 14f; also ll. 698–9*n*.

vi *318–20*. *determine*] settle the issue. *repeat*] repetition. *As . . . once*] since in any case it would be impossible to repeat it immediately. *prevention*] anticipation.

As not of power, at once; nor odds appeared
In might or swift prevention; but the sword
Of Michael from the armoury of God
Was given him tempered so, that neither keen
Nor solid might resist that edge: it met
The sword of Satan with steep force to smite
Descending, and in half cut sheer, nor stayed,
But with swift wheel reverse, deep entering shared
All his right side; then Satan first knew pain,
And writhed him to and fro convolved; so sore
The griding sword with discontinuous wound
Passed through him, but the ethereal substance closed
Not long divisible, and from the gash
A stream of nectarous humour issuing flowed

vi *320–3*. Cp. *Jer.* l 25: 'The Lord hath opened his armoury, and hath brought forth the weapons of his indignation.' Such magical accoutrements almost always have an emblematic or symbolic value. Cp. Aeneas' god-given armour, that breaks the mortal blade of Turnus; or the sword of justice, stolen from Jupiter, that Astraea gives to Arthegall: 'Of most perfect metall it was made, / Tempred with Adamant ... there no substance was so firme and hard, / But it would pierce or cleave, where so it came; / Ne any armour could his dint out ward, / But wheresoever it did light, it throughly shard' (*F.Q.* V i 10).

vi *325*. Overgoing Virgil: Turnus' sword merely shatters in fragments (*Aen.* xii 741).

vi *326*. *shared*] cut into parts; cut off.

vi *327*. *first*] *pace* Empson (54), this need not conflict with Sin's statement that Satan already felt pain at the assembly of v 767ff; see ii 752–61*n*.

vi *328–34*. 'Milton has here three ideas which Psellus also connects closely: the demon's pain when his substance is cut, his quick and thorough healing, and his "panorganic" substance' (West 146f). Cp. Ficino, *Ex Michaele Psello de daemonibus* (Lyons 1577) vi 360f: 'The body of the demon is through its whole self naturally sensitive in accordance with its individual parts and without medium sees, hears, touches, suffers. It suffers with contact and division like a solid body, but ... when it is cut soon is recreated in itself again and coalesces like water and air. ... Yet meanwhile it suffers while divided, for which cause it fears the edge of the sword.' *convolved*] contorted. *griding*] piercing, cutting, or scraping through, so as to cause intense rasping pain. *discontinuous*] The medical definition of a wound was 'dissolution of continuity'.

vi *331–4*. From a wound in a man there would flow blood: namely, the sanguine humour or fluid, produced by digestion of ordinary food and giving rise in turn to a sanguine disposition. But angels, who eat nectar (v 633), bleed a *nectarous humour* ... / *Sanguine*. For 'sanguine' as the purest temperament, and the temperament of unfallen man, see Klibansky 103,

Sanguine, such as celestial spirits may bleed,
And all his armour stained ere while so bright.
Forthwith on all sides to his aid was run
By angels many and strong who interposed
Defence, while others bore him on their shields
Back to his chariot; where it stood retired
From off the files of war; there they him laid
Gnashing for anguish and despite and shame
To find himself not matchless, and his pride
Humbled by such rebuke, so far beneath
His confidence to equal God in power.
Yet soon he healed; for spirits that live throughout
Vital in every part, not as frail man
In entrails, heart or head, liver or reins,
Cannot but by annihilating die;
Nor in their liquid texture mortal wound
Receive, no more than can the fluid air:
All heart they live, all head, all eye, all ear,
All intellect, all sense, and as they please,
They limb themselves, and colour, shape or size
Assume, as likes them best, condense or rare.
    Mean while in other parts like deeds deserved
Memorial, where the might of Gabriel fought,
And with fierce ensigns pierced the deep array
Of Moloc furious king, who him defied,
And at his chariot wheels to drag him bound
Threatened, nor from the holy one of heaven
Refrained his tongue blasphemous; but anon

105, 110f. Cp. Homer's gods, who bleed ichor (*Il.* v 339); M. prefers to hint at a connection with the best human humour.
vi *335. was run*] In imitation of Latin syntax (*cursum est*).
vi *344–54.* Angels have no organs, since their substance is homogeneous or 'uncompounded' (i 425); see ll. 328–34*n*.
vi *355. the might of Gabriel*] Homeric diction for 'mighty Gabriel': see v 371*n*.
vi *357–62.* Gilbert suggests a resemblance with a grotesque battle between devils and saracens in Boiardo (*Italica* xx (1943) 132–4); and in a general way it is true that M.'s angelic war begins by resembling the chivalric combats of Renaissance romantic epics. But because it is more impressionistic and economical and functional, it always avoids their 'long and tedious havoc' (ix 30). See 698–9*n* below. *furious king*] For his earlier appearances see i 392–6 and ii 43–108.
vi *359–60.* Cp. *2 Kings* xix 22: 'Whom hast thou reproached and blasphemed? . . . the Holy One of Israel.' *blasphemed*] Stressed on the second syllable.

Down cloven to the waist, with shattered arms
And uncouth pain fled bellowing. On each wing
Uriel and Raphael his vaunting foe,
Though huge, and in a rock of diamond armed,
Vanquished Adramelec, and Asmadai,
Two potent thrones, that to be less than Gods
Disdained, but meaner thoughts learned in their flight,
Mangled with ghastly wounds through plate and mail,
Nor stood unmindful Abdiel to annoy
The atheist crew, but with redoubled blow
Ariel and Arioc, and the violence
Of Ramiel scorched and blasted overthrew.
I might relate of thousands, and their names
Eternize here on earth; but those elect
Angels contented with their fame in heaven

vi *362. uncouth*] strange, unknown.

vi *363–8.* With angelic objectivity, *Raphael* can refer to himself easily in the third person; Adam and Eve, it should be remembered, do not know his name. (Searching out the names of angels is a fallen kind of curiosity.) Raphael's opponent was presumably *Asmadai* (Asmodeus); a later encounter between the same two, in Biblical times, is alluded to at iv 168. It is equally appropriate that the solar intelligence *Uriel* should take on *Adramelec*, a pagan sun-god mentioned in *2 Kings* xvii 31. For the identification of the rebel angels with heathen gods, see i 364–75*n*. A medieval scheme, which M. does not seem to have followed regularly, made Asmodeus leader of the fourth order of an evil hierarchy. See West 157; also Burton, *Anatomy of Melancholy* I ii 1 ii. *diamond*] See ll. 354–5*n*.

vi *366. gods*] See i 116–7*n*.

vi *370. atheist*] impious.

vi *371–2. Ariel and Arioc*] In the Bible, *Ariel* (Lion of God) is properly a name for Jerusalem (*Is.* xxix 1f); but West (152–4) traces a separate history from *1 Enoch* through the inferior O.T. translations of Aquila and Symmachus (who use it for an avatar of Mars worshipped at Arina) to the Cabbalists Agrippa, Fludd and Kircher (who apply it to the spirit of earth). *Arioc*] originally the 'Arioch king of Ellasar' of *Gen.* xiv 1, against whom Abraham fought, he became known as the 'spirit of revenge' in Renaissance demonology (West 154). The name means 'Lion-like'. *Ramiel* is one of those angels who fall by fornication with the daughters of men, in *1 Enoch* vi 7. *violence . . . Ramiel*] For the rhetoric see l. 355*n* and v 371*n*.

vi *374–5. elect / Angels*] Biblical diction: see *1 Tim.* v 21. Gilbert scents a contradiction, here, of 363–5; since Raphael has just related his own exploit. But looked at more sympathetically, the passage can be seen as a beautiful dramatic irony. Raphael is both modest and consistent, since he never tells Adam and Eve his name. On the other hand, it is known to us—necessarily, or we should not appreciate the point.

Seek not the praise of men: the other sort
In might though wondrous and in acts of war,
Nor of renown less eager, yet by doom
Cancelled from heaven and sacred memory,
Nameless in dark oblivion let them dwell.
For strength from truth divided and from just,
Illaudable, naught merits but dispraise
And ignominy, yet to glory aspires
Vain glorious, and through infamy seeks fame:
Therefore eternal silence be their doom.
   And now their mightiest quelled, the battle swerved,
With many an inroad gored; deformed rout
Entered, and foul disorder; all the ground
With shivered armour strown, and on a heap
Chariot and charioteer lay overturned
And fiery foaming steeds; what stood, recoiled
O'er-wearied, through the faint Satanic host
Defensive scarce, or with pale fear surprised,
Then first with fear surprised and sense of pain
Fled ignominious, to such evil brought
By sin of disobedience, till that hour
Not liable to fear or flight or pain.
Far otherwise the inviolable saints
In cubic phalanx firm advanced entire,
Invulnerable, impenetrably armed:
Such high advantages their innocence
Gave them above their foes, not to have sinned,
Not to have disobeyed; in fight they stood
Unwearied, unobnoxious to be pained

vi *379*. See i 82*n*, 361–3*n*; v 658–9*n*.
vi *382*. *illaudable*] unworthy of praise.
vi *391*. *what*] those who.
vi *393*. *Defensive scarce*] scarcely capable of making any defence.
vi *394*. *Then first*] See 327*n*.
vi *395–7*. Unlike the obedient angels, who are *invulnerable* (l. 400), the rebels have grown 'gross' with sinning (l. 661), and are liable to pain from their wounds; see ll. 328–34*n*.
vi *398*. *saints*] elect (angels), as at ll. 47 and 374f; see iii 330*n*.
vi *399*. *cubic phalanx*] The shape of virtue and stability; see i 550*n*. It is idle to debate whether a cube proper or a square is meant here; since M. himself did not have to decide that question. Even if the angels moved as if on a single plane surface, their spears could adumbrate a tidy enough cube, after the manner of illustrations in seventeenth-century arts of war, such as Wallhausen's *Art militaire de la cavalerie*.
vi *404*. *unobnoxious*] not liable, not exposed (*OED* 1).

By wound, though from their place by violence moved.
Now night her course began, and over heaven
Inducing darkness, grateful truce imposed,
And silence on the odious din of war:
Under her cloudy covert both retired,
Victor and vanquished: on the foughten field
Michael and his angels prevalent
Encamping, placed in guard their watches round,
Cherubic waving fires: on the other part
Satan with his rebellious disappeared,
Far in the dark dislodged, and void of rest,
His potentates to council called by night;
And in the midst thus undismayed began.
O now in danger tried, now known in arms
Not to be overpowered, companions dear,
Found worthy not of liberty alone,
Too mean pretence, but what we more affect,
Honour, dominion, glory, and renown,
Who have sustained one day in doubtful fight
(And if one day, why not eternal days?)
What heaven's lord had powerfulest to send
Against us from about his throne, and judged
Sufficient to subdue us to his will,
But proves not so: then fallible, it seems,

vi *406*. The evening of Day 3 of the poem's action; see Introduction, 'Chronology' (p. 444).

vi *407*. Editors compare Horace, *Sat.* I v 9: *iam nox inducere terris / umbras . . . parabat.* But *induce* = 'lead on; bring in; spread as a covering' was perfectly idiomatic Eng. See *OED* s.v. *Induce* 1, 2, 7.

vi *410. foughten field*] battle-field.

vi *411. prevalent*] victorious.

vi *413*. The cherubim, who excel in knowledge, are customarily given the role of sentinels: cp. iv 778ff, xii 590ff.

vi *415. dislodged*] moved his position (military term); cp. v 669.

vi *416*. There was Homeric precedent for this nocturnal council of war in *Il.* ix – the council called by Agamemnon after defeat by Hector.

vi *421. mean pretence*] low ambition; but also 'base false pretence'. *affect*] aspire to; but also 'assume a false appearance of'. Raphael is an excellent vessel for M.'s irony.

vi *423–4*. Empson (41) is certainly right to see this passage as a serious theological argument about the 'claims of God': if they can match God's might in battle, even to the extent of surviving unsubdued, the rebels have as much right as he to such titles as *eternal*. The fallacy is that so far the rebel party has not encountered God at all, but only angels. See i 623–4*n*.

Of future we may deem him, though till now
Omniscient thought. True is, less firmly armed,
Some disadvantage we endured and pain,
Till now not known, but known as soon contemned,
Since now we find this our empyreal form
Incapable of mortal injury
Imperishable, and though pierced with wound,
Soon closing, and by native vigour healed.
Of evil then so small as easy think
The remedy; perhaps more valid arms,
Weapons more violent, when next we meet,
May serve to better us, and worse our foes,
Or equal what between us made the odds,
In nature none: if other hidden cause
Left them superior, while we can preserve
Unhurt our minds, and understanding sound,
Due search and consultation will disclose.
He sat; and in the assembly next upstood
Nisroc, of principalities the prime;
As one he stood escaped from cruel fight,
Sore toiled, his riven arms to havoc hewn,
And cloudy in aspect thus answering spake.
Deliverer from new lords, leader to free
Enjoyment of our right as gods; yet hard
For gods, and too unequal work we find
Against unequal arms to fight in pain,

vi *429*. *Of future*] in future (submerged idiom, building on phrases such as 'of late'); but also 'about what will happen in the future' (*OED*, s.v. *Future* sb. B 2 b).
vi *430*. Unless there is an oversight on M.'s part, Satan cannot have thought God 'omniscient' at v 682f, when he tried to keep the rebellion secret. If, that is to say, the secrecy there was genuine, and not a mere pretence to encourage the troops. But it may be futile to look for consistency in Satan.
vi *436*. *soon closing*] See ll. 328–34*n*.
vi *440*. *worse*] injure, make worse.
vi *444*. *sound*] healthy; also 'search into'.
vi *447*. One of the passages in which M. seems to think in terms of a regular antihierarchy of evil. See West 134 and 157, and cp. ll. 363–8*n*. The meanings of the Heb. name *Nisroc* given in Stephanus' *Dictionary*–'Flight' or 'Delicate temptation' (Starnes 268)–are in accordance with the flinching attitude portrayed here. Nisroch was the Assyrian idol which Sennacherib was worshipping when he was murdered (*2 Kings* xix 37, *Is.* xxxvii 38).
vi *452*. *gods*] Used vaguely and ambiguously, in a sense that varies shiftily from 'autonomous beings' to 'angels'. See i 116–17*n*.

Against unpained, impassive; from which evil
Ruin must needs ensue; for what avails
Valour or strength, though matchless, quelled with pain
Which all subdues, and makes remiss the hands
Of mightiest. Sense of pleasure we may well
Spare out of life perhaps, and not repine,
But live content, which is the calmest life:
But pain is perfect misery, the worst
Of evils, and excessive, overturns
All patience. He who therefore can invent
With what more forcible we may offend
Our yet unwounded enemies, or arm
Our selves with like defence, to me deserves
No less than for deliverance what we owe.
Whereto with look composed Satan replied.
Not uninvented that, which thou aright
Believest so main to our success, I bring;
Which of us who beholds the bright surface
Of this ethereous mould whereon we stand,
This continent of spacious heaven, adorned
With plant, fruit, flower ambrosial, gems and gold,
Whose eye so superficially surveys
These things, as not to mind from whence they grow
Deep under ground, materials dark and crude,
Of spiritous and fiery spume, till touched
With heaven's ray, and tempered they shoot forth

vi *455. impassive*] not liable to suffering, impassible. *OED* gives no instance earlier than this.
vi *458. remiss*] slack.
vi *464–8.* Veiling a threat: 'Come up with something new, or we'll change our leader.' *offend*] attack; hurt. *to me*] Supply 'it seems'.
vi *471. main*] highly important.
vi *472–81.* Cp. the sun's generation of precious stones by its subterranean action on condensed dew at iii 608–12 above. Here minerals are formed similarly, by the action of *heaven's ray* (the celestial equivalent of sunshine) upon *spume*, the exhalation of the celestial earth. See E. H. Duncan's exposition in *Osiris* xi (1954) 388, which finds a source in Aristotle's *Meteorologica* (341^b and 348^a). 'Here is the scheme of chaos and cosmos, with a physical sense of the ominous minerals lying beneath the flowers and the gold. . . . The cunning choice of *toucht*, *temperd*, *shoot*, and *opening* anticipates what follows; gunpowder is invented in the images before it occurs in the narrative' (Svendsen 119f).
vi *472. surface*] Stressed on the second syllable.
vi *475. ambrosial*] See ii 245*n*.
vi *478. crude*] raw; at an early stage of growth.

So beauteous, opening to the ambient light.
These in their dark nativity the deep
Shall yield us pregnant with infernal flame,
Which into hollow engines long and round
Thick-rammed, at the other bore with touch of fire
Dilated and infuriate shall send forth
From far with thundering noise among our foes
Such implements of mischief as shall dash
To pieces, and o'erwhelm whatever stands
Adverse, that they shall fear we have disarmed
The thunderer of his only dreaded bolt.
Nor long shall be our labour, yet ere dawn,
Effect shall end our wish. Mean while revive;
Abandon fear; to strength and counsel joined
Think nothing hard, much less to be despaired.
He ended, and his words their drooping cheer
Enlightened, and their languished hope revived.
The invention all admired, and each, how he

vi *483*. *infernal*] Bentley objected to the word, on the grounds that Satan does not yet know his punishment; and Empson[2] 158 has Satan extrapolating from 'the previous day's hints about hell'. But only Raphael intends the allusion to hell here; Satan means simply 'flame belonging to the region below, the *deep*'.

vi *484–90*. Newton found sources in Ariosto's account of the invention of firearms in *Orl. Fur.* ix 28f and 91, and (more plausibly) in Spenser's mention of 'that divelish yron Engin wrought / In deepest Hell, and framd by *Furies* skill, / With windy Nitre and quick Sulphur fraught, / And ramd with bullet round, ordaind to kill' (*F.Q.* I vii 13). Cp. also Daniel, *Civil Wars* vi 26f. But the attitude was understandably a common one. Erasmo di Valvasone had introduced the invention of cannon into his angelic war: see Kirkconnell 81. *the other bore*] the other cylindrical perforation; the touch-hole. *touch of fire*] contact with fire; but also 'touch-powder, the fine gunpowder placed over the touch-hole'. The wit of the description, which is so charged with ambiguity that it applies with equal force both to breech-loading and to muzzle-loading firearms, seems to have made little impact on critics even of the highest calibre. The two chains of discourse are: 'materials that rammed into one end of hollow engines (the breech) at the other end (the muzzle) shall send forth implements' and 'materials that rammed into (the muzzle of) hollow engines and dilated with touch-powder at the touch-hole, shall send etc.'

vi *484*. *hollow*] The first three edns have 'hallow', an obsolete or dialectal form.

vi *494*. *counsel*] judgment.

vi *496*. *cheer*] mood, spirits.

vi *498*. The zeugma is easily missed, since the second *admired*, in the sense

To be the inventor missed, so easy it seemed
Once found, which yet unfound most would have thought
Impossible: yet haply of thy race
In future days, if malice should abound,
Some one intent on mischief, or inspired
With devilish machination might devise
Like instrument to plague the sons of men
For sin, on war and mutual slaughter bent.
Forthwith from council to the work they flew;
None arguing stood, innumerable hands
Were ready, in a moment up they turned
Wide the celestial soil, and saw beneath
The originals of nature in their crude
Conception; sulphurous and nitrous foam
They found, they mingled, and with subtle art,
Concocted and adusted they reduced
To blackest grain, and into store conveyed:
Part hidden veins digged up (nor hath this earth
Entrails unlike) of mineral and stone,
Whereof to found their engines and their balls

'marvelled' has to be supplied. Throughout this passage M. uses the most extravagant possible figures of rhetoric, not excluding even vicious ones, such as bomphiologia (excessively lofty diction). See ll. 698–9*n*.

vi *509–15*. An epitome of 'mineralogical and lapidary lore' (Svendsen 121). As Svendsen points out, it is strategically important that the materials for gunpowder should exist in heaven. M. wishes to portray matter as morally neutral. 'It is the fallen angels who must mingle, concoct, adust.' *originals of nature*] original elements. Sulphur is mentioned as one of the originals not simply because it is an ingredient of gunpowder, but also because in alchemy it was the father of minerals and metals (mercury being the mother: see iii 601–5*n* and Caron 161). *crude*] Cp. l. 478. *nitrous foam*] Cp. the 'nitre' that blows Satan up at ii 937; also the 'nitrous powder' (gunpowder) to which he is compared at iv 815. Potassium nitrate (saltpetre) is an ingredient of gunpowder. Cp. also 'spume' at l. 479. *concocted*] prepared by heating (an alchemical term; but also a physiological term denoting a phase of digestion). *adusted*] scorched, dried up with heat (an alchemical term; but also a physiological term referring to a certain corruption of humours by drying).

vi *515–16*. Necessary information for Adam and Eve, since there was no mining before the Fall. See i 684–92*n*.

vi *518*. *found*] cast, mould. *engines*] pieces of ordnance; the word was quite usually applied to offensive weapons of all kinds, but especially to those of large size.

Of missive ruin; part incentive reed
Provide, pernicious with one touch to fire.
So all ere day-spring, under conscious night
Secret they finished, and in order set,
With silent circumspection unespied.
Now when fair morn orient in heaven appeared
Up rose the victor angels, and to arms
The matin trumpet sung: in arms they stood
Of golden panoply, refulgent host,
Soon banded; others from the dawning hills
Looked round, and scouts each coast light-armed scour,
Each quarter, to descry the distant foe,
Where lodged, or whither fled, or if for fight,
In motion or in halt: him soon they met
Under spread ensigns moving nigh, in slow
But firm battalion; back with speediest sail
Zophiel, of cherubim the swiftest wing,
Came flying, and in mid air aloud thus cried.
   Arm, warriors, arm for fight, the foe at hand,
Whom fled we thought, will save us long pursuit
This day, fear not his flight; so thick a cloud

vi *519–20.* The rhetorical point of these lines is their bomphiologia or excessively inflated diction. Cannon were a mean subject, grotesquely unworthy of such high-flown learned wit. *missive*] missile (adj.). *incentive*] kindling (wrongly connected with Lat. *incendere*, to burn). The 'incentive reed' is simply the match. *pernicious*] quick; also 'destructive' (the pun is between separate words, from different Lat. roots). *touch*] The same bad pun as at l. 485.

vi *521. dayspring*] early dawn. *conscious*] Perhaps 'aware and interested', but certainly 'guilty' (*OED* 4 b). Night is personified as an accessory sharing the guilty knowledge.

vi *524.* The morning of Day 3 of the poem's action; see Introduction, 'Chronology' (p. 444).

vi *532. halt*] *Ed I* and *Ed II* have 'alt', a common seventeenth-century spelling that possibly allows a secondary sense depending on the idiom *in alt*='in an excited frame of mind' (*OED* s.v. *Alt*[2] b).

vi *533–4.* Apparently courageous stoicism; but the slow pace turns out to be a necessary camouflage: see l. 555.

vi *535.* West (155) in disgust gives up the search for a definite source for *Zophiel* (Spy of God) among a tangle of misprints, mistranslations and mistransliterations in Agrippa and Fludd.

vi *539. cloud*] Incidentally imitates Virgil's *nubes belli* (*Aen.* x 809), but the main allusion is to the 'clouds . . . to whom the mist of darkness is reserved for ever' of *2 Pet.* ii 17: namely, false teachers who 'speak great swelling words of vanity'.

He comes, and settled in his face I see
Sad resolution and secure: let each
His adamantine coat gird well, and each
Fit well his helm, gripe fast his orbed shield,
Borne even or high, for this day will pour down,
If I conjecture aught, no drizzling shower,
But rattling storm of arrows barbed with fire.
So warned he them aware themselves, and soon
In order, quit of all impediment;
Instant without disturb they took alarm,
And onward move embattled; when behold
Not distant far with heavy pace the foe
Approaching gross and huge; in hollow cube
Training his devilish enginery, impaled
On every side with shadowing squadrons deep,
To hide the fraud. At interview both stood
A while, but suddenly at head appeared
Satan: and thus was heard commanding loud.
   Vanguard, to right and left the front unfold;
That all may see who hate us, how we seek
Peace and composure, and with open breast
Stand ready to receive them, if they like
Our overture, and turn not back perverse;
But that I doubt, however witness heaven,

vi *541. sad*] sober, serious. *secure*] confident, free from apprehension.
vi *542–6.* See *Eph.* vi 14–17 for this spiritual armour against 'fiery darts', and cp. l. 213*n*.
vi *543. gripe*] seize, grip.
vi *545. conjecture*] prognosticate, interpret the signs. Fenton's proposed emendation of *aught* to 'right' is unnecessary.
vi *548. impediment*] hindrance, obstruction; also 'baggage'.
vi *549. instant*] pressing, urgent (adj.); though in a secondary chain of discourse it is used adverbially = instantly. *disturb*] disturbance. *took alarm*] responded to the call to arms; took up action stations.
vi *550. embattled*] formed in order of battle.
vi *552. hollow cube*] the outward form of virtue (see l. 399*n* and i 550*n*) emblematically conceals a hollow and devilishly aggressive interior.
vi *553. Training*] pulling. *enginery*] artillery; see 518*n*. *impaled*] enclosed for defence (military term).
vi *555. at interview*] in mutual view (*OED* s.v. *Interview* 2). A rare usage.
vi *560. composure*] settlement. *breast*] heart (*OED* I 5 a); broad front of a moving company (*OED* I 7).
vi *562. overture*] A pun between 'opening of negotiations for a settlement' (*OED* 3) and 'aperture, hole' (*OED* 1)–the 'bore' (485) or 'hideous orifice' (577) of the cannon.

Heaven witness thou anon, while we discharge
Freely our part; ye who appointed stand
Do as you have in charge, and briefly touch
What we propound, and loud that all may hear.
  So scoffing in ambiguous words he scarce
Had ended; when to right and left the front
Divided, and to either flank retired.
Which to our eyes discovered new and strange,
A triple mounted row of pillars laid
On wheels (for like to pillars most they seemed
Or hollowed bodies made of oak or fir,
With branches lopped, in wood or mountain felled)
Brass, iron, stony mould, had not their mouths
With hideous orifice gaped on us wide,
Portending hollow truce; at each behind

vi *566.* The pun on *touch* has been made so often (ll. 479, 484–90*n*, 520) that it now seems as laboured as the ones on 'discharge' (l. 564) and 'loud'. Since frequent puns are quickly felt to be extravagant and excessive, the figure is highly appropriate in the present context. See ll. 698–9*n*. This strategic purpose behind the puns was missed by Landor when he cleverly said that 'the first overt crime of the refractory angels was *punning*' (*Works*, ed. T. E. Welby (1927–36) v 258).
vi *568.* Following the punctuation of *Ed I. Ed II* wrongly moves the comma to the end of the line.
vi *569–70.* A recognized stratagem in the warfare of the time; see H. H. Scudder in *N & Q* cxcv (1590) 335.
vi *572. triple-mounted*] The ordnance the rebel angels have made are 'organs' or *orgues*–weapons consisting of several barrels fired simultaneously. In the seventeenth century these were chiefly used in siege war; see *EB* xvii 238. There have to be *three* barrels to underline the antithesis with Messiah's 'three-bolted thunder' (l. 764).
vi *572–8.* Just as the cubic battle formation of the devils is deceptive and hollow (ll. 552–5), so also are the *pillars* of their ordnance. The column, like the cube, was an emblem of virtue; see Tervarent 107. Scudder (*art. cit.* 569–70*n*) cites a contemporary historical instance of the use of fake cannon as a tactical stratagem.
vi *576. Brass . . . mould*] made of brass, etc.
vi *578–94.* The sustained physiological imagery (e.g. *belched, embowelled, entrails, disgorging, glut;* cp. *concocted* and *adusted* at 514) amounts almost to a Freudian allegory about alimentary and anal aggression. Devils were often portrayed defecating or vomiting. See, e.g., the mural of the Campo Santo at Pisa (flames issuing from mouth, belly and anus) and Lorch's engraving, illus. Cohn, Fig. 2 (vomiting, in accordance with *Rev.* xvi 13). The passage abounds in diction that is indecorously low. *hollow*] insincere, false;

A seraph stood, and in his hand a reed
Stood waving tipped with fire; while we suspense,
Collected stood within our thoughts amused,
Not long, for sudden all at once their reeds
Put forth, and to a narrow vent applied
With nicest touch. Immediate in a flame,
But soon obscured with smoke, all heaven appeared,
From those deep throated engines belched, whose roar
Embowelled with outrageous noise the air,
And all her entrails tore, disgorging foul
Their devilish glut, chained thunderbolts and hail
Of iron globes, which on the victor host
Levelled, with such impetuous fury smote,
That whom they hit, none on their feet might stand,
Though standing else as rocks, but down they fell
By thousands, angel on archangel rolled;
The sooner for their arms, unarmed they might
Have easily as spirits evaded swift
By quick contraction or remove; but now
Foul dissipation followed and forced rout;
Nor served it to relax their serried files.
What should they do? If on they rushed, repulse
Repeated, and indecent overthrow
Doubled, would render them yet more despised,
And to their foes a laughter; for in view
Stood ranked of seraphim another row
In posture to displode their second tire
Of thunder: back defeated to return
They worse abhorred. Satan beheld their plight,

and concave; see l. 566*n.* *suspense*] in a state of mental suspense; undecided. *amused*] puzzled, absorbed; deceived as to the enemy's real designs (military: *OED* 5) *narrow vent*] at one level, the touch-hole. *embowelled*] disembowelled (*OED* I 2); or filled the bowels of (*OED* II 3). *glut*] surfeit, excessive flow of bile.

vi *594*. The only line in *PL* 'that might be read to signify an archangelic order' (West 133f). Usually M. uses the term *archangel* to connote personal rank rather than membership of an order.

vi *597*. For the ability of angels to change their size and shape, see i 423–31*n*.

vi *598*. *dissipation*] dispersal, scattering.

vi *601*. *indecent*] unbecoming, uncomely.

vi *605*. *posture*] A military term denoting any one of the particular positions in weapon drill–cp. Gervase Markham, *The souldiers accidence* (1625) 24: 'The three Postures or words of Command, which are used for the Musquet in the face of the enemie . . . are these–1. Make readie. 2. Present. 3. Give fire.' *tire*] volley, broadside.

And to his mates thus in derision called.
O friends, why come not on these victors proud?
Ere while they fierce were coming, and when we,
To entertain them fair with open front
And breast, (what could we more?) propounded terms
Of composition, straight they changed their minds,
Flew off, and into strange vagaries fell,
As they would dance, yet for a dance they seemed
Somewhat extravagant and wild, perhaps
For joy of offered peace: but I suppose
If our proposals once again were heard
We should compel them to a quick result.
To whom thus Belial in like gamesome mood,
Leader, the terms we sent were terms of weight,
Of hard contents, and full of force urged home,
Such as we might perceive amused them all,
And stumbled many, who receives them right,
Had need from head to foot well understand;
Not understood, this gift they have besides,
They show us when our foes walk not upright.
So they among themselves in pleasant vein
Stood scoffing, highthened in their thoughts beyond
All doubt of victory, eternal might
To match with their inventions they presumed
So easy, and of his thunder made a scorn,
And all his host derided, while they stood
A while in trouble; but they stood not long,
Rage prompted them at length, and found them arms
Against such hellish mischief fit to oppose.
Forthwith (behold the excellence, the power
Which God hath in his mighty angels placed)
Their arms away they threw, and to the hills

vi *611–12. open front*] candid face (*OED* s.v. *Front* I 2); also 'front line': 'Divided, and to either flank retired' (l. 570). For the pun on *breast*, see l. 560*n*. *propound*] propose.
vi *614. vagaries*] frolics; fantastic or capricious actions. So Aeneas taunts Meriones with dancing to avoid his spear-throw at *Il.* xvi 617f.
vi *620–7. Belial*, who was described as 'timorous' at ii 117, is in the angelic war 'celebrated for nothing but that scoffing speech' (Addison). The puns are all obvious, except perhaps for that in *understand* = comprehend, also 'prop up, support' (*OED* I 9). *amused them*] engaged their whole attention; cp. 581. *stumbled*] puzzled; tripped up.
vi *635*. Cp. Virgil, *Aen.* i 150: *furor arma ministrat.*
vi *639–66*. Cp. the simile of the hill 'torn from Pelorus, or the shattered side / Of thundering Aetna' at i 230ff, or the comparison of Satan to a

(For earth hath this variety from heaven
Of pleasure situate in hill and dale)
Light as the lightning glimpse they ran, they flew,
From their foundations loosening to and fro
They plucked the seated hills with all their load,
Rocks, waters, woods, and by the shaggy tops
Up lifting bore them in their hands: amaze,
Be sure, and terror seized the rebel host,
When coming towards them so dread they saw
The bottom of the mountains upward turned,
Till on those cursed engines' triple-row
They saw them whelmed, and all their confidence
Under the weight of mountains buried deep,
Themselves invaded next, and on their heads
Main promontories flung, which in the air
Came shadowing, and oppressed whole legions armed,
Their armour helped their harm, crushed in and bruised
Into their substance pent, which wrought them pain
Implacable, and many a dolorous groan,
Long struggling underneath, ere they could wind
Out of such prison, though spirits of purest light,
Purest at first, now gross by sinning grown.
The rest in imitation to like arms
Betook them, and the neighbouring hills uptore;
So hills amid the air encountered hills

displaced mountain at vi 195ff. MacCaffrey 88–90 rightly treats these and similar passages as images of the chaos, tamed in creation, into which cosmos is always liable to relapse. M. here makes the most direct of his many allusions to the war of the Giants against Jupiter – the chief pagan analogue of the angelic rebellion. In the Giant War hills were used as missiles, and at the end several Giants remained buried to form the volcanoes of later time (see i 197–200*n*, 230–7*n*). Among M.'s closest models is Claudian: with ll. 644–7 cp. the wonderfully detailed account of hill throwing in *Gigantomachia* 70f: 'Enipeus, gathered up with its beetling crags, scatters its waters over yon giant's shoulders.' Claudian, too, presents the war as a return to the confusion of chaos. *amaze*] bewilderment; stupefaction, panic.

vi *650. triple-row*] the 'triple-mounted pillars'; see l. 572*n*.

vi *653. invaded*] attacked.

vi *654. main*] whole, solid (*OED* 4 b).

vi *655. oppressed*] weighed down.

vi *664–7.* The anthropomorphic scene is hard to imagine because of the difficulties of scale. That this effect is intended as an alienation device seems clear from *Be sure*, with its recall from the second-order fictive sequence to Adam and Eve in the first-order sequence.

Hurled to and fro with jaculation dire,
That under ground they fought in dismal shade;
Infernal noise; war seemed a civil game
To this uproar; horrid confusion heaped
Upon confusion rose: and now all heaven
Had gone to wrack, with ruin overspread,
Had not the almighty Father where he sits
Shrined in his sanctuary of heaven secure,
Consulting on the sum of things, foreseen
This tumult, and permitted all, advised:
That his great purpose he might so fulfil,
To honour his anointed Son avenged
Upon his enemies, and to declare
All power on him transferred: whence to his Son
The assessor of his throne he thus began.
   Effulgence of my glory, Son beloved,
Son in whose face invisible is beheld
Visibly, what by deity I am,
And in whose hand what by decree I do,
Second omnipotence, two days are past,
Two days, as we compute the days of heaven,
Since Michael and his powers went forth to tame
These disobedient; sore hath been their fight,

vi *665. jaculation*] hurling.
vi *666.* Following the punctuation of *Ed I*. *Ed II* wrongly adds comma after *ground*.
vi *670.* Surpassing the effect of the first day's fighting. Cp. 218 above.
vi *673. sum of things*] 'Universe' is the usual explanation, by analogy with Lucretius' phrase *summarum summa* (v 362); but a closer Latin original (if such be desired) is *summa rerum*, 'highest public interest', and in any case 675 makes it clear that M. also intends 'goal of things' (*OED* s.v. *Sum* 13). Cp. *Natur* 35, and Ovid, *Met.* ii 300, *rerum consule summae*.
vi *674. advised*] after consideration, deliberately.
vi *679. assessor*] sharer. The term is used of one who sits beside another, participating in his status and position.
vi *680–2.* Cp. *Heb.* i 3, 'the brightness of his glory, and the express image of his person'; also *Col.* i 15, 'the image of the invisible God'.
vi *684. Second omnipotence*] No less an oxymoron than 'invisible . . . Visibly' at l. 681f.
vi *685.* For the nature of time in heaven, see v 579–82*n*. In spite of the difficult theology involved M. is bound to continue computing the days of the action, even when it does not take place on earth, for the sake of his numerological structure. See ll. 4–11*n*, 698–9*n*, v 579–82*n*; also Introduction, 'Chronology'.

As likeliest was, when two such foes met armed;
For to themselves I left them, and thou know'st,
Equal in their creation they were formed,
Save what sin hath impaired, which yet hath wrought
Insensibly, for I suspend their doom;
Whence in perpetual fight they needs must last
Endless, and no solution will be found:
War wearied hath performed what war can do,
And to disordered rage let loose the reins,
With mountains as with weapons armed, which makes
Wild work in heaven, and dangerous to the main.
Two days are therefore past, the third is thine;
For thee I have ordained it, and thus far

vi *689. thou know'st*] This has been ridiculed, on the ground that the Son is omniscient (see Peter 13, Ricks 19). But if the tone of the phrase is rightly imagined–'*thou* knowest, thou of all beings, thou by whose agency I created them, thou who sharest with me the secrets of creation'–it will be seen to have the right sublime intimacy. Of course, the more general objection stands: that any attempt to verbalize God must fail. Only, the degree of unsuccess seems to count for something.
vi *690–1*. For the status of Satan and Michael see v *660n*. Their equality continues, because sin has so far affected Satan only *insensibly* (imperceptibly).
vi *698–9*. Christ is now to put an end to the confusion and chaos of the first two days' fighting. Note the answering change to a steadier and more exalted style: the *wild work* was portrayed in an appropriately grotesque manner. See ll. 357–62*n*, 498*n* and 566*n*. The delay of Messiah's entry into the war, which so offends Empson, could scarcely have been avoided by M.; for it was Scriptural (see *De doctrina* i 7, Columbia xv 105, on Rev. xii 7f) and in any case it was necessary if there was to be any angelic war. There was also an arithmological reason: namely, that the dyad of the two days' fighting symbolized rebellion and excess and division, whereas the triad of the third day symbolizes virtue and limitation and order and a return to the principle of unity (Bongo 95ff; Fowler 5f). Typologically, the reference would be to Christ's rising on the third day (e.g. *Luke* xiii 32, 'the third day I shall be perfected'): Messiah's defeat of Satan here foreshadows the later victory of the resurrection. *main*] whole, universe.
vi *700–9*. Empson's thesis (e.g. *Milton's God* 41f) is largely built on the argument that God's delay in finishing the war amounted to intentional deception of Satan about his omnipotence. Here precisely the opposite reason is given for the delay: namely, that it will make possible a manifest distinction between the power of angels and the power of Christ. The distinction turns out to be so clear that to keep his rebellion intellectually respectable Satan has to forget about the third day's fighting altogether: see, e.g., i 169–71*n*.

Have suffered, that the glory may be thine
Of ending this great war, since none but thou
Can end it. Into thee such virtue and grace
Immense I have transfused, that all may know
In heaven and hell thy power above compare,
And this perverse commotion governed thus,
To manifest thee worthiest to be heir
Of all things, to be heir and to be king
By sacred unction, thy deserved right.
Go then thou mightiest in thy Father's might,
Ascend my chariot, guide the rapid wheels
That shake heaven's basis, bring forth all my war,
My bow and thunder, my almighty arms
Gird on, and sword upon thy puissant thigh;
Pursue these sons of darkness, drive them out
From all heaven's bounds into the utter deep:
There let them learn, as likes them, to despise
God and Messiah his anointed king.
He said, and on his Son with rays direct
Shone full, he all his Father full expressed
Ineffably into his face received,
And thus the filial Godhead answering spake.

vi *701. suffered*] In the sense 'allowed', followed by a clause introduced by 'that', was a common construction (*OED* s.v. *Suffer* II 14 a). But *suffered that*='waited patiently, endured, so that' leads to a possible secondary chain of discourse.
vi *706.* 'And that all may know this insurrection (controlled thus by your power alone) to manifest....'
vi *708. heir*] Cp. v 720 ('heir of all my might'), and see *Heb.* i 2: 'His Son, whome he hath appointed heir of all things, by whom also he made the worlds.'
vi *709.* For the anointing of the Messiah, see v 603–6*n*, 664*n*.
vi *712. war*] A synecdoche for 'weapons of war'. Whether or not M. invented the figure, it was soon after a popular one; cp. Dryden (*Aen.* viii 572: 'His broken Axeltrees, and blunted War'); Addison, *Cato* i 4 ('th'em-battled Elephant, / Loaden with war'); etc.
vi *715. sons of darkness*] Contrast v 716, where the angels generally were 'sons of morn'.
vi *716. utter*] outer.
vi *718.* The literal meaning of *Messiah* is *anointed king*.
vi *720–1.* Cp. x 63–7, and see *2 Cor.* iv 6: 'God, who commanded the light to shine out of darkness, hath shined in our hearts, to give the light of the knowledge of the glory of God in the face of Jesus Christ.'

O Father, O supreme of heavenly thrones,
First, highest, holiest, best, thou always seek'st
To glorify thy Son, I always thee,
As is most just; this I my glory account,
My exaltation, and my whole delight,
That thou in me well pleased, declar'st thy will
Fulfilled, which to fulfil is all my bliss.
Sceptre and power, thy giving, I assume,
And gladlier shall resign, when in the end
Thou shalt be all in all, and I in thee
For ever, and in me all whom thou lovest:
But whom thou hatest, I hate, and can put on
Thy terrors, as I put thy mildness on,
Image of thee in all things; and shall soon,
Armed with thy might, rid heaven of these rebelled,
To their prepared ill mansion driven down
To chains of darkness, and the undying worm,
That from thy just obedience could revolt,
Whom to obey is happiness entire.
Then shall thy saints unmixed, and from the impure

vi *724–34*. Following the thought, and to some extent the diction, of *John* xvii 1–23, Jesus' prayer at the last supper: 'Thou hast given him power. . . . I have glorified thee on the earth. . . . And now, O Father, glorify thou me . . . that they might have my joy fulfilled in themselves . . . I in them, and thou in me.' Cp. also *Matt.* iii 17 ('my beloved Son, in whom I am well pleased'). The argument whether this passage is Arian or Trinitarian (Kelley 120, etc.) seems both endless and pointless. Even if every single text used here were interpreted to Arian effect in *De doctrina* i 5, M. could hardly have expected readers of *PL* to know this. The texts were comparatively uncontroversial ones and they are not provided here with any context of dogmatic theology.
vi *731–2*. See iii 339–43*n*, and cp. *1 Cor.* xv 24, 28: 'Then cometh the end, when he shall have delivered up the kingdom to God, even the Father; when he shall have put down all rule and all authority and power. . . . And when all things shall be subdued unto him, then shall the Son also himself be subject unto him that put all things under him, that God may be all in all.'
vi *734*. 'Do not I hate them, O Lord, that hate thee? and am not I grieved with those that rise up against thee?' (*Ps.* cxxxix 21).
vi *738*. The grim obverse of Christ's promise, 'In my Father's house are many mansions: if it were not so, I would have told you. I go to prepare a place for you' (*John* xiv 2). *mansion*] dwelling. Cp. *Nativity Ode* 140.
vi *739*. See i 48*n*, and cp. *Jude* 6: 'And the angels which kept not their first estate, but left their own habitation, he hath reserved in everlasting chains under darkness unto the judgment of the great day.' At *Mark* ix 44 hell is 'where their worm dieth not'.

Far separate, circling thy holy mount
Unfeigned hallelujahs to thee sing,
Hymns of high praise, and I among them chief.
So said, he o'er his sceptre bowing, rose
From the right hand of glory where he sat,
And the third sacred morn began to shine
Dawning through heaven: forth rushed with
    whirlwind sound

vi *744*. At ii 243 submission means to Mammon a prospect of singing 'forced hallelujahs'.
vi *748*. Day 4 of the poem's action, though only the third *morn*; see Introduction, 'Chronology'. M. has so arranged the action that the number 4, which is a form of the holy *tetractys*, denoted the sacred day when the triumph of Messiah is celebrated.
vi *749–59*. The principal image of the poem, which has been prepared for by many partial anticipations. See, e.g., Satan's counterfeit chariot at ll. 100–3 and 338; the seven archangels of the cosmic chariot (see iii 656*n*); and the many mentions of this and other chariots (i 311, ii 887, iii 394, 522, vi 211, 358, 390, 711). Messiah's chariot is a 'triumphal chariot' (l. 881), so that his ascent of it constitutes a factitive claim to sovereignty. The triumph of a god or allegorical abstraction was one of the principal motifs of Renaissance and Baroque art, and it generally included as one of its most prominent features a chariot or mobile throne; see the relevant ch. in E. Van Marle, *Iconographie de l'art profane* ii (The Hague 1932); É. Mâle, 'Les triomphes' in *Revue de l'art ancien et moderne* (1906); and C. Lorgues-Lapouge, 'Triomphes renaissants' in *L'Oeil* xxxv (1957) 27–35. The Triumph of Christ was a distinct subject, an example of which is illustrated *ibid.* 32. M.'s chariot of sovereignty, however, is unusually mysterious and mystical, even if the distinct detail of the portrayal may mislead us into thinking otherwise. His principal source is Ezekiel's apocalyptic vision of God in a machine (i 4–6, 16, 26–8, x 12, 16): 'Behold, a whirlwind . . . a great cloud, and a fire infolding itself, and a brightness was about it, and out of the midst thereof as the colour of amber . . . four living creatures. . . . And every one had four faces and every one had four wings. . . . The appearance of the wheels and their work was like unto the colour of a beryl: and they four had one likeness: and their appearance and their work was as it were a wheel in the middle of a wheel. . . . the firmament that was over their heads was the likeness of a throne, as the appearance of a sapphire stone. . . . the appearance of a man above upon it. And I saw as the colour of amber . . . as the appearance of the bow that is in the cloud in the day of rain. . . . And their whole body, and their backs, and their hands, and their wings, and the wheels, were full of eyes round about, even the wheels that they four had. . . . And when the cherubims went, the wheels went by them.' These verses had generally been interpreted in a cosmic sense, its various tetrads being identified with the four elements, the four seasons, etc., but also with the four cardinal

The chariot of paternal deity,
Flashing thick flames, wheel within wheel undrawn,
It self instinct with spirit, but convoyed
By four cherubic shapes, four faces each
Had wondrous, as with stars their bodies all
And wings were set with eyes, with eyes the wheels
Of beryl, and careering fires between;
Over their heads a crystal firmament,
Whereon a sapphire throne, inlaid with pure
Amber, and colours of the showery arch.
He in celestial panoply all armed
Of radiant urim, work divinely wrought,

virtues, after the usual manner of expansion of the *tetractys* (see, e.g., Jerome, *Comm. in Ezech.*, Migne xxv 22ff; Valeriano 549; Bongo 243). But M. underlines the cosmic aspect by adding *stars* (l. 754) to the Biblical *firmament*. Here, no less than in the overtly hexaemeral parts of *PL*, M. presents his distinctive vision of a nature that is a vehicle for divinity. Messiah's chariot is nothing less than the cosmic chariot of *Timaeus* 41E and *Laws* 899A. A less obvious source is the golden chariot of the king in *Song of Sol.* iii 9f, which seems to have been a prominent subject of meditation in the mystical thought of the time. See, e.g., G. Foliot, *Expositio in Canticum Canticorum* (1643) 174f, where, however, the chariot is interpreted as a symbol of the Church, or the New Covenant. For other allusions to King Solomon and his gold in *PL* see i 403*n*.

The throne on the 'firmament' is with a special appropriateness placed at the sovereign centre of the heavens, by its placement at the numerical centre of the whole poem (by line-count, *Ed I* only; see l. 761*n*, iv 30*n*; also Qvarnström, *passim*, and Fowler, Index s.v. *Central Position of Sovereignty*). In his description of the ideal Christian poet in *Reason of Church-Government*, M. singles out the power 'to celebrate in glorious and lofty Hymns the throne and equipage of Gods Almightinesse' (Yale i 817). Rupert of Deutz had anticipated M. in combining the divine chariot with the angelic rebellion (McColley 36–8). (The theology underlying this use of an apocalyptic vision to portray the earliest events of the redemptive history has still to be worked out.) In view of the alchemical implications of *radiant urim* (see l. 761*n*) it is interesting to compare a stanza in one of Cowley's *Pindarique Odes* (1668), describing Elijah's chariot: ''Twas gawdy all, and rich in every part, / Of *Essences* of *Gems*, and *Spirit* of *Gold* / Was its *substantial mold*; / Drawn forth by *Chymique Angels* art. . . .' (ed. Waller p. 205).

vi *752. instinct*] animated, impelled.

vi *761. urim*] see *Exod.* xxviii 30: 'And thou shalt put in the breastplate of judgment the Urim and the Thummim; and they shall be upon Aaron's heart, when he goeth in before the Lord.' For the symbolism of Aaron's breastplate of priesthood, see iii 594–605*nn* above. As Qvarnström explains, *urim* was not only a sacerdotal emblem and a symbol of virtue, but was also

Ascended, at his right hand Victory
Sat, eagle-winged, beside him hung his bow
And quiver with three-bolted thunder stored,
And from about him fierce effusion rolled
Of smoke and bickering flame, and sparkles dire;
Attended with ten thousand thousand saints,

identified with the Philosopher's Stone; Tancke called it 'the right, true sun itself . . . the right *Urim* and fiery Carbuncle'. Thus, Messiah's armour carries on the cosmic image of the preceding lines and again asserts his sovereign claim as creator. The one true alchemist, he wears the stone that in Fludd's philosophy mediates between God and the material world. Note that in the arrangement of *Ed I* the stone of judgment justly divides the poem's central paragraph – a pattern that Qvarnström shows to have a precedent in Benlowes's *Theophila.* The centralization is emphasized structurally by such features as the speeches of equal length on either side of the midpoint. Messiah's speeches at ll. 723–45 and 801–23 are both of 23 lines, 23 being a number that symbolized both divine vengeance upon sinners (on the basis of Vulg. *Num.* xxv 9) and the consummation of the salvation of man (the 3 of perfect faith in the Trinity + the 10 of the Old Covenant or Decalogue + the 10 of the New Covenant); see Bongo 441–3. For the idea that Christ's judgment is delivered from a central position in the cosmos, see Panofsky's discussion of 'the equation of the astrological notion, *medium coeli*, with the theological notion, *medium coeli et terrae*, presumed to be the seat of the Judge' (Panofsky 262); and cp. iv 30*n* and 1013–15*n*. The centricity of Christ was an idea current in seventeenth-century mystical theology. In Fludd's system, e.g., the divine Word is the centre of *mens*; see C. H. Josten, 'Robert Fludd's Theory of Geomancy', *JWI* xxvii (1964) 329.

vi *762–3*. The eagle, bird of Jupiter, and therefore a symbol of imperial majesty (Valeriano 228f), was sometimes placed at the feet of Victory, who normally had wings (Ripa 516). M. condenses these two attributes into a single image.

vi *764*. The Jehovah of the Bible has his thunder; but there is a secondary allusion to the thunderbolt of the Jupiter of the Giant War. *three-bolted*] See l. 572*n*.

vi *765*. Cp. *Ps.* xviii 8: 'There went up a smoke out of his nostrils, and fire out of his mouth devoured: coals were kindled by it.'

vi *766*. *bickering*] darting, flashing.

vi *767*. Cp. *Rev.* v 11: 'And I beheld, and I heard the voice of many angels round about the throne and the beasts and the elders: and the number of them was ten thousand times ten thousand, and thousands of thousands.' Note that while the rebels are indeterminate 'multitudes' (l. 31), the elect are numbered in multiples of ten. See v 588, 610–12*n*, 898–903*n*; also Bongo 659f and 667, where large numbers generated by ten are treated as virtuous and unsearchable, whereas innumerable multitudes are evil and opposed to unity. For the elect angels as 'saints', see l. 398*n*.

He onward came, far off his coming shone,
And twenty thousand (I their number heard)
Chariots of God, half on each hand were seen:
He on the wings of cherub rode sublime
On the crystalline sky, in sapphire throned.
Illustrious far and wide, but by his own
First seen, them unexpected joy surprised,
When the great ensign of Messiah blazed
Aloft by angels borne, his sign in heaven:
Under whose conduct Michael soon reduced
His army, circumfused on either wing,
Under their head embodied all in one.
Before him power divine his way prepared;
At his command the uprooted hills retired
Each to his place, they heard his voice and went

vi *769*. Cp. *Ps.* lxviii 17: 'The chariots of God are twenty thousand, even thousands of angels: the Lord is among them, as in Sinai, in the holy place.' M.'s disposition of the chariots in two wings not only puts Messiah in the sovereign central position, but arrives at the number ten thousand, which expresses philosophically the supreme perfection of the angels (Bongo 658; cp. previous note).

vi *771*. So in *Ps.* xviii 10 'He rode upon a cherub, and did fly: yea, he did fly upon the wings of the wind' (cp. *2 Sam.* xxii 11). *sublime*] set aloft, high up.

vi *772*. 'And above the firmament that was over their heads was the likeness of a throne, as the appearance of a sapphire stone' (*Ezek.* i 26). The *crystálline sky* or heaven was the sphere next to the firmament; see vii 271*n*.

vi *773–4*. Though Messiah was clearly visible from a distance, his own army were the first to see him.

vi *776*. Alluding to the prophecy of *Matt.* xxiv 30: 'And then shall appear the sign of the Son of man in heaven: and then shall all the tribes of the earth mourn, and they shall see the Son of man coming in the clouds of heaven with power and great glory.'

vi *777*. *reduced*] led back (*OED* I 2 b); but there may also be a secondary sense, 'took back to their origin' (*OED* I 4 a, citing the *De Imitatione* iii 59, 'Grace reducith all thinges to god, of whom thei wellith oute groundely and originally').

vi *779*. For Messiah as 'the head of the body, the Church', see *Col.* i 18, and cp. v 606*n*.

vi *780–4*. In a general way these lines are to be related to Isaiah's prophecy (xl 3f) of a divine advent, which is similarly expressed in terms of moralized landscape: 'Prepare ye the way of the Lord, make straight in the desert a highway for our God. Every valley shall be exalted, and every mountain and hill shall be made low: and the crooked shall be made straight, and the rough places plain.'

Obsequious, heaven his wonted face renewed,
And with fresh flowerets hill and valley smiled.
This saw his hapless foes but stood obdured,
And to rebellious fight rallied their powers
Insensate, hope conceiving from despair.
In heavenly spirits could such perverseness dwell?
But to convince the proud what signs avail,
Or wonders move the obdurate to relent?
They hardened more by what might most reclaim,
Grieving to see his glory, at the sight
Took envy, and aspiring to his highth,
Stood re-embattled fierce, by force or fraud
Weening to prosper, and at length prevail
Against God and Messiah, or to fall
In universal ruin last, and now
To final battle drew, disdaining flight,
Or faint retreat; when the great Son of God
To all his host on either hand thus spake.
   Stand still in bright array ye saints, here stand
Ye angels armed, this day from battle rest;
Faithful hath been your warfare, and of God
Accepted, fearless in his righteous cause,
And as ye have received, so have ye done
Invincibly; but of this cursed crew
The punishment to other hand belongs,
Vengeance is his, or whose he sole appoints;
Number to this day's work is not ordained

vi *785. obdured*] hardened. On God's hardening of the heart of sinners, see iii 197–200*n*.
vi *788*. Imitating Virgil's famous apostrophe at Juno's malevolence: *tantaene animis caelestibus irae?*' (*Aen*. i 11).
vi *789–91*. So Pharaoh's heart was hardened (*Exod*. xiv 4), in spite of the miraculous plagues. *by . . . reclaim*] Theologically exact; sinners were supposed to be hardened by precisely the kind and just treatment that 'ought rather to soften the hearts of sinners' (*De doctrina* i 8; Columbia xv 81).
vi *801*. So at *Exod*. xiv 13 Moses tells the children of Israel to stand and watch the destruction of the Egyptians.
vi *808*. The belief that vengeance on sinners was a divine prerogative, not delegated lightly, expressed often in the Bible (*Deut*. xxxii 35, *Ps*. xciv 1, *Rom*. xii 19, *Heb*. x 30), was one of the finest elements in Hebrew religion.
vi *809–10*. The rebels are to be confronted, not by the numerous multitude of the faithful, but by Messiah alone (l. 820). One is not a number, because as the divine monad it is 'itself not a number, but the source and origin of numbers' (Macrobius, *In somn. Scip*. I vi 7f). See Bongo 13–61 *passim*, where the idea is developed at quite unusual length; significantly, it is

Nor multitude, stand only and behold
God's indignation on these godless poured
By me, not you but me they have despised,
Yet envied; against me is all their rage,
Because the Father, to whom in heaven supreme
Kingdom and power and glory appertains,
Hath honoured me according to his will.
Therefore to me their doom he hath assigned;
That they may have their wish, to try with me
In battle which the stronger proves, they all,
Or I alone against them, since by strength
They measure all, of other excellence
Not emulous, nor care who them excels;
Nor other strife with them do I vouchsafe.
  So spake the Son, and into terror changed
His countenance too severe to be beheld
And full of wrath bent on his enemies.
At once the four spread out their starry wings
With dreadful shade contiguous, and the orbs
Of his fierce chariot rolled, as with the sound
Of torrent floods, or of a numerous host.
He on his impious foes right onward drove,

applied (15) to Lucifer's illusion of autonomy. For the opposition of unity and multitude in *PL* see i 338ff, v 610–2*n*, vi 767*n*, etc. In another sense, *number . . . is not ordained* to Day 4 of the poem's action because the tetrad is a form of the *tetractys*, which is *omnium numerorum radix et exordium* (Giorgio 50ᵛ, *cit.* Fowler 276).

vi *815.* 'And lead us not into temptation, but deliver us from evil: For thine is the kingdom, and the power, and the glory, for ever' (*Matt.* vi 13).

vi *820–3.* This censure of the rebel angels for their narrow conception of excellence is one of the main supports for Steadman's theory that *PL* sets out a definite hierarchy of virtues. Cp. i 144, 273, ii 232, etc.; and see Steadman 93.

vi *827. four*] The 'four cherubic shapes' of l. 753. At l. 755 they had wings set with eyes, the regular iconographical attribute of cherubim, authorized by *Ezek.* x 12. *starry wings*] These are less usual; they may be intended to emphasize the cosmic nature of Messiah's equipage (see ll. 749–59*n*).

vi *828. contiguous*] Explained by *Ezek.* i 9, where the wings of the cherubim moving the chariot are said to be 'joined one to another'.

vi *830.* 'I heard the noise of their wings, like the noise of great waters' (*Ezek.* i 24).

vi *831.* In *Ezekiel* (i 12) the steadiness of the cherubim's progress is repeatedly emphasized: 'And they went every one straight forward: whither the spirit was to go, they went; and they turned not when they went.' Cp. i 9, x 22.

Gloomy as night; under his burning wheels
The steadfast empyrean shook throughout,
All but the throne it self of God. Full soon
Among them he arrived; in his right hand
Grasping ten thousand thunders, which he sent
Before him, such as in their souls infixed
Plagues; they astonished all resistance lost,
All courage; down their idle weapons dropt;
O'er shields and helms, and helmed heads he rode
Of thrones and mighty seraphim prostrate,

vi *832. burning wheels*] Cp. the 'fervid wheels' of the chariot in which the Son rides to the creation, at vii 218; and see l. 846*n*.

vi *833–4.* Conflicting with Satan's claim at i 105, to have shaken the throne itself. The allusion is to *Is.* xiii 12f: 'I will make a man more precious than fine gold; even a man than the golden wedge of Ophir. Therefore I will shake the heavens, and the earth shall remove out of her place, in the wrath of the Lord of hosts, and in the day of his fierce anger'–verses that have resonance time and again in distant parts of the poem. See, e.g., the allusion to Solomon's golden triumphal chariot (ll. 749–59*n*); and the sovereign position of Ophir at xi 400.

vi *836. ten thousand*] See l. 767*n*. *thunders*] see l. 764*n*.

vi *838. plagues*] Probably in the Latinizing sense 'blow, stroke, wound' (*OED* 1), though the more general current meaning 'afflicting visitation of divine anger' might be adequate. A secondary allusion to the Egyptian plagues has been rendered obvious by such earlier allusions as l. 801. *astonished*] bewildered, stupefied.

vi *840–1.* As Verity pointed out, the imagery of these lines, like that of the supplementary account at iii 393–6, closely resembles M.'s description in *An Apology Against a Pamphlet* of the zeal that is sometimes needed to 'astonish the proud resistance of carnall, and false Doctors'. Against new heresies and old corruptions, 'Zeale whose substance is ethereal, arming in compleat diamond ascends his fiery Chariot drawn with two blazing Meteors figur'd like beasts, but of a higher breed then any the Zodiack yields, resembling two of those four which *Ezechiel* and S. *John* saw, the one visag'd like a Lion to expresse power, high autority and indignation, the other of count'nance like a man to cast derision and scorne upon perverse and fraudulent seducers; with these the invincible warriour Zeale shaking loosely the slack reins drives over the heads of Scarlet Prelats, and such as are insolent to maintaine traditions, brusing their stiffe necks under his flaming wheels. Thus did the true Prophets of old combat with the false; thus Christ himselfe the fountaine of meeknesse found acrimony anough to be still galling and vexing the Prelaticall Pharisees' (Yale i 900f). *prostrate*] Stressed on the second syllable.

That wished the mountains now might be again
Thrown on them as a shelter from his ire.
Nor less on either side tempestuous fell
His arrows, from the fourfold-visaged four,
Distinct with eyes, and from the living wheels
Distinct alike with multitude of eyes,
One spirit in them ruled, and every eye
Glared lightning, and shot forth pernicious fire
Among the accursed, that withered all their strength,
And of their wonted vigour left them drained,
Exhausted, spiritless, afflicted, fallen.
Yet half his strength he put not forth, but checked
His thunder in mid volley, for he meant
Not to destroy, but root them out of heaven:
The overthrown he raised, and as a herd
Of goats or timorous flock together thronged

vi *842*. What before had caused them 'many a dolorous groan' (l. 658) now seems preferable to the wrath of Messiah. Cp. *Rev.* vi 16, where the damned at the Last Judgment cry 'to the mountains and rocks, Fall on us, and hide us from the face of him that sitteth on the throne, and from the wrath of the Lamb'.

vi *845*. Cp. Ezekiel's vision of the wheels (x 14): 'every one had four faces: the first face was the face of a cherub, and the second face was the face of a man, and the third the face of a lion, and the fourth the face of an eagle.'

vi *846*. In Ezekiel's vision the wheels set with eyes (x 12) are living creatures, though not necessarily members of an order of angels. In cabbalistic literature, however, wheels constituted the second of the angelic orders. West (157f) finds significance in M.'s regular association of wheels with cherubim, the second order of the Dionysian hierarchies (see vii 218 and 224 below), especially in view of the fact that Agrippa actually identified cherubim and wheels. But the association in *PL* is perhaps accounted for by the assignment of wheels to cherubim in *Ezek.* x 9. Nor should one forget the quite unesoteric iconographical tradition in which wheels were the attributes of the order of thrones (see Didron ii 92, 98, 103). *Distinct*] adorned (poetic).

vi *847*. A heavier point is required after *eyes*.

vi *849*. *pernicious*] destructive, fatal; but perhaps also 'swift'–in *Ezek.* i 13 the living creatures shoot forth lightning.

vi *856–7*. Earlier editors should not be ridiculed for trying to justify the baseness of the simile with Homeric precedent: M. might at least have agreed that it lowers the rebels drastically. *goats*] Alludes to the parable of the sheep and the goats in *Matt.* xv, especially 33 and 41. At the Last Judgment the goats are to be banished 'into everlasting fire, prepared for the devil and his angels'.

Drove them before him thunderstruck, pursued
With terrors and with furies to the bounds
And crystal wall of heaven, which opening wide,
Rolled inward, and a spacious gap disclosed
Into the wasteful deep; the monstrous sight
Strook them with horror backward, but far worse
Urged them behind; headlong themselves they threw
Down from the verge of heaven, eternal wrath
Burnt after them to the bottomless pit.
   Hell heard the unsufferable noise, hell saw
Heaven ruining from heaven and would have fled
Affrighted; but strict fate had cast too deep
Her dark foundations, and too fast had bound.
Nine days they fell; confounded Chaos roared,
And felt tenfold confusion in their fall
Through his wild anarchy, so huge a rout
Encumbered him with ruin: hell at last
Yawning received them whole, and on them closed,

vi *858. thunderstruck*] Used both literally and figuratively. It may also be relevant that the word was specifically applied to ecclesiastical censure (*OED* 2 b; cp., e.g., Henry More, *Apocalypsis apocalypseos* (1680) 132: 'Gregory the seventh, when he had excommunicated the Emperor Henry the fourth, said, he was *fulmine afflatus* thunder-struck by him'); particularly in view of ll. 840–1*n*.
vi *859*. Combining *Job* vi 4 ('the terrors of God do set themselves in array against me') with *Is.* li 20 ('thy sons have fainted . . . they are full of the fury of the Lord, the rebuke of thy God'). *furies*] Has also, however, a classical overtone, suggesting the avenging deities sent from Tartarus to punish wrong.
vi *861. rolled*] turned on its axis. Cp. the automated gate of heaven, v 254–6 and *n*.
vi *862. wasteful*] desolate, uninhabited, void.
vi *866*. Continuity is here established with the events of the flashback of i 44–9, which are there said to have come to their conclusion nine days before the first-order time of Bk i. See Introduction, 'Chronology'.
vi *868. ruining*] falling headlong.
vi *871*. An important line for the poem's chronology; see Introduction. On the meaning of this time interval, see i 50–83*n*.
vi *873. rout*] disreputable crowd; or defeat.
vi *874. Encumbered*] burdened; blocked up; involved; harassed. *ruin*] fall, destruction; or failure. Cp. ii 995f where Chaos tells Satan how at the fall of the angels he heard 'ruin upon ruin, rout on rout, / Confusion worse confounded'.
vi *875*. 'Therefore hell hath enlarged herself, and opened her mouth without

Hell their fit habitation fraught with fire
Unquenchable, the house of woe and pain.
Disburdened heaven rejoiced, and soon repaired
Her mural breach, returning whence it rolled.
Sole victor from the expulsion of his foes
Messiah his triumphal chariot turned:
To meet him all his saints, who silent stood
Eye witnesses of his almighty acts,
With jubilee advanced; and as they went,
Shaded with branching palm, each order bright,
Sung triumph, and him sung victorious king,
Son, heir, and Lord, to him dominion given,
Worthiest to reign: he celebrated rode
Triumphant through mid heaven, into the courts
And temple of his mighty Father throned
On high: who into glory him received,
Where now he sits at the right hand of bliss.
  Thus measuring things in heaven by things on earth
At thy request, and that thou mayst beware
By what is past, to thee I have revealed
What might have else to human race been hid;

measure: and their glory, and their multitude, and their pomp, and he that rejoiceth, shall descend into it.' (*Is.* v 14).

vi *876–7*. 'It is better for thee to enter into life maimed, than having two hands to go into hell, into the fire that never shall be quenched (*Mark* ix 43).

vi *877*. *house . . . pain*] For the diction, see ii 823*n*.

vi *880–3*. See i 169–71*n* and ii 993–7*n* for Satan's and Chaos' versions of the expulsion. Only now does the extent of Messiah's triumph emerge.

vi *882–92*. The whole scene is apocalyptic in conception and even in imagery. Thus the *palm* (emblematic of victory) resembles that carried by the servants of God in *Rev*. vii 9 and the triumph song is like the one in *Rev*. v 12, while the reception into glory at *the right hand of bliss* recalls the Ascension after the Atonement (*Heb*. i 3). In other words, at the mid-point of *PL* M. not only loops back to the first point of the action, but also forwards to subsequent stages of the redemptive history (see MacCaffrey 57, where a similar point is made). *Sung triumph*] at a Roman triumph, the soldiers returning with the victorious general shouted '*Io triumphe*' as they entered the Capitol. The Renaissance tradition of festival triumphs was of course based on Roman precedent; see C. Lorgues-Lapouge in *L'Oeil* xxxv (1957) 27–35, also ll. 749–59*n*.

vi *884–8*. In *Rev*. xii 9f, immediately after the 'old serpent' Satan is cast out from heaven a loud voice is heard celebrating Christ's victory. *jubilee*] joyful shouting, sound of jubilation.

The discord which befell, and war in heaven
Among the angelic powers, and the deep fall
Of those too high aspiring, who rebelled
With Satan, he who envies now thy state,
Who now is plotting how he may seduce
Thee also from obedience, that with him
Bereaved of happiness thou mayst partake
His punishment, eternal misery;
Which would be all his solace and revenge,
As a despite done against the most high,
Thee once to gain companion of his woe.
But listen not to his temptations, warn
Thy weaker; let it profit thee to have heard
By terrible example the reward
Of disobedience; firm they might have stood,
Yet fell; remember, and fear to transgress.

THE END OF THE SIXTH BOOK

Paradise Lost

BOOK VII

The Argument

Raphael at the request of Adam relates how and wherefore this world was first created; that God, after the expelling of Satan and his angels out of

vi *900–7*. Raphael is evidently a good enough judge of Satan's character to recognize at least two of the passions, envy and despite, that we know–on M.'s authority–to actuate him; see iv 115 and ix 126–8. The Lat. proverb *Solamen miseris socios habuisse doloris* had been the devils' motive for corrupting man in Marlowe, *Faustus* 480. These lines contain the warning referred to in v Argument, which according to many critics Raphael never delivered. Empson 151 complains that the terms of the warning are insufficiently specific. But perhaps we should rather admire the delicacy with which Raphael refrains from usurping Adam's prerogatives in any way. A hint should be enough: to give detailed information or instructions would mean limiting Adam's independent role.
vi *909*. *weaker*] supply 'vessel'. The allusion is to *1 Pet.* iii 7: 'Likewise, ye husbands, dwell with them according to knowledge, giving honour unto the wife, as unto the weaker vessel, and as being heirs together of the

heaven, declared his pleasure to create another world and other creatures to dwell therein; sends his son with glory and attendance of angels to perform the work of creation in six days: the angels celebrate with hymns the performance thereof, and his re-ascension into heaven.

Descend from heaven Urania, by that name
If rightly thou art called, whose voice divine
Following, above the Olympian hill I soar,
Above the flight of Pegasean wing.
The meaning, not the name I call: for thou
Nor of the Muses nine, nor on the top
Of old Olympus dwell'st, but heavenly born,

grace of life; that your prayers be not hindered.' Ironically, the verse occurs in a homily on duties of wives and husbands, which, if they were performed, would unquestionably counteract any tendency to uxoriousness.

vii *1–50*. The third of the four invocations in *PL*, the others being i 1–49, iii 1–55, and ix 1–47. For their rhetoric, see Condee; for their structural disposition, ix 1–47*n*.

vii *1–7*. Only in this invocation is M.'s Muse ever named; the departure here being apparently for the sake of a decorum. For *Urania* (Celestial) was anciently the Muse of Astronomy, and as such she has an obvious right to preside over the part of the poem primarily concerned with the macrocosm, Bks vii–viii (*Ed II*; *Ed I* Bk vii). M.'s denial that his Urania is one *of the Muses nine*, however, directs attention to a more recent, single Muse. Since Du Bartas's *L'Uranie*, the name had been used for the specifically Christian Muse of the divine poetry movement; see L. B. Campbell, 'The Christian Muse', *HLB* viii (1935), and cp. Drummond's *Urania, or Spiritual Poems*. M.'s hesitation about using the name is unusual, and conveys the seriousness of his determination to transcend pagan forms of thought. The classical Muse was only *named* Urania; but M. wants to call upon a truly celestial being. Cp. Tasso's invocation, *Gerus. Lib.* i 2: 'O heavenly Muse, that not with fading bays / Deckest thy brow by the Heliconian spring, / But sittest crowned with stars' immortal rays / In Heaven, where legions of bright angels sing' (tr. Fairfax). *Descend*] Because from this point onward the course of the poem is steadily downwards; see ll. 12–25*n*. *the Olympian hill*] Mt Olympus, a resort of the classical Muses, like Helicon, the 'Aonian mount' of i 15; M. has therefore to diminish it by calling it a mere hill. (The distinction between hill and mountain, though comparatively recent, was quite clear in M.'s time.)

vii *1*. Some copies *Ed I* omit comma after *Urania*.

vii *3*. Some copies *Ed I* omit comma after *Following*.

vii *4*. The winged horse Pegasus was regularly an emblem for the inspired poet. Consult R. J. Clements, '*Picta Poesis*,' Temi e testi vi (Rome 1960) 51f, 55f, 229f; and for a typical example see Lebey-Batilly, *Emblemata* (Frankfurt 1596), Emblem 49. After striking the Muses' spring from Helicon, Pegasus flew up to the heavens; hence he could symbolize the poet

Before the hills appeared, or fountain flowed,
Thou with eternal Wisdom didst converse,
Wisdom thy sister, and with her didst play
In presence of the almighty Father, pleased
With thy celestial song. Up led by thee
Into the heaven of heavens I have presumed,
An earthly guest, and drawn empyreal air,

soaring above ordinary sources of inspiration. To aspire to top Pegasus is thus a sublime piece of overgoing. More usually, Pegasus was itself the Christian aspiration; cp. *Mirror for Magistrates*, 'Tragedy of the Poet Collingbourn', 176–8: 'Like Pegasus a Poet must have wynges, / To flye to heaven, thereto to feede and rest: / He must have knoweledge of eternal thynges.'
vii *8–12*. In the tremendous eighth chapter of *Proverbs*, Wisdom the daughter of God is said to have been brought forth 'when there were no fountains... Before the mountains were settled': 'Then I was by him, as one brought up with him: and I was daily his delight, rejoicing (Vulgate *ludens*) always before him' (*Prov.* viii 24–5, 30). The Wisdom of *Proverbs* claims to have been present when the Lord 'prepared the heavens... when he set a compass upon the face of the depth' (viii 27); and in *Wisdom of Solomon* vii–viii a Wisdom 'conversant with God', and privy to all the mysteries of natural philosophy, is conceived almost as a Muse–'in all ages entering into holy souls, she maketh them... prophets' (vii 27). The idea of Wisdom as a divine consort proved amenable to Platonic development and was popular in the Renaissance. But we should note that Wisdom is not M.'s Muse but the *sister* of his Muse. Fletcher[2] 112 draws an explanation from a rabbinical source, Ben Gerson, according to whom two spirits, Wisdom and Understanding, accompanied God at the creation. His theory, that M.'s Muse is an aspect of the Holy Spirit, is convincingly demolished by Kelley (115–18), who in turn proposes a theory almost equally untenable–that M. invokes some unspecified attribute of God the Father. It seems far more likely that M.'s Muse is the Logos, the agency of creation and the Son of God. For we know that M. rejected the usual identification of the Wisdom of *Prov.* viii with Christ (see *De doctrina* i 7, Columbia xv 13) and that he believed both Wisdom and Christ to have been present at the Creation with their Father. A similar conclusion is arrived at in Robins 157–75.
vii *11*. Some copies *Ed I* omit comma after *Father*.
vii *12–25*. Matching the ascending movement in the invocation of iii 13–22, we have here a descent; the central eminence of Messiah's triumph is past. For the downward course of the last part of the poem, see MacCaffrey 58f.
vii *14–15*. The air of the 'first region' (iii 562–4) was normally fatal to mortals: see Svendsen 88 and *n*. It was well known in M.'s time that at high altitudes men could suffer from the thinness of the air. Cp. xii 76–8, where Adam expects the presumptuous builders of the Tower of Babel to be

Thy tempering; with like safety guided down
Return me to my native element:
Lest from this flying steed unreined, (as once
Bellerophon, though from a lower clime)
Dismounted, on the Aleian field I fall
Erroneous there to wander and forlorn.
Half yet remains unsung, but narrower bound
Within the visible diurnal sphere;
Standing on earth, not rapt above the pole,
More safe I sing with mortal voice, unchanged
To hoarse or mute, though fallen on evil days,
On evil days though fallen, and evil tongues;
In darkness, and with dangers compassed round,

famished of breath. *Thy tempering*] air tempered by you; but also implying that the Muse had been tempering, attuning, raising the poet himself to a high pitch.

vii *16. native element*] earth.

vii *17–20.* When Bellerophon tried to fly to heaven upon Pegasus, Jupiter sent an insect to sting the horse and throw the rider. According to Conti, Bellerophon fell on the Aleian plain, the 'field of error', and wandered blind and lonely till his death (*Mythologiae* ix 4, p. 953; following a tradition traceable only in part to Calepinus' and Stephanus' Dictionaries: see Starnes 240f). Among many interpretations of the myth listed by Conti, the most relevant is a euhemeristic one–that Bellerophon was an astronomer, who ascended into the heavens in the sense that he explored the stars. *clime*] region: note the pun. *erroneous*] Both 'wandering' and 'straying from the ways of wisdom'. In the former sense, probably rare enough to be felt as a Latinism.

vii *19.* Some copies *Ed I* omit comma after *Dismounted*.

vii *20. Ed I* wrongly has comma after *Erroneous*.

vii *21. Half. . . unsung*] A clear indication that M. means us to see the poem's invocations as disposed structurally according to a two-part division. See ix 1–47*n*. But Richardson and Newton were perhaps also right in taking the line to refer to the bisection of Raphael's episode.

vii *22.* That is, within the astronomical universe, which appears to revolve around the earth with a *diurnal* motion or period of about a day.

vii *23. rapt*] entranced, enraptured. *pole*] Either the celestial pole or (more probably) synecdoche for the sky.

vii *25–8.* The obfuscated syntax conceals a topical allusion to M.'s dangerous situation during the persecutions that immediately followed the Restoration. See John Toland's early biography (reprinted in Darbishire 175–7) for M.'s leaving his house near St James's Park and going into temporary retirement.

vii *25. days*] Some copies *Ed I* have 'tongues'.

vii *27. In darkness*] Refers to M.'s blindness; cp. iii 45.

And solitude; yet not alone, while thou
Visit'st my slumbers nightly, or when morn
Purples the east: still govern thou my song,
Urania, and fit audience find, though few.
But drive far off the barbarous dissonance
Of Bacchus and his revellers, the race
Of that wild rout that tore the Thracian bard
In Rhodope, where woods and rocks had ears
To rapture, till the savage clamour drowned
Both harp and voice; nor could the Muse defend
Her son. So fail not thou, who thee implores:
For thou art heavenly, she an empty dream.
Say goddess, what ensued when Raphael,

vii *29*. *nightly*] So iii 31f and ix 21–4. See Jonathan Richardon's *Life*, reprinted Darbishire 291: 'that he frequently Compos'd lying in Bed in a Morning . . . I have been Well inform'd, that when he could not Sleep, but lay Awake whole Nights, he Try'd; not One Verse could he make; at Other times flow'd *Easy his Unpremeditated Verse*, with a certain *Impetus* and *Aestro*, as Himself seem'd to Believe. Then, at what Hour soever, he rung for his Daughter to Secure what Came.' For the diction cp. *Ps*. xvii 3: 'Thou hast proved mine heart; thou hast visited me in the night.'
vii *31*. Not necessarily implying an esoteric intention. Any serious writer might similarly have adapted Horace's advice (*Sat*. I x 73f): *neque te ut miretur turba labores, / contentus paucis lectoribus*, which in context was an encouragement to write bluntly and with integrity. In *Eikonoklastes*, Pref., Yale iii 339f, M. speaks of 'readers; few perhaps, but those few, such of value and substantial worth, as truth and wisdom, not respecting numbers and bigg names, have bin ever wont in all ages to be contented with.' Some copies *Ed I* have colon after *few*.
vii *32–8*. Orpheus was generally a type of the inspired poet; but also particularly appropriate to the present context because of his life of isolation. The myth of his dismemberment by Thracian women during orgies of Bacchus seems to have focused some of M.'s deepest fears: cp. the even more intense application in *Lycidas* 58–63. *Rhodope*] A mountain range in Thrace. *woods and rocks*] Because in Ovid's account of the myth these were enthralled by the *Threicius vates* and mourned his loss–though they also provided the instruments for his murder (*Met*. xi 1–60). *drowned*] The word has a secondary overtone, since Orpheus' head was thrown into the Hebrus river. *harp*] The lyre given to Orpheus by Apollo or Mercury.
vii *36*. Some copies of *Ed I* omit comma after *rapture*.
vii *39*. Some copies *Ed I* omit comma after *heavenly*. *she*] The heroic Muse Calliope, Orpheus' mother.
vii *40*. Some copies *Ed I* omit comma after *goddess*.

The affable archangel, had forewarned
Adam by dire example to beware
Apostasy, by what befell in heaven
To those apostates, lest the like befall
In Paradise to Adam or his race,
Charged not to touch the interdicted tree,
If they transgress, and slight that sole command,
So easily obeyed amid the choice
Of all tastes else to please their appetite,
Though wandering. He with his consorted Eve
The story heard attentive, and was filled
With admiration, and deep muse to hear
Of things so high and strange, things to their thought
So unimaginable as hate in heaven,
And war so near the peace of God in bliss
With such confusion: but the evil soon
Driven back redounded as a flood on those
From whom it sprung, impossible to mix
With blessedness. Whence Adam soon repealed
The doubts that in his heart arose: and now
Led on, yet sinless, with desire to know
What nearer might concern him, how this world
Of heaven and earth conspicuous first began,
When, and whereof created, for what cause,
What within Eden or without was done

vii *41.* A variant of the formula is 'sociable spirit' (v 221). Adam thanks Raphael for his affability at viii 648–50. Some copies *Ed I* omit comma after *archangel.*

vii *47. that sole command*] i.e. 'not to taste that only tree / Of knowledge'; see iv 421–4*n.*

vii *50. consorted*] associated, espoused, united as consorts.

vii *52. admiration*] amazement. Some copies *Ed I* omit the comma immediately following.

vii *56.* Some copies *Ed I* have comma after *confusion.*

vii *57–9.* Cp. Belial on 'the ethereal mould / Incapable of stain' (ii 138–41). *redounded*] flowed back.

vii *59. repealed*] abandoned (*OED* 2); cp. Henry More, *Psychathanasia* (1647), II ii 23: 'Therefore repeal / This grosse conceit, and hold as reason doth reveal.'

vii *61.* In view of the common opinion that the M. was antiscientific, it is worth noting that he here explicitly judges Adam's cosmological enquiry to be blameless.

vii *63. conspicuous*] visible; implying the distinction between the astronomical 'visible diurnal sphere' (l. 22) and the empyreal 'heaven of heavens' (l. 13).

Before his memory, as one whose drouth
Yet scarce allayed still eyes the current stream,
Whose liquid murmur heard new thirst excites,
Proceeded thus to ask his heavenly guest.
   Great things, and full of wonder in our ears,
Far differing from this world, thou hast revealed
Divine interpreter, by favour sent
Down from the empyrean to forewarn
Us timely of what might else have been our loss,
Unknown, which human knowledge could not reach:
For which to the infinitely good we owe
Immortal thanks, and his admonishment
Receive with solemn purpose to observe
Immutably his sovereign will, the end
Of what we are. But since thou hast vouchsafed
Gently for our instruction to impart
Things above earthly thought, which yet concerned
Our knowing, as to highest wisdom seemed,
Deign to descend now lower, and relate
What may no less perhaps avail us known,
How first began this heaven which we behold
Distant so high, with moving fires adorned
Innumerable, and this which yields or fills
All space, the ambient air wide interfused

vii *66–9*. So Dante thirsts for further information from Virgil at *Purg.* xviii 4. The conception of the epistemological desire as thirst for a *fons sapientiae* goes back at least to patristic commentaries on *Ps.* xlii 1f ('As the hart panteth after the water brooks ... My soul thirsteth for God'). *drouth*] thirst. *current*] flowing.
vii *72*. Cp. Virgil, *Aen.* iv 378, where Mercury is *interpres divum*, coming from Jupiter with a dread command. In the Jewish Cabala Mercury was often identified with Raphael; see Cirlot 271.
vii *79*. See *Eccles.* xii 13: 'Fear God, and keep his commandments: for this is the whole duty of man.' But many of M.'s readers would appreciate the irony that in Calvin's Catechism the first question and answer were: 'What is the principal and Chiefe Ende of Man's Life?–To know God' (see Fletcher ii 95).
vii *83*. *seemed*] seemed good (*OED* II 7 e)–a usage rare enough for us to notice secondary chains of discourse, e.g. 'as to highest seemed wise'. Note also seemed = 'was suitable' (*OED* I 1 b). Some copies *Ed I* omit comma after *knowing*.
vii *88–9*. Cp. ii 842, 'buxom air'. The air *yields* to solid bodies or *fills* the space they leave vacant.

Embracing round this florid earth, what cause
Moved the creator in his holy rest
Through all eternity so late to build
In chaos, and the work begun, how soon
Absolved, if unforbid thou mayst unfold
What we, not to explore the secrets ask
Of his eternal empire, but the more
To magnify his works, the more we know.
And the great light of day yet wants to run
Much of his race though steep, suspense in heaven
Held by thy voice, thy potent voice he hears,

vii *90–2.* It is curious that M. should put Adam's question so absurdly–as if he were to ask, like a child, what moved the prime mover. In *De Doctrina* i 7 (Columbia xv 3) M. calls it 'the height of folly' to enquire into 'the actions of God before the foundation of the world'. He rejects even the usual assumption that God 'was occupied with election and reprobation, and with decreeing other things relative to these subjects'. For 'it is not imaginable that God should have been wholly occupied from eternity in decreeing that which was to be created in a period of six days'. The Occasional Cause commonly assigned for creation–the dispeopling of heaven–is explicitly rejected at ll. 145–9. *florid*] flowery; or perhaps in a broader sense, 'resplendent'.

vii *93–4.* Note the interest in the exact duration of the work. *Absolved*] accomplished, finished; not a Latinism.

vii *93.* Some copies *Ed I* omit comma after *begun.*

vii *97.* Job. xxxvi 24: 'Remember that thou magnify his work.' Adam knows that he may be asking for the forbidden knowledge, so that he has to tread circumspectly, making clear his motive. On the other hand, M. minimises the limitation on knowledge to which *Genesis* commits him, by showing that the permissible ration is far from meagre (Burden 114f). Some copies *Ed I* omit comma after *works.*

vii *98–100.* The appeal to continue a narration was an epic commonplace, going back to Homer, *Od.* xi 372–6. Since the sun's course is *steep* it must be near the end of its race; but Adam is no doubt mindful of the apparent deceleration produced by atmospheric refraction (see iv 541*n*). In a secondary chain of discourse the same phenomenon becomes by a pathetic fallacy the sun's reluctance to end Raphael's narration. *suspense*] certainly both 'attentive' (*OED* 1) and 'hanging' (*OED* 4); perhaps also 'undecided (whether to set)' (*OED* 2). Underlying these meanings is a philosophical allusion to the anakuklesis or change in the course of the sun that was anciently supposed to accompany entry into a new World Cycle (here a cycle of decay); see Plato, *Politicus* 268E, *Rep.* ed. Adams ii 298, and, for Spenser's similar use of *Josh.* x 12–14, Fowler 42. M. had explicitly mentioned the transition to a new Cycle at v 583 above. Cp. also x 687ff below, where the sun turns aside in disgust at man's sin.

And longer will delay to hear thee tell
His generation, and the rising birth
Of nature from the unapparent deep:
Or if the star of evening and the moon
Haste to thy audience, night with her will bring
Silence, and sleep listening to thee will watch,
Or we can bid his absence, till thy song
End, and dismiss thee ere the morning shine.
Thus Adam his illustrious guest besought:
And thus the godlike angel answered mild.
This also thy request with caution asked
Obtain: though to recount almighty works
What words or tongue of seraph can suffice,
Or heart of man suffice to comprehend?
Yet what thou canst attain, which best may serve
To glorify the maker, and infer
Thee also happier, shall not be withheld
Thy hearing, such commission from above
I have received, to answer thy desire
Of knowledge within bounds; beyond abstain

vii *103*. The deep was *unapparent* (invisible, secret) before creation not only because it was dark, but also because chaos was without form.

vii *105*. *audience*] assembly of listeners. But Adam is also courteously acknowledging Raphael's position, since the formal interviews held by an ambassador were *audiences* in another sense.

vii *106*. *watch*] remain awake.

vii *108*. Adam's majesty is carried so modestly that he avoids saying outright that he will dismiss Raphael. Just as the antecedent of *we* could be Adam *and* Eve, so *dismiss* could = 'release', with *song* as subject.

vii *112–14*. *words or tongue*] Bentley wanted this to read 'words from tongue', but as Empson[2] 161 points out this would lose 'the completeness of the statement; "How can any stage in the production of the speech of seraphs be adequate; how can they find words, and if they could how could their tongues pronounce them?" But besides this, the merit of *or* is its fluidity; the way it allows "words from tongue" to be suggested without pausing for analysis, without holding up the single movement of the line.' Cp. *1 Cor.* ii 9: 'Eye hath not seen, nor ear heard, neither have entered into the heart of man, the things which God hath prepared for them that love him.'

vii *113*. In Isaiah's vision of the Lord's glory it was a seraph who purified his mouth with fire (*Is.* vi 6).

vii *116*. *infer*] render, induce, procure (*OED* 1). *the*] thy *Ed I*, some copies.

To ask, nor let thine own inventions hope
Things not revealed, which the invisible king,
Only omniscient, hath suppressed in night,
To none communicable in earth or heaven:
Enough is left besides to search and know.
But knowledge is as food, and needs no less
Her temperance over appetite, to know
In measure what the mind may well contain,
Oppresses else with surfeit, and soon turns
Wisdom to folly, as nourishment to wind.
Know then, that after Lucifer from heaven
(So call him, brighter once amidst the host
Of angels, than that star the stars among)
Fell with his flaming legions through the deep
Into his place, and the great Son returned
Victorious with his saints, the omnipotent
Eternal Father from his throne beheld
Their multitude, and to his Son thus spake.
At least our envious foe hath failed, who thought

vii *121. inventions*] reasonings; cp. *Eccles.* vii 29: 'God hath made man upright; but they have sought out many inventions.' An allusion to scientific inventions (discoveries) is possible; cp. in this connection viii 76. *hope*] hope for.

vii *122–3.* Cp. *1 Tim.* i 17, 'the King eternal, immortal, invisible, the only wise God'; also Horace, *Odes* III xxix 29–32: *prudens futuri temporis exitum / caliginosa nocte premit deus, / ridetque si mortalis ultra / fas trepidat.*

vii *124. none*] Cp. *Matt.* xxiv 36: 'But of that day and hour knoweth no man, no, not the angels of heaven, but my Father only.' For the bounds set to man's knowledge of the astronomical universe, see viii 70ff below.

vii *126–30.* The metaphor implicit in earlier uses of savoury (see, e.g., v 84–5*n*) is now made an explicit simile. Cp. Davenant, *Gondibert* (1651) II viii 22: 'For though Books serve as Diet of the Minde; / If knowledg, early got, self vallew breeds, / By false digestion it is turn'd to winde; / And what should nourish, on the Eater feeds.'

vii *126. as*] a *Ed I*, some copies.

vii *132.* Cp. v 658f, and see i 82*n* and 361–3 on Satan's loss of his original name. In ancient times Lucifer was a name for the planet Venus when it appeared as a morning star. The symbolic possibilities of the connection between Satan and the morning star were well worked at the outset of Raphael's narration: see v 700–14*n*.

vii *135. his place*] Biblical diction; cp. *Acts* i 25: 'This ministry and apostleship, from which Judas by transgression fell, that he might go to his own place.'

vii *136. saints*] angels; cp. vi 398*n*, 767.

vii *139. least*] Perhaps to be amended to 'last', though the case for this is not so clear-cut as Adams 94 suggests.

All like himself rebellious, by whose aid
This inaccessible high strength, the seat
Of deity supreme, us dispossessed,
He trusted to have seized, and into fraud
Drew many, whom their place knows here no more;
Yet far the greater part have kept, I see,
Their station, heaven yet populous retains
Number sufficient to possess her realms
Though wide, and this high temple to frequent
With ministeries due and solemn rites:
But lest his heart exalt him in the harm
Already done, to have dispeopled heaven
My damage fondly deemed, I can repair
That detriment, if such it be to lose

vii *141*. For the inaccessible highest heaven, see v 643*n*.
vii *142*. *us dispossessed*] The absolute construction when not in the nominative case would perhaps be felt as a Latinism; though there were many precedents in Middle English usage. Cp., e.g., Wyclif's *Matt.* xxviii 13, 'they han stolen him us slepinge'.
vii *143*. *fraud*] faithlessness.
vii *144*. 'He that goeth down to the grave shall come up no more. He shall return no more to his house, neither shall his place know him any more' (*Job* vii 9f). Some copies *Ed I* omit comma after *many*.
vii *145*. *greater part*] On different estimates of the proportion of loyal to disloyal angels see ii 692*n*.
vii *145–56*. See ll. 90–2*n*. The repeopling of heaven is a 'convenient' feature of the creation of man, but M. goes out of his way to insist that that does not make creation 'necessary'. God's works are all 'executed freely according to his own good pleasure' (*De doctrina* i 5; Columbia xiv 187). Thus it would be wrong to speak of *repair* of *detriment*. Note that Raphael does not make God say 'I will create *so that* Satan's heart may not exalt him'; thus Empson (56, 87) is wrong to interpret the passage as meaning that God creates us 'to spite the devils'. Raphael nowhere advances any theory about the cause of man's creation. Being an angel, however, he would no doubt be interested in the idea, afterwards patristic, that men supply the places of the fallen angels. See St Augustine, *Civ. Dei* xxii 1: 'Gathering so many unto this grace as should supply the places of the fallen angels, and so preserve (and perhaps augment) the number of the heavenly inhabitants.' For Augustine this is an instance of God's ability to turn apparent evil into eventual good. Dr Johnson and A. H. Gilbert (132–4) see a discrepancy between the present passage and others that speak of a rumour of man's creation having been 'rife' before the fall of the angels (e.g. ii 345–53). But this can be explained as an attempt to render God's foreknowledge and providence. See ix 136–8*n*.
vii *151*. Some copies *Ed I* omit comma after *done*.

Self-lost, and in a moment will create
Another world, out of one man a race
Of men innumerable, there to dwell,
Not here, till by degrees of merit raised
They open to themselves at length the way
Up hither, under long obedience tried,
And earth be changed to heaven, and heaven to
earth,
One kingdom, joy and union without end.
Mean while inhabit lax, ye powers of heaven,
And thou my Word, begotten Son, by thee
This I perform, speak thou, and be it done:
My overshadowing spirit and might with thee
I send along, ride forth, and bid the deep
Within appointed bounds be heaven and earth,
Boundless the deep, because I am who fill

vii *154*. *Self-lost*] Cp. St Augustine, *Civ. Dei* xxii 1: 'Nor had there been any evil at all, but that those spirits . . . procured such evil unto themselves by sin.' *moment*] The theory that creation was instantaneous, and that all living creatures not immediately developed were nevertheless present from the first as *rationes seminales*, was Augustinian. See the *De Genesi* i 1–3, and consult the useful account in Ellrodt 77ff. Here 155f looks almost like a rationalisation of Augustine's doctrine in protogenetic terms.
vii *156–60*. See v 496–500*n*. Some copies *Ed I* omit comma after *innumerable*.
vii *161*. *without*] For accentuation on the first syllable indicating emphasis, see B. A. Wright in *N& Q* cciii (1958) 202f.
vii *162*. *inhabit lax*] spread out; live spaciously; annex the principalities of the rebel third. The phrase imitates Cicero, *De domo sua* xliv 115: *habitare laxe et magnifice voluit*.
vii *162*. Some copies of *Ed I* have semicolon after *heaven*.
vii *163–4*. M.'s Arianism did not lead him to question Christ's role as the Neoplatonic Logos (Word), the agency of creation, nor his special generation before the rest of creation. See iii 170*n*, v 601*n*; *John* i 1–3; and *De doctrina* i 7, Columbia xv 5: 'Creation is that act whereby God the Father produced every thing that exists by his Word and Spirit.' In the same ch. M. argues at some length that Christ was the instrumental, though not the principal, cause of creation (*ibid*. xv 6–10).
vii *165–6*. *spirit*] M. would privately mean God's 'will' or his 'divine power, rather than any person' of the Trinity (*De doctrina* i 7, Columbia xv 5, 13). *overshadowing*] The angel Gabriel said to Mary 'the power of the Highest shall overshadow thee' (*Luke* i 35). Cp. also *Gen*. i 2: 'And the Spirit of God moved upon the face of the waters.'
vii *168*. Set in a metrically prominent place, *fill* 'aligns the plenitude of God against the emptiness of opposing forces' (MacCaffrey 105, contrasting ii 932).

Infinitude, nor vacuous the space.
Though I uncircumscribed my self retire,
And put not forth my goodness, which is free
To act or not, necessity and chance
Approach not me, and what I will is fate.
So spake the almighty, and to what he spake
His Word, the filial Godhead, gave effect.
Immediate are the acts of God, more swift
Than time or motion, but to human ears
Cannot without process of speech be told,
So told as earthly notion can receive.
Great triumph and rejoicing was in heaven
When such was heard declared the almighty's will;

vii *168–73*. The basis for Saurat's hypothesis that M. held a 'retraction theory' of creation, and believed God to have produced the universe by a simple act of withdrawal. Saurat's theory is dismantled by R. J. Z. Werblowski in *JWI* xviii (1955) 90–113 and in Kelley 209–11. The *De Doctrina* has nothing about creation by retraction, while the present passage seems to imply a theory almost diametrically opposed. It says that space is not void; and that it is infinite because God, who fills it, is. It also asserts that the chaotic character of the deep (where Chance governs; see ii 909f) does not show God being circumscribed by randomness–only choosing not to extend his creative form-giving goodness. According to Fletcher ii 173 all the ideas in the passage could have been derived from Magirus' standard school textbook of natural philosophy. See also Howard 169f, Robins 47f. In 'Milton and the Creation,' *JEGP* lxi (1962), J. H. Adamson suggests that the corollary of an *ex Deo* theory of Creation is a deiform nature, and a theological justification for the appreciation of beauty.
vii *173*. In hell Satan attempted in Stoic fashion to assert the supremacy of Fate; see i 116–7*n*. God here explains, however, that there is no Fate other than his own decree. The devils sometimes admitted this–especially Belial (ii 197–9). In *De doctrina* i 2 (Columbia xiv 27) M. as usual insists on the subordination of all laws to God's untrammelled decree: 'There are some who pretend that nature or fate is this supreme Power: but the very name of nature implies that it must owe its birth to some prior agent, or, to speak properly, signifies in itself nothing; but means either the essence of a thing, or that general law which is the origin of every thing, and under which every thing acts; on the other hand, fate can be nothing but a divine decree emanating from some almighty power.'
vii *176–9*. Raphael here implies that his account of creation will be a myth, like his narration of the angelic war (cp. v 571–6). On instantaneous creation see l. 154*n* above. The topic was one that invited speculation, then as now. Augustinian commentators on *Genesis* explained the six days of creation as a manifestation of what had really been performed instantaneously. Cp. Bacon's distinction between two emanations of virtue from God in creation:

Glory they sung to the most high, good will
To future men, and in their dwellings peace:
Glory to him whose just avenging ire
Had driven out the ungodly from his sight
And the habitations of the just; to him
Glory and praise, whose wisdom had ordained
Good out of evil to create, in stead
Of spirits malign a better race to bring
Into their vacant room, and thence diffuse
His good to worlds and ages infinite.
So sang the hierarchies: mean while the Son
On his great expedition now appeared,
Girt with omnipotence, with radiance crowned
Of majesty divine, sapience and love
Immense, and all his Father in him shone.
About his chariot numberless were poured
Cherub and seraph, potentates and thrones,
And virtues, winged spirits, and chariots winged,
From the armoury of God, where stand of old
Myriads between two brazen mountains lodged
Against a solemn day, harnessed at hand,
Celestial equipage; and now come forth

by power he instantaneously created the confused matter of the universe; by wisdom he disposed it in the orderly works of the six days (*Advancement of Learning* I vi 2). *process*] Stressed on the second syllable. *notion*] understanding.

vii *182–3*. Modelled on the angels' song in *Luke* ii 14; because that accompanied the beginning of the New Creation, as this does the old. Cp. also *Job* xxxviii 7, where 'the morning stars sang together, and all the sons of God shouted for joy' at the creation.

vii *183*. Some copies *Ed I* have semicolon after *peace*.

vii *191*. *worlds*] world *Ed I*, some copies.

vii *194*. *Girt with omnipotence*] Presumably refers to 'thunders' such as those of vi 836. Cp. *Ps*. xviii 39: 'thou hast girded me with strength'.

vii *195*. For the particular association of Christ with *Sapience*, see ll. 8–12*n*; also Ellrodt 166ff.

vii *196*. See iii 139–40*n*.

vii *197*. *poured*] Cp. vi 830.

vii *200*. Cp. *Jer*. l 25: 'The Lord hath opened his armoury.'

vii *201*. Cp. Zechariah's vision (vi 5, 1) of chariots that were 'spirits of the heavens, which go forth from standing before the Lord of all the earth': 'behold, there came four chariots out from between two mountains; and the mountains were mountains of brass.'

vii *203*. *equipage*] retinue, apparatus for the expedition. But there may also be a sombre overtone; since 'equipage' often meant apparatus of war, and

Spontaneous, for within them spirit lived,
Attendant on their Lord: heaven opened wide
Her ever during gates, harmonious sound
On golden hinges moving, to let forth
The king of glory in his powerful Word
And Spirit coming to create new worlds.
On heavenly ground they stood, and from the shore
They viewed the vast immeasurable abyss
Outrageous as a sea, dark, wasteful, wild,
Up from the bottom turned by furious winds
And surging waves, as mountains to assault
Heaven's highth, and with the centre mix the pole.
  Silence, ye troubled waves, and thou deep, peace,
Said then the omnific Word, your discord end:
  Nor stayed, but on the wings of cherubim
Uplifted, in paternal glory rode
Far into chaos, and the world unborn;
For chaos heard his voice: him all his train
Followed in bright procession to behold
Creation, and the wonders of his might.
Then stayed the fervid wheels, and in his hand

the *solemn day* (l. 202) is left so indeterminate that it could refer to the day of judgment.

vii *204*. For the animated chariots, cp. *Ezek.* i 20, and see vi 846*n*.

vii *205–8*. Cp. *Ps.* xxiv 7: 'Lift up your heads, O ye gates; and be ye lift up, ye everlasting doors; and the King of glory shall come in.' There is an obvious contrast with the gates of hell, which opened with a 'jarring sound' to give Satan his very different view of the *abyss*, at ii 879ff. The syntax of these lines is discussed by Lewis (46). On the self-opening gates see v 254–6*n*.

vii *208–9*. Cp. ll. 163–5. Notice how *word* and *spirit* are made subordinate to God.

vii *210–15*. 'The earth is the Lord's, and the fulness thereof; the world, and they that dwell therein. For he hath founded it upon the seas, and established it upon the floods' (*Ps.* xxiv 1f). *Outrageous*] excessive, unrestrained. *wasteful*] desolate, excessive. See ii 961*n*. *Up . . . bottom*] Probably alludes to the sea upheaved *a sedibus imis* by the winds, but calmed by Neptune, in Virgil, *Aen.* i 84ff, 106ff, 124ff; if so, there is a contrast with Death's Neptune role in the pseudo-creation at x 295. Like *mountains*, *centre* and *pole* belong to the vehicle of the simile; chaos itself is without place (ii 894).

vii *217*. *omnific*] all-creating. *OED* gives no instance earlier than this.

vii *218*. *cherubim*] Those of Messiah's triumphal chariot; see ll. 197–9 and vi 846*n*.

vii *224*. *fervid*] burning. Cp. the 'burning wheels' of the chariot, at vi 832.

He took the golden compasses, prepared
In God's eternal store, to circumscribe
This universe, and all created things:
One foot he centred, and the other turned
Round through the vast profundity obscure,
And said, Thus far extend, thus far thy bounds,
This be thy just circumference, O world.
Thus God the heaven created, thus the earth,
Matter unformed and void: darkness profound
Covered the abyss: but on the watery calm
His brooding wings the spirit of God outspread,

In Ezekiel's vision the mystical chariot is repeatedly described as burning. *the*] his *Ed I*, some copies.

vii *225–30*. Cf. l. 170, where by contrast God calls himself 'uncircumscribed'. The notion of a divine geometrical construction stems originally from *Prov*. viii 27 ('When he prepared the heavens, I was there: when he set a compass upon the face of the depth'), where an abstract circle–Vulgate *gyrus*–is meant. Biblical commentators, however, made the compass a concrete one (see Fletcher[2] 108), so that in *Par*. xix 40f Dante could speak of God as him 'who turned his compass (*sesto*) round the confines of the universe'. For visual art, the history of the motif of God circumscribing the world with compasses is summarised and traced back to the *Bible moralisée* in Klibansky 339*n*. In view of the variant in which God holds both compasses and scales, it is of interest to recall that in *PL* the divine scales have already appeared, at iv 997ff. The image implied an anthropomorphic conception of God as an architect, planning the universe according to the principles of number and proportion (see Wittkower 15, 101). Cp. also *Job* xxxviii 11: 'Hitherto shalt thou come, but no further: and here shall thy proud waves be stayed.' For a list of articles containing speculations about how M. could have known the familiar compass image, see Svendsen 258f.

vii *227*. Empson[2] 167 builds a great deal on the assumption that this line implies that the angels are not created. But M. is here speaking of the visible universe, and even specifically of *things*. From *De doctrina* i 7 (Columbia xv 32f) we know that he believed the angels to have been created long before the material world.

vii *233*. *Matter unformed*] The 'first matter' of v 472. Plato's account of creation from formless substance (*Tim*. 50ff) had from patristic times been synthesized with that given in *Genesis*. The authoritative work, which influenced M. a good deal, was Philo's *De opificio mundi*. In *De doctrina* i 7 (Columbia xv 19) M. explicitly rejects the doctrine of creation *ex nihilo*. *darkness*] Cp. ii 962, where Night is Chaos' consort.

vii *235*. Gen. i 2: 'And the earth was without form, and void; and darkness was upon the face of the deep. And the Spirit of God moved upon the face of the waters.' See i 17–22*n* above for M.'s use of *brooding* to translate the Heb. word wrongly rendered in A.V. 'moved'; and cp. *De doctrina* i 7

And vital virtue infused, and vital warmth
Throughout the fluid mass, but downward purged
The black tartareous cold infernal dregs
Adverse to life: then founded, then conglobed
Like things to like, the rest to several place
Disparted, and between spun out the air,
And earth self balanced on her centre hung.
   Let there be light, said God, and forthwith light
Ethereal, first of things, quintessence pure
Sprung from the deep, and from her native east
To journey through the airy gloom began,
Sphered in a radiant cloud, for yet the sun
Was not; she in a cloudy tabernacle

(Columbia xv 13), *Spiritus Dei incubabat.* In the same place M. argues that by *spirit* is meant God's 'divine power, rather than any person'; or that, if a person is meant, it can have been 'only a subordinate minister: God is first described as creating the heaven and the earth; the Spirit is only represented as moving upon the face of the waters already created'.

vii *236–42. virtue*] influence, power. *vital warmth*] Perhaps building on Plato's myth about God making the body of the cosmos from fire and earth (*Tim.* 31B–C), Neoplatonists had come to speak of a 'primal heat' of creation (see, e.g., Ficino 1468). In the interest of stability and amity, fire and earth required the bond of two intermediate elements, for reasons explained in *Tim.* 31f; cp. Macrobius, *In somn. Scip.* I vi 22–41. The present passage recalls Ovid's account of the separation of four elements, in *Met.* i 21–31, or Lucretius' in *De rerum nat.* v 438ff; but M. has added psychological overtones. Thus, the *infernal dregs* are *black* and *Adverse to life* because earth was associated with melancholy. M. here accepts the common Christian evaluation of that temperament as evil (see Klibansky *passim*). *conglobed*] formed (the earth) into a ball; placing the other elements in order about it.

vii *242.* 'He stretcheth out the north over the empty place, and hangeth the earth upon nothing' (*Job* xxvi 7). Cp. Ovid, *Met.* i 12f: *circumfuso pendebat in aere tellus / ponderibus librata suis*; *Nativity Ode* 117–24; also iv 1000 and v 578f ('earth now rests / Upon her centre poised') above.

vii *243–9.* Developing the passage on the primogeniture of light at iii 8–12. See *Gen.* i 3: 'And God said, Let there be light: and there was light.' 'Patristic theory had by Milton's time pretty much accounted for the difficulty implicit in the delayed creation of the heavenly bodies by calling the first light "informed", though real, and by assigning its perfection in form to the fourth day' (Svendsen 64). Light was 'not one of the four warring elements of chaos but a fifth element (quintessence)' (Fletcher ii 191). See iii 1–55*n*, 6*n*, and 716*n* above. *Ethereal*] of the nature of ether, the highest purest and subtlest element; celestial. Cp. iii 7, 'pure ethereal stream'.

vii *248–9.* Negotiating the difficulty that light is mentioned on the first day of creation, but the heavenly bodies not till the fourth (*Gen.* i 16–19 and

Sojourned the while. God saw the light was good;
And light from darkness by the hemisphere
Divided: light the day, and darkness night
He named. Thus was the first day even and morn:
Nor passed uncelebrated, nor unsung
By the celestial choirs, when orient light
Exhaling first from darkness they beheld;
Birth-day of heaven and earth; with joy and shout
The hollow universal orb they filled,
And touched their golden harps, and hymning praised
God and his works, creator him they sung,
Both when first evening was, and when first morn.
   Again, God said, Let there be firmament

see previous note). In *De doctrina* i 7 (Columbia xv 29–31) M. admits the impossibility of our conceiving 'light independent of a luminary', but attempts to distinguish between visible light and the perpetual invisible light of the heaven of heavens. See John Swan, *Speculum mundi* (*cit.* Svendsen 64), where the controversy about presolar light is summarized. Swan believed the light to be 'no spirituall Light', but shared St Thomas Aquinas' view that it was 'an informed light, which on the fourth day had its perfect form'. Swan refers to an idea utilized by M. (at ll. 245f above) when he writes that 'this first Light was made in motion, and was created in the Eastern part of that Hemisphere in which Man was made.' *tabernacle*] in *Ps.* xix 4 God sets 'a tabernacle for the sun' in the sequence of days and nights.

vii *249–52.* 'And God saw the light, that it was good: and God divided the light from the darkness. And God called the light Day, and the darkness he called Night. And the evening and the morning were the first day' (*Gen.* i 4f). *even and morn*] An important phrase from the point of view of the poem's chronology, since it indicates that M. is to follow the Hebrew system and 'to account the naturall day from evening to evening' (Willet 4). The interpretation of the phrase as it occurs in *Gen.* i 5 had been so controversial that M. could not have used it casually; and indeed it later becomes clear that he has systematically followed St Jerome's exegesis. For he consistently takes 'evening' to stand for 'night' (and not for 'day', as Sts Ambrose and Chrysostom held); see ll. 255 and 582f, also Introduction, 'Chronology'.

vii *256–60.* When God 'laid the foundations of the earth . . . the morning stars sang together, and all the sons of God shouted for joy' (Job xxxviii 4, 7). The *first* evening of creation is the evening that begins Day 14 of the poem's action. See Introduction, 'Chronology' (p. 444).

vii *261–9.* 'And God said, Let there be a firmament in the midst of the waters . . . And God made the firmament, and divided the waters which were under the firmament from the waters which were above the firmament . . . And God called the firmament Heaven' (*Gen.* i 6–8). The 'waters . . . above the

Amid the waters, and let it divide
The waters from the waters: and God made
The firmament, expanse of liquid, pure,
Transparent, elemental air, diffused
In circuit to the uttermost convex
Of this great round: partition firm and sure,
The waters underneath from those above
Dividing: for as earth, so he the world
Built on circumfluous waters calm, in wide
Crystalline ocean, and the loud misrule
Of Chaos far removed, lest fierce extremes
Contiguous might distemper the whole frame:
And Heaven he named the firmament: so even
And morning chorus sung the second day.
The earth was formed, but in the womb as yet
Of waters, embryon immature involved,

firmament' were the subject of one of the greatest controversies of pre-Newtonian cosmology. See Svendsen 56–60, where M.'s model is shown to be a highly eclectic one. In his interpretation of the firmament as a penetrable atmosphere (cp. iii 574) rather than a hard shell, M. agrees with the sceptical Raleigh, Petavius and Thomas Vaughan. On the other hand, he will not join them in explaining away the *circumfluous waters* as clouds; and he retains an outer 'firm opacous globe' at iii 418. The diction of the passage has many technical overtones: e.g., *expanse* implies Lat. *expansum*, the correct rendering–as various cosmologists had explained; see Svendsen 59–of the Hebrew word translated as 'firmament' in A.V. (though A.V. marg. has 'expansion'). *liquid*] Often a poetical Latinism, but here more technical in flavour. Cp. Burton, *Anatomy of Melancholy* II ii 3, on Tycho's view that the spheres are not 'hard, impenetrable, subtile, transparent, etc., or making music, as Pythagoras maintained of old, and Robert Constantine of late, but still, quiet, liquid, open'. *round* and *world*] universe.

vii *271. Crystalline ocean*] Cp. iii Arg. and 518–19*n*; and see H. F. Robins in *PMLA* lxix (1954) 904. Robins distinguishes the crystalline ocean from the crystalline sphere; Svendsen does not. This uncertainty seems a faithful rendering of seventeenth-century confusions.

vii *272–3*. In chaos, opposed qualities war directly, since they are not attached to elements and separated out. *distemper*] The primary sense is 'disturb the order and mixture of the elements' (*OED* v^1); but there is a secondary overtone of 'mix with water; impair by dilution' (*OED* v^2).

vii *274. heaven*] the atmosphere. The Hebrew world picture also included a starry heaven, and a 'third heaven' inhabited by the angels.

vii *275. chorus*] The early edns treat as a proper name. *second day*] Day 15 of the poem's action.

vii *277. embryon*] embryo. *involved*] enfolded, enveloped.

Appeared not: over all the face of earth
Main ocean flowed, not idle, but with warm
Prolific humour softening all her globe,
Fermented the great mother to conceive,
Satiate with genial moisture, when God said
Be gathered now ye waters under heaven
Into one place, and let dry land appear.
Immediately the mountains huge appear
Emergent, and their broad bare backs upheave
Into the clouds, their tops ascend the sky:
So high as heaved the tumid hills, so low
Down sunk a hollow bottom broad and deep,
Capacious bed of waters: thither they
Hasted with glad precipitance, uprolled
As drops on dust conglobing from the dry;
Part rise in crystal wall, or ridge direct,
For haste; such flight the great command impressed
On the swift floods: as armies at the call
Of trumpet (for of armies thou hast heard)
Troop to their standard, so the watery throng,

vii *279–82.* At l. 236 we had 'vital warmth', the *primus calor* of the Neoplatonic cosmogony; now is added the genial moisture of creation, the *primus humor.* On the conception of a generative ocean in Renaissance Neoplatonism, see Wind (117*n*), who cites Boyle's *The Sceptical Chymist.* *Main*] uninterrupted. *prolific*] generative; fertilizing. *genial*] generative.

vii *283–91.* Cp. Gen. i 9f: 'And God said, Let the waters under the heaven be gathered together unto one place, and let the dry land appear . . . And God called the dry land Earth; and the gathering together of the waters called he Seas.' Cp. also *Ps.* civ 6–8: 'The waters stood above the mountains. At thy rebuke they fled; at the voice of thy thunder they hasted away. They go up by the mountains; they go down by the valleys unto the place which thou hast founded for them.' *Immediately*] Cp. 243 ('forthwith'), and see ll. 176ff on the instantaneousness of God's acts. *So high*] For a tradition that the seas' depths and the mountains' heights exactly correspond, see Nicolson[3] 20. *tumid*] swollen.

vii *292. conglobing*] Cp. l. 239. The repetition of the rare word clarifies the parallel between the separation of the elements at large and the separation of terrestrial earth and water.

vii *293.* Repeated in the division of the Red Sea into 'two crystal walls' at xii 197–itself a type of the power of God's grace.

vii *296.* Anticipating the charge of anachronism: the simile would not have made Raphael's narration any more intelligible to Adam and Eve, if he had not already recounted the angelic war in Bk vi. By such alienations M. encourages us to scrutinize what his Paradise includes and excludes.

Wave rolling after wave, where way they found,
If steep, with torrent rapture, if through plain,
Soft ebbing; nor withstood them rock or hill,
But they, or under ground, or circuit wide
With serpent error wandering, found their way,
And on the washy ooze deep channels wore;
Easy, ere God had bid the ground be dry,
All but within those banks, where rivers now
Stream, and perpetual draw their humid train.
The dry land, earth, and the great receptacle
Of congregated waters he called seas:
And saw that it was good, and said Let the earth
Put forth the verdant grass, herb yielding seed,
And fruit tree yielding fruit after her kind;
Whose seed is in her self upon the earth.
He scarce had said, when the bare earth, till then
Desert and bare, unsightly, unadorned,
Brought forth the tender grass whose verdure clad
Her universal face with pleasant green,
Then herbs of every leaf, that sudden flowered
Opening their various colours, and made gay
Her bosom smelling sweet: and these scarce blown,
Forth flourished thick the clustering vine, forth crept
The swelling gourd, up stood the corny reed

vii *299. rapture*] force of movement (*OED* 2). Cp. Chapman, *Od.* xiv 427f: 'That 'gainst a rock, or flat, her keel did dash / With headlong rapture.'
vii *297–306.* The first falling of the rivers to the sea is with Du Bartas an elaborate set piece; see 'The Third Day of the First Week', ll. 135ff. *train*] The metaphor of a trailed robe was old enough to be unemphatic. Cp. e.g., Countess of Pembroke, *Psalms* (1586) lxxviii 20f: 'All that rich land, where over Nilus trailes / Of his wett robe the slymy seedy train.'
vii *302.* By itself, *error* might just be a simple Latinism ('winding course'), but with *serpent* it unmistakably belongs to the large class of instances of the word used as reminders of the Fall (Ricks 110 following Stein 66f).
vii *307–12.* 'And God called the dry land Earth; and the gathering together of the waters called he Seas: and God saw that it was good. And God said, Let the earth bring forth grass, the herb yielding seed, and the fruit tree yielding fruit after his kind, whose seed is in itself, upon the earth: and it was so' (*Gen.* i 10f). *congregated waters*] Cp. Vulgate *Gen.* i 10, *congregationesque aquarum.*
vii *317–18.* The odours are from the account of the third day's creation in *2 Esdras* vi 44.
vii *321. swelling*] The *Ed I* and *Ed II* reading 'smelling' is clearly a misprint; for once an emendation of Bentley's is acceptable. *corny reed*] Cp. v 23, 'balmy reed'. But also perhaps corny=Latin *corneus*, horny. 'The horn

Embattled in her field: and the humble shrub,
And bush with frizzled hair implicit: last
Rose as in dance the stately trees, and spread
Their branches hung with copious fruit; or gemmed
Their blossoms: with high woods the hills were
crowned,
With tufts the valleys and each fountain side,
With borders long the rivers. That earth now
Seemed like to heaven, a seat where gods might dwell,
Or wander with delight, and love to haunt
Her sacred shades: though God had yet not rained
Upon the earth, and man to till the ground
None was, but from the earth a dewy mist
Went up and watered all the ground, and each
Plant of the field, which ere it was in the earth
God made, and every herb, before it grew
On the green stem; God saw that it was good.
So even and morn recorded the third day.
Again the almighty spake: Let there be lights

reed stood upright among the undergrowth of nature, like a grove of spears or a battalion with its spikes aloft' (Hume, comparing Virgil, *Aen.* iii 22f: *tumulus, quo cornea summo / virgulta et densis hastilibus horrida myrtus.*

vii *322. Embattled*] Cp. iv 980–2, where the 'ported spears' of the angelic guard are compared with heads of corn blown in the wind. *and*] considerations of diction and scansion suggest that *Ed I* 'add' may be preferable; see Adams 102f. *humble*] low-growing.

vii *323.* A characteristically Bartasian or Sylvestrian conceit. Cp. the famous line 'And perriwig with wooll the bald-pate woods'. *frizzled*] curled crisply. *implicit*] entangled, interwoven.

vii *325. gemmed*] budded, put forth (*OED* 1). Possibly rare enough to be felt as a Latinism (*gemmare*=to bud).

vii *331–4.* 'The Lord God had not caused it to rain upon the earth, and there was not a man to till the ground. But there went up a mist from the earth, and watered the whole face of the ground' (*Gen.* ii 5f). Note however that after man was put in Paradise at least *showers* of rain fell, even before the Fall; see iv 646.

vii *335–7.* Cp. Gen. ii 4f: 'The Lord God made . . . every plant of the field before it was in the earth, and every herb of the field before it grew.' *ere*] some commentators, notably Philo and St Augustine, took this passage to mean that creation was instantaneous, but comprised in the first instance generic forms or *rationes seminales*. See, e.g., Philo, *Legum allegoria* i 22–4.

vii *338. recorded*] bore witness to (*OED* III 10) or rendered in song (*OED* I 2 b). *third day*] Day 16 of the poem's action.

vii *339–45.* 'And God said, Let there be lights in the firmament of the heaven to divide the day from the night; and let them be for signs, and for seasons,

High in the expanse of heaven to divide
The day from night; and let them be for signs,
For seasons, and for days, and circling years,
And let them be for lights as I ordain
Their office in the firmament of heaven
To give light on the earth; and it was so.
And God made two great lights, great for their use
To man, the greater to have rule by day,
The less by night altern: and made the stars,
And set them in the firmament of heaven
To illuminate the earth, and rule the day
In their vicissitude, and rule the night,
And light from darkness to divide. God saw,
Surveying his great work, that it was good:
For of celestial bodies first the sun
A mighty sphere he framed, unlightsome first,
Though of ethereal mould: then formed the moon
Globose, and every magnitude of stars,
And sowed with stars the heaven thick as a field:
Of light by far the greater part he took,
Transplanted from her cloudy shrine, and placed
In the sun's orb, made porous to receive
And drink the liquid light, firm to retain
Her gathered beams, great palace now of light.

and for days, and years: And let them be for lights in the firmament of the heaven to give light upon the earth' (*Gen.* i 14f). For the determining of time by the lights, see iii 579–81 above. *expanse*] More accurate than A.V: 'firmament'; see ll. 261–9*n*. For the use of the stars see iv 661–73*n*.

vii *346–52*. 'And God made two great lights; the greater light to rule the day, and the lesser light to rule the night: he made the stars also. And God set them in the firmament of the heaven to give light upon the earth. And to rule over the day and over the night, and to divide the light from the darkness' (*Gen.* i 16–18). *altern*] in turns, alternately. *vicissitude*] reciprocal succession.

vii *355*. *unlightsome*] dark. A rare word, which had been used is a similar context by Chapman in *Hymnus in Noctem*, 30–2: 'When unlightsome, vast, and indigest / The formelesse matter of this world did lye' Night 'fildst every place with [her] Divinitie.'

vii *356*. *ethereal mould*] aether, regarded as the material of the sun's body. Cp. *Nativity Ode* 138, 'earthly mould'.

vii *360*. *cloudy shrine*] the 'cloudy tabernacle' (l. 248) in which light moved before the sources of light were created.

vii *361–3*. Controversy about the sun's density and permeability, opacity and diaphanousness, was rife in M.'s day; see e.g. Riccioli i 93.

Hither as to their fountain other stars
Repairing, in their golden urns draw light,
And hence the morning planet gilds her horns;
By tincture or reflection they augment
Their small peculiar, though from human sight
So far remote, with diminution seen.
First in his east the glorious lamp was seen,
Regent of day, and all the horizon round
Invested with bright rays, jocund to run
His longitude through heaven's high road: the grey
Dawn, and the Pleiades before him danced

vii *364–9.* Svendsen 68f draws attention to M.'s deliberate accumulation here of alternative views about the origin of stellar light. She cites the *Speculum mundi*: 'The sunne . . . is indeed the chief fountain from whence the whole world receiveth lustre . . . some Philosophers and Astronomers have been of opinion that the fixed starres shine not but with borrowed light from the sunne. . . . But according to the minds of the best Authours . . . the starres are called lights, as well as the sunne. . . . For if they had not their proper and peculiar light (being so farre distant from inferiour bodies) it is thought they could not alter them in such sort as they sometimes do.' It was believed as late as Kepler that the planets were self-luminous; see Dreyer 411. *tincture*] infusion of a quality; imbuing with an active principle emanating from elsewhere (*OED* 5 b, 6 b), but also secondarily referring to the alchemical elixir or 'universal tincture' (*OED* 6 a)–see iii 607 above for the sun's exhalation of 'elixir'. *peculiar*] A semi-technical term for inherent or 'proper' light, as opposed to light 'strange' or borrowed.
vii *366. her*] Venus'. *Ed I* has 'his', with Lucifer as the implied antecedent, introducing an inappropriate association that M. did well to remove. *horns*] Alludes to the horned appearance of Venus (*cornuta*) when near to conjunction–as we know her to be at present, from various astronomical data given in Bks iv and v above; see v 166–70*n*. An added aptness lies in the fact that Venus' House Taurus was often represented with gilded horns. Note that it is just possible for Venus to be at conjunction in Taurus, when Sol is in Aries (as here: see iii 555–61*n*). In the *thema coeli* or state of the heavens at creation, the planets were supposed to have occupied their own houses. But Venus was more usually placed in Libra than in Taurus. For a list of contemporary published observations of the phases of Venus, including Galileo's, see Riccioli i 484.
vii *372–3.* Cp. *Ps.* xix 5, where the sun 'rejoiceth as a strong man to run a race'. *longitude*] course round the ecliptic–equatorial circle. For the identity of the ecliptic and the equator in the prelapsarian cosmos, see x 651–706*n*.
vii *374–5.* 'Canst thou bind the sweet influences of Pleiades, or loose the bands of Orion?'(*Job* xxxviii 31). Note that while *Dawn* goes before the sun

Shedding sweet influence: less bright the moon,
But opposite in levelled west was set
His mirror, with full face borrowing her light
From him, for other light she needed none
In that aspect, and still that distance keeps
Till night, then in the east her turn she shines,
Revolved on heaven's great axle, and her reign
With thousand lesser lights dividual holds,
With thousand thousand stars, that then appeared
Spangling the hemisphere: then first adorned
With their bright luminaries that set and rose,
Glad evening and glad morn crowned the fourth day.

in his diurnal motion, the *Pleiades* do not. For they are situated in the constellation Taurus, which before the Fall was also the sign Taurus; and the sun is here still in Aries, the preceding sign (see x 329 and iii 555–61*n*; creation was at the vernal equinox). Thus the Pleiades dance *before* the sun only in the sense that they occupy his next position in the *annual* motion round the ecliptic. Almost imperceptibly, the seasonal movement is gathering way.

Hughes, following Newton, compares Guido Reni's painting *Aurora*, which he describes as showing nymphs who represent the Pleiades alongside the sun's chariot. Unfortunately, Reni's nymphs are not the Pleiades but the Hours–as their spaced-out arrangement shows: cp. Ovid, *Met.* ii 26: *positae spatiis aequalibus Horae*. They number seven because the four Hours or Seasons were commonly accompanied by the three Graces (see Hieatt 111). The painting bears some relation, however, to another Ovidian passage, *Met.* ii 112ff, that was used by M. at vi 2–4 above. See Cesare Gnudi and Gian Carlo Cavalli, *Guido Reni* (Florence 1955) 66.

vii *375–9*. Svendsen 72f finds a contradiction between the moon of this passage and the self-luminous moons of viii 150 (see ll. 364–9*n*). But M. says only that 'proper light' is unnecessary in this one *aspect* of opposition. The point of the passage lies in an allusion to a theory of Anastasius Synaita's, that 'when God made these two luminaries, the greater–namely the sun–he placed immediately at the east of the firmament; but the moon at the west' (*In hexaemeron* iv; Migne *P.G.* lxxix 890–914). Hence it was full moon at creation, and the sun and the moon were in an aspect of opposition (180° apart). Bede and many other theologians held that since the moon was created perfect, it must have been full on the fourth day of creation. For a synthesis of this theory with the placement of the sun in Aries at creation, see Riccioli ii 232. *aspect*] Stressed on the second syllable.

vii *382. dividual*] divided, shared.

vii *385. set and rose*] In that order; since the Biblical day begins with evening. See Introduction, 'Chronology' (p. 444).

vii *386*. The fourth day is crowned in a formal or ceremonial sense in that it occupies the sovereign central place among the days of creation, and also

And God said, Let the waters generate
Reptile with spawn abundant, living soul:
And let fowl fly above the earth, with wings
Displayed on the open firmament of heaven.
And God created the great whales, and each
Soul living, each that crept, which plenteously
The waters generated by their kinds,
And every bird of wing after his kind;
And saw that it was good, and blessed them, saying,
Be fruitful, multiply, and in the seas
And lakes and running streams the waters fill;
And let the fowl be multiplied on the earth.
Forthwith the sounds and seas, each creek and bay
With fry innumerable swarm, and shoals
Of fish that with their fins and shining scales
Glide under the green wave, in schools that oft
Bank the mid sea: part single or with mate
Graze the sea weed their pasture, and through groves
Of coral stray, or sporting with quick glance

the central 17th place among the 33 days of the poem's action (see Introduction, 'Chronology'; and, for numerological precedents, Fowler, Index, s.v. *Central position of sovereignty*). The reason for so dignifying the fourth day is that the luminaries created then are 'regent' (371 above). Commentators often gave *Gen.* i 18 an elaborate mystical treatment. See, e.g., Anastasius' anagogies, in which sun and moon are not only Adam and Eve but also *Sol iustitiae* and Holy Church (Migne *P.G.* lxxix 890–914); also Henry More, *Conjectura Cabbalistica.*

vii *387–98.* Cp. *Gen.* i 20–2: 'Let the waters bring forth abundantly the moving creature that hath life, and fowl that may fly above the earth in the open firmament of heaven. And God created great whales, and every living creature that moveth, which the waters brought forth abundantly, after their kind, and every winged fowl after his kind: and God saw that it was good. And God blessed them, saying, Be fruitful, and multiply, and fill the waters in the seas, and let fowl multiply in the earth.' *Reptile*] crawling animal. Vulgate *Gen.* i 20 has *producant aquae reptile animae viventis*, Tremellius *reptilia animantia.* *soul*] animate existence. *crept*] Takes in *Gen.* i 20 A.V. marg., or *Ps.* civ 24f: 'The earth is full of thy riches. So is this great and wide sea, wherein are things creeping innumerable.'

vii *402. schools*] sculles *Ed I* and *Ed II.*

vii *403. Bank*] form a shelving elevation rising almost to the surface of the sea (a verbal use of *OED* sb^{1} I 5).

vii *404.* Not merely a piscatory modulation of the pastoral mode: the fishes' diet has an ideological bearing. See x 710–14*n*.

Show to the sun their waved coats dropped with gold,
Or in their pearly shells at ease, attend
Moist nutriment, or under rocks their food
In jointed armour watch: on smooth the seal,
And bended dolphins play: part huge of bulk
Wallowing unwieldy, enormous in their gait
Tempest the ocean: there leviathan
Hugest of living creatures, on the deep
Stretched like a promontory sleeps or swims,
And seems a moving land, and at his gills
Draws in, and at his trunk spouts out a sea.
Mean while the tepid caves, and fens and shores

vii *406–10.* A subdued allegoria in which the colour-patterns of the fish are likened to various heraldic patterns or *coats*. Thus *waved*, though it may also directly express the appearance of fish glimpsed through the waves, at the level of the vehicle means 'divided undy or wavy'; see Sir G. Mackenzie, *The Science of Herauldry* (Edinburgh 1680) 26: '*Waved* is so call'd, from the *waves* of the Sea, which it represents, and is therefore called *undê*, and is used for signifying that the Bearer got his Arms for service done at sea.' *dropped* (spotted) *with gold*] The whole phrase was heraldically possible; the Grayndores, e.g., bore 'Party ermine and vert, the vert dropped with gold'. Similarly *bended* means not only 'striped, banded' but also 'bendy, having a bend': e.g. John Bossewell, *Workes of armorie* (1572) ii 85: 'One greate difference betwene Armes Bended, and these Armes . . . In Armes Bendee the colours contained in the shielde are equally divided. *attend*] wait for. Bended (*curvus*) was the ancient stock epithet for *delphinus*, especially for the Dolphin constellation; see R. H. Allen, *Star Names* (New York 1963) p. 199. *smooth*] smooth water. Probably this substantive use had a nautical tang: cp. *OED* s.v. *Smooth*, sb. 1 c, 'a stretch of comparatively smooth or calm water in a rough sea'. Although the earliest *OED* instance in this sense is 1840, it would make the dolphins' habitat so much more appropriate that coincidence seems unlikely.
vii *415. seems . . . land*] This reminds the reader of the deceptiveness of leviathan in the simile of i 200–8. Here, however, the illusion is not dangerous. *tempest*] disturb violently.
vii *417–21.* Just possibly alluding to the ancient question whether the egg came before the bird or vice versa, which had been debated by Plutarch (*Symposiacs*), by Macrobius (*Saturnalia*) and more recently by Hendrik Van der Putte (*Ovi encomium*); see D. C. Allen in *MLN* lxiii (1948) 264. The account of creation given by the mystical alchemists has too prominent a place in *PL* for M. to decide the question otherwise than in favour of the Orphic primal egg. See, however, i 17–22 above. *kindly*] natural. *disclosed*] set free; hatched. *callow*] unfeathered. *fledge*] fledged, fit to fly. *summed their pens*] brought their plumage to completion. The past participle 'summed' (as at *PR* i 14) was a technical term in falconry;

Their brood as numerous hatch, from the egg that
 soon
Bursting with kindly rupture forth disclosed
Their callow young, but feathered soon and fledge
They summed their pens, and soaring the air sublime
With clang despised the ground, under a cloud
In prospect; there the eagle and the stork
On cliffs and cedar tops their eyries build:

cp. George Turberville, *The Booke of Faulconrie* (1575) p. 117: 'When . . . hir principal feathers be ful sommed.' M.'s use of 'summed' as an active verb in this sense, however, may be a departure from prose usage. *soaring*] reaching, flying up through. *sublime*] aloft, high up.

vii *422–3. clang*] harsh scream; resonant cry. Probably poetic, in imitation of Latin *clangor* or Greek *κλαγγή*; cp. Chapman, *Il.* x 244: 'By her clange they knew . . . it was a hern.' *ground . . . prospect*] The ground seemed under a cloud of birds. Perhaps, however, there is a secondary prolepsis: in future prospect earth is under a cloud, metaphorically.

vii *423–46.* The seven birds named all symbolized virtues. It will be observed that M. repeatedly draws attention to these emblematic qualities; so that the passage is as far as possible from being a simple catalogue.

vii *423–30.* The eagle is named first as the sovereign of birds. It could symbolize divine grace, or human generosity, majesty, or elevation of thought– even spiritual illumination (see, e.g., Valeriano 234, and consult Tervarent 6, Cirlot 87–9). 'Doth the eagle mount up at thy command, and make her nest on high? She dwelleth and abideth on the rock, upon the crag of the rock, and the strong place' (*Job* xxxix 27f). The stork, on the other hand, was an emblem of impartial justice (cp. Arnold Freitag's emblem, illustrated Scoular Plate 9), of gratitude, of filial piety and of enmity to the snake (Valeriano 203–6, Tervarent 97). Its habit of building its *eyrie* in the towering fir (*Ps.* civ 17) signified *animus divinis intentus* (Valeriano 207). Eagle and stork are respectively notable examples of the sub-classes of those that wing *loosely* (separately) and those that fly in formation. Thus the eagle was proverbially solitary (Valeriano 231), while the stork was an emblem of military discipline because of its unanimity of movement (Valeriano 206, with woodcut illustrating the wedge formation). *Intelligent* (cognizant) *of seasons*] see *Jer.* viii 7: 'The stork in the heaven knoweth her appointed times; and the turtle and the crane and the swallow observe the time of their coming; but my people know not the judgment of the Lord.' *caravan*] company travelling together for security. *mutual wing* probably refers to St Basil's belief that storks use their wings to support their aged parents (Robin 63f). But cp. a similar tradition about migrating birds originating in Pliny and attached by the encyclopedists either to the *crane* or the wild-goose: namely, that they take it in turns to head the flight wedge, and fly each with his beak resting on the bird in front (Svendsen 158). Strictly

Part loosely wing the region, part more wise
In common, ranged in figure wedge their way,
Intelligent of seasons, and set forth
Their airy caravan high over seas
Flying, and over lands with mutual wing
Easing their flight; so steers the prudent crane
Her annual voyage, borne on winds; the air
Floats, as they pass, fanned with unnumbered plumes:
From branch to branch the smaller birds with song
Solaced the woods, and spread their painted wings
Till even, nor then the solemn nightingale
Ceased warbling, but all night tuned her soft lays:
Others on silver lakes and rivers bathed
Their downy breast; the swan with arched neck
Between her white wings mantling proudly, rows
Her state with oary feet: yet oft they quit
The dank, and rising on stiff pennons, tower
The mid aerial sky: others on ground
Walked firm; the crested cock whose clarion sounds

speaking, all these references to migration are prolepses or dramatic ironies, since earth has no seasons until after the Fall. Cp. l. 374f above for a similar prolepsis.

vii *430–2. The prudent crane*] An emblem of diligence and vigilance, the crane belonged like the stork to the sub-class of formation-fliers. Its military propensities have already been mentioned at i 576; cp. also *Prol vii* (Yale i 304). *floats*] undulates.

vii *434. painted wings*] Imitates Virgil, *Aen.* iv 525, *pictae volucres*, in a passage immediately preceding Dido's suicide.

vii *435–6.* The nightingale, to which the central place among the seven named birds is given, is also prominent elsewhere in *PL*: see iii 38–40, iv 602–4, 648, v 40, and viii 518–20. It was the bird 'most musical, most melancholy' (*Il Penseroso* 62). Perhaps because it signified music, poetry and nocturnal meditation (Valeriano 275f), perhaps too because it sang in the dark, M. seems to have made of it a highly personal symbol. But it should also be recalled that in the seventeenth century there was an extensive poetic cult of the nightingale. On this, see L. C. Martin's note to Crashaw's 'Musicks Duell', *The Poems* (Oxford 1927) p. 439f.

vii *438.* The *swan*, like the nightingale, was a symbol of music and poetry, and often signified purity of soul. *mantling*] forming a mantle. Note also, however, that in falconry mantling was a technical term for the perched bird's practice of stretching alternate wings over the corresponding leg for exercise.

vii *441. dank*] pool, mere. *tower* soar aloft into (*OED* I 5).

The silent hours, and the other whose gay train
Adorns him, coloured with the florid hue
Of rainbows and starry eyes. The waters thus
With fish replenished, and the air with fowl,
Evening and morn solemnised the fifth day
  The sixth, and of creation last arose
With evening harps and matin, when God said,
Let the earth bring forth soul living in her kind,
Cattle and creeping things, and beast of the earth,
Each in their kind. The earth obeyed, and straight
Opening her fertile womb teemed at a birth
Innumerous living creatures, perfect forms,
Limbed and full grown: out of the ground up rose
As from his lair the wild beast where he wons
In forest wild, in thicket, brake, or den;
Among the trees in pairs they rose, they walked:
The cattle in the fields and meadows green:
Those rare and solitary, these in flocks

vii *444–5. other*] i.e., the peacock. *starry eyes*] Clearly indicates that the peacock is here a symbol of night, to offset the *cock*, herald of day (see Ripa 210f, Klibansky 313*n*). Morally, the cock was often an emblem of vigilance, the peacock of marital concord.
vii *448. fifth day*] Day 18 of the poem's action.
vii *449.* The account of the sixth day of creation (Day 19) is not an eye-witness report, for according to viii 229 Raphael was on that day absent on a mission to the gates of hell.
vii *450–8.* 'And God said, Let the earth bring forth the living creature after his kind, cattle, and creeping thing, and beast of the earth after his kind: and it was so' (*Gen.* i 24).
vii *450. matin*] morning (*OED* II 3 and III 5 b); but with a secondary allusion to the Office of Matins, which was said either early in the morning or on the preceding evening. The latter practice was based on the *Genesis* formula 'evening and morning were one day'.
vii *451. soul*] foul *Ed I* and *Ed II*; the emendation is Bentley's. With *soul living* cp. 'living soul' (l. 388); in any case, the fowl were created on the fifth day, not the sixth. Adams 94f ingeniously suggests retaining 'foul' as a common variant spelling of 'foal' = young quadruped. But foal would not have the requisite generality of meaning; and besides, the creatures are 'full grown' (l. 456).
vii *454. teemed*] produced, bore.
vii *457. wons*] lives, stays.
vii *461–2. Those* presumably refers to the *wild* beasts, *these* to the *cattle* or domestic livestock (*OED*, *Cattle* II 4), which in turn are divided between those in *flocks* (sheep, goats) and those in *herds* (cows). *rare*] keeping far

Pasturing at once, and in broad herds upsprung.
The grassy clods now calved, now half appeared
The tawny lion, pawing to get free
His hinder parts, then springs as broke from bonds,
And rampant shakes his brinded mane; the ounce,
The libbard, and the tiger, as the mole
Rising, the crumbled earth above them threw
In hillocks; the swift stag from underground
Bore up his branching head: scarce from his mould
Behemoth biggest born of earth upheaved
His vastness: fleeced the flocks and bleating rose,
As plants: ambiguous between sea and land
The river horse and scaly crocodile.
At once came forth whatever creeps the ground,
Insect or worm; those waved their limber fans
For wings, and smallest lineaments exact
In all the liveries decked of summer's pride
With spots of gold and purple, azure and green:
These as a line their long dimension drew,
Streaking the ground with sinuous trace; not all

apart, spread out at wide intervals (*OED* 2 a, 3 a). *broad herds*] Homeric diction; cp. *Il.* xi 679, *αἰπόλια πλατέ' αἰγῶν.*
vii *463–70.* The parallel with Lucretius ii 991–8 suggested by Hughes is not close. Coleridge following Newton compared Raphael's paintings of the Creation in the Loggie of the Vatican, but thought the motif unworthy of poetic expression. There may be more than pictorial naivety, however, in the lion's imprisoned hindquarters. Expounding an image of Adargatis–the earth goddess from whom all life emerges when she is quickened by the rays of the sun, Valeriano 14 remarks: *Sed enim ipsa Leonis effigies utrumque referre videtur hieroglyphicum*: *quippe quae anterioribus partibus Solem exscribit, posterioribus vero Terram.* Note that the animal named first is the sovereign of beasts; cp. l. 423, where the eagle was the first-named of the birds. *brinded*] brindled, brownish, marked with streaks of a different colour. *ounce*] In M.'s time the term was applied to various feline beasts of moderate size, but principally to the lynx; cp. iv 344. *libbard*] leopard.
vii *471.* 'Behold now behemoth, which I made with thee' (*Job* xl 15). The Hebrew word 'behemoth' is interpreted in Geneva margin as 'the elephant, or some other'; l. 474 shows that M. rejected Bochart's alternative, the hippopotamus.
vii *473. ambiguous*] of doubtful classification; or hesitating.
vii *474. river horse* for 'hippopotamus' would not be felt as etymological word-play; the usage was current until the nineteenth century.
vii *475. creeps*] The first instance given in *OED* of this rare transitive use.
vii *476. worm*] Includes serpents, and the grubs, maggots and caterpillars that after the Fall became pests.

Minims of nature; some of serpent kind
Wondrous in length and corpulence involved
Their snaky folds, and added wings. First crept
The parsimonious emmet, provident
Of future, in small room large heart enclosed,
Pattern of just equality perhaps
Hereafter, joined in her popular tribes
Of commonalty: swarming next appeared
The female bee that feeds her husband drone

vii *482. minim*] A form of life of the least importance or size. Usually contemptuous, as in Lancelot Andrewes, *Sermons* (1629) p. 279: 'They be the base people, the minims of the world.' The source of the expression, which is alluded to here, is Vulg. *Prov.* xxx 24: *Quattuor sunt minima terrae, et ipsa sunt sapientiora sapientibus.* On the interest taken in small animals and insects in the seventeenth century, see Scoular 81–117, 'Much in Little'.
vii *483. corpulence*] bulk; not to be taken with *involved*, as Hughes. *involved*] coiled: a past tense, not a participle.
vii *484.* The notion of winged serpents is traced by D. C. Allen, *MLN* lix (1944) 538, through the natural historians back to *Is.* xxx 6 ('fiery flying serpent') and Herodotus ii 75. Belief in the existence of dragons, which it must have been very hard to distinguish from winged serpents, was almost universal; but Allen may be right to refer the passage to a more scientific context. The pterodactyl of more recent zoology is a winged reptile.
vii *485. parsimonious*] careful (a neutral, not a dyslogistic term). Cp. *Prol vii* (Yale i 304), where we are told that our 'domestic economy owes much to the ants'. *emmet*] ant. 'The ants are a people not strong, yet they prepare their meat in the summer' (*Prov.* xxx 25); therefore 'Goe to the emmote o sluggard' (Douay version *Prov.* vi 6).
vii *486. large heart*] This phrase does not quite translate Virgil's description of bees as having *ingentis animos angusto in pectore* (*Georg.* iv 83). As at i 444 above and Coverdale and A.V. *1 Kings* iv 29, it meant 'capacious intellect; wisdom' (see *OED* s.v. *Large* A II 3 c).
vii *487–9.* As Svendsen 150–2 shows, both the prudence and the 'commonalty' (democracy) of ants were common information among the encyclopedists; while the idea that ants have no kings went back to Aristotle. Since this lack manifestly did not lead to anarchy, the ants were used as examples of successful republicanism. *perhaps*] Either because Raphael cannot be certain about future events, or because he is unconvinced about the justice (rightness) of republicanism.
vii *490–2.* The bee pairs with the ant in exemplifying civil merits. It need not serve, however, as a complementary example of the alternative, monarchic virtues, as is sometimes said. Indeed, in his controversy with Salmasius (who had used the example of the bee to defend monarchy), M. presses the argument that most bees 'have republics'; see Svendsen 152f. The belief that worker bees were female and drones male was general.

Deliciously, and builds her waxen cells
With honey stored: the rest are numberless,
And thou their natures know'st, and gavest them names,
Needless to thee repeated; nor unknown
The serpent subtlest beast of all the field,
Of huge extent sometimes, with brazen eyes
And hairy mane terrific, though to thee
Not noxious, but obedient at thy call.
Now heaven in all her glory shone, and rolled
Her motions, as the great first mover's hand
First wheeled their course; earth in her rich attire
Consummate lovely smiled; air, water, earth,
By fowl, fish, beast, was flown, was swam, was walked
Frequent; and of the sixth day yet remained;
There wanted yet the master work, the end

vii *493*. For the naming of the animals see vi 73–6 and viii 342–54.

vii *495–8*. Note how the serpent is singled out for special mention last of all the beasts, and next to man: coincidence, presumably, as far as Raphael is concerned, though design on M.'s part. Cp. *Gen.* iii 1: 'Now the serpent was more subtil than any beast of the field which the Lord God had made.' *mane*] Virgil describing the serpent that killed Laocoon has *iubaeque sanguineae superant undas*; *iuba* can mean either 'mane' or 'crest'. The destruction of Troy, in which Virgil's maned serpents played a crucial part, is in *PL* often used as a mythic analogue of the Fall; see, e.g., i 1–49*n*. Cp. also the description of the serpent animated by Satan at ix 496ff.

vii *500*. *motions*] movements of the heavenly bodies.

vii *502–3*. For the rhetoric, cp. Shakespeare, *Hamlet* III i 160: 'The courtier's, soldier's, scholar's, eye, tongue, sword'. Curtius 286f traces this scheme from the medieval Latin *versus rapportati* to German Baroque. See also *ibid.* 285, on the piling up of words by 'verse-filling asyndeton': M.'s present intention is to render the teeming abundance of life. *consummate*] completed, perfect. *was ... walked*] Not an impersonal Latin construction (*pace* Hughes), but an ordinary English passive; see, e.g., *OED* s.v. *Walk* III 17, 15.

vii *504*. *frequent*] crowded; abundantly. Not a Latinism.

vii *505–11*. The idea that man's upright posture distinguishes him from other animals, and indicates his special destiny, was a commonplace of hexaemeral literature. It had the authority of various classical authors (Plato, *Tim.* 90A; Cicero, *De nat. deor.* ii 56; etc.); but Ovid's version (*Met.* i 76–86) is closest to M.'s: 'A living creature of finer stuff than these, more capable of lofty thought, one who could have dominion over all the rest, was lacking yet. . . . And, though all other animals are prone, and fix their gaze upon the earth, he gave to man an uplifted face and bade him stand erect and turn his

Of all yet done; a creature who not prone
And brute as other creatures, but endued
With sanctity of reason, might erect
His stature, and upright with front serene
Govern the rest, self-knowing, and from thence
Magnanimous to correspond with heaven,
But grateful to acknowledge whence his good
Descends, thither with heart and voice and eyes
Directed in devotion, to adore
And worship God supreme, who made him chief
Of all his works: therefore the omnipotent
Eternal Father (for where is not he
Present) thus to his Son audibly spake.
  Let us make now man in our image, man
In our similitude, and let them rule
Over the fish and fowl of sea and air,
Beast of the field, and over all the earth,
And every creeping thing that creeps the ground.
This said, he formed thee, Adam, thee O man
Dust of the ground, and in thy nostrils breathed
The breath of life; in his own image he

eyes to heaven.' Cp. also iv 288 above. *front*] forehead, face; or composure. *magnanimous*] great-souled, nobly ambitious, lofty of purpose; for the Aristotelian and medieval background of this elusive term, see R. A. Gauthier, *Magnanimité: l'ideal de la grandeur dans la philosophie païenne et dans la théologie chrétienne*, Bibliothèque Thomiste xxviii (Paris 1951).

vii *518*. 'Previously, however, to the creation of man, as if to intimate the superior importance of the work, the Deity speaks like to a man deliberating: *Gen.* i.26. "God said, Let us make man in our own image, after our own likeness"' (*De doctrina* i 7, Columbia xv 37).

vii *519–23*. 'Let us make man in our image, after our likeness: and let them have dominion over the fish of the sea, and over the fowl of the air, and over the cattle, and over all the earth, and over every creeping thing that creepeth upon the earth' (*Gen.* i 26). Broadbent 198*n* notices M.'s avoidance of the distinction between *Imago* and *Similitudo Dei*.

vii *524–8*. 'And the Lord God formed man of the dust of the ground, and breathed into his nostrils the breath of life; and man became a living soul' (*Gen.* ii 7). M.'s formulation suggests that he here sides with St Chrysostom, who thought that man's soul was created *after* his body, against Origen (who thought it *earlier* created) and St Thomas Aquinas (*simultaneously*). Note the three degrees–as Willet 32 calls them–of man's creation: 'The forming of his bodie, the giving of it life, the endewing of him with a reasonable soule.' *image ... Express*] Cp. *Heb.* i 3: 'Who being the brightness of his glory, and the express image of his person, and upholding all things by the word of his power . . . purged our sins.'

Created thee, in the image of God
Express, and thou becamest a living soul.
Male he created thee, but thy consort
Female for race; then blessed mankind, and said,
Be fruitful, multiply, and fill the earth,
Subdue it, and throughout dominion hold
Over fish of the sea, and fowl of the air,
And every living thing that moves on the earth.
Wherever thus created, for no place
Is yet distinct by name, thence, as thou know'st
He brought thee into this delicious grove,
This garden, planted with the trees of God,
Delectable both to behold and taste;
And freely all their pleasant fruit for food
Gave thee, all sorts are here that all the earth yields,
Variety without end; but of the tree
Which tasted works knowledge of good and evil,
Thou mayst not; in the day thou eat'st, thou diest;
Death is the penalty imposed, beware,
And govern well thy appetite, lest Sin
Surprise thee, and her black attendant Death.
Here finished he, and all that he had made

vii *529–30*. 'So God created man in his own image, in the image of God created he him; male and female created he them' (*Gen.* i 27). *consort*] Stressed on the second syllable.
vii *530–4*. Cp. *Gen.* i 28: 'And God blessed them, and God said unto them, Be fruitful, and multiply, and replenish the earth, and subdue it: and have dominion over the fish of the sea', etc.
vii *535–8*. See *Gen.* ii 8, 15: 'And the Lord God planted a garden eastward in Eden; and there he put the man whom he had formed. . . . And the Lord God took the man, and put him into the garden of Eden to dress it and to keep it'; also *2 Esdras* iii 6: 'And thou leddest him into paradise, which thy right hand had planted, before ever the earth came forward.' M. follows the literal interpretation of Josephus (*Antiq.* i 1), that Adam was created outside Paradise; rather than the figurative interpretation, that Adam was put in Paradise merely in the sense of being stationed there. Cp. viii 296ff. *delicious*] delightful.
vii *539–41*. 'And out of the ground made the Lord God to grow every tree that is pleasant to the sight, and good for food' (*Gen.* ii 9). For the notion that Paradise contained every species of tree, cp. iv 138–43*n* and v 339–41*n*.
vii *542–5*. Cp. *Gen.* ii 16f, and contrast x 210 below, where the penalty is mitigated. See viii 323–33*n*.
vii *547*. *attendant*] Does this imply that Raphael is not privy to the guilty secret of Death's true relation with Sin?
vii *548–50*. Cp. *Gen.* i 31.

Viewed, and behold all was entirely good;
So even and morn accomplished the sixth day:
Yet not till the creator from his work
Desisting, though unwearied, up returned
Up to the heaven of heavens his high abode,
Thence to behold this new created world
The addition of his empire, how it showed
In prospect from his throne, how good, how fair,
Answering his great idea. Up he rode
Followed with acclamation and the sound
Symphonious of ten thousand harps that tuned
Angelic harmonies: the earth, the air
Resounded, (thou remember'st, for thou heard'st)
The heavens and all the constellations rung,
The planets in their station listening stood,
While the bright pomp ascended jubilant.
Open, ye everlasting gates, they sung,
Open, ye heavens, your living doors; let in
The great creator from his work returned
Magnificent, his six days' work, a world;
Open, and henceforth oft; for God will deign
To visit oft the dwellings of just men

vii *552. unwearied*] This carefully obviates any false conclusion from *Gen.* ii 2, where God is said to have rested on the seventh day (Burden 9).
vii *553. heaven of heavens*] the empyrean; cp. l. 13.
vii *557–81.* Messiah's triumphal return from creation is closely correspondent to his return from the expulsion of the rebels at vi 880–92.
vii *557.* The thought is Platonic, and M. may have in mind *Timaeus* 37C–D, where God rejoices in the life of the newly-created universe and its resemblance to the perfect paradeigma.
vii *559. symphonious*] harmonious; sounding in concert. *ten thousand*] See vi 767*n*. *tuned*] uttered, gave vent to.
vii *561–3.* Cp. iv 680–8. But after the Fall the sound of the heavens will become inaudible: see *Nativity Ode* 125f and *Solemn Music* 19–21. Cp. *Job* xxxviii 7: 'The morning stars sang together, and all the sons of God shouted for joy.' The word texture of the present passage is discussed in Rajan 114. *station*] stations *Ed I.* A technical term in astronomy for the apparent arrest of a planet at its apogee or perigee; but here applied to quite a different set of limiting positions–the places of the planets in the *thema coeli* or disposition of the heavens at creation.
vii *564. pomp*] triumphal procession.
vii *565–7.* 'Lift up your heads, O ye gates; and be ye lift up, ye everlasting doors; and the King of glory shall come in' (*Ps.* xxiv 7). For the *living doors* of M.'s heaven, see v 254–6*n*, vi 861, and 205–8 above.

Delighted, and with frequent intercourse
Thither will send his winged messengers
On errands of supernal grace. So sung
The glorious train ascending: he through heaven,
That opened wide her blazing portals, led
To God's eternal house direct the way,
A broad and ample road, whose dust is gold
And pavement stars, as stars to thee appear,
Seen in the galaxy, that Milky Way
Which nightly as a circling zone thou seest
Powdered with stars. And now on earth the seventh
Evening arose in Eden, for the sun
Was set, and twilight from the east came on,
Forerunning night; when at the holy mount

vii *571*. Cp. iii 528–37.
vii *575–81*. *blazing portals*] The immediate connection with the *Milky Way* shows that these can only be the 'Portals of the Sun', the tropical signs Capricorn and Cancer that mark the limits of the solar path. See Porphyry, *De antro nymph.* 28; Helpericus of Auxerre, *De computo* 2 (Migne, cxxxvii 25); and Macrobius, *In Somn. Scip.* I xii 1f: 'The Milky Way girdles the zodiac, its great circle meeting it obliquely so that it crosses it at the two tropical signs, Capricorn and Cancer. Natural philosophers named these the 'portals of the sun' because the solstices lie athwart the sun's path on either side, checking farther progress and causing it to retrace its course across the belt beyond whose limits it never trespasses. Souls are believed to pass through these portals when going from the sky to the earth and returning from the earth to the sky. For this reason one is called the portal of men and the other the portal of gods: Cancer, the portal of men, because through it descent is made to the lower regions; Capricorn, the portal of gods, because through it souls return to their rightful abode of immortality, to be reckoned among the gods.' Thus the route taken by the returning creator continues the solar symbolism associated throughout *PL* with the triumphant Messiah. Marjorie Nicolson (*ELH* ii (1935) 12, 24) classes this description of the Milky Way with other pieces of 'Galilean' astronomy; but in itself the theory of stellar composition was as old as Democritus: see Macrobius, *ibid.* I xv 6. Cp. Ovid, *Met.* i 170, where the Milky Way is the route by which 'the gods fare to the halls and royal dwelling of the mighty Thunderer'; also iv 976 above, where Satan refers contemptuously to triumphs on the 'road of heaven star-paved'. *galaxy*] Specifically the Milky Way. *zone*] belt, band; region of the sky.
vii *581–4*. Chronologically a crucial passage, since it clearly indicates that the 'evenings' of *PL* are to be reckoned from sunset. See ll. 249–52*n* and Introduction, 'Chronology' (p. 444). *seventh / Evening*] The evening that begins Day 20 of the poem's action.

Of heaven's high-seated top, the imperial throne
Of Godhead, fixed for ever firm and sure,
The filial power arrived, and sat him down
With his great Father (for he also went
Invisible, yet stayed [:] such privilege
Hath omnipresence) and the work ordained,
Author and end of all things, and from work
Now resting, blessed and hallowed the seventh day,
As resting on that day from all his work,
But not in silence holy kept; the harp
Had work and rested not, the solemn pipe,
And dulcimer, all organs of sweet stop,
All sounds on fret by string or golden wire
Tempered soft tunings; intermixed with voice
Choral or unison: of incense clouds
Fuming from golden censers hid the mount.

vii *584–5. holy mount*] See v 643*n*.
vii *588–90.* The early edns begin parentheses with opening brackets both after *Father* (l. 588) and after *stayed* (l. 589); and have comma after *ordained* (l. 590). Editors usually remove the first of these opening brackets, with the result that the subject changes, so that it is the Father who *rests*, and is the *Author and end*. The allusion to *Heb.* xii 2, however, strongly suggests that *The filial power* is at least jointly in apposition to *Author and end*. I conclude that the parenthesis more probably runs from *for* (l. 588) to *omnipresence* (l. 590), and that opening bracket after *stayed* is an error for colon or comma. For the Father's universal presence, cp. l. 517f.
vii *592.* 'And God blessed the seventh day, and sanctified it: because that in it he had rested from all his work which God created and made' (*Gen.* ii 3). *hallowed*] Introduced from the variant account in A.V. *Exod.* xx 11.
vii *594–9.* Even by the standards of the time, M.'s portrayal of the music of heaven is unusually concrete and specific. A defence of music on the Sabbath is incidentally implied. Note the comprehensiveness of the classification of instruments. The *harp* takes precedence because it was played by David the type of Christ. As the context indicates, the *dulcimer* is here not the stringed instrument usually called by that name, but the Hebrew 'bagpipe' (Gk. συμφωνία). Consult Spaeth 40*n* and *OED* s.v. *Dulcimer* 1 b; and see *Dan.* iii 5: 'At what time ye hear the sound of the cornet, flute, harp, sackbut, psaltery, dulcimer, and all kinds of musick, ye fall down and worship the golden image that Nebuchadnezzar the king hath set up' (A.V. margin 'symphony'). *frets*] The ridges dividing the finger-board of guitar-like stringed instruments, so as to regulate the fingering. *string . . . wire*] both the gut strings of instruments such as the lute, and the wire strings of such as the cittern. *tunings*] musical sounds.
vii *600. censers*] In no way Papist in association, but taken direct from the Jewish Temple (Broadbent 157), or rather from *Rev.* viii 3. 'It would appear

Creation and the six days' acts they sung,
Great are thy works, Jehovah, infinite
Thy power; what thought can measure thee or tongue
Relate thee; greater now in thy return
Than from the giant angels; thee that day
Thy thunders magnified; but to create
Is greater than created to destroy.
Who can impair thee, mighty king, or bound
Thy empire? Easily the proud attempt
Of spirits apostate and their counsels vain
Thou hast repelled, while impiously they thought
Thee to diminish, and from thee withdraw
The number of thy worshippers. Who seeks
To lessen thee, against his purpose serves
To manifest the more thy might: his evil
Thou usest, and from thence createst more good.
Witness this new-made world, another heaven
From heaven gate not far, founded in view
On the clear hyaline, the glassy sea;
Of amplitude almost immense, with stars
Numerous, and every star perhaps a world

that all allegories whatever are likely to seem Catholic to the general reader. . . . Catholicism is allegorical' (Lewis[2] 322).
vii *601–32*. A 'hymn of the creation' is included in Act i of Draft iii of M.'s outline for a tragedy on Paradise Lost; see Introduction, 'Composition' (p. 420).
vii *601*. The angels' praise harmonizes with M.'s own, just as on the chronologically later occasion described in Bk iii. See iii 410–15*n*.
vii *604–7*. Implying a hierarchy of virtues in which creativity takes precedence over strength or power or fortitude. Cp. iii 267–9*n*, vi 820–3*n*, and see Steadman 93. *giant angels*] Throughout *PL*, but especially in Bks i and vi, the war against the rebel angels is compared with its mythic analogue, Jupiter's war against the Giants.
vii *613–6*. That God's creativity manifests itself in the power to use evil for good is a central theme of *PL*: cp, e.g., i 216–9 and xii 469–73; and see Lewis 66 and Rajan 45f. Contrast Satan's determination to pervert good to evil (i 164f).
vii *619*. *hyaline*] The *θάλασσα ὑαλίνη* of *Rev*. iv 6, the 'sea of glass like unto crystal' before the throne of God. It is the same as the waters above the firmament: see l. 271*n* and iii 518–9*n*; also Svendsen 55f. 'Hyaline' is wrongly treated as a proper name in the early edns.
vii *620–2*. For the idea of other inhabited worlds see iii 565–71*n*. Here the possibility is presented as an expression of God's continued and unsearchable creativity. *immense*] infinite; immeasurable.

Of destined habitation; but thou know'st
Their seasons: among these the seat of men,
Earth with her nether ocean circumfused,
Their pleasant dwelling place. Thrice happy men,
And sons of men, whom God hath thus advanced,
Created in his image, there to dwell
And worship him, and in reward to rule
Over his works, on earth, in sea, or air,
And multiply a race of worshippers
Holy and just: thrice happy if they know
Their happiness, and persevere upright.
  So sung they, and the empyrean rung,
With halleluiahs: thus was Sabbath kept.
And thy request think now fulfilled, that asked
How first this world and face of things began,
And what before thy memory was done
From the beginning, that posterity
Informed by thee might know; if else thou seek'st
Aught, not surpassing human measure, say.

THE END OF THE SEVENTH BOOK

vii *622–3.* Either 'you know whether their seasons are compatible with habitation' or 'you know the seasons when they are destined for habitation'. The latter meaning seems the primary one, in view of the probable allusion to *Acts* i 7: 'It is not for you to know the times or the seasons, which the Father hath put in his own power.'
vii *624. nether ocean*] the ocean of the nether world earth, in antithesis to the waters above the firmament. In ancient geography, Oceanus was a great river encompassing the disc of the earth.
vii *629.* 'Thou madest him to have dominion over the works of thy hands; thou hast put all things under his feet' (*Ps.* viii 6).
vii *631–2.* Alluding to Virgil's exclamation over the happiness of simple peasants: 'O happy husbandmen! too happy, should they come to know their blessings! for whom, far from the clash of arms, most righteous Earth, unbidden, pours forth from her soil an easy sustenance' (*Georg.* ii 458–60). *persevere*] continue in a state of grace (a technical term in theology). In M.'s time the main stress in *persevere* was moving from the second to the third syllable; he consistently used the more modern form. Cp. the elaboration of this warning at viii 639ff.
vii *634. halleluiah*] 'praise ye the Lord' (*Ps.* cxlvi: A.V. margin 'Halleluiah'); italicized in the early edns.
vii *636. face*] outward form.
vii *639.* The belief that the *artes* had their origin in the relics of Adam's

Paradise Lost

BOOK VIII

The Argument

Adam inquires[1] concerning celestial motions, is doubtfully answered, and exhorted to search rather things more worthy of knowledge: Adam assents, and still desirous to detain Raphael, relates to him what he remembered since his own creation, his placing in Paradise, his talk with God concerning solitude and fit society, his first meeting and nuptials with Eve, his discourse with the angel thereupon; who after admonitions repeated departs.

The angel ended, and in Adam's ear
So charming left his voice, that he awhile
Thought him still speaking, still stood fixed to hear;
Then as new waked thus gratefully replied.
What thanks sufficient, or what recompense
Equal have I to render thee, divine
Historian, who thus largely hast allayed
The thirst I had of knowledge, and vouchsafed
This friendly condescension to relate
Things else by me unsearchable, now heard
With wonder, but delight, and, as is due,
With glory attributed to the high
Creator; something yet of doubt remains,

prelapsarian wisdom was a common tenet of seventeenth-century theological art-theory. See Curtius, *Excursus* xxii, especially p. 556. There is a good deal about this topic in Goulart's Commentary on Du Bartas. See, e.g., Lodge's translation, p. 138: 'From him it is as from a living source, that this current of celestiall science floweth unto us'; and cp. L'Isle's version (1595), p. 45: 'From him had we first our Arts and Sciences derived.'
viii *Argument* 1. *Adam inquires*] Adam then inquires *Ed I*.
viii *1–4*. Bks vii and viii of *Ed II* form a single book in *Ed I*. *Ed I* vii 641, which corresponds to *Ed II* viii 4, reads *To whom thus Adam gratefully replied*. The three opening lines of *Ed II* viii may have been added to provide in terms of action for the inevitable pause between books. *charming*] enchanting, spell-binding. *still stood fixed*] After digressions in classical epics, audiences often remain similarly rapt. Cp. e.g., Homer, *Od.* xiii 1; Apollonius, *Argonaut.* i 512–16. The latter passage is the more immediate model; for there the silence ensues after Orpheus has sung the story of creation, to dispel thoughts of strife.
viii *12*. The accentuation *attribùted* continued to be possible, at least in verse, as late as the nineteenth century.

Which only thy solution can resolve.
When I behold this goodly frame, this world
Of heaven and earth consisting, and compute
Their magnitudes, this earth a spot, a grain,
An atom, with the firmament compared

viii *14. solution*] explanation.
viii *15. frame*] universe; see v 154*n*.
viii *15–38.* Adam proposes to Raphael essentially the same problem proposed to him by Eve at iv 657f; though he carries it to a higher level of abstraction. It was a topic of the schools, which M. had already touched in *Prol vii* (Yale i 292). There he maintains that the heavens cannot exist simply for the material convenience of man, but that they call for meditation and study and reverence: 'Can we indeed believe, my hearers, that the vast spaces of boundless air are illuminated and adorned with everlasting lights, that these are endowed with such rapidity of motion and pass through such intricate revolutions, merely to serve as a lantern for base and slothful men, and to light the path of the idle and the sluggard here below?' Here, however, the question is given a new precision; so that the problem of the wastefulness of an anthropocentric universe is focused in the problem of the incomprehensible distribution of kinetic energy entailed by the geocentric system. Cp. M.'s own doubt at iv 592–5, 'whether the prime orb, / Incredible how swift, had thither rolled / Diurnal, or this less voluble earth / By shorter flight to the east....' For the velocities thought to be involved and their bearing on the Copernican hypothesis, which had been taken up by Kepler, Gilbert, Galileo and others, see iv 592–7*n*. Burton's discussion of 'that main paradox, of the earth's motion, now so much in question' at *Anat. of Mel.* II ii 3 covers very similar ground; dwelling on the impossible velocities with which the heavens must move in a geocentric system, and quoting Gilbert's exclamation 'what fury is that... that shall drive the heavens about with such incomprehensible celerity in twenty-four hours'.

Burden (116) comments that Adam is here almost a sceptical astronomer reasoning falsely about final causes. Far from concentrating on the glorification of God Adam in effect indicts providence; showing that this sphere of knowledge is beyond his capacity. It seems that at least part of astronomy (or a certain kind of astronomical speculation) may come within the category of forbidden knowledge; not because M. is against science, but because some knowledge is of 'no avail' for man. Raphael's volte face at l. 122 will indicate that what avails is not the intricate choice of one particular cosmological model but the enjoyment of our own station in the universe (cp. ll. 160–87).
viii *15. goodly frame*] Cp. *Hamlet* II ii 317: 'It goes so heavily with my disposition that this goodly frame, the earth, seems to me a sterile promontory.'
viii *16. Ed I* and *Ed II* wrongly have comma after *compute*.

And all her numbered stars, that seem to roll
Spaces incomprehensible (for such
Their distance argues and their swift return
Diurnal) merely to officiate light
Round this opacous earth, this punctual spot,
One day and night; in all their vast survey
Useless besides, reasoning I oft admire,
How nature wise and frugal could commit
Such disproportions, with superfluous hand
So many nobler bodies to create,
Greater so manifold to this one use,
For aught appears, and on their orbs impose
Such restless revolution day by day
Repeated, while the sedentary earth,
That better might with far less compass move,
Served by more noble than her self, attains
Her end without least motion, and receives,
As tribute such a sumless journey brought

viii *19. numbered*] numerous (the same rare usage as at vi 229: cp. Shakespeare, *Cymbeline* I vi 36, 'the number'd beach'); but perhaps also alluding to *Ps.* cxlvii 4: 'He telleth the number of the stars; he calleth them all by their names.'

viii *22. officiate*] supply, minister. Implying that the stars are ordained (like the angels) to minister to men.

viii *23. opacous*] opaque. *punctual*] point-like, minute (*OED* II 3 a). The idea that the earth is a mere point compared with the heavens is perennial. It was constantly reiterated in encyclopedias and astronomical works from the late Middle Ages onwards (e.g., Alexander Neckham: *tanta est firmamenti quantitas ut ipsi totalis terra collata quasi punctum esse videatur*), but, as Svendsen 40 shows, some scholars are reluctant to admit that it was not a Copernican discovery. In M.'s time the commonplace was given, however, an almost novel turn: the question became 'How big would earth seem, viewed from the heavens?' See Riccioli i 57, where the answer of Cleomedes (*c.* 50 A.D.) is quoted: from the sun, the earth would seem a point; from the stars, it would be invisible. The question of size was now related, moreover, to the question of plurality of worlds. Thus, Tycho Brahe would never believe that the huge stars 'were made to no other use than this that we perceive, to illuminate the earth, a point insensible in respect of the whole' (Burton, *Anat. of Mel.* II ii 3). Note also that Adam introduces the traditional encyclopedia paradox about little earth's centrality as matter for *doubt* (l. 13) rather than for wonder.

viii *25. admire*] wonder, marvel.

viii *32. sedentary*] Not only 'motionless' but also 'slothful': cp. *Prol. vii*, *loc. cit.* ll. 15–38*n*.

Of incorporeal speed, her warmth and light;
Speed, to describe whose swiftness number fails.
 So spake our sire, and by his countenance seemed
Entering on studious thoughts abstruse, which Eve
Perceiving where she sat retired in sight,
With lowliness majestic from her seat,
And grace that won who saw to wish her stay,
Rose, and went forth among her fruits and flowers,
To visit how they prospered, bud and bloom,
Her nursery; they at her coming sprung
And touched by her fair tendance gladlier grew.
Yet went she not, as not with such discourse
Delighted, or not capable her ear
Of what was high: such pleasure she reserved,
Adam relating, she sole auditress;
Her husband the relater she preferred
Before the angel, and of him to ask
Chose rather; he, she knew would intermix
Grateful digressions, and solve high dispute
With conjugal caresses, from his lip
Not words alone pleased her. O when meet now
Such pairs, in love and mutual honour joined?
With goddess-like demeanour forth she went;
Not unattended, for on her as queen

viii *37. incorporeal speed*] Cp. l. 110, 'Speed almost spiritual'. *warmth*] Not merely heat, but also the fomenting 'influence' of iv 669.

viii *45–7.* By making the flowers respond so to Eve's coming, M. is in effect casting her in the role of a Venus. Cp. Marino, *Adone* iii 65: 'Plants bleached and yellowed by the sun became all green, and every flower opened and lifted its head.' Eve's Venus role is further developed at ll. 59–63. *visit*] inspect (*OED* II 9). *Her nursery*] her nursing; objects of her care. *tendance*] attention, care.

viii *48–56.* Eve has to be absent for the discussion of marital relations that follows later in the book, but M. is anxious that her departure should not be taken to imply that women are by nature unsuited to intellectual pursuits. He may also have felt a need to square his account with *1 Cor.* xiv 35: 'And if they will learn any thing, let them ask their husbands at home: for it is a shame for women to speak in the church.'

viii *59–63. pomp*] train, procession. The Graces were attendants upon Venus, with whom M. more than once identifies Eve. Cp. l. 46f and v 381. *shot* is intransitive, with *darts* as its subject; since darts were an attribute, not of the *Graces*, but of Venus herself, or of Cupid (Tervarent 186f; an alleged exception in Titian's *The Blinding of Amor* is dismissed by Wind at 76f). On the potential danger of the *darts of desire*, which for the first half of l. 63 remain unspecified and ambiguous, see Stein 91 and Ricks 98.

A pomp of winning graces waited still,
And from about her shot darts of desire
Into all eyes to wish her still in sight.
And Raphael now to Adam's doubt proposed
Benevolent and facile thus replied.
 To ask or search I blame thee not, for heaven
Is as the book of God before thee set,
Wherein to read his wondrous works, and learn
His seasons, hours, or days, or months, or years:
This to attain, whether heaven move or earth,
Imports not, if thou reckon right, the rest
From man or angel the great architect
Did wisely to conceal, and not divulge
His secrets to be scanned by them who ought
Rather admire; or if they list to try
Conjecture, he his fabric of the heavens

viii *65. facile*] easy of converse; mild.
viii *67–9.* For the traditional and at first theological metaphor of the cosmos as the *book of God* or 'book of nature' setting forth the wisdom of the creator, see Curtius 320f, 339, 344, etc. By M.'s time it was commonly secularized; but it still often occurred in its original mystical form, as here. Note that many of the creatures mentioned in Bk vii (e.g. bees, ants, behemoth, leviathan) were the same with those singled out as important pages of the book of nature (Curtius 222f).
viii *69.* Cp. vii 340–52; and *Gen.* i 14, where the 'lights in the firmament' are 'for signs, and for seasons, and for days, and years'.
viii *71–84.* McColley, 'Milton's Dialogue on Astronomy: the Principal Immediate Sources', *PMLA* lii (1937) 759f, thinks that this passage expresses radical opposition to the scientific movement of the time. But Svendsen 77f and Schultz convincingly show that M.'s true targets are dubious speculation and corrupted learning. In *First Defence* 1 (Columbia vii 67), indeed, M. defends astronomers 'who should be trusted in their own faculties' against the attack of Salmasius. The relativity of the centre of the universe, and of the motion of heavenly bodies, including the earth, had been asserted by Nicholas of Cusa (*De docta ignorantia* ii 11; tr. Heron (1954) 107ff); by taking up some such position it would not be difficult for an intelligent theologian of M.'s time to remain detached from the cosmological controversy.
viii *74. scanned*] criticized, passed judgment on; discussed minutely. So Calvin on *Deut.* xiii 76, tr. Golding (1583): 'When men will needs scanne of Gods workes and providence according to their owne reason: they shall finde thinges to grudge at.'
viii *75. admire*] wonder.
viii *76.* Cp. Vulg. *Eccles.* iii 11: *Cuncta fecit bona in tempore suo, et mundum tradidit disputationi eorum, ut non inveniat homo opus, quod operatus est Deus ab initio usque ad finem.*

Hath left to their disputes, perhaps to move
His laughter at their quaint opinions wide
Hereafter, when they come to model heaven
And calculate the stars, how they will wield
The mighty frame, how build, unbuild, contrive
To save appearances, how gird the sphere
With centric and eccentric scribbled o'er,
Cycle and epicycle, orb in orb:
Already by thy reasoning this I guess,
Who art to lead thy offspring, and supposest
That bodies bright and greater should not serve
The less not bright, nor heaven such journeys run,
Earth sitting still, when she alone receives
The benefit: consider first, that great
Or bright infers not excellence: the earth

viii *78. wide*] astray, mistaken; not an ellipsis.

viii *80. calculate*] compute the number of (*OED* 1); predict the motions of (*OED* 2); arrange, frame (*OED* 4, 5).

viii *82. To save appearances*] Or 'to save the phenomena', a term of the Schools, meaning 'to reconcile the observed facts with some theory they appear to disagree with'. Cp. Bacon, *Essays* (1625), 'Of Superstition': 'Astronomers, which did faigne Eccentricks and Epicycles, and such Engines of Orbs, to save the Phenomena; though they knew, there were no such Things.' For the history of the term see Karl Hammerle, '*To Save Appearances* (*Par. L.*, VIII 82), ein Problem der Scholastick', *Anglia* lxii (1938) 368–72.

viii *83. centric and eccentric*] See iii 573–6*n*. Note that the terms *eccentric* and *epicycle* come in a logical expository sequence. In the Ptolemaic system, observed irregularities in the motion of the heavenly bodies were accounted for first by hypothesizing slight displacements from the earth of the centres of orbit (hence the eccentric circles); secondly–since this was insufficient for planets other than the sun–by adding epicycles, smaller circles whose centres ride on the circumferences of the main eccentric circles and carry the planets. 'In the case of the outer planets (Mars, Jupiter, Saturn) the epicycle corresponds to the motion of the Earth, and the eccentric main circle to that of the planet concerned. For the inner planets (Mercury, Venus) this situation is reversed, and it is the main circle that contains the annual revolution' (Price 99). Copernicus still required as many as thirty-four auxiliary circles, to account for the varying velocities of the planets; see Dreyer 331, 343.

viii *90–1. excellence*] Raphael's dissociation of size and brightness from excellence is perhaps to be related to the underlying hierarchy of virtues and qualities in *PL*, discussed by Steadman. Cp. vi 820–3, where a distinction between modes of excellence is developed. *infers*] implies, entails.

viii *91–9.* Raphael's argument is doubly *a fortiori*: 'even if the sun (the chief luminary) ministers, and even if he ministers merely to Earth, it is not

Though, in comparison of heaven, so small,
Nor glistering, may of solid good contain
More plenty than the sun that barren shines,
Whose virtue on it self works no effect,
But in the fruitful earth; there first received
His beams, unactive else, their vigour find.
Yet not to earth are those bright luminaries
Officious, but to thee earth's habitant.
And for the heaven's wide circuit, let it speak
The maker's high magnificence, who built
So spacious, and his line stretched out so far;
That man may know he dwells not in his own;
An edifice too large for him to fill,
Lodged in a small partition, and the rest
Ordained for uses to his Lord best known.
The swiftness of those circles attribute,
Though numberless, to his omnipotence,
That to corporeal substances could add
Speed almost spiritual; me thou think'st not slow,
Who since the morning hour set out from heaven
Where God resides, and ere mid-day arrived
In Eden, distance inexpressible
By numbers that have name. But this I urge,

unfitting'. Cp. Marlowe, *Doctor Faustus* 620: the heavens were 'made for man, therefore is man more excellent'. *barren*] W. B. Hunter (*MLR* xliv (1949) 89) compares Proclus' description of the sun as 'shadowless and unreceptive of generation'. Because the sun already contains a plenitude of life, it requires no addition from its own virtuous beams.
viii *99. officious*] dutiful; attentive; efficacious in performing its function.
viii *102.* Cp. *Job* xxxviii 5, where God asks, concerning the earth, 'Who hath laid the measures thereof, if thou knowest? or who hath stretched the line upon it?'
viii *107. circles*] orbital courses. *attribute*] Stressed on the first syllable.
viii *108. numberless*] Probably qualifies swiftness (cp. ll. 36–8, 'a sumless journey . . . to describe whose swiftness number fails'); though the number of stars that have to move in a geocentric universe, and therefore the great number of *circles*, is conceivably also alluded to (cp. ll. 28, 80).
viii *110. Speed almost spiritual*] Cp. l. 37. The notion that speed is spiritual depends on the ancient and medieval belief that the spheres were moved by intelligences or spirits. See especially Ficino's Commentary on Plotinus' *Enneads* ii 1–3, where an extended analogy is traced between the movement of the heavens and the movement of the soul in thought.
viii *114–18.* With an unexpected change of direction Raphael disengages himself from the Ptolemaic position. The contrast between conversation with M.'s angels and with, say, Marlowe's, is very striking. Marlowe's

Admitting motion in the heavens, to show
Invalid that which thee to doubt it moved;
Not that I so affirm, though so it seem
To thee who hast thy dwelling here on earth.
God to remove his ways from human sense,
Placed heaven from earth so far, that earthly sight,
If it presume, might err in things too high,
And no advantage gain. What if the sun
Be centre to the world, and other stars
By his attractive virtue and their own
Incited, dance about him various rounds?

Mephistophilis glumly casts his vote for the traditional world picture (*Doctor Faustus* 653–87), whereas Raphael is detached, provocative, agile, intellectually stimulating.

viii *117–22.* The elusiveness of Raphael's position reflects the difficulty M. must have felt in making a final decision in favour of any one of the many alternative planetary systems available. He had little enthusiasm for the Ptolemaic system, but, as Rajan 152f rightly stresses, the main struggle was between the Copernican system and the Tychonic or geoheliocentric. Throughout the present dialogue the diction is often ingeniously designed to allow simultaneous reference to more than one of these alternative systems; e.g., the first part of Raphael's speech (ll. 85–114) refers to the Tychonic system as well as to the Ptolemaic, so that Rajan regrets M.'s omission of the Tychonic system needlessly. Grant McColley, 'Milton's Dialogue on Astronomy', *PMLA* lii (1937) 728–62, is useful for its reference of *PL* to the context of contemporary scientific controversy, and particularly for its demonstration of a close relation with Bishop Wilkin's *Discourse that the Earth May be a Planet* (1640) and Ross's *The New Planet no Planet.* McColley is not at all convincing, however, in his view that M.'s purpose was to reprimand the Royal Society by criticizing the speculations of one of its secretaries. On the contrary, the opinions of Wilkins seem fairly evenly distributed between Adam and Raphael, while on the main issue of heliocentricity we find Wilkins on the 'right' side.

viii *122–3. What if the sun / Be centre*] Appropriately the word *sun* is placed in the centre of the 113–line paragraph. But this is no evidence of numerology in the pattern of stressed syllables (as Whaler takes it to be); only of line-count numerology. See Introduction, 'Numerology'; also Fowler, Index, s.v. *Central Position of Sovereignty.* *world*] universe.

viii *124.* For the theory that the planets are impelled by the magnetic influence of the sun, see iii 583–6*n.* *attractive virtue*] influence or power of attraction.

viii *125.* For the image of a cosmic dance, see iii 579–81*n.* *rounds*] A pun between 'circles' (*OED* II 6) and 'dances in which the performers move in a ring' (*OED* III 11). Cp. *Comus* 114.

Their wandering course now high, now low, then hid,
Progressive, retrograde, or standing still,
In six thou seest, and what if seventh to these
The planet earth, so steadfast though she seem,
Insensibly three different motions move?
Which else to several spheres thou must ascribe,

viii *126. wandering*] Literally translates Gk πλανήτης, from which *planet* is derived. Common poetic diction.
viii *127. retrograde*] Apparently moving from east to west, that is, in a direction contrary to the order of the zodiacal signs.
viii *128. six*] Saturnus, Jupiter, Mars, Venus, Mercurius and Luna. Since Copernicus, the main subject debated by astronomers was whether the earth or the sun constituted the seventh planet.
viii *130. three different motions*] The three motions attributed to the earth by Copernicus: namely, diurnal rotation, annual orbital revolution about the sun and a 'third motion' or 'motion in declination'. The last of these, 'whereby the axis of the earth describes the surface of a cone in [about] a year, moving in the opposite direction to that of the earth's centre', was unnecessarily introduced to account for 'the fact, that the axis of the earth, notwithstanding the annual motion, always points to the same spot on the celestial sphere' (Dreyer 329, 328). Later, Tycho Brahe was able to dispense with this third motion (*ibid.* 361). It is important not to join Hughes in confusing 'motion in declination' with the much slower resultant of axial and orbital annual revolutions, which in the fallen world causes precession of the equinoxes (a motion with a period, in Copernicus' estimation, of some 25,798 years). For Raphael is speaking in a prelapsarian world in which ecliptic and equator coincide, so that there is no equinoctial point to precess. (Contrast iii 483 above, where M. can refer to 'trepidation', because the digression is in 'real' or seventeenth-century time.) Before the Fall, the period of 'motion in declination' was presumably exactly equal to the period of annual orbital revolution. On the beginning of the distinction between ecliptic and equator, see x 651–706*n*; also Introduction, 'M.'s Universe'.
viii *131–2.* Meaning 'if you don't ascribe motion to the earth, then to account for the observed phenomena you will have to posit a number of spheres moving in contrary directions'. In the ancient and medieval planetary systems the motion of each planet was explained as the resultant of the circular motions of several concentric spheres (for a simple account, consult Crombie i 80f). *thwart obliquities*] The zodiac was frequently referred to as the 'thwart circle'; see, e.g., Robert Recorde, *The castle of knowledge* (1556) 30: 'The Zodiak (whiche many doo call the Thwarte circle).' It seems very probable, therefore, that M. intends an allusion to the inclination of the ecliptic circle; though from Raphael's point of view there is as yet no obliquity in this sense. The allusion is thus a dramatic irony: Adam would take the phrase to refer to the obliquity of the equator–ecliptic with respect

Moved contrary with thwart obliquities,
Or save the sun his labour, and that swift
Nocturnal and diurnal rhomb supposed,
Invisible else above all stars, the wheel
Of day and night; which needs not thy belief,
If earth industrious of her self fetch day
Travelling east, and with her part averse
From the sun's beam meet night, her other part
Still luminous by his ray. What if that light
Sent from her through the wide transpicuous air,
To the terrestrial moon be as a star

to the horizon (which in the Ptolemaic system was a fixed frame of reference), or to mean simply 'awkward indirections'. For the inclining of the ecliptic to the equator after the Fall, see x 651–706*n*, 668–80*n*.

viii *134*. The accuracy and subtlety of this line is generally missed. *rhomb* is from Gk. ῥόμβος, a magic wheel, and refers to the imaginary *primum mobile* or tenth sphere, which in the medieval planetary system revolved diurnally about the earth with incredible swiftness, carrying the interior spheres of the stars and planets with it. But 'rhomb' more obviously means 'rhombus, lozenge-shape'; a sense that has precise though secondary relevance here. In diagrams illustrating the Ptolemaic system, the triangle of the sun's rays, together with the triangle of the umbra or darkest central part of the earth's shadow, formed an elongated rhombus (well described as *Nocturnal and diurnal*), which was to be thought of as rotating about its own centroid or the earth's centre, like a pair of spokes of a parti-coloured wheel. Based on such illustrations were certain more mystical diagrams showing the intersection of 'the pyramid of light' with 'the pyramid of shadows'. A particularly interesting example is the geometrical development of the *tetractys* in Kircher, *Musurgia* ii 450, where the rhombus of intersection of the two 'pyramids' extends beyond the heavens to the *circulus universorum*. Cp. iii 556f above, and see v 758–9*n*.

viii *137*. *industrious*] Contrast the 'sedentary earth' of the Ptolemaic system, l. 32.

viii *140–5*. *that light*] the light from the earth's *other part . . . luminous* by the rays of the sun. Cp. Burton, *Anat. of Mel.* II ii 3: 'If the earth move, it is a planet, and shines to them in the moon, and to the other planetary inhabitants, as the moon and they do to us upon the earth: but shine she doth, as Galileo, Kepler, and others prove, and then *per consequens*, the rest of the planets are inhabited, as well as the moon.' This curious argument, in which Burton follows Kepler more or less faithfully, is based on the anthropocentric assumption that there is no point in having planets or satellites that shine, unless they shine for creatures similar to men. Kepler shares this assumption with Adam and Eve (see ll. 24f and iv 568) and with Raphael himself (ll. 153–8). For seventeenth-century speculations about the plurality of worlds, see iii 565–71*n*.

Enlightening her by day, as she by night
This earth? Reciprocal, if land be there,
Fields and inhabitants: her spots thou seest
As clouds, and clouds may rain, and rain produce
Fruits in her softened soil, for some to eat
Allotted there; and other suns perhaps
With their attendant moons thou wilt descry
Communicating male and female light,
Which two great sexes animate the world,
Stored in each orb perhaps with some that live.
For such vast room in nature unpossessed
By living soul, desert and desolate,
Only to shine, yet scarce to contribute
Each orb a glimpse of light, conveyed so far
Down to this habitable, which returns
Light back to them, is obvious to dispute.

viii *144–5*. Cp. i 290f, where Galileo can 'descry new lands, / Rivers or mountains in her spotty globe'.
viii *145–6*. In M.'s time, reported changes or movements of the spots of the moon were often ascribed to the effects of a lunar atmosphere; see Riccioli i 207½ [*sic*], 'De Novis Maculis Lunae, eiusque Asperitatibus, Vallibus, Cavernis, Montibus, Collibus etc.', where, however, the movements are attributed to lunar libration or to faulty observation. The theory that the spots were clouds, rather than surface features revealed by gaps in the clouds, was held, e.g., by Julius Caesar Lagalla. Raphael seemed to commit himself to that view at v 418–20 more definitely than he does here.
viii *148*. The idea that the fixed stars are suns with their attendant planets went back to Nicholas of Cusa. It was accepted by, e.g., Bruno, and rejected by Kepler; and in M.'s time was a topic of much speculation and controversy.
viii *150*. In Pliny, *Nat. hist.* i 129f the sun is 'a masculine star, burning up and absorbing everything' while the moon is 'a feminine and delicate planet': a sexual differentiation that was taken over from mythology. But the context makes it clear that Raphael refers to the fact that while the light of suns is 'peculiar', that of moons or planets is mostly reflected; cp. vii 368. The passage thus has a bearing on Raphael's teaching about relations between the sexes at ll. 561ff. It is also possible that M. may intend a more covert allusion to a Gnostic polarity in which 'male light' was mental light and 'female light' physical.
viii *151–2*. i.e., animate the universe, each orb of which is perhaps inhabited.
viii *154*. *desert*] Stressed on the second syllable.
viii *155*. *contribute*] Stressed on the first syllable.
viii *157*. *this habitable*] Probably imitates the Gk idiom ἡ οἰκουμένη, 'the inhabited (world), the Greek world'.
viii *158*. *obvious to dispute*] open to dispute. M. had himself formally disputed it at Cambridge; see the passage from *Prol vii* quoted in ll. 15–38*n*.

But whether thus these things, or whether not,
Whether the sun predominant in heaven
Rise on the earth, or earth rise on the sun,
He from the east his flaming road begin,
Or she from west her silent course advance
With inoffensive pace that spinning sleeps
On her soft axle, while she paces even,
And bears thee soft with the smooth air along,
Solicit not thy thoughts with matters hid,
Leave them to God above, him serve and fear;
Of other creatures, as him pleases best,
Wherever placed, let him dispose: joy thou
In what he gives to thee, this Paradise
And thy fair Eve; heaven is for thee too high
To know what passes there; be lowly wise:
Think only what concerns thee and thy being;
Dream not of other worlds, what creatures there
Live, in what state, condition or degree,
Contented that thus far hath been revealed
Not of earth only but of highest heaven.
To whom thus Adam cleared of doubt, replied.
How fully hast thou satisfied me, pure
Intelligence of heaven, angel serene,
And freed from intricacies, taught to live,

viii *162–6.* Raphael's personification of sun and earth has the effect of setting up a large-scale metaphor in which the issues of astronomical and of social sexual hierarchy are subtly related. *inoffensive*] harmless; also in the Latin sense 'unobstructed'.

viii *166.* M. provides for the stock anti-Copernican argument that rotation of the earth would cause violent winds, by having the atmosphere move with the earth. Cp. Riccioli i 51.

viii *167.* The extent and the tenor of Raphael's conversation with Adam shows that the forbidden fruit is not scientific knowledge *per se*, but that scientific knowledge like any other kind may come within the forbidden category (Burden 121f). *solicit*] disturb, make anxious (*OED* I 1).

viii *168.* 'Let us hear the conclusion of the whole matter: Fear God, and keep his commandments: for this is the whole duty of man' (*Eccles* xii 13).

viii *176.* Speculation about the nature of the inhabitants of other planets was rife in M.'s day, and covered a range of topics that have since become the province of science fiction. Kepler, e.g., at one time wondered whether aliens were rational, whether they had souls to be saved and whether they or men were lords of creation.

viii *181.* Some copies of *Ed I* wrongly have full stop after *serene.* *Intelligence*] spirit; intellectual being.

The easiest way, nor with perplexing thoughts
To interrupt the sweet of life, from which
God hath bid dwell far off all anxious cares,
And not molest us, unless we our selves
Seek them with wandering thoughts, and notions vain.
But apt the mind or fancy is to rove
Unchecked, and of her roving is no end;
Till warned, or by experience taught, she learn,
That not to know at large of things remote
From use, obscure and subtle, but to know
That which before us lies in daily life,
Is the prime wisdom, what is more, is fume,
Or emptiness, or fond impertinence,
And renders us in things that most concern
Unpractised, unprepared, and still to seek.
Therefore from this high pitch let us descend
A lower flight, and speak of things at hand
Useful, whence haply mention may arise
Of something not unseasonable to ask
By sufferance, and thy wonted favour deigned.
Thee I have heard relating what was done

viii *183–97*. M. has far more than scientific curiosity in mind here. Like the Cambridge Platonists, he is concerned that the understanding should be kept clear of all the phantasms of the imagination (*fancy*) as well as all the idle speculations of the intellect (*mind*). Cp. John Smith, *Discourses* (1673) 4 and 21: 'The reasons why, notwithstanding all our acute reasons and subtile disputes, Truth prevails no more in the world, is, we so often disjoyn *Truth* and true Goodness, which in themselves can never be disunited. . . . Our own *Imaginative Powers*, which are perpetually attending the highest acts of our Souls, will be breathing a gross dew upon the pure Glass of our Understandings.' For the fancy as a source of evil, cp. v 102–19 above. Restored to its context of seventeenth-century speculative thought, the present speech might well appear not an attack on science but a plea for science of a more practical and sensible kind. Bush cites Ralph Cudworth's sermon to the House of Commons, 31 March 1647: 'We think it a gallant thing to be fluttering up to heaven with our wings of knowledge and speculation: whereas the highest mystery of a divine life here, and of perfect happiness hereafter, consisteth in nothing but mere obedience to the divine will.'
viii *194*. *fume*] something unsubstantial, transient, imaginary (*OED* II 5); something which goes to the head and clouds the reason (*OED* II 6). Some copies *Ed I* have semicolon after *wisdom*.
viii *195*. *fond impertinence*] foolish irrelevance.
viii *197*. *to seek*] deficient; as at *Comus* 366.
viii *202*. *By sufferance*] by permission; probably implying 'by divine permission'.

Ere my remembrance: now hear me relate
My story, which perhaps thou hast not heard;
And day is yet not spent; till then thou seest
How subtly to detain thee I devise,
Inviting thee to hear while I relate,
Fond, were it not in hope of thy reply:
For while I sit with thee, I seem in heaven,
And sweeter thy discourse is to my ear
Than fruits of palm-tree pleasantest to thirst
And hunger both, from labour, at the hour
Of sweet repast; they satiate, and soon fill,
Though pleasant, but thy words with grace divine
Imbued, bring to their sweetness no satiety.
  To whom thus Raphael answered heavenly meek,
Nor are thy lips ungraceful, sire of men,
Nor tongue ineloquent; for God on thee
Abundantly his gifts hath also poured
Inward and outward both, his image fair:
Speaking or mute all comeliness and grace
Attends thee, and each word, each motion forms.
Nor less think we in heaven of thee on earth
Than of our fellow servant, and inquire
Gladly into the ways of God with man:
For God we see hath honoured thee, and set
On man his equal love: say therefore on;
For I that day was absent, as befell,

viii *211–16*. So Virgil's Menalcas compliments Mopsus by comparing his song to the slaking of thirst in summer heat, at *Ecl.* v 45–7. But M.'s introduction of the notion of satiety develops the alimentary / epistemological analogy of *PL* v 84, 400–500, etc.; so that ix 248, with its implication that Adam's converse is in danger of satiating Eve, acquires an ominous resonance. Cp. *Ps.* xix 103: 'How sweet are thy words unto my taste!'
viii *213. from*] Either 'when I come from' or 'caused by'.
viii *218*. Cp. *Ps.* xlv 2: 'Grace is poured into thy lips: therefore God hath blessed thee for ever.'
viii *221*. The doctrine of man's *outward* imaging of God was developed in the first description of Adam and Eve, at iv 289–95; though 'it was chiefly with respect to the soul that Adam was made in the divine image' (*De doctrina* i 7, Columbia xv 45). It is difficult to see how the present passage could be thought to make M. an anthropomorphite (Warburton's sneer).
viii *225*. When the author of *Revelation* tried to worship the angel who interpreted his vision, the latter prevented him: 'for I am thy fellowservant, and of thy brethren the prophets' (*Rev.* xxii 9).
viii *229*. The sixth day of creation, and Day 19 of the poem's action. See ll. 242–4*n*, and Introduction, 'Chronology', p. 444 above.

Bound on a voyage uncouth and obscure,
Far on excursion toward the gates of hell;
Squared in full legion (such command we had)
To see that none thence issued forth a spy,
Or enemy, while God was in his work,
Lest he incensed at such eruption bold,
Destruction with creation might have mixed.
Not that they durst without his leave attempt,
But us he sends upon his high behests
For state, as sovereign king, and to inure
Our prompt obedience. Fast we found, fast shut
The dismal gates, and barricadoed strong;
But long ere our approaching heard within
Noise, other than the sound of dance or song,

viii *230. uncouth*] unfamiliar, unaccustomed.
viii *232.* For other instances of the angels' practice of adopting square formations, see i 758 and vi 62; and for the significance of the shape see i 550*n*.
viii *233–40.* Apparently an unsatisfactory passage, betraying the poet's difficulties and afterthoughts. No sooner has a reason been given for the expedition than M. seems to think it makes God look less than omnipotent, so that a qualification is hurried in: 'Not that. . . .' But the new formulation is if possible worse; as Empson 110 puts it, 'Raphael . . . assumes God gave him a job at the time merely to disappoint him.' We should remember, however, that Raphael is supposed to be concerned to give Adam just the right impression about things he is unable to understand. It may be, too, that M. means to portray Raphael as expressing a very strong wish that he had been present at man's creation. One way to do that would be to exaggerate the tediousness of the obedience that took him elsewhere. The main reason for Raphael's absence–to provide an occasion for the present episode–must of course remain unmentioned.
viii *238–40. state*] ceremony. That there is no point to the angel's errands is precisely their point; for they are tests of obedience. Burden 124f compares St Augustine's view that God is insulted when a higher reason than his will is required–a view with which Calvin (*Inst.* I xiv 1) agreed.
viii *241. barricadoed*] barred securely. Sin later (ii 877–84) unbarred the gates; but to close them again excelled her power, so that she had to leave them open. The point of this detail, as well as of the chronological array discussed in the following note, is evidently to express the total absence of evil from the original state of creation. When Satan begins his mission, however, evil is already admitted (though not yet sin).
viii *242–4.* M. assimilates Virgil's famous image of Aeneas terrified outside the gate of Tartarus, listening to 'groans and the sound of the savage lash, then the clank of iron and dragging of chains' (*Aen.* vi 557–9). Cp. Ariosto, *Orl. Fur.* xxxiv 4, where Astolfo hears the air 'torn with sobs and howls and everlasting mourning, sure sign that it was hell'. The present passage

Torment, and loud lament, and furious rage.
Glad we returned up to the coasts of light
Ere Sabbath evening: so we had in charge.
But thy relation now; for I attend,
Pleased with thy words no less than thou with mine.
So spake the godlike power, and thus our sire.
For man to tell how human life began
Is hard; for who himself beginning knew?
Desire with thee still longer to converse
Induced me. As new waked from soundest sleep
Soft on the flowery herb I found me laid
In balmy sweat, which with his beams the sun
Soon dried, and on the reeking moisture fed.
Straight toward heaven my wondering eyes I turned,
And gazed a while the ample sky, till raised

helps to date the week of creation with respect to the infernal events with which the poem opens. Thus the fact that the gate is barred is evidence that the 6th day of creation lies letween Days 13 and 22 of the poem's action. Some assume that the *furious rage* Raphael heard must be the raging of the assembled host of rebels at i 666, since the devils prostrate on the lake were silent (i 83) and stupefied (i 281) before Satan spoke to Beelzebub. This would put the creation of man on the 22nd day of the poem's action (see Introduction, 'Chronology', p. 445): a timing that would have some numerological fitness in view of the microcosmic properties of 22 (Bongo 439f, Fowler 285*n*), and some dramatic fitness in view of the fact that the poem begins *in medias res* on that day. On the other hand, we would expect the devils to be tormented during their stupor, so that there is no real obstacle to the more probable supposition that the 6th day of creation, and Raphael's excursion, took place on Day 19. Henry More tells us that demons begin their punishment by falling into 'an unquiet sleep, full of furious tormenting Dreams' (*The Immortality of the Soul* III xviii 10).

viii *246. sabbath-evening*] the evening that began the sabbath, the seventh day of rest after the creation of man. M., like the Hebrews, reckoned the day from sunset. See Introduction, 'Chronology' (p. 444).

viii *247. relation*] narration.

viii *249.* In *Ed I* the episode that follows was symmetrically placed with respect to Eve's narration of *her* origin. For it occurred as vii 886–1157, being followed by three complete books; just as Eve's narration was preceded by three books. For other instances of symmetry about the centre of *PL*, see vi 761*n*.

viii *256. reeking*] steaming. On the sun's sustenance from vapours, see v 423–6. But there the vapours of the whole earth were meant, so that the present line becomes a magnificent piece of microcosmic grandiloquence.

viii *258. gazed*] The transitive use was poetic.

By quick instinctive motion up I sprung,
As thitherward endeavouring, and upright
Stood on my feet; about me round I saw
Hill, dale, and shady woods, and sunny plains,
And liquid lapse of murmuring streams; by these,
Creatures that lived, and moved, and walked, or flew,
Birds on the branches warbling; all things smiled,
With fragrance and with joy my heart o'erflowed.
My self I then perused, and limb by limb
Surveyed, and sometimes went, and sometimes ran
With supple joints, and lively vigour led:
But who I was, or where, or from what cause,
Knew not; to speak I tried, and forthwith spake,
My tongue obeyed and readily could name
What e'er I saw. Thou sun, said I, fair light,
And thou enlightened earth, so fresh and gay,
Ye hills and dales, ye rivers, woods, and plains,
And ye that live and move, fair creatures, tell,
Tell, if ye saw, how came I thus, how here?
Not of my self; by some great maker then,
In goodness and in power pre-eminent;
Tell me, how may I know him, how adore,

viii *260.* On Adam's upright posture, see vii 505–11*n*.
viii *263. lapse*] gliding flow. Probably a Latinism: the present instance is the earliest cited in *OED* for this sense.
viii *265. warbling*] singing sweetly.
viii *266.* Richardson and Ricks speculate about what this line would mean if the comma before it had been put at various places in the middle. But we may rest content with the deliberately naïf zeugma of the line as it stands; the syntax is not, here, particularly fluid.
viii *268. went*] walked.
viii *269. and*] as *Ed I.*
viii *272.* Whereas *Gen.* ii 19 says only 'whatsoever Adam called every living creature, that was the name thereof', M. agreed with most commentators in an Augustinian assumption of Adam's ability to administer the true names of things. M.'s version, however, is relatively simple and literal; see ll. 343–56*n*. Note that the sun is the first entity addressed by Adam. Cf. the hymn to the sun at v 171ff, and see Broadbent 166f, where the importance of the sun as a divine symbol in *PL* is rightly stressed.
viii *277.* Willet 36 gives it as the first purpose of the naming of the beasts 'that man seeing his excellent creation farre surpassing all other, might thereby be stirred up to praise his Creator'.
viii *280–2.* Smith 162 draws attention to the manner in which 'the Latinized elliptical construction' of ll. 280–1 'suddenly resolves itself with ease and grace' in l. 282.

From whom I have that thus I move and live,
And feel that I am happier than I know.
While thus I called, and strayed I knew not whither,
From where I first drew air, and first beheld
This happy light, when answer none returned,
On a green shady bank profuse of flowers
Pensive I sat me down; there gentle sleep
First found me, and with soft oppression seized
My drowsed sense, untroubled, though I thought
I then was passing to my former state
Insensible, and forthwith to dissolve:
When suddenly stood at my head a dream,
Whose inward apparition gently moved
My fancy to believe I yet had being,
And lived: one came, methought, of shape divine,
And said, Thy mansion wants thee, Adam, rise,
First man, of men innumerable ordained
First father, called by thee I come thy guide
To the garden of bliss, thy seat prepared.
So saying, by the hand he took me raised,
And over fields and waters, as in air

viii *281*. Cp. St Paul's Mars' hill sermon on the Unknown God, *Acts* xvii 28: 'For in him we live, and move, and have our being, as certain also of your own poets have said, For we are also his offspring.'
viii *282*. A dramatic irony, in view of vii 631f, 'thrice happy if they know / Their happiness'. Throughout *PL* happiness is a resonant and often ironic term. Cp. especially v 74, where Satan tempting Eve uses the word three times, yet tells her she may be 'Happier'.
viii *288*. *oppression*] the action of weighing down; gentle pressure. Normally the word had a much more violent sense–as it has in the description of Adam's satiety after the Fall, at ix 1044; see Ricks 115.
viii *291*. Lewis 46 suggests that the ambiguous syntax here renders the 'crumbling of consciousness'.
viii *292–5*. For the dream psychology implied, see v 100–13 above, where fancy forms imaginations of external things represented by the senses; and cp. ll. 460–1. *dream*] Not merely a synecdoche for 'figure seen in a dream'; M. is imitating Homer, *Il*. ii 8, 16, etc., where *Oneiros* is a dream personified. *stood . . . head*] An allusion to the position taken up by the false dream sent by Zeus to Agamemnon, *ibid*. 20.
viii *296–9*. According to *Gen*. ii 8 and 15, Adam was created outside Paradise and only afterwards placed in it. See vii 535–8*n* above. *mansion*] dwelling-place, home. An allusion to *John* xiv 2 ('In my Father's house are many mansions. . . . I go to prepare a place for you') is possible. *wants*] lacks. *seat*] residence; or throne.

Smooth sliding without step, last led me up
A woody mountain; whose high top was plain,
A circuit wide, enclosed, with goodliest trees
Planted, with walks, and bowers, that what I saw
Of earth before scarce pleasant seemed. Each tree
Loaden with fairest fruit that hung to the eye
Tempting, stirred in me sudden appetite
To pluck and eat; whereat I waked, and found
Before mine eyes all real, as the dream
Had lively shadowed: here had new begun
My wandering, had not he who was my guide
Up hither, from among the trees appeared
Presence divine. Rejoicing, but with awe
In adoration at his feet I fell
Submiss: he reared me, and Whom thou sought'st I am,
Said mildly, author of all this thou seest
Above, or round about thee or beneath.
This Paradise I give thee, count it thine
To till and keep, and of the fruit to eat:
Of every tree that in the garden grows
Eat freely with glad heart; fear here no dearth;
But of the tree whose operation brings

viii *302.* For the accentuation *wìthout*, implying emphasis, see ii 892*n* above.
viii *303–5.* For a fuller account of the geography of Paradise, cp. iv 132ff.
viii *308. tempting*] Here an innocent word, which takes on in the course of the poem an increasingly moral significance. Cp. esp. ix 595, where the dramatic irony is emphatic. All the trees are made provocative here, so that the forbidden tree may not seem specially so (Burden 127).
viii *311. lively*] realistically, to the life.
viii *316. Submiss*] submissive. Those who wish to will of course find a Latinism (*submissus*=cast down); unnecessarily. *whom . . . am*] The inversion throws enough stress on *I am* to make an allusion to *Exod.* iii 14. There God answers Moses' enquiry about his name with the words 'I AM THAT I AM. . . . Thus shalt thou say unto the children of Israel, I AM hath sent me unto you.'
viii *320–2.* 'And the Lord God took the man, and put him into the garden of Eden to dress it and to keep it. And the Lord God commanded the man, saying, Of every tree of the garden thou mayest freely eat' (*Gen.* ii 15f). *till*] A.V. has 'dress', and does not introduce the idea of tilling until after the Fall, at iii 23; but M., who refuses to consider work as a punishment, follows the Heb., Septuagint and Vulg. versions, where the same word is used in both places.
viii *323–33.* Cp. *Gen.* ii 17: 'But of the tree of the knowledge of good and evil, thou shalt not eat of it: for in the day that thou eatest thereof thou

Knowledge of good and ill, which I have set
The pledge of thy obedience and thy faith,
Amid the garden by the tree of life,
Remember what I warn thee, shun to taste,
And shun the bitter consequence: for know,
The day thou eat'st thereof, my sole command
Transgressed, inevitably thou shalt die;
From that day mortal, and this happy state
Shalt loose, expelled from hence into a world
Of woe and sorrow. Sternly he pronounced
The rigid interdiction, which resounds
Yet dreadful in mine ear, though in my choice
Not to incur; but soon his clear aspect
Returned and gracious purpose thus renewed.
Not only these fair bounds, but all the earth
To thee and to thy race I give; as lords
Possess it, and all things that therein live,

shalt surely die.' *From that day mortal* is more careful diction than may at first appear. Since patristic times, Biblical commentators had puzzled over an apparent discrepancy in the Genesis account of the Fall, in that 'mere bodily death, as it is called, did not follow the sin of Adam on the self-same day, as God had threatened' (*De doctrina* i 12, Columbia xv 203). One way out of the difficulty was to distinguish between different 'degrees of death', namely guiltiness, spiritual death, bodily death and eternal death (*De doctrina* i 12–14, Columbia xv 202–50; see Willet 35 for a similar classification). The first two of these followed Adam's transgression immediately, as M. shows in his description of the results of eating the fruit, ix 1010ff below. Willet like M. follows St Jerome's interpretation 'that Adam began in the same day to die, not actually, but because then he became mortall and subject to death ... So Symmachus readeth, thou shalt be mortall. Many of the Fathers speculated that if Adam had not sinned he would have been immortal (see, e.g., Augustine, *Civ. Dei* xiv 1. Cp. M.'s speculation in *PL* v 497; and see *De doctrina* i 8 (Columbia xv 91): 'God, at least after the fall of man (*post lapsum saltem hominis*), limited human life to a certain term.' *operation*] effect. The warning is recalled by the echo of this word at ix 1012.

viii *329*. Cp. iii 95 above. As Lewis 68 stresses, the fruit has for M.'s good characters no intrinsic magic: it is important only as a pledge of obedience.

viii *332. loose*] break up, do away with (*OED* 7); violate (*OED* 8); also 'lose', which previous editors have assumed to be the only word indicated, in spite of the awkwardness of its accord with *state*. *Ed I* and *Ed II* have the form 'loose', which could indicate either word.

viii *334. interdiction*] prohibition.

viii *336. incur*] (Intrans.) become liable (*OED* I 2).

viii *337. purpose*] discourse.

viii *338–41*. Cp. *Gen.* i 28; see vii 530–4*n*.

Or live in sea, or air, beast, fish, and fowl.
In sign whereof each bird and beast behold
After their kinds; I bring them to receive
From thee their names, and pay thee fealty
With low subjection; understand the same
Of fish within their watery residence,
Not hither summoned, since they cannot change
Their element to draw the thinner air.
As thus he spake, each bird and beast behold
Approaching two and two, these cowering low
With blandishment, each bird stooped on his wing.

viii *343–56.* For other references to the naming of the beasts, cp. l. 276; also vi 73–6, vii 493. The present account illustrates most of the five causes of the ceremony assigned by Willet (36): '1. that man seeing his excellent creation farre surpassing all other, might thereby be stirred up to praise his Creator. 2. that their might be a triall of Adams wisdome: *he brought them to see how he would call them.* 3. that by this meanes the Hebrewe language, wherein those names were given, might be founded. 4. that mans authoritie and dominion over the creatures might appeare: *for howsoever man named every living creature, so was the name thereof.* 5. that man finding among all the creatures no helpe or comfort meete for him: v. 20. might have a greater desire thereunto, and more lovingly embrace his helper, which should be brought to him.' Adam's wisdom was shown particularly in the effortless suddenness of his perceptions: cp. *De doctrina* i 7, Columbia xv 53: 'Certainly without extraordinary wisdom he could not have given names to the whole animal creation with such sudden intelligence, *Gen.* ii 20.' St Thomas Aquinas had held that Adam had an angelic understanding, capable of moving through objects to concepts instantly (*Summa Theol.* I xciv 2–4; see MacCaffrey 36–8).

The naming of the creatures had a strong topical interest, for in M.'s time, after such 'natural' classifications of species as Cesalpino's and Jung's, the movement towards morphological systematisation gathered momentum and was soon to culminate in the work of Linnaeus. In 1682 John Ray could list as many as 18,000 species of plants alone. On Adam's endowment with science, see vii 639*n*, The ability to name implied great knowledge, for 'names were given at the first according to the severall properties and nature of creatures' (Willet 37)–a doctrine that seems to have owed as much to Plato, *Crat.* 422, as to *Genesis.* Names could still be regarded magically; thus Bacon prophesied that when man 'shall be able to call the creatures by their true names he shall again command them' (*Of the Interpretation of Nature*).

viii *350. two and two*] A grim reminder of the next mythic gathering of the beasts, 'two and two unto Noah into the ark' (*Gen.* vii 9).

viii *351. stooped*] caused to bow down; brought to the ground (*OED* II 7); but with a secondary allusion to the intrans. sense, common of birds of

I named them, as they passed, and understood
Their nature, with such knowledge God endued
My sudden apprehension: but in these
I found not what me thought I wanted still;
And to the heavenly vision thus presumed.
O by what name, for thou above all these,
Above mankind, or aught than mankind higher,
Surpassest far my naming, how may I
Adore thee, author of this universe,
And all this good to man, for whose well being
So amply, and with hands so liberal
Thou hast provided all things: but with me
I see not who partakes. In solitude
What happiness, who can enjoy alone,
Or all enjoying, what contentment find?
Thus I presumptuous; and the vision bright,
As with a smile more brightened, thus replied.
What call'st thou solitude, is not the earth
With various living creatures, and the air
Replenished, and all these at thy command
To come and play before thee, know'st thou not
Their language and their ways, they also know,
And reason not contemptibly; with these
Find pastime, and bear rule; thy realm is large.
So spake the universal Lord, and seemed
So ordering. I with leave of speech implored,
And humble deprecation thus replied.
Let not my words offend thee, heavenly power,
My maker, be propitious while I speak.

prey: 'descend swiftly upon, swoop down on' (*OED* I 6)–foreshadowing postlapsarian carnivorousness. See xi 182–90*nn*.

viii *357*. Adam follows the order of natural theology, in proceeding from the names of the creatures to the name of their creator–an order to which the contentious Warburton took needless exception.

viii *371*. *Replenished*] abundantly stocked (*OED* I 1).

viii *373*. For evidence that M. read Lactantius on the relation between human and animal nature, see *Commonplace Book*, Yale i 373. It was a widespread Jewish belief that before the Fall Adam understood the language of the beasts: see Josephus, *Antiq.* I i 4 ('all the living creatures had one language'); Philo, *Quaest. in Gen.* i 32; *Jubilees* iii 28. The original language was usually supposed, understandably enough, to have been Hebrew; but sometimes Syriac or Greek or Aramaic. See Charles ii 17. *know*] have understanding or knowledge.

viii *379*. Cp. Abraham's apprehensive preface to a bold request, at *Gen.* xviii 30: 'Oh let not the Lord be angry, and I will speak'.

Hast thou not made me here thy substitute,
And these inferior far beneath me set?
Among unequals what society
Can sort, what harmony or true delight?
Which must be mutual, in proportion due
Given and received; but in disparity
The one intense, the other still remiss
Cannot well suit with either, but soon prove
Tedious alike: of fellowship I speak
Such as I seek, fit to participate
All rational delight, wherein the brute
Cannot be human consort; they rejoice
Each with their kind, lion with lioness;
So fitly them in pairs thou hast combined;
Much less can bird with beast, or fish with fowl
So well converse, nor with the ox the ape;
Worse then can man with beast, and least of all.
Whereto the almighty answered, not displeased.
A nice and subtle happiness I see
Thou to thy self proposest, in the choice

viii *384–9.* An extended musical allegoria. For true harmony, there has to be the right mathematical proportion–a proportion that is here punningly described as reciprocal. Thus, in a stringed instrument the strings should bear a due ratio of length and frequency. But the human string is too strained (*intense*) and therefore high in pitch; while the animal string is too *remiss*, i.e., low in pitch. The moral or psychological meanings of *intense* and *remiss*, which give the allegoria its force, are perhaps to be considered as a dramatic irony (it is not the animals who prove remiss, in the event). *sort*] fit, be in harmony.
viii *390. participate*] impart, share out (*OED* I 2).
viii *392–7.* i.e., 'Animals rejoice with their own species. Less converse is possible across the major divisions between kinds; indeed, even with more closely related species it is difficult. How much less converse is possible, therefore, between man and beast.' Intercourse would certainly be difficult between the emasculated ox, which drew Diana's car, and the ape, proverbially lascivious (Carroll 19, 92). Note how the choice of examples introduces notions of moral restraint and psychological adjustment; cp. Adam's phrase *rational delight* (l. 391).
viii *396. converse*] consort, associate familiarly.
viii *398.* Burden 31f notices how God plays out the scene with Adam as if he did not know he was going to create Eve. Providence must never be allowed to appear deterministic; though from the point of view of a human character he may seem to improvise.
viii *399. nice*] fastidious; but with 'over-refined, luxurious', even 'wanton', as overtones.

Of thy associates, Adam, and wilt taste
No pleasure, though in pleasure, solitary.
What think'st thou then of me, and this my state,
Seem I to thee sufficiently possessed
Of happiness, or not? Who am alone
From all eternity, for none I know
Second to me or like, equal much less.
How have I then with whom to hold converse
Save with the creatures which I made, and those
To me inferior, infinite descents
Beneath what other creatures are to thee?
He ceased, I lowly answered. To attain
The highth and depth of thy eternal ways
All human thoughts come short, supreme of things;
Thou in thy self art perfect, and in thee
Is no deficience found; not so is man,
But in degree, the cause of his desire
By conversation with his like to help,
Or solace his defects. No need that thou
Shouldst propagate, already infinite;
And through all numbers absolute, though one;

viii *402. in pleasure*] in a state of pleasure. Eden was often explained as meaning 'pleasure'.
viii *406–7.* Cp. Horace, *Odes* I xii 17f: *unde nil maius generatur ipso, / nec viget quicquam simile aut secundum.* Hughes compares Aristotle, *Nic. Ethics* 1154[b], on God's 'single and simple pleasure' in unchanging immobile activity.
viii *413.* 'O the depth of the riches both of the wisdom and knowledge of God! how unsearchable are his judgments, and his ways past finding out!' (*Rom.* xi 33).
viii *416–19.* As Howard 160 shows, Adam's awareness of this *deficience* makes him the proegumenic or impulsive helping cause of the Fall. For his need for companionship leads to the creation of Eve, who in turn will provide the procatarctic cause, or occasion. See iii 120*n* above. At *Eud. Ethics* 1244[b] Aristotle says that a god 'needing nothing . . . will not need a friend, nor have one, supposing that he does not need one'; at 1245[b] he argues against the position that a virtuous man should imitate the divine by dispensing with his friends. *But*] except.
viii *420.* Ridiculously taken as evidence of Arianism by Kelley 121–as ll. 405–7 above were taken by Verity. There was no necessary connection between the theology of the monad and rejection of the doctrine of the Trinity.
viii *421.* Editors have seen this line as a 'quibble' between *numbers* in antithesis to *one*, and *numbers* in the Latin sense 'parts', as in such idiomatic phrases as *perfectum . . . omnibus numeris* (Cicero, *De nat. deor.* ii 13) or *liber numeris omnibus absolutus* (Pliny, *Epistles* ix 38). But the primary meaning

But man by number is to manifest
His single imperfection, and beget
Like of his like, his image multiplied,
In unity defective, which requires
Collateral love, and dearest amity.
Thou in thy secrecy although alone,
Best with thy self accompanied, seek'st not
Social communication, yet so pleased,
Canst raise thy creature to what highth thou wilt
Of union or communion, deified;
I by conversing cannot these erect
From prone, nor in their ways complacence find.
Thus I emboldened spake, and freedom used
Permissive, and acceptance found, which gained
This answer from the gracious voice divine.
  Thus far to try thee, Adam, I was pleased,
And find thee knowing not of beasts alone,
Which thou hast rightly named, but of thy self,
Expressing well the spirit within thee free,
My image, not imparted to the brute,
Whose fellowship therefore unmeet for thee

is that the divine monad contains all other numbers, and is therefore complete and perfect (*absolute, OED* II 4, 5) through them all. Bongo 13f explains that the monad is like God because it is the fountain and origin of all numbers, as God is the origin of created being. His extended analogy opens with a distinction between divine and created singleness that closely resembles M.'s. Whereas creaturely singleness (*single imperfection*) means the absence of a second member of the species, God's oneness means universality: *Unus si dicatur, non numeri, sed universitatis est nomen.* See vi 809–10*n.*
viii *426. collateral*] parallel, ranking side by side with, accompanying.
viii *427–8.* The paradox perhaps imitates Cato's famous description of Scipio Africanus: *Numquam minus solum esse, quam cum solus esset*' (Cicero, *De re pub.* I xvii 27, cp. *De offic.* III i 1).
viii *431. deified*] absorbed in the divine nature. A theological term for 'the elevation of the human soul to a supernatural state' by sanctifying grace; see Corcoran 103. Although *union* and *communion* could be taken as general terms distinguishing degrees of separateness or plurality in the relationship, it is difficult not to see references to mystical union and Holy Communion (Eucharist). See v 438–9*n*, on similar use of *transubstantiate.*
viii *432.* For the symbolic significance of the human posture, see vii 505–11.
viii *433. complacence*] object or source of pleasure; cp. iii 276, where the Father's 'sole complacence' is Messiah. The original accentuation *còmplacence* occurred certainly as late as 1675: as in many cases, M. prefers the newer pronunciation.
viii *435. permissive*] allowed.

Good reason was thou freely shouldst dislike,
And be so minded still; I, ere thou spakest,
Knew it not good for man to be alone,
And no such company as then thou saw'st
Intended thee, for trial only brought,
To see how thou couldst judge of fit and meet:
What next I bring shall please thee, be assured,
Thy likeness, thy fit help, thy other self,
Thy wish exactly to thy heart's desire.
He ended, or I heard no more, for now
My earthly by his heavenly overpowered,
Which it had long stood under, strained to the highth
In that celestial colloquy sublime,
As with an object that excels the sense,
Dazzled and spent, sunk down, and sought repair
Of sleep, which instantly fell on me, called
By nature as in aid, and closed mine eyes.
Mine eyes he closed, but open left the cell
Of fancy my internal sight, by which

viii *445*. 'And the Lord God said, It is not good that the man should be alone' (*Gen.* ii 18).
viii *448*. God's motive is Scriptural: see ll. 343–56*n*, and cp. *Prov.* xvii 3, *John* vi 6.
viii *450. fit help*] Recalls *Gen.* ii 18, 'I will make him an help meet for him'. *other self*, however, is a classical term for a close friend (Lat. *alter ego*, Gk ἕτερος αὐτός); cp. x 128. In *De doctrina* i 10 (Columbia xv 163) M. gives the reasons for Eve's creation in the same order: 'God gave a wife to man at the beginning to the intent that she should be his help and solace and delight.' If she ceases to be such, he argues, then the husband should have no hesitation in divorcing her. Ever the Biblical theologian, M. invariably stressed the relational aspect of marriage.
viii *452–86*. 'And the Lord God caused a deep sleep to fall upon Adam, and he slept: and he took one of his ribs, and closed up the flesh instead thereof; And the rib, which the Lord God had taken from man, made he a woman, and brought her unto the man' (*Gen.* ii 21f).
viii *453. earthly*] Supply 'nature'. For the difficulty of sustaining conversation with God, see *Dan.* x 17: 'How can the servant of this my lord talk with this my lord? for as for me, straightway there remained no strength in me, neither is there breath left in me.'
viii *460–1. cell / Of fancy*] The *cellula phantastica*; see v 109*n*. For the action of fancy in producing dreams, see v 100–13*n*, and cp. viii 294. The present passage perhaps rationalizes the open-eyed trance of *Num.* xxiv 4: 'He hath said, which heard the words of God, which saw the vision of the Almighty, falling into a trance, but having his eyes open.'

Abstract as in a trance methought I saw,
Though sleeping, where I lay, and saw the shape
Still glorious before whom awake I stood,
Who stooping opened my left side, and took
From thence a rib, with cordial spirits warm,
And life-blood streaming fresh; wide was the wound,
But suddenly with flesh filled up and healed:
The rib he formed and fashioned with his hands;
Under his forming hands a creature grew,
Manlike, but different sex, so lovely fair,
That what seemed fair in all the world, seemed now
Mean, or in her summed up, in her contained
And in her looks, which from that time infused
Sweetness into my heart, unfelt before,
And into all things from her air inspired

viii *462. Abstract*] withdrawn, separated. The soul was believed to become separated from the body in the state of 'ecstasy', when meditating on divine truths. *trance*] Follows Septuagint *Gen.* ii 21, ἔκστασιν, where A.V. has only 'deep sleep'.
viii *465–6*. Cp. iv 484. *Gen.* ii 21 does not specify from which side the rib was taken; but most commentators thought the left, since that was nearer Adam's heart. M. clinches the allusion to this pathetic theory by his use of the term *cordial* [i.e. cardiac] *spirits*, a rather old-fashioned synonym for 'vital spirits' (on which see v 484*n*). Willet (37), who thinks it needless to specify the left side, considers it more important to note that Eve was formed 'not out of his head, that shee should not be proud'. Perhaps the birth of Sin, described in *PL* ii, is meant to contrast in this respect with the birth of Eve. See, however, ii 752–61*n*.
viii *469. fashioned*] The early edns have 'fashoned', a spelling introduced, and abandoned, in the seventeenth century (cp. Fr. *façonner*).
viii *471–4*. So Marino, of the beautiful but fatally destructive Helen: 'So well does beauty's aggregate / In that fair face summed up unite, / Whatever is fair in all the world / Flowers in her' (*Adone* ii 173).
viii *471*. Poetic and difficult syntax. M. probably means to imply that Eve is the archetype of a whole sex; so that *sex* is in apposition to *creature*: 'a sex like man, yet also distinct'. But it may well be that both syntax and rhythm were beautifully complicated by the presence of a contemporary (and shortlived) predicative quasi-adj. use of sex='feminine' (*OED* 1 f); cp. Dryden, *Cymon and Iphigeneia* 367f (ed. Kinsley iv 1750): 'She hugg'd th'Offender, and forgave th'Offence, / Sex to the last!'
viii *476. air*] Radically ambiguous, two main possibilities being separable: (1) mien, look; (2) breath, *OED* I 9, as in Shakespeare, *Winter's Tale* V iii 77f: 'Still me thinkes / There is an ayre comes from her.' (2) gains support from the fact that in M.'s time the physical sense of *inspired* ('breathed') was still current.

The spirit of love and amorous delight.
She disappeared, and left me dark, I waked
To find her, or for ever to deplore
Her loss, and other pleasures all abjure:
When out of hope, behold her, not far off,
Such as I saw her in my dream, adorned
With what all earth or heaven could bestow
To make her amiable: on she came,
Led by her heavenly maker, though unseen,
And guided by his voice, nor uninformed
Of nuptial sanctity and marriage rites:
Grace was in all her steps, heaven in her eye,
In every gesture dignity and love.
I overjoyed could not forbear aloud.
This turn hath made amends; thou hast fulfilled
Thy words, creator bounteous and benign,
Giver of all things fair, but fairest this
Of all thy gifts, nor enviest. I now see
Bone of my bone, flesh of my flesh, my self
Before me; woman is her name, of man
Extracted; for this cause he shall forego
Father and mother, and to his wife adhere;
And they shall be one flesh, one heart, one soul.

viii *478*. Editors compare *Sonnet XXIII*, but the motif was not a rare one.
viii *481*. *out of hope*] beyond hope.
viii *488*. Cp. Shakespeare, *Troilus* IV iv 118, 'The lustre in your eye, heaven in your cheek', of Cressida. Again an ominous analogue for Eve.
viii *490*. *aloud*] Supply 'saying'.
viii *494*. *enviest*] grudge, give reluctantly. Continuing the thought of 'thou hast fulfilled'.
viii *495–9*. See *Gen.* iii 23f: 'And Adam said, This is now bone of my bones and flesh of my flesh: she shall be called Woman, because she was taken out of Man. Therefore shall a man leave his father and his mother, and shall cleave unto his wife: and they shall be one flesh.' In *Matt.* xix 4–6 and *Mark* x 6–8 these verses are made the basis of Jesus' doctrine of marriage as *henosis* or union in one flesh. *my self*] See l. 450*n*. *adhere*] A.V. has 'cleave' but Vulg. *adhaerebit*.
viii *499*. The Biblical expression 'one flesh' is replaced by the familiar Platonic tripartite division into parts, in order to preclude any misunderstanding. Cp. Willet 39: 'They shall be one flesh, not onely in respect of carnall copulation . . . for so bruit beasts may bee said to be one flesh: but is respect of their perpetuall societie, the conjunction both of their bodies and minds.' *flesh*] Corresponds to the Platonic concupiscible part, as *heart* to the irascible and *soul* to the rational.

She heard me thus, and though divinely brought,
Yet innocence and virgin modesty,
Her virtue and the conscience of her worth,
That would be wooed, and not unsought be won,
Not obvious, not obtrusive, but retired,
The more desirable, or to say all,
Nature her self, though pure of sinful thought,
Wrought in her so, that seeing me, she turned;
I followed her, she what was honour knew,
And with obsequious majesty approved
My pleaded reason. To the nuptial bower
I led her blushing like the morn: all heaven,

viii *500. divinely brought*] Cp. l. 485 and see *Gen.* ii 22.
viii *501. modesty*] As Burden 46f points out, the modesty has nothing to do with guilt but springs from a sense of the exclusiveness of the relationship. M.'s difficulty is that many of the passions he wishes to write about only have an imaginable existence in fallen communities larger than two.
viii *502. conscience*] consciousness; inward knowledge.
viii *504. obvious*] open to influence. So H. Brooke, *Fool of Quality* iii 13, as late as 1809: 'She was artless and obvious to seduction.'
viii *508.* Alluding to *Heb.* xiii 4: 'Marriage is honourable in all, and the bed undefiled: but whoremongers and adulterers God will judge.' The source of Eve's knowledge about honour was explained at l. 487 above. In expressing the notion that honour antedated the Fall, M. must have recalled Guarini's famous distinction between the *verace onor* of the Golden Age and the false honour of later times (*Pastor Fido* iv 10)–itself a correction of the First Chorus of Tasso's *Aminta*, which had declared the Golden Age free from honour altogether. Lewis (119f) agrees with Tasso, disliking the suggestion here of sexual shame in the unfallen Eve; though he grants that a spiritual modesty may be entirely appropriate. Empson 104f, 107 wonders if it is possible to make a distinction between a blameless sexual pleasure at the blushes of others, and an offensive sense of mastery. While the answer in respect of our fallen world must clearly be negative, I suspect that M. is trying to sustain some such distinction in respect of the world before the Fall. He would naturally wish all imaginable desires to have their innocent counterparts: in particular, perhaps, a desire for 'sweet reluctant amorous delay' (iv 311).
viii *509. obsequious*] compliant; without any suggestion of undue servility. The oxymoron was not so violent as it has become. Cp. Spenser, *Epithalamion* 306f: 'In proud humility; / Like unto Maia, when as Jove her tooke.'
viii *511. blushing*] Here we have to make allowance for what seems a general change in sensibility since the seventeenth century. Englishmen of that time had a strong taste for disdain or denial on the lady's part, so that however much M. was on the side of fruition, he was bound to share a little in the

And happy constellations on that hour
Shed their selectest influence; the earth
Gave sign of gratulation, and each hill;
Joyous the birds; fresh gales and gentle airs
Whispered it to the woods, and from their wings
Flung rose, flung odours from the spicy shrub,
Disporting, till the amorous bird of night
Sung spousal, and bid haste the evening star
On his hill top, to light the bridal lamp.
Thus I have told thee all my state, and brought
My story to the sum of earthly bliss
Which I enjoy, and must confess to find
In all things else delight indeed, but such
As used or not, works in the mind no change,

feeling that 'willing kisses yield no joy' (Stanley, *Poems and Translations*, ed. G. M. Crump (Oxford 1962) 55). Burden's view (47) is that the 'sole propriety' of wedded love, its exclusive privacy, must give rise to a modesty that had nothing to do with guilt.

viii *513*. The happy *influence* of the constellations is introduced not only to clarify the analogy between generation of a universe and generation of its microcosm (cp. the 'sweet influence' of the Pleiades at the creation, vii 375), but also to stress that until the Fall Adam and Eve enjoyed every benefit of astral influence. Their natures and sexual adjustment being perfect, they lack any excuse for error. The evil influence of stars and planets begins at x 657–64, when the macrocosm is altered as a result of the Fall.

viii *514*. So in Homer, *Il.* xiv 347ff, earth gives signs of joy at the coition of Zeus and Hera. See iv 499–501*n* above. *gratulation*] joy; congratulation.

viii *515*. *gales*] Simply 'winds'; see iv 156*n*. The play on *airs*=melodies, which is underlined by *sung* in l. 519, was noticed by M.'s first commentator, Patrick Hume; see Ricks 106.

viii *516*. For the *wings* of the personified *airs*, cp. iv 156ff; also *Comus* 989, 'And west winds with musky wing'.

viii *518*. *amorous bird of night*] the nightingale; cp. v 40f.

viii *519*. *evening star*] The planet Venus, here mythologized as Hesperus; cp. iv 605 above. The *hill top* recalls Virgil, *Ecl.* viii 30, or Catullus, *Carm.* lxii 1–4: *Vesper adest, iuvenes, consurgite: Vesper Olympo / expectata diu vix tandem lumina tollit. / surgere iam tempus, iam pingues linquere mensas, / iam veniet virgo, iam dicetur Hymenaeus.* In epithalamial tradition, the rising of Venus was the occasion for lighting the *bridal lamp* and conducting the bride to the bridegroom. In view of the considerable epithalamic element in *PL* (cf. iv 710–18, 741–70, xi 588–95) it is interesting that a marriage song is included in M.'s second draft of a tragedy on Paradise Lost. The tragedy was to have 'Evening Star' among its dramatis personae (see Introduction, 'Composition'; also Gilbert 19).

Nor vehement desire, these delicacies
I mean of taste, sight, smell, herbs, fruits, and flowers,
Walks, and the melody of birds; but here
Far otherwise, transported I behold,
Transported touch; here passion first I felt,
Commotion strange, in all enjoyments else
Superior and unmoved, here only weak
Against the charm of beauty's powerful glance.
Or nature failed in me, and left some part
Not proof enough such object to sustain,
Or from my side subducting, took perhaps
More than enough; at least on her bestowed
Too much of ornament, in outward show
Elaborate, of inward less exact.
For well I understand in the prime end
Of nature her the inferior, in the mind
And inward faculties, which most excel,
In outward also her resembling less
His image who made both, and less expressing
The character of that dominion given
O'er other creatures; yet when I approach
Her loveliness, so absolute she seems
And in her self complete, so well to know
Her own, that what she wills to do or say,
Seems wisest, virtuousest, discreetest, best;

viii *526. vehement*] A highly significant word here, in view of its derivation from *vehe-mens* 'lacking in mind'. Cp. ii 954 and Argument to Bk ix.
viii *527–8.* Note the absence of any mention of touch, in Renaissance thought the lowest and most physical of the five senses (see Kermode² *passim*). In the nuptials, on the contrary, touch is prominent (l. 530). See ll. 579–85*n*.
viii *530–1. Transported*] put in an ecstasy. But there may be an ominous overtone ('banished'), in view of the contiguity of *passion*, not usually an innocent word. *Commotion*] mental perturbation; strong excitement.
viii *535. proof*] of tried power of resistance, impervious.
viii *536. subducting*] taking away from its place, subtracting.
viii *539–44. exact*] perfect, consummate, finished, refined (*OED* I 1, 2). As soon as Adam has taken the forbidden fruit, however, he tells Eve 'now I see thou art exact of taste, / And elegant, of sapience no small part' (ix 1017f). Cp. also the question of the Chorus at *SA* 1025–30: 'Is it for that such outward ornament / Was lavished on their sex, that inward gifts / Were left for haste unfinished, judgment scant, / Capacity not raised to apprehend / Or value what is best / In choice, but oftest to affect the wrong?' Most of the commentators on *Genesis* agreed that Eve was a less perfect image of God than Adam was; see Williams 87.
viii *547. absolute*] entire, perfect, independent.

All higher knowledge in her presence falls
Degraded, wisdom in discourse with her
Looses discountenanced, and like folly shows;
Authority and reason on her wait,
As one intended first, not after made
Occasionally; and to consummate all,
Greatness of mind and nobleness their seat
Build in her loveliest, and create an awe
About her, as a guard angelic placed.
To whom the angel with contracted brow.
  Accuse not nature, she hath done her part;
Do thou but thine, and be not diffident
Of wisdom, she deserts thee not, if thou
Dismiss not her, when most thou need'st her nigh,
By attributing overmuch to things
Less excellent, as thou thy self perceiv'st.
For what admir'st thou, what transports thee so,
An outside? Fair no doubt, and worthy well

viii *551–2*. The dramatic irony is strong: Adam is betraying a tendency to mistake the appointed hierarchy of relationships that we know will prove fatal. 'The higher falls, and other falls inevitably follow' (MacCaffrey 69). Note, however, that Adam's continuation makes it clear that the tendency is meanwhile held in check, so that it does not yet constitute a defect. All we can say is that the 'balanced perfection' of life before the Fall 'becomes less stable: the knife-edge between man's "disposition to do good" and his "liability to fall", as Milton puts it in *De doctrina*, is sharpened through Books v, vii and viii' (Broadbent 197).
viii *553*. Proleptic of the argument between Adam and Eve at ix 205–385. *Looses*] 'goes to pieces; comes unstuck' (cp. *OED* 5, quotation of 1526). Or perhaps 'loses' is intended. The *Ed I* and *Ed II* spelling 'Looses' could indicate either word.
viii *556*. *Occasionally*] accidentally–i.e., as a result of the contingency of Adam's need for companionship. *consùmmate*] complete.
viii *557*. *Greatness of mind*] magnanimity, on which see vii 505–11*n*.
viii *561–70*. We are reminded of this warning, after the Fall, by Christ's censure at x 145–56. *nature*] Here 'God' or 'God's work in forming your nature'. Adam might conceivably–even after Raphael's account of the creation–have thought of nature as responsible for a fault in his constitution (l. 534); but he certainly knew that it was specifically God who subducted from his side (ll. 398 and 536). We have already, therefore, reached a point at which there can be talk of accusing God. *diffident*] mistrustful. *wisdom*] Not simply Adam's own wisdom, but also the eternal Wisdom of vii 9f etc.; thus Raphael is in effect saying 'Have faith in God'. *attributing*] Stressed on the third syllable.

Thy cherishing, thy honouring, and thy love,
Not thy subjection: weigh with her thy self;
Then value: oft times nothing profits more
Than self esteem, grounded on just and right
Well managed; of that skill the more thou know'st,
The more she will acknowledge thee her head,
And to realities yield all her shows:
Made so adorn for thy delight the more,
So awful, that with honour thou mayst love
Thy mate, who sees when thou art seen least wise.
But if the sense of touch whereby mankind
Is propagated seem such dear delight
Beyond all other, think the same vouchsafed
To cattle and each beast; which would not be

viii *569*. Cp. the verses used in the Prayer Book marriage service, *Eph.* v 28f ('So ought men to love their wives as their own bodies. He that loveth his wife loveth himself. For no man ever yet hated his own flesh; but nourisheth and cherisheth it, even as the Lord the church') and *1 Pet.* iii 7 ('Likewise, ye husbands, dwell with them according to knowledge, giving honour unto the wife, as unto the weaker vessel, and as being heirs together of the grace of life; that your prayers be not hindered').
viii *570*. *Not thy subjection*] Cp. the similar sentiment expressed in M.'s own voice at ix 1182–6.
viii *573*. *that skill*] Not 'self-esteem', as Verity and Hughes, but 'the skill of managing well just and right'.
viii *574*. *head*] Alludes to *1 Cor.* xi 3: 'The head of every man is Christ; and the head of the woman is the man; and the head of Christ is God.' A similar hierarchic conception underlies the Scriptural passages alluded to at l. 569.
viii *575*. *Ed I* has semicolon after *shows*.
viii *576*. *adorn*] Apparently M.'s coinage, on the analogy of Italian *adorno*, the contracted form of *adornato* (adorned).
viii *577*. *honour*] Raphael carefully distinguishes between different senses of the term. Here the sense is not that of l. 569, but is related rather to that of l. 508 (on which see *n*).
viii *579–85*. See ll. 527–8*n*. Throughout the exchange between Raphael and Adam, M. assumes familiarity with the Neoplatonic ordering of different kinds of love and with the related ordering of the five senses in the Banquet of Sense tradition. Cp., e.g., Chapman, *Ovids banquet of sence* St. 92: 'Pure love (said she) the purest grace pursues, / And there is contact, not by application / Of lips or bodies, but of bodies vertues.' Touch, which Chapman's Ovid calls 'the sences Emperor', was the fifth course of the Banquet, often associated–as it is here–with coitus; see *Commonplace Book* (Yale i 369*n*), also Kermode[2] 97f. Not far in the background, too, is the *quinque linea amoris* scheme of erotic poetry; on which see Hutton in *MLN* lvii (1942) 657–61.

To them made common and divulged, if aught
Therein enjoyed were worthy to subdue
The soul of man, or passion in him move.
What higher in her society thou find'st
Attractive, human, rational, love still;
In loving thou dost well, in passion not,
Wherein true love consists not; love refines
The thoughts, and heart enlarges, hath his seat
In reason, and is judicious, is the scale
By which to heavenly love thou mayst ascend,
Not sunk in carnal pleasure, for which cause
Among the beasts no mate for thee was found.
  To whom thus half abashed Adam replied.

viii *588. passion*] This must be wrong, because it entails the overthrow of the reason. On the medieval Christian condemnation of passionate sexual love, even within marriage, see Lewis[2] 15f. Although this attitude had changed by M.'s time, it had by no means been replaced by formal approval of passion. According to generally received doctrine, passion was never experienced until after the Fall. Raphael's frown, therefore, is entirely understandable: for a horrified moment, indeed, he may even have thought that the Fall was already under way. And though Adam's answer reassures him, clearly the 'liability to fall' is now in fact considerable. See Broadbent 197f, on the inadequacy of M.'s psychology to the task of rendering the metaphysical transition from innocence to guilt.
viii *589–94*. Raphael here expounds the very familiar Neoplatonic distinction between divine or celestial love; human or terrestrial love; and bestial love. The first (M.'s *heavenly love*) is the love of the contemplative, belonging to mind alone. The second (*true love*) is the force that drives a man to propagate the earthly image of divine beauty, but may also, in its ideal form, lead him to the first–as Spenser describes in his first *Hymn*. The third (*sunk . . . pleasure*) is experienced by him who 'stoops to debauchery, or, even worse, abandons for sensual pleasures a contemplative state already attained' (Panofsky[2] 143). Cp. *Comus* 1003–11; also the conclusion of *Dam*.
viii *590. heart enlarges*] Probably 'makes wise'; see vii 486*n*.
viii *591. scale*] Not the scale or ladder of nature (v 509), but the Neoplatonic ladder of love. The proximity of *judicious*, however, and the fairly recent 'weigh with her thyself' (l. 570), support the suspicion of an ambiguity in which the scale is a balance and Adam's soul is weighed against Eve's. For the importance of the balance symbol in *PL*, see iv 997–1004*n*.
viii *595*. Adam is only *half abashed*, for he goes on to give a spirited defence of his love. One is presumably to conclude that it is still rational and unfallen; so that Raphael's unsympathetic sharpness has been occasioned by an anxiety without present foundation. The occasion can hardly, in view of ll. 624–9, have been angelic bias against the mystery of human marriage with its involvement of physical sex. Nevertheless, the conversation of

Neither her outside formed so fair, nor aught
In procreation common to all kinds
(Though higher of the genial bed by far,
And with mysterious reverence I deem)
So much delights me as those graceful acts,
Those thousand decencies that daily flow
From all her words and actions mixed with love
And sweet compliance, which declare unfeigned
Union of mind, or in us both one soul;
Harmony to behold in wedded pair
More grateful than harmonious sound to the ear.
Yet these subject not; I to thee disclose
What inward thence I feel, not therefore foiled,
Who meet with various objects, from the sense
Variously representing; yet still free
Approve the best, and follow what I approve.
To love thou blamest me not, for love thou say'st
Leads up to heaven, is both the way and guide;

Raphael and Adam does in some respects resemble a debate between Heavenly Love and Human Love, in which the angel / man distinction is intensified into an antithesis. In this connection it is interesting that in the first three drafts of M.'s projected drama on the Fall, there is a character called 'Heavenly Love'. See Introduction, 'Composition'.

viii *598. genial*] 'nuptial'; see iv 712*n.* i.e., 'I value marital sex higher than animal coition'–also, perhaps, 'I value marital sex higher than you do'.

viii *599. mysterious*] such as is due to a mystery; the only instance of this sense given by *OED*. The relation of one flesh is described as a 'great mystery' in *Eph.* v 32. *Eph.* v sets out a theology of sex, based on an analogy between the love of a husband for his wife, and the love of Christ for the Church.

viii *600. Ed I* has comma after *me*.

viii *601. decencies*] instances of comeliness or of propriety.

viii *604*. Cp. l. 499. In stressing the union of souls, Adam is appealing to the value of friendship, which was regarded as superior to sexual love.

viii *607*. i.e., 'These (the thousand decencies, etc.) do not put me in subjection to her.'

viii *608. foiled*] overcome; also defiled, polluted; dishonoured. Adam admits to feeling passion, but not to yielding to it. The distinction is fine enough for the precariousness of his position to be felt.

viii *609–11*. i.e., 'Though my senses present me with a variety of objects, and these under a variety of forms, I am not committed to approve any of them unless I choose.' But the speech is ominous if the echo of Ovid, *Met.* vii 20f is caught: 'I see the better, I approve it too: / The worse I follow' (tr. Sandys). See Douglas Bush in *JEGP* lx (1961) 639. Cp. v 117–9: 'Evil into the mind of god or man / May come and go, so unapproved, and leave / No spot

Bear with me then, if lawful what I ask;
Love not the heavenly spirits, and how their love
Express they, by looks only, or do they mix
Irradiance, virtual or immediate touch?
  To whom the angel with a smile that glowed
Celestial rosy red, love's proper hue,
Answered. Let it suffice thee that thou know'st
Us happy, and without love no happiness.
Whatever pure thou in the body enjoy'st
(And pure thou wert created) we enjoy
In eminence, and obstacle find none
Of membrane, joint, or limb, exclusive bars:
Easier than air with air, if spirits embrace,
Total they mix, union of pure with pure

or blame behind.' The interplay between *subject* (l. 607) and *objects* (l. 609) is thematic; cp. Jonson's antithesis in *Hymenaei* (ed. Herford and Simpson vii 209): 'It is a noble and just advantage, that the things subjected to understanding have of those which are objected to sense. . . .'

viii *617*. Expression of love by looks would be essential or *virtual* contact; expression by irradiance, *immediate*. A division was made logically between 'real' and 'virtual' causes.

viii *618–20*. Raphael may be blushing at a successful riposte of Adam's ('"Come now, what do you know about this? Have you got any sex?"' as Empson 105 paraphrases); but it seems more likely that the riposte is unsuccessful, and that the angel's smile glows red because that is the colour of angelic ardour (cp. iv 977f). Certainly M. and Raphael go on to insist proudly on the closeness and totality of angelic coitus, much as angelic digestion was flaunted at v 433ff. The tone of 'In eminence' (l. 624, q.v.) is not modest but superior; it is a point of honour with the servants of Love that their several modes of expression should fall short neither in fulness nor in pureness.

viii *624–9*. Cp. Henry More, *The immortality of the soul* (1659) III ix 4, p. 421, where the angels are imagined as 'reaping the lawful pleasures of the very *Animal* life, in a far higher degree than we are capable of in this World. . . . Wherefore they cannot but enravish one anothers Souls, while they are mutual Spectators of the perfect pulchritude of one anothers persons, and comely carriage, of their graceful dancing, their melodious singing and playing.' On the fluidity and penetrability of angelic bodies, see i 423–31*n* and vi 328–34*n*.   *In eminence*] superlatively, in a superior way. As Burden 158f remarks, M.'s tactic in introducing angelic sexuality was to establish the innocence of sexuality in general, and to relate it to the theme of the transmutation of flesh to spirit. One might add that he was specifically countering the disparagement of sex as a merely animal activity. Cp. Donne's approach in 'Air and Angels'.

Desiring; nor restrained conveyance need
As flesh to mix with flesh, or soul with soul.
But I can now no more; the parting sun
Beyond the earth's green cape and verdant isles
Hesperean sets, my signal to depart.
Be strong, life happy, and love, but first of all
Him whom to love is to obey, and keep
His great command; take heed lest passion sway
Thy judgment to do aught, which else free will
Would not admit; thine and of all thy sons
The weal or woe in thee is placed; beware.
I in thy persevering shall rejoice,

viii *628. restrained conveyance*] restricting, confined, limited mode of expression or communication (*OED*, s.v. *Conveyance* I 5, 9, 14). Angelic natures exhibit no differentiation into flesh and soul, so that their love is simple and complete. 'The angels which are in heaven' 'neither marry, nor are given in marriage' (*Mark* xii 25), because they have no need of an institutionalised or organic channel of expression. For the use of *conveyance* in a sacramental sense, cp. Hooker, *Eccles. Pol.* V lxvii 4: 'those mysteries should serve as conducts of life and conveyances of his body and blood unto them'. Cp. also Donne, 'The Ecstasy', where the souls acknowledge that their bodies 'Did us, to us, at first convey'.

viii *631–2.* Cp. iv 354 and 592, where the sun sets 'Beneath the Azores'. Here the *green cape* is Cape Verde and the *verdant isles* the Cape Verde Islands. Stephanus' entry runs: 'Hesperium ceras . . . Africae extremum promontorium . . . Hodie vocant Caput viride. vulgo, *Le cap verd*' (*cit.* Starnes 314). *Hesperian* should be grouped with *sets*; it is impossible to imagine a rhythm and juncture that would allow it to be taken with *isles* as Hughes proposes. Thus its primary meaning must be 'western' (*OED* A 1). At the same time, the context exerts a strong pull in the direction of a secondary allusion to the Hesperian Isles; cp. iii 567f above. Perhaps at a tertiary level the sun is even a Hesperian fruit; vegetable as well as potable gold (iii 607–8*n*, iv 217–21*n*). *Signal*] see v 229 and 376 for the term set to Raphael's mission.

viii *633. Be strong*] Recalls the exhortation of *Josh.* i 6.

viii *634–5.* Cp. *1 John* v 3: 'For this is the love of God, that we keep his commandments.'

viii *637–8.* Note how Adam's posterity and its destiny, *of . . . woe*, is carried within the personal pronoun of which he is the antecedent, *thine . . . thee. admit*] allow.

viii *639–40.* However, 'joy shall be in heaven over one sinner that repenteth, more than over ninety and nine just persons' that persevere (*Luke* xv 7). *persevering*] A theological term, meaning 'continuance in a state of grace'; cp. vii 632.

And all the blest: stand fast; to stand or fall
Free in thine own arbitrament it lies.
Perfect within, no outward aid require;
And all temptation to transgress repel.
So saying, he arose; whom Adam thus
Followed with benediction. Since to part,
Go heavenly guest, ethereal messenger,
Sent from whose sovereign goodness I adore.
Gentle to me and affable hath been
Thy condescension, and shall be honoured ever
With grateful memory: thou to mankind
Be good and friendly still, and oft return.
So parted they, the angel up to heaven
From the thick shade, and Adam to his bower.

THE END OF THE EIGHTH BOOK

viii *640–1*. Cp. *1 Cor.* vii 37: 'Nevertheless he that standeth stedfast in his heart, having no necessity, but hath power over his own will, and hath so decreed in his heart that he will keep his virgin, doeth well.' Raphael echoes the drift of his commission at v 235, which in turn echoes the words of God the Father at iii 99. *arbitrament*] free choice; absolute decision.
viii *642*. *require*] look for (*OED* III 9); ask (*OED* I 2; II 5, 6).
viii *646*. *ethereal*] celestial, heavenly.
viii *648*. Cp. vii 41, 'affable archangel'.
viii *651*. *oft return*] But Raphael will not return in the poem (except in the sense that v 222, e.g., referred to a chronologically later visit); instead, the less affable archangel, Michael, will come to expel Adam and Eve from Paradise. For the diction, cp. Virgil, *Ecl.* v 65, addressing the dead Daphnis: *sis bonus o felixque tuis*; also *Lycidas* 183f: 'thou art the genius of the shore / . . . and shalt be good / To all that wander in that perilous flood.'
viii *653*. Since Adam's bower has been described as 'of thickest covert . . . inwoven shade' (iv 693, cp. v 367), the line is heavy with overtones. The angel leaves the thick shade of the lower world for the light of heaven; but Adam is bound for ever darker shade. Within a few lines we shall come to a mention of Sin's 'shadow Death' (ix 12). 'Shade' and 'shadow' are among the poem's most resonant words: they are gradually transformed from innocence (iv 138, 141, 245, 325, 532), through evil associations (iv 1015, ix 185, x 249), back to hope of salvation (xii 233, 291, 303).

Paradise Lost

BOOK IX

The Argument

Satan having compassed the earth, with meditated guile returns as a mist by night into Paradise, enters into the serpent sleeping. Adam and Eve in the morning go forth to their labours, which Eve proposes to divide in several places, each labouring apart: Adam consents not, alleging the danger, lest that enemy, of whom they were forewarned, should attempt her found alone: Eve loth to be thought not circumspect or firm enough, urges her going apart, the rather desirous to make trial of her strength; Adam at last yields: the serpent finds her alone; his subtle approach, first gazing, then speaking, with much flattery extolling Eve above all other creatures. Eve wondering to hear the serpent speak, asks how he attained to human speech and such understanding not till now; the serpent answers, that by tasting of a certain tree in the garden he attained both to speech and reason, till then void of both: Eve requires him to bring her to that tree, and finds it to be the tree of knowledge forbidden: the serpent now grown bolder, with many wiles and arguments induces her at length to eat; she pleased with the taste deliberates a while whether to impart thereof to Adam or not, at last brings him of the fruit, relates what persuaded her to eat thereof: Adam at first amazed, but perceiving her lost, resolves through vehemence of love[1] to perish with her; and extenuating the trespass eats also of the fruit: the effects thereof in them both; they seek to cover their nakedness; then fall to variance and accusation of one another.

No more of talk where God or angel guest
With man, as with his friend, familiar used

ix *Argument*[1] *vehemence of love*] Note the root meaning of Lat. *vehementia*, 'mindlessness'; see viii 526*n*, and cp. 431 below.
ix *1–47*. The fourth and last of the poem's invocations, the others being i 1–49, iii 1–55 and vii 1–50. This, unlike the others, avoids direct address to the divine Muse; possibly in response to the increased *distance* (l. 9) of heaven in the part of the poem it introduces. In *Ed II*, the placing of the invocations draws attention to the poem's two-part structure. Thus, if **i** denotes a book with an invocation, we have the following array:

i 2 **i** 4 5 6 || **i** 8 **i** 10 11 12

(*Ed II*). The first part, broadly speaking, deals with the fall of the angels, the second with the fall of man. For other indications of a binary structure, with simple balance about the mid-point at the end of vi, see vii 20*n* and vi 761*n*. But the positions of the invocations were originally determined by the subtler, four-part structure of *Ed I*; and it is only in terms of that structure that they can be fully understood: **i** 2 | **i** 4 5 6 || **i** | **i** 9 10 (*Ed I*). If invocations are taken to be inceptions of new parts of the poem, as, strictly speaking, they

To sit indulgent, and with him partake
Rural repast, permitting him the while
Venial discourse unblamed: I now must change
Those notes to tragic; foul distrust, and breach

ought to be, then the total numbers of books composing the four parts run: 2 | 4 || 1 | 3. Now this arrangement makes good sense numerologically. For, first, it divides the ten books of *Ed I* into the four numbers composing the creative number principle, the divine *tetractys* (1, 2, 3, 4). Secondly, it reorders the number of the *tetractys* to give a sequence running from the evil and rebellious *dyad*, through the *tetrad* of the ordered world (4 elements, 4 humours, 4 virtues, etc.; see Bongo 193f), through the *monad* fountain of creation, to the *triad* of mediation between God and the fallen world. (For these number symbolisms, see Hopper, Fowler.). Properly considered, the content of the books will be seen to be appropriate to their numerological arrangement: e.g., the origin of creation is related in vii (monad); while i–ii (*dyad*) are given over to the portrayal of evil and disorder.

ix *1–9*. See Ricks 69–72 on the meanings underlying the alliterative crescendo *discourse ... distrust ... disloyal ... disobedience ... distance and distaste. heaven* is put where we would expect *God*, to introduce the notion of space and physical distance. Before the Fall it was no matter that heaven was far from earth; 'but the distance is now moral and spiritual, and not merely material'. The force of *distaste* depends on the frequency with which 'the Fall is described as the *tasting* of the apple. The real structure of the phrase is of a brilliantly unspoken pun. On the part of man, *taste*; on the part of Heaven, *distaste*.' See also l. 9*n*.

ix *1–4*. See viii 651*n*. God talked with Adam after putting him in Paradise (viii 316–51). There was no mention in Bk viii of any common meal between man and God; nevertheless, it seems illegitimate to escape, by supplying 'spoke' after *God* (Verity) or by arguing that God was present in his angel (Richardson, more plausibly), from M.'s obscure implication that before the Fall there could be some meal with God less tragic than Holy Communion. The implication is that the subject of the present book is to be a feast of a different kind: namely, Adam's disloyal feast with Eve and Satan. See l. 9*n*. *Rural*] pastoral, in contrast to the *tragic* melody about to be played; but alluding also to the alfresco character of the meal partaken by Adam and his *angel guest* Raphael in v. *Exod.* xxxiii 11 authorized the notion of God speaking to man 'face to face, as a man speaketh unto his friend'.

ix *2. familiar*] Carries, in addition to its modern meaning, the sense 'on a family footing'. Its use here is also enriched by the overtone 'familiar angel' = 'guardian angel' (*OED* A 2 d).

ix *5. Venial*] allowable, permissible (*OED* A 3; a rare usage).

ix *6*. In the medieval tradition that regarded tragedies as stories *de casibus virorum illustrium*, the fall of Adam had an important place. It comes second, e.g., with the fall of Lucifer first, in Chaucer's *Monk's Tale*. Newton

Disloyal on the part of man, revolt,
And disobedience: on the part of heaven
Now alienated, distance and distaste,
Anger and just rebuke, and judgment given,
That brought into this world a world of woe,
Sin and her shadow Death, and Misery
Death's harbinger: sad task, yet argument

thought that M. intended here to announce a change to a less lofty style: 'what follows is more of the *tragic* strain than of the *epic*'. But all *PL* is epic; and there is no lowering of diction in the part of the poem that follows. Scaliger praised the epic genre for containing all genres within itself. Thus, the earlier portrayal of Paradise was pastoral (see, e.g., iv 328*n*), while in the part to follow, which takes us out of the Golden Age into a world of woe, there is an appropriate move from the pastoral to the tragic mode. Yet the poem remains epic and (as ll. 13f below explicitly affirm) there is no drop in heroic elevation. *distrust*] Recalls Raphael's warning at viii 562: 'be not diffident / Of wisdom'. *breach*] Primarily 'break-up of friendly relations' (*OED* I 5 b); but also, elliptically, 'violation (of God's commandment)'.

ix *9. distaste*] dislike, aversion. A secondary meaning, 'disrelish, dislike of food', keeps up the feast theme, which recurs throughout the book and is given a very prominent place in the present invocation (cp. ll. 3f, 37–9). After the Fall, M. returns to the theme with a clinching statement at x 687f: 'At that tasted fruit / The sun, as from Thyestean banquet, turned'. See also ll. 1–9*n*.

ix *10–19*. Burden (11f), developing a point made by Newton, calls this passage 'a characteristic exercise in close discrimination, turning on anger'. Achilles is *stern* in his *wrath* because he refused any covenant with Hector; whereas Messiah, more heroically, is not implacable in his anger. He issued his sole commandment 'sternly' (viii 333); but when it is disobeyed, he works for reconciliation. Similarly, God's anger is distinguished from *Neptune's ire* and *Juno's* (which merely 'perplexed' Odysseus and Aeneas) in that it is expressed in justice rather than in victimisation. The Christian epic, by contrast with the pagan, unravels perplexity; cf. xii 275f: 'Erewhile perplexed . . . but now I see'. *Perplexed*] tormented, plagued; also confused, bewildered. *Cytherea's son*] The periphrasis is to emphasise that Juno's persecution of Aeneas had a petty motive in her envy of Venus, as a result of Paris' fatal judgment.

ix *11*. Cp. xi 627 for a very similar play on *world*. Cp. *Rom.* v 12, 'by one man sin entered into the world'.

ix *12–13*. Bentley objected to the image of *Misery* as *Death's harbinger*, on the ground that misery often invokes death in vain. But, as Burden 6f points out, the image springs naturally from the idea of different stages of death, which was developed to explain the apparent non-fulfilment of Gen. ii 17. See viii 323–33*n* above. *Sin and her shadow Death* do not enter the world, at least in

Not less but more heroic than the wrath
Of stern Achilles on his foe pursued
Thrice fugitive about Troy wall; or rage
Of Turnus for Lavinia disespoused,
Or Neptun's ire or Juno's, that so long
Perplexed the Greek and Cytherea's son;
If answerable style I can obtain
Of my celestial patroness, who deigns
Her nightly visitation unimplored,
And dictates to me slumbering, or inspires
Easy my unpremeditated verse:
Since first this subject for heroic song
Pleased me long choosing, and beginning late;
Not sedulous by nature to indite

the fable, until x 230ff, but the present invocation refers to the whole of the fourth part of *PL*; see ll. 1–47*n*.

ix *16*. M.'s selection of the pursuit of Achilles as an episode representative of the *Iliad* is by no means casual. It works, in a way, to Homer's disadvantage; in the *Poetics* Aristotle selects this very episode as an example of epic's admitting what would be ridiculous in another genre. M.'s implication is that his Christian epic need have no recourse to such dubious material.

ix *17*. *disespoused*] Makes Turnus' claim to Lavinia as strong as possible, so that Virgil's hero Aeneas is presented in a somewhat discreditable light.

ix *20*. *answerable*] equal, equivalent; corresponding (*OED* II 3, 5); but with the secondary sense 'accountable' (*OED* I 1) continuing the theme of responsibility from the preceding contrast between God's accountable anger and the mere passions of pagan epic.

ix *21–4*. *celestial patroness*] The heavenly Muse, Urania; see vii 1–7*n*. Hanford (415) finds M.'s emphasis here on the unconsciousness of his inspiration significant, and believes that he thought himself actually possessed. *nightly*] on the nocturnal composition of *PL*, see vii 29*n*. *dictates*] Stressed on the first syllable.

ix *26*. For an account of the genesis of *PL*, see Introduction, 'Composition' (pp. 419–23).

ix *27–41*. Cp. i 16, where M. parodies Ariosto's claim to originality. It was true that both ancient and modern epics had always had war, or at least fighting, as a principal ingredient. (So has *PL*, in the first half of the poem; but in the second this subject is transcended.) M. now glances unfavourably at the typical matter of the romantic epic, whereas ll. 10–19 were solely concerned with classical epic. The claim to originality is expressed in a form itself unusual in epic (though there were precedents, such as Spenser's *Faerie Queene*). Thus Johnson felt that M.'s 'extrinsick paragraphs' of autobiographical digression were incorrect; though he was prepared to defend them on the ground of their popularity: 'Since the end of poetry is pleasure,

Wars, hitherto the only argument
Heroic deemed, chief mastery to dissect
With long and tedious havoc fabled knights
In battles feigned; the better fortitude
Of patience and heroic martyrdom
Unsung; or to describe races and games,
Or tilting furniture, emblazoned shields,

that cannot be unpoetical with which all are pleased.' *argument*] matter, subject.
ix *29*. *mastery*] (Spelled 'maistrie') art, skill. *dissect*] Both ancient and Italian epic poets were given to describing wounds with a minuteness and technicality that would have been more appropriate in text books of anatomy.
ix *30–1*. M. frequently insists on the authenticity of his matter, implying its superiority in this respect to legendary or mythical subjects. Cp., e.g., i 746f and iv 706. Yet at one time he seriously considered writing an Arthurian epic (see, e.g., *Dam* 162–78), so that he evidently did not hold–or did not always hold–feigned matter in contempt. The extent and continuance of his interest in early British history is shown by the *History of Britain*, as well as by the British subjects for epic projected in *Trin. MS.* *feigned*] fictional.
ix *31–2*. Clearly implying a hierarchy of heroic virtues, in which patience is to be regarded as occupying a superior place to that of fortitude. See Steadman 94, and cf. iii 267–9*n*, vi 820–3*n* and vii 604–7*n* above. These are tragic rather than heroic values (Burden 59).
ix *33*. *describe . . . games*] Games were de rigueur in classical epic; see Homer, *Od.* viii 83ff and *Il.* xxiii 262ff, Apollonius Rhodius ii 1ff, Virgil, *Aen.* v 104ff, Statius, *Theb.* vi 255ff, Quintus Smyrnaeus iv 171ff and Nonnus xxxvii 103ff, and consult H. A. Harris, *Greek Athletes and Athletics* (1964), Ch. 3. Such passages perhaps seemed objectionable to M. as much for their irrelevance as for their triviality. Johnson, commenting on the spareness of *PL*, says: 'Here are no funeral games, nor is there any long description of a shield' (*Lives*). M. does touch on games, at ii 528ff and iv 551f; but in both instances briefly, not sedulously. By such means he achieved a real advantage of compression over most earlier epic poets.
ix *34–7*. Referring to chivalric epics such as those of Boiardo, Ariosto, Tasso and Spenser. Sidney's *Arcadia* has particularly elaborate descriptions of *Impreses* (heraldic devices, often with accompanying mottos), as has Trissino's *La Italia liberata* (Rome 1547). See, e.g., *Arc.* (1590) I xvii 1: '*Phalantus* was all in white, having in his bases, and caparison imbroidered a waving water: at each side whereof he had nettings cast over, in which were divers fishes naturally made, and so pretily, that as the horse stirred, the fishes seemed to strive, and leape in the nette. But the other knight . . . was all in black, with fire burning both upon his armour, and horse. His *impresa* in his shield, was a fire made of Juniper, with this word, *More easie, and more*

Impreses quaint, caparisons and steeds;
Bases and tinsel trappings, gorgeous knights
At joust and tournament; then marshalled feast
Served up in hall with sewers, and seneschals;
The skill of artifice or office mean,
Not that which justly gives heroic name
To person or to poem. Me of these
Nor skilled nor studious, higher argument
Remains, sufficient of it self to raise
That name, unless an age too late, or cold

sweete.' *Bases*] cloth housings of horses. *tinsel trappings*] Cp. the description of Florimell in *F.Q.* III i 15: 'All her steed with tinsell trappings shone.' *tournament*] The spelling in the early edns, 'torneament', may possibly be Miltonic, and intended to give an Italian flavour.

ix *37–9*. The *sewer* superintended the seating of guests and the tasting and serving of the dishes; while the *seneschal* was a steward with wider responsibilities. *artifice*] mechanic art, applied art. M. means that it is beneath the dignity of epic to teach etiquette and social ceremony and heraldry. Yet he did not dislike chivalric epics; or, if he did, he made an exception in the case of Tasso, whom he quite often echoes (see, e.g., 147–51*n*), and of Spenser–as we know from *Areopagitica* (Yale ii 516). The mention of the *feast* as a subject has strong overtones here, since M. himself is at the moment in transition from the feast with Raphael to the forbidden Thyestean feast; see 1–4*n*, 9*n*.

ix *41*. *Me . . . remains*] Imitates Latin *me manet*.

ix *44*. *That name*] i.e., of epic. M.'s argument is not only high enough for epic, but high enough to raise the very name of epic and set a new standard.

ix *44–7*. M. mentions three defects of nature that might prevent his success. First, the decline of culture, and the general progressive corruption of nature. Cp. *Reason of Church-Government* ii Pref. (Yale i 814), where M. thinks of something 'adverse' in 'the fate of this age' as a possible obstacle to epic-writing. In the poem *Naturam non pati senium* and in *Prol vii*, however, he had opposed the view that the earth is decaying. A cosmic pessimism that drew its strength both from apocalyptic theories of history and from recent astronomical thought was current in M.'s time, and in the generation preceding had been even commoner. See J. L. Lievesay in *MLN* lix (1944). The theory went that change in the declination of the sun, since Ptolemy's measurements, marked a deterioration in nature (cp. *F.Q.* V Proem 7) which would eventually bring the end of the world. Secondly, *cold / Climate* might be an obstacle. Cp. *Reason of Church-Government*, *ibid.*, 'that there be nothing advers in our climate'; also *Mans* 24–9, where M. modestly asks indulgence for his poetry, on the ground that he has been 'poorly nourished under the frozen Bear'. On the wide distribution and scientific basis for this theory of the inferiority of the north, see Z. S. Fink in *MLQ* ii (1941) 67–80 and T. B. Stroup in *MLQ* iv (1943) 185–9. Burton, e.g.,

Climate, or years damp my intended wing
Depressed, and much they may, if all be mine,
Not hers who brings it nightly to my ear.
  The sun was sunk, and after him the star
Of Hesperus, whose office is to bring
Twilight upon the earth, short arbiter
Twixt day and night, and now from end to end
Night's hemisphere had veiled the horizon round:
When Satan who late fled before the threats
Of Gabriel out of Eden, now improved
In meditated fraud and malice, bent
On man's destruction, maugre what might hap
Of heavier on himself, fearless returned.
By night he fled, and at midnight returned
From compassing the earth, cautious of day,
Since Uriel regent of the sun descried
His entrance, and forewarned the cherubim

believed that 'cold air in the other extreme is almost as bad as hot. . . . In those northern countries, the people are therefore generally dull, heavy. . . . these cold climes are more subject to natural melancholy' (*Anatomy of Melancholy* I ii 2 v). Thirdly, M.'s own age (*years*). *Ed I* did not appear in print until M. was fifty-eight years old.

While the present passage is certainly autobiographical, it should be noticed that it also relates to x 651ff, where such phenomena as climate and variable declination are shown to have their origin in the Fall. Not even a personal aside is allowed to be entirely digressive. *climate*] Both in the sense 'region' (the place, as *age* is the time, of his life) and in the modern sense. *wing*] Cp. iii 13, vii 4.

ix *48–9. star / Of Hesperus*] the planet Venus; cp. iv 605. *office*] contrast 'office mean' at l. 39. The offices described in M.'s epic are cosmic ones, not mere domestic duties or political places.

ix *50–1.* Twilight maintains an even balance between light and darkness; but only briefly. So also the precarious stasis of prelapsarian life cannot long be sustained. For twilight as an expression of the balance theme that runs throughout *PL*, see iv 354–5*n* and 998–1015*nn*.

ix *53. late*] i.e., at the end of Bk iv, a week earlier.

ix *54. improved*] intensified, made worse (*OED* 4).

ix *58. midnight*] On the eighth night (l. 67), after his journey of ll. 63–6.

ix *59.* Cp. iii 440–1, and see *Job* i 7: 'And the Lord said unto Satan, Whence comest thou? Then Satan answered the Lord, and said, From going to and fro in the earth, and from walking up and down in it.'

ix *60.* For Uriel's regency of the sun, see iii 648 above; for his report of having seen Satan's entrance, iv 564–75.

That kept their watch; thence full of anguish driven,
The space of seven continued nights he rode
With darkness, thrice the equinoctial line

ix *62. thence . . . driven*] As recounted at the end of Bk iv. There seems to be no support in the text for taking this phrase to refer to a separate attempt by Satan to return on the first night following his expulsion.
ix *63. seven continued nights*] From the night of the first temptation (iv 800ff), the night preceding Day 24, to the night preceding Day 31. (For the reckoning of the days of *PL* from sunset, see Introduction, 'Chronology' (p. 444 above); also vii 249–52*n*). Thus Satan accomplishes the preliminaries of his successful second temptation in a week, which travesties the divine week of creation. This symmetry not only renders the contrast between good and evil, but also the dyadic doubling of the singleness of creation that makes moral choice necessary. Spenser's formal application of a similar idea is discussed in Fowler 7f. Cp. ll. 136–8, where Satan draws attention to (but falsely denies) the correspondence between the times of creation and destruction. *continued*] by keeping to earth's shadow Satan contrives to experience a whole week of darkness. The first of these continued nights runs midnight 24–midnight 25; the second, midnight 25–midnight 26 . . . and the seventh, midnight 30–midnight 31.
ix *64–6.* Satan's repeated girdling of the earth, which is scarcely authorized by Job i 7 (see l. 59*n*), is essentially an astronomical modulation of a motif found in religious iconography, particularly in certain types of the Virgin of the Immaculate Conception. In these, the infernal serpent is shown wrapped round a lunar or terrestrial globe and spurned by the Virgin. See Manuel Trens, *María. Iconografía de la Virgen en el arte español* (Madrid 1946) 144–6 and 173, Figs 83f, 99. Each day of the unnatural week of uncreation has to be turned into night by a journey that keeps Satan in the shadow of the earth. On three occasions, this is achieved simply by going round the equator (*equinoctial line*) from east to west, always keeping ahead of the sun. On the other four, Satan is supposed to follow great circles or colures, taking in the poles. These lines are usually taken at their face value; but a moment's reflection will show that the journey is strictly speaking impossible. For, before the Fall, ecliptic and equator coincided, so that the earth's axis was always perpendicular to the direction of the sun. Since the sun is larger than the earth, it follows, therefore, that the poles were never in darkness. We must choose one of two possibilities: (1) oversight on M.'s part–unlikely, in view of his accuracy elsewhere in astronomical matters; (2) deliberate prolepsis and dramatic irony, looking forward to the tilting of the poles at x 669. Satan is as it were describing a fallen world; in contrast to Christ's describing of the universe at vii 226–32. *each colure*] The two colures were great circles, intersecting at right angles at the poles and dividing the equinoctial circle into four equal parts. One colure passed through the solstitial points of the ecliptic, the other through the equinoctial points. Since the solstitial and equinoctial points did not exist before the Fall, M.'s mention

He circled, four times crossed the car of Night
From pole to pole, traversing each colure;
On the eighth returned, and on the coast averse
From entrance or cherubic watch, by stealth
Found unsuspected way. There was a place,
Now not, though sin, not time, first wrought the
    change,
Where Tigris at the foot of Paradise

of colures must again be either oversight or prolepsis. The division of the nights into three and four continues the parody of the week of creation; for it symbolizes the body-forming power of seven. See Macrobius, *In somn. Scip.* I vi 22–44, where the division is discussed at length. *car of night*] Simply the dark part of earth or the shadow of earth. But there is a distorted echo, in the vehicle earth provides for Night, of the bright cosmic vehicle of Messiah (vi 749–59*n*).

ix *67–8*. The midnight before Day 32; see Introduction, 'Chronology' (p. 444). On the *eighth* night Satan is to descend into a serpent; whereas on the eighth day of Passion Week Christ rose. The association of eight with resurrection, and consequently with baptism, was very familiar: see Simson 21, 40, 48, 144; Hopper 114; and Fowler 53. The symbolism can be observed in the octagonal design of many Gothic columns and baptismal fonts. *coast averse*] side turned away. *entrance . . . watch*] To the east of Paradise (iv 542); the river enters from the north (iv 223). For the north as the direction from which evil comes, see v 689*n*.

ix *70*. At first sight this line seems to have an allegorical meaning only: the change is a moral or spiritual one. xi 829–38, however, will show that there is also a literal and historical sense. As in many other instances the effect of the Fall is to reduce the significant to the merely factual. Conversely, the line indicates that the geography of Paradise is not only physical. Sin bars natural access to the fountain of life, but Christ will reopen it to believers: see xi 278–9*n*.

ix *71–5*. For a fuller account of the landscape, see iv 223–232 and *nn*. *mist*] Probably not a mist in the ordinary sense, but a fountain rising by capillary attraction. M. obeys *Gen.* ii 10 to the letter in making the undivided fountain of Paradise come, not from a source, but from a river. On the other hand, he takes an unusual step in calling the undivided river *Tigris*. In *Gen.* ii 14, Tigris (Hiddekel) is the name of one of the four distributaries, and in M.'s time, though nomenclatures and geographical identifications of the rivers abounded in great profusion (Willet 29ff summarizes a dozen schemes), Tigris does not seem to have been singled out as the source river. Hughes says that M. had the authority of Josephus, *Antiq.* I i 3; but this is not so. (St Ambrose, however, attributes to Josephus a theory that the *Euphrates* was the source.) The undivided river was usually allegorized as Grace, or the Water of Life; whereas the Tigris was either Self-mastery (being over against the Assyria of pleasure) or Courage. See, e.g., Philo, *Quaest. in Gen.*

Into a gulf shot under ground, till part
Rose up a fountain by the tree of life;
In with the river sunk, and with it rose
Satan involved in rising mist, then sought
Where to lie hid; sea he had searched and land
From Eden over Pontus, and the pool
Maeotis, up beyond the river Ob;
Downward as far antarctic; and in length
West from Orontes to the ocean barred
At Darien, thence to the land where flows
Ganges and Indus: thus the orb he roamed
With narrow search; and with inspection deep
Considered every creature, which of all
Most opportune might serve his wiles, and found

i 12f. The main drift of the present passage, however, is clear enough: the mode of Satan's entry indicates that evil enters life at its very origin, and that even Baptism does not free us from its taint. The point is further made at x 20 that not even the caution of angels could exclude evil and temptation. The angelic guard is there described as 'wondering' at Satan's successful entry: perhaps they do not grasp how primordially the choice of good and evil is instilled into the very stream of life. On the Tigris' source on Mt Niphates, see iii 742*n* above. Its subterranean course is from Lucan's *Pharsalia*: '*Tigris*, soon swallowed by the thirsty earth, / Finds there a buriall where it had its birth' (tr. Heylyn iii 143).

ix *76–82*. Satan's journey, already described in astronomical terms, is now retraced geographically. In his north–south circles he passed *Pontus* (Pontus Euxinus, the Black Sea), the *pool / Maeotis* (Palus Maeotis, the Sea of Azov) and the Siberian *River Ob*, which flows north into the Gulf of Ob and from there into the Arctic Ocean; in his westward circling of the equinoctial line, he crossed the Syrian River *Orontes*, then the Pacific ('peaceful') *Ocean barred* by the Isthmus of *Darien* (Panama). Note that every landscape feature mentioned is a sea or river; probably in order to suggest Satan's gradual insinuation into the water of life. In this connection it is significant that St Jerome, St Ambrose, St Epiphanius and others identified the *Ganges* with Pison, one of the four rivers of Paradise of *Gen.* ii 10. The seven features are divided four and three, just as the circlings of the globe were (see ll. 64–6*n* above); only here the north–south features number three, the east–west features four. The geographical journey is thus an anti-creation, just as the astronomical journey was. *barred*] Alludes to the creation-myth at *Job* xxxviii 10f: at the separation of land and sea God 'set bars and doors' to the ocean.

ix *84*. Roughly corresponding to the forming and naming of the species in the week of creation. See l. 63*n* above.

The serpent subtlest beast of all the field.
Him after long debate, irresolute
Of thoughts revolved, his final sentence chose
Fit vessel, fittest imp of fraud, in whom
To enter, and his dark suggestions hide
From sharpest sight: for in the wily snake,
Whatever sleights none would suspicious mark,
As from his wit and native subtlety
Proceeding, which in other beasts observed
Doubt might beget of diabolic power
Active within beyond the sense of brute.
Thus he resolved, but first from inward grief
His bursting passion into plaints thus poured:
  O earth, how like to heaven, if not preferred

ix *86*. In *Gen.* iii 1 the serpent's subtlety is directly connected with the temptation: 'Now the serpent was more subtil than any beast of the field which the Lord God had made. And he said unto the woman, Yea, hath God said, Ye shall not eat of every tree of the garden?'
ix *87*. *irresolute*] undecided.
ix *88*. *sentence*] judgment, decision.
ix *88–9*. *chose / Fit vessel*] Highly ironic, for it is only the divine potter who chooses vessels, 'one vessel unto honour, and another unto dishonour' (*Rom.* ix 20–4; cp. *Acts* ix 15, *2 Tim.* ii 21). The implication is that the final sentence on the serpent and on Satan will be that they are 'vessels of wrath fitted to destruction' (*Rom.* ix 22). See also v 348*n* above on 'fit vessels pure'.
ix *89*. Patrick Hume rightly perceived that M. is using a horticultural image here, but wrongly interpreted *imp* as the serpent stock on which *fraud* is grafted. In reality an imp is a shoot or slip, so that the serpent is fraud's scion or extension. The image implies that from the little slip represented by the serpent the Fall will grow and a whole new tree (world) of evil. There is possibly an allusion to St Paul's use of grafting as a symbol of Incorporation in Christ in *Rom.* xi.
ix *90*. *suggestions*] temptations.
ix *95*. *Doubt*] suspicion.
ix *99*. Raphael too thought the earth *like to heaven*. cp. vii 329.
ix *99–178*. Rajan 103f compares Satan's earlier plaints at iv 32ff: 'This time he addresses the earth instead of the sun and, just as the sun once reminded him of the glory he had lost, the earth now suggests to him the glory he is to recover.' (Satan must convince himself that earth is superior, in order to enhance the glory he wins by destroying it.) A consistent offsetting against the earlier soliloquy works to amplify Satan's decline. The contrast is even underlined structurally; the present soliloquy is succeeded by a serpent metamorphosis, whereas the earlier was preceded by metamorphosis to a cherub. The two soliloquies correspond almost exactly in length.

More justly, seat worthier of gods, as built
With second thoughts, reforming what was old!
For what god after better worse would build?
Terrestrial heaven, danced round by other heavens
That shine, yet bear their bright officious lamps,
Light above light, for thee alone, as seems,
In thee concentring all their precious beams
Of sacred influence: as God in heaven
Is centre, yet extends to all, so thou
Centring receivest from all those orbs; in thee,
Not in themselves, all their known virtue appears
Productive in herb, plant, and nobler birth
Of creatures animate with gradual life
Of growth, sense, reason, all summed up in man.

ix *101–2. second thoughts*] Satan's bad theology; an omniscient and provident God cannot be said to make mistakes or to correct them.
ix *103–13.* The case for a geocentric hypothesis, put at viii 86–114 by Raphael in the role of *advocatus diaboli*, is now put in a perverse form by Satan. Man's microcosmic nature no longer speaks 'the maker's high magnificence', but becomes instead an occasion for pride. *bright officious lamps*] Echoes Raphael's 'bright luminaries / Officious' (viii 98f; see ix 48–9*n*). Satan's use of *officious* may, however, be edged with contempt, for a reason suggested at 154f below. *as seems*] Avoids any suggestion of diabolic confirmation of anthropocentricity, such as Marlowe's Mephistophilis had accorded the conservative cosmology of an earlier generation. *in thee, / Not in themselves*] Corresponds to Raphael's 'the sun that barren shines, / Whose virtue on itself works no effect, / But in the fruitful earth' (viii 94–6); though the application is very different. Satan makes use of the same point at the height of the temptation, ll. 721f. For the productive effect of stellar influence, see also iii 608–12*n*; and for the sacredness of light iii 1–55*n*.
ix *103.* On the stellar motions as a dance, see iii 579–81*n*. *Terrestrial heaven* means 'heaven on earth', whereas *heavens* means 'spheres'. Such rapid semantic transitions, concealed by surface harmonies and fluent unbroken syntax, are characteristic of Satan's sophistical style.
ix *108–9.* Again a confusion of thought: receiving is not really like extending. The idea that 'God is an infinite sphere, whose centre is everywhere, whose circumference nowhere' was widespread among Renaissance Neoplatonists. For a particularly fine expression of it, see Nicholas of Cusa, *De docta ignorantia* ed. E. Hoffmann and R. Klibansky (1932) 104.
ix *112–13. gradual*] arranged in grades or steps; *growth, sense* and *reason* are the activities of the vegetable, animal and rational souls in man respectively. Plant life exhibited the first, and animal life the first and second; but only man and a few of the higher animals combined all three.

With what delight could I have walked thee round,
If I could joy in aught, sweet interchange
Of hill, and valley, rivers, woods and plains,
Now land, now sea, and shores with forest crowned,
Rocks, dens, and caves; but I in none of these
Find place or refuge; and the more I see
Pleasures about me, so much more I feel
Torment within me, as from the hateful siege
Of contraries; all good to me becomes
Bane, and in heaven much worse would be my state.
But neither here seek I, no nor in heaven
To dwell, unless by mastering heaven's supreme;
Nor hope to be my self less miserable
By what I seek, but others to make such
As I, though thereby worse to me redound:
For only in destroying I find ease

ix *114*. *Ed I* has no comma after *round*.

ix *115*. Satan's one remaining joy lies in destruction: see ll. 477–9. For the pleasure demons take in landscape, see Henry More, *The immortality of the soul* (1659) III iv 7.

ix *116–18*. The landscape features include several pairs of *contraries*–which, however, are pleasant, unlike those in Satan's mind (ll. 121f). Thus *hill* opposes *valley*, *woods plains* and *land sea*. The patterning of the items, which is complex, includes yet another use of the sovereign central position. Thus the *forest crowned* is physically above the *shore* in the central position, between *land* and *sea*, in the central line of the three composing the list. Note that the first line repeats exactly the centralized pattern of viii 275: 'Ye hills and dales, ye rivers, woods, and plains'.

ix *119*. *place or refuge*] Bentley wanted 'place of refuge', but M. obviously means to depart from this idiom just far enough to add a further meaning. Newton rightly paraphrases: '*I in none of these find place* to dwell in *or refuge* from divine vengeance.'

ix *120–2*. Since Satan is surrounded by *pleasures*, and carries *torment* within him, the *siege / Of contraries* is the 'beleaguering' of pain by its contrary; a novel version of the allegorical siege, in which it was usually Satan, with pleasure as his ally, who beleaguered the human soul. But siege could also mean 'throne', so that there may be a punning allusion to Satan's having brought *torment* (cp. iv 75) from his hellish kingdom of opposites, where he rules over all that is contrary to Paradise.

ix *122–3*. Closely corresponding to iv 109f. Satan's state would be worse in heaven, presumably, because the contraries there would be more intense.

ix *126–8*. Confirming Raphael's interpretation of Satan's motives, at vi 900–7.

ix *129–30*. Cp. ll. 115 and 477–9.

To my relentless thoughts; and him destroyed,
Or won to what may work his utter loss,
For whom all this was made, all this will soon
Follow, as to him linked in weal or woe,
In woe then; that destruction wide may range:
To me shall be the glory sole among
The infernal powers, in one day to have marred
What he almighty styled, six nights and days
Continued making, and who knows how long
Before had been contriving, though perhaps
Not longer than since I in one night freed
From servitude inglorious well-nigh half
The angelic name, and thinner left the throng
Of his adorers: he to be avenged,
And to repair his numbers thus impaired,
Whether such virtue spent of old now failed
More angels to create, if they at least
Are his created, or to spite us more,

ix *133. Follow*] i.e., follow man to destruction; a shrewd prediction, which is fulfilled at x 651ff. See also ix 782–4*n*. A heavier stop is needed after *woe*.

ix *136–8*. Satan here anticipates a difficulty felt by many commentators in the *Genesis* account of creation: namely, that an omnipotent God should require time to create; see vii 154*n* and 176–9*n* above. For the structural symmetry between the periods of creation and destruction, see ix 63*n* above. How Satan learned the time required for creation is not clear: perhaps this piece of information formed part of the rumour mentioned at ii 346, perhaps Uriel told him, perhaps it is evident to any angelic intelligence that such a work must take six days, perhaps M. nodded.

ix *138–9. Who . . . contriving*] For M.'s opinion of the folly of speculating that God spent an eternity predestining election and reprobation, see vii 90–2*n*. The flaw in that line of thought is exploited here by Satan, whose insinuation is that God's creative efforts were laborious.

ix *139–43*. Implying lack of providence on God's part, as well as the contingency of creation on Satan's initiative. This suggestion is flatly contradicted not only by the one immediately before it, but also by the fact of the existence of an ancient rumour of creation, referred to, e.g., by Beelzebub at ii 346. (*Pace* Gilbert, 132f, who sees the inconsistency as M.'s, not Satan's.) *well nigh half*] An exaggeration; see ii 692*n*.

ix *144–7*. Contemplation of nature, which even to Satan is clear evidence of God's creativity, again leads him inexorably to the awkward matter of his own creatureliness; see iv 43*n* and iii 740*n*. He has to resist the implication of his own words by adding the hasty proviso *if . . . created*. *virtue*] power.

ix *147*. *Ed I* omits comma after *created*.

ix *147–51*. See iv 359*n*. Satan means only to be contemptuous that the

Determined to advance into our room
A creature formed of earth, and him endow,
Exalted from so base original,
With heavenly spoils, our spoils: what he decreed
He effected; man he made, and for him built
Magnificent this world, and earth his seat,
Him lord pronounced, and, O indignity!
Subjected to his service angel wings,
And flaming ministers to watch and tend
Their earthly charge: of these the vigilance
I dread, and to elude, thus wrapped in mist
Of midnight vapour glide obscure, and pry
In every bush and brake, where hap may find
The serpent sleeping, in whose mazy folds
To hide me, and the dark intent I bring.
O foul descent! That I who erst contended
With gods to sit the highest, am now constrained
Into a beast, and mixed with bestial slime,
This essence to incarnate and imbrute,

human race, vile and dust-born as it is, should be favoured by God (cp. ii 350) and given the rebels' possessions or offices (*OED* s.v. *Spoils* I 1–4). But unwittingly he prophesies also the exaltation of human nature through the Incarnation and Christ's second victory over Satan, in which human nature was very often referred to as 'spoil' ('the armour or body of the slain': *OED* II 5–6). Cp. iii 250f, where Christ himself prophesies: 'I shall rise victorious, and subdue / My vanquisher, spoiled of his vaunted spoil'. Both the contempt for man's material origin and the prophecy of Christ's victory have analogues in a speech of Tasso's Satan, *Gerus. lib.* iv 10f. *original*] origin.

ix *154–7*. Cp. *Ps.* xci 11 ('he shall give his angels charge over thee') and *Heb.* i 14 ('ministering spirits, sent forth to minister for them who shall be heirs of salvation'). *flaming ministers*] Cp. xi 101, where the cherubim are 'flaming warriors'; and see *Ps.* civ 4.

ix *158*. *wrapped*] spelt 'wrapt', which could conceivably also indicate rapt='carried' (*OED* 6).

ix *164*. *constrained*] compressed, contracted (*OED* 7); forced (*OED* 1) But the image of l. 89 above might be taken to support a third meaning: forced out; produced by effort; produced in opposition to nature (*OED* 3).

ix *166*. With Satan's reluctance to *incarnate* his essence, however briefly, contrast Christ's willingness to undertake the permanent incarnation of his incomparably purer essence (iii 227ff; see Ricks 73). For the angels' 'ethereal' or 'empyreal' *essence* or substance, cp. i 117, 138, and v 499, and see vi 328–34*nn*. Gilbert 93 argues that there is an internal inconsistency at this point, since no indication is given that this is not the first time Satan has taken the form of a beast. But perhaps he has to become *incarnate* in a way

That to the highth of deity aspired;
But what will not ambition and revenge
Descend to? Who aspires must down as low
As high he soared, obnoxious first or last
To basest things. Revenge, at first though sweet,
Bitter ere long back on it self recoils;
Let it; I reck not, so it light well aimed,
Since higher I fall short, on him who next
Provokes my envy, this new favourite
Of heaven, this man of clay, son of despite,
Whom us the more to spite his maker raised
From dust: spite then with spite is best repaid.
    So saying, through each thicket dank or dry,
Like a black mist low creeping, he held on
His midnight search, where soonest he might find
The serpent: him fast sleeping soon he found
In labyrinth of many a round self rolled,
His head the midst, well stored with subtle wiles:
Not yet in horrid shade or dismal den,
Nor nocent yet, but on the grassy herb

he never was before, in order to be able actually to speak through the serpent. The lion, tiger and toad were mute.

ix *170. obnoxious . . . to*] open to the influence of; exposed to (*OED* 4).

ix *172–4. recoils* and *well aimed* and *fall short* belong to an allegoria that recalls the cannon simile used by Satan in his first soliloquy; see iv 13–19*n*. Throughout Satan's speeches his aggressiveness is indirectly suggested in this way by his choice of imagery. *higher*] i.e., when I aim higher, at God, I fall short.

ix *175*. For spite and envy as Satan's motives, see ii 379–85, iv 358–92 and 381–5*n*. St Augustine explained Satan's motives similarly, in *Civ. Dei* xiv 11: 'that proud, and therefore envious angel . . . envying man's constancy'.

ix *180*. The analogue usually cited, Homer, *Il.* i 359, is not very close. Perhaps M. had in mind *Gen.* ii 6, 'there went up a mist from the earth'; which would make Satan's disguise particularly effective. But the loyal cherubim also move like mist: cp. xii 629–32. Hughes cites Sylvester's *Du Bartas*: 'As in liquid clouds (exhaled thickly), / Water and Ayr (as moist) do mingle quickly, / The evill Angells slide too easily, / As subtle spirits into our fantasie.'

ix *185. horrid*] bristling; frightful, dreadful. Not a Latinism. *dismal*] sinister; dark, gloomy.

ix *186. Nor nocent*] Not nocent *Ed I*, a possible but uneuphonious reading: both 'nor harmful' (*OED* A 1) and 'nor guilty; innocent' (*OED* A 2). The phrase is heavily charged, for it refers not only to the serpent's becoming morally harmful when Satan possesses it, but also to its 'guilty' part in the

Fearless unfeared he slept: in at his mouth
The devil entered, and his brutal sense,
In heart or head, possessing soon inspired
With act intelligential; but his sleep
Disturbed not, waiting close the approach of morn.
Now when as sacred light began to dawn
In Eden on the humid flowers, that breathed
Their morning incense, when all things that breathe,
From the earth's great altar send up silent praise
To the creator, and his nostrils fill
With grateful smell, forth came the human pair
And joined their vocal worship to the choir
Of creatures wanting voice, that done, partake
The season, prime for sweetest scents and airs:
Then commune how that day they best may ply
Their growing work: for much their work outgrew

Fall, and to its change of habit and habitat (as a result of the curse of x 163–81), when it becomes physically harmful. *grassy herb*] cp. Virgil, *Ecl.* v 26, *graminis . . . herbam.*
ix *187. at his mouth*] Because the soul was often said to enter and leave the body by that orifice. See Didron ii 173f.
ix *188. brutal*] animal.
ix *190. act intelligential*] (the power of) intelligent action. A precise phrase, since in Aristotelian thought the term 'act' was reserved for rational agents, and denied to both animals and children; see *Eud. Ethics* 1224[a].
ix *191. close*] concealed.
ix *192.* The morning of Day 32; see Introduction, 'Chronology' (p. 444). For the sacredness of light, see iii 1–6*nn.* *whenas*] when.
ix *195–7.* Closely considered, *altar* might be thought to constitute a dramatic irony; for it can have no purpose other than sacrifice. Cp. *Gen.* viii 21 and *Lev.* i 9, where God is said to enjoy the 'sweet savour' of burnt offerings. However, one should also remember, in this connection, the Penitential Psalm, li 17: 'The sacrifices of God are a broken spirit.' Of the latter, *praise* might be the prelapsarian equivalent.
ix *198–200. choir . . . wanting voice*] Less paradoxical than it has come to seem: 'choir' commonly meant any orderly band or group of people or even of objects (*OED* 6). However, the modern meaning is probably present in a secondary way, just as *airs* suggests 'melodies' (see Ricks 106); both the voiceless *creatures* and the *season* almost succeed in uttering audible praise. *prime*, in this ecclesiastical context, must have something of its force at v 170 ('the first canonical Hour': see v 18–25*n* and 170*n*).
ix *199.* A heavier stop is needed after *voice.*
ix *201. commune*] Stressed on the first syllable. Both distributions of stress were common, and both were used by M. In view of ll. 195–7*n*, it may be relevant that *commune* could mean 'take communion'.

The hands' dispatch of two, gardening so wide.
And Eve first to her husband thus began.
  Adam, well may we labour still to dress
This garden, still to tend plant, herb and flower,
Our pleasant task enjoined, but till more hands
Aid us, the work under our labour grows,
Luxurious by restraint; what we by day
Lop overgrown, or prune, or prop, or bind,
One night or two with wanton growth derides
Tending to wild. Thou therefore now advise
Or hear what to my mind first thoughts present,
Let us divide our labours, thou where choice

ix *204*. Note that Eve speaks *first*, something she has not previously done. The point is underlined by *first thoughts* (l. 213). Contrast v 17ff and esp. iv 408–10, where Adam's right to the initiative seems insisted on.
ix *205–384*. As Burden 86ff points out, the main lines of this debate are determined by the logical requirements of M.'s matter. Eve has to be alone intentionally, and Adam has to condone her being alone, in order that both may be fully responsible for their Fall. There must be nothing accidental about the events: man's own actions must constitute at each stage the 'cause'.
ix *206*. *Ed I* misprints full stop after *flower*.
ix *207–8*. *till ... us*] Forestalls any accusation of improvidence on God's part. The work may be too great for Adam and Eve; but this has been foreseen and provided for by the command to 'be fruitful, and multiply' (*Gen*. i 22, 28; *PL* vii 531).
ix *209–12*. M. was committed by *Gen*. i 28 to the view that even prelapsarian nature had to be 'subdued'. *luxurious*] luxuriant (*OED* 4). *wanton*] profuse (*OED* 7); unmanageable. But both words are also meant to suggest their less innocent moral meanings. Nature has a continual tendency to wildness that Eve is perhaps already beginning to experience almost as a moral temptation. *wild*] (Vb.) grow wild, or make wild.
ix *213*. *hear*] bear *Ed II*: probably a misprint; though it is by no means an impossible reading (bear = tolerate). Having given Adam the choice between considering for himself or listening to her, Eve chooses for him by immediately going on to present her own scheme.
ix *214*. *Pace* John Crowe Ransom, *God without Thunder* (1931) 133f, the division of labour referred to here has little directly to do with that of the political economist or the efficiency expert. (Though it is true that, in so far as she argues about means without considering ends, Eve resembles, in a general way, the modern technocrat. Note that Adam (l. 241) soon brings the debate back to the 'end of human life'.) The division should rather be seen as an expression of the *dyad*, the divisive principle, moral or cosmic, in the Pythagorean system. Cp. the separation of Redcrosse and Una in *F.Q.* I ii 9, and see Fowler 7f.

Leads thee, or where most needs, whether to wind
The woodbine round this arbour, or direct
The clasping ivy where to climb, while I
In yonder spring of roses intermixed
With myrtle, find what to redress till noon:
For while so near each other thus all day
Our task we choose, what wonder if so near
Looks intervene and smiles, or object new
Casual discourse draw on, which intermits
Our day's work brought to little, though begun
Early, and the hour of supper comes unearned.
    To whom mild answer Adam thus returned.
Sole Eve, associate sole, to me beyond
Compare above all living creatures dear,
Well hast thou motioned, well thy thoughts employed
How we might best fulfil the work which here

ix *216–19*. Eve 'doesn't care what he does, and she knows very well what she will do' (Ricks 144). After the argument we see her exactly where she had first insisted she was going–in the *spring of roses intermixed / With myrtle* (cp. ll. 426–31). Note also, however, the contrast between the two pairs of plants mentioned. The *ivy* need only be directed to climb the 'married elm', for it to make an emblem of true love like that used above at v 215f. *Woodbine*-honeysuckle has a similar meaning, which M. further specifies by locating the plant at the nuptial bower (*arbour*). Cp. Vaughan, 'Upon the Priorie Grove', 13f: 'Only the Woodbine here may twine, / As th'Embleme of her Love, and mine'; also Stanley, *Poems and Translations*, ed. Crump (1962) 26, 'Love's innocence'. Shakespeare combined both emblems at *Midsummer Night's Dream* IV i 48–51: Titania embracing her lover says: 'So doth the woodbine the sweet honeysuckle / Gently entwist; the female ivy so / Enrings the barky fingers of the elm. / O! how I love thee; how I dote on thee!' Eve, on the other hand, is determined to leave the bower for a pair of plants associated by Ovid with a goddess' defence of her virtue; see ll. 426–33*nn* below. Emblematically, she is abandoning the interdependence of true love for the independence of a dangerous adventure. *spring*] grove of young trees. *redress*] raise again to an erect position (horticultural: *OED* 1 a). In the event, however, Eve '"her self, though fairest unsupported Flour" will be "drooping unsustained"' (Ricks 146).

ix *222–5*. On the irony here, that after separation an *object new* (the snake) will draw on far from *Casual discourse* and bring to nothing much more than their day's work, see Ricks *ibid*.

ix *225*. The irony is very exact. Not only will their *supper* be *unearned*, as things turn out, but even *the hour of supper*; since their crime carries sentence of death 'that day' (viii 331).

ix *227*. *Sole Eve*: i.e., sole mother; see *Gen*. iii 20.

ix *229*. *motioned*] proposed.

God hath assigned us, nor of me shalt pass
Unpraised: for nothing lovelier can be found
In woman, than to study household good,
And good works in her husband to promote.
Yet not so strictly hath our Lord imposed
Labour, as to debar us when we need
Refreshment, whether food, or talk between,
Food of the mind, or this sweet intercourse
Of looks and smiles, for smiles from reason flow,
To brute denied, and are of love the food,
Love not the lowest end of human life.
For not to irksome toil, but to delight
He made us, and delight to reason joined.
These paths and bowers doubt not but our joint hands
Will keep from wilderness with ease, as wide
As we need walk, till younger hands ere long
Assist us: but if much converse perhaps
Thee satiate, to short absence I could yield.
For solitude sometimes is best society,
And short retirement urges sweet return.
But other doubt possesses me, lest harm
Befall thee severed from me; for thou know'st
What hath been warned us, what malicious foe
Envying our happiness, and of his own
Despairing, seeks to work us woe and shame
By sly assault; and somewhere nigh at hand
Watches no doubt, with greedy hope to find
His wish and best advantage, us asunder,
Hopeless to circumvent us joined, where each
To other speedy aid might lend at need;
Whether his first design be to withdraw
Our fealty from God, or to disturb

ix *245. wilderness*] uncultivated condition. On the progressive increase of wildness in *PL*, see ll. 209–12*n* and MacCaffrey 131f.

ix *247. converse*] Stressed on the second syllable.

ix *249.* Cp. *PR* i 302. Cicero's aphorism, *numquam minus solus quam cum solus* (*De rep.* I xvii 27 and *De off.* III i 1); was said by Cowley to have become 'a very vulgar saying' ('Of Solitude'). Defended by Sir George MacKenzie in *A moral essay, preferring solitude to publick employment* (Edinburgh 1665), Cicero's position was an antique strong-point of some strategic importance in the long campaign fought through the seventeenth and eighteenth centuries between the devotees of retirement and of public life.

ix *250.* Poetic syntax: Adam cannot bear to think of a long *retirement*, and so, touchingly, he adds *short*, though it works against the logical prose meaning of the rest of the line.

ix *262. fealty*] The feudal obligation of vassal to lord; fidelity.

Conjugal love, than which perhaps no bliss
Enjoyed by us excites his envy more;
Or this, or worse, leave not the faithful side
That gave thee being, still shades thee and protects.
The wife, where danger or dishonour lurks,
Safest and seemliest by her husband stays,
Who guards her, or with her the worst endures.
To whom the virgin majesty of Eve,
As one who loves, and some unkindness meets,
With sweet austere composure thus replied.
Offspring of heaven and earth, and all earth's lord,
That such an enemy we have, who seeks
Our ruin, both by thee informed I learn,
And from the parting angel overheard
As in a shady nook I stood behind,
Just then returned at shut of evening flowers.
But that thou shouldst my firmness therefore doubt
To God or thee, because we have a foe
May tempt it, I expected not to hear.
His violence thou fear'st not, being such,
As we, not capable of death or pain,
Can either not receive, or can repel.
His fraud is then thy fear, which plain infers
Thy equal fear that my firm faith and love

ix *265. Or this, or worse*] whether this, or worse (be his first design). The creation of Eve from Adam's side is described at viii 465ff: she was taken from the side nearer his heart, and so from the *faithful* side.
ix *267–9.* In accordance with the adoption of a tragic mode (see l. 6 above), the style has become noticeably sententious; cp. ll. 232–4, etc. Adam's abstract generalizations not only demonstrate his full moral responsibility, but also conceal bitter ironies. In the present case, we know that Adam will endure the worst with Eve in a sense very different from that he intends–not faithfully, but desperately.
ix *270. virgin*] chaste, innocent; *virgin majesty* is a formula, but not only a formula. As the Fall nears, Eve's innocence and integrity are expressed more and more in sexual terms. Cp. ll. 216–19 above, and 396, 466–31, etc. below. For the tradition that Satan tempted Eve sexually, see Svendsen 277.
ix *272. Ed II* erroneously has comma after *replied.*
ix *273.* Contrast the informality of l. 205: Eve is now standing on her dignity.
ix *276.* Eve's knowledge of the prohibition was often stressed by commentators; see Williams 114. The warning referred to here is viii 633–43; though Eve was also present when Raphael gave his more specific warning at vi 900ff. *overheard*] Taken by some to imply eavesdropping, a sign of moral deterioration in Eve; but this is perhaps a forced interpretation.
ix *278. shut*] the time of shutting (poetic).

Can by his fraud be shaken or seduced;
Thoughts, which how found they harbour in thy breast
Adam, misthought of her to thee so dear?
To whom with healing words Adam replied.
Daughter of God and man, immortal Eve,
For such thou art, from sin and blame entire:
Not diffident of thee do I dissuade
Thy absence from my sight, but to avoid
The attempt it self, intended by our foe.
For he who tempts, though in vain, at least asperses
The tempted with dishonour foul, supposed
Not incorruptible of faith, not proof
Against temptation: thou thy self with scorn
And anger wouldst resent the offered wrong,
Though ineffectual found: misdeem not then,
If such affront I labour to avert
From thee alone, which on us both at once
The enemy, though bold, will hardly dare,
Or daring, first on me the assault shall light.
Nor thou his malice and false guile contemn;
Subtle he needs must be, who could seduce
Angels, nor think superfluous others' aid.
I from the influence of thy looks receive

ix *287. seduced*] See l. 270*n*.

ix *288–9.* The syntax is defended against Peter by Ricks (34f), who is surely right in treating it as a rendering of the disjointedness of actual speech. Thus there is a shift of construction between *Thoughts, which* and the more direct *how found they. . . .* The indignant, sharp word-play in *misthought*–'not thoughts, *mis*-thoughts rather'–confirms this interpretation. *Ed I* has comma after *breast*.

ix *291.* The formula used by Adam exactly balances the formula Eve used at 273; for she was created out of *man*, as Adam was out of 'earth'. But it is a *healing word*, in that it implies that for him to mistrust her would be to mistrust his own substance. *Eve* implies 'mother of all living' (Gen. iii 20); so that the line has an internal symmetry. But the primary sense depends on another Hebrew meaning of *Eve*: 'subject unto thee': it is to this, as much as to *immortal*, that *such* in the following line refers. The point that Eve is in a way Adam's daughter makes unexpected sense of M.'s puzzling statement in the *De doctrina* that the first sin included parricide (see ll. 1003–4*n*); for Eve killed Adam by persuading him to eat the forbidden fruit.

ix *292. entire*] unblemished, blameless; not a Latinism.

ix *293. diffident*] mistrustful. One of the preoccupations of Bk ix is mistrust, with its various forms and objects; cp. e.g., ll. 6, 355, 357.

ix *296. asperses*] spatters; falsely charges (*OED* 4).

ix *298. faith*] fidelity.

Access in every virtue, in thy sight
More wise, more watchful, stronger, if need were
Of outward strength; while shame, thou looking on,
Shame to be overcome or over-reached
Would utmost vigour raise, and raised unite.
Why shouldst not thou like sense within thee feel
When I am present, and thy trial choose
With me, best witness of thy virtue tried.
  So spake domestic Adam in his care
And matrimonial love; but Eve, who thought
Less attributed to her faith sincere,
Thus her reply with accent sweet renewed.
  If this be our condition, thus to dwell
In narrow circuit straitened by a foe,
Subtle or violent, we not endued
Single with like defence, wherever met,
How are we happy, still in fear of harm?
But harm precedes not sin: only our foe
Tempting affronts us with his foul esteem

ix *310. Access*] addition, increase. It was a fundamental doctrine of Renaissance Neoplatonism that love inspires the lover to virtue: 'Such is the powre of that sweet passion, / That it all sordid basenesse doth expell, / And the refyned mynd doth newly fashion / Unto a fairer forme, which now doth dwell / in his high thought, that would it selfe excell; which he beholding still with constant sight, / Admires the mirrour of so heavenly light' (Spenser, *An Hymne of Love* 190–6). Especially in Petrarchan poetry, this effect was above all ascribed to the glance of the beloved; Sidney's Astrophil, e.g., exclaims: 'O eyes . . . / Whose beames be joyes, whose joyes all vertues be' (*Astrophil and Stella* xlii). Thus Adam should be regarded as wooing Eve, at this point, with the arguments of a love poet.
ix *312–14.* Just as the influence of love would increase Adam's *virtue* or power, so shame also would increase his *vigour* (rigorous force) and join it to his virtue. Love and shame were thought of as contrary passions.
ix *318. domestic*] concerned about the wellbeing of the family.
ix *319. Ed I* has comma after *love.*
ix *320. Less*] too little; a Latinism. *attributed*] Stressed on the third syllable. *sincere*] pure, morally uncorrupted, or true. *Fides sincera* was a watchword or semitechnical theological term among the Reformers.
ix *322–41.* Unless Eve is right here, M. appears to be contradicting the rejection of cloistered virtue in *Areopagitica* (Waldock 22). But the point of the present speech is that Eve is already being tested: since her dream she has been drawn in the direction of excessive strength and curiosity.
is *328–30. affronts*] The primary meaning is 'insults' or 'causes to feel ashamed, put to the blush'; but a secondary meaning, 'sets face to face' is played on by *front*= face. In this connection, see l. 358*n* below.

Of our integrity: his foul esteem
Sticks no dishonour on our front, but turns
Foul on himself; then wherefore shunned or feared
By us? Who rather double honour gain
From his surmise proved false, find peace within,
Favour from heaven, our witness from the event.
And what is faith, love, virtue unassayed
Alone, without exterior help sustained?
Let us not then suspect our happy state
Left so imperfect by the maker wise,
As not secure to single or combined;
Frail is our happiness, if this be so,
And Eden were no Eden thus exposed.

ix *329. integrity*] Like 'entire' (l. 292) and 'unite' (l. 314), emphasises the completeness, unity and wholesomeness–in short, the monadic quality–of innocent virtue. See l. 214*n*.

ix *334.* But it is not from the *event* (result) that the true believer ought to expect *witness*, for that would be justification by works. Rather 'the Spirit itself beareth witness . . . that we are the children of God' (*Rom.* viii 16). With modern punctuation there would be a comma after *witness.*

ix *335.* Cp. *Areopagitica* (Yale ii 527): in the absence of freedom to encounter temptation 'what were vertue but a name?' *faith, love, virtue*] Alluding to the Neoplatonic Triad of Fidius, Alciati's *Fidei symbolum* (Embl. ix, p. 55–7); on which see P. L. Williams in *JWI* iv (1941). In the Triad of Fidius, Veritas and Virtus appear with linked hands, united by a third, Amor. Thus the answer to Eve's rhetorical question is, They are an emblem of integrity and faithfulness, if only they stay together with linked hands. In view of Miss Williams's demonstration that the Triad of Fidius is related to Pico's triad of human nature (*intellectus, ratio* and *voluntas* or the passionate part), it is significant that many passages in *PL* suggest that Adam allegorically represents *intellectus* or *mens*, Eve *ratio* or *anima*. See ll. 358*n*, 360–1*n*, and 385–6*n*. One suspects that the present scene is intended in part as a tableau, in which Intellectus and Ratio adopt appropriate roles and exhibit even the physical arrangement (see ll. 385f) of the Triad of Fidius emblem.

We should not assume that because in *Areopagitica* M. rejects 'cloistered virtue' he therefore approves Eve's sentiments here, in the very different context of an unfallen world. At least before the Fall it hardly has the same force to say 'how much we . . . expell of sin, so much we expell of virtue' (*Areopagitica*, Yale ii 527). At the same time, M. would naturally want to involve his own cherished convictions and aspirations in Eve's dangerous individualism; both for the sake of idealizing her, and in the interests of self-discovery.

ix *339.* Some copies of *Ed II* have an illegible point (not semicolon) after *combined. Ed I* has full stop.

ix *341. no Eden*] i.e., no pleasure, the literal Hebrew meaning of 'Eden'.

To whom thus Adam fervently replied.
O woman, best are all things as the will
Of God ordained them, his creating hand
Nothing imperfect or deficient left
Of all that he created, much less man,
Or aught that might his happy state secure,
Secure from outward force; within himself
The danger lies, yet lies within his power:
Against his will he can receive no harm.
But God left free the will, for what obeys
Reason, is free, and reason he made right,
But bid her well beware, and still erect,
Lest by some fair appearing good surprised
She dictate false, and misinform the will
To do what God expressly hath forbid.
Not then mistrust, but tender love enjoins,
That I should mind thee oft, and mind thou me.

ix *342. fervently*] Often taken as a euphemism for 'angrily', but Adam is 'first incensed' only at l. 1162.
ix *343. O woman*] Not a cold form of address but a reminder of the ontological relation instituted between man and wo-man. The implication is that Eve has been pressing for an unsuitable form of liberty (Burden 88).
ix *347–8. secure, / Secure*] The repetition has a certain ironic force. By the second *secure*, Adam means only 'safe, carefree' (*OED* A II 3 c); but Eve is being conspicuously *secure* in another sense: 'over-confident' (*OED* A I 1 a). It is a key word in *PL*, related to the faith / distrust complex. Cp. e.g., l. 371 below, and 339, iv 791 above; and see l. 293*n* above.
ix *351–6*. Cp. *Areopagitica*: 'Many there be that complain of divin Providence for suffering *Adam* to transgresse, foolish tongues! when God gave him reason, he gave him freedom to choose, for reason is but choosing; he had bin else a meer artificiall *Adam*, such an Adam as he is in the motions [puppet-shows]' (Yale ii 527); where however, the application is almost exactly contrary. *still erect*] always attentive; but also with a glance at *right* = upright.
ix *354*. So Eve is in the event *surprised* by Satan: see l. 551.
ix *358. mind thee . . . mind thou me*] The repetition of *mind* ('admonish' and 'pay heed to') punningly brings into play the third of the divisions of human nature that provide the psychological scheme of the present passage. We have already had Reason and Will, and now we get a hint that Adam himself stands for Mind. The same threefold division was alluded to more obliquely in the Triad of Fidius at l. 335. Note that in the Triad, Mind (Veritas) and Reason (Virtus) are opposed face to face, because it is the function of Reason to reflect obediently, and to translate into practical terms, the truth contemplated by Mind. (See Williams, *art. cit.* l. 335*n*.) This reflexive relation seems to be rendered in the symmetry of the present

Firm we subsist, yet possible to swerve,
Since reason not impossibly may meet
Some specious object by the foe suborned,
And fall into deception unaware,
Not keeping strictest watch, as she was warned.
Seek not temptation then, which to avoid
Were better, and most likely if from me
Thou sever not: trial will come unsought.
Wouldst thou approve thy constancy, approve
First thy obedience; the other who can know,
Not seeing thee attempted, who attest?
But if thou think, trial unsought may find

line: *I . . . thee . . . thou me*. Throughout *PL* repetitive figures, especially those developed on a large scale, are used to express a responsive relation of obedient love. See, e.g., iv 639–56*n* (Adam and Eve); iii 131, 145, 227 (God and Messiah); and x 1098–1104*n* (God and man).

ix *360–1*. Since it is Eve who meets the *specious object* (in the shape of the serpent), these lines give the clearest possible indication that Eve is allegorically cast in the role of Reason, *ratio*, the faculty that chooses and directs the will. Cp. ll. 351f, and see *Areopagitica* (Yale ii 527): 'reason is but choosing'. This symbolism was by no means peculiar to M.; on the contrary, in a cruder form it was so commonplace as to be the subject of a chapter in a school textbook, Valeriano's *Hieroglyphica* (xiv 26, p. 176 *Sensus a Voluptate, Mens a Sensu Decepta*; also 27, p. 177). It goes back to St Augustine (*Enarr. in Ps.* xlviii), for whom, whoever, *caro nostra Eva est, quae seducit virum, id est, rationem*. Valeriano's version of the allegory, in which Eve represents *sensus* and Adam *intellectus*, may be regarded as logically intermediate between St Augustine's and M.'s. The ultimate source of the tradition is probably Philo, *De opificio* 165 (Loeb i 131).

ix *361*. Ordinary reasoning on *a priori* grounds would let Adam see that it would take an *object* to tempt them. See ll. 413*n* below.

ix *367*. *approve*] demonstrate; make proof of; test.

ix *370–5*. One of the most critical passages in the whole poem. Waldock 34 goes as far as to attribute the Fall to Adam's failure to assume full responsibility here–an interpretation that comes very close to Eve's accusation in ll. 1155–61. With more penetration, Burden 89ff suggests that M. has a theological difficulty: If Adam was not deceived (*1 Tim.* ii 14) how could his judgment at this point fail, unless God had been improvident in creating him? The answer may be that Adam, the image of God, here experiences the same kind of dilemma as God himself in iii 100ff. He sees the risk of letting Eve go perfectly well, as l. 361 shows; so that his judgment does not fail. But to keep Eve in passive obedience would be to lose her (with l. 372 cp. iii 110). Eve, already in the grip of temptation, has put Adam in an impossible position, transmitting to him the pressure, the excessive motion, put

Us both securer than thus warned thou seem'st,
Go; for thy stay, not free, absents thee more;
Go in thy native innocence, rely
On what thou hast of virtue, summon all,
For God towards thee hath done his part, do thine.
So spake the patriarch of mankind, but Eve
Persisted, yet submiss, though last, replied.
With thy permission then, and thus forwarned
Chiefly by what thy own last reasoning words
Touched only, that our trial, when least sought,
May find us both perhaps far less prepared,
The willinger I go, nor much expect
A foe so proud will first the weaker seek;
So bent, the more shall shame him his repulse.
Thus saying, from her husband's hand her hand
Soft she withdrew, and like a wood-nymph light
Oread or dryad, or of Delia's train,

on her by Satan. Perhaps, however, more emphasis should be laid on symbolic meanings of the separation. If Adam symbolizes intellect or *mens*, and Eve *ratio* (or perhaps *voluntas*), then the separation may be a loss of integration. Man fails to inform and support his moral choices with intellect and wisdom.

ix *371. securer*] more careless, more over-confident. Cp. ll. 347–8.

ix *377. submiss*] submissive. 'Eve persisted; yet she replied submissively (even if she insisted on having the last word).' The balanced words and phrases, and the successive qualifications, render the contradictions entering human nature, as well as miming Eve's persistence. Burden 92 comments that Eve, being unfallen, is submissive even when having the last word.

ix *383*. Whether or not the dramatic irony here is intentional, it is certainly difficult at this point to regard Eve as altogether the weaker of the two.

ix *385–6*. Clasped hands are an emblem of faith, troth, or concord, so that Eve withdrawing hers is symbolically breaking trust. The bond thus so broken will not be fully restored until xii 648. See l. 335*n* on the Triad of Fidius or *Fidei symbolum*, in which Veritas (*mens*) and Virtus (*ratio*) clasp hands. Ricks (90) thought that *Soft* may go with *hand*, secondarily, as a enhancing suggestion; but this is unlikely, since a monosyllabic adjective hardly ever follows a monosyllabic noun in English. *light*] Not merely 'nimble' (*OED* IV 15), but in the context clearly also 'unsteady, fickle' (*OED* IV 16). A true ambiguity; for the moral condition of Eve is at this point uncertain and in process of alteration.

ix *387. Oreads*] mountain nymphs, such as attended on Diana. *dryads*] wood nymphs. Neither class of nymphs were immortal; the dryads and hamadryads perished with the trees over which they presided.

ix *387–92*. The simile is so discriminating that it consists mainly of qualifications. Eve is like the immortal Diana (called *Delia* from Delos, her

Betook her to the groves, but Delia's self
In gait surpassed and goddess-like deport,
Though not as she with bow and quiver armed,
But with such gardening tools as art yet rude,
Guiltless of fire had formed, or angels brought.
To Pales, or Pomona thus adorned,

secluded island birthplace and refuge–see x 293–6*n*) in outward bearing (*deport*), but lacks the *quiver* of counsel (on which see Valeriano 525f). Instead she has gardening tools; but only *rude* ones, since before the Fall mechanical arts dependent on the invention of fire were unknown (see v 396*n*). *Guiltless of*] inexperienced in, unskilled in (*OED*'s first instance in this sense); but with a secondary allusion to the association of fire with man's guilt. Only as a result of the Fall did it become necessary for him to have some means of warming himself: see x 1078–81*n*. There may also be an allusion to the fire stolen from heaven by Prometheus, in a myth which was regarded as one of the main pagan distortions of the history of the Fall.

ix *393–6*. The previous simile was based on *gait*, this on equipment. In respect of the *gardening tools* she carries, Eve resembles *Pales*, the Roman goddess of pastures; *Pomona*, the nymph or goddess of fruit-trees (often represented sitting on a basket of flowers and fruit, holding in her hand apples); and *Ceres*, the goddess of corn and agriculture. The qualifications are again very precise. Pomona might be thought a morally favourable analogue, since Ovid described her as shutting herself in her orchard to escape male attentions, and as carrying 'no javelin, but the curved pruning-hook with which now she repressed the too luxuriant growth' (*Met.* xiv 628–36). M., however, specifically refers to her seduction by the disguised Vertumnus (*ibid.* 654ff). *fled*] Used ironically, for Pomona only fled Vertumnus until his guileful persuasions awakened 'answering passion' (*ibid.* 771). Ceres was occasionally represented with a plough, but far more usually with a lighted torch–the fire explicitly excluded at l. 392 above. The torch was the one she used to search for her daughter Proserpina, after Proserpina had been abducted by Pluto, in what was another of the main mythic analogues to the Fall. *Jove* is brought in not merely to shift the time back before the Fall to Ceres' virginity and its loss, but also to allude to his incestuous seduction of Proserpina, in the form of a serpent. For an inverted use of the same myths, in which Proserpina is the prelapsarian Eve and Ceres the postlapsarian, see iv 268–72 above; the inversion serves to render the deterioration taking place in Eve, or perhaps to move the action on to an atemporal plane altogether.

The present simile, like that immediately preceding, is three-fold; and refers, like it, to two sub-deities and one major goddess. But the simile of ll. 387–92 compared Eve to deities who preside over wild places, while observing that she nevertheless carried the tools of cultivation; this compares her to deities who preside over domesticated nature, while alluding to the

Likeliest she seemed, Pomona when she fled
Vertumnus, or to Ceres in her prime,
Yet virgin of Proserpina from Jove.
Her long with ardent look his eye pursued
Delighted, but desiring more her stay.
Oft he to her his charge of quick return
Repeated, she to him as oft engaged
To be returned by noon amid the bower,
And all things in best order to invite
Noontide repast, or afternoon's repose.
O much deceived, much failing, hapless Eve,
Of thy presumed return! Event perverse!
Thou never from that hour in Paradise
Found'st either sweet repast, or sound repose;
Such ambush hid among sweet flowers and shades
Waited with hellish rancour imminent
To intercept thy way, or send thee back

loss of virginity and sexual restraint. On wildness as a category in *PL*, see l. 245*n* above.

ix *394*. *Likeliest*] Likest *Ed I*, a paler word preferred by Newton and subsequent editors. But according to the principle whereby, other things being equal, the reading with the less usual word is favoured, one should prefer *Likeliest*, 'portraying most accurately' (*OED* s.v. *Likely* A 1). As a term of art criticism it is specially appropriate in the context of an iconographical simile. For comparable elision or synaloepha, see, e.g., l. 505 below.

ix *395*. Apart from the secondary reference to the time of day (see ll. 200*n* and *401n*), *prime* means simply 'in her best time; before the loss of Proserpina brought cares and suffering upon her'. There is no need to join Bentley and Empson in asking whether goddesses experience old age; though one must admire the latter's comment: 'the very richness of the garden makes it heavy with autumn. Ceres when virgin of the queen of Hell was already in her full fruitfulness upon the world; Eve is virgin of sin from Satan and of Cain, who in the Talmud was his child' (Empson[2] 185f).

ix *401*. For *noon* as the critical time of judgment in *PL*, see iv 30*n*; also ll. 739–40*n*.

ix *404–5*. 'Adam was not deceived, but the woman being deceived was in the transgression' (*1 Tim.* ii 14). Ricks 97 notices that at first we take *failing* absolutely, as part of a general apostrophe about Eve. 'But then the next line–"Of thy presum'd return!"–declares that she is *deceived in* the one present circumstance: her presumed return. So the lines are both tragically prophetic and dramatically momentary.' *event perverse*] adverse event, outcome. *hapless*] By parting from Adam Eve makes herself more exposed to the effects of chance. But the present exclamation is something of a trap for the unwary reader: Eve's fall will not just be bad luck. See l. 421*n*.

Despoiled of innocence, of faith, of bliss.
For now, and since first break of dawn the fiend,
Mere serpent in appearance, forth was come,
And on his quest, where likeliest he might find
The only two of mankind, but in them
The whole included race, his purposed prey.
In bower and field he sought, where any tuft
Of grove or garden-plot more pleasant lay,
Their tendance or plantation for delight,
By fountain or by shady rivulet
He sought them both, but wished his hap might find
Eve separate, he wished, but not with hope
Of what so seldom chanced, when to his wish,

ix *411. innocence . . . faith . . . bliss*] A triad of qualities that would be felt to correspond with the more ontological triad given at l. 335, 'faith, love, virtue'. Innocence is a condition of the virtuous part, as bliss or joy of the appetitive.

ix *413. Mere serpent*] plain serpent; i.e., he seemed just an ordinary serpent. M. is not specially concerned to exclude the half-humanized serpent common in Gothic paintings of the temptation (e.g. Hugo van der Goes' *Fall of Man*); though he would no doubt have agreed with Willet (48) that in human form Satan could never have deceived Eve, since she 'knewe well enough, that her selfe and Adam, were all mankind.' The point is a subtler one, to which commentators on Genesis iii devoted a good deal of space: namely, whether the serpent was a true serpent possessed, or only the appearance of a serpent. Thus Willet, like M., rejects the theory of Thomas Cajetan, 'who by a continued allegorie, by the serpent, would have the devill understood: that there was neither serpent in trueth nor in shew that appeared to Eva, but this tentation was altogether internall and spirituall: for by this meanes, the whole storie of the creation may as well be allegorized, and so the truth of the narration called in question, and beside, whereas the divell internally tempteth onley two wayes, either by alluring the sense by some object, or else by mooving and working the phantasie, our parents before their fall could not be so tempted, having no inordinate motion.' He also rejects St Cyril's opinion, 'that it was not a true serpent, but a shewe onely and apparition' (ll. 45f). M.'s phrase is very carefully drafted; 'serpent in appearance', e.g., without the *mere*, might have been taken to imply that he agreed with St Cyril.

ix *418–19*. The *garden plot* would be a *tendance* (object of care), the *grove* a *plantation*.

ix *421–5. wished . . . hap / wished . . . hope / wish . . . hope*] The sinuous verbal pattern here seems to Adams (89) 'verbal frippery', to Ricks (38), more subtly, a net woven by Satan.

ix *421*. In Satan's world picture, events usually occur either by necessity or by chance (*hap*). Cp. iv 530 and vii 172.

Beyond his hope, Eve separate he spies,
Veiled in a cloud of fragrance, where she stood,
Half spied, so thick the roses bushing round
About her glowed, oft stooping to support
Each flower of slender stalk, whose head though gay
Carnation, purple, azure, or specked with gold,
Hung drooping unsustained, them she upstays
Gently with myrtle band, mindless the while,
Her self, though fairest unsupported flower,
From her best prop so far, and storm so nigh.
Nearer he drew, and many a walk traversed
Of stateliest covert, cedar, pine, or palm,
Then voluble and bold, now hid, now seen
Among thick-woven arborets and flowers

ix *426–31*. See ll. 216–9*n*, and cp.ll. 628f. *roses . . . myrtle*] The two were associated in the festival of Venus; myrtle, to commemorate an occasion when wanton satyrs surprised Venus bathing, and the naked goddess hid behind a myrtle tree (Ovid, *Fasti* iv 138ff; for the Renaissance use of Faunus and satyr to symbolise Excess or Concupiscence or even Satan, see Fowler[3] 101). The rose, particularly when the focus is on the head as distinct from the leaves, as here, was a symbol of human frailty and of the mutability of mortal happiness (see Valeriano lv 1, *Imbecillitas humana*, 638f; also Ripa, s.v. *Amicitia*, where the rose signifies 'the pleasures of friendship, so long as a union of will is maintained'). Thus Eve's supporting the rose with myrtle should be read as an emblem of the dependence of unfallen bliss upon conjugal virtue. Her activity is the moral one of keeping up the marriage. For an iconographical use of the *myrtus coniugalis* in a similar sense, see Panofsky[2] 161f. Specifically sexual interpretations of the present passage (virginity supported by virtue, passion restrained by modesty, etc.) are not ruled out, but must clearly be subordinate. *Half spied*] for a moment we are allowed to think Eve concealed by the fragrance: see Ricks 95f. *purple, azure . . . gold*] the colours of Minerva, the virgin goddess. Cp. *Comus* 448 where in a similar situation the Lady carries a Minerva-shield of 'chaste austerity'. *mindless*] heedless; see l. 358*n*.

ix *432–3*. The syntax and the images of the preceding lines have worked to identify Eve very closely with the roses (note the ambiguous agreements, and such echoes as *stooping / drooping*); and now the identification is made explicit. Cp. iv 270, where Proserpina (and by implication Eve) was 'Herself a fairer flower' when she was carried off by the king of hell. *though fairest*] This implies condemnation of Adam: was it not his duty to prop this flower above all? Adam as Eve's prop returns to the emblems of ll. 216–19.

ix *435*. For the trees, cp. iv 139.

ix *436*. *voluble*] Punning between 'gliding easily with an undulating movement' (*OED* I 3) and 'glib, fluent' (*OED* II 5 a). Neither meaning is a Latinism.

Embordered on each bank, the hand of Eve:
Spot more delicious than those gardens feigned
Or of revived Adonis, or renowned
Alcinous, host of old Laertes' son,
Or that, not mystic, where the sapient king
Held dalliance with his fair Egyptian spouse.

ix *438. Embordered*] (Spelled 'Imborderd') set as a border. But the aptness of the image depends on some degree of fusion with 'Imbordured', a heraldic term meaning 'furnished with a bordure (a bearing all round the escutcheon, in the shape of a hem) of the same tincture as the rest of the field'. *hand*] handiwork; as one might say with respect to a painting—or an embroidery.

ix *439–43*. 'The Circumstances of these Gardens of *Adonis* being to Last but a very little while, which even became a Proverb among the Ancients, adds a very Pathetick propriety to the Simile: Still More, as that 'tis not the Whole Garden of *Eden* which is Now spoken of, but that One *Delicious Spot* where *Eve* was, This *Flowrie Plat* and This was of her Own Hand, as those Gardens of *Adonis* were always of the Hands of those *Lovely Damsels*, Less Lovely yet than She' (Richardson 416). Ricks 133–5 convincingly argues that the relevance of the comparison to the Garden of Solomon (*Song of Sol.* vi 2) depends on an analogy between the *sapient king* and Adam: both were wise, both uxorious and both beguiled by 'fair idolatresses' (i 444–6). Only the analogy was not M.'s. It goes back at least to St Augustine; see *Civ. Dei* xiv 11: 'As . . . Solomon . . . yielded worship to idols [not] of his own erroneous belief, but was brought unto that sacrilege by his wives' persuasions: so is it to be thought, that the first man did not yield to his wife in this transgression of God's precept, as if he thought she spoke the truth; but only being compelled to it by this social love to her.' *sapient*] A heavily thematic word in *PL*; at ix 1015–8 it again occurs associated with 'dalliance', and used in a way that brings out its root meaning in Latin, 'knowledge gained by tasting'. The Garden of Adonis and the Garden of Alcinoüs (cp. v 341) were *feigned* because only mythical (*mystical*) and pagan. These comparisons belong to a line of thought that in part went back to Lactantius; see Williams 108. For a late and popular mythographic expression, see the anonymous *Observationum libellus* (attached to Conti's *Mythologiae*), s.v. *Adonidis horti*: *Imo vox ipsa Graeca* ἡδονη *quae voluptatem significat, ab Hebraea Eden deducta videtur. Unde et* Adonis *fictitius poetarum, et Adonis sive Edonis regio* (*quae Edene est*) *sed vitiose a peregrinis Graecis pronuntiata, pro Edenis vel Edene*' ((Lyons 1653) Sig. Iii 1r). *revived*] Because after being killed by a boar Adonis was restored to life every year during the season of growth. It is just possible that M. alludes specifically to Spenser's addition to the myth: namely, that Venus keeps Adonis hidden in a secret garden (*F.Q.* III vi). Cp. *Comus* 998–1002. *Laertes' son*] The sapient king Odysseus; much-travelled as he was, when he saw the Garden of Alcinoüs he marvelled (Homer, *Od.* vii 112–35). The periphrasis is to bring in *Laertes*,

Much he the place admired, the person more.
As one who long in populous city pent,
Where houses thick and sewers annoy the air,
Forth issuing on a summer's morn to breathe
Among the pleasant villages and farms
Adjoined, from each thing met conceives delight,
The smell of grain, or tedded grass, or kine,
Or dairy, each rural sight, each rural sound;
If chance with nymph-like step fair virgin pass,
What pleasing seemed, for her now pleases more,
She most, and in her look sums all delight.
Such pleasure took the serpent to behold
This flowery plat, the sweet recess of Eve
Thus early, thus alone; her heavenly form

who resigned his kingship to take up gardening; unlike Satan, who keeps his crown and destroys the Garden.

Note that, like several other similes in ix, this consists of three parts arranged AAB (i.e., two pagan analogues, one sacred). See ll. 393–6*n* above. The pattern may only be for climax, or it may be intended to express the opposition of Monad and Dyad. It may also be worth noting that according to Pico della Mirandola the 1 : 2 ratio symbolizes the relation of the reason to the concupiscible faculty (see i 73–43*n*, Fowler 281*n*).

ix *444*. Ricks 135–8 points out that while this single-line sentence applies to Satan, it is also very apt for Solomon–and for Adam, whose tendency was to admire Eve too much (viii 567f, ix 1178f). Here, as at v 40–8, a passage also based on *Song of Solomon*, Satan takes Adam's place syntactically.

ix *445–54*. There seems at first little need to connect this simile with the autobiographical event reflected in *Elegia VII*. It is common sense to suppose that M. sometimes took walks in inhabited country places. But the girl in *Elegia VII* affected him deeply; and when he never saw her again his grief was like 'the grief of Hephaestus for his lost heaven'. Note that the simile is based on pastoral assumptions: hell is like a city, Paradise like the country. One has to be a very devoted member of the devil's party to stop short at sympathy with the townsman's need for a holiday and his appreciation of beauty – without reflecting how mean it would be for him to take advantage of the country girl's innocence. The contrast of smells recalls that made on the occasion of Satan's entry into Paradise (iv 168). *annoy*] affect injuriously. *tedded*] spread out to dry. *kine*] cows; Emma 34 notes that archaic plurals are uncommon in M. *nymphlike*] Keeps in play the comparison of l. 387 above. *for*] because of.

ix *456*. *plat*] patch, piece of ground.

ix *457–8*. Bentley sneered at *soft*, on the ground that if Eve's form were softer than *angelic*, she would be altogether fluid and 'no fit Mate for her Husband'; and Empson[2] 153f also finds the word 'vague' and conflicting 'with concrete details already settled'. But it is ingenuous to suppose that

Angelic, but more soft, and feminine,
Her graceful innocence, her every air
Of gesture or least action overawed
His malice, and with rapine sweet bereaved
His fierceness of the fierce intent it brought:
That space the evil one abstracted stood
From his own evil, and for the time remained
Stupidly good, of enmity disarmed,
Of guile, of hate, of envy, of revenge;
But the hot hell that always in him burns,
Though in mid heaven, soon ended his delight,
And tortures him now more, the more he sees
Of pleasure not for him ordained: then soon
Fierce hate he recollects, and all his thoughts
Of mischief, gratulating, thus excites.

soft must always mean 'physically yielding and flexible'. Much more appropriate in the present context is the sense 'gentle; free from severity or rigour' (*OED* II 8). 'Emotionally impressionable' (*OED* III 13) is just possible as an overtone. *form*] beauty; or simply 'appearance' (*OED* I 1 a).

ix *459–66*. The resemblance to the Elder Brother's account of the power of chastity and its effect on outward form (*Comus* 450ff) is very marked; see G. D. Hildebrand in *N & Q* cxcvii (1952) 246. The idea in common is that while virtue makes corporeality immortal, lust 'lets in defilement to the inward parts', so that 'the soul grows clotted by contagion, / Imbodies and imbrutes' (*Comus* 466–8; cp. l. 166 above, where Satan was constrained to *imbrute* himself in the serpent). Thus Satan is *abstracted* not only in the sense 'absent in mind' but also 'separated, removed from matter'–turned momentarily, in fact, 'to the soul's essence' (*Comus* 462). This line of thought is reinforced by the play *evil one . . . own evil*, which in the pronunciation of M.'s time would be a fully-fledged pun (see Dobson ii 676 and 694). For a moment Satan's evil becomes a separate thing, rather than a quality of himself. Conversely, even Eve's outward *form* is heavenly. *air*] manner; mien. For M.'s concrete embodiment of such abstract qualities as have the power to affect the mind, see MacCaffrey 67.

ix *467*. See i 255*n* and iv 20–3*n*.

ix *468*. No mere hyperbole: M. had it on the authority of Job i 6 and ii 1 that Satan is sometimes summoned to heaven.

ix *470–9*. Cp. ll. 129f. This passage seems at first to contain a very damaging admission, for at ii 365f and 400ff Beelzebub, speaking for Satan, had held out hope that the devils might possess earth and enjoy its 'soft delicious air'. But perhaps Satan did not deceive his followers; he may only now be discovering how far pleasure is bound up with goodness, and hence *not for him ordained*.

ix *472*. *gratulating*] expressing joy at the event (of meeting Eve).

Thoughts, whither have ye led me, with what sweet
Compulsion thus transported to forget
What hither brought us, hate, not love, nor hope
Of Paradise for hell, hope here to taste
Of pleasure, but all pleasure to destroy,
Save what is in destroying, other joy
To me is lost. Then let me not let pass
Occasion which now smiles, behold alone
The woman, opportune to all attempts,
Her husband, for I view far round, not nigh,
Whose higher intellectual more I shun,
And strength, of courage haughty, and of limb
Heroic built, though of terrestrial mould,
Foe not informidable, exempt from wound,
I not; so much hath hell debased, and pain
Enfeebled me, to what I was in heaven.
She fair, divinely fair, fit love for gods,

ix *480.* See l. 421*n*, and cp. l. 160, 'where hap may find'. As Burden 93f points out, *occasion* (opportunity) is a key word in Satan's ideology of chance and necessity. For a general account of the concept *Occasio* and its relation to *Fortuna*, see Panofsky² 72 and H. R. Patch, *The Goddess Fortuna in Mediaeval Literature* (Cambridge, Mass. 1927) pp. 115ff.

ix *481. opportune*] liable, exposed (rare in this sense: a genuine Latinism; cp. *opportunus*); secondarily, 'convenient as to time and place'.

ix *482–8.* An important passage, since it provides evidence that Satan would have avoided Adam and Eve if they had stayed together. The point of separation is thus seen to have been critical. See ll. 404–5*n* above, and cp. l. 1145 below. *intellectual*] mind (*OED* B 1). *higher*] Because allegorically Adam corresponds to *Mens*, Eve to *Ratio*; see ll. 358*n*, 360–1*n*. Adam is no doubt also to be thought of as a man having (as it happens) higher intellectual powers than Eve; cp. in this connection viii 541. But M. was perfectly capable of noticing that a woman sometimes has a better intellect than her husband, and he held that in such cases the man should submit to the woman (*Tetrachordon*; Yale ii 589). He thought the differentiation of sexual roles less fundamental than the 'superior and more naturall law . . . that the wiser should govern the lesse wise'. Thus it is quite possible that he intended the tragedy of Eve's fall to typify (among other things) the tragedy of a people betrayed by its intellectuals and leaders. *courage*] spirit.

ix *485. terrestrial mould*] Cp. 'formed of earth' (l. 149) and 'man of clay' (l. 176); Satan despises man's material substance.

ix *486.* Cp. l. 283 and see vi 327 for Satan's discovery that his own exemption had expired.

ix *489–93.* As with the first temptation, M. comes very near to presenting the second as a seduction. See v 40–1*n* and cp. v 48. For a poetic precedent for sexual union between Satan and Eve, see ii 727–8*n*. Sylvester's Du Bartas

Not terrible, though terror be in love
And beauty, not approached by stronger hate,
Hate stronger, under show of love well feigned,
The way which to her ruin now I tend.
    So spake the enemy of mankind, enclosed
In serpent, inmate bad, and toward Eve
Addressed his way, not with indented wave,
Prone on the ground, as since, but on his rear,
Circular base of rising folds, that towered
Fold above fold a surging maze, his head
Crested aloft, and carbuncle his eyes;
With burnished neck of verdant gold, erect
Amidst his circling spires, that on the grass

244 similarly describes the serpent 'as a false Lover that thick snares hath laid. / T'intrap the honour of a fair young Maid'. *tend*] turn my energies, apply myself.

ix *496–504*. *Gen.* iii 14 makes it clear only that the serpent has gone on its belly since the curse after the Fall; Biblical commentators disagreed as to the serpent's earlier gait. Three principal theories may be distinguished: (1) the serpent always went on his belly, but after the Fall this became a curse; (2) the serpent previously went upright, and began to go on its belly after the curse; (3) the serpent assumed an upright posture only while being used as an instrument by Satan (see the summary of these theories in Willet 47, 52). M. rejects (1) but does not decide between (2) and (3), for his account of the curse at x 175ff does not touch this point; while his description of the un-possessed serpent at iv 347–9 is ambiguous. *indented*] zigzagged. *maze*] The train of error is labyrinthine and elusive; cp. ii 651, where Sin has 'many a scaly fold'. M. here fuses two traditional images of Error (monster and labyrinth), which were merely juxtaposed by Spenser (*F.Q.* I i 11–15). *carbuncle* or reddish eyes denoted rage; cp. Shakespeare, *Coriolanus* V i 64f. But a precious stone in a *crested* serpent's head may also allude to Philostratus, *Life of Apollonius* iii 8, where we are told that there was just such a stone, from just such a serpent, in Gyges' ring. The Gyges legend has a grim relevance, for Eve, like Candaules' wife, has been shown naked by her husband; will be angry at his weakness in allowing her to be dishonoured (1155–61 below); and will arrange his death. The carbuncle in particular may be specified in the interest of having a chthonic antitype to the arch-chemic stone of the sun (see iii 596–601*nn*). More certain is the allusion to *Ezek.* xxviii 13: 'Thou hast been in Eden the garden of God; every precious stone was thy covering, the sardius, topaz, and the diamond, the beryl, the onyx, and the jasper, the sapphire, the emerald, and the carbuncle, and gold', a verse that is applied to Satan by St Augustine in *Civ. Dei* xi 15. *spires*] coils, spirals (not a Latinism). *redundant*] copious overflowing (perhaps a Latinism in this sense); possibly also 'wavelike' (which would certainly be a Latinism), and 'abundant to excess'.

Floated redundant: pleasing was his shape,
And lovely, never since of serpent kind
Lovelier, not those that in Illyria changed
Hermione and Cadmus, or the god
In Epidaurus; nor to which transformed
Ammonian Jove, or Capitoline was seen,
He with Olympias, this with her who bore
Scipio the height of Rome. With tract oblique

ix *505–10.* No doubt M. was aware of the tradition that Eve was charmed by the serpent's beauty (see John Salkeld, *A treatise of paradise* (1617), 218, *cit.* Hughes); and Empson[2] 175 is probably right in taking the simile to imply in some sense 'that Eve turned into a snake and became Satan's consort.' Or, at least, that she is tempted to imbrute herself like him. But another application of the simile is possible. Cadmus was metamorphosed into a serpent first; and only after he had embraced his wife Hermione (Harmonia) in his new form–an act that filled all who watched with horror–did she too change (Ovid, *Met.* iv 572–603). In the same way (though less innocently) Eve is the cause of a change in her spouse Adam. *changed*] Modern punctuation would introduce a comma, but this would resolve an ambiguity. As it stands the line can be an inversion of 'Hermione and Cadmus changed (i.e. became) serpents'; cp. x 540f. *Hermione,* not an Ovidian form, occurs in Stephanus; see Starnes 243f. M. almost certainly intends an allusion to Vulcan's fatal gift to Hermione, which made all her children impious and wicked. *the god / In Epidaurus*] Aesculapius, the god of healing, who restored so many to life that he aroused the anger of Pluto the king of hell. Once when an embassy from Rome came to Epidaurus to ask help, Aesculapius changed into a serpent 'raised breast-high', and accompanied the Romans in that form (Ovid, *Met.* xv 626–744).

ix *508. Ammonian Jove*] Jupiter Ammon, the 'Lybian Jove' of iv 277. In his account of the parentage of Alexander the Great, Plutarch relates that his ostensible father Philip of Macedonia withdrew his love from *Olympias* because she was given to sleeping with a serpent; only to be told by the Delphic oracle that the serpent was a form of Jupiter Ammon. *Capitoline*] Jupiter Capitolinus, so called from his temple at Rome, the capitol.

ix *510. Scipio*] Scipio Africanus, the height of Rome because the greatest Roman. *tract*] course. Svendsen 169f cites Camerarius' *The Living Librarie*: '*Philo* and the Hebrewes say, That the Serpent signifieth allegorically, Lecherie. *Alexander* the Great held for certaine, That his mother *Olympias* was gotten with child of him by a Serpent, which the superstitious Pagans called *Jupiters* Genius. Wherefore having upon a time written to his mother thus; King *Alexander* the sonne of *Jupiter Ammon*, saluteth his mother *Olympias*. . . . The like is reported of *Scipio Africanus*; *C.Oppius* that hath written his life, *Titus Livius*, *Gellius*, and *Julius Higinus* doe say, That a great Serpent lay with *Scipios* mother, and was seene often in her chamber, and when any bodie came in, he would vanish away. *Valerius*

At first, as one who sought access, but feared
To interrupt, sidelong he works his way.
As when a ship by skilful steersman wrought
Nigh river's mouth or foreland, where the wind
Veers oft, as oft so steers, and shifts her sail;
So varied he, and of his tortuous train
Curled many a wanton wreath in sight of Eve,
To lure her eye; she busied heard the sound
Of rustling leaves, but minded not, as used
To such disport before her through the field,
From every beast, more duteous at her call,
Than at Circean call the herd disguised.
He bolder now, uncalled before her stood;
But as in gaze admiring: oft he bowed
His turret crest, and sleek enamelled neck,
Fawning, and licked the ground whereon she trod.
His gentle dumb expression turned at length
The eye of Eve to mark his play; he glad
Of her attention gained, with serpent tongue
Organic, or impulse of vocal air,
His fraudulent temptation thus began.
　Wonder not, sovereign mistress, if perhaps

Maximus also speaketh of it.' So also E. Topsell, *The historie of serpents* (1608) 5.

ix *521–6.* The intention of this passage is not to bait Eve by making her a sorceress, as Empson[2] 176 suggests. Circe was in M.'s time regarded allegorically as a type of the Excess that leads to the imbruting of man; see M. Y. Hughes, 'Spenser's Acrasia and the Renaissance Circe', *JHI* iv (1943) 381–99. Homer's Circe changed men into wolves and lions who surprised Odysseus' company by *fawning* on them like dogs (*Od.* x 212–19).

ix *523. bolder*] A difference is made in the serpent's behaviour so that there may be a clue for Eve, if only she chooses to pay attention to it.

ix *525. enamelled*] of variegated colour (*OED* 3).

ix *530. organic*] instrumental, serving as an instrument (*OED* 1, rare). The serpent lacks the organs that ordinarily produce human speech, so that Satan has to use its tongue as an instrument, or else pulses of air. *impulse*] A pun: both 'motion, thrust' (*OED* 1) and 'strong suggestion from a spirit' *OED* 3 a; cp. Roger Coke, *Elements of power and subjection* (1660) 177: 'If he by chance offend by the impulse of the Devil, let him make amends therefore.' The means by which the serpent spoke were much discussed by the Biblical commentators; see Williams 116f.

ix *532–48.* Cp. v 38ff, the dream temptation, whose themes the present speech develops. The flattery of Eve as a goddess, however, is an addition. Such flattery was common in Renaissance poems on the Fall; but M. gives it a contemporary immediacy: see D. S. Berkeley, 'Précieuse Gallantry and the

Thou canst, who art sole wonder, much less arm
Thy looks, the heaven of mildness, with disdain,
Displeased that I approach thee thus, and gaze
Insatiate, I thus single, nor have feared
Thy awful brow, more awful thus retired.
Fairest resemblance of thy maker fair,
Thee all things living gaze on, all things thine
By gift, and thy celestial beauty adore
With ravishment beheld, there best beheld
Where universally admired; but here
In this enclosure wild, these beasts among,
Beholders rude, and shallow to discern
Half what in thee is fair, one man except,
Who sees thee? (And what is one?) Who shouldst
    be seen
A goddess among gods, adored and served
By angels numberless, thy daily train.
  So glozed the tempter, and his proem tuned;
Into the heart of Eve his words made way,
Though at the voice much marvelling; at length
Not unamazed she thus in answer spake.
What may this mean? Language of man pronounced

Seduction of Eve', *N&Q* cxcvi (1951) 337–9. The contemptuous references to Eve's *retired* . . . *rude* environment flout the pastoral values M. insisted on in a recent simile; see ll. 445–54*n*. The offer of a *numberless* multitude of admirers in exchange for Adam's single admiration makes explicit a fundamental opposition underlying much of the poem's number symbolism. See vi 809–10*n*. Satan's appeal to Eve's pride is in accordance with the central Christian tradition concerning the causes of the Fall; see Lewis 68, citing St Augustine on the desire for independent selfhood. By l. 790, Eve is lost in thoughts of her own 'godhead'. Burden 141 comments on Satan's use of *sovereign*, a word that calls up the whole hierarchical cosmic order, in which Eve's role is in fact quite a different one.

ix *549. glozed*] fawned, flattered, spoke smoothly and speciously. *proem*] prelude.

ix *553–66.* Eve's speech touches on one of the puzzles of the Genesis account for seventeenth-century commentators: namely, 'how without fear or doubt she could discourse with such a creature, or hear a serpent speak, without suspicion of imposture' (Sir Thomas Browne, *Pseudodoxia epidemica* i 1). M. has already provided partial answers, by making the prelapsarian serpent harmless (ll. 185f) and beautiful (ll. 504ff), and by arranging for Eve to be aware of the existence and powers of angels. All these explanations had been resorted to by the commentators: see Willet 47. M. is unusually favourable to Eve, however, in making her ask the serpent (shrewdly enough) how it came by its voice. The Eve of Scriptural exegesis, on the contrary, is

By tongue of brute, and human sense expressed?
The first at least of these I thought denied
To beasts, whom God on their creation-day
Created mute to all articulate sound;
The latter I demur, for in their looks
Much reason, and in their actions oft appears.
Thee, serpent, subtlest beast of all the field
I knew, but not with human voice endued;
Redouble then this miracle, and say,
How camest thou speakable of mute, and how
To me so friendly grown above the rest
Of brutal kind, that daily are in sight?
Say, for such wonder claims attention due.
To whom the guileful tempter thus replied.
Empress of this fair world, resplendent Eve,
Easy to me it is to tell thee all
What thou command'st, and right thou shouldst be obeyed:
I was at first as other beasts that graze
The trodden herb, of abject thoughts and low,
As was my food, nor aught but food discerned
Or sex, and apprehended nothing high:
Till on a day roving the field, I chanced
A goodly tree far distant to behold
Loaden with fruit of fairest colours mixed,
Ruddy and gold: I nearer drew to gaze;
When from the boughs a savoury odour blown,
Grateful to appetite, more pleased my sense

carried away by the words, and makes no enquiry into their source, whether a good or a bad spirit.

ix *558. demur*] hesitate about. Cp. vii 485ff on the emmet's wisdom; or viii 374, where Adam's God says that the beasts 'reason not contemptibly'.

ix *563. speakable*] capable of speech; *OED*'s earliest instance of this rare usage. *of*] from being.

ix *560.* For the serpent's subtlety, see *Gen.* iii 1, *2 Cor.* xi 3. *I knew* establishes Eve's responsibility (Burden 101). She has been put on her guard against subtlety by Raphael's narration; cp. l. 307.

ix *572. abject*] mean-spirited (*OED* A 3). There is some irony here; since, after the Fall and the curse, the serpent will be literally 'cast down' and subject like the *herb* to being *trodden*.

ix *578–88.* Cp. ll. 740–2, where Eve experiences similar sensations.

ix *579. savoury*] appetizing; edifying; see v 84–5*n* on a very similar pun in Eve's account of the first temptation. Note that Satan has already connected thought and eating by a piece of casual syntax at ll. 572f.

Than smell of sweetest fennel or the teats
Of ewe or goat dropping with milk at even,
Unsucked of lamb or kid, that tend their play.
To satisfy the sharp desire I had
Of tasting those fair apples, I resolved
Not to defer; hunger and thirst at once,
Powerful persuaders, quickened at the scent
Of that alluring fruit, urged me so keen.
About the mossy trunk I wound me soon,
For high from ground the branches would require
Thy utmost reach or Adam's: round the tree
All other beasts that saw, with like desire
Longing and envying stood, but could not reach.
Amid the tree now got, where plenty hung
Tempting so nigh, to pluck and eat my fill
I spared not, for such pleasure till that hour
At feed or fountain never had I found.
Sated at length, ere long I might perceive
Strange alteration in me, to degree
Of reason in my inward powers, and speech

ix *581–3*. Again a simile with an AAB pattern (see ll. 439–43*n*): the comparison is with one plant, and the teats of two species of animals. Milk from the teat and *fennel* were supposed to be favourite foods of serpents. Fennel was said to renew the serpent in spring, either by inducing it to cast its skin, or by sharpening its sight. See Pliny, *Nat. hist.* viii 99, xx 254; and cp. M.'s *An Apology against a Pamphlet* (Yale i 909): 'to see clearer then any fenell rub'd Serpent'. Note also, however, that fennel was an emblem of flattery; see *OED* 3, citing, e.g., Robert Greene: 'Woman's weeds, fennel I mean for flatterers' (*A quip for an upstart courtier* (1592)).
ix *585*. The identification of the forbidden fruit as an apple may have been drawn from the Ursinian (Heidelberg) Catechism; see Fletcher ii 96. But it was also a popular belief.
ix *586*. *defer*] delay.
ix *588*. As Burden 133 points out, Satan is lying when he describes the forbidden fruit as specially *alluring*. See iv 221–2*n* and v 53*n*.
ix *590–1*. Even when giving a simple estimate of height, Satan manages to insinuate an image of man's disobedience. But M., more subtle still, simultaneously makes the point in favour of divine providence, that if the fruit was so difficult of access there was no chance of its being plucked without a firm decision.
ix *595–601*. See v 45–90*n*. In this second temptation, the appearances of the first are traced back to their causes. How did the dream tempter know the effect of the fruit? Because, it turns out, he had once been an abject serpent.
ix *599*. *to degree*] to a certain amount; the idea of a degree as a step or stage in an ascent is secondarily present.

Wanted not long, though to this shape retained.
Thenceforth to speculations high or deep
I turned my thoughts, and with capacious mind
Considered all things visible in heaven,
Or earth, or middle, all things fair and good;
But all that fair and good in thy divine
Semblance, and in thy beauty's heavenly ray
United I beheld; no fair to thine
Equivalent or second, which compelled
Me thus, though importune perhaps, to come
And gaze, and worship thee of right declared
Sovereign of creatures, universal dame.
So talked the spirited sly snake; and Eve
Yet more amazed unwary thus replied.
Serpent, thy overpraising leaves in doubt
The virtue of that fruit, in thee first proved:
But say, where grows the tree, from hence how far?
For many are the trees of God that grow
In Paradise, and various, yet unknown
To us, in such abundance lies our choice,
As leaves a greater store of fruit untouched,
Still hanging incorruptible, till men
Grow up to their provision, and more hands

ix *602.* The use the serpent makes of his newly acquired reason is not to glorify God, but to engage in *speculations high*–no doubt of the kind dismissed by Raphael as unprofitable at viii 173–8; *deep* speculations recalls the 'causes deep' of creation that Uriel said were hid by God as his secrets (iii 707).
ix *605. middle*] the space between.
ix *609.* Echoing Horace *Odes* I xii 18, *nec viget quicquam simile aut secundum*: praise appropriate only to God. Cp. viii 406f, where God in fact described himself in precisely these terms.
ix *612. dame*] mistress (*OED* I 1).
ix *613. spirited*] indued with an animating spirit, stirred up (*OED* s.v. *Spirit*, vb. I 2 d and 3); also energetic, enterprising (*OED* s.v. *Spirited*, a. 2 b). The sense 'possessed by a spirit', if it is operative, may be an extension original with M.
ix *616. virtue*] power. Eve is flirting: 'If you pay silly compliments like that, the tree can't have done much for your reason.' *proved*] tested by experiment.
ix *618–24.* There is no single and complete syntactic line: *in such . . . choice* must be attached in turn to the word group before and the one after. *trees of God*] Biblical diction; cp. *Ps.* civ 16.
ix *623. to their provision*] to what is already (providentially) provided for them.

Help to disburden nature of her birth.
  To whom the wily adder, blithe and glad.
Empress, the way is ready, and not long,
Beyond a row of myrtles, on a flat,
Fast by a fountain, one small thicket past
Of blowing myrrh and balm; if thou accept
My conduct, I can bring thee thither soon.
  Lead then, said Eve. He leading swiftly rolled
In tangles, and made intricate seem straight,
To mischief swift. Hope elevates, and joy
Brightens his crest, as when a wandering fire,
Compact of unctuous vapour, which the night
Condenses, and the cold environs round,
Kindled through agitation to a flame,
Which oft, they say, some evil spirit attends
Hovering and blazing with delusive light,
Misleads the amazed night-wanderer from his way
To bogs and mires, and oft through pond or pool,
There swallowed up and lost, from succour far.

ix *624. birth*] the early edns have the unusual spelling 'bearth'.

ix *627. myrtles*. See 426–31*n* above. Read emblematically, the *row of myrtles* is the obstacle of Eve's virtue. In view of the strong element of sexual seduction in M.'s presentation of the temptation, however, it may be that the myrtles (not to speak of the *fountain*, *thicket* and *balm*) also have an anatomical sexual symbolism. For this see Valeriano 639 or Liceti 377 (myrtle as female *pudenda*).

ix *629. blowing*] blooming.

ix *630. conduct*] Ostensibly 'guidance' (*OED* I 1); but in reality, as we know, 'management' (*OED* II 5, 6).

ix *632. made*] *Ed I* misprints 'make'.

ix *634–42*. Cp. *Com* 433. See Svendsen (108) who explains that Renaissance meteorologists 'regularly treated *ignis fatuus* and *ignis lambens* together, and nearly always as emblems of self-deception'. She quotes Swan's *Speculum mundi*: 'These kinds of lights are often seen in Fennes and Moores, because there is always great store of unctuous matter fit for such purposes. ... Wherefore the much terrified, ignorant, and superstitious people may see their own errours in that they have deemed these lights to be walking spirits. ... They are no spirits, and yet lead out of the way, because those who see them are amazed, and look so earnestly after them that they forget their way' (*ibid.* 109). See also Lerner 306, with the correction of Ricks 126. The implication of the simile is that Eve is led astray because she lacks the guidance of intellect, which would have obviated her amazement. *amazed*] Recalls Eve's amazement at l. 614 above.

ix *635. compact of*] composed of.

So glistered the dire snake, and into fraud
Led Eve our credulous mother, to the tree
Of prohibition, root of all our woe;
Which when she saw, thus to her guide she spake.
  Serpent, we might have spared our coming hither,
Fruitless to me, though fruit be here to excess,
The credit of whose virtue rest with thee,
Wondrous indeed, if cause of such effects.
But of this tree we may not taste nor touch;
God so commanded, and left that command
Sole daughter of his voice; the rest, we live
Law to our selves, our reason is our law.

ix *643–5*. Discussed persuasively by Ricks (75f), who notices the silent pun in *root*; the oxymoron *credulous mother*; the accuracy of *tree / Of prohibition* (not Latinism, but literal truth: 'of all prohibitions'); and the 'calculated brutality' of *snake*, in *PL* an unusual variant for serpent. Burden points out that the forbidden tree is never described by M. as attractive or provocative except when appetite is perversely aroused; hence the present description is flat and bare. The passive use of *fraud*–'the state of being deceived; error' or 'injury, detriment'–is an extension perhaps original with M.; cp. Latin *fraus*. Cp. vii 143 and *PR* i 372.

ix *647–50*. On the dramatic irony or unspoken puns, see Ricks 73f. To Eve the words are mere jaunty levity, to us they are truer than she knows–*excess* in a darker sense is not far off. *virtue*] Another pun, between 'power' and 'virtuousness'.

ix *651*. Cp. l. 663, where Eve, as in *Gen.* iii 3, refers to a prohibition against even touching the fruit. The Prohibition itself, however, was only against eating: see *Gen.* ii 17. Some Biblical commentators held that Eve was unwarrantably adding to God's precept, but M. evidently agreed with Willet 49 that Eve 'faithfully expoundeth the meaning of the precept', for he harmonizes the two formulas and uses them almost indifferently. Thus at l. 925 Adam speaks of the 'ban to touch'; and at vii 46 so does M., *in persona auctoris*.

ix *653*. *daughter of his voice*] Perhaps a Hebraism for 'voice sent from heaven' (a revelation of less weight than God's own voice), and Eve is perhaps palliating the prohibition; see W. Hunter in *MLQ* ix (1948) 279f. But a more salient feature of the passage is that Eve has omitted one of God's daughters. vii 8–12 made it clear that God has *two* daughters, Wisdom and Urania (perhaps Logos), so that *Sole daughter* is a dramatic irony. Eve slights an obedience she ought to acknowledge. She is not as independent as she claims, for she owes allegiance to Wisdom, and hence to Adam.

ix *654*. Cp. *Rom.* ii 14: 'When the Gentiles, which have not the law, do by nature the things contained in the law, these, having not the law, are a law unto themselves.'

To whom the tempter guilefully replied.
Indeed? Hath God then said that of the fruit
Of all these garden trees ye shall not eat,
Yet lords declared of all in earth or air?
To whom thus Eve yet sinless. Of the fruit
Of each tree in the garden we may eat,
But of the fruit of this fair tree amidst
The garden, God hath said, Ye shall not eat
Thereof, nor shall ye touch it, lest ye die.
She scarce had said, though brief, when now more bold
The tempter, but with show of zeal and love
To man, and indignation at his wrong,
New part puts on, and as to passion moved,
Fluctuates disturbed, yet comely and in act
Raised, as of some great matter to begin.
As when of old some orator renowned

ix *655–8*. Closely following *Gen.* iii 1; but with a very different effect, since we know that Satan is well aware of the terms of the prohibition. Hence *guilefully*.

ix *659*. *yet sinless*] Important, not only for its indication that (at least as far as M.'s intention is concerned) we are not to think of Eve as corrupted by the first temptation in any way that involves guilt, but also for its more elusive implication that there are different degrees of corruption or proximity to the place of sin. If an Eve who has accepted Satan's 'conduct . . . into fraud' (ll. 630, 643) is still sinless, then presumably an Eve who presses her will on Adam and separates from him, while certainly also sinless, might similarly, though to a lesser degree, be led by an evil proclivity.

ix *663*. See l. 651*n*. Commentators generally agreed that in saying 'lest ye die' (*Gen.* iii 3; Vulgate, even more strikingly, *ne forte moriamini*) Eve was hedging: what God actually said was 'thou shalt surely die' (*Gen.* ii 17; see Willet 48). Similarly *this fair tree amidst / The garden* (l. 661; *Gen.* iii 3) is a vague evasion of the morally definitive 'tree of the knowledge of good and evil'.

ix *668*. *Fluctuates*] undergoes changes of form; is unstable (*OED* 2 a); but perhaps with the additional overtone 'undulates' (Latinism).

ix *670–6*. A very intricate simile; since three strands of meaning – oratorical, theatrical and theological – are kept going simultaneously, in addition to the one being illustrated. Thus *part* means 'part of the body', 'dramatic role' and 'moral act' (*OED* II 11); *motion* means 'gesture', 'mime' (or 'puppet-show') and 'instigation, persuasive force, inclination' (*OED* 7, 9); while *act* means 'action', 'performance of a play' and 'the accomplished deed itself, as distinct from the mere motion' (*OED* 2). The implication is that Satan, besides talking persuasively, is acting a part; and that each feature of his performance could be given an unattractive definition, if only Eve

In Athens or free Rome, where eloquence
Flourished, since mute, to some great cause addressed,
Stood in himself collected, while each part,
Motion, each act won audience ere the tongue,
Sometimes in highth began, as no delay
Of preface brooking through his zeal of right.
So standing, moving, or to highth upgrown
The tempter all impassioned thus began.
O sacred, wise, and wisdom-giving plant,
Mother of science, now I feel thy power
Within me clear, not only to discern
Things in their causes, but to trace the ways
Of highest agents, deemed however wise.
Queen of this universe, do not believe
Those rigid threats of death; ye shall not die:
How should ye? By the fruit? It gives you life
To knowledge. By the threatener? Look on me,
Me who have touched and tasted, yet both live,
And life more perfect have attained than fate

cared to use the terms of moral theology. *since mute*] Because eloquence has declined; but also (literally, not hyperbolically) because the serpent now no longer speaks. *in himself collected*] completely in control of himself. The phrase imitates the Ital. idiom *in se raccolto*, but also precisely defines the inwardness of the serpent's self-command: *in himself* being in mild antithesis to *while each* (outward serpentine) *part*. Cicero's first oration against Catiline is an instance of the beginning without preface (*in highth*). *audience*] attention.

ix *679–80*. Having endowed the tree with power ('virtue': ll. 616, 649), Satan now animates it: the step to Eve's worship at ll. 835f is a short one. Contrast the many earlier presentations of the tree as no more than a pledge of obedience (iii 95*n*, iv 428, viii 325, etc.). *science*] knowledge.

ix *682*. See l. 602*n* above. The knowledge and wisdom Satan offers consists in exploration of God's forbidden secrets (cp. iii 707), and in scepticism about the wisdom of *highest agents* (Burden 105).

ix *685*. Cp. *Gen.* iii 4f: 'The serpent said unto the woman, Ye shall not surely die: For God doth know that in the day ye eat thereof, then your eyes shall be opened, and ye shall be as gods, knowing good and evil.'

ix *687–90*. The early edns have a question mark after *knowledge* and a comma after *threatener*, but this is evidently an error. The antithesis between fruit and *threatener* requires that the latter, like the former, shall be interrogative. *threatener* is a metrical dissyllable, spelled 'threatner'. *To*] in addition to.

ix *689–90*. Satan has to invoke in one sentence both Necessity and Chance (the two powers acknowledged in his ideology), to escape using such awkward terms as commandment, obedience and natural law. Throughout

Meant me, by venturing higher than my lot.
Shall that be shut to man, which to the beast
Is open? Or will God incense his ire
For such a petty trespass, and not praise
Rather your dauntless virtue, whom the pain
Of death denounced, whatever thing death be,
Deterred not from achieving what might lead
To happier life, knowledge of good and evil;
Of good, how just? Of evil, if what is evil
Be real, why not known, since easier shunned?
God therefore cannot hurt ye, and be just;
Not just, not God; not feared then, nor obeyed:
Your fear it self of death removes the fear.

the temptation he encourages Eve to wish for an absolute freedom, unconditioned by the organic limitations of human nature. To this end, he represents the differentiation of species as a chance affair–a matter of *lot*; enforced, however, by Fate, to produce the bondage from which Eve is to be liberated. Burden 143 compares Grotius, *Adamus exul* 1075–80, where Satan uses a necessitarian argument, though a much cruder one.
ix *692. incense*] kindle, excite.
ix *694.* Satan's deceptions are here concentrated on a single word. He renders the concept of *virtue* so uncertain that the word comes to mean no more than 'courage, manliness': a possible significance (see *OED* i 7), but here a narrow and perverse one. Empson (159), rightly wishing to give the most sublime explanation of Eve's motives, thinks she is moved by this argument of Satan's above the others: 'She feels the answer to this elaborate puzzle must be that God wants her to eat the apple, since what he is really testing is not her obedience but her courage.' This is plausible; especially since virtue (though in a wider sense) is after all the specific concern of Eve as *ratio* (see l. 335*n*). Adam, however, would have known that the virtue of obedience takes precedence.
ix *695.* Again Satan acts the part of innocence. At ii 781–816 Sin explained the nature of Death to him in some detail, and we were told that 'the subtle fiend his lore / Soon learned'.
ix *698–9.* If the knowledge is of good, how is it just to prohibit it? The matter of the prohibition is dangerous ground for Satan, so that he has to argue even more quickly and elliptically than usual. Here occurs the most egregious logical fallacy in the speech: the alteration of the meaning of *knowledge* in the middle of a sorites. (In order that evil may be *shunned*, it is not at all necessary that it should be *known* in the sense of the prohibition.) The distinction between theoretical knowledge and knowledge in the sense of 'miserable experience' (Willet 50) was a standard one in commentaries on *Gen.* iii.

Why then was this forbid? Why but to awe,
Why but to keep ye low and ignorant,
His worshippers; he knows that in the day
Ye eat thereof, your eyes that seem so clear,
Yet are but dim, shall perfectly be then
Opened and cleared, and ye shall be as gods,
Knowing both good and evil as they know.
That ye should be as gods, since I as man,
Internal man, is but proportion meet,
I of brute human, ye of human gods.
So ye shall die perhaps, by putting off
Human, to put on gods, death to be wished,
Though threatened, which no worse than this can
bring.

ix *703–9*. 'For God doth know that in the day ye eat thereof, then your eyes shall be opened, and ye shall be as gods, knowing good and evil' (*Gen.* iii 5). The argument that God's prohibition was made out of envy and a desire to protect his own vested interest had often been assigned to the serpent. M. Nicolson (*PQ* vi (1927) 17) usefully compares Henry More's *Conjectura Cabbalistica*: 'God indeed loves to keep his creatures in awe . . . but he knows very well that if you take your liberty with us, and satiate yourselves freely with your own will, your eyes will be wonderfully opened . . . so that you will . . . like God know all things whatsoever whether good or evil.' Her conclusion, however, that 'the ethical import of the fall is that man followed his instincts and will, not his reason' is too simple. M. is unambiguous that to Eve Satan's words seem *impregned / With reason* (l. 737f). In other words, Eve follows what she thinks is reason: she is not shown, in the first instance, as giving way to instinct or will, but rather as being *deceived* (cf. 404 above, and see *1 Tim.* ii 14). Her error, more subtly, lies in her failure to reflect or respond faithfully to wisdom or intellect (mind); for the duty of *ratio* is to translate the mind's contemplations of truth into practical terms. Thus Eve is not abandoning reason, exactly, but the 'higher intellect' (l. 483).

ix *710–12*. Cp. ll. 932–7, where Adam reasons similarly. In the event, however, God turns out to have ordained a different *proportion*; not *Change from serpent*: *Change from man* :: *Man* : *Angel*, but rather *Angel* : *Man* :: *Change to serpent* : *Change to fallen man*. For Satan's punitive metamorphosis see x 507ff. *internal man*] see l. 600; the serpent's pretence is that his 'inward powers' are human.

ix *713–15*. Satan offers a travesty of Christian mortification and death to sin; cp. *1 Cor.* xv 53, or *Col.* iii 1–15, esp. 2f and 9f: 'Set your affection on things above . . . For ye are dead, and your life is hid with Christ in God. . . . ye have put off the old man with his deeds; And have put on the new man, which is renewed in knowledge after the image of him that created him.'

And what are gods that man may not become
As they, participating godlike food?
The gods are first, and that advantage use
On our belief, that all from them proceeds;
I question it, for this fair earth I see,
Warmed by the sun, producing every kind,
Them nothing: if they all things, who enclosed
Knowledge of good and evil in this tree,
That whoso eats thereof, forthwith attains
Wisdom without their leave? And wherein lies
The offence, that man should thus attain to know?
What can your knowledge hurt him, or this tree
Impart against his will if all be his?
Or is it envy, and can envy dwell
In heavenly breasts? These, these and many more
Causes import your need of this fair fruit.
Goddess humane, reach then, and freely taste.
He ended, and his words replete with guile
Into her heart too easy entrance won:
Fixed on the fruit she gazed, which to behold

ix *716–17. participating*] sharing; partaking of. Both language and thought echo v 493–500, where Raphael holds out hope of a permissible evolution, until eventually 'men / With angels may participate'. Thus the choice before Eve is not made to lie between aspiration and stasis, but between the right aspiration and the wrong (Burden 144).
ix *720–2.* A perverse form of the argument advanced by Raphael–at viii 93ff; after Eve had left the table–about the fruitfulness of the earth compared with the sun (not with God). See Rajan 161. *they*] 'produce' understood.
ix *722–5.* The dualistic implication of these lines completely contradicts the earlier monotheistic arguments; throughout, Satan's speech lacks any steady metaphysical orientation. Satan here assumes the magical operation of the tree; see Lewis 68.
ix *728. impart*] communicate; bestow, give a share in.
ix *729–32.* See ll. 10–19*n* and 703–9*n*, and cp. Virgil, *Aen.* i 11, *tantaene animis caelestibus irae?* Burden 142ff comments that Satan presents the choice to Eve as one between Fate and 'free virtue' (ii 551 above); he is inviting her to participate in a Satanic or pagan epic–complete with machinery of jealous gods–about her 'own heroic deeds' (ii 549). *import*] occasion (*OED* I 4).
ix *732. goddess humane*] human goddess. Satan must now be very sure to risk so wild an oxymoron. The paradox is only partially softened by a secondary sense 'gracious goddess'.
ix *735–43.* Cp. *Gen.* iii 6: 'When the woman saw that the tree was good for food, and that it was pleasant to the eyes, and a tree to be desired to make one wise, she took of the fruit thereof, and did eat.' The forbidden fruit is

Might tempt alone, and in her ears the sound
Yet rung of his persuasive words, impregned
With reason, to her seeming, and with truth;
Mean while the hour of noon drew on, and waked
An eager appetite, raised by the smell
So savoury of that fruit, which with desire,
Inclinable now grown to touch or taste,
Solicited her longing eye; yet first
Pausing a while, thus to her self she mused.
   Great are thy virtues, doubtless, best of fruits,

now for the first time described as specially attractive and tempting to man (Burden 134). It would have been improvident or provoking of God to have allowed it to seem so before; but now Eve's heart is corrupted. Note that Eve is deceived into following what seems to her the *truth*: she does not follow her appetite in the first instance; see ll. 703–9*n*. Burden cites the Puritan divine Thomas Cartwright (1535–1603) on the precedence of the heart's corruption before the abuse of sight and taste (which he regarded as outward causes of the Fall). *impregned*] impregnated. *savoury*] Not only 'appetizing' but also, secondarily, 'edifying'. For earlier uses of the word in similar contexts, see l. 579*n* above; also v 84–5*n*. *inclinable*] disposed. This can only describe Eve's *desire*, hardly the fruit; in the sense 'amenable' it seems not to have been applied to inanimate objects. *now*] Implies that Eve never before desired to touch or taste the fruit. We have thus reached the second of the three phases of sin recognized in the moral theology of M.'s day: *Suggestio*, *Delectatio* and *Consensus*.

ix *739–40*. Burden (134ff) has it that the fact that Eve would always be hungry at *noon* contributes to the crisis. The increased appetitive urge is not, of course, evil in itself–even Raphael got hungry at this time (v 301 and 436ff); but M. means to run excitingly close to a tragedy of necessity. It seems likely, however, that M. intends noon, as such an apparently temporal specification is often intended in Scripture, 'not as an indication of time, but for the sake of its ethical significance' (Auerbach 7; cp. MacCaffrey 52). This significance is to be found in the common symbolism whereby noon was the critical time of judgment; see iv 30*n*. There was also a tradition, going back at least to Hugh of St-Victor, that the Fall actually occurred, like the Expulsion and the death of Christ, at the Biblical sixth hour (see Bongo 280, also xii 1*n*).

ix *743–4*. The pause is indispensable: Eve must have time to resolve deliberately before acting (Burden 136, citing Hobbes's analysis of the conversion of appetite into will).

ix *745*. *Ed II* wrongly has full stop after *fruits*. *virtues*] powers. *doubtless*] without question; certainly.

ix *745–79*. The resemblances between Eve's speech and earlier speeches of

Though kept from man, and worthy to be admired,
Whose taste, too long forborne, at first assay
Gave elocution to the mute, and taught
The tongue not made for speech to speak thy praise:
Thy praise he also who forbids thy use,
Conceals not from us, naming thee the tree
Of knowledge, knowledge both of good and evil;
Forbids us then to taste, but his forbidding
Commends thee more, while it infers the good
By thee communicated, and our want:
For good unknown, sure is not had, or had
And yet unknown, is as not had at all.
In plain then, what forbids he but to know,
Forbids us good, forbids us to be wise?
Such prohibitions bind not. But if death
Bind us with after-bands, what profits then
Our inward freedom? In the day we eat
Of this fair fruit, our doom is, we shall die.
How dies the serpent? He hath eaten and lives,
And knows, and speaks, and reasons, and discerns,
Irrational till then. For us alone
Was death invented? Or to us denied
This intellectual food, for beasts reserved?
For beasts it seems: yet that one beast which first
Hath tasted, envies not, but brings with joy
The good befallen him, author unsuspect,
Friendly to man, far from deceit or guile.
What fear I then, rather what know to fear
Under this ignorance of good and evil,
Of God or death, of law or penalty?

Satan's are too obvious to list separately. She has trusted Satan's account of the fruit, and consequently argues from false premises–such as its magical power.

ix *748*. *elocution*] utterance (*OED* 3); eloquence, oratory (*OED* 2).

ix *758*. *In plain*] in plain terms, plainly (*OED* s.v. *Plain* a.[1] A V 19 a).

ix *761*. *after-bands*] subsequent bonds (possibly a coinage: only instance in *OED*).

ix *766–7*. The irony here is strong, for we know from the divine colloquy of Bk iii that death *was* invented for man.

ix *771*. *author unsuspect*] Eve means 'informant not subject to suspicion'; it may be an irony that *author* could also mean 'inventor' or 'instigator, prompter'.

ix *773*. 'What fear I, then–or rather (since I'm not allowed to know anything) what do I know that is to be feared?'

Here grows the cure of all, this fruit divine,
Fair to the eye, inviting to the taste,
Of virtue to make wise: what hinders then
To reach, and feed at once both body and mind?
    So saying, her rash hand in evil hour
Forth reaching to the fruit, she plucked, she ate:
Earth felt the wound, and nature from her seat
Sighing through all her works gave signs of woe,
That all was lost. Back to the thicket slunk
The guilty serpent, and well might, for Eve
Intent now wholly on her taste, naught else
Regarded, such delight till then, as seemed,
In fruit she never tasted, whether true
Or fancied so, through expectation high
Of knowledge, nor was godhead from her thought.
Greedily she engorged without restraint,

x7 76. *cure of all*] The primary meaning is 'remedy of all (this ignorance, etc.)', the ironic secondary meaning 'charge, duty, of all (men)'. Whether an older meaning of *cure* (care, trouble) is also operative, is more difficult to say. See *OED* s.v. *Cure* I 2, 3 and II 7, and cp. Latin *cura*= grief.

ix 777. The fruit is now *inviting*, and therefore a provocation; see ll. 735–43*n*.

ix 778. *Of virtue to make wise*] Primarily 'having power to make wise'; secondarily and ironically 'to make experienced, wise after the event, instead of virtuous'.

ix 781. *ate*] spelt 'eat' in the early edns, and possibly pronounced 'et' (still a correct alternative to 'ate' in unstressed positions).

ix 782–4. Cp. ll. 1000–4 below, where nature gives a 'second groan' at Adam's fall; also x 651–719, where the changes in nature occasioned by the Fall are described in more detail. The effect was anticipated by Satan at ll. 132f above: 'all this will soon / Follow, as to him linked in weal or woe'. The thought, which goes back to *Rom*. viii 22 ('the whole creation groaneth and travaileth in pain') was common in poetry: Hughes cites instances as far apart as Gower, *Mirrour* 26,810ff and Joseph Beaumont, *Psyche* vi 254. Nature's sigh is only a *sign* (portent) of mutability, because the changes themselves will not take place until man's case has been heard and judged. Sylvester's Du Bartas 254–75 ('The Furies'), one of the most elaborate and interesting accounts of the changes in nature at the Fall, puts them after the Expulsion.

ix 789. *fancied*] See ll. 735–43*n*.

ix 790. *god-head*] See ll. 532–48*n*.

ix 791–2. Svendsen (128) cites Sebastian Franck, *The Forbidden Fruit, or a Treatise of the Tree of Knowledge of Good and Evil which Adam at First, and as yet All Mankind doe eate death* (1640): like Eve, all men 'doe eate death, and yet ... thinke themselves to eate life, and hope to be Gods'. She offers

And knew not eating death: satiate at length,
And heightened as with wine, jocund and boon,
Thus to her self she pleasingly began.
O sovereign, virtuous, precious of all trees
In Paradise, of operation blest
To sapience, hitherto obscured, infamed,
And thy fair fruit let hang, as to no end
Created; but henceforth my early care,
Not without song, each morning, and due praise
Shall tend thee, and the fertile burden ease
Of thy full branches offered free to all;
Till dieted by thee I grow mature
In knowledge, as the gods who all things know;
Though others envy what they cannot give;

the interesting suggestion that Eve here devours in a manner reminiscent of Death himself: 'the release of inordinate appetite into the world brings on the insatiable devourer of all men'. *knew . . . death*] knew not that she was eating death; imitating a Greek construction in which verbs of knowing or perceiving are followed by a participle. But also 'she was unaware, while she ate death' or even 'she *knew*; not eating (immediate) death'. *satiate*] contrast the temperate eating of v 451f.

ix *793*. The only 'heightening' effect achieved is inebriation (Burden 145). It should be recalled that fermented wine was unknown before the Fall; see v 345*n*. At least since the time of St Bernard, drunkenness has always been a convenient symbol of the loss of rationality resulting from the Fall. Bersuire in one of his allegorizations specifies that 'by wine can be understood the human will; for . . . the human will burns with desire' (*Reductorium morale* VIII iii 33). *boon*] jolly, convivial. Eve's new state is characterized by a gaiety shockingly trivial and inappropriate.

ix *795*. *virtuous, precious*] the positive for the superlative; a classicism. Richardson instances Homer, *Il.* v 381 (δῖα θεάων), Virgil *Aen.* iv 576 (*sancte deorum*).

ix *796–7*. *operation*] agency; efficacy (*OED* 2, 3). 'Of efficacy in producing sapience'. As l. 1018 will show more clearly, *sapience* contains a word-play similar to that in 'savour' at l. 579 and v 84f; though here the wit is appropriately even more learned and laborious. 'Sapience' is derived from Latin *sapientia* (discernment, taste), and ultimately from *sapere* (to taste). *infamed*] defamed.

ix *800*. Eve proposes to offer the tree the morning orisons she has till now kept for God; cp. e.g., v 145.

ix *804–7*. Eve parrots Satan's argument at ll. 722–5 (that God cannot have put knowledge in the tree if he forbids its use), and gets it wrong. *gods*] God; Eve has learned from Satan to use the vaguer pagan form (cp. l. 718 above). *others*] i.e., God. Eve's language is now full of lapses in logic and evasions in theology.

For had the gift been theirs, it had not here
Thus grown. Experience, next to thee I owe,
Best guide; not following thee, I had remained
In ignorance, thou open'st wisdom's way,
And giv'st access, though secret she retire.
And I perhaps am secret; heaven is high,
High and remote to see from thence distinct
Each thing on earth; and other care perhaps
May have diverted from continual watch
Our great forbidder, safe with all his spies
About him. But to Adam in what sort
Shall I appear? Shall I to him make known
As yet my change, and give him to partake
Full happiness with me, or rather not,
But keep the odds of knowledge in my power
Without copartner? So to add what wants
In female sex, the more to draw his love,
And render me more equal, and perhaps,
A thing not undesirable, sometime
Superior; for inferior who is free?
This may be well: but what if God have seen,
And death ensue? Then I shall be no more,
And Adam wedded to another Eve,
Shall live with her enjoying, I extinct;
A death to think. Confirmed then I resolve,
Adam shall share with me in bliss or woe:

ix *810. access*] Stressed on the second syllable. *secret*] uncommunicative, not given to revelation (*OED* A 2 a); secluded from observation (*OED* A 1 c); abstruse, mystical (*OED* A 1 g).
ix *811–13. secret*] hidden. See *Job* xxii 13f, *Is.* xlvii 10 and *Ps.* x 11 ('He hath said in his heart, God hath forgotten: he hideth his face; he will never see it').
ix *815. safe*] safely remote; a usage that Pearce felt to have only colloquial warrant.
ix *821–30.* Eve's decision now lies only between one selfish purpose and another: the motive of desire for sexual domination is ranged against fear and jealousy. The idea of Eve's jealousy is traced to rabbinical sources by D.C. Allen in *MLN* lxiii (1948) 262f; and to Christian commentators in Williams 123.
ix *821–2.* The first suggestion we have had that Eve feels any inadequacy.
ix *824. A thing not undesirable*] The parenthesis is probably to be taken as a piece of solemn self-deception: Eve really thinks it very desirable indeed that she should be almost always superior. Contrast the first description of Adam and Eve, 'not equal, as their sex not equal seemed' (iv 296).

So dear I love him, that with him all deaths
I could endure, without him live no life.
   So saying, from the tree her step she turned,
But first low reverence done, as to the power
That dwelt within, whose presence had infused
Into the plant sciential sap, derived
From nectar, drink of gods. Adam the while
Waiting desirous her return, had wove
Of choicest flowers a garland to adorn
Her tresses, and her rural labours crown,
As reapers oft are wont their harvest queen.
Great joy he promised to his thoughts, and new
Solace in her return, so long delayed;
Yet oft his heart, divine of something ill,
Misgave him; he the faltering measure felt;

ix *832–3*. The first explicit expression of love from Eve–and the first false expression. For in effect she is planning to kill Adam to ease her own mind. Note the confusion of her thought: in reality there is no question of Eve's living without Adam, since if she loses him it will be because she is dead. The lines perhaps echo Horace, *Odes* III ix 24: *tecum vivere amem, tecum obeam libens*. If so, the point would not just be that Horace's poem is a dialogue, and Eve is having a dialogue with herself. There would be an allusion to the contrast between Lydia's professed willingness to die *for* Calais, if only he can survive her (ll. 15f), and her less noble readiness to die *with* her old flame. Eve's attitude lies all on the latter side of this contrast; the former has not even occurred to her as a possibility. The allusion would have some chance of being recognized by M.'s earlier readers, as Horace's poem was extremely popular in the seventeenth century. There were translations or imitations by Jonson, Herrick, Stanley, Ashmore (three), Hannay, John Hall, Collop and Flatman; see Marianne Mays, 'Some Themes and Conventions in Caroline Lyrics' (Oxford B. Litt. thesis).
ix *835–6*. 'She who thought it beneath her dignity to bow to Adam or to God, now worships a vegetable. She has at last become "primitive" in the popular sense' (Lewis 122). Empson 155 argues that Eve really prays to the power, not the tree; but the same could be said of primitive man.
ix *837*. *sciential*] endowed with knowledge.
ix *842*. This simile returns us to earlier comparisons of Eve with the agricultural goddesses Pales, Pomona and Ceres (ll. 393–6). The irony is powerful; for when Eve comes she bears no natural crop in her hand.
ix *845*. Eve had previously been 'due at her hour'; see v 303.   *divine*] prophet, diviner, soothsayer (*OED* 1); perhaps secondarily a Latinism (*divinus*, prophetic).
ix *846*. Primarily the rhythm of his own heart, the *faltering measure* may also be nature's 'signs of woe' (l. 783). Cp. Sin's attraction by a feeling of sympathy at x 245–7.

And forth to meet her went, the way she took
That morn when first they parted; by the tree
Of knowledge he must pass, there he her met,
Scarce from the tree returning; in her hand
A bough of fairest fruit that downy smiled,
New gathered, and ambrosial smell diffused.
To him she hasted, in her face excuse
Came prologue, and apology to prompt,
Which with bland words at will she thus addressed.
Hast thou not wondered, Adam, at my stay?
Thee I have missed, and thought it long, deprived
Thy presence, agony of love till now
Not felt, nor shall be twice, for never more
Mean I to try, what rash untried I sought,
The pain of absence from thy sight. But strange
Hath been the cause, and wonderful to hear:
This tree is not as we are told, a tree
Of danger tasted, nor to evil unknown
Opening the way, but of divine effect
To open eyes, and make them gods who taste;
And hath been tasted such: the serpent wise,

ix *851. smiled*] Ricks (59) thinks that M. is here enlivening the metaphor: the smile is one of heartless indifference. But Burden 138 remarks that the bough is fair and smiling to Adam because from his point of view it is a nondescript bough like any other. It is attractive until he knows it to be from the forbidden tree; see ll. 735–43*n*.

ix *852. ambrosial*] A dramatic irony: to Adam the bough is 'fragrant', but to Eve the sap of the forbidden tree has seemed literally 'drink of gods' (l. 838).

ix *853–4*. The expression on Eve's face is visible in advance as she approaches, and so is like the *prologue* (i.e., prologue-speaker) of a play. But it also remains on her face as she speaks, to help out her words, and so is like the prompter of the play. The actor prompted is apology: i.e., justification or defence personified (not 'expression of regret'). The simile has an exact counterpart in the theatrical simile of ll. 670–6, during the temptation of Eve.

ix *856–85*. In view of this subtly persuasive speech, which leaves hardly any stop unpulled, it is strange that both Tillyard (263) and Waldock (46, 48) found it possible to advance the thesis that Adam decides to eat the fruit without being tempted by Eve. It is less surprising that they were undeterred by l. 999 ('fondly overcome with female charm'): that is only M.'s conscious and deliberate statement of his intention with respect to Adam's fall.

ix *864*. 'If' is to be understood after *danger*.

Or not restrained as we, or not obeying,
Hath eaten of the fruit, and is become,
Not dead, as we are threatened, but thenceforth
Endued with human voice and human sense,
Reasoning to admiration, and with me
Persuasively hath so prevailed, that I
Have also tasted, and have also found
The effects to correspond, opener mine eyes,
Dim erst, dilated spirits, ampler heart,
And growing up to godhead; which for thee
Chiefly I sought, without thee can despise.
For bliss, as thou hast part, to me is bliss,
Tedious, unshared with thee, and odious soon.
Thou therefore also taste, that equal lot
May join us, equal joy, as equal love;
Lest thou not tasting, different degree
Disjoin us, and I then too late renounce
Deity for thee, when fate will not permit.
   Thus Eve with countenance blithe her story told;
But in her cheek distemper flushing glowed.
On the other side, Adam, soon as he heard
The fatal trespass done by Eve, amazed,
Astonied stood and blank, while horror chill
Ran through his veins, and all his joints relaxed;
From his slack hand the garland wreathed for Eve

ix *868*. *Or . . . or*] either . . . or.
ix *874*. *tasted*] experienced, tested (*OED* I 2, 3).
ix *881*. *lot*] A word redolent of Satanic ideology; cp. l. 690. Eve is inviting Adam to subject himself to fortune and necessity.
ix *883*. An implicit admission that she has offended against the principle of degree.
ix *885*. Eve pretends readiness to renounce a deity she does not have; but, as we know from l. 830, she is in reality not even prepared to renounce her claim on Adam after she dies.
ix *886*. *blithe*] Cp. the description of the serpent as 'spirited' (l. 613).
ix *887*. *distemper*] Either 'intoxication' (*OED* 4 d; cp. l. 793 above) or 'a disordered condition, due to disturbance of the temperament of the bodily humours'.
ix *890*. Cp. *Job* xvii 8: 'Upright men shall be astonied at this'; also Virgilian passages such as *Aen.* ii 120f: *obstipuere animi, gelidusque per ima cucurrit / ossa tremor.* *astonied*] bewildered; stunned, benumbed, paralysed. *blank*] resourceless; discomfited; deprived of speech (*OED* 5); pale (*OED* 1): these two senses are separated at l. 894.

Down dropped, and all the faded roses shed:
Speechless he stood and pale, till thus at length
First to himself he inward silence broke.
  O fairest of creation, last and best
Of all God's works, creature in whom excelled
Whatever can to sight or thought be formed,
Holy, divine, good, amiable or sweet!
How art thou lost, how on a sudden lost,
Defaced, deflowered, and now to death devote?
Rather how hast thou yielded to transgress
The strict forbiddance, how to violate
The sacred fruit forbidden! Some cursed fraud
Of enemy hath beguiled thee, yet unknown,
And me with thee hath ruined, for with thee

ix *893. faded*] The first instance of decay in Paradise. There may be an allusion to Statius, *Theb.* vii 149f, where Bacchus, frightened by the impending destruction of Thebes, drops his thyrsus, and 'unimpaired grapes' fall from his head. Adam has earlier been cast as Bacchus (iv 279 above); and M. may mean to contrast the unimpaired grapes and the faded roses. See E. M. W. Tillyard, *TLS* (1 July 1949) 429. The image derives iconographical precision from the fact that roses were a symbol of human frailty, or of the mutability of happiness. (Contrast the innocent Eve's support of roses with myrtle bands, and see ll. 426–31*n*.) Thus, the fall of the garland conveys the idea that Adam is losing his hold on happiness; perhaps, in part, through a slackness of grip not entirely caused by the relaxation of horror.
ix *899. amiable*] kind; lovable, lovely.
ix *901. Defaced*] Stein 8 cites a definition of sin in *De doctrina* i 12: 'a diminution of the majesty of the human countenance, and a conscious degradation of mind'. *deflowered*] Primarily metaphorical, though in a literal sense it would apply to the suggested seduction of Eve by Satan (see l. 270*n*). The word has many other resonances; for Eve has been carefully portrayed as 'the gatherer and guardian of flowers, "her self, though fairest unsupported Flour"' (Ricks 140). *devote*] cursed, consigned to destruction.
ix *905.* Adam as yet only suspects some connection between Satan and the serpent Eve told him about at ll. 867ff. As Burden 160 notes, the shrewdness of his guess and his grasp of the implications show the superiority of his intellect.
ix *906–7.* The principal strands of meaning are: 'firm my resolution is to die with thee', 'assuredly my resolution is to die with thee' and '(if I stay) with thee my resolution [in the theological sense] is certain to die away'. Adam's 'vehemence' of love is excessive, but M. means it to be moving too. It is precisely the comparative goodness of Adam's motives in acting wrongly that amplifies the extent of our own fall. Waldock's thesis testifies to the success of at least one phase of this tactic.

Certain my resolution is to die;
How can I live without thee, how forgo
Thy sweet converse and love so dearly joined,
To live again in these wild woods forlorn?
Should God create another Eve, and I
Another rib afford, yet loss of thee
Would never from my heart; no no, I feel
The link of nature draw me: flesh of flesh,

ix *908–9.* Adam is not deceived (*1 Tim.* ii 14). 'He did not believe what his wife said to him to be true, but yielded because of the social bond (*socialis necessitudo*) between them' (Lewis 67, citing Augustine, *Civ. Dei* xiv 11); an interpretation confirmed by 998 below. Because Adam is not prepared to make an independent stand he consciously surrenders to the false assumption underlying Eve's speech at ll. 879–85: namely, that separation is unthinkable. As before, Eve is pressing for what Adam cannot refuse her, except by opting for a love and a purpose larger than human. He now fails to choose separation, just as at ll. 342–75 he failed to resist it. Burden 163ff connects this passage with the prose expression of M.'s views on marriage and divorce in *Tetrachordon*. In a sense Adam becomes corrupt because he refuses to divorce Eve: because he wants solace at any price. Williams 123 notes the important fact that the commentators agreed that 'since Original Sin is an effect of Adam's sin, the human race would not have been involved if only Eve had sinned'. *sweet converse*] Ironic in view of the recriminations that are to close the book.

ix *910.* Verity, Brooks 273f, and Margaret Giovannini in *Explicator* xii (Oct. 1953), take the wildness of the woods to be subjective; G. Koretz retorts in *Explicator* (June 1954) that Paradise was already a 'wilderness of sweets' (v 294) 'wild above rule or art' (v 297) before the Fall. Only, the wilderness that was sweet before now becomes desolate and *forlorn*.

ix *911–13.* Waldock 47 argues that these lines show Adam to be acting out of love for this Eve in particular. This need not be denied; but it is also very likely that M. introduces the possibility of *another Eve* to avoid the appearance of improvidence on the part of his God. Adam must not be forced to fall by an awareness that there can never be anyone but Eve to solace his loneliness and be a help meet for him.

ix *914–15.* See viii 495–9*n*. By making Adam use the Dominical institution of the married state of one flesh to counter the prohibition, M. has fined down the choice to the point of sublimity. Adam's disobedience surpasses the virtue of most fallen men. On the other hand, M. would certainly have thought it wrong to interpret the Biblical terms as Adam does. In *Tetrachordon* (Yale ii 599ff) M. rejects the view that the expression 'flesh of my flesh' (*Gen.* ii 23) refers to a natural and indissoluble bond of marriage. It has rather to be taken metaphorically, he argues, as meaning a state of love, solace and mutual fitness. Significantly, Adam in the present passage refers only to the bond of flesh and of *heart* (l. 913), not to that of soul (contrast

Bone of my bone thou art, and from thy state
Mine never shall be parted, bliss or woe.
 So having said, as one from sad dismay
Recomforted, and after thoughts disturbed
Submitting to what seemed remediless,
Thus in calm mood his words to Eve he turned.
 Bold deed thou hast presumed, adventurous Eve,
And peril great provoked, who thus hath dared
Had it been only coveting to eye
That sacred fruit, sacred to abstinence,
Much more to taste it under ban to touch.
But past who can recall, or done undo?
Not God omnipotent, nor fate, yet so
Perhaps thou shalt not die, perhaps the fact
Is not so heinous now, foretasted fruit,
Profaned first by the serpent, by him first
Made common and unhallowed ere our taste;
Nor yet on him found deadly, he yet lives,

viii 499). In any case, Burden 167 remarks, the power of nature is only an excuse if no power above nature's is acknowledged. See also l. 1044*n*.
ix *919. seemed*] M. does not endorse Adam's decision. Since Eve is an unbeliever, there was the remedy of divorce (Burden 168ff).
ix *920. calm*] There is nothing excited or inadvertent about Adam's entry into sin, for he was 'not deceived' (see ll. 998f and *n*). Here he seems to have fallen into the stoicism or 'apathy' earlier characterized as devilish; cp. ii 564.
ix *921.* Adam responds to Eve's presentation of her deed as epic, and therefore worthy of admiration (Burden 146). Contrast Eve's correct response (tragic horror) to the 'venturous' act of the tempter, when he tasted the forbidden fruit in her dream, v 65. *adventurous*] Spelled 'adventrous': prosodically a trisyllable.
ix *922. hath*] hast *Ed I*. The *Ed II* reading makes the thought more general; see B. A. Wright in *RES* n.s. v (1954) 170. Adams 92 gives good reasons for preferring 'hast'.
ix *924.* As in l. 902, the fruit is described quite flatly: it has lost its attraction. See l. 851*n* above.
ix *925. ban to touch*] See l. 651*n*.
ix *927. yet so*] even so. Burden 172f notes the close alternation of God and fate. Adam has adopted the satanic ideology.
ix *928. Perhaps*] Adam joins Eve in evasiveness about the terms of God's commandment: see l. 663*n* above. *fact*] crime (*OED* I c: in the seventeenth century the commonest sense).
ix *930.* Instead of exploring the enemy's 'fraud', as ll. 904f held out hope he might, Adam now uncritically accepts Eve's recension of the serpent's story.

Lives, as thou saidst, and gains to live as man
Higher degree of life, inducement strong
To us, as likely tasting to attain
Proportional ascent, which cannot be
But to be gods, or angels demi-gods.
Nor can I think that God, creator wise,
Though threatening, will in earnest so destroy
Us his prime creatures, dignified so high,
Set over all his works, which in our fall,
For us created, needs with us must fail,
Dependent made; so God shall uncreate,
Be frustrate, do, undo, and labour loose,
Not well conceived of God, who though his power
Creation could repeat, yet would be loth
Us to abolish, lest the adversary
Triumph and say; Fickle their state whom God
Most favours, who can please him long; me first
He ruined, now mankind; whom will he next?
Matter of scorn, not to be given the foe,
However I with thee have fixed my lot,
Certain to undergo like doom, if death
Consort with thee, death is to me as life;

ix *936. Proportional ascent*] on Adam's Satanic reasoning here, see ll. 710–12*n* above. Note that Adam does not merely comply with Eve's wishes, but displays a definite ambition of his own.
ix *941–2.* On the involvement of nature in the Fall, see ll. 782–4*n*. Adam's theology disintegrates as fast as Eve's: he is already attributing to God an unjust compunction.
ix *944. loose,* the spelling in the early edns, could indicate either 'loose'– 'undo' (*OED* 2); 'break up, do away with' (*OED* 7)–or 'lose'. In the first case *labour* would have its common seventeenth-century meaning 'work performed' (*OED* 3, 4).
ix *947–8.* Cp. *Deut.* xxxii 27. For *adversary*=Satan, see vi 282*n*. Scan *Triúmph.*
ix *949.* Adversary or not, Adam is working himself into the Satanic role.
ix *952. lot*] On the ideological implications, see l. 881*n*.
ix *953. Certain*] resolved. Perhaps a Latinism on the analogy of *certus*, but the word was sometimes used in the sense 'resolved' in prose (see *OED* I 5 b) and there is also a possibility that *Certain* may have the commoner meaning 'sure' (*OED* I 6). *doom*] Three separate meanings are possible: judgment, sentence of punishment (*OED* 2); irrevocable destiny, adverse fate (*OED* 4 a); ruin, death (*OED* 4 b). Burden 173 holds that Adam uses the word in the second, the fallen angels' sense; cp. ii 550, 'doom of battle'.
ix *954.* Whereas Satan asserts his resolution in terms such as 'evil be thou my good' (iv 110), Adam's antinomies are less abstract and fundamental.

So forcible within my heart I feel
The bond of nature draw me to my own,
My own in thee, for what thou art is mine;
Our state cannot be severed, we are one,
One flesh; to lose thee were to lose my self.
So Adam, and thus Eve to him replied.
O glorious trial of exceeding love,
Illustrious evidence, example high!
Engaging me to emulate, but short
Of thy perfection, how shall I attain,
Adam, from whose dear side I boast me sprung,
And gladly of our union hear thee speak,
One heart, one soul in both; whereof good proof
This day affords, declaring thee resolved,
Rather than death or aught than death more dread
Shall separate us, linked in love so dear,
To undergo with me one guilt, one crime,
If any be, of tasting this fair fruit,
Whose virtue, for of good still good proceeds,
Direct, or by occasion hath presented
This happy trial of thy love, which else
So eminently never had been known.

ix 956. *bond of nature*] Cp. 'link of nature' (l. 914), and see ll. 908–9*n* and 914–15*n*.

ix 956. The 'link of nature' (l. 914) has now become a *bond*–in allusion to the 'bondage' of marriage with an unbeliever in *1 Cor.* vii 15 (Burden 172f).

ix 959. The *Ed I* and *Ed II* spelling 'loose' could indicate either 'lose' or 'loose'.

ix 961. *exceeding*] Ostensibly 'extremely great', but 'excessive' is present as a dramatic irony. Steadman 92 holds that Satan, Eve and Adam all display certain moral virtues in excess.

ix 962. *evidence*] manifestation (*OED* I 2, II 3); but in view of *trial*, probably complicated by the legal connotation 'proof; witness'.

ix 967. *One heart, one soul*] Contrast the relationship as it was before the Fall–'Union of mind, or in us both one soul' (viii 604). Intellect (*mens*) has been displaced by the more passionate *heart*.

ix 974. *Direct . . . occasion*] i.e. directly or indirectly.

ix 975. *trial*] Cp. l. 961. Eve's insistence on a test of love was common in literary treatments of the Fall. Hughes compares Grotius, *Adamus exul* ll. 1398–1468, and Andreini, *L'Adamo caduto* III i (Kirkconnell 180–4, 254–7).

ix 976. *eminently*] conspicuously, notably (*OED* 2, 3). There is also a blasphemous play on the theological sense of the word (*OED* 4). God was said to possess the excellences of human character not *formally* (in the ordinary, creaturely sense of their formal definition) but *eminently* (in a higher sense). At first there may indeed seem to be a true analogy between Adam's offer to

Were it I thought death menaced would ensue
This my attempt, I would sustain alone
The worst, and not persuade thee rather die
Deserted, than oblige thee with a fact
Pernicious to thy peace, chiefly assured
Remarkably so late of thy so true,
So faithful love unequalled; but I feel
Far otherwise the event, not death, but life
Augmented, opened eyes, new hopes, new joys,
Taste so divine, that what of sweet before
Hath touched my sense, flat seems to this, and harsh.
On my experience, Adam, freely taste,
And fear of death deliver to the winds.
So saying, she embraced him, and for joy
Tenderly wept, much won that he his love
Had so ennobled, as of choice to incur
Divine displeasure for her sake, or death.
In recompense (for such compliance bad
Such recompense best merits) from the bough
She gave him of that fair enticing fruit
With liberal hand: he scrupled not to eat
Against his better knowledge, not deceived,
But fondly overcome with female charm.
Earth trembled from her entrails, as again
In pangs, and nature gave a second groan,
Sky loured and muttering thunder, some sad drops

undergo death, and Christ's. But the analogy is really a contrast. M. has carefully indicated that love was not with Christ the dominating motive: 'above . . . shone / Filial obedience' (iii 268–9).

ix *980. oblige*] make liable to a penalty (*OED* II 5 a). *fact*] crime, deed.

ix *981. chiefly assured*] i.e., especially since I have been assured.

ix *984. event*] result, outcome.

ix *989*. Primarily 'cast away your fear of death'; but there is a horrible dramatic irony if the line is connected with the image of Death sniffing from far away 'the smell / Of mortal change on earth' (x 267–81).

ix *994. compliance*] unworthy submission, conformity (*OED* II 6); see ll. 908–9*n*, and cp. *Gen*. iii 17: 'Because thou hast hearkened unto the voice of thy wife, and hast eaten of the tree . . . cursed is the ground.'

ix *996*. The fruit is now again *enticing* to Adam, because his heart, and consequently also his appetite, are now corrupt; see ll. 735–43*n*, 851*n*, 924*n*.

ix *998–9*. In accordance with *1 Tim*. ii 14. For the implications of this summary author-comment, see ll. 856–85*n* and 908–9*n*.

ix *1000–1*. For nature's first groan, see ll. 782–4 and *n*.

ix *1002*. The first thunderstorm. Until now there have only been gentle showers in Paradise (iv 646).

Wept at completing of the mortal sin
Original; while Adam took no thought,
Eating his fill, nor Eve to iterate
Her former trespass feared, the more to soothe
Him with her loved society, that now
As with new wine intoxicated both
They swim in mirth, and fancy that they feel
Divinity within them breeding wings
Wherewith to scorn the earth: but that false fruit
Far other operation first displayed,
Carnal desire inflaming, he on Eve
Began to cast lascivious eyes, she him

ix *1003–4*. The only occurrence in *PL* of the term Original Sin. The doctrine denoted is discussed in *De doctrina* i 11 (Columbia xv 180ff). There Original Sin, 'the sin which is common to all men', is defined as 'that which our first parents, and in them all their posterity committed, when, casting off their obedience to God, they tasted the fruit of the forbidden tree' (*ibid.* 181). The comprehensiveness of the first sin is next defined, in terms that have had some interest for critics of *PL*: 'If the circumstances of this crime are duly considered, it will be acknowledged to have been a most heinous offence, and a transgression of the whole law. For what sin can be named, which was not included in this one act? It comprehended at once distrust in the divine veracity, and a proportionate credulity in the assurances of Satan; unbelief; ingratitude; disobedience; gluttony; in the man excessive uxoriousness, in the woman a want of proper regard for her husband, in both an insensibility to the welfare of their offspring, and that offspring the whole human race; parricide, theft, invasion of the rights of others, sacrilege, deceit, presumption in aspiring to divine attributes, fraud in the means employed to attain the object, pride, and arrogance' (*ibid.* 181–3). The sin was original in the sense that 'all sinned in Adam' – the Pauline doctrine, for which M. cites the authority of *Rom.* v 12–21 and offers the explanation that it is the 'principle' or 'method' of God's justice to visit penalties 'incurred by the violation of things sacred' on the whole of the sinner's posterity (*ibid.* 185). M. thought this principle to be entirely just, and to be acknowledged as such in a multitude of pagan testimonies (*ibid.* 191).
ix *1008*. On the intoxication consequent on the Fall, see l. 793*n*.
ix *1010*. The illusion of divinity breeds the *wings* appropriate to a god or angel. Cp. Eve's dream, in which she actually takes flight with her angel tempter (v 86–90).
ix *1012*. *operation*] Either the 'influence, action' of the fruit, or a 'vital process' in Adam and Eve (*OED* 3, 4).
ix *1013*. Beginning the account of the 'formal cause' of the Fall, the cause through which the Fall is what it is. The 'form' of man's disobedience is the change in his nature that accompanies sin: it can be illustrated only by its effects. See Howard 163f.

As wantonly repaid; in lust they burn:
Till Adam thus gan Eve to dalliance move.
   Eve, now I see thou art exact of taste,
And elegant, of sapience no small part,
Since to each meaning savour we apply,
And palate call judicious; I the praise
Yield thee, so well this day thou hast purveyed.
Much pleasure we have lost, while we abstained
From this delightful fruit, nor known till now
True relish, tasting; if such pleasure be
In things to us forbidden, it might be wished,
For this one tree had been forbidden ten.
But come, so well refreshed, now let us play,

ix *1017–20.* The fullest development of one of the poem's most central thematic word-play complexes, that on tasting and discerning: *exact of taste, / And elegant* is a grotesque travesty of Eve's discriminating avoidance of 'inelegant' mixtures of tastes in her preparation of supper for Raphael (v 332–6). At the same time, *exact of taste* has also a more figurative sense: before the Fall Adam remarked that nature had perhaps bestowed on Eve 'too much of ornament, in outward show / Elaborate, of inward less exact [perfect, refined]' (see viii 539–44*n*); whereas now he calls her discernment perfect. It seems that mind can no longer be distinguished from lower faculties of perception.   *elegant*] refined, delicate – a word that would normally be applied to literary taste; so that Adam implies that Eve has made cookery a fine art, and by doing so betrays his confusion of values. For the play in *sapience*, see ll. 796–7*n*; Schultz 10 traces it to St Bernard, who writes that Eve 'transgressed, with the fruit of ill-savour, the Apostle's rule *sapere ad sobrietatem*'.   *savour*] tastiness (*OED* 1 b); understanding (*OED* 5); see v 84*n*.
ix *1019.* *we*] *Ed II* misprints 'me'.
ix *1021.* *purveyed*] provided, made provision.
ix *1023.* *known*] i.e., have known.
ix *1026.* *For*] instead of. The wish will come true when under the Covenant there are ten commandments.
ix *1027.* Cp. *Exod.* xxxii 6f: 'The people sat down to eat and to drink, and rose up to play [taken at *1 Cor.* x 7 to mean *fornicate*]. And the Lord said unto Moses, Go, get thee down; for thy people, which thou broughtest out of the land of Egypt, have corrupted themselves.'
ix *1027–45.* Lewis (69) thinks that the contrast between this indulgence and earlier pictures of unfallen sexual activity is a failure: 'He has made the unfallen already so voluptuous and kept the fallen still so poetical that the contrast is not so sharp as it ought to have been.' But M. may have wanted to steal one of the devil's best tunes, and so deliberately made sex before the Fall as exciting as possible. Here, by contrast, the foreplay is perfunctory, even crude: 'now let us play'.   *seized*] (l. 1037) is a word that would have been

As meet is, after such delicious fare;
For never did thy beauty since the day
I saw thee first and wedded thee, adorned
With all perfections, so inflame my sense
With ardour to enjoy thee, fairer now
Than ever, bounty of this virtuous tree.
    So said he, and forbore not glance or toy
Of amorous intent, well understood
Of Eve, whose eye darted contagious fire.
Her hand he seized, and to a shady bank,
Thick overhead with verdant roof embowered
He led her nothing loth; flowers were the couch,
Pansies, and violets, and asphodel,
And hyacinth, earth's freshest softest lap.
There they their fill of love and love's disport
Took largely, of their mutual guilt the seal,
The solace of their sin, till dewy sleep
Oppressed them, wearied with their amorous play.

unthinkable in the earlier passages; contrast, e.g., viii 508–11. Williams 125 notes that a Jewish idea that the first effect of the fruit was to stimulate lust was taken over by certain Christian commentators on *Genesis*.

ix *1029–41*. Addison compares Homer, *Il.* xiv, where Hera, bent on deceiving Zeus, comes to him with Aphrodite's zone, and seems more charming to him than ever before. Lines 1029f correspond closely to *Il.* xiv 327f, while the flowers of the present passage have *hyacinth* in common with those of the couch prepared by Earth for Zeus and Hera (cp. also the flowers of the nuptial bower, iv 697–703 above). In view of the comparison of Eve to 'Ceres in her prime, / Yet virgin of Proserpina from Jove' at ll. 395f above, it is possible that M. also means to recall an adjacent line in the Homeric passage (xiv 326) comparing Hera favourably with Demeter (Ceres).

ix *1029–33*. Echoing the pagan sensuality of the similarly fatal Paris in Homer, *Il.* iii 442ff, xiv 313ff. See Douglas Bush in *JEGP* lx (1961) 640.

ix *1033*. Before the Fall Eve was adorned with virtues; now it is the tree that is virtuous. See l. 778*n* on a similar transfer; and cp. ll. 616, 649, 745 and 795.

ix *1038. embowered*] Recalls, but by no means implies, the nuptial bower of iv 690–711 etc. The indefinite article in the preceding line indicates that Adam and Eve now copulate casually, wherever they happen to be.

ix *1042–4*. The impudent woman of *Prov.* vii entices a youth to adultery with similar words: 'Come, let us take our fill of love until the morning: let us solace ourselves with loves.' As Burden 166 notes, *solace* is here debased in meaning. It is for the first time applied to mere physical sex; the deeper solace of relationship in true love having disappeared. See ll. 914–15*n* above.

Soon as the force of that fallacious fruit,
That with exhilarating vapour bland
About their spirits had played, and inmost powers
Made err, was now exhaled, and grosser sleep
Bred of unkindly fumes, with conscious dreams
Encumbered, now had left them, up they rose
As from unrest, and each the other viewing,
Soon found their eyes how opened, and their minds
How darkened; innocence, that as a veil
Had shadowed them from knowing ill, was gone,

ix *1046–51*. Contrast the 'airy light' sleep of unfallen man, bred of 'temperate vapours bland' (v 3–7). *bland*] Here means 'pleasing to the senses', whereas at v 5 it meant 'genial'. *unkindly*] unnatural. *fumes*] vapours or exhalations rising from the stomach to the brain; especially often used of the vapours that result from drinking alcohol. Fumes are to some degree inevitable, but their quality is critical. It is the grosser fumes that produce sleep. See Vives, *De anima et vita* (Basel 1538) 109f: *Non potest quidem tolli omnino ea effumigatio, quae a ventriculo ascendit ad caput: sed eius densitas ad certum aliquem modum efficit somnum, subtilitas vigiliam, hoc est solutionem sensuum.* Vives goes on to treat sleep as an image of death: an idea that may well be relevant to the present passage (see 1052–9*n* on the degrees of death). *conscious*] guilty.

ix *1052–9*. Cp. *Gen.* iii 7: 'The eyes of them both were opened, and they knew that they were naked.' Before the Fall Eve needed no veil even when a third was present, for she was 'virtue-proof' (see v 384 and *n*). Iconographically, nudity in most cases signified simplicity, integrity and virtue. This was also the usual emphasis in ancient authors; cp., e.g., Horace, *Odes* I xxiv 6f: *Pudor et Iustitiae soror, / incorrupta Fides, nudaque Veritas.* In the terms of traditional moral theology, this *nuditas virtualis* (symbol of innocence) has been replaced by *nuditas criminalis*. See Panofsky[2] 156. *shame*] For Horace a good quality, for M. a bad one, shame was the first of the four degrees of death distinguished by theologians; see *De doctrina* i 12 (Columbia xv 202f), and viii 323–33*n* above. Note that the number of virtues lost, four, was itself a number that symbolised virtue (the *tetractys*; the four cardinal virtues; etc.): see ll. 1074–6*n*. *he covered*] Perhaps cp. *Ps.* cix 29: 'Let mine adversaries be clothed with shame, and let them cover themselves with their own confusion, as with a mantle.' Editors usually let in heavy punctuation between *shame* and *he*, but the absence of punctuation in the early edns is essential to M.'s ambiguity. He wants to leave us in doubt whether honour or shame is doing the covering; because prelapsarian honour did not cover, but the honour we know does. Cp. the discrimination between true and false honour in Guarini's *Pastor Fido* iv 9, and see iv 289*n* above, on 'with native honour clad'. Cp. also x 216ff, where Christ clothes man both inwardly and outwardly. In a lesser ambiguity, Adam covers in response to Eve's guilty shame.

Just confidence, and native righteousness
And honour from about them, naked left
To guilty shame he covered, but his robe
Uncovered more, so rose the Danite strong
Herculean Samson from the harlot-lap
Of Philistean Dalilah, and waked
Shorn of his strength, they destitute and bare
Of all their virtue: silent, and in face
Confounded long they sat, as strucken mute,
Till Adam, though not less than Eve abashed,
At length gave utterance to these words constrained.
O Eve, in evil hour thou didst give ear
To that false worm, of whomsoever taught
To counterfeit man's voice, true in our fall,
False in our promised rising; since our eyes
Opened we find indeed, and find we know
Both good and evil, good lost, and evil got,
Bad fruit of knowledge, if this be to know,
Which leaves us naked thus, of honour void,
Of innocence, of faith, of purity,
Our wonted ornaments now soiled and stained,
And in our faces evident the signs
Of foul concupiscence; whence evil store;

ix *1059–63.* See *Judges* xvi for the story of Samson's betrayal by Delilah. *Danite*] Samson's father Manoah is said to be of the tribe of Dan, at *Judges* xiii 2. Dalilah is in its first syllable nearer to the Greek form. The comparison between Adam and Samson was traditional; cp., e.g., Willet 48.
ix *1059. more. So*] *Ed I. Ed II* misprints 'more, so'.
ix *1061. Philistean Dalilah*] see *SA* 216*n*.
ix *1067.* See ll. 1029–41*n*. When Zeus woke after Hera had seduced him, he was similarly resentful. See Ricks 103: Adam's 'cry proclaims that the word evil is derived from Eve, and that evil derives from her.' The name *Eve* was in the Bible only given after the Fall (*Gen.* iii 20). There was a great deal of speculation as to its significance; see Willet 54; also l. 291*n* above.
ix *1070–4.* Cp. *De doctrina* i 10 (Columbia xv 115): 'It was called the tree of knowledge of good and evil from the result; for since Adam tasted it, we not only know evil, but we know good only by means of evil.' The point that Adam by his transgression got no wisdom, but only the miserable experience or 'experimental knowledge' of evil, was often made by commentators; see, e.g., Willet 43, where it is ascribed to St Augustine.
ix *1074–6.* Again the quadrate of virtue. The four ornaments are essentially the same as those of ll. 1054–7: *honour* and *innocence* are repeated, and *faith* corresponds to 'confidence', *purity* to 'righteousness'. Cp. Willet 38 on a different arithmological treatment of the *ornaments* of Eve: a Hebrew 'curiosity' in which they were reckoned twenty-four in number.

Even shame, the last of evils; of the first
Be sure then. How shall I behold the face
Henceforth of God or angel, erst with joy
And rapture so oft beheld? Those heavenly shapes
Will dazzle now this earthly, with their blaze
Insufferably bright. O might I here
In solitude live savage, in some glade
Obscured, where highest woods impenetrable
To star or sunlight, spread their umbrage broad
And brown as evening: cover me ye pines,
Ye cedars, with innumerable boughs
Hide me, where I may never see them more.
But let us now, as in bad plight, devise
What best may for the present serve to hide
The parts of each from other, that seem most
To shame obnoxious, and unseemliest seen,
Some tree whose broad smooth leaves together sewed,
And girded on our loins, may cover round

ix *1079. last*] least.

ix *1083. earthly*] earthly nature; cp. viii 453.

ix *1085–90.* The archetypal poem of retirement. Revulsion from vice was of course an obvious motive in the literature of retirement and solitude. See Henry Vaughan, 'Retirement' (*Works*, ed. Martin (1914) ii 642); Thomson, 'Hymn on Solitude'; Grainger, 'Ode on Solitude'; etc. Often this motive took a specifically sexual turn; as, e.g., in Marvell's 'The Garden' 25f: 'When we have run our Passions heat, / Love hither makes his best retreat.' At the same time, the *woods impenetrable / To star or sun-light* distinctly recall Statius' dark grove of Sleep, *nulli penetrabilis astro, / lucus iners* (*Theb.* x 85f) and Spenser's labyrinthine wood of Error, 'Whose loftie trees . . . / Did spred so broad, that heavens light did hide, / Not perceable with power of any starre' (I i 7). Adam's guilty impulse to retirement is by no means approved of by M. *umbrage*] shade (*OED 1*); foliage (*OED* 2 c). *brown*] See iv 246*n* on 'Embrowned'. *them*] i.e., the *shapes* of l. 1082.

ix *1091–8.* 'And the eyes of them both were opened, and they knew that they were naked; and they sewed fig leaves together, and made themselves aprons' (*Gen.* iii 7; marg. 'things to gird about'). M. took the shame mentioned in this verse to have arisen from the pollution of the 'whole man': '"their mind and conscience is defiled": whence arises shame' (*De doctrina* i 12; Columbia xv 205). *obnoxious*] exposed (*OED* 1 a); objectionable (*OED* 6). *sewed*] Taken to mean plaited, so that the simile of the Indian *cincture* at l. 1117 is exact.

ix *1092–3.* So *Ed I. Ed II* wrongly transposes *for* and *from.*

Those middle parts, that this new comer, shame,
There sit not, and reproach us as unclean.
So counselled he, and both together went
Into the thickest wood, there soon they chose
The fig-tree, not that kind for fruit renowned,
But such as at this day to Indians known
In Malabar or Decan spreads her arms
Branching so broad and long, that in the ground
The bended twigs take root, and daughters grow
About the mother tree, a pillared shade
High overarched, and echoing walks between;
There oft the Indian herdsman shunning heat
Shelters in cool, and tends his pasturing herds

ix *1097*. In view of the context it may be relevant to note that *comer* was a horticultural term, = 'springer'.

ix *1100–10*. The banyan or Indian fig had been described at length by Pliny, Raleigh and encyclopedists such as Bartholomew, so that a source is hard to assign (see Svendsen 31f). But Gerard's description is probably as close as any to the present passage: 'The ends thereof hang downe, and touch the ground, where they take roote and grow in such sort that those twigs become great trees; and these being growen up to the like greatnes, do cast their branches and twiggie tendrels unto the earth, where they likewise take hold and roote. . . . Of one tree is made a great wood, or desart of trees, which the Indians do use for coverture against the extreme heate of the sunne. . . . Some likewise use them for pleasure, cutting downe by a direct line a long walke, or as it were a vault, through the thickest part, from which also they cut certaine loope holes or windowes in some places, to the end to receive thereby the fresh coole aire that entereth therat; as also for light, that they may see their cattle. . . . The first or mother of this wood or desart of trees, is hard to be knowne from the children' (*Herball* (1597) 1330f). Svendsen 135 treats this fig-bower as a 'deep interior sanctuary'. But it seems more probable that M. intends a contrast with the prelapsarian nuptial bower of iv 690–708. The Indian herdsman is put in because he is primitive and pagan, and perhaps also because his work is connected with fallen man's non-vegetarian diet. Similarly the Amazonian targe is carried over from Gerard because before the Fall man never thought of fighting, let alone woman. The proliferating tree is a tree of error: it is an objective correlative of the proliferating sin that will ramify through Adam's and Eve's descendants. In this connection, cp. Thomas Becon's allegorization of the fig-tree: 'As this Tree (saith he) so did Man grow straight and upright towards God, untill such time as he had transgressed and broken the Commandment of his Creatour; and then like unto the boughes of this tree, he beganne to bend downeward, and stouped toward the earth, which all the rest of *Adam's* posteritie have done, rooting themselves therein and fastening themselves to this corrupt world' (*cit.* Svendsen 136 from Raleigh).

At loop-holes cut through thickest shade: those leaves
They gathered, broad as Amazonian targe,
And with what skill they had, together sewed,
To gird their waist, vain covering if to hide
Their guilt and dreaded shame; O how unlike
To that first naked glory. Such of late
Columbus found the American so girt
With feathered cincture, naked else and wild
Among the trees on isles and woody shores.
Thus fenced, and as they thought, their shame in part
Covered, but not at rest or ease of mind,
They sat them down to weep, nor only tears
Rained at their eyes, but high winds worse within
Began to rise, high passions, anger, hate,
Mistrust, suspicion, discord, and shook sore
Their inward state of mind, calm region once
And full of peace, now tossed and turbulent:
For understanding ruled not, and the will
Heard not her lore, both in subjection now
To sensual appetite, who from beneath
Usurping over sovereign reason claimed
Superior sway: from thus distempered breast,
Adam, estranged in look and altered style,
Speech intermitted thus to Eve renewed.
Would thou hadst hearkened to my words, and stayed
With me, as I besought thee, when that strange
Desire of wandering this unhappy morn,

ix *1117. cincture*] A wittily exact word. Besides meaning 'belt' (*OED* 3 a), it is the term applied in architecture to the fillet that divides the shaft of a column from the capital and base (*OED* 3 b); thus the comparison of Eve's savage posterity to pillars is carried on from ll. 1105f.

ix *1122.* The microcosm–macrocosm analogy not only universalizes the change in human nature, but also prepares for the meteorological disturbances to be treated in the next book. With the stormy tears which here *rain* down, contrast Eve's gentle tears before the Fall (v 130). For a corresponding contrast in the macrocosm, see 1002*n* above. *high winds*] Cp., in the external world, the violent winds of x 695ff and the 'gentle gales' before the Fall (e.g. iv 156).

ix *1127–31.* Cp. 351–6. This model, too, has a universalizing effect–man's fall means the corruption of the state as well as of the individual psyche. For a similar politico-legal *allegoria* of the Fall, see iii 176*n* and 204ff.

ix *1132–3. estranged*] changed, rendered remote from his normal condition, made unlike himself (*OED* 4). *style*] tone; but see also Introduction, 'Prosody' (p. 439 above).

I know not whence possessed thee; we had then
Remained still happy, not as now, despoiled
Of all our good, shamed, naked, miserable.
Let none henceforth seek needless cause to approve
The faith they owe; when earnestly they seek
Such proof, conclude, they then begin to fail.
　To whom soon moved with touch of blame thus Eve.
What words have passed thy lips, Adam severe,
Imput'st thou that to my default, or will
Of wandering, as thou call'st it, which who knows
But might as ill have happened thou being by,
Or to thy self perhaps: hadst thou been there,
Or here the attempt, thou couldst not have discerned
Fraud in the serpent, speaking as he spake;
No ground of enmity between us known,
Why he should mean me ill, or seek to harm.
Was I to have never parted from thy side?
As good have grown there still a lifeless rib.
Being as I am, why didst not thou the head
Command me absolutely not to go,
Going into such danger as thou saidst?
Too facile then thou didst not much gainsay,

ix *1140–2.* Referring to Eve's argument of ll. 332–6 above. *approve*] demonstrate practically, give proof of (*OED* 3). The rhythm mimes the sense; for *Let . . . owe* can be read as the first half of a common metre stanza (alternate iambic tetrameters and trimeters); but if *when . . . fail* is read as the second half of the stanza, it tails away into ineffectual sententiousness. *owe*] 'be under obligation to render' (*OED* I 2) or 'possess' (*OED* I 1 a).
ix *1144. What . . . lips*] Echoes Odysseus' disapproval of a speech of Agamemnon's, *Il.* xiv 83.
ix *1146–50.* Belied by Satan's admission at l. 483 that he shuns Adam's 'higher intellectual'. M. is enforcing the point that temptation should be dealt with by intellectual discernment, nor merely by emotional resistance or exertion of the will. Burden 81 notices Eve's use of *happened*, redolent of the Satanic ideology of mischance.
ix *1155. head*] Alludes to *1 Cor.* xi 3: 'The head of every man is Christ; and the head of the woman is the man; and the head of Christ is God.' Eve, having implied in ll. 1146–50 that Adam is no wiser than she is, now blames him nevertheless for not guiding her. Thus she empties headship of its true meaning, and makes it mere status in a hierarchy of power and command. Contrast iv 442f.
ix *1158–61.* It is true that Adam permitted her to go: see ll. 372 and 378 above. But then, to command her 'absolutely not to go' (l. 1156) would have made her stay 'not free' (l. 372). Whether Adam was *Too facile* is harder to say: *facile* in the sense 'courteous, mild, gentle' (*OED* 4) he certainly

Nay didst permit, approve, and fair dismiss.
Hadst thou been firm and fixed in thy dissent,
Neither had I transgressed, nor thou with me.
   To whom then first incensed Adam replied,
Is this the love, is this the recompense
Of mine to thee, ingrateful Eve, expressed
Immutable when thou wert lost, not I,
Who might have lived and joyed immortal bliss,
Yet willingly chose rather death with thee:
And am I now upbraided, as the cause
Of thy transgressing? Not enough severe,
It seems, in thy restraint: what could I more?
I warned thee, I admonished thee, foretold
The danger, and the lurking enemy
That lay in wait; beyond this had been force,
And force upon free will hath here no place.
But confidence then bore thee on, secure
Either to meet no danger, or to find
Matter of glorious trial; and perhaps
I also erred in overmuch admiring
What seemed in thee so perfect, that I thought
No evil durst attempt thee, but I rue
That error now, which is become my crime,
And thou the accuser. Thus it shall befall

was; whether he was 'easily led, compliant' (*OED* 5) is controversial; see ll. 370–5*n* above. In view of the falsity of the rest of Eve's arguments, it seems that this accusation is also unjust, and that Adam's culpable errors begin only at l. 906.

ix *1164. ingrateful*] ungrateful. *expressed*] revealed by external actions (*OED* II 7).

ix *1166. joy*] enjoy.

ix *1175. confidence*] unfounded assurance, overboldness, presumption (*OED* 4, citing Hooker: 'Their confidence, for the most part, riseth from too much credit given to their own wits'). *secure*] over-confident (*OED* I 1).

ix *1177. matter*] pretext, occasion (*OED* 13).

ix *1178–86.* The admiration confessed by Adam at viii 540–59. There he spoke–to Raphael's displeasure–of 'greatness of mind and nobleness' creating 'an awe / About her, as a guard angelic placed'. The passage clearly indicates a psychological interpretation of the Fall. Marjorie Nicolson compares Henry More's interpretation of Adam and Eve as Intellect and Will. This is a useful comparison, but M.'s scheme may not have been identical. Indeed, if his Eve were human will, the phrase *her will* (l. 1184) would be a type fallacy. See further in ll. 703–9*n* above.

Him who to worth in women overtrusting
Lets her will rule; restraint she will not brook,
And left to her self, if evil thence ensue,
She first his weak indulgence will accuse.
  Thus they in mutual accusation spent
The fruitless hours, but neither self-condemning,
And of their vain contest appeared no end.

THE END OF THE NINTH BOOK

Paradise Lost

BOOK X

The Argument

Man's transgression known, the guardian angels forsake Paradise, and return up to heaven to approve their vigilance, and are approved, God declaring that the entrance of Satan could not be by them prevented. He sends his Son to judge the transgressors, who descends and gives sentence accordingly; then in pity clothes them both, and re-ascends. Sin and Death sitting till then at the gates of hell, by wondrous sympathy feeling the success of Satan in this new world, and the sin by man there committed, resolve to sit no longer confined in hell, but to follow Satan their sire up to the place of man: to make the way easier from hell to this world to and fro, they pave a broad highway or bridge over chaos, according to the track that Satan first made; then preparing for earth, they meet him proud of his success returning to hell; their mutual gratulation. Satan arrives at Pandemonium, in full assembly relates with boasting his success against man; instead of applause is entertained with a general hiss by all his audience, transformed with himself also suddenly into serpents, according to his doom given in Paradise; then deluded with a show of the forbidden tree springing up before them, they greedily reaching to take of the fruit, chew dust and bitter ashes. The proceedings of Sin and Death; God foretells the final victory of his Son over them, and the renewing of all things; but for the present commands his angels to

ix *1183. women*] Bentley emended to 'woman', but the transition from plural to singular can be defended, either as artful imitation on M.'s part (for a Latin precedent see Terence, *Eun.* II i 10) or as artless impatience on Adam's.
ix *1188. fruitless*] Enlivened by the thematic pun made explicit at l. 648. *neither self-condemning*] Cp. the Fourth Draft of M.'s projected Paradise Lost tragedy, where 'Adam then and Eve return accuse one another but especially Adam lays the blame to his wife, is stubborn in his offence'.
ix *1189. contest*] Stressed on the second syllable.

make several alterations in the heavens and elements. Adam more and more perceiving his fallen condition heavily bewails, rejects the condolement of Eve; she persists and at length appeases him: then to evade the curse likely to fall on their offspring, proposes to Adam violent ways which he approves not, but conceiving better hope, puts her in mind of the late promise made them, that her seed should be revenged on the serpent, and exhorts her with him to seek peace of the offended Deity, by repentance and supplication.

Meanwhile the heinous and despiteful act
Of Satan done in Paradise, and how
He in the serpent, had perverted Eve,
Her husband she, to taste the fatal fruit,
Was known in heaven; for what can scape the eye
Of God all-seeing, or deceive his heart
Omniscient, who in all things wise and just,
Hindered not Satan to attempt the mind
Of man, with strength entire, and free will armed,
Complete to have discovered and repulsed
Whatever wiles of foe or seeming friend.
For still they knew, and ought to have still remembered
The high injunction not to taste that fruit,
Whoever tempted; which they not obeying,

x *1–16.* Rhetorically, these lines function both as *principium*, stating the subject of the book, and as *initium*, introducing the first scene. They also sum up the theological content of Bk iii, which will receive specific application in the present book, in the exchanges between the Father and the Son (ll. 34–84 below) and between the Son and Adam (ll. 124ff). Note the structural symmetry whereby the divine decrees of the third book are balanced by those of the third last. Addison remarks that the book 'has a greater variety of Persons in it than any other in the whole Poem. The Author upon the winding up of his Action introduces all those who had any Concern in it, and shews with great Beauty the influence which it had upon each of them. It is like the last Act of a well written Tragedy, in which all who had a part in it are generally drawn up before the Audience, and represented under those Circumstances in which the determination of the Action places them' (*Spectator*, No. 357; ed. Bond iii 329f).
x *5–7.* Showing the impossibility of Eve's illusory hope of concealment at ix 811–16. For the all-seeing eye of God, cp. iii 534 and 578, with *n.* On the eye as an ancient and Renaissance hieroglyph of Justice, see Wind (186f), who discusses the application of it in Alberti's emblem, with its threatening allusion to the Day of Judgment, which will come 'in the twinkling of an eye' (*1 Cor.* xv 52).
x *10. Complete*] fully equipped or endowed (qualifying *mind*).
x *12. still*] always, ever.
x *14.* Scan by stressing *which* and *not*, with *obeying* a dissyllable by synaloepha.

Incurred, what could they less, the penalty,
And manifold in sin, deserved to fall.
Up into heaven from Paradise in haste
The angelic guards ascended, mute and sad
For man, for of his state by this they knew,
Much wondering how the subtle fiend had stolen
Entrance unseen. Soon as the unwelcome news
From earth arrived at heaven gate, displeased
All were who heard, dim sadness did not spare
That time celestial visages, yet mixed
With pity, violated not their bliss.
About the new-arrived, in multitudes
The ethereal people ran, to hear and know
How all befell: they towards the throne supreme
Accountable made haste to make appear
With righteous plea, their utmost vigilance,
And easily approved; when the most high
Eternal Father from his secret cloud,
Amidst in thunder uttered thus his voice.
  Assembled angels, and ye powers returned
From unsuccessful charge, be not dismayed,
Nor troubled at these tidings from the earth,
Which your sincerest care could not prevent,
Foretold so lately what would come to pass,
When first this tempter crossed the gulf from hell.

x *16. manifold*] multiplied; alluding to *Ps.* xxxviii 19: 'they that hate me wrongfully are multiplied'; and perhaps also to *Ps.* xvi 4: 'their sorrows shall be multiplied that hasten after another god'. In both cases, early English versions used 'manifolded' to translate Vulg. *multiplicati.* The epithet should be connected with the fundamental opposition in the number symbolism of *PL* between good unity and evil multiplicity; see vi 767*n* and 809–10*n*. It is now apparent why (from a philosophical point of view) so much emphasis was laid on the separation or *division* of Adam and Eve: it was to enact their 'manifolding'. For M.'s analysis of the manifold character of the first sin itself, see ix 1003–4*n*.

x *18. angelic guards*] the cherubim of iv 550ff and ix 61f.

x *28–31.* Double syntax: either 'liable to be called to answer for their responsibilities (*OED* s.v. *Accountable* 1) they hastened . . . to make appear their vigilance', or 'they hastened . . . to make their vigilance appear explicable (*OED* s.v. *Accountable* 5)'. *approved*] confirmed (qualifying *vigilance*).

x *32–3.* For the imagery, cp. *Rev.* iv 5, and see ii 264–5*n* and iii 375–82*n*.

x *34–62.* Burden 40 notes that, like all the divine speeches, this initiates action; eliciting an immediate response from the Son (l. 85 below).

x *39. gulf*] From *Luke* xvi 26.

I told ye then he should prevail and speed
On his bad errand, man should be seduced
And flattered out of all, believing lies
Against his maker; no decree of mine
Concurring to necessitate his fall,
Or touch with lightest moment of impulse
His free will, to her own inclining left
In even scale. But fallen he is, and now
What rests but that the mortal sentence pass
On his transgression, death denounced that day,
Which he presumes already vain and void,
Because not yet inflicted, as he feared,
By some immediate stroke; but soon shall find

x *40. then*] i.e., at iii 92f. *speed*] be successful.

x *43–4*. See iii 113–23*n* on God's rejection of any Predestinarian account of his decrees that would lay him open to the charge of necessitating evil. *concurring*] cooperating (with man's free will).

x *45–7*. On the balance image, which is one of the most fully developed in the poem, see iv 997–1004*n*; *moment* belongs to the figure, for it was a term specifically applied to the smallest increment that could affect the equilibrium of a balance; see vi 239*n*. *impulse*] Cp. iii 120, 'without least impulse . . . of fate', and see *n*. *inclining*] Cp. ix 742, where Eve's desire is 'inclinable'. The metaphor of the true balance gains point from the iconographical tradition whereby in the weighing of souls at the last judgement the devils tried to cheat by leaning on one of the scales. Empson 116f rightly finds it noteworthy that we should here be reminded of the incident at the end of Bk iv, when God moved the Balance 'to expose mankind to the tempter'. But the discrepancy is only apparent. If man had been protected from the tempter, then there would have been real interference with the free action of the scales of justice.

x *48. rests*] remains.

x *49–53*. See viii 323–33*n* on the literalistic interpretation of *Gen.* ii 17, 'in the day that thou eatest thereof', which necessitated an allegorical interpretation of 'thou shalt surely die'. Cp. Adam's wishful argument of ix 927–37. *ere day end*] The fact that Christ descends to judge man at sunset (l. 92ff) seems to imply that in one sense the day of the Fall is to be regarded as ending at that hour. This accords with the reckoning of the Hebrew day from sunset to sunset (see Introduction, 'Chronology', p. 444). Later, however, Adam can refer to the night as still belonging to the day of the Fall (see l. 773*n*), and a midnight-to-midnight reckoning–even a sunrise-to-sunrise reckoning–appears to be followed. It would seem that Adam fearfully holds back the *terminus ad quem* of the day of reckoning, until at last he realizes the figurative meaning of the prohibition, at l. 1050.

Forbearance no acquittance ere day end.
Justice shall not return as bounty scorned.
But whom send I to judge them? Whom but thee
Vicegerent Son, to thee I have transferred
All judgment, whether in heaven, or earth, or hell.
Easy it might be seen that I intend
Mercy colleague with justice, sending thee
Man's friend, his mediator, his designed
Both ransom and redeemer voluntary,
And destined man himself to judge man fallen.
So spake the Father, and unfolding bright
Toward the right hand his glory, on the Son
Blazed forth unclouded deity; he full
Resplendent all his Father manifest
Expressed, and thus divinely answered mild.
Father Eternal, thine is to decree,
Mine both in heaven and earth to do thy will
Supreme, that thou in me thy Son beloved
Mayst ever rest well pleased. I go to judge

x *53. acquittance*] satisfaction or settlement of a debt. 'Omittance is not quittance' was a proverb; cp. *As You Like It* III v 133.
x *54.* 'My just dealing must not meet a return of generosity scorned'–i.e. not without further satisfaction. There is some difficulty in the diction, as a result of M.'s wish to continue the commercial metaphor with *return*.
x *56–7.* Cp. *John* v 22: 'The Father judgeth no man, but hath committed all judgment unto the Son'; and see *De doctrina* i 5 (Columbia xiv 251): 'The Son . . . was entitled to the name of God both in the capacity of a messenger and of a judge.'
x *58. might*] may *Ed I*.
x *59–62. colleague*] allied, united for a common purpose. For the alliance of mercy with justice cp. iii 131–4 and 407; also *Nativity Ode* 141–6. *Ps.* lxxxv 10 is usually cited, but that verse concerns four qualities (mercy and truth, righteousness and peace), not two. Justice and mercy as a pair recall rather the imperial virtues, Iustitia and Clementia; on which see Frances A. Yates, 'Queen Elizabeth as Astraea', *JWI* x (1947) 67. The double syntax–l. 62 can be read either 'himself a man, destined to judge man' (primary) or 'destined to judge man himself, man fallen'–mimes the close identification of Christ with man; for the pronoun has now Christ, now mankind, as its antecedent. See also *De doctrina* i 15 (Columbia xv 285): 'The mediatorial office of Christ is that whereby . . . he voluntarily performed, and continues to perform, on behalf of man, whatever is requisite for obtaining reconciliation with God, and eternal salvation.'
x *64–7.* Cp. the similar passages, all based on *Heb.* i 3, at iii 138–42, 384–9; vi 680–4, 719–21 above; and see *nn*.
x *70–1.* Echoing *Matt.* iii 17.

On earth these thy transgressors, but thou know'st,
Whoever judged, the worst on me must light,
When time shall be, for so I undertook
Before thee; and not repenting, this obtain
Of right, that I may mitigate their doom
On me derived, yet I shall temper so
Justice with mercy, as may illustrate most
Them fully satisfied, and thee appease.
Attendance none shall need, nor train, where none
Are to behold the judgment, but the judged,
Those two; the third best absent is condemned,
Convict by flight, and rebel to all law
Conviction to the serpent none belongs.
  Thus saying, from his radiant seat he rose
Of high collateral glory: him thrones and powers,
Princedoms, and dominations ministrant
Accompanied to heaven gate, from whence
Eden and all the coast in prospect lay.
Down he descended straight; the speed of gods
Time counts not, though with swiftest minutes winged.

x *74*. Alluding, like iii 284, to *Gal.* iv 4: 'When the fulness of the time was come, God sent forth his Son, made of a woman, made under the law.' The Son's undertaking was made at iii 227–65.

x *75–9*. Burden (39f) sees this part of the speech as apologetics, laying a theoretical foundation for the incident of Christ's clothing of Adam and Eve (ll. 211–21) that *Genesis* lacks. *derived*] channelled (*OED* I 1); diverted (*OED* I 2); imparted, passed on by descent (*OED* I 4); not a Latinism. *illustrate*] (Stressed on the second syllable) make clear; display to advantage (*OED* 3, 6). *Them* primarily refers to *Justice* and *mercy*, whose demands are satisfied; but in a secondary chain of discourse it could refer to Adam and Eve, who constitute a debt to God (*thee*) that is 'paid off' (*OED* s.v. *Satisfy* I 1, debt as object).

x *82–4*. *the third*] Satan. On the distribution of guilt between Satan and the serpent, see ll. 164–74*n*. *Convict*] convicted. *Conviction*] Has both the legal sense (proof of guilt: *OED* I) and the theological (the condition of being convinced of sin: *OED* 8). As an animal lacking reason, the serpent can have no heightened awareness of sin.

x *85–9*. Cp. the departure of Messiah to the Creation, vii 192–215.

x *86*. *collateral*] side by side (*OED* A 1); or conceivably 'subordinate' (*OED* A 3).

x *86–7*. On the roll-call of titles, see v 601*n*.

x *89*. *coast*] region; or perhaps 'side (of the world)'; cp. iii 739, vi 529.

x *90–1*. Either 'however swift he may be, Time cannot count the speed of gods' or 'though their speed is winged with minutes–takes place in time–Time cannot count it'. Cp. viii 110, 'Speed almost spiritual'. *with* ...

Now was the sun in western cadence low
From noon, and gentle airs due at their hour
To fan the earth now waked, and usher in
The evening cool when he from wrath more cool
Came the mild judge and intercessor both
To sentence man: the voice of God they heard
Now walking in the garden, by soft winds
Brought to their ears, while day declined, they heard,
And from his presence hid themselves among
The thickest trees, both man and wife, till God
Approaching, thus to Adam called aloud.
  Where art thou Adam, wont with joy to meet

minutes winged] Iconographically precise, for there was a type of Time–here deliberately overgone–which showed him with four wings to represent the seasons, and twelve feathers the months. See Panofsky[2] 79 and Fig. 50. Cowley 252 describes the descent of an angel similarly: 'Slow *Time* admires, and knows not what to call / The *Motion*, having no *Account* so *small.*' Cp. also vii 176f: 'Immediate are the acts of God, more swift / Than time or motion.' The parallel between the two descents of Christ is of the first importance; for it gives formal expression to the idea that the new creation is now beginning; the second task of Christ the second Adam.

x *92–102*. See *Gen.* iii 8: 'They heard the voice of the Lord God walking in the garden in the cool of the day: and Adam and his wife hid themselves from the presence of the Lord God amongst the trees of the garden.' Christ did not come at *noon*, the hour of the Fall, because symbolically that was the time of destructive judgment (see iv 30*n*); but neither may he wait until the sun has quite gone down on his wrath, in view of *Eph.* iv 26. *cadence*] falling; sinking; probably a Latinism, though there are prose instances. *gentle airs*] Picks up 'wind', the A.V. marginal alternative to 'cool', in *Gen.* iii 8. Ricks 107 traces a secondary musical chain of discourse in *airs* and *cadence*. *evening*] Day 33.

x *101*. *God*] Christ assumes the divine title while on earth, since there he is 'Vicegerent' (l. 56). Cp. *De doctrina* i 5, (Columbia xiv 251): 'The name of God is ascribed to judges, because they occupy the place of God to a certain degree in the administration of judgment.'

x *102–8*. Following *Gen.* iii 9, but greatly developing God's pretence of ignorance. No doubt this is to give Adam and Eve every chance to be candid. *obvious*] 'standing in the way' (*OED* 1) or 'plain, palpable' (*OED* 4). *change*] Followed so closely by *chance* this strongly recalls the First Collect after the Offertory: 'the changes and chances of this mortal life'. *chance* is a very deliberate and pointed choice of word: God knows perfectly well that Adam and Eve are absent by design, and that they have become subject to chance in a sense much graver than is ostensibly intended here. He is giving them an opening for confession. See ix 404–5*n*, 421*n*, 480–1*nn*.

My coming seen far off? I miss thee here,
Not pleased, thus entertained with solitude,
Where obvious duty erewhile appeared unsought:
Or come I less conspicuous, or what change
Absents thee, or what chance detains? Come forth.
He came, and with him Eve, more loath, though first
To offend, discountenanced both, and discomposed;
Love was not in their looks, either to God
Or to each other, but apparent guilt,
And shame, and perturbation, and despair,
Anger, and obstinacy, and hate, and guile.
Whence Adam faltering long, thus answered brief.
  I heard thee in the garden, and of thy voice
Afraid, being naked, hid myself. To whom
The gracious judge without revile replied.
  My voice thou oft hast heard, and hast not feared,
But still rejoiced, how is it now become
So dreadful to thee? That thou art naked, who
Hath told thee? Hast thou eaten of the tree
Whereof I gave thee charge thou shouldst not eat?
  To whom thus Adam sore beset replied.
O heaven! In evil strait this day I stand
Before my judge, either to undergo
My self the total crime, or to accuse
My other self, the partner of my life;
Whose failing, while her faith to me remains,
I should conceal, and not expose to blame
By my complaint; but strict necessity
Subdues me, and calamitous constraint
Lest on my head both sin and punishment,
However insupportable, be all
Devolved; though should I hold my peace, yet thou
Wouldst easily detect what I conceal.
This woman whom thou madest to be my help,
And gavest me as thy perfect gift, so good,
So fit, so acceptable, so divine,

x *112. apparent*] evident.

x *116–8.* Closely following *Gen.* iii 10. *revile*] reviling.

x *119–23.* See *Gen.* iii 11: 'And he said, Who told thee that thou wast naked? Hast thou eaten of the tree, whereof I commanded thee that thou shouldest not eat?' *still*] always.

x *128. other self*] Cp. viii 450.

x *135. devolved*] caused to fall upon (*OED* I 3 c); also 'caused to pass to another, by legal succession, especially through the deficiency of one previously responsible' (*OED* I 3 a, b).

That from her hand I could suspect no ill,
And what she did, whatever in it self,
Her doing seemed to justify the deed;
She gave me of the tree, and I did eat.
  To whom the sovereign presence thus replied.
Was she thy God, that her thou didst obey
Before his voice, or was she made thy guide,
Superior, or but equal, that to her
Thou didst resign thy manhood, and the place
Wherein God set thee above her made of thee,
And for thee, whose perfection far excelled
Hers in all real dignity: adorned
She was indeed, and lovely to attract
Thy love, not thy subjection, and her gifts
Were such as under government well seemed,
Unseemly to bear rule, which was thy part
And person, hadst thou known thy self aright.

x *141–3.* A less reputable version of Adam's enthusiastic speech to Raphael at viii 548–50: 'So well to know / Her own, that what she wills to do or say, / Seems wisest, virtuousest, discreetest, best.' Similarly Raphael's rebuke, with its insistence on headship, has its parallel in Christ's, ll. 144–56.
x *143. She*] Carries very heavy stress from its position in the line–appropriately to its rhetorical force as the summation of ll. 137–42. The verse closely follows *Gen.* iii 12: 'The woman whom thou gavest to be with me, she gave me of the tree, and I did eat.'
x *144.* Burden (90f) will not allow Waldock's sneer that the speech which follows presents a false official version of the facts. He argues that M. started (at least in order of logical priority) with this summary synoptic view, and then expanded it into the series of actions that have just ensued.
x *147. equal*] Cp. ix 823–5, where fallen Eve wondered if she would keep the fruit to herself, to make her 'more equal, and perhaps . . . sometime / Superior'.
x *149–50.* See *1 Cor.* xi 8f: 'For the man is not of the woman; but the woman of the man. Neither was the man created for the woman; but the woman for the man.'
x *151. real*] royal, regal (*OED* s.v. *Real* a.[1]); perhaps secondarily 'true, actual' (*OED* s.v. *Real* a.[2]).
x *154–5.* See *1 Tim.* ii 12.
x *155–6.* Christ analyses the error as a wrong choice of role. *part*] dramatic part, role. If the allegorical interpretation advanced at ix 360–1*n* above is accepted, then *thy part* will be seen to mean also 'your part of human nature, i.e., the intellect'. *person*] character (in a play). Cp. *PR* ii 240, 'some active scene / Of various persons, each to know his part', or Jeremy Taylor, *A course of sermons* (1653), 'put on a person and act a part'. Not a Latinism.

So having said, he thus to Eve in few:
Say woman, what is this which thou hast done?
To whom sad Eve with shame nigh overwhelmed,
Confessing soon, yet not before her judge
Bold or loquacious, thus abashed replied.
The serpent me beguiled and I did eat.
Which when the Lord God heard, without delay
To judgment he proceeded on the accused

x *157. in few*] in few words; not a Latinism. Cp. Shakespeare, *Hamlet* I iii 126; *II Henry IV* I i 112.

x *159–61*. M. carefully gives a lead as to how we should imagine the brief answer spoken. He does this sympathetically, making Eve immediately responsive to Christ. She experiences certain of the emotions of contrition, or at least of attrition, much more readily than Adam. See ix 1188*n* but also ll. 989–1008 below.

x *162*. Repeating A.V. *Gen.* iii 13, with only a slight alteration of word order.

x *164–74*. See ix 186*n*. Burden (54f) thinks that M. is in difficulty here, and that he betrays uneasiness at Christ's seeming injustice to the helpless serpent. The mysteriousness of the curse is not enough to remove its injustice; so that Satan too must be made to grovel on his belly, in the entirely invented episode of ll. 508ff. This is possible; though it is hardly to be supposed that M. would consciously have dissented from the view of, say, Mercerus (Willet 52), that 'God curseth the serpent because he was Sathans organe and instrument: and this standeth with Gods justice to punish the instrument with the principall [the authority cited is *Lev.* xx 15, 'if a man lie with a beast, he shall surely be put to death: and ye shall slay the beast']. . . . And though the serpent had no understanding, yet God curseth him for mans instruction, that he might see how much this their action in seducing him, was displeasing to God.' There was more difference of opinion as to the exact meaning of the curse (for which see following *n*). Some referred the whole curse to the serpent, others to Satan 'by way of allegorie', while others again understood it literally of the serpent and mystically of Satan, and a fourth group (to which Calvin belonged) gave the first part of the curse to the serpent and the last part to Satan. M.'s lines embrace the views of almost all these groups. For *at last* seems at l. 171 to refer to the last part of the curse, though at l. 190 it turns out to refer also to the 'last things', the final reckoning with Satan. Similarly, ll. 182–9 applies the curse allegorically or 'mysteriously' to Satan, and ll. 176–81 can be taken to apply literally to the serpent (particularly since at ix 496ff we saw it upright and 'not . . . / Prone on the ground, as since'); yet the curse seems to be applied literally to Satan at ll. 508ff, where he and the other devils actually fall prone and eat dust. *unable*] Probably qualifies *serpent*. *no further*] At this stage Adam and Eve have no knowledge of the verification of the oracle, in the redemptive history (see ll. 182–9); that the serpent is an instrument, Adam has already a shrewd idea (see ix 904f).

Serpent though brute, unable to transfer
The guilt on him who made him instrument
Of mischief, and polluted from the end
Of his creation; justly then accursed,
As vitiated in nature: more to know
Concerned not man (since he no further knew)
Nor altered his offence; yet God at last
To Satan first in sin his doom applied,
Though in mysterious terms, judged as then best:
And on the serpent thus his curse let fall.
  Because thou hast done this, thou art accursed
Above all cattle, each beast of the field;
Upon thy belly grovelling thou shalt go,
And dust shalt eat all the days of thy life.
Between thee and the woman I will put
Enmity, and between thine and her seed;
Her seed shall bruise thy head, thou bruise his heel.
  So spake this oracle, then verified
When Jesus son of Mary second Eve,
Saw Satan fall like lightning down from heaven,
Prince of the air; then rising from his grave
Spoiled principalities and powers, triumphed
In open show, and with ascension bright
Captivity led captive through the air,
The realm it self of Satan long usurped,

mysterious] mystical. Adam's still formidable intellect will have given him an inkling of the inner meaning of the curse by ll. 1030ff.

x *175–81*. See *Gen.* iii 14f: 'And the Lord God said unto the serpent, Because thou hast done this, thou art cursed above all cattle, and above every beast of the field; upon thy belly shalt thou go, and dust shalt thou eat all the days of thy life: And I will put enmity between thee and the woman, and between thy seed and her seed; it shall bruise thy head, and thou shalt bruise his heel.'

x *183. second Eve*] Cp. v 386f.

x *184*. When the disciples returned from preaching and reported that they had subjected devils through Jesus' name, he said 'I beheld Satan as lightning fall from heaven' (*Luke* x 18).

x *185*. Cp. *Eph.* ii 2: 'In time past ye walked . . . according to the prince of the power of the air.'

x *186*. Cp. *Col.* ii 14f, where Christ is said to have put the condemnation of the Law out of the way, 'nailing it to his cross; And having spoiled principalities and powers, he made a shew of them openly, triumphing over them in it.'

x *188*. Cp. *Ps.* lxviii 18: 'Thou hast ascended on high, thou hast led captivity captive'; applied to Christ at *Eph.* iv 8.

Whom he shall tread at last under our feet;
Even he who now foretold his fatal bruise,
And to the woman thus his sentence turned.
Thy sorrow I will greatly multiply
By thy conception; children thou shalt bring
In sorrow forth, and to thy husband's will
Thine shall submit, he over thee shall rule.
On Adam last thus judgment he pronounced.
Because thou hast hearkened to the voice of thy wife,
And eaten of the tree concerning which
I charged thee, saying: Thou shalt not eat thereof,
Cursed is the ground for thy sake, thou in sorrow
Shalt eat thereof all the days of thy life;
Thorns also and thistles it shall bring thee forth
Unbid, and thou shalt eat the herb of the field,
In the sweat of thy face shalt thou eat bread,
Till thou return unto the ground, for thou
Out of the ground wast taken, know thy birth,
For dust thou art, and shalt to dust return.
So judged he man, both judge and saviour sent,
And the instant stroke of death denounced that day

x *190*. See *Rom.* xvi 20, a proof text for the mystical interpretation of the curse on the serpent: 'And the God of peace shall bruise [margin 'tread'] Satan under your feet shortly.'

x *192*. The order of the curses is of vital importance. See *De doctrina* i 14, (Columbia xv 253): 'In pronouncing the punishment of the serpent, previously to passing sentence on man, [God] promised that he would raise up from the seed of the woman one who should bruise the serpent's head, Gen. iii 15. and thus anticipated the condemnation of mankind by a gratuitous redemption.' Cp. the analogous order of subjects in the divine conversation in Bk iii; see iii 173–202*n*.

x *197–202*. Cp. *Gen.* iii 17: 'And unto Adam he said, Because thou hast hearkened unto the voice of thy wife, and hast eaten of the tree, of which I commanded thee, saying, Thou shalt not eat of it; cursed is the ground for thy sake; in sorrow shalt thou eat of it all the days of thy life'.

x *203–8*. Cp. *Gen.* iii 18–9: 'Thorns also and thistles shall it bring forth to thee; and thou shalt eat the herb of the field; In the sweat of thy face shalt thou eat bread, till thou return unto the ground; for out of it wast thou taken: for dust thou art, and unto dust shalt thou return.' *know thy birth*] This is puzzling, since Adam has already been told by Raphael that he was formed of 'dust of the ground' (vii 525).

x *210–1*. On the terms of the prohibition, see viii 323–33*n*. Christ removes the fear that physical death will follow the eating of the fruit on the same day, by his mention of 'all the days' of Adam's life (l. 202). *denounced*] proclaimed, implying a warning.

Removed far off; then pitying how they stood
Before him naked to the air, that now
Must suffer change, disdained not to begin
Thenceforth the form of servant to assume,
As when he washed his servants' feet so now
As father of his family he clad
Their nakedness with skins of beasts, or slain,
Or as the snake with youthful coat repaid;
And thought not much to clothe his enemies:
Nor he their outward only with the skins
Of beasts, but inward nakedness, much more
Opprobrious, with his robe of righteousness,
Arraying covered from his Father's sight.
To him with swift ascent he up returned,
Into his blissful bosom reassumed

x *211–19.* Burden 39 notes how Christ's pity is immediately active.

x *213.* The *change* in the air is at ll. 692–706.

x *214.* Cp. *Phil.* ii 7: 'made himself of no reputation, and took upon him the form of a servant, and was made in the likeness of men'.

x *215.* *Ed I* has comma after *feet.*

x *216.* *father*] See *Heb.* ii 13: 'the children which God hath given me'.

x *216–23.* See *Gen.* iii 21. Willet 54f mentions, only to reject, the view that God slew beasts and clothed Adam and Eve 'to betoken . . . the cloathing of the nakednesse of the soule by repentance'. Reasons he accepts include: to show man how to care for his body; to cover his nakedness with what the Chaldee paraphrase calls *vestimenta honoris*; to teach man he may kill for clothing; and to remind him of mortality. If the animals are *slain*, then in this the first instance of actual death, Christ is the immediate cause (see *ere thus was . . . judged*, l. 229). The mention of the *snake's* slough probably alludes to a neat theory in the *Targum*, ascribed to Jonathan ben Uzziel, that man's needs were by a poetic justice met from the skin of the serpent that had occasioned them. Christ's clothing man with a robe of righteousness was a commonplace of religious poetry; cp., e.g., George Herbert, 'Sunday': 'The brightnesse of that day / We sullied by our foul offence: / Wherefore that robe we cast away, / Having a new at his expence, / Whose drops of bloud paid the full price, / That was requir'd to make us gay, / And fit for Paradise.' The Biblical source is *Is.* lxi 10: 'My soul shall be joyful in my God; for he hath clothed me with the garments of salvation, he hath covered me with the robe of righteousness, as a bridegroom decketh himself with ornaments, and as a bride adorneth herself with her jewels.' Cp. ix 1054–9, where Adam and Eve discover themselves to have lost the veils of innocence, confidence, righteousness and honour.

x *219.* *enemies*] See *Rom.* v 10: 'If, when we were enemies, we were reconciled to God by the death of his Son, much more, being reconciled, we shall be saved by his life.'

In glory as of old, to him appeased
All, though all-knowing, what had passed with man
Recounted, mixing intercession sweet.
Meanwhile ere thus was sinned and judged on earth,
Within the gates of hell sat Sin and Death,
In counterview within the gates, that now
Stood open wide, belching outrageous flame
Far into chaos, since the fiend passed through,
Sin opening, who thus now to Death began.
O son, why sit we here each other viewing
Idly, while Satan our great author thrives
In other worlds, and happier seat provides
For us his offspring dear? It cannot be
But that success attends him; if mishap,
Ere this he had returned, with fury driven
By his avengers, since no place like this
Can fit his punishment, or their revenge.
Methinks I feel new strength within me rise,
Wings growing, and dominion given me large
Beyond this deep; whatever draws me on,
Or sympathy, or some connatural force

x *230*. Addison disapproved of the long allegory that follows, thinking it improper for epic. But Newton illuminatingly remarks that much of M.'s poem 'lies in the invisible world. . . . The actions of Sin and Death are at least as probable as those ascribed to the good or evil Angels.' Such allegories were fairly common in literary treatments of the Fall. Hughes cites Samuel Pordage; and there is a very elaborate example indeed in Sylvester's Du Bartas II i 3, 'The Furies', where Dearth, War and Sickness, all with their attendant abstractions, come in procession with their 'steely Cars' across 'th'ever-shaking nine-fold steely bars / Of Stygian Bridge'.
x *231*. See ii 649, where Sin and Death sit 'before the gates' of hell, 'on either side'.
x *232*. The gates have been open since Sin's failure to shut them, at ii 883f. *outrageous*] fierce; enormous; immoderate.
x *236*. *author*] parent; inventor.
x *241*. *avengers*] avenger *Ed I*. *like*] i.e., so well as.
x *244*. Cp. ix 1009f, where Adam and Eve, newly intoxicated by their fall, 'fancy that they feel / Divinity within them breeding wings'. The three sets of wings are bred simultaneously, for the sub-plot concerning Sin is not a separate action, but a treatment of the main action in a different mode and from a different point of view. M. discreetly indicates this at l. 229, by noticing the simultaneity of Sin's rise and man's fall.
x *246–9*. *or . . . or*] either . . . or. *sympathy*] affinity by virtue of which two entities might influence one another, regardless of distance. Philemon Holland defined the term as meaning 'a fellow-feeling, used in *Pliny*, for the

Powerful at greatest distance to unite
With secret amity things of like kind
By secretest conveyance. Thou my shade
Inseparable must with me along:
For Death from Sin no power can separate.
But lest the difficulty of passing back
Stay his return perhaps over this gulf
Impassable, impervious, let us try
Adventurous work, yet to thy power and mine
Not unagreeable, to found a path
Over this main from hell to that new world
Where Satan now prevails, a monument
Of merit high to all the infernal host,
Easing their passage hence, for intercourse,
Or transmigration, as their lot shall lead.
Nor can I miss the way, so strongly drawn
By this new felt attraction and instinct.

agreement or amitie naturall in divers sencelesse things, as betweene yron and the loadstone' (Pliny's *Historie of the world* (1634) tom. ii, A 6^{v}). Lewis (66) thinks that Sin here shows her deluded ignorance, by mistaking for sympathy with Satan what is really God's summons of his hell-hounds 'to lick up the draff and filth' made by the Fall (see ll. 616–40). From another point of view, the feeling of sympathy is to be related to Adam's feeling of sympathy with Eve, which gave him a premonition of her Fall (Burden 167f; see ix 845f). *conveyance*] communication.

x *252–323*. A great work of building was traditionally an ingredient of epic; the building of Carthage in Virgil *Aen.* i 423ff is probably the most famous instance. *PL* has several such works. God performs a single work of creation in vii, and this is doubled in the two devilish works, Pandaemonium (i) and the bridge over chaos. The latter forms a close antitype to God's creation out of chaos, as Tillyard notes in *SP* xxxviii (1941) 269.

x *253–4*. See *Luke* xvi 26 on the 'great gulf' fixed between the elect and the reprobate 'so that they which would pass from hence to you cannot; neither can they pass to us, that would come from thence'. *impervious*] affording no passage (*OED* 1).

x *255*. *Adventurous*] Spelt 'Adventrous', and scanned as a trisyllable.

x *256*. *found*] build; establish. Not a Latinism.

x *257*. *main*] ocean, expanse; i.e., chaos.

x *260–1*. Sin inevitably uses the terms of the satanic ideology; speaking of *lot* as the determining factor. Cp. Eve at ix 881 and Adam at ix 952. *intercourse*] communication to and fro between two places. *transmigration*] permanent migration from one place to another.

x *263*. *instinct*] Stressed on the second syllable.

Whom thus the meagre shadow answered soon.
Go whither fate and inclination strong
Leads thee, I shall not lag behind, nor err
The way, thou leading, such a scent I draw
Of carnage, prey innumerable, and taste
The savour of death from all things there that live:
Nor shall I to the work thou enterprisest
Be wanting, but afford thee equal aid.
So saying, with delight he snuffed the smell
Of mortal change on earth. As when a flock
Of ravenous fowl, though many a league remote,
Against the day of battle, to a field,
Where armies lie encamped, come flying, lured
With scent of living carcasses designed
For death, the following day, in bloody fight.
So scented the grim feature, and upturned
His nostril wide into the murky air,
Sagacious of his quarry from so far.
Then both from out hell gates into the waste
Wide anarchy of chaos damp and dark
Flew diverse, and with power (their power was great)
Hovering upon the waters; what they met

x *264. meagre*] emaciated (*OED* 1); Death was usually represented as an almost fleshless skeleton.

x *266. err*] mistake.

x *267. draw*] inhale (*OED* II 23).

x *268–70. savour of death*] For the word play see ix 1017–20*n*, and for a resemblance between Death and Eve, ix 791–2*n*.

x *271. Ed II* wrongly has comma after *aid*.

x *273–8.* Satan is similarly compared to a vulture at iii 431ff. The prolepsis here (*living carcasses*) may have been suggested by Pliny, *Nat. hist.* x 7: *triduo antea volare eos ubi cadavera futura sunt*, or by one of several passages based on this in encyclopedists such as Aldrovandus. As in the simile at ll. 307–11, an implied correspondence between tenor and vehicle is the numerousness, in each case, of those who are to die.

x *279. feature*] form, shape (*OED* 1 c); cp. *Areopagitica* (Yale ii 549), 'an immortall feature of loveliness and perfection'.

x *281. Sagacious*] acute of perception (especially by smell). Cp. Eve, who is 'exact of taste', ix 1017.

x *283. anarchy*] Cp. ii 988, vi 873.

x *284. diverse*] turning in opposite directions. The parenthesis discriminates between God's creation and that of Sin and Death: the latter have power, but not goodness.

x *285–8.* Contrast vii 235–40, where the spirit of God hovered over the same deep, but made it a 'watery calm', and 'purged / The black tartareous cold

Solid or slimy, as in raging sea
Tossed up and down, together crowded drove
From each side shoaling towards the mouth of hell.
As when two polar winds blowing adverse
Upon the Cronian sea, together drive
Mountains of ice, that stop the imagined way
Beyond Petsora eastward, to the rich
Cathaian coast. The aggregated soil
Death with his mace petrific, cold and dry,
As with a trident smote, and fixed as firm
As Delos floating once; the rest his look

infernal dregs'. *shoaling*] crowding together, assembling in swarms (*OED* v.[3] 2).

x *289–93. Cronian Sea*] the Arctic Ocean, better known as the *mare concretum*– an apt choice, therefore, in view of the solidifying work Death is soon to engage in. *the imagined way*] A north east passage to Cathay had been searched for by Hudson in 1608; but he was unable to find an opening through the ice. *Petsora* or Pechora is a river in N. Russia, mentioned by M. in his *Brief History of Muscovia*. Cathay (see xi 388) was regarded as a separate empire from China, to the north. *rich*] Makes the point of the simile clear: Cathay is so desirable that it stands for the objective of human effort, Paradise. Nevertheless, the simile is an intricate one, whose logical structure includes the unusual feature of double tenors carried on a single vehicle (due to the fact that Sin's actions are allegorical). Thus Cathay in the vehicle corresponds in one tenor to Paradise on earth, in the other to paradise in heaven. The Cronian ice–i.e., the structure of fallen human nature–is like the *bridge* built to make access from the earthly Paradise to hell easy; but it also constitutes a *barrier* making man's ascent to paradise above difficult. See ll. 321–4*n*.

x *293–6. mace petrific*] Cp. Marlowe, *Dido*, II i 115, 'pale Death's stony mace'. The mace conveys utter destruction, yet at the same time travesties the creative sovereignty of Christ; see Cirlot 186. Whereas the spirit of God infused 'vital warmth' into the 'fluid mass' of chaos (vii 236f), Death chooses cold and dry–the qualities inimical to life–for his work. *Delos*] An island raised by the trident of Neptune, to provide a refuge where Latona might give birth to Apollo and Diana; a floating island, until Jupiter fastened it with chains to the bottom of the sea. Delos has already been connected with Paradise, the refuge of Adam and Eve, at v 265 and ix 387, so that the implication is that Death's effect is as irrevocable as Jupiter's chains of necessity. *As with a trident*] Highly ambivalent: on the one hand the implied comparison with Neptune the controller of waves suggests peace, on the other, the trident was an attribute of Satan (its triple form symbolizing the infernal trinity).

x *296–8*. The Gorgons turned to stone all whom they looked at; see ii 611*n*. But it is not clear why Death treats some of the material of chaos with his

Bound with Gorgonian rigor not to move,
And with asphaltic slime; broad as the gate,
Deep to the roots of hell the gathered beach
They fastened, and the mole immense wrought on
Over the foaming deep high arched, a bridge
Of length prodigious joining to the wall
Immovable of this now fenceless world
Forfeit to Death; from hence a passage broad,
Smooth, easy, inoffensive down to hell.
So, if great things to small may be compared,
Xerxes, the liberty of Greece to yoke,

mace, and the rest with his look. Bentley and Empson[2] 154 have some elusive objection to M.'s mixture of concrete and abstract in this zeugma: a mixture which is of course the staple of allegory. *asphaltic slime*] asphaltus, jew's pitch; used by the devils at i 729. M. no doubt selected this particular cement less for its black colour and connection with the Dead Sea (l. 562) than for the association of *Ecclus.* xiii 1: 'He that toucheth pitch shall be defiled therewith' (a verse that had become proverbial; cp. Spenser, *Shepheardes Calender*, May 74). *slime*] In A.V. *Gen.* xi 3 'slime' translates the Hebrew word for pitch (Vulgate *bitumen*). *rigor*] numbness, stiffness. *OED* cites no instance of the form *rigor mortis* earlier than 1839. On a possible source (which however does not help with the interpretation of the passage) see Tillyard in *SP* xxxviii (1941) 267.

x *300*. The bridge is fastened to hell, as God's work, the universe, is fastened to heaven (ii 1051).

x *302–3*. The *wall* is 'the utmost orb / Of this frail world', the firm opaque outer shell to which we were told at ii 1024–31 the bridge was fastened. In spite of the wall, the world is without defence (*fenceless*) against Death.

x *305*. *inoffensive*] not giving offence (i.e., to society: the passage is designed for conformists), and 'not causing stumbling; free from obstacles' (Lat. *inoffensus*). The word also continues the play on *fence*. Cp. *Matt.* vii 13: 'Enter ye in at the strait gate: for wide is the gate, and broad is the way, that leadeth to destruction, and many there be which go in thereat.'

x *306*. See ii 921–2*n*.

x *307–11*. Starnes and Talbert (285) show the source to be not Herodotus vii 33 but Stephanus: *Xerxes, Persarum rex fuit filius Darii . . . Graeciae bellum intulit . . . tantum autem habuit navium apparatum, ut totum Hellespontum operiret, et Asiam Europae ponte coniungeret.* Susa was the winter seat of the Persian kings; it was sometimes called *Memnonia*, after Memnon, son of Tithonus and Aurora, who lived there. The comparison has many points of similarity, widely varying in degree of subtlety. Death and Xerxes both build bridges, both intend to subdue whole nations, are both proud and both strike the deep (295 above; Zerxes had the Hellespont scourged because his first bridge was destroyed by a storm). Less obviously, both are doomed to fail

From Susa his Memnonian palace high
Came to the sea, and over Hellespont
Bridging his way, Europe with Asia joined,
And scourged with many a stroke the indignant waves.
Now had they brought the work by wondrous art
Pontifical, a ridge of pendent rock
Over the vexed abyss, following the track
Of Satan, to the self same place where he
First lighted from his wing, and landed safe
From out of chaos to the outside bare
Of this round world: with pins of adamant
And chains they made all fast, too fast they made
And durable; and now in little space
The confines met of empyrean heaven
And of this world, and on the left hand hell
With long reach interposed; three several ways
In sight, to each of these three places led.
And now their way to earth they had descried,
To Paradise first tending, when behold
Satan in likeness of an angel bright
Betwixt the Centaur and the Scorpion steering

in spite of initial successes. But the simile gains most force from a silent allusion to the well-known story that Xerxes wept while reviewing his army, at the thought that within a century such multitudes would all be dead. Note how much of the imagery is drawn from military contexts, in passages concerned with evil agents.

x *313. Pontifical*] bridge-making. A learned pun on Lat. *pons* and *facere*; but the usual sense of the word, 'episcopal', must obviously be intended too. The implication that the priesthood are as good at making the way easy to hell as Sin and Death draws ironic force from the fact that the Pope's title *pontifex* was interpreted as meaning that his role was one of bridge-builder between the present world and the world to come (Cirlot 31, citing St Bernard).

x *314. vexed*] disturbed by storms; see vii 212–5.

x *316. First lighted*] See iii 418–22.

x *321–4.* Previously, the *confines* (common boundaries) of heaven and the *world* (universe) met without interruption; but now the way to hell is interposed; see ll. 289–93*n*. The three ways are: the stair to heaven (iii 510ff), the passage through the opaque outer sphere of the universe down to earth (iii 526ff) and the new bridge. *left*] the sinister evil side, to which the reprobate are put, in the parable of the sheep and the goats (*Matt.* xxv 33).

x *327.* On Satan's disguise, see iii 634*n*.

x *328–9.* Verity and Hughes repeat Newton's canard that Satan, to avoid discovery by Uriel, keeps at as great a distance as possible from him, so that, since the sun is in Aries, Satan steers between 'two constellations which lay

His zenith, while the sun in Aries rose:
Disguised he came, but those his children dear
Their parent soon discerned, though in disguise.
He after Eve seduced, unminded slunk
Into the wood fast by, and changing shape
To observe the sequel, saw his guileful act
By Eve, though all unweeting, seconded
Upon her husband, saw their shame that sought

in a quite different part of the Heavens'. But if Satan were hiding from Uriel in Aries, he would steer in Libra, the sign in opposition to Aries. And besides, if he were invisible to Uriel he would need no disguise. The real reason for steering *betwixt the Centaur* (Sagittarius) *and the Scorpion* is rather that the only constellation noticeably spread over these two signs is Anguis, the serpent held by Ophiuchus. (This can easily be verified by a glance at any celestial globe, or at a figured star map such as Dürer's.) Anguis has its head in Libra, and extends through Scorpio into Sagittarius. Accordingly, Satan enters the world in Libra (see iii 551–61*n*), but leaves it between Scorpio and Sagittarius. Cp. ii 707–11*nn* on a similar allusion to Ophiuchus. The sun is in *Aries* not because it had strong astrological influence in the sign of its exaltation (Svendsen 83), but because it was situated in that sign in the *thema coeli* that prevailed from the creation to the Fall (see iii 555–61*n*). The present verse is the most explicit indication M. has given us that the state of his universe before the Fall corresponds to the traditional vernal schema. It is therefore of crucial importance to the interpretation of such passages as iii 555ff and iv 267f, 354f. The information that a point between Scorpio and Sagittarius is at Satan's zenith clearly indicates that the time in Paradise is between 2.00 a.m. and 4.00 a.m. (or, assuming Sol to be in the centre of Aries, 3.00 a.m.) on Day 33, the day after the Fall. It should be noted that Sin and Death are not observing Satan from Paradise, so that the present passage must not be taken to imply that the sun is rising there. Satan, flying straight up from Paradise (*steering / His zenith*), is between Scorpio and Sagittarius, i.e., at an aspect of 120°–150° to the sun in Aries; hence the horizon of reference cannot possibly be that of Paradise (where his aspect to a rising sun would be 90°). See further l. 773*n*. The emendation of *rose* to *rode* proposed by Bentley is quite unnecessary. From the vantage-point of Sin and Death, the sun might well seem to rise from beyond the earth; just as at iii 558–60 Aries seemed to Satan (in a similar position) to bear Andromeda 'Beyond the horizon'. Sin and Death, we are told, follow 'the track that Satan first made' (x Argument).

x *332. after Eve seduced*] For the Lat. construction cp. i 573, 'since created man'. *unminded*] unnoticed; perhaps secondarily expressing the removal of mind from the serpent when Satan changes his shape.

x *334. sequel*] consequence.

x *335. unweeting*] unconsciously. *seconded*] repeated; or supported, followed up.

Vain covertures; but when he saw descend
The Son of God to judge them terrified
He fled, not hoping to escape, but shun
The present, fearing guilty what his wrath
Might suddenly inflict; that past, returned
By night, and listening where the hapless pair
Sat in their sad discourse, and various plaint,
Thence gathered his own doom, which understood
Not instant, but of future time. With joy
And tidings fraught, to hell he now returned,
And at the brink of chaos, near the foot
Of this new wondrous pontifice, unhoped
Met who to meet him came, his offspring dear.
Great joy was at their meeting, and at sight
Of that stupendous bridge his joy increased.
Long he admiring stood, till Sin, his fair
Enchanting daughter, thus the silence broke.
O parent, these are thy magnific deeds,
Thy trophies, which thou view'st as not thine own,
Thou art their author and prime architect:
For I no sooner in my heart divined,
My heart, which by a secret harmony
Still moves with thine, joined in connection sweet,
That thou on earth hadst prospered, which thy looks
Now also evidence, but straight I felt
Though distant from thee worlds between, yet felt
That I must after thee with this thy son;

x *337. covertures*] Both the garments of ix 1110–14 and the dissimulations and excuses of x 116ff (see *OED* s.v. *Coverture* 3 and 7f).

x *342. night*] Evidently the night during which Adam's complaint is uttered; see ll. 716ff.

x *344–5.* Referring to Adam's recollection and interpretation of the curse, at ll. 1030ff. The full stop after *time* in the early edns makes *understood* a verb in the past tense, with its subject omitted. If there were a comma only, *understood* could be a participle, and the passage would flow more easily.

x *347. foot*] the end of the slope or hump of the bridge. See *OED*, s.v. *Foot* V 18 b.

x *348. pontifice*] bridge (*OED* [2]) or priest (*OED* [1]); see l. 313*n*. The ambiguity is accentuated rather than resolved by *foot* in the preceding line.

x *331. stupendous*] The early edns have 'stupendious', the accepted form until the latter seventeenth century.

x *352.* The double-cross juncture after *increased*, followed by a spondee, mimes Satan's admiring pause.

x *358. secret harmony*] The 'sympathy' or 'connatural force' of ll. 246–9; see *n* there.

Such fatal consequence unites us three:
Hell could no longer hold us in her bounds,
Nor this unvoyageable gulf obscure
Detain from following thy illustrious track.
Thou hast achieved our liberty, confined
Within hell gates till now, thou us empowered
To fortify thus far, and overlay
With this portentous bridge the dark abyss.
Thine now is all this world, thy virtue hath won
What thy hands builded not, thy wisdom gained
With odds what war hath lost, and fully avenged
Our foil in heaven; here thou shalt monarch reign,
There didst not; there let him still victor sway,
As battle hath adjudged, from this new world
Retiring, by his own doom alienated,
And henceforth monarchy with thee divide
Of all things parted by the empyreal bounds,
His quadrature, from thy orbicular world,

x *364. consequence*] cause-effect relationship.

x *365.* For the falsity of this boast, see i 209–13*n* and iii 80–6*n*. The trinity Satan-Sin-Death is an antitype of the divine Trinity, so that l. 365 may be seen as a parody of *Matt.* xvi 18 ('the gates of hell shall not prevail') and of similar Biblical texts applied to Christ's resurrection.

x *370. fortify*] grow strong (intrans.: *OED* I 6); strengthen structurally (trans., *OED* I 1), referring to the bridge, is perhaps secondarily operative.

x *371. portentous*] prodigious (*OED* 2); but also 'portending a calamity (to man)' (*OED* 1).

x *372–3.* A parody of Justification.

x *372. virtue*] power; courage–the commonest senses when the word is used by evil agents. See i 320, ix 616*n*, 647–50*n*, 778*n* and 694*n*.

x *374. odds*] advantage.

x *375. foil*] defeat.

x *378. doom*] judgment.

x *379.* See *n* on iv 111: 'Divided empire with heaven's king I hold.'

x *381.* Cp. ii 1048, and see *Rev.* xxi 16, on the New Jerusalem: 'The city lieth foursquare, and the length is as large as the breadth: and he measured the city with the reed, twelve thousand furlongs. The length and the breadth and the height of it are equal.' The *world* (universe) is repeatedly referred to in *PL* as *orbicular*: cp., e.g., iii 718 (Uriel on the creation). Sin's subtle sneer depends on the notion that the sphere is a more perfect form than the cube, since more capacious, and on the fact that the square and the circle are incommensurate. But there is probably also a dramatic irony, depending on a common development of the same arithmological doctrine. The mysterious integration of spirit and matter in man's nature was often symbolized by the squaring of the circle (see Fowler 267), so that the present passage may allude

Or try thee now more dangerous to his throne.
  Whom thus the prince of darkness answered glad.
Fair daughter, and thou son and grandchild both,
High proof ye now have given to be the race
Of Satan (for I glory in the name,
Antagonist of heaven's almighty king)
Amply have merited of me, of all
The infernal empire, that so near heaven's door
Triumphal with triumphal act have met,
Mine with this glorious work, and made one realm
Hell and this world, one realm, one continent
Of easy thorough-fare. Therefore while I
Descend through darkness, on your road with ease
To my associate powers, them to acquaint
With these successes, and with them rejoice,
You two this way, among these numerous orbs
All yours, right down to Paradise descend;
There dwell and reign in bliss, thence on the earth
Dominion exercise and in the air,
Chiefly on man, sole lord of all declared,
Him first make sure your thrall, and lastly kill.
My substitutes I send ye, and create
Plenipotent on earth, of matchless might

to the Incarnation, when a perfect man will combine sovereignty over both the square and the orbicular worlds.

x *382. try*] find by experience to be (*OED* 13); 'extract by refining with fire' (*OED* 3) may be operative as a secondary irony.

x *384. son and grandchild*] Because he is the offspring of Satan's incestuous relations with his daughter Sin.

x *386–7. Satan* literally means 'adversary'.

x *390.* The work of Sin and Death is probably to be regarded as a triumphal work in the specific sense that the bridge constitutes a triumphal arch.

x *397. these*] those *Ed I.*

x *397–8.* Not so much a parallel with Satan's descent 'amongst innumerable stars' (iii 565) as a contrast with Christ's triumphal and creative descent into chaos at vii 180ff; see MacCaffrey 61.

x *399–402.* Cp. ii 839–44, and see *Rom.* v 14, 17, 21: 'death reigned from Adam to Moses'; 'by one man's offence death reigned by one'; 'as sin hath reigned unto death, even so might grace reign through righteousness unto eternal life by Jesus Christ our Lord.' *thrall*] See *John* viii 34: 'Whosoever committeth sin is the servant of sin.' But we should also note the echo of man's commission at *PL* viii 338ff, which implies that Sin and Death are now to institute a whole new estate of subjugated man.

x *404. Plenipotent*] possessing full authority. Cp. God's commission of Messiah, iii 317ff.

Issuing from me: on your joint vigour now
My hold of this new kingdom all depends,
Through Sin to Death exposed by my exploit.
If your joint power prevails, the affairs of hell
No detriment need fear, go and be strong.
   So saying he dismissed them, they with speed
Their course through thickest constellations held
Spreading their bane; the blasted stars looked wan,
And planets, planet-strook, real eclipse
Then suffered. The other way Satan went down
The causey to hell gate; on either side
Disparted chaos over built exclaimed,
And with rebounding surge the bars assailed,
That scorned his indignation: through the gate,
Wide open and unguarded, Satan passed,
And all about found desolate; for those
Appointed to sit there, had left their charge,

x *407*. Cp. *Rom.* v 12: 'By one man sin entered into the world, and death by sin; and so death passed upon all men, for that all have sinned.'

x *408*. *prevails*] prevail *Ed I*–a reading that Adams prefers because the subjunctive is more Latinate.

x *409*. So Moses gives Joshua his commission to lead the people of Israel to take possession of the Promised Land, at *Deut.* xxxi 7f (cp. xi 8). But the joke is on Satan; for, after the redemption, death will indeed for man be the way to a promised paradise. The whole triumph tradition was based on Roman models. Appropriately, therefore, *detriment* alludes to the charge given to the two consuls at Rome, when supreme power was conferred on them in times of crisis: *Videant consules ne quid respublica detrimenti capiat.* Note that this commission, temporary like Satan's, conferred no powers *de iure*. Thus, if the consuls put anyone to death, they could later plead the commission; but they would still have to justify their action legally.

x *412–13*. The wild figures here approach the chaotic bomphiologia of Bk vi (on which see vi 698–9*n*). *blasted*] breathed on balefully–specifically applied to the influence of a malignant planet (see *OED* s.v. *Blast* II 7 and *Blasted* 1), so that the inverted application here, to the effect *on* stars, would be felt as a radical dislocation of meaning. Similarly with *planets, planet-strook* (planet-struck, 'stricken by the malign influence of an adverse planet'); though here a preposterous pun may also be intended (planets struck by planets). *real eclipse*] Usually an eclipse is only an observational phenomenon, but in this case the obscuration is real.

x *415*. *causey*] causeway, raised way over wet ground; sometimes applied to an arched viaduct; see ll. 300f.

x *418*. i.e., the bars scorned Chaos' indignation. Cp. Virgil, *Georg.* ii 161f, where the ocean is *indignatum* at the Lucrine breakwater.

x *420*. i.e., Sin and Death.

Flown to the upper world; the rest were all
Far to the inland retired, about the walls
Of Pandaemonium, city and proud seat
Of Lucifer, so by allusion called,
Of that bright star to Satan paragoned.
There kept their watch the legions, while the grand
In council sat, solicitous what chance
Might intercept their emperor sent, so he
Departing gave command, and they observed.
As when the Tartar from his Russian foe
By Astracan over the snowy plains
Retires, or Bactrian sophy from the horns
Of Turkish crescent, leaves all waste beyond
The realm of Aladule, in his retreat
To Tauris or Casbeen. So these the late
Heaven-banished host, left desert utmost hell
Many a dark league, reduced in careful watch
Round their metropolis, and now expecting
Each hour their great adventurer from the search
Of foreign worlds: he through the midst unmarked,
In show plebeian angel militant
Of lowest order, passed; and from the door

x *423. inland*] Two words in *Ed I*.
x *425–6. paragoned*] compared, placed side by side. On the comparison of Satan to the morning star, see v 700–14*n* and vii 132*n*.
x *427. the grand*] The 'great seraphic lords and cherubim' of the secret conclave at i 794ff.
x *428. solicitous*] anxious, concerned.
x *431–9. Astracan*] A Tartar kingdom and capital city near the mouth of the Volga, often referred to in M.'s *Brief History of Muscovia*. *Bactrian*] Persian. *sophy*] shah, Persian king. *horns . . . crescent*] Refers not only to the Turkish ensign, but also to their battle formations; cp. the similar play in Dryden, *Annus Mirabilis* (1667), St. 125: 'Their huge unwieldy Navy wasts away: / So sicken waning Moons too neer the Sun, / And blunt their crescents on the edge of day.' *Aladule*] greater Armenia. *Tauris* (mod. Tabriz) is in the extreme north-west of Persia; *Casbeen*] Kazvin, north of Teheran. The simile is a complex one. Physically, the *snowy plains* remind us of the 'frozen continent' of hell at ii 587, where the devils are haled for punishment 'at certain revolutions', and so prepares us for the punitive metamorphosis soon to follow. Morally, the grand devils are being compared to Saracens (cp. i 348, ii 1–4, etc.): either barbarians (Tartars) or proud but ineffective rulers (sophies). The last point is underlined with a sarcastic pun; for *sophy* meant 'sage' (*OED* 3) as well as 'shah' (*OED* 2). *Many a*] Requires synaloepha. *reduced*] led back.

Of that Plutonian hall, invisible
Ascended his high throne, which under state
Of richest texture spread, at the upper end
Was placed in regal lustre. Down a while
He sat, and round about him saw unseen:
At last as from a cloud his fulgent head
And shape star bright appeared, or brighter, clad
With what permissive glory since his fall
Was left him, or false glitter: all amazed
At that so sudden blaze the Stygian throng
Bent their aspect, and whom they wished beheld,
Their mighty chief returned: loud was the acclaim:
Forth rushed in haste the great consulting peers,
Raised from their dark divan, and with like joy
Congratulant approached him, who with hand
Silence, and with these words attention won.
Thrones, dominations, princedoms, virtues, powers,
For in possession such, not only of right,
I call ye and declare ye now, returned
Successful beyond hope, to lead ye forth
Triumphant out of this infernal pit
Abominable, accursed, the house of woe,

x 444. *Plutonian*] pertaining to Pluto, ruler of the classical underworld. First instance in *OED*.

x 445. *state*] canopy (*OED* II 20 b). For an earlier description of Satan's glittering throne, see ii 1–4.

x 448. *saw unseen*] One motive of Satan's invisible entry is evidently to check on the loyalty of his followers.

x 450–2. Satan's original form is recalled, so that his metamorphosis to a serpent (ll. 511ff) will have maximum effect. On the 'process of alternating inflation and deflation of the devils' see Broadbent 110. *permissive*] permissible; permitted (by God). Cp. i 591ff.

x 450. *star bright*] Hyphenated in *Ed I*.

x 453. *Stygian throng*] Cp. 'Stygian council', ii 506.

x 454. *aspect*] Stressed on the second syllable.

x 457. *divan*] oriental council of state; continuing the Saracen implication of ll. 431–9.

x 458. *Congratulant*] expressing congratulation (Latinism; cp. *congratulantes*).

x 460. Cp. ii 11–14, v 772, and see v 601*n*. Empson 79 suggests that M.'s repetition of the roll-call of titles is sardonic: that Satan is no longer morally conscious enough to see the irony of this claim to have provided victims for them to rule.

x 465. *house of woe*] For the diction see ii 823*n*.

And dungeon of our tyrant: now possess,
As lords, a spacious world, to our native heaven
Little inferior, by my adventure hard
With peril great achieved. Long were to tell
What I have done, what suffered, with what pain
Voyaged the unreal, vast, unbounded deep
Of horrible confusion, over which
By Sin and Death a broad way now is paved
To expedite your glorious march; but I
Toiled out my uncouth passage, forced to ride
The untractable abyss, plunged in the womb
Of unoriginal Night and Chaos wild,
That jealous of their secrets fiercely opposed
My journey strange, with clamorous uproar
Protesting fate supreme; thence how I found
The new created world, which fame in heaven
Long had foretold, a fabric wonderful
Of absolute perfection, therein man
Placed in a paradise, by our exile
Made happy: him by fraud I have seduced
From his creator, and the more to increase
Your wonder, with an apple; he thereat
Offended, worth your laughter, hath given up
Both his beloved man and all this world,
To Sin and Death a prey, and so to us,
Without our hazard, labour, or alarm,

x *466*. The angelic dignities need no longer be merely titular, as Satan suggested they were at v 773f.
x *469–502*. This summary of the action to date is one of the strongest pieces of evidence in support of Burden's contention that there is a 'satanic epic' running parallel to M.'s. Satan is inviting the devils (and the reader) to think of him as the hero of a falsely heroic epic in which they too may participate.
x *471*. *unreal*] Because formless, and therefore not fully material.
x *475*. *uncouth*] unfamiliar, strange; solitary (*OED* 2b, 5).
x *477–9*. *unoriginal*] uncreated (only instance in *OED*). See ii 962 where Night is 'eldest of things'. Neither Night nor Chaos in fact opposed Satan; and Chaos even helped him. See especially ii 1004–9.
x *481–2*. For the rumour, see i 651–4*n*, ii 346–52*n*, vii 145–56*n*.
x *484*. *exile*] Stressed on the second syllable.
x *485*. On the Satanic view that because 'the apple has no intrinsic magic... the breach of the prohibition becomes a small matter' see Lewis 68.
x *485–90*. Gilbert 20 compares M.'s Fourth Draft of a tragedy on Paradise Lost (see Introduction, 'Composition', p. 421 above): 'Here again may appear Lucifer relating, and insulting in what he had done to the destruction of man.'

To range in, and to dwell, and over man
To rule, as over all he should have ruled.
True is, me also he hath judged, or rather
Me not, but the brute serpent in whose shape
Man I deceived: that which to me belongs,
Is enmity, which he will put between
Me and mankind; I am to bruise his heel;
His seed, when is not set, shall bruise my head:
A world who would not purchase with a bruise,
Or much more grievous pain? Ye have the account
Of my performance: what remains, ye gods,
But up and enter now into full bliss.
  So having said, a while he stood, expecting
Their universal shout and high applause
To fill his ear, when contrary he hears
On all sides, from innumerable tongues
A dismal universal hiss, the sound
Of public scorn; he wondered, but not long
Had leisure, wondering at himself now more;
His visage drawn he felt to sharp and spare,
His arms clung to his ribs, his legs entwining
Each other, till supplanted down he fell
A monstrous serpent on his belly prone,
Reluctant, but in vain, a greater power
Now ruled him, punished in the shape he sinned,
According to his doom: he would have spoke,

x *496. that*] i.e., that part of the curse; see ll. 164–74*n*.
x *508. dismal*] dreadful, sinister, gloomy. See i 60*n*.
x *511–14.* Cp. the metamorphosis of Cadmus in Ovid, *Met.* iv 572–603, already alluded to at ix 506 above; Lucan, *Phars.* ix 700ff; and P. Fletcher, *Purple Island* vii 11. Dante had carried the evocation of horror through serpentine metamorphoses to considerable lengths in *Inf.* xxiv and xxv. *clung*] drawn together, shrunk, shrivelled (participle; *OED* s.v. *Clung* 2).
x *513. supplanted*] tripped up, made to stumble (*OED* 1); caused to fall from a position of power or virtue (*OED* 2). See Ricks 64f: 'The applied moral meaning is in the background, and provides the grim irony with which Satan is always seen–Satan, on whom always evil "recoils". . . . Satan is the great supplanter: "He set upon our fyrst parentes in paradyse, and by pride supplanted them" (More, 1522).'
x *515. Reluctant*] writhing.
x *517.* The *doom* (judgment) referred to is the curse on the serpent (see ll. 164–74*n*), which is now accomplished literally. Nevertheless, the metamorphosis should not be seen merely as a punishment, but also as a divine judgment of Satan's character, and a repudiation of the false ideal of heroism that has just been set forth. At the moment of acclaim Satan is revealed

But hiss for hiss returned with forked tongue
To forked tongue, for now were all transformed
Alike, to serpents all as accessories
To his bold riot: dreadful was the din
Of hissing through the hall, thick swarming now
With complicated monsters head and tail,
Scorpion and asp, and amphisbaena dire,
Cerastes horned, hydrus, and ellops drear,

in his true brutishness as the monstrous opponent of heroic virtue; see Steadman 101f. As a peripeteia, the episode is highly dramatic: just when the devils seem about to become heroes in Satan's epic (see ll. 469–502*n*) they turn out instead to be monsters in God's. Hughes cites Boehme: after 'the divine light went out of the Devils, they lost their beauteous forme and Image, and became like Serpents, Dragons, Wormes, and evill Beasts: as may be seen by *Adam's* Serpent.'

x *523. complicated*] compound, composite (*OED* 4); tangled (*OED* 2).

x *524–6.* The *amphisbaena* is a serpent with a head at either end, according to Lucan (*Phars.* ix 719) with eyes like lamps; it is the subject of a paper by G. C. Druce in *Arch. Journ.* lxvii, No. 268; 2nd ser. xvii, No. 4, pp. 285–317. The *cerastes* has four horns on its head, shaped like a ram's. The *hydrus* (not to be confused with the many-head hydra) is a water-snake, enemy of the crocodile; its venom causes dropsy. The *ellops*, though sometimes identified as the swordfish, is mentioned as a serpent in Pliny, *Nat. hist.* xxxii 5, while the *dipsas* causes raging thirst by its bite. On all these serpents, see Robin; White 174–85; and Svendsen (35f), who gives illustrations from popular authorities such as Bartholomew, Batman, Topsell (*The historie of serpents* (1608)) and Swan. Hughes, drawing on the more high-powered natural history of Aldrovandus (which carried over a good deal of moralization from the bestiaries and medieval encyclopedias) assigns complex emblematic significances to the serpents: e.g., the amphisbaena could stand for inconstancy and adultery. Seven serpents are named, with cerastes (symbolic of power-lust) in the central position of sovereignty, so that it would be tempting to correlate them with the deadly sins. But M. has given far too little descriptive differentiation of the serpents for this approach to be made with any confidence. More likely he intended the passage simply as a counterpart to ix 185ff. Cp. in this connection Sylvester's Du Bartas I vi: 'O wert thou pleas'd to form / Th'innammel'd *Scorpion*, and the *Viper*-worm, / Th'horned *Cerastes*, th' *Alexandrian Skink*, / Th'*Adder*, and *Drynas* (full of odious stink) / Th'*Eft*, *Snake*, and *Dipsas* (causing deadly Thirst): / Why hast thou arm'd them with a rage so curst? / Pardon, good God, pardon me; 't was our pride, / Not thou, that troubled our first happy tyde, / And in the Childehood of the World, did bring / Th' *Amphisbena* her double banefull sting'; with side-note: 'Why God created such noysom and dangerous creatures: Sin the occasion of the hurt they can do us.' The serpents are actual species, and M. is grappling with the problem how Providence

And dipsas (not so thick swarmed once the soil
Bedropped with blood of Gorgon, or the isle
Ophiusa) but still greatest he the midst,
Now dragon grown, larger than whom the sun
Ingendered in the Pythian vale on slime,
Huge Python, and his power no less he seemed
Above the rest still to retain; they all
Him followed issuing forth to the open field,
Where all yet left of that revolted rout
Heaven-fallen, in station stood or just array,
Sublime with expectation when to see
In triumph issuing forth their glorious chief;
They saw, but other sight instead, a crowd
Of ugly serpents; horror on them fell,
And horrid sympathy; for what they saw,
They felt themselves now changing; down their arms,
Down fell both spear and shield, down they as fast,
And the dire hiss renewed, and the dire form
Catched by contagion, like in punishment,
As in their crime. Thus was the applause they meant,
Turned to exploding hiss, triumph to shame
Cast on themselves from their own mouths. There stood
A grove hard by, sprung up with this their change,
His will who reigns above, to aggravate
Their penance, laden with fair fruit, like that

can allow them to exist. The early edns italicize the names of the serpents as technical terms.

x *526–7*. When Perseus was bringing back the severed head of Medusa, drops of blood fell to earth, and that is why Libya is full of serpents. See Ovid, *Met.* iv 617–20; also Lucan, *Phars.* ix 699ff, where the asp, cerastes, dipsas and amphisbaena are all mentioned as having been produced in this way.

x *528*. *Ophiusa*] Literally 'full of serpents'; a name anciently given to several islands, including Rhodes and one of the Balearic group.

x *529–32*. Cp. *Elegia VII*, and for the birth of *Python* from the *slime* remaining after the flood see Ovid, *Met.* i 438–40. M. cannot allude to Python without introducing also the slaying of Python by Apollo. Similarly, Satan's *dragon* shape is that of the 'old dragon' of Christian apocalypse; see *Rev.* xii 9: 'the great dragon was cast out, that old serpent, called the Devil, and Satan'.

x *535*. i.e., either on guard or drawn up for review.

x *536*. *Sublime*] uplifted.

x *546*. *exploding*] Used both in its modern sense and 'driving off the stage'.

x *546*. 'As they were increased, so they sinned against me: therefore will I change their glory into shame' (*Hos.* iv 7).

x *550*. *penance*] punishment (*OED* 5). *fair*] so in *Ed I*; erroneously omitted in *Ed II*.

Which grew in Paradise, the bait of Eve
Used by the tempter: on that prospect strange
Their earnest eyes they fixed, imagining
For one forbidden tree a multitude
Now risen, to work them further woe or shame;
Yet parched with scalding thirst and hunger fierce,
Though to delude them sent, could not abstain,
But on they rolled in heaps, and up the trees
Climbing, sat thicker than the snaky locks
That curled Megaera: greedily they plucked
The fruitage fair to sight, like that which grew
Near that bituminous lake where Sodom flamed;
This more delusive, not the touch, but taste
Deceived; they fondly thinking to allay
Their appetite with gust, instead of fruit

x 555. *furder*] further.
x 556. The Tantalus-like thirst of the devils, together with other echoes at ll. 432, 537 and 560, suggests that the present passage bears some close relation to that describing the punishment of the devils at ii 596ff. The punishment by metamorphosis, like the others, is administered periodically; see ll. 575ff, and i 193–5*n*. For a similar view see John M. Steadman, 'Tantalus and the Dea Sea Apples' in *JEGP* lxiv (1965) 35–40. Steadman shows that 'the apples of the Tantalus myth are cross grafted with those of the Dead Sea and the tree of knowledge'. In this grafting operation M. had possibly been anticipated by Edward Browne. Tantalus' doom, it should be noted, is like that of the devils a talion punishment.
x 560. *Megaera*] one of the Furies or Eumenides who punish sin; thus at ii 596 it is 'harpy-footed Furies' who hale the devils off for their periodic punishments. The Furies are often described as snaky-haired.
x 562. *bituminous lake*] The Dead Sea, beside which lies Sodom. The allusion is to Josephus, *Wars* IV viii 4, where it is said that traces still remain of the divine fire that burnt Sodom; such as 'ashes growing in their fruits, which fruits have a colour as if they were fit to be eaten; but if you pluck them with your hands, they dissolve into smoke and ashes'. Svendsen 28f shows that this passage was widely drawn on by the encyclopedists. M. himself refers to the tradition as if it were a commonplace, in *Eikonoklastes* (Yale iii 552). At a more fundamental level, however, the present passage depends on *Deut.* xxxii 32f: 'Their vine is of the vine of Sodom, and of the fields of Gomorrah: their grapes are grapes of gall, their clusters are bitter: Their wine is the poison of dragons, and the cruel venom of asps.' By the 'vine of Sodom' (which was identified with the fruit described by Josephus) Moses was taken to mean that the people of Israel had become corrupt and rotten at the core.
x 565. *gust*] relish.

Chewed bitter ashes, which the offended taste
With spattering noise rejected: oft they assayed,
Hunger and thirst constraining, drugged as oft,
With hatefulest disrelish writhed their jaws
With soot and cinders filled; so oft they fell
Into the same illusion, not as man
Whom they triumphed once lapsed. Thus were they plagued
And worn with famine, long and ceaseless hiss,
Till their lost shape, permitted, they resumed,
Yearly enjoined, some say, to undergo
This annual humbling certain numbered days,
To dash their pride, and joy for man seduced.
However some tradition they dispersed

x *566–70.* In literal enactment of the curse of l. 178, that the serpent 'dust shalt eat'. See ll. 164–74*n*. Topsell 16 discusses a popular fallacy that serpents eat nothing but dust.

x *568. drugged*] nauseated (first instance in *OED* in this sense). Richardson explains the word as 'a metaphor taken from the general nauseousness of drugs'.

x *571–2.* i.e., 'did not as man (whom they conquered) fall once'; secondarily, 'not like man, whom they triumphed over, once he was fallen'. See *OED* s.v. *Triumph* 2 c.

x *574.* See l. 451 and *n*.

x *578–84.* See Apollonius Rhodius, *Argonaut.* i 503–9, where Orpheus sings how Ophion and Eurynome daughter of Ocean ruled Olympus until the one yielded to Cronos (*Saturn*), the other to Rhea (*Ops*). Their two successors then ruled the Titans 'while Zeus still . . . dwelt in the Dictaean cave'. Starnes and Talbert (269), correcting Verity and Hughes, argue that M. is fusing Apollonius' Ophion with another, a friend of Cadmus, one of those born from the serpent's teeth, *ideoque et nomen habet a serpente, qui Graece ὄφις dicitur* (Stephanus, *Thesaurus*). But the identification of Apollonius' Ophion as a serpent is better explained simply as an allusion to *De raptu Proserpinae* iii 332–56. Claudian there describes a dreadful grove hung with Jupiter's spoils from the Giant War: 'Here hang the gaping jaws and monstrous skins of the Giants; affixed to trees their faces still threaten horribly, and heaped up on all sides bleach the huge bones of slaughtered serpents. Their stiffening sloughs smoke with the blow of many a thunderbolt, and every tree boasts some illustrious name.' Among them 'spoiled Ophion weighs down those branches' (348). Not only does this allusion follow naturally after the punitive grove of 547ff (indeed, M.'s 'There stood / A grove hard by' directly translates Claudian's *lucus erat prope*), but it satisfactorily deflates the triumph of the devils by recalling their defeat under the type of Giants. (For the casting of the devils in the role of rebel Giants, see i 50–83*n*, 197–200*n*.) Thus, while the devil-inspired tradition

Among the heathen of their purchase got,
And fabled how the serpent, whom they called
Ophion with Eurynome, the wide-
Encroaching Eve perhaps, had first the rule
Of high Olympus, thence by Saturn driven
And Ops, ere yet Dictaean Jove was born.
Mean while in Paradise the hellish pair
Too soon arrived, Sin there in power before,
Once actual, now in body, and to dwell
Habitual habitant; behind her Death
Close following pace for pace, not mounted yet
On his pale horse: to whom Sin thus began.
  Second of Satan sprung, all conquering Death,
What think'st thou of our empire now, though earned

claims precedence over Jupiter, M.'s allusion shows Jupiter supreme. The association of Ophion with Satan was traditional; see Sandys[2] 27: 'Pherecides the Syrian writes how the Divels were throwne out of heaven by *Jupiter* (this fall of the Gyants perhaps an allusion to that of the Angells) the chiefe called *Ophioneus*, which signifies Serpentine: having after made use of that creature to poyson *Eve* with a false ambition.' Empson 175, following Bentley, takes part of M.'s meaning to be that the serpent was Eve's husband, and that she was *wide-Encroaching* (cp. *Eurynome*=wide-ruling) in the sense that her children are all mankind. But as Pearce cautions, the tradition is presented by M. as a false slander of our parent. See ix 505–10*n* above. *purchase*] plunder, prey, spoil (*OED* II 8); but also 'annual return or rent' (*OED* II 10)–alluding to the *annual* punishment of the devils (ll. 575f). *Dictaean*) The Cretan mountain where Jupiter spent his childhood was called Dicte, and Dictaeus was one of his surnames.

x *586–7*. Sin had already been present potentially (*in power*); but once committed (*once actual*) it was present in a fuller sense as a *body*–'the body of sin' in St Paul's phrase. Cp. *Rom.* vi 6: 'Our old man is crucified with him, that the body of sin might be destroyed, that henceforth we should not serve sin.' *Actual* sin (the result of a free act of will) is to be distinguished from original sin (the general state of sinfulness to which fallen man is subject). See *De doctrina* i 11 (Columbia xv 199): 'The second thing in sin, after evil concupiscence, is the crime itself, or the act of sinning, which is commonly called Actual Sin.'

x *589–90*. Cp. *Rev.* vi 8: 'I looked, and behold a pale horse: and his name that sat on him was Death, and Hell followed with him. And power was given unto them over the fourth part of the earth; to kill with sword, and with hunger, and with death, and with the beasts of the earth.' Death is *not mounted yet* because the Last Things are not yet happening. The reason cannot be (as Greenwood has it) because Death has not yet exercised his power, since there were already perhaps dead animals at l. 217 above, and certainly a dead plant at ix 893.

With travail difficult, not better far
Than still at hell's dark threshold to have sat watch,
Unnamed, undreaded, and thy self half starved?
Whom thus the Sin-born monster answered soon.
To me, who with eternal famine pine,
Alike is hell, or Paradise, or heaven,
There best, where most with ravine I may meet;
Which here, though plenteous, all too little seems
To stuff this maw, this vast unhide-bound corpse.
To whom the incestuous mother thus replied.
Thou therefore on these herbs, and fruits, and flowers
Feed first, on each beast next, and fish, and fowl,
No homely morsels, and whatever thing
The scythe of time mows down, devour unspared,
Till I in man residing through the race,
His thoughts, his looks, words, actions all infect,
And season him thy last and sweetest prey.
This said, they both betook them several ways,
Both to destroy, or unimmortal make
All kinds, and for destruction to mature
Sooner or later; which the almighty seeing,
From his transcendent seat the saints among,
To those bright orders uttered thus his voice.
See with what heat these dogs of hell advance
To waste and havoc yonder world, which I
So fair and good created, and had still
Kept in that state, had not the folly of man

x *601. unhide-bound*] (Only instance in *OED*): since Death is emaciated, he might be expected to be hidebound, like an emaciated horse; but on the contrary his skin is loose and capacious. See *OED* s.v. *Hidebound* I 1: 'Of cattle: Having the skin clinging closely to the back and ribs . . . as a result of bad feeding and consequent emaciation.'

x *602. incestuous*] See ii 790ff.

x *606*. Before the Fall, Raphael held out hope that 'tract of time' might improve man into spirit; but now time is a destroyer. On Time's scythe, and on the personification of Time generally, see Panofsky² 69–94.

x *611. unimmortal*] First instance in *OED*. M. is probably coining negative forms, to emphasize the insubstantiality of Death. Cp. *unhide-bound* (l. 601), *unnamed. undreaded* (l. 595).

x *616. dogs of hell*] Cp. the 'hell hounds' about Sin's middle at ii 653ff.

x *617. havoc*] devastate, make havoc of. The order 'havoc!' was originally the signal for general pillage. Cp. *Julius Caesar* III i 270–3; 'And Caesar's spirit, ranging for revenge, / With Ate by his side come hot from hell, / Shall in these confines with a monarch's voice / Cry "Havoc!" and let slip the dogs of war'.

Let in these wasteful furies, who impute
Folly to me, so doth the prince of hell
And his adherents, that with so much ease
I suffer them to enter and possess
A place so heavenly, and conniving seem
To gratify my scornful enemies,
That laugh, as if transported with some fit
Of passion, I to them had quitted all,
At random yielded up to their misrule;
And know not that I called and drew them thither
My hell-hounds, to lick up the draff and filth
Which man's polluting sin with taint hath shed
On what was pure, till crammed and gorged, nigh burst
With sucked and glutted offal, at one sling
Of thy victorious arm, well-pleasing Son,
Both Sin, and Death, and yawning grave at last
Through chaos hurled, obstruct the mouth of hell
For ever, and seal up his ravenous jaws.
Then heaven and earth renewed shall be made pure
To sanctity that shall receive no stain:
Till then the curse pronounced on both precedes.
He ended, and the heavenly audience loud

x *621*. God's providential use of evil is a frequent theme in *PL*: cp. i 162ff, 210ff; vii 613ff; xii 470ff; and see Lewis 66.

x *623*. *enter and possess*] Legal diction.

x *624*. *conniving*] taking no notice; pretending ignorance (*OED* 1).

x *627*. *quitted*] yielded, handed over (*OED* I 5 b).

x *630*. *draff*] refuse, dregs, lees. Often used figuratively, in such phrases as 'the draffs of filthy errors'.

x *633*. Cp. *1 Sam*. xxv 29: 'The souls of thine enemies, them shall he sling out, as out of the middle of a sling.'

x *635–6*. Cp. ii 734, 805ff, and see *Hos*. xiii 14 ('O death, I will be thy plagues; O grave, I will be thy destruction'), *1 Cor*. xv 54, and *Rev*. xx 14 ('death and hell were cast into the lake of fire. This is the second death').

x *638–9*. Alluding to the apocalyptic vision of *2 Pet*. iii 7–13: 'The heavens and the earth, which are now, by the same word are kept in store, reserved unto fire against the day of judgment. . . . We, according to his promise, look for new heavens and a new earth, wherein dwelleth righteousness.' *heaven and earth*] the universe. Burden 40 notes the positive activity in the darkest of God's speeches. Even the curse is imposed in order to cleanse the world.

x *640*. *curse*] Probably that of *Gen*. iii 17: 'Cursed is the ground for thy sake.' *precedes*] not 'prevails' (as Bush) but 'goes before'.

Sung hallelujah, as the sound of seas,
Through multitude that sung: Just are thy ways,
Righteous are thy decrees on all thy works;
Who can extenuate thee? Next, to the Son,
Destined restorer of mankind, by whom
New heaven and earth shall to the ages rise,
Or down from heaven descend. Such was their song,
While the creator calling forth by name
His mighty angels gave them several charge,
As sorted best with present things. The sun

x *642*. Cp. v 872f, and see *Rev*. xix 6: 'I heard as it were the voice of a great multitude, and as the voice of many waters, and as the voice of mighty thunderings, saying, Alleluia: for the Lord God omnipotent reigneth.'
x *644*. Cp. *Rev*. xvi 7: 'True and righteous are thy judgments.' Note that M. reserves this explicit approval for perhaps the most appalling of all God's decrees.
x *645*. *extenuate*] disparage; diminish in honour (*OED* II 5).
x *647–8*. *the ages*] the millennium, the golden ages. Cp. xii 549, 'ages of endless date'. *Or down*] see *Rev*. xxi 2: 'I John saw the holy city, new Jerusalem, coming down from God out of heaven.'
x *650*. Possibly the seven spirits of iii 648ff.
x *651*. Belief in nature's involvement in man's corruption was general in M.'s time; see ix 782–4*n*. The present passage may be regarded as a more detailed treatment of nature's 'signs of woe' at the Fall. On the microcosmic implication Svendsen writes: 'The first result was earth's wound; the next man's passion; then into the cosmos for the stupendous distortion (it was labor even for angels); and last back to earth and within Adam, now like Satan "inly racked". These tremendous arcs bind the universe and the poem together and contribute to the sense of visual image and cosmic rhythm.' More obviously, the repeated cutting has the effect of establishing the closest possible relation between macrocosm and microcosm. *sorted*] associated; consorted (*OED* III 19).
x *651–706*. A passage of great importance for the understanding of the world picture of *PL*. It shows clearly that the cosmic system used throughout most of the poem is not–in spite of many scholarly statements to the contrary–the Ptolemaic system. Instead, it is a theoretical system, of ideal simplicity, in which the ecliptic and the equatorial circles coincide. On the earth of such a system, every point must be an equinoctial point, and there can be neither solstices nor seasons. Spring, in fact, is *perpetual*. The system we ourselves know, and try to describe in our Ptolemaic, Copernican, or other astronomies, is purely an accident of the Fall, and therefore obtains only in the part of the poem subsequent to the present passage. The originality and energy with which M. imagines a complete prelapsarian astronomy, and applies it throughout the larger part of *PL* with the most inventive consistency, are beyond praise. The physical implications of the initial assumption

Had first his precept so to move, so shine,
As might affect the earth with cold and heat
Scarce tolerable, and from the north to call
Decrepit winter, from the south to bring
Solstitial summer's heat. To the blank moon
Her office they prescribed, to the other five
Their planetary motions and aspects
In sextile, square, and trine, and opposite,
Of noxious efficacy, and when to join
In synod unbenign, and taught the fixed
Their influence malignant when to shower,
Which of them rising with the sun, or falling,
Should prove tempestuous: to the winds they set
Their corners, when with bluster to confound

about prelapsarian regularity are followed out even in quite minute details. The geographical location of Paradise, e.g., is conceived in terms of the 'special case' astronomy (see iv 209–16*n*). Other passages depending on the system include iii 555–61, iv 354f, 776–80, v 18–25 and x 328–9. Of particular importance are the many expressions of what I have called the equinoctial theme: balancings of night and day, light and darkness (see iv 997–1004*n*). This theme acquires a literal force and validity from the prelapsarian astronomical system. See Introduction, 'Milton's Universe'.

x *655*. The portrayal of Winter as an old man or woman was a commonplace of iconography; see, e.g., Ripa 475. It depended on the ancient correlation of ages of man with seasons of the year; on which see Klibansky 10 *et passim*.

x *656*. *blank*] white, pale.

x *675*. *other five*] i.e., planets; as at v 177.

x *658–61*. Astrological determinism has its beginning. For the terms used see Ptolemy, *Tetrabiblos* i 13: *sextile* is an aspect of 60°, *square* (or quartile) of 90°, *trine* of 120° and *opposite* (opposition) of 180°. Of these, trine and sextile are harmonious, quartile and opposition disharmonious. *Synod* (conjunction) is not formally recognized as an aspect by Ptolemy; hence its separate place here. *aspects*] Stressed on the second syllable.

x *661–2*. Contrast the 'sweet influence' of the *fixed* stars when they were first created (vii 375). The present action is conceived as a detailed revision of the creation. Burden 184 observes that words such as *taught* constantly remind us that the changes in the macrocosm are neither random nor uncontrolled, but consequent on deliberate decrees of God.

x *663–4*. i.e., which cosmical risings and acronycal settings are signs of bad weather. Meteorological lore relating to the rising and setting of particular constellations was a considerable ingredient in such works as Aratus' *Phaenomena*, Ovid's *Fasti* and Manilius' *Astronomicon*.

x *665–6*. i.e., to *confound* the four elements; *thunder* implying Fire and *shore* Earth.

Sea, air, and shore, the thunder when to roll
With terror through the dark aerial hall.
Some say he bid his angels turn askance
The poles of earth twice ten degrees and more
From the sun's axle; they with labour pushed
Oblique the centric globe: some say the sun
Was bid turn reins from the equinoctial road
Like distant breadth to Taurus with the Seven
Atlantic Sisters, and the Spartan Twins
Up to the tropic Crab; thence down amain
By Leo and the Virgin and the Scales,
As deep as Capricorn, to bring in change
Of seasons to each clime; else had the spring
Perpetual smiled on earth with vernant flowers,
Equal in days and nights, except to those
Beyond the polar circles; to them day
Had unbenighted shone, while the low sun
To recompense his distance, in their sight
Had rounded still the horizon, and not known

x *668–80.* Starting from M.'s 'special case' cosmic system, the universe as we now know it can be arrived at either by tilting the axis of earth about 23·5°, or else by altering the inclination of the sun's course by a corresponding amount. (Not by 'shifting the centre of the sun's orbit' as Svendsen 71; only the *plane* of the orbit is moved, not its centre.) Naturally the first alternative corresponds to the heliocentric theory and the second to the geocentric; and M. avoids any decision between them. *centric globe*] earth. *like distant breadth*] a similar number of degrees of declination. The northern (summer) departure of the sun, which immediately followed on the Fall, is traced out in detail: up to the tropic sign Cancer, when the sun is 23·5° North, then back down again to the equator (*equinoctial road*), reached when the sun enters Libra (*the Scales*). The winter departure is indicated more summarily, by the mention of the southern tropic sign, Capricorn. Aries is presumably omitted because the sun is already in that sign (l. 329): the northern detour is *to* Taurus. M. could also have cited Hyginus' description of Taurus (*Poet. astron.* iii 20): *Taurus ad ortum signorum dimidia parte collocatus. . . . Genua eius a reliquo corpore dividit circulus Aequinoctialis.* *Seven / Atlantic Sisters*] the Pleiades, mythologically the daughters of Atlas. Astronomically, they are situated in the constellation Taurus. Their introduction in the present passage is to clinch an earlier prolepsis; see vii 374–5*n* above. *Spartan Twins*] the zodiacal sign Gemini; mythologically Castor and Pollux, sons of King Tyndarus of Sparta. *amain*] at full speed.

x *678–9. clime*] region. In the cosmography of M.'s day each hemisphere was divided into seven horizontal strips called climes. For the perpetual *spring* before the Fall, see iv 268*n*.

Or east or west, which had forbid the snow
From cold Estotiland, and south as far
Beneath Magellan. At that tasted fruit
The sun, as from Thyestean banquet, turned
His course intended; else how had the world
Inhabited, though sinless, more than now,
Avoided pinching cold and scorching heat?
These changes in the heavens, though slow, produced
Like change on sea and land, sideral blast,
Vapour, and mist, and exhalation hot,
Corrupt and pestilent: now from the north

x *686. Estotiland*] Modern N.E. Labrador. The name was sometimes used vaguely.
x *687. Magellan*] In Heylyn's map of the Americas, modern Argentina is called *Magellonica*, after the Portuguese explorer Magellan.
x *687–9.* Thyestes seduced Aerope, the wife of Atreus his brother. In revenge, Atreus pretended to be reconciled and invited Thyestes to a banquet, but served up to him the flesh of one of his children. The act was thought so horrible that the sun was said to have changed course to avoid observing it. See, e.g., Seneca, *Thyestes* 776ff. On the feast motif in *PL*, see ix 9*n* above. Scan *Thyéstean*.
x *693. sideral*] coming from the stars (*OED* 2). Probably the *sideral blast is* the malign blasting effect of the stars already referred to at l. 412.
x *694. exhalation hot*] Probably 'meteor'. Meteors were believed to be ignited bodies of vapour.
x *695–706.* Repeating 'in miniature' the attack of Sin and Death upon the abyss (MacCaffrey 90). Whiting 121f believes that the only wind-chart giving all the winds mentioned by M. is in Jansson's *Novus atlas* (1647–62), a splendid publication in eleven volumes, concerning which M. is known to have made an enquiry. Here *Boreas* is the N.N.E. wind; *Caecias* E.N.E.; *Argestes* W.N.W.; *Thrascias* N.N.W.; *Notus* S.; *Afer* (Africus) S.W.; *Eurus* E.S.E.; *Zephir* (Zephirus) W.; *Sirocco* S.E.; *Libecchio* S.W. *brazen dungeon*] Alludes to the prison in which Aeolus keeps the winds enclosed, in Virgil, *Aen.* i 50ff. *flaw*] sudden squall of wind. *Serraliona*] Modern Sierra Leone. *thwart*] Previously the winds have all been more or less N. or S.; but now *lateral* (E.–W.) winds join the battle. Most of the names of the winds are classical; but *Levant* is vernacular (in nautical jargon, a raw east wind in the Mediterranean was a Levanter), *ponent* (setting, west) perhaps a Latinizing or Gallicizing coinage, and *Sirocco* and *Libecchio* Italian. The conflict of all the winds was a reversion to chaos that had often been used as a symbol of the chaotic state of human passion. Cp. Spenser, *F.Q.* IV ix 23, where the conflict of four different erotic dispositions is compared to that of winds: 'As when Dan Aeolus . . . / Sends forth the winds out of his hidden threasure, / Upon the sea to wreake his fell intent; / They breaking forth with crude unruliment, / From all foure parts of heaven doe rage full sore, / And tosse

Of Norumbega, and the Samoed shore
Bursting their brazen dungeon, armed with ice
And snow and hail and stormy gust and flaw,
Boreas, and Caecias and Argestes loud
And Thrascias rend the woods and seas upturn;
With adverse blast upturns them from the south
Notus and Afer black with thunderous clouds
From Serraliona; thwart of these as fierce
Forth rush the Levant and the ponent winds
Eurus and Zephir, with their lateral noise,
Sirocco, and Libecchio, thus began
Outrage from lifeless things; but Discord first
Daughter of Sin, among the irrational,
Death introduced through fierce antipathy:
Beast now with beast gan war, and fowl with fowl,
And fish with fish; to graze the herb all leaving,
Devoured each other; nor stood much in awe
Of man, but fled him, or with countenance grim
Glared on him passing: these were from without
The growing miseries, which Adam saw
Already in part, though hid in gloomiest shade,
To sorrow abandoned, but worse felt within,
And in a troubled sea of passion tossed,

the deepes, and teare the firmament, / And all the world confound with wide uprore, / As if in stead thereof they Chaos would restore.' Cp. also ix 1122f above: 'high winds worse within / Began to rise, high passions.'

x *696. Norumbega*] The name vaguely given to S.E. Canada and the N.E. part of the U.S.A.; while *Samoedia*, which is mentioned in M.'s *Brief History of Muscovia*, was a region corresponding to the extreme N.E. of modern Siberia.

x *710–14*. Contrast the unhurried play of the animals before the Fall, iv 340ff. For *herb* as the prelapsarian diet, see *Gen.* i 30: 'To every beast of the earth, and to every fowl of the air, and to every thing that creepeth upon the earth, wherein there is life, I have given every green herb for meat.' *but fled*] Contrasting awe before the Fall with fear after it.

x *718*. The correspondence between passion and macrocosmic disorder is now introjected to become subjective metaphor. Cp. *Is.* lvii 20: 'The wicked are like the troubled sea, when it cannot rest, whose waters cast up mire and dirt.' The Sea of Troubles topic could be traced through St Augustine's *Enarr. in Ps.* cvii (*Migne* xxxvii 1425f), Chaucer's *Man of Law's Tale*, medieval and Renaissance Fortune iconography, *Hamlet* III i 59, Quarles, *Emblemes* (Cambridge 1643) iii 11 (on *Ps.* lxix 15, 'Let not the water-flood overflow me') and Vaughan's 'The Storm'. An erotic variant of the topic, found e.g. in Petrarch, *Rime* clxxxix and Spenser, *F.Q.* III iv 8–10

Thus to disburden sought with sad complaint.
O miserable of happy! Is this the end
Of this new glorious world, and me so late
The glory of that glory, who now become
Accurst of blessed, hide me from the face
Of God, whom to behold was then my highth
Of happiness: yet well, if here would end
The misery, I deserved it, and would bear
My own deservings; but this will not serve;
All that I eat or drink, or shall beget,
Is propagated curse. O voice once heard
Delightfully, *Increase and multiply*,
Now death to hear! For what can I increase
Or multiply, but curses on my head?
Who of all ages to succeed, but feeling
The evil on him brought by me, will curse
My head, Ill fare our ancestor impure,
For this we may thank Adam; but his thanks
Shall be the execration; so besides
Mine own that bide upon me, all from me
Shall with a fierce reflux on me redound,

('Huge sea of sorrow and tempestuous grief'), stems from Horace *Odes* I v.

x *720.* Broadbent 80 notices that 'the characters of *Paradise Lost* do not soliloquize until they have fallen; unfallen speech and gesture are directed always to another person, on the supreme model of light inter-reflected by Father and Son.' This the first of all complaints is made the subject of critical discriminations similar to those occasioned by the other genres worked into the poem (see ix 16*n*, 30–1*n*, etc.). Here, just causes of complaint are distinguished from unjust, Christian from unrepentant and unreasoning sorrow.

x *722.* Adam is probably meant here to have fallen into bad theology. He was not the glory of the world, but the 'glory of God' (*1 Cor.* xi 7).

x *728–9. propagated*] extended (*OED* 4); handed down from one generation to another (*OED* 1 d). Food prolongs life and thus extends the curse; while begetting children hands it on. Note also that eating and sex are jointly the concerns of the concupiscible faculty, which was often regarded as the especial field of operation of concupiscence or the 'body of sin' (*De doctrina* i 11, Columbia xv 193). Thus the eating and begetting itself might quite properly be called a *curse*.

x *730.* Cp. vii 530f, and see *Gen.* i 28.

x *736. For . . . Adam*] To Addison this seemed a colloquialism.

x *738–40. Mine own*] i.e., curses. On the repetition of *me* see l. 832*n*. *redound*] Both in the physical sense 'flow back; overflow' (*OED* 4, 1 b) and the figurative 'recoil, come back' (of disgrace: *OED* 8).

On me as on their natural centre light
Heavy, though in their place. O fleeting joys
Of Paradise, dear bought with lasting woes!
Did I request thee, Maker, from my clay
To mould me man, did I solicit thee
From darkness to promote me, or here place
In this delicious garden? As my will
Concurred not to my being, it were but right
And equal to reduce me to my dust,
Desirous to resign, and render back
All I received, unable to perform
Thy terms too hard, by which I was to hold
The good I sought not. To the loss of that,
Sufficient penalty, why hast thou added
The sense of endless woes? Inexplicable
Thy justice seems; yet to say truth, too late,
I thus contest; then should have been refused
Those terms whatever, when they were proposed:
Thou didst accept them; wilt thou enjoy the good,
Then cavil the conditions? And though God
Made thee without thy leave, what if thy son
Prove disobedient, and reproved, retort,

x *740–1*. In the primary chain of discourse *light* means 'alight'; in the secondary, 'not heavy'. The curses might be expected to be light at their natural centre, since the force that returned them is there null. In view of the topicality of the science and the intricacy of the conceit we must suppose M. to have intended Adam's wit to seem positively Metaphysical.

x *743–4*. The complaint condemned in *Is.* xlv 9: 'Woe unto him that striveth with his Maker! Let the potsherd strive with the potsherds of the earth. Shall the clay say to him that fashioneth it, What makest thou? or thy work, He hath no hands?'

x *748*. *equal*] just.

x *754*. *endless woes*] As Burden 186f remarks, it is unthinkable that such generalization of grief should have been approved by M., who always preferred to introduce rational discriminations. Adam, however, is not yet properly repentant.

x *758*. *thou*] Adam takes first God's part, then his own, in an imaginary debate.

x *760–5*. Cp. *Is.* xlv 10: 'Woe unto him that saith unto his father, What begettest thou? or to the woman, What hast thou brought forth?' Here, as at 743f, M. alludes to a Biblical curse, with an effect of dramatic irony. Even better than Adam, we can see how the curse of *Gen.* iii 14–19 will proliferate. *election*] choice; but with the theological sense–predestination–as a strong overtone.

Wherefore didst thou beget me? I sought it not:
Wouldst thou admit for his contempt of thee
That proud excuse? Yet him not thy election,
But natural necessity begot.
God made thee of choice his own, and of his own
To serve him, thy reward was of his grace,
Thy punishment then justly is at his will.
Be it so, for I submit, his doom is fair,
That dust I am, and shall to dust return:
O welcome hour whenever! Why delays
His hand to execute what his decree
Fixed on this day? Why do I overlive,
Why am I mocked with death, and lengthened out
To deathless pain? How gladly would I meet
Mortality my sentence, and be earth
Insensible, how glad would lay me down
As in my mother's lap? There I should rest
And sleep secure; his dreadful voice no more
Would thunder in my ears, no fear of worse
To me and to my offspring would torment me

x *762.* Following the punctuation of *Ed I*. *Ed II* has no point after *not*.
x *769. doom*] judgment.
x *770.* Alluding to the conclusion of God's curse on Adam at *Gen.* iii 19: 'Dust thou art, and unto dust shalt thou return.'
x *773. this day*] Newton and Verity hold that this is a careless error, because the night of the day of the Fall was mentioned at l. 342, and the sun's subsequent rising at l. 329. But M. puts so much weight on the exact terms of the prohibition (both here and at ll. 49ff, 210f, and 1048ff) that we must count it extremely improbable that he should be vague about his chronology at precisely the stage most crucial from this point of view. Admittedly, the night following the Fall and Christ's judgment was mentioned at l. 342. But there is no reason why the present action should not be regarded as taking place on that same night, for l. 329 does not refer to a sunrise over Eden at all (see ll. 328–9*n*). Adam can speak of death delaying, since the day of the Fall *is* already over, reckoning in the Hebrew manner from sunset to sunset (see Introduction, 'Chronology'). But, lacking faith, he fears that God may be following some other system of reckoning whereby the day will not end until sunrise. Later, he overlooks a third system, whereby the 24-hour period starting with the noon of the Fall (ix 739) will not have run out until the 'hour precise' of the Expulsion, at xii 589. The completion of each period of reckoning of 'that day' brings with it a new peripeteia, and a fuller understanding of the depth of God's judgment. See ll. 49–53*n*, 854–9*n*, 923 and 1050*n*.
x *778. mother's lap*] Cp. xi 536. Exclamation mark is probably intended after *lap*.

With cruel expectation. Yet one doubt
Pursues me still, lest all I cannot die,
Lest that pure breath of life, the spirit of man
Which God inspired, cannot together perish
With this corporeal clod; then in the grave,
Or in some other dismal place who knows
But I shall die a living death? O thought
Horrid, if true! Yet why? It was but breath
Of life that sinned; what dies but what had life
And sin? The body properly hath neither.
All of me then shall die: let this appease
The doubt, since human reach no farther knows.
For though the Lord of all be infinite,
Is his wrath also? Be it, man is not so,
But mortal doomed. How can he exercise
Wrath without end on man whom death must end?
Can he make deathless death? That were to make
Strange contradiction, which to God himself

x *783. all I*] all of me; cp. l. 792.

x *786–92.* Adam argues that since it was his spirit that sinned, and since death is the punishment for sin, it would be unjust for his body to die and not his spirit. See *De doctrina* i 13 (Columbia xv 227), where M. rejects 'the sophistical distinction, that although the whole man dies, it does not therefore follow that the whole of man should die'; also *ibid.* 219: 'What could be more absurd than that the mind, which is the part principally offending, should escape the threatened death; and that the body alone, to which immortality was equally allotted, before death came into the world by sin, should pay the penalty of sin by undergoing death, though not implicated in the transgression?' and *ibid.* 217–9: 'The death of the body is the loss or extinction of life. The common definition, which supposes it to consist in the separation of soul and body, is inadmissible. For what part of man is it that dies when this separation takes place? Is it the soul? This will not be admitted by the supporters of the above definition. Is it then the body? But how can that be said to die, which never had any life of itself? Therefore the separation of soul and body cannot be called the death of man.' M.'s belief in the joint extinction and joint resurrection of man's body and mind was not an eccentric heresy, but good Biblical theology; see the discussions in Kelley 13, G. Williamson, *SP* xxxii (1935) 553–79, corrected in N. H. Henry, *SP* xlviii (1951) 248. *living death*] *mors aeterna*, the fourth degree of death; on which see *De doctrina, ibid.* 251, also *De doctrina* i 33 *passim*. *yet why*] Why should this doubt (782) pursue me? *appease*] allay.

x *798–801.* Adam's theology is again at fault. While it is true that 'the power of God is not exerted in things which imply a contradiction' (*De doctrina* i 2, Columbia xiv 49), allowance should have been made for the possibility–which M. believed to be in fact the case–that man first dies, then is brought

Impossible is held, as argument
Of weakness, not of power. Will he draw out,
For anger's sake, finite to infinite
In punished man, to satisfy his rigour
Satisfied never; that were to extend
His sentence beyond dust and nature's law,
By which all causes else according still
To the reception of their matter act,
Not to the extent of their own sphere. But say
That death be not one stroke, as I supposed,
Bereaving sense, but endless misery
From this day onward, which I feel begun
Both in me, and without me, and so last
To perpetuity; ay me, that fear
Comes thundering back with dreadful revolution
On my defenceless head; both death and I
Am found eternal, and incorporate both,

to life again at the day of judgment (e.g. *De doctrina* i 13, Columbia xv 249). *argument*] evidence, manifestation.

x *801*. In the early edns comma is wrongly inserted after *he*.

x *804–8*. As at ll. 798–801, Adam tries to comfort himself with an argument drawn from the Schools. Here the appeal is to an axiom, given in Stahlius' *Axiomata* (1651) xiv 4 in the form *Quod recipitur, per modum recipientis*. The axiom goes back through St. Thomas Aquinas (e.g. *Summa* I lxxxix 4) to Aristotle (*De anima* 424ª); it was usually applied to the way in which things are received into the mind or the senses. Here Adam means that God would be going beyond a natural law about agents acting according to the capacities of their subjects, not their own.

x *810*. 'The second death, or the punishment of the damned, seems to consist partly . . . in eternal torment, which is called the punishment of sense' (*De doctrina* i 33, Columbia xvi 371).

x *813*. Cp. *Hamlet* III i 65–8: 'To sleep: perchance to dream: ay, there's the rub; / For in that sleep of death what dreams may come / . . . Must give us pause.'

x *816*. *Am*] Bentley objected to the use of a singular verb with a plural subject; but, as Darbishire[2] 305f points out, Adam is realizing that death has become one with himself. His own body and 'the body of this death' (*Rom.* vii 24) share a single identity and a single verb. M. had a precedent for the device in Spenser, *F.Q.* II xi 45f, where the antecedents of the pronouns are just uncertain enough to attract the attention momentarily. Arthur shares pronouns with Maleger, because Maleger is the body of sin in him. *incorporate*] united in one body (*OED* I 1); also 'embodied, having a bodily form' (*OED* II 3); referring to the doctrine of the 'body of sin'; cp. l. 587, and see *n*.

Nor I on my part single, in me all
Posterity stands cursed: fair patrimony
That I must leave ye, sons; O were I able
To waste it all my self, and leave ye none!
So disinherited how would ye bless
Me now your curse! Ah, why should all mankind
For one man's fault thus guiltless be condemned,
If guiltless? But from me what can proceed,
But all corrupt, both mind and will depraved,
Not to do only, but to will the same
With me? How can they then acquitted stand
In sight of God? Him after all disputes
Forced I absolve: all my evasions vain,
And reasonings, though through mazes, lead me still
But to my own conviction: first and last
On me, me only, as the source and spring

x *817*. Not only are Death and I double, two in one, but so also am I, since I am both myself and my descendants. Cp. *2 Esdras* vii 48. *single*] 'one; solitary; unmarried; simple; free from duplicity'. In addition to the obvious resonances, there is a number symbolism: Adam reflects on his dyadic state (see vi 809–10*n*).

x *825*. Without holding the extreme Calvinist doctrine of Total Depravity, M. believed in a 'general depravity of the human mind', *communis*. . . .*mentis humanae pravitas* (*De doctrina* i 11, Columbia xv 194f).

x *826–7*. Cp. *Rom.* i 32: 'Who knowing the judgment of God, that they which commit such things are worthy of death, not only do the same, but have pleasure in them that do them.'

x *827*. *Ed I* omits *then*.

x *828–44*. Adam at last reaches full conviction of his sin; but being unable yet to pass to contrition, the next stage of repentance, he falls instead into despair. See *De doctrina* i 19 (Columbia xv 385): 'We may distinguish certain progressive steps in repentance; namely, conviction of sin, contrition, confession, departure from evil, conversion to good.' The present passage should be compared with Satan's similar fall into conscience-stricken despair, at iv 86–113; the progressive steps in repentance 'belong likewise in their respective degrees to the repentance of the unregenerate' (*De doctrina*, *ibid.*).

x *829*. It is didactically effective to have God's ways acknowledged to be just, by the man best placed of all to detect any injustice in the treatment accorded his species.

x *832*. Cp. Virgil, *Aen.* ix 427, where Nisus exposes himself to the Rutulians in an attempt to save Euryalus, acknowledging his own guilt with the cry *me, me, adsum, qui feci, in me convertite ferrum*; or *1 Sam.* xxv 24, where Abigail to save Nabal cries 'Upon me, my lord, upon me let this iniquity be'. Broadbent 151f notes that Adam here repeats 'the central ploce on

Of all corruption, all the blame lights due;
So might the wrath. Fond wish! Couldst thou support
That burden heavier than the earth to bear
Than all the world much heavier, though divided
With that bad woman? Thus what thou desirest
And what thou fear'st, alike destroys all hope
Of refuge, and concludes thee miserable
Beyond all past example and future,
To Satan only like both crime and doom.
O conscience! into what abyss of fears
And horrors hast thou driven me; out of which
I find no way, from deep to deeper plunged!
    Thus Adam to himself lamented loud
Through the still night, not now, as ere man fell,
Wholesome and cool, and mild, but with black air
Accompanied, with damps and dreadful gloom,
Which to his evil conscience represented
All things with double terror: on the ground
Outstretched he lay, on the cold ground, and oft
Cursed his creation, death as oft accused
Of tardy execution, since denounced
The day of his offence. Why comes not death,

"me"' in Christ's speech at iii 236 ('Behold me then, me for him, life for life'): 'This is the spring of self-sacrifice which Adam and Eve draw on after the Fall to recover sanity and love.' Cp. l. 738, and contrast the Satanic travesty at ll. 494–8.

x *834*. i.e., would that the wrath, similarly, were confined to me.

x *835–6. world*] universe; not merely a repetition of *earth*.

x *840. future*] Stressed on the second syllable.

x *841*. Having heard God's distinction between Satan's sin and Adam's at iii 129ff, we know this to be the false perspective of despair.

x *842*. But at iii 194–7 God said that he would place his 'umpire conscience' within man 'as a guide', and that, if man listened, he would arrive safe in the end. Conscience appears among the *dramatis personae* in M.'s drafts of a tragedy on the Fall.

x *849–50*. 'Guiltiness'. . . is accompanied or followed by terrors of conscience' (*De doctrina* i 12, Columbia xv 205).

x *853. denounced*] proclaimed as a warning, announced.

x *854–9*. Adam still thinks he can expect the terms of the prohibition to be fulfilled literally, by his physical death. When this fails to occur, he begins to discover the mysteriousness of divine justice. He is to learn that it is tempered with mercy, but that its decrees are nevertheless eventually accomplished, though in an unexpected way. See l. 773*n*. *acceptable*] Stressed on the first syllable.

Said he, with one thrice acceptable stroke
To end me? Shall truth fail to keep her word,
Justice divine not hasten to be just?
But death comes not at call, justice divine
Mends not her slowest pace for prayers or cries.
O woods, O fountains, hillocks, dales and bowers,
With other echo late I taught your shades
To answer, and resound far other song.
Whom thus afflicted when sad Eve beheld,
Desolate where she sat, approaching nigh,
Soft words to his fierce passion she assayed:
But her with stern regard he thus repelled.
  Out of my sight, thou serpent, that name best
Befits thee with him leagued, thy self as false
And hateful; nothing wants, but that thy shape,
Like his, and colour serpentine may show
Thy inward fraud, to warn all creatures from thee
Henceforth; lest that too heavenly form, pretended
To hellish falsehood, snare them. But for thee
I had persisted happy, had not thy pride
And wandering vanity, when least was safe,
Rejected my forewarning, and disdained
Not to be trusted, longing to be seen
Though by the devil himself, him overweening
To over-reach, but with the serpent meeting
Fooled and beguiled, by him thou, I by thee,
To trust thee from my side, imagined wise,
Constant, mature, proof against all assaults,
And understood not all was but a show
Rather than solid virtue, all but a rib

x *860–1.* The echo here is of the morning hymn of Adam and Eve; cp. especially v 202–4.
x *867.* Some commentators interpreted Eve's name etymologically in the sense 'serpent'.
x *872. pretended*] stretched in front as a covering (*OED* I 1).
x *873–4. Ed I* has comma after *heart* and no comma after *dying*.
x *875–9* Adam takes a firm enough line now on Eve's wish to work separately. With this harsh account of her motives, cp. ix 335–86 and *nn.*
x *884–8. sinister*] left; corrupt, evil, base. Stressed on the second syllable. For the true implication to be drawn from the side of Eve's origin, see viii 465–6*n.* But here M. provides the recriminating Adam with fit ammunition: mere stock antifeminist lore. Svendsen 184 illustrates the notion that woman is formed from a bent rib, and therefore crooked, from such misogynistic works as the *Malleus maleficarum* and Swetnam's *The Araignment of Lewde, Idle, Froward, and Unconstant Women* (1615). Willet 38, citing

Crooked by nature, bent, as now appears,
More to the part sinister from me drawn,
Well if thrown out, as supernumerary
To my just number found. O why did God,
Creator wise, that peopled highest heaven
With spirits masculine, create at last
This novelty on earth, this fair defect
Of nature, and not fill the world at once
With men as angels without feminine,
Or find some other way to generate
Mankind? This mischief had not then befallen,
And more that shall befall, innumerable
Disturbances on earth through female snares,
And strait conjunction with this sex: for either
He never shall find out fit mate, but such
As some misfortune brings him, or mistake,
Or whom he wishes most shall seldom gain
Through her perverseness, but shall see her gained
By a far worse, or if she love, withheld
By parents, or his happiest choice too late
Shall meet, already linked and wedlock-bound
To a fell adversary, his hate or shame:
Which infinite calamity shall cause
To human life, and household peace confound.
    He added not, and from her turned, but Eve

Mercerus and Calvin, argues that Eve must have been made from an extra rib for Adam to have been perfectly created in the first instance. This rib was 'supernumerarie ... above the usuall number or ribbes created of purpose by the Lord, not as a superfluous or monstrous part, but as necessarie for the creation of the woman, which God intended'. The supernumerary syllable at the end of 887 may be intended mimetically; see Sprott 58f.

x *888–95.* Another ancient piece of antifeminism; cp. Euripides, *Hippolytus* 616ff. *defect / Of nature*] Aristotle had said in the *De generatione* ($735^{a}25$, $767^{a}35$, $775^{a}15$) that the female is a defective male. See Fletcher ii 177, and Fr. W. T. Costello in *Ren N* viii (1955) 179–84, on a seventeenth-century discussion of the point, in Keckermann's *Physica*. Keckermann discusses whether the human female, being a defect of nature, is monstrous; but decides not, on the grounds that women are common, monsters rare.

x *898–908.* Those who attempt to find autobiographical allusions here ought first to reckon with the exaggerated extremity of Adam's prognostications. The almost comical multiplication of griefs accords with his present despair, but hardly with M.'s own more rational view. Throughout the present passage M. deliberately assigns to Adam culpable sentiments and erroneous opinions.

x *899. fit mate*] Contrast viii 450, and see *Gen.* ii 18.

Not so repulsed, with tears that ceased not flowing,
And tresses all disordered, at his feet
Fell humble, and embracing them, besought
His peace, and thus proceeded in her plaint.
  Forsake me not thus, Adam, witness heaven
What love sincere, and reverence in my heart
I bear thee, and unweeting have offended,
Unhappily deceived; thy suppliant
I beg, and clasp thy knees; bereave me not,
Whereon I live, thy gentle looks, thy aid,
Thy counsel in this uttermost distress,
My only strength and stay: forlorn of thee,
Whither shall I betake me, where subsist?
While yet we live, scarce one short hour perhaps,
Between us two let there be peace, both joining,
As joined in injuries, one enmity
Against a foe by doom express assigned us,
That cruel serpent: on me exercise not
Thy hatred for this misery befallen,
On me already lost, me than thy self
More miserable; both have sinned, but thou
Against God only, I against God and thee,
And to the place of judgment will return,
There with my cries importune heaven, that all
The sentence from thy head removed may light
On me, sole cause to thee of all this woe,
Me me only just object of his ire.
  She ended weeping, and her lowly plight,
Immovable till peace obtained from fault
Acknowledged and deplored, in Adam wrought
Commiseration; soon his heart relented

x *923*. See ll. 773*n*, 1050*n*.
x *926*. *doom*] The judgment of ll. 179–81. Appropriately it is Eve who reminds Adam of this, since the enmity was to be specifically between the *woman* and the serpent. Cp. *Gen*. iii 15: 'I will put enmity between thee and the woman.'
x *931*. Echoing iv 299, where the natures of man and woman are distinguished in similar terms: 'He for God only, she for God in him.' Cp. also the Penitential Psalm, *Ps*. li 4: 'Against thee, thee only, have I sinned.'
x *936*. On an important resonance in the repeated *me*, see l. 832*n*.
x *937–40*. The difficulty in the syntax seems to arise from M.'s wish to have *Immovable* qualify *plight* as well as *Adam*. In addition to the two chains of discourse thus set up there is a third, in which *her lowly plight*=humbly pledged herself. In that case it is Eve who cannot be moved from Adam's feet, until he forgives her.

Towards her, his life so late and sole delight,
Now at his feet submissive in distress,
Creature so fair his reconcilement seeking,
His counsel whom she had displeased, his aid;
As one disarmed, his anger all he lost,
And thus with peaceful words upraised her soon.
  Unwary, and too desirous, as before,
So now of what thou know'st not, who desir'st
The punishment all on thy self; alas,
Bear thine own first, ill able to sustain
His full wrath whose thou feel'st as yet least part,
And my displeasure bear'st so ill. If prayers
Could alter high decrees, I to that place
Would speed before thee, and be louder heard,
That on my head all might be visited,
Thy frailty and infirmer sex forgiven,
To me committed and by me exposed.
But rise, let us no more contend, nor blame
Each other, blamed enough elsewhere, but strive
In offices of love, how we may lighten
Each other's burden in our share of woe;
Since this day's death denounced, if aught I see,
Will prove no sudden, but a slow-paced evil,
A long day's dying to augment our pain,
And to our seed (O hapless seed!) derived.
  To whom thus Eve, recovering heart, replied.
Adam, by sad experiment I know
How little weight my words with thee can find,
Found so erroneous, thence by just event
Found so unfortunate; nevertheless,

x *950–1.* Cp. ll. 834–7; Adam can grasp more clearly than Eve what the sentence of God may involve. Notice how he brings her back to rational discourse, to what she knows.
x *957.* Note the difference in Adam's attitude to the fault he denied at ix 1170ff. He may now be thought to exaggerate the degree of his own guilt.
x *959. elsewhere*] Either 'heaven' or the 'place of judgment' of l. 932 etc.
x *962–4.* Adam sees that the terms of the prohibition were not merely literal. Cp. ll. 854–9 and see *n*; also l. 773*n*.
x *965. derived*] imparted, passed on by descent, as in l. 77.
x *969. event*] consequence.
x *970. unfortunate*] Cp. l. 965, 'hapless seed'. Burden 181f comments on Adam's and Eve's concern for the ideology of the tragedy they see themselves as acting. Eve understands that the event is *just*, but wrongly imagines that the effect on posterity is a necessary or *certain woe* (l. 980). The necessitarian tragedy of pagan literature has become possible. Looked at from another

Restored by thee, vile as I am, to place
Of new acceptance, hopeful to regain
Thy love, the sole contentment of my heart
Living or dying, from thee I will not hide
What thoughts in my unquiet breast are risen,
Tending to some relief of our extremes,
Or end, though sharp and sad, yet tolerable,
As in our evils, and of easier choice.
If care of our descent perplex us most,
Which must be born to certain woe, devoured
By death at last, and miserable it is
To be to others cause of misery,
Our own begotten, and of our loins to bring
Into this cursed world a woeful race,
That after wretched life must be at last
Food for so foul a monster, in thy power
It lies, yet ere conception to prevent
The race unblest, to being yet unbegot.
Childless thou art, childless remain:
So death shall be deceived his glut, and with us two
Be forced to satisfy his ravenous maw.
But if thou judge it hard and difficult,
Conversing, looking, loving, to abstain
From love's due rights, nuptial embraces sweet,

point of view, the present phase is one in which God's justice is recognized, but not his mercy. Consequently the justice seems inflexible and rigid.

x *978. As in*] considering we are in. Possibly a Latinism; Richardson compares Cicero, *Epist. fam.* xii 2 (*nonnihil, ut in tantis malis, est profectum*) and iv 9.

x *979. descent*] descendants. *perplex*] torment (a key word in *PL*: see ix 10–19*n*.)

x *982.* Some copies of *Ed I* have full stop after *misery*.

x *987. prevent*] cut off beforehand; preclude, render impossible (*OED* II 6, 8). At a time when the rate of puerperal and infant mortality was high and the expectation of life short, and when in consequence the begetting of as many children as possible was generally regarded as a sacred duty, Eve's sentiment would seem reprehensible, even shocking. M. uses violent strategies to bring home the seriousness of man's fallen state – and the cosmic role of hope.

x *989–90.* All previous editors have moved *So Death* back to the end of l. 989, in the interests of metrical regularity. But this may be philistinism. The line division as its stands in *Ed I*, *Ed II*, and three subsequent edns is perhaps intended to mime first the deficiency of childlessness (l. 989 defective), then the glut denied to Death (l. 990 hypermetrical).

And with desire to languish without hope,
Before the present object languishing
With like desire, which would be misery
And torment less than none of what we dread,
Then both our selves and seed at once to free
From what we fear for both, let us make short,
Let us seek death, or he not found, supply
With our own hands his office on our selves;
Why stand we longer shivering under fears,
That show no end but death, and have the power,
Of many ways to die the shortest choosing,
Destruction with destruction to destroy.
 She ended here, or vehement despair
Broke off the rest; so much of death her thoughts
Had entertained, as dyed her cheeks with pale.
But Adam with such counsel nothing swayed,
To better hopes his more attentive mind
Labouring had raised, and thus to Eve replied.
 Eve, thy contempt of life and pleasure seems
To argue in thee something more sublime
And excellent than what thy mind contemns;
But self-destruction therefore sought, refutes
That excellence thought in thee, and implies,
Not thy contempt, but anguish and regret
For loss of life and pleasure overloved.

x *995. without*] On the first-syllable accentuation, implying emphasis, see ii 892*n*. Cp. Dante, *Inf.* iv 42, 'without hope we live in desire'.
x *996. object*] Eve.
x *1007. vehement*] passionate; usually explained etymologically as *vehe-* lacking + *mens* mind. Cp. 'mindless' at ix 431, and see ix 358*n*.
x *1013–24.* In 'Milton and the Mortalist Heresy', *SP* xxxii (1935) 553–79, esp. 576f, G. Williamson relates these lines to a contemporary controversy about suicide; citing Charleton's defence of Epicurus on self-homicide and John Adams's *Essay concerning Self-Murther* (1700), where M. is said to have made 'the first man argue against self-murder from the Light of Nature'. The passage may also be taken more broadly, with Horrell 420f and perhaps also with Broadbent 98, as a discrimination between Stoic extremity (exemplified earlier by the devils of ii 562–9) and Christian patience. In his *Commonplace Book*, under the head 'Death self-inflicted', M. notes treatments of suicide in Dante (*Inf.* xiii) and in Sidney's *Arcadia* ('whether lawfull, disputed with exquisite reasoning': Yale i 371). M. himself regarded suicides as moved by a 'perverse hatred of self' (*De doctrina* ii 8, Columbia xvii 201), and thought they should be placed in the class denoted in *Ps.* lv 23: 'Bloody and deceitful men shall not live out half their days' (*ibid.* i 8, Columbia xv 93). Cp. also *SA* 505ff.

Or if thou covet death, as utmost end
Of misery, so thinking to evade
The penalty pronounced, doubt not but God
Hath wiselier armed his vengeful ire than so
To be forestalled; much more I fear lest death
So snatched will not exempt us from the pain
We are by doom to pay; rather such acts
Of contumacy will provoke the highest
To make death in us live: then let us seek
Some safer resolution, which methinks
I have in view, calling to mind with heed
Part of our sentence, that thy seed shall bruise
The serpent's head; piteous amends, unless
Be meant, whom I conjecture, our grand foe
Satan, who in the serpent hath contrived
Against us this deceit: to crush his head
Would be revenge indeed; which will be lost
By death brought on our selves, or childless days
Resolved, as thou proposest; so our foe
Shall scape his punishment ordained, and we
Instead shall double ours upon our heads.
No more be mentioned then of violence
Against our selves, and wilful barrenness,
That cuts us off from hope, and savours only
Rancour and pride, impatience and despite,
Reluctance against God and his just yoke
Laid on our necks. Remember with what mild
And gracious temper he both heard and judged
Without wrath or reviling; we expected
Immediate dissolution, which we thought
Was meant by death that day, when lo, to thee

x *1024–8.* Adam delivers the fruits of the labouring of his 'more attentive mind' at ll. 786–816. *doom*] judgment. *make death in us live*] Cp. 'living death' l. 788 and see *n.*

x *1030–40.* The curse of ll. 164–81 is brought in here because (as Burden 178f remarks, citing Calvin, *Inst.* II xiii 2) it was pronounced in the first place in order to prevent Eve from giving way to despair. The dawning perception of man's (and implicitly Christ's) role is also a vital part of Adam's progression to true repentance and faith. Burden 31ff notes that Adam's rejection of suicide, and acceptance of the role predetermined by the curse, are experienced as free choices; whereas Satan's wilful serpent role is by x 510 involuntary.

x *1045. reluctance*] the act of struggling *against* something; resistance (*OED* 1).

x *1050.* Notice how Adam's understanding of the mysterious, figurative

Pains only in child-bearing were foretold,
And bringing forth, soon recompensed with joy,
Fruit of thy womb: on me the curse aslope
Glanced on the ground, with labour I must earn
My bread; what harm? Idleness had been worse;
My labour will sustain me; and lest cold
Or heat should injure us, his timely care
Hath unbesought provided, and his hands
Clothed us unworthy, pitying while he judged;
How much more, if we pray him, will his ear
Be open, and his heart to pity incline,
And teach us further by what means to shun
The inclement seasons, rain, ice, hail and snow,
Which now the sky with various face begins
To show us in this mountain, while the winds
Blow moist and keen, shattering the graceful locks
Of these fair spreading trees; which bids us seek
Some better shroud, some better warmth to cherish
Our limbs benumbed, ere this diurnal star
Leave cold the night, how we his gathered beams
Reflected, may with matter sere foment,

sense of Christ's sentence (ll.1031ff) is bound up with recognition of the figurative terms of the original prohibition (on which see viii 323–33*n*). He now grasps that the day of the Fall ended at sunset after all (see ll. 49–53*n*, 773*n*), and that it is now another day, Day 33. There is, however, a further surprise in store for him in this connection; see xii 588–9*n*.

x *1052–3. soon recompensed*] Alludes to *John* xvi 21: 'A woman when she is in travail hath sorrow, because her hour is come: but as soon as she is delivered of the child, she remembereth no more the anguish, for joy that a man is born into the world'–Christ's metaphor for the joy there will be at his victory. *Fruit of thy womb*] A similar allusion to Christ, *via Luke* i 42.

x *1053–5.* Referring to Christ's words at ll. 201–5.

x *1060–81.* M. restores technology to its rightful context, by making it a matter of Christ's instruction, according to human needs. Adam's vision of a modest technological progress is sustained by the surrounding expressions of confidence in Christ's mercy: because God is merciful, life can continue and considerations of human convenience become appropriate. Nevertheless, as Broadbent 103 points out, it is only after the Fall that Adam has to think about applied science at all. See v 349*n*, 396*n*.

x *1060–1.* Biblical diction: cp. *Ps.* xxiv 4, cxix 36, 112; *1 Pet.* iii 12.

x *1066. shattering*] Cp. *Lycidas* 5.

x *1068. shroud*] shelter (*OED* sb[1]3); also 'loppings of a tree, branches cut off' (*OED* sb.[3]), continuing the thought of the preceding line more concretely.

x *1070–80.* M. blends hard primitivism and soft primitivism in his account of man's earliest state. The rationalistic explanation of the discovery of fire

Or by collision of two bodies grind
The air attrite to fire, as late the clouds
Justling or pushed with winds rude in their shock
Tine the slant lightning, whose thwart flame driven down
Kindles the gummy bark of fir or pine,
And sends a comfortable heat from far,
Which might supply the sun: such fire to use,
And what may else be remedy or cure
To evils which our own misdeeds have wrought,
He will instruct us praying, and of grace
Beseeching him, so as we need not fear
To pass commodiously this life, sustained

as a first step in civilization is characteristic of hard primitivism (see Panofsky[2] 41). But this whole logical development is made here to depend on a disturbance of the macrocosm caused by the Fall and the loss of the Golden Age, so that the world view is ultimately soft-primitivistic.
x *1070. how*] Follows *seek* (l. 1067).
x *1071. foment*] cherish; but alluding also to Lat. *fomes* (tinder). Adam's formidable intellect seems at first to be capable of envisaging quite a sophisticated method of making fire: focusing the sun's rays onto dry combustibles with a parabolic mirror. *Reflected*, however, could mean simply 'deflected' (*OED* I 1); in which case refraction through any transparent solid that will act as a lens need be all that is involved. (Cowley (81) could even imagine a 'Burning-Glass of Ice'.) Note the secondary sense in *Reflected*, appeased (*OED* I 2 b: see foll. *n*, and iv 30*n*).
x *1073. attrite*] Primarily 'ground down by friction' (*OED* 1); but the word had also a common technical theological sense which is highly appropriate in the present context: 'having an imperfect sorrow for sin, a bruising that does not amount to the utter crushing of contrition' (*OED* s.v. *Attrite* 2 and *Attrition* 4, citing Tucker: 'Three stages in the passage from vice to virtue: attrition, contrition, and repentance'). The diction of the present line shows the working of Adam's mind in the direction of true contrition, a stage that he has reached by ll. 1091 and 1103.
x *1074. Justling*] jostling. A spelling and perhaps a phonetic variant.
x *1075–8. Tine*] A variant form of *tind*: ignite. *thwart*] transverse. Lightning is given as the origin of fire in Lucretius, v 1091–4.
x *1078–81. supply*] take the place of (*OED* 11). *of*] for. Before the Fall man was 'guiltless of fire': see v 349*n*, 396*n*, ix 387–92*n*. M. has at several points found it hard to imagine prelapsarian mundane activities not dependent on technology; once he had even to invoke angels to get out of the difficulty. For he was committed to the view that arts as we know them exist to repair the damage caused by the Fall (a view that was commonplace in the Renaissance, though seldom more eloquently expressed than by Thomas Wilson in the Pref. to his *Arte of Rhetorique* (1560)).

By him with many comforts, till we end
In dust, our final rest and native home.
What better can we do, than to the place
Repairing where he judged us, prostrate fall
Before him reverent, and there confess
Humbly our faults, and pardon beg, with tears
Watering the ground, and with our sighs the air
Frequenting, sent from hearts contrite, in sign
Of sorrow unfeigned, and humiliation meek.
Undoubtedly he will relent and turn
From his displeasure; in whose look serene,
When angry most he seemed and most severe,
What else but favour, grace, and mercy shone?
So spake our father penitent, nor Eve
Felt less remorse: they forthwith to the place
Repairing where he judged them prostrate fell
Before him reverent, and both confessed
Humbly their faults, and pardon begged, with tears
Watering the ground, and with their sighs the air
Frequenting, sent from hearts contrite, in sign
Of sorrow unfeigned, and humiliation meek.

THE END OF THE TENTH BOOK

x *1088–92.* Having passed on from conviction of sin Adam, now *contrite* (cp. 1103), is ready for confession, the third stage of repentance. See ll. 828–44*n*. *Frequenting*] filling, crowding (*OED* 6; not a Latinism).

x *1090.* Cp. *Is.* xvi 9: 'I will water thee with my tears, O Heshbon'; and perhaps Virgil, *Aen.* xi 191, *spargitur et tellus lacrimis.*

x *1091.* Another allusion to the Penitential Psalm: 'The sacrifices of God are a broken spirit: a broken and a contrite heart, O God, thou wilt not despise' (*Ps.* li 17).

x *1096–7.* At last, explicit recognition of God's *mercy* is joined to recognition of his justice. God's mercy is the subject of the whole speech ll. 1046–96; but the word itself is held back until the last line. (See iii 134: 'mercy first and last shall brightest shine'.) In the next line, 1097, Adam is for the first time called *penitent.* No doubt M. wanted to draw attention to the sequence of phases: recognition of God's mercy leads to repentance, just as the latter leads to faith. See *De doctrina* i 19 (Columbia xv 387): 'Repentance, in regenerate man, is prior to faith.'... Therefore that sense of the divine mercy, which leads to repentance, ought not to be confounded with faith, as it is by the greater number of divines.'

x *1098–1104.* Repeating ll. 1086–92, modulated into narrative discourse (only the last two verses remain identical). The same device was used at iv 641–56.

Paradise Lost

BOOK XI

The Argument

The Son of God presents to his Father the prayers of our first parents now repenting, and intercedes for them: God accepts them, but declares that they must no longer abide in Paradise; sends Michael with a band of cherubim to dispossess them; but first to reveal to Adam future things: Michael's coming down. Adam shows to Eve certain ominous signs; he discerns Michael's approach, goes out to meet him: the angel denounces their departure. Eve's lamentation. Adam pleads, but submits: the angel leads him up to a high hill, sets before him in vision what shall happen till the flood.

Thus they in lowliest plight repentant stood
Praying, for from the mercy-seat above
Prevenient grace descending had removed
The stony from their hearts, and made new flesh
Regenerate grow instead, that sighs now breathed
Unutterable, which the spirit of prayer
Inspired, and winged for heaven with speedier flight

xi *1. stood*] There is no literal contradiction of 'prostrate' at x 1099, since *stood* means 'remained' (*OED* I 15 d; cp. 'stand free', 'stand alone'). In a secondary chain of discourse, *in lowliest plight . . . stood* extends such idioms as 'stood in need' (*OED* s.v. *Stand* IV 46). The apparent contradiction is treated as a deliberate paradox by John E. Parish in *English Miscellany*, ed. M. Praz, xv (Rome 1964) 89–102. Adam and Eve are prostrate in sin, but raised by regeneration.
xi *2. mercy-seat*] The solid gold covering laid on the Ark of the Covenant, God's resting-place. In *Exod.* xxv 18 it is described as having two cherubim of gold at its ends; and these were interpreted as a type of intercession in heaven. Cp. i 381–7 and see *n.*
xi *3. Prevenient*] antecedent to human action (*OED* 2). Prevenient grace precedes the determination of the human will, which remains free, nevertheless, to accept or reject it. It is the condition and the initiation of all activity leading to justification. The doctrine was based on such texts as *Ps.* lix 10 (Vulg.: *Deus meus, misericordia eius praeveniet me*), *Rom.* viii 30 and *2 Tim.* i 9.
xi *4.* Cp. *Ezek.* xi 19: 'And I will give them one heart, and I will put a new spirit within you; and I will take the stony heart out of their flesh, and will give them an heart of flesh.'
xi *5–7.* Cp. *Rom.* viii 26: 'Likewise the Spirit also helpeth our infirmities: for we know not what we should pray for as we ought: but the Spirit itself maketh intercession for us with groanings which cannot be uttered.'

Than loudest oratory: yet their port
Not of mean suitors, nor important less
Seemed their petition, than when the ancient pair
In fables old, less ancient yet than these,
Deucalion and chaste Pyrrha to restore
The race of mankind drowned, before the shrine
Of Themis stood devout. To heaven their prayers
Flew up, nor missed the way, by envious winds
Blown vagabond or frustrate: in they passed
Dimensionless through heavenly doors; then clad
With incense, where the golden altar fumed,

xi *8. port*] bearing.

xi *10–14.* Deucalion is a mythic analogue to Noah. Advised by his father Prometheus, he built an ark and escaped the universal flood. When the waters subsided, he and his wife Pyrrha consulted the oracle of Themis; and their prayers were effectual, for they were told how to repair the loss of mankind by throwing behind them stones, which became men and women. Bentley and Empson[2] 179f perversely take *less ancient* to imply that *Genesis* is an old fable too. But M. can hardly have meant that. What he says is that the pagan *ancient pair* is *less ancient* than the Biblical ancient pair. In narratives professing to describe the origin of the present human race, juniority brings discredit. The introduction of the Deucalion myth is particularly appropriate to the context of Adam's repentance, because it was allegorized as a symbol of conversion. See, e.g., the interpretation in George Sandys[2] 33: '*God is said in the Gospell* to be able of stones to raise up children unto Abraham: *the sence not unlike, though diviner*; *meaning the ingrafting of the Gentiles into his faith, hardned in sinne through ignorance and custome*. So the giving us hearts of flesh insteed of those of stone, *is meant by our conversion*' (cp. esp. l. 4).

xi *14–16.* No doubt the 'violent cross wind' of iii 487, which 'blows . . . / Into the devious air', and from there into Limbo, those given to 'painful superstition and blind zeal' (iii 452).

xi *17–18. Dimensionless*] without physical extension (*OED* 1 a), because spiritual, not material. See *Ps.* cxli 2: 'Let my prayer be set forth before thee as incense; and the lifting up of my hands as the evening sacrifice'; also *Rev.* viii 3: 'And another angel came and stood at the altar, having a golden censer; and there was given unto him much incense, that he should offer it with the prayers of all saints upon the golden altar which was before the throne.' Dismissing M. M. Ross's complaint that the heaven of *PL* is too Catholic, Broadbent 157 points out that its equipment comes 'from the Jewish temple direct, not via a Roman cathedral'. Broadbent thinks that M. vacillates between an apocalyptic and an emblematic heaven. But if we grant M.'s initial premise about the corporeality of spirits, the appointments of his heaven will seem quite appropriate and consistent.

By their great intercessor, came in sight
Before the Father's throne: them the glad Son
Presenting, thus to intercede began.
 See Father, what first fruits on earth are sprung
From thy implanted grace in man, these sighs
And prayers, which in this golden censer, mixed
With incense, I thy priest before thee bring,
Fruits of more pleasing savour from thy seed
Sown with contrition in his heart, than those
Which his own hand manuring all the trees
Of Paradise could have produced, ere fallen
From innocence. Now therefore bend thine ear
To supplication, hear his sighs though mute;
Unskilful with what words to pray, let me
Interpret for him, me his advocate
And propitiation, all his works on me
Good or not good ingraft, my merit those
Shall perfect, and for these my death shall pay.
Accept me, and in me from these receive
The smell of peace toward mankind, let him live
Before thee reconciled, at least his days

xi *19. intercessor*] Christ; see *Heb.* ix 24; 'Christ is . . . entered . . . into heaven itself, now to appear in the presence of God for us.'
xi *24.* Cp. the 'golden vials full of odours, which are the prayers of saints' (*Rev.* v 8).
xi *26.* The 'sweet savour' of acceptable sacrifices or peace-offerings is a commonplace in the Bible (e.g. *Ezek.* xx 41). There is also a semantic resonance with *savoury* used of man's sacramental or forbidden fruit at v 84, 401, ix 741.
xi *26–30.* Varying the metaphor of the parable of the sower, in *Mark* iv 14–20, with the help of *Heb.* xiii 15: 'Let us offer the sacrifice of praise to God continually, that is, the fruit of our lips giving thanks to his name.' *manuring*] cultivating.
xi *31.* 'The Spirit itself maketh intercession for us with groanings which cannot be uttered' (*Rom.* viii 26).
xi *32–44.* The emphatic repetition of *me* (the rhetorical figure ploce) helps to connect the passage with Christ's similar offer of atonement at iii 236ff. See x 832*n*.
xi *32.* Some copies of *Ed I* omit comma.
xi *33.* Cp. *1 John* ii 1f: 'We have an advocate with the Father, Jesus Christ the righteous: And he is the propitiation for our sins.'
xi *35. engraft*] Keeps up the horticultural metaphor, and alludes to the Pauline allegory of regeneration and incorporation in Christ as a grafting, in *Rom.* xi 16ff.

Numbered, though sad, till death, his doom (which I
To mitigate thus plead, not to reverse)
To better life shall yield him, where with me
All my redeemed may dwell in joy and bliss,
Made one with me as I with thee am one.
To whom the Father, without cloud, serene.
All thy request for man, accepted Son,
Obtain, all thy request was my decree:
But longer in that Paradise to dwell,
The law I gave to nature him forbids:
Those pure immortal elements that know

xi *40–1. doom*] judgment. Cp. x 76, 'that I may mitigate their doom'. From the divine stand-point, death is a mercy, not a punishment. *numbered*] limited. But *at least his days numbered* is not entirely explicable as an allusion to *Ps.* xc 12: 'teach us to number our days, that we may apply our hearts unto wisdom.' The broad sense is Let man be reconciled with the monad–made one with me (l. 44)– and belong with the numbered good, instead of with the unnumbered evil (see vi 767*n*). In the Bible, 'numbered' often means 'elect': see, e.g., *Exod.*, xxx 12, 'then shall they give every man a ransom for his soul unto the Lord, when thou numberest them'. But one suspects that M. here also hints at the number symbolism governing the days of the poem's action.

xi *43–4*. Cp. *John* xvii 11, 21–3: 'Holy Father, keep through thine own name those whom thou hast given me, that they may be one, as we are. . . . that they also may be one in us.'

xi *45. without cloud*] without darkening of his countenance (*OED* s.v. *Cloud* II 10; cp. iii 262 above); but alluding also to the clouds of mystery from which God speaks to angels or to men (see *Num.* xi 25, *Mark* ix 7; and cp. iii 378ff, vi 28). On the accentuation *wìthout*, implying emphasis, see ii 892*n*.

xi *49–57*. The Expulsion is not presented as a punishment, but as a further physically inevitable consequence of the change in man's nature at the Fall. Ironically, Adam earlier (x 805) appealed to 'nature's law' against what he considered God's harshness; whereas now it turns out that God is merciful, yet cannot change the harsh consequences of natural law. *purge him off*] Cp. ii 138–42, where Belial predicts that if the devils returned to heaven 'the ethereal mould / Incapable of stain would soon expel / Her mischief, and purge off the baser fire'. Cp. *Lev.* xviii 25: 'The land is defiled: therefore I do visit the iniquity thereof upon it, and the land itself vomiteth out her inhabitants.' On the 'purer air' of Paradise, see iv 153*n*. 'Of pure now purer' there is countered by *of incorrupt / Corrupted* here. *distempered*] disturbed the proper proportion of humours or elements; disturbed the condition of the air, weather, etc. Dissolution was thought to be held at bay only by a proper tempering of conflicting qualities, so that decay and death were physical consequences of sin.

No gross, no unharmonious mixture foul,
Eject him tainted now, and purge him off
As a distemper, gross to air as gross,
And mortal food, as may dispose him best
For dissolution wrought by sin, that first
Distempered all things, and of incorrupt
Corrupted. I at first with two fair gifts
Created him endowed, with happiness
And immortality: that fondly lost,
This other served but to eternize woe;
Till I provided death; so death becomes
His final remedy, and after life
Tried in sharp tribulation, and refined
By faith and faithful works, to second life,
Waked in the renovation of the just,
Resigns him up with heaven and earth renewed.
But let us call to synod all the blest
Through heaven's wide bounds; from them I will not hide
My judgments, how with mankind I proceed,
As how with peccant angels late they saw;
And in their state, though firm, stood more confirmed.
He ended, and the Son gave signal high
To the bright minister that watched, he blew

xi 59. *fondly*] foolishly.
xi 64. *faithful works*] Cp. 'faith not void of works', xii 427. M. shared the general Protestant belief in the doctrine of Justification by Faith. See *De doctrina* i 22 (Columbia xvi 39): 'We are justified by faith without the works of the law, but not without the works of faith.' In the long progression of stages in regeneration, repentance has been achieved, and we are now entering the stage of faith. See x 828–44*n*, 1096–7*n*.
xi 65. Cp. 'the resurrection of the just', *Luke* xiv 14.
xi 66. 'Nevertheless we, according to his promise, look for new heavens and a new earth, wherein dwelleth righteousness' (*2 Pet.* iii 13).
xi 67. *synod*] assembly. Cp. the synod of gods at vi 156, and the synod of stars at x 661.
xi 73–6. Perhaps also the 'ethereal trumpet' that gave the signal for battle at vi 60. *Oreb*] Horeb; referring to the occasion when God descended to the sound of a trumpet, to deliver the Ten Commandments on Mt Sinai (*Exod.* xix 16; see vi 56–60*n*). *general doom*] the Last Judgment; see *1 Thess.* iv 16: 'The Lord himself shall descend from heaven with a shout, with the voice of the archangel, and with the trump of God: and the dead in Christ shall rise first.' The concern with renovation in the passage immediately preceding accords with an allusion also to *1 Cor.* xv 52: 'The trumpet

His trumpet, heard in Oreb since perhaps
When God descended, and perhaps once more
To sound at general doom. The angelic blast
Filled all the regions: from their blissful bowers
Of amarantin shade, fountain or spring,
By the waters of life, where'er they sat
In fellowships of joy: the sons of light
Hasted, resorting to the summons high,
And took their seats; till from his throne supreme
The almighty thus pronounced his sovereign will.
    O sons, like one of us man is become
To know both good and evil, since his taste
Of that defended fruit; but let him boast
His knowledge of good lost, and evil got,
Happier, had it sufficed him to have known
Good by it self, and evil not at all.
He sorrows now, repents, and prays contrite,
My motions in him, longer than they move,

shall sound, and the dead shall be raised incorruptible, and we shall be changed.' Cp. *Nativity Ode* 157ff.

xi *77.* On the *regions* or layers of atmosphere distinguished in the meteorology of M.'s time, see i 515–16*n*, iii 562*n*. *blissful bowers*] Empson 108 rightly compares the nuptial bower of Adam and Eve.

xi *78. amarantin*] On the unwithering amarant, symbol of immortality, see iii 353–7*n*.

xi *79. waters of life*] Cp. the 'fount of life' and 'river of bliss' at iii 357–9, and see *nn*.

xi *84–98.* Cp. *Gen.* iii 22f: 'And the Lord God said, Behold, the man is become as one of us, to know good and evil: and now, lest he put forth his hand, and take also of the tree of life, and eat, and live for ever: Therefore the Lord God sent him forth from the garden of Eden.' Empson 108 detects 'a mysterious tone of connivance'; but Burden's explanation (7f) is to be preferred: namely, that M. fears that the *Genesis* speech will sound like a confession of inadvertency, and so makes his God speak even more ironically. Cp. Willet (55), who believes 'with Mercerus and Calvin, that God speaketh ironically', or with Rupert of Deutz that Adam 'was so farre from being as God, but he was almost become as the divill'.

xi *86. defended*] forbidden (*OED* I 3 a).

xi *90. contrite*] Stressed on the second syllable. Sorrow for sin and contrition are separate stages of repentance; see x 828–44*n*, 1073*n*.

xi *91. motions*] inward promptings, stirrings of the soul, impulses. Used in a semi-technical way, in theological or homiletic contexts, of God's working in the soul (*OED* 9 b, citing Walton: 'God . . . mark'd him with . . . a blessing of obedience to the motions of his blessed Spirit').

His heart I know, how variable and vain
Self-left. Lest therefore his now bolder hand
Reach also of the tree of life, and eat,
And live for ever, dream at least to live
For ever, to remove him I decree,
And send him from the garden forth to till
The ground whence he was taken, fitter soil.
    Michael, this my behest have thou in charge,
Take to thee from among the cherubim
Thy choice of flaming warriors, lest the fiend
Or in behalf of man, or to invade
Vacant possession some new trouble raise:
Haste thee, and from the Paradise of God
Without remorse drive out the sinful pair,

xi *91–3.* The syntax seems to be difficult because *I know* is held back, mimetically, *longer* even than *His heart.* The sense is: 'I know his heart will outlast these impulses to good, and I know how variable and vain it will become if left to itself.'

xi *98. fitter soil*] A curious expression, since it seems to imply the Scholastic distinction between the *donum supernaturale* of Adam's superadded 'original righteousness' and the *pura naturalia* or ordinary properties of human nature *per se* (see N. P. Williams, *The Ideas of the Fall and of Original Sin* (1927) 363). The ground from which Adam was taken (vii 535–8*n* above) is the dust of *pura naturalia*; from now on this is the nature he will have to work with.

xi *99. Michael*] See vi 44*n.* 'It would not have been so proper for the *sociable spirit Raphael* to have executed this order: but as Michael was the principal Angel employ'd in driving the rebel Angels out of Heaven, so he was the most proper to expel our first parents too out of Paradise' (Newton). There is also the consideration that Michael is the apocalyptic angel; for the visions shown to Adam are essentially apocalyptic visions of history. Michael's name occurs in the *dramatis personae* of M.'s first draft of a tragedy on the Fall (see p. 419 above).

xi *102. Or . . . or*] either . . . or.   *in behalf of man*] At first this seems surprising, and justly seized on by Empson([2] 165) as evidence of Satan's nobility in the eyes of God. But *in behalf of* quite usually meant 'with regard to; in respect of' in M.'s time (Adams 119). And in any case, the passage is ironic.

xi *102–3. invade . . . possession*] encroach on my property while it has no possessor. In law, 'vacant effects' were 'such as are abandoned for want of an Heir, after the Death or Flight of their former Owner' (Bailey, 1730, *cit. OED* s.v. *Vacant* A 1 c). Continuing the ironic tone of the previous paragraph: see ll. 84–98*n.*

xi *105. without remorse*] The angels feel pity readily, as v 566 and x 25 show. But Burden 36 points out that remorse would here be wrong, since it would imply injustice on the part of God.

From hallowed ground the unholy, and denounce
To them and to their progeny from thence
Perpetual banishment. Yet lest they faint
At the sad sentence rigorously urged
For I behold them softened and with tears
Bewailing their excess, all terror hide.
If patiently thy bidding they obey,
Dismiss them not disconsolate; reveal
To Adam what shall come in future days,
As I shall thee enlighten, intermix
My Covenant in the woman's seed renewed;
So send them forth, though sorrowing, yet in peace:
And on the east side of the garden place,
Where entrance up from Eden easiest climbs,
Cherubic watch, and of a sword the flame
Wide waving, all approach far off to fright,
And guard all passage to the tree of life:
Lest Paradise a receptacle prove
To spirits foul, and all my trees their prey,
With whose stolen fruit man once more to delude.
He ceased; and the archangelic power prepared
For swift descent, with him the cohort bright
Of watchful cherubim; four faces each

xi *106. denounce*] proclaim, often with an implication of warning (*OED* 3).
xi *108. faint*] lose heart; become depressed (*OED* 1).
xi *111. excess*] transgression; outrage (*OED* 3, 4).
xi *115–16.* i.e., intermix the theme of the Covenant, the bond between the God of Israel and his people, whereby they paid sacrificial dues–later the spiritual bond, whereby righteousness, made perfect by the gift of grace, was the offering.
xi *118–22.* 'So he drove out the man; and he placed at the east of the garden of Eden Cherubims, and a flaming sword which turned every way, to keep the way of the tree of life' (*Gen.* iii 24); cp. xii 590ff. On cherubim as guards of Paradise, see iv 549–50*n*; on the *sword* see xii 643*n*.
xi *123. receptacle*] Stressed on the third syllable.
xi *128–9.* For the source of the four-faced cherubim in *Ezekiel*, see vi 749–59*n* above. *double Janus*] *Ianus quadrifrons*, the four-headed variant of the ancient god Janus, who presided over gates. The comparison is particularly appropriate in view of the fact that man is going out into a world of change, seasonal and historical. For the four heads of Janus, like the four doors of his temple, were interpreted as meaning the four seasons of the year (Valeriano 384). See A. H. Gilbert in *PMLA* liv (1939) 1026–30, where St Augustine's connection of the four faces with the four quarters of the earth is cited.

Had, like a double Janus, all their shape
Spangled with eyes more numerous than those
Of Argus, and more wakeful than to drowse,
Charmed with Arcadian pipe, the pastoral reed
Of Hermes, or his opiate rod. Mean while
To resalute the world with sacred light
Leucothea waked, and with fresh dews embalmed
The earth, when Adam and first matron Eve
Had ended now their orisons, and found
Strength added from above, new hope to spring
Out of despair, joy, but with fear yet linked;
Which thus to Eve his welcome words renewed.
  Eve, easily may faith admit, that all
The good which we enjoy, from heaven descends;
But that from us aught should ascend to heaven
So prevalent as to concern the mind
Of God high-blest, or to incline his will,
Hard to belief may seem; yet this will prayer,
Or one short sigh of human breath, upborne
Even to the seat of God. For since I sought
By prayer the offended Deity to appease,
Kneeled and before him humbled all my heart,
Methought I saw him placable and mild,

xi *129–33*. Cp. *Ezek*. i 18, where the cherubim have rings 'full of eyes'. *Argus* was set to guard Io, because he had a hundred eyes which watched by turns; but Mercury lulled all the eyes to sleep with his reed pipe (Ovid, *Met.* i 682–4) and finally with his *virga somnifera* (*ibid.* 671f, 716). Like Janus, Argus was interpreted as a temporal or astronomical symbol; in the words of Pontanus 'Argus is Heaven; aethereall fires his eyes, / That wake by turnes; and Starres that set and rise' (Sandys[2] 37).
xi *134–5*. *Leucothea*] the Roman Mater Matuta, goddess of the dawn. She is in place here because, as Ovid tells us, she 'keeps handmaidens afar from the thresholds of her temple' (*Fasti* vi 479ff). *embalmed*] Now with a sinister overtone: the earth is decaying.
xi *137*. *Ed I* has comma after *found*.
xi *139*. Burden 199 remarks that M. balances cause for woe very carefully against cause for joy. The idea of the 'fortunate Fall' does not cancel out tragedy. Some copies of *Ed I* have comma after *linked*.
xi *141*. *faith*] The first mention, indicating a new phase in Adam's regeneration. For the previous phases, see x 828–44*n*, 1073*n*, 1096–7*n*; xi 3*n*, 91*n*.
xi *142*. Cp. *Jam.* i 17: 'Every good gift and every perfect gift is from above, and cometh down from the Father of lights, with whom is no variableness, neither shadow of turning.' *Ed I* has no point after *descends*.
xi *144*. *prevalent*] efficacious, influential, powerful (*OED* 1).
xi *148*. *seat*] The mercy-seat of l. 2 above.

Bending his ear; persuasion in me grew
That I was heard with favour; peace returned
Home to my breast, and to my memory
His promise, that thy seed shall bruise our foe;
Which then not minded in dismay, yet now
Assures me that the bitterness of death
Is past, and we shall live. Whence hail to thee,
Eve rightly called, Mother of all Mankind,
Mother of all things living, since by thee
Man is to live, and all things live for man.
  To whom thus Eve with sad demeanour meek.
Ill worthy I such title should belong
To me transgressor, who for thee ordained
A help, became thy snare; to me reproach
Rather belongs, distrust and all dispraise:
But infinite in pardon was my judge,
That I who first brought death on all, am graced
The source of life; next favourable thou,
Who highly thus to entitle me vouchsafest,
Far other name deserving. But the field
To labour calls us now with sweat imposed,
Though after sleepless night; for see the morn,
All unconcerned with our unrest, begins
Her rosy progress smiling; let us forth,
I never from thy side henceforth to stray,
Where'er our day's work lies, though now enjoined
Laborious, till day droop; while here we dwell,
What can be toilsome in these pleasant walks?

xi *154–8*. Referring to the curse on the serpent at x 175–81; the implication of which–removal 'far off' of the 'instant stroke of death' (x 210f)–Adam had been too dismayed to grasp, until the maturer reflections of x 962f and 1030–40. At first he expected to die, according to the literal terms of the prohibition, on 'that day' when he transgressed. See viii 323–33*n*, x 773*n*. Now, however, he errs on the other side; like Agag (who said 'surely the bitterness of death is past' just before Samuel hewed him in pieces, *1 Sam.* xv 32f) he has spoken too soon. The bitterness of the Expulsion and of the historical consequences of the Fall lie ahead.
xi *158*. Adam addresses Eve with the 'holy salutation used / Long after to blest Mary, second Eve' (v 386f), since it is as a type of Mary that Eve has the promise applied to her.
xi *159*. 'And Adam called his wife's name Eve; because she was the mother of all living' (*Gen.* iii 20).
xi *162*. *sad*] serious.
xi *165*. *help*] See x 899*n*.
xi *171–2*. Referring to the curse of Adam, x 205 and *Gen.* iii 19.

Here let us live, though in fallen state, content.
So spake, so wished much-humbled Eve, but fate
Subscribed not; nature first gave signs, impressed
On bird, beast, air, air suddenly eclipsed
After short blush of morn; nigh in her sight
The bird of Jove, stooped from his airy tower,
Two birds of gayest plume before him drove:
Down from a hill the beast that reigns in woods,
First hunter then, pursued a gentle brace,
Goodliest of all the forest, hart and hind;
Direct to the eastern gate was bent their flight.
Adam observed, and with his eye the chase
Pursuing, not unmoved to Eve thus spake.
O Eve, some further change awaits us nigh,
Which heaven by these mute signs in nature shows
Forerunners of his purpose, or to warn
Us haply too secure of our discharge
From penalty, because from death released
Some days; how long, and what till then our life,
Who knows, or more than this, that we are dust,
And thither must return and be no more.
Why else this double object in our sight
Of flight pursued in the air and o'er the ground
One way the self-same hour? Why in the east
Darkness ere day's mid-course, and morning light
More orient in yon western cloud that draws

xi *182–90. signs*] Not 'signs of the Fall; the blight now beginning to fall on all nature' as Hughes (those signs were perceptible to Adam back at x 715), but specifically omens. In all three omens described, the sovereign of a realm of creation displays his power in a changed and grimmer form. The sun in eclipse darkens the air; the eagle (*bird of Jove*) stoops on two other birds; and the lion pursues a hart and a hind (contrast the harmless lion of iv 343, but cp. the earlier anticipation of fallen animality when Satan stalks his prey at iv 402ff). The direction of the chase shows that the omens foreshadow the Expulsion (cp. esp. xii 638f): the two beasts, like the two birds, correspond to the human couple.
xi *185. stooped*] having swooped (a technical term in falconry); see viii 351*n*. *tower*] lofty flight; soaring (but cp. *L'Allegro* 43). *Ed I* and *Ed II* have the form 'tour', common in the seventeenth century. A pun with tour=circuit (*OED* 12) is possible.
xi *196. secure*] confident; over-confident.
xi *204*. Cp. *Is.* xvi 3: 'Execute judgment; make thy shadow as the night in the midst of the noonday.'
xi *205. orient*] bright; but punning on the sense 'eastern', here paradoxical. The light in the west is the glory of Michael's 'cohort bright' (l. 127),

O'er the blue firmament a radiant white,
And slow descends, with something heavenly fraught.
He erred not, for by this the heavenly bands
Down from a sky of jasper lighted now
In Paradise, and on a hill made alt,
A glorious apparition, had not doubt
And carnal fear that day dimmed Adam's eye.
Not that more glorious, when the angels met
Jacob in Mahanaim, where he saw
The field pavilioned with his guardians bright;
Nor that which on the flaming mount appeared
In Dothan, covered with a camp of fire,
Against the Syrian king, who to surprise
One man, assassin-like had levied war,
War unproclaimed. The princely hierarch
In their bright stand, there left his powers to seize
Possession of the garden; he alone,
To find where Adam sheltered, took his way,
Not unperceived of Adam, who to Eve,
While the great visitant approached, thus spake.
Eve, now expect great tidings, which perhaps
Of us will soon determine, or impose
New laws to be observed; for I descry
From yonder blazing cloud that veils the hill
One of the heavenly host, and by his gait
None of the meanest, some great potentate

already placed to drive Adam and Eve to the east gate. Note also that Michael was associated with the west wind (Valeriano 549).
xi *209. jasper*] See iii 363–4*n*, and *Rev.* iv 3, where God in judgment is 'to look upon like a jasper and a sardine stone'. *lighted*] descended (*OED* v.[1] II 6), arrived (*OED* v.[1] II 10 b); but also 'shone' (*OED* v.[2] 1).
xi *210. alt*] a halt. A military term usually occurring only in the phrase 'to make alt'. (Alt='alto; high flight' was a different word.)
xi *212. carnal fear*] fleshly fear; the animal's terror of the spiritual.
xi *213–15.* See *Gen.* xxxii 1–2. On account of the meeting Jacob called the place *Mahanaim*, meaning 'Armies' or 'Camps' (cp. M.'s *pavilioned*).
xi *216–20.* See *2 Kings* vi 13–17. *one man*] Elisha, whom the king of Syria besieged Dothan to catch. When Elisha's servant told him of this he was unconcerned; at his prayer God opened the servant's eyes 'and, behold, the mountain was full of horses and chariots of fire round about Elisha'.
xi *220. hierarch*] A title also of Raphael; cp. v 468.
xi *221. stand*] station, place of standing (*OED* II 11); but in view of the recent omen of the eagle (ll. 185f) the special application in falconry–'an elevated resting place of a hawk' (*OED* II 14)–may have a grim relevance.
xi *227. determine*] make an end.

Or of the thrones above, such majesty
Invests him coming; yet not terrible,
That I should fear, nor sociably mild,
As Raphael, that I should much confide,
But solemn and sublime, whom not to offend,
With reverence I must meet, and thou retire.
He ended; and the archangel soon drew nigh,
Not in his shape celestial, but as man
Clad to meet man; over his lucid arms
A military vest of purple flowed
Livelier than Meliboean, or the grain
Of Sarra, worn by kings and heroes old
In time of truce; Iris had dipped the woof;
His starry helm unbuckled showed him prime
In manhood where youth ended; by his side
As in a glistering zodiac hung the sword,
Satan's dire dread, and in his hand the spear.
Adam bowed low, he kingly from his state

xi *232–3*. Cp. *Ps.* xciii 1: 'The Lord reigneth, he is clothed with majesty; the Lord is clothed with strength, wherewith he hath girded himself: the world also is stablished, that it cannot be moved.' The allusion suggests that Michael's clothing, described at ll. 240–8, embodies aspects of deity.

xi *233*. The punctuation of *Ed I*; *Ed II* has question mark after *coming*.

xi *234*. Cp. v 221, where Raphael is called 'the sociable spirit'; and see l. 99*n* above.

xi *240–8*. Contrast the description of Raphael's wings at v 277–85, and see *n* there. Raphael's wings were regal purple, gold and blue, but Michael's *vest* is only purple. He comes without wings, because he is to talk about terrestrial matters, about fallen mundane history, and because he is to prepare Adam for a more lowly role. There is also the reason that spiritual forms now frighten Adam (l. 212). *Meliboean*] The vividness of purple from Meliboea on the coast of Thessaly was anciently famous. A cloak of *purpura Meliboea* is a prize of honour in Virgil, *Aen.* v 251. *grain*] Cp. v 285 and see *n.* *Sarra*] Tyre, famous for its dye; see *2 Chron.* ii 14. *Iris . . . woof*] Cp. *Comus* 83, 'sky-robes spun out of Iris' woof'. *Iris*, because the iris flower was the *lilium purpureum*; but also–as in *Nativity Ode* 143–because the rainbow is a sign of God's Covenant or *truce* with his people. See ll. 879ff. *zodiac*] Michael's belt is compared with the belt of the celestial sphere occupied by the zodiacal constellations. (Hughes's obscure suggestion that *zodiac* meant 'belt' in Greek seems to be without foundation). The zodiac is brought in because the belt, like the *helm*, is *starry*; but also because the zodiac corresponds to the specifically post-lapsarian course of the sun–Michael's mission relates to the new order of things. On the sword, see vi 250–1*n*.

xi *249–51*. The abrupt beginning contrasts with the more leisurely meeting

Inclined not, but his coming thus declared.
  Adam, heaven's high behest no preface needs:
Sufficient that thy prayers are heard, and Death,
Then due by sentence when thou didst transgress,
Defeated of his seizure many days
Given thee of grace, wherein thou mayst repent,
And one bad act with many deeds well done
Mayst cover: well may then thy Lord appeased
Redeem thee quite from Death's rapacious claim;
But longer in this Paradise to dwell
Permits not; to remove thee I am come,
And send thee from the garden forth to till
The ground whence thou wast taken, fitter soil.
  He added not, for Adam at the news
Heart-strook with chilling gripe of sorrow stood,
That all his senses bound; Eve, who unseen
Yet all had heard, with audible lament
Discovered soon the place of her retire.
  O unexpected stroke, worse than of death!
Must I thus leave thee Paradise? Thus leave
Thee native soil, these happy walks and shades,
Fit haunt of gods? Where I had hope to spend,
Quiet though sad, the respite of that day
That must be mortal to us both. O flowers,
That never will in other climate grow,
My early visitation, and my last
At even, which I bred up with tender hand
From the first opening bud, and gave ye names,

of Adam with Raphael, when it was Adam who spoke first. Cp. v 358–71 and see *n.* *state*] dignity of demeanour (*OED* II 18).

xi *254. Defeated . . . seizure*] Either 'frustrated, cheated in his attempt to seize' or (looking forward to *redeem* at 258) 'deprived, dispossessed of what he had seized, his seisin' (*OED* s.v. *Defeat* 5 and 7a, b; *Seizure* 1 a and 2). The diction is legal. See viii 323–33*n*, x 773*n*.

xi *256–7.* Cp. *1 Pet.* iv 8.

xi *258. quite*] Either 'completely' or 'free, clear, rid of' (adj., since obsolete). It is hard to say whether the adverb or the adjective forms the primary chain of discourse.

xi *259–62.* In accordance with the solemnity of his commission, Michael delivers the divine decree verbatim (see ll. 96–8). As Newton remarks, it is on these words that the whole catastrophe of the poem depends.

xi *264. Heart-strook*] heart-stricken. *gripe*] grip, spasm.

xi *267. retire*] withdrawal (*OED* 1).

xi *272. respite*] delay; extension (*OED* I 1).

Who now shall rear ye to the sun, or rank
Your tribes, and water from the ambrosial fount?
Thee lastly nuptial bower, by me adorned
With what to sight or smell was sweet; from thee
How shall I part, and whither wander down
Into a lower world, to this obscure
And wild, how shall we breathe in other air
Less pure, accustomed to immortal fruits?
Whom thus the angel interrupted mild.
Lament not Eve, but patiently resign
What justly thou hast lost; nor set thy heart,
Thus over-fond, on that which is not thine;
Thy going is not lonely, with thee goes
Thy husband, him to follow thou art bound;
Where he abides, think there thy native soil.
Adam by this from the cold sudden damp
Recovering, and his scattered spirits returned,
To Michael thus his humble words addressed.

xi *278–9.* On seventeenth-century interest in the naming and classification of species, see viii 343–56*n*. *ambrosial fount*] More definite than iv 240, where we are told that the fountain of Paradise 'ran nectar'. In visual art, the fountain of Paradise was very often a Fountain of Life, shown as an architecturally elaborate well to connect it with the well of living water of *John* iv 10 (cp. l. 416 below). (See, e.g., Jan Gossart's *Adam and Eve* in the Queen's Collection; and the Bedford Book of Hours, B. M. Add. MS. 18850 fol. 14, where the fountain flows out as four distributaries.) On its significance see ix 71–5*n* above. Since the Expulsion must deprive Adam of natural access to immortality, the courses of the rivers are changed after the Fall; see iv 237–8*n*; ix 71–5*n*; xi 829–38*n*.
xi *283. to*] compared with.
xi *284–5. Less pure*] See ll. 49–57*n* above, on the need for 'gross [to be purged] to air as gross'. Bentley asked, more grossly still, what the fruits have to do with Eve's breathing; provoking a fine reply from Empson ([2] 162): 'In the tired repeated rhythm of the last two lines, she leaves floating, as things already far off, all that makes up for her the "atmosphere" of Paradise.' But M. may well have meant this nostalgic effect, moving as it is, to be yet another test of our discrimination. If it were true that Eve was *accustomed* exclusively to *immortal fruits*, she would not now be leaving Paradise (contrast i 2, 'mortal taste'). Michael's interruption, indeed, may be provoked by her insensitivity in venturing to mention fruit at this juncture.
xi *287. patiently*] See ll. 360–4*n*.
xi *289. over-fond*] Two words in *Ed I*.
xi *293–4. damp*] dazed or stupefied condition; depression of spirits (*OED* 4, 5). It was the scattering of Adam's animal *spirits*, the spirits controlling sensation (iv 805, v 484) that had 'his senses bound' at l. 265.

Celestial, whether among the thrones, or named
Of them the highest, for such of shape may seem
Prince above princes, gently hast thou told
Thy message, which might else in telling wound,
And in performing end us; what besides
Of sorrow and dejection and despair
Our frailty can sustain, thy tidings bring,
Departure from this happy place, our sweet
Recess, and only consolation left
Familiar to our eyes, all places else
Inhospitable appear and desolate,
Nor knowing us nor known: and if by prayer
Incessant I could hope to change the will
Of him who all things can, I would not cease
To weary him with my assiduous cries:
But prayer against his absolute decree
No more avails than breath against the wind,
Blown stifling back on him that breathes it forth:
Therefore to his great bidding I submit.
This most afflicts me, that departing hence,
As from his face I shall be hid, deprived
His blessed countenance; here I could frequent,
With worship, place by place where he vouchsafed
Presence divine, and to my sons relate;
On this mount he appeared; under this tree
Stood visible, among these pines his voice
I heard, here with him at this fountain talked:
So many grateful altars I would rear
Of grassy turf, and pile up every stone
Of lustre from the brook, in memory,

xi *296–8.* Only after the Fall does Adam bother about the social status of the different ranks of angels.

xi *307–10.* The first of Adam's many errors in his dialogue with Michael. We know from the parable of Luke xviii 5–7 that importunate prayers are in fact effective. *can*] knows (*OED* I 1); the secondary sense 'is able' helps to make the irony clear.

xi *316.* Cp. Cain's response to his curse: 'Behold, thou hast driven me out this day from the face of the earth; and from thy face shall I be hid; and I shall be a fugitive and a vagabond in the earth' (*Gen.* iv 14).

xi *315–33.* Newton contrasts Adam's reasons for regret with Eve's. But this is unfair to Eve. Adam's speech is more considered, and in any case he has to make the necessary errors about local devotion, in order to provoke Michael's instruction of ll. 335ff.

xi *325–6.* The patriarchs were accustomed to raise altars wherever God appeared to them.

Or monument to ages, and thereon
Offer sweet smelling gums and fruits and flowers:
In yonder nether world where shall I seek
His bright appearances, or footstep trace?
For though I fled him angry, yet recalled
To life prolonged and promised race, I now
Gladly behold though but his utmost skirts
Of glory, and far off his steps adore.
   To whom thus Michael with regard benign.
Adam, thou know'st heaven his, and all the earth.
Not this rock only; his omnipresence fills
Land, sea, and air, and every kind that lives,
Fomented by his virtual power and warmed:
All the earth he gave thee to possess and rule,
No despicable gift; surmise not then
His presence to these narrow bounds confined
Of Paradise or Eden: this had been
Perhaps thy capital seat, from whence had spread
All generations, and had hither come
From all the ends of the earth, to celebrate
And reverence thee their great progenitor.
But this pre-eminence thou hast lost, brought down
To dwell on even ground now with thy sons:
Yet doubt not but in valley and in plain
God is as here, and will be found alike
Present, and of his presence many a sign

xi *327*. Burnt offerings would not be appropriate for Paradise. See x 1078–81*n*; also *Gen.* iv 3, where Cain makes an offering of fruit.
xi *329*. Following *Ed I*: *Ed II* misplaces a hyphen: 'foot step-trace'.
xi *331*. *promised race*] the race whose destiny it is to bruise Satan; see x 175–92.
xi *332–3*. For the dazzling *skirts* of God cp. iii 380 and see iii 375–82*n*.
xi *335–54*. Michael corrects Adam's new-found fallacious enthusiasm for local devotions, pious superstitions and tradition generally. In M.'s view all such enthusiasm is definitely postlapsarian, and, it seems, to be closely associated with depression of spirits. For the omnipresence of the God of *PL* see vii 168f. Cp. *Jer.* xxiii 24, 'Do not I fill heaven and earth? saith the Lord.' *Not this rock only*] Alludes to Jesus' warning to the woman of Samaria: 'The hour cometh, when ye shall neither in this mountain, nor yet at Jerusalem, worship the Father' (John iv 21). But M.'s substitution of *rock* for *mountain* (Vulg. *monte*, Gk. ὄρει) clearly strikes at the successors of St Peter, the rock, for their excessive reliance on tradition and their belief that God's presence is in some sense *confined* within the *narrow bounds* of the institutional church. *Fomented*] cherished, nurtured. *virtual*] potent, exerting influence. The omnipresence of God is the theme of *Ps.* cxxxix, which tradition ascribed to Adam himself (see Charles ii 17).

Still following thee, still compassing thee round
With goodness and paternal love, his face
Express, and of his steps the track divine.
Which that thou mayst believe, and be confirmed
Ere thou from hence depart, know I am sent
To shew thee what shall come in future days
To thee and to thy offspring; good with bad
Expect to hear, supernal grace contending
With sinfulness of men; thereby to learn
True patience, and to temper joy with fear
And pious sorrow, equally inured
By moderation either state to bear,
Prosperous or adverse: so shalt thou lead
Safest thy life, and best prepared endure
Thy mortal passage when it comes. Ascend
This hill; let Eve (for I have drenched her eyes)
Here sleep below while thou to foresight wakest,

xi *355*. The purpose of the vision is to *confirm* Adam's faith. In *De doctrina* i 25 (Columbia xvi 67–9) M. traces the 'progressive steps' and the causes leading to 'assurance of salvation, and the final perseverance of the saints': 'Both regeneration and increase are accompanied by confirmation, or preservation in the faith, which is also the work of God.' Faith is the theme of Bk xi, as repentance was the theme of Bk x. See x 828–44*n*, 1073*n*, 1096–7*n*.
xi *357*. On the precedents for Adam's vision of the future, see l. 423*n*.
xi *360–4*. *pious sorrow*] Burden (189) takes this to mean 'pity', and concludes that the darker attitude to be learned is pity and terror: the correct response to the series of tragedies Adam is shown. *True patience*] By implication to be distinguished from the false stubborn philosophical patience of ii 569 and ix 920. Burden cites Calvin, *Inst.* III viii 8, where true Christian patience is contrasted with the impracticable 'too exact and rigid patience' of the Stoics and the puritans. Originally, however, *moderation* was itself a Stoic and Aristotelian principle assimilated by Christianity. Hughes recalls that Petrarch wrote a book *De remediis utriusque fortunae.*
xi *366*. *mortal passage*] death. As Burden 189f remarks, the ascent of the mount of contemplation and of truth is the legitimate ascent that contrasts with the false easy ascent by flying (v 87).
xi *367*. *drenched*] Probably 'administered medicine to' (*OED* 1); though normally the word would refer to medicine drunk, as at ii 73–4. In view of the other references earlier to Mercury's 'opiate rod' in connection with Michael's cherubim (l. 133), it may be relevant that in Cabbalistic thought Michael was sometimes identified with Mercury (Valeriano 549C; but see vii 72*n* above.
xi *368–9*. *foresight*] vision of the future. The resemblance with viii 40ff, where Eve retired to leave Adam and Raphael alone, is superficial; in any case,

As once thou slept'st, while she to life was formed.
   To whom thus Adam gratefully replied.
Ascend, I follow thee, safe guide, the path
Thou lead'st me, and to the hand of heaven submit,
However chastening, to the evil turn
My obvious breast, arming to overcome
By suffering, and earn rest from labour won,
If so I may attain. So both ascend
In the visions of God: it was a hill
Of Paradise the highest, from whose top
The hemisphere of earth in clearest ken
Stretched out to the amplest reach of prospect lay.
Not higher that hill nor wider looking round,
Whereon for different cause the tempter set
Our second Adam in the wilderness,
To show him all earth's kingdoms and their glory.
His eye might there command wherever stood
City of old or modern fame, the seat
Of mightiest empire, from the destined walls

Eve is here to have her own series of dreams (see xii 595). A deeper link, to which Michael himself draws attention, is with viii 452–78, where Adam slept yet remained conscious during the creation of Eve. This link is based on a typological correspondence. Earlier, Adam had a vision of the creation of the first Eve; now he is to have a vision of the 'race' leading up to the second Eve and the second creation. Burden 188 notes that the instruction of Adam makes him typical man, whereas before he was only archetypal. At the end of the poem he will go out into the world with the kind of historical knowledge ordinary fallen men have.

xi *372. submit*] Broadbent (98) sees submission as a characteristic note of M.'s portrayal of Christian patience, distinguishing it from 'stoical apathy'. cp. xii 597.

xi *374. obvious*] exposed, vulnerable (*OED* 2).

xi *375–6.* Combining echoes of *Heb.* iv 11 and *Phil.* iii 11; with the implication that his aim is resurrection.

xi *377–84.* MacCaffrey 61 includes this vista among the poem's series of synoptic godlike visions; noting that the episodes that follow are conceived as static tableaux. But see ll. 429–47*n* for a different opinion. M. here alludes to the ascent of Ezekiel: 'The hand of the Lord was upon me, and brought me thither. In the visions of God brought he me into the land of Israel, and set me upon a very high mountain, by which was as the frame of a city on the south' (*Ezek.* xl 1–2). Cp. *Matt.* iv 8, where the devil to tempt Christ 'taketh him up into an exceeding high mountain, and sheweth him all the kingdoms of the world, and the glory of them'; also *PR* iii 251ff. *ken*] sight, view (*OED* 3).

xi *380. Ed I* omits *the*.

Of Cambalu, seat of Cathaian khan
And Samarchand by Oxus, Temir's throne,
To Paquin of Sinaean kings, and thence
To Agra and Lahor of great mogul
Down to the golden Chersonese, or where
The Persian in Ecbatan sat, or since
In Hispahan, or where the Russian czar

xi *387–8. Cambalu*] Stressed on the first syllable, Cambaluc, capital of Cathay. M. uses the popular form. Its walls are *destined* because they will exist, but do not yet.
xi *388–95.* The Asian kingdoms are arranged symmetrically according to an elaborately centralized Baroque pattern. *Chersonese*, the only place without a visible ruler, occupies nevertheless the central position of sovereignty. Next to it come the mogul's and the Persian's realms, each with a pair of capitals; then the Sinaean kings' and the czar's, each with a single capital. Finally, on each flank there is a pair of realms associated with the khans and the sultans respectively. Each of these except *Turchestan* has its capital. Thus: *Cambalu* and *Samarchand*; *Paquin*; *Agra* and *Lahor*; (CHERSONESE-OPHIR); *Ecbatan* and *Hispahan*; *Mosco*; *Bizance* and (*Turchestan*). Or: 1. Cathay and 2. Tartary; 3. China; 4. the mogul's empire; 5. (CHERSONESE-OPHIR); 6. Persia; 7. Russia; 8. Byzantium and 9. (Turkestan). The reason why the golden Chersonese should be assigned the place of sovereignty will only become evident when the pattern is repeated with the African realms that follow (see ll. 396–407*n*).
xi *388–9. Samarchand*] Samarkand, near the *Oxus* river, the capital of Timur, Marlowe's Tamburlaine. *khan*] The title given to Genghis Khan's successors, who during the Middle Ages ruled not only the Tartar and Mongol tribes but also Cathay. They were known in Europe as the great khans (chams) either of Cathay or (as in the case of Timur) of Tartary.
xi *390. Paquin*] Pekin, capital of China, which was regarded as a separate kingdom from Cathay (see x 289–93*n*). *Sinaean*] Chinese.
xi *391.* Two areas of northern India. *Agra*] A kingdom in the centre, whose capital, a city of the same name, is described by Heylyn as 'the Seat Royall, of late times, of the Great Monguls'. *Lahor*] Lahore, in the Punjab, to the north-west. *great mogul*] The designation, among Europeans, of the emperor of eastern India.
xi *392. golden Chersonese*, so called from its wealth, was in *India extra Gangem*, the extreme east part of the continent – what would now be called Malacca in the Malay Peninsula. Josephus identified it with the Ophir which supplied King Solomon with gold (*Antiq.* VIII vi 4); see ll. 396–407*n*, 400*n* below.
xi *393–4. Ecbatan*] Ecbatana, the ancient summer capital of the Persian kings; Ispahan became a capital city in the sixteenth century, when the Safavid dynasty moved their residence there from Kazvin.

In Mosco, or the sultan in Bizance,
Turchestan-born; nor could his eye not ken
The empire of negus to his utmost port
Ercoco and the less maritime kings
Mombaza, and Quiloa, and Melind,

xi *395–6. Mosco*] Moscow. *Bizance*] Byzantium, Constantinople, capital of the Turkish sultan. *Turchestan-born*] The sultans belonged to a tribe that came originally from Turkestan, a region in central Asia between Mongolia and the Caspian. Note that Turkestan, having no capital city associated with it, falls into a somewhat separate category from the other realms. See l. 405*n* below.

xi *396–407. nor . . . ken*] Signalizes a transition to the African continent. Here the kingdoms form a pattern which resembles that formed by the Asian kingdoms in several respects (see ll. 388–95*n*). Again there are nine, and again the last falls into a distinct category (here because it is European). Thus: 1. Abyssinia; 2. Mombaza; 3. Quiloa; 4. Melind; 5. SOFALA-OPHIR; 6. Congo; 7. Angola; 8. Almanzor's Barbary; 9. (Rome). The central position is occupied by Sofala, which, like Chersonese in the earlier pattern, is *thought Ophir*. It becomes clear that the idea underlying both patterns is the attribution of secret sovereignty to Ophir. This is partly to be explained by the connection between Ophir and King Solomon, the only Biblical ruler named or implied anywhere in the passage. Solomon was the just divider, so that he is associated here with the fifth position among the rulers, since the fifth digit divides the others justly (Fowler 34, citing Iamblichus, etc.). Moreover, the 'incorruptible' five, in its pentacle (pentagram) form, was Solomon's mystic seal or knot. M.'s emphasis on the vacancy of the central seat of sovereignty, however, suggests that his intention is also larger and deeper. The pattern reflects both the absence of true sovereignty in the natural world, and the unseen sovereignty of Christ. This symbolism would be based on a verse in the Forty-fifth *Psalm*, which was interpreted typologically as a prophecy of the majesty and grace of Christ's kingdom: 'upon thy right hand did stand the queen in gold of Ophir' (*Ps.* xlv 9); cp. *Is.* xiii 12f: 'I will make a man more precious than fine gold; even a man than the golden wedge of Ophir. Therefore I will shake the heavens, and the earth shall remove out of her place, in the wrath of the Lord of hosts, and in the day of his fierce anger.' Thus the centrality of Ophir here repeats the structure of the poem as a whole (see Introduction, 'Numerology, p. 441 above). On the just centrality of Solomon's Temple *in meditullio mundi*, see Giorgio 158^{v}.

xi *397–8.* The Abyssinian empire; *negus* was the hereditary title of the emperors. *Ercoco*, mod. Arkiko, is a port on the Red Sea. Scan *marìtime. Ed I* spells 'Maritine', *Ed II* 'Maritim', both current forms until the eighteenth century.

xi *399. Mombaza*] Mombasa. *Melind*] Malindi. *Quiloa*] Kilwa. The first two are on the coast of Kenya, the last, of Tanzania.

And Sofala thought Ophir, to the realm
Of Congo, and Angola farthest south;
Or thence from Niger flood to Atlas mount
The kingdoms of Almansor, Fez and Sus,
Morocco and Algiers, and Tremisen;
On Europe thence, and where Rome was to sway
The world: in spirit perhaps he also saw
Rich Mexico the seat of Motezume,

xi *400. Sofala*] (M. chooses to stress on the first syllable.) The name of a port in what is now Mozambique. From its wealth it was supposed (as Purchas and even the sceptical Heylyn inform us) to be the land of Ophir. The purity of the gold of Ophir was proverbial, and is given a typical moral application by Sir Thomas Browne in *Christian Morals* i 28: 'There is dross, alloy, and embasement in all human tempers; and he flieth without wings, who thinks to find ophir or pure metal in any.' Ophir gold is repeatedly mentioned in connection with the building of Solomon's Temple, so that it became endowed with the meaning 'wise sovereignty'. This symbolism was confirmed by *Gen.* ii 11 and x 29, where Ophir is connected through Havilah with Pison, the river of Paradise that according to Philo signifies Prudence (see Fowler[2] 290). Thus Adam's view is of the moral course of the river: a prospect of wise government and of the secret lordship of Christ through the ages (see ll. 396–407).

xi *402–4. Almanzor*] Mansur ('Victorious') was the surname of countless Mohammedan princes; but the one known to European writers as Almanzor was Ibn Abi'Amir Mahommed, the Caliph of Cordova (939–1002). The five territories named were all parts of Barbary. *Sus*] Province of Morocco. *Tremisen*] Tlemcen, part of Algeria.

xi *405.* The numerological placement of Barbary and Rome in a position similar to that of Byzantium (New Rome) and Turkestan in the earlier array (see ll. 388–95*n*, 396–407*n*) probably implies an uncomplimentary analogy between Papal and Saracen empires. The point is made in a different way by the ambiguous *sway*. True sovereignty lies not in external secular power, but in the power of the invisible incorruptible 'true Church'.

xi *406. in spirit*] Even from this vantage-point Adam could not physically see the other hemisphere.

xi *407–11.* Montezuma's empire had been spoiled by Cortez and Atahuallpa's Peruvian empire, with its capital Cuzco, had been spoiled by Pizarro; but Manoa, the fabulous El Dorado (more gold of sovereignty), capital of Guiana, remained as yet unplundered by the Spanish. Three territories, because the monster *Geryon* that Hercules slew had three bodies and heads. Geryon was Dante's guardian of the fraudulent; but M. calls the Spanish his sons because Spenser had built up Geryon as a type of political tyranny in *F.Q.* V x 8ff: '*Geryon*, / He that whylome in Spaine so sore was dred, / For his huge powre and great oppression.' Guiana would be of topical interest in 1667, when the British colony founded in 1663 between the

And Cusco in Peru, the richer seat
Of Atabalipa, and yet unspoiled
Guiana, whose great city Geryon's sons
Call El Dorado: but to nobler sights
Michael from Adam's eyes the film removed
Which that false fruit that promised clearer sight
Had bred; then purged with euphrasy and rue
The visual nerve, for he had much to see;
And from the well of life three drops instilled.
So deep the power of these ingredients pierced,
Even to the inmost seat of mental sight,
That Adam now enforced to close his eyes,
Sunk down and all his spirits became entranced:
But him the gentle angel by the hand
Soon raised, and his attention thus recalled.
Adam, now ope thine eyes, and first behold

Copenam and Maroni rivers was ceded to the Netherlands by the Peace of Breda, in exchange for New York. *Motezume*] A more correct form than the Spanish Montezuma.

xi *411–12*. So Homer's Pallas clears Diomedes' eyes (*Il.* v 127); Virgil's Venus, Aeneas' (*Aen.* ii 604); and Tasso's Michael, Goffredo's (*Gerus. Lib.* xviii 92f).

xi *413–15*. For Satan's promise to open Eve's eyes, see ix 706–9. The falsity of his comparison of the fruit to eye-quickening fennel at ix 581 is recalled by the need here for Michael to apply two herbs to *cure* its effects. *euphrasy*] eyebright. Both euphrasy and *rue* are mentioned in Gerard's *Herball* as remedies for restoring or quickening the sight. But there were many such remedies, and M.'s selection of these particular ones is the result of a deliberate choice. The name 'euphrasy' is from Gk. εὐφρασία, 'cheerfulness', while the bitter 'rue' puns on rue=sorrow, pity, or repentance (a pun so common that no fewer than five instances are given in *OED* s.v. *Rue* sb.[2] 1 b). In other words the herbs are correlates of the 'joy' and 'pious sorrow' that Michael told Adam to temper, at ll. 361f. Note, however, that the tempering is connected with the operation of the *well of life*: true Christian patience depends on grace and repentance. See, however, a different interpretation in Svendsen 130f.

xi *416*. Cp. *Ps.* xxxvi 9: 'With thee is the fountain of life: in thy light shall we see light.' *well of life*] See ll. 278–9*n*. *three drops*] A masterfully assimilated structural signpost; see xii 5*n*.

xi *418*. Cp. M.'s appeal to his Muse to 'shine inward' and 'plant eyes' in his mind, at iii 51–5.

xi *421*. In *Dan.* x 8–14, one assisted by 'Michael, one of the chief princes' shows Daniel a 'great vision' of the future; positioning him first with 'an hand'.

xi *423*. Here the second of the poem's major episodes begins (the first being

The effects which thy original crime hath wrought
In some to spring from thee, who never touched
The excepted tree, nor with the snake conspired,
Nor sinned thy sin, yet from that sin derive
Corruption to bring forth more violent deeds.
His eyes he opened, and beheld a field,
Part arable and tilth, whereon were sheaves
New reaped, the other part sheep-walks and folds;
In the midst an altar as the landmark stood

Raphael's account of the war in heaven, in Bks v and vi; see v 563–4*n*). Johnson commented: 'Both are closely connected with the great action; one was necessary to Adam as a warning, the other as a consolation.' M. deliberately challenges comparison with the closely comparable episode in Virgil, *Aen.* vi 756ff, where Aeneas is shown a vision merely of Rome's future. The kind of poetry to which the next part of *PL* belongs, namely Biblical history or paraphrase, had often been attempted in English. Among the most successful examples were Drayton's *Noahs Flood* and *Moses His Birth and Miracles*; Sylvester's Du Bartas (from II i 4 onwards); Sandys's *Paraphrases*; and Cowley's *Davideis*. By comparison with all of these except the last, M.'s history is far more highly organized, both logically and theologically.

ope thine eyes] Barbara K. Lewalski's 'Structure and the Symbolism of Vision in Michael's Prophecy,' *PQ* xlii (1963) shows how M. uses improvement of sight as a symbol of the different stages of faith (inner vision). Many of those shown to Adam in his visions–Abel, Enoch, Noah, Abraham, Joseph, Moses and David, for example–appear in the great roll-call of examples of faith in *Heb.* xi.

xi *425*. Michael does not distinguish the sins of Adam and Eve; he addresses an undifferentiated Adam-Eve, just as God refers to 'man' at iii 130 (Burden 77).

xi *427*. *sinned thy sin*] Biblical diction; cp. *Exod.* xxxii 30, *1 John* v 16. *Ed II* omits the second *sin*; probably by an oversight, since the change makes the line metrically defective.

xi *429–47*. The first of the six scenes shown to Adam is Cain's murder of Abel (*Gen.* iv). On the general character of the visions, see ll. 377–84*n*. It may be questioned, however, if MacCaffrey is right in likening them to tableaux; they seem much more like brief tragedies, in which a single dramatic passage of intense movement is selected. As Burden 188 remarks, Adam's role as observer exemplifies the role M.'s reader is expected to learn–except that the reader will avoid, it is to be hoped, some of Adam's crasser errors.

xi *432*. *an altar as the landmark*] Not merely because it is prominently visible, but also because the landmark (boundary, mark, limit) was a symbol of the Law and the Covenant (see ll. 115–16*n*). The spelling in the early edns, 'Ith' midst', probably gives a correct indication of the necessary elision.

Rustic, of grassy sward; thither anon
A sweaty reaper from his tillage brought
First fruits, the green ear, and the yellow sheaf,
Unculled, as came to hand; a shepherd next
More meek came with the firstlings of his flock
Choicest and best; then sacrificing, laid
The inwards and their fat, with incense strewed,
On the cleft wood, and all due rites performed.
His offering soon propitious fire from heaven
Consumed with nimble glance, and grateful steam;
The other's not, for his was not sincere;
Whereat he inly raged, and as they talked,
Smote him into the midriff with a stone
That beat out life; he fell, and deadly pale
Groaned out his soul with gushing blood effused.
Much at that sight was Adam in his heart
Dismayed, and thus in haste to the angel cried.
O teacher, some great mischief hath befallen
To that meek man, who well had sacrificed;
Is piety thus and pure devotion paid?
To whom Michael thus, he also moved, replied.
These two are brethren, Adam, and to come
Out of thy loins; the unjust the just hath slain,
For envy that his brother's offering found

xi *434*. The omission of names is no doubt so that Adam will not know which of his sons is to turn out a murderer. *sweaty*] in accordance with the curse of x 25.
xi *436*. *unculled*] unselected; God's preference for Abel's 'choicest' sacrifice is not arbitrary.
xi *441*. *fire from heaven*] An astonishingly common sign that a sacrifice was acceptable; see *Lev*. ix 24; *Judges* vi 21; *1 Kings* xviii 38; *1 Chron*. xxi 26; *2 Chron*. vii 1. *nimble*] swift. *glance*] oblique impact; flash.
xi *445*. See Allen[2] 178, and cp. Cowley, *Davideis* i, note 16: 'Neither is it declared in what manner [Cain] slew his *Brother*: And therefore I had the Liberty to chuse that which I thought most probable; which is, that he knockt him on the head with some great stone, which was one of the first ordinary and most natural weapons of Anger. That this stone was big enough to be the *Monument* or *Tombstone* of *Abel*, is not so *Hyperbolical*, as what *Virgil* says in the same kind of *Turnus*, "*saxum circumspicit ingens, / Saxum antiquum ingens, campo qui forte jacebat / Limes agro positus.*"'
xi *450–2*. Adam makes the wrong response to the first tragedy of death, distrusting God's justice (Burden 190).
xi *453*. *he also moved*] The effect of tragedy is to move the spectator; see, e.g., Sidney, *An Apologie for Poetrie*, in G. Gregory Smith, *Elizabethan Critical Essays* (1904) i 177f.

From heaven acceptance; but the bloody fact
Will be avenged, and the other's faith approved
Lose no reward, though here thou see him die,
Rolling in dust and gore. To which our sire.
  Alas, both for the deed and for the cause!
But have I now seen death? Is this the way
I must return to native dust? O sight
Of terror, foul and ugly to behold,
Horrid to think, how horrible to feel!
  To whom thus Michael. Death thou hast seen
In his first shape on man; but many shapes
Of death, and many are the ways that lead
To his grim cave, all dismal; yet to sense
More terrible at the entrance than within.
Some, as thou saw'st, by violent stroke shall die,
By fire, flood, famine, by intemperance more
In meats and drinks which on earth shall bring
Diseases dire, of which a monstrous crew
Before thee shall appear; that thou mayst know

xi *457. fact*] crime (*OED* 1 c; the commonest meaning in the seventeenth century).

xi *458–9*. Throughout the visions, the theme of faith will be prominent; for their purpose is to confirm Adam. See l. 355*n*. With the thought here, cp. *Lycidas* 64–84.

xi *465*. As Burden 191 remarks, Adam is now feeling terror, part of the proper response to tragedy. See ll. 495–7*n*.

xi *466. Michael*] Here a trisyllable, in accordance with the slow gravity of the passage.

xi *469–70. his grim cave*] M.'s cave of death is like the underworld of the ancients. The classic description in Virgil, *Aen.* vi emphasized the access through a cavern (236ff) and the terrors *at the entrance* (*vestibulum ante ipsum primisque in faucibus Orci*, 273). Cp. also Sackville's Induction to *A Mirror for Magistrates* (1563). *dismal*] dreadful.

xi *471–2*. The first vision showed the effect of the Fall on irascible passions, leading to death by 'violent deeds' (ll. 423, 428). The second is to show the effect on concupiscible appetites, leading to death by disease. At the entrance to Virgil's hell *pallentesque habitant Morbi . . . et malesuada Fames ac turpis Egestas, / terribiles visu formae* (vi 275ff). These are all on the opposite side of the threshold (*adverso in limine*) from War and Strife. (Spenser had made a similar psychological application of this dichotomy in *F.Q.* II vii 24ff.) All this does not, however, explain why the second vision should take the specific form of a catalogue of diseases. The reason seems to lie in a simple numerological decorum. For the second digit often symbolized the body; see Fowler 9, citing Valeriano 456: *Dualis numerus mystico significato corpoream indicat naturam.*

What misery the inabstinence of Eve
Shall bring on men. Immediately a place
Before his eyes appeared, sad, noisome, dark,
A lazar-house it seemed, wherein were laid
Numbers of all diseased, all maladies
Of ghastly spasm, or racking torture, qualms
Of heart-sick agony, all feverous kinds,
Convulsions, epilepsies, fierce catarrhs,
Intestine stone and ulcer, colic pangs,
Demoniac frenzy, moping melancholy
And moon-struck madness, pining atrophy,
Marasmus, and wide-wasting pestilence,
Dropsies, and asthmas, and joint-racking rheums.
Dire was the tossing, deep the groans, despair
Tended the sick busiest from couch to couch;
And over them triumphant death his dart
Shook, but delayed to strike, though oft invoked
With vows, as their chief good, and final hope.
Sight so deform what heart of rock could long
Dry-eyed behold? Adam could not, but wept,

xi *476. inabstinence*] Perhaps a Miltonic coinage: *OED* gives no earlier instance.

xi *477–90.* In 'The Furies' (II i 3) Sylvester's Du Bartas describes several regiments of personified diseases, but all under a military allegory. *lazar-house*] hospital; especially (but not necessarily) a leper-house. *all feverous kinds*] Careful diction, for the classification of fevers was a great question at the time. See Svendsen 179 and cp. Sylvester's Du Bartas 265, where two paragraphs are devoted to fever 'whose inconstant fury / Transforms her ofter then Vertumnus can, / To *Tertian, Quartan,* and *Quotidian,* / And *Second* too'. *colic pangs*: paroxysmal griping belly pains. *moon-struck madness*] lunacy. *pining*] causing to pine. *Marasmus*] wasting away of the body.

xi *485–7.* Not in *Ed I.*

xi *491.* For Death's dart see ii 672, 786.

xi *492. oft invoked*] Cp. x 858 ('Death comes not at call'). Verity compares Sophocles, *Phil.* 797f, Horace, *Odes* II xviii 38ff; but Pliny, *Nat. hist.* VII I 167 is closer: *Tot morbi, tot metus, tot curae, totiens invocata morte ut nullum frequentius sit votum.*

xi *493. chief good*] An early use of the converted noun 'chief' in translating *summum bonum* (Emma 43).

xi *494.* For the stony heart of the unregenerate see l. 4.

xi *495–7.* Echoing *Macbeth* V vii 42–7, where Macbeth, on hearing that Macduff is not 'of woman born' exclaims: 'Accursed be that tongue that tells me so, / For it hath cow'd my better part of man.' The echo is more than

Though not of woman born; compassion quelled
His best of man, and gave him up to tears
A space, till firmer thoughts restrained excess,
And scarce recovering words his plaint renewed.
  O miserable mankind, to what fall
Degraded, to what wretched state reserved!
Better end here unborn. Why is life given
To be thus wrested from us? Rather why
Obtruded on us thus? Who if we knew
What we receive, would either not accept
Life offered, or soon beg to lay it down,
Glad to be so dismissed in peace. Can thus
The image of God in man created once
So goodly and erect, though faulty since,
To such unsightly sufferings be debased
Under inhuman pains? Why should not man,
Retaining still divine similitude
In part, from such deformities be free,
And for his maker's image sake exempt?
  Their maker's image, answered Michael, then

a verbal reminiscence, for one of the chief themes of *Macbeth* is the drying-up of the 'milk of human kindness,' i.e., the hardening of the heart against *compassion*. Cp. also *Henry V* IV vi 31, 'all my mother came into my eyes'; and *Hamlet* IV vii 190, 'the woman will be out'. Compassion, or pity, is the second part of the response to tragedy. For the first part, terror, see l. 465.

xi *504–6*. See ll. 360–4*n*. Adam makes the wrong, Stoic response to tragedy. Cp. Seneca, *De consolat.* xxii 3: '*Non mehercules quisquam illam* [*vitam*] *accepisset, nisi daretur inscientibus.*' Also Drummond, *A Cypress Grove* (ed. Kastner ii 80): 'O! who if before hee had a beeing, hee could have knowledge of the manie-fold Miseries of it, would enter this woefull Hospitall of the World, and accept of life upon such hard conditiones?'

xi *509. erect*] See vii 505–11*n*.

xi *511–25*. Catholic theologians held that the *imago Dei* was obscured, but not lost, by the Fall; whereas the *similitudo Dei* was utterly destroyed, but restored by Baptism. (The *imago Dei* was often identified with man's intellectual nature.) Protestant theologians tended to emphasise the disfiguring of the *imago Dei* more strongly. M. himself held that 'some remnants of the divine image still exist in us' (*De doctrina* i 12, Columbia xv 209: a liberal version of the Protestant position). These he thought to be visible in the human understanding and free-will: he particularly instances the wisdom and holiness of many of the heathen. Here, *maker's image* (l. 515) seems to refer to the *similitudo Dei*, while *God's likeness* (which is also *their own*, l. 521) is the *imago Dei*. Contrast iv 291ff.

xi *515–19*. The account of the change in human nature at the Fall began at

Forsook them, when themselves they vilified
To serve ungoverned appetite, and took
His image whom they served, a brutish vice,
Inductive mainly to the sin of Eve.
Therefore so abject is their punishment,
Disfiguring not God's likeness, but their own,
Or if his likeness, by themselves defaced
While they pervert pure nature's healthful rules
To loathsome sickness, worthily, since they
God's image did not reverence in themselves.
  I yield it just, said Adam, and submit.
But is there yet no other way, besides
These painful passages, how we may come
To death, and mix with our connatural dust?
  There is, said Michael, if thou well observe
The rule of not too much, by temperance taught
In what thou eat'st and drink'st, seeking from thence
Due nourishment, not gluttonous delight,
Till many years over thy head return:
So mayst thou live, till like ripe fruit thou drop
Into thy mother's lap, or be with ease
Gathered, not harshly plucked, for death mature:
This is old age; but then thou must outlive

ix 1013 (see *n*); the numerous diseases Adam has just seen are supposed the proliferating consequences of that initial change.
xi *516. vilified*] reduced to a lower standing (*OED* 1).
xi *519. Inductive*] giving rise to (*OED* 2).
xi *526.* The need for submission and patience is a constant theme of the present book; see above, Argument, 112 and 551.
xi *528. passages*] deaths (*OED* 2 b).
xi *531. rule . . . much*] Alludes to the ancient maxim μηδὲν ἄγαν, which is said to have been written up in the temple at Delphi by Cleobulus. Plato quotes it in *Protag.* 343B. M. writes often on the topic of moderation; see *Elegia VI* 59f, *Il Penseroso* 46, *Comus* 762ff and *SA* 553ff.
xi *535–7.* The comparison goes back to Cicero, *De senectute* 19. *mother's lap*] Cp. Adam's use of the same phrase in a similar connection at x 778.
xi *538–46.* The description of old age is a highly traditional one; cp., e.g., Shakespeare's 'mere oblivion / Sans teeth, sans eyes, sans taste, sans everything' (*As You Like It* II vii 165f); or Everyman's abandonment by Strength, Beauty and Five-Wits. In the correlation of Ages of Man with humours, *melancholy* was often assigned to the fourth period, old age; and the airy, sanguine humour to the second, *youth.* See Klibansky 122, 149 and 293. Sanguine was of course the preferred humour, supposed, usually, to have prevailed before the Fall; whereas melancholy, the worst humour, was regarded as especially characteristic of the corruption that followed (*ibid.*

Thy youth, thy strength, thy beauty, which will change
To withered weak and gray; thy senses then
Obtuse, all taste of pleasure must forego,
To what thou hast, and for the air of youth
Hopeful and cheerful, in thy blood will reign
A melancholy damp of cold and dry
To weigh thy spirits down, and last consume
The balm of life. To whom our ancestor.
   Henceforth I fly not death, nor would prolong
Life much, bent rather how I may be quit
Fairest and easiest of this cumbrous charge,
Which I must keep till my appointed day
Of rendering up, and patiently attend
My dissolution. Michael replied,
   Nor love thy life, nor hate; but what thou livest
Live well, how long or short permit to heaven:
And now prepare thee for another sight.
   He looked and saw a spacious plain, whereon

103, 105, 110f; see vi 331–4*n* above). According to one authority, melancholy was born out of the breath of the serpent (see Klibansky 79f). In this connection it is interesting that Satan entered the serpent as a 'midnight vapour' (ix 159); foreshadowing the *melancholy damp* that is to weigh Adam's spirits. *damp*] depression of spirits (*OED* 5); but also, apparently, 'vapour' (in the physiological sense), an extension of the normal application of the word to external exhalations and vapours (*OED* 1, 2).

xi *551–2*. *Ed I* has here only the one line, 'Of rendering up. Michael to him replied'. The insertion gives added emphasis to the thematic idea of patient resignation (see l. 526*n*). *attend*] wait for. Cp. *Job* xiv 14: 'If a man die, shall he live again? all the days of my appointed time will I wait, till my change come.'

xi *553–4*. Again a wrong response of Adam's–here his emotional embracing of death–is corrected by Michael; true patience is more detached (Burden 193). Cp. Martial, *Epig*. X xlvii 13, *summum nec metuas diem nec optes*; Horace, *Odes* I ix 9, *permitte divis cetera*; and Seneca, *Epist*. xxiv 29, lxv 18. The use of *permit* with an indirect object is not a departure from idiomatic English syntax (see *OED* s.v. *Permit* I 1).

xi *556–97*. The third vision apparently shows mankind in a more fortunate condition. This is appropriate from the point of view of number symbolism, for three is fortunate. It is also a Marriage Number (being formed from the union of Odd and Even); hence much of the vision is taken up with nuptials.

xi *556–73*. Cain's descendant Lamech had three sons: Jabal 'the father of such as dwell in tents, and of such as have cattle', Jubal 'the father of all such as handle the harp and organ', and Tubalcain 'an instructor of every artificer in brass and iron' (*Gen*. iv 19–22). Broadbent 105 notes that Tubalcain's smelting imitates that of the devils building Pandaemonium; and the same

Were tents of various hue; by some were herds
Of cattle grazing: others, whence the sound
Of instruments that made melodious chime
Was heard, of harp and organ; and who moved
Their stops and chords was seen: his volant touch
Instinct through all proportions low and high
Fled and pursued transverse the resonant fugue.
In other part stood one who at the forge
Labouring, two massy clods of iron and brass
Had melted (whether found where casual fire
Had wasted woods on mountain or in vale,
Down to the veins of earth, thence gliding hot
To some cave's mouth, or whether washed by stream
From underground) the liquid ore he drained
Into fit moulds prepared; from which he formed
First his own tools; then, what might else be wrought
Fusile or graven in metal. After these,
But on the hither side a different sort

point might be made in connection with Jubal and the organ (cp. i 708ff). The invention of the arts is given elaborate treatment in Sylvester's Du Bartas II i 4, 'The Handy-Crafts'; though from a point of view closer to Adam's than to Michael's–the characteristic tone is unreflecting exclamation: 'Happy device'! Cp. also Marvell's 'Musicks Empire', Sts 2f: '*Jubal* first made the wilder Notes agree; / And *Jubal* tuned Musicks *Jubilee*: / He call'd the *Ecchoes* from their sullen Cell, / And built the Organs City where they dwell. // Each sought a consort in that lovely place; / And Virgin Trebles wed the manly Base. / From whence the Progeny of numbers new / Into harmonious Colonies withdrew.'

xi *562–3. Instinct*] impelled, as at ii 937 (*OED* s.v. *Instinct* ppl. a; perhaps a Latinism). *proportions*] The art of music was regarded as essentially based on numerical proportions. Perhaps M. alludes to the ancient accounts of the invention of music, which relate that Pythagoras discovered the proportions when he heard blacksmiths beating a hot iron (Macrobius, *In somn. Scip.* II i 9ff, ed. Stahl 186f, with refs). *fugue*] Derived from Ital. *fuga*=flight. M. brings this out with *Fled*; no doubt to remind us that Jubal's race is the fugitive race of Cain; see ll. 608f.

xi *566–70. casual*] accidental, chance (*OED* 1). M. follows the account of the discovery of metals in Lucretius, *De rerum nat.* v 1241–68.

xi *573–80.* The descendants not of Cain but of Seth. According to Eutychius, they lived in the mountains *neighbouring* Paradise itself, and therefore on the *hither* side of the plain (whereas Cain dwelt 'on the east of Eden', *Gen.* iv 16). Josephus (*Antiq.* I ii 3) and others made them the inventors of physics and astronomy; hence their study is *God's works / Not hid.* Being children of light they presumably avoid meddling with God's secret hidden causes.

xi *573. Fusile*] melted or cast.

From the high neighbouring hills, which was their seat,
Down to the plain descended: by their guise
Just men they seemed, and all their study bent
To worship God aright, and know his works
Not hid, nor those things last which might preserve
Freedom and peace to men: they on the plain
Long had not walked, when from the tents behold
A bevy of fair women, richly gay
In gems and wanton dress; to the harp they sung
Soft amorous ditties, and in dance came on:
The men though grave, eyed them, and let their eyes
Rove without rein, till in the amorous net
Fast caught, they liked, and each his liking chose;
And now of love they treat till the evening star
Love's harbinger appeared; then all in heat
They light the nuptial torch, and bid invoke
Hymen, then first to marriage rites invoked;
With feast and music all the tents resound.
Such happy interview and fair event
Of love and youth not lost, songs, garlands, flowers,
And charming symphonies attached the heart
Of Adam, soon inclined to admit delight,
The bent of nature; which he thus expressed.
  True opener of mine eyes, prime angel blest,
Much better seems this vision, and more hope
Of peaceful days portends, than those two past;
Those were of hate and death, or pain much worse,
Here nature seems fulfilled in all her ends.
  To whom thus Michael. Judge not what is best
By pleasure, though to nature seeming meet,

xi *579. last*] lost *Ed I*, corrected in *Errata*.

xi *581–92*. Cp. *Gen.* vi 1f and see l. 622*n*. M. treated the same subject again in a very similar fashion in *PR* 153ff.

xi *588–9. treat*] deal, discuss. *evening star*] Venus, whose appearance was also the signal for the lighting of the 'bridal lamp' at viii 519f, at the nuptials of Adam and Eve. But the pagan god Hymen was not invoked by them.

xi *594. youth not lost*] Adam is particularly open to influence on this score, since Michael told him at ll. 538ff that he must lose his own youth.

xi *595. symphonies*] harmonies, concords; part-songs (*OED* 2, 4). Cp. the 'dulcet symphonies' that accompanied the building of Pandaemonium at i 712.

xi *599–602*. Burden 193f notes that Adam has again gone wrong by trusting his feelings. He fails to grasp the falsity of the god invoked, or to see that the marriages are based on *heat* (l. 589) and *delight* (l. 596), instead of on rational choice. As at viii 530 (after a scene not entirely dissimilar) he is 'transported'.

Created, as thou art, to nobler end
Holy and pure, conformity divine.
Those tents thou saw'st so pleasant, were the tents
Of wickedness, wherein shall dwell his race
Who slew his brother; studious they appear
Of arts that polish life, inventors rare,
Unmindful of their maker, though his Spirit
Taught them, but they his gifts acknowledged none.
Yet they a beauteous offspring shall beget;
For that fair female troop thou saw'st, that seemed
Of goddesses, so blithe, so smooth, so gay,
Yet empty of all good wherein consists
Woman's domestic honour and chief praise;
Bred only and completed to the taste
Of lustful appetance, to sing, to dance,
To dress, and troll the tongue, and roll the eye.
To these that sober race of men, whose lives
Religious titled them the sons of God,

xi *605–6.* As the Catechism reminds us, the chief end of man is to know God and enjoy him. The joy of the third vision, however, is a delight at the fulfilment of merely natural ends–*Here Nature seems fulfilled.*
xi *607–8.* 'I had rather be a doorkeeper in the house of my God, than to dwell in the tents of wickedness' (*Ps.* lxxxiv 10).
xi *611–12.* The arts of the children of Cain provided an occasion for many commentators on *Genesis* to discuss the problems presented to the Christian theologian by the existence of secular culture. Calvin, e.g., applied his doctrine of General Grace to account for the inspiration of the heathen.
xi *618. completed*] Perhaps 'accomplished; equipped'; but these senses seem to have been rare before *PL.* M. may intend an academic metaphor: 'graduated' (*OED* 13 b).
xi *619. appetence*] desire.
xi *620. troll*] wag.
xi *621–2.* Referring to *Gen.* vi 1f: 'And it came to pass, when men began to multiply on the face of the earth, and daughters were born unto them, That the sons of God saw the daughters of men that they were fair; and they took them wives of all which they chose.' Some early commentators took these verses to mean that the fallen angels lay with the daughters of men (e.g. Philo, Clement of Alexandria and Tertullian), and M. himself allows us to dally with this surmise in an ambiguous passage at iii 461ff. But now, in the down-to-earth demythologizing Bk xi, it turns out that that was only another of the vanities and follies bound for Limbo. On the discarded theory, which certain later commentators treated as heretical, see D. C. Allen in *MLN* lxi (1946) 78. West 129f rightly rejects the idea that M. at any time seriously entertained the angel perversion theory; but he misses the joke of iii 461ff. See l. 642*n*.

Shall yield up all their virtue, all their fame
Ignobly, to the trains and to the smiles
Of these fair atheists, and now swim in joy,
(Erelong to swim at large) and laugh; for which
The world erelong a world of tears must weep.
 To whom thus Adam of short joy bereft.
O pity and shame, that they who to live well
Entered so fair, should turn aside to tread
Paths indirect, or in the mid way faint!
But still I see the tenor of man's woe
Holds on the same, from woman to begin.
 From man's effeminate slackness it begins,
Said the angel, who should better hold his place
By wisdom, and superior gifts received.
But now prepare thee for another scene.
 He looked and saw wide territory spread

xi *624. trains*] snares, enticements.
xi *625–7. swim in joy*] An idiomatic expression; cp. 'swim in mirth' at ix 1009 above. The word play in *swim* and in *The world . . . must weep* looks forward to the Flood in the fifth vision, where it is repeated (l. 757). Erelong] soon.
xi *631*. This line is numerologically in the *mid way* of the *Paths indirect* of the first, destroyed world. For it is at the mid-point between the first line of the first vision (l. 423) and the last line of the fifth (the Flood: l. 839).
xi *632–6*. Again Adam makes the wrong response, by putting the blame on Eve. Burden 196 remarks how continuously the theme of the poem is applied to marriage. It is true that M. gives a considerable place to marriage, both in itself and as representative of the larger community. But here, as often elsewhere, M. really intends a psychological statement about the relation of intellect and emotions. The explanation of *woman* as meaning 'woe to man' was proverbial, and is given by some of the commentators on *Gen.* ii 23 or iii 20.
xi *638–711*. The tetrad commonly symbolized Friendship and Concord, so that M.'s fourth vision shows the corresponding evil, Strife. Cp. Spenser's treatment of Ate in his fourth book, and see Fowler 24–6 on the background of ancient number symbolism. M. repeats the point in miniature by giving four separate vignettes within the vision: foraging (ll. 646–50); tournament (ll. 651–5); siege (ll. 656–9); and council (ll. 660–71). The whole vision bears a close relation to Homer's elaborate account of the shield of Achilles (which had panoramic representations on it of conflict at a place of assembly, a siege, an attack on shepherds and a battle; see *Il.* xviii 490–540), as well as to Virgil's imitation in *Aen.* viii 626–728, a description of the shield of Vulcan given to Aeneas by his mother, with its prophetic images of Rome's future. Both ancient shields included representations of Discord or Strife personified.

Before him, towns, and rural works between,
Cities of men with lofty gates and towers,
Concourse in arms, fierce faces threatening war,
Giants of mighty bone, and bold emprise;
Part wield their arms, part curb the foaming steed,
Single or in array of battle ranged
Both horse and foot, nor idly mustering stood;
One way a band select from forage drives
A herd of beeves, fair oxen and fair kine
From a fat meadow ground; or fleecy flock,
Ewes and their bleating lambs over the plain,
Their booty; scarce with life the shepherds fly,
But call in aid, which makes a bloody fray;
With cruel tournament the squadrons join;
Where cattle pastured late, now scattered lies
With carcasses and arms the ensanguined field
Deserted: others to a city strong

xi *641. concourse*] hostile encounter.

xi *642. Giants*] A shade more than a figure of speech, in view of the tradition that the offspring of the *sons of God* were Giants. See l. 622*n*. *emprise*] chivalric enterprise, martial prowess.

xi *643–4.* Establishing an analogy with the warlike devils of ii 531f. As Broadbent 96 notes, M. has far more chivalry in hell and fallen earth than in heaven. He never loses an opportunity of chilling martial ardours.

xi *651. makes*] So *Ed II*. *Ed I* 'tacks' is almost certainly an error: tacks= 'attacks' (aphetic form) is syntactically difficult, while tacks='joins' would be unidiomatic with *fray*. On the other hand, if 'tacks' were idiomatic, as Adams 99 claims, the objection that it is too technical would carry little weight, in view of the high concentration of technical military terms in those parts of the poem that are concerned with the fallen world.

xi *654. ensanguined*] blood-stained (first instance in *OED*).

xi *655–71.* The just man is Enoch. From *Gen.* v 21–4, *Heb.* xi 5 and *Jude* 14 we learn that Enoch was 365 years of age (less than half the common patriarchal span) when he was translated by God. The details of Enoch's translation are not Scriptural, and it is possible that they may have been drawn from visual sources. The translation in a cloud agrees with the account of Enoch's vision translation in *Enoch* xiv 8f: 'Clouds invited me and a mist summoned me, and the course of the stars and the lightnings sped and hastened me, and the winds in the vision caused me to fly and lifted me upward, and bore me into heaven' (Charles ii 197). Unfortunately, however, these verses are not among the fragments of *The Book of Enoch* that could have been accessible to M. Nevertheless a good deal was known about *Enoch* in M.'s time, from quotations in patristic authors; indeed, the book was much discussed and quoted. This fact is of some importance as a key to the form of *PL* xi–xii. For the visions shown by Michael are from one

Lay siege, encamped; by battery, scale, and mine,
Assaulting; others from the wall defend
With dart and javelin, stones and sulphurous fire;
On each hand slaughter and gigantic deeds.
In other part the sceptred heralds call
To council in the city gates: anon
Gray-headed men and grave, with warriors mixed,
Assemble, and harangues are heard, but soon
In factious opposition, till at last
Of middle age one rising, eminent
In wise deport, spake much of right and wrong,
Of justice, of religion, truth, and peace,
And judgment from above: him old and young
Exploded and had seized with violent hands,
Had not a cloud descending snatched him thence
Unseen amid the throng: so violence
Proceeded, and oppression, and sword-law
Through all the plain, and refuge none was found.
Adam was all in tears, and to his guide
Lamenting turned full sad; O what are these,
Death's ministers, not men, who thus deal death
Inhumanly to men, and multiply
Ten thousand fold the sin of him who slew
His brother; for of whom such massacre
Make they but of their brethren, men of men?
But who was that just man, whom had not heaven
Rescued, had in his righteousness been lost?
  To whom thus Michael. These are the product
Of those ill mated marriages thou saw'st:

point of view a late contribution to the Enoch vision-literature tradition. Enoch, too, was a prophet of the future, and his visions, like M.'s, foretold the Deluge and God's judgments upon sin. M. would naturally have a great interest in the *Book of Enoch* because it was very largely concerned with the origin of evil. It also contained much useful angelic mythology. See ll. 700–10*n*. *exploded*] shouted down; drove away with hoots.

xi *656*. *scale*] ladder. Not a Latinism.

xi *661*. *city gates*] A common place for councils in Biblical times; see, e.g., *Gen*. xxxiv 20, *Zech*. viii 16.

xi *678*. Continuing the allusion to Enoch's visions. One of his prophecies was that 'the Lord cometh with ten thousands of his saints, To execute judgment upon all' (*Jude* 14f).

xi *683*. *Ed I* has semicolon after *Michael*.

xi *683–8*. For the Giant offspring of the sons of God and the daughters of Cain, see ll. 621–2*n*, 642*n*. The subject is treated at length in *Enoch* vi-vii, a passage that was paraphrased in many patristic authors.

Where good with bad were matched, who of themselves
Abhor to join; and by imprudence mixed,
Produce prodigious births of body or mind.
Such were these giants, men of high renown;
For in those days might only shall be admired,
And valour and heroic virtue called;
To overcome in battle, and subdue
Nations, and bring home spoils with infinite
Manslaughter, shall be held the highest pitch
Of human glory, and for glory done
Of triumph, to be styled great conquerors,
Patrons of mankind, gods, and sons of gods,
Destroyers rightlier called and plagues of men.
Thus fame shall be achieved, renown on earth,
And what most merits fame in silence hid.
But he the seventh from thee, whom thou beheld'st
The only righteous in a world perverse,
And therefore hated, therefore so beset
With foes for daring single to be just,
And utter odious truth, that God would come
To judge them with his saints: him the most high
Rapt in a balmy cloud with winged steeds

xi *689–90*. A strong piece of evidence in support of Steadman's thesis that M. systematically distinguishes two hierarchies of heroic virtues: the Christian one based on goodness and the Satanic on might. See ii 5*n*, vi 41–3*n*, 820–3*n*.
xi *692–3*. See ll. 643–4*n*.
xi *698*. Cp. *Gen*. vi 4: 'There were giants in the earth in those days; and also after that, when the sons of God came in unto the daughters of men, and they bare children to them, the same became mighty men which were of old, men of renown.'
xi *700–10*. Enoch is called 'the seventh from Adam' in *Jude* 14. The cloud with winged steeds is puzzling (see ll. 665–71*n*); though it may simply be based on the description of Elijah's translation at *2 Kings* ii 11. (Enoch and Elijah were often associated.) *walk with God*) Cp. *Gen*. v 24. *climes of bliss*] Cp. the 'happy climes that lie / Where Day never shuts his eye', of which the Attendant Spirit speaks in *Comus* 978f. Enoch's translation was a controversial issue in M.'s time: commentators on Genesis discussed whether Enoch escaped death, whether he was preserved in some terrene paradise and whether he would come again to be slain by Antichrist. (The various opinions are conveniently summarised in Willet 71f.) The translation was generally regarded as a type of Resurrection, or of the Ascension. Thus the Geneva Bible gloss is that Enoch was taken 'to shew that there was a better life prepared, and to be a testimonie of the immortalitie of soules and bodies'.

Did, as thou saw'st, receive, to walk with God
High in salvation and the climes of bliss,
Exempt from death; to show thee what reward
Awaits the good, the rest what punishment;
Which now direct thine eyes and soon behold.
He looked, and saw the face of things quite changed,
The brazen throat of war had ceased to roar,
All now was turned to jollity and game,
To luxury and riot, feast and dance,
Marrying or prostituting, as befell,
Rape or adultery, where passing fair
Allured them; thence from cups to civil broils.
At length a reverend sire among them came,

xi *708. High*] Cp. 665, 'rising'. Cope's thesis about a cycle of metaphoric rises and falls running through the poem is nowhere more evidently true. The just man Enoch is raised up on high, whereas the corrupt sons of God 'Down to the plain descended' (l. 576).
xi *710.* Punctuation as in *Ed I. Ed II* erroneously has question-mark after *punishment.*
xi *712–53.* Not only was five a Marriage Number (being the sum of two and three, the first female and the first male numbers in the Pythagorean system) but it was also the number of the senses and of sensuality. Consequently the fifth vision opens with the corruption of sexual manners. This point is reinforced by the series of five pairs of actions given in ll. 714–17. More important, however, is the symbolism whereby five stood for Justice (see Hopper 86, 115, 180; Fowler 34f). For it is in accordance with this symbolism that the Deluge now descends on human corruption.
xi *712. Ed I* semicolon after *changed* is preferable.
xi *714. luxury*] lust.
xi *717. passing fair*] Punning between 'surpassing, pre-eminent beauty' and 'woman passing by' (see *OED* s.v. *Passing* ppl. a. 3, 1; *Fair* sb.[2] 4, 2).
xi *719–53.* M.'s account of Noah and the Flood is faithful to *Gen.* vi 9–ix 17, with only a few divagations into the commentators; see Allen[2] 153f, where is is improbably suggested that the length and literal orthodoxy of M.'s account are due to the special doubts that had been cast on the historical truth of the Flood in his time. Noah's remonstrations with the rioters are mentioned in Josephus, *Antiq.* I iii 1. The loose sexual morals of antediluvian society are implied in *Luke* xvii 26f: 'As it was in the days of Noe, so shall it be also in the days of the Son of man. They did eat, they drank, they married wives, they were given in marriage, until the day that Noe entered into the ark, and the flood came.' They had occasionally provided a subject for visual representations, as in Hoet's engraving for the Cambridge Bible of 1660 (Fig. 15 in Allen[2]). The Flood itself, was, of course one of the great

And of their doings great dislike declared,
And testified against their ways; he oft
Frequented their assemblies, whereso met,
Triumphs or festivals, and to them preached
Conversion and repentance, as to souls
In prison under judgments imminent:
But all in vain: which when he saw, he ceased
Contending, and removed his tents far off;
Then from the mountain hewing timber tall,
Began to build a vessel of huge bulk,
Measured by cubit, length, and breadth, and highth,
Smeared round with pitch, and in the side a door
Contrived, and of provisions laid in large
For man and beast: when lo a wonder strange!
Of every beast, and bird, and insect small
Came sevens, and pairs, and entered in, as taught
Their order: last the sire, and his three sons
With their four wives; and God made fast the door.
Meanwhile the south-wind rose, and with black wings

subjects of visual art; its prominence in that field, as in literature and theology, may be put down to the effectiveness with which it focused the apocalyptic fears of the time. Its prominence in *PL* in particular, however, has this additional reason, that it provides a complete analogue of the Fall: it too is the loss of a world because of sin.

xi *721*. Cp. *Heb.* xi 7: 'By faith Noah, being warned of God of things not seen as yet, moved with fear, prepared an ark to the saving of his house; by the which he condemned the world.'

xi *723–5*. Cp. *1 Pet.* iii 18–21: Christ was 'put to death in the flesh, but quickened by the Spirit: By which also he went and preached unto the spirits in prison; Which sometime were disobedient, when once the long-suffering of God waited in the days of Noah, while the ark was a preparing, wherein few, that is, eight souls were saved by water. The like figure whereunto even baptism doth also now save us . . . by the resurrection of Jesus Christ.'

xi *730*. Cp. *Gen.* vi 15.

xi *734*. The inclusion of *insects* is not Biblical, and shows M. to be in agreement with the more modern of the commentators on Genesis. In the most elaborate of all treatments of the ark, Athanasius Kircher's *Arca Noe* (Amsterdam 1675), we still find the view that insects arise from putrefaction or spontaneous generation; so that they could safely be excluded (Allen[2] 185, 153).

xi *738–53*. Based on Ovid's description of Deucalion's flood in *Met.* i 262–347. The close relation between Deucalion and Noah was a commonplace of Biblical Poetics. But it could be used either to prove or to disprove the truth of pagan myth, either to prove or disprove the historicity of the Bible.

Wide hovering, all the clouds together drove
From under heaven; the hills to their supply
Vapour, and exhalation dusk and moist,
Sent up amain; and now the thickened sky
Like a dark ceiling stood; down rushed the rain
Impetuous, and continued till the earth
No more was seen; the floating vessel swum
Uplifted; and secure with beaked prow
Rode tilting o'er the waves, all dwellings else
Flood overwhelmed, and them with all their pomp
Deep under water rolled; sea covered sea,
Sea without shore; and in their palaces
Where luxury late reigned, sea monsters whelped
And stabled; of mankind, so numerous late,
All left, in one small bottom swum embarked.
How didst thou grieve then, Adam, to behold
The end of all thy offspring, end so sad,
Depopulation; thee another flood,
Of tears and sorrow a flood thee also drowned,
And sunk thee as thy sons; till gently reared
By the angel, on thy feet thou stood'st at last,

Allen[2] 176f discusses the modification that was currently taking place in the kind of truth attributed to the Flood narrative. The Ovidian passage has the south wind producing rain by its action on heavy clouds (implying a meteorological theory that, as Svendsen 97 shows, was still given credence in the seventeenth century); the image of the *sea without shore*; and a marvellous topsy-turvy panorama–very popular in M.'s time–of sea creatures taking the place of land creatures (*Met.* i 293–303). Sylvester's Du Bartas (I ii *ad fin.*; p. 57) develops the image at some length: 'The Sturgeon, coasting over Castles, muses / (Under the Sea) to see so many houses, / The *Indian* Manat and the Mullet float / O'r Mountain tops where yearst the bearded Goat / Did bound and brouz: the crooked Dolphin scuds / O'r th' highest branches of the hugest Woods,' etc. So does Drayton, but with more force: 'The Grampus, and the Whirlpoole, as they rove, / Lighting by chance upon a lofty Grove / Under this world of waters, are so much / Pleas'd with their wombes each tender branch to touch, / That they leave slyme upon the curled Sprayes, / On which the Birds sung their harmonious Layes' (*Noahs Floud* 729–34). Cp. also Cowley, *Davideis* i (ed. Waller 263). *supply*] assistance (*OED* I 1). *exhalation*] mist, vapour. *stabled*] Punning between 'lived as in a stable' and 'stuck in the mud' (*OED* vb.[2] 2 b, vb.[3]). *bottom*] boat.

xi *750–2.* As Broadbent 103 notices, this image brings to its logical conclusion a line of satire that began with the description of Pandaemonium's splendours.

xi *756–7.* See ll. 625–7*n*.

Though comfortless, as when a father mourns
His children, all in view destroyed at once;
And scarce to the angel uttered'st thus thy plaint.
   O visions ill foreseen! Better had I
Lived ignorant of future, so had borne
My part of evil only, each day's lot
Enough to bear; those now, that were dispensed
The burden of many ages, on me light
At once, by my foreknowledge gaining birth
Abortive, to torment me ere their being,
With thought that they must be. Let no man seek
Henceforth to be foretold what shall befall
Him or his children, evil he may be sure,
Which neither his foreknowing can prevent,
And he the future evil shall no less
In apprehension than in substance feel
Grievous to bear: but that care now is past,
Man is not whom to warn: those few escaped
Famine and anguish will at last consume
Wandering that watery desert: I had hope
When violence was ceased, and war on earth,
All would have then gone well, peace would have
   crowned
With length of happy days the race of man;
But I was far deceived; for now I see
Peace to corrupt no less than war to waste.
How comes it thus? Unfold, celestial guide,
And whether here the race of man will end.
To whom thus Michael. Those whom last thou saw'st
In triumph and luxurious wealth, are they
First seen in acts of prowess eminent
And great exploits, but of true virtue void;
Who having spilt much blood, and done much waste
Subduing nations, and achieved thereby
Fame in the world, high titles, and rich prey,

xi *765–6*. 'Take therefore no thought for the morrow: for the morrow shall take thought for the things of itself. Sufficient unto the day is the evil thereof' (*Matt.* vi 34).

xi *770–3*. Adam now falls into the error of despair, brought on by a false deterministic doctrine of Predestination.

xi *773–4*. *neither . . . and*] Editors explain this as an imitation of the 'elegant' Latin idiom *neque . . . et*. But is it likely that Adam would be elegant in his despair? 'Neither . . . and' is good but ungrammatical English: see many examples in *OED* s.v. *Neither* A 1 g.

xi *790*. *true virtue*] See ll. 689–90*n*.

Shall change their course to pleasure, ease, and sloth,
Surfeit, and lust, till wantonness and pride
Raise out of friendship hostile deeds in peace.
The conquered also, and enslaved by war
Shall with their freedom lost all virtue lose
And fear of God, from whom their piety feigned
In sharp contest of battle found no aid
Against invaders; therefore cooled in zeal
Thenceforth shall practise how to live secure,
Worldly or dissolute, on what their lords
Shall leave them to enjoy; for the earth shall bear
More than enough, that temperance may be tried:
So all shall turn degenerate, all depraved,
Justice and temperance, truth and faith forgot;
One man except, the only son of light
In a dark age, against example good,
Against allurement, custom, and a world
Offended; fearless of reproach and scorn,
Or violence, he of their wicked ways
Shall them admonish, and before them set
The paths of righteousness, how much more safe,
And full of peace, denouncing wrath to come
On their impenitence; and shall return
Of them derided, but of God observed
The one just man alive; by his command
Shall build a wondrous ark, as thou beheld'st,
To save himself and household from amidst
A world devote to universal rack.
No sooner he with them of man and beast
Select for life shall in the ark be lodged,
And sheltered round, but all the cataracts

xi *797–806.* One of the few passages in the poem which editors are probably justified in regarding as direct topical allusion. See particularly Hughes, who thinks the passage can be read as 'an attack upon the time-servers in his own party . . . the record of disillusion from the mood in which he painted England in *Areopagitica*'. The lines about feigned zeal cooling in adversity, which sound particularly *ad hominem*, refer to a problem dealt with more fully in *SA*. *contest*] Stressed on the second syllable.

xi *798. lose*] The *Ed I* and *Ed II* spelling 'loose' could indicate either 'lose' or 'loose' ('relax').

xi *815. denouncing*] proclaiming.

xi *821. devote*] doomed (*OED* s.v. *Devoted* 3). *rack*] (Variant of 'wreck') destruction.

xi *824–7.* Cp. *Gen.* vii 11: 'The same day were all the fountains of the great deep broken up, and the windows of heaven were opened.' *cataracts*]

Of heaven set open on the earth shall pour
Rain day and night, all fountains of the deep
Broke up, shall heave the ocean to usurp
Beyond all bounds, till inundation rise
Above the highest hills: then shall this mount
Of Paradise by might of waves be moved
Out of his place, pushed by the horned flood,
With all his verdure spoiled, and trees adrift
Down the great river to the opening gulf,
And there take root an island salt and bare,
The haunt of seals and orcs, and sea-mews' clang.
To teach thee that God attributes to place
No sanctity, if none be thither brought
By men who there frequent, or therein dwell.
And now what further shall ensue, behold.

where A.V. has 'windows' (marg. 'flood-gates'), Vulgate and Tremellius have *cataractae*.

xi *829–38*. As Allen notes, the fate of Paradise was a topic much discussed by the commentators. The Flood might naturally be expected to have changed the landscape, and Pererius argued that Paradise must have been destroyed altogether. Kircherus, on the other hand, held that it remained exactly where it was: he ridicules the idea that it was carried off to the Armenian mountains, or into the Antarctic, or to the Torrid Zone to become the Isle of Zealand (see Allen[2] 153f, 191). The present passage helps to explain the puzzling account of the entry of the Tigris into Paradise, at ix 69ff ('There was a place, / Now not, though sin, not time, first wrought the change'); though of course it would be simple-minded to conclude that M.'s point was geological and not theological. The *great river*, then, is the ordinary, mundane, present-day Tigris or Euphrates (cp. *Gen.* xv 18, 'the great river, the river Euphrates'). After all the splendid exotic geographical suggestions in such passages as iv 280ff, after all the esoteric theories about the locations of the terrene Paradise, the matter is settled for us and we come down to this: a bare island in the Persian Gulf. The lesson in the concluding lines is a simple homiletic Protestant one, that the existence of Paradise is inward and spiritual, and not to be superstitiously localized. MacCaffrey 88 rightly connects the *gulf* with the gulf of chaos, and finds analogues for the uprooted mountain in those of hell (i 230ff, ii 539ff). The *horned flood* probably echoes a Virgilian description of the mighty Tiber, *corniger Hesperidum fluvius regnator aquarum* (*Aen.* viii 77). But the phrase also occurs in Jonson, as well as in Browne, *Britannia's pastorals* ii 5 (a copy of which is extant with annotations thought by some to be M.'s holograph). *orcs*] not merely whales, but also leviathans, devouring monsters (*OED* 2, citing Sylvester's Du Bartas: 'Insatiate Orque, that even at one repast / Almost all creatures in the World would waste'). Cp. i 201ff above, where Satan is an orc. *sea-mew*] gull. *clang*] harsh scream; see vii 422–3*n*.

He looked, and saw the ark hull on the flood,
Which now abated, for the clouds were fled,
Driven by a keen north-wind, that blowing dry
Wrinkled the face of deluge, as decayed;
And the clear sun on his wide watery glass
Gazed hot, and of the fresh wave largely drew,
As after thirst, which made their flowing shrink
From standing lake to tripping ebb, that stole
With soft foot towards the deep, who now had stopped
His sluices, as the heaven his windows shut.
The ark no more now floats, but seems on ground
Fast on the top of some high mountain fixed.
And now the tops of hills as rocks appear;
With clamour thence the rapid currents drive
Towards the retreating sea their furious tide.

xi *840–69*. The appropriateness of the position of the sixth vision is obvious. Six was the number of the days of Creation, so that it was generally a creation symbol (see Bongo 264ff). This decorum is underlined by the connection drawn with the first creation in ll. 852–4. Six was also the number of the ages of the world's duration; the sixth age being reckoned from the coming of Christ to the Last Day. Consequently six symbolized the salvation of man, of which the Covenant with Noah is the type (Bongo 280). See further in xii 1*n* below.

xi *840–3*. The diction may possibly reflect a recollection of phrases from Sidney–'the carkas of the shippe . . . hulling there . . . bloud had (as it were) filled the wrinckles of the seas visage'–in a chapter of the 1590 *Arcadia* (I i) that sets out a myth of the Fall. See Tillyard in *TLS* (6 Mar. 1953) 153. Cp. also Cowley's description of the Flood, in which 'The face of shipwrackt Nature naked lay' (*Davideis* i, ed. Waller 263). More obviously, the wind is the one that clears the clouds in *Gen.* viii 1, or in Ovid, *Met.* i 328 (where it is specified to be the *north-wind*). *hull*] drift. *north-wind*] the word was often hyphenated in the seventeenth century.

xi *844–6*. On the sun's drinking, see v 423–6*n*. Note the half-pun, whereby *face* and *gazed* lead us to take *glass*=mirror, until *fresh* . . . *thirst* shows this to be wrong. The shift in meaning is a profound one. As a self-reflecting mirror (emblematic of vanity) the world is wrinkled and old, but as an instrument of communion with God it becomes *fresh* again.

xi *849*. Cp. *Gen.* viii 2: 'The fountains also of the deep and the windows of heaven were stopped, and the rain from heaven was restrained', and see ll. 824–7*n*.

xi *851*. Deliberately avoiding the localization of *Gen.* viii 4, 'upon the mountains of Ararat'.

xi *852–4*. Cp. the receding waters at the Creation, vii 285ff. The connection implies that 'one whole world' (l. 874) has been destroyed, and that God is creating afresh a New Creation based on the Covenant.

Forthwith from out the ark a raven flies,
And after him, the surer messenger,
A dove sent forth once and again to spy
Green tree or ground whereon his foot may light;
The second time returning, in his bill
An olive leaf he brings, pacific sign:
Anon dry ground appears, and from his ark
The ancient sire descends with all his train;
Then with uplifted hands, and eyes devout,
Grateful to heaven, over his head beholds
A dewy cloud, and in the cloud a bow
Conspicuous with three listed colours gay,
Betokening peace from God, and Covenant new.
Whereat the heart of Adam erst so sad
Greatly rejoiced, and thus his joy broke forth.
O thou who future things canst represent
As present, heavenly instructor, I revive
At this last sight, assured that man shall live
With all the creatures, and their seed preserve.
Far less I now lament for one whole world
Of wicked sons destroyed, than I rejoice
For one man found so perfect and so just,
That God vouchsafes to raise another world
From him, and all his anger to forget.
But say, what mean those coloured streaks in heaven,
Distended as the brow of God appeased,
Or serve they as a flowery verge to bind
The fluid skirts of that same watery cloud,
Lest it again dissolve and shower the earth?
To whom the archangel. Dextrously thou aim'st;
So willingly doth God remit his ire,

xi *864*. On the pun in *Grateful* ('feeling gratitude' and 'pleasing') see Ricks 114.

xi *865–7*. See Svendsen 98. *three . . . colours*] The primary colours red, yellow and blue. *listed*] arranged in bands. *Covenant*] See *Gen.* ix 13–15: 'I do set my bow in the cloud, and it shall be for a token of a covenant between me and the earth. . . . the waters shall no more become a flood to destroy all flesh.' For Michael's commission to 'intermix' God's Covenant in the visions, see ll. 115f above, with *n*.

xi *868*. *erst*] previously.

xi *870*. *who*] that *Ed I*.

xi *880*. *distended*] expanded (i.e., not contracted in anger).

xi *881*. In modern usage, *Or* might be preceded by a dash, to indicate that a sudden afterthought is being introduced.

Though late repenting him of man depraved,
Grieved at his heart, when looking down he saw
The whole earth filled with violence, and all flesh
Corrupting each their way; yet those removed,
Such grace shall one just man find in his sight,
That he relents, not to blot out mankind,
And makes a Covenant never to destroy
The earth again by flood, nor let the sea
Surpass his bounds, nor rain to drown the world
With man therein or beast; but when he brings
Over the earth a cloud, will therein set
His triple-coloured bow, whereon to look
And call to mind his Covenant: day and night,
Seed time and harvest, heat and hoary frost
Shall hold their course, till fire purge all things new,
Both heaven and earth, wherein the just shall dwell.

THE END OF THE ELEVENTH BOOK

xi *886–7*. Cp. *Gen.* vi 6, where God's reason for causing the Flood is that 'it repented [him] that he had made man on the earth, and it grieved him at his heart'.
xi *888–9*. Cp. *Gen.* vi 11: 'The earth also was corrupt before God, and the earth was filled with violence.'
xi *890*. 'But Noah found grace in the eyes of the Lord' (*Gen.* vi 8).
xi *892–901*. Cp. *Gen.* ix 14–16, viii 22. M. conspicuously omits the lifting of the curse on the ground (*Gen.* viii 21); probably not so much for the reason Burden gives–to avoid having God change his mind–as because the curse on the ground has in part been interpreted by M. as occasioning a macrocosmic change to the mutable astronomical world of our own experience. See x 623–40, where we are told that mutability will continue until the last things: 'Till then the curse pronounced on both [heaven and earth] precedes.' That divine pronouncement was immediately followed by the movement of the sun, and by such other macrocosmic changes 'as sorted best with present things' (x 651). *triple-coloured*] Cp. l. 866. Svendsen 98 mentions a belief that while the blue of the rainbow shows the Flood is past, the fiery colour shows what is yet to come. This idea stems ultimately from *2 Pet.* iii 6f, which links the final conflagration with the Flood, in a criticism of those who take the continuance of the world too much for granted: 'The world that then was, being overflowed with water, perished: But the heavens and the earth, which are now, by the same word are kept in store, reserved unto fire against the day of judgment and perdition of ungodly men.' The verses that follow develop an apocalyptic vision of the Last Day when 'the elements shall melt with fervent heat', but when those within

Paradise Lost

BOOK XII

The Argument

The angel Michael continues from the Flood to relate what shall succeed; then, in the mention of Abraham, comes by degrees to explain, who that seed of the woman shall be, which was promised Adam and Eve in the Fall;[1] his incarnation, death, resurrection, and ascension; the state of the Church till his second coming. Adam greatly satisfied and recomforted by these relations and promises descends the hill with Michael; wakens Eve, who all this while had slept, but with gentle dreams composed to quietness of mind and submission. Michael in either hand leads them out of Paradise, the fiery sword waving behind them, and the cherubim taking their stations to guard the place.

As one who in his journey baits at noon,
Though bent on speed, so here the archangel paused
Betwixt the world destroyed and world restored,
If Adam aught perhaps might interpose;

the Covenant may 'look for new heavens and a new earth, wherein dwelleth righteousness' (13f). The view that the present world will in a literal sense perish by fire was more general in M.'s time than in ours. He himself sets out what is known about the expected event from Scripture in *De doctrina* i 33 (Columbia xvi 369–71). Cp. viii 334–5*n*. It is fitting that an apocalypse should end the visions of the first 'world' (xii 6).

xii *Argument*[1]. *The angel Michael . . . in the Fall*] *Ed I* has 'thence from the Flood relates, and by degrees explains, who that seed of the woman shall be'.

xii *1–5*. Added when the tenth book of *Ed I* became the eleventh and twelfth of *Ed II*. Thus, *Ed II* xi 901 = *Ed I* x 896, and *Ed II* xii 6 = *Ed I* x 897. Note that *Ed I* does not even start a fresh paragraph to mark the pause in the archangel's journey. The paragraphs beginning at xii 1 and 6 are both new with *Ed II*.

xii *1*. *baits*] stops for rest. *noon*] the point of transition between one world and another, as the subsequent lines make clear. The transition is specifically like noon because noon is the 'sixth hour' of the Biblical day. A great deal of mystical speculation had been based on the tradition that the Fall, the Expulsion and the death of Christ all took place at the sixth hour. Bongo, who discusses the matter at some length (pp. 279–81) draws from these harmonies the conclusion that six is the number of salvation. See ll. 466–7*n*; also ix 739–40*n*. Note that the six visions which have just been shown to Adam correspond to the hours of Michael's journey in the exact metaphor of the present line. The visions cover the period of the Age of Adam (ll. 466–7*n*), so that the metaphorical noon here sees Adam's death, in

Then with transition sweet new speech resumes.
  Thus thou hast seen one world begin and end;
And man as from a second stock proceed.
Much thou hast yet to see, but I perceive
Thy mortal sight to fail; objects divine
Must needs impair and weary human sense:
Henceforth what is to come I will relate,
Thou therefore give due audience, and attend.
This second source of men, while yet but few;
And while the dread of judgment past remains
Fresh in their minds, fearing the Deity,
With some regard to what is just and right
Shall lead their lives, and multiply apace,
Labouring the soil, and reaping plenteous crop,
Corn wine and oil; and from the herd or flock,
Oft sacrificing bullock, lamb, or kid,
With large wine-offerings poured, and sacred feast,
Shall spend their days in joy unblamed, and dwell
Long time in peace by families and tribes
Under paternal rule; till one shall rise

accordance with the terms of the prohibition; just as the real noon of l. 589 will see his expulsion from Paradise into the mortal world.

xii 5. Apparently M. felt it necessary to add an explicit commentary on the structure in *Ed II*. The *transition* is *sweet* in the sense that honey of doctrine can be extracted from it. It is a transition from the first to the second *world*, from the first to the *second stock* (l. 7) and from the first to the *second source* (l. 13). It corresponds to a movement from the first to the second of the 'three drops' instilled into Adam's eyes at xi 416, and it is marked formally by a change from vision to narration. See further in ll. 466–7*n*.

xii *7. stock*] An ambiguity, referring not only to the literal replacement of one source of the human line of descent (Adam) by another (Noah), but also to the grafting of mankind onto the stem of Christ, according to the Pauline allegory of regeneration (*Rom.* xi). The covenant with Noah was a type of the New Covenant.

xii *13.* Some copies *Ed I*, probably correctly, have comma after *few*.

xii *16–24.* Since Richardson, editors have compared the Ovidian Age of Silver (*Met.* i 113ff); but the correspondence is not very close.

xii *18. labouring*] tilling, cultivating (*OED* I 1).

xii *19. Corn wine and oil*] Often associated in O.T. expositions of the law of tithes: see, e.g., *Deut.* xiv 23, *Neh.* x 39. But the phrase seems specifically to echo the Prayer Book version of *Ps.* iv 8 (7), as it was used in the Office of Compline: 'Thou hast put gladness in my heart: since the time that their corn and wine and oil increased.'

xii *24–63.* Nimrod is not connected with the builders of the Tower in *Genesis*, which merely has 'Cush begat Nimrod: he began to be a mighty

Of proud ambitious heart, who not content
With fair equality, fraternal state,
Will arrogate dominion undeserved
Over his brethren, and quite dispossess
Concord and law of nature from the earth,
Hunting (and men not beasts shall be his game)
With war and hostile snare such as refuse
Subjection to his empire tyrannous:
A mighty hunter thence he shall be styled
Before the Lord, as in despite of heaven,
Or from heaven claiming second sovereignty;

one in the earth. He was a mighty hunter before the Lord: wherefore it is said, Even as Nimrod the mighty hunter before the Lord. And the beginning of his kingdom was Babel' (*Gen.* x 8–10). The connection is made, however, in Josephus, *Antiq.* I iv 2f, where we also learn the derivation of *Babel* (cp. l. 62), the composition of the Tower (ll. 41–3) and the fact that Nimrod 'changed the government into tyranny'. On this basis the commentators (especially St Jerome) developed Nimrod into an archetype of the tyrant, and made him replace the patriarchal *paternal rule* by *dominion* and *empire.* But M.'s presentation of Nimrod has also a republican tinge, for which we have been prepared by the preceding Senecan idyll of virtuous primitive governors (see Hughes in Yale iii 118f, citing Seneca, *Epist.* lxxxi). The appeal to Natural Law against the claim of the tyrannical ruler is republican (though by no means exclusively so), and so is the ideal of a *fraternal state.* Throughout the present passage there are resonances with *The Tenure of Kings and Magistrates*, some of which are noted below.

xii *29*. Cp. St Basil's definition of a tyrant, cited in *The Tenure*: 'A Tyrant whether by wrong or by right comming to the Crown, is he who regarding neither Law nor the common good, reigns onely for himself and his faction' (Yale iii 212). Cp. also *ibid.* 202, M.'s denial of the natural right of kings, and his insistence that their power is committed to them in trust by the people.

xii *30–3*. A metaphorical interpretation of Nimrod's hunting was frequent among the commentators. See, e.g., Willet 117, applying *Lam.* iv 18. Cp. *Eikonoklastes*: 'The Bishops could have told him, that *Nimrod*, the first that hunted after Faction is reputed, by ancient Tradition, the first that founded Monarchy; whence it appeares that to hunt after Faction is more properly the Kings Game' (Yale iii 466; similarly at 598). Cp. also Dryden, *The Hind and the Panther* i 282f.

xii *34–5*. The commentators found *Before the Lord* (*Gen.* x 9) a puzzling phrase. M. chooses to take it (with Vatablus and Mercerus) in a constitutional sense; cp. *The Tenure* (Yale iii 204): 'To say Kings are accountable to none but God, is the overturning of all Law.'

And from rebellion shall derive his name,
Though of rebellion others he accuse.
He with a crew, whom like ambition joins
With him or under him to tyrannize,
Marching from Eden towards the west, shall find
The plain, wherein a black bituminous gurge
Boils out from under ground, the mouth of hell;
Of brick, and of that stuff they cast to build
A city and tower, whose top may reach to heaven;
And get themselves a name, lest far dispersed
In foreign lands their memory be lost
Regardless whether good or evil fame.
But God who oft descends to visit men
Unseen, and through their habitations walks
To mark their doings, them beholding soon,
Comes down to see their city, ere the tower
Obstruct heaven towers, and in derision sets
Upon their tongues a various spirit to raze

xii *36.* Starnes and Talbert (267) note that the explanation of *Nimrod* as derived from Hebrew *mârad* and = Latin *rebellis* is given in Charles Estienne's *Dictionarium*: perhaps the best prop to their shaky argument that M. drew from there the material for the present passage.

xii *41–4. The plain*] In Shinar. For this and the direction of the journey cp. *Gen.* xi 2, and see iii 466–8*n* above. The materials of the Tower–brick with bitumen as mortar–are specified in *Gen.* xi 3; where A.V. translates the Hebrew word rendered *bitumen* in Vulgate as 'slime' (a common synonym at the time: see *OED* s.v. *Slime* 1 b). M.'s *hell* is not under the earth; but bitumen has a symbolic connection with hell (see x 296–8 and *n*). Bentley and Empson ([2] 155) with an odd crassness insist on taking the location literally. *gurge*] whirlpool (first instance in *OED*; almost certainly a Latinism: *gurges* = abyss, whirlpool). *cast*] set themselves with resolution.

xii *45–6.* 'And they said, Go to, let us build us a city and a tower, whose top may reach unto heaven; and let us make us a name, lest we be scattered abroad upon the face of the whole earth' (*Gen.* xi 4).

xii *52. Obstruct heaven towers*] Ironic, surely; in spite of Empson[2] 155 to the contrary. *in derision*] Cp., e.g, *Ps.* ii 4: 'He that sitteth in the heavens shall laugh: the Lord shall have them in derision.'

xii *53–8.* In the seventeenth century it was generally believed that the separation of language into distinct individual languages had its beginning at the confusion of tongues at Babel. At a time when synthetic universal languages were much canvassed, the Babel story had a strong fascination. Sir Thomas Urquhart, for example, presents his universal language as a return to a total expression such as no language has been capable of since Babel; see his *Most exquisite Jewel* and *Logopandecteision*. M. himself writes in his *Logic*

Quite out their native language, and instead
To sow a jangling noise of words unknown:
Forthwith a hideous gabble rises loud
Among the builders; each to other calls
Not understood, till hoarse, and all in rage,
As mocked they storm; great laughter was in heaven
And looking down, to see the hubbub strange
And hear the din; thus was the building left
Ridiculous, and the work Confusion named.
  Whereto thus Adam fatherly displeased.
O execrable son so to aspire
Above his brethren, to himself assuming
Authority usurped, from God not given:
He gave us only over beast, fish, fowl
Dominion absolute; that right we hold
By his donation; but man over men
He made not lord; such title to himself
Reserving, human left from human free.
But this usurper his encroachment proud
Stays not on man; to God his tower intends
Siege and defiance: wretched man! What food
Will he convey up thither to sustain
Himself and his rash army, where thin air

(i 24, Columbia xi 220) that 'languages, both that first one which Adam spoke in Eden, and those varied ones also possibly derived from the first, which the builders of the tower of Babel suddenly received, are without doubt divinely given'. See D. C. Allen in *PQ* xxviii (1949) 11. *various*] causing differences; unstable; going in different directions. *jangling noise*] Sylvester's phrase (Du Bartas 320).

xii *62. Confusion named*] Cp. A.V. *Gen.* xi 9, 'Therefore is the name of it called Babel'; marginal gloss 'that is, Confusion'. Josephus develops this popular but false etymology in *Antiq.* I iv 3.

xii *66.* Broadbent 112 compares Satan's establishment as king (e.g. ii 466f) in spite of the republican sentiments he expresses at v 790ff.

xii *73–4.* In *Antiq.* I iv 2 Josephus gives a relatively full account of Nimrod's motives. He persuaded the people on the plain of Shinar not to ascribe their happiness to God but to their own courage, because he wanted to turn them from the fear of God and to 'avenge himself on God for destroying their forefathers'.

xii *76–8.* The upper air was not for mortals: see iii 562*n*. Throughout *PL* the atmosphere is a symbol of degree–i.e., of both moral and natural station. Cp., e.g., the 'purer air' of Paradise (iv 153) and the 'thinner air' that fish are unable to breathe (viii 348). The importance of the idea to M. may be gauged from its prominence in his Third Draft of a tragedy on the Fall (see Introduction, 'Composition', p. 419 above).

Above the clouds will pine his entrails gross,
And famish him of breath, if not of bread?
  To whom thus Michael. Justly thou abhorr'st
That son, who on the quiet state of men
Such trouble brought, affecting to subdue
Rational liberty; yet know withal,
Since thy original lapse, true liberty
Is lost, which always with right reason dwells
Twinned, and from her hath no dividual being:
Reason in man obscured, or not obeyed,
Immediately inordinate desires
And upstart passions catch the government
From reason, and to servitude reduce
Man till then free. Therefore since he permits
Within himself unworthy powers to reign
Over free reason, God in judgment just
Subjects him from without to violent lords;
Who oft as undeservedly enthral
His outward freedom: tyranny must be,
Though to the tyrant thereby no excuse.
Yet sometimes nations will decline so low
From virtue, which is reason, that no wrong,

xii *80–101*. This whole passage may recall the style of the regicide tracts. But it follows closely St Augustine's thought in *Civ. Dei* xix 15, where we read that man was made lord 'only over the unreasonable, not over man, but over beasts . . . justly was the burden of servitude laid upon the back of transgression. And therefore in all the Scriptures we never read the word *servant*, until such time as that just man Noah laid it as a curse upon his offending son. So that it was guilt, and not nature that gave original unto that name.' Hence the derivation of servitude, whose mother is sin, the 'first cause of man's subjection to man: which notwithstanding comes not to pass but by the direction of the highest, in whom is no injustice' (*ibid.*, alluding to *John* viii 34). For the connection between psychological and political enslavement, cp. ix 1127–31 and see *n.* *right reason*] conscience; a great watch-word in seventeenth-century theological controversies (see vi 41–3*n*). Cp. 'rectified' reason, *Articles of Peace* (Yale iii 330). *Twinned*] Implies not only a close relation but also a reflective relation in which free will is a true image of reason. In Neoplatonic systems such as Pico's, the mind (*intellectus*) was supposed to have such a reflective relationship with the faculty of choice (*ratio*). *dividual*] separate, distinct. The passage has an obvious bearing on the separation of Adam and Eve immediately before the Fall: without Adam's *reason*, Eve's *liberty* led only to *upstart passions*. Cp. iii 108–10, ix 351f.

xii *95–6*. Cp. iv 393, where necessity is called 'the tyrant's plea'.

But justice, and some fatal curse annexed
Deprives them of their outward liberty,
Their inward lost: witness the irreverent son
Of him who built the ark, who for the shame
Done to his father, heard this heavy curse,
Servant of servants, on his vicious race.
Thus will this latter, as the former world,
Still tend from bad to worse, till God at last
Wearied with their iniquities, withdraw
His presence from among them, and avert
His holy eyes; resolving from thenceforth
To leave them to their own polluted ways;
And one peculiar nation to select
From all the rest, of whom to be invoked,
A nation from one faithful man to spring:
Him on this side Euphrates yet residing,
Bred up in idol-worship; O that men
(Canst thou believe?) should be so stupid grown,
While yet the patriarch lived, who scaped the flood,
As to forsake the living God, and fall
To worship their own work in wood and stone
For gods! Yet him God the most high vouchsafes

xii *101–14*. Because Ham the son of Noah looked on the nakedness of his drunken father, and told his brothers about it, his own son Canaan was cursed: 'Cursed be Canaan; a servant of servants shall he be unto his brethren' (*Gen.* ix 25).
xii *111–13*. Another new beginning from another faithful 'remnant'. In *De doctrina* M. distinguishes the 'general or national election' of Israel from the eternal predestination or election of an individual. (Hughes tells us that M. 'condemns the Calvinistic doctrine of individual election to personal salvation'. In fact what M. condemns is the doctrine of Reprobation, not of Election. There is nothing wrong with predestinating glory.) See especially *De doctrina* i 4, (Columbia xiv 96–100). *peculiar*] special, particular; cp. *Deut.* xiv 2: 'For thou art an holy people unto the Lord thy God, and the Lord hath chosen thee to be a peculiar people unto himself, above all the nations that are upon the earth.'
xii *114–15*. On Abraham's origins, see *Joshua* xxiv 2: 'Thus saith the Lord God of Israel, Your fathers dwelt on the other side of the flood in old time, even Terah, the father of Abraham, and the father of Nachor: and they served other gods.'
xii *117*. *the patriarch*] Noah, who lived for 350 years after the Flood, according to *Gen.* ix 28.
xii *120*. *most high*] The name used in Melchizedek's blessing of Abraham, *Gen.* xiv 19.

To call by vision from his father's house,
His kindred and false gods, into a land
Which he will show him, and from him will raise
A mighty nation, and upon him shower

xii *121–34*. For the calling of Abraham and God's covenant with him, see *Gen.* xii and *Acts* vii. The departure from idolatry is stressed in *Judith* v 6–9. *all nations*] Cp. *Gen.* xii 3: 'In thee shall all families of the earth be blessed.' *firm believes*] Cp. Heb. xi 8, 'By faith Abraham, when he was called to go out into a place which he should after receive for an inheritance, obeyed; and he went out, not knowing whither he went.' The irony is strong in view of the imminence of Adam's expulsion: he will shortly be challenged by the need to have a similar faith. *thou canst not*] the object is too divine for Adam in his present state; see l. 9. The *ford* is probably M.'s inference from the information given in *Gen.* xi 31: *Ur* was on one bank of the Euphrates and *Haran* (see iv 209–16*n*) on the other, to the N.W. *servitude*] slaves and servants collectively (putting the abstract for the concrete).
xii *135–51*. The account of the journey is based on *Gen.* xii 5f; of the promise, on *Josh.* xiii 5f. *Hamath*] Marks the N. border, the 'great sea' the W. border, and the wilderness of Zin the S. border of the Promised Land in *Num.* xxxiv 3–8. *Josh.* xiii 5f itself mentions Mt *Hermon* and the district of *Hamath* as boundaries. *as I point them*] In all his panoramic views, M. is most careful to establish a clear perspective: the places are not only visualized, but visualized from one particular standpoint. *on the shore*] Mt *Carmel's* position, as certain as destiny, is something to swear an oath on in *Jer.* xlvi 18: 'As I live, saith the King, whose name is the Lord of hosts, Surely as Tabor is among the mountains, and as Carmel by the sea, so shall he come.' Thus the very landscape is prophetic of sure deliverance. *double-founted*] The fallacious belief that the *Jordan* is formed by the confluence of two fountains Jor and Dan is still subscribed to in George Sandys's *Relation* (1615), which M. seems to have used (though the tradition went back to St. Jerome, as Hughes notes). The river is mentioned as the E. border of Canaan in *Num.* xxxiv 12. *Senir* seems to have been thought of by M. as a ridge running E. from Mt Hermon; the allusion is to *1 Chron.* v 23. Note that nine places are named in the Promised Land: the incorruptible number of heavenly things (see Fowler 270ff). Also, that among these nine Jordan has the eighth position – a position appropriate to its connection with baptism, since eight is the number of baptism and regeneration (*ibid.* 53; Bongo 330f). It may be for the purpose of drawing attention to this numerological arrangement that M. twice announces he is giving *names*, at ll. 140 and 142f (notice also, however, an echo of Virgil, *Aen.* vi 776). The central place of sovereignty is occupied by *Hermon*, because of its connection with King Solomon (see *Song of Sol.* iv 8, and cf. xi 396–407*n* above). See also St Augustine's mystical interpretation of the dew of Hermon (*Ps.* cxxxiii 3) as the grace of God: 'The light set on high is Christ, whence is the dew of Hermon.'

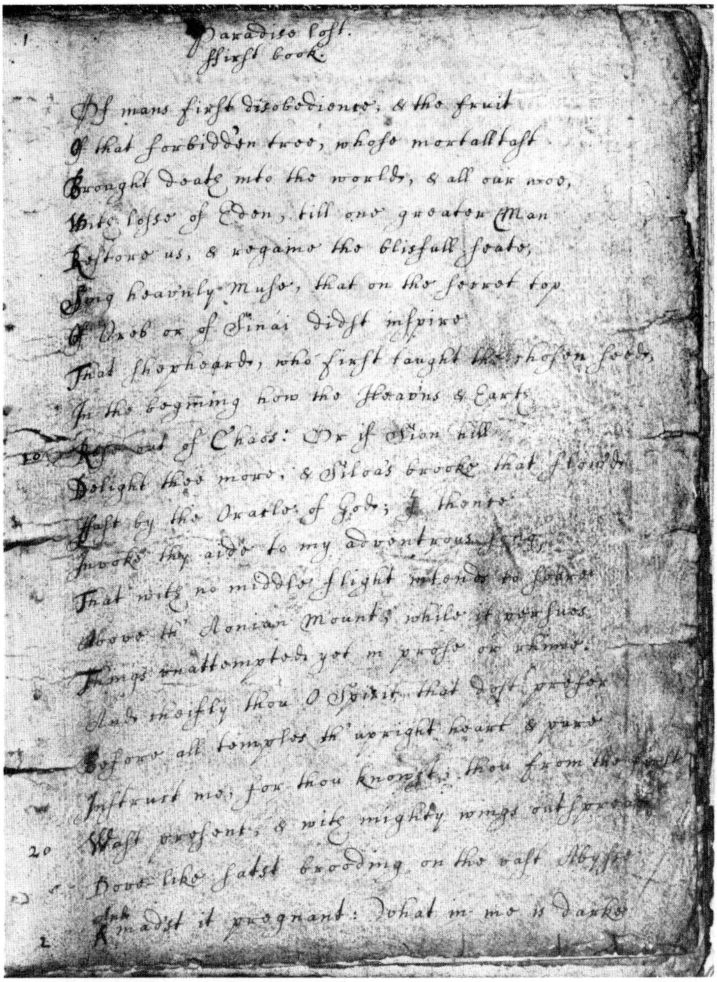

Plate 5 Paradise Lost. Pierpont Morgan manuscript

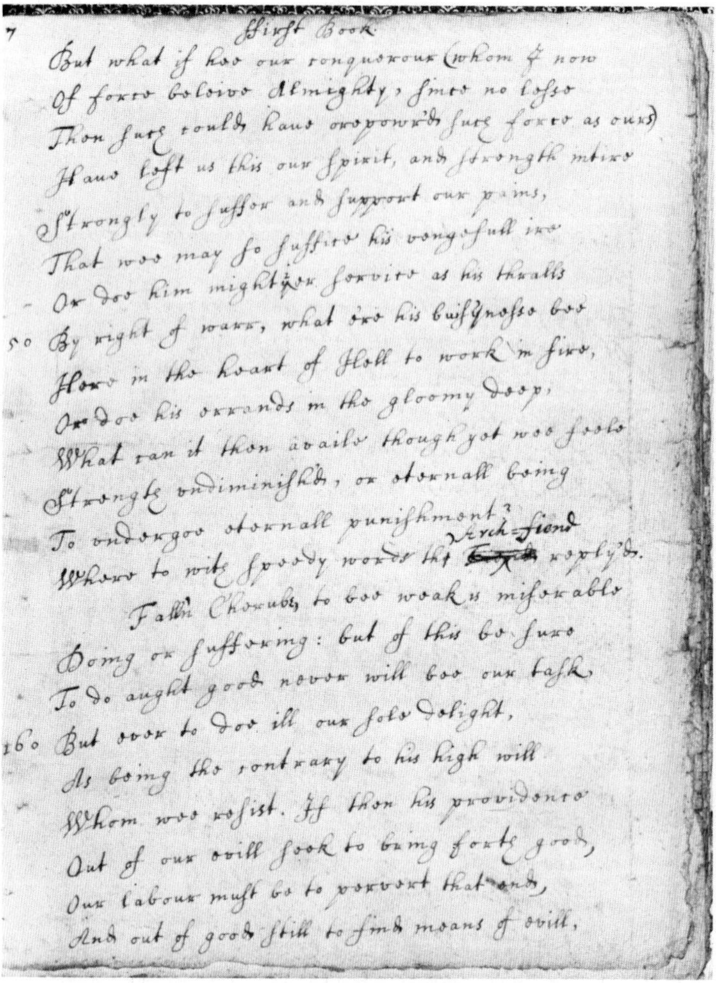
7 First Book

But what if hee our conquerour (whom I now
Of force beleive Almighty, since no lesse
Then such could have orepowr'd such force as ours)
Have left us this our spirit, and strength intire
Strongly to suffer and support our pains,
That wee may so suffice his vengefull ire
Or doe him mightier service as his thralls
By right of warr, what ere his buisinesse bee
Here in the heart of Hell to work in fire,
Or doe his errands in the gloomy deep;
What can it then availe though yet wee feele
Strength undiminisht, or eternall being
To undergoe eternall punishment?
Whereto with speedy words th' Arch-fiend reply'd.
Fall'n Cherube, to bee weak is miserable
Doing or suffering: but of this bee sure
To do aught good never will bee our task
But ever to doe ill our sole delight,
As being the contrary to his high will
Whom wee resist. If then his providence
Out of our evill seek to bring forth good,
Our labour must be to pervert that end,
And out of good still to find means of evill,

Plate 6 Paradise Lost. Pierpont Morgan manuscript

His benediction so, that in his seed
All nations shall be blest; he straight obeys,
Not knowing to what land, yet firm believes:
I see him, but thou canst not, with what faith
He leaves his gods, his friends, and native soil
Ur of Chaldaea, passing now the ford
To Haran, after him a cumbrous train
Of herds and flocks, and numerous servitude;
Not wandering poor, but trusting all his wealth
With God, who called him, in a land unknown.
Canaan he now attains, I see his tents
Pitched about Sechem, and the neighbouring plain
Of Moreh; there by promise he receives
Gift to his progeny of all that land;
From Hamath northward to the desert south
(Things by their names I call, though yet unnamed)
From Hermon east to the great western sea,
Mount Hermon, yonder sea, each place behold
In prospect, as I point them; on the shore
Mount Carmel; here the double-founted stream
Jordan, true limit eastward; but his sons
Shall dwell to Senir, that long ridge of hills.
This ponder, that all nations of the earth
Shall in his seed be blessed; by that seed
Is meant thy great deliverer, who shall bruise
The serpent's head; whereof to thee anon
Plainlier shall be revealed. This patriarch blest,
Whom faithful Abraham due time shall call,
A son, and of his son a grandchild leaves,
Like him in faith, in wisdom, and renown;
The grandchild with twelve sons increased, departs
From Canaan, to a land hereafter called

xii *147–51*. The promise to Abraham (*Gen.* xii 1–3) renews the promise implicit in the curse on the serpent; see x 180ff.

xii *152*. *Abraham*] 'Father of a great multitude'; see *Gen.* xvii 5, with A.V. marg. gloss; and cp. *Gal.* iii 9: 'So then they which be of faith are blessed with faithful Abraham.'

xii *153*. The *son* is Isaac, the *grandchild* Jacob.

xii *155–63*. *Gen.* xlv and xlvi tell how Jacob went down to Egypt at the bidding of the *younger son* Joseph. The *seven mouths* of the Nile contrast with the nine places of the Promised Land (see ll. 135–51*n*), because seven is the number of mortality and mutability. The opposition between seven and nine was very common; and so was that between Egypt (symbolizing body, flesh, sin, this world) and the Promised Land (mind, spirit, regeneration, heaven). See Fowler, App. i *passim*.

Egypt, divided by the river Nile;
See where it flows, disgorging at seven mouths
Into the sea: to sojourn in that land
He comes invited by a younger son
In time of dearth, a son whose worthy deeds
Raise him to be the second in that realm
Of Pharao: there he dies, and leaves his race
Growing into a nation, and now grown
Suspected to a sequent king, who seeks
To stop their overgrowth, as inmate guests
Too numerous; whence of guests he makes them slaves
Inhospitably, and kills their infant males:
Till by two brethren (those two brethren call
Moses and Aaron) sent from God to claim
His people from enthralment, they return
With glory and spoil back to their promised land.
But first the lawless tyrant, who denies
To know their God, or message to regard,
Must be compelled by signs and judgments dire;
To blood unshed the rivers must be turned,
Frogs, lice and flies must all his palace fill
With loathed intrusion, and fill all the land;
His cattle must of rot and murrain die,
Botches and blains must all his flesh emboss,
And all his people; thunder mixed with hail,
Hail mixed with fire must rend the Egyptian sky
And wheel on the earth, devouring where it rolls;
What it devours not, herb, or fruit, or grain,
A darksome cloud of locusts swarming down
Must eat, and on the ground leave nothing green:
Darkness must overshadow all his bounds,
Palpable darkness, and blot out three days;

xii *164–8.* Following *Exod.* i. *sequent king*] Named as Busiris at i 307, in the comparison of the devils to the Pharaoh's 'Memphian chivalry'. *overgrowth*] excessive growth (*OED* 1).

xii *172. spoil*] Jewels and clothes extorted as a 'loan' when the Egyptians were anxious to see the Israelites leave as soon as possible (*Exod.* xii 36).

xii *173. denies*] refuses.

xii *173–90.* The brief account of the plagues is in general based on *Exod.* vii–xii. The chariot image in l. 183, however, is M.'s own, and should be referred to the central image of the poem, the chariot of cosmic justice (see vi 749–59*n*, and cp. i 311). The locust plague has appeared earlier, in the simile at i 338–43.

xii *188. palpable*] Cp. Vulgate *Exod.* x 21: *Sint tenebrae super terram Aegypti, tam densae, ut palpari queant.*

Last with one midnight stroke all the first-born
Of Egypt must lie dead. Thus with ten wounds
The river-dragon tamed at length submits
To let his sojourners depart, and oft
Humbles his stubborn heart, but still as ice
More hardened after thaw, till in his rage
Pursuing whom he late dismissed, the sea
Swallows him with his host, but them lets pass
As on dry land between two crystal walls,
Awed by the rod of Moses so to stand
Divided, till his rescued gain their shore:
Such wondrous power God to his saint will lend,
Though present in his angel, who shall go
Before them in a cloud, and pillar of fire,
By day a cloud, by night a pillar of fire,
To guide them in their journey, and remove
Behind them, while the obdurate king pursues:
All night he will pursue, but his approach

xii *191. The*] This *Ed I.* Röstvig 187 remarks that the description of the Pharaoh as 'the great dragon that lieth in the midst of his rivers' in *Ezek.* xxix 3 is the foundation for his typological interpretation as Sin.

xii *192.* M. uses Pharaoh as the classic example of one whose heart was hardened, in *De doctrina* i 8 (Columbia xv 71), and compares his blindness to that of King Charles, in *Eikonoklastes* (Yale iii 516).

xii *193–4.* Svendsen 99 notes that according to Swan's *Speculum mundi* snow 'melting on the high hilles, and after frozen againe, becommeth so hard, that it is a stone, and is called Christall.'

xii *197.* Cp. the youthful *Psalm cxxxvi* 49f: 'The floods stood still like walls of glass, / While the Hebrew bands did pass.' Both passages may have been influenced by the phrase 'walls of crystal' in Sylvester's account of the parting of the Red Sea (Du Bartas 454). But much more important is the connection with the division of the waters at the Creation (vii 293 above: 'Part rise in crystal wall'). See *Exod.* xiv 16, 21f.

xii *199.* As the Nile 'divided' Egypt (l. 157), so Moses' rod *Divided* the water. Division, when auspicious, was usually a symbol of justice and creative power; see Fowler 34, 206.

xii *200–5.* Cp. *Exod.* xiii 21f. *present in his angel*] See *De doctrina* i 5 (Columbia xiv 287–9), where M. develops at length the point that God never went himself with the Israelites, since that would have destroyed them; but that he sent 'a representation of his name and glory in the person of some angel'. *saint*] Often applied, in the seventeenth century, to O.T. personages. *obdurate*] Stressed on the second syllable; there is elision or synaloepha with *the.*

xii *206–14.* See *Exod.* xiv, and cp. i 306ff. *defends*] wards off, averts

Darkness defends between till morning watch;
Then through the fiery pillar and the cloud
God looking forth will trouble all his host
And craze their chariot wheels: when by command
Moses once more his potent rod extends
Over the sea; the sea his rod obeys;
On their embattled ranks the waves return,
And overwhelm their war: the race elect
Safe towards Canaan from the shore advance
Through the wild desert, not the readiest way,
Lest entering on the Canaanite alarmed
War terrify them inexpert, and fear
Return them back to Egypt, choosing rather
Inglorious life with servitude; for life
To noble and ignoble is more sweet
Untrained in arms, where rashness leads not on.
This also shall they gain by their delay
In the wide wilderness, there they shall found
Their government, and their great senate choose
Through the twelve tribes, to rule by laws ordained:
God from the mount of Sinai, whose grey top
Shall tremble, he descending, will himself
In thunder lightning and loud trumpets' sound
Ordain them laws; part such as appertain
To civil justice, part religious rites

(*OED* I 1); hinders (*OED* I 2). *war*] soldiers in fighting array (perhaps poetic diction; first example in this sense in *OED*).

xii *216–19*. The explanation given in *Exod.* xiii 17f. The actual route took a detour south to avoid the warlike Philistines. The Civil War is compared to the wandering in the desert, in *Eikonoklastes* (Yale iii 580).

xii *224–6*. For the election of the Seventy Elders see *Num.* xi 16–25 and *Exod.* xxiv. *senate*] M.'s choice of the term probably implies that he saw the Seventy as the beginning of the Sanhedrin, which he refers to as a senate in *The Ready and Easy Way* (Columbia vi 128), and takes as a model for contemporary senates. The Jewish constitution was at the time fairly often proposed as a pattern commonwealth; though such proposals by no means met with general acceptance. Hobbes, e.g., 'expressly repudiated the view of Moses as the institutor of a conciliar government' (Hughes, Yale iii 89*n*, citing *Leviathan* iii 42).

xii *227–30*. Cp. *Exod.* xix 16–20.

xii *229*. In this case the modern spelling possibly obscures a piece of double syntax. The early edns have 'trumpets' (without apostrophe), so that *sound* may at first be felt as a verb.

Of sacrifice, informing them, by types
And shadows, of that destined seed to bruise
The serpent, by what means he shall achieve
Mankind's deliverance. But the voice of God
To mortal ear is dreadful; they beseech
That Moses might report to them his will,
And terror cease; he grants what they besought
Instructed that to God is no access
Without mediator, whose high office now
Moses in figure bears, to introduce
One greater, of whose day he shall foretell,
And all the prophets in their age the times
Of great Messiah shall sing. Thus laws and rites
Established, such delight hath God in men
Obedient to his will, that he vouchsafes
Among them to set up his tabernacle,

xii *232–4.* Cp. *Heb.* viii 5: earthly priests 'serve unto the example and shadow of heavenly things, as Moses was admonished of God when he was about to make the tabernacle: for, See, saith he, that thou make all things according to the pattern showed to thee in the mount.'

xii *235–8.* See *Exod.* xx 19: frightened by the thunder and lightning and trumpeting, the Israelites said to Moses: 'Speak thou with us, and we will hear: but let not God speak with us, lest we die.'

xii *238. what they besought*] *Ed I* has 'them their desire' followed by comma.

xii *238–44.* 'For Moses truly said unto the fathers, A prophet shall the Lord your God raise up unto you of your brethren, like unto me; him shall ye hear in all things whatsoever he shall say unto you' (*Acts* iii 22, citing *Deut.* xviii 15–19. Moses was regarded as a *figure* of Christ in his capacity as mediator. Cp. *De doctrina* i 15 (Columbia xv 287): 'The name and office of mediator is in a certain sense ascribed to Moses, as a type of Christ.' *laws and rites*] Described in typological terms in *Heb.* ix 19–23 (e.g. 'without shedding of blood is no remission').

xii *247–56.* The description of the Tabernacle in general follows *Exod.* xxv–xxvi; but mindful of his theme Michael adds from *Heb.* ix 4 the identification of the testimony as *The records of his Covenant.* The early edns indicate elision of the medial vowel of *Covenant.* *cedar*] not in *Exod.*; but cp. *Num.* xxiv 5–6, where tabernacles are compared to cedar trees. *mercy-seat*] see xi *2n.* *representing / The heavenly fires*] Josephus has several passages interpreting the details of the Tabernacle as cosmological symbols. See esp. *Antiq.* III vi 7, on the candlestick ('It terminated in seven heads, in one row, all standing parallel to one another; and these branches carried seven lamps, one by one, in imitation of the number of the planets'); *ibid.* III vii 7 ('By branching out the candlestick into seventy parts, he secretly intimated the *Decani*, or seventy divisions of the planets; and as to the seven lamps upon the candlesticks, they referred to the course

The holy one with mortal men to dwell:
By his prescript a sanctuary is framed
Of cedar, overlaid with gold, therein
An ark, and in the ark his testimony,
The records of his Covenant, over these
A mercy-seat of gold between the wings
Of two bright cherubim, before him burn
Seven lamps as in a zodiac representing
The heavenly fires; over the tent a cloud
Shall rest by day, a fiery gleam by night,
Save when they journey, and at length they come,
Conducted by his angel to the land
Promised to Abraham and his seed: the rest
Were long to tell, how many battles fought,
How many kings destroyed, and kingdoms won,
Or how the sun shall in mid heaven stand still
A day entire, and night's due course adjourn,
Man's voice commanding, sun in Gibeon stand,
And thou moon in the vale of Aialon,
Till Israel overcome; so call the third
From Abraham, son of Isaac, and from him
His whole descent, who thus shall Canaan win.
Here Adam interposed. O sent from heaven,
Enlightener of my darkness, gracious things
Thou hast revealed, those chiefly which concern
Just Abraham and his seed: now first I find

of the planets, of which that is the number'); and *De bellis* V v 5. These passages would be precious to M., as providing a means of unifying the astronomical and historical parts of his poem.

xii *256–8*. See *Exod.* xl 34–8.

xii *260*. For the promise to Abraham cp. ll. 137ff, and see *nn*.

xii *263–7*. See *Josh.* x 12f: 'Then spake Joshua to the Lord in the day when the Lord delivered up the Amorites before the children of Israel, and he said in the sight of Israel, Sun, stand thou still upon Gibeon; and thou, Moon, in the valley of Ajalon. And the sun stood still, and the moon stayed, until the people had avenged themselves upon their enemies. Is not this written in the book of Jasher? So the sun stood still in the midst of heaven, and hasted not to go down about a whole day.' The incident is often treated as an example of the power of Faith; as in Spenser, *F.Q.* I x 20, where it is linked (in the 1609 edn at least) with Moses' parting of the Red Sea–when Fidelia wished, 'She would commaund the hastie Sunne to stay, / Or backward turne his course from heauens hight; / Sometimes great hostes of men she could dismay, / Dry-shod to passe, she parts the flouds in tway.' Note that one of the themes projected in the *Trin. MS* is 'Joshua in Gibeon'. *Israel*] Jacob (see *Gen.* xxxii 28).

Mine eyes true opening, and my heart much eased,
Erewhile perplexed with thoughts what would become
Of me and all mankind; but now I see
His day, in whom all nations shall be blest,
Favour unmerited by me, who sought
Forbidden knowledge by forbidden means.
This yet I apprehend not, why to those
Among whom God will deign to dwell on earth
So many and so various laws are given;
So many laws argue so many sins
Among them; how can God with such reside?
To whom thus Michael. Doubt not but that sin
Will reign among them, as of thee begot;
And therefore was law given them to evince
Their natural pravity, by stirring up
Sin against law to fight; that when they see
Law can discover sin, but not remove,
Save by those shadowy expiations weak,
The blood of bulls and goats, they may conclude

xii *274. true opening*] Alludes to the serpent's false or ironic promise that the forbidden fruit will open man's eyes. Cp. xi 412ff.

xii *277.* The dramatic irony depends on familiarity with Christ's claim that 'before Abraham was I AM'. See *John* viii 56: 'Your father Abraham rejoiced to see my day: and he saw it, and was glad.' Adam means only that he can imagine the time of Abraham: he thinks the promise will be realised then. But he will learn that the blessing of ll. 147f contains another mystery still to be unfolded.

xii *285–306.* A statement of the relation of Law to Justification by Faith that covers central ground common to all Protestant theologians. This, together with the conciseness of the passage, puts the assigning of sources out of the question. The following texts, however, are somewhere in the background: *Rom.* iii 20, iv 22–5, v 1, 13, 17, 21, vii 7f, viii 15, x 5; *Heb.* vii 19, ix 13f, x 1–5; *Gal.* iii 4.

xii *287. evince*] Primarily 'make manifest' (*OED* 5), but secondarily 'overcome, subdue' (*OED* 1).

xii *288. pravity*] depravity.

xii *290.* Cp. *Rom.* iii 19f: The Law makes all guilty before God 'for by the law is the knowledge of sin'.

xii *291.* See ll. 238–44*n*. The Law being only a type, its sacrifices could not be efficacious like Christ's. See *Heb.* x 1: 'For the law having a shadow of good things to come, and not the very image of the things, can never with those sacrifices which they offered year by year continually make the comers thereunto perfect.'

Some blood more precious must be paid for man,
Just for unjust, that in such righteousness
To them by faith imputed, they may find
Justification towards God, and peace
Of conscience, which the law by ceremonies
Cannot appease, nor man the moral part
Perform, and not performing cannot live.
So law appears imperfect, and but given
With purpose to resign them in full time
Up to a better Covenant, disciplined
From shadowy types to truth, from flesh to spirit,
From imposition of strict laws, to free
Acceptance of large grace, from servile fear
To filial, works of law to works of faith.
And therefore shall not Moses, though of God
Highly beloved, being but the minister
Of law, his people into Canaan lead;
But Joshua whom the gentiles Jesus call,
His name and office bearing, who shall quell
The adversary serpent, and bring back
Through the world's wilderness long wandered man
Safe to eternal paradise of rest.
Meanwhile they in their earthly Canaan placed

xii *293*. Cp. *1 Pet.* i 18f: 'Ye know that ye were not redeemed with corruptible things, as silver and gold, from your vain conversation received by tradition from your fathers; But with the precious blood of Christ, as of a lamb without blemish and without spot.'
xii *294*. Cp. *1 Pet.* iii 18.
xii *297–8*. Cp. *Gal.* ii 16.
xii *300–6*. The thought follows *Gal.* iii 22–6. *but*] only. *resign*] consign; yield up with confidence (*OED* 2).
xii *307–11*. See *Deut.* xxxiv, *Josh.* i. In *De doctrina* i 26 (Columbia xvi 111) we find what is almost a prose version of the present passage. The Law fails to promise what faith in God through Christ has attained, eternal life: 'Thus the imperfection of the law was manifested in the person of Moses himself; for Moses, who was a type of the law, could not bring the children of Israel into the land of Canaan, that is, into eternal rest; but an entrance was given to them under Joshua, or Jesus.' *Jesus*] The Greek equivalent of *Joshua*; appearing as such in *Acts* vii 45 etc. Starnes 261 compares the wording of the entry on Joshua in Charles Estienne's *Dictionarium*: *Iosue, et Iesus, idem est nomen . . . Iosue, Typum Iesu Christi non solum in gestis, verum etiam in nomine genens, transiit Iordanem'*.
xii *313*. Clearly implying, like l. 190, a typological or mystical application of the O.T.; see Røstvig 187.

Long time shall dwell and prosper, but when sins
National interrupt their public peace,
Provoking God to raise them enemies:
From whom as oft he saves them penitent
By judges first, then under kings; of whom
The second, both for piety renowned
And puissant deeds, a promise shall receive
Irrevocable, that his regal throne
For ever shall endure; the like shall sing
All prophecy, that of the royal stock
Of David (so I name this king) shall rise
A son, the woman's seed to thee foretold,
Foretold to Abraham, as in whom shall trust
All nations, and to kings foretold, of kings
The last, for of his reign shall be no end.
But first a long succession must ensue,
And his next son for wealth and wisdom famed,
The clouded ark of God till then in tents
Wandering, shall in a glorious temple enshrine.
Such follow him, as shall be registered
Part good, part bad, of bad the longer scroll,
Whose foul idolatries, and other faults
Heaped to the popular sum, will so incense
God, as to leave them, and expose their land,
Their city, his temple, and his holy ark
With all his sacred things, a scorn and prey
To that proud city, whose high walls thou saw'st
Left in confusion, Babylon thence called.

xii *316*. *but*] except.
xii *320*. Cp. *Judges* ii 16.
xii *321–4*. David received a promise from the prophet Nathan, that 'thine house and thy kingdom shall be established for ever before thee: thy throne shall be established for ever' (*2 Sam.* vii 16).
xii *324–30*. In many O.T. passages (such as *Is.* xi 10 and *Ps.* lxxxix 36), the royal line or the seed of David has a Messianic significance. *Luke* i 32 applies this to Jesus: 'He shall be great, and shall be called the Son of the Highest: and the Lord God shall give unto him the throne of his father David.' For the promise to Adam, see x 180ff; for the confirming of it to Abraham, xii 125f and 147ff.
xii *332–4*. i.e. Solomon, who built the Temple to give the ark its first fixed location (*1 Kings* v–viii; *2 Chron.* ii–v). The building of the Temple was the occasion of yet another divine Covenant (*1 Kings* ix 1–9): hence its relevance here.
xii *338*. *Heaped . . . sum*] added to the sum of the people's faults.
xii *339–43*. See *2 Chron.* xxxvi, *2 Kings* xvii 24ff.

There in captivity he lets them dwell
The space of seventy years, then brings them back,
Remembering mercy, and his Covenant sworn
To David, stablished as the days of heaven.
Returned from Babylon by leave of kings
Their lords, whom God disposed, the house of God
They first re-edify, and for a while
In mean estate live moderate, till grown
In wealth and multitude, factious they grow;
But first among the priests dissension springs,
Men who attend the altar, and should most
Endeavour peace: their strife pollution brings
Upon the Temple it self: at last they seize
The sceptre, and regard not David's sons,
Then lose it to a stranger, that the true
Anointed king Messiah might be born
Barred of his right; yet at his birth a star

xii *344–7*. For the Babylonian captivity, see *Jer.* xxv 12 and xxxiii 20–6, where the return is related to the Covenant with David, and made as sure as the succession of day and night. Cp. the promise to David, *Ps.* lxxxix 29: 'His seed also will I make to endure for ever, and his throne as the days of heaven.' M.'s close juxtaposition of *seventy years* and *days of heaven* is possibly meant to recall Josephus' interpretation of the seventy parts of the candlestick of the Tabernacle as meaning 'the *Decani*, or seventy divisions of the planets' in the zodiac (see ll. 247–56*n*, and *Antiq.* III vii 7).
xii *348–50*. The rebuilding of Jerusalem is the subject of the Book of Ezra, and of *Neh.* i–vi; the Persian *kings* are Cyrus, Artaxerxes and Darius. *disposed*] put into a favourable mood (*OED* I 6).
xii *353–8*. *2 Macc.* iv–vi relates the *strife* between the intriguing priests Jason (Joshua), Menelaus (Onias) and Simon, which led indirectly to Antiochus' sacking Jerusalem and polluting the Temple. Two years later Greek forms of worship were imposed and the Temple at Jerusalem was rededicated to Jupiter Olympius. M. would see these events as an exemplum of the Church's betrayal with an obvious bearing on the history of his own time.
xii *356*. *they*] Refers to the Asmonean family, who held the high priesthood 153–35 B.C. One of them seized *the sceptre* to become Aristobulus I, thus ending the Israelite theocracy (see Josephus, *Antiq.* XIII xi 1).
xii *357*. *David's sons*] The descendants of David whose genealogy is traced in *Matt.* i and *Luke* iii.
xii *358*. *a stranger*] Antipater the Idumean (father of Herod the Great), who was made Procurator of Judaea by Julius Caesar in 47 B.C. (Josephus, *Antiq.* XIV viii 5).
xii *360–9*. Combining details from *Matt.* ii and *Luke* ii. *Barred*] Legal diction. *solemn*] holy (*OED* 1); awe-inspiring (*OED* 7). *thither*] To Bethlehem. *squadroned*] Cp. *Nativity Ode* 21. *power*] a deliberate

Unseen before in heaven proclaims him come,
And guides the eastern sages, who inquire
His place, to offer incense, myrrh, and gold;
His place of birth a solemn angel tells
To simple shepherds, keeping watch by night;
They gladly thither haste, and by a choir
Of squadroned angels hear his carol sung.
A virgin is his mother, but his sire
The power of the most high; he shall ascend
The throne hereditary, and bound his reign
With earth's wide bounds, his glory with the heavens.
He ceased, discerning Adam with such joy
Surcharged, as had like grief been dewed in tears,
Without the vent of words, which these he breathed.
O prophet of glad tidings, finisher
Of utmost hope! Now clear I understand
What oft my steadiest thoughts have searched in vain,
Why our great expectation should be called
The seed of woman: virgin Mother, hail,
High in the love of heaven, yet from my loins
Thou shalt proceed, and from thy womb the Son

formulation; cp. *De doctrina* i 14 (Columbia xv 281), where *Luke* i 35 ('The Holy Ghost shall come upon thee, and the power of the Highest shall overshadow thee') is taken to mean 'the power and spirit of the Father himself'.
xii *369–71*. The diction recalls Virgil's prophecy with respect to Augustus in *Aen.* i 287 (*imperium Oceano, famam qui terminet astris*), but the idea is probably of a terrestrial reign of Christ, prophesied in *Is.* ix 7, *Rev.* ii 25–7, etc. See particularly *Ps.* ii 8, where the kingdom stretches to 'the uttermost parts of the earth'; and *Dan.* vii 13–22, where its glory and dominion is everlasting. In *De doctrina* i 33 (Columbia xvi 359–63) M. writes at some length about this earthly kingdom of glory, which is to begin with Christ's second advent; he distinguishes it from the kingdom of grace, which began with the first advent. It is possible, however, that the present passage combines both kingdoms. See further in v 496–500*n*.
xii *373*. *Surcharged*] overwhelmed (*OED* 4).
xii *375–85*. As Burden 197f notes, Michael's first account of Christ is partly couched in epic terms, and Adam errs in his response by expecting an ordinary epic hero. To correct this response Michael will stress Christ's tragic role. *finisher*] 'one who reaches the end' (*OED* s.v. *Finish* v. 5); but there is also an irony, for Adam does not yet understand in what sense *Christ* is the 'finisher of our faith' (*Heb.* xii 2).
xii *379*. *seed of woman*] See x 179–81; still another facet of the promise becomes clear to Adam. *hail*] Cp. xi 158 and see *n*. Here ll. 379–82 is a catena of phrases from the angel's address to Mary at the Annunciation, Luke i 31–5.

Of God most high; so God with man unites.
Needs must the serpent now his capital bruise
Expect with mortal pain: say where and when
Their fight, what stroke shall bruise the victor's heel.
 To whom thus Michael. Dream not of their fight,
As of a duel, or the local wounds
Of head or heel: not therefore joins the Son
Manhood to Godhead, with more strength to foil
Thy enemy; nor so is overcome
Satan, whose fall from heaven, a deadlier bruise,
Disabled not to give thee thy death's wound:
Which he, who comes thy saviour, shall recure,
Not by destroying Satan, but his works
In thee and in thy seed: nor can this be,
But by fulfilling that which thou didst want,
Obedience to the law of God, imposed
On penalty of death, and suffering death,
The penalty to thy transgression due,
And due to theirs which out of thine will grow:
So only can high justice rest apaid.

xii *383. capital*] on the head (*OED* I 1); fatal (*OED* 2 d).
xii *386–7.* With the Fathers, and later with the medieval hymnists, the *duel* was a favourite image for what led to Christ's victory on the cross. (The idea has been studied by Bishop Aulén in *Den kristna försöningstanken*, of which there is an abridged English version by A. G. Hebert, *Christus Victor* (1931).) In M.'s view it is a misleading image, because insufficiently spiritual: there can be no conflict so equal and uncertain as a duel, with a being so transcendent as Christ (cp. *De doctrina* i 9, Columbia xv 104; also *PR* i 173ff).
xii *393. recure*] heal, cure.
xii *394–5.* Cp. *1 John* iii 8: 'For this purpose the Son of God was manifested, that he might destroy the works of the devil.'
xii *395–465.* Cp. iii 208ff. A speech of some importance, since it sets out the basis of the faith that Adam must have, before he can go out into the world as a justified sinner. As an attempt to define the Faith and distil the definition into a few lines, it must, perhaps inevitably, be considered a failure. There are too many technical theological terms condensed into too little emotional space. But if the passage is looked at in the context of the rest of Adam's confirmation course, it will be seen to have the proper complementary, even crowning, function. Its abstract and spiritual terms irrupt into the Jewish history as if from another level of discourse. Notice, however, the continuity of pace: Michael's narration has been steadily becoming more summary.
xii *401. apaid*] satisfied.

The law of God exact he shall fulfil
Both by obedience and by love, though love
Alone fulfil the law; thy punishment
He shall endure by coming in the flesh
To a reproachful life and cursed death,
Proclaiming life to all who shall believe
In his redemption, and that his obedience
Imputed becomes theirs by faith, his merits
To save them, not their own, though legal works.
For this he shall live hated, be blasphemed,
Seized on by force, judged, and to death condemned
A shameful and accurst, nailed to the cross
By his own nation, slain for bringing life;
But to the cross he nails thy enemies,
The law that is against thee, and the sins
Of all mankind, with him there crucified,
Never to hurt them more who rightly trust
In this his satisfaction; so he dies,
But soon revives, Death over him no power
Shall long usurp; ere the third dawning light
Return, the stars of morn shall see him rise
Out of his grave, fresh as the dawning light,

xii *403–4.* 'Love worketh no ill to his neighbour: therefore love is the fulfilling of the law' (*Rom.* xiii 10).
xii *406. cursed death*] See *Gal.* iii 13, citing *Deut.* xxi 23.
xii *409–10.* In the Protestant doctrine of Justification by Faith Imputation had an important part to play. It was held that Christ's righteousness and obedience were *imputed* to the believer. Thus by a legal fiction the sinner's misdeeds were covered by the merits of Christ. See *De doctrina* i 22 (Columbia xvi 24ff). *though legal*] though their works were in accordance with the law (there being no justification by works).
xii *412.* See iii 240*n*.
xii *416.* 'Blotting out the handwriting of ordinances that was against us, which was contrary to us, and took it out of the way, nailing it to his cross' (*Col.* ii 14).
xii *419. satisfaction*] Another theological term, meaning generally payment of a penalty due to God on account of man's sin. Here Christ's vicarious satisfaction is meant.
xii *422. stars of morn*] A complex phrase. Primarily, M. is using the morning star in a familiar way as an image of Christ's resurrection. (Based on the fact that the morning star is the same as the evening star that set to rise again, this symbolism goes back at least to Rabanus Maurus.) Secondarily, however, the stars may be angels; in which case *see* becomes literal and personal. Cp. v 708ff, where Satan has the face of the morning star. The opposition of true and false morning stars was also a patristic idea.

Thy ransom paid, which man from Death redeems,
His death for man, as many as offered life
Neglect not, and the benefit embrace
By faith not void of works: this Godlike act
Annuls thy doom, the death thou shouldst have died,
In sin for ever lost from life; this act
Shall bruise the head of Satan, crush his strength
Defeating Sin and Death, his two main arms,
And fix far deeper in his head their stings
Than temporal death shall bruise the victor's heel,
Or theirs whom he redeems, a death like sleep,
A gentle wafting to immortal life.
Nor after resurrection shall he stay
Longer on earth than certain times to appear
To his disciples, men who in his life
Still followed him; to them shall leave in charge
To teach all nations what of him they learned
And his salvation, them who shall believe
Baptising in the profluent stream, the sign
Of washing them from guilt of sin to life
Pure, and in mind prepared, if so befall,
For death, like that which the redeemer died.
All nations they shall teach; for from that day
Not only to the sons of Abraham's loins
Salvation shall be preached, but to the sons
Of Abraham's faith wherever through the world;
So in his seed all nations shall be blest.
Then to the heaven of heavens he shall ascend
With victory, triumphing through the air

xii *424. Thy*] Implies that Adam is being addressed as representative of fallen man.

xii *425–6.* Hinting at the doctrine of Election. See iii 173–202 ('saved who will').

xii *427. faith . . . works*] See xi 64*n*.

xii *433. temporal death*] The death of the body, which is described as a temporary sleep in *1 Thess.* iv 13–15.

xii *442. profluent*] flowing in a full stream; often figuratively, 'abundant'. M. thought baptism should be performed with running water; cp. *De doctrina* i 28 (Columbia xvi 169): 'Baptism, wherein the bodies of believers who engage themselves to pureness of life are immersed in running water [*in profluentem aquam*], to signify their regeneration by the Holy Spirit, and their union with Christ in his death, burial, and resurrection.'

xii *446–50.* The promise to Abraham (ll. 25f and 147ff) is now given a more precise spiritual interpretation, after *Gal.* iii 8 etc.

xii *452. triumphing*] Stressed on the second syllable.

Over his foes and thine; there shall surprise
The serpent, prince of air, and drag in chains
Through all his realm, and there confounded leave;
Then enter into glory, and resume
His seat at God's right hand, exalted high
Above all names in heaven; and thence shall come,
When this world's dissolution shall be ripe,
With glory and power to judge both quick and dead,
To judge the unfaithful dead, but to reward
His faithful, and receive them into bliss,
Whether in heaven or earth, for then the earth
Shall all be paradise, far happier place
Than this of Eden, and far happier days.
So spake the archangel Michael, then paused,
As at the world's great period; and our sire
Replete with joy and wonder thus replied.

xii *454*. Cp. *Rev.* xx 1f. *prince of air*] See *PR* i 39–41 and ii 117.
xii *458–65*. Cp. the earlier account of the Second Coming, at iii 321ff. Empson (127) thinks that *Whether in heaven or earth* indicates that M. is doubtful about the idea of the Millennium. But the phrase hardly puts an alternative. It is rather equivalent to 'both in heaven and on earth'. There are, however, two chains of discourse. If a backward syntactic link is made, it is the comprehensiveness of the Last Judgment that is being expressed: angels as well as men are to be judged (iii 331–5), the living as well as the dead. But when we come to make the primary forward link, the point is that bliss will be general, so that the distinction between heaven and earth is insignificant. Some will be received here, others there. *to judge both quick and dead*] Echoes the Apostles' Creed (or *Acts* x 42, *2 Tim.* iv 1 and *1 Pet.* iv 5).
xii *466–7*. This is Michael's second pause: the first was at xii 2. The three divisions of Adam's instruction are meant to correspond to the 'three drops' of the well of life placed in his eyes (see xi 416, xii 5*n*). Here the pause is compared with the world's period, whereas at xii 1f the comparison was with noon, the sixth hour. The underlying connection between the two time indications is a number symbolism. See Cowley 184: 'The ordinary *Traditional opinion* is, that the world is to last six thousand years . . . and that the *seventh Thousand* is to be the *Rest* or *Sabbath* of *Thousands*.' Diurnal and millennial divisions correspond, because 'one day is with the Lord as a thousand years' (*2 Pet.* iii 8, where the context is a prophecy of the Last Judgment). The tradition of six periods of redemptive history went back to St Augustine, *Civ. Dei* xxii 30. There the ages run: (1) Adam to the Flood, (2) the Flood to Abraham, (3) Abraham to David, (4) David to the Captivity, (5) the Captivity to the Nativity of Christ, and (6) the present

O goodness infinite, goodness immense!
That all this good of evil shall produce,
And evil turn to good; more wonderful
Than that which by creation first brought forth
Light out of darkness! Full of doubt I stand,

age, from the first to the second coming of Christ. M. adopts this scheme almost exactly. Thus the structure of the episode may be expressed in the form of a table:

Drop 1	*Drop 2*	*Drop 3*
xi 429–901	*xii 1–467*	*xii 468–605*
six-part vision	four narrations, divided by Adam's interpositions at xii 63, 270, 375, 469	narration
	SIX DAYS OR AGES OF HISTORY	
Age of Adam	four ages, from the Flood to the coming of Christ	Age of Second Adam, ending with the Second coming

xii *469–78*. In tracing the various aspects or 'causes' of the Fall, we have at last come to the Final Cause or end of the Fall: namely a greater *glory* for God and an opportunity for him to show his surpassing love through the sacrifice of Christ (Howard 165). On God's power to turn evil to good, cf. such passages as i 215ff, and see Lewis 66. The history of the idea of the Fortunate Fall is traced by A. O. Lovejoy in 'Milton and the Paradox of the Fortunate Fall', *ELH* iv (1937) 161–79. M.'s special contribution to the idea is an infusion of hard realism. He never allows us to lose sight of the plain misery brought by the Fall. We may rejoice in God's grace, not that man gave him occasion to exercise it. From the classic statement in the Hymn *O felix culpa* (Missal, *Exultet* for Holy Saturday), the idea of the Fortunate Fall is often referred to as a paradox; but it is noticeable that M. avoids paradox in its expression here. Contrast Salandra, *Adamo caduto* ii 14, where the expression is extravagantly paradoxical. Addison was right, however, to remark that at the end of the poem Adam is left triumphant in the depth of misery, while Satan is miserable in the height of his triumph. Some paradox is inherent in the story. Burden (37) notices the bearing of v 497–503, Raphael's prophecy of man's transmutation to spirit, on the present passage. He draws the inference that fallen man is not better off than if he had remained obedient; but perhaps the emphasis intended is rather that God's will for man is to be fulfilled in spite of the Fall, though in a more

Whether I should repent me now of sin
By me done and occasioned, or rejoice
Much more, that much more good thereof shall spring,
To God more glory, more good will to men
From God, and over wrath grace shall abound.
But say, if our deliverer up to heaven
Must reascend, what will betide the few
His faithful, left among the unfaithful herd,
The enemies of truth; who then shall guide
His people, who defend? Will they not deal
Worse with his followers than with him they dealt?
Be sure they will, said the angel; but from heaven
He to his own a Comforter will send,
The promise of the Father, who shall dwell
His Spirit within them, and the law of faith
Working through love, upon their hearts shall write,
To guide them in all truth, and also arm
With spiritual armour, able to resist
Satan's assaults, and quench his fiery darts,
What man can do against them, not afraid,
Though to the death, against such cruelties
With inward consolations recompensed,
And oft supported so as shall amaze
Their proudest persecutors: for the Spirit
Poured first on his apostles, whom he sends

difficult and surprising way. The present passage ironically echoes i 162ff, where Satan announced his intention of opposing Providence's bringing forth of good out of evil. This is perhaps the most important of a long sequence of echoes between the first and second halves of the poem, discussed by J. R. Watson in *EC* xiv (1964) 148–55.

xii *478*. Cp. *Rom.* v 20 ('where sin abounded, grace did much more abound') and *2 Cor.* iv 15.

xii *486*. *Comforter*] The Holy Spirit. See *John* xiv 18 and xv 26: 'When the Comforter is come, whom I will send unto you from the Father, even the Spirit of truth, which proceedeth from the Father, he shall testify of me.' M. believed that the Holy Spirit was either God the Father himself, or his divine power; see *De doctrina* i 6.

xii *488–9*. Cp. *Rom.* iii 27 ('of works? Nay: but by the law of faith'); *Gal.* v 6 ('neither circumcision availeth any thing, nor uncircumcision; but faith which worketh by love'); and *Heb.* viii 10.

xii *491*. *spiritual armour*] Alluding to the allegory in *Eph.* vi 11–17. The most important part of the armour is Faith (vi 16): 'Above all, taking the shield of faith, wherewith ye shall be able to quench all the fiery darts of the wicked.'

xii *495*. Cp. *SA* 663–6: 'consolation from above: / Secret refreshings'.

xii *497–502*. Referring to events narrated, e.g., in *Acts* ii and x.

To evangelize the nations, then on all
Baptized, shall them with wondrous gifts endue
To speak all tongues, and do all miracles,
As did their Lord before them. Thus they win
Great numbers of each nation to receive
With joy the tidings brought from heaven: at length
Their ministry performed, and race well run,
Their doctrine and their story written left,
They die; but in their room, as they forewarn,
Wolves shall succeed for teachers, grievous wolves,
Who all the sacred mysteries of heaven
To their own vile advantages shall turn
Of lucre and ambition, and the truth
With superstitions and traditions taint,
Left only in those written records pure,
Though not but by the Spirit understood.

xii *505*. The metaphor is Pauline: see *1 Cor.* ix 24, *2 Tim.* iv 7, *Heb.* xii 1.
xii *507–8*. 'For I know this, that after my departing shall grievous wolves enter in among you, not sparing the flock' (*Acts* xx 29). Cp. the simile comparing Satan to a wolf in the fold, at iv 183–7 above; also *Lycidas* 113ff and *Cromwell* 14 ('hireling wolves whose gospel is their maw'). The whole passage that follows, down to l. 537, should be regarded, not as an attack on the Church of Rome or of England, but as a general condemnation of everything in the Church that is not built by Faith. See, however, Schultz 127, who argues that M.'s portrayal of Antichrist is specifically directed against Rome.
xii *511*. See *1 Pet.* v 2: 'Feed the flock of God which is among you, taking the oversight thereof. . . not for filthy lucre, but of a ready mind.' M. wrote a tract on the subject, the *Considerations touching the likeliest means to remove hirelings out of the Christian Church* (Yale vii).
xii *511–22*. It was an important article of Protestant belief that in doctrinal matters the ultimate arbiter is individual conscience rather than mere authority. Those to the left of the Anglican position even held, with Henry Robinson, that 'there is no *medium* between an implicite faith, and that which a mans owne judgement and understanding leads him to' (*cit.* Yale ii 543*n*). (Implicit faith was unquestioning acceptance of the doctrines of the Church, on the authority of the higher clergy.) M. often expresses contempt for dependence on patristic and other authorities, the 'muddy pool of conformity and tradition' (*Areopagitica*, Yale *ibid.*) Cp. *De doctrina* i 30 (Columbia xvi 281): 'We are expressly forbidden to pay any regard to human traditions, whether written or unwritten' (citing *Deut.* iv 2 etc.). See also *1 Cor.* ii 14f: 'the natural man receiveth not the things of the Spirit of God: for they are foolishness unto him: neither can he know them, because they are spiritually discerned. But he that is spiritual judgeth all things.'

Then shall they seek to avail themselves of names,
Places and titles, and with these to join
Secular power, though feigning still to act
By spiritual, to themselves appropriating
The Spirit of God, promised alike and given
To all believers; and from that pretence,
Spiritual laws by carnal power shall force
On every conscience; laws which none shall find
Left them enrolled, or what the Spirit within
Shall on the heart engrave. What will they then
But force the spirit of grace it self, and bind
His consort liberty; what, but unbuild
His living temples, built by faith to stand,
Their own faith not another's: for on earth
Who against faith and conscience can be heard
Infallible? Yet many will presume:
Whence heavy persecution shall arise
On all who in the worship persevere
Of spirit and truth; the rest, far greater part,
Well deem in outward rites and specious forms
Religion satisfied; truth shall retire

xii *515–24*. The corruption of the Church through its pursuit of *Secular power* is a subject M. had dealt with at large in *Of Reformation* (Yale i). In *De doctrina* i 30 (Columbia xvi 281) he condemns the enforcement of obedience to human opinions or authority (*sanctiones quascunque . . . et dogmata*): no modern church or magistrate is entitled 'to impose on believers a creed nowhere found in Scripture, or which is merely inferred from thence by human reasons carrying with them no certain conviction.' *laws which . . . engrave*] laws neither written in Scripture nor in the individual conscience (*Jer.* xxxi 33). Cp. *Doctrine and Discipline*, Pref. (Yale ii 237), 'A Law not onely writt'n by *Moses*, but character'd in us by nature . . . which Law is to force nothing against the faultles proprieties of nature.'
xii *526*. Cp. *2 Cor.* iii 17: 'Now the Lord is that Spirit: and where the Spirit of the Lord is, there is liberty.'
xii *527*. Cp. *1 Cor.* iii 17: 'The temple of God is holy, which temple ye are.'
xii *528–30*. Not aimed exclusively at the Church of Rome. Infallibility was often held to reside in the edicts of the Oecumenical Councils and in articles of faith common to the whole Church. Yet, even though the doctrine of Papal Infallibility was not devised until 1870, there can be no doubt that Rome is M.'s *main* target here. In *A Treatise of Civil Power* he writes that the 'Pope assumes infallibility over conscience and scripture' (Columbia vi 8).
xii *532–3*. Cp. *John* iv 23: 'True worshippers shall worship the Father in spirit and in truth.'
xii *534*. *Well*] Will *Ed I*.

Bestuck with slanderous darts, and works of faith
Rarely be found: so shall the world go on,
To good malignant, to bad men benign,
Under her own weight groaning till the day
Appear of respiration to the just,
And vengeance to the wicked, at return
Of him so lately promised to thy aid
The woman's seed, obscurely then foretold,
Now amplier known thy saviour and thy Lord,
Last in the clouds from heaven to be revealed
In glory of the Father, to dissolve
Satan with his perverted world, then raise
From the conflagrant mass, purged and refined,
New heavens, new earth, ages of endless date
Founded in righteousness and peace and love
To bring forth fruits joy and eternal bliss.
He ended; and thus Adam last replied.
How soon hath thy prediction, seer blest,
Measured this transient world, the race of time,
Till time stand fixed: beyond is all abyss,

xii *536*. *works of faith*] Cp. l. 427 and see *n*.
xii *537*. Some copies *Ed I* omit comma after *on*.
xii *539*. Cp. *Rom.* viii 22: 'For we know that the whole creation groaneth and travaileth in pain together until now.'
xii *539–51*. Note how *groaning* refers back to nature's groans at the Fall of Adam and Eve (ix 783, 1001), while *respiration* looks forward to a new breath, like that by which life was first inspired in man (vii 526, cf. i 7). The day of judgment is called *day . . . of respiration* because of *Acts* iii 19: 'Repent ye therefore, and be converted, that your sins may be blotted out, when the times of refreshing shall come from the presence of the Lord', where *refreshing* translates Gk. ἀνάψυξις (Vulg. *refrigerium*, but elsewhere sometimes transl. *respiratio*). M. may also, however, be thinking of A.V. *Esther* iv 14: 'Then shall there enlargement [marg. 'respiration'] and deliverance arise to the Jews from another place.' *respiration*] opportunity for breathing again; rest (*OED* 3). The whole passage should be compared with ll. 446ff and with iii 321ff; all three are apocalyptic prophecies drawing on the same Biblical texts. The promise to Eve (x 179ff) is here given a final gloss, this time an eschatological one.
xii *546*. *dissolve*] annihilate, destroy (*OED* 6, 7).
xii *548*. *purged and refined*] Cp. xi 900f and see *n*.
xii *551*. Having begun with the immediate 'effects' of touching the forbidden tree (xi 424), Michael now ends with the final *fruits* Cp. i 1ff.
xii *555*. Cp. the vision of *Rev.* x 6, in which an angel swore 'that there should be time no longer'. Some copies *Ed I* have semicolon after *fixed*.

Eternity, whose end no eye can reach.
Greatly instructed I shall hence depart,
Greatly in peace of thought, and have my fill
Of knowledge, what this vessel can contain;
Beyond which was my folly to aspire.
Henceforth I learn, that to obey is best,
And love with fear the only God, to walk
As in his presence, ever to observe
His providence, and on him sole depend,
Merciful over all his works, with good
Still overcoming evil, and by small
Accomplishing great things, by things deemed weak
Subverting worldly strong, and worldly wise
By simply meek; that suffering for truth's sake
Is fortitude to highest victory,
And to the faithful death the gate of life;
Taught this by his example whom I now
Acknowledge my redeemer ever blest.
To whom thus also the angel last replied:
This having learned, thou hast attained the sum
Of wisdom; hope no higher, though all the stars
Thou knew'st by name, and all the ethereal powers,
All secrets of the deep, all nature's works,
Or works of God in heaven, air, earth, or sea,
And all the riches of this world enjoyed'st,
And all the rule, one empire; only add

xii *559. vessel*] Not the Pauline metaphor for the body (as at *1 Thess.* iv 4); implying rather the limitations of human nature as a created entity: cp. *Jer.* xviii 4, xlviii 38, *Rev.* ii 27, etc. For the submission of the intellect, cp. Adam's speech to Raphael, beginning viii 179ff.

xii *561–73.* Steadman 99f argues that Adam has learned the correct form of the virtues of obedience and *fortitude* from the example of Messiah. Stripped of virtue in the Fall (ix 1062f) he recovers it through regeneration.

xii *561. to obey is best*] Cp. *1 Sam.* xv 22, 'to obey is better than sacrifice'.

xii *565. Merciful*] Cp. *Ps.* cxlv 9, 'his tender mercies are over all his works.'

xii *566. overcoming evil*] Cp. *Rom.* xii 21, 'overcome evil with good'.

xii *567. things deemed weak*] Cp. *1 Cor.* i 27: 'God hath chosen the weak things of the world to confound the things which are mighty'.

xii *576–81.* Cp. the exhortation of Raphael at viii 167–78. *secrets of the deep*] Recalls Uriel's speech about the impossibility of any created mind comprehending the wisdom that hid the causes of God's works (iii 705ff). Cp. also *Job* xxviii 28, 'the fear of the Lord, that is wisdom'.

xii *581–7.* Cp. *2 Pet.* i 5–7: 'Add to your faith virtue; and to virtue knowledge; And to knowledge temperance; and to temperance patience; and to patience godliness; And to godliness brotherly kindness; and to brotherly kindness charity.' M., however, subtracts godliness and brotherly love, and

Deeds to thy knowledge answerable, add faith,
Add virtue, patience, temperance, add love,
By name to come called Charity, the soul
Of all the rest: then wilt thou not be loath
To leave this Paradise, but shalt possess
A paradise within thee, happier far.
Let us descend now therefore from this top
Of speculation; for the hour precise
Exacts our parting hence; and see the guards,
By me encamped on yonder hill, expect

adds *deeds*; giving seven conditions of fruitfulness. These he arranges with some care; e.g. *virtue* is given fourth place, because the tetrad is a form of the *tetraktys*, which in Pythagorean symbolism is the fountain of virtue. Significantly, this puts virtue in the sovereign central place, so that we might say of Adam, as Cowley 195 of Brutus, 'Virtue was thy *Lifes* Center'–an emphasis which M. balances by asserting (after *1 Cor.* xiii) the primacy of *love* or *charity*. The seven qualities constitute a complete world or microcosm, which is seen as replacing the earthly Paradise (love as the animating soul of a world was a common idea in Platonic cosmogonies).
xii *587. paradise within*] contrast the 'hell within' of Satan, iv 20ff. G. C. Taylor, *PQ* xxviii (1949) 208, compares the title of Robert Croft's *A Paradice within us; or the Happie Mind* (1640), a book of consolation which gives pious and practical advice about how to attain an internal paradise of health and integration and spiritual comfort. Croft's exhortations are couched in terms not unlike Michael's: 'Let us possesse our minds with livelinesse, quicknesse, perspicacity, and gallantness of spirit, with moderation, Temperance, Humility, Meekenesse, Tranquility, Mildnesse, with Contentation, Fortitude, Cherefulnesse, with Humanity, Affability, Love, Kindnesse, and with all Joy and Happinesse. . . . So as to enjoy even a Paradice of delights and happinesse within us.'
xii *587*. Some copies *Ed I* omit comma after *thee*.
xii *588–9. top / Of speculation*] vantage-point (*OED* s.v. *Speculation* I 2 c); but also 'height of theological speculation'. *hour precise*] The emphasis on the time (noon) is for two reasons. First, noon is the termination of the twenty-four-hour period beginning at the noon of the Fall (ix 739), so that the 'day' referred to in the Prohibition (viii 329–32) is in one sense only now accomplished. Hence, by a last bitter peripeteia, the terms of the Prohibition acquire yet another meaning: Adam and Eve die, in the sense of leaving Paradise for the mortal world, on 'that day' when they sinned. Secondly, noon was the sixth hour, the actual time of the Expulsion, according to Hugh of St-Victor; but also the hour of the Fall, as well as of the Crucifixion (see Bongo 280; also x 1050*n*, xii 1*n*). Thus the Expulsion becomes itself a Janus image, looking back to the Fall and forward to the Crucifixion and Redemption of man.
xii *591–3. expect / Their motion*] await deployment, transfer, marching

Their motion, at whose front a flaming sword,
In signal of remove, waves fiercely round;
We may no longer stay: go, waken Eve;
Her also I with gentle dreams have calmed
Portending good, and all her spirits composed
To meek submission: thou at season fit
Let her with thee partake what thou hast heard,
Chiefly what may concern her faith to know,
The great deliverance by her seed to come
(For by the woman's seed) on all mankind.
That ye may live, which will be many days,
Both in one faith unanimous though sad,
With cause for evils past, yet much more cheered
With meditation on the happy end.
He ended, and they both descend the hill;
Descended, Adam to the bower where Eve
Lay sleeping ran before, but found her waked;

orders (military diction; see *OED* s.v. *Motion* 5). *remove*] Sustains the military diction: 'departure' (*OED* 5 b, citing Markham, 1622, 'he may then cause the Drumme-major to beat a remove'). *flaming sword*] See l. 643*n*.

xii *594–605*. Michael's final summing-up emphasizes the two themes of the visions: *submission* (or resignation) and *faith*. The two are balanced carefully here in the single phrase *one faith unanimous though sad*: Adam is to look in resignation at the Fall and its consequences, but in faith forward to Christ's victory and the unification of God and man. Throughout the final books of the poem, the opposition of the two themes has received a subtle and constantly renewed expression at the formal level. For the terms of the Prohibition and the terms of the promise to Eve have both received continual reinterpretations and enlargements balanced one against the other. Thus M. imitates the psychological process whereby Adam's understanding of the curse and of the promise grows; yet at the same time imparts a numinous sense of the mysteriousness of God's providence. Michael's last speech gives each series of interpretations its final term, but with a difference. The Expulsion is a matter of fact, the bruising of the serpent a matter of faith. Hence M.'s balance of the two series is itself an expression of his faith in the literal truth of the promise.

xii *601*. (*For by the woman's seed*)] for it will be by one born of a virgin (l. 368). Some copies of *Ed I* have comma after *mankind*.

xii *602*. *many days*] Adam lived to be 930 years of age (*Gen.* v 5).

xii *603*. Some copies *Ed I* omit comma after *unanimous*.

xii *604*. *With cause for*] with good reason; in view of.

xii *607*. Some copies *Ed I* omit comma after *descended*.

xii *608*. Apparently in contradiction to the Argument, where 'Adam . . . wakens Eve'.

And thus with words not sad she him received.
Whence thou return'st, and whither went'st, I know;
For God is also in sleep, and dreams advise,
Which he hath sent propitious, some great good
Presaging, since with sorrow and heart's distress
Wearied I fell asleep: but now lead on;
In me is no delay; with thee to go,
Is to stay here; without thee here to stay,
Is to go hence unwilling; thou to me
Art all things under heaven, all places thou,
Who for my wilful crime art banished hence.
This further consolation yet secure
I carry hence; though all by me is lost,
Such favour I unworthy am vouchsafed,
By me the promised seed shall all restore.
So spake our mother Eve, and Adam heard
Well pleased, but answered not; for now too nigh
The archangel stood, and from the other hill
To their fixed station, all in bright array
The cherubim descended; on the ground
Gliding meteorous, as evening mist
Risen from a river o'er the marish glides,
And gathers ground fast at the labourer's heel
Homeward returning. High in front advanced,

xii *611*. Cp. *Num.* xii 6: 'If there be a prophet among you, I the Lord will make myself known unto him in a vision, and will speak unto him in a dream.' The authorities on the various types of dream were Artemidorus (*Oneirocritica*) and Macrobius (*In somn. Scip.* I iii 2–17). The prophetic vision (Lat. *visio*) was defined as a dream that 'actually comes true' (*ibid.* 9).
xii *615–23*. Cp. x 738–40 and see *n.* Eve has submissively assimilated Michael's exhortation at xi 292: 'where [Adam] abides, think there thy native soil'. There is also a resonance with Eve's song at iv 634–56 (every time of day is pleasing with, none without, Adam).
xii *626. archangel*] Two words in some copies *Ed I.*
xii *629–32. meteorous*] (=*meteoric*, from Gk μετέωρος): pertaining to the region of mid-air (*OED* 1 a). In the seventeenth century the term 'meteor' was applied to almost any atmospheric phenomenon, but especially to luminous bodies and exhalations such as fireballs, shooting stars, comets and the *ignis fatuus*. *marish*] marsh. Richardson 533, with the approval of Ricks 109 returns to the derivative meaning of *meteorous* ('raised on high'), and contrasts the raised (and, one might add, luminous) mist of the good angels with the 'black mist low creeping' of Satan at ix 180. Clearly this is right, so far as it goes; but it is too simple. For, as Svendsen 107–12 points out in a fascinating if incompletely perspicuous discussion of the passage, Satan has also been compared to a delusively bright mist, at ix

The brandished sword of God before them blazed
Fierce as a comet; which with torrid heat,
And vapour as the Lybian air adust,
Began to parch that temperate clime; whereat
In either hand the hastening angel caught
Our lingering parents, and to the eastern gate
Led them direct, and down the cliff as fast
To the subjected plain; then disappeared.
They looking back, all the eastern side beheld
Of Paradise, so late their happy seat,
Waved over by that flaming brand, the gate

633–41. And the guardian cherubim almost seem like demons at l. 644 (see *n*). As Svendsen 111 puts it: 'Adam's sin has made the Cherubim so, has altered their relation to him.' Or, at least sin *may* make the cherubim seem so, if they are not viewed with the eyes of faith. For Svendsen is wrong to contrast the situation of the labourer with that of Adam and Eve. Fallen man is indeed by God's curse a *labourer* (though the mention of *heel* balances this curse as ever with the promise of *Gen.* iii 15). And the hour of the Expulsion is a time of transition from the immortal to the mortal world, just as the labourer at *evening* passes from light to darkness. True, the mist is dreadful; but we know that 'to the faithful death [is] the gate of life' (l. 571): Michael has shown Adam that, though he is exiled, he may eventually, like the labourer, return home.

xii *633–6. adust*] scorched, burnt up; dried up with heat; parched. Swan and Gadbury tell us that a comet in the shape of a sword signifies war and the destruction of cities (Svendsen 92f). Again it requires faith to see a distinction between this comparison with a comet and the comparison of Satan with a comet at ii 706–11. The *Libyan air* simile alludes to a common gloss of the 'flaming sword' of *Gen.* iii 24, which explained it as the '*torrida zona*, the parching countrie under the aequinoctiall' (Willet 54). This explanation is not St Thomas Aquinas's (*pace* Hughes), but goes back to Tertullian; it depended on a belief that the torrid zone was uninhabitable. On the equatorial location of the terrene Paradise, see iv 280–5*n* above. Cp. also the separate account of the beginning of climatic extremes, at x 651ff.

xii *637–8*. The physical detail is transferred from Gen. xix 16, which describes the angels' conduct of Lot and his family from doomed Sodom. There is a resonance also with l. 648.

xii *640*. 'We have descended with Adam and Eve to our own mundane world' (MacCaffrey 59). *subjected*] underlying, placed underneath (*OED* s.v. *Subjected* 1); submissive, obedient (*OED* 2). On submission as a theme of xii see ll. 594–605*n*.

xii *643*. Cp. *Gen.* iii 24, 'a flaming sword which turned every way'. M. here, as at xi 120 ('of a sword the flame / Wide waving') follows the Chaldee Paraphrast in understanding a literal sword 'which by the shaking seemeth to glitter as the flame of fire' (Willet 57).

With dreadful faces thronged and fiery arms:
Some natural tears they dropped, but wiped them
soon;
The world was all before them, where to choose
Their place of rest, and providence their guide:
They hand in hand with wandering steps and slow,
Through Eden took their solitary way.

THE END

xii *644*. W. B. Hunter in *MLR* xliv (1949) 89–91 cites John Petters, *Volatiles from the History of Adam and Eve* (1674): 'By this flaming sword etc. is meant an order of evil Angels, appointed also to guard the way to the tree of life'; and Svendsen (107) thinks that the *dreadful faces* make the cherubim 'strangely like Satan and his cohorts'. But it seems better to take 'dreadful' as a subjective description: guilt is a not uncommon cause of fear. Besides, even if the cherubim were objectively dreadful, that would not make them evil.

xii *645*. Burden 200 notes the careful balance of woe and joy.

xii *647*. Note that *providence* can be the object of *choose*: decisions of faith lie ahead.

xii *648*. The joining of hands is a hieroglyph of the pledging of faith. Svendsen 111f cites Camerarius, who 'in *The Living Librarie* collects numerous examples of such symbolism from Alexander of Alexandria, Numa Pompilius, and others to show the joining of hands as a consecration of faith.' She traces several earlier symbolic uses of hand imagery in *PL*, but perhaps the strongest echoes here are of iv 321 ('hand in hand they passed'), of the separation at ix 385f ('from her husband's hand her hand / Soft she withdrew') and of the corrupt sexuality in ix 1037 ('Her hand he seized'). There has been endless controversy about the propriety of the epithets; from which the main points to emerge are that *wandering* implies 'erring' and *slow* 'reluctant'. Thus the line could be said to counterbalance previous consolations and make terror the last passion left in the mind of the reader, were it not for the hope resting in the clasped hands. As often in *PL*, the positive aspect is the implicit one. The iconography of the Expulsion is discussed from a different point of view in M. Y. Hughes, 'Some Illustrators of Milton: the Expulsion from Paradise', in *JEGP* lx (1961). Some copies *Ed I* omit comma after *slow*.

xii *649*. Eden refers not to Paradise but to the country round it: see i 4 and iv 209–16*n*. Cp. *Ps*. cvii 4: 'They wandered in the wilderness in a solitary way; they found no city to dwell in.' But those who heard the echo of this psalm would also remember the continuation: 'Then they cried unto the Lord . . . And he led them forth by the right way, that they might go to a city of habitation.'

Paradise Regained

Edited by

JOHN CAREY

94 Paradise Regained

Date. 1667–70. Edward Phillips records that *PR* 'was begun and finisht and Printed after the other [*PL*] was publisht [i.e. 1667], and that in a wonderful short space considering the sublimeness of it; however it is generally censur'd to be much inferiour to the other, though he [M.] could not hear with patience any such thing when related to him' (Darbishire 75–6). *PR* was licensed 2 Jul. 1670, and entered on the Stationers' Register 10 Sep. (French v 17). Thomas Ellwood, rightly or wrongly, considered himself in some part responsible for the engendering of *PR:* he relates that, on returning to M. an MS of *PL* which M. had lent him, he said 'Thou hast said much here of *Paradise lost*; but what hast thou to say of *Paradise found*? He made me no answer, but sate some time in a Muse'. This incident is not datable, but may have occurred about Aug. 1665. 'And when afterwards I went to wait on him there[in London] . . . he shewed me his Second Poem, called *Paradise Regained*; and in a pleasant tone said to me, *This is owing to you*; *for you put it into my head by the question you put to me at* Chalfont; *which before I had not thought of*' (*History of the Life of Thomas Ellwood* (1714) 233–4).
Publication. *1671* (for details of this volume see headnote to *SA*, p. 332 above).
Modern criticism. The most thorough studies of *PR* are Pope and Lewalski. Pope undertakes an examination of the temptation tradition from the gospel onwards, noting the similarities and the differences between M.'s and previous treatments.

In the order of the three temptations M., unlike most medieval and Renaissance theologians and artists, follows *Luke* iv 1–13, rather than *Matt.* iv 1–11, which reverses the second and third. However, he follows *Matt.* in placing the three temptations after Christ's forty-day fast. In *Luke* Christ is 'forty days tempted of the devil'. Many biblical commentators assumed that there were other temptations, not mentioned by the evangelists: M. introduces two–the banqueting scene and the storm–not found in previous accounts.

In adopting the view that Christ underwent temptation only as a man, and hence did not use divine power to drive the devil away, M. was in agreement with a long line of theologians from Ambrose on (see the emphasis on Christ's manhood in *PR* i *4*, *36–7*, *122*, *150–67*, etc.). He stops short, however, of the extreme form of this theory, which was that Christ was tempted inwardly 'by his own corruption' (as the theologian Diodati put it, in opposing this interpretation): M.'s temptations are orthodox in their externality. Where M. does deviate from the majority of exegetes is in refusing Christ both foreknowledge of the temptation (in this, however, Paraeus had preceded him), and power over his own appetite (see *PR* i *290–3*, ii *245–59*).

The equation between the fall of man and the temptation of Christ is another of M.'s traditional properties. From patristic times it had been common to argue that the three sins Christ refused to commit were the three Adam had committed (gluttony, vainglory, avarice), and contained within themselves all other sins (see i *154–5*, *161–2*, ii *132–43*). M. innovates by making the temptations to all these sins occur on the second day of the temptation (see ii *337–65n*, and iii *25–30n*), and for the sake, Pope thinks, of drama and surprise, he turns the pinnacle scene from a temptation to vainglory into a murderous identity test. The storm, which he introduces beforehand, can be regarded as a temptation by violence which, as Satan points out (iv *477–83*), prefigures the passion (see, however, iv *464–83n*).

During the Middle Ages and the Renaissance it was widely assumed that Satan's chief object in attempting to seduce Christ was to find out if he really was the Son of God or, if he was, whether by nature or merely by grace. The first and the last temptations were seen as attempts to elicit from Christ an acknowledgement of his divinity, and some theologians argued also that Satan's impudent assertion that he owned the world (in the temptation of the kingdoms) was intended to provoke a counter-claim from Christ. A number of Protestant theologians (including Calvin, Knox and Taylor) rejected this whole hypothesis, however, and argued that Satan had no doubt that the Christ he was tempting was the promised Messiah. Modern critics disagree about M.'s view. Pope and Lewalski consider that M.'s Satan really is confused by the term 'Son of God' (iv *517–20*). Pope also thinks that Christ deliberately withholds evidence of his identity from Satan, but Lewalski argues that Christ is almost as much in the dark as Satan most of the time: to see Christ undergoing temptation with full consciousness of his divinity would be to destroy the dramatic conflict of *PR*. Allen (110–21) regards Satan's uncertainty about Christ's identity as a pretence, citing i *356* (but see note to this line), *475–7* (an admission which may, however, be a mere stratagem of Satan's) and iv *525* (but compare iv *535–6*). For diplomatic reasons, says Allen, Satan maintains the illusory doubt. The real doubt that lurks in his mind, though, is about his own failing powers as a corrupter. What motivates him is fear (see i *66*, *94–5*, iv *195*). His claim that he is beyond fear (iii *206*) is quickly contradicted (iii *220*), and his fear, turning to panic, drives him, as Allen sees it, to the violence of the storm and of the pinnacle, though he had assured his followers that he would not use force (i *97*). What uncertainty there is in the poem, Allen insists, is not in Satan but in the disciples (ii *11–12*), in Mary (ii *70*) and in Christ who, in his divine nature knows his identity and foresees his course, but in his human nature is often uncertain of both. During the poem he crosses and recrosses the boundary between the two natures: by himself he is uncertain (i *287–93*), but confronted by Satan he flares into divine certainty (ii *383–4*, iv *151*, *178–81*, *190–1*).

Stein[2], like Allen, stresses Satan's limitations: compared with the Satan of *PL* he is a severely diminished antagonist. His understanding is weakened (see ii *337–65n*): Christ's speech, ii *473–80*, would otherwise be enough to make clear to him the futility of offering the kingdoms-of-the-world temptation: but Satan is blinded by his obsession with power–all his temptations, even that of learning, are offered in terms of power. Stein, however, agrees with Pope that one of Satan's objectives is to discover Christ's identity.

Lewalski's main thesis is that *PR* is an example of 'that Epick form whereof . . . the book of Job [is] a brief model', as M. put it in *Reason of Church Government* (Columbia iii 237, Yale i 183). She firmly opposes Tillyard (316) who claims that *PR* 'is not an epic . . does not try to be an epic, and . . . must not be judged by any kind of epic standard'. She first surveys the history of the idea of the *Book of Job* as epic from patristic times to the seventeenth century, discovering that the dominant tradition emphasized *Job* i and ii and scanted the dialogues that follow, so that the two councils in heaven and the trials inflicted on Job by Satan came to be regarded as the main elements in the story. These, she claims, are the basis of *PR*'s structure: M. writes his brief epic on the Jobean model. Lewalski also undertakes an extended survey of the genre of the biblical brief epic, enlarging upon B.O. Kurth's attempt in *M. and Christian Heroism* (Berkeley 1959) to relate M.'s heroic ideals in *PR* to contemporary English biblical poems. She finds that the heavenly and hellish councils, the geographical catalogue of worldly kingdoms, the detailed descriptions of particular cities, the account of the hero's reading and education, the choice of a 'peaceful' New Testament subject (along with the intimation that it is vastly superior to the old heroic themes), and the four-book division, were common features of the genre during the humanist period. M., unlike most of the humanist writers in the genre, does not take over and Christianize the pagan supernatural nomenclature (Olympus, Avernus etc.), and he manages to give Christ's character much of the psychological interest previously found only in Old Testament heroes subject to human doubts and frailties, like Du Bartas's Judith and Robert Aylett's David. The only previous example Lewalski finds of a brief biblical epic which uses the *Book of Job* as its structural model but does not take Job as its subject is Robert Aylett's *Joseph* (1623). The only previous example she finds of a brief epic which takes the temptation as its subject is Jacobus Strasburgus's *Oratio Prima* (1565).

The two issues central to *PR*'s dramatic action, in Lewalski's view, are Christ's identity and his mission. Christ and Satan begin more or less in ignorance of both. Neither understands that Christ is the 'first-begot' who drove Satan from heaven and Christ has only partial knowledge of his future roles (i *221–3, 254, 264–7*). To clarify the first issue Lewalski peruses the christology of the *De doctrina* and concludes that there, and presumably in *PR*, M. conceives of an incarnate Christ who has really emptied himself of divine understanding and will (Columbia xiv 275, 343) and who can therefore be educated and illuminated by the Father (Columbia xv 275, *PR* i *291–3*). Christ, she argues, withstands each of the temptations with his limited, human understanding, and then merits a special illumination after each (e.g. *PR* i *355–6, 460–4*, ii *381–4*, iv *146–53, 561*) bringing him to perfect and divine understanding of the aspect of himself that has been under attack in the previous temptation. Protestant commentators, and M. himself in the *De doctrina*, saw Christ's mission as threefold: he was to be prophet (or teacher, a role for which the Old Testament types were Moses and Elijah), king (over his church and his heavenly kingdom: the types were David and

Solomon) and priest (by his sacrificial death and intercession for man: the types were Job and Melchisedec). A number of commentaries, including those of William Perkins and Thomas Taylor, linked the three temptations with these three aspects of the mediatorial office. Lewalski argues that *PR* deals with each aspect in turn, and that they are basic to its structure. So is the typology, since Christ defines himself in relation to the earlier types, both Old Testament and classical (Socrates, Hercules etc.) and Satan's strategy is to get Christ to identify himself with inferior types (e.g. the oracles, i *393–6*, and Balaam, i *490–2*, inferior types of the prophetic office, and Alexander, Caesar, Pompey, Scipio, iii *31–42*, David, iii *152–3*, *370–5*, iv *106–8*, and Judas Maccabaeus, iii *165*, inferior types of the kingly office). By reading all *PR*'s Old Testament and classical allusions in a typological perspective Lewalski brings added point and force to many of Christ's and Satan's speeches. At times she overstates her case, as when she insists that Hercules, who is not explicitly mentioned during the banquet–wealth temptation at all, is present by inference since aspects of the temptation resemble features of the story of Hercules' choice in Xenophon's *Memorabilia* II i 21–33. Also her interpretation of *PR*'s structure as dependent on Christ's three roles imports an imbalance into the poem since the roles of prophet and king are discussed and exemplified in detail but the priestly role is hardly introduced except in the brief storm-tower sequence: commentators, laying particular emphasis on the Temple setting, had often seen Christ's temptation on the pinnacle as foreshadowing his defeat of Sin and Death at the crucifixion (see iv *549n*).

Stein[2] is concerned to show that *PR* attempts a dramatic definition of 'heroic knowledge'. The poem juxtaposes what he considers to be the two competing theories of knowledge in the seventeenth century: Satan, the empiric, advocates knowledge derived externally from sense impression and used for power: Christ, the Platonic, represents pure thought, inaccessible to the senses. His contest with Satan is a preparation for acting transcendence in the world by uniting intuitive knowledge with proved intellectual and moral discipline. In reply J. M. Steadman, *UTQ* xxxi (1962) 416–30, claims that Stein emphasises Christ's knowledge at the expense of his rejection. The method of systematic rejection, an important structural feature of the second temptation, and its 'ethical ladder' of the voluptuous, ethical and contemplative lives, should he considers be traced not to Plato but to Aristotle's *Nicomachean Ethics*.

Merritt Hughes, *SP* xxxv (1938) 254–77, had previously drawn attention to the Aristotelian element in *PR*. Reacting against the view of the Christ of *PR* as the self-portrait of a defeated old man who had come to regret that he had tried 'to influence men's deeds instead of enlightening their minds' (Tillyard 309), Hughes insists upon the positive element in M.'s Christ. Christ's character is the result of the effort of Renaissance critics and poets to create a purely exemplary hero in heroic poetry by Christianizing the Aristotelian ideal of the magnanimous man, an effort which came to a head in the Arthur of Spenser's *F.Q.*, and which can be traced in such critical

Gul. Faithorne ad Vivum
Delin. et sculpsit.
Ioannis Miltoni Effigies Ætat: 62.
1670.

Plate 7 Milton aged about 62. Engraving by William Faithorne. From *The History of Britain*, 1670

Plate 8 Bust of Milton. Plaster cast of original in Christ's College. Cambridge, attributed to Edward Pierce

works as Tasso's *Del Poema Eroico* and *Della Virtù Eroica*. This effort produced a contemplative as opposed to an active hero, who renounces the world and masters his passions by reason. Kermode[4] agrees, but points out that the heroic ideal of M.'s Christ is in no sense derived from Tasso: M. had been working it out from the time of *Passion*, where Christ is 'Most perfect hero'. Christ's long contemplative withdrawal in *PR* is like that M. underwent at Horton and praised in Cromwell (Columbia viii 212–15); his patient endurance of suffering is of the kind exemplified in M.'s sonnet on his blindness and praised by the chorus in *SA* 1287–96; his renunciation of ambition and glory is what M. commended in Fairfax (Columbia viii 217–19) and what Phoebus preached in *Lycidas* 76–84. The renunciation of glory is of particular importance, and from this viewpoint Scipio (see *PR* ii *199–200*, iii *34–5*, *101–3*) is M.'s model. Lewalski (242–9) rather than identifying the Christ of *PR* with one particular classical ideal, argues that he assimilates principles common to the Stoics, the Academics, and the Peripatetics, especially in his definition of the ideal kingship over self (*PR* ii *457–83*), and that certainly some of his attitudes are quite un-Aristotelian. She agrees with Samuel (69–95) that ultimately Christ relates himself most closely to the Socratic-Platonic philosopher. M. M. Mahood, *Poetry and Humanism* (1950) pp. 225–37, reading the poem in the light of M.'s 'almost obsessive' longing for fame in the past, also places great weight on Christ's renunciation: 'This reorientation of "that last infirmity of noble mind" is the central theme of *PR*.'

In a later study Tillyard[3] agrees with Hughes's modification of his autobiographical approach to *PR*. The most thoroughgoing autobiographical reading is that of W. Menzies, *E & S* xxix (1948) 80–113, who explains that M. is both Christ and Satan in *PR*, and that the poem's debate 'is connected directly with the poet's own experience, his past life, and his actual circumstances'. (The theory is naively applied: e.g. the repudiation of classical learning is accounted for by the fact that 'M. was finding it more and more difficult to remember Greek'.)

Examinations of the structure of *PR* have been neither very numerous nor apart from Lewalski's (see above) very fruitful. Dick Taylor, *Tulane Studies in English* iv (1954) 57–90, advances the notion that all M.'s major poems share a structural pattern: the trial and proof of the protagonist, followed by an extension of grace accompanied by a miraculous event. A. H. Sackton, *UTSE* xxxiii (1954) 33–45, draws attention to the frequency of parallelism and contrast in *PR*: the baptismal scene, for example, is presented in three contrasting accounts (i *18–32*, *70–85*, *273–86*), and the repeated assaults and rebuttals of the second day's temptations form a structure of contrasts, in that Christ's replies are not merely negative but combine a positive with a negative theme, opposing true values to false (e.g. ii *466–7*, iii *60–2*, *400–2*, iv *143–5*, *288–92*). A. S. P. Woodhouse, *UTQ* xxv (1956) 167–82, finds symmetry in the framing of the major temptation between the two minor ones, and suggests, not very convincingly, that the way the division into books cuts across the scheme of the three temptations is a device for preventing this symmetry from becoming too mechanical. Roy Daniells, *M., Mannerism and Baroque* (Toronto 1963) pp. 194–208, likens this architecture of a threefold design dominated by a central element to that of a baroque church. L. E. Orange, *Southern Quarterly* ii (1964) 190–201, maintains that Satan's strategy of temptation is based on the seven deadly sins and that these, therefore, underlie *PR*'s structure: his demonstration of this theory wears very thin, however, as does L. S. Cox's argument, *ELH* xxviii (1961) 225–43, that the poem's structure is largely dependent on the development of recurrent imagery of food and of words. Samuel 70–1 concludes that the sequence of temptations follows, in reverse order, Socrates' scale of the five kinds of men and governments outlined in Plato's *Republic*.

At any rate the gradual advance through growing climaxes to the climax of the tower can be viewed as a counterpoint to the basic tripartite structure. Lewalski 330–1 suggests that since the kingdoms temptation deals first with private, then with public themes (the shift coming at iii *152*), one might distinguish four rather than three basic structural divisions. Still another structural counterpoint within the kingdoms temptation, overlaying this two-part division, is its organisation according to the traditional tripartite scale of ethical goods, *Voluptaria* (the banquet), *Activa* (wealth, glory, Parthia, Rome), and *Contemplativa* (learning).

A small but shrewd structural point is made by H. H. Petit, *Papers of the Michigan Academy* xliv (1958) 365–9: as Christ is second Adam, so Mary is 'second Eve' (*PL* v 387, x 183), hence the emphasis upon her humility, faith and obedience in *PR* ii, contrasting with Eve's rash pride, doubts and disobedience in *PL* ix. The last line of *PL* leaves Adam and Eve together, and the last line of *PR* does the same for second Adam and second Eve.

Christ's stance, and the style of his speeches, have come in for some adverse comment. Northrop Frye, *MP* liii (1956) 227–38, puts the case most strongly, remarking on the similarity between *PR* and *Comus* in that dramatically Christ, like the Lady, is an increasingly unsympathetic figure–'a pusillanimous quietist in the temptation of Parthia, an inhuman snob in the temptation of Rome, a peevish obscurantist in the temptation of Athens'. 'Comus and Satan get our dramatic attention because they show such energy and resourcefulness; the tempted figures are either motionless or unmoved and have only the ungracious dramatic function of saying No. Yet, of course, the real relation is the opposite of the apparent one: the real source of life and freedom and energy is in the frigid figure at the centre.' W. W. Robson (Kermode[3] 124–37) comments on Christ's plain and unpoetical vocabulary, and on the greater degree of 'presence' which Satan's speeches have by contrast. The difference was part of M.'s intention, Robson assumes: Christ was meant to be the paragon of surly virtue, hence his condemnation of the multitude (iii *50*) and of Greek philosophy (iv *291–318*). These speeches, however, and others of Christ's, amount to errors of feeling and taste, and, coupled with the tonelessness and desiccation of the verse Christ speaks, lead to a failure of incarnation. Robson concludes that M. did not succeed in combining the sacred figure and the epic hero. In reply

F. W. Bateson (Kermode[3] 138–40) defends the bare and ascetic style of much of *PR*, particularly the 'condensed and laconic art' of i *497–502*: the stylistic brilliance of such lines 'arises from, is indeed a function of, their context'. G. A. Wilkes, *English Studies* xliv (1963) 35–8, suspects that Christ's speeches have seemed so unpalatable to critics because they are delivered from set moral positions: the 'oration from a given moral standpoint' was one of the conventions of the minor sacred epic of the Renaissance, and is found in Du Bartas, *La Judith* and Drayton, *Noah's Flood*. Even if M. was influenced by this 'convention', however, the question of whether the style of the resultant speeches can be defended still remains. Louis Martz's contention, in *The Paradise Within* (New Haven 1964) pp. 171–211, that the style of the major part of *PR* is that of Virgil's *Georgics*, converted by M. from a didactic mode to a channel for religious meditation, can hardly be taken seriously in the absence of corroboratory analysis and comparison. As Lewalski 38 remarks, the expository form of the *Georgics* and their explicit abnegation of heroic subject and tone (iii 1–48) contrast sharply with the narrative / dramatic form and heroic claims of *PR*.

A determined attempt to interpret *PR* as an ecclesiastical parable is made by Howard Schultz, *M. and Forbidden Knowledge* (New York 1955). He reads Christ's condemnation of heathen philosophy as a contribution to the learned ministry controversy, similar to that made by M. in his tract *The Likeliest Means to Remove Hirelings out of the Church* (1659), where it is argued that learning, beyond knowledge of languages and of Scripture, is inessential to a minister. Schultz takes the banquet temptation to represent the lure of Popish idolatry; and the offer of earthly monarchy, the junction of civil and ecclesiastical power which M. detested. This narrowing, or sharpening, of the poem's significance is contested by E. L. Marilla, *Studia Neophilologica* xxvii (1955) 179–91, who insists that *PR* is 'inspired primarily by dynamic interest in the "practical" problems of the temporal world', and that it recommends an acute and unrelaxing awareness of the spiritual significance of man as a way through those problems. Marilla's view is essentially a reaffirmation of J. H. Hanford's, *SP* xv (1918) 176–84. Another attempt, beside Schultz's, to place *PR* in a context of seventeenth-century religious controversy, is that of M. Fixler, *M. and the Kingdoms of God* (1964). Fixler regards *PR* as M.'s reaction to the worst excesses of Puritan apocalyptic materialism: Satan treats the messianic prophecies in what was considered to be the spirit of Jewish messianism as opposed to the orthodox Christian interpretation of spiritual typology: this can be taken as M.'s comment upon the seventeenth-century revival of Jewish (i.e. temporal) messianism, and upon its intrusion into contemporary English life (e.g. in the expectations of the Fifth Monarchists).

Finally two critics, R. D. Miller, *MLN* xv (1900) 403–9, and D. Daube, *RES* xix (1943) 204–9, emphasise the historical aspect of the temptations: they represent things that were real problems to the historical Jesus. Modern biblical scholars, Daube remarks, are inclined to believe that the question of whether Jesus ought to assume political leadership and fight Rome, or whether he ought to choose strength in weakness, did play a tremendous part in his life. The temptations were subjective, internal: the scriptural narrative, with its real devil, is merely a symbolical version. M., in accepting this version at its face value, has, Miller thinks, misunderstood the temptations. They are presented, in *PR*, not as a psychological series but as the expedients of a resourceful devil: thus 'the various attempts of Satan are seemingly without connection, the transitions are lame, and the unity of the poem is lost'.

Style and rhetoric. That the style of *PR* is flatter and drier than that of *PL* is a common complaint, but it is also terser and tenser and, though less involved, often as delicately managed. The sentence length is abbreviated: the average in *PR* i, for example, is 7 lines. Satan's opening period in the hellish debate (i *44–69*) and Christ's musings on his youth (i *201–26*) are joint longest in this book. Satan's panoramas also extend the normal sense-unit. Rome has a sentence of 19 lines (iv *61–79*) and Athens, the climax of the temptations, reaches a peak with consecutive sentences of 25 and 24 lines (iv *236–84*). Brevity of sense-unit is a frequent mark of Christ's retorts (e.g. i *421–41* has 8 sentences: the most fragmented set of 21 lines in *PR*). Laconism features prominently in his speeches (e.g. i *335–6*; 'the same I now' i *354*; 'thou canst not more' i *496*; ii *317–8*, *321–2*; 'I never liked thy talk, thy offers less' iv *171*; 'the Son of God went on / And stayed not, but in brief him answered thus. / Me worse than wet thou find'st not' iv *485–6*). It seems an inherited characteristic (see the Father's 'This is my son beloved, in him am pleased' i *85*), and Satan quickly picks it up (see his sharp rejoinder 'By miracle he may' i *337*). Monosyllabic lines, rare in *PL*, are relatively plentiful in *PR*: *PR* i has 28 (an average of 1 in 18 lines); ii has 15, iii, 14 and iv, 34. Satan as the simple rustic has 4 in 23 lines (i *321–45*), the disciples ('Plain fishermen') 2 in 28 (ii *30–57*). Satan also uses them for the sake of insistence (ii *368*, *377*; iv *517*, *518*, *520*), and Christ for his steely parries (iii *396*, *398*, *407*; iv *152*, *153* and, the culmination of the action, iv *561*). When Satan makes his appeal to Christ's compassion, the monosyllabic lines cluster more thickly than anywhere else in the poem (iii *204*, *206*, *209*, *220*, *223*, *224*).

Satan, Christ and the narrator all use word-play: e.g. Satan's 'Pretends' (i *73*), 'deserted' (ii *316*); Christ's 'arm . . . arms' (iii *387–8*); and the narrator's 'consistory' (i *42*), 'ravens . . . ravenous' (ii *267–9*) and 'crude' (ii *349*). Satan's sardonic jocularity turns to other kinds of verbal sleight as well, e.g. his definition of 'eternal' (iv *391–2*) and his sneering 'highest is best' as he sets Christ on the highest pinnacle of the Temple (iv *553*). His professional interest in ambiguity (see i *434–5*) comes out, crucially, in his questioning of the title 'Son of God' (iv *517–21*); and the poem culminates in Christ's ambiguous 'Tempt not the Lord thy God' (iv *561*, see footnote), which Satan at any rate, since he falls not only 'smitten with amazement' (iv *562*) at Christ's balancing-feat but also 'struck with dread' (iv *576*), seems to interpret as a revelation of Christ's own godhead, whether Christ meant it like that or not. The poem's style often accommodates less obvious verbal intricacies. When God reminds Gabriel how he foretold the virgin birth to Mary 'doubting how these things could be' (i *137*) the doubt seems momentarily Gabriel's, not Mary's–an impression prearranged by God's announcement that he is about to offer Gabriel verification (i *130–3*). When we are told that Christ, entering the wilderness, had not 'marked' (observed) the way he came, so that 'return / Was difficult, by human steps untrod' (i *297–8*), the last phrase, at first sight merely conveying an unexciting attribute of deserts, becomes, when a measure of emphasis is allowed to 'human', suggestive of the twofold nature of the figure who has trodden *this* desert, and the idea of non-human steps, once present, allows a shade of the meaning 'left footprints upon' to get into 'marked'. The ordering of i *303–7* persuades the reader that he is being given an account of Christ's various habitat, only to reveal, in the last three words, that no such account is available: thus M. is able to fill in the gaps in his source and leave them scrupulously open at the same time. Verbs are fairly often connectable with more than one object (direct or indirect) and adjectives with more than one noun, so that undertones of meaning emerge. For example, iii *86–7* 'Rolling in brutish vices, and deformed, / Violent or shameful death their due reward' permits 'deformed' to adhere to 'vices', suggesting perversion (particularly in the Tiberius context), or to 'death', suggesting physical misshapenness; and 'Rolling in' can extend from 'vices' to 'death', bringing a glimpse of agonized contortions. The apparent grammatical slip in iv *583* ('him' should strictly refer to the last figure named, Satan, but obviously refers to the Son of God) is actually a splendid dismissal of Satan, now fallen, from the poem. He ceases to count even as a grammatical referent, and 'him' jumps slightingly back across his name to that of the victor. Lewalski's detection of ironic *double-entendre* in i *383* is surely valid (see footnote), and Christ's comment on the relationship between God and man, 'of whom what could he less expect / Than glory and benediction' (iii *126–7*), gives 'less' a similar duplicity: God, foreseeing all, knows how little 'glory and benediction' he is to receive from ungrateful mankind. Words which alter or complete meanings in one line are quite commonly placed at the beginning of the next line, with gains in delay and emphasis. Satan is fond of this expedient: 'single none / Durst ever, who returned, and dropped not here / His carcase' (i *323–5*) gathers a more horrible surprise from the intrusion of 'His carcase' upon what seemed the completed meaning of 'dropped' (fell exhausted); and 'whom I know / Declared the Son of God' (i *384–5*) throws a dubious weight upon declaration, as opposed to proof. Verbal echoes sound across the poem to encourage particular comparisons: the 'full frequence' of devils imitates the 'full frequence' of angels (i *128* and ii *130*), and Satan's scornful use of 'rudiments' (iii *245*) harks back to God's plans for Christ (i *157*).

Movement within *PR* is scarce. The flights to mountain-top and pinnacle are exceptional. For the most part the adversaries are locked in cerebral combat, and Christ's immobility is repeatedly stressed (e.g. iv *18–20*). Stylistically this stillness is reflected in the preference for participles rather than other parts of the verb. The past participle freezes action into posture: e.g. 'on him *baptized*' (i *29*), 'by the head / *Broken*' (i *60–1*), 'whom he suspected *raised*' (i *124–5*), 'wet *returned* from field at eve' (i *318*), 'our Saviour answered thus *unmoved*' (iii *386*), 'sturdiest oaks / Bowed their stiff necks, *loaden* with stormy blasts, / Or *torn* up sheer' (iv *417–9*). It is introduced in contexts where its only function seems to be to withdraw the action from the immediate and the present: e.g. 'with words *thus uttered* spake' (i *320*), 'Among daughters of men the fairest *found*' (ii *154*), 'With sound of harpies' wings, and talons *heard*' (ii *403*). It also defines characters by reference to their past and stable rather than their present and uncertain roles: e.g. 'His first-begot' (i *89*), 'this new-declared' (i *121*), 'King of Israel born' (i *254*), 'composed of lies' (i *407*), 'the new-baptized' (ii *1*). Often it gives a clipped quality to the style, particularly where one would expect some expansion, as at the annunciation, 'Hail highly favoured, among women blest' (ii *68*), and in Mary's ponderings, 'From Egypt home returned . . . Full grown to man, acknowledged . . . in public shown, / Son owned' (ii *79–85*). The present participle, though less stationary, reduces the swift or sudden to the continuous or gradual: e.g. 'With dread *attending*' (i *53*), 'on him *rising* / Out of the water' (i *80*), 'the spirit *leading*' (i *189*), 'Now *missing* him' (ii *9*), 'So spake the old serpent *doubting*' (ii *147*), '*Suffering*, *abstaining*, quietly *expecting*' (iii *192*), '*Appearing*, and *beginning* noble deeds' (iv *99*), '*Spreading* and *overshadowing* all the earth' (iv *148*). It, too, helps to sleek the style: e.g. 'a star . . . in heaven *appearing* / Guided' (i *249–50*), 'they found the place, / *Affirming* it thy star' (i *252–3*) (Mary, again, is the speaker). Sometimes it is hedged by past participles to reduce what activity it has, as in the description of Roman games: 'by their sports to blood *inured* / Of *fighting* beasts, and men to beasts *exposed*' (iv *139–40*), where what one would expect to be action-filled is almost motionless. At other times it is coupled with the past participle so that its active force is counter-balanced by passivity: e.g. 'Hated of all, and hating' (iv *97*), 'men divinely taught, and better teaching' (iv *357*)–Christ's correction of Satan's 'teaching not taught' (iv *220*). The present participle 'unconniving' (i *363*) seems to be M.'s only coinage in *PR*.

Another mannerism which establishes balance and stasis is the pairing of adjectives, nouns and verbs with 'and' or 'or'. This is extremely popular in *PR* i but very common in the later books too, especially in Satan's speeches. It is particularly noticeable when, as often, it edges on pleonasm: e.g. 'defeated and repulsed' (i *6*), 'aghast and sad' (i *43*), 'Distracted and surprized' (i *108*), 'care / And management' (i *111–2*), 'pre-ordained and fixed' (i *127*), 'path or road' (i *322*), 'town or village' (i *332*) etc. The triple grouping of adjectives, nouns, or verbs, though less in evidence than pairing, is still a very distinct feature of all four books: e.g. 'obscure, / Unmarked, unknown' (i *24–5*), 'good, or fair, / Or virtuous' (i *381–2*), 'holy wise and pure' (i *486*), 'found him, viewed him, tasted him' (ii *131*), 'cottage, herd or sheep-cote' (ii *288*), 'virtue, valour, wisdom' (ii *431*) 'Passions, desires, and fears' (ii *467*) etc. Both devices imply leisure and expansiveness and thus counteract any suggestion of haste which the abbreviated participial syntax might introduce.

In spite of M.'s comment upon Satan's 'persuasive rhetoric' (iv *4*), his speeches are no more marked by rhetorical figures than Christ's, or the narrator's, and no one in *PR* uses the various repetitive figures as freely as they are employed in *PL* or *SA*. The narrator's opening paragraph (i *1–7*) is bound together by traductio, anaphora, agnomination and ploce ('sung . . . By one man's disobedience . . . sing . . . mankind . . . By one man's obedience . . . temptation . . . tempter'), and he is later responsible for some of the most closely schematized moments in the poem: e.g. ii *9–12* (which includes one of the few examples of anadiplosis), ii *287–8*, iv *13* (epanalepsis), iv *565–71* ('foiled . . . fall . . . fell . . . foil . . . fell . . . fall'). Ploce, the most common figure, is used by everyone, including Mary (i *233*, *238–9*). She, like the disciples, is more fond of rhetoric than Belial, a plain speaker who limits himself to a modest anaphora (ii *170–1*). Traductio comes next in frequency to ploce and is, with it, the habitual weapon in the Christ / Satan exchanges: e.g. iii *44–107*, where Christ, picking up Satan's five uses of 'glory' and 'inglorious' in the previous speech, replies with 'glory' or 'glorious' eleven times, and Satan follows (iii *109–20*) with 'glory' or 'glorified' eight times; and iv *182–7*, where Christ's four uses of 'given' or 'giver' parry Satan's 'give . . . given . . . give . . . gift' (iv *163–9*). Traductio is so natural to Christ that he uses it even in meditation (e.g. ii *249–51* 'need . . . needing', ii *258* 'fed . . . feed'), and so does his mother (ii *71–2* 'birth . . . bore . . . born'). Satan attempts to rouse Christ by climax, 'Thy actions to *thy words* accord, *thy words* / To thy large *heart* give utterance due, thy *heart* / Contains of good, wise, just, the perfect shape' (iii *9–11*), and Christ mimics the figure in reply, 'Thou neither dost persuade me to seek wealth / For *empire's* sake, nor *empire* to affect / For *glory's* sake . . . For what is *glory* but the blaze of fame, / The *people's praise*, if always *praise* unmixed? / And what the *people* . . .' (iii *44–9*). Satan employs anadiplosis once or twice in his arguments (i *404–5*, iv *90–1*, iv *382–3*); Christ, only once, and then in his joyful meditation upon the revelation which accompanied his baptism, 'me his, / Me his beloved Son' (i *284–5*; cp. his anaphora eight lines earlier, 'Me him . . . Me him'). More usually the distinction between Christ's rhetoric and Satan's, where any distinction can be made, is that Christ turns to rigorously intellectual and argumentative ends figures which Satan introduces to incite or to move. Compare Satan's emotional epistrophe (i *377–9*) or the ploce, traductio and epizeuxis which make iii *203–24* one of the most elaborately patterned passages in the poem, with what is probably *PR*'s most tightly figured section, the opening of Christ's reply to the learning-temptation (iv *286–92*), with its two epanalepses within four lines (unparalleled elsewhere in the poem).

By the time the rhetorical figuring wears thinnest, in Satan's panoramas, the poem has started to take on a richness of which its opening movements are bare. It derives this partly from the exotic name catalogues which cluster round each of the later temptations (ii *347*, *360–1*; iii *270–93*, *316–21*; iv

70–9, 257, 259, 271: M. uses the unusual and grandiose 'Melesigenes' (see iv *259n*) to help Athens vie with the splendid nomenclature of Rome). The first of these catalogues is at ii *20–4*: another enlivens the hellish consistory (ii *186–8*). Christ's replies, as usual, show their command of the Satanic armoury by exploiting this device for their own ends (ii *446*, iv *117–8*) so as to prove that width of knowledge and a generous imagination are not the tempter's prerogatives. Similes also grow less rare as the poem proceeds (though never plentiful). Christ's 'like a fawning parasite' (i *452*) is apparently the only example in the first book. Belial's wistful memory of women 'passing fair / As the noon sky' (ii *155–6*) is almost alone in the second, if we exclude a number of typological parallels, as is Satan's 'shading cool / Interposition, as a summer's cloud' (iii *221–2*) in the third. By comparison the fourth book is richly illustrated. Besides the epic similes which colour its opening (iv *10–20*) and its climax (iv *563–75*), and Christ's employment of the biblical tree and stone (iv *147–50*), it has Christ's beautifully aloof dismissal of the erudite, 'collecting toys, . . . As children gathering pebbles on the shore' (iv *328–30*), his scorn for a style less spare than his own, 'swelling epithets thick-laid / As varnish on a harlot's cheek' (iv *343–4*), Satan's admission that Christ has stood 'as a rock / Of adamant, and as a centre, firm' (iv *533–4*: an image which looks back to Christ as rock in iv *18*), the fairytale Temple, 'like a mount / Of alabaster, topped with golden spires' (iv *547–8*) and the angelic prophecy of Satan's fall from heaven, 'like an autumnal star / Or lightning' (iv *619–20*). Asyndeton and polysyndeton, grudgingly admitted into the first book (e.g. i *117, 178–9, 413–4*) help the progressive enrichment by a more liberal appearance in the second (ii *81, 131, 422, 460, 464*), and grow to their most spacious proportions in the last (e.g. iv *36–8, 386–8*).

The spectacular visual aids with which Satan drives home his points–the banquet, the Parthian army, Rome, Athens–grow successively more actual. Contrasted with the first bleak stones-into-bread temptation, the banquet (ii *340–367*) might seem resplendently solid, but M.'s description of it is carefully remote, and its instantaneous disappearance (ii *402–3*) as well as the suspiciously supernatural setting, 'the haunt of wood-gods or wood-nymphs', help to shift it, in the reader's mind, to the realm of mirage and illusion, in spite of M.'s insistence that it is 'no dream' (ii *337*). It is in part the generous concessiveness of the description which dissipates its actuality: 'beasts of chase, *or* fowl of game, / In pastry built, *or* from the spit *or* boiled', 'And all the while harmonious airs were heard / Of chiming strings, *or* charming pipes'. The repetition, or . . . or, leaves us to make up our own minds, so that instead of forming a defined image we remain in doubt about what was actually seen and heard. Similarly total inclusiveness lands us back at the generality of the generic: '*all* fish from sea or shore, / Freshet, or purling brook, of shell or fin', cannot be grasped like 'cod' or 'oyster', but retain the mistiness of mere 'fish', like the later 'fruits and flowers'. The concentration upon the names of the fish, 'exquisitest named', which at the same time witholds those names, and the switching of the reader's attention from the table to his atlas, 'Pontus and Lucrine bay, and Afric coast', and then to myth and finally to romance, are other ruses of M.'s to prevent the banquet hardening into anything eatable, while 'more distant', 'feigned' and 'fabled' conspire to smudge what outline the scene had, some time before it finally vanishes. Even the smells, often thought blind M.'s strong point, contradict and confuse: early spring scents ('Flora's earliest smells') would be swamped by the spicier 'Arabian odours'. To reply that epic decorum demands that this whole description should be remote and general is to ignore the kitchen-worthy 'pastry', the one bit of the banquet Christ could have got his teeth into. Besides, low terms ('waggons') and technical terms ('Cuirassiers') are not expelled from the Parthian-army description (iii *303–45*). This description, with its detailed observation of 'steel bows', 'coats of mail' and 'elephants endorsed with towers / Of archers', provides more palpable ingredients than the banquet, but keeps itself just beyond the range of exact vision by some of the same subterfuges. Confusion, as with the banquet's odours, is introduced by the contradiction of 'All horsemen' and 'Nor wanted clouds of foot'; the same unsettling concessiveness appears in the repetition of 'or' and 'nor' in *327–34*, and first the atlas (*316–21*) then the romances (*337–43*) deflect the eye from the army, while giving a vague impression of pomp and splendour. The few details of dress and armour are counteracted by sweeping strokes which seem to block in the general shapes of the formations, 'rhombs and wedges, and half-moons and wings' and 'clouds', but which actually, by the words used, turn the attention to a variety of non-military contexts. 'Coats of mail' is blurred by zeugma which merges it into an abstraction, 'In coats of mail and military pride'. 'Numbers numberless' designedly thwarts the numerical imagination, and 'The field all iron cast a gleaming brown' applies a wash into which any previously-grasped details vanish. And the reader's understanding is dimmed by what seem to be incompatible military operations going on at the same time. What is happening to the Parthian army? According to Satan it is just leaving its quarters in Ctesiphon to march the 1,200-odd miles to the border province of Sogdiana where the Scythians are proving troublesome: 'they issued forth' and 'The city gates outpoured' back up this impression. But a moment later the army is not in march formation but in 'forms of battle ranged' with 'each horn' extended, and engaging in battle with some unspecified 'pursuers'. When the reader entered the geographical catalogue at *316* he was with an army just marching out of a friendly city. When he leaves it six lines later he is with an army deployed for battle and engaged. Later he is returned to the pioneers and the baggage train, still apparently strung out on the column of march.

The Roman panorama (iv *27–85*) is, by contrast, situated in almost painstakingly specific surroundings, 'Another plain, long but in breadth not wide; / Washed by the southern sea, and on the north / To equal length backed with a ridge of hills . . . in the midst / Divided by a river'. The pace swiftly changes to a pelting generality, however, with 'Porches and theatres, baths, aqueducts, / Statues and trophies, and triumphal arcs, / Gardens and groves', which leaves the eye behind in despair after the pictorially precise opening. From this welter Satan's pointing finger rescues two particulars, 'there the Capitol thou seest' and 'there Mount Palatine', though the first is deprived of architectural immediacy by personification, and the second quickly slides back into the muddled splendour, 'Turrets and terraces, and glittering spires'. After this the uncertain picture breaks up into suggestions of myth, 'Houses of gods', and of illusion, 'my airy microscope', and into its raw materials, 'cedar, marble, ivory or gold', to be lost at length in the usual geographical fanfare, with one last glimpse of 'Dusk faces with white silken turbans wreathed' on the roads out of Rome.

The last vision, Athens (iv *238–80*), though the least gorgeous, is the most defined. Specification is constant throughout it: '*Look* ... Westward much nearer by south-west, *behold* / Where on the Aegean shore a city stands', '*See there* the olive-grove of Academe', '*There* flowery hill Hymettus', '*there* Ilissus rolls', 'Lyceum *there*, and painted Stoa next', 'Socrates, *see there* his tenement'. Unlike the contradictory scents of the first vision, the three sounds of Athens blend into a lulling but insistent accompaniment to the sight-seeing: the murmur of bees on Hymettus, the whispering river, and the nightingale which 'Trills her thick-warbled notes the summer long'.

The progress from remoteness to definition in the four visions, making the poem gradually more alive for eye and ear, is in part matched by the flowering of the wilderness between the first book and the last. Starting as a place of 'dark shades and rocks' (i *194*) and 'stones' (i *343*), a 'barren waste' (i *354*), it ends up 'fresh and green', its plants and trees dripping with water, and birds singing 'in bush and spray' (iv *433–8*); Eden is 'raised in the waste wilderness'. However the delineation of the wilderness is less neat than this implies. Christ calls it 'barren' (i *354*), and the seventeenth-century sense of this, applied to land, is given by the *OED* as 'producing little or no vegetation; not fertile, sterile, unproductive, bare'. The only other occurrence of the word in the poem is at iii *264* where it is applied to the Persian desert, 'barren desert fountainless and dry'. Travellers in the wilderness are said to die of 'hunger' and 'drouth' (i *325*), and in it Christ says he suffers 'thirst / And hunger' (iv *120–1*). Yet the wilderness is also, richly wooded, (i *305–6*, *502*, ii *246*, *263*, iv *416–7*) and damp (i *306*, *318*, iv *406*, *411–12*), supporting an abundance of wildlife (i *310–13*, *501–2*), grassy (ii *282*) and, to all appearances, suitable for raising sheep (i *315*, ii *287*). It most resembles the wood in which the Lady of *Comus* wanders: both represent spiritual pilgrimage, each has its false shepherd, each is called a maze (*PR* ii *246* 'this woody maze', *Comus* 180 'the blind mazes of this tangled wood'), the Lady rests on 'a grassy turf' (*Comus* 279), Christ on a 'grassy couch' (*PR* ii *282*). It seems possible that M.'s attempt to amalgamate the allegorical 'woody maze' and the bare, rocky desert which later grows green has obscured both elements of the combination.

The echoes of other writers are not very frequent in *PR*. Scraps of Virgilian phraseology are turned to account on seven or eight occasions, and there are half a dozen recollections each of Giles Fletcher and Shakespeare (see footnotes). Spenserian diction lends colour to passages of chivalric comparison (e.g. 'prowest' and 'paynim' iii *342–3*) or nationalistic eloquence 'fulmined' iv *270*), and the disciples are made into a fishy pastoral by fusing the first line of Spenser's *Shepheardes Calender* with Phineas Fletcher's imitation of it in his *Piscatory Eclogues* (see ii *27n*).

THE FIRST BOOK

I who erewhile the happy garden sung,
By one man's disobedience lost, now sing
Recovered Paradise to all mankind,
By one man's firm obedience fully tried
Through all temptation, and the tempter foiled
In all his wiles, defeated and repulsed,
And Eden raised in the waste wilderness.
Thou spirit who led'st this glorious eremite

¶ i *1. I who erewhile*] Echoes *Aen.* i 1–4 (lines probably by Virgil, but later excised, in which he takes his farewell of pastoral and rural poetry): *Ille ego, qui quondam gracili modulatus avena / carmen. . . .*, and Spenser's imitation, *F.Q.* I introd. 1–4: 'Lo! I, the man whose Muse whylome did maske, / As time her taught, in lowly Shephards weeds, / Am now enforst, a farre unfitter taske, / For trumpets sterne to chaunge mine Oaten reeds.' Lewalski 6 comments: 'by the allusion to *PL* as a poem about a "happy garden", M. seems to imply that he has now graduated from pastoral apprentice work to the true epic subject.' She quotes (116–7) openings of other biblical epics which imitate these Virgilian lines.

i *2–4*. Cp. *Rom.* v 19: 'For as by one man's disobedience many were made sinners, so by the obedience of one shall many be made righteous.'

i *7*. Cp. *Isa.* li 3: 'He will comfort all her waste places; and he will make her wilderness like Eden, and her desert like the garden of the Lord', and Spenser, *Virgil's Gnat* 369–70: 'I carried am into waste wildernesse, / Waste wildernes, amongst Cymerian shades.'

i *8. spirit*] Pope 27–9 considers that M. here follows the orthodox line in interpreting the unspecified 'spirit' of *Luke* iv 1 as the Holy Ghost. As M. Kelley, *SP* xxxii (1935) 221–34, remarks, however, the fact that M. here invokes the 'spirit' means that it is unlikely it is to be taken as the Holy Ghost, since M. in *De doctrina* insists that the Holy Ghost should not be invoked. Robins 173 suggests that what is here referred to is Christ's own spirit, given to him at the time of his baptism, when the power and virtue of the Father were bestowed upon the Son and symbolized by the descending dove.

i *8–9. eremite . . . desert*] Greek ἐρημίτης (hermit) means, literally, 'desert-dweller'.

Into the desert, his victorious field
Against the spiritual foe, and brought'st him thence
By proof the undoubted Son of God, inspire,
As thou art wont, my prompted song else mute,
And bear through highth or depth of nature's bounds
With prosperous wing full summed to tell of deeds
Above heroic, though in secret done,
And unrecorded left through many an age,
Worthy t' have not remained so long unsung.
  Now had the great proclaimer with a voice
More awful than the sound of trumpet, cried
Repentance, and heaven's kingdom nigh at hand
To all baptized: to his great baptism flocked
With awe the regions round, and with them came
From Nazareth the son of Joseph deemed
To the flood Jordan, came as then obscure,
Unmarked, unknown; but him the Baptist soon
Descried, divinely warned, and witness bore

i *9. victorious field*] The concept of the temptation as a martial combat was, as Pope 115–20 demonstrates, a well-established aspect of the tradition, and though Michael cautions Adam against it, *PL* xii 386–95, it is employed throughout *PR* (see i 158, 174; iv 562–70 etc.). The final anthem, iv 604–9, draws the parallel between this duel on earth and the previous one in heaven.
i *12. As thou art wont*] Robins 168 takes these words to mean that the Muse of *PR* is the same as that of *PL*, and he identifies this Muse (Urania), in spite of the sex being female, with the Logos. Newton, in the 'Life' prefixed to his 1778 edn of *PL*, reports that M.'s third wife said that 'her husband used to compose his poetry chiefly in winter, and on his waking in a morning would make her write down sometimes twenty or thirty verses; and being asked whether he did not often read Homer and Virgil, she understood it as an imputation upon him for stealing from these authors, and answered with eagerness that he stole from nobody but the Muse who inspired him, and being asked by a lady present who the Muse was, replied it was God's grace and the Holy Spirit that visited him nightly'. Cp. *PL* i 6–22*n*.
i *14. full summed*] wanting none of its feathers; a term from falconry.
i *16. unrecorded*] not in the modern sense, since they were recorded in the gospels, but 'unsung'. 'Record' was particularly used of birdsong in the seventeenth century.
i *18. great proclaimer*] John the Baptist.
i *20*. Cp. *Matt.* iii 2: 'Repent ye: for the kingdom of heaven is at hand.'
i *23. son of Joseph deemed*] Cp. *Luke* iii 23: 'being (as was supposed) the son of Joseph'.
i *26. divinely warned*] Cp. *John* i 33: 'And I knew him not; but he that sent me to baptize with water, the same said unto me, Upon whom thou shalt

As to his worthier, and would have resigned
To him his heavenly office, nor was long
His witness unconfirmed: on him baptized
Heaven opened, and in likeness of a dove
The Spirit descended, while the Father's voice
From heaven pronounced him his beloved Son.
That heard the adversary, who roving still
About the world, at that assembly famed
Would not be last, and with the voice divine
Nigh thunder-struck, the exalted man, to whom
Such high attest was given, a while surveyed
With wonder, then with envy fraught and rage
Flies to his place, nor rests, but in mid air
To council summons all his mighty peers,
Within thick clouds and dark tenfold involved,
A gloomy consistory; and them amidst
With looks aghast and sad he thus bespake.
  O ancient powers of air and this wide world,
For much more willingly I mention air,
This our old conquest, than remember hell
Our hated habitation; well ye know
How many ages, as the years of men,
This universe we have possessed, and ruled
In manner at our will the affairs of earth,

see the Spirit descending, and remaining on him, the same is he which baptizeth with the Holy Ghost.'

i *30–2*. Cp. *Matt.* iii 16–7: 'He saw the Spirit of God descending like a dove: And lo a voice from heaven, saying, This is my beloved Son, in whom I am well pleased.'

i *33*. *adversary*] Satan (which means 'adversary' in Hebrew). *still*] continually.

i *33–4*. Cp. *Job* i 7: 'And the Lord said unto Satan, Whence comest thou? Then Satan answered the Lord and said, From going to and fro in the earth, and from walking up and down in it.'

i *37*. *attest*] attestation.

i *39*. *place*] home; cp. *Job* vii 10: 'He shall return no more to his house, neither shall his place know him any more.' *mid air*] Cp. *Eph.* ii 2, the origin of the belief that the devils inhabit and rule over the air, where Satan is called 'Prince of the power of the air'.

i *42*. *consistory*] An ironic reference to the ecclesiastical senate in which the Pope presides over the body of Cardinals, and to the bishop's court for ecclesiastical cases in the Anglican church. Each of these bodies had the title 'consistory'.

i *48*. *as the years of men*] By human computation.

Since Adam and his facile consort Eve
Lost Paradise deceived by me, though since
With dread attending when that fatal wound
Shall be inflicted by the seed of Eve
Upon my head, long the decrees of heaven
Delay, for longest time to him is short;
And now too soon for us the circling hours
This dreaded time have compassed, wherein we
Must bide the stroke of that long-threatened wound,
At least if so we can, and by the head
Broken be not intended all our power
To be infringed, our freedom and our being
In this fair empire won of earth and air;
For this ill news I bring, the woman's seed
Destined to this, is late of woman born,
His birth to our just fear gave no small cause,
But his growth now to youth's full flower, displaying
All virtue, grace and wisdom to achieve
Things highest, greatest, multiplies my fear.
Before him a great prophet, to proclaim
His coming, is sent harbinger, who all
Invites, and in the consecrated stream
Pretends to wash off sin, and fit them so
Purified to receive him pure, or rather
To do him honour as their king; all come,
And he himself among them was baptized,
Not thence to be more pure, but to receive
The testimony of heaven, that who he is
Thenceforth the nations may not doubt; I saw
The prophet do him reverence; on him rising
Out of the water, heaven above the clouds

i *51. facile*] easily led.

i *53. attending*] waiting (qualifies 'me'). *when*] until. *wound*] Cp. *Gen.* iii 15: 'And I will put enmity between thee and the woman, and between thy seed and her seed; it shall bruise thy head, and thou shalt bruise his heel.'

i *56.* Cp. *Ps.* xc 4: 'A thousand years in thy sight are but as yesterday.'

i *57. circling hours*] Cp. *PL* vi 3; echoing *Aen.* i 234: *volventibus annis.*

i *60–1. by the head / Broken*] by the prophecy about my head being broken.

i *62. infringed*] broken (Latin *infrangere*).

i *73. pretends*] claims. Satan, in his sarcasm, gives the word something also of its modern sense (already current in the seventeenth century).

i *74.* Cp. *1 John* iii 3: 'Every man that hath this hope in him purifieth himself, even as he is pure.'

i *80. on him rising*] when he rose.

Unfold her crystal doors, thence on his head
A perfect dove descend, whate'er it meant,
And out of heaven the sovran voice I heard,
This is my son beloved, in him am pleased.
His mother then is mortal, but his sire
He who obtains the monarchy of heaven,
And what will he not do to advance his son?
His first-begot we know, and sore have felt,
When his fierce thunder drove us to the deep;
Who this is we must learn, for man he seems
In all his lineaments, though in his face
The glimpses of his father's glory shine.
Ye see our danger on the utmost edge
Of hazard, which admits no long debate,
But must with something sudden be opposed,
Not force, but well-couched fraud, well-woven snares,
Ere in the head of nations he appear
Their king, their leader, and supreme on earth.
I, when no other durst, sole undertook
The dismal expedition to find out
And ruin Adam, and the exploit performed
Successfully; a calmer voyage now
Will waft me; and the way found prosperous once
Induces best to hope of like success.

i *82. doors*] Cp. *Ps.* lxxviii 23: 'Though he had commanded the clouds from above, and opened the doors of heaven.'

i *83. dove*] Cp. *Matt.* iii 16: 'And he saw the Spirit of God descending like a dove.' *whate'er it meant*] M. in *De doctrina* I vi (Columbia xiv 367) is similarly doubtful: 'The descent therefore and appearance of the Holy Spirit in the likeness of a dove, seems to have been nothing more than a representation of the ineffable affection of the Father for the Son, communicated by the Holy Spirit under the appropriate image of a dove, and accompanied by a voice from heaven declaratory of that affection.'

i *87. obtains*] holds (Latin *obtinere*) a sense common from the fifteenth-century.

i *89–91.* As W. G. Rice, *Papers of the Michigan Academy* xxii (1936) 495–6 notes, these lines lend support to the theory that Satan's attempt to discover Christ's real nature is an element of the poem's action. A possible reply is that Satan is here speaking in public, so his words cannot be taken at their face value.

i *94–5. the utmost edge / Of hazard*] Echoes *All's Well* III iii 6: 'to th'extreme edge of hazard'.

i *97. couched*] concealed.

i *100.* Cp. *PL* ii 430–66, where Satan volunteers to undertake the journey to earth.

He ended, and his words impression left
Of much amazement to the infernal crew,
Distracted and surprised with deep dismay
At these sad tidings; but no time was then
For long indulgence to their fears or grief:
Unanimous they all commit the care
And management of this main enterprise
To him their great dictator, whose attempt
At first against mankind so well had thrived
In Adam's overthrow, and led their march
From hell's deep-vaulted den to dwell in light,
Regents and potentates, and kings, yea gods
Of many a pleasant realm and province wide.
So to the coast of Jordan he directs
His easy steps; girded with snaky wiles,
Where he might likeliest find this new-declared,
This man of men, attested Son of God,
Temptation and all guile on him to try;
So to subvert whom he suspected raised
To end his reign on earth so long enjoyed:
But contrary unweeting he fulfilled
The purposed counsel pre-ordained and fixed
Of the Most High, who in full frequence bright
Of angels, thus to Gabriel smiling spake.
Gabriel this day by proof thou shalt behold,
Thou and all angels conversant on earth
With man or men's affairs, how I begin
To verify that solemn message late,
On which I sent thee to the virgin pure
In Galilee, that she should bear a son
Great in renown, and called the Son of God;
Then told'st her doubting how these things could be

i *113. dictator*] Z. S. Fink, *JEGP* xl (1941) 482–8, takes this title in its seventeenth-century political sense of a person or council granted unlimited but temporary power in a time of national emergency. Harrington in *Oceana* included a dictator as a necessary part of a commonwealth, but M., in his *Ready and Easy Way*, did not. Satan's ineffectiveness as a dictator in *PR* amounts, in Fink's estimation, to a comment about political theory.
i *117. gods*] As in *PL* M. identifies the pagan gods with the fallen angels.
i *120. girded with snaky wiles*] In contrast to *Isa.* xi 5: 'righteousness shall be the girdle of his loins', and *Eph.* vi 14: 'having your loins girt about with truth'.
i *128. frequence*] attendance.
i *129. Gabriel*] guardian of Eden in *PL* iv, and the angel of the Annunciation.
i *134–40.* Cp. *Luke* i 26–38.

To her a virgin, that on her should come
The Holy Ghost, and the power of the Highest
O'ershadow her: this man born and now upgrown,
To show him worthy of his birth divine
And high prediction, henceforth I expose
To Satan; let him tempt and now assay
His utmost subtlety, because he boasts
And vaunts of his great cunning to the throng
Of his apostasy; he might have learnt
Less overweening, since he failed in Job,
Whose constant perseverance overcame
Whate'er his cruel malice could invent.
He now shall know I can produce a man
Of female seed, far abler to resist
All his solicitations, and at length
All his vast force, and drive him back to hell,
Winning by conquest what the first man lost
By fallacy surprised. But first I mean
To exercise him in the wilderness,

i *146. apostasy*] the apostate angels.

i *147. overweening*] arrogance. *Job*] the first of five references to him in *PR* (see i 369, 425; iii 64–7, 95). The *Book of Job* was the model M. suggested for the 'brief' epic (Columbia iii 237, Yale i 813). Hughes[2] 264 considers that M. may have been indebted to it in *PR* conceptually as well as structurally: 'Job had come to be recognized as the greatest exemplar of the Christian version of Aristotle's high-mindedness or magnanimity.' Possibly, too, M. thought that the *Book of Job* was epic in its verse form: C.W. Jones, *SP* xliv (1947) 209–27 draws attention to the belief held by Jerome, Origen and others of the Fathers that Hebrew poetry was metrical in a Greek sense: Jerome, in the introduction to his translation of *Job*, says that the verse part is mainly in hexameters.

Lewalski 112 quotes from Gregory *Moralia in Job* as a precedent for relating Job and Christ as heroes exhibited by God: 'God's saying to Satan in figure, *Hast thou considered my servant Job*, is His exhibiting in his despite the Only-Begotten Son as an object of wonder in the form of a servant.'

i *152–3*. The distinction between 'solicitations' and 'force' foreshadows that between the earlier trials and those of the storm and the pinnacle, which entail violence.

i *156. exercise*] Cp. *De doctrina* i 8 (Columbia xv 86–7): 'A good temptation is that whereby God tempts even the righteous for the purpose of proving them, not as though he were ignorant of the disposition of their hearts, but for the purpose of exercising (*exercendam*) or manifesting their faith or patience.'

There he shall first lay down the rudiments
Of his great warfare, ere I send him forth
To conquer Sin and Death the two grand foes,
By humiliation and strong sufferance:
His weakness shall o'ercome Satanic strength
And all the world, and mass of sinful flesh;
That all the angels and ethereal powers,
They now, and men hereafter may discern,
From what consummate virtue I have chose
This perfect man, by merit called my Son,
To earn salvation for the sons of men.
  So spake the eternal Father, and all heaven
Admiring stood a space; then into hymns
Burst forth, and in celestial measures moved,
Circling the throne and singing, while the hand
Sung with the voice, and this the argument.
  Victory and triumph to the Son of God
Now ent'ring his great duel, not of arms,
But to vanquish by wisdom hellish wiles.
The Father knows the Son; therefore secure
Ventures his filial virtue, though untried,
Against whate'er may tempt, whate'er seduce,
Allure, or terrify, or undermine.
Be frustrate all ye stratagems of hell,
And devilish machinations come to nought.
  So they in heaven their odes and vigils tuned:
Meanwhile the Son of God, who yet some days

i *157–8. the rudiments / Of his great warfare*] Echoes Virgil, *Aen.* xi 156–7 *bellique . . . rudimenta.*

i *159. Sin and Death*] Cp. *PL* ii 648–73 and x 585–609.

i *161.* Cp. *1 Cor.* i 27: 'God hath chosen the weak things of the world to confound the things which are mighty.'

i *165–7.* A. P. Fiore, *Franciscan Studies* xv (1955) 48–59, 257–82, in his study of M.'s soteriology, relates these lines to the definition of redemption in the *De doctrina* (Columbia xv 252–3). This definition, however, does *not* raise the question of Christ's 'merit'. Cp. *PL* iii 308–9 and vi 43.

i *171. hand*] the hand which played upon a stringed instrument.

i *172. argument*] subject, theme.

i *176. The Father knows the Son*] Cp. *John* x 15: 'As the Father knoweth me, even so know I the Father.' *secure*] without anxiety.

i *180. frustrate*] frustrated; a common form from the fifteenth century to the seventeenth.

i *182. vigils*] night hymns.

Lodged in Bethabara where John baptized,
Musing and much revolving in his breast,
How best the mighty work he might begin
Of saviour to mankind, and which way first
Publish his godlike office now mature,
One day forth walked alone, the spirit leading
And his deep thoughts, the better to converse
With solitude, till far from track of men,
Thought following thought, and step by step led on,
He entered now the bordering desert wild,
And with dark shades and rocks environed round,
His holy meditations thus pursued.
  O what a multitude of thoughts at once
Awakened in me swarm, while I consider
What from within I feel myself, and hear
What from without comes often to my ears,
Ill sorting with my present state compared.
When I was yet a child, no childish play
To me was pleasing, all my mind was set
Serious to learn and know, and thence to do
What might be public good; myself I thought
Born to that end, born to promote all truth,
All righteous things: therefore above my years,
The Law of God I read, and found it sweet,
Made it my whole delight, and in it grew

i *184. Bethabara*] Cp. *John* i 28: 'These things were done in Bethabara beyond Jordan, where John was baptizing.'
i *189. spirit*] See i 8*n. 1671* has a semicolon at the end of the line which is probably an error, though not corrected in the *Errata.* The sense seems to require no stop.
i *193. desert*] Though this is clearly the desert near Bethabara, i 350–4 and ii 306–14 appear to identify it with the wilderness of Beersheba where Hagar wandered and into which Elijah retreated, and with the wilderness of Sin where the Israelites were fed with manna. M. seems to have regarded the whole desert area of the near East as a single wilderness (see i 350–4*n*).
i *200. sorting*] corresponding.
i *204. What might be public good*] Schultz 80 reviews the traditional application of utility as a criterion of learning, which Christ's qualification here implies, and points to a similar emphasis in *Of Education.*
i *204–5.* Cp. *John* xviii 37: 'To this end was I born, and for this cause came I into the world, that I should bear witness unto the truth.'
i *206–7. above my years*] Perhaps echoing *Aen.* ix 311: *Ante annos animumque gerens curamque virilem* (with a man's mind and a spirit beyond his years).
i *208. delight*] Cp. *Ps.* i 2: 'But his delight is in the law of the Lord.'

To such perfection, that ere yet my age
Had measured twice six years, at our great feast
I went into the Temple, there to hear
The teachers of our Law, and to propose
What might improve my knowledge or their own;
And was admired by all, yet this not all
To which my spirit aspired, victorious deeds
Flamed in my heart, heroic acts, one while
To rescue Israel from the Roman yoke,
Thence to subdue and quell o'er all the earth
Brute violence and proud tyrannic power,
Till truth were freed, and equity restored:
Yet held it more humane, more heavenly first
By winning words to conquer willing hearts,
And make persuasion do the work of fear;
At least to try, and teach the erring soul
Not wilfully misdoing, but unware
Misled; the stubborn only to subdue.
These growing thoughts my mother soon perceiving
By words at times cast forth inly rejoiced,
And said to me apart, High are thy thoughts
O son, but nourish them and let them soar
To what highth sacred virtue and true worth
Can raise them, though above example high;
By matchless deeds express thy matchless sire.
For know, thou art no son of mortal man,
Though men esteem thee low of parentage,
Thy father is the eternal King, who rules
All heaven and earth, angels and sons of men,
A messenger from God foretold thy birth
Conceived in me a virgin, he foretold
Thou shouldst be great and sit on David's throne,
And of thy kingdom there should be no end.
At thy nativity a glorious choir
Of angels in the fields of Bethlehem sung

i *209–14*. Cp. *Luke* ii 46–50, where Christ, at Passover time, astonishes the doctors of the Law with his 'understanding and answers'.

i *214*. *admired*] wondered at.

i *226*. *subdue*] *1671* has 'destroy', corrected to 'subdue' in the *Errata*. Cp. *Luke* ix 56: 'For the Son of man is not come to destroy men's lives.'

i *233*. *express*] make apparent.

i *238–54*. The details are taken from *Matt.* i–ii and *Luke* i–ii.

i *239–41*. Cp. *Luke* i 32–3: 'He shall be great . . . and the Lord God shall give unto him the throne of his father David . . . and of his kingdom there shall be no end.'

To shepherds watching at their folds by night,
And told them the Messiah now was born,
Where they might see him, and to thee they came,
Directed to the manger where thou lay'st,
For in the inn was left no better room:
A star, not seen before in heaven appearing
Guided the wise men thither from the east,
To honour thee with incense, myrrh, and gold,
By whose bright course led on they found the place,
Affirming it thy star new-graven in heaven,
By which they knew thee King of Israel born.
Just Simeon and prophetic Anna, warned
By vision, found thee in the Temple, and spake
Before the altar and the vested priest,
Like things of thee to all that present stood.
This having heard, straight I again revolved
The Law and prophets, searching what was writ
Concerning the Messiah, to our scribes
Known partly, and soon found of whom they spake
I am; this chiefly, that my way must lie
Through many a hard assay even to the death,
Ere I the promised kingdom can attain,
Or work redemption for mankind, whose sins'
Full weight must be transferred upon my head.
Yet neither thus disheartened or dismayed,
The time prefixed I waited, when behold
The Baptist, (of whose birth I oft had heard,
Not knew by sight) now come, who was to come
Before Messiah and his way prepare.
I as all others to his baptism came,
Which I believed was from above; but he
Straight knew me, and with loudest voice proclaimed
Me him (for it was shown him so from heaven)
Me him whose harbinger he was; and first
Refused on me his baptism to confer,
As much his greater, and was hardly won;

i *255. Just*] Cp. *Luke* ii 25: 'And the same man was just.' *prophetic*] Cp. *Luke* ii 36: 'And there was one Anna, a prophetess.'

i *258*. This is the last line of Mary's speech.

i *264. Through many a hard assay*] Echoes *F.Q.* II i 35: 'Through many hard assayes'.

i *266–7*. Cp. *Isa.* liii 6: 'The Lord hath laid on him the iniquity of us all.'

i *270–89*. M. follows the accounts in *Matt.* iii, *Luke* iii and *Mark* i.

i *279. hardly won*] persuaded with difficulty.

But as I rose out of the laving stream,
Heaven opened her eternal doors, from whence
The Spirit descended on me like a dove,
And last the sum of all, my Father's voice,
Audibly heard from heaven, pronounced me his,
Me his beloved Son, in whom alone
He was well pleased; by which I knew the time
Now full, that I no more should live obscure,
But openly begin, as best becomes
The authority which I derived from heaven.
And now by some strong motion I am led
Into this wilderness, to what intent
I learn not yet, perhaps I need not know;
For what concerns my knowledge God reveals.
  So spake our morning star, then in his rise,
And looking round on every side beheld
A pathless desert, dusk with horrid shades;
The way he came not having marked, return
Was difficult, by human steps untrod;
And he still on was led, but with such thoughts
Accompanied of things past and to come
Lodged in his breast, as well might recommend
Such solitude before choicest society.
Full forty days he passed, whether on hill
Sometimes, anon in shady vale, each night
Under the covert of some ancient oak,
Or cedar, to defend him from the dew,
Or harboured in one cave, is not revealed;
Nor tasted human food, nor hunger felt
Till those days ended, hungered then at last
Among wild beasts: they at his sight grew mild,

i *281. eternal doors*] Cp. *Ps.* xxiv 7: 'everlasting doors'.

i *286–7. the time / Now full*] Cp. *Gal.* iv 4: 'When the fulness of time was come, God sent forth his Son.'

i *291–3.* Cp. *De doctrina* i 5 (Columbia xiv 316–7): 'Even the Son, however, knows not all things absolutely', and *Mark* xiii 32: 'But of that day and that hour knoweth no man, no, not the Son, but the Father.'

i *294. morning star*] Cp. *Rev.* xxii 16, where Jesus says 'I am . . . the bright and morning star'.

i *296. horrid*] bristling (Latin *horridus*).

i *310–13.* Pope 108–10 explains that it was part of the doctrinal tradition of the temptation story that the wild beasts did not molest Christ because he was perfect man. Cp. *Mark* i 3, the only mention of the wild beasts in the gospel accounts, also Giles Fletcher, *Christ's Victory and Triumph* i 40–1, where the animals frolic round Christ, the lion licking his feet and the lamb

Nor sleeping him nor waking harmed, his walk
The fiery serpent fled, and noxious worm,
The lion and fierce tiger glared aloof.
But now an aged man in rural weeds,
Following, as seemed, the quest of some stray ewe,
Or withered sticks to gather; which might serve
Against a winter's day when winds blow keen,
To warm him wet returned from field at eve,
He saw approach, who first with curious eye
Perused him, then with words thus uttered spake.
Sir, what ill chance hath brought thee to this place
So far from path or road of men, who pass
In troop or caravan, for single none
Durst ever, who returned, and dropped not here
His carcase, pined with hunger and with drouth?
I ask the rather, and the more admire,
For that to me thou seem'st the man, whom late
Our new baptizing prophet at the ford
Of Jordan honoured so, and called thee Son
Of God; I saw and heard, for we sometimes
Who dwell this wild, constrained by want, come forth

and tiger standing side by side. Fletcher, like M., is here influenced by various Old Testament prophecies, e.g. *Ezek.* xxxiv 25, *Isa.* xi 6–9 and lxv 25.
i *312. noxious*] harmful. The line is based on *Micah* vii 17.
i *314. an aged man in rural weeds*] Hughes[2] 256 compares Satan's disguise with that of the fiend who 'in likeness of a man of religion' tries to bring Sir Bors into 'error and wanhope' in Malory, *Morte d'Arthur* xvi 13. Sources more usually suggested are Spenser, *F.Q.* I i 29, where Archimago appears as 'An aged Sire, in long blacke weedes yclad, / His feete all bare, his beard all hoarie gray', and Giles Fletcher, *Christ's Victory and Triumph* ii 15, where Satan comes to tempt Christ disguised as 'an aged Syre . . . slowely footing'. Pope 42–7 notes that from the fourteenth-century to the eighteenth writers and artists frequently assume that Satan comes into the wilderness in disguise: there was no general agreement about the disguise adopted. The most common was that of a benevolent old hermit, but he also appears as an old man of mean appearance, an old man richly dressed, and a handsome young man. Some artists and writers gave him three different disguises, one for each temptation (as M. seems to: see ii 298–300 and iv 449).
i *315–6.* Satan's apparent occupations relate to his usual occupation, looking for lost souls (strayed sheep) to burn. Cp. *John* xv 6: 'If a man abide not in me he is cast forth as a branch, and is withered; and men gather them, and cast them into the fire, and they are burned.'
i *324–5. dropped . . . carcase*] Cp. *Num.* xiv 29: 'Your carcases shall fall in this wilderness.' *pined*] wasted away.
i *326. admire*] wonder.

To town or village nigh (nighest is far)
Where aught we hear, and curious are to hear,
What happens new; fame also finds us out.
To whom the Son of God. Who brought me hither
Will bring me hence, no other guide I seek.
By miracle he may, replied the swain,
What other way I see not, for we here
Live on tough roots and stubs, to thirst inured
More than the camel, and to drink go far,
Men to much misery and hardship born;
But if thou be the Son of God, command
That out of these hard stones be made thee bread;
So shalt thou save thyself and us relieve
With food, whereof we wretched seldom taste.
He ended, and the Son of God replied.
Think'st thou such force in bread? Is it not written
(For I discern thee other than thou seem'st)
Man lives not by bread only, but each word
Proceeding from the mouth of God; who fed
Our fathers here with manna; in the mount
Moses was forty days, nor eat nor drank,
And forty days Elijah without food
Wandered this barren waste, the same I now:
Why dost thou then suggest to me distrust,

i *332. nighest*] the nearest town or village.
i *334. fame . . . out*] rumour (Latin *fama*) reaches us too.
i *339. stubs*] stumps of plants, shrubs or trees.
i *342–50.* The original of this dialogue is *Luke* iv 3–4.
i *344. save thyself*] See ii 245–59*n*.
i *349–50.* Cp. *Deut.* viii 3: 'He . . . fed thee with manna . . . that he might make thee know that man doth not live by bread only, but by every word that proceedeth out of the mouth of the Lord.'
i *350–4.* Cp. *Exod.* xxiv 18: 'Moses was in the mount forty days', when he received the commandments on Mt Sinai. It was, as Pope 110–12 shows, a well-documented branch of the tradition that identified the wilderness of the temptation with the desert in which the Jews wandered for forty years, and Moses and Elijah fasted for forty days. The typological appropriateness of this identification leads M. to adopt it. Other commentators, with more realistic geography, made the temptation-wilderness that between Jerusalem and Jericho.
i *353.* In *1 Kings* xix 8 Elijah travels to Mt Horeb for forty days and nights without food.
i *355. distrust*] Pope 56–64 notes that M., in making the first temptation not one of gluttony but of distrust in God, follows Calvin and the Protestant theologians, (see iv 110–20*n*). He presents Eve's temptation (*PL* ix 703–5)

Knowing who I am, as I know who thou art?
Whom thus answered the Arch-fiend now undisguised.
'Tis true, I am that spirit unfortunate,
Who leagued with millions more in rash revolt
Kept not my happy station, but was driven
With them from bliss to the bottomless deep,
Yet to that hideous place not so confined
By rigour unconniving, but that oft
Leaving my dolorous prison I enjoy
Large liberty to round this globe of earth,
Or range in the air, nor from the heaven of heavens
Hath he excluded my resort sometimes.
I came among the sons of God, when he
Gave up into my hands Uzzean Job
To prove him, and illustrate his high worth;
And when to all his angels he proposed

as one of the same kind, thus preserving the traditional equation between those temptations Christ withstood and those to which Adam and Eve succumbed.

i *356. Knowing who I am*] Woodhouse 171–2 takes these words as proof that Satan's alleged doubt about Christ's identity is not real but 'assiduously fostered': 'He will not let himself acknowledge the truth'. E. L. Marilla, *Studia Neophilologica* xxvii (1955) 184, also assumes that this line destroys the theory that the temptations are Satan's attempt to establish Christ's identity. However, 'Knowing who I am' can merely mean 'Knowing that I am the Son of God': in this sense Satan knows who Christ is: what worries him is the meaning of that title.

i *363. unconniving*] unwinking, ever-vigilant; this is the only recorded example of the word; cp. Lat. *inconivus*.

i *368–76.* Cp. *Job* i 6: 'The sons of God came to present themselves before the Lord, and Satan came also among them', and *1 Kings* xxii 20–2: 'And the Lord said, Who shall persuade Ahab, that he may go up and fall at Ramoth-gilead? And one said on this manner, and another said on that manner. And there came forth a spirit, and stood before the Lord, and said, I will persuade him. And the Lord said unto him, Wherewith? And he said, I will go forth, and I will be a lying spirit in the mouth of all his prophets.' The same encounter is related in *2 Chron.* xviii 19–22. The identification of this 'lying spirit' with Satan, and the coupling of the cases of Ahab and Job, may have been suggested by the margin of the A.V. which, at *2 Chron.* xviii 20, refers to *Job* i 6, or, as A. I. Carlisle, *RES* n.s. v (1954) 249–55, thinks, by Ludwig Lavater, *In Libros Chronicorum*, to which M. refers in *Trin. MS* when discussing *1 Kings* xxii.

i *369. Uzzean*] Cp. *Job* i 1: 'There was a man in the land of Uz whose name was Job.'

To draw the proud king Ahab into fraud
That he might fall in Ramoth, they demurring,
I undertook that office, and the tongues
Of all his flattering prophets glibbed with lies
To his destruction, as I had in charge.
For what he bids I do; though I have lost
Much lustre of my native brightness, lost
To be beloved of God, I have not lost
To love, at least contemplate and admire
What I see excellent in good, or fair,
Or virtuous, I should so have lost all sense.
What can be then less in me than desire
To see thee and approach thee, whom I know
Declared the Son of God, to hear attent
Thy wisdom, and behold thy godlike deeds?
Men generally think me much a foe
To all mankind: why should I? they to me
Never did wrong or violence, by them
I lost not what I lost, rather by them
I gained what I have gained, and with them dwell
Copartner in these regions of the world,
If not disposer; lend them oft my aid,
Oft my advice by presages and signs,
And answers, oracles, portents and dreams,

i *372. fraud*] the state of being defrauded or deluded (Latin *fraus*); this sense of the word is not found outside M.

i *373. they demurring*] while they hesitated.

i *375. glibbed*] made smooth.

i *378. brightness*] Cp. *PL* i 591–2, vii 132–3.

i *379–80.* Cp. *PL* ii 482–3.

i *383. What can be then less in me than desire*] This line has caused some difficulty. C. L. Barnes, *N & Q* clvi (1929) 440 and clvii (1929) 251, thought 'less' an error for 'more'; but E. Bensly, *N & Q* clvii (1929) 177–8, explains the meaning as 'How can I feel anything less than a desire too . . .'. Lewalski 351 agrees with Bensly, but praises the ironic *double-entendre*: the word-arrangement suggests the opposite and truer meaning, that there can be nothing Satan desires less than thus to confront and listen to Christ.

i *385. attent*] attentive; a common seventeenth-century form.

i *393–6.* Cp. ll. 430–3, 446–51, 455–64. The orthodox patristic view, put forward by Lactantius, *Divine Institutes* ii 16 and Eusebius, *Praeparatio Evangelica* ii, was that the fallen angels inhabited the shrines of the pagan oracles and made pronouncements in the names of the classical deities. In this they were aided by an ability to travel in spirit to any point on the earth's surface in a moment of time, and also by a foreknowledge of certain events retained from prelapsarian days.

Whereby they may direct their future life.
Envy they say excites me, thus to gain
Companions of my misery and woe.
At first it may be; but long since with woe
Nearer acquainted, now I feel by proof,
That fellowship in pain divides not smart,
Nor lightens aught each man's peculiar load.
Small consolation then, were man adjoined:
This wounds me most (what can it less) that man,
Man fall'n shall be restored, I never more.
  To whom our Saviour sternly thus replied.
Deservedly thou griev'st, composed of lies
From the beginning, and in lies wilt end;
Who boast'st release from hell, and leave to come
Into the heaven of heavens; thou com'st indeed,
As a poor miserable captive thrall,
Comes to the place where he before had sat
Among the prime in splendour, now deposed,
Ejected, emptied, gazed, unpitied, shunned,
A spectacle of ruin or of scorn
To all the host of heaven; the happy place
Imparts to thee no happiness, no joy,
Rather inflames thy torment, representing
Lost bliss, to thee no more communicable,
So never more in hell than when in heaven.
But thou art serviceable to heaven's King.
Wilt thou impute to obedience what thy fear
Extorts, or pleasure to do ill excites?
What but thy malice moved thee to misdeem
Of righteous Job, then cruelly to afflict him

i *401. That fellowship . . . smart*] Cp. the Latin tag *solamen miseris socios habuisse doloris*, Englished in *Lucrece* 790 as 'fellowship in woe doth woe assuage'. Seneca, *De Consolatione* xii 5, considers that the solace that comes from having company in misery smacks of ill-will.

i *407. composed of lies*] In *John* viii 44 Satan is called 'a liar, and the father of it'.

i *410–20.* Though up to this point in the poem Christ has apparently no recollection of his heavenly existence before the incarnation, these lines seem to imply that memory is returning, or that God has granted illumination (see i 293). Lewalski 212, however, calls Christ's speech 'an imaginative recreation of the scene based upon traditional (Christian) exegesis of the Job story', and believes that Christ does not recollect his encounters with Satan in heaven until the tower temptation.

i *413. prime*] foremost.

i *420.* Cp. *PL* ix 467–70.

i *423.* Cp. *PL* i 160.

With all inflictions, but his patience won?
The other service was thy chosen task,
To be a liar in four hundred mouths;
For lying is thy sustenance, thy food.
Yet thou pretend'st to truth; all oracles
By thee are given, and what confessed more true
Among the nations? that hath been thy craft,
By mixing somewhat true to vent more lies.
But what have been thy answers, what but dark
Ambiguous and with double sense deluding,
Which they who asked have seldom understood,
And not well understood as good not known?
Who ever by consulting at thy shrine
Returned the wiser, or the more instruct
To fly or follow what concerned him most,
And run not sooner to his fatal snare?
For God hath justly given the nations up
To thy delusions; justly, since they fell
Idolatrous, but when his purpose is
Among them to declare his providence
To thee not known, whence hast thou then thy truth,
But from him or his angels president
In every province, who themselves disdaining

i *428.* Cp. i 368–76*n*, and *1 Kings* xxii 6: 'Then the king of Israel gathered the prophets together, about four hundred men, and said unto them, Shall I go against Ramoth-gilead to battle, or shall I forbear? And they said, Go up.'

i *433. vent*] utter.

i *434–5.* Cp. Cicero, *Of Divination* ii 56, of the oracle of Apollo: 'Chrysippus filled a whole volume with your oracles; of these some, as I think, were false; some came true by chance, as happens very often even in ordinary speech; some were so intricate and obscure that their interpreter needs an interpreter and the oracles themselves must be referred back to the oracle; and some so equivocal that they require a dialectician to construe them.'

i *446–7. whence . . . But from him*] Aquinas, *Summa* II ii 172 (6) says, citing Balaam as an example, that the pagan prophets were not always inspired by devils but sometimes by God, and so spoke truth: thus, he explains, the Sibyl foretold Christ's coming. Even when they were inspired by devils, he adds, they sometimes told the truth, either through the intervention of good spirits, or by virtue of the devils' own nature which was created by the Holy Spirit, or because God used the devils to make the truth known and revealed divine mysteries to them through the agency of angels.

i *447–8. angels president / In every province*] Cp. *De doctrina* I ix (Columbia xv 102–3): 'It appears also probable that there are certain angels appointed to preside over nations, kingdoms and particular districts.'

To approach thy temples, give thee in command
What to the smallest tittle thou shalt say
To thy adorers; thou with trembling fear,
Or like a fawning parasite obey'st;
Then to thyself ascrib'st the truth foretold.
But this thy glory shall be soon retrenched;
No more shalt thou by oracling abuse
The Gentiles; henceforth oracles are ceased,
And thou no more with pomp and sacrifice
Shalt be inquired at Delphos or elsewhere,
At least in vain, for they shall find thee mute.
God hath now sent his living oracle
Into the world, to teach his final will,
And sends his spirit of truth henceforth to dwell
In pious hearts, an inward oracle
To all truth requisite for men to know.
   So spake our Saviour; but the subtle Fiend,
Though inly stung with anger and disdain,
Dissembled, and this answer smooth returned.
   Sharply thou hast insisted on rebuke,
And urged me hard with doings, which not will
But misery hath wrested from me; where
Easily canst thou find one miserable,
And not enforced oft-times to part from truth;
If it may stand him more in stead to lie,
Say and unsay, feign, flatter, or abjure?
But thou art placed above me, thou art Lord;
From thee I can and must submiss endure
Check or reproof, and glad to scape so quit.
Hard are the ways of truth, and rough to walk,
Smooth on the tongue discoursed, pleasing to the ear,
And tunable as sylvan pipe or song;
What wonder then if I delight to hear
Her dictates from thy mouth? Most men admire
Virtue, who follow not her lore: permit me
To hear thee when I come (since no man comes)
And talk at least, though I despair to attain.

i 454. *retrenched*] done away with.

i 455. *oracling*] A rare word but not M.'s coinage; first recorded 1656.

i 456. *oracles are ceased*] Cp. *Nativity Ode* 173, and *Micah* v 12.

i 458. *Delphos*] Cp. *Nativity Ode* 178.

i 462. *spirit of truth*] Cp. *John* xvi 13: 'Howbeit, when he, the Spirit of truth, is come, he will guide you into all truth.'

i 466. *disdain*] anger, vexation.

i 477. *scape so quit*] escape with so light a quittance as a reproof.

Thy father, who is holy, wise and pure,
Suffers the hypocrite or atheous priest
To tread his sacred courts, and minister
About his altar, handling holy things,
Praying or vowing, and vouchsafed his voice
To Balaam reprobate, a prophet yet
Inspired; disdain not such access to me.
  To whom our Saviour with unaltered brow.
Thy coming hither, though I know thy scope,
I bid not or forbid; do as thou find'st
Permission from above; thou canst not more.
  He added not; and Satan bowing low
His grey dissimulation, disappeared
Into thin air diffused: for now began
Night with her sullen wing to double-shade
The desert, fowls in their clay nests were couched;
And now wild beasts came forth the woods to roam.

THE SECOND BOOK

  Meanwhile the new-baptized, who yet remained
At Jordan with the Baptist, and had seen
Him whom they heard so late expressly called
Jesus Messiah Son of God declared,
And on that high authority had believed,

i *490–2.* When Balak, King of Moab, urged Balaam to curse the Israelites, he replied, *Num.* xxiii 20: 'Behold, I have received commandment to bless: and he hath blessed; and I cannot reverse it.' Fixler 254 notes that, while Christian writers maintained an attitude of unrelieved blackness towards Balaam, Jewish tradition was mixed, regarding him at times as a prophet on a level with Moses.

i *494. scope*] drift, purpose.

i *495–6.* Cp. *PL* iv 1006–9.

i *498. grey dissimulation*] Perhaps an echo of Ford, *Broken Heart* IV ii 101: 'Lay by thy whining grey dissimulation.'

i *499. Into thin air diffused*] Echoes Virgil's account of the disappearance of Mercury, *Aen.* iv 278: *procul in tenuem ex oculis evanuit auram* (vanished into thin air, far from the eyes of men).

i *500. sullen*] dark in colour. The 'sullen wing' probably echoes *Aen.* viii 369: *Nox ruit et fuscis tellurem amplectitur alis* (night rushes down and clasps the earth with dusky wings). *double-shade*] Cp. *Comus* 335 and Ovid, *Met.* xi 549–50: 'The shadows of the pitchy clouds hide all the sky and double the darkness of the night.'

And with him talked, and with him lodged, I mean
Andrew and Simon, famous after known
With others though in Holy Writ not named,
Now missing him their joy so lately found,
So lately found, and so abruptly gone,
Began to doubt, and doubted many days,
And as the days increased, increased their doubt:
Sometimes they thought he might be only shown,
And for a time caught up to God, as once
Moses was in the mount, and missing long;
And the great Thisbite who on fiery wheels
Rode up to heaven, yet once again to come.
Therefore as those young prophets then with care
Sought lost Elijah, so in each place these
Nigh to Bethabara, in Jericho
The city of palms, Aenon, and Salem old,
Machaerus and each town or city walled
On this side the broad lake Genezaret,
Or in Perea, but returned in vain.
Then on the bank of Jordan, by a creek:
Where winds with reeds, and osiers whisp'ring play

ii *6. lodged*] Cp. *John* i 39: 'They came and saw where he dwelt, and abode with him that day.'
ii *15. Moses . . . missing long*] Cp. *Exod.* xxxii 1: 'And when the people saw that Moses delayed to come down out of the mount, the people gathered themselves together unto Aaron and said . . . as for this Moses . . . we wot not what is become of him.'
ii *16. Thisbite*] Elijah, called 'the Tishbite' in *1 Kings* xvii 1. The city of Thisbe, or Thesbon, was east of Jordan, in Gilead. *on fiery wheels*] Cp. *2 Kings* ii 11: 'Behold, there appeared a chariot of fire, and horses of fire, and parted them both asunder; and Elijah went up by a whirlwind into heaven.'
ii *17. yet . . . to come*] Cp. *Mal.* iv 5: 'Behold, I will send you Elijah the prophet before the coming of the great and dreadful day of the Lord.'
ii *18–19.* Cp. *2 Kings* ii 15–17; after Elijah's translation 'fifty strong men' of the 'sons of the Prophets' searched for him 'three days, but found him not'.
ii *20–21. Jericho . . . palms*] Cp. *Deut.* xxxiv 3: 'Jericho, the city of palm trees'.
ii *21. Aenon . . . Salem old*] Cp. John iii 23: 'And John was also baptizing in Aenon near to Salim, because there was much water there': 'old' probably means that M. identifies this 'Salim' with the Salem of *Gen.* xiv 18, of which Melchizedek was king.
ii *22. Machaerus*] A fortress in Peraea, in the desert east of the Dead Sea, the traditional scene of John the Baptist's execution.
ii *23. lake Genezaret*] the Sea of Galilee.

Plain fishermen, no greater men them call,
Close in a cottage low together got
Their unexpected loss and plaints outbreathed.
Alas, from what high hope to what relapse
Unlooked for are we fallen, our eyes beheld
Messiah certainly now come, so long
Expected of our fathers; we have heard
His words, his wisdom full of grace and truth,
Now, now, for sure, deliverance is at hand,
The kingdom shall to Israel be restored:
Thus we rejoiced, but soon our joy is turned
Into perplexity and new amaze:
For whither is he gone, what accident
Hath rapt him from us? will he now retire
After appearance, and again prolong
Our expectation? God of Israel,
Send thy Messiah forth, the time is come;
Behold the kings of the earth how they oppress
Thy chosen, to what highth their power unjust
They have exalted, and behind them cast
All fear of thee, arise and vindicate
Thy glory, free thy people from their yoke,
But let us wait; thus far he hath performed,
Sent his anointed, and to us revealed him,
By his great prophet, pointed at and shown,
In public, and with him we have conversed;
Let us be glad of this, and all our fears
Lay on his providence; he will not fail
Nor will withdraw him now, nor will recall,
Mock us with his blest sight, then snatch him hence,
Soon we shall see our hope, our joy return.
Thus they out of their plaints new hope resume
To find whom at the first they found unsought:
But to his mother Mary, when she saw

ii *27*. Cp. Spenser, *Shep. Cal.* January 1: 'A shepeheards boye, (no better doe him call,)', and Phineas Fletcher's imitation, which M. is imitating, *Piscatory Eclogues* iii 1 'A fisher-lad (no higher dares he look)'.
ii *34. full . . . truth*] Cp. *John* i 14: 'And the Word was made flesh, and dwelt among us, . . . full of grace and truth.'
ii *36. The kingdom . . . restored*] In *Acts* i 6 the disciples ask the resurrected Jesus: 'Wilt thou at this time restore again the kingdom to Israel?'
ii *40. rapt*] snatched.
ii *44. the kings of the earth . . . oppress*] Cp. *Ps.* ii 2: 'The kings of the earth set themselves . . . against the Lord.'

Others returned from baptism, not her son,
Nor left at Jordan, tidings of him none;
Within her breast, though calm; her breast though
    pure,
Motherly cares and fears got head, and raised
Some troubled thoughts, which she in sighs thus clad.
  O what avails me now that honour high
To have conceived of God, or that salute
Hail highly favoured, among women blest;
While I to sorrows am no less advanced,
And fears as eminent, above the lot
Of other women, by the birth I bore,
In such a season born when scarce a shed
Could be obtained to shelter him or me
From the bleak air; a stable was our warmth,
A manger his; yet soon enforced to fly
Thence into Egypt, till the murderous king
Were dead, who sought his life, and missing filled
With infant blood the streets of Bethlehem;
From Egypt home returned, in Nazareth
Hath been our dwelling many years, his life
Private, unactive, calm, contemplative,
Little suspicious to any king; but now
Full grown to man, acknowledged, as I hear,
By John the Baptist, and in public shown,
Son owned from heaven by his Father's voice;
I looked for some great change; to honour? no,
But trouble, as old Simeon plain foretold,
That to the fall and rising he should be
Of many in Israel, and to a sign
Spoken against, that through my very soul
A sword shall pierce, this is my favoured lot,

ii *61–2. not her son . . . none*] He did not return from baptism, he had not remained at Jordan, and there was no news of him.
ii *67. salute*] greeting; i.e. *Luke* i 28: 'Hail, thou that art highly favoured, the Lord is with thee: blessed art thou among women.'
ii *76. king*] Herod.
ii *82. suspicious*] worthy of suspicion.
ii *87–91.* Cp. i 255–6, and *Luke* ii 34–5: 'And Simeon blessed them, and said unto Mary his mother, Behold, this child is set for the fall and rising again of many in Israel; and for a sign which shall be spoken against; (Yea, a sword shall pierce through thy own soul also,) that the thoughts of many hearts may be revealed.'
ii *90. Spoken against*] decried.

My exaltation to afflictions high;
Afflicted I may be, it seems, and blest;
I will not argue that, nor will repine.
But where delays he now? some great intent
Conceals him: when twelve years he scarce had seen,
I lost him, but so found, as well I saw
He could not lose himself; but went about
His Father's business; what he meant I mused,
Since understand; much more his absence now
Thus long to some great purpose he obscures.
But I to wait with patience am inured;
My heart hath been a storehouse long of things
And sayings laid up, portending strange events.
  Thus Mary pondering oft, and oft to mind
Recalling what remarkably had passed
Since first her salutation heard, with thoughts
Meekly composed awaited the fulfilling:
The while her son tracing the desert wild,
Sole but with holiest meditations fed,
Into himself descended, and at once
All his great work to come before him set;
How to begin, how to accomplish best
His end of being on earth, and mission high:
For Satan with sly preface to return
Had left him vacant, and with speed was gone
Up to the middle region of thick air,
Where all his potentates in council sat;

ii *92. exaltation*] Donne, *Sermons* ed. E. M. Simpson and G. R. Potter (Berkeley 1958) ix 193, points out that 'in pure, and Originall Hebrew, the word [Mary] signifies *Exaltation*, and whatsoever is best in the kinde thereof'.
ii *94. argue*] dispute (that she may be both afflicted and blessed).
ii *96–100.* See i 209–15.
ii *97–8. so found . . . himself*] I found him in such circumstances that I realized he was able to take care of himself.
ii *99. His Father's business*] Cp. *Luke* ii 49, 51: 'Wist ye not that I must be about my Father's business? . . . but his mother kept all these sayings in her heart.' *mused*] wondered.
ii *101. obscures*] hides the reason for.
ii *103–4.* Cp. *Luke* ii 19: 'Mary kept all these things, and pondered them in her heart.'
ii *106. what . . . passed*] what had passed that was worthy of notice.
ii *115. preface*] Used in the literal sense of the Latin *praefatio* ('a saying before'); the only recorded example of the word in this sense. M. means that before Satan left he said he would return.
ii *116. vacant*] at leisure.

There without sign of boast, or sign of joy,
Solicitous and blank he thus began.
Princes, heaven's ancient sons, ethereal thrones,
Demonian spirits now, from the element
Each of his reign allotted, rightlier called,
Powers of fire, air, water, and earth beneath,
So may we hold our place and these mild seats
Without new trouble; such an enemy
Is risen to invade us, who no less
Threatens than our expulsion down to hell;
I, as I undertook, and with the vote
Consenting in full frequence was empowered,
Have found him, viewed him, tasted him, but find
Far other labour to be undergone
Than when I dealt with Adam first of men,
Though Adam by his wife's allurement fell,
However to this man inferior far,
If he be man by mother's side at least,
With more than human gifts from heaven adorned,
Perfections absolute, graces divine,
And amplitude of mind to greatest deeds,
Therefore I am returned, lest confidence
Of my success with Eve in Paradise
Deceive ye to persuasion over-sure
Of like succeeding here; I summon all
Rather to be in readiness, with hand
Or counsel to assist; lest I who erst
Thought none my equal, now be overmatched.
So spake the old serpent doubting, and from all
With clamour was assured their utmost aid
At his command; when from amidst them rose

ii *120 blank*] resourceless, nonplussed.
ii *122–4*. See *Il Penseroso* 93–6.
ii *130. frequence*] assembly.
ii *131. tasted*] examined, tried out; a frequent seventeenth-century sense.
ii *138. absolute*] finished, complete.
ii *139. amplitude of mind*] The critics who read the Christ of *PR* as an Aristotelian ideal treat this phrase as synonymous with Aristotle's 'magnanimity'. Cp. Cicero, *Tusculan Disputations* ii 26: 'Make this your aim: consider that largeness of soul (*amplitudinem animi*) ... which best shows itself in scorn and contempt for pain, is the one fairest thing in the world, and all the fairer should it be independent of popular approval.'
ii *147. old serpent*] Cp. *Rev*. xii 9 and xx 2: 'That old serpent, called the Devil, and Satan.'

Belial the dissolutest spirit that fell,
The sensualest, and after Asmodai
The fleshliest incubus, and thus advised.
  Set women in his eye and in his walk,
Among daughters of men the fairest found;
Many are in each region passing fair
As the noon sky; more like to goddesses
Than mortal creatures, graceful and discreet,
Expert in amorous arts, enchanting tongues
Persuasive, virgin majesty with mild
And sweet allayed, yet terrible to approach,
Skilled to retire, and in retiring draw
Hearts after them tangled in amorous nets.
Such object hath the power to soften and tame
Severest temper, smooth the rugged'st brow,
Enerve, and with voluptuous hope dissolve,
Draw out with credulous desire, and lead
At will the manliest, resolutest breast,
As the magnetic hardest iron draws.
Women, when nothing else, beguiled the heart
Of wisest Solomon, and made him build,
And made him bow to the gods of his wives.

ii *150. Belial*] See *PL* i 490–3*n* and ii 109–17*n*.
ii *151. Asmodai*] This and the form used in *PL* vi 365 'Asmadai' are closer to Hebrew *Aschemedai* ('the destroyer') than the more usual form 'Asmodeus' in *PL* iv 168 and *Tobit* iii 8. In *Tobit* Asmodeus is an evil spirit who loves Sarah and slaughters her seven husbands in turn: he is thus regarded as the personification of lust.
ii *152. incubus*] a demon specialising in the seduction of women. Augustine, *De Civitate Dei* xv 23 admits their existence.
ii *160.* See *PL* ix 490–1.
ii *161–2.* See *PL* viii 504–5.
ii *163. object*] This word seems to retain some of its older meaning, 'something put in the way so as to interrupt or obstruct a person's course', which is not recorded after the mid-sixteenth century.
ii *164. temper*] temperament. *smooth . . . brow*] See *Il Penseroso* 58.
ii *166. credulous desire*] Perhaps echoing Horace, *Odes* IV i 30, where the ageing lover speaks of his *spes animi credula mutui* (credulous hope of mutual love).
ii *168. magnetic*] magnet; a form confined to the seventeenth century.
ii *169–71.* Cp. *1 Kings* xi 4–8: 'For it came to pass, when Solomon was old, that his wives turned away his heart after other gods . . . Then did Solomon build an high place for Chemosh, the abomination of Moab . . . And likewise did he for all his strange wives, which burnt incense and sacrificed unto their gods.'

To whom quick answer Satan thus returned.
Belial, in much uneven scale thou weigh'st
All others by thyself; because of old
Thou thyself dot'st on womankind, admiring
Their shape, their colour, and attractive grace,
None are, thou think'st, but taken with such toys.
Before the flood thou with thy lusty crew,
False titled Sons of God, roaming the earth
Cast wanton eyes on the daughters of men,
And coupled with them, and begot a race.
Have we not seen, or by relation heard,
In courts and regal chambers how thou lurk'st,
In wood or grove by mossy fountain-side,
In valley or green meadow to waylay
Some beauty rare, Calisto, Clymene,
Daphne, or Semele, Antiopa,
Or Amymone, Syrinx, many more
Too long, then lay'st thy scapes on names adored,
Apollo, Neptune, Jupiter, or Pan,
Satyr, or Faun, or Sylvan? But these haunts
Delight not all; among the sons of men
How many have with a smile made small account
Of beauty and her lures, easily scorned
All her assaults, on worthier things intent!
Remember that Pellean conqueror,
A youth, how all the beauties of the East

ii *178–81.* It seems probable that Satan is not referring to the incident recorded in *Gen.* vi 2, since the orthodox interpretation of that verse, as R. H. West, *MLN* lxv (1950) 187–91, remarks, identified the 'Sons of God' who coupled with the 'daughters of men' as the descendants of Seth, and M. accepts this interpretation in *PL* xi 573–87.

ii *186–8.* These nymphs seduced or pursued by pagan gods are all from Ovid: Calisto was one of Diana's nymphs, seduced by Jove, *Met.* ii 409; Clymene, an oceanid, mother of Phaethon, *Met.* i 757; Daphne, a nymph changed into a laurel when pursued by Apollo, *Met.* i 452; Semele, mother of Bacchus by Jove, *Met.* iii 253; Antiopa, seduced by Jove disguised as a satyr, *Met.* vi 110; Syrinx, a nymph pursued by Pan and turned into a reed, *Met.* i 690; Amymone, a nymph loved by Neptune, *Am.* I x 5. Justin Martyr, *Apologia Prima* 9 and 25, explains that the lustful classical gods were really fallen angels.

ii *189. Too long*] too many to mention.

ii *191. haunts*] habits.

ii *196. Pellean conqueror*] Alexander the Great, born at Pella, capital of Macedonia. After the battle of the Issus and the capture of Darius' wife and daughters, Alexander, according to Plutarch, *Life* 21, treated the women

He slightly viewed, and slightly overpassed;
How he surnamed of Africa dismissed
In his prime youth the fair Iberian maid.
For Solomon he lived at ease, and full
Of honour, wealth, high fare, aimed not beyond
Higher design than to enjoy his state;
Thence to the bait of women lay exposed;
But he whom we attempt is wiser far
Than Solomon, of more exalted mind,
Made and set wholly on the accomplishment
Of greatest things; what woman will you find,
Though of this age the wonder and the fame,
On whom his leisure will vouchsafe an eye
Of fond desire? Or should she confident,
As sitting queen adored on beauty's throne,
Descend with all her winning charms begirt
To enamour, as the zone of Venus once
Wrought that effect on Jove, so fables tell;
How would one look from his majestic brow
Seated as on the top of virtue's hill,
Discount'nance her despised, and put to rout
All her array; her female pride deject,
Or turn to reverent awe! For beauty stands
In the admiration only of weak minds
Led captive; cease to admire, and all her plumes
Fall flat and shrink into a trivial toy,
At every sudden slighting quite abashed:
Therefore with manlier objects we must try
His constancy, with such as have more show

with honour and respect, so that they lived 'as though in sacred and inviolable virgins' chambers instead of in an enemy's camp'. Alexander considered 'the mastery of himself a more kingly thing than the conquest of his enemies': seeing the other captive Persian beauties 'he merely said jestingly that Persian women were torments to the eyes' and 'passed them by as though they were lifeless images for display'.

ii *199. he surnamed of Africa*] Scipio Africanus: Livy xxvi 50 relates that after the fall of New Carthage, 210 B.C., Scipio gave back a beautiful Spanish captive to the young man to whom she was betrothed, Allucius of the Celtiberians.

ii *205–6. wiser far / Than Solomon*] Cp. *Matt.* xii 42: 'Behold, a greater than Solomon is here.'

ii *214–5.* In *Iliad* xiv 214–351 Jove surrenders to Juno when she comes wearing the girdle ('zone') of Venus.

ii *222–3.* The image is based on Ovid's peacock, *Ars Amatoria* i 627, which displays its plumes only when praised.

Of worth, of honour, glory, and popular praise;
Rocks whereon greatest men have oftest wrecked;
Or that which only seems to satisfy
Lawful desires of nature, not beyond;
And now I know he hungers where no food
Is to be found, in the wide wilderness;
The rest commit to me, I shall let pass
No advantage, and his strength as oft assay.
He ceased, and heard their grant in loud acclaim;
Then forthwith to him takes a chosen band
Of spirits likest to himself in guile
To be at hand, and at his beck appear,
If cause were to unfold some active scene
Of various persons each to know his part;
Then to the desert takes with these his flight;
Where still from shade to shade the Son of God
After forty days' fasting had remained,
Now hung'ring first, and to himself thus said.
Where will this end? Four times ten days I have passed
Wandering this woody maze, and human food
Nor tasted, nor had appetite: that fast
To virtue I impute not, or count part
Of what I suffer here; if nature need not,
Or God support nature without repast
Though needing, what praise is it to endure?
But now I feel I hunger, which declares,
Nature hath need of what she asks; yet God
Can satisfy that need some other way,
Though hunger still remain: so it remain
Without this body's wasting, I content me,
And from the sting of famine fear no harm,
Nor mind it, fed with better thoughts that feed
Me hung'ring more to do my Father's will.

ii *235. grant*] assent.
ii *242. shade to shade*] one night to the next.
ii *245–59*. This speech makes it clear that Christ's fast was not a miracle performed by him as man, but by God, with him as object. Christ, as man, was not in control of his appetite. The miraculous nature of the fast cannot, therefore, be used, as G. W. Whiting, *MLN* lxvi (1951) 12–16, attempts to use it, as proof that the hero of *PR* is Christ in his divine nature, rather than in his human nature. Lewalski 202–3 makes the point that, since Christ first feels hunger at this juncture, he was not hungry during the stones-into-bread temptation (i 342–4).
ii *255. so*] provided that.
ii *259*. Cp. *John* iv 34: 'My meat is to do the will of him that sent me.'

It was the hour of night, when thus the Son
Communed in silent walk, then laid him down
Under the hospitable covert nigh
Of trees thick interwoven; there he slept,
And dreamed, as appetite is wont to dream,
Of meats and drinks, nature's refreshment sweet;
Him thought, he by the brook of Cherith stood
And saw the ravens with their horny beaks
Food to Elijah bringing even and morn,
Though ravenous, taught to abstain from what they brought;
He saw the prophet also how he fled
Into the desert, and how there he slept
Under a juniper; then how awaked,
He found his supper on the coals prepared,
And by the angel was bid rise and eat,
And eat the second time after repose,
The strength whereof sufficed him forty days;
Sometimes that with Elijah he partook,
Or as a guest with Daniel at his pulse.
Thus wore out night, and now the herald lark
Left his ground-nest, high towering to descry
The Morn's approach, and greet her with his song:
As lightly from his grassy couch uprose
Our Saviour, and found all was but a dream,
Fasting he went to sleep, and fasting waked.
Up to a hill anon his steps he reared,
From whose high top to ken the prospect round,

ii *262–3. hospitable covert . . . trees thick interwoven*] Cp. Horace, *Odes* II iii 9–11, where pine and poplar interweave their branches to provide *umbram hospitalem*.

ii *266–9.* Cp. *1 Kings* xvii 5–6: 'For he went and dwelt by the brook Cherith, that is before Jordan. And the ravens brought him bread and flesh in the morning, and bread and flesh in the evening; and he drank of the brook.'

ii *270–6.* Cp. *1 Kings* xix 4–8. Elijah, threatened by Jezebel, flees into the wilderness. As he sleeps under a juniper tree: 'An angel touched him, and said unto him, Arise and eat. And he looked, and behold, there was a cake baken on the coals, and a cruse of water at his head.' Elijah eats, sleeps again, is again woken by the angel, eats a second time 'and went in the strength of that meat forty days and forty nights unto Horeb the mount of God.'

ii *278.* Cp. *Dan.* i 3–21, where Daniel refuses to eat the food provided for the children of the Hebrew nobility by order of King Nebuchadnezzar, preferring instead his simple diet of 'pulse' (lentils, beans, etc.).

ii *279. herald lark*] Cp. *Romeo and Juliet* III v 6: 'the lark, the herald of the morn'.

If cottage were in view, sheep-cote or herd;
But cottage, herd or sheep-cote none he saw,
Only in a bottom saw a pleasant grove,
With chant of tuneful birds resounding loud;
Thither he bent his way, determined there
To rest at noon, and entered soon the shade
High-roofed and walks beneath, and alleys brown
That opened in the midst a woody scene,
Nature's own work it seemed (Nature taught Art)
And to a superstitious eye the haunt
Of wood-gods and wood-nymphs; he viewed it round,
When suddenly a man before him stood,
Not rustic as before, but seemlier clad,
As one in city, or court, or palace bred,
And with fair speech these words to him addressed.
 With granted leave officious I return,
But much more wonder that the Son of God
In this wild solitude so long should bide
Of all things destitute, and well I know,
Not without hunger. Others of some note,
As story tells, have trod this wilderness;
The fugitive bond-woman with her son
Outcast Nebaioth, yet found he relief
By a providing angel; all the race
Of Israel here had famished, had not God
Rained from heaven manna, and that prophet bold

ii *289. bottom*] dell.

ii *295.* This line raises a difficulty, as Woodhouse 179–82 points out. If the 'pleasant grove' (l. 289) was only the work of Satan's 'art', why does Christ succumb to the temptation it offers and decide to rest in its shade? A possible answer is that it was not the 'grove' but the 'woody scene' in its 'midst'–Satan's setting for his banquet–which was created by 'art'. This could not be seen from outside the wood.

ii *302. officious*] eager to please (Latin *officiosus*).

ii *308–10.* Hagar and her son Ishmael were cast out by Sarah, *Gen.* xxi 9–21. Ishmael would have died had not an angel shown Hagar a well. M. here calls Ishmael by the name of his eldest son, Nebaioth.

ii *309. he*] Most editors print 'here', the second edn reading.

ii *310–12.* Cp. *Exod.* xvi 35: 'And the children of Israel did eat manna forty years, until they came to a land inhabited.'

ii *312–4.* See ii 270–6*n*. M. apparently confuses Thebez (Tubas, north-east of Mt Ephraim) where Abimelech was slain (*Judges* ix 50–5), with Thisbe or Thesbon in Gilead, Elijah's birthplace.

Native of Thebez wandering here was fed
Twice by a voice inviting him to eat.
Of thee these forty days none hath regard,
Forty and more deserted here indeed.
To whom thus Jesus; What conclud'st thou hence?
They all had need, I as thou seest have none.
How hast thou hunger then? Satan replied,
Tell me if food were now before thee set,
Wouldst thou not eat? Thereafter as I like
The giver, answered Jesus. Why should that
Cause thy refusal, said the subtle Fiend.
Hast thou not right to all created things,
Owe not all creatures by just right to thee
Duty and service, nor to stay till bid,
But tender all their power? Nor mention I
Meats by the law unclean, or offered first
To idols, those young Daniel could refuse;
Nor proffered by an enemy, though who
Would scruple that, with want oppressed? behold
Nature ashamed, or better to express,
Troubled that thou shouldst hunger, hath purveyed
From all the elements her choicest store
To treat thee as beseems, and as her Lord
With honour, only deign to sit and eat.

ii *313. Thebez*] This spelling is supplied by the *1671 Errata*; *1671* has 'Thebes'; the change is presumably to ensure a disyllabic pronunciation.

ii *318–9.* Lewalski 203 notices that Satan's response ironically echoes Christ's own conclusion (ii 252–3) that the hunger is itself evidence of need.

ii *324.* Cp. *Heb.* i 2: 'His Son, whom he hath appointed heir of all things.' Satan had similarly reminded Eve that she was mistress of creation (*PL* ix 532–40).

ii *327–8. Nor . . . unclean*] M. Fixler, *MLN* lxx (1955) 573–7, notes that the banquet (ii 342–7), since it includes shell-fish, would be forbidden by the Mosaic dietary laws. Satan's assurance that it is not unclean, repeated ii 369, may be viewed as an attempt to make Jesus reject these laws (as M. rejects them in the *De doctrina*)–such a rejection would give Satan a lead as to Christ's real identity. Alternatively, if Christ refuses the banquet because it contains forbidden foods, he seems to subject himself (and his church) to the dietary prohibitions of the law which he has come to supersede. 'Christ's way out of the dilemma is to refuse the banquet simply on the basis of the giver', (Lewalski 217).

ii *329.* Cp. *Dan.* i 8: 'But Daniel purposed in his heart that he would not defile himself with the portion of the king's meat, nor with the wine which he drank.'

He spake no dream, for as his words had end,
Our Saviour lifting up his eyes, beheld
In ample space under the broadest shade
A table richly spread, in regal mode,
With dishes piled, and meats of noblest sort
And savour, beasts of chase, or fowl of game,
In pastry built, or from the spit, or boiled,

ii *337–65*. M.'s introduction of this banqueting scene finds no support either in Scripture or in the tradition. Pope 70–9 regards it as an attempt to preserve the equation between the temptations of Adam and Eve and those of Christ (cp. ll. 348–9). Eve was guilty of greed (wanting the apple to satisfy her appetite) and covetousness (wanting it as a beautiful object): see *PL* ix 739–43 and 735–6. The second of these is paralleled in *PR* during the temptation of the kingdoms (see iv 110–21*n*), where the primary appeal is made to a desire for glory and opulence. The first is not paralleled by the temptation to turn stones into bread (see i 355*n*), so M. inserts the banquet scene to parallel it: here the primary appeal is made to the desire for food. In order to complete the coincidence, it is made evident (ll. 245–59) that Christ has not been feeling the effects of hunger for forty days, and that the power which has sustained him is still sustaining him to the extent of miraculously satisfying the essential demands of the flesh. Thus, like Eve, he longs for food but does not actually require it (see ll. 252–4). Kermode[4] 323–5 suggests that another reason for the introduction of this non-canonical temptation may be the contrast it makes with Christ's final reward (iv 588–90) where the food is 'celestial', 'divine' and 'ambrosial': here the attractions are sensual, and the sensual impact proceeds from the eye, the highest (ii 338), through smell (350–1) and ear (362–3), to the lowest, touch and taste (369–71). Stein[2] 60 sees the banquet as Satan going back on his announced intention not to tempt appetite with what exceeds the natural and apparently lawful (ii 229–30). What the attempt reveals, then, is Satan's loss of understanding: he is compulsively evil. 'What he says and does reflects an essential loss, which is the more marked because of his brilliant surface competence and awareness.' Lewalski (203–4) referring to Christ's role as second Israel (a commonplace among the typologists) sees the lush banquet as a visible embodiment of the presumptous demand of the Israelites, 'Can the Lord furnish a table in the wilderness?' (*Ps.* lxxviii 19). Christ, by refusing, demonstrates that he will perfect and fulfil the old type, the carnal Israel. Satan's banquet is frequently compared with that in Tasso, *Jerusalem Delivered* x 64, with which Armida tempts her lovers. T. H. Banks, *PMLA* lv (1940) 773–6, considers that Christ is tempted not so much to eat as to claim his own godhead by accepting as his due the offering of the fruits of the earth: the temptation lies not in the luxury but in the fact that the gift is presented (332–6) as Nature's tribute to her Lord.

Grisamber-steamed; all fish from sea or shore,
Freshet, or purling brook, of shell or fin,
And exquisitest name, for which was drained
Pontus and Lucrine bay, and Afric coast.
Alas how simple, to these cates compared,
Was that crude apple that diverted Eve!
And at a stately sideboard by the wine
That fragrant smell diffused, in order stood
Tall stripling youths rich-clad, of fairer hue
Than Ganymede or Hylas, distant more
Under the trees now tripped, now solemn stood
Nymphs of Diana's train, and Naiades
With fruits and flowers from Amalthea's horn,
And ladies of the Hesperides, that seemed
Fairer than feigned of old, or fabled since

ii *344. Grisamber*] ambergris, used in cooking as well as perfumery. The form was a fairly common one in the seventeenth century.
ii *345. Freshet*] small stream.
ii *347. Pontus*] the Black Sea. Pliny ix 19–20 remarks on the swiftness with which all kinds of fish come to perfection in this sea, and says that it is particularly famous for tunny fish. *Lucrine bay*] a lagoon near Naples, famed for its oysters, which Horace mentions, *Epodes* ii 49, *Satires* II iv 32.
ii *349. crude*] raw, uncooked. *diverted*] seduced.
ii *353. Ganymede*] See *Elegia VII 21n.* *Hylas*] Apollonius Rhodius, *Argonautica* i 1207–39, tells how a nymph falls in love with the beautiful boy, Hylas, as he is drawing water for his master Hercules at her spring, and draws him to the depths.
ii *356. Amalthea's horn*] the cornucopia. Ovid, *Fasti* v 115–28, tells how the nymph Amalthea owned a she-goat which suckled the infant Jupiter on Mt Ida, 'but she broke a horn on a tree and was shorn of half her charm. The nymph picked it up, wrapped it in fresh herbs, and carried it, full of fruit, to the lips of Jove. He, when he gained the kingdom of heaven ... made his nurse and her horn of plenty into stars.'
ii *357. ladies of the Hesperides*] See *Comus* 980–1*n*. M. here uses 'Hesperides' as a name for the garden of the Hesperides, as does Shakespeare, *Love's Labour's Lost* IV iii 341.
ii *358–61*. Hughes[2] 256–7 reads these lines as M.'s confession of his indebtedness to the grail romances, particularly Malory's *Morte d'Arthur*, an indebtedness suggested by Tillyard 319. Pope 116–19 sees M. associating Christ's prowess in overcoming temptation with feats of knight-errantry (see i 9*n*), and notes that John Knox, in his exposition upon the temptations of Christ, had put a formal, quasi-chivalric challenge into Christ's mouth. Cp. M.'s mention of his reading in 'those lofty Fables and Romances, which recount in solemne cantos the deeds of Knighthood founded by our victorious Kings; & from hence had in renowne all over Christendome' (Columbia

Of faëry damsels met in forest wide
By knights of Logres, or of Lyonesse,
Lancelot or Pelleas, or Pellenore,
And all the while harmonious airs were heard
Of chiming strings, or charming pipes and winds
Of gentlest gale Arabian odours fanned
From their soft wings, and Flora's earliest smells.
Such was the splendour, and the tempter now
His invitation earnestly renewed.
  What doubts the Son of God to sit and eat?
These are not fruits forbidden, no interdict
Defends the touching of these viands pure,
Their taste no knowledge works, at least of evil,
But life preserves, destroys life's enemy,
Hunger, with sweet restorative delight.
All these are spirits of air, and woods, and springs,
Thy gentle ministers, who come to pay
Thee homage, and acknowledge thee their Lord:
What doubt'st thou Son of God? Sit down and eat.
  To whom thus Jesus temperately replied:
Said'st thou not that to all things I had right?
And who withholds my power that right to use?

iii 304, Yale i 891). Lewalski 223–4 makes the point that by including beautiful women in the temptation Satan goes against his previous decision (ii 225–7): the inclusion extends the Christ / Adam parallel, since undue susceptibility to woman was Adam's particular sin.

ii *360. Logres*] Loegria: England east of Severn and south of Humber. *Lyonesse*] between Land's End and the Scillies: now submerged.

ii *361. Lancelot*] 'Head of all Christian knights', as Sir Ector calls him in Malory, *Morte d'Arthur* xxi 13, the lover of Guinivere; besotted by wine, he was twice led to sleep with the fair Elaine, thinking her Guinivere. *Pelleas*] lover of Ettare. Some traditions make him one of the four knights of the Round Table to achieve the Grail. *Pellenore*] King of the Isles, eventually killed by Sir Gawain. Lewalski 225 thinks the allusion should be to his son Percival, who was offered after a three-day fast a banquet with 'all manner of meetes that he cowde thynke on' by a fair gentlewoman (actually 'the mayster fyende of helle' in disguise). He was saved from serious sin with the lady only by making the sign of the cross, which caused the scene to vanish (*Morte d'Arthur* xiv 9–10).

ii *364*. Cp. *PL* iv 162–3.

ii *365. Flora*] goddess of flowers.

ii *369. fruits forbidden*] The temptation of Eve is again recalled, see ii 324*n*.

ii *370. Defends*] forbids.

Shall I receive by gift what of my own,
When and where likes me best, I can command?
I can at will, doubt not, as soon as thou,
Command a table in this wilderness,
And call swift flights of angels ministrant
Arrayed in glory on my cup to attend:
Why shouldst thou then obtrude this diligence,
In vain, where no acceptance it can find,
And with my hunger what hast thou to do?
Thy pompous delicacies I contemn,
And count thy specious gifts no gifts but guiles.
    To whom thus answered Satan malcontent:
That I have also power to give thou seest,
If of that power I bring thee voluntary
What I might have bestowed on whom I pleased,
And rather opportunely in this place
Chose to impart to thy apparent need,
Why shouldst thou not accept it? but I see
What I can do or offer is suspect;
Of these things others quickly will dispose
Whose pains have earned the far-fet spoil. With that
Both table and provision vanished quite
With sound of harpies' wings, and talons heard;
Only th' importune tempter still remained,
And with these words his temptation pursued.
    By hunger, that each other creature tames,
Thou art not to be harmed, therefore not moved;
Thy temperance invincible besides,

ii *381–6.* Cp. *Ps.* lxxviii 19: 'They said, Can God furnish a table in the wilderness?' Martz (187) detects a hint of the communion table. Lewalski 218 agrees, and adds: 'Christ's own "table in the wilderness" alludes typologically to such future manifestations of his proper "banquet" as the angelic repast which is to celebrate his victory over Satan at the conclusion . . . the feeding of the multitude in the wilderness in reprise and fulfilment of the manna type, and the Eucharistic banquet.'
ii *391. no gifts*] M. in the *Apology*, decrying the traces of Roman Catholicism in the Anglican liturgy, speaks of 'enemies . . . whose guifts are no guifts, but the instruments of our bane' (Columbia iii 354, Yale i 939).
ii *401. far-fet*] far fetched.
ii *402–3.* Recalling the stage direction to *Tempest* III iii 83, 'enter Ariel like a harpy; claps his wings upon the table; and with a quaint device, the banquet vanishes'; also *Aen.* iii 225–8, where harpies snatch away the Trojans' meal.
ii *404. importune*] importunate, persistent.
ii *408. besides*] in other respects as well.

For no allurement yields to appetite,
And all thy heart is set on high designs,
High actions; but wherewith to be achieved?
Great acts require great means of enterprise,
Thou art unknown, unfriended, low of birth,
A carpenter thy father known, thyself
Bred up in poverty and straits at home;
Lost in a desert here and hunger-bit:
Which way or from what hope dost thou aspire
To greatness? whence authority deriv'st,
What followers, what retinue canst thou gain,
Or at thy heels the dizzy multitude,
Longer than thou canst feed them on thy cost?
Money brings honour, friends, conquest, and realms;
What raised Antipater the Edomite,
And his son Herod placed on Judah's throne;
(Thy throne) but gold that got him puissant friends?
Therefore, if at great things thou wouldst arrive,
Get riches first, get wealth, and treasure heap,
Not difficult, if thou hearken to me,
Riches are mine, fortune is in my hand;
They whom I favour thrive in wealth amain,
While virtue, valour, wisdom sit in want.
  To whom thus Jesus patiently replied;
Yet wealth without these three is impotent,
To gain dominion or to keep it gained.
Witness those ancient empires of the earth,
In highth of all their flowing wealth dissolved:
But men endued with these have oft attained
In lowest poverty to highest deeds;
Gideon and Jephtha, and the shepherd lad,
Whose offspring on the throne of Judah sat
So many ages, and shall yet regain
That seat, and reign in Israel without end.

ii *416. hunger-bit*] Cp. *Job* xviii 12: 'His strength shall be hunger-bitten.'
ii *422.* Cp. Horace, *Epistles* I vi 36–7: 'Of course a wife and dowry, credit and friends, birth and beauty, are the gift of Queen Money.'
ii *423–4.* Josephus, *Antiquities* xiv 1 mentions Antipater's great wealth and rise to power, and stresses as the main reason for Herod's obtaining control over Judaea his promise of money to Mark Antony.
ii *426–7.* Cp. Mammon's advice to Guyon, *F.Q.* II vii, to gain honour through riches, and Horace's ironic *O cives, cives, quaerenda pecunia primum est, Epistles* I i 53.
ii *429. Riches are mine*] Cp. *Hag.* ii 8: 'The silver is mine, and the gold is mine, saith the Lord of hosts.'

Among the heathen, (for throughout the world
To me is not unknown what hath been done
Worthy of memorial) canst thou not remember
Quintius, Fabricius, Curius, Regulus?
For I esteem those names of men so poor
Who could do mighty things, and could contemn
Riches though offered from the hand of kings.
And what in me seems wanting, but that I
May also in this poverty as soon
Accomplish what they did, perhaps and more?

ii *439. Gideon*] his reply, when commanded by God to lead Israel against the Midianites was 'O my Lord, wherewith shall I save Israel? behold my family is poor in Manasseh, and I am the least in my father's house', *Judges* vi 15. Lewalski 252 argues that he is not merely a type of poverty here but also of Christ's repudiation of kingship (see *Judges* viii 23). *Jephtha*] champion of Israel against the Ammonites: he had been disinherited and banished in his youth, *Judges* xi 2–3. The Fathers and later exegetes saw his sacrifice of his daughter as typifying Christ's sacrifice on the cross. Lewalski 253 thinks he is used here to emphasize the sacrificial aspect of kingship. *shepherd lad*] David. God 'took him from the sheepfolds: from following the ewes', and 'brought him to feed Jacob his people', *Ps* lxxviii 70–1. 'Christ sees himself as second David because he also expects to obtain the throne of Israel after overcoming great difficulties' (Lewalski 252).
ii *443–9.* Hughes[2] 267 refers to Tasso, *Del Poema Eroico*, where it is maintained that, while the first earthly honour previously belonged to the Roman worthies like the Curtii, Decii and Marcelli, the heroic spirit of such men is merely 'a shadow and a figure' of the divine love which Christ brought into the world.
ii *446. Quintius*] Lucius Quinctius Cincinnatus, a historical figure, though details of his career were derived from popular poetry. In 458 B.C., according to tradition, when Minucius was besieged by the Aequi, Cincinnatus was appointed dictator, dispatched to the rescue, defeated the Aequi, resigned his dictatorship after fifteen days and returned to farm beyond the Tiber. *Fabricius*] Gaius Fabricius Luscinus, hero of the war with Pyrrhus, consul 282 and 278 B.C. There are several stories of his poverty, austerity and incorruptibility: he rejected bribes from Pyrrhus and also the offers of Pyrrhus' would-be poisoners. *Curius*] Manius Curius Dentatus. He conquered the Samnites and Sabines (290 B.C.) and Pyrrhus (275 B.C.). The rhetorical accounts of his incorruptibility and frugality derive largely from Cato, who idealized him. *Regulus*] Marcus Atilius Regulus: captured by the Carthaginians in the first Punic War (255 B.C.), he was sent to Rome with terms. On his advice they were rejected. He insisted on returning to Carthage with the answer, and died in captivity. The story of his death by torture was a national legend, and is celebrated by Horace, *Odes* III v, but is probably untrue. Augustine, *De Civitate Dei* v 18,

Extol not riches then, the toil of fools,
The wise man's cumbrance if not snare, more apt
To slacken virtue, and abate her edge,
Than prompt her to do aught may merit praise.
What if with like aversion I reject
Riches and realms; yet not for that a crown,
Golden in show, is but a wreath of thorns,
Brings dangers, troubles, cares, and sleepless nights
To him who wears the regal diadem,
When on his shoulders each man's burden lies;
For therein stands the office of a king,
His honour, virtue, merit, and chief praise,
That for the public all this weight he bears.
Yet he who reigns within himself, and rules
Passions, desires, and fears, is more a king;
Which every wise and virtuous man attains:
And who attains not, ill aspires to rule
Cities of men, or headstrong multitudes,
Subject himself to anarchy within,
Or lawless passions in him which he serves.
But to guide nations in the way of truth
By saving doctrine, and from error lead
To know, and, knowing worship God aright,
Is yet more kingly, this attracts the soul,
Governs the inner man, the nobler part,
That other o'er the body only reigns,
And oft by force, which to a generous mind
So reigning can be no sincere delight.
Besides to give a kingdom hath been thought
Greater and nobler done, and to lay down

linked together Regulus, Quintius and Fabricius as examples of virtue surpassing that of most Christians.

ii *453. toil*] snare.

ii *458. for that*] because. M. makes it clear that it is not the cares and responsibilities of kingship that Christ fears.

ii *466–8.* Cp. *Prov.* xvi 32 which, as Hughes[2] 271 points out, Leone Ebreo cites in the *Dialoghi d'Amore* when outlining the familiar neo-Platonic case that the hero is the man who vanquishes himself, and in whom 'sensuality has quite ceased to disturb virtuous reason'. Horace, *Odes* II ii 9–12 makes a similar point: 'You will rule a broader realm by subduing a greedy heart than you would by joining Libya to distant Gades.'

ii *480. sincere*] pure.

ii *481–2.* Perhaps echoing Seneca, *Thyestes* 529: *Habere regnum casus est, virtus dare* (To have a kingdom is chance; to give one, virtue).

Far more magnanimous, than to assume.
Riches are needless then, both for themselves,
And for thy reason why they should be sought,
To gain a sceptre, oftest better missed.

THE THIRD BOOK

So spake the Son of God, and Satan stood
A while as mute confounded what to say,
What to reply, confuted and convinced
Of his weak arguing, and fallacious drift;
At length collecting all his serpent wiles,
With soothing words renewed, him thus accosts.
I see thou know'st what is of use to know,
What best to say canst say, to do canst do;
Thy actions to thy words accord, thy words
To thy large heart give utterance due, thy heart
Contains of good, wise, just, the perfect shape.
Should kings and nations from thy mouth consult,
Thy counsel would be as the oracle
Urim and Thummim, those oraculous gems
On Aaron's breast: or tongue of seers old
Infallible; or wert thou sought to deeds
That might require the array of war, thy skill
Of conduct would be such, that all the world
Could not sustain thy prowess, or subsist
In battle, though against thy few in arms.
These godlike virtues wherefore dost thou hide?
Affecting private life, or more obscure
In savage wilderness, wherefore deprive
All earth her wonder at thy acts, thyself

ii *483. magnanimous*] Hughes[2] 258–9, seeing M.'s Christ as a Christianization of the Aristotelian magnanimous man, refers to *De doctrina* ii 9 (Columbia xvii 240–3) where Christ's rejection of the world in *Matt.* iv is cited as an example of magnanimity.

iii *14. Urim and Thummim*] As R. J. Beck, *N & Q* n.s. iv (1957) 27–9, remarks, none of the half-dozen references to these oracular gems in the Old Testament makes their exact nature clear, and other authorities (e.g. Josephus, *Antiquities* iii 8–9, Philo, *Life of Moses* ii) are contradictory. *Num.* xxvii 21 shows that they were used in divination, and *Exod.* xxviii 30 that they were in Aaron's breastplate. Urim means 'light' and Thummin, 'truth', the plurals being intensive.

iii *16. sought to*] called upon for.

The fame and glory, glory the reward
That sole excites to high attempts the flame
Of most erected spirits, most tempered pure
Ethereal, who all pleasures else despise,
All treasures and all gain esteem as dross,
And dignities and powers all but the highest?
Thy years are ripe, and over-ripe, the son
Of Macedonian Philip had ere these
Won Asia and the throne of Cyrus held
At his dispose, young Scipio had brought down
The Carthaginian pride, young Pompey quelled
The Pontic king and in triumph had rode.
Yet years, and to ripe years judgment mature,
Quench not the thirst of glory, but augment.
Great Julius, whom now all the world admires

iii *25–30.* Cp. Cicero, *De officiis* I viii 26: 'It is in the greatest souls and in the most brilliant geniuses that we usually find ambitions for civil and military authority, for power and for glory, springing up'; also M.'s reference in the *Defensio Secunda* to 'what itself conquers the most excellent of mortals . . . glory' (Columbia viii 218–9), and *Lycidas* 70–2.

Pope 67–9 notes that M. breaks with tradition by including the temptation to vainglorious presumption ('glory') among the kingdoms-of-the-world temptations: a seventeenth-century reader would have expected it to be the temptation presented on the pinnacle of the temple, since this was the view taken by all orthodox theologians. Glory following wealth is, however, the order of temptations in *F.Q.* ii, where the persuasions of Mammon give way to Philotime (Vainglory).

iii *27. erected*] elevated, exalted: an obsolescent sense: *PL* i 679 is the last instance of it recorded in *OED*.

iii *31. Thy years are ripe*] According to *Luke* iii 23, Christ's baptism took place when he was about thirty.

iii *31–4.* Alexander won the battle of the Issus (333 B.C.) when he was twenty-three, and he was twenty-five when, at Arbela, he overthrew the Persian empire founded by Cyrus.

iii *34–5.* Scipio drove the Carthaginians from Spain when he was twenty-seven (207 B.C.). He was thirty-two when he won his greatest victory, at Zama.

iii *35–6.* Satan exaggerates. Pompey was forty when he overthrew Mithridates (66 B.C.), and forty-five when he celebrated his triumph in Rome.

iii *37. to*] in addition to.

iii *39–42.* Plutarch, *Life of Caesar* xi 3 tells how Caesar, as a young man, burst into tears on reading the exploits of Alexander, and when asked the reason, replied: 'Do you not think it is matter for sorrow that while Alexander, at my age, was already king of so many peoples, I have as yet achieved no brilliant success.'

The more he grew in years, the more inflamed
With glory, wept that he had lived so long
Inglorious: but thou yet art not too late.
  To whom our Saviour calmly thus replied.
Thou neither dost persuade me to seek wealth
For empire's sake, nor empire to affect
For glory's sake by all thy argument.
For what is glory but the blaze of fame,
The people's praise, if always praise unmixed?
And what the people but a herd confused,
A miscellaneous rabble, who extol
Things vulgar, and well weighed, scarce worth the praise,
They praise and they admire they know not what;
And know not whom, but as one leads the other;
And what delight to be by such extolled,
To live upon their tongues and be their talk,
Of whom to be dispraised were no small praise?
His lot who dares be singularly good.
The intelligent among them and the wise
Are few, and glory scarce of few is raised.
This is true glory and renown, when God,
Looking on the earth, with approbation marks
The just man, and divulges him through heaven
To all his angels, who with true applause

iii *47–51.* Cp. Seneca, *Epistles* cii 17: 'There is this difference between renown and glory: the latter depends upon the judgments of the many, but renown on the judgments of good men'; and Cicero, *Tusculan Disputations* v 36: 'Popular glory is not to be coveted for its own sake nor obscurity feared . . . Can anything be more foolish than to suppose that those whom individually one despises as illiterate mechanics, have ideas of value collectively? The wise man will . . . reject the distinctions bestowed by the people'; also Giles Fletcher, *Christ's Triumph over Death* 31: 'Fraile Multitude, whose giddy lawe is list, / And best applause is windy flattering, / Most like the breath of which it doth consist, / No sooner blowne, but as soone vanishing, / As much desir'd, as little profiting, / That makes the men that have it oft as light / As those that give it . . .'

Hughes[2] 260 finds in Alessandro Piccolomini's *Della Institution Morale* vi 9 and viii 17, a foretaste of M.'s Christ's almost Hobbesian exaggeration of the aristocratic element in the Aristotelian magnanimous man's renunciation of the world.

iii *56.* An echo of Jonson, *Cynthia's Revels* III iii 15–6 'of such / To be disprais'd is the most perfect praise'. Jonson is himself echoing Seneca, *De remediis fortuitorum* vii 1: *Malis displicere laudari est.*

iii *62. divulges*] makes known.

Recount his praises; thus he did to Job,
When to extend his fame through heaven and earth,
As thou to thy reproach may'st well remember,
He asked thee, Hast thou seen my servant Job?
Famous he was in heaven, on earth less known;
Where glory is false glory, attributed
To things not glorious, men not worthy of fame.
They err who count it glorious to subdue
By conquest far and wide, to overrun
Large countries, and in field great battles win,
Great cities by assault: what do these worthies,
But rob and spoil, burn, slaughter, and enslave
Peaceable nations, neighbouring, or remote,
Made captive, yet deserving freedom more
Than those their conquerors, who leave behind
Nothing but ruin wheresoe'er they rove,
And all the flourishing works of peace destroy,
Then swell with pride, and must be titled gods,
Great benefactors of mankind, deliverers,
Worshipped with temple, priest, and sacrifice;
One is the son of Jove, of Mars the other,
Till conqueror Death discover them scarce men,
Rolling in brutish vices, and deformed,
Violent or shameful death their due reward.
But if there be in glory aught of good,
It may by means far different be attained
Without ambition, war, or violence;
By deeds of peace, by wisdom eminent,
By patience, temperance; I mention still
Him whom thy wrongs with saintly patience borne,

iii *67*. Cp. *Job* i 8: 'And the Lord said unto Satan, Hast thou considered my servant Job, that there is none like him in the earth, a perfect and an upright man, one that feareth God, escheweth evil?'
iii *81. titled gods*] The Roman emperors were generally accorded the title 'divine' by the Senate. Cp. also *Acts* xii 21–2: 'Herod . . . made an oration unto them. And the people gave a shout, saying, It is the voice of a god, and not of a man.'
iii *82. benefactors*] Cp. *Luke* xxii 25: 'The kings of the Gentiles . . . are called benefactors.'
iii *84*. Alexander was made out to be the son of Jupiter Ammon, and Scipio of Jupiter Capitolinus (see *PL* ix 508–10): Romulus was called son of Mars.
iii *86. brutish vices*] Alexander was an alcoholic, and his early death in 323 B.C. was often attributed to this.
iii *91–2. wisdom . . . patience, temperance*] Cp. *2 Pet.* i 6 'And [add] to knowledge temperance; and to temperance patience'.

Made famous in a land and times obscure;
Who names not now with honour patient Job?
Poor Socrates (who next more memorable?)
By what he taught and suffered for so doing,
For truth's sake suffering death unjust, lives now
Equal in fame to proudest conquerors.
Yet if for fame and glory aught be done,
Aught suffered; if young African for fame
His wasted country freed from Punic rage,
The deed becomes unpraised, the man at least,
And loses, though but verbal, his reward.
Shall I seek glory then, as vain men seek
Oft not deserved? I seek not mine, but his
Who sent me, and thereby witness whence I am.
  To whom the tempter murmuring thus replied.
Think not so slight of glory; therein least
Resembling thy great Father: he seeks glory,
And for his glory all things made, all things
Orders and governs, nor content in heaven
By all his angels glorified, requires
Glory from men, from all men good or bad,
Wise or unwise, no difference, no exemption;
Above all sacrifice, or hallowed gift
Glory he requires, and glory he receives
Promiscuous from all nations, Jew, or Greek,
Or barbarous, nor exception hath declared;
From us his foes pronounced glory he exacts.

iii *98. unjust*] Socrates was condemned for corrupting the youth and maligning the gods of the state. He could easily have escaped, but chose to die rather than act in a lawless way (his reasons for the choice are recorded in full in Plato's *Crito*). Lewalski 240, quoting Justin Martyr, *First Apology* v, points out that behind Christ's words is a tradition of commentary which saw Socrates' death for truth's sake as a foreshadowing of Christ's, and his teaching as prefiguring Christ's doctrine.
iii *101. young African*] Scipio, who landed in Africa in 204 B.C. and forced the Carthaginians to recall Hannibal from Italy.
iii *106–7. not mine, but his / Who sent me*] Cp. *John* vii 18: 'He that speaketh of himself seeketh his own glory: but he that seeketh his glory that sent him, the same is true', and viii 50: 'I seek not mine own glory.'
iii *111. for his glory all things made*] Cp. *Rev.* iv 11, where the elders falling down and casting their crowns before 'him that sat on the throne' cry: 'Thou art worthy, O Lord, to receive glory and honour and power; for thou hast created all things, and for thy pleasure they are and were created.'
iii *119. barbarous*] non-Hellenic.

To whom our Saviour fervently replied.
And reason; since his word all things produced,
Though chiefly not for glory as prime end,
But to show forth his goodness, and impart
His good communicable to every soul
Freely; of whom what could he less expect
Than glory and benediction, that is, thanks,
The slightest, easiest, readiest recompense
From them who could return him nothing else,
And not returning that would likeliest render
Contempt instead, dishonour, obloquy?
Hard recompense, unsuitable return
For so much good, so much beneficence.
But why should man seek glory? who of his own
Hath nothing, and to whom nothing belongs
But condemnation, ignominy, and shame?
Who for so many benefits received
Turned recreant to God, ingrate and false,
And so of all true good himself despoiled,
Yet, sacrilegious, to himself would take
That which to God alone of right belongs;
Yet so much bounty is in God, such grace,
That who advance his glory, not their own,
Them he himself to glory will advance.
So spake the Son of God; and here again
Satan had not to answer, but stood struck
With guilt of his own sin, for he himself
Insatiable of glory had lost all,
Yet of another plea bethought him soon.
Of glory as thou wilt, said he, so deem,
Worth or not worth the seeking, let it pass:
But to a kingdom thou art born, ordained
To sit upon thy father David's throne;
By mother's side thy father, though thy right

iii *121. fervently*] The adverb distinguishes this reply from Christ's others; he grows heated because his Father's name is called in question.
iii *138. recreant*] The primary meaning is 'confessing oneself overcome or vanquished'. M. in the *Doctrine and Discipline of Divorce* (1643) uses the word for the first time, according to *OED*, in the sense 'unfaithful to duty, false, apostate', as here.
iii *140. sacrilegious*] Cp. *De doctrina* ii 4 (Columbia xvii 116–7): 'Sacrilege . . . consists in . . . the appropriation to private uses of things dedicated to God.'
iii *146. had . . . answer*] had no answer.
iii *154. By mother's side thy father*] The genealogy of Christ in the gospels

Be now in powerful hands, that will not part
Easily from possession won with arms;
Judaea now and all the promised land
Reduced a province under Roman yoke,
Obeys Tiberius; nor is always ruled
With temperate sway; oft have they violated
The Temple, oft the Law with foul affronts,
Abominations rather, as did once
Antiochus: and think'st thou to regain
Thy right by sitting still or thus retiring?
So did not Maccabeus: he indeed
Retired unto the desert, but with arms;

(*Matt.* i 1–16, *Luke* iii 23–38) is traced through Joseph back to David and beyond. David is referred to as Christ's 'father' (ancestor) in *Luke* i 32, and Christ is frequently addressed as 'son of David' in the gospels (cp. *Rev.* xxii 16: 'I Jesus ... am the root and the offspring of David'). It is not asserted in the gospels that Mary was of the house of David, though the assumption that she was was common in the seventeenth century. Jewish law did not, in any case, recognize descent through the mother, so Satan's qualification is a slighting one: after all, he suggests, Christ is not son of Joseph; perhaps, then, not descended from David.

iii *157–60.* Judaea was annexed to Syria by Quirinius, Roman governor of Syria, in A.D. 6. Tiberius (A.D. 14–37) retained Pilate as governor from 25–36, in spite of various acts of tyranny (cp. *Luke* xiii 1: 'the Galileans, whose blood Pilate had mingled with their sacrifices'). Josephus, *Antiquities* xviii 3, tells how Pilate planted armed soldiers, disguised as Jews, in the mob at Jerusalem, and when the mob began to abuse him the soldiers 'laid about them with much greater vigour than Pilate had commanded', killing many who had not been abusive as well as those who had.

iii *160. oft*] Satan is exaggerating. Pompey, however, had violated the Holy of Holies in Jerusalem in 63 B.C.

iii *163. Antiochus*] In 169 B.C. Antiochus Epiphanes stole all the holy vessels from the Temple, the altar, candlesticks and hangings, scaled off the gold facing of the building, and forced the Jews to build shrines for idols and pollute the temple by sacrificing swine and unclean beasts. *1 Macc.* i 20–63 and Josephus, *Antiquities* xii 5, have accounts of the desecration.

iii *165–70.* The national resistance to Antiochus Epiphanes began in 166 B.C. in the obscure town of Modin and centred round Judas Maccabeus, a Levite, whose heroic struggle with Antiochus resulted in the founding of the Asmonaean dynasty. Lewalski 262 notes that in traditional biblical exegesis Judas' defeat of Antiochus was regarded as a type of Christ's conquest over Antichrist.

iii *166. Retired unto the desert*] Cp. *1 Macc.* v 24–8: 'And Judas . . . passed over Jordan and went three days' journey in the wilderness . . . and Judas and his army turned suddenly by the way of the wilderness unto Bosora.'

And o'er a mighty king so oft prevailed,
That by strong hand his family obtained,
Though priests, the crown, and David's throne usurped,
With Modin and her suburbs once content.
If kingdom move thee not, let move thee zeal,
And duty; zeal and duty are not slow;
But on occasion's forelock watchful wait.
They themselves rather are occasion best,
Zeal of thy Father's house, duty to free
Thy country from her heathen servitude;
So shalt thou best fulfil, best verify
The prophets old, who sung thy endless reign,
The happier reign the sooner it begins,
Reign then; what canst thou better do the while?
To whom our Saviour answer thus returned.
All things are best fulfilled in their due time,
And time there is for all things, Truth hath said:
If of my reign prophetic writ hath told,
That it shall never end, so when begin
The Father in his purpose hath decreed,
He in whose hand all times and seasons roll.
What if he hath decreed that I shall first
Be tried in humble state, and things adverse,
By tribulations, injuries, insults,
Contempts, and scorns, and snares, and violence,
Suffering, abstaining, quietly expecting
Without distrust or doubt, that he may know

iii *171. kingdom*] kingship.
iii *172–4. occasion's forelock*] Proverbially occasion (opportunity) had a forelock which had to be grasped because she was bald behind. In *F.Q.* II iv 12, where the proverb is acted out, Guyon grasps it. *zeal and duty . . . are occasion best*] Here Satan slightly changes the meaning of 'occasion' from 'opportunity' to 'reason, cause'–an equally well-established meaning in the seventeenth century.
iii *175. Zeal of thy Father's house*] Christ's disciples, *John* ii 17, regarded his expulsion of the money-changers from the Temple as a fulfilment of the prophecy in *Ps.* lxix 9: 'The zeal of thine house hath eaten me up.'
iii *178. endless*] Cp. *Isa.* ix 7: 'Of the increase of his government and peace there shall be no end.'
iii *183. time . . . for all things*] Cp. *Eccles.* iii 1: 'To every thing there is a season, and a time to every purpose under the heaven.'
iii *187.* Cp. *Acts* i 7: 'It is not for you to know the times or the seasons, which the Father hath put in his own power.'

What I can suffer, how obey? Who best
Can suffer, best can do; best reign, who first
Well hath obeyed; just trial ere I merit
My exaltation without change or end.
But what concerns it thee when I begin
My everlasting kingdom, why art thou
Solicitous, what moves thy inquisition?
Know'st thou not that my rising is thy fall,
And my promotion will be thy destruction?
To whom the tempter inly racked replied.
Let that come when it comes; all hope is lost
Of my reception into grace; what worse?
For where no hope is left, is left no fear;
If there be worse, the expectation more
Of worse torments me than the feeling can.
I would be at the worst; worst is my port,
My harbour and my ultimate repose,
The end I would attain, my final good.
My error was my error, and my crime
My crime; whatever for itself condemned,
And will alike be punished; whether thou
Reign or reign not; though to that gentle brow
Willingly I could fly, and hope thy reign,
From that placid aspect and meek regard,
Rather than aggravate my evil state,
Would stand between me and thy Father's ire,

iii *194–6. Who best . . . Well hath obeyed*] Cp. *Matt.* xx 26–7: 'Whosoever will be great among you, let him be your minister; And whosoever will be chief among you, let him be your servant'; also Mucius Scaevola's boast, Livy ii 12, before thrusting his hand into the flames: 'Both to do and to endure valiantly is the Roman way.' Among the various classical authorities for the maxim that the most obedient servant makes the best master are Plato, *Laws* iv 715, 762, Aristotle, *Politics* iii 4, Cicero, *De Legibus* iii 2 and Seneca, *De Ira* ii 15.

iii *204–22.* Arnold Stein, *ELH* xxiii (1956) 117–21, quoting this 'masterly exhibition of dramatic art', claims that the language and rhythm reveal Satan's 'real self' overcoming the 'dramatic self'. Stein thinks that Satan is ready 'to turn weakness into strength', to create a new drama and a new protagonist who will be Saviour to Satan, though in fact 'no offer is made, and no pause to permit a counter-offer' – a fact which tells against those who interpret the speech as merely another stratagem of Satan's, a histrionic approach which, as H. J. Laskowsky, *Thoth* iv (1963) 24–9, sees it, he tries when sophistry has failed. Lewalski 258 reads the speech as mere 'rhetorical craft': an attempt to corrupt Christ by urging him to hasten to his own kingdom (see iii 223–4).

(Whose ire I dread more than the fire of hell)
A shelter and a kind of shading cool
Interposition, as a summer's cloud.
If I then to the worst that can be haste,
Why move thy feet so slow to what is best,
Happiest both to thyself and all the world,
That thou who worthiest art shouldst be their king?
Perhaps thou linger'st in deep thoughts detained
Of the enterprise so hazardous and high;
No wonder, for though in thee be united
What of perfection can in man be found,
Or human nature can receive, consider
Thy life hath yet been private, most part spent
At home, scarce viewed the Galilean towns,
And once a year Jerusalem, few days'
Short sojourn; and what thence couldst thou observe?
The world thou hast not seen, much less her glory,
Empires, and monarchs, and their radiant courts,
Best school of best experience, quickest in sight
In all things that to greatest actions lead.
The wisest, unexperienced, will be ever
Timorous and loth, with novice modesty,
(As he who seeking asses found a kingdom)
Irresolute, unhardy, unadventurous:
But I will bring thee where thou soon shalt quit
Those rudiments, and see before thine eyes
The monarchies of the earth, their pomp and state,
Sufficient introduction to inform
Thee, of thyself so apt, in regal arts,

iii *221–2.* Frye 237 maintains that *PL* iii 385–6 shows that this is the direct opposite of Christ's true nature: cp. however *Isa.* xxv 4–5: 'For thou hast been . . . a shadow from the heat . . . even the heat with the shadow of a cloud.' Rachel Trickett, *E & S* (1978) 35 cites *Macbeth* III iv 110–12.
iii *234. once a year*] Cp. *Luke* ii 41: 'Now his parents went to Jerusalem every year at the feast of the passover.'
iii *242. he who . . . found a kingdom*] Saul. In *1 Sam.* ix 1–x 1, Kish, Saul's father, loses his asses, and Saul, looking for them, comes to Samuel who, forewarned by God, anoints him with the words, 'Is it not because the Lord hath anointed thee to be captain over his inheritance?' Saul's 'novice modesty' shows itself in his initial reaction, ix 21. Lewalski 265 thinks Satan is implying that Christ may, if he is backward like Saul, be, like Saul, at length rejected by God for disobedience.
iii *245. rudiments*] initial stages.
iii *247. inform*] train.

And regal mysteries; that thou may'st know
How best their opposition to withstand.
With that (such power was given him then) he took
The Son of God up to a mountain high.
It was a mountain at whose verdant feet
A spacious plain outstretched in circuit wide
Lay pleasant; from his side two rivers flowed,
Th' one winding, the other straight, and left between
Fair champaign with less rivers interveined,
Then meeting joined their tribute to the sea:
Fertile of corn the glebe, of oil and wine,
With herds the pastures thronged, with flocks the hills,
Huge cities and high-towered, that well might seem
The seats of mightiest monarchs, and so large
The prospect was, that here and there was room
For barren desert fountainless and dry.
To this high mountain-top the tempter brought
Our Saviour, and new train of words began.
Well have we speeded, and o'er hill and dale,
Forest and field, and flood, temples and towers
Cut shorter many a league; here thou behold'st

iii *249. regal mysteries*] either 'state secrets' or 'the skills of government'. 'Mystery' could mean either 'secret' or 'skill' in the seventeenth century. A contrast is suggested with *Matt.* xiii 11: 'It is given unto you to know the mysteries of the kingdom of heaven.'
iii *250. their*] that of the 'monarchies' (l. 246).
iii *252. a mountain high*] Cp. *Matt.* iv 8: 'an exceeding high mountain', *Luke* iv 5: 'an high mountain'. Though the Bible does not specify which mountain it was, the candidate most favoured by tradition was Mt Quarantania, which rises from the plain of Jericho. It seems likely that M. has Mt Niphates in mind: he had made Satan alight on this in *PL* iii 742. Strabo, *Geography* XI xii 4, describing the Taurus range, writes 'it rises higher, and bears the name Niphates, and somewhere here are the sources of the Tigris'. The source of the Tigris is, in fact, on the southern slope of Niphates: there was a tradition that it was identical with that of the Euphrates (cp. Boethius, *De Consol.* v 1 *Tigris et Euphrates uno se fonte resolvunt*). This would fit M.'s 'from his side two rivers flowed' (l. 255).
iii *256. winding . . . straight*] Strabo XI xii 3, distinguishing the Euphrates from the Tigris, says that the Euphrates flows 'with winding stream'. Pliny vi 31 says that 'Tigris' is the Persian word for 'arrow', and that it is so called because of its swift, straight course.
iii *257. champaign*] open, flat land; here Mesopotamia.
iii *258. meeting*] The Tigris and Euphrates meet and flow into the Persian Gulf.

Assyria and her empire's ancient bounds,
Araxes and the Caspian lake, thence on
As far as Indus east, Euphrates west,
And oft beyond; to south the Persian bay,
And inaccessible the Arabian drouth:
Here Nineveh, of length within her wall
Several days' journey, built by Ninus old,
Of that first golden monarchy the seat,
And seat of Salmanassar, whose success
Israel in long captivity still mourns;
There Babylon the wonder of all tongues,
As ancient, but rebuilt by him who twice
Judah and all thy father David's house
Led captive, and Jerusalem laid waste,
Till Cyrus set them free; Persepolis,

iii *270–3.* On Niphates Christ and Satan stand at the tip of a huge horn of land (representing the Assyrian empire as it was at the zenith of Assyrian power, about 722–636 B.C.). The horn widens and curves away southwards and eastwards, ending at the Indus, the great river which flows south into the Arabian Sea. The horn's southern (convex) side runs from the tip along the Euphrates and then along the northern shores of the Persian Gulf and the Arabian Sea. Part of its concave side is formed by the Araxes, which flows eastward from central Armenia into the Caspian. Whiting 124 thinks that M. was using Tables iv–vii of Ptolemy's *Geographia* (1605).
iii *274. drouth*] desert. Usually a variant form of 'drought'. *OED* records no other instance of the word in M.'s sense in modern English.
iii *275–9. Nineveh*] The great capital of Assyria (cp. *Jonah* iii 3 'an exceeding great city of three days' journey') lies in the middle of the tip of the horn of land which Christ and Satan survey, about 250 miles south-east of Niphates. Ninus was its eponymous founder. Shalmaneser (Salmanassar) captured Samaria and carried the ten northern tribes of Israel into captivity *c.* 722 B.C. and, *2 Kings* xvii 6, 'placed them in Halah and Habor by the river of Gozan and in the cities of the Medes'.
iii *280–3.* Babylon, on the Euphrates, about 600 miles from Niphates on the convex side of the horn, was originally built by Belus and Semiramis, father and wife of Ninus, and was rebuilt by Nebuchadnezzar from 604 B.C. onwards (*Dan.* iv 30), after which it became one of the wonders of the ancient world. Nebuchadnezzar twice sacked Jerusalem and led its inhabitants into captivity: once in the reign of Jehoiakim (*c.* 596 B.C.), and again in 586 in the reign of Zedekiah (*2 Kings* xxiv 13–5 and xxv 11, *2 Chron.* xxxvi 6–20). J. E. Parish, *N & Q* ccix (1964) 337, notes that 'the wonder of all tongues' is a pun: M. in *PL* xii 342–3 had identified Babylon with the Babel of *Genesis*.
iii *284–7.* Cyrus was founder of the Persian empire, and united the Medes and the Persians by the capture of Ecbatana, capital of Media, a city whose massive fortifications are described in *Judith* i 2–4. (Looking south-east

His city there thou seest, and Bactra there;
Ecbatana her structure vast there shows,
And Hecatompylos her hundred gates,
There Susa by Choaspes, amber stream,
The drink of none but kings; of later fame
Built by Emathian, or by Parthian hands,
The great Seleucia, Nisibis, and there
Artaxata, Teredon, Ctesiphon,
Turning with easy eye thou may'st behold.
All these the Parthian, now some ages past,

from Niphates, Ecbatana would be seen about 250 miles beyond Nineveh). Then, in 538 B.C., he took Babylon and freed the Israelites from the power of Belshazzar (*Dan.* v, *Ezra* i 1–8). His summer capital, Persepolis, was in southern Persia (more or less in line with Nineveh, viewed from Niphates, but 600 miles beyond). Bactra was capital of the Persian province of Bactria, now Balkh in Afghanistan, near to the furthest end of the concave side of the horn, viewed from Niphates, and about 1500 miles away. Hecatompylos (which means 'hundred-gated') was a city in Parthia, but its site is not known.

iii *288–9.* Susa (Shushan), winter-palace of the Persian kings, stood on the banks of the Choaspes. From Niphates it would lie in the same direction as Persepolis, but about 300 miles nearer. Herodotus i 188 says that when Cyrus marched he carried with him water from the Choaspes 'whereof alone, and of none other, the king drinks. This water of the Choaspes is boiled, and very many four-wheeled waggons drawn by mules carry it in silver vessels'; M. is also indebted here to Athenaeus, *Deipnosophists* xii 515: 'Agathocles . . . says that in Persia there is water called "golden" . . . and none may drink of it save only the king and his eldest son.'

iii *290. Emathian*] Macedonian.

iii *291–2. Seleucia*] Founded by Alexander's general Seleucus Nicator, after Alexander's death. It lay on the Tigris, about 350 miles up river, near the modern Baghdad, and was called 'the great' to distinguish it from other Seleucid foundations of the same name. *Nisibis*] On a tributary of the Euphrates, in Mesopotamia, only about 100 miles south-east of Niphates. *Artaxata*] The ancient capital of Armenia, on the Araxes. *Teredon*] Near the confluence of the Tigris and Euphrates. *Ctesiphon*] On the east bank of the Tigris, opposite Seleucia: for some time it was the Parthian capital. Cp. Josephus, *Antiquities* xviii 9: 'Ctesiphon, a Greek city, near Seleucia, where the king [of Parthia] wintered every year, and where the greatest part of his treasures are deposited.' Starnes and Talbert (305) suggestively quote Stephanus, *Ctesiphon . . . magnitude est adeo, ut Parthorum multitudinem et apparatum omnem recipiat* (Ctesiphon . . . so great in size that it can contain the Parthian host and all its equipment).

iii *294–7.* About 250 B.C. Arsaces invaded Parthia, then a province of the Seleucid empire which had its capital at Antioch on the Orontes. He was

By great Arsaces led, who founded first
That empire, under his dominion holds
From the luxurious kings of Antioch won.
And just in time thou com'st to have a view
Of his great power; for now the Parthian king
In Ctesiphon hath gathered all his host
Against the Scythian, whose incursions wild
Have wasted Sogdiana; to her aid
He marches now in haste: see, though from far,
His thousands, in what martial equipage
They issue forth, steel bows, and shafts their arms
Of equal dread in flight, or in pursuit;
All horsemen, in which fight they most excel;
See how in warlike muster they appear,
In rhombs and wedges, and half-moons, and wings.
He looked and saw what numbers numberless
The city gates outpoured, light-armed troops

expelled by Seleucus II about 238, but his brother Tiridates, who took the name Arsaces, recaptured Parthia and founded the Arsacid line of Parthian kings. The Parthian empire remained very limited in extent until the final decay of the Seleucid empire after the death of Antiochus Epiphanes in 165 B.C. 'Luxurious' is not an adjective deserved by the Seleucid kings generally though Antiochus Epiphanes certainly deserved it: Satan is allowing his reputation to colour that of his predecessors, or is perhaps thinking of the reputation of the city of Antioch, which had in its suburbs the park of woods and waters known as the paradise of Daphne, the beauty and lax morals of which were celebrated all over the western world.
iii *301–2*. The Scythians were the barbarians who lived north-east of the Caspian and north of the Aral Sea. They eventually overran the province of Sogdiana, the area round the mouth and lower reaches of the Oxus, which flows into the south-east corner of the Aral Sea. The watcher from Niphates could, theoretically, look to his left across the waist of the Caspian to the Aral Sea beyond. Even by the shortest possible route the distance from Ctesiphon to this area would be over 1200 miles.
iii *306*. The Parthians were notoriously skilful mounted archers, and were particularly noted for the accuracy with which they could fire backwards while in retreat.
iii *309. rhombs*] lozenge-shaped or diamond-shaped formations.
iii *311–40*. M. seems to recall several details from Ammianus Marcellinus, who has a most vivid account of the battle with the Parthians near Maranga, in which Julian was killed, xxv i 11–19: 'All their companies were clad in iron, and all parts of their bodies were covered with thick plates, so fitted that the stiff joints conformed with those of their limbs . . . their entire bodies were covered with metal. . . . Hard by the archers (for that nation has especially trusted in this art from the very cradle) were bending their

In coats of mail and military pride;
In mail their horses clad, yet fleet and strong,
Prancing their riders bore, the flower and choice
Of many provinces from bound to bound;
From Arachosia, from Candaor east,
And Margiana to the Hyrcanian cliffs
Of Caucasus, and dark Iberian dales,
From Atropatia and the neighbouring plains
Of Adiabene, Media, and the south

flexible bows. . . . Behind them gleaming elephants, with their awful figures and savage, gaping mouths. . . . If they perceived their forces were giving way, as they retreated they would shoot their arrows back like a shower of rain and keep the enemy from a bold pursuit.' xxv iii 11: 'They sent forth such a shower of arrows that they prevented their opponents from seeing the bowmen.' Perhaps the details came to M. by way of Montaigne, *Essays* ii 9, who paraphrases Marcellinus (Florio's translation): 'They had (saith he) their horses stiffe and strong, covered with thick hides and themselves armed from head to foot, with massie iron plates so artificially contrived, that where the joynts are, there they furthered the motion, and helped the stirring. A man would have said, they had been men made of yron.' Lewalski 120–2 regards these lines as a reworking of a *topos* common in biblical epic, the detailed description of a pagan metropolis. Nearest to M.'s picture, in her opinion, is the view of Memphis in Girolamo Fracastoro's *Joseph* (printed in Du Bartas[2] 818).

iii *316–21*. The components of the great horn of land which Christ is viewing are named anti-clockwise, beginning at the south-east corner with Arachosia, a province west of the Indus, in modern Baluchistan, then moving northwards to Candaor in Afghanistan, then west from Afghanistan to Margiana (modern Khorasan) and Hyrcania, which lies a little further west, skirting the south-east shore of the Caspian, and, further west still, Iberia, a region of the Caucasus west of the Caspian and north of Araxes (Purchas, *Pilgrimes* iii 110 speaks of the 'palpable darkness' of this thickly wooded region). Moving south across Araxes again we come to Atropatia, the northern province of Media, and then, to the west, Adiabene, one of the plains around Nineveh. Travelling away from Niphates again to the south, we come to Susiana, the most southerly Parthian province, bordering on the Persian Gulf, and Balsara, a port on the Chatt-el-Arab (united Tigris and Euphrates), the modern Basra. The juxtaposition of 'Hyrcanian' and 'Caucasus' was probably suggested to M. by a recollection of Virgil, *Aen.* iv 365–7.

iii *326*. Cp. the approaching army in Euripides, *Phoenissae* 110, 'the glare of brass flashes all over the plain', and Plutarch's description of the Parthians at Carrhae, *Life of Crassus* xxiv: 'They dropped the coverings of their armour, and were seen to be themselves blazing in helmets and breastplates, their Margianian steel glittering keen and bright and their horses clad in plates of bronze and steel.'

Of Susiana to Balsara's haven.
He saw them in their forms of battle ranged,
How quick they wheeled, and flying behind them shot
Sharp sleet of arrowy showers against the face
Of their pursuers, and overcame by flight;
The field all iron cast a gleaming brown,
Nor wanted clouds of foot, nor on each horn,
Cuirassiers all in steel for standing fight;
Chariots or elephants endorsed with towers
Of archers, nor of labouring pioneers
A multitude with spades and axes armed
To lay hills plain, fell woods, or valleys fill,
Or where plain was raise hill, or overlay
With bridges rivers proud, as with a yoke;
Mules after these, camels and dromedaries,
And waggons fraught with utensils of war.
Such forces met not, nor so wide a camp,
When Agrican with all his northern powers
Besieged Albracca, as romances tell;
The city of Gallaphrone, from thence to win
The fairest of her sex Angelica
His daughter, sought by many prowest knights,
Both paynim, and the peers of Charlemagne.

iii *327. clouds of foot*] Echoes *Aen.* vii 793: *nimbus peditum.*
iii *328. Cuirassiers*] heavy cavalry armed with the cuirass (metal armour extending from neck to waist).
iii *329. endorsed*] both in the sense 'carrying on their backs' and in the sense 'confirmed, strengthened', (to 'endorse' meant to write on the back of a document, indicating its validity). Ben Jonson has the same word play in his epigram on the Earl of Newcastle's horsemanship, *Underwood* liii 11–12: 'Nay, so your Seate his beauties did endorse, / As I began to wish myselfe a horse.'
iii *337–43.* In Boiardo, *Orlando Innamorato* I x–xiv, Agrican, King of Tartary, brings 2,200,000 men to Albracca, the stronghold of Gallaphrone, King of Cathay and father of Angelica, whom Agrican loves. Roland and the French paladins are involved, and Lewalski (267) considers that the parallel 'identifies Parthia with great and misused military force, for the *Orlando Innamorato* records that many of Charlemagne's knights were enticed to this siege through Angelica's deceit and thereby defaulted in their proper service to their king'.
iii *342. prowest*] most valiant: a favourite superlative of Spenser, who uses it coupled with 'knight' or 'knightly' six times in *F.Q.*
iii *343. paynim*] pagan: another favourite Spenserian word, used twentyfive times in *F.Q.*

Such and so numerous was their chivalry;
At sight whereof the Fiend yet more presumed,
And to our Saviour thus his words renewed.
That thou mayst know I seek not to engage
Thy virtue, and not every way secure
On no slight grounds thy safety; hear, and mark
To what end I have brought thee hither and shown
All this fair sight; thy kingdom though foretold
By prophet or by angel, unless thou
Endeavour, as thy father David did,
Thou never shalt obtain; prediction still
In all things, and all men, supposes means,
Without means used, what it predicts revokes.
But say thou wert possessed of David's throne
By free consent of all, none opposite,
Samaritan or Jew; how couldst thou hope
Long to enjoy it quiet and secure,
Between two such enclosing enemies
Roman and Parthian? Therefore one of these
Thou must make sure thy own, the Parthian first
By my advice, as nearer and of late
Found able by invasion to annoy
Thy country, and captive lead away her kings
Antigonus, and old Hyrcanus bound,
Maugre the Roman: it shall be my task
To render thee the Parthian at dispose;
Choose which thou wilt by conquest or by league.
By him thou shalt regain, without him not,
That which alone can truly reinstall thee
In David's royal seat, his true successor,

iii *344. chivalry*] cavalry.

iii *347–9. I seek not . . . thy safety*] It is not my aim to arouse your courage without making provision for your safety.

iii *358. opposite*] opposing.

iii *359. Samaritan or Jew*] The Jews of Judaea and Galilee did not regard the Samaritans as pure Jews, since Samaria had been colonized by alien races. Jews had 'no dealings with the Samaritans' (*John* iv 9).

iii *366–7.* Satan is inaccurate. The Parthians were allies of Antigonus: with their support he overran Judaea and captured Jerusalem. He took prisoner his uncle, the seventy-year-old Hyrcanus II, and Herod's brother Phasaelus, killed the latter and cut off the ears of the former to disqualify him from priestly office, carrying him off to Seleucia. After a three-year reign Antigonus was defeated and captured by Herod, who bribed Antony to have him executed (37 B.C.). These events are related in Josephus, *Antiquities* xiv 13–16.

iii *368. Maugre*] in spite of.

Deliverance of thy brethren, those ten tribes
Whose offspring in his territory yet serve
In Habor, and among the Medes dispersed,
Ten sons of Jacob, two of Joseph lost
Thus long from Israel; serving as of old
Their fathers in the land of Egypt served,
This offer sets before thee to deliver.
These if from servitude thou shalt restore
To their inheritance, then, nor till then,
Thou on the throne of David in full glory,
From Egypt to Euphrates and beyond
Shalt reign, and Rome or Caesar not need fear.
To whom our Saviour answered thus unmoved.
Much ostentation vain of fleshly arm,
And fragile arms, much instrument of war
Long in preparing, soon to nothing brought,
Before mine eyes thou hast set; and in my ear
Vented much policy, and projects deep
Of enemies, of aids, battles and leagues,
Plausible to the world, to me worth naught.
Means I must use thou say'st, prediction else
Will unpredict and fail me of the throne:
My time I told thee, (and that time for thee
Were better farthest off) is not yet come;

iii *374–6.* See ll. 275–9*n*. The Habor was a tributary of the Euphrates, and the land around it, Gozan, was under Parthian domination in the time of Christ. It lay only about 150 miles south of Niphates, nearer than any of the regions previously mentioned by Satan.
iii *377. two of Joseph*] The ten tribes included Ephraim and Manasses, named after the sons of Joseph.
iii *384. From Egypt to Euphrates*] Cp. *Gen.* xv 18, where God makes a covenant with Abraham, promising to give his sons dominion from Nile to Euphrates, also *1 Kings* iv 21: 'And Solomon reigned over all kingdoms from the river [Euphrates] unto the land of the Philistines, and unto the border of Egypt.'
iii *387.* Cp. *2 Chron.* xxxii 8: 'With him is an arm of flesh; but with us is the Lord our God to help us, and to fight our battles', also Jer. xvii 5: 'Cursed is the man that trusteth in man, and maketh flesh his arm'; M.'s phrase echoes Spenser, *F.Q.* III iv 27 'So feeble is the powre of fleshly arme.'
iii *395. fail me of the throne*] To 'fail of' means to come short of attaining, but M.'s construction with an imitation of the Latin dative pronoun ('me') is singular: *OED* gives no instance of it.
iii *396–7. My time . . . is not yet come*] Cp. *John* vii 6: 'My time is not yet come'–Jesus' reply to his brothers when they tell him to show himself to the world.

When that comes think not thou to find me slack
On my part aught endeavouring, or to need
Thy politic maxims, or that cumbersome
Luggage of war there shown me, argument
Of human weakness rather than of strength.
My brethren, as thou call'st them; those ten tribes,
I must deliver, if I mean to reign
David's true heir, and his full sceptre sway
To just extent over all Israel's sons;
But whence to thee this zeal, where was it then
For Israel, or for David, or his throne,
When thou stood'st up his tempter to the pride
Of numb'ring Israel, which cost the lives
Of threescore and ten thousand Israelites
By three days' pestilence? such was thy zeal
To Israel then, the same that now to me.
As for those captive tribes, themselves were they
Who wrought their own captivity, fell off
From God to worship calves, the deities
Of Egypt, Baal next and Ashtaroth,
And all the idolatries of heathen round,
Besides their other worse than heathenish crimes;
Nor in the land of their captivity
Humbled themselves, or penitent besought
The God of their forefathers; but so died
Impenitent, and left a race behind
Like to themselves, distinguishable scarce

iii *401. Luggage*] Commonly used in the seventeenth century to mean the baggage of an army.

iii *409–12.* Cp. *1 Chron.* xxi 1–14: 'And Satan stood up against Israel, and provoked David to number Israel . . . And God was displeased with this thing; therefore he smote Israel . . . So the Lord sent pestilence upon Israel: and there fell of Israel seventy thousand men.'

iii *414–9.* Jeroboam divided the northern tribes from Judah and Benjamin and founded the kingdom of Samaria. He set up calves in Bethel and in Dan, in imitation of the two calves worshipped by the Egyptians, and said 'Behold thy gods, O Israel, which brought thee up out of the land of Egypt' (*1 Kings* xii 25–33). Ahab built an altar for Baal, and married Jezebel, a Zidonian princess (*1 Kings* xvi 31–2); Ashtoreth, goddess of the moon, was the Zidonian Venus. For Baal and Ashtoreth (Ashtaroth is the plural form), see *Nativity Ode* 197–201 and *PL* i 419–24.

iii *419. worse than heathenish crimes*] The worship of Baal entailed human sacrifice (cp. *Jer.* xix 5).

From Gentiles, but by circumcision vain,
And God with idols in their worship joined.
Should I of these the liberty regard,
Who freed, as to their ancient patrimony,
Unhumbled, unrepentant, unreformed,
Headlong would follow; and to their gods perhaps
Of Bethel and of Dan? No, let them serve
Their enemies, who serve idols with God.
Yet he at length, time to himself best known,
Rememb'ring Abraham by some wondrous call
May bring them back repentant and sincere,
And at their passing cleave the Assyrian flood,
While to their native land with joy they haste,
As the Red Sea and Jordan once he cleft,
When to the promised land their fathers passed;
To his due time and providence I leave them.
So spake Israel's true King, and to the Fiend
Made answer meet, that made void all his wiles.
So fares it when with truth falsehood contends.

THE FOURTH BOOK

Perplexed and troubled at his bad success
The tempter stood, nor had what to reply,
Discovered in his fraud, thrown from his hope,
So oft, and the persuasive rhetoric
That sleeked his tongue, and won so much on Eve,
So little here, nay lost; but Eve was Eve,
This far his over-match, who self-deceived

iii *425. circumcision vain*] Cp. *Rom.* ii 25: 'If thou be a breaker of the law, thy circumcision is made uncircumcision.'

iii *430.* The awkwardly compressed syntax has frequently been commented on, and various unlikely emendations (e.g. 'fall unto' for 'follow; and to') suggested.

iii *431–2.* Cp. *Jer.* v 19: 'Like as ye have forsaken me, and served strange gods in your land, so shall ye serve strangers in a land that is not yours.'

iii *436. Assyrian flood*] Euphrates; cp. Isaiah's prophecy, *Is.* xi 15–16: 'The Lord . . . with his mighty wind shall . . . shake his hand over the river . . . and make men go over dryshod. And there shall be an highway for the remnant of his people, which shall be left, from Assyria; like as it was to Israel in the day that he came up out of the land of Egypt.'

iii *438.* The cleaving of the Red Sea is narrated in *Exod.* xiv 21–2, and that of Jordan in *Josh.* iii 14–17.

And rash, beforehand had no better weighed
The strength he was to cope with, or his own:
But as a man who had been matchless held
In cunning, over-reached where least he thought,
To salve his credit, and for very spite
Still will be tempting him who foils him still,
And never cease, though to his shame the more;
Or as a swarm of flies in vintage-time,
About the wine-press where sweet must is poured,
Beat off, returns as oft with humming sound;
Or surging waves against a solid rock,
Though all to shivers dashed, the assault renew,
Vain battery, and in froth or bubbles end;
So Satan, whom repulse upon repulse
Met ever; and to shameful silence brought,
Yet gives not o'er though desperate of success,
And his vain importunity pursues.
He brought our Saviour to the western side
Of that high mountain, whence he might behold
Another plain, long but in breadth not wide;

iv *8. better*] than Eve.

iv *15–17*. Cp. *Il.* xvi 641, where Homer compares warriors round Sarpedon's body to flies round a milk can, and Ariosto, *Orlando Furioso* xiv 109, where the Moors attack the Christians as flies swarm over milking pails or left-overs of food. Arnold Stein, *ELH* xxiii (1956) 123, sees in M.'s wine image 'a striking anticipatory symbol of the sacerdotal role not yet entered in'.

iv *18–20*. Cp. *Il.* xv 618–22: 'They abode firm-fixed . . . like a crag, sheer and great, hard by the grey sea, that abideth the swift paths of the shrill winds, and the swelling waves that belch forth against it; even so the Danaans withstood the Trojans steadfastly, and fled not', and *Aen.* vii 586–90: 'He, like an unmoved ocean-cliff resists; like an ocean-cliff, which, when a great crash comes, stands steadfast in its bulk amid many howling waves; in vain the crags and foaming rocks roar about it, and the sea-weed, dashed upon its sides, is whirled back.'

iv *27. Another plain*] The plain of Latium in central Italy, lying south and west of the Apennines, which screen it from the north ('Septentrion') winds, and with Rome, on the Tiber, at its centre. S. Kliger, *PMLA* lxi (1946) 474–91, connects M.'s panoramic view of Rome and her power with the literary tradition which saw in Rome the *urbs aeterna*, and more particularly with two examples of this tradition–Anchises's speech in *Aen.* vi and Claudian's eulogy in *On Stilicho's Consulship* iii. There was a long-standing Christian attempt, running through Augustine, Lactantius, Tertullian, Prudentius, Dante and others, to take over this pagan tradition and convert the *urbs aeterna* into an *urbs sacra*. Kliger sees Christ's stern rebuke of Satan (iv 147–51) as a drastic rejection of this compromise.

Washed by the southern sea, and on the north
To equal length backed with a ridge of hills
That screened the fruits of the earth and seats of men
From cold Septentrion blasts, thence in the midst
Divided by a river, of whose banks
On each side an imperial city stood,
With towers and temples proudly elevate
On seven small hills, with palaces adorned,
Porches and theatres, baths, aqueducts,
Statues and trophies, and triumphal arcs,
Gardens and groves presented to his eyes
Above the height of mountains interposed.
By what strange parallax or optic skill
Of vision multiplied through air, or glass
Of telescope, were curious to inquire:
And now the tempter thus his silence broke.
The city which thou seest no other deem
Than great and glorious Rome, queen of the earth
So far renowned, and with the spoils enriched
Of nations; there the Capitol thou seest
Above the rest lifting his stately head
On the Tarpeian rock, her citadel
Impregnable, and there Mount Palatine
The imperial palace, compass huge, and high
The structure, skill of noblest architects,
With gilded battlements, conspicuous far,
Turrets and terraces, and glittering spires.
Many a fair edifice besides, more like
Houses of gods (so well I have disposed

iv *40. parallax*] apparent displacement of an object caused by actual change in the position of the observer.

iv *42. were curious to inquire*] As Pope 112–4 remarks, many commentators *did* inquire how Satan could have shown Christ all the kingdoms of the world from a single mountain-top. M.'s telescopic explanation (iv 56–7) had been anticipated by Cornelius Jansen and Francis Luca. Another popular theory was that the kingdoms were mere mirages or visions.

iv *49. Tarpeian rock*] The steepest precipice on the Capitoline hill. The citadel occupied the commanding northern summit of the Capitoline.

iv *50–1. Mount Palatine / The imperial palace*] During the empire a large part of the Palatine hill was gradually covered by the expanding imperial palace. What now remains on the Palatine, occupying its centre, are the ruins of Domitian's palace, which M. would have seen when he visited Rome. Satan may be referring to Augustus' second palace, rebuilt after the fire of A.D. 3, or to the Domus Tiberiana.

My airy microscope) thou mayst behold
Outside and inside both, pillars and roofs
Carved work, the hand of famed artificers
In cedar, marble, ivory or gold.
Thence to the gates cast round thine eye, and see
What conflux issuing forth, or entering in,
Praetors, proconsuls to their provinces
Hasting or on return, in robes of state;
Lictors and rods the ensigns of their power,
Legions and cohorts, turms of horse and wings:
Or embassies from regions far remote
In various habits on the Appian road,
Or on the Aemilian, some from farthest south,
Syene, and where the shadow both way falls,

iv *57. microscope*] *OED* gives this as the first instance of 'microscope' in a transferred sense: the peculiarity of M.'s 'microscope' is that it can see 'Outside and inside both'. Marjorie Nicolson, *JELH* ii (1935) 1–11, considers that M.'s blindness prevented him from understanding the real nature of the microscope. While microscopes were known in England between 1625 and 1660, they did not come into common use until after 1660. She thinks that M., from vague accounts of the new instrument, misunderstood its function. Kester Svendsen, *MLN* lxiv (1949) 525–7, draws attention to a passage in Leonard and Thomas Digges's *Pantometria* (1591) I xxi, which describes a system of lens arrangement that produces the same effects as Satan's 'microscope'.
iv *59. hand*] handiwork.
iv *63. Praetors, proconsuls*] Under the empire there were sixteen praetors (magistrates), each of whom was allowed a year of provincial government following his term of office in Rome. Proconsuls were governors of senatorial provinces.
iv *65. Lictors*] attendants who accompanied Roman dignitaries and carried bundles of rods to symbolize the officials' power to punish criminals.
iv *66. cohorts*] tenth parts of a legion. *wings*] Roman cavalry fought on the flanks of the infantry, and its formations became known as wings. A 'turm' (Latin *turma*) was the tenth part of a wing, about thirty in number. 'Turm' is found in English usage from the fifteenth century.
iv *68–9. Appian . . . Aemilian*] The Via Appia, built by Appius Claudius 312 B.C., was the main road running south from Rome to Brindisi. The Via Aemilia, built by Aemilius Lepidus, went from Rimini to Piacenza.
iv *69–70. farthest south, Syene*] Assouan, on the first cataract of the Nile, at the extreme south of the Roman sphere of influence. Tacitus, *Ann.* ii 61, speaks of it as one of the former 'limits of the Roman empire'.
iv *70–1. where the shadow both way falls, Meroe*] Cp. Pliny ii 75: 'In Meroe–this is an inhabited island in the river Nile 5000 stades from Syene, and is the

Meroe Nilotic isle, and more to west,
The realm of Bocchus to the Blackmoor sea;
From the Asian kings and Parthian among these,
From India and the golden Chersoness,
And utmost Indian isle Taprobane,
Dusk faces with white silken turbans wreathed:
From Gallia, Gades, and the British west,
Germans and Scythians, and Sarmatians north
Beyond Danubius to the Tauric pool.
All nations now to Rome obedience pay,
To Rome's great emperor, whose wide domain
In ample territory, wealth and power,
Civility of manners, arts, and arms,
And long renown thou justly mayst prefer
Before the Parthian; these two thrones except,
The rest are barbarous, and scarce worth the sight,
Shared among petty kings too far removed;

capital of the Ethiopian race–the shadows disappear twice a year, when the sun is in the 18th degree of Taurus and in the 14th of Leo. There is a mountain named Maleus in the Indian tribe of the Oretes, near which shadows are thrown southward in summer and northward in winter.' As Whiting 88–9 notes, M. seems to have read the second sentence as if it also referred to Meroe.

iv 72. *realm of Bocchus*] Mauretania; Bocchus was king of it at the time of the Jugurthine war: he surrendered his son-in-law Jugurtha to the Romans in 106 B.C. *Blackmoor sea*] that part of the Mediterranean bordering on Mauretania, the land of the moors or 'blackamoors'. It is called *Africum Pelagus* in Ortelius, but Horace, *Odes* II vi 3–4 calls it *Maura unda*, which may have suggested the name M. uses.

iv 74. *golden Chersoness*] In *PL* xi 392 the spelling is 'Chersonese'; here M. may be avoiding rhyme with 'these'. The Malay peninsula was called 'golden' to distinguish it from the 'Tauric Chersonese' (the Crimea): Josephus, *Antiquities* viii 6, says that it was formerly called Ophir, and that Solomon sent a fleet there to bring back gold. 'Chersonese' is from the Greek word for a peninsula.

iv 75. *Taprobane*] G. W. Whiting, *RES* xiii (1937) 209–12, produces evidence from Ortelius, *Theatrum Orbis Terrarum* and elsewhere to show that 'Taprobane' usually meant Sumatra. J. D. Gordon, *RES* xviii (1942) 319, notes that Ariosto, *Orlando Furioso* xv 17, mentions *l'aurea Chersonesso* (a form near to M.'s) and Taprobane together in the same stanza.

iv 77. *Gallia*] France. *Gades*] Cadiz.

iv 78. *Scythians*] See iii 301–2*n*. *Sarmatians*] the barbarians living north of the Scythians, divided from them by the Don: they occupied Poland and Russia west of the Volga.

iv 79. *Tauric pool*] Sea of Azov.

These having shown thee, I have shown thee all
The kingdoms of the world, and all their glory.
This emperor hath no son, and now is old,
Old, and lascivious, and from Rome retired
To Capreae an island small but strong
On the Campanian shore, with purpose there
His horrid lusts in private to enjoy,
Committing to a wicked favourite
All public cares, and yet of him suspicious,
Hated of all, and hating; with what ease
Endued with regal virtues as thou art,
Appearing, and beginning noble deeds,
Might'st thou expel this monster from his throne
Now made a sty, and in his place ascending
A victor people free from servile yoke!
And with my help thou mayst; to me the power
Is given, and by that right I give it thee.
Aim therefore at no less than all the world,
Aim at the highest, without the highest attained
Will be for thee no sitting, or not long
On David's throne, be prophesied what will.
  To whom the Son of God unmoved replied.
Nor doth this grandeur and majestic show

iv *90–4.* Tiberius (42 B.C.–A.D. 37) retired from active government in A.D. 26 and took up residence the following year on Capri, attracted to it, according to Suetonius, *Caesars* iii 40 and Tacitus, *Ann.* iv 67, because a landing could only be made on one small beach, and it was otherwise surrounded by sheer cliffs and deep water. Suetonius, iii 43–5, and Tacitus, vi 1, both describe Tiberius' progressive degradation on Capri. Lewalski 122 cites a parallel passage from Beaumont's *Psyche* ix 225–6, 229, in which Satan calls forth Tiberius from the globe wherein he is displaying all the kingdoms to Christ, upbraids him for mismanagement and offers Christ his place.
iv *95. a wicked favourite*] Sejanus. Tiberius grew suspicious of him, and finally denounced him to the Senate which condemned the fallen favourite to death A.D. 31.
iv *102. victor people*] The *1671 Errata* removes a comma from between these words.
iv *103–4.* Cp. *Luke* iv 6: 'And the devil said unto him, All this power will I give thee, and the glory of them: for that is delivered unto me; and to whomsoever I will I give it.'
iv *110–20.* Pope 56–66 remarks that the emphasis on luxury and physical pleasure in these lines is in keeping with the treatment of the temptations by Protestant theologians (see i 355*n*) who, as they regarded the first temptation as one not of gluttony but of distrust in God, were obliged to inter-

Of luxury, though called magnificence,
More than of arms before, allure mine eye,
Much less my mind; though thou should'st add to tell
Their sumptuous gluttonies, and gorgeous feasts
On citron tables or Atlantic stone;
(For I have also heard, perhaps have read)
Their wines of Setia, Cales, and Falerne,
Chios and Crete, and how they quaff in gold,
Crystal and myrrhine cups embossed with gems

pret the kingdoms-of-the-world temptation as an attempt to excite bodily appetite, as well as the longing for honour, wealth, dominion and power. Thus the devil in Bale's *Temptation of Our Lord*, after enumerating the actual regions he is preparing to hand over to Christ, and dwelling on their 'ryches, their honor, their wealth', goes on to persuade him that 'Here are fayre women, of countenaunce ameable, / With all kyndes of meates, to the body dylectable', and Giles Fletcher, *Christ's Victory and Triumph* i 49–59, describes the temptation of the kingdoms allegorically as a house with four stories: on the first are wine and alluring ladies, on the second and third, 'avarice' and 'ambitious honour'.

iv *115*. *citron tables*] The wood of the African citrus was in great demand among wealthy Romans for table-tops, as Pliny xiii 29–30 relates, partly because it was very hard and spilt wine would not mark it, and partly because it had beautiful graining, either in stripes (tiger wood) or in rounds (panther wood) or in clusters (parsley wood). *Atlantic stone*] The meaning is not certain. 'Atlantic' derives from the Libyan Mt Atlas (and was thence applied to the sea near the W. shore of Africa, afterwards extending to the whole ocean). M. may, then, mean marble from the Atlas mountains, or he may be referring again to the citrus wood, which looked like marble and grew on the slopes of Atlas (cp. Pliny xiii 29: 'adjoining Mt Atlas is Mauretania, which produces a great many citrus trees').

iv *117*. *Setia*] Sezza, near Rome, mentioned for its wines by Martial xiii 23. *Cales, and Falerne*] Cales, and the Falernian vineyards, were in Campania, near Vesuvius. Cp. Horace, *Odes* I xxxi 9: 'trim the vine with Calenian pruning-knife', and Virgil, *Georg*. ii 96: 'Falernian wine vaults'.

iv *118*. *Chois*] Island off the Ionian coast, the source of expensive, sweet Greek wines. Horace looks forward to a jar of Chian wine, *Odes* III xix 5.

iv *119*. *Crystal and myrrhine cups*] Cp. Pliny xxxiii 2: 'out of the same earth we have dug myrrhine (*murrina*) and crystal (*crystallina*), things which their mere fragility rendered costly. . . . Nor was this enough: we drink out of a crowd of precious stones, and set our cups with emeralds', and Juvenal, *Sat*. vi 155–6, who says that two of the things spoilt women will squander their husbands' money on are crystal and myrrhine cups. Of the materials M. mentions only gold would be embossed and decorated with jewels. Pliny thought that the basic material of myrrhine cups was a fossil; Propertius IV v 26 regarded it as porcelain from Parthia. It is now thought

And studs of pearl, to me should'st tell who thirst
And hunger still: then embassies thou show'st
From nations far and nigh; what honour that,
But tedious waste of time to sit and hear
So many hollow compliments and lies,
Outlandish flatteries? Then proceed'st to talk
Of the emperor, how easily subdued,
How gloriously; I shall, thou say'st, expel
A brutish monster: what if I withal
Expel a devil who first made him such?
Let his tormentor conscience find him out,
For him I was not sent, nor yet to free
That people victor once, now vile and base,
Deservedly made vassal, who once just,
Frugal, and mild, and temperate, conquered well,
But govern ill the nations under yoke,
Peeling their provinces, exhausted all
By lust and rapine; first ambitious grown
Of triumph that insulting vanity;
Then cruel, by their sports to blood inured
Of fighting beasts, and men to beasts exposed,
Luxurious by their wealth, and greedier still,
And from the daily scene effeminate.
What wise and valiant man would seek to free
These thus degenerate, by themselves enslaved,

that these cups, though they reached Rome via Parthia, came from China and were made of a rare sort of clay.

iv *130. conscience*] Cp. Tacitus, *Ann.* vi 6, where Tiberius writes to the Senate: 'May all the gods and goddesses destroy me more miserably than I feel myself to be daily perishing, if I know at this moment what to write to you.' Tacitus comments: 'Tiberius was not saved by his elevation or his solitude from having to confess the anguish of his heart.'

iv *133. Deservedly made vassal*] It was a favourite theory of M.'s that those who became slaves to their own passions deservedly and frequently allowed themselves to be enslaved politically. Cp. *History of Britain*: 'But when God hath decreed servitude on a sinful nation, fitted by their own vices for no condition but servile, all Estates of Government are alike unable to avoid it'; also *Defensio Secunda*: 'by the wonted judgment, and as it were by the just retribution of God, it comes to pass, that the nation, which has been incapable of governing and ordering itself, and has delivered itself up to the slavery of its own lusts, is itself delivered over, against its will, to other masters' (Columbia x 198 and viii 250–1).

iv *136. Peeling*] pillaging.

iv *142. scene*] stage show, theatrical performance; a common seventeenth-century sense.

Or could of inward slaves make outward free?
Know therefore when my season comes to sit
On David's throne, it shall be like a tree
Spreading and overshadowing all the earth,
Or as a stone that shall to pieces dash
All monarchies besides throughout the world,
And of my kingdom there shall be no end:
Means there shall be to this, but what the means,
Is not for thee to know, nor me to tell.
　To whom the tempter impudent replied.
I see all offers made by me how slight
Thou valu'st, because offered, and reject'st:
Nothing will please the difficult and nice,
Or nothing more than still to contradict:
On the other side know also thou, that I
On what I offer set as high esteem,
Nor what I part with mean to give for naught;
All these which in a moment thou behold'st,
The kingdoms of the world to thee I give;
For given to me, I give to whom I please,
No trifle; yet with this reserve, not else,

iv *147–50*. Christ sees himself (and, as Lewalski 279 points out, Christian exegesis up to M.'s day had consistently seen him) as the fulfilment of the two visions in *Dan.* iv 10–12 and ii 31–5: Nebuchadnezzar's dream of the tree that 'reached unto heaven, and the sight thereof to the end of all the earth', and his vision of a stone which smashed the metal image of the kingdoms and 'became a great mountain, and filled the whole earth'.
iv *151*. Cp. *Luke* i 33: 'And of his kingdom there shall be no end.'
iv *153*. *Is not for thee to know*] Pope 39 remarks that the phrase suggests that M. was working under the influence of the tradition that Christ deliberately withheld from Satan all evidence of his own identity. It is not necessary to assume, however, that Christ is aware of his own identity all along: Allen's theory that he has moments of illumination (see headnote) would explain flashes of confidence like this one.
iv *157*. *the*] C. W. Brodribb, *TLS* (17 May, 1941) 239–41, and some eighteenth-century critics, would prefer to read 'thee', thus turning a general statement into a particular one. There is no authority or necessity for this emendation. *nice*] over-fastidious.
iv *164*. As Pope 67 and Gilbert[2] 606 remark, the glory of Athens is not offered as one of the gifts of Satan, or as one of the kingdoms which he can personally bestow upon Christ. He presents his bargain at the conclusion of the temptation of Rome. Thoroughly as M. castigates classical philosophy and literature, he does not place them under the direct control of the devil.
iv *165–7*. Cp. *Matt.* iv 9: 'All these things will I give thee, if thou wilt fall down and worship me.' Arnold Stein, *ELH* xxiii (1956) 126, considers that

On this condition, if thou wilt fall down,
And worship me as thy superior lord,
Easily done, and hold them all of me;
For what can less so great a gift deserve?
Whom thus our Saviour answered with disdain.
I never liked thy talk, thy offers less,
Now both abhor, since thou hast dared to utter
The abominable terms, impious condition;
But I endure the time, till which expired,
Thou hast permission on me. It is written
The first of all commandments, Thou shalt worship
The Lord thy God, and only him shalt serve;
And dar'st thou to the Son of God propound
To worship thee accursed, now more accursed
For this attempt bolder than that on Eve,
And more blasphemous? which expect to rue.
The kingdoms of the world to thee were given,
Permitted rather, and by thee usurped,
Other donation none thou canst produce:
If given, by whom but by the King of kings,
God over all supreme? If given to thee,
By thee how fairly is the giver now
Repaid! But gratitude in thee is lost
Long since. Wert thou so void of fear or shame,
As offer them to me the Son of God,
To me my own, on such abhorred pact,
That I fall down and worship thee as God?
Get thee behind me; plain thou now appear'st
That Evil One, Satan for ever damned.

Satan is not really tempting Christ to accept this price: 'A bargainer like Satan does not expect a customer uninterested in the merchandise to become interested on hearing the full price. . . . If this *is* the Son of God, and is successfully provoked, then Satan may learn, however sadly, the fact.' Lewalski 260, however, regards Satan's move as 'a desperate face-saving maneuver: recognizing that Christ has regarded all his offers as "slight" and valueless, he here attempts to prove their value by citing their high price'.

iv *174–6.* Cp. *Luke* iv 8: 'And Jesus answered and said unto him, Get thee behind me, Satan: for it is written, Thou shalt worship the Lord thy God, and him only shalt thou serve', where Christ is quoting *Deut.* vi 13.

iv *184. donation*] grant, bestowal of property.

iv *191. To me my own*] Pope 37 comments that the phrase is ambiguous. It may mean 'the kingdoms you have offered me for my own', as well as 'my own kingdoms': Christ is not provoked into making a direct claim.

To whom the Fiend with fear abashed replied.
Be not so sore offended, Son of God;
Though Sons of God both angels are and men,
If I to try whether in higher sort
Than these thou bear'st that title, have proposed
What both from men and angels I receive,
Tetrarchs of fire, air, flood, and on the earth
Nations besides from all the quartered winds,
God of this world invoked and world beneath;
Who then thou art, whose coming is foretold
To me so fatal, me it most concerns.
The trial hath endamaged thee no way,
Rather more honour left and more esteem;
Me naught advantaged, missing what I aimed.
Therefore let pass, as they are transitory,
The kingdoms of this world; I shall no more
Advise thee, gain them as thou canst, or not.
And thou thyself seem'st otherwise inclined
Than to a worldly crown, addicted more
To contemplation and profound dispute,
As by that early action may be judged,
When slipping from thy mother's eye thou went'st
Alone into the Temple; there was found
Amongst the gravest Rabbis disputant
On points and questions fitting Moses' chair,
Teaching not taught; the childhood shows the man,
As morning shows the day. Be famous then
By wisdom; as thy empire must extend,
So let extend thy mind o'er all the world,
In knowledge, all things in it comprehend,
All knowledge is not couched in Moses' law,
The Pentateuch or what the prophets wrote,
The Gentiles also know, and write, and teach

iv *197*. Cp. *Rom.* viii 14: 'For as many as are led by the Spirit of God, they are the sons of God'.

iv *201*. *Tetrarchs*] rulers of fourth parts: here, of one of the four elements.

iv *203*. Satan is called 'the god of this world' in *2 Cor.* iv 4.

iv *215*. See i 209–14*n*.

iv *219*. *Moses' chair*] the chair from which the doctors expounded the law. *Matt.* xxiii 2: 'The scribes and Pharisees sit in Moses' seat.'

iv *221–2*. *Be famous then / By wisdom*] Pope 67 finds M. the first writer to include learning among the temptations.

iv *226*. *Pentateuch*] the first five books of the Old Testament, containing the Mosaic Law.

To admiration, led by nature's light;
And with the Gentiles much thou must converse,
Ruling them by persuasion as thou mean'st,
Without their learning how wilt thou with them,
Or they with thee hold conversation meet?
How wilt thou reason with them, how refute
Their idolisms, traditions, paradoxes?
Error by his own arms is best evinced.
Look once more ere we leave this specular mount
Westward, much nearer by south-west, behold
Where on the Aegean shore a city stands
Built nobly, pure the air, and light the soil,
Athens the eye of Greece, mother of arts
And eloquence, native to famous wits
Or hospitable, in her sweet recess,
City or suburban, studious walks and shades;
See there the olive-grove of Academe,
Plato's retirement, where the Attic bird
Trills her thick-warbled notes the summer long,
There flowery hill Hymettus with the sound

iv *228. To admiration*] admirably.
iv *229–35.* Schultz 227, viewing the whole temptation in an ecclesiastical context (see headnote), remarks that Satan's two arguments for philosophy as *ancilla theologiae*–that it would make one socially acceptable, hence escaping contempt, and that it would be useful for refuting heresy–were the arguments constantly used by the conservative side in the learned-ministry controversy.
iv *234. idolisms*] idolatries: first found in Sylvester (Du Bartas 632).
iv *235. evinced*] conquered.
iv *236. specular mount*] lookout mountain; according to *OED*, the first instance of 'specular' (Latin *specula*= watchtower) in the sense 'affording an extensive view'.
iv *240. the eye*] the seat of intelligence or light. *OED* first records this idiom in Hakluyt *Voyages* (1582) of Oxford and Cambridge. It is also found in *Justin* V viii 4 and Aristotle *Rhet.* III x 7 of Athens and Sparta.
iv *244. Academe*] The Academy was a gymnasium, enlarged as a public park by Cimon, about a mile north-west of Athens. It was planted with olive trees. Plato used to walk there with his pupils, and from it his school of philosophy took its name.
iv *245. the Attic bird*] the nightingale; near the Academy was Colonus, celebrated by Sophocles, *Oedipus at Colonus* 671, as the haunt of nightingales.
iv *247. Hymettus*] A line of hills to the south-east of Athens; the thyme-covered slopes are famous for their honey.

Of bees' industrious murmur oft invites
To studious musing; there Ilissus rolls
His whispering stream; within the walls then view
The schools of ancient sages; his who bred
Great Alexander to subdue the world,
Lyceum there, and painted Stoa next:
There thou shalt hear and learn the secret power
Of harmony in tones and numbers hit
By voice or hand, and various-measured verse,
Aeolian charms and Dorian lyric odes,
And his who gave them breath, but higher sung,
Blind Melesigenes thence Homer called,
Whose poem Phoebus challenged for his own.
Thence what the lofty grave tragedians taught
In chorus or iambic, teachers best

iv *249. Ilissus*] A little river which rises on the slopes of Hymettus and flows to the south of the city.
iv *251. his*] Aristotle's, tutor to Alexander.
iv *253. Lyceum*] Originally a sanctuary of Apollo Lyceius, the Lyceum was a park to the E. of the city, beyond the Diocharean Gate (not, then, 'within the walls'). Aristotle and his pupils used to stroll up and down its walks, hence the name of their school, the 'peripatetics' (strollers). *Stoa*] covered colonnade. The Athenian agora had more than one, but one, on the north side, was, according to Pausanias I iii 1, XIV vi 3, decorated with frescoes by famous artists and known as the 'painted stoa': this was where the founder of the 'Stoics', Zeno, taught.
iv *257. Aeolian*] The island of Lesbos belonged to the Aeolians, and the songs of Sappho and Alcaeus were in the Aeolic dialect. In *Odes* III xxx 13–4, Horace boasts that he introduced the *Aeolium carmen* into Italy. *charms*] songs (Latin *carmen*). *Dorian*] Pindar's odes and hymns are written in the Dorian dialect.
iv *259. Melesigenes*] Not used as a title for Homer by any Greek or Latin poet; presumably M. invented it, referring to the fact that, according to one tradition, Homer was born near the river Meles in Ionia. It was common among the ancients to represent Homer as the source of all poetry. Aelian, *Var. Hist.* xiii 22, says Galaton the painter drew Homer as a fountain with other poets receiving water from his mouth. *thence*] from his blindness. The pseudo-Herodotean *Life of Homer* explained ὅμηρος as a Cumaean word meaning 'blind'.
iv *260.* An epigram in the *Greek Anthology* ix 455, entitled 'What Apollo would say about Homer' perpetuates the tradition that Apollo envied Homer's poetry. It reads: 'The song is mine, but divine Homer wrote it down.'
iv *262. chorus or iambic*] In Greek tragedy the dialogue is written in iambics, the chorus in various metres.

Of moral prudence, with delight received
In brief sententious precepts, while they treat
Of fate, and chance, and change in human life;
High actions, and high passions best describing:
Thence to the famous orators repair,
Those ancient, whose resistless eloquence
Wielded at will that fierce democraty,
Shook the Arsenal and fulmined over Greece,
To Macedon, and Artaxerxes' throne;
To sage philosophy next lend thine ear,
From heaven descended to the low-roofed house
Of Socrates, see there his tenement,
Whom well inspired the oracle pronounced

iv *264. brief sententious precepts*] Cp. Quintilian X i 68, on the style of M.'s favourite Euripides: *sententiis densus* (thick with maxims).
iv *269. democraty*] democracy. M.'s form, nearer to the Greek δημοκρατία, was common in the seventeenth century.
iv *270. Shook the Arsenal*] E. C. Baldwin, *PQ* xviii (1939) 218–22, refers to Dionysius of Halicarnassus, *Epistle to Ammoeus* i 15–22, for the information that Demosthenes 'shook' the great Arsenal or dockyard which Philo of Eleusis constructed at Piraeus in that, on his advice, the building of it was suspended from 339–338 B.C. so that public funds might be freed for use against Philip of Macedon. B. A. Wright, *N & Q* n.s. v. (1958) 199–200, accepting the fact that it is Philo's dockyard that is meant, interprets 'shook' as 'brandished, as the symbol of Athenian naval power'. *fulmined*] sent forth lightning and thunder: the first recorded use of the verb is *F.Q.* III ii 5. M. is echoing Aristophanes' satiric identification of Pericles with the Olympian Zeus in *Acharnians* 530: 'He lightened, thundered and confounded Hellas.' It was Pericles who endeavoured to inspire the Athenians while the Spartans were ravaging outside their gates, and while the Athenian fleet was away supporting the Egyptian revolt against the Persian king Artaxerxes, allied to Sparta.
iv *273. From heaven descended*] Cp. Cicero, *Tusculan Disputations* V iv 10 'Socrates on the other hand was the first to call philosophy down from the heavens and set her in the cities of men and bring her also into their homes and compel her to ask questions about life and morality'. Cicero is referring to the scientific pretentiousness of pre-Socratic thought (cp. *Phaedo* 96–9, where Socrates tells Cebes of his youthful enthusiasm for scientific philosophy, and how he eventually decided he must give up investigating 'realities', and investigate 'conceptions' instead). When Satan speaks of the descent of philosophy from heaven he means something more than Cicero does, and something he hopes will be more tempting to Christ. *low-roofed house*] In Aristophanes, *Clouds* 92, the dwelling of Socrates is pointed out as a 'little house'.
iv *275–6.* Cp. Plato, *Apology* 21, where Socrates at his trial tells how his

Wisest of men; from whose mouth issued forth
Mellifluous streams that watered all the schools
Of Academics old and new, with those
Surnamed Peripatetics, and the sect
Epicurean, and the Stoic severe;
These here revolve, or, as thou lik'st, at home,
Till time mature thee to a kingdom's weight;
These rules will render thee a king complete
Within thyself, much more with empire joined.
To whom our Saviour sagely thus replied.
Think not but that I know these things, or think

friend Chaerephon asked the Delphic oracle if there were any men wiser than Socrates, and how the oracle replied that there was no one wiser.

iv *276–8.* Cp. Quintilian I x, who calls Socrates the 'fountain' of philosophers.

iv *278. old and new*] There were three phases of Academic philosophy: old, under Plato (d. 347 B.C.); middle, under Arcesilas (d. 271 B.C.); new, under Carneades (d. 128 B.C.).

iv *279. Peripatetics*] See l. 253*n*.

iv *280. Epicurean*] Epicurus, 341–270 B.C., reacting against Plato and Aristotle, based his ethical doctrine not on logic and metaphysics but on sensation–the only touchstone of truth, as he saw it. Thus his moral philosophy is a qualified hedonism. He became the loved and venerated head of a little community of men and women who lived a life of simple pleasure, drinking water and eating barley-bread. The accusations of debauchery which the Stoics brought against this community are probably mere venomous slander. *Stoic*] See *Comus* 706*n*.

iv *286–7.* J. H. Hanford, *SP* xv (1918) 183–4, remarks that M. 'cannot bring himself to say quite flatly that Jesus Christ was ignorant' of pagan philosophy. In fact, Christ's reply is plain evidence of knowledge.

iv *286–321.* M. introduces the temptation of learning, without any precedent, in order to maintain the parallel between the temptations of the first and second Adam (cp. Adam's thirst for unnecessary knowledge, against which Raphael warns him, *PL* viii 66–178). There has been frequent expression of surprise that M. should be false to his earlier affiliations. Irene Samuel, *PMLA* lxiv (1949) 709–23, stresses, however, the constancy of M.'s attitude to learning throughout his life. Not only Raphael's reply to Adam about astronomy and Michael's restriction of the 'sum Of wisdom' (*PL* viii 66–178 and xii 575–87), but also M.'s insistence on the 'plainness and brightness' of truth in *Of Reformation* (Columbia iii 33, Yale i 566), and his commendation of the 'plain unlearned man that lives well by that light which he has' in *Animadversions* (Columbia iii 162–3, Yale i 720) and of the man 'learned without letters' in *Defensio prima* (Columbia vii 69), are quite in harmony, she argues, with Christ's words here. What Christ insists on, as Miss Samuel sees it, is what M. had always insisted on:

I know them not; not therefore am I short
Of knowing what I ought: he who receives
Light from above, from the fountain of light,
No other doctrine needs, though granted true;

the adequacy of the human spirit, with or without particular books, in the quest for all knowledge essential to the good life. Stein[2] 97 takes the same view as Miss Samuel. Plainly, however, Miss Samuel's argument applies better to ll. 286–90 than to the specific condemnation of Greek philosophy as 'false' and 'built on nothing firm', which follows. This certainly does seem, as G. F. Sensabaugh, *SP* xliii (1946) 258–72, feels, out of key with the ideals and enthusiasms of *Of Education*. Sensabaugh thinks M. did change his educational philosophy between the 1640s and the Restoration, and that this was the result of the process by which he forced his mind into a systematized scheme of Christian thought–a process which produced the *De doctrina*. In this work he ostensibly lifts his whole educational policy from the secular to the religious plane, though there is a tendency, particularly in Book ii, to retain an ethical system drawn largely from classical and Renaissance thought, while asserting the all-sufficiency of Scripture. Perhaps Christ's speech should be read in this light, or as that of a *dramatis persona*, in which case the difficulties of fitting what he says to M.'s own beliefs disappear, and all that is needed is a reason for the placing of this anti-Hellenic speech in the mouth of the historical Christ. The reason is not far to seek. The gradual Hellenisation of Judaea had been in train since Antiochus violated the Holy of Holies (167 B.C.) and forbade circumcision. Hellenisation was part of Herod's policy too.

Schultz 92 notes that 'almost any of the Fathers or their modern imitators could have matched M.'s school-by-school criticism of pagan philosophy', with its 'labour-saving device of rejecting only the *summum bonum* of each sect'. He refers particularly to Clement, *Protrepticus* v–vii, Tertullian, *De praescriptione haereticorum* vii, and Lactantius, *De falsa sapientia* (*Divine Institutes* iii 5–23–this source is also suggested by J. Horrell, *RES* xviii (1943) 423–4): among more modern works, Philippe de Mornay's *De la vérité de la chrétienne religion*, which Sidney translated, and George Hakewill's *Apology* (see *Natur* headnote). E. Newmeyer, *Bulletin of the N.Y. Public Library* lxvi 485–98, adds to this list Theodore Beza's *Job Expounded*: Beza, following Josephus, maintains that Abraham taught the Egyptians, and that Greek philosophy, derived from Egypt, was therefore a corrupt residue of Abraham's superior learning. Lewalski 120 notes that in Quarles' *Job Militant*, a meditation upon the varieties of false felicity which seduce other men but not Job includes Athenian learning.

iv *288–90*. Lewalski 291–5 shows that in assuming a radical distinction between knowledge (*scientia*), which derives from the study of the things of the world, and wisdom (*sapientia*) which comes only from above, M.'s Christ is defending a Christian commonplace prevalent from Augustine's time through to the seventeenth century.

But these are false, or little else but dreams,
Conjectures, fancies, built on nothing firm.
The first and wisest of them all professed
To know this only, that he nothing knew;
The next to fabling fell and smooth conceits,
A third sort doubted all things, though plain sense;
Others in virtue placed felicity,
But virtue joined with riches and long life,
In corporal pleasure he, and careless ease,
The Stoic last in philosophic pride,
By him called virtue; and his virtuous man,
Wise, perfect in himself, and all possessing,
Equal to God, oft shames not to prefer,
As fearing God nor man, contemning all
Wealth, pleasure, pain or torment, death and life,
Which when he lists, he leaves, or boasts he can,

iv *294. that he nothing knew*] In Plato, *Apology* 21–3, Socrates, having told of the answer of the Delphic oracle (see 275–6*n*), adds that he went round Athens interviewing reputedly wise people, and eventually concluded that he was indeed the wisest, but only because he alone knew that he knew nothing. Lewalski 126–7 quotes from Quarles, *Job Militant* xi a passage on the uselessness of knowledge without wisdom, 'Which made that great Philosopher avow, / He knew so much, that he did nothing know'.
iv *295. The next to fabling fell*] An objection to Plato, as Kermode[4] 328 notes, which is ultimately Platonic. In *Id Plat* 38 M. calls Plato *fabulator maximus*: allegories and myths are frequent in the dialogues.
iv *296. third sort*] the Sceptics, founded by Pyrrho of Elis, *c.* 360–270 B.C. Because they believed the impossibility of knowing things in their own nature, and held that against every statement the contrary might be advanced with equal reason, they thought it necessary to preserve an attitude of intellectual suspense and imperturbability.
iv *297–8. Others . . . riches and long life*] the Peripatetics; Aristotle taught that man's happiness is the activity of soul according to virtue in a mature life, requiring as conditions moderate bodily health and external goods of fortune.
iv *299. he*] Epicurus; a jaundiced view: see l. 280*n*.
iv *300–6*. M. may be influenced in his arguments against Stoicism by Cicero's account and systematic refutation of it, *De finibus* iii–iv. Schultz 92 and 261 lists later denunciations in Cyprian and Lactantius and, in the seventeenth century, Samuel Gardiner, William Rawley, Anthony Burges and others. The Stoics divided humanity into two classes: wise or virtuous, unwise or wicked. The wise man alone, they claimed, is free, rich, beautiful, skilled to govern, capable of giving or receiving a benefit. His happiness is in no way inferior to that of Zeus ('Equal to God'). The so-called goods of life ('Wealth, pleasure') are to him indifferent. He will have self-control

For all his tedious talk is but vain boast,
Or subtle shifts conviction to evade.
Alas what can they teach, and not mislead;
Ignorant of themselves, of God much more,
And how the world began, and how man fell
Degraded by himself, on grace depending?
Much of the soul they talk, but all awry,
And in themselves seek virtue, and to themselves
All glory arrogate, to God give none,
Rather accuse him under usual names,
Fortune and Fate, as one regardless quite
Of mortal things. Who therefore seeks in these
True wisdom, finds her not, or by delusion
Far worse, her false resemblance only meets,
An empty cloud. However many books
Wise men have said are wearisome; who reads
Incessantly, and to his reading brings not
A spirit and judgment equal or superior,
(And what he brings, what needs he elsewhere seek)
Uncertain and unsettled still remains,
Deep-versed in books and shallow in himself,
Crude or intoxicate, collecting toys,

even in the midst of pain. Suicide is allowable for him, if the circumstances should call for it ('life, Which when he lists, he leaves'). Cp. *De doctrina* ii 10 (Columbia xvii 253) where M. lists as one of the opposites of true patience, 'a stoical apathy; for sensibility to pain, and even lamentations, are not inconsistent with true patience; as may be seen in Job and the other saints, when under the pressure of affliction'.
iv *308. subtle shifts*] It is to the personal characteristics of Chrysippus that the hair-splitting and formal pedantry of the Stoics can be traced; because of this they became known as the Dialecticians.
iv *314–5.* So Cicero, *De natura deorum* iii 36, argues that man has a right to take pride in his own wisdom and virtue as proceeding from himself and not, like external things, a gift of the gods: 'Our virtue is a just ground for others' praise and a right reason for our own pride, and this would not be so if the gift of virtue came to us from a god and not from ourselves.'
iv *321. cloud*] See *Passion 56n.*
iv *321–2.* Cp. *Eccles.* xii 12 'Of making many books there is no end; and much study is a weariness of the flesh.'
iv *322–30.* Kermode[4] 328 suggests that Seneca, *Epistle* lxxxviii, which treats of intemperate learning and the tenuous relationship of learning to virtue may be among M.'s sources: his rejection of the classics is not independent of classical authority. Augustine's dismissal of the Gentile philosophers, *De civitate Dei* xviii 41, may also have contributed.
iv *328. crude*] unable to digest.

And trifles for choice matters, worth a sponge;
As children gathering pebbles on the shore.
Or if I would delight my private hours
With music or with poem, where so soon
As in our native language can I find
That solace? All our Law and story strewed
With hymns, our psalms with artful terms inscribed,
Our Hebrew songs and harps in Babylon,
That pleased so well our victor's ear, declare
That rather Greece from us these arts derived;
Ill imitated, while they loudest sing
The vices of their deities, and their own
In fable, hymn, or song, so personating
Their gods ridiculous, and themselves past shame.
Remove their swelling epithets thick-laid
As varnish on a harlot's cheek, the rest,
Thin-sown with aught of profit or delight,
Will far be found unworthy to compare
With Sion's songs, to all true tastes excelling,

iv *329. worth a sponge*] fit to be expunged, erased.

iv *335. artful terms*] artistic expressions; language that shows technical skill.

iv *336–7.* Cp. *Ps.* cxxxvii 1–3: 'By the rivers of Babylon, there we sat down, yea, we wept, when we remembered Zion. . . . For they that carried us away captive required of us a song . . . saying, Sing us one of the songs of Zion.'

iv *337. declare*] show.

iv *338. Greece from us these arts derived*] Schultz 89–90 and 260–1 notes that Josephus, *Antiquities* I viii 2, had traced learning from Abraham through the Egyptians to the Greeks: Philo of Alexandria had allegorized Moses until he could find the teachings of Plato in the Old Testament: Clement of Alexandria, Eusebius and other Fathers had affirmed the Jewish origin of learning; by the seventeenth century the idea was a commonplace.

iv *344.* Echoing *Hamlet* III i, 'The harlot's cheek, beautied with plast'ring art'.

iv *346–7. unworthy to compare With Sion's songs*] Among previous claims in English for the supremacy of Hebrew poetry Kermode[4] 329 cites Wither, *Preparation to the Psalter*, and Falkland's verses on Sandys's version of the Psalms. Schultz 91, 261 adds similar claims from Daniel Featley, *Characters of Heavenly Wisdom* and Felltham, *Resolves*. Cp. also Sidney, *Defence* (*Works* ed. A. Feuillerat (Cambridge 1923) iii 9) 'the chiefe [poets] both in antiquitie and excellencie, were they that did imitate the unconceivable excellencies of God. Such were David, in his Psalmes, Salomon in his song of songs, in his Ecclesiastes, and Proverbes. Moses and Debora in their Hymnes, and the wryter of Jobe', and M. himself, in *Reason of Church-Government* (Columbia iii 238, Yale i 816): 'But those frequent songs throughout the

Where God is praised aright, and godlike men,
The Holiest of Holies, and his saints;
Such are from God inspired, not such from thee;
Unless where moral virtue is expressed
By light of nature not in all quite lost.
Their orators thou then extoll'st, as those
The top of eloquence, statists indeed,
And lovers of their country, as may seem;
But herein to our prophets far beneath,
As men divinely taught, and better teaching
The solid rules of civil government
In their majestic unaffected style
Than all the oratory of Greece and Rome.
In them is plainest taught, and easiest learnt,
What makes a nation happy, and keeps it so,
What ruins kingdoms, and lays cities flat;
These only with our Law best form a king.
So spake the Son of God; but Satan now
Quite at a loss, for all his darts were spent,
Thus to our Saviour with stern brow replied.
Since neither wealth, nor honour, arms nor arts,
Kingdom nor empire pleases thee, nor aught
By me proposed in life contemplative,
Or active, tended on by glory, or fame,
What dost thou in this world? The wilderness

law and prophets beyond all these, not in their divine argument alone, but in the very critical art of composition may be easily made appear over all the kinds of Lyrick poesy, to be incomparable.'

iv *347*. *tastes*] *OED* records this as the first instance in the sense 'faculty of perceiving what is excellent in art or literature.'

iv *351*. *Unless*] catches up 'unworthy' (l. 346): pagan thought is not unworthy if it discovers moral truth, inspired by the light of nature. This view finds scriptural support in texts like *Rom*. ii 14–5: 'The Gentiles, which have not the law. . . . Which shew the work of the law written in their hearts.' M. quotes this in support of his contention, in the *De doctrina* (Columbia xv 208–11), that 'it cannot be denied . . . that some remnants of the divine image still exist in us, not wholly extinguished by the spiritual death. This is evident . . . from the wisdom and holiness of many of the heathen, manifested both in words and deeds.'

iv *354*. *statists*] statesmen.

iv *361–4*. Cp. *De doctrina* ii 17 (Columbia xvii 412–3): 'The observance of the divine commandments is the source of prosperity to nations . . . It renders them flourishing and wealthy and victorious . . . *Deut*. xxviii 1 etc.–a chapter which should be read again and again by those who have the direction of political affairs.'

For thee is fittest place, I found thee there,
And thither will return thee, yet remember
What I foretell thee, soon thou shalt have cause
To wish thou never hadst rejected thus
Nicely or cautiously my offered aid,
Which would have set thee in short time with ease
On David's throne; or throne of all the world,
Now at full age, fulness of time, thy season,
When prophecies of thee are best fulfilled.
Now contrary, if I read aught in heaven,
Or heaven write aught of fate, by what the stars
Voluminous, or single characters,
In their conjunction met, give me to spell,
Sorrows, and labours, opposition, hate,
Attends thee, scorns, reproaches, injuries,
Violence and stripes, and lastly cruel death,
A kingdom they portend thee, but what kingdom,
Real or allegoric I discern not,

iv *382–8.* Schultz 54 reviewing the orthodox opposition to divinatory astrology, notes that Satan's pretence to it here stamps it as devilish. It was still widely practised in seventeenth century England, and controversy about it was lively, the anti-astrologists drawing for ammunition upon such biblical texts as *Jer.* x 2: 'Learn not the way of the heathen, and be not dismayed at the signs of heaven.' In 1624 Bishop Carleton published his *Astrologomania*, refuting Sir Christopher Heydon's *Defence of Judicial Astrology*. Eighteenth-century critics regarded Satan's speech as an allusion to the presumption of the Italian astrologer Cardano (1501–76), who cast Christ's horoscope. It is as well, however, to recall M.'s reservation in *De doctrina* ii 5 (Columbia xvii 151): 'All study of the heavenly bodies, however, is not unlawful or unprofitable; as appears from the journey of the wise men,and still more from the star itself, divinely appointed to announce the birth of Christ, *Matt.* ii 1, 2.'

iv *384. Voluminous*] forming a large volume, or book. *single characters*] regarded as single letters in this volume.

iv *385. conjunction*] When two stars or planets were in conjunction they were in the same sign of the zodiac, and apparently close together; this was one of the unfavourable astrological 'aspects'. *spell*] See *Il Penseroso* 170*n*.

iv *387. Attends*] L. H. Kendall, *N & Q* n.s. iv (1957) 523, notes approvingly that B. A. Wright in his ed. of M.'s *Poems* (1956) emends to 'Attend', for the sake of grammar. A plural subject and singular verb is, however, quite common in seventeenth-century English, especially when, as here, there is a singular noun in close proximity.

Nor when, eternal sure, as without end,
Without beginning; for no date prefixed
Directs me in the starry rubric set.
   So saying he took (for still he knew his power
Not yet expired) and to the wilderness
Brought back the Son of God, and left him there,
Feigning to disappear. Darkness now rose,
As daylight sunk, and brought in louring night
Her shadowy offspring unsubstantial both,
Privation mere of light and absent day.
Our Saviour meek and with untroubled mind
After his airy jaunt, though hurried sore,
Hungry and cold betook him to his rest,
Wherever, under some concourse of shades
Whose branching arms thick intertwined might shield
From dews and damps of night his sheltered head,
But sheltered slept in vain, for at his head
The tempter watched, and soon with ugly dreams
Disturbed his sleep; and either tropic now
'Gan thunder, and both ends of heaven, the clouds
From many a horrid rift abortive poured
Fierce rain with lightning mixed, water with fire

iv *391–2.* Satan is being ironic: an eternal kingdom can have no end, but neither can it have a beginning.
iv *393. rubric*] manual containing laws or rules; the word derived from the red colour of captions in law books and liturgical works, which made them stand out from the surrounding black lettering. So M. imagines stars standing out against the sky.
iv *402. jaunt*] develops from 'jaunce' (prance of a horse), and means 'a tiring journey' from its first usage (*Romeo and Juliet* II v 26) until the end of the seventeenth century, when the 'pleasure-trip' meaning begins to develop.
iv *407–25.* J. M. Steadman, *MP* lix (1961) 81–8, sees M. complying with a commonplace in the literature of spiritual warfare by including the storm, as an adversity symbol, to complement the other temptations of prosperity and demonstrate the dual aspect of the world's assault on the Christian warrior. Lewalski 311–12 reads the storm as a foreshadowing of the violent upheavals of nature recorded at Christ's death (*Matt.* xxvii 51–2), and takes 'shrouded' (l. 419) as a reference to Christ's burial and the 'hellish furies' (l. 422) as suggesting the descent into hell.
iv *409. tropic*] apparently used loosely to mean 'part of the sky' or 'point of the compass': *OED* does not instance this use, or any appropriate sense.
iv *411. abortive*] destructive of life.
iv *412–13. water with fire . . . reconciled*] Cp. Aeschylus, *Agamemnon* 650–2: 'fire and sea, formerly the bitterest of enemies, swore alliance and for proof

In ruin reconciled: nor slept the winds
Within their stony caves, but rushed abroad
From the four hinges of the world, and fell
On the vexed wilderness, whose tallest pines,
Though rooted deep as high, and sturdiest oaks
Bowed their stiff necks, loaden with stormy blasts,
Or torn up sheer: ill wast thou shrouded then,
O patient Son of God, yet only stood'st
Unshaken; nor yet stayed the terror there,
Infernal ghosts, and hellish furies, round
Environed thee, some howled, some yelled, some shrieked,
Some bent at thee their fiery darts, while thou
Sat'st unappalled in calm and sinless peace.
Thus passed the night so foul till morning fair
Came forth with pilgrim steps in amice grey;
Who with her radiant finger stilled the roar
Of thunder, chased the clouds, and laid the winds,
And grisly spectres, which the Fiend had raised
To tempt the Son of God with terrors dire.
And now the sun with more effectual beams
Had cheered the face of earth, and dried the wet
From drooping plant, or dropping tree; the birds
Who all things now behold more fresh and green,
After a night of storm so ruinous,
Cleared up their choicest notes in bush and spray
To gratulate the sweet return of morn;
Nor yet amidst this joy and brightest morn
Was absent, after all his mischief done,
The Prince of Darkness, glad would also seem
Of this fair change, and to our Saviour came,

of it destroyed the hapless Greek fleet.' *ruin*] 'fall', as well as 'destruction': both were common seventeenth-century senses.
iv *414. caves*] Cp. *Aen.* i 52–4, where Aeolus keeps the 'struggling winds and roaring gales' imprisoned in a vast cavern.
iv *415. hinges*] cardinal points of the compass (Latin *cardo*, a hinge).
iv *419. shrouded*] sheltered.
iv *420. only*] alone.
iv *422–3.* Cp. *Richard III* I iv 58–9: 'With that, methoughts, a legion of foul fiends / Environ'd me about, and howled in my ears.'
iv *426–7.* See *Comus* 188–9, *Lycidas* 187. *amice*] hood or cape made or lined with grey fur.
iv *432. more effectual*] than those of the early morning sun.
iv *437. Cleared up*] made clear, brightened.
iv *438. gratulate*] give thanks for.

Yet with no new device, they all were spent,
Rather by this his last affront resolved,
Desperate of better course, to vent his rage,
And mad despite to be so oft repelled.
Him walking on a sunny hill he found,
Backed on the north and west by a thick wood,
Out of the wood he starts in wonted shape;
And in a careless mood thus to him said.
   Fair morning yet betides thee Son of God,
After a dismal night; I heard the rack
As earth and sky would mingle; but myself
Was distant; and these flaws, though mortals fear them
As dangerous to the pillared frame of heaven,
Or to the earth's dark basis underneath,
Are to the main as inconsiderable,
And harmless, if not wholesome, as a sneeze
To man's less universe, and soon are gone;
Yet as being oft-times noxious where they light
On man, beast, plant, wasteful and turbulent,
Like turbulencies in the affairs of men,
Over whose heads they roar, and seem to point,
They oft fore-signify and threaten ill:

iv *449. wonted shape*] Pope 49–50 notes the ambiguity; the phrase may mean 'his own shape (with wings, cloven hooves etc.), with no disguise' or 'his usual disguise': if the second, the old man of i 314 must be regarded as the same man (though in different clothes) as the courtier ('Not rustic as before') of ii 298–300. There was support among artists and writers before M. either for Satan's continuing his disguise to the end, or for his throwing it off before the last temptation. Miss Pope favours the idea that Satan here retains his disguise (i.e. appears as a man), and points to the phrase 'without wing / Of hippogrif' (ll. 541–2).
iv *452. rack*] *OED* gives this as the only instance of the word in the sense 'crash as of something breaking'. The meaning 'destruction' was common in the seventeenth century, however (cp. *PL* xi 817), and would fit here.
iv *453. earth and sky . . . mingle*] Echoes *Aen.* i 133–4: *caelum terramque . . . miscere.*
iv *454. flaws*] squalls.
iv *455. pillared*] Cp. *Job* xxvi 11: 'The pillars of heaven tremble.'
iv *457. main*] universe.
iv *464–83.* Satan's emphasis on portents here and elsewhere (e.g. iii 152–3, iv 380–93), and the care with which he dissociates himself from the storm (iv 452–4) and interprets it as intended for Christ (465–6), lead Dick Taylor, *UTQ* xxiv (1955) 359–76, to the conclusion that the storm scene is not a mere exhibition of enraged violence but an essential part of the second temptation – Satan is tempting Christ to take the storm as a portent, a sign

This tempest at this desert most was bent;
Of men at thee, for only thou here dwell'st.
Did I not tell thee, if thou didst reject
The perfect season offered with my aid
To win thy destined seat, but wilt prolong
All to the push of fate, pursue thy way
Of gaining David's throne no man knows when,
For both the when and how is nowhere told,
Thou shalt be what thou art ordained, no doubt;
For angels have proclaimed it, but concealing
The time and means: each act is rightliest done,
Not when it must, but when it may be best.
If thou observe not this, be sure to find,
What I foretold thee, many a hard assay
Of dangers, and adversities and pains,
Ere thou of Israel's sceptre get fast hold;
Whereof this ominous night that closed thee round,
So many terrors, voices, prodigies
May warn thee, as a sure foregoing sign.
So talked he, while the Son of God went on
And stayed not, but in brief him answered thus.
Me worse than wet thou find'st not; other harm
Those terrors which thou speak'st of, did me none;
I never feared they could, though noising loud
And threat'ning nigh; what they can do as signs
Betokening, or ill-boding, I contemn
As false portents, not sent from God, but thee;
Who knowing I shall reign past thy preventing,
Obtrud'st thy offered aid, that I accepting
At least might seem to hold all power of thee,
Ambitious spirit, and would'st be thought my God,
And storm'st refused, thinking to terrify
Me to thy will; desist, thou art discerned
And toil'st in vain, nor me in vain molest.
To whom the Fiend now swoll'n with rage replied:
Then hear, O Son of David, virgin-born;

of God's will that he should assume power under Satan's auspices. Taylor draws attention to the intense contemporary interest in portents around 1666, and thinks it may have influenced M. Though iv 365–6 and 443–6 seem to discredit Taylor's theory, he claims that these passages merely exemplify M.'s consistent practice of describing Satan, incident by incident, as at a loss at the failure of each stratagem (cp. ii 119–20, iii 2–4, 145–8, iv 1–6).

iv 467. *Did I not tell thee*] i.e. in iv 375ff. M. here begins his sentence as a question but continues it as an affirmation.

iv 481. *ominous*] full of omens.

For Son of God to me is yet in doubt,
Of the Messiah I have heard foretold
By all the prophets; of thy birth at length
Announced by Gabriel with the first I knew,
And of the angelic song in Bethlehem field,
On thy birth-night, that sung thee Saviour born.
From that time seldom have I ceased to eye
Thy infancy, thy childhood, and thy youth,
Thy manhood last, though yet in private bred;
Till at the ford of Jordan whither all
Flocked to the Baptist, I among the rest,
Though not to be baptized, by voice from heaven
Heard thee pronounced the Son of God beloved.
Thenceforth I thought thee worth my nearer view
And narrower scrutiny, that I might learn
In what degree or meaning thou art called
The Son of God, which bears no single sense;
The Son of God I also am, or was,
And if I was, I am; relation stands;
All men are Sons of God; yet thee I thought
In some respect far higher so declared.
Therefore I watched thy footsteps from that hour,
And followed thee still on to this waste wild;
Where by all best conjectures I collect
Thou art to be my fatal enemy.
Good reason then, if I beforehand seek
To understand my adversary, who
And what he is; his wisdom, power, intent,
By parle, or composition, truce, or league
To win him, or win from him what I can.
And opportunity I here have had
To try thee, sift thee, and confess have found thee
Proof against all temptation as a rock
Of adamant, and as a centre, firm
To the utmost of mere man both wise and good,
Not more; for honours, riches, kingdoms, glory

iv *518*. Cp. *Job* i 6: 'Now there was a day when the sons of God came to present themselves before the Lord, and Satan came also among them.'
iv *520*. *All men are Sons of God*] Cp. *Matt.* vi 9: 'After this manner therefore pray ye: Our Father . . .'
iv *524*. *collect*] infer.
iv *525*. *fatal*] in the sense 'fated' as well as 'deadly'.
iv *529*. *parle*] parley. *composition*] treaty, truce.
iv *534*. *adamant*] See *SA* 134*n*. *centre*] pivot; the unmoving point around which a body turns.

Have been before contemned, and may again:
Therefore to know what more thou art than man,
Worth naming Son of God by voice from heaven,
Another method I must now begin.
   So saying he caught him up, and without wing
Of hippogrif bore through the air sublime
Over the wilderness and o'er the plain;
Till underneath them fair Jerusalem,
The holy city lifted high her towers,
And higher yet the glorious Temple reared
Her pile, far off appearing like a mount
Of alabaster, topped with golden spires:
There on the highest pinnacle he set

iv *538–40.* Satan's words suggest that the pinnacle episode is to be an attempt to discover Christ's identity, not a temptation to vainglory or presumption (see iii 25–30*n*). M.'s handling of this episode represents his most spectacular break with tradition, as Pope 80–107 demonstrates.
iv *542. hippogrif*] fabulous creature, front half griffin, rear half horse. It appears frequently in Ariosto, *Orlando Furioso*, and in IV xviii carries Astolfo to the moon. See 449*n*.
iv *545. towers*] Sandys 156–7, describing Jerusalem, mentions several towers: 'Upon a steepe rocke . . . stood the tower of Baris . . . but Herod . . . built thereon a stately strong Castle, having at every corner a tower' (156), 'Mariamnes Tower . . . that of Phaseolus . . . in the North wall [of Herod's palace] on a lofty hill stood the tower Hippic, eighty foure cubits high: fouresquare, and having two spires at the top', and on the north the outer wall 'fortified with ninety Towers, two hundred cubits distant from each other' (157).
iv *548. alabaster . . . golden spires*] Josephus speaks of the gold and white appearance of the Temple, *Jewish War* V v 6: 'The outward front of the temple . . . was covered all over with massive plates of gold, and reflected at the first rising of the sun a very fiery splendour, and made those who forced themselves to look upon it turn their eyes away. . . . But it appeared to strangers, when they were approaching it at some distance, like a mountain covered with snow, for where it was not gilt, it was exceeding white.'
iv *549. highest pinnacle*] The nature of the 'pinnacle' (the word *is* used in *Matt.* iv 5 and *Luke* iv 9) was, as Pope 85–9 explains, much debated. Some commentators, like Diodati, held that it was merely a flat roof: thus Christ was quite free to stand or throw himself down, and the temptation was purely one of presumption. Others made it a balustrade or a peaked gable or a spire. Fuller and Chemnitius quote Josephus, *Jewish War* V v 6, who records that the Temple roof 'had sharp points to prevent any pollution of it by birds sitting upon it'. Of those who take 'pinnacle' to mean 'point' or 'spire', however, it appears that only Thomas Bilson goes on to suggest that Christ's ability to stand upon such a point was a deliberate display of

The Son of God; and added thus in scorn:
    There stand, if thou wilt stand; to stand upright
Will ask thee skill; I to thy Father's house
Have brought thee, and highest placed, highest is best,
Now show thy progeny; if not to stand,
Cast thyself down; safely if Son of God:
For it is written, He will give command
Concerning thee to his angels, in their hands
They shall uplift thee, lest at any time
Thou chance to dash thy foot against a stone.

his miraculous powers. The others explain either that Satan held him to prevent his falling, or that there was room for a man to stand; and they often add that Christ could perfectly well have climbed down and escaped by the stairs. Bilson's view ran counter to the doctrine that Christ was undergoing temptation as a man, and that a display of his miraculous powers was just what Satan wanted to provoke. It is clear that M.'s pinnacle is too small for a man to stand firmly, and that Satan does not hold Christ: Satan expects him to fall (l. 571), and tells him to stand only 'in scorn' (l. 550). M.'s view might seem near to Bilson's, therefore. But 'uneasy station' (l. 584) implies that the standing was not miraculous but a balancing feat. Perhaps M. remembers Josephus's description of the royal portico to the south of the Temple, which looked over the ravine of Kedron: 'the valley was very deep, and its bottom could not be seen if you looked from above into the depth, the high elevation of the portico stood upon that height, that if anyone looked down from the top of the roof to those depths, he would be giddy, while his sight could not reach down to such an abyss', *Antiquities* XV xi 5. E. Cleveland, *MLQ* xvi (1955) 232–6, thinks the pinnacle symbolic of the cross, and Satan's speech (ll. 551–9) a foreshadowing of the scornful questioning at the crucifixion. Lewalski (309–10) shows that this symbolism was a traditional feature of biblical commentary. John Knox, Joseph Hall and others regarded the violent transportation to the tower as prefiguring the crucifixion, and Satan's words as a foretaste of the taunts of the crowd.

iv 555. *Cast thyself down*] In the gospel account, *Luke* iv 9–11, Satan intends Christ to choose; the temptation is to presumption. In M. it is clear Satan thinks Christ has no choice: he expects him to fall, and is amazed when he stands (ll. 562, 571). 'Cast thyself down' is therefore sarcastic: Christ's fall, as Satan sees it, will settle the problem of his identity: if he is not merely perfect man, but something more, angels will save him: if he is merely perfect man, he will die.

iv 556–9. *He will give . . . stone*] Frye 237 finds irony in Satan's quotation from *Ps.* xci 11–12, since the next verse reads: 'Thou shalt tread upon the lion and adder: the young lion and the dragon shalt thou trample under feet': Satan is the dragon Christ is to trample upon. The irony is present in M.'s source, *Luke* iv 10–11, where Satan uses the same quotation.

To whom thus Jesus: Also it is written,
Tempt not the Lord thy God, he said and stood.
But Satan smitten with amazement fell

iv *560–1. Also it is written, Tempt not the Lord thy God*] Cp. *Luke* iv 12: 'And Jesus answering said unto him, It is said, Thou shalt not tempt the Lord thy God', where Jesus is quoting *Deut.* vi 16: 'Ye shall not tempt [i.e. make trial of, test] the Lord your God.'

As Pope 83, 103, sees it, since Satan has deliberately placed Christ in a position where, as man, he cannot stand (see however, iv 549*n*), there is no question of his 'making trial' of God by casting himself down, so his reply cannot be taken in the usual sense. It must mean 'Tempt not *me*', and must amount to a claim to, or revelation of, his own divinity. Some early commentators, chiefly Church Fathers, had interpreted the reply in *Luke* in this way, but as a doctrine it had never won general acceptance, and Thomas Taylor, among other seventeenth-century exegetes, refutes it.

G. G. Loane, *N & Q* clxxv (1938) 184–5, also thinks that Christ's reply in M. (though not in *Luke*) can be taken to mean 'Tempt not *me*', but considers that it could also be taken in the normal sense (i.e. as meaning 'I cannot cast myself down, because that would be to make trial of God, and we are commanded not to'). It is, then, an ambiguous reply, and Loane finds this odd after Christ's denunciation of the ambiguity of the oracles (i 435). More recently Frye (237) and Lewalski (316) have agreed that the reply, in M., is ambiguous.

Stein[2] 128–9, however, rejects the idea that Christ's reply can mean 'Tempt not *me*': for Christ to reveal his own divinity would be to give in, at last, to Satan's pressure. Instead Stein assumes that Christ does not speak the reply at all: it is spoken by God through Christ: 'the full revelation occurs, the miracle of epiphany, theophany, but not as an act of will, not from the self'. Stein's solution is perhaps unnecessarily ingenious. It could be argued that Christ takes Satan's sarcastic 'There stand' at its face value, stands on his 'uneasy station' by a supreme display of nerve, and gives as his reason for doing so his unwillingness to make trial of God. His reply would then mean the same as it does in *Luke* (and *Deuteronomy*), and would entail no claim to divinity (a claim which the M. who wrote *De doctrina* might wish to avoid). Even if Christ had performed a miracle by standing it would not in itself have been a revelation of his divinity, since miracles can be performed by men, as they had been by Moses and were later by the apostles. Alternatively it could be argued that if a miracle does occur it is not Christ but God who performs it: thus Christ suddenly finds himself able to stand, and makes his reply. This explanation is adopted by Dick Taylor, *Tulane Studies in English* iv (1954) 57–90, and Lewalski 316. But '*uneasy* station' (l. 584) seems decisively against the theory that any miracle occurs.

iv *562. fell*] Pope 11 notes that no other writer states that Satan fell after his final defeat: the traditional accounts follow *Luke* iv 13 in saying that Satan, when he had 'ended all the temptation, . . . departed from him for a season'.

As when Earth's son Antaeus (to compare
Small things with greatest) in Irassa strove
With Jove's Alcides, and oft foiled still rose,
Receiving from his mother Earth new strength,
Fresh from his fall, and fiercer grapple joined,
Throttled at length in the air, expired and fell;
So after many a foil the tempter proud,
Renewing fresh assaults, amidst his pride
Fell whence he stood to see his victor fall.
And as that Theban monster that proposed
Her riddle, and him, who solved it not, devoured;
That once found out and solved, for grief and spite
Cast herself headlong from the Ismenian steep,
So struck with dread and anguish fell the Fiend,
And to his crew, that sat consulting, brought

In visual art, on the other hand, it was quite common for the artist to depict Satan as reeling or falling. Perhaps M. was influenced by iconography, or by Fletcher's *Christ's Victory and Triumph* i 49, where the allegorical figure of Presumption 'tombles headlong' from the tower at the end of the second temptation, or, as Hughes[2] 256 suggests, by the fall of Malory's fiend in the *Morte d'Arthur* xiv 9 who, when Sir Percivale has resisted all his wiles, goes away at last 'with the wind roaring and yelling'.

iv *563–8.* Antaeus was a giant, son of Ge (Earth), who fought with Hercules (called 'Alcides' after his grandfather Alcaeus, and 'Jove's' because he was the son of Jove). Antaeus drew strength from his mother every time he fell, and Hercules had to hold him in the air and strangle him. In the Renaissance this contest was frequently treated as an allegory of the victory of the spirit over the flesh; Hercules was a common type of Christ (see *Nativity Ode* 227–8*n*). Lewalski 128 finds precedent for M.'s parallel between Hercules / Antaeus and Christ / Satan the tempter, in Sedulius, *Carmen Paschale* ii 199–200. Starnes and Talbert 238 claim that the account of the incident in Conti (paraphrased in Stephanus) is 'very suggestive' of M.'s language.

iv *563–4. to compare . . . greatest*] Echoes Virgil, *Ecl.* i 24: *Sic parvis componere magna solebam* (Thus I used to compare great things with small).

iv *564. Irassa*] L. R. Farnell, *TLS* (1 Oct. 1931) 754, points out that nowhere else in ancient literature could M. have found the name Antaeus brought into connection with the Libyan town 'Irassa' except in Pindar, *Pyth.* ix 106. Farnell thinks that the piling of divine epithets on Aristaeus in this ode (64–5) may have suggested the 'swelling epithets' of iv 343.

iv *572–5.* The Sphinx threw itself from the acropolis at Thebes (above the river Ismenus) when Oedipus gave the right answer, 'Man', to its riddle, 'Which creature goes first on four, then on two, and finally on three legs?'

Joyless triumphals of his hoped success,
Ruin, and desperation, and dismay,
Who durst so proudly tempt the Son of God.
So Satan fell and straight a fiery globe
Of angels on full sail of wing flew nigh,
Who on their plumy vans received him soft
From his uneasy station, and upbore
As on a floating couch through the blithe air,
Then in a flowery valley set him down
On a green bank, and set before him spread
A table of celestial food, divine,
Ambrosial, fruits fetched from the tree of life,
And from the fount of life ambrosial drink,
That soon refreshed him wearied, and repaired
What hunger, if aught hunger had impaired,
Or thirst, and as he fed, angelic choirs
Sung heavenly anthems of his victory
Over temptation, and the tempter proud.
True image of the Father whether throned

iv *578. triumphals*] tokens of triumph: the first recorded instance of the noun in this sense: previously it had meant 'triumph', 'triumphal chariot' or 'triumphal ode'.
iv *581. globe*] Cp. Fletcher, *Christ's Triumph after Death* 13: 'Out thear flies / A globe of winged Angels, swift as thought', which is the first recorded instance of 'globe' in the sense 'compact body of persons' (one of the meanings of the Latin *globus*).
iv *582. angels*] Kermode[4] 324 notes that the following passage is M.'s development of a hint in *Matt.* iv 11: 'Angels came and ministered unto him': Fletcher, *Christ's Victory on Earth* 61, also has choiring angels who bring a banquet to Christ.
iv *583. vans*] wings. M. is the first (here and in *PL* ii 927) to use 'van' to mean 'wing'. 'Fan' is found meaning 'wing' in mid-seventeenth-century poetry: M. adopts the form nearer to the Italian *vanni*. Cp. Fletcher, *Christ's Victory on Earth* 38: 'But him the Angels on their feathers caught / And to an ayrie mountaine nimbly bore.'
iv *589. Ambrosial*] belonging to heaven or paradise: the first recorded instance of this sense is *Comus* 16. *the tree of life*] J. M. Steadman, *RES* n.s. xi (1960) 348–91, draws attention to the multiple significance of this tree: it is the reward of obedience, a meaning given to it as early as the Jerusalem Targum on *Gen.* ii 9; it is a symbol of eternal life, as M. says in *De doctrina* (Columbia xv 114–5); and as it was indigenous to paradise, Christ's participation in its fruits signifies that he has regained the paradise that Adam lost, and parallels Adam's participation in the fruits of the tree of knowledge.

In the bosom of bliss, and light of light
Conceiving, or remote from heaven, enshrined
In fleshly tabernacle, and human form,
Wandering the wilderness, whatever place,
Habit, or state, or motion, still expressing
The Son of God, with godlike force endued
Against the attempter of thy Father's throne,
And thief of Paradise; him long of old
Thou didst debel, and down from heaven cast
With all his army, now thou hast avenged
Supplanted Adam, and, by vanquishing
Temptation, hast regained lost Paradise,
And frustrated the conquest fraudulent:
He never more henceforth will dare set foot
In Paradise to tempt; his snares are broke:
For though that seat of earthly bliss be failed,
A fairer Paradise is founded now
For Adam and his chosen sons, whom thou
A Saviour art come down to reinstall.
Where they shall dwell secure, when time shall be
Of tempter and temptation without fear.
But thou, infernal serpent, shalt not long
Rule in the clouds; like an autumnal star
Or lightning thou shalt fall from heaven trod down
Under his feet: for proof, ere this thou feel'st
Thy wound, yet not thy last and deadliest wound
By this repulse received, and hold'st in hell

iv *597–8*. Cp. *John* i 9 and 18: 'the true Light . . . which is in the bosom of the Father'. *light of light / Conceiving*] taking on light from the Father (Light).

iv *605*. *debel*] suppress by war (Latin *debellare*): first recorded in mid-sixteenth century.

iv *611*. Cp. *Ps.* cxxiv 7: 'The snare is broken and we are escaped.'

iv *612*. *be failed*] is absent, has disappeared.

iv *617*. The line is inverted.

iv *619*. *autumnal star*] One of the names given to Sirius: here, however, M. seems to mean a comet or meteor (cp. *PL* ii 708–11).

iv *620–1*. Cp. *Luke* x 18: 'And he said unto them, I beheld Satan as lightning fall from heaven'; and *Mal.* iv 3: 'Ye shall tread down the wicked . . . under the soles of your feet.'

iv *622*. *thy last and deadliest wound*] Cp. *Rev.* xx 10: 'And the devil that deceived them was cast into the lake of fire and brimstone, where the beast and the false prophet are, and shall be tormented day and night for ever and ever.'

No triumph; in all her gates Abaddon rues
Thy bold attempt; hereafter learn with awe
To dread the Son of God: he all unarmed
Shall chase thee with the terror of his voice
From thy demoniac holds, possession foul,
Thee and thy legions, yelling they shall fly,
And beg to hide them in a herd of swine,
Lest he command them down into the deep
Bound, and to torment sent before their time.
Hail Son of the Most High, heir of both worlds,
Queller of Satan, on thy glorious work
Now enter, and begin to save mankind.
Thus they the Son of God our Saviour meek
Sung victor, and from heavenly feast refreshed
Brought on his way with joy; he unobserved
Home to his mother's house private returned.

iv *624. Abaddon*] Cp. *Rev.* ix 11: 'And they had a king over them, which is the angel of the bottomless pit, whose name in the Hebrew tongue is Abaddon, but in the Greek tongue hath his name Apollyon.' In *Job* xxvi 6 'Abaddon' is used as a name for hell. In his version of *Ps.* lxxxviii 47 (p. 318) M. translates it as 'perdition'.

iv *628. holds*] strongholds. Cp. *Rev.* xviii 2: 'Babylon the great is fallen, is fallen, and is become the habitation of devils, and the hold of every foul spirit.'

iv *630.* In *Matt.* viii 28–32 Christ meets two people 'possessed with devils', and the devils cry out 'Art thou come hither to torment us before the time?' There is a herd of swine nearby, and the devils ask 'If thou cast us out, suffer us to go away into the herd of swine'. Christ does so, and the swine 'ran violently down a steep place into the sea, and perished in the waters'.

iv *636. meek*] Cp. *Matt.* xi 29: 'I am meek, and lowly in heart.'

Bibliography of References Cited

Unless otherwise stated, the place of publication is London.

ADAMS, JAMES, ed. *The Republic of Plato*. 2 vols. Cambridge 1929.

ADAMS, ROBERT MARTIN. *Ikon: John Milton and the Modern Critics*. Ithaca, N.Y. 1955.

ALCIATI, ANDREA. *Emblemata*. Lyons 1600.

ALLEN, DON CAMERON. *The Harmonious Vision: Studies in Milton's Poetry*. Baltimore, Md. 1954.

ALLEN[2]. *The Legend of Noah: Renaissance Rationalism in Art, Science, and Letters*. Urbana, Ill. 1963.

ARTHOS, J. *On a Masque Presented at Ludlow Castle*. Ann Arbor, Mich. 1954.

AUERBACH, ERICH. *Mimesis: The Representation of Reality in Western Literature*. New York 1957.

BACON, FRANCIS. *The Philosophical Works*, ed. Ellis and Spedding, re-ed. John M. Robertson. 1905.

BANKS, T. H. 'The Meaning of "Gods" in *Paradise Lost*', *MLN* liv, 1939.

BARKER, ARTHUR E., ed. *Milton: Modern Essays in Criticism*. New York 1965.

BATESON, F. W. *English Poetry*. 1950.

BENTLEY, RICHARD. *Milton's Paradise Lost*. 1732.

BERNHEIMER, RICHARD. *Wild Men in the Middle Ages: A Study in Art, Sentiment and Demonology*. Cambridge, Mass. 1952.

BONGO, PIETRO. *Numerorum mysteria*. Bergamo 1591.

BRETT, R. L. *Reason and Imagination*. Oxford 1960.

BROADBENT, JOHN B. *Some Graver Subject: An Essay on 'Paradise Lost'*. 1960.

BROADBENT[2]. 'Milton's Hell', *ELH* xxi, 1954.

BROOKS, CLEANTH and HARDY, J. E. *Poems of Mr John Milton*. 1957.

BROWNE, WILLIAM. *Poems*, ed. G. Goodwin. 1894.

BURDEN, DENNIS. *The Logical Epic*. 1967.

BUSH, DOUGLAS. *Milton: Poetical Works*. 1966.

CARON, M. and HUTIN, S. *The Alchemists*. 1961.

CARROLL, W. M. *Animal Conventions in English Renaissance Non-Religious Prose 1550–1600*. New York 1954.

CARTARI, VINCENZO. *Imagines deorum*. Lyons 1581.

CAXTON, WILLIAM. *Mirrour of the World*, ed. O. H. Prior. *EETS* 1913.

CHAMBERS, A. B. 'Chaos in *Paradise Lost*', *JHI* xxiv, 1963.

CHARLES, R. H. ed. *The Apocrypha and Pseudepigrapha of the Old Testament.* 2 vols. Oxford 1913.
CIRLOT, J. E. *A Dictionary of Symbols*, tr. Jack Sage. 1962.
CLARK, D. L. *John Milton at St Paul's School.* New York 1948.
COHN, NORMAN. *The Pursuit of the Millennium.* 1962.
COLUMBIA. *The Works of John Milton*, ed. F. A. Patterson *et al.* New York 1931–8.
CONDEE, R. W. 'The Formalized Openings of Milton's Epic Poems.' *JEGP* l, 1951.
CONTI, NATALE. *Mythologiae, sive explicationis fabularum, Libri decem.* Lyons 1653.
COPE, JACKSON I. *The Metaphoric Structure of 'Paradise Lost'.* Baltimore 1962.
CORCORAN, Sister M. I. *Milton's Paradise with Reference to the Hexaemeral Background.* Chicago, Ill. 1945.
CORMICAN, L. A. 'Milton's Religious Verse', in *From Donne to Marvell*, ed. Boris Ford. Pelican Guide to English Literature, vol. iii. 1956.
COWLEY, ABRAHAM. *Poems*, ed. A. R. Waller. Cambridge 1905.
CROMBIE, A. C. *Augustine to Galileo.* 2 vols. 1961.
CURRY. *Essays in Honour of Walter Clyde Curry*, ed. H. Craig. Nashville, Tenn. 1954.
CURTIUS, ERNST ROBERT. *European Literature and the Latin Middle Ages*, tr. Willard R. Trask. 1953.
DAICHES, DAVID. *Milton.* 1957.
DAICHES[2]. 'The Opening of *Paradise Lost*', in *The Living Milton*, ed. Frank Kermode. 1960.
DARBISHIRE, HELEN, ed. *The Early Lives of Milton.* 1932.
DARBISHIRE[2], ed. *The Poetical Works of John Milton.* 2 vols. Oxford 1952–5.
DARBISHIRE[3], ed. *The Manuscript of Milton's 'Paradise Lost' Book I.* Oxford 1931.
DAVIE, DONALD. *Articulate Energy: An Inquiry into the Syntax of English Poetry.* 1955.
DAVIE[2]. 'Syntax and Music in *Paradise Lost*', in *The Living Milton*, ed. Frank Kermode. 1960.
DIDRON, A. N. *Christian Iconography.* 2 vols. 1886.
DIEKHOFF, J. S. 'The Text of *Comus*', *PMLA* lii, 1937.
DOBSON, ERIC. *English Pronunciation 1500–1700.* 2 vols. Oxford 1957.
DORIAN, D. C. *The English Diodatis.* New Brunswick, N.J. 1950.
DRAYTON, MICHAEL. *Works*, ed. J. William Hebel. Oxford 1961.
DREYER, J. L. E. *A History of Astronomy from Thales to Kepler.* 1953.
DRUMMOND, WILLIAM. *The Poems*, ed. W. C. Ward. 2 vols. n.d.

DU BARTAS. *Devine Weekes and Workes*, tr. Joshua Sylvester. 1613.

DU BARTAS[2]. *Devine Weekes and Workes*, tr. Joshua Sylvester. 1621.

DUNCAN, E. H. 'The Natural History of Metals and Minerals in the Universe of Milton's *Paradise Lost*', *Osiris* xi, 1954.

EISENSTEIN, S. *The Film Sense*, tr. and ed. J. Leyda. New York 1957.

EISLER, R. *The Royal Art of Astrology*. 1946.

ELLRODT, ROBERT. *Neoplatonism in the Poetry of Spenser*. Travaux d'Humanisme et Renaissance, xxxv. Geneva 1960.

EMMA, RONALD D. *Milton's Grammar*. The Hague 1964.

EMPSON, WILLIAM. *Milton's God*. 1961.

EMPSON[2]. *Some Versions of Pastoral*. 1950.

EMPSON[3]. *The Structure of Complex Words*. 1952.

EVANS, W. M. *Henry Lawes*. New York 1941.

FERRY, ANNE D. *Milton's Epic Voice: The Narrator in 'Paradise Lost'*. Cambridge, Mass. 1963.

FICINO, MARSILIO. *Opera omnia*. Basel 1576.

FINLEY, J. H. 'Milton and Horace', *Harvard Studies in Classical Philology* xlviii, 1937.

FIXLER, M. *Milton and the Kingdoms of God*. 1964.

FLETCHER, HARRIS F. *The Intellectual Development of John Milton*. Vol. i: *The Institution to 1625: From the Beginnings Through Grammar School*. Vol. ii: *The Cambridge University Period 1625–32*. Urbana, Ill. 1956–61.

FLETCHER[2]. *Milton's Rabbinical Readings*. Urbana, Ill. 1930.

FLETCHER[3], ed. *Milton's Complete Poetical Works in Photographic Facsimile*. Urbana, Ill. 1943.

FOWLER, ALASTAIR D. S. *Spenser and the Numbers of Time*. 1964.

FOWLER[2]. 'The River Guyon', *MLN* lxxv, 1960.

FOWLER[3]. 'The Image of Mortality: *The Faerie Queene*, II. i–ii', *HLQ* xxiv, 1961.

FREEMAN, ROSEMARY. *English Emblem Books*. 1948.

FRENCH, J. MILTON, ed. *The Life Records of John Milton*. New Brunswick, N.J. 1949–58.

FRYE, NORTHROP. 'The Typology of *Paradise Regained*', *MP* liii, 1956.

GILBERT, ALLAN H. *On the Composition of 'Paradise Lost': A Study of the Ordering and Insertion of Material*. Chapel Hill, N.C. 1947.

GILBERT[2]. 'The Temptation in *Paradise Regained*', *JEGP* xv, 1916.

GIORGIO, FRANCESCO. *De harmonia mundi totius cantica tria*. Paris 1545.

GOULART, SIMON. *A learned summary upon the famous poeme of W. of Saluste* [i.e. Du Bartas], tr. T. L[odge]. 1621.

GRIERSON, H. J. C., ed. *The Poems of John Milton*. 1925.

HANFORD, JAMES HOLLY. 'That Shepherd, Who First Taught the Chosen Seed', *UTQ* viii, 1939.

HANFORD[2]. *A Milton Handbook*. New York 1947.

HANFORD[3]. *John Milton, Englishman*. 1950.

HARDING, D. P. 'Milton and the Renaissance Ovid', *Illinois Studies in Language and Literature*, xxx, 1946.

HARTWELL, K. E. *Lactantius and Milton*. Cambridge, Mass. 1929.

HENINGER, S. K. 'The Implications of Form for *The Shepheardes Calender*', *Studies in the Renaissance* ix, 1962.

HERRICK, ROBERT. *The Poetical Works of Robert Herrick*, ed. L. C. Martin. Oxford 1956.

HEYLYN, PETER. *Cosmographie In Four Bookes*. 1652.

HIEATT, A. KENT. *Short Time's Endless Monument: The Symbolism of the Numbers in Edmund Spenser's 'Epithalamion'*. New York 1960.

HOPPER, VINCENT F. *Medieval Number Symbolism*. New York 1938.

HORRELL, JOSEPH. '*Milton, Limbo, and Suicide*', *RES* xviii, 1942.

HORWOOD, A. J., ed. *A Commonplace Book of John Milton*. Camden Society. 1876.

HOWARD, LEON. '"The Invention" of Milton's "Great Argument": A Study of the Logic of "God's Ways to Men"', *HLQ* ix, 1945.

HUGHES, MERRITT Y., ed. *John Milton: Complete Poems and Major Prose*. New York 1957.

HUGHES[2]. 'The Christ of *Paradise Regained* and the Renaissance Poetic Tradition', *SP* xxxv, 1938.

HUIZINGA, J. *The Waning of the Middle Ages*. 1955.

HUNTLEY, FRANK L. 'Milton, Mendoza, and the Chinese Land-ship' *MLN* lxix, 1954.

HUNTLEY[2]. 'A Justification of Milton's "Paradise of Fools" (P.L. III 431–499)', *ELH* xxi, 1954.

JERRAM, C. S., ed. *The 'Lycidas' and the 'Epitaphium Damonis'*. 1878.

JOHNSON, F. R. *Astronomical Thought in Renaissance England*. Baltimore, Md. 1937.

JONSON, BENJAMIN. *Works*, ed. C. H. Herford and P. and E. Simpson. Oxford 1925–50.

KELLEY, MAURICE. *This Great Argument: a Study of Milton's 'De Doctrina Christiana' as a Gloss upon 'Paradise Lost'*. Princeton, N.J. 1941.

KERMODE, FRANK. 'Adam Unparadised', in *The Living Milton*, ed. Frank Kermode. 1960.

KERMODE[2]. 'The Banquet of Sense', *Bulletin of the John Rylands Libr.* xliv, 1961.

KERMODE[3], ed. *The Living Milton*. 1960.

KERMODE[4]. 'Milton's Hero', *RES*, iv, 1953.

KIRKCONNELL, WATSON. *The Celestial Cycle . . . with Translations of the Major Analogues.* Toronto 1952.

KLIBANSKY, RAYMOND, and others. *Saturn and Melancholy.* 1964.

KROUSE, F. M. *Milton's Samson and the Christian Tradition.* Princeton 1949.

LERNER, L. D. 'The Miltonic Simile', *EC* iv, 1954.

LEWALSKI, B. K. *Milton's Brief Epic.* Providence, R. I. 1966.

LEWIS, C. S. *A Preface to Paradise Lost.* 1942.

LEWIS[2]. *The Allegory of Love.* Oxford 1951.

LOVEJOY, ARTHUR O. *The Great Chain of Being: A Study of the History of an Idea.* New York 1960.

MACCAFFREY, ISABEL G. '*Paradise Lost*' *as* '*Myth*'. Cambridge, Mass. 1959.

MCCOLLEY, GRANT. '*Paradise Lost*': *An Account of Its Growth and Major Origins.* Chicago 1940.

MACKELLAR, W., ed. *The Latin Poems of John Milton.* Cornell Studies in English, No. xv. New Haven, Conn. 1930

MÂLE, EMILE. *The Gothic Image: Religious Art in France of the Thirteenth Century*, tr. Dora Nussey. 1961.

MARLOWE, CHRISTOPHER. *Works*, ed. C. F. Tucker Brooke. Cambridge 1910.

MARTZ, L. *The Paradise Within.* New Haven, Conn. 1964.

MASSON, DAVID, ed. *The Poetical Works of John Milton.* 1890.

MASSON[2]. *The Life of John Milton.* 1881.

MAXWELL, J. C. '"Gods" in *Paradise Lost*', *N & Q* cxciii, 1948.

MORE, HENRY, *Conjectura Cabbalistica. Or, a conjectural essay of Interpreting the minde of Moses, according to a Threefold cabbala.* 1653.

MORE[2]. *The immortality of the soul.* 1659.

NELSON, L. *Baroque Lyric Poetry.* New Haven, Conn. 1961.

NICOLSON, MARJORIE H. 'Milton and the Conjectura Cabbalistica', *PQ*, vi, 1927.

NICOLSON[2]. 'A World in the Moon', *Smith College Studies in Modern Languages*, xvii, 1936.

NICOLSON[3]. *The Breaking of the Circle: Studies in the Effect of the* '*New Science*' *Upon Seventeenth Century Poetry.* Evanston, Ill. 1950.

NICOLSON[4]. *Science and Imagination.* Ithaca, N.Y. 1956.

NORWOOD. *Studies in Honour of Gilbert Norwood*, ed. M. E. White. Toronto 1952.

ORAS, ANTS. *Milton's Editors and Commentators from Patrick Hume to Henry John Todd 1695–1801: A Study in Critical Views and Methods.* Tartu 1930.

OVID. See under SANDYS[2].

PANOFSKY, ERWIN. *Meaning in the Visual Arts.* New York 1955.

PANOFSKY². *Studies in Iconology*. New York and Evanston, Ill. 1962.
PARKER, W. R. *Milton's Contemporary Reputation*. Columbus, Ohio. 1940.
PARKER². *Milton's Debt to Greek Tragedy in 'Samson Agonistes'*. Baltimore, Md. 1937.
PARROTT. *Essays in Dramatic Literature. The Parrott Presentation Volume*, ed. H. Craig. Princeton, N.J. 1935.
PATRIDES, C. A. ed. *Milton's 'Lycidas': The Tradition and the Poem*. New York 1961.
PEARCE, Z. *A Review of the Text of 'Paradise Lost'*. 1733.
PETER, JOHN. *A Critique of 'Paradise Lost'*. 1960.
POPE, E. M. *'Paradise Regained', The Tradition and the Poem*. Baltimore 1947.
PRICE, DEREK J., ed. *The Equatorie of the Planetis*. Cambridge 1955.
PRINCE, F. T. *The Italian Element in Milton's Verse*. Oxford 1954.
QVARNSTRÖM, G. *Poetry and Numbers: On the Structural Use of Symbolic Numbers. Scripta minora Regiae Societatis Humaniorum Litterarum Lundensis*. Lund 1966.
RAJAN, B. *'Paradise Lost' and the Seventeenth Century Reader*. 1962.
RAJAN², ed. *John Milton: 'Paradise Lost' Books I and II*. 1964.
RANDOLPH, THOMAS. *Works*, ed. W. C. Hazlitt. 1875.
READ. *Studies for William A. Read*, ed. N. M. Caffee and T. A. Kirby. Baton Rouge, La. 1940.
RÉAU, LOUIS. *Iconographie de l'art Chrétien*. 3 vols. Paris 1956.
RICCIOLI, GIOVANNI-BATTISTA, S. J. *Almagesti novi . . . tomus primus*. 2 parts. Bologna 1651.
RICHARDSON, JONATHAN, sen. and jun. *Explanatory Notes on 'Paradise Lost'*. 1734.
RICKS, CHRISTOPHER. *Milton's Grand Style*. Oxford 1963.
RIPA, CESARE. *Iconologia*. Rome 1603.
ROBIN, P. ANSELL. *Animal Lore in English Literature*. 1932.
ROBINS, HARRY F. *If This Be Heresy: A Study of Milton and Origen*. Illinois Studies in Lang. and Lit., No. li. Urbana, Ill. 1963.
ROBSON, W. W. 'The Better Fortitude', in *The Living Milton*, ed. Frank Kermode. 1960.
ROSEN, EDWARD, ed. *Three Copernican Treatises*. New York 1959.
RØSTVIG, MAREN-SOFIE. *The Happy Man: Studies in the Metamorphoses of a Classical Ideal*. Vol. i: *1600–1700*. Oslo 1962.
RØSTVIG². *The Hidden Sense*. Oslo 1963.
SAMLA. *SAMLA Studies in English*, ed. J. Max Patrick. Gainesville, Fla. 1953.
SAMUEL, IRENE. *Plato and Milton*. Ithaca, N.Y. 1947.
SANDYS, GEORGE. *A relation of a journey*. 1615.

SANDYS[2]. *Ovid's Metamorphosis. Englished Mythologiz'd and Represented in Figures* by G[eorge] S[andys]. 1632.

SCHULTZ, HOWARD. *Milton and Forbidden Knowledge*. New York 1955.

SCOTT. *Fred Newton Scott Anniversary Papers*, Chicago, Ill. 1929.

SCOULAR, KITTY W. *Natural Magic: Studies in the Presentation of Nature in English Poetry from Spenser to Marvell*. Oxford 1965.

SELDEN, JOHN. *De Dis Syris*. 1617.

SHAWCROSS, J. T. 'The Establishment of a Text of Milton's Poems through a Study of *Lycidas*'. *Bibliographical Society of America Papers* lvi, 1962.

SHAWCROSS[2]. 'Certain Relationships of the Manuscripts of *Comus*'. *Bibliographical Society of America Papers* liv, 1960.

SIMS, JAMES H. *The Bible in Milton's Epics*. Gainesville, Fla. 1962.

SIMSON, OTTO VON. *The Gothic Cathedral: Origins of Gothic Architecture and the Medieval Concept of Order*. New York and Evanston, Ill. 1964.

SMART, JOHN, ed. *The Sonnets of Milton*. Glasgow 1921.

SMITH, HALLETT. 'No Middle Flight', *HLQ* xv, 1951–2.

SPAETH, SIGMUND. *Milton's Knowledge of Music*. Ann Arbor, Mich. 1963.

SPROTT, S. ERNEST. *Milton's Art of Prosody*. Oxford 1953.

STARNES, DEWITT T. and TALBERT, ERNEST WILLIAM. *Classical Myth and Legend*. Chapel Hill 1955.

STEADMAN, JOHN M. 'Heroic Virtue and the Divine Image in *Paradise Lost*', *JWI* xxii, 1959.

STEIN, ARNOLD. *Answerable Style: Essays on 'Paradise Lost'*. Minneapolis, Minn. 1953.

STEIN[2]. *Heroic Knowledge*. Minneapolis, Minn. 1957.

STEPHANUS, CAROLUS. *Dictionarium historicum, geographicum, poeticum*. Geneva 1621.

SUMMERS, JOSEPH H. *The Muse's Method: An Introduction to 'Paradise Lost'*. 1962.

SVENDSEN, KESTER. *Milton and Science*. Cambridge, Mass. 1956.

SYLVESTER'S DU BARTAS. See DU BARTAS.

TAYLOR, GEORGE C. *Milton's Use of Du Bartas*. Cambridge, Mass. 1934.

TAYLOR[2]. *A Tribute to George Coffin Taylor*, ed. A. Williams. Chapel Hill, N.C. 1952.

TERVARENT, GUY DE. *Attributs et symboles dans l'art profane 1450–1600* Travaux d'humanisme et renaissance, No. xxix. Geneva 1958.

TILLEY, M. P. *A Dictionary of Proverbs in England in the Sixteenth and Seventeenth Centuries*. Ann Arbor, Mich. 1950.

TILLYARD, E. M. W. *Milton*. 1930.

TILLYARD[2]. *The Miltonic Setting, Past and Present*. Cambridge 1938.

TILLYARD[3]. *Studies in Milton*. 1951.

TODD, H. J., ed. *The Poetical Works of John Milton*. 1801.

TUVE, ROSEMOND. *A Reading of George Herbert.* 1952.
TUVE². *Images and Themes in Five Poems by Milton.* Oxford 1957.
VALERIANO, PIERIO. *Hieroglyphica, sive de sacris Aegyptiorum aliarumque gentium literis, Commentariorum Libri LVIII. ... Accesserunt loco auctarii, Hieroglyphicorum Collectanea, ex veteribus et recentioribus auctoribus descripta, et in sex libros digesta.* Frankfort 1613.
VERITY, A. W. ed. *Milton: 'Paradise Lost'.* Cambridge 1910.
VISIAK, E. H., ed. *Milton's 'Lament for Damon'.* 1935.
WALDOCK, A. J. A. *'Paradise Lost' and Its Critics.* Cambridge 1961.
WARTON, THOMAS, ed. *Poems upon Several Occasions ... by John Milton.* 1791.
WEST, R. H. *Milton and the Angels.* Athens, Ga. 1955.
WHALER, JAMES. 'Counterpoint and Symbol: An Inquiry into the Rhythm of Milton's Epic Style', *Anglistica* vi, 1956.
WHITE, T. H. *The Bestiary: A Book of Beasts.* New York 1960.
WHITING, GEORGE W. *Milton's Literary Milieu.* New York 1964.
WHITING². *Milton and this Pendant World.* Austin, Texas 1958.
WILLET, ANDREW. *Hexapla ... Sixfold Commentary upon Genesis.* 1608.
WILLIAMS, ARNOLD. *The Common Expositor: An Account of the Commentaries on Genesis 1527–1633.* Chapel Hill, N.C. 1948.
WILSON KNIGHT, G. *The Burning Oracle.* Oxford 1939.
WIND, EDGAR. *Pagan Mysteries in the Renaissance.* 1958.
WIND². *Bellini's Feast of the Gods.* Cambridge, Mass, 1948.
WITTKOWER, RUDOLF. *Architectural Principles in the Age of Humanism.* 1962.
WOODHOUSE, A. S. P. 'Theme and Pattern in *Paradise Regained*', *UTQ.* xxv, 1956.
WRIGHT, B. A. '"Shade" for "Tree" in Milton's Poetry', *N & Q* cciii, 1958.
WRIGHT², ed. *Milton's Poems.* 1959.
YALE. *The Complete Prose Works of John Milton,* ed. Douglas Bush *et al.* New Haven, Conn. 1953–.

Index of Titles and First Lines

Titles are given in italic type.

A book was writ of late called *Tetrachordon* 305
Adhuc madentes rore squalebant genae 24
Ad Joannem Rousium Oxoniensis Academiae Bibliothecarium 299
Ad Leonoram Romae canentem 254
Ad Patrem 148
Ad Salsillum poetam Romanum aegrotantem. Scazontes 257
Ah Constantine, of how much ill was cause 283
A little onward lend thy guiding hand 346
Altera Torquatum cepit Leonora poetam 256
‘Αμαθεῖ γεγράφθαι χειρὶ τήνδε μὲν εἰκόνα 291
Among the holy mountains high 318
And to be short, at last his guide him brings 283
Angelus unicuique suus (sic credite gentes) 255
Answer me when I call 404
Apologus De Rustico et Hero 13
‘*Apology for Smectymnuus*’, *Translations from* 284
Arcades 155
‘*Areopagitica*’, *Translation from title-page of* 288
Ariosto, Note on 155
Avenge O Lord thy slaughtered saints, whose bones 411

Because you have thrown off your prelate lord 296
Before the starry threshold of Jove’s court 175
Be not thou silent now at length 312
Bless’d is the man who hath not walked astray 402
Blest pair of sirens, pledges of heaven’s joy 162
Brutus far to the west, in the ocean wide 324

Canzone 93
Captain or colonel, or knight in arms 285
Carmina Elegiaca 10
Circumcision, Upon the 166
Credula quid liquida sirena Neapoli iactas 257
Cromwell, our chief of men, who through a cloud 326
Cum simul in regem nuper satrapasque Britannos 33
Curre per immensum subito mea littera pontum 53
Cyriack Skinner Upon his Blindness, To Mr 414
Cyriack, this three years’ day these eyes, though clear 414
Cyriack, whose grandsire on the royal bench 413

Daughter to that good Earl, once President 286
Defensio Pro Populo Anglicano, Epigram from 325
Defensio Secunda, Verses from 409
De Idea Platonica quemadmodum Aristoteles intellexit 66
de virtute loquutus 409

Dicite sacrorum praesides nemorum deae 66
Diodati, e te'l dirò con maraviglia 94
Donna leggiadra il cui bel nome honora 91

Elegia prima ad Carolum Diodatum 18
Elegia secunda. In Obitum Praeconis Academici Cantabrigiensis 31
Elegia tertia. In Obitum Praesulis Wintoniensis 49
Elegia quarta 53
Elegia quinta. In adventum veris 80
Elegia sexta 113
Elegia septima 69
Epitaphium Damonis 267
Epitaph on the Marchioness of Winchester, An 126
Erewhile of music, and ethereal mirth 119
et nos 416

Fairfax, whose name in arms through Europe rings 322
Fair Infant, On the Death of a 14
Fix here ye overdated spheres 254
Fly envious Time, till thou run out thy race 165
Founded in chaste and humble poverty 283

Gaudete scombri, et quicquid est piscium salo 409
Gemelle cultu simplici gaudens liber 300
Giovane piano, e semplicetto amante 95
Goddess of shades, and huntress, who at will 324
God in the great assembly stands 311

Haec ego mente olim laeva, studioque supino 231
Haec quoque Manse tuae meditantur carmina laudi 261
Hail native language, that by sinews weak 75
Harry whose tuneful and well-measured song 292
Hence loathed Melancholy 132
Hence vain deluding Joys 140
Here lies old Hobson, Death hath broke his girt 124
Here lieth one who did most truly prove 125
Heu quam perpetuis erroribus acta fatiscit 61
Himerides nymphae (nam vos et Daphnin et Hylan 269
History of Britain', Translations from 'The 323
Horace, Lib. I, The Fifth Ode of 96
How lovely are thy dwellings fair 314
How soon hath time the subtle thief of youth 147

Iam pius extrema veniens Iacobus ab arcto 36
Iapetionidem laudavit caeca vetustas 35
I did but prompt the age to quit their clogs 294
Ignavus satrapam dedecet inclytum 11
Il Penseroso 139
In Effigiei eius Sculptor 291
In Inventorem Bombardae 35
In Obitum Praesulis Eliensis 24
In Obitum Procancellarii Medici 27
In Proditionem Bombardicam 33
In Quintum Novembris 36
In se perpetuo Tempus revolubile gyro 81

Ισραὴλ ὅτε παῖδες, ὅτ' ἀγλαὰ φῦλ' 'Ιακώβου 229
I who erewhile the happy garden sung 1077

Jehovah to my words give ear 405
Jesting decides great things 284

Lady, that in the prime of earliest youth 287
L'Allegro 130
Laughing to teach the truth 284
Lawrence of virtuous father virtuous son 410
Let us with a gladsome mind 7
Look nymphs, and shepherds look 156
Lord General Cromwell, To the 325
Lord General Fairfax at the siege of Colchester, On the 321
Lord God that dost me save and keep 319
Lord how many are my foes 403
Lord in thine anger do not reprehend me 406
Lord my God to thee I fly 406
Low in a mead of kine under a thorn 324
Lycidas 232

Mansus 260
Masque presented at Ludlow Castle, 1634, A 168
Methought I saw my late espoused saint 415
Mitto tibi sanam non pleno ventre salutem 113
Moestus eram, et tacitus nullo comitante sedebam 49

Nativity, On the Morning of Christ's 97
Naturam non pati senium 61
New Forcers of Conscience, On the 295
Nondum blanda tuas leges Amathusia noram 70
Now the bright morning Star, Day's harbinger 90
Nunc mea Pierios cupiam per pectora fontes 149

Ὦ ἄνα εἰ ὀλέσῃς με τὸν ἔννομον, οὐδέ τιν' ἄνδρων 13
O fairest flower no sooner blown but blasted 14
Of man's first disobedience, and the fruit 458
'*Of Reformation*', *Translations from* 283
O Jehovah our Lord how wondrous great 408
O musa gressum quae volens trahis claudum 258
O nightingale, that on yon bloomy spray 90

Paradise Lost 419
Paradise Regained 1063
Parere fati discite legibus 27
Passion, The 119
Per certo i bei vostr'occhi, Donna mia 95
Philosophus ad regem 12
Psalms i-viii 402
Psalms lxxx-lxxxviii 306
Psalm cxiv, A Paraphrase on 6
Psalm cxiv (Greek) 229
Psalm cxxxvi 7
Purgatorem animae derisit Iacobus ignem 34

Qual in colle aspro, al imbrunir di sera 92
Quem modo Roma suis devoverat impia diris 35
Quis expedivit Salmasio suam Hundredam 325

Ready and Easy Way', From the title-page of 'The 416
'*Reason of Church-Government', Translation from* 284
Ridonsi donne e giovani amorosi 93
Rusticus ex malo sapidissima poma quotannis 13

Samson Agonistes 330
Shakespeare, On 122
Siccine tentasti caelo donasse Iacobum 33
Sir Henry Vane the Younger, To 327
Solemn Music, At a 161
Song. On May Morning 90
Sonnet I 88
Sonnet II 91
Sonnet III 92
Sonnet IV 94
Sonnet V 95
Sonnet VI 95
Sonnet VII 146
Sonnet VIII. When the assault was intended to the City 284
Sonnet IX 287
Sonnet X. To the Lady Margaret Ley 286
Sonnet XI 305
Sonnet XII 293
Sonnet XIII. To Mr H. Lawes, on his Airs 292
Sonnet XIV 298
Sonnet XV. On the late Massacre in Piedmont 411
Sonnet XVI 329
Sonnet XVII 409
Sonnet XVIII 412
Sonnet XIX 415
Surge, age surge, leves, iam convenit, excute somnos 10

Tandem, care, tuae mihi pervenere tabellae 18
'*Tenure of Kings and Magistrates', Translation from* 323
Te, qui conspicuus baculo fulgente solebas 31
'*Tetrachordon', Translation from* 288
Then passed he to a flowery mountain green 283
There can be slain 323
This is the month, and this the happy morn 101
This is true liberty when freeborn men 288
This rich marble doth inter 127
Thou shepherd that dost Israel keep 308
Thy gracious ear, O Lord, incline 317
Thy land to favour graciously 315
Time, On 165
'Tis you that say it, not I, you do the deeds 284
To God our strength sing loud, and clear 310
Tu mihi iure tuo Iustiniane vale 155

University Carrier, On the 124

Vacation Exercise in the College, At a 75
Vane, young in years, but in sage counsel old 328

What needs my Shakespeare for his honoured bones 123
What slender youth bedewed with liquid odours 96
When faith and love which parted from thee never 298
When I consider how my light is spent 330
When I die, let the earth be rolled in flames 284
When the blest seed of Terah's faithful son 6
Whom do we count a good man, whom but he 291
Why do the Gentiles tumult, and the nations 402

Ye flaming powers and winged warriors bright 166
Yet once more, O ye laurels, and once more 239